# Basic Managerial Finance

Second Edition

*

# Basic Managerial Finance

Second Edition

ERWIN ESSER NEMMERS
Northwestern University

ALAN E. GRUNEWALD
Michigan State University

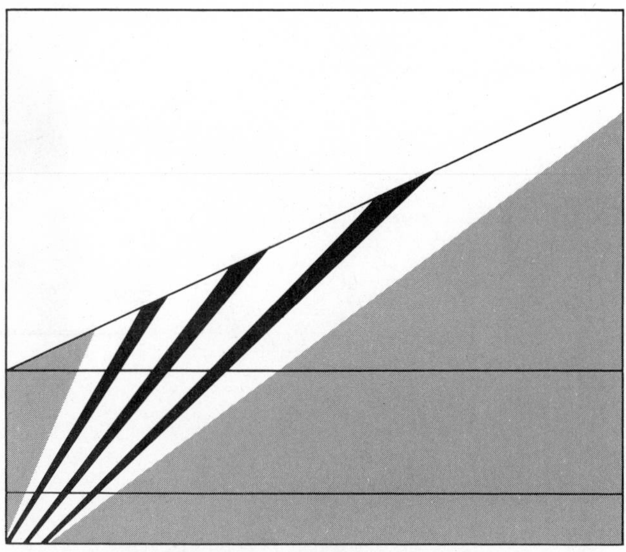

**West Publishing Company**

St. Paul • New York • Boston
Los Angeles • San Francisco

Printed in the United States of America

Library of Congress Cataloging in Publication Data

Nemmers, Erwin Esser, 1916–
Basic managerial finance.

In previous ed. Grunewald's name appeared first on title page.
Includes bibliographies.

1. Corporations—Finance. I. Grunewald, Alan E., joint author. II. Title.
HG4011.N43 1975 658.1'5 74–17164

**ISBN 0–8299–0025–X**

Basic Man.Finance 2d Ed. C & B

# PREFACE

The reception accorded the first edition of *Basic Managerial Finance* indicates general agreement with our position that development of both the institutional framework of finance and the theoretical and quantitative tools useful in finance is necessary in order to properly equip the financial manager to reach decisions aimed at maximizing the market value of his firm.

Another prime goal of this book is flexibility in several dimensions. This flexibility is achieved through the use of appendices to many of the chapters. One dimension of this flexibility is to permit the instructor to place emphasis on these areas of finance which fit the purposes of the course in the curriculum at his school. Another important dimension of flexibility is the level at which the text is used. We suspect that most first courses in finance involve students who have had courses in economics and accounting but not in statistics and only limited work in mathematics. The text without appendices serves this use very well. Only in the text of Chapter 10 on risk do we call for some knowledge of statistics. On the other hand, students with some training in statistics and mathematics are well served by the appendices.

Another dimension of flexibility is that this book can be used in a one-term first course by omission of some or all of the appendices. Or the two-term course can be served by including the appendices. Finally, the entire book can serve the basic finance course in the MBA program.

We believe this text to be the most comprehensive available, both as to the topics covered and as to methodology.

In the last several years finance has undergone many changes, and the impact of these changes, colors this revision. The highly volatile interest rates has shaken conventional practices as long-term, and short-term interest rates have developed a greater spread than at any time in modern history in 1971–1972 and then merged in 1973 only to develop the opposite spread in 1974. Inflation has reached proportions previously unknown to the United States. Rates on junior securities (preferred stock) moved lower than on senior securities (bonds) and now appear to be returning to the normal relationship. The academic world has struggled with these and other problems while the business world has called attention to the omission by theory of important variables.

Both of the authors are active in the business community. One is also a director of several companies (large and small) and a legal specialist in practice before the SEC. This book reflects experiences and insights on the "firing line." Businessmen are willing, even eager, to examine developments in financial theory. Once the legs under conventional practices have been shot away—as they have been—everyone joins the search for new principles.

Several related publications enhance the effectiveness of the textbook. The *Instructor's Manual* includes answers to the questions and problems at the end of each chapter and has extensive examination materials. The *Programmed Study Guide* is for student use and includes an outline of the text, a graduated set of problems for each chapter with many step-by-step solutions, and self-exercise examination and review questions and answers. The student using the *Programmed Study Guide* can work from the problems with solutions to the problems at the end of each chapter of the text. The text problems will in turn prepare the student to solve the remaining problems in the *Guide*. E.E. in the text, contains actual financial documents such as voting trust agreement, loan contract, complete underwriting documents such as agreement among selected dealers, and agreement among underwriters.

The enlargement of the small type in the first edition will undoubtedly find favor with the users of this revised edition.

We have spent a major part of our effort on carefully weaving the institutional and theoretical threads of finance more tightly together. All time series have been updated, and regulatory and other changes since the first edition are reflected in this edition. Recent advances in theory have been incorporated. The selected references at the end of each chapter have been brought up to date, previous problems have been altered, and new end-of-chapter problems added as have compound interest tables.

Special thanks are due to those who did very effective reviewing of our manuscript: Professors William Beranek of the University of Pittsburgh, Irwin Harvey of the University of Georgia, and Oscar Goodman of Roosevelt University. We fear slighting by mistaken omission some of the many professors who have made more limited contributions and hence do not append a list.

The typing assistance of Mrs. Ann Cost of Northwestern University and Karl E. Grunewald of Michigan State University is acknowledged with pleasure and sincere thanks.

ERWIN ESSER NEMMERS
Evanston, Illinois
ALAN E. GRUNEWALD
East Lansing, Michigan

# TABLE OF CONTENTS

*Part Two*

## THE MANAGEMENT OF WORKING CAPITAL



*Part Three*

## PROFITABILITY, RISK, AND THE FINANCIAL ENVIRONMENT

*Part Six*

**LONG–TERM FINANCING**

†

# PART ONE

# The Finance Function–

# An Overview

*

# 1
# The Financial Manager and the Firm

The financial manager is the focus of this book. As we forge the tools of finance, such as the techniques of analysis, financial planning, forecasting and monitoring the firm's activities, we will take the viewpoint of the financial manager. But, at appropriate times we will view the firm through the eyes of its sources of funds—its lenders, trade creditors, and owners.

To present a realistic view of financial decision making we begin by characterizing the firm as a system described in terms of a financial model that shows how the financial elements of the firm fit together. The objective of the financial manager, and thus of the model, is maximization of the market value of the firm.

## THE FINANCIAL MANAGER AND THE ECONOMY

The financial manager is a key member of the top management team. Observation of the real world shows that the effects of his decisions are felt throughout the firm. Though the final decision on all financial matters rests with the owners—the board of directors in the case of a corporation

—the financial manager has a major role in planning and raising the funds needed by the firm and then putting those funds to work profitably. The decisions he makes directly affect the fortunes of the firm and have an impact on the welfare of the economy.

Because business firms are responsible for the allocation of the largest portion of our nation's labor, raw materials, and capital resources, the more efficient the performance of the financial manager, the more prosperous both the firm and the economy will be. Thus we will study problems such as whether to expand plant capacity or increase inventories as well as methods used to compare the profitability of various investment proposals. New developments of recent years in the field of financial management suggest that further improvements will come rapidly.

Since the first manned flights to the moon, people are more aware than ever of the earth's limited resources. The old view that somewhere or somehow a new discovery will enhance the supply of our resources necessary to provide for future generations has been replaced by a strong emphasis on ecology. We cannot subscribe to the cynical view that in future years we will all be dead and the shortage of resources will be someone else's problem. We can no longer ignore the evidence around us: the exhaustion of natural gas supplies, which forces utilities to limit the number of new customers; electrical power shortages in the summer; polluted air, streams, and lakes; and millions of hungry people. The unfilled needs and wants of people in all societies are growing. We see all around us rapidly increasing demands on scarce and dwindling resources. The need for an efficient allocation of resources is greater than ever before. And it will be greater tomorrow than today.

Over the years many forms of organization have been developed. Of all these the business firm [1] remains the most efficient allocator of human and natural resources because it must meet the test of survival in the marketplace. Firms strive to survive, and in the process, to make a profit. Profit maximization as a goal has guided both economists and businessmen for decades, while the notions of ecology and social responsibility have only recently gained importance. The significance of the notions of ecology and social responsibility lies in their obvious relevance to the long-run interests of the firm and society. The firm must look beyond immediate profit and be involved in environmental issues such as clean air and water, nondiscriminatory hiring practices, fair wages to its employees, education, and consumer confidence in its products.

However, conflicts are bound to arise between the firm and society over *intermediate* goals designed to achieve a long-term objective, such as a higher standard of living. Is it more important to close *this* paper mill *today* thereby halting its pollution of the environment but also its income producing activity than to *wait* several years? Or is it more important

---

[1] Most business firms are privately owned. In others the federal government has a substantial interest such as in Comsat or Amtrak. In still others the government may be the sole stockholder—for example, the Volkswagen Works in West Germany before going public.

to build a college addition *today*? The real dispute is over priorities. Often problems are oversimplified. Thus the particular paper mill may choose to close rather than make an uneconomic investment in pollution-control equipment. But this may idle a community since, given the options offered by today's technology, no new paper mill would locate there. In such a situation what losses does society bear, what losses does the firm bear, and what losses do individuals bear?

## THE FIRM AS A SYSTEM

A firm may be viewed as a system operating in an environment and having three subsystems—production, distribution, and finance. If we think of this system as a "black box," we realize that inputs to this box can, from the point of view of the firm, be controllable variables, such as the levels of receivables and inventory to carry, and noncontrollable variables, such as the levels of interest rates and the rate of inflation. The outputs from the box are the results of the system which then act upon the input variables.

In our study of the firm as an allocator of resources, we are concerned with what goes on inside that black box in relation to the finance subsystem: its organization, its function, and its contribution to the prosperity of the firm and the welfare of society. We will be seeking optimal values for controllable variables and studying the impact of noncontrollable variables on possible solutions.

The finance function within this system is a pattern of activity based on an organizational framework. Decisions are made, actions taken, and results flow from the actions. These results are then monitored, and reports are sent back to the decision point where new decisions are made based on the feedback of information.

All decisions relating to the finance function might be classified into three types: investment, financing, and dividend. These three areas must be related to each other in allocating the firm's resources so as to produce the greatest private and social good.

*Investment.* This area concerns allocation of resources among new projects. The returns from these projects lie in the *future* but their costs must be paid *today*. Further, the return-over-cost expected in the future must be measured against the risk assumed in reaching for that profit. Meanwhile funds for the proposed projects may be diverted from what the firm is presently doing with these funds or may be raised by the sale of new securities.

*Financing.* This area involves the capital structure of the firm—the percentage of the firm's financing obtained through debt (long- or short-term), preferred stock, common stock, and retained earnings.

*Dividend.* This area involves the timing and the percentage of earnings to be paid out in dividends to preferred and common stockholders. That portion not paid out is retained earnings, an important source of further financing.

## MAXIMIZATION OF THE MARKET VALUE OF THE FIRM

The test of the firm's *stewardship*, or efficient use, of funds under its control is the value of the firm—how much people are willing to pay for the company as measured by the prices they bid for its securities. The more efficiently a firm allocates its resources, the higher the earnings available to security holders will be in relation to risk.

The introduction of the concept of *risk* distinguishes modern financial management. Older economic theory holds that firms will strive to maximize profits: that marginal revenue equals marginal cost, but that firms operate in a world of certainty. Every firm is forced by its competition to produce as efficiently as possible, and those operating very efficiently will earn maximum profits and serve society by being the mechanism for allocating resources optimally.

While economics emphasizes profit maximization as a guide to explaining firm behavior, finance focuses on maximizing the value of the firm. For example, a firm can increase total profits simply by issuing common stock and buying short-term government bonds with the proceeds, but because this transaction will lower the *rate* of earning of the firm's assets, the prices of the firm's securities will fall.

Second, a firm can obtain financing from a variety of sources—from suppliers, from banks, by issuing bonds, by issuing common stock or by retaining earnings. For example, borrowing large sums from a bank may appear cheap in terms of interest paid and increased earnings per share, but the risk of the company not being able to repay the bank loan will also be increased. Stockholders may then sell their shares, driving down the market price. The signal of the market to the firm would be that the firm is not utilizing its borrowing power efficiently. The risk complexion of a firm is affected by the manner in which the firm is financed: the relative proportions of debt and ownership funds used.

Third, a firm has the opportunity to invest in a variety of proposals, each promising a different percent return on the capital invested in the proposal but representing a different degree of risk. The firm might select a proposal promising a high yield but also representing a high degree of risk. Upon learning of the decision, stockholders may sell their shares if they feel that the firm's earnings prospects do not warrant the degree of risk involved. Again, the signal of the market to the firm would be that its allocation of resources is not as efficient as possible. The risk complexion of a firm is affected by the composition of its assets: the relative proportions of cash, receivables, inventory, and plant and equipment, and the type of projects in which each of these assets is invested.

Thus we take maximization of the value of the firm as the guiding objective of our financial management model—an objective that reflects both the ability of the firm to earn a return on its assets and the risk the firm has assumed in reaching for those earnings. This means maximization of the market value of *all* outstanding securities. However, our primary focus is on maximizing the value of the common stock, which is the ultimate test of the efficiency with which the firm is allocating its resources among the competing uses available and risks they entail. If the value of the firm's common stock is high, this means that profits are high relative to risk, which in turn will mean a high value for the firm's bonds and preferred stock.

Maximization of the value of the firm requires integration of the financing, purchasing, production, and marketing functions of the firm. The finance function, as we have said, encompasses the investment, financing, and dividend decisions that determine the risk-return character of the firm. Investors place a value on this risk-return package by the prices they are willing to pay for the firm's securities.

These notions may be expressed in the form of a stock valuation model in which the risk-return complexion of the firm is a function of the investment, financing, and dividend decisions and where the value per share of common stock is in turn a function of the risk-return complexion of the firm.

$$\text{Risk, return} = g[\text{Investment, Financing, Dividend}]$$

and

$$\text{Value per share of common stock} = f[\text{Risk, Return}].$$

### Maximization versus Satisficing

Firms are organized to produce and distribute goods and services in anticipation of generating *earnings*—sales minus costs (including taxes). The profit motive is the engine that drives the economy. Individuals commit their funds and talents to those endeavors and at those times that attractive earnings can reasonably be expected. Consumers choose among goods and services by weighing their utilities and prices, but earnings expectations allocate resources among firms and within firms. Funds flow to industries where earnings expectations are high, and the individual firm allocates its available funds to projects that promise the best rate of return, always considering the risk involved.

A necessary condition for all this to take place is that the firm survive through time.[2] Survival requires an organization that is capable of cooperative effort, that has an awareness that the firm exists in an ongoing society and economy, that operates in a changing technological environment, and that generates the profits that are necessary to cover the risks of doing business in an uncertain environment. People are unwilling to expose their capital to a chance of loss unless there is a proportionate prospect of a return. Thus risk-taking is a genuine cost of business operations —one that must be covered if the firm is to continue to fulfill its function of supplying society with desirable goods and services at fair prices. There is no conflict between the goals of maximizing market value of the firm and satisficing. Those who say they seek satisficing simply have a greater risk aversion than those who say they seek maximization. Those satisficing simply maximize at a lower level of risk.

---

[2] Economics texts tend to stress profit maximization, but business leaders frequently speak of the importance of a satisfactory profit. See R. N. Anthony, "The Trouble with Profit Maximization," *Harvard Business Review*, 38 (November–December 1960), pp. 126–134; and P. F. Drucker, "Business Objectives and Survival Needs," *Journal of Business*, 31 (April 1958), pp. 81–90.

### Management Goals versus Stockholder Goals

The intermediate goals of management and stockholders can be and frequently are at variance,[3] though their long-run objectives usually coincide. In a firm whose stock is widely distributed any individual outside stockholder (not part of management) can have little influence on a given decision. Ownership and control are separated. This often gives rise to a conflict of goals.

Stockholders may prefer that the firm assume more risk by financing with debt to increase earnings; management may prefer to play it safe by using retained earnings. The stockholder can diversify his portfolio, but it is harder for management to diversify its job security risk. Stockholders may prefer a higher cash dividend to provide more spendable income; management may prefer a larger cash balance to give it greater maneuverability. Stockholders may prefer a correct statement of earnings and financial condition to evaluate their investments properly; management may prefer to overstate their earnings (say, to float a new stock issue at a better price) or understate them (reduce pressures for wage increases) or alternate both of these practices in order to show a consistent earnings growth pattern.[4] These conflicts are almost always resolved in favor of management's views. Stockholder revolts are rare, and even more rarely do they succeed.[5]

Though a separation of ownership and management functions exists, the conflict of their views can be overemphasized. The pecuniary interests of both groups are reasonably similar.[6] The stockholdings of top management of major companies such as GM, IBM, du Pont, and so on, are larger than commonly supposed. A considerable portion of top management's compensation is provided by stock options in lieu of salary. In fact, in many cases stock compensation, dividends, bonuses, and capital gains outweigh the compensation received in the form of a fixed salary.

### Liquidity versus Profitability

Another basic conflict facing the financial manager is liquidity versus profitability. A firm may be highly profitable and yet go into bankruptcy because it is unable to meet commitments when due. With the urge to reach for earnings the firm may leave itself with insufficient liquid reserves to meet an unexpectedly heavy drain of cash: an uninsured catastrophe may occur and require funds; payments on accounts receivable may decline sharply, thus depriving the firm of a substantial cash inflow; or a planned loan from a bank may not materialize.

---

[3] G. Donaldson, "Financial Goals: Management vs. Stockholders," *Harvard Business Review*, 41 (May–June 1963), pp. 116–129.

[4] This is euphemistically called "income smoothing."

[5] With the rising earnings and stock prices of the 1960s, proxy contests were rather rare. Relative calm prevailed in the executive suites; in 1971 that calm was broken. A rash of proxy fights broke out as stockholders became dissatisfied with sagging profits and stock prices. See *The Wall Street Journal*, May 14, 1971, p. 26.

[6] W. G. Lewellen, "Management and Ownership in the Large Firm," *Journal of Finance*, 24 (May 1969), pp. 299–322.

The financial manager can drive down the risk of a shortage of liquid funds by increasing the percentage of the firm's assets held in cash or near cash items. But this result can be achieved only at the expense of the profitability of the firm—that is, through reducing the percentage of assets that are "earning" assets.

Some *increase* in liquidity may actually improve the profitability of the firm by lowering the interest rate charged by lenders. With a lowered interest rate costs are reduced and profits increased. The firm that has backed itself into a corner of illiquidity finds itself with an increased *cost* of borrowed money and an increased *risk* of bankruptcy.

## WIDENING HORIZONS OF FINANCIAL MANAGERS

Adequate funds are a prerequisite to launching a business venture. Countless firms have failed because of insufficient capital. In the post-World War II period perhaps the most notable example was the Tucker Motor Car Company, which failed before mass production could get started because of lack of capital and the firm's inability to secure the necessary suppliers. Of course, once the firm is organized[7] and a profitable level of operations is achieved, adequate capital does not guarantee continued profitability. Success is a continuum, made up of a stream of decisions regarding the raising of capital, maintenance of liquidity, and the investment of funds in income-producing assets (plant, equipment, real estate, or even other companies). W. C. Durant, the organizer of General Motors in 1908, lost control of the company in 1920–1921 when a working capital crisis brought Morgan and du Pont money into the firm. But Ford, through financial maneuvering, managed to retain control of his company when faced with a similar working capital crisis. The failure of the Public Bank in Detroit in 1967 resulted from the emphasis on large prospective earnings. Many high-risk loans were made in an effort to generate large earnings, but the risks proved too large for the bank. When borrowers started defaulting, the equity cushion was insufficient to absorb the losses. The bank failed, and its assets and liabilities were taken over by another Detroit bank. One afternoon the Public Bank closed its doors at the regular time and opened the next morning as the Bank of the Commonwealth.

The financial manager today is concerned with many broad policy areas. The growth of large-scale enterprise, rapid technological change, shortened product life cycles, shifts in products and markets, heavy tax rates, and narrowing profit margins have led the financial manager to see his role in the business enterprise in terms of an ever-widening horizon.

---

[7] See *The Wall Street Journal*, April 30, 1971, pp. 1 ff. for information about how Viatron Computer Systems Corp. lost $30 million on sales of only $2.5 million. Viatron's blunders included losing track of $6 million in debts, expanding production during a sluggish economy, pricing its computer terminal too low, and making its biggest shipments to a customer that could not or would not pay. Its stock was issued in 1969 at $15 per share, soared to $61, and fell to about $1 before the company went into bankruptcy.

## ORGANIZATIONAL FRAMEWORK FOR FINANCIAL MANAGEMENT

The finance function is not a standardized operation. It varies from firm to firm, depending on the size of the company and industry. In small firms the owner generally handles the acquisition of funds and management of its capital. He arranges for needed loans, extends credit, collects receivables, draws up a cash budget, and manages the cash account. Little delegation of functions exists. There may be little formal planning, and cash crises are often frequent. Funds at what the owner considers a reasonable cost are scarce.

In medium-sized firms specialization becomes apparent. The top financial officer may be called treasurer, controller, or vice-president of finance. His role varies with the policy of the firm and his own abilities. He may be responsible for the credit and collection department, the accounting department, the annual reports, or the capital budgeting program.

In a large firm, the top financial manager is likely to be a vice-president of finance,[8] reporting directly to the president, and in many cases he may be on the board of directors. He has the responsibility for financial policy and planning. Under him may be the treasurer and controller. The treasurer is responsible for arranging to meet the liquidity needs of the firm, and the controller serves as the chief monitor of the overall performance of the firm. In some large firms all financial responsibilities are divided between a treasurer and controller.

Important among the responsibilities of the financial executive is long-range planning: estimating industry trends, forecasting revenues and costs, evaluating ways of raising needed capital, and budgeting. The financial manager participates in decisions involving dividend policy, the acquisition of other firms, the refinancing of maturing debt, and the introduction of a major new product. Managing the firm's working capital (such as, arranging for short-term loans), supervising the extension of credit and the collection of receivables, preparing the cash budget, and disbursing funds occupy the major portion of the financial manager's time. Thus, to fulfill his position competently, he needs a good background in accounting, a thorough understanding of financial management, and an intimate knowledge of the operations of the firm whose activities he is guiding. A knowledge of operations research methods, management information systems, and computer science is also important.

## LEGAL FRAMEWORK FOR FINANCIAL MANAGEMENT

The financial manager needs to understand the implications of firms operating as proprietorships, partnerships, or corporations, because the legal form of an organization will substantially affect such things as the risk borne by the residual owners, the ability of the firm to raise outside funds from such sources as banks, issuing debt and stock, restrictions on the payment of profits to owners, and taxes. But first let us

---

[8] A third of the firms in *Fortune*'s list of the 500 largest firms have established the position of vice-president of finance. See J. R. Krum, "Who Controls Finance in the Giants," *Financial Executive*, 38 (March 1970), pp. 20–29.

consider the economic importance of the different forms of a business organization.

In the fields of agriculture, forestry, and fisheries, in transportation, and in wholesale and retail trade, the vast majority of businesses are proprietorships. In the field of manufacturing, proprietorships and corporations account for about 45 percent and 48 percent respectively, of the number of businesses. But corporations are responsible for more than 98 percent of the volume, the remainder being split between proprietorships and partnerships. In wholesale and retail trade, corporations account for about 19 percent of the businesses but do 79 percent of the volume. Proprietorships account for about 71 percent of the businesses and do only 17 percent of the volume.[9]

### Sole Proprietorship

A *sole proprietorship* is a business owned and operated by a single individual. Control is shared with no one. The owner formulates policy, puts the plans into operation, assumes the total risk of loss, and receives all profit. He is solely liable for the debts of the firm. Even his personal assets may be seized if those of the firm are not sufficient to meet the firm's obligations. The liability of the owner is unlimited, but he also has sole control. Despite this unlimited liability feature, most businesses operate as sole proprietorships.

A sole proprietorship is treated under law as part of the owner's assets. Thus, the profits of the firm are considered under the federal income tax law as income to the owner, whether the latter draws a salary or leaves all of the profits in the business. The sole proprietorship itself pays no federal income tax.

The sole proprietorship is restricted to small operations that can be financed with the limited funds of the owner and short-term bank loans. Long-term funds, if any, are likely to come from a mortgage, either on the real estate of the firm or on the house of the proprietor. Because of the small size of the firm the owner is usually planner, financier, action man, and controller all in one. Organizational ease, flexibility, and the avoidance of the double taxation imposed on a corporation,[10] make the sole proprietorship the most common type of firm despite unlimited liability. But its life cycle is short. A sole proprietorship terminates with the death of the owner. Sometimes a new owner takes over the business, but frequently the operation disappears with the owner's death.

### Partnership

In many ways a partnership[11] is like a sole proprietorship but it has several owners.

---

[9] *Statistics of Income*, 1970, U.S. Business Income Tax Returns, U.S. Treasury Department, Internal Revenue Service (Washington D.C., Government Printing Office, 1973), pp. 4 ff.

[10] In the case of a corporation, income tax is paid first on the profit of the corporation and then on the dividends received by the owners.

[11] See the Uniform Partnership Act, National Conference of Commissioners on Uniform State Laws, Chicago.

A *general partnership* may be established by an oral or written agreement stating who the partners are and by additional provisions, such as the business to be conducted and the assets to be contributed by each of the partners. A general partnership also can come into being when two or more people *act* as partners in the operation of a business enterprise for profit, even though neither of the partners considers that there is a partnership.

Control of the business is shared among the general partners. Each can bind the others in dealings of the firm. A foolish contract made by one general partner cannot be disavowed by the remaining general partners.

The general partnership form carries with it unlimited liability. Should difficulty arise, each partner may be held responsible to the full extent of even his personal assets for the obligations of the firm. The partnership agreement may state in what proportion the obligations of the partnership are to fall among the partners, but such a provision is not binding on outside creditors. All general partners are "jointly and severally" liable, which means that the partners are collectively and individually liable to the full extent of all their assets for the debts of the firm. If one partner cannot meet his proportionate share of the partnership obligations, the remaining partner or partners are required to meet them. Of course, such a partner has recourse against any remaining assets of the defaulting partner, but generally no assets remain.

The general partnership is not considered a legal entity and is not taxed separately under the income tax law; rather, each partner pays personal income tax on his share of partnership earnings even if he has not yet received that share. Profits are divided equally unless otherwise specified in the partnership agreement.

Partnerships can generally engage in larger-scale ventures than sole proprietorships because of their ability to draw on the capital of several people. The number of partners is usually restricted by the unlimited liability feature. Individuals are reluctant to enter into an association that involves committing all of their assets as a pledge for obligations incurred by others even though it may be in behalf of the business.

A general partnership legally terminates with the death of one of the general partners. The agreement is also terminated if a member withdraws, becomes bankrupt, or becomes mentally incompetent. Partnership agreements frequently provide for the formation of a new partnership should the old one be dissolved as a result of one of these events.

Sometimes it is desirable to admit a new partner. The position of a deceased partner may need to be filled, the firm may require capital, or another key member may be required. Each partner must approve the admission of the new member. Naturally, the unlimited liability feature makes existing partners of a firm understandably reluctant to admit new partners unless they have complete trust and confidence in the new member.

*Limited Partnership* The hazards of unlimited liability can be reduced for some (but not all) of the partners through a *limited partnership* agreement, which must be in writing and recorded as a public document in the county where the business is conducted. Such a firm must have at least one general partner, who has unlimited liability, and may have one or more limited partners, whose liabilities are limited to the amounts of their contributions. In short, limited partners are primarily investors in the firm. To retain limited liability status, a limited partner may not permit his name to be used in the business name unless he is identified as a limited partner, and he may not conduct business for the firm or participate in the firm's management. If he engages in any of these activities, he will be held to be a general partner with unlimited liability. The interest of a limited partner is transferable to another person without dissolving the partnership. Death or insanity of a limited partner does not dissolve the partnership.

### Corporation

The corporate form is suited to the needs of medium-sized and large firms. The most significant feature of a corporation is the limited liability of the owners. Once a stockholder pays to the corporation the full par value of the shares, or the stated value in the event that the stock carries no par value, the shares become fully paid and nonassessable. Neither the original purchaser nor any subsequent purchaser is liable for additional capital to meet the debt of the corporation.

Limited liability for shareholders results because the corporation is considered a legal entity and has an existence separate from the owners. Each stockholder is the owner of that part of the corporation represented by his proportion of all the shares, but none owns the corporation's assets. The property of the corporation is held in the corporate name; the firm can act in its own name, can sue, and can be sued. The death of any shareholder does not affect the life of the corporation. The corporation, unless the charter or law of the state regarding incorporation specifies otherwise, has perpetual life. Business operations may cease and nothing more than a shell may remain, but the corporation continues to exist as long as it retains its charter.

Limited shareholder liability and the ease of share transfer have enabled corporations to raise the large sums of money required to finance the vast industrial organizations of today. Stockholders are willing to invest limited sums of money to finance a business, and creditors are willing to lend large sums of money when there exists a large base of equity funds to protect against loss. The stockholders commit their funds and assume the risks in the hope of earning a good return on their investments. Lenders seek a fair rate of interest on their funds and the return of their capital at maturity.

It may seem strange that a bank will lend more money to a corporation with its limited liability than it would to a partnership with the same amount of equity funds and unlimited liability. Two reasons are (1) the bank or other creditor feels no compunction about exhausting the corporation if that is necessary to effect repayment of a loan but would not proceed so swiftly to bankrupt a group of individuals, and (2) the bank or other creditor can get a complete accounting statement of a corporation, but in the case of a partnership any statement of the individual affairs of the partners beyond the accounts of the firm is uncertain and, even if obtained, changes quickly and calls for a probing that is distasteful to all concerned.

A corporation is formed when one or more persons, called *incorporators,* file *articles of incorporation* in a particular state. If the firm is small and its operations will be carried on in only one state, the organization is usually incorporated in that state. If the firm is to operate in several states, such factors as the incorporation tax, the annual franchise tax, the provisions of the incorporation laws, and the extent to which these laws have been tested and defined in the courts are considered in selecting the state of incorporation.

The articles of incorporation are filed with the Secretary of State of the state of incorporation. Once the articles are certified, they are the *charter,* which is a contract between the state and the firm and between the firm and its stockholders. The charter must specify, at the least, the corporation's name, the name and address of the registered agent of the corporation, the purpose of the corporation, the amount of authorized capital stock including number of shares and their par or no-par value, and the name of the incorporators. Some state laws require that before business can actually be transacted a minimum capital must be paid into the firm.

The final step before the corporation begins to transact business is the adoption of the bylaws by the incorporators, directors, or stockholders. The *bylaws* are the rules by which the internal affairs of the firm are to be managed. They are subordinate to the charter and are not publicly recorded. The bylaws contain provisions relating to time, place, and purpose of stockholders' meetings; number, qualifications, and term of office of directors; timing of directors' meetings; the designated officers and their duties; stock transfer arrangements; and many other items.

The corporation is subject to federal corporate income tax laws as a separate entity.[12] Profits are fully taxed, whether they are paid out in dividends or not. Stockholders also pay income tax on the portion of earnings paid out in dividends. Thus, corporate profits paid out in dividends are taxed both at the corporate level and at the shareholder level, resulting in double taxation. This tax policy has influenced corporations to both (1) use more debt in financing because interest is tax deductible to the corporation and (2) to finance a larger percentage of their capital expenditures out of retained earnings than would be the case if there were no double taxation.[13] Figure 1–1 outlines the financial control structure of a corporation.

---

[12] Subchaper S of the *Internal Revenue Code* permits corporations meeting specific conditions to elect to be taxed as partnerships; they are then known as "Subchapter S corporations." *Internal Revenue Code,* § 1371. This legislation was passed in order to provide tax relief for corporate businesses with no more than 10 stockholders.

[13] In 1972 Canada took the first step to eliminate the distortion caused by double taxation of a corporation with a provision that Canadian-controlled corporations can annually deduct the first $50,000 of dividends paid to stockholders in determining corporate income subject to the corporate income tax. Any unused dividend deduction of one year can be carried forward to future years. Similarly to reduce corporate taxation, Sweden and Japan have established special depreciation allowances. In the case of Sweden, any asset other than buildings can be depreciated in five years or less.

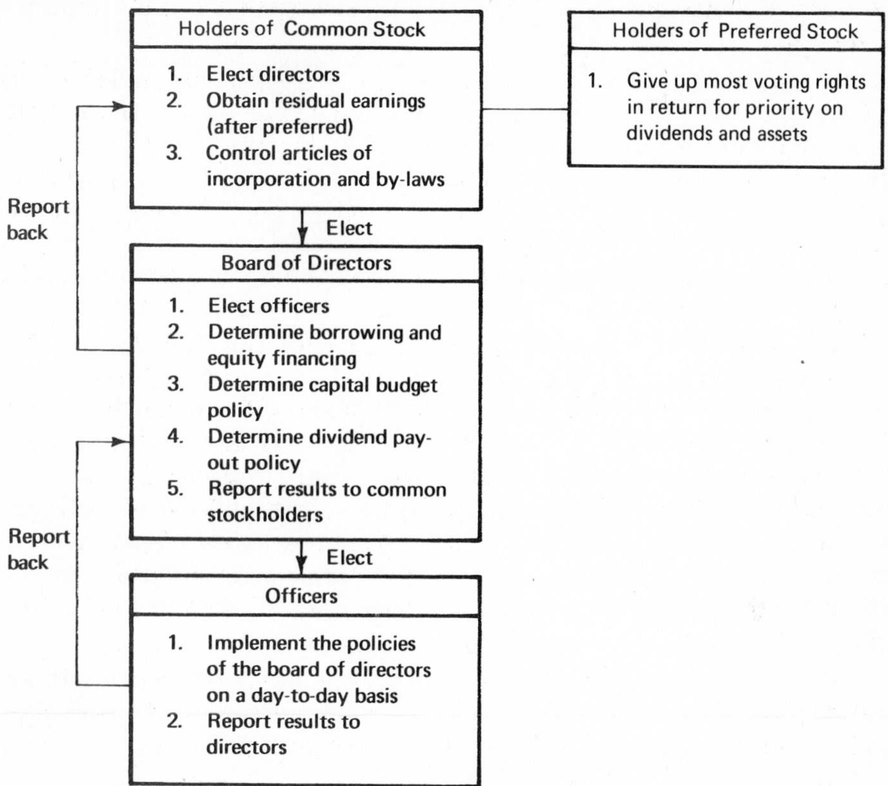


Figure 1–1 The financial control structure of a corporation.

## SUMMARY

The welfare of society requires efficient allocation of resources. The business firm generally does this job well. The value of the firm is measured by the prices investors are willing to pay for its securities, and these prices indicate how well a particular firm is doing its job.

The goal of the financial manager is maximization of the value of the firm. Achievement of this goal requires the financial manager to integrate financing, investment, and dividend decisions. In his daily activities the financial manager, whether his title is treasurer, controller, or vice-president of finance, must provide for the liquidity needs of the firm and be concerned with its profitability. The financial manager's reach for profits is constrained by the firm's need for liquidity. Also in reaching for profits he must consider the element of risk. Risk and return are the major elements influencing the value of the firm.

As a long-run objective management and stockholders may agree on maximization of the value of the firm, but they may be at variance concerning intermediate goals. Stockholders may prefer that the firm reach for higher earnings by assuming more risk, and management may prefer to play it safe. Stockholders may prefer a correct statement of earnings and financial condition, and management may prefer either more favorable or less favorable financial statements depending on the current situation. Almost all of these conflicts are resolved in favor of management.

The major forms of business organization are the sole proprietorship, the partnership, and the corporation. Most businesses are sole proprietorships, but corporations are responsible for most of the volume. The proprietorship and partnership are easily organized. But limited life and the unlimited liability feature make these forms unsuitable for large-scale operations. Limited liability, the ease of share transference, and long life enable the corporation to raise large sums to engage in major ventures.

### Study Questions

1. Why must each of us be concerned with the efficient allocation of economic resources?
2. Discuss risk-taking as a cost of doing business.
3. Compare the process of resource allocation in a free economy, in a planned economy, and in an efficiently run firm.
4. Contrast the activities of planning, organizing, executing, and controlling in the small and the large firm.
5. Discuss some of the implications of a firm's financial decisions upon the economy.
6. The establishment of a standard set of solutions to financial problems which is operational and will lead to good results is not possible. Discuss.
7. Give the three major decisions into which all the decisions related to the finance function can be classified. Describe each.
8. Distinguish between the financial management model and the elementary economic model.
9. Why do we take maximization of the market value of the firm as the objective of our financial management model, and what is the significance of this objective to society?
10. At what points are the intermediate goals of management and stockholders frequently at variance?
11. Generally it is not possible for an industrial organization to be highly liquid and highly profitable at the same time. Discuss. Is the same true for an individual managing his own investment assets? What exists in the economy that prevents liquidity and profitability from being jointly available?
12. Why is the proprietorship an ideal type of business organization for the small venture?
13. Contrast the characteristics of the sole proprietorship, the partnership, and the corporation.
14. Without the limited liability feature of corporations large-scale enterprise could not exist. Discuss this statement.

### Problems

1. Study the histories of several well-known firms that have failed, such as Penn Central, Four Seasons Nursing Homes, or Viatron Computer Systems Corp., and ascertain the extent to which the failure can be ascribed to financial decisions.

2. Examine a random sample of annual reports of industrial and public utility firms that indicate the occupation of each of its directors. Note the number and position of those representing the finance area.

3. Tom, Dick, and Harry plan to enter the computer field making electronic components for major manufacturers. Each has a strong technical background and feels confident of the success of the firm. The three, however, are weak in finance and ask you to classify the following terms so they will know whether the terms are balance sheet or income statement items and, if balance sheet items, whether they are current asset, current liability, fixed asset or net worth items. Check the glossary of financial terms at the end of the text if you are unsure of the definition of a current asset and current liability.

a. cash
b. plant and equipment
c. sales
d. raw material costs
e. accounts payable
f. cost of goods sold
g. inventory: raw material
h. bank loan (90 day note)
i. common stock
j. profit
k. retained earnings
l. inventory: finished goods.

4. A new firm, Star Merchandising, is to be launched with a capital of $2 million, which will be adequate to acquire the necessary building and equipment.

Working capital will be obtained initially through bank borrowing and credit from suppliers. Sales the first year are expected to average $800,000 monthly. The cost of goods sold is estimated at 70 percent of the selling price. The firm expects to break even the first month. A 30-day inventory of goods must be maintained. Cash is held at 2 percent of monthly sales. Star sells on a net 30-day basis, but its suppliers extend terms of net 60 days.

Draw up a balance sheet of Star Merchandising as of the opening day of business ready to sell merchandise and another after 30 days. Accounts payable are $736,000 and $800,000, respectively. Ignore taxes and accrued items such as depreciation. Do you have any advice for these young men? Does it appear that the firm is already slow at the end of these 30 days?

At the beginning of the second year sales are expected to jump to $1.8 million monthly but no profit has been earned. Toward the latter part of the year the firm expects to begin earning substantial profit and estimates it will close the year with earnings of $1.5 million.

Draw up the balance sheet of the firm after several months of operation into the second year (ignoring profits) and at the close of the second year. Building and equipment will be renewed as they are depreciated and for purposes of this problem may be ignored. Accounts payable are $1.3 million on each date. Do you have any further advice for these young men? Is it substantially different from your earlier advice?

### Selected References

Anthony, R. N., "The Trouble with Profit Maximization," *Harvard Business Review,* 38 (November–December 1960), pp. 126–134.

Branch, Ben, "Corporate Objectives and Market Performance," *Financial Management,* 2 (Summer 1973), pp. 24–29.

Dewing, A. S., *The Financial Policy of Corporations,* vol. 1, 5th ed. New York: Ronald Press Company, 1953, Chap. 1.

Donaldson, G., "Financial Goals: Management vs. Stockholders," *Harvard Business Review,* 41 (May–June 1963), pp. 116–129.

Drucker, P. F., "Business Objectives and Survival Needs," *Journal of Business,* 31 (April 1958), pp. 81–90.

Forrester, J. W., *Industrial Dynamics,* Cambridge, Mass.: M. I. T. Press, 1962, Chaps. 1 and 2.

Krum, J. R., "Who Controls Finance in the Giants?" *Financial Executive,* 38 (March 1970), pp. 20–29.

Lewellen, W. G., "Management and Ownership in the Large Firm," *Journal of Finance,* 24 (May 1969), pp. 299–322.

Moag, J. S., W. T. Carleton, and E. M. Lerner, "Defining the Finance Function: A Model-Systems Approach," *Journal of Finance,* 22 (December 1967), pp. 543–555.

Weston, J. F., *The Scope and Methodology of Finance,* Englewood Cliffs, N. J.: Prentice-Hall, Inc., 1966.

———, "New Themes in Finance," *Journal of Finance,* 29 (March 1974), pp. 237–243.

# 2

# The Flow of Funds in a Firm

## FLOW OF FUNDS SYSTEM

A firm may be likened to a living organism and characterized as a system. Each major activity of the firm, such as production, distribution, or finance, may be compared to a vital organ. The flow of funds—means of payment—through the firm may be thought of as the life blood of the organism. Figure 2–1 shows the flows of the firm.

Taking a snapshot to stop the flow action, we can consider the assets of the firm as economic values (a stock concept) of the firm in various forms. The dollar is the unit of measure.[1] With this graphic representation, the flow of funds (flow of economic values) from one asset to another may be analyzed.

The concept of the flow of funds is vital to understanding both the analysis and management of a firm's working capital: cash, accounts re-

[1] Because of instability of its purchasing power, the dollar is not a scientific unit of measurement. A ruler that one day has 12 inches and some days later only 9 inches would be a quite unacceptable measuring device. But in business we assume the purchasing power of the dollar remains stable.

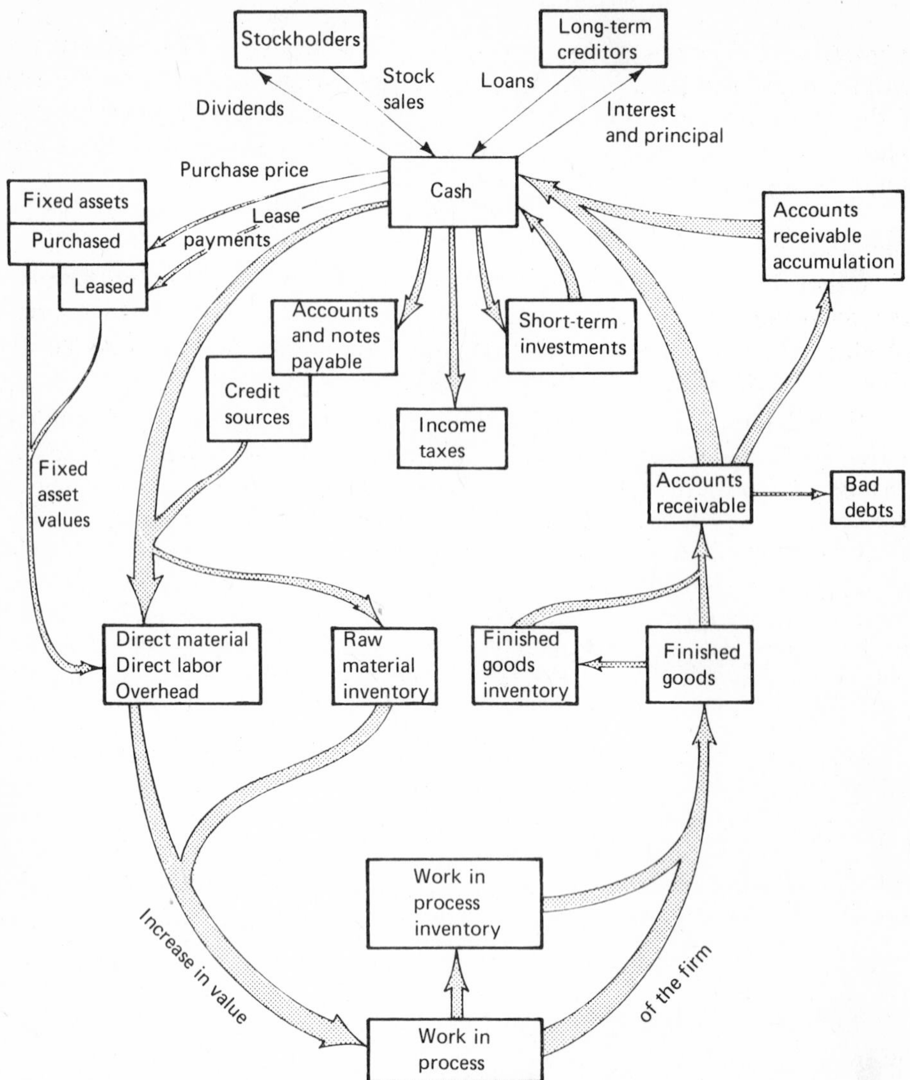


Figure 2–1 The flow of funds through a firm.

ceivable, and inventory. Most firms have substantial sums invested in working capital, investments that require important decisions from the financial manager. The skill with which he makes these decisions will have a direct influence on the value of the firm.

For example, if a firm faces declining sales but continues producing at a previously set level, inventory will rise. This may lead to large losses from the overhanging inventory, and, as a result, the earnings and value of the firm will decline. Or a firm may be growing rapidly, with its expansion financed largely from the firm's cash balances. This reduction in liquidity may increase risks and cause stockholders to sell, driving down the price of the firm's stock and thus the value of the firm.

Funds enter the firm in the form of cash or credit, are converted into goods and services, and then are reconverted into cash through the sale of goods and services. The process is then repeated. The risk-return[2] complexion of the firm is determined in part by the decisions on the size of the investment (how much funds?), each asset category (cash, receivables, and so on), and the speed of the flow of funds (conversion of economic values) from one asset category to another.

### Cash: The Focal Point of the Flow of Funds

Generally the first cash available to the firm is provided by the owners: proprietor, partners, or original stockholders. Once the firm is established, credit may be obtained from suppliers, additional cash may be obtained through a bank loan, and needed equipment may be leased.

If the firm is a manufacturing operation, cash and credit are applied to the purchase of raw materials, labor, supplies, heat, light, and so on. Through manufacturing, the raw materials are converted into work in process and then into finished goods. With the sale of the merchandise, the finished goods are converted into accounts receivable, and collection of the receivables reinstates the cash to begin a new cycle. As the process continues and if no losses occur, the sum of the economic values of the firm will be higher at the end of the period than at the beginning. The increase in funds represents the profit the firm earned through its goods-creating activities.

However, the cash position of the firm may be higher or lower at the end of the period than at the beginning, regardless of the profit. The firm's cash balance will rise if the cash inflows of the period exceed the cash outflows of the same period. If the reverse is true, the cash balance will fall. On the other hand, profit or loss, and hence the increase or decrease in the total value of the firm, depends on whether sales (both cash and credit sales) plus other revenue for the period exceed the cost of operation.

As the flow of funds proceeds from one stage to another, a portion of the flow may be shunted into work-in-process inventory, finished-goods inventory, or accounts receivable accumulation. If the production, distribution, and collection flows were fully synchronized there would be no need for these reservoirs of raw materials, work in process, or finished goods. However, purchasing of materials, sale of the merchandise, and collection of receivables usually occur at different rates. It may be cheaper to purchase in large quantities and store raw materials to meet future production needs rather than to gear purchasing to production. Or it may be more economical to produce in long production runs and build up finished-goods inventory to meet future sales than to vary production at the same rate that the sale of goods is varying. Collection policies may be relaxed or trade terms lengthened to meet competition, causing receivables to increase. Consequently, there are reservoirs of raw materials, work in process, finished goods, and accounts receivable to permit the activities of purchas-

---

[2] The firm has alternative combinations of risk and return available. With many higher risk projects, the *expected* return is higher. Lower risk projects offer lower returns. For example credit terms of 60 days rather than 30 days may increase sales volume and (perhaps) profit, but these will be achieved by selling to marginal customers with a higher bad debt risk.

ing, production, sales, and collection to be carried on at different rates. The levels in each reservoir (funds invested) are like water in a bathtub. When the flows from the faucet into the bathtub and the flow out through the waste-pipe are altered, the level of the water in the bathtub changes. A change in the amount of funds invested in a particular asset may depend on either outside economic forces, such as a change in raw material prices, or inside decisions, such as a decision to increase production or change credit terms.

When the economic values return to the cash form, they can be used to pay trade creditors, make interest and principal payments, pay income taxes, declare dividends, purchase plant and equipment, and begin the process all over again. If more cash is available than required to continue the purchasing-manufacturing-sale process, the excess can be invested temporarily in short-term securities. If a greater amount of funds is needed than can be withdrawn from the cash account (allowing for a necessary minimum cash balance), additional funds can be obtained through the sale of short-term investments, through a bank loan, or through the sale of bonds or stock.

### Subsidiary Funds Flow Circuits

The mainstream of the flow consists of cash and credit through inventory to receivables, and back into cash. A portion of the cash may be deflected to acquire short-term investments, to pay income taxes, and to reduce accounts payable. There are also two subsidiary flows: (1) the two-way flow from long-term creditors and owners to the firm and back again, and (2) the flow of funds into plant and equipment and their recapture through a noncash charge of depreciation against cost of goods sold. This flow occurs as long as the firm is producing and selling goods—even if it is merely breaking even on profits. But this flow is reduced by the extent of any loss, and if the loss exceeds the depreciation charge, funds are actually flowing out of the firm.

A glance back at Figure 2–1 will reveal a difference between these two subsidiary flows. The first is completely separate from the mainstream of the flow of funds. It is outside the flow of cash, inventory, receivables, and back to cash. The second, though outside the mainstream, is still part of it. The funds invested in plant and equipment are converted into the value of the product.

The combined minimum level of cash, inventory, and receivables is called *permanent working capital.* This is the amount of working capital necessary for the firm to conduct its normal level of operations. Since the level of activity fluctuates, it is difficult to determine the efficient level of permanent working capital. Thus, when operations expand and the firm requires additional plant and equipment, working capital is frequently tapped as a source of funds to finance, at least in part, the needed assets. And as funds flow from working capital into fixed assets, the firm becomes less liquid.

### Policy Decisions and the Cash Balance

Decisions in practically every area of the firm have an impact on the flow of cash—in or out—and hence on the cash balance. For example, a decision by a seasonal business to lower *operating* costs by leveling out production will require the *carrying* costs of a larger average inventory. Cash will flow out earlier to purchase labor and materials for the build-up of finished goods in inventory. Or, expanding sales by granting more liberal credit terms will result in a rise in receivables and a decrease in cash that is available to replace the inventory sold but not yet paid for. Conversely, initiation of a stringent credit policy and tough collection procedures will cause a spurt in the cash inflow. But purchasing in larger quantities to reduce the number of orders and freight costs will cause the average inventory level to rise and the cash balance to fall. Acquiring modern machinery to reduce operating costs will result in a major cash expenditure. Profits may rise *over a long period* due to the reduced costs, but the cash balance goes down *immediately.* A decision to borrow from the bank or to sell bonds, while increasing the firm's liabilities, will immediately increase its cash balance. The sale of common stock will also increase the cash balance. The purchase of inventory by means of trade credit bypasses the necessity for immediate cash payment. The cash balance of the purchasing firm is temporarily higher than it would be if the goods were bought cash on delivery.

These illustrations highlight the fact that almost every decision will have an impact on the cash flows of the firm and hence on the cash balance. As management seeks to maximize the value of the firm, the need to provide the means to meet maturing obligations serves as a constraint on the urge for profits.

### Depreciation as a Funds Generator

Unless purchased on an installment plan, plant and equipment purchases are paid for in cash shortly after delivery. These fixed assets are used up over a period of time known as their useful life. The accounting charge made in any period for the use of fixed assets is called *depreciation expense.* It is presently a noncash charge—the cash went out at the time of purchase. When combined with the cash costs of operation—such as materials, labor, heat, light, and administration—this noncash charge determines the total cost of producing the goods for a given period. When the merchandise is sold, the difference between the selling price and the total *cash* cost represents the net *inflow* of cash due to operations for the period. The amount of net cash inflow will exceed the profit by the amount of the depreciation charge. It is in this sense that depreciation expense is referred to as a source of funds.

Funds flow into the firm through cash resulting from sales. When the selling price is higher than the cash costs of producing the goods, the result is a net inflow of funds; when cash costs exceed the selling price, the result is a net outflow of funds. It is only through the successful operation of the firm, therefore, that depreciation is a generator of funds. If plant and equipment remain idle, no goods being produced and sold, depreciation can be charged, but no funds will flow into the enterprise except through income tax refund due to a loss. "Funds" is a *stock* concept, not a flow. It is the "*flow* of funds" that conveys the notion of the change in the economic values of the firm from one form to another.

The relation among cash, funds, depreciation, and values can be illustrated through an example. Assume that the Blue Refining Company has just completed its first petroleum cracking plant at a cost of $1 million. The plant's useful life is estimated at ten years. The depreciation charge is, therefore, $100,000 per year under straight-line depreciation. Table 2–1 is the income statement at the close of the first year's operation.

**TABLE 2–1. The Blue Refining Company**
**Income Statement**
**January 1, 1972 to December 31, 1972**

| | | |
|---|---|---|
| Sales | | $400,000 |
| Less cost of: | | |
| Labor, materials, overhead | $180,000 | |
| Depreciation | 100,000 | 280,000 |
| Profit before taxes | | $120,000 |

With all sales on a cash basis, the total funds inflow is $400,000 for the year. Costs total $280,000, leaving a profit of $120,000. For simplicity we assume there are no income taxes. Of the $280,000 only $180,000 represents cash outlays. The other $100,000 is a noncash charge representing depreciation on the plant and equipment. The funds for these assets were paid out earlier and are now being recouped.

If we examine the company balance sheets at the start and at the end of the year (Table 2–2), the balance sheet footings increase by $120,000, the amount of the profit for the period.

TABLE 2–2. The Blue Refining Company
Comparative Balance Sheet

| *Assets* | December 31 | | *Liabilities and Net Worth* | December 31 | |
|---|---|---|---|---|---|
| | 1972 | 1971 | | 1972 | 1971 |
| Cash | $ 270,000 | $ 50,000 | Accounts payable | $ 100,000 | $ 100,000 |
| Inventory | 150,000 | 150,000 | | | |
| Plant and Equipment | 1,000,000 | 1,000,000 | | | |
| Less accumulated depreciation | 100,000 | 0 | Common stock | 1,100,000 | 1,100,000 |
| Net plant and equipment | 900,000 | 1,000,000 | Retained earnings | 120,000 | 0 |
| Total assets | $1,320,000 | 1,200,000 | Total liabilities and net worth | $1,320,000 | $1,200,000 |

[A9802]

The profit represents the additional value that flowed into the firm from customers buying the product. This increase in the value of the firm is specifically recognized by the $120,000 retained earnings entry. In addition to this net inflow of values there is a rearrangement of values on the asset side of the balance sheet.

Since no reinvestment took place in either plant and equipment or inventory expansion, and since accounts receivable could not increase because all sales were for cash, the net inflow accumulated in the cash account, which rose from $50,000 to $270,000, and represents the amount of the profit plus the depreciation charged.

The funds statement (Table 2–3) shows the sources of the inflow and the outflow of funds, that is, the net amount of funds generated and the use to which the funds were put. Sales produced $400,000, *cash* expenses were $180,000, and, since no additional investments were made, the entire amount of the net funds inflow of $220,000 is lodged in the cash account.

TABLE 2–3. The Blue Refining Company
Funds Statement
For Year 1972

| | |
|---|---|
| Funds generated from sales | $400,000 |
| Cash expenses | – 180,000 |
| Funds generated from operations | $220,000 |
| Increase in cash | $220,000 |
| Increase in inventory, plant, and equipment | 0 |
| Funds applied | $220,000 |
| Cash reconciliation | |
| Cash, Jan. 1, 1972 | $ 50,000 |
| Profit | 120,000 |
| Depreciation charge | 100,000 |
| Cash, Jan. 1, 1973 | $270,000 |

## DYNAMICS OF THE FLOW OF FUNDS

The model of the flow of funds of a manufacturing operation just introduced is a stable system with continuous flows. In reality the flow of funds through the system is dynamic, that is, the rates of flow in the various stages fluctuate. Thus, a continuing problem within a firm is to balance the rate of production with the rate of sales to achieve an optimum return, that is, to maintain the amount of funds invested in cash, receivables, and inventory at such levels as to maximize profit.

The reason there are wide fluctuations in the various working capital account levels is because the information feedback system does not function perfectly. The information may be bad, not timely, or the decisions delayed or wrong. Before examining in detail the dynamic functioning of the flow of funds system, let us look at several information feedback systems. The following discussion is designed not only to show what happens in a firm when the information feedback system functions inadequately, but also to help us understand the difficult task of the financial manager in balancing the working capital of the firm.

### Information Feedback Systems

A thermostat is an example of a closed-loop information feedback system. The thermostat receives information concerning room temperature; when the temperature falls below a set point, it starts the furnace. The temperature rises and the furnace is stopped as the room temperature reaches a predetermined point; the temperature then begins to fall and the cycle continues.

The solar system is another example. Study of the solar system leads to a better understanding of its functioning, which in turn leads to more accurate predictions regarding such solar phenomena as eclipses. Yet, the increased knowledge of its functioning on the part of observers does not influence the way the solar system operates. The same is not true of an information feedback system in a firm. Improved knowledge of its functioning can result in changes in its operation. Individuals will tailor their actions to new knowledge or will seek to modify the structure if the system cannot be improved by the new information.

Figure 2–2 illustrates a simple information feedback system for a firm.

### Fluctuations in Sales and Working Capital Accounts

Starting at the retail level, note that if sales increase sharply, the initial impact is a decline in the finished-goods inventory and an increase in receivables. If management has some way of knowing that the jump in sales is only temporary, production will only be increased for the period necessary to accommodate the temporary bulge in sales. In turn the increase in sales can be financed by drawing down the cash position temporarily. If the new higher level of sales is expected to continue over an extended period of time, additional financing will be necessary. A higher level of inventories will be required at all stages, and receivables will automatically expand with the larger sales volume. In any event, if management is able to make predictions particularly as to the rate of sales, the rate of activity in purchasing and production can be kept in balance, with the result that cash and inventories will be maintained at appropriate levels.

In practice, when sales rise unexpectedly the decision often is not immediately made to increase purchases of raw materials and to step up production. Delays are inevitable. Those who have responsibility for making the decision wait to determine whether the increase in sales is temporary or not. In the interval, the finished-goods inventory continues to drop. At some point, either management becomes convinced that the rise in sales is of a permanent nature or during the wait-and-see period the finished-goods inventory drops to an uncomfortably low level. In either event a rush of purchase and production orders goes out to raise the level of the finished-goods inventory to its former level—or even higher to meet the increased sales. The result is a production rate substantially but temporarily above that which would be required to support

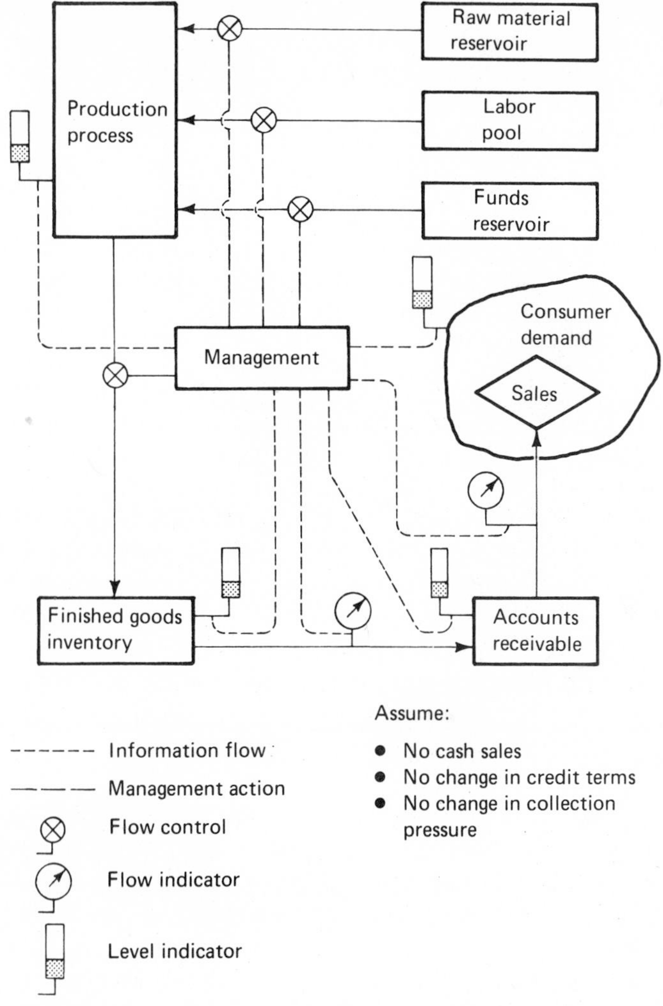


Figure 2–2 Simple information feedback system.

the higher level of sales were no restoration of inventories required at the same time as a buildup. To finance the sudden rise in the production level, the cash balance will fall sharply and accounts payable will rise. Additional outside financing may be necessary. If sales continue at the new level, production will again drop from its peak to a normal but higher level. The purchase of raw materials will follow a pattern similar to the finished-goods variation just described.

An inverse series of events follows a decline in sales. Management will probably wait to determine whether the drop is of a lasting nature. During this period production continues at the same level. In the interval of reduced sales and declining cash, the finished-goods inventory begins to accumulate. As sales fall and inventory accumulates, management becomes increasingly concerned. The resources of the firm are going into goods that are not selling. At some point the decision must be made to cut production. Both production and purchases of raw materials are sharply reduced below the level necessary to sustain the current value of sales. Then, as sales continue at a rate above the sharply reduced production rate, excess inventories are worked off. With the sale of excess finished-goods inventory the production rate can be increased to meet the current level of sales.

The delay in the key decision results from an unclear view of the future. To adjust production to every slight change in sales would be disruptive and costly but to wait too long might mean lost sales and profit (when sales rise) or excess inventory and potential losses from write-offs (when sales fall).

We will now trace the implications for working capital of these fluctuations in sales with their resultant amplified changes in the production rate. A rise in sales is accompanied by an increase in receivables. Normally cash will decline. Funds are flowing into the receivables. The firm may obtain outside financing to restore cash to its former level. A step-up in production will require an increased rate of raw materials purchases, raising the level of accounts payable. If the firm is already straining the credit available to it, delayed payment on its accounts payable may be the only course open to it. A continually expanding firm, even with good profits, is frequently in a poor working capital position because rising sales mean an increased amount of receivables, and increased production to meet those sales requires increased purchases of raw materials, covered in part by increased credit from suppliers. The increased profits, though good, are frequently not sufficient to finance all the expanding firm's needs for cash.

A declining sales trend produces the opposite effect. Receivables are reduced as sales decline; the funds flow into the cash balance. Production is adjusted downward, raw material purchases fall and accounts payable decline as suppliers are paid off. The net effect is an improved working capital position, ironically brought about by reduced sales and profitability. Losses, however, would be an offset to the improvement in working capital.

## IMPACT OF THE DEPRECIATION CHARGE ON THE FLOW OF FUNDS

Management's actions are restricted to adapting the firm to its environment. In this situation planning is essential. Important areas of planning include cash budgeting; capital budgeting, or the allocation of funds among alternative capital investment projects; and arranging for future financing needs. In each of these areas depreciation policy is an important element because of its impact on earnings and cash flow.

When sales take place, funds flow into the firm. The amount of depreciation charged over an accounting period significantly affects the amount of taxable profit and hence the amount of income tax due. The net amount of funds generated during the period is reduced by the taxes paid. Since depreciation is a cost, it qualifies as a deduction from income but does not require a cash outlay. The funds were expended when the fixed assets were purchased. Thus a firm is able through depreciation taken for tax purposes to influence the timing of its income tax liability and therefore the time pattern of its cash outlays over a span of years.

The firm is interested in deferring income taxes because present dollars are more valuable than future dollars. Present money is more valuable than future money because a dollar invested today will earn interest. Consequently, a dollar to be received in one year must be worth something less than a dollar today. A firm's tax depreciation policy can be an effective instrument for increasing present funds at the expense of future funds by reducing present income taxes but increasing *future* income taxes. Thus the gain in deferring income taxes is the interest earned during the period of deferral. There is no reduction of the income tax itself in the deferral process if we assume that income tax rates do not change.

### Straight-line versus Accelerated Depreciation

Management has a choice as to depreciation methods at the time of purchase of an asset. We will compare two methods: *straight-line depreciation* and depreciation using the *sum-of-the-years'-digits method.* Under the straight-line method, the depreciation charge for each year is the same and is computed by dividing the cost of the equipment, reduced by the salvage value, by the life of the asset in years. Under the sum-of-the-years'-digits method, the annual depreciation charge declines each year and is computed by multiplying the cost of the equipment, reduced by the salvage value, by a fraction whose numerator is the remaining years of life of the equipment at the start of each year and whose denominator is the sum of the number of years of life of the asset at the time the asset was acquired.[3]

Following straight-line depreciation in our Blue Refining example, $100,000 of depreciation would be charged each year for 10 years. With the sum-of-the-years'-digits method the charge the first year would be 10/55 of $1 million, or $181,818. Calling the alternatives of straight-line and the sum-of-the-years'-digits methods slow and fast depreciation, respectively, we trace the effect on profits and the flow of funds in the first year of operation in Table 2–4. Note that even though profits after income taxes would be significantly *reduced* in the first year through the charging of accelerated depreciation, the flow of funds would be *increased* because the income tax outflow is reduced.

### Depreciation as a Tax Shield

Depreciation is a tax shield for a profitable firm since depreciation charges against income do not affect the net inflow of funds from operations before income taxes but can be taken as a deduction to reduce income taxes. Table 2–4 shows fast depreciation reduced income taxes in the first year by $32,800 (from $48,000 to $15,200), which results in an increase of *net* cash inflow by $32,800 (from $172,000 to $204,800). By

---

[3] For example, an asset with a life of four years is acquired. To determine the denominator, we sum the years 1 to 4, which equals 10. The numerator is the remaining years of life of the asset at the start of each year. The first year depreciation would be 4/10, the second year 3/10, the third year 2/10, and the fourth year 1/10 times the cost of the asset less the salvage value. But for the straight-line method, depreciation would be 1/4 each year.

TABLE 2–4.* The Blue Refining Company
Comparative Funds Statements under Fast and Slow Depreciation

| | *Fast depreciation* | | *Slow depreciation* | |
|---|---|---|---|---|
| Sales | | $400,000 | | $400,000 |
| Less cost of: | | | | |
| Labor, materials, overhead | $180,000 | | $180,000 | |
| Depreciation | 182,000 ** | 362,000 | 100,000 | 280,000 |
| Operating income | | 38,000 | | 120,000 |
| Less income tax (40%) | | 15,200 | | 48,000 |
| Profits after taxes | | 22,800 | | 72,000 |
| Add back depreciation | | 182,000 | | 100,000 |
| Net cash inflow | | $204,800 | | $172,000 |

* Based on Tables 2–1 and 2–2.
* * Rounded. First year's depreciation.

the same token, fast depreciation *reduced* after-tax profits by $49,200 ($72,000 to $22,800), which is the result of the increase in depreciation of $82,000 (from $100,000 to $182,000), less the tax saving of $32,800 ($48,000 to $15,200). The net inflow of funds at the end of the period before income taxes will be the same regardless of the amount charged for depreciation. But the amount remaining after income taxes will be affected by the amount of depreciation charged. The higher the depreciation charged, the greater the total operating expense and the lower the income tax liability. Since funds not paid out in taxes remain with the firm, depreciation serves to shield the firm's cash inflow from the reach of the tax collector.

The use of fast depreciation only postpones the tax liability and the accompanying necessary cash outflow. In later years when the depreciation charge is low, the income tax liability and the cash outflow will rise. In the interval the firm—assuming corporate tax rates do not rise—has an interest-free loan. By using fast depreciation, the firm reduces risk while gaining an interest-free loan that does not appear on the balance sheet and is not really a loan, but rather a contingent liability for future income taxes if future earnings are forthcoming. The reduction of risk lies in improved liquidity.

If the firm is growing rapidly and new assets are being acquired faster than the old ones are being retired, the firm is able to defer income taxes for as long as it grows. If the firm can grow indefinitely, then fast depreciation results in a permanent interest free loan by the government to the firm in the amount of the difference between the tax liabilities under slow and fast depreciation.

## SUMMARY

Cash is the focal point of the flow of funds through the system. The funds flow from cash through raw material purchases, work in process, finished-goods inventory, accounts receivable, and back to cash. Inventories are maintained to permit purchasing, production, and sales to be carried on at different rates. Changes in the levels of cash, inventories, receivables, and payables will depend upon the relative rates of purchasing, production, distribution, and collection from customers of the firm and payment to creditors of the firm.

Sales (or other revenues) are the source of funds inflow. When cash costs of production and income taxes are deducted, the balance represents the net inflow of funds. The same figure may be obtained by starting with net profit and adding back depreciation. Depreciation is sometimes referred to as a source of funds.

The method of depreciation adopted influences the reported earnings figure and the flow of funds. Accelerated depreciation will result in high charges in the early years, with profits reduced but cash inflow increased. The increased "costs" reduce the tax liability. Under straight-line depreciation "costs" would be less, taxable profits higher, the tax liability higher, and net cash inflow would be reduced in the early years. Firms adopt accelerated depreciation to obtain the larger net funds inflow in the early years, which is an interest-free "loan" by the government against future tax liability that may become due.

### Study Questions

1. Can an economy be characterized as a system, and a firm as a subsystem to that system? Explain.
2. Why is cash important to a firm?
3. Distinguish between cash, funds, and profit.
4. What are the advantages and disadvantages to a toy manufacturer, the bulk of whose sales occur shortly before the Christmas holidays, of following a level production plant compared to producing just prior to the anticipated arrival of orders?
5. Under what conditions can depreciation be referred to as a source of funds?
6. Explain in detail why small changes in sales volume frequently cause major changes in the production rate.
7. A rapidly growing but profitable firm is frequently in poor financial condition. Explain this phenomenon.
8. A barely profitable firm in a declining industry may currently be in excellent financial health. Explain this phenomenon.
9. How does depreciation serve as a tax shield? How is it possible to increase the charge for depreciation, reduce net income, and increase the inflow of funds?
10. Why do we say cash is the focal point of the flow of funds? What are the subsidiary flows?

### Problems

1. Develop your own model of a flow of funds system for a firm.

2. Two firms of reasonably similar quality in the same industry both report earnings of $1 per share and are selling at $20 per share. Company Fast uses accelerated depreciation and Company Slow uses straight-line depreciation.

Develop illustrative figures for the two companies and demonstrate which company would be the more attractive investment.

**3.** Business and financial publications frequently carry announcements of a change in a company's policy that will sharply influence its flow of funds. Develop a list of reasonable company actions that could have an effect on its flow of funds and trace that effect. Refer to the periodicals and see how many of the policy changes listed can be located in the business world. Observe the size of the company and the industry in which the policy changes are being effected. Do you detect any patterns?

**4.** Examine the annual reports of a selected number of companies over several years. Do you note any major changes in cash, receivables, inventory, or payables? Can you account for these changes? Where did the funds flow to and where did they come from?

**5.** Show by example that the higher the tax rate, the more desirable the adoption of some method of accelerated depreciation over straight-line depreciation.

**6.** The president of Mercury, Inc., is puzzled. Profit last year was $300,000 and yet cash rose by $500,000 from $100,000 to $600,000. He asks you to explain.

Mercury only buys and sells for cash. Books are kept on a cash basis but depreciation is recognized. Examining the books of the firm you obtain the following information:

Sales amounted to $2.9 million.

Cash expenses were $2.4 million.

Inventory, plant, and equipment remained unchanged.

Cash at the beginning of the year January 1, 1972 was $100,000.

Depreciation charge for the year was $200,000.

To explain the situation to the president, draw up a funds statement and a cash reconciliation.

**7.** Suppose that in December, Mercury (Problem 6) had purchased $100,000 worth of equipment for cash. Would the funds generated and the funds-applied totals be affected by this transaction? Which numbers on your funds statement and cash reconciliation would be affected?

**8.** A company president writing in the annual report states that Ultronics is "financing new plant and equipment requirements out of retained earnings and depreciation." Interpret this statement.

### Selected References

Bodenhorn, D., "A Cash-Flow Concept of Profit," *Journal of Finance,* 19 (March 1964), pp. 16–31.

Bonini, C. P., R. K. Jaedicke, and H. M. Wagner, *Management Controls,* New York: McGraw-Hill, Inc., 1964.

Dearden, J., "Can Management Information Be Automated?" *Harvard Business Review,* 42 (March–April 1964), pp. 128–135.

Englemann, K., "The 'Internal-Cash-Generation' Phenomenon," *Financial Analysts Journal,* 17 (September–October 1961), pp. 37–40.

Helfert, E. A., *Techniques of Financial Analysis,* Homewood, Ill.: Richard D. Irwin, Inc., 3d ed., 1972, chap. 1.

McDonough, A. M., and L. J. Garrett, *Management Systems,* Homewood, Ill.: Richard D. Irwin, Inc., 1965.

McLean, J. H., "Depreciation: Its Relationship to Funds," *Financial Analysts Journal*, 19 (May–June 1963), pp. 73–78.

Paton, W. A., "The 'Cash-Flow' Illusion," *Accounting Review*, 38 (April 1963), pp. 243–251.

Rayman, R. A., "An Extension of the System of Accounts: The Segregation of Funds and Value," *Journal of Accounting Research*, 7 (Spring 1969), pp. 53–89.

Staubus, G. J., "Alternative Asset Flow Concepts," *Accounting Review*, 41 (July 1966), pp. 397–412.

# 3

# Financial Analysis: the Basis of Effective Management

We characterize a firm as a system designed to produce goods and services. That system consists of a portfolio of assets and liabilities whose total value is to be maximized by the decisions of management.

Knowledge of the current financial position of the firm and planning is analogous to a driver consulting a road map for the best route to his destination. The driver must know his current location and his destination in order to use the map. The purpose of the financial plan is to adjust the firm's portfolio of assets and liabilities over time so as to best anticipate future events and maximize the value of the firm.

## TOOLS OF FINANCIAL ANALYSIS

The heart of financial analysis lies in easily computed ratios relating various items of the balance sheet and income statement. The financial manager seeks to draw meaning from these financial ratios or tools of analysis. He needs experience, insight, and imagination. Working with the material gives experience, but insight and imagination are harder to attain. The individual must know his own capacity and limitations and work within them.

Before proceeding with our discussion of ratios several comments are in order. Even casual observation will reveal that financial analysis is a skill widely practiced by financial managers, creditors of all kinds, and investors. Thus the topic merits the considerable attention we accord it. But financial analysis also has many deficiencies. In this regard the student is urged to consider with particular care the following remarks, the discussion later in this chapter on the hazards in the use of ratios, and Appendixes A and B to this chapter, which deal with the influence of managerial decision-making on reported earnings and financial reporting by diversified firms respectively.

First, though financial analysis may be used with some confidence to evaluate the financial position of a firm in relation to similar firms and to measure the progress of a firm toward some particular goals such as improved liquidity and higher income relative to sales, the predictive powers of financial analysis are open to serious question. Predicting the future earnings of a firm and its financial condition (solid, weak, bankrupt) some years hence using ratios is a very hazardous activity. And yet it is precisely the future that is of greatest concern to those analyzing the financial statements of a firm: the financial manager trying to decide whether to build a new plant, the creditor trying to decide whether to extend a large loan, the investor trying to decide whether to buy a large block of stock.

Second, the arithmetic precision with which a particular ratio can be computed may blind the analyst to the weakness of the input data used for the ratio computation. This may cause the analyst to place undue reliance on the ratio result. Worse yet, the analyst may become enamored with ratio computation and lose sight of the purpose of the analysis. Ratio computation may become an end in itself.

Third, no ratio standing alone has any particular meaning. Only groups of ratios computed at various points in time can, in conjunction with numerous related qualitative factors such as the honesty and shrewdness of management, provide an analyst with insight into a firm's current and potential earning and financial condition.

Below we group ratios into four classifications. The purpose of such a classification is to help the student remember the ratios, nothing more. We, dislike, as do others, such a classification. It is artificial and does not in itself aid the analyst in selecting the proper ratios to evaluate a particular situation. But it is a convenient device.

### Classification of Ratios

Financial ratios may be grouped into four classifications:

1. *Liquidity:* to measure ability of the firm to meet obligations maturing within a year.

2. *Leverage:* to measure the firm's use of fixed-charge financing obligations (bonds, leases, preferred stock).

3. *Activity:* to measure the intensity of the firm's resource utilization.

4. *Profitability:* to measure management's ability to generate profits.

Every analysis has a purpose and the ratios selected must meet that purpose.

### Purpose of a Financial Analysis

On going to work for a new firm we might first assess its overall financial condition by computing all the ratios in these four categories. The lack of an objective and the absence of any method of relating the ratios to obtain a composite value are weaknesses of this approach.

*Working Capital* A financial manager planning over a short time horizon and a trade creditor or banker making a seasonal loan are primarily interested in the firm's liquidity or bill-paying ability. The short-term ability of a firm to pay its bills is best judged by studying the working capital of the firm. The analysis will include the current and quick ratios (liquidity ratios) and inventory turnover and the ratio of receivables to average daily credit sales (activity ratios).

*Investment Position* When making long-term plans for the firm or as an outsider considering the purchase of the firm's bonds or stock, we will be particularly interested in the cash-generating ability of the firm and profitability of the firm. Here we would use the debt-to-equity ratio and times interest earned (leverage ratios), asset turnover (activity ratio), and margin of profit and return on investment (profitability ratios). A stock investor and the financial manager would also consider the price-earnings ratio (PER), dividend yield (market ratios) and payout ratio in this category.

*Depth of Analysis* A relation should exist between the amount of funds involved in the financing and the thoroughness of the analysis by the financial manager and the investor; the greater the sum, the more thorough should be the analysis. A relation should also exist between the risk of the firm and the completeness of the analysis: the more risky, the more thorough should be the analysis.

## BALANCE SHEET ANALYSIS

The basic documents used in analyzing the financial condition of a business firm are the balance sheet and income statement. We study these financial statements because the quantitative data contained therein are helpful in making decisions that are economic rather than emotional. The balance sheet tells us the current financial condition of the firm but not the firm's future condition. But through the study of a series of past balance sheets, clues as to future balance sheets can be developed.

### The Balance Sheet: A "Snapshot" of the Firm

The balance sheet is a "snapshot" of the firm at a given point in time. The drawing up of a balance sheet is one way to convey the financial characteristics of a firm and to provide a basis for analyzing its strengths and weaknesses. Since it represents the firm as viewed pursuant to one set of accounting rules, other balance sheets could be prepared using other accounting rules.

It is essential that the financial analyst understand the accounting principles underlying the balance sheet, and since much analysis involves comparison of a series of balance sheets, it is vital that consistency be maintained in the accounting from one balance sheet to the next.

### Information Available

Three major classifications of information are found on the balance sheet: *current asset and liability data*, *plant and property items*, and *capital structure*—total long-term financing. Ratios based on this information may be grouped in a number of ways depending on the purpose of the analysis. We present them in terms of evaluating the working capital and investment positions of the firm, and consider both purposes in this chapter.

One major financial factor not found on the balance sheet is earning power. Earnings are the basis for the long-run survival of the firm and one side of the coin in determining the value of the firm—the other side is risk. Thus the entire next chapter is devoted to an analysis of earning power.

### Distinguishing between Cash and Profit [1]

When a dollar is started on its way through the firm's system it is anticipated that when it returns to the cash account it will bring with it an added amount. If only the dollar returns, the firm will be covering its out-of-pocket costs but will be running at a deficit to the extent of the noncash charges such as depreciation. If the dollar returns carrying with it an amount sufficient to cover the firm's cash and noncash costs, the firm will be just breaking even. If the dollar comes back with an amount beyond this, the excess is profit.

One feature that distinguishes the cash flow and profit is that cash is a readily identifiable money unit, whereas profit is a book figure representing the excess of revenue over all of the firm's cash and noncash costs that may be properly allocated to that period—the net inflow of economic values.[2] The task of the accountant is to determine the ex-

---

[1] Businessmen sometimes complain to their accountants that they have made a given amount of profit for the year but have less money in the bank. See W. E. Stone, "The Funds Statement as an Analysis Tool," *Accounting Review*, 34 (January 1959), pp. 127–130.

[2] A funds statement, as presented in Table 3–7, highlights the difference between cash and earnings and shows what happens to funds (values) generated by profitable activities.

penses to be charged to the period. Cash expenses are usually easily allocated.[3] It is the noncash charges that cause difficulty.

Noncash charges include depreciation, the bad-debt charge (an expense charged against income but with no outflow of cash), and the charging of prepaid expense. A five-year insurance policy, for example, may be purchased and paid for in cash, with one fifth of the cost of the policy charged against income each year.

A number of cash flows do not affect the income statement. These flows include dividend disbursements, payments for materials and supplies previously purchased on credit, and collection of receivables. The receipt of funds from a loan or sale of securities would swell the inflow of cash but would not represent profit. The payment for supplies would cause a large outflow of cash but also would not affect profit. Frequently the payment date disrupts the correspondence between cash flow and profit, a good example being the payment of wages and salaries at year end. In determining the profit for a year, the cost of the labor inputs is properly allocated to that year, but if workers are paid every two weeks, the cash may actually not be paid out until 10 days after the close of the year. The cash would flow out on pay day, but the costs for the first few days of the pay period would be reflected on the income statement for the previous year.

### Illustrative Analysis

To illustrate the analysis that a financial manager would conduct to determine the financial strength and earning power of his firm and gain insight into developing trends, we use the firm of Blu-Tronics, Inc., a manufacturer of electrical distribution equipment. We begin with the analysis of the comparative balance sheet (Table 3–1)

## SHORT-TERM ANALYSIS: WORKING CAPITAL POSITION

The working capital position of a firm is evaluated through the use of several ratios that measure liquidity. These ratios deal with cash and current items; which are assets that in the normal course of business are converted into cash within one year. These ratios also deal with current liabilities, which are debts of the firm payable within one year.

### Liquidity Ratios; Working Capital

*Current Ratio* The current ratio is the ratio of current assets to current liabilities. Current assets (CA) include cash, bank balances, marketable securities being held as a short-term substitute for cash, accounts receivable, and inventories. Current liabilities (CL) include accounts pay-

---

[3] The question with research and similar outlays is whether to expense or capitalize them.

TABLE 3–1. Blu-Tronics, Inc. Comparative Balance Sheet

| *Assets* | *December 31* 1973 | *December 31* 1972 | *Liabilities and stockholders' investment* | *December 31* 1973 | *December 31* 1972 |
|---|---|---|---|---|---|
| Current assets | | | Current liabilities | | |
| Cash | $ 155,000 | $ 400,000 | Accounts payable | $ 1,432,000 | $ 685,000 |
| Accounts receivable (net) | 3,113,000 | 1,780,000 | Notes payable | 2,389,000 | 1,600,000 |
| Inventories | 7,698,000 | 4,760,000 | Accrued items | 813,000 | 567,000 |
| Total current assets | $10,966,000 | $6,940,000 | Federal and state income taxes | 1,065,000 | 416,000 |
| Plant and equipment | 4,317,000 | 3,711,000 | Installments due within one year on long-term promissory notes payable | 120,000 | 120,000 |
| Less depreciation | 1,462,000 | 1,164,000 | | | |
| Net fixed assets | $ 2,855,000 | $2,547,000 | Total current liabilities | $ 5,819,000 | $3,388,000 |
| | | | Long-term promissory notes | 2,160,000 | 2,280,000 |
| | | | Stockholders' investment, common stock par value $1 | 832,000 | 761,000 |
| | | | Additional paid-in capital | 1,036,000 | 194,000 |
| | | | Retained earnings | 3,974,000 | 2,864,000 |
| | | | Total net worth | $ 5,842,000 | $3,819,000 |
| Total assets | $13,821,000 | $9,487,000 | Total liabilities and net worth | $13,821,000 | $9,487,000 |

able, notes payable, bank loans, that portion of long-term debt that will mature within one year, and various accrued items. The comparative balance sheet for Blu-Tronics, Inc. (Table 3–1) shows the following current ratios:

$$\text{Current ratio} = \frac{CA}{CL} = \begin{cases} \dfrac{\$10{,}966{,}000}{\$5{,}819{,}000} = 1.9 & (1973) \\[2ex] \dfrac{\$6{,}940{,}000}{\$3{,}388{,}000} = 2.0 & (1972) \end{cases}$$

A current ratio of 1.9 means that for every $1 of current liabilities the firm has $1.90 of current assets.

The current ratio is widely used but it is only a rough measure and can be misleading. For example, Blu-Tronics, Inc., seeking to improve its current ratio in 1972 might just before the balance sheet date pay off $300,000 of current liabilities with cash. Though this action might temporarily leave the firm short of cash its current ratio would rise to 2.1.[4]

Since the current ratio includes inventory and receivables there exist other possibilities for misjudging the actual liquidity position of the firm. The inventory may not be easily salable. If it consists of toys and the balance sheet date is August 31, the inventory is probably highly salable because most toys are sold in the months just before Christmas. An acceptable current ratio would indicate a favorable liquidity position. With the firm carrying a large inventory of toys on December 31, the same ratio would indicate a poorer working capital position. In judging the liquidity position of his firm the financial manager must estimate the salability of the inventory. Receivables, while not normally causing difficulty because of their nearness to cash, also deserve some attention. At times items become uncollectible. A firm with many smaller accounts is less vulnerable to large losses than a firm with a few very large accounts. It is customary to show a bad-debt reserve against receivables but not a reserve against inventory because this is more difficult to determine.

A low current ratio indicates a weak liquidity position. The firm may experience difficulty in meeting its maturing obligations. The poor ratio may be due to heavy losses, excessive financing on a short-term basis, or the practice of using current funds to finance fixed assets. A current ratio that is too high might indicate that management is overly concerned with liquidity and sacrificing earnings for short-term safety.

*Quick Ratio* The quick ratio is the ratio of current assets minus inventory to current liabilities.[5] This is a more stringent test than the cur-

[4] This practice is called "window dressing." Banks have been known to engage in this practice by reciprocally making large deposits just before statement date and withdrawing them after the date. The purpose is to increase the total size of the assets of the institution since in some financial circles a large total assets figure is a mark of strength. Banks sometimes still advertise their total assets in gold letters on the front window.

[5] This is sometimes known as the *acid test ratio.* This is the accepted definition. The Council of Economic Advisors in a study of corporate liquidity defined the quick ratio as

rent ratio. The focus is on the cash and near-cash coverage of the current liabilities. The Blu-Tronics, Inc., comparative balance sheet (Table 3–1) shows the following quick ratios:

$$\text{Quick ratio} = \frac{\text{CA} - \text{Inv.}}{\text{CL}} = \begin{cases} \dfrac{\$10{,}966{,}000 - \$7{,}698{,}000}{\$5{,}819{,}000} = 0.6 & (1973) \\[2ex] \dfrac{\$6{,}940{,}000 - \$4{,}760{,}000}{\$3{,}388{,}000} = 0.6 & (1972) \end{cases}$$

A quick ratio of 0.6 means that in 1972 for every dollar of current liabilities the firm has 60 cents of near-cash items.

The farther removed an asset is from cash, the less liquid. Receivables are one step from cash, inventory two steps. But these are not even steps. The nearness of inventory to receivables (and then cash) depends on its salability. If it is salable, it is near to receivables, if it is not, it is far from receivables. The range of liquidity for inventory is wider than for receivables. In receivables, the firm has a claim to cash that it can legally press—the customer is under obligation to pay. In inventory, the firm has a claim only to the ownership of the merchandise. It has the right to sell the goods for whatever the market will pay; if the market will pay nothing, the firm does not have a right to collect anything. Thus the step between cash and receivables is quite small, while that between receivables and inventory may be quite large.

*Percentage Composition of the Working Capital* This is the percentage each component of the current assets bears to the total. By definition, current assets are assets convertible to cash in one year. But since some are more liquid than others, determination of the percentage each bears to the total will provide some insight into the firm's liquidity position, as shown in Table 3–2.

TABLE 3–2. Blu-Tronics, Inc.

Comparative Analysis of Working Capital *

| | *December 31* | |
|---|---|---|
| *Current assets* | *1973* | *1972* |
| Cash | 1.4% | 5.8% |
| Accounts receivable | 28.4 | 25.6 |
| Inventory | 70.2 | 68.6 |
| | 100.0% | 100.0% |

* Based on Table 3–1.

cash plus government securities to total current liabilities. See *Economic Report of the President*, 1971, U.S. Government Printing Office, Washington, D.C., p. 171.

Blu-Tronics' current and quick ratios for 1973 and 1972 indicate a declining liquidity situation. But there is more. The current and quick ratios, while showing relatively little change from 1972 to 1973, hide the drop in cash and the increase in receivables and inventory.

*Cash to Average-Daily-Purchases Ratio* This is the ratio of cash and near-cash items to the average daily payments of accounts payable. The balance sheet for 1973 shows \$1,432,000 of accounts payable. The firm's 1973 income statement (Table 3–3) shows a cost of goods sold (COGS) of \$15,158,000. Postulating that raw materials represent 60 percent of COGS, purchases are roughly \$9 million per year, or daily purchases are \$25,000 (\$9 million/360 days). Thus, cash equals 6.2 days' purchases:

$$\frac{\text{Cash}}{\text{Average daily purchases}} = \frac{\$155{,}000}{\$25{,}000} = 6.2 \text{ days}$$

Relating the average monthly purchases of \$750,000 (\$25,000 x 30) to 1973 year-end accounts payable of \$1,432,000, we find Blu-Tronics is taking about 60 days on the average to pay its suppliers. Summarizing the 1973 working capital position of Blu-Tronics we find that the current ratio is marginal—1.9, but that the quick ratio of 0.6, the low percentage of cash to total current assets and average daily purchases, and the large amount of payables on the books all indicate that the firm is in a poorer liquidity position than indicated by the current ratio.

In evaluating the liquidity position of a firm the sophisticated financial manager will also consider the firm's reserve borrowing power and financial strength of the insiders. If these sources are strong the firm can operate with a lower cash balance relative to its daily requirements than other firms.

### Working Capital Efficiency Ratios

Working capital efficiency ratios evaluate the efficiency with which the firm is managing the funds invested in working capital. For example, the inventory-turnover ratio gives clues as to the salability of the inventory. It is a measure of the work the firm is getting out of the funds invested in inventory.

*Inventory-Turnover* This ratio represents the relation of cost of goods sold (COGS) to inventory (either ending inventory or average of beginning and ending inventory). The inventory turnover of Blu-Tronics, Inc., using ending inventory is as follows:

| | 1973 | 1972 |
|---|---|---|

$$\text{Inventory turnover} = \frac{\text{COGS}}{\text{Inv}} = \begin{cases} \dfrac{\$15{,}158{,}000}{\$7{,}698{,}000} = 2.0\times & \text{(1973)} \\[2ex] \dfrac{\$10{,}780{,}000}{\$4{,}760{,}000} = 2.3\times & \text{(1972)} \end{cases}$$

The COGS figures are obtained from Table 3–3, the ending inventory figures from Table 3–1. An inventory-turnover ratio of 2.0 times means each dollar of inventory is converted to sales 2.0 times per year. The higher the turnover ratio, the greater the profit—provided gross margin does not change. Gross margin = (Sales − COGS)/Sales. A dollar of inventory that can be converted to sales 4 times and yield a gross profit of 10 cents each time will produce an annual gross profit of 40 cents; if the inventory turnover were only 1, the gross profit would be 10 cents.

TABLE 3–3. Blu-Tronics, Inc.
Comparative Income Statement

| | *Year Ending December 31* | |
|---|---|---|
| | *1973* | *1972* |
| Net sales | $21,425,000 | $15,007,000 |
| Costs and expenses | | |
| Cost of goods sold | 15,158,000 | 10,780,000 |
| Selling and administrative expenses | 2,825,000 | 2,204,000 |
| Interest expense | 242,000 | 153,000 |
| Total cost and expenses | $18,225,000 | $13,137,000 |
| Profit before taxes on income | $ 3,200,000 | $ 1,870,000 |
| Taxes on income | | |
| Federal | $ 1,440,000 | $ 807,000 |
| State | 170,000 | 93,000 |
| Net profit | $ 1,590,000 | $ 970,000 |

The inventory-turnover ratio can help us evaluate the significance of a rise or decline in the percent of inventory to total current assets. A sharp increase in inventory as a percent of current assets with sales rising rapidly presents a different picture than a rise in inventory as a percent of current assets with sales declining. In the first case the firm with a growing demand for its product is shifting cash and near-cash resources into inventory to meet the rising sales volume. True, the firm is becoming less liquid: it has less cash on hand to meet its short-term obligations. But its inventory is selling rapidly and there need be little concern for large inventory losses. The firm can count on converting merchandise to cash through sales in the normal course of business. In the second case the firm also is becoming less liquid. But the factors accompanying that increasing illiquidity are different. Cash and near-cash resources are being locked into inventory that is becoming less marketable. The ability of the firm to meet its short-term debts is deteriorating as sales drop and inventory mounts. Should this trend continue the earnings of the firm will decline as it is forced to liquidate inventory at reduced prices to obtain cash.

To modify the uniqueness that may result from basing calculations on a single balance sheet date, inventory turnover is often calculated by taking the average of the inventory at the beginning and at the end of the year.

$$\text{Inventory turnover} = \frac{\text{COGS}}{(\text{Inv } 12/31/73 + \text{Inv } 12/31/72)/2}$$

$$= \frac{\$15{,}158{,}000}{(\$7{,}698{,}000 + \$4{,}760{,}000)/2} = 2.4 \times$$

*Receivables in Terms of Daily Credit Sales* The ratio of receivables to average daily credit sales is the average collection period. This is a measure of the relative size of the receivables account, the collectibility of the receivables, and the firm's credit policy enforcement standard. *Credit policy* refers to the terms of sale the vendor extends to customers. With a credit policy of net 30 days (meaning the vendor's customer must pay his bill without discount within 30 days), we would probably inquire into the operation of the credit department and its enforcement of the firm's credit standards if receivables outstanding represent 60 days' credit sales.

The ratio of receivables to average daily credit sales is calculated in two steps. First, we calculate the average daily credit sales. Assume that 80 percent of Blu-Tronics' sales are on credit. In 1973 sales were $21,425,000, and in 1972 sales were $15,007,000. We use a 360-day year for ease of computation.

$$\text{Daily credit sales} = \begin{cases} \dfrac{\$17{,}140{,}000}{360} = \$48{,}000 \quad (1973) \\[2ex] \dfrac{\$12{,}006{,}000}{360} = \$33{,}000 \quad (1972) \end{cases}$$

Second, divide the average daily credit sales into the year-end receivables.

$$\begin{array}{l} \text{Days credit sales} \\ \text{outstanding} \\ \text{as receivables} \end{array} = \frac{\text{Receivables}}{\text{Average daily credit sales}} = \begin{cases} \dfrac{\$3{,}113{,}000}{\$48{,}000} = 65 \text{ days} \quad (1973) \\[2ex] \dfrac{\$1{,}780{,}000}{\$33{,}000} = 54 \text{ days} \quad (1972) \end{cases}$$

At year-end 1973, Blu-Tronics had receivables equivalent to 65 days credit sales, up from 54 days in 1972. As the firm increased its sales from 1972 to 1973, it also became more liberal in its credit and collection policies. Receivables rose faster than sales. Paralleling this situation, inventory turnover declined. If we assume Blu-Tronics' credit sales are on the basis of net 30 days, then the level of receivables outstanding is significantly above its appropriate level.

## LONG–TERM ANALYSIS: INVESTMENT CHARACTERISTICS

One set of ratios is available to measure the protection that the firm offers long-term creditors. These solvency ratios consist of two subsets: one measures protection of assets, and the other measures protection of earnings. They also measure the extent to which leverage has been used. Another set of investment ratios measures the performance of the firm in the stock market.

### Solvency Ratios

*Debt Coverage* Debt coverage is shown in the ratio of debt to total assets. This *debt-to-assets ratio* measures the relative use made of creditor funds to finance the firm and is of interest to both creditors and owners. The advantage of this ratio over the other two to be discussed is that it focuses attention on the percent of creditor funds used to finance the firm. It indicates the financial risk the firm has assumed where financial risk is defined in terms of the variability in earnings available to the common stock because of the use of debt.

For large firms where current liabilities are a small percent of total assets, short-term debt and current liabilities can be omitted in the calculation of the debt-to-assets ratio. For smaller firms where the current liabilities account is relatively large (there frequently being no long-term debt) the debt-to-assets ratio is calculated on the basis of total debt to total assets.

$$\text{Percentage of debt financing} = \frac{\text{Creditor funds}}{\text{Total assets}}$$

| | 1973 | 1972 |
|---|---|---|
| $= \frac{\$5{,}819{,}000 + \$2{,}160{,}000}{\$13{,}821{,}000}$ | = 57.7% | |
| $= \frac{\$3{,}388{,}000 + \$2{,}280{,}000}{\$9{,}487{,}000}$ | = | 59.7% |

In 1973 creditors supplied 57.7 percent of the funds, a decline from 59.7 percent for 1972. The working capital position of the firm deteriorated, but its long-term financing position improved.

A widely used ratio calculated to measure the relative proportions of creditor and equity funds is the *debt-to-equity ratio*, which shows the creditor funds in terms of the stockholder equity funds—preferred stock, common stock, capital surplus, and retained earnings.

$$\text{Debt-to-equity relationship} = \frac{\text{Creditor funds}}{\text{Equity funds}}$$

| | 1973 | 1972 |
|---|---|---|
| $= \dfrac{\$7{,}979{,}000}{\$5{,}842{,}000} =$ | 1.37 | |
| $= \dfrac{\$5{,}668{,}000}{\$3{,}819{,}000} =$ | | 1.48 |

These figures tell us that in 1973, creditors supplied $1.37 for every dollar supplied by stockholders and that in 1972, they supplied $1.48 for every dollar supplied by stockholders.

For creditors, the lower the percent of creditor funds the better. This is because the equity funds, or net worth, serve as a buffer to absorb any shrinkage in the value of the assets. Any increase in the value of the assets increases the buffer for the creditors.[6] Creditors want to receive prompt payment, and if they are bondholders, they want to receive punctually the promised interest and the repayment of principal at maturity. For example, with creditor funds representing 20 percent of the value of the assets it would be possible for the assets to shrink by 80 percent before the creditors would begin to suffer a loss of principal (assuming the assets are worth their book value). In contrast, if creditors supplied 70 percent of the funds employed, the value of the assets need shrink by but 30 percent before the claims of the creditors against the firm would begin to be impaired.

Whether a given debt-to-equity relationship depicts a favorable or unfavorable condition depends on the industry, the stability of earnings, the trend, and the investment interests of the analyst. A low percentage of debt to equity is favorable from the creditor's position. A large margin of protection provides safety. The same low percentage of debt, however, may be viewed as quite unsatisfactory by shareholders. They may see a neglected opportunity for using low-cost debt to acquire capital equipment that could earn a high return.

*Times Interest Earned* The ratio of earnings before interest and taxes (*EBIT*) to interest charges measures the protection the earnings afford the bondholders. If, for example, times interest earned is 5, this means interest charges have been earned 5 times over and earnings could decline 80 percent and still be sufficient to meet interest charges. Lease payments also constitute a fixed charge and generally should be included in the calculation if the firm has leased assets and the lease contract is not subject to cancellation by the firm. The ratio then is known as *times fixed charges earned.*

[6] And also is attractive to creditors who hold convertible bonds or warrants.

The importance of earnings to all long-term investors, whether bondholders or stockholders, can be seen by considering the basis of the firm's value. Goods can be classified into two groups: consumers' goods and producers' goods. The value of the former is direct because of its ability to satisfy people's needs and wants. Producers' goods have value only to the extent that they can profitably produce goods to be used to make other goods. The value of producers' goods is indirect. There is no necessary relation between cost and value. The cost to a firm to acquire a certain item of equipment is not its value. The value of the capital good will depend on the earnings the firm is able to generate with it. The purchase price represents historical cost, and this is the amount recorded on the balance sheet. The value of the capital item depends on its earning power which is usually quite different from its historical cost. Hence we wish to determine not only the "book" asset protection, as shown on the balance sheet and based on historical cost, but also the earnings protection. Earnings measure the actual value of the assets.

To illustrate, imagine a hotel built in the middle of the Sahara desert at a cost of $1 million. Hypothesizing a dearth of guests, the hotel would be worthless. The inability of the assets to earn a return renders them so. What both management and investors want are earning assets, not costly assets.

Returning to the Blu-Tronics example (Table 3–3), we can compute the following:

$$\text{Times fixed charges earned} = \frac{\text{EBIT}}{\text{Fixed charges}}$$

$$= \begin{cases} \dfrac{\$3{,}442{,}000}{\$242{,}000} = 14\times & (1973) \\[2ex] \dfrac{\$2{,}023{,}000}{\$153{,}000} = 13\times & (1972) \end{cases}$$

In 1973 Blu-Tronics earned its fixed charges 14 times and in 1972, 13 times. EBIT could drop by roughly 93 percent from the 1973 level before the firm would not be covering charges.

Where two or more debt issues are outstanding, the correct procedure to follow in computing the times interest earned figure on the junior issue is the overall method. Divide the total interest charges on all issues into the earnings available either before or after deduction of federal income taxes. Though total earnings before taxes is available for the payment of interest charges, some analysts prefer deducting income taxes from the earnings available for the payment of fixed charges before computing times fixed charges. They believe this method yields a more conservative figure, which it does. Others do not deduct federal income taxes, and we also recommend not deducting income taxes. However, firms may also have preferred stock outstanding, and preferred dividends are not a tax deductible expense. The financial manager seeking to obtain comparable figures of different firms—some with only debt outstanding, others with debt and preferred stock, and still others with only preferred stock—must deduct income taxes before calculating times interest and preferred dividends earned to make the ratios for all firms comparable, as is done in Table 3–4.

TABLE 3–4. Total Interest and Preferred Dividend Coverage Calculation

| | | |
|---|---|---|
| EBIT | | $100,000 |
| Interest on bonds | $40,000 | |
| Net after interest | $60,000 | |
| Federal income tax (50 percent rate) | | 30,000 |
| Total after taxes available for interest and dividends | | $ 70,000 |
| Preferred dividends | $10,000 | |
| Total interest and preferred dividend charges | | $ 50,000 |
| Total interest and preferred dividend charge coverage after taxes $= \frac{\$70,000}{\$50,000} =$ | | 1.4 × |

Though bondholders are naturally most interested in the earnings coverage for their securities, if a junior debt issue is outstanding, the senior bondholders will also be concerned with the earnings coverage on the junior bonds. If the firm is unable to meet the interest payments on the junior debt, such default would seriously affect the senior issue. The market value of both issues would decline sharply.

As financial managers, we should know how businessmen determine the proper amount of debt to carry and what standards are employed. Some executives believe that any debt is too much. Most businesses, however, borrow at one time or another, and the financial community over time has evolved conservative standards of debt capacity for particular industries. The firm may follow the advice of its investment banker regarding the appropriate amount of debt to carry. Another approach is to follow the industry standards. A third approach is to borrow as much as possible. Regardless of the approach, the key measures employed in establishing the debt capacity of the borrower will be the debt-to-equity relationship and the ratio of times fixed charges earned.

Initially the ability of a firm to meet its interest charges is dependent upon its cash position. Earnings might not cover charges and the firm could still meet its obligations with a substantial cash balance. However, losses mean a net outflow of economic values, and the firm will find it increasingly difficult to meet its interest payments under continuing deficits. This drain will ultimately exhaust the cash balance. The fundamental support for the fixed charges is earnings. Therefore when a firm is not earning its fixed charges, though interest payments continue, the market value of all outstanding issues of the firm declines.

### Earnings, Market Price, and the Common Stockholder

The residual owners of the firm are interested in the earnings remaining after all claims and charges are paid. The major distinction between bondholders and common stockholders is that the former look to the amount of EBIT as a cushion to protect the quality of their investment while the latter look to the remaining earnings after all charges as a source of dividends and the basis for future dividends, dividend increases, and appreciation in market price. An important figure is *earnings per share*,[7] found by dividing earnings available to the common shareholder by the number of shares outstanding. For Blu-Tronics, earnings per share were $1.91 for 1973 and $1.27 for 1972 with dividends of 60 cents and 50 cents per share, respectively. The safety of the current dividend and the possibility of an increase are always of interest to the financial manager and to investors, particularly holders of common stock. For Blu-Tronics, the pay-out ratios, or the ratios of dividends to earnings, are 31 percent ($0.60/$1.91) for 1973 and 39 percent ($0.50/$1.27) for 1972. A measure of the expensiveness of the shares is the *price-earnings ratio.* It is calculated by dividing the earnings per share into the market price. The price-earnings ratio is widely used by investors as a guide when considering the purchase of the common stock of a company. Assuming that the market price of Blu-Tronics is $40 per share, the price-earnings ratio would be 21 ($40/$1.91), which is above the average for a common stock. If the stock was expected to earn $4 the following year, the price-earnings ratio based on anticipated earnings would be only 10 ($40/$4).

The *dividend yield* is the relationship of the current dividend to market price. The current dividend yield is 1.5 percent ($0.60/$40). If an investor expected the earnings of the firm to double, a stock selling at only 21 times current earnings would be quite cheap. If and when the market realized that the earnings were going to double, the price might easily be bid up to $60 per share.

The *earnings-price ratio* is frequently computed to compare the earnings the firm is yielding on its common stock. It is the reciprocal of the price-earnings ratio. The earnings-price ratio makes direct comparison of rates possible. In our illustration the stockholder is receiving a 4.8 percent earnings return ($1.91/$40).

The ratio of earnings available to the common shareholders to the common stock equity is an important measure of stockholder return on investment. The amount the firm is able to earn on its total assets and the percentages of debt, preferred and common equity (common stock, capital surplus, and retained earnings) used to finance the firm determine the earnings available for the common stock. The first concept is called *earning power*, and the second, *financial leverage.* Earning power is

[7] The flowering of diversified firms through conglomerate mergers and internal growth has created serious problems regarding the information content of reported earnings per share. One important use of financial data is to extrapolate so as to predict the future. Such extrapolation is particularly hazardous when the earnings per share grow as a result of the merger of two firms. When the price-earnings ratio of the acquiring firm exceeds that of the firm acquired, the indicated growth in earnings per share may be purely transitory, given that the share exchange is effected on the basis of market price. See Appendix B on financial reporting by diversified firms. Also see A. J. Curley, "Conglomerate Earnings per Share: Real and Transitory Growth," *Accounting Review*, 46 (July 1971), pp. 519–528.

the relationship of net operating income to operating assets and is discussed fully in Chapter 4.

Financial leverage comes into play when a firm finances part of its asset requirements by obtaining funds from those willing to accept a fixed return on their capital contribution. The amount the firm earns on its assets beyond what it must pay the suppliers of these funds accrues to the common stockholders. When the firm earns less than it must pay to its capital suppliers, the earnings available to the common stockholders are reduced proportionately. This is called *reverse leverage.* Thus, as the *EBIT* of a firm fluctuates from year to year, the earnings available to the holders of common stock will fluctuate more widely when part of the firm's asset requirements are financed by debt and preferred stock than when the firm is financed entirely by common equity. Financial leverage will be discussed in detail in later chapters.

### Use and Hazards in the Use of Ratios

Many items appear on the balance sheet and income statement, and the computation of many ratios is possible. The analyst should have a reason for computing whatever ratios he selects. Too many ratios are apt to be confusing; a few well-chosen ones will be enlightening.

When analyzing a firm, trend is important as well as current condition. Evaluation of trend requires that the same ratio be compared at different points in time. A financially weak firm growing stronger presents an entirely different picture than a financially strong firm declining in financial strength. But watch for turning points. Recognition of turning points is the mark of a great analyst. For much of the time, it is safe to predict the continuation of a trend. But the big money is made and lost at the turning points.

Note that a ratio is made up of two numbers, the numerator and the denominator. A change in the ratio from one period to the next can be caused by a change in the numerator, the denominator, or both, and the cause of the change in the ratio will affect the significance of the change. For example, if a firm has a current ratio of greater than 1 to 1, the current ratio can be improved by increasing current assets or by decreasing current liabilities.[8] An increase in current assets relative to current liabilities as a result of highly profitable operations in the last year is indicative of a real improvement in the working capital position of the firm. But if just before the balance sheet date management pays off overdue creditors, with the intention of allowing current liabilities to again accumulate after the balance sheet date, the improved current ratio will not be reflecting solid improvement. The quick ratio, however, will reflect the cash disbursement. If the current ratio is less than 1 to 1, management can improve the current ratio through increasing current liabilities by the same amount as current assets, for example, by buying inventory on credit. The quick ratio though would point up the real change that had taken place. The working capital position of the firm

[8] As long as the ratio is above 1, increasing both numerator and denominator by the same amount will cause a decline in the current ratio, while decreasing both by the same amount will cause an increase in the current ratio.

as reflected in the current and quick ratios is also substantially affected by changes in fixed assets and in long-term debt and equity. The use of working capital to finance fixed asset acquisitions will reduce the current and quick ratios, while the sale of bonds and stock will improve them. Table 3–5 gives a summary of financial ratios.

TABLE 3–5. Summary of Financial Ratios

1. Current Ratio $= \dfrac{\text{Current Assets}}{\text{Current Liabilities}}$

2. Quick Ratio $= \dfrac{\text{Current Assets—Inventory}}{\text{Current Liabilities}}$

3. Cash to Average Daily Purchases Ratio $= \dfrac{\text{Cash}}{\text{Annual Purchases/360}}$

4. Inventory Turnover $= \dfrac{\text{Cost of Goods Sold}}{\text{(Beginning Inventory + Ending Inventory)/2}}$

   or $\dfrac{\text{Cost of Goods Sold}}{\text{Ending Inventory}}$

5. Days' Credit Sales Outstanding as Receivables * $= \dfrac{\text{Receivables}}{\text{Credit Sales/360}}$

6. Percentage of Debt Financing $= \dfrac{\text{Creditor Funds}}{\text{Total Assets}}$

7. Debt-to-Equity Relationship $= \dfrac{\text{Creditor Funds}}{\text{Equity Funds}}$

8. Times Fixed Charges Earned $= \dfrac{\text{Earnings Before Interest and Taxes [EBIT]}}{\text{Fixed Charges}}$

9. Return on Investment + $= \dfrac{\text{Net Operating Income}}{\text{Operating Assets}}$

10. Operating Margin + $= \dfrac{\text{Net Operating Income}}{\text{Sales}}$

11. Asset Turnover + $= \dfrac{\text{Sales}}{\text{Operating Assets}}$

12. Return on Common + $= \dfrac{\text{Net Profit}}{\text{Net Worth}}$

13. Earnings per Share + $= \dfrac{\text{Earnings Available to the Common}^{\dagger}}{\text{Number of Shares Outstanding}}$

14. Dividend Yield + $= \dfrac{\text{Current Annual Dividend}}{\text{Market Price}}$

15. Payout Ratio + $= \dfrac{\text{Dividends per Share}}{\text{Earnings per Share}}$

16. Book Value per Common Share + $= \dfrac{\text{Net Worth}}{\text{Shares Outstanding}}$

17. Price-Earnings Ratio + $= \dfrac{\text{Earnings per Share}^{\dagger}}{\text{Market Price}}$

* Average collection period.
+ Also covered in the following chapter.
† Last 12-months earnings or projected earnings.

[A9804]

**Industry Standards**

Comparative ratio data may be obtained from a wide variety of sources. These include the industry ratios of Dun & Bradstreet Inc., Robert Morris Associates (a national association of bank loan officers), the Federal Trade Commission (FTC), the Securities and Exchange Commission (SEC), and trade associations. The most well-known and widely used source is Dun & Bradstreet, which computes 14 ratios for 125 lines of business. For each of the ratios, the upper, median, and lower quartile is given. With this information one can quickly determine where a particular firm ranks in relation to its industry; comparisons can be made for each of the 14 ratios. The computation of a firm's ratios and comparison of these with the industry figures is simple. The judgmental questions are whether the firm is representative of the industry, and whether the industry ratios reflect sound financial practice under the current economic conditions.

Table 3–6 presents liquidity, activity, leverage, and profitability ratios for several selected industries. An analysis of the data reveals some interesting information.

A current ratio of 2 to 1 is a rule of thumb. Observe in Table 3–6 the diverse industry groups whose median quartile figures are approximately 2 to 1: home furnishings, malt liquor, toys. There are deviations (petroleum, 1.72 to 1) but they are not as wide as one might expect. The current ratio for all manufacturing corporations at the end of 1969 was just a shade above 2 to 1.[9] It had declined from a high of over 3 to 1 approximately 20 years earlier. Corporate liquidity declined noticeably in 1969 and 1970. The absence of depressions and the growth of inflation since 1965 have caused firms to reduce their high liquidity after World War II and shift resources into inventories and plant and equipment.

Blu-Tronics, with a current ratio of 2 to 1 in 1972, is in the lower end of the scale for its industry group—electric transmission and distribution equipment. The lower quartile figure is 1.95.

As might be expected, the collection period in days is widely different for the various industry groups, reflecting different trade terms. Blu-Tronics had a 54-day average collection period for 1972, a little better than the industry average of 62 days. By 1973 however Blu-Tronics was up to 65 days. Also as might be expected the inventory turnover ratio varies widely from industry to industry; 16.4 times for malt liquor down to 4.6 for electric transmission equipment. Similarly, total debt to tangible net worth (which measures financial leverage) varies widely: 171.5 percent for electric appliance wholesalers down to 69.1 percent for petroleum refining. Blu-Tronics had a ratio of 148 percent in 1972 compared to the industry median of 81.8 percent. By 1973 Blu-Tronics ratio had dropped to 137 percent. Note that the net profits on tangible net worth figures for various industries are remarkably uniform. (See, for example, the median quartile figures.) The figures for Blu-Tronics are

[9] Economic Report of the President, 1971, p. 173.

**TABLE 3–6. Key Financial Ratios * for Selected Industries, 1971**

| Line of Business (and number of concerns reporting) | Current assets to current debt | Net profits on net sales | Net profits on tangible net worth | Net profits on net working capital | Net sales to tangible net worth | Net sales to net working capital | Collection period | Net sales to inventory | Fixed assets to tangible net worth | Current debt to tangible net worth † | Total debt to tangible net worth | Inventory to net working capital | Current debt to inventory | Funded debts to net working capital |
|---|---|---|---|---|---|---|---|---|---|---|---|---|---|---|
| | Times | Per cent | Per cent | Per cent | Times | Times | Days | Times | Per cent | Per cent | Per cent | Per cent | Per cent | Per cent |
| Department Stores (259) | 4.47 | 2.92 | 9.28 | 11.81 | 4.69 | 5.98 | — | 7.1 | 11.7 | 22.4 | 51.9 | 57.6 | 44.1 | 16.3 [a] |
| | 2.89 | 1.55 | 5.42 | 7.05 | 3.13 | 4.15 | — | 5.6 | 26.0 | 42.1 | 82.0 | 76.9 | 69.8 | 32.2 [b] |
| | 2.06 | 0.52 | 1.61 | 2.05 | 2.37 | 3.05 | — | 4.3 | 54.2 | 70.6 | 128.1 | 107.5 | 101.9 | 66.2 [c] |
| Electrical Appliances, TV & Radio Sets (92) ** | 2.76 | 2.03 | 12.45 | 13.76 | 8.32 | 9.48 | 30 | 8.3 | 3.9 | 48.0 | 113.6 | 70.0 | 73.9 | 11.6 [a] |
| | 1.91 | 1.22 | 7.69 | 8.81 | 6.12 | 7.34 | 42 | 5.9 | 7.5 | 103.4 | 171.5 | 117.7 | 96.6 | 21.8 [b] |
| | 1.48 | 0.72 | 4.23 | 5.24 | 4.56 | 5.13 | 52 | 4.8 | 18.7 | 182.6 | 258.2 | 162.6 | 128.6 | 54.6 [c] |
| Furniture & Home Furnishings (79) ** | 3.76 | 2.80 | 11.15 | 13.95 | 6.06 | 7.38 | 37 | 7.7 | 4.9 | 32.5 | 81.4 | 55.4 | 65.0 | 12.0 [a] |
| | 2.35 | 1.43 | 7.02 | 8.10 | 4.23 | 5.15 | 48 | 6.3 | 11.8 | 67.4 | 113.1 | 85.8 | 101.4 | 30.0 [b] |
| | 1.66 | 0.63 | 2.93 | 3.57 | 2.90 | 3.39 | 67 | 4.6 | 27.3 | 120.9 | 177.9 | 114.8 | 136.8 | 51.0 [c] |
| Books: Publishing, Publishing & Printing (57) ** | 3.64 | 6.86 | 12.65 | 20.03 | 2.73 | 4.49 | 48 | 6.9 | 14.3 | 21.3 | 38.3 | 38.2 | 66.1 | 7.5 [a] |
| | 2.59 | 4.71 | 8.15 | 11.10 | 1.94 | 2.77 | 68 | 4.1 | 36.0 | 45.4 | 57.8 | 65.6 | 95.4 | 25.8 [b] |
| | 2.09 | 1.90 | 2.56 | 4.45 | 1.31 | 2.06 | 96 | 3.0 | 56.2 | 64.3 | 106.4 | 89.1 | 165.2 | 54.2 [c] |
| Electric ** Transmission & Distribution Equipment (64) | 3.83 | 4.14 | 11.99 | 14.99 | 3.82 | 4.73 | 48 | 5.5 | 29.7 | 27.8 | 50.3 | 67.0 | 53.0 | 20.0 [a] |
| | 2.93 | 2.58 | 7.15 | 8.73 | 2.59 | 3.14 | 62 | 4.2 | 41.9 | 42.9 | 81.8 | 77.4 | 78.7 | 42.8 [b] |
| | 1.95 | (2.49) | (2.87) | (4.03) | 1.88 | 2.66 | 81 | 3.1 | 62.3 | 77.4 | 166.1 | 93.8 | 105.5 | 80.4 [c] |
| Electronic Components & Accessories (95) ** | 3.55 | 4.41 | 10.18 | 16.19 | 3.89 | 5.40 | 51 | 6.3 | 31.8 | 31.0 | 58.0 | 58.5 | 59.3 | 26.5 [a] |
| | 2.55 | 1.83 | 5.04 | 6.45 | 2.45 | 3.55 | 59 | 4.6 | 55.1 | 43.0 | 86.7 | 79.3 | 84.6 | 54.8 [b] |
| | 1.78 | (3.60) | (10.28) | (12.19) | 1.97 | 2.63 | 73 | 3.3 | 79.0 | 80.7 | 139.1 | 94.2 | 135.7 | 87.5 [c] |
| Malt Liquors (26) †† | 2.79 | 5.15 | 14.22 | 63.37 | 4.21 | 15.79 | 11 | 21.6 | 55.4 | 17.9 | 46.3 | 33.4 | 118.1 | 64.5 [a] |
| | 2.12 | 1.91 | 6.83 | 32.14 | 2.61 | 10.45 | 14 | 16.4 | 75.6 | 27.9 | 59.5 | 59.1 | 162.4 | 97.5 [b] |
| | 1.56 | 0.60 | 1.49 | 4.57 | 2.16 | 6.64 | 27 | 11.6 | 102.6 | 37.9 | 98.9 | 88.2 | 194.0 | 133.0 [c] |
| Petroleum Refining (51) †† | 2.04 | 6.89 | 10.93 | 56.41 | 3.36 | 12.20 | 38 | 13.4 | 83.9 | 24.8 | 50.4 | 51.8 | 138.8 | 62.0 [a] |
| | 1.72 | 4.87 | 8.73 | 37.70 | 1.91 | 7.86 | 49 | 10.5 | 101.5 | 35.4 | 69.1 | 76.8 | 188.1 | 141.6 [b] |
| | 1.41 | 1.99 | 5.70 | 13.68 | 1.37 | 5.35 | 70 | 7.7 | 118.1 | 54.2 | 121.2 | 134.4 | 240.4 | 196.5 [c] |
| Toys, Amusement & Sporting Goods (63) †† | 3.93 | 5.36 | 17.55 | 22.38 | 5.04 | 6.31 | 46 | 6.9 | 14.7 | 28.4 | 60.8 | 54.4 | 62.7 | 17.8 [a] |
| | 2.37 | 2.52 | 8.68 | 10.51 | 3.43 | 4.26 | 59 | 4.9 | 27.1 | 58.4 | 111.8 | 86.8 | 92.0 | 34.0 [b] |
| | 1.69 | 1.00 | 4.19 | 5.76 | 2.67 | 3.31 | 82 | 4.0 | 57.0 | 106.8 | 180.7 | 126.2 | 138.1 | 65.0 [c] |

SOURCE: Dun & Bradstreet, Key Business Ratios in 125 Lines, 1971. Used by permission.

* Rounded.

† Tangible net worth is stockholder's equity minus any intangible assets such as goodwill.

** Wholesaling.

†† Manufacturing.

[a] Upper quartile. With all figures for a given ratio ranked from highest to lowest, the upper quartile figure represents the ratio figure one-fourth of the way below the highest figure.

[b] Median quartile—the ratio figure mid-way between the highest and the lowest figures.

[c] Lower quartile—the ratio figure one-fourth of the way above the lowest figure.

far above the industry average: 25.4 percent [10] for 1972 versus an average of 8.92 percent. Evidently Blu-Tronics' high leverage is paying off.

One set of figures important to all long-term investors is not given in Table 3–6—times interest earned. Comparative figures must be obtained from other sources. Blu-Tronics covered their charges 13 times

[10] See Chapter 4, p. 71.

in 1972. Authorities in the field of security analysis recommend the following average figures: public utilities, 4 times; railroads, 5 times; industrials 7 times, and retail firms 5 times.[11]

## SOURCE AND APPLICATION OF FUNDS STATEMENT

Information regarding developing trends may also be obtained by studying the balance sheet changes over some time period. A *source and application of funds statement* reveals the changes that have taken place in assets, liabilities, and stockholders' equity. The period selected should correspond with the purpose of the analysis. If our concern is with the short-term changes that occur as the firm goes through its seasonal period, we would choose a span of months covering the season. If we are interested in the longer-term changes that occur as the firm goes through its cyclical swing, we would choose the span of years covering the cycle. If our interest is in the growth or decline of the firm, we would choose the span of time covering such fundamental changes in the position of the firm.

Frequently the source and application of funds statement will show the change in working capital in summary form. The changes in working capital are netted with the net working capital figure presented for the beginning and the end of the period. By eliminating short-term financing movements and the purchase and sales circuit flow of funds, attention is focused on the major sources and applications of funds. In our example we show all changes in the current asset items in order to present a more complete picture of what transpired between balance sheet dates.

The source and application of funds statement does not show the path traced by the balance sheet amounts from the level at the beginning of the period to the level at the end of the period. The path may not be a smooth path though the analysis implicitly assumes it is. If the path is important, intermediate periods must be selected for analysis, if the analyst has reason to believe that there were major deviations from the smooth line.

### Preparing the Source and Application of Funds Statement

To prepare the source and application of funds statement, first calculate the changes that have taken place in the asset, liability, and net worth items. Then classify and sort the net change in each account according to whether it is a source or a use of funds. Among the uses of funds are: (1) increases in assets, (2) decreases in liabilities, and (3) decreases in net worth. The balance sheet items representing sources of funds are those that provide the firm with the power of purchase. They are: (1) decreases in assets, (2) increases in liabilities, and (3) increases in net worth. A decrease in cash is a source of funds. In addition, we need certain items from the income statement, such as deprecia-

[11] Benjamin Graham, David L. Dodd, Sidney Cottle, and Charles Tatham, *Security Analysis*, 4th ed. (New York: McGraw-Hill Inc., 1962), p. 373.

tion (source), earnings (source), and dividends (use). The funds statement of Blu-Tronics, Inc. is given in Table 3–7.

TABLE 3–7. Blu-Tronics, Inc.
Comparative Statement of Source and Application of Funds *

| | *Year ended December 31* | |
|---|---|---|
| | *1973* | *1972* |
| *Source of Funds* | | |
| Operations | | |
| Net earnings for the year | $1,590,000 | $ 970,000 |
| Add depreciation of plant and equipment that did not require use of funds | 325,000 | 264,000 |
| Total from operations | $1,915,000 | $1,234,000 |
| Proceeds from sale of common stock | 913,000 | |
| Additional long-term borrowing | | 1,240,000 |
| Increase in current liabilities | 2,431,000 | 866,000 |
| Decrease (increase) in cash | 244,000 | (57,000) |
| | $5,503,000 | $3,283,000 |
| *Application of Funds* | | |
| Cash dividends to stockholders | $ 480,000 | $ 381,000 |
| Payment on long-term notes payable | 120,000 | |
| Additions to property, plant, equipment (net) | 627,000 | 872,000 |
| Increase in accounts receivable | 1,334,000 | 327,000 |
| Increase in inventories | 2,940,000 | 1,721,000 |
| Miscellaneous, net | 2,000 | (18,000) |
| | $5,503,000 | $3,283,000 |

* The 1973 figures may be obtained from Table 3–1. Those for 1972 require a 1971 balance sheet.

### Analysis of the Source and Application of Funds Statement

In 1973 the majority of the funds came from an increase in current liabilities ($2,431,000), earnings ($1,590,000), and sale of common stock ($913,000). These funds were used primarily to increase working capital—a $2,940,000 increase in inventory and a $1,334,000 increase in receivables. In 1972 one major source was long-term borrowing—$1,240,000—and major uses were in inventories of $1,721,000 and additions to plant of $872,000.

Blu-Tronics represents a substantial growth firm. If we were to calculate the balance sheet changes over a longer period of time, we would find that a major portion of the firm's funds were supplied by retained earnings and by long- and short-term creditors and that these funds were used primarily to increase receivables and inventory. Cash balances remained low and plant and equipment increased only moderately.

## SUMMARY

Ratios are the tools of analysis. The basic statements normally analyzed are the balance sheet, income statement, and statement of source and application of funds. The short-term creditor, since his loan will be repaid from accounts receivable and through conversion of inventory to cash in the normal course of business, looks primarily to the current and quick ratios, the percentage that cash, receivables, and inventory bear to total working capital, the amount of cash in terms of average daily purchases, inventory turnover, and days' credit sales outstanding. He looks for liquidity.

Long-term suppliers of funds are interested in the return the firm is earning on its total invested capital. They look primarily to the debt-to-equity relationship, times charges earned, and the prospects for long-term earnings. A good working capital position can be quickly dissipated through large losses.

The concerns of holders of common stock are earnings and dividends. They are interested in both the return on total capital of the firm and the return on common equity. The price-earnings ratio tells the holder of common stock how much the market is currently willing to pay for each dollar of earnings.

### *Study Questions*

1. The earnings figure is whatever management desires. Discuss.
2. To eliminate the wide variability in accounting treatment, it would be reasonable for the Securities and Exchange Commission to impose a uniform standard of financial statements on all industrial firms. Discuss.
3. Why does management place such emphasis on the earnings figure? Why do stockholders also focus on the earnings figure?
4. Why is it in the national interest for financial statements to reflect fairly the operations of a firm?
5. How would the analysis of a firm's financial statements differ if conducted by a short-term creditor? a long-term creditor? or a stockholder?
6. What are the ratios that measure the liquidity position of the firm? Can one "poor" ratio be offset by another "good" ratio? Of what value are industry standards?
7. What are the dangers indicated by weak liquidity ratios?
8. How can increasing a firm's inventory turnover improve its profitability? its working capital position?
9. In what fields of business enterprise would you expect (a) a high margin of profit, (b) a low margin of profit, (c) a low times fixed charges earned ratio, (d) a high price-earnings ratio, (e) a low dividend yield, (f) a high dividend yield, (g) a high inventory turnover, (h) a low inventory turnover, and (i) a high debt-to-equity relationship?
10. What is the difference between cost and value? Why do individuals desire valuable items rather than costly ones? How does society benefit from this preference for value over costs?
11. What is leverage? How can it benefit the stockholder?

12. How does summarizing the changes in liquidity in the source and application of funds statement aid in the financial analysis of a firm?
13. What are the major differences among the balance sheet, the income statement, and the source and application of funds statement?
14. In what sense is a decrease in cash a source of funds?

### Problems

1. The Knotty Pine Lumber Company at the beginning of the heavy building season on April 30 has current assets of $300,000 and current liabilities of $600,000. Compute the current ratio after giving effect to each of the following transactions. Cumulate the transactions.

a. $50,000 of additional inventory was purchased on credit.

b. An additional $200,000 of cash was borrowed on a short-term loan from the friendly banker.

What do yon notice about the current ratio? Through increasing short-term financing do you think management can ever make it reach 1? surpass 1? Why not?

On August 31, the firm has current assets of $500,000 and current liabilities of $500,000. Compute the current ratio after giving effect to each of the following transactions. Cumulate the transactions.

c. A $100,000 bank loan is paid off with cash.

d. $200,000 of inventory is acquired on credit.

e. Income taxes of $50,000 are paid.

What do you notice about the current ratio? What is the mathematical principle involved?

On December 31, the firm has current assets of $200,000 and current liabilities of $100,000. Compute the current ratio after giving effect to each of the following transactions. Cumulate the transactions.

f. $400,000 of cash is borrowed from the friendly banker.

g. $200,000 of additional inventory is acquired on credit. What do you notice about the current ratio? Through increasing short-term financing would it ever reach 1? Why not? What are the implications of the mechanics for computing the current ratio to the financial executive in the management of working capital?

2. Using the December 31 Knotty Pine Lumber Company figures of current assets ($400,000) and current liabilities ($200,000), compute the current ratio and net working capital after giving effect to each of the following transactions. *Do not* cumulate.

a. Several new trucks are purchased for $20,000 cash.

b. $40,000 of new machinery is purchased on a short-term note.

c. A dividend of $10,000 is paid (assume accrued dividends on the balance sheet).

d. $5,000 of accounts receivable is collected.

e. $15,000 of short-term Treasury securities is purchased.

f. A $50,000 mortgage is taken out on the building to increase cash.

g. $20,000 of accounts payable is paid off.

h. Old machinery is sold for $10,000 cash.

i. A long-term note of $20,000 is paid off.

Contrast the answers to g and i. What is the reason for the disparity? What implications for working capital management do you see?

3. The balance sheet and income statement for 1973 and 1972 of the Mini-Machines Company appear in Table 3–8 and Table 3–9.

TABLE 3–8. Mini-Machines Company

Balance Sheet

| | December 31 | | | December 31 | |
|---|---|---|---|---|---|
| | 1973 | 1972 | | 1973 | 1972 |
| Current Assets | | | Current Liabilities | | |
| Cash | $ 437,000 | $ 396,000 | Accounts payable | $ 705,000 | $ 598,000 |
| Marketable securities | 377,000 | 570,000 | Loans | 195,000 | 174,000 |
| Accounts receivable (net) | 803,000 | 574,000 | Accrued items | 279,000 | 296,000 |
| Inventories | 390,000 | 297,000 | | | |
| Prepaid insurance, etc. | 46,000 | 93,000 | | | |
| Total current assets | $2,053,000 | $1,930,000 | Total current liabilities | $1,179,000 | $1,068,000 |
| Fixed Assets | | | Long-term debt | $ 659,000 | $ 599,000 |
| Land | $ 65,000 | $ 57,000 | Capital stock | | |
| Building and equipment | 5,742,000 | 4,495,000 | 530,000 shares outstanding | 1,311,000 | — |
| | $5,807,000 | $4,552,000 | 356,000 shares outstanding | — | 862,000 |
| Less depreciation | 2,708,000 | 2,248,000 | | | |
| Net fixed assets | $3,099,000 | $2,304,000 | Retained earnings | $2,011,000 | $1,716,000 |
| Goodwill less amortization | $ 8,000 | $ 11,000 | Net Worth | $3,322,000 | $2,578,000 |
| Total assets | $5,160,000 | $4,245,000 | Total liabilities and net worth | $5,160,000 | $4,245,000 |

TABLE 3–9. Mini-Machines Company
Income Statement

| | Year ending December 31 | |
|---|---|---|
| | 1973 | 1972 |
| Sales | $4,348,000 | $3,673,000 |
| Costs and expenses | | |
| Costs of goods sold | 2,742,000 | 2,205,000 |
| Depreciation | 460,000 | 423,000 |
| Operating costs | 3,202,000 | 2,628,000 |
| Operating profit | 1,146,000 | 1,045,000 |
| Amortization of goodwill | 3,000 | 3,000 |
| Interest expense | 24,000 | 18,000 |
| Total operating and nonoperating expenses | $3,229,000 | $2,649,000 |
| | $1,019,000 | $1,024,000 |
| Other income | $ 35,000 | $ 36,000 |
| Net before income tax | $1,154,000 | $1,060,000 |
| Income tax | $ 528,000 | $ 483,000 |
| Net profit | $ 626,000 | $ 577,000 |
| Other information | 1973 | 1972 |
| Earnings per share | $ 1.18 | $ 1.62 |
| Dividends per share | 0.50 | 0.46 |
| Market price per share | $40.00 | $30.00 |
| All sales are made on credit. | | |

**Note:** A rights offering resulting in the increase in stock outstanding was made in early 1973. All per share figures are adjusted.

a. From the Mini-Machines Company financial statements compute the following for the years 1973 and 1972: (1) current ratio, (2) quick ratio, (3) percentage composition of current assets, (4) cash in terms of average daily purchases, (5) inventory turnover (using ending inventory), (6) days' credit sales outstanding (materials are 60% of cost of goods sold), (7) long-term debt-to-equity ratio, (8) times interest charges earned, (9) earnings and dividends per share (verify the figures), (10) price-earnings ratio, and (11) dividend yield.

b. What does your analysis regarding the financial condition of this company reveal?

c. Compute the long-term debt-to-equity ratio using the market value of the equity (number of shares of stock outstanding times market price) instead of book equity. What does this tell you about "cost" and "value"? What can you surmise from the market's valuation of this company?

d. Compare Mini-Machines with the industry standards for computer companies. Where does Mini-Machines stand?

**4.** Prepare a funds statement for Mini-Machines for 1973. The accountant had scrambled his notes but tells you there were some direct charges to earnings which did not go through the income statement. Comment on the statement of funds.

5. The financial manager of the Puzzle Corporation, upon hearing that the firm's president just completed a course in financial management, submitted to him a year-end balance sheet (Table 3–10) and additional items of information with a note suggesting that the completion of the balance sheet would be a good opportunity for him to demonstrate his knowledge and at the same time to get in some practice.

TABLE 3–10. Puzzle Corporation
Balance Sheet
December 31, 1973

| Assets | | Liabilities and net worth | |
|---|---|---|---|
| Cash | | Accounts payable | |
| Accounts receivable | | Long-term debt | |
| Inventory | | Common stock | $250,000 |
| Plant and equipment | $800,000 | Surplus | 550,000 |

*Additional Information:* Day's credit sales outstanding, 30, based on a 360-day year; interest at the rate of 5 percent, or $5,000, was paid on the long-term debt; debt-to-equity ratio, 0.75 to 1; operating asset turnover, (sales to operating assets), 2; quick ratio, 1 to 1; current ratio 1.2 to 1; all sales are on credit.

Unfortunately, the president did not do his lessons well and asks you as his assistant to complete the balance sheet.

6. Analyze the financial data in Table 3–11 and Table 3–12 taken from the 1973 statements of the Elixir Drug Co. Industry averages for the drug industry are given below for purposes of comparison (Table 3–13).

a. Compute the indicated ratios for Elixir.

b. Compare your ratio results with the industry averages to detect possible management policy errors.

TABLE 3–11. Elixir Drug Co.
Balance Sheet
December 31, 1973

| | | | |
|---|---|---|---|
| Cash | $ 96,000 | Accounts payable | $ 42,000 |
| Receivables | 74,000 | Notes payable | 5,000 |
| Inventory | 90,000 | Other current liabilities | 30,000 |
| Total current assets | $260,000 | Total current liabilities | $ 77,000 |
| | | Long-term debt | 23,000 |
| Fixed assets (net) | 104,000 | Net worth | 264,000 |
| Total assets | $364,000 | Total liabilities and net worth | $364,000 |

TABLE 3–12. Elixir Drug Co.
Income Statement
For Year Ended December 31, 1973

| | | |
|---|---|---|
| Sales | | $450,000 |
| Costs | | |
| Cost of Sales | $124,000 | |
| Distribution and marketing | 146,000 | |
| Research | 25,000 | |
| Administrative and other | 45,000 | 340,000 |
| Profit before income tax | | $110,000 |
| Income tax | | 50,000 |
| Net profit | | $ 60,000 |

TABLE 3–13. Ratios and Averages for Drug Industry

| | *Elixir* | *Industry Average* |
|---|---|---|
| Current ratio | | 2.2 × |
| Sales to inventory | | 6.0 × |
| Days' credit sales outstanding as receivables | | 55 days |
| Total debt to net worth | | 54.9% |
| Sales to total assets | | 1.3 × |
| Sales to net worth | | 2.1 × |
| Net profit to sales | | 4.8% |
| Net profit to total assets | | 8.4% |
| Net profit to net worth | | 13.0% |

### Selected References


Altman, E. I., "Financial Ratios, Discriminant Analysis and the Prediction of Corporate Bankruptcy," *Journal of Finance,* 23 (September 1968), pp. 589–609.

Bierman, H., Jr., "Measuring Financial Liquidity," *Accounting Review,* 35 (October 1960), pp. 628–632.

Foulke, R. A., *Practical Financial Statement Analysis,* 6th ed. New York: McGraw-Hill, Inc., 1968.

Grunewald, A. E., "Computer-Assisted Investment Analysis," *Business Topics,* (Spring 1967), pp. 11–19.

Helfert, E. A., *Techniques of Financial Analysis,* 3d ed. Homewood, Ill.: Richard D. Irwin, Inc., 1972.

Hobgood, G., "Increased Disclosure in 1969 Annual Reports," *Financial Executive,* 38 (August 1970), pp. 24–33.

Horrigan, J. O., "A Short History of Financial Ratio Analysis," *Accounting Review,* 43 (April 1968), pp. 284–294.

Jaedicke, R. K., and R. T. Sprouse, *Accounting Flows: Income, Funds, and Cash,* Englewood Cliffs, N. J.: Prentice-Hall, Inc., 1965.

McFarland, W. B., "Review of Funds Flow Analysis," *Harvard Business Review*, 41 (September–October 1963), pp. 162 ff.

Mason, P., "'Cash Flow' Analysis and Funds Statements," *Journal of Accountancy*, 111 (March 1961), pp. 59–72.

Murray, Roger, "Lessons for Financial Analysis," *Journal of Finance*, 26 (May 1971), pp. 327–332.

Spacek, L., "The Merger Accounting Dilemma," *Financial Executive*, 38 (February 1970), pp. 38 ff.

Spencer, C. H., and T. S. Barnhisel, "A Decade of Price-Level Changes—The Effect on the Financial Statements of Cummins Engine Company," *Accounting Review*, 40 (January 1965), pp. 144–153.

## *Appendix A*

## INFLUENCE OF MANAGERIAL DECISIONS ON REPORTED EARNINGS

A firm that maintains its books on a cash basis, pays for all items in cash, does not grant credit, and does not have any noncash charges can fairly accurately equate an increase in cash at the end of the year over the starting balance with the profit earned for the period, assuming no loans were made or repaid and no equipment was purchased. This method of operation, with its accompanying method of cash accounting exists only as a textbook illustration. Most firms require some fixed assets, thereby giving rise to depreciation charges; credit frequently is granted; and materials are usually purchased on open-book account. With the growth of the business, bookkeeping is shifted from cash to accrual accounting. The result is a wide disparity between the amount of net cash inflow and the profit earned for the period.

The amount of earnings reported is not the result of a foolproof or tamperproof set of accounting principles. Nor are all managements interested in a fair presentation of the facts. Both the revenue to be reported and the costs to be allocated to an accounting period can be substantially [12] influenced by managerial decision. The partner of a large public accounting firm states that, given the books of the company, he can double the earnings in a year's time.[13] Let us look first at revenues and then at costs.

A manufacturing firm upon delivery and acceptance of its goods will consider the sale complete and recognize the revenue; the revenue is recorded in the period in which the total performance is completed. In some industries, however, a project may extend over several years. The practice of recognizing profit only in the year of completion might result in a succession of periods in which losses are reported, followed by a period in which a substantial profit is reported. To avoid this, the practice has developed of recognizing profit as work progresses based on the percentage of work completed. The ship-building industry is an example. A firm will prorate to each year of construction a portion of the total estimated profit on the contract based on a percentage of the work completed during the period. Management is required to estimate the total profit to be earned on the

---

[12] "What Are Earnings? The Growing Credibility Gap," *Forbes*, 99 (May 15, 1967), pp. 28–31. Also see "CPA Audits & Gobbledygook Guides," *Wall Street Journal*, June 7, 1967, p. 16; "Up and Down Wall Street," *Barron's*, June 5, 1967, p. 21 and November 15, 1971, p. 29 (regarding Playboy Enterprises), and December 13, 1971, p. 29 (regarding Fedders Corporation).

[13] "What Are Earnings? The Growing Credibility Gap," *Forbes*, 99 (May 15, 1967), p. 30.

contract and the percentage of work completed. Though the total contract price may be known, the future costs are only estimates.

When the activities of a firm are proceeding normally, revenues are generated from operations and a profit is earned. Part of the profit may be distributed to the owners and the remainder credited to retained earnings. Occasionally, unusual gains may arise because of the sale of securities, land holdings, or an unprofitable subsidiary, or unusual losses may arise as a result of damage from fire, hurricanes, and so on. These extraordinary gains or losses may either be carried through the income statement or reflected directly against surplus. The method selected will influence the amount of reported earnings. The management of the Hupp Corporation in its acquisition and subsequent disposal of Hercules Engine chose the best of both worlds.[14] Upon acquiring Hercules Engine at less than book value, Hupp took the difference into earnings, but when Hercules was later disposed of at less than the cost, the loss was tagged as a special charge for that year.

A firm with overseas subsidiaries affords management still another opportunity for influencing reported profit. Most firms issue consolidated reports in which the full earnings of the subsidiary are included. Some firms however—for example, Otis Elevator—include only remitted dividends. For many years IBM also included only the remitted dividends but a number of years ago switched to a fully consolidated basis. Finally, a firm selling major items such as cemetery lots (Savoy Industries) or mobile franchised ice cream units (Tastee Freez) [15] on the installment basis can account for the income generated by the transactions in two ways. The firm can take all the earnings from the sale immediately as income (though the customer may have as much as five years to pay) or spread the earnings over the life of the installment sale.

The manner in which costs are recognized and calculated is also significant in influencing the reported profit figure. Important are the areas of depreciation; inventory valuation; research and development expenses; taxes on subsidiary profits; pension costs and retirement allowances; and with an acquisition, the treatment of goodwill, depreciation base, and the loss carry-over of the acquired company. Based on an actual case, *Forbes,* following conservative and liberal methods of accounting, determined that the earnings of an actual company could be either $1.99 or $3.14 per share.[16]

Given the depreciation method, the estimates of the useful life of the asset and its salvage value will also affect the amount of depreciation charged and hence profit reported. The charges will be higher or lower depending on management's estimate of a shorter or longer useful life and a lower or higher salvage value. Further, the practice of basing depreciation on historical cost during a long period of rising prices misleads one as to future earnings since the assets must be replaced at higher prices. Although accounting convention and the Internal Revenue Service do not permit the calculation of depreciation on the basis of replacement costs, some firms have made a special effort in their annual reports to point to the inflated nature of the reported profits.

First in, first out (FIFO), last in, first out (LIFO), and average cost are three methods of valuing inventory. In periods of generally rising prices, FIFO

---

[14] Over $1 million was added to earnings in the span of four years (in three of these years earnings were boosted by 10 percent or more). A net loss of $1.3 million resulted from the sale. See *Barron's* "Up and Down Wall Street," June 5, 1967, p. 21.

[15] Tastee Freez became overextended and went into receivership.

[16] "What Are Earnings? The Growing Credibility Gap" *Forbes*, 99 (May 15, 1967), pp. 28–31.

will produce a larger profit figure than LIFO. The inventory acquired earlier carries a lower cost than that acquired later. Feeding this lower-cost inventory into profit determination through following FIFO will result in a wider margin between cost and revenue, producing larger profit. Should management decide to shift from FIFO to LIFO, reported earnings would in the future be reduced from what they would have been had the firm continued to follow the FIFO method.

Research expenditures may be charged off as expense or capitalized and carried to the balance sheet. The capitalization of these expenditures can be justified, since they will contribute to earnings in future years.[17] However, it is difficult to estimate the period of years over which these values should be amortized. The way in which the issue is decided will affect reported earnings.

When a merger takes place, the management of the acquiring company has a golden opportunity to influence the firm's reported earnings. If the merger is effected through accounting as a purchase, goodwill arises which may be charged immediately to surplus or written off against income in the current year or over a period of time. Recently these possibilities have been limited by new rules to be discussed in Chapter 23. The alternative to purchase accounting is to combine by a pooling of interest, in which case the balance sheets of the two companies are simply combined. But this raises new possibilities for manipulation.[18]

## *Appendix B*

## FINANCIAL REPORTING BY DIVERSIFIED FIRMS

Financial statements are the springboard for internal or external analysis of a firm. The tools of analysis are ratios and other analytical techniques discussed in Chapters 3 and 4. The work of the analyst consists of comparing and predicting. Comparison is a necessary prelude to prediction. The analyst compares the performance of the firm to overall economic conditions, to industry averages, to other firms in the industry, and to prior performance of the firm over a period of months or years. For these comparisons to serve as the basis of reliable prediction, the financial statements must present relevant information regarding the firm's financial position and its operating results. There is little problem when a firm has only one product sold in one market.

But the real world is not that simple. Many firms produce a wide variety of products that sell in many markets. Westinghouse produces electrical appliances and machinery and even pollution-control equipment and nuclear devices; National Distillers produces liquor and chemicals; Gulf & Western operates in eleven major groups. Countless firms sell in both domestic and foreign markets. Thus, a set of consolidated general purpose statements—balance sheet, income statement, and source and application of funds statement—may not contain all the information necessary about a firm's financial position and operating results to permit comparison and prediction using our analytical tools.

To illustrate the difficulty of using consolidated financial statements, suppose as investors we are interested in predicting next year's earnings of a firm that has three divisions operating in unrelated markets. The earnings of the divi-

---

[17] On similar grounds it has been suggested that advertising outlays be capitalized rather than expensed.

[18] "Up and Down Wall Street," *Barron's*, February 14, 1972, p. 29 (regarding Browning-Ferris Industries).

sions and the consolidated earnings for the previous five years are presented in Table 3–14.

TABLE 3–14. Divisional and Consolidated Earnings

| | Year | | | | | |
|---|---|---|---|---|---|---|
| Division | 1 | 2 | 3 | 4 | 5 | 6 (est) |
| A | $ 100 | $ 200 | $ 400 | $ 800 | $1000 | ? |
| B | 1000 | 1200 | 1100 | 1000 | 1000 | ? |
| C | 900 | 800 | 900 | 900 | 1000 | ? |
| Consolidated | $2000 | $2200 | $2400 | $2700 | $3000 | ? |

Based on the *consolidated* income statement we might predict $3300 in year 6 by simple extrapolation. But with divisional detail available we see the actual is likely to be around $3000 and could even drop to $2900—a reversal of trend. Table 3–14 clearly illustrates the difficulty of extrapolating the past performance of a firm as an entity on the basis of a consolidated statement unless all divisions have substantially similar past earnings patterns and are likely to show a similar performance in the future.

With no information regarding the factors responsible for the growth trend in this company an investor cannot ascertain the conditions that would cause the trend to reverse. But if financial statements contain sufficient detail enabling an investor to understand the *composition* of the earnings growth trend then he is in a better position to anticipate future earnings.

In October 1970, the Securities and Exchange Commission (SEC) ruled that larger publicly held companies must break down their total revenue and income before income taxes by line of business and report the percentages attributable to each line on Form 10–K beginning with the year 1972. The detail must be shown for any line of business that accounts for 10 percent or more of total revenue or earnings. For firms of less than $50 million revenue, the specified percentage is 15 percent.

One problem is that the SEC rules do not require these same disclosures be made in the firm's annual report to its shareholders. Though the information is available to the public at the SEC office [19] in Washington D. C., shareholders are largely dependent on annual reports.

A significant increase occurred in 1970 in the number of firms voluntarily providing a divisional breakdown in their annual report to shareholders.[20] Many firms (over half) showed contributions to revenue by divisions, but substantially fewer (about a fourth) showed contribution to earnings by division.[21] But many firms declined to disclose revenue and earnings on anything other than a total basis. Despite the obvious benefits to investors, these firms for competitive or other reasons refrained.

---

[19] Copies of Form 10–K may be requested at reproduction cost by letter as well as by personal visit to the SEC reference room.

[20] E. Hobgood, "Segmented Disclosure in 1970 Annual Reports," *Financial Executive*, 39 (August 1971), pp. 18–22.

[21] Singer, for example, reports revenue and earnings by major product category—Consumer Products, Industrial Products, Information Systems, Aerospace and Marine Systems, Education and Training Products—and revenue by geographic area—United States, Canada, Europe, and so on. See the Singer Company's *Annual Report*, 1970, p. 1. Also see the ITT 1970 *Annual Report*, p. 3.

The full disclosure problem is one of growing importance both to financial managers faced with recommending the format of the financial statements and the external user required to rely on general purpose statements in the making of investment decisions.[22] The growth in the merger and diversification movement in recent years has further emphasized the problem. Publicly held companies have acquired firms in widely diverse industries creating what has been termed a conglomerate company. Other companies adverse to growth by acquisition have diversified extensively through internal growth. Both movements have made the task of the outside analyst increasingly difficult.

Each time a company absorbs a publicly held firm, the acquired firm stops publishing financial statements. This impairs the ability of investors to draw reliable conclusions about the remaining firms in the industry and about the conglomerate itself and weakens the sound functioning of the securities markets—the objective of much securities legislation.

In the absence of a legal requirement that specific revenue and earnings contribution information be furnished in a firm's annual report, some diversified firms will continue experimenting with reporting revenue and operating results of their lines of business. Other firms will continue to decline to report by division. Here the investor must be particularly careful about extrapolating any overall trend. Industry trends for the various components of a company are about all that can be studied.

---

[22] See Hobgood, p. 22, for some biting comments on the state of the art of reporting to shareholders.

# 4

# Earning Power and the Magic of Leverage

Conditions change and with them a firm's bill-paying ability and profitability. Changing conditions will affect the firm's flow of receipts and disbursements and leave the bill-paying ability of the firm at the end of the period different from what it was at the opening. Further, changing conditions will affect the firm's sales and costs and will produce a record of profitability that will directly affect the market value of the firm. To plan the firm's future, the financial manager must be able (1) to assess the firm's current position and (2) to understand the impact of changing economic conditions. The purpose of these opening chapters is to develop these twin capabilities.

In the previous chapters we studied how the flow of funds of a firm is affected by changing economic conditions and learned how to evaluate a firm's investment position. In this chapter we examine the process by which a firm generates earnings and learn how to measure its earning ability.

We have observed how earnings fluctuate with revenue and how both the level and the volatility of earnings are affected by the extent to which the firm is levered. The magic of leverage is that whereas sales may jump 10 percent, profits may jump 30 percent.

*Leverage* may be defined as earning more by the use of assets than the firm pays as fixed costs and as earning more by the use of borrowed funds than the firm pays as a fixed charge. The former is known as *operating* leverage; the latter as *financial* leverage. The fixed cost and the fixed charge are comparable to the fulcrum of a lever. For a given fluctuation in revenue the presence of fixed costs will amplify the fluctuation of earnings per share and the presence of debt will also amplify the fluctuation of earnings. The analysis of the relationships between revenue, fixed and variable costs, and profit is known as *cost-volume-profit analysis.*

## EARNING POWER

*Earning power* is the ability of the firm to earn a return on its operating assets. A more descriptive term is *return on investment.* This rate is a good measure of management performance. Common stockholder return on investment is the rate earned on the common equity—common stock, capital surplus, and retained earnings.

### Return on Investment (ROI)

Return on operating asset investment, which we shorten to return on investment (ROI), is the measure of the firm's annual net operating income to the investment committed to generate this income.[1] We define *net operating income* (NOI) as earnings before interest and income taxes produced by our mainline operating assets. Excluded are nonoperating income items such as rent on a leased warehouse or interest on long-term investments. We wish to focus on the income generated by our operating assets undistorted by the manner in which the firm is financed or taxed.[2] We define *operating assets* as the total of those assets—net of depreciation and bad debts—employed in the ordinary course of business. Excluded are securities held as long-term investment, vacant land held for speculative purposes, leased property no longer direct-

[1] Return on assets refers to the left-hand side of the balance sheet. An alternative measure of profitability as defined by some analysts is return on part of the right-hand side of the balance sheet: net profit after taxes plus bond interest divided by net worth plus long-term debt. The difference is the exclusion of current liabilities.

[2] Some firms follow the practice of including interest and dividend income in the numerator figure. The related assets are then also generally included in the denominator figure. Income taxes also give rise to variation in the calculation of return on investment. Some analysts deduct taxes from net operating income on the grounds that management is sufficiently able to control its tax bill. Others take net operating income before taxes on the ground that there is little control possible for the firm over its income taxes (the practice we shall follow). NOI = EBIT if no nonoperating income and expense items are present.

ly employed in operations, and so on. For Blu-Tronics we have (from Tables 3–1 and 3–3):

$$\underset{\text{(Based on year-end assets)}}{\text{Return on investment}} = \frac{\text{Net operating income}}{\text{Operating assets}}$$

| | 1973 | 1972 |
|---|---|---|
| $\dfrac{\$3,442,000}{\$13,821,000} =$ | 24.9% | |
| $\dfrac{\$2,023,000}{\$9,487,000} =$ | | 21.3% |

In 1973, Blu-Tronics earned 24.9 percent on its invested capital and in 1972, 21.3 percent. Now let us examine the factors that influence the return on investment figures. The larger the spread between sales and costs, the greater the profit. The ratio of *NOI* to sales is operating margin. For Blu-Tronics the computation is (from Table 3–3):

$$\text{Operating margin} = \frac{\text{Net operating income}}{\text{Sales}}$$

| | 1973 | 1972 |
|---|---|---|
| $\dfrac{\$3,442,000}{\$21,425,000} =$ | 16.1% | |
| $\dfrac{\$2,023,000}{\$15,007,000} =$ | | 13.5% |

For every dollar of sales Blu-Tronics generated in 1973, only 83.9 cents was required to begin its way through the flow of funds system; for 1972, 86.5 cents was required. Conversely, in 1973 for every dollar of sales generated by the system, 16.1 cents was retained in net operating income, but in 1972 only 13.5 cents.

ROI is also influenced by the amount of operating assets. The smaller the asset investment necessary to generate a given level of sales, the more desirable it is. The ratio of sales to operating assets is known as *asset turnover*. For Blu-Tronics we have:

$$\text{Asset turnover} = \frac{\text{Sales}}{\text{Operating assets}}$$

| | 1973 | 1972 |
|---|---|---|
| $\dfrac{\$21,425,000}{\$13,821,000} =$ | 1.55 × | |
| $\dfrac{\$15,007,000}{\$9,487,000} =$ | | 1.58 × |

Combining operating margin and the asset turnover ratio, we have ROI.

$$\text{Return on investment} = \frac{\text{Net operating income}}{\text{Sales}} \times \frac{\text{Sales}}{\text{Operating assets}}$$

$$= \frac{\text{Net operating income}}{\text{Operating assets}}$$

The relationship of margin times asset turnover, though yielding the same figure as ROI calculated directly, highlights the elements comprising the final figure. In Figure 4–1 these elements are broken down along two analytic streams that depict the earnings-generating mechanism of a firm.

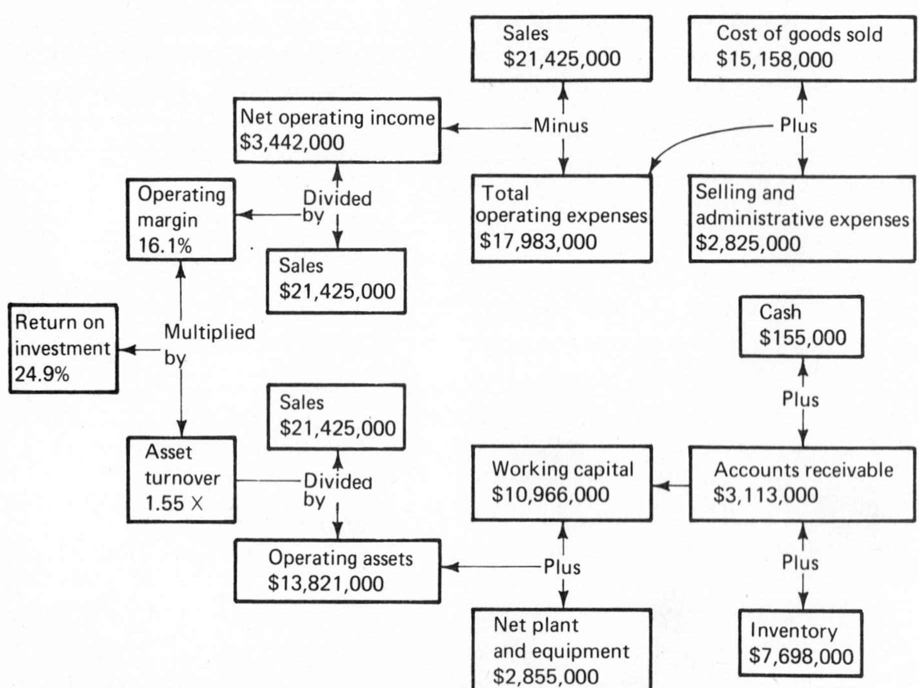


Figure 4–1 Relation of elements that determine return on investment. The figures are those of the Blu-Tronics example for 1973.

#### Earning Power of Blu-Tronics and Methods of Increasing ROI

The ROI for Blu-Tronics was higher in 1973 than in 1972—24.9 percent versus 21.3 percent. The higher 1973 return is due to a wider margin. Asset turnover slowed, but margin widened sufficiently to compensate for this and to raise ROI. If the margin had remained the same, the ROI would have dropped because of the reduced asset turnover.

Figure 4–1 suggests five actions that lead to an increase in ROI. Starting at the top of the figure, one action is to reduce cost of sales. With sales volume remaining the same, net operating income will rise and so will ROI. A second action is to increase the selling price, but not so much that the drop in volume offsets the larger spread between selling price and cost. The result will be an increase in NOI as long as the wider margin is more than sufficient to offset any reduced asset turnover. Third, we can reduce selling price to gain a larger volume. If the increase in volume and asset turnover is more than sufficient to compensate for the reduced margin, ROI will rise. A fourth action is to reduce the investment in working capital and fixed assets. Generating the same sales and net operating income with a smaller capital investment will raise ROI. Fifth, increasing the sales volume without a change in prices while keeping total investment constant will increase the NOI and ROI.

### Return on Common Stock

Increasing the productivity of a firm's assets is one way to increase the returns on common stock. Another way is to finance the firm by using debt and preferred and common stock in such combination that common stock earns as high a return as possible without assuming undue risk. The usual measure of return on common stock relates net profit available to the common stock to the common equity (net worth minus any preferred outstanding). For Blu-Tronics, which has no preferred, the computation is:

$$\text{Return on common stock (Based on year-end net worth)} = \frac{\text{Net profit}}{\text{Net worth}}$$

| | 1973 | 1972 |
|---|---|---|
| $\frac{\$1{,}590{,}000}{\$5{,}842{,}000}$ = | 27.2% | |
| $\frac{\$970{,}000}{\$3{,}819{,}000}$ = | | 25.4% |

The higher this rate, the larger the earnings per common share, which is the first figure common stockholders examine. For Blu-Tronics the computation is:

$$\text{Earnings per common share (EPS)} = \frac{\text{Net profit}}{\text{Shares outstanding}}$$

| | 1973 | 1972 |
|---|---|---|
| $\frac{\$1{,}590{,}000}{832{,}000 \text{ shares}}$ = | $1.91 per share | |
| $\frac{\$970{,}000}{761{,}000 \text{ shares}}$ = | | $1.27 per share |

To illustrate the income advantage gained from financial leverage,[3] we need the book value per common share figure. For Blu-Tronics we have:

$$\text{Book value per common share} = \frac{\text{Common net worth}}{\text{Shares outstanding}}$$

| | 1973 | 1972 |
|---|---|---|
| $= \dfrac{\$5{,}842{,}000}{832{,}000 \text{ shares}} =$ | \$7.02 per share | |
| $= \dfrac{\$3{,}819{,}000}{761{,}000 \text{ shares}} =$ | | \$5.02 per share |

Blu-Tronics in 1973 had \$4,669,000 (from Table 3–1: \$2,389,000 + \$120,000 + \$2,160,000) of short- and long-term notes outstanding on which it paid \$242,000 interest, or about 5 percent on the average. Substituting common stock for this debt would eliminate the interest charges but increase the number of shares outstanding. If Blu-Tronics could sell stock at \$23 per share—about 12 times 1973 earnings and 3 times book value—it would have to sell 203,000 shares (\$4,669,000/\$23). Table 4–1 recasts the 1973 income statement to effect this refinancing. With a reduction in the debt-to-equity relationship of 1.36-to-1 to 0.32-to-1 the result is a drop in earnings per share (EPS) from \$1.91 to \$1.65, because Blu-Tronics is operating under favorable leverage. In 1973 Blu-Tronics earned 24.9

TABLE 4–1. Blu-Tronics, Inc.
Abbreviated Statement of Net Earnings Showing Effect of Financial Leverage

| | Year ended December 31 | |
|---|---|---|
| | 1973 (actual debt) | *Pro forma* (no short- and long-term notes) |
| Earnings before taxes (after interest) | \$3,200,000 | \$3,442,000 |
| Income taxes—1973 actual | 1,610,000 | |
| *Pro forma*—income taxes increased by 50% × \$242,000 | | 1,731,000 |
| Net earnings | \$1,590,000 | \$1,711,000 |

Earnings per common share:

1973 actual: $\dfrac{\$1{,}590{,}000}{832{,}000} = \$1.91$ *Pro forma:* $\dfrac{\$1{,}711{,}000}{1{,}035{,}000} = \$1.65$

[3] The older term is "trading on the equity" and has direct reference to the use of the owner's equity in property as a base for borrowing.

percent before interest and taxes on its investment. Part of this investment is financed with borrowed funds for which the firm pays only 5 percent. The difference between what the firm earns on its assets and what it pays for debt goes to the benefit of the common shareholder. In 1973 Blu-Tronics earned 27.2 percent on net worth after taxes. Calculating for 1973 on the basis of earnings after taxes but before interest (EATBI), we find the return on total long-term invested capital to be:[4]

$$\text{After taxes but before interest return on total long-term invested capital} = \frac{\text{EATBI}}{\text{Total long-term invested capital}} = \frac{\$1{,}832{,}000}{\$8{,}002{,}000} = 22.9\%$$

Comparing the 27.2 percent return on common stockholder net worth with the 22.9 percent return on total invested capital, we see the effect of favorable leverage. Both operating and financial leverage also work in reverse; that is, when the fixed cost rate is *above* the average earning on assets or the fixed charge rate is above the average earning on debt plus equity, the difference comes out of the pocket of the common stockholder.

#### Industry Characteristics

Out of total receipts of $1,680 billion and net income of $93 billion in 1969, Figure 4–2 shows the percent that went to each industrial group. Manufacturing for example accounted for 42.2 percent of total receipts and 48.4 percent of total income; wholesaling accounted for 13.1 percent of total receipts and only 5.9 percent of total income.

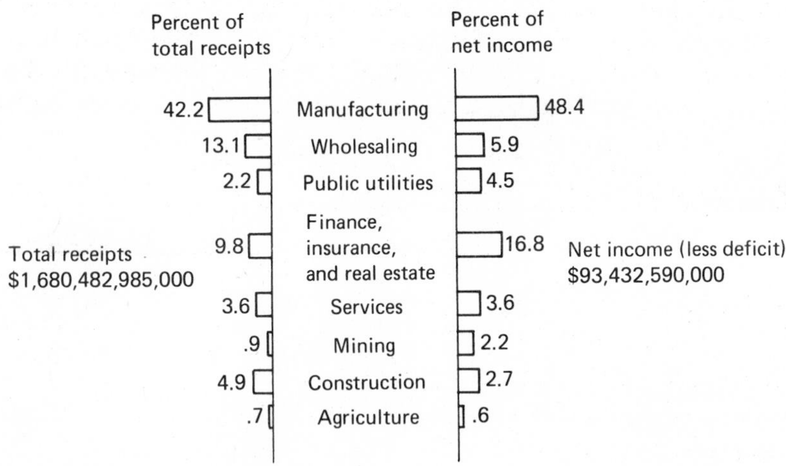


Figure 4–2 Percent distribution of total receipts and net income for selected categories.

U. S. Treasury Department, Internal Revenue Service, *Statistics of Income, 1969*, Corporation Income Tax Returns (Washington, D. C.: Government Printing Office, 1973), pp. 14ff.

---

[4] Note the switch in performance measure and the accompanying changes in definitions, from return on investment to return on long-term invested capital. The comparison of return on common equity with the before-tax return on operating assets to show the power of financial leverage would not have been appropriate, since an amount equivalent to a substantial portion of the current liabilities would have been included in the denominator figure, thus reducing the rate and overstating the effect of leverage.

Table 4–2 presents the earnings configuration for various industry groups. Note that differences in respective returns on investment are not as great as the differences in operating characteristics. How is this possible? The answer lies in the balancing of asset turnover and net operating margin. Electric and gas utilities, for example, require a heavy investment in fixed assets, whereas retailing entails a much smaller investment. The respective asset turnover ratios are 0.3 times and 2.6 times. The utilities have a 19.0 percent margin and retail trade only 3.0 percent. The wider margin of the utilities permits them to meet the costs of the large amount of funds needed for financing their fixed assets. But the slow asset turnover makes them about as profitable (in 1969) as retail trade: 6.1 percent versus 8.1 percent. If retailing with its high asset turnover had a margin approximating that of utilities, retailing would produce tremendous profits, ROI would be high. Funds would

TABLE 4–2. Return on Investment and Financial Leverage in Selected Industries (billions of dollars)

| | Mining | Manufacturing | Transportation | Electricity and gas | Retail trade | Total services |
|---|---|---|---|---|---|---|
| *Abbreviated income statement* | | | | | | |
| I. Sales | $15.4 | $689.9 | $54.9 | $ 36.3 | $267.6 | $57.2 |
| II. Earnings before interest and taxes | 2.1 | 52.5 | 3.5 | 6.9 | 8.4 | 4.0 |
| III. Earnings before taxes and after interest | 1.8 | 42.8 | 1.7 | 4.2 | 6.2 | 2.6 |
| IV. Interest | 0.3 | 9.7 | 1.8 | 2.7 | 2.2 | 1.4 |
| V. Net profit | 1.2 | 24.6 | 1.3 | 2.4 | 4.5 | 2.3 |
| *Abbreviated balance sheet* | | | | | | |
| VI. Current debt | 5.2 | 150.3 | 15.2 | 12.4 | 42.0 | 17.2 |
| VII. Long-term debt | 5.1 | 122.2 | 32.4 | 55.9 | 18.0 | 19.1 |
| VIII. Preferred stock | 0.3 | 6.4 | 0.7 | 6.4 | 0.9 | 0.4 |
| IX. Common equity | 12.0 | 293.1 | 34.4 | 36.9 | 41.6 | 17.4 |
| Total equity | 12.3 | 299.5 | 35.1 | 43.3 | 42.5 | 17.8 |
| X. Total financing | $22.8 | $572.1 | $82.9 | $111.9 | $102.8 | $54.4 |
| *Industry standards* | | | | | | |
| Net operating margin † (II/I) | 13.7% | 7.6% | 6.4% | 19.0% | 3.0% | 7.0% |
| Asset turnover (I/X) | 0.7 × | 1.2 × | 0.7 × | 0.3 × | 2.6 × | 1.0 × |
| Debt and preferred stock to common equity (VI + VII + VIII/IX) | 0.9 × | 0.9 × | 1.4 × | 2.0 × | 1.5 × | 2.1 × |
| Times interest charges earned (II/IV) | 7.0 × | 5.4 × | 1.9 × | 2.5 × | 3.8 × | 2.8 × |
| Return on investment (II/X) | 9.2% | 9.2% | 4.2% | 6.1% | 8.1% | 7.2% |
| Return on common equity (V/IX) | 10.0% | 8.4% | 3.8% | 6.5% | 10.8% | 13.2% |

SOURCE: U.S. Treasury Department, Internal Revenue Service, *Statistics of Income, 1969 Corporation Income Tax Returns* (Washington, D.C.: Government Printing Office, 1973), Table 2, Active Corporation Returns, pp. 14ff.

† To be distinguished from margin of profit: sales less cost of goods sold divided by sales.

flow into the field and drive the return down to a competitive level given the risk. This is what has actually happened and accounts for the small margin of profit in that field.

Funds flow into industries that offer an attractive risk-return combination until there is rough equality with the opportunities offered in other industries. However, the market's assessment of risk and return fluctuates. Thus, the process is dynamic and there is a constant movement of funds.

Table 4–2 also shows the *return on common equity*. Except for manufacturing and transportation, the return on common equity (after tax) exceeds the ROI (before tax). The use of financial leverage has paid off. Note also the large amount of debt and preferred relative to common equity but the low times interest charges earned figures of transportation and electric and gas companies compared to mining and manufacturing. And yet utility securities carry a high investment rating. This is due to the stability of utility revenue. In contrast, mining and manufacturing with high times interest earned ratios do not carry such a high investment rating on their senior securities because revenues are volatile.

### Summary of Financial Ratios

To conclude our discussion of financial statement analysis we summarize the ratios in Table 4–3. We classify them according to purpose of analysis: working capital position and investment characteristics. Letters indicate the type of ratio: liquidity (*Q*), activity (*A*), leverage (*L*), profitability (*P*), market (*M*). Accompanying each ratio is a number indicating a likely value for that ratio if computed for a large manufacturing firm. These ratios are a rough reference guide. The exact numerical value of a specific ratio will be influenced by the financial policies of the company, the industry to which the firm belongs, the level of economic activity, and the condition of the stock market.

TABLE 4–3. Guideline Ratios for Large Manufacturing Firms

| | |
|---|---|
| A. *Working capital ratios* | |
| 1. Current ratio (*Q*) | 2/1 |
| 2. Quick ratio (*Q*) | 1/1 |
| 3. Inventory turnover (*A*) | 6× |
| 4. Average collection period (*A*) | 50 days |
| B. *Investment characteristic ratios* | |
| 5. Long-term debt to equity (*L*) | 0.3/1 |
| 6. Times fixed charges earned (*L*) | 10× |
| 7. Operating margin (*P*) | 5% |
| 8. Operating asset turnover (*A*) | 1.5× |
| 9. Return on operating assets * (*P*) | 13% |
| 10. Return on net worth (*P*) | 13% |
| 11. Price-earnings ratio (*M*) | 14× |
| 12. Dividend yield (*M*) | 4% |
| 13. Payout ratio | 60% |

* Earning power.

[B3]

For any given company "favorable ratios" will attract lenders and investors. Lenders will be eager to extend credit at favorable interest rates and investors will be anxious to buy the firm's stock, thereby pushing up the price. The result will be increased profitability (lower interest rates and higher price-earnings ratios mean lower costs) and an increase in the value of the firm. Thus the financial manager in seeking to maximize the value of the firm must be alert to ways of improving the data contained in the firm's financial statement.

## OPERATING LEVERAGE: IMPACT ON NOI

The operating costs of every firm may be classified into fixed and variable to determine the break-even point and to conduct an operating leverage analysis—a study of how NOI varies with changes in revenue. The fluctuation in NOI is known as *business risk*. The greater the change in NOI for a given change in revenue, the greater the degree of *operating leverage*.

Fixed costs are assumed not to change with the *level* of production but with production *capacity*.[5] Depreciation charges, property taxes, insurance, and officers' salaries are examples.

Variable costs are assumed to change in direct proportion to the level of production.[6] Should the level of output rise by 10 percent, variable costs will also rise 10 percent. Raw materials, direct wages, and some supplies are examples.

### Relation between Fixed and Variable Costs

Since fixed costs are assumed not to vary with output, the amount allocated to each unit produced varies inversely (but not linearly) with the volume of output. In contrast, variable costs per unit tend to remain constant although in economic theory variable unit costs at first decline and then rise. Thus, since the fixed cost per unit falls as output rises, whereas variable cost per unit remains constant, the total cost per unit falls, at least over a considerable range.

Table 4–4 shows changes in output and total and unit costs, both fixed and variable, where variable cost per unit is constant. Note that

---

[5] This is "received doctrine" in some quarters. In the real world, fixed costs do change with the level of production. Thus officers' salaries are changed, insurance costs change, property taxes change, and so on. However, we will explain received doctrine so the reader can examine it.

[6] Again this is "received doctrine" in some quarters. In the real world as layoffs happen (1) in union shops the "stretch out" of work occurs, and (2) even in nonunion shops the "team effort" is destroyed. In both cases direct labor cost per unit rises. It is a convenient myth that variable costs change in direct proportion to the level of production.

although total costs are linear (as we will see in Figure 4–3), fixed cost per unit and total cost per unit are curves.

TABLE 4–4. Birch Bark Canoe Company
Linear Relationship among Changes in Volume, Output Total, and Unit Costs of Product Produced and Sold *

| | *Fixed costs* | | *Variable costs* | | *Combined costs* | |
|---|---|---|---|---|---|---|
| *Sales in units* | *total* | *per unit* | *total* | *per unit* | *total* | *per unit* |
| 10,000 | $60,000 | $6.00 | $ 4,000 | $0.40 | $ 64,000 | $6.40 |
| 50,000 | 60,000 | 1.20 | 20,000 | 0.40 | 80,000 | 1.60 |
| 100,000 | 60,000 | 0.60 | 40,000 | 0.40 | 100,000 | 1.00 |
| 150,000 | 60,000 | 0.40 | 60,000 | 0.40 | 120,000 | 0.80 |
| 200,000 | 60,000 | 0.30 | 80,000 | 0.40 | 140,000 | 0.70 |

* Everything produced is immediately sold.

The movement of these three costs may be presented mathematically and graphically. Let $C_f$ equal total fixed cost and the parameter $F$ the fixed cost for any level of production.

$$C_f = F \tag{4–1}$$

Let $C_v$ equal total variable cost, $v$ variable cost per unit, and $x$ the number of units produced.

$$C_v = vx \tag{4–2}$$

Let $C_t$ equal total cost and

$$C_t = C_f + C_v \tag{4–3}$$

Substitute Eq. (4–1) and Eq. (4–2) in Eq. (4–3).

$$C_t = F + vx \tag{4–4}$$

### Determination of the Break-even Point

For each dollar of revenue, a portion must be applied to cover variable cost. The balance is applied to cover fixed cost. After fixed and variable costs are covered, the remainder is NOI. Should the margin of revenue be just sufficient to cover fixed and variable costs, the firm will be operating at the break-even point. For example, suppose the firm in Table 4–4 sells its product for \$1 each. The total revenue function, $R$, is then price per unit times $x$, the number of units sold, or

$$R = px \tag{4–5}$$

The firm receives 60 cents above variable cost for each item sold, which can be applied to fixed cost. By selling 100,000 items at 60 cents above variable cost we arrive at \$60,000 and total fixed cost is covered. The break-even point is 100,000 units.

The volume required to achieve the break-even point is determined by the amount of fixed cost to be recovered and the margin over variable cost. The rate at which the fixed cost will be recovered is determined by the percent that variable cost represents of each dollar of revenue. In our example variable cost represents 40 cents of each dollar of revenue. Fixed cost would be recovered at the rate of 60 cents for each dollar of revenue.

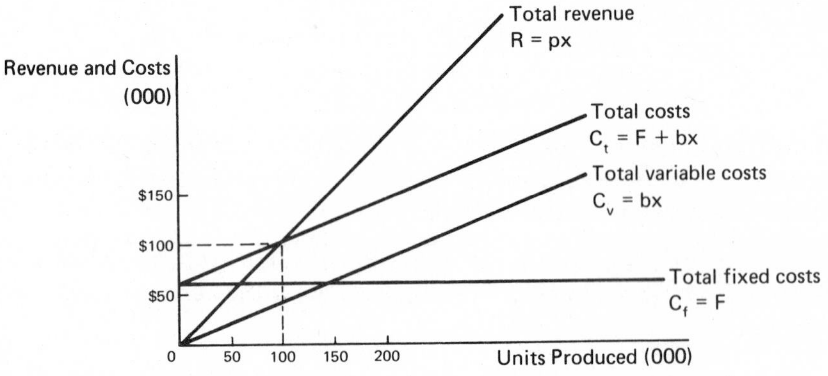


Figure 4–3 Break-even chart for cost data of Table 4–4.

Once the break-even point is reached, profits will climb more quickly with a further rise in sales if variable cost takes only 40 cents per dollar of revenue than if they take 50 cents per dollar of revenue. But should revenue decline, profits will also fall more precipitously.

The break-even point in units ($x_b$) may be computed directly from Eqs. (4–4) and (4–5):

$$\text{Total revenue} = \text{total costs}$$

$$px = F + vx \tag{4–6}$$

Solving Eq. (4–6) for $x_b$

$$x_b = \frac{F}{p - v} \tag{4–7}$$

Multiplying both sides of Eq. (4–7) by $p$ we have ($px_b$), the break-even point in dollars.

$$px_b = \frac{F}{1 - (v/p)} \tag{4–8}$$

Note that $v/p$ is the variable cost per dollar of revenue. Thus, the break-even point in dollars is equal to fixed cost divided by profit contribution per dollar of revenue (the complement of variable cost per dollar of revenue) and occurs where

$$R = \frac{\text{Fixed cost}}{1 - \text{Variable cost per dollar of revenue}} \tag{4–9}$$

These relationships are shown graphically in Figure 4–3. Observe that, because we have straight-line functions, the profit contribution per dollar of revenue is a linear function.

The slope of the total cost line is $v$, but the break-even point is changed if $v$ or $p$, or both $v$ and $p$, are changed, unless they happen to be offsetting changes.

#### Limitations of Break-even Analysis

Break-even analysis suffers from six limitations.

1. It generally assumes an unlimited demand for the firm's product at a fixed price and constant returns to scale.

2. It requires a strict classification of all costs into fixed and variable.

3. It assumes either a single product or an invariant product mix in the case of a multiple product firm.

4. In a dynamic environment major reliance must be placed on judgment in determining the necessary information inputs to the break-even analysis.

5. The planning horizon of the analysis is short and reflects the status quo.

6. Profits are not a simple residual but controllable to a considerable degree by management.

These limitations are discussed in detail in Chapter 8 but are included here to alert the reader to the dangers of basing decisions on casual break-even analysis.

The test of a method or technique is whether it leads to correct decisions. Where the probability is high that the break-even analysis will not lead to correct decisions, it should be abandoned.

### Nonlinear Break-even Analysis

Relationships in the business world are seldom linear, as depicted in Figure 4–3. For example, increased dollar sales can usually be obtained by reducing selling price. Because of economies and diseconomies of scale, variable cost per unit may at first fall and then rise over some range of output. Thus, in almost all cases it is necessary to abandon the linear assumption in break-even analysis and to work with nonlinear relationships, as shown in Figure 4–4.

Profit is maximized at the volume where marginal revenue equals marginal cost. Marginal revenue is the slope of the total revenue curve, whereas marginal cost is the slope of the total cost curve. This is illustrated in Figure 4–4. Only if we have at least one nonlinear relation (either total revenue or total cost), will we have an upper and a lower break-even point.[7]

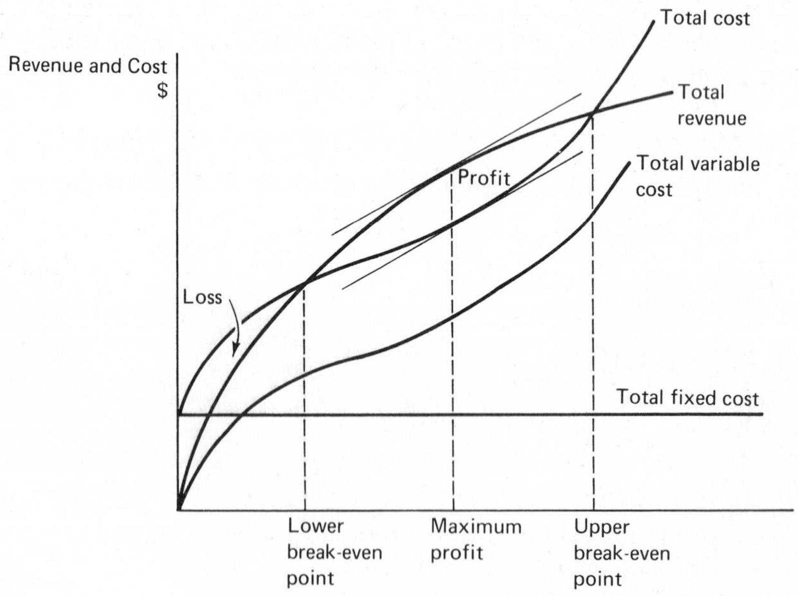


Figure 4–4 Nonlinear break-even chart.

---

[7] A fallacious argument is sometimes advanced that the use of linear assumptions is warranted because we are only interested in a narrow range of output variation and over this range relations may be approximately linear. The fallacy lies in assuming we should confine our decision alternatives to a narrow range of volume.

### Computing Operating Leverage

Operating leverage is a point measure, and since we are dealing with linear total relationships, the measure will describe the same relationship

TABLE 4–5. Les Doe Inc.
Impact of Increase in Selling Price on Operating Leverage and Break-even Point

| | Current situation | | Increase in units sold | |
|---|---|---|---|---|
| | Plant A | Plant B | Plant A Higher leverage | Plant B Lower leverage |
| Sales, in units | 300,000 | 300,000 | 330,000 | 330,000 |
| (A) Revenue, \$0.90/unit | \$270,000 | — | \$297,000 | — |
| (B) Revenue, \$1/unit | — | \$300,000 | — | \$330,000 |
| Variable cost, \$0.80/unit | 240,000 | 240,000 | 264,000 | 264,000 |
| Fixed cost | 20,000 | 20,000 | 20,000 | 20,000 |
| Net operating income | \$ 10,000 | \$ 40,000 | \$ 13,000 | \$ 46,000 |
| Increase in revenue | | | 10% | 10% |
| Increase in net operating income | | | 30% | 15% |
| Degree of operating leverage * | 3 to 1 | 1.5 to 1 | — | — |
| Break-even point, units | 200,000 | 100,000 | — | — |

* Increase in net operating income/increase in revenue.

[A9841]

at a given point for any percentage change in revenue. If we have tables such as Table 4–5, we can easily compute the degree of operating leverage at a point by using the following formula:

$$\begin{array}{c}\text{Degree of operating leverage}\\ \text{at sale of } x \text{ units}\end{array} = \frac{\text{Percent change in } NOI}{\text{Percent change in revenue}}$$

The degree of operating leverage at a point can also be calculated directly by the formula

$$\begin{array}{l}\text{Degree of operating leverage}\\ \text{at sale of } x \text{ units}\end{array} = \frac{x(p - v)}{x(p - v) - F}.$$

where

$x$ = number of units produced and sold
$p$ = selling price per unit
$v$ = variable cost per unit
$F$ = total fixed cost

Thus, for Plant A, Table 4–4, we have:

$$\begin{array}{l}\text{Degree of operating leverage}\\ \text{at 300,000 units}\end{array} = \frac{300{,}000(\$0.90 - \$0.80)}{300{,}000(\$0.90 - \$0.80) - \$20{,}000} = 3.0$$

The degree of operating leverage may also be computed when we know the break-even point:[8]

$$\text{Degree of operating leverage at sale of } x \text{ units} = \frac{x}{x - (\text{Break-even point in units})}$$

For the example presented in Table 4–5 we have

$$\text{Degree of operating leverage at sale of 300,000 units} = \frac{300{,}000}{300{,}000 - 200{,}000} = 3$$

This formulation shows the direct relationship between the break-even point and the degree of operating leverage at a selected level of unit output. The closer that level is to the break-even point the higher the degree of operating leverage.

Note that as the spread between price and variable cost narrows, the denominator goes to zero and the degree of operating leverage increases rapidly.[9]

## FINANCIAL LEVERAGE: IMPACT ON RESIDUAL EARNINGS[10]

Financial leverage is introduced into the capital structure (total of bonds and ownership interests) when funds are obtained on a fixed-return basis. Then any variation in earnings before interest and taxes (EBIT)[11] is magnified on earnings per share (EPS). The greater the de-

---

[8] To obtain this expression solve

$$\text{Break-even point in units} = x_b = \frac{F}{p-v} \qquad \text{(from Eq. 4-7)}$$

for $F$, namely $F = x_b(p-v)$, and substitute for $F$ in

$$\text{Degree of operating leverage at sale of } x \text{ units} = \frac{x(p-v)}{x(p-v)-F}$$

and simplify

[9] The degree of operating leverage at the break-even point is not defined, since $x(p - v) - F = 0$ at this point.

[10] Earnings available to the common stockholder.

[11] Note the switch from net operating income to earnings before interest and taxes. Since we are interested in the impact of different combinations of bond and stock financing on earnings per share, we focus on *all* income before taxes available to all long-term security holders. It is necessary to use income before taxes, since bond interest is a deductible expense and preferred and common stock dividends are not. Note further that the emphasis is on earnings per share. We are no longer concerned with measuring operating performance, but, rather, with the effect on earnings per share that flow from different combinations of debt and stock financing given the income generated by the assets.

gree of financial leverage, the wider the fluctuation in EPS for any variation in EBIT. The fluctuations in EPS are known as *financial risk*. For example, in Table 4–6 Birch Bark Canoe Company, in a misguided effort to remain profitable in a declining industry, decides to refinance, going from all common stock financing of 250,000 shares of $4 par common to $600,000 of 5 percent bonds and 100,000 shares of $4 par common equity.

A 10 percent drop in EBIT results in a 14.3 percent drop in EPS; a 50 percent drop in EBIT from $90,000 to $45,000 results in a 75 percent drop in EPS. Using the same figures, except postulating a rising earnings trend going from $45,000 EBIT to $90,000 EBIT, we have a 100 percent increase in EBIT resulting in a 300 percent increase in EPS.

TABLE 4–6. Birch Bark Canoe Company
Balance Sheet after Substituting Bonds for Part of Common Stock

| Assets | | |
|---|---|---|
| | $ 600,000 | bonds—5% |
| | $ 400,000 | common stock, $4 par, 100,000 shares |
| $1,000,000 | $1,000,000 | |

Earnings in three successive years

| | *1st year* | *2d year* 10% drop in EBIT | *3d year* Additional 50% drop in EBIT |
|---|---|---|---|
| EBIT | $100,000 | $90,000 | $45,000 |
| Bond interest | 30,000 | 30,000 | 30,000 |
| Earnings before taxes | $ 70,000 | $60,000 | $15,000 |
| Taxes (50 percent rate) | 35,000 | 30,000 | 7,500 |
| Earnings after taxes | $ 35,000 | $30,000 | $ 7,500 |
| EPS | $0.35 | $0.30 | $0.075 |
| Change in EBIT * | — | −10% | −50% |
| Change in EPS * | — | −14.3% | −75% |

* Change is from the first to the second year and the second to the third year.

Had Birch Bark continued with 100 percent common stock financing, 250,000 shares of $4 par stock outstanding, the respective EPS would be 20, 18, and 9 cents for the three years in Table 4–6. EPS of 20 cents is determined as follows: [$100,000—($100,000 × 50%)]/250,000 shares. To compute EPS of 18 cents and 9 cents see Table 4–6. The EPS decline would be in direct proportion to the drop in EBIT.

### Computing Financial Leverage

Similar to operating leverage, financial leverage is also a point measure. Since we are dealing with linear relationships, the measure will describe the same relationship of a percentage change in earnings per share (EPS) at a given earnings before interest and taxes (EBIT) point for any percentage change in EBIT. From Table 4–6 we can compute the degree of financial leverage at EBIT of \$100,000 by using the expression

$$\text{Degree of financial leverage at EBIT of \$100,000} = \frac{\text{Percent change in EPS}}{\text{Percent change in EBIT}} = \frac{14.3\%}{10.0\%} = 1.43$$

The degree of financial leverage can be determined directly knowing only the specified level of EBIT and interest by using the expression[12]

$$\text{Degree of financial leverage at specified level of EBIT} = \frac{\text{EBIT}}{\text{EBIT} - \text{I}}$$

where $I$ = interest on debt in dollars.

For Birch Bark Canoe, Table 4–6, we have

$$\text{Degree of financial leverage at EBIT of \$100,000} = \frac{\$100{,}000}{\$100{,}000 - \$30{,}000} = \frac{\$100{,}000}{\$70{,}000} = 1.43$$

---

[12] Derived as follows:

$$\text{EPS} = \frac{(\text{EBIT} - I)(1 - t)}{N}$$

where $t$ is the corporate income tax rate, $N$ is the number of common shares outstanding, and *EPS*, *EBIT*, and $I$ are as defined above.

Since $I$ is a constant, the change in EPS is given by

$$\Delta\text{EPS} = \frac{\Delta\text{EBIT}(1 - t)}{N} \quad \text{where } \Delta \text{ denotes "change in."}$$

The percentage change in EPS is the ratio of the change in EPS to the given EPS:

$$\frac{\Delta\text{EBIT}(1 - t)/N}{(\text{EBIT} - I)(1 - t)/N} = \frac{\Delta\text{EBIT}}{\text{EBIT} - I}$$

The percentage change in EBIT is the ratio of the change in EBIT to the given EBIT or $\Delta$ EBIT/EBIT. Then the ratio of the percentage change in EPS to the percentage change in EBIT at the specified level of EBIT is given by

$$\frac{\Delta\text{EBIT}/(\text{EBIT} - I)}{\Delta\text{EBIT}/\text{EBIT}} = \frac{\Delta\text{EBIT}}{\text{EBIT} - I} \cdot \frac{\text{EBIT}}{\Delta\text{EBIT}} = \frac{\text{EBIT}}{\text{EBIT} - I}$$

This expression shows how the fixed interest charge acts as a fulcrum causing financial leverage. Other things equal, increasing the interest charge will raise the degree of financial leverage, and vice versa. In terms of the times interest charges earned ratio, the lower the coverage the higher the financial leverage.

## OPERATING AND FINANCIAL LEVERAGE TOGETHER

Financial and operating leverage combine to produce a wider percentage change in earnings for a given percentage change in revenue. The example of Hi-Flyer, Inc. (Table 4–7) indicates how a 10 percent increase in revenue is magnified to a 60 percent increase in NOI by operating leverage, and further magnified to 66⅔ percent increase in earnings available to the common stock by financial leverage. The same variability holds on the down side.

Normally, it would not seem desirable to finance a high operating leverage firm with large amounts of debt, but the controlling factor is variability of revenue. A stable firm, such as an electric utility, can advantageously combine high operating and financial leverage. Producing above the break-even point with little probability of falling below it, the risk assumed by the firm is small. The absence of substantial revenue variation means the net available for the common stock will not fluctuate widely and will not impart a speculative character to the common stock.

TABLE 4–7. Hi-Flyer, Inc.
Effect of a 10 Percent Increase in Revenue on
Earnings Available to the Common Stock

| | | | *Increase (%)* |
|---|---|---|---|
| Sales, units | 300,000 | 330,000 | |
| Revenues, $1/unit | $300,000 | $330,000 | 10 |
| Variable costs, $0.60/unit | $180,000 | $198,000 | |
| Fixed costs | $100,000 | $100,000 | |
| Net operating income | $20,000 | $32,000 | 60 |
| Interest | $2,000 | $2,000 | |
| | $18,000 | $30,000 | |
| Taxes (50%) | $9,000 | $15,000 | |
| Net available to the common stock | $9,000 | $15,000 | 66⅔ |

A firm in the steel business would not find it desirable to impose substantial financial leverage on its high operating leverage position because revenues fluctuate too widely. Even if the firm could operate most of the time above the break-even point, a large amount of financial leverage would impart a speculative character to the common shares. For the same reason, a textile firm with relatively large variable costs would not find it desirable to assume a large amount of debt.

The degree of operating leverage can be combined with the degree of financial leverage to compute the total leverage effect on earnings available to the common stock for a given change in sales.[13] That is,

$$\text{Combined degree of leverage at sale of } x \text{ units} = \frac{x(p - v)}{x(p - v) - F - I}$$

For Hi-Flyer, Inc., Table 4–6, we have

$$\text{Combined degree of leverage at sale of 300,000 units} = \frac{300{,}000(\$1.00 - \$0.60)}{300{,}000(\$1.00 - \$0.60) - \$100{,}000 - \$2{,}000}$$

$$= 6.6\tfrac{2}{3}$$

At the 300,000 unit level of sales, a 10 percent change in sales will cause a 66⅔ percent change in earnings available to the common stock; that is, the change in earnings available to the common stock will be 6.6⅔ times as great as the change in sales.

## SUMMARY

Return on investment is a function of operating margin times asset turnover and is a measure of management's ability to operate the firm. By studying the components of return on investment we can understand how a firm generates earnings. Operating leverage results from the presence of fixed costs that magnify net operating income fluctuations flowing from small variations in revenue. The larger the fixed costs relative to the variable costs, the greater the degree of operating leverage measured at a point and the closer we are to the break-even point. Increasing the break-even point will increase the degree of operating leverage. The degree of operating leverage may be computed if we know the break-even point. At the break-even point the excess of revenue over variable cost is just sufficient to cover fixed costs. Break-even analysis, whether assuming linear or nonlinear relationships, has numerous limitations.

The return to shareholders can be raised through financing a portion of the asset requirements with debt. Financial leverage is favorable when the firm is able to earn more on its assets than it is paying for borrowed funds, and unfavorable when the converse is true.

---

[13] The combined degree of leverage at a specified level of sales is equal to the degree of operating leverage times the degree of financial leverage (respectively from n. 8 and n. 12 above

$$\text{Combined degree of leverage} = \frac{x(p-v)}{x(p-v)-F} \quad \frac{EBIT}{EBIT-I}$$

Since EBIT $= x(p-v-)-F$ we can write

$$\text{Combined degree of leverage} = \frac{x(p-v)}{x(p-v)-F} \quad \frac{x(p-v)}{x(p-v)-F-I}$$

$$= \frac{x(p-v)-F}{x(p-v)-F-I}$$

Generally, it is undesirable to finance a firm with high operating leverage by means of high financial leverage. The main consideration is the stability of revenues. Public utilities can successfully combine high rates of operating and financial leverage.

The return on investment among the industry groups tends to be equalized by economic forces. The slow asset turnover of the firms in the utility field is compensated by a wide margin. In the retail field the asset turnover is rapid but the profit margin is narrow.

### *Study Questions*

1. Enterprise return on investment is frequently employed as one test of the quality of management. Discuss. What other measures would you use to obtain a fair appraisal of management?
2. Would return on net worth be a better test of management efficiency than return on investment?
3. Why are stockholders' interests pointed to a generous return on their investment? Is this in the national interest?
4. What is the justification for saying that maximization of firm value is positive and liquidity needs are negative?
5. What factors or conditions would you seek to change if you wished to improve the operating margin of your firm; the asset turnover? Which factors would you most likely be able to influence? Does your answer depend upon the industry you have in mind? How?
6. What factors or conditions would you seek to change if you wished to improve the return on net worth? What factors would you most likely be able to influence? Does your answer depend upon the industry you have in mind? How?
7. How do you explain the flow of investible funds from one field of economic activity to another? How can legislation stimulate or impede such flow? Give current examples on both sides.
8. What industry characteristics account for the varying turnover rates and profit margins in various areas of business activity? Do these help to explain the movement of investible funds? How?
9. What is the relation between debt financing and financial leverage? Develop a simple example illustrating the financial leverage phenomenon. Introduce the dynamic dimension into your illustration by postulating given changes in EBIT.
10. What is the relation between fixed costs and operating leverage? Develop a simple example illustrating the operating leverage phenomenon. Introduce the dynamic dimension into your illustration by postulating given changes in sales.
11. What data would you as a financial manager require to develop a break-even chart? What information would you hope to gain from your break-even analysis? How would this help you in reaching sound financial decisions?
12. Contrast the indifference point and the break-even point. How can knowing these points help you reach sound financial decisions? Why is it impossible to know these points with certainty? The indifference point is developed in Appendix D below.

13. What are the circumstances under which a firm's total costs will vary in direct proportion to changes in output? What industries seem to have such cost characteristics? Do they tend to have a high or low break-even point?

14. Referring to question 13, answer the same questions for firms whose total costs vary hardly at all with changes in output.

15. Assuming other things equal, what will be the effect of the following decisions on a firm's break-even point and on its degree of operating leverage: (a) selling prices are increased; (b) a new plant is purchased that will increase depreciation charges by $50,000; (c) a new materials flow system is introduced that will reduce variable costs by 1 cent per unit?

16. The accountant for three small firms wishes to compare their operating characteristics but finds he has only partial data. He asks you to supply the missing information.

| *Company* | *Sales* | *Operating assets* | *Operating margin* | *Return on investment* |
|---|---|---|---|---|
| F | $1,000 | — | 24% | 6% |
| S | — | $1,000 | 1% | 4% |
| J | $6,000 | $3,000 | — | 10% |

What are the industries to which firms F, S, and J are likely to belong?

## Problems

1. Melody Milk, Inc., organized to manufacture and sell a new dietary drink known as DD, has just completed its first year of operation. The financial statements are presented in Tables 4–8 and 4–9.

TABLE 4–8. Melody Milk, Inc.
Balance Sheet (year end)

| *Assets* | | *Liabilities* | |
|---|---|---|---|
| Cash | $ 2,000 | Accounts payable | $10,000 |
| Accounts receivable | 10,000 | Notes payable (6%) | 5,000 |
| Inventory | 6,000 | Long-term debt (6%) | 5,000 |
| Plant and equipment (net) | 22,000 | Common stock, $6 par | $ 6,000 |
| | | Retained earnings | 14,000 |
| Total assets | $40,000 | Total liabilities and net worth | $40,000 |

TABLE 4–9. Melody Milk, Inc.
Income Statement (annual)

| | |
|---|---|
| Sales | $120,000 |
| Cost of goods sold | 93,400 |
| Gross profit | $ 26,600 |
| Selling and administrative expenses | 18,600 |
| Earnings before interest and taxes | $ 8,000 |
| Interest | 600 |
| Earnings before taxes | $ 7,400 |
| Income tax (50%) | 3,000 |
| Net profit | $ 4,400 |
| Other information: | |
| Selling price of DD | $2.50 per package |
| Fixed cost (total) other than interest and taxes | $ 50,000 |
| Variable cost other than interest and income taxes | $1.50 per package |

a. Using the formula $x_b = F/(p - v)$ compute the break-even point in units. Determine the break-even point in dollars.

b. Compute NOI at the 60,000 package level. Assume sales rise by 50 percent to 90,000 packages. Now recompute NOI. What is the percentage increase in NOI? Assume sales rise 100 percent to 120,000 packages. Recompute NOI. What is the percentage rise in NOI?

c. Using the formula [Degree of operating leverage at sale of $x$ units] = $\%\Delta$NOI/$\%\Delta$ sales, compute the degree of operating leverage at the 60,000 package level for a 50 percent and a 100 percent increase in sales.

d. Draw a break-even chart of the firm.

e. The management of Melody Milk plans to expand. Determine the new break-even point in units and dollars if fixed costs rise from $50,000 to $54,000 and variable costs fall from $1.50 to $1.30 per package.

f. Calculate earnings per share at 0, $10,000, and $20,000 debt levels for combinations of $1000, $5000, and $10,000 *EBIT*. Assume an interest rate of 6%, an income tax rate of 50 percent and that additional shares could be sold or repurchased at $40 per share net to the firm to replace dollars of debt.

g. The material required to work this and the following part is contained in Appendix D, which follows these problems. Using the figures determined in (f), prepare an indifference chart.

h. Using the formula $(x - B)\ (1 - t)/S_1 = x(1 - t)/S_2$ calculate the indifference point and determine the EPS at this point.

2. Using Figure 4–1 trace the effect of (other things equal): (a) a 10 percent drop in cost of goods sold, (b) a 5 percent increase in total operating expenses, (c) a 10 percent drop in net operating income, (d) an $855,000 drop in net plant, (e) a $1 million increase in net working capital. Do not cumulate.

3. Calculate the return on investment, giving effect to each of the shifts in the items in problem 2. Do not cumulate.

**4.** Classify the following costs as fixed ($F$), variable ($V$), and partially fixed and partially variable ($F/V$). Be sure you can support your answer.

(a) Raw materials, (b) electric power, (c) president's salary, (d) heat, (e) direct wages, (f) wages of supervisory plant personnel, (g) property taxes, (h) fire insurance, (i) obsolescence, (j) cleaning and janitor supplies.

**5.** Picture a break-even chart such as shown in Figure 4–3. Match the statements in column II with those in column I. Assume other things equal. Assume also the firm is operating above the break-even point. More than one statement in column II may apply to one statement in column I. Statements in column II may be used more than once. Reference to Appendix C will be helpful.

| Column I | Column II |
|---|---|
| a. An increase in selling price. | i. Increases the break-even point. |
| b. An increase in fixed cost. | ii. Increases the degree of operating leverage. |
| c. An increase in variable cost per unit. | iii. Decreases the break-even point. |
| d. A decrease in selling price. | iv. Decreases the degree of operating leverage. |
| e. A decrease in fixed cost. | v. No effect on the break-even point. |
| f. A decrease in variable cost per unit. | vi. No effect on the degree of operating leverage. |
| | vii. Changes the slope of the total revenue curve. |
| | viii. Changes the slope of the total cost curve. |
| | ix. No effect on the slope of the total revenue curve. |
| | x. No effect on the slope of the total cost curve. |

### *Selected References*


Hobbs, J. B., "Volume-Mix-Price/Cost Budget Variance Analysis: A Proper Approach," *Accounting Review*, 39 (October 1967), pp. 905–913.

Hugon, J. H., "Breakeven Analysis in Three Dimensions," *Financial Executive*, 33 (December 1965), pp. 22–26.

Jaedicke, R. K., and A. A. Robichek, "Cost-Volume-Profit Analysis under Conditions of Uncertainty," *Accounting Review*, 39 (October 1964), pp. 917–926.

Kelvie, W. E., and J. M. Sinclair, "New Technique for Breakeven Charts," *Financial Executive*, 36 (June 1968), pp. 31–43.

Morrison, T. A., and E. Kaczka, "A New Application of Calculus and Risk Analysis to Cost-Volume-Profit Changes," *Accounting Review*, 44 (April 1969), pp. 330–343.

Pfahl, J. K., D. T. Crary, R. H. Howard, "The Limits of Leverage," *Financial Executive*, 38 (May 1970), pp. 48–56.

Raun, D. L., "The Limitations of Profit Graphs, Breakeven Analysis, and Budgets," *Accounting Review*, 39 (October 1964), pp. 927–945.

———, "Product-Mix Analysis by Linear Programming," *NAA—Management Accounting*, 47 (September 1965—August 1966), pp. 3–13.

Reinhardt, V. E., "Break Even Analysis for Lockheed's Tri-Star: An Application of Financial Theory," *Journal of Finance*, 28 (September 1973), pp. 821–838.

Robbins, S., and E. Foster, Jr., "Profit-Planning and the Finance Function," *Journal of Finance*, 12 (December 1957), pp. 451–467.

## *Appendix C*

### SENSITIVITY ANALYSIS OF COST-VOLUME-PROFIT RELATIONSHIP[14]

Besides the break-even point the financial manager is interested in estimating profits at various levels of operation. The lower the break-even point, the better the chance of operating at a profit. We are also interested in exploring the effects on NOI and the break-even point of changes in the selling price per unit, in the variable cost per unit and in total fixed cost.

Beginning with revenue, a change in the selling price will change the slope of the total revenue line. An increase in selling price will lower the break-even point and lower the degree of operating leverage at a given level of output. An increase in the selling price with the variable cost per dollar of revenue constant means that a greater amount is left to cover fixed cost. Thus, for a given change in units sold there will be a smaller percentage change in NOI when the selling price is higher because we start from a larger base.

For example, refer back to Table 4–5, which shows the data of Les Doe Inc., a firm that currently has two plants, A and B, supplying two markets, in each of which it sells 300,000 units. Fixed and variable costs are the same at both plants: $20,000 and 80 cents per unit. The output of Plant A is sold at 90 cents per unit and that of Plant B at $1 per unit. Now suppose each plant increases its production and sales by 10 percent. There is a 30 percent increase in NOI at Plant A, the higher leverage plant, and 15 percent at Plant B, the lower leverage plant. At sales of 300,000 units the degree of operating leverage of Plant A is 3 and of Plant B it is 1.5. Plant A has a smaller profit contribution per dollar of revenue to cover fixed costs: only 10 cents versus 20 cents for Plant B. Also at the level of 300,000 units, Plant A is closer to its break-even point than is Plant B; 200,000 units versus 100,000 units. Conversely Plant B has the lower break-even point. The sale of fewer units is required to cover Plant B's fixed costs.

Similarly, a change in the variable cost per unit will change the slope of the total cost line. A decrease in the variable cost per unit will lower the break-even point and lower the degree of operating leverage at a given level of output. More remains per dollar of revenue after paying variable costs to cover fixed costs. Conversely, an increase in the variable cost per unit will raise the break-even point and raise the operating leverage at a given point. This is equivalent to reducing the price per unit and keeping fixed cost steady. An increase in fixed cost will raise the break-even point and raise the degree of operating leverage at any given level of output above the break-even point. The increase in fixed cost does not change the slope of the revenue or total cost lines but does increase the degree of operating leverage. For any given level of output, that given level is now closer to the break-even point.

*Fixed versus Variable Cost* Firms frequently have the opportunity to reduce variable cost per unit by adding assets that increase fixed cost. If they just offset each other so there is no change in the break-even point, then the degree

---

[14] The reader is reminded that we are assuming linear revenue and linear cost functions.

of operating leverage will not change. But assuming the firm is operating above the break-even point, the higher fixed-cost lower-variable cost per unit arrangement will be more profitable. If the increase in fixed cost less than offsets the decrease in variable cost per unit, decreasing the break-even point, then the degree of operating leverage for any given level of operation will fall. Conversely, if the increase in fixed cost more than offsets the decrease in variable cost per unit, increasing the break-even point, the degree of operating leverage for any given level of operation will rise. In either event if the firm is operating above the break-even point the higher fixed cost option will yield a higher NOI.

For example, assume Les Doe Inc. has a third plant C, which produces and sells 300,000 units at $1 each. Variable cost is 90 cents per unit and total fixed cost $20,000. Table 4–10 shows the degree of operating leverage at the 300,000 unit of sales mark is 3 to 1. Now suppose the firm, after estimating a 10 percent increase in sales, considers the purchase of some equipment that will reduce the variable cost to 80 cents per unit. Table 4–11 shows the impact on Les Doe's operating leverage and break-even point if fixed cost rises to $30,000, $40,000, and $50,000.

If an increase in fixed cost of $10,000 reduces variable cost to 80 cents per unit, operating leverage declines to 2 to 1, and the break-even point to 150,000 units. Compare Tables 4–10 and 4–11. If an increase in fixed cost of $20,000 is needed to reduce variable cost to 80 cents per unit, there is no change in operating leverage or break-even point compared to the original $20,000 fixed cost and 90 cent variable cost per unit combination. But the firm has twice as much NOI under the $40,000 fixed cost—an 80 cent variable cost per unit arrangement when there is no volume increase. If an increase in fixed cost of $30,000 is needed to get a variable cost of 80 cents per unit, operating leverage rises to 6 to 1, the break-even point rises to 250,000 units and there is no improvement in NOI unless volume increases.

TABLE 4–10. Les Doe Inc.
Operating Leverage Computation with Present Equipment

| | Level of Operations | |
|---|---|---|
| | Current | 10% Volume Increase |
| Sales, units | 300,000 | 330,000 |
| Revenue, $1/unit | $300,000 | $330,000 |
| Variable cost, $0.90/unit | 270,000 | 297,000 |
| Fixed cost | 20,000 | 20,000 |
| Net operating income | $ 10,000 | $ 13,000 |
| Increase in revenue | — | 10% |
| Increase in net operating income | — | 30% |
| Degree of operating leverage | 3 to 1 | — |
| Break-even point, units | 200,000 | — |

TABLE 4–11. Les Doe Inc.

Operating Leverage Computation with New Equipment—*Pro forma* Computations

| | Equipment Plan<br>Variable unit costs cut 10 cents | | | | | |
|---|---|---|---|---|---|---|
| | $10,000 Added Fixed Cost<br>Level of Operations | | $20,000 Added Fixed Cost<br>Level of Operations | | $30,000 Added Fixed Cost<br>Level of Operations | |
| | Current | 10% Volume Increase | Current | 10% Volume Increase | Current | 10% Volume Increase |
| Sales, units | 300,000 | 330,000 | 300,000 | 330,000 | 300,000 | 330,000 |
| Revenue, $1/unit | $300,000 | $330,000 | $300,000 | $330,000 | $300,000 | $330,000 |
| Variable cost, $0.80/unit | 240,000 | 264,000 | 240,000 | 264,000 | 240,000 | 264,000 |
| Fixed cost | 30,000 | 30,000 | 40,000 | 40,000 | 50,000 | 50,000 |
| Net operating income | 30,000 | 36,000 | 20,000 | 26,000 | 10,000 | 16,000 |
| Increase in revenue | — | 10% | — | 10% | — | 10% |
| Increase in net operating income | — | 20% | — | 30% | — | 60% |
| Degree of operating leverage * | 2 | — | 3 | — | 6 | — |
| Break-even point, units | 150,000 | — | 200,000 | — | 250,000 | — |

* Increase in net operating income/increase in revenue.

*Analysis of Variability* Table 4–12 illustrates the impact of different degrees of operating leverage on NOI of the same dispersion of sales levels.

With sales of 300,000 units Les Doe Inc. can generate the same NOI, $30,000, using different combinations of fixed and variable costs. But at other sales levels, the different cost combinations achieve different levels of NOI. Operating leverage is at work.

TABLE 4–12. Les Doe Inc.
Analysis of Net Operating Income Variability

| State of Nature<br>Probability | Recession<br>0.20 | Normal<br>0.60 | Boom<br>0.20 |
|---|---|---|---|
| Project K (lower leverage) | | | |
| Sales, units | 240,000 | 300,000 | 360,000 |
| Revenue, $1/unit | $240,000 | $300,000 | $360,000 |
| Variable cost, 80¢/unit | 192,000 | 240,000 | 288,000 |
| Fixed cost | 30,000 | 30,000 | 30,000 |
| Net operating income | 18,000 | 30,000 | 42,000 |
| Degree of operating leverage | | 4 | |
| Project S (higher leverage) | | | |
| Sales, units | 240,000 | 300,000 | 360,000 |
| Revenue, $1/unit | $240,000 | $300,000 | $360,000 |
| Variable cost, 70¢/unit | 168,000 | 210,000 | 252,000 |
| Fixed cost | 60,000 | 60,000 | 60,000 |
| Net operating income | 12,000 | 30,000 | 48,000 |
| Degree of operating leverage | | 6 | |

The probabilities of achieving specific levels of NOI under the two cost structures are graphed in Figure 4–5. The expected NOIs of both distributions are identical, but the higher operating leverage project creates a wider variation in possible NOI levels than does the lower operating leverage project. Other things equal, we prefer the tighter distribution represented by Project K.

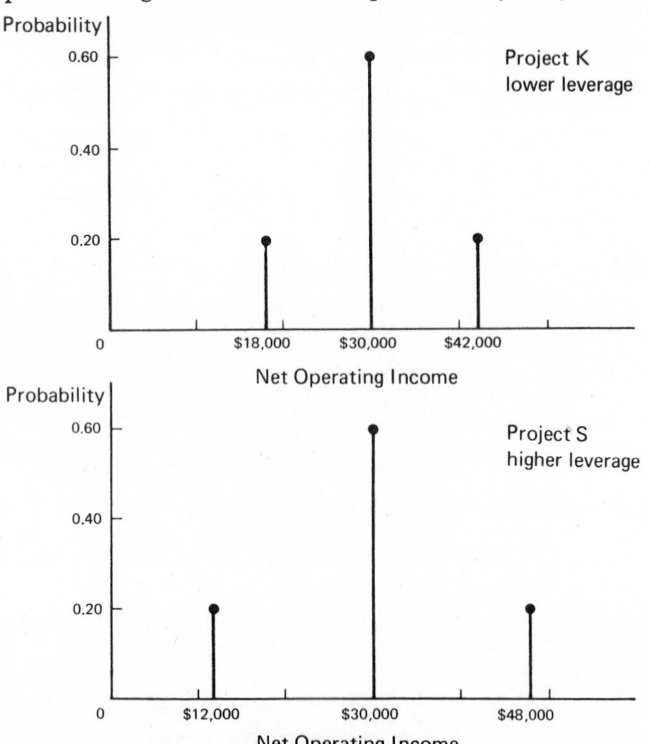


Figure 4–5 Les Doe Inc. Variations in net operating income due to different operating leverages.

***Appendix D***

## DETERMINATION OF THE DEBT-EQUITY INDIFFERENCE POINT

One reason for considering financial leverage is to select the appropriate debt-equity financing mix. Leverage can be favorable or unfavorable. What we want to know is the effect on EPS of various combinations of debt and equity. The indifference point is the EBIT level at which EPS are the same regardless of the debt-to-equity combination, given the total amount of funds to be employed and the interest rate on the bonds. A change in either the total funds or the interest rate will change the indifference point which is established by equating the debt-equity combination to a pure common stock structure:

$$\frac{(x - B)(1 - t)}{S_1} = \frac{x(1 - t)}{S_2}$$

where

$x$ = EBIT indifference point in dollars
$S_1$ = number of common shares outstanding when financing is through bonds and common stock
$S_2$ = number of common shares outstanding under pure common stock financing
$B$ = bond interest in dollars[16]
$t$ = corporate income tax rate (50 percent)

For a combination of bonds and preferred where $S_7$ equals the number of common shares outstanding when financing through bonds and preferred, we have the formula

$$\frac{(x - B)(1 - t) - P}{S_7} = \frac{x(1 - t)}{S_2}$$

In the Birch Bark Canoe example (Table 4–6) $600,000 of 5 percent bonds was substituted for $600,000 of common stock (150,000 shares of $4 par) leaving $400,000 of common stock (100,000 shares of $4 par).

Solving our Birch Bark Canoe problem for the indifference point, we have

$$\frac{(x - 30{,}000)(1 - 0.50)}{100{,}000} = \frac{x(1 - 0.50)}{250{,}000}$$

$$\frac{0.50x - 15{,}000}{100{,}000} = \frac{0.50x}{250{,}000}$$

$$x = \$50{,}000 \text{ EBIT indifference point.}$$

EPS at the indifference point = $0.10.

---

[16] For preferred stock instead of bonds, where $S_3$ equals the number of common shares outstanding when financing is through preferred and common stock and $P$ equals preferred stock dividends in dollars, we have

$$\frac{x(1 - t) - P}{S_3} = \frac{x(1 - t)}{S_2}$$

To determine the EPS at the indifference point, divide the EBIT at the indifference point by the number of shares at the starting point (here 100,000 shares).

At EBIT of $50,000 the EPS is 10 cents regardless of the portions of debt and common stock. This is shown graphically in Figure 4–6. Note that the greater the degree of financial leverage, the steeper the slope of the line. This means that for any given change in EBIT the greater the financial leverage, the greater the change in EPS. One limit is 100 percent debt resulting in an infinite slope, an infinite increase in EPS for a given increase in EBIT. At the other extreme the limit is a 100 percent common stock capital structure; the increase in EPS is directly proportional to the increase in EBIT.

Continuing with Birch Bark, in the third year (Table 4–6) earnings are $45,000 which is below the indifference point of $50,000 and the outlook for sales gains is gloomy. Birch Bark decides to hit the merger trail and acquires several firms engaged in oceanography and changes its name to Birch Bark Hydro-onics, Inc. Upon these announcements the price of the stock shoots from a price of $1.20 per share or 16 times current earnings, ($1.20/$0.075) to $4.50 or 60 times earnings. Birch Bark requires an additional $600,000 to carry out its expansion plans and seeks the indifference point before making a decision whether to use additional 5 percent debt or common stock. This point can be calculated by using a formula which compares a capital structure with added debt to one with the current amount of debt.

$$\frac{(x - B_1 - B_2)(1 - t)}{S_4} = \frac{(x - B_1)(1 - t)}{S_5}$$

where

$B_1$ = bond interest in dollars on currently outstanding debt
$B_2$ = bond interest in dollars on additional debt
$S_4$ = number of common shares outstanding if bonds are issued
$S_5$ = number of common shares outstanding if stock is issued

and $x$ and $t$ are defined as before.

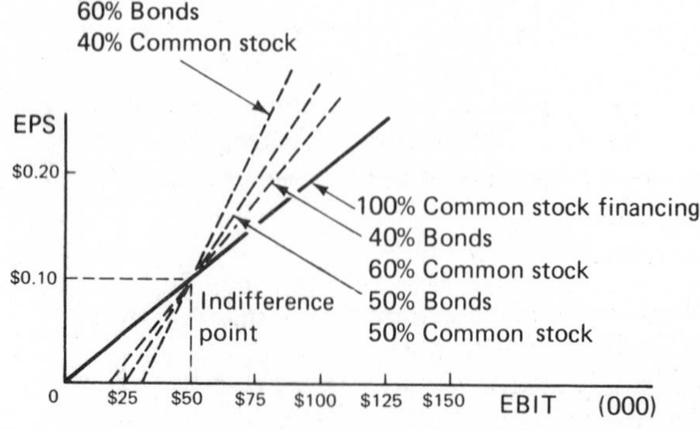


Figure 4–6 Indifference point and financial leverage using Birch Bark Canoe example (Table 4–6).

With Birch Bark able to sell the additional stock at $4 per share [17] and issue bonds at 5 percent, these alternative financing plans for raising $600,000 are reflected in the *pro forma* balance sheets shown in Table 4–13. The starting base is the $600,000 of 5 percent bonds and $400,000 common stock.

TABLE 4–13. Birch Bark Hydro-onics, Inc.
*Pro Forma* Balance Sheets

| *Additional bonds* | | *Additional stock* | |
|---|---|---|---|
| Assets | $1,200,000 Bonds—5%<br>$ 400,000 Common stock, $4 par, 100,000 shares | Assets | $ 600,000 Bonds—5%<br>$1,000,000 Common stock, $4 par, 250,000 shares |
| $1,600,000 | $1,600,000 | $1,600,000 | $1,600,000 |

Determination of the EBIT indifference point then becomes

$$\frac{(x - \$30{,}000 - \$30{,}000)(1 - 0.50)}{100{,}000} = \frac{(x - \$30{,}000)(1 - 0.50)}{250{,}000}$$

$$x = \$80{,}000$$

EPS at the indifference point = $0.10

The EPS at the indifference point is computed as follows:
[($80,000 − $30,000) × 0.50]/250,000 shares.

If Birch Bark is able to sell the additional shares for $6 per share, only 100,000 shares need be issued. The effect is to raise the EBIT indifference point to $90,000, but at this level EPS would be 15 cents. The higher the price at which the common stock can be sold the higher the indifference point. If the shares could be sold for only $2 per share, 300,000 additional shares would have to be issued to raise the needed $600,000. The EBIT indifference point would be lowered to $70,000, but EPS at this level would drop to 5 cents per share. Also the higher the rate of interest the higher the indifference point and the higher must be the EBIT to be in the favorable leverage range.

### Financial Planning and the Significance of the Indifference Point

When planning the financing of a firm the nearness of the indifference point to the profit-loss break-even point is important. We will be favorably inclined toward debt financing if our projected EBIT are expected to remain substantially above the indifference point. Referring to our Birch Bark example, if we anticipate EBIT substantially above $80,000, we might consider financing the additional $600,000 through bonds. If there is a reasonable chance EBIT may drop below $80,000, it would be desirable to scale down the debt financing, since such a drop would put us in the unfavorable leverage range. More important, if EBIT drops just somewhat further to below $60,000, ($1.2 million × 5%) we are in the loss range.

While it is uncomfortable to be operating below the indifference point—we are earning less per common share than if we had financed the firm more conservatively—it is not fatal. But if we drop into the loss range, continued losses are fatal. The line that represents profit and loss can be likened to the line that separates nonfreezing from freezing temperatures. Cherry blossoms may not develop quickly if the temperature should fall close to the freezing mark, but a few degrees below freezing for any period is fatal.

[17] Net after all selling charges and to allow for "underpricing."

If the additional $600,000 were financed through common stock, the EBIT indifference point would still be $80,000, but only after earnings dropped below $30,000 would we be in the loss column. The risk of severe financial difficulties is much less under the common stock financing plan than under the bond borrowing plan if we expect our EBIT in the future to fluctuate around $80,000. If we expect future EBIT to be in the $100,000 range and upward, with little or no chance of falling below the $60,000 level, bond financing would be the route to take, provided we are reasonably certain that investors will not consider the bond financing as too risky. It is not just what *is* likely to happen that is important but what investors *think* is likely to happen.

In considering bond financing the financial manager must weigh the expected market reaction and its effect on the market price of the firm's stock if he is to realize the goal of maximizing the value of the firm. If investors consider the bond financing too risky, the price-earnings ratio applied to the shares will be lowered proportionately more than the increase in earnings per share so on balance the market price per share and the value of the firm will drop. Here a decision to finance with bonds would not be correct.

On the other hand investors may feel the bond financing carries relatively little risk. The price-earnings ratio may be reduced only slightly or even be increased if it is anticipated that the growth in earnings per share will be accelerated. In either event the price per share and the value of the firm will be increased. Here a decision to finance with bonds would be correct.

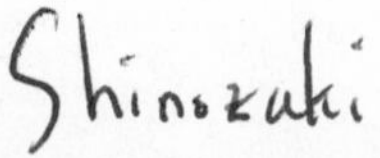

# PART TWO

# The Management of Working Capital

*

# 5
# The Money Management System

Money means power—power over resources. The long-run value of a firm depends in part on how wisely the firm manages its money assets.[1]

A firm requires cash to pay its bills in order to continue production. The financial manager cannot time cash inflows to coincide with required cash outflows. Thus, the firm must hold liquid balances—cash and assets readily convertible into cash—to absorb the drain of a cash outflow greater than the cash inflow over some period of time. But holding cash and short-term securities is costly; cash does not produce goods and services and the return on short-term securities is low. Thus, if the financial manager is to maximize the value of the firm he must: (1) weigh the need for liquid balances against their opportunity cost (the rate that could be earned on the funds in the best alternative use), and (2) fix the proportion of these liquid balances that should be held in the form of cash and the proportion that should be held in short-term securities. This is what the management of money is all about.

---

[1] Viewing the firm as a system, the money management system is a subsystem of the firm, as are the inventory and receivables systems.

Part Two of this book, on management of working capital, is aimed at minimizing liquidity requirements and maintaining levels of receivables and inventory that result in maximum value of the firm: high return on investment with minimum risk. Chapters 6 and 7 will deal with the management of inventory and receivables.

The present chapter examines the role of controlling all liquid resources of the firm—cash and assets rapidly convertible into cash. The availability of credit is a major factor in the management of the money assets of a firm and influences both the size of the cash reserves and the type of the investments used to absorb excess cash.

The generation of profits is heavily a function of the utilization of fixed assets and has a long-term horizon. The financial manager requires long-range plans setting forth the time pattern for the use and expansion of facilities and product development. In the automobile industry several years elapse between the original design on the drawing board and the first car rolling off the assembly line. In the aircraft industry the interval is even longer. At the same time that longer-range activities are proceeding, the firm has current production activities, utilizing existing assets and conducting the day-to-day activities necessary to keep the production process running. This requires working capital—cash, inventory, receivables.

## THE FIRM'S INVESTMENT IN CASH

To some extent cash and inventory management pose similar problems. The financial manager holds the minimum cash necessary to keep operations flowing smoothly so maximum funds can be invested in plant or used to reduce indebtedness. There is, however, an important difference between cash and inventory. The outflow of cash is more controllable, and expenditures are planned, but the inflow is partially noncontrollable and subject to more variation. With inventory the reverse is true. The inflow is largely planned and controllable, but the outflow (finished goods) is dependent upon the desires of the customer and is more uncontrollable.

### Industry Overview

The percentage that working capital bears to total assets varies widely among different industry groups. Table 5–1 reveals that in wholesale and retail trade, working capital comprises 70 and 65 percent, respectively, of total assets. By contrast the utility industry holds only 8 percent of total assets in working capital. In manufacturing the figure is 47 percent. But when we take cash as a percent of working capital (Table 5–2), public utilities are near the top and retail and wholesale trade at the bottom. Manufacturing drops to 12 percent.[2] Manufacturing and

[2] Since we show working capital as a percent of total assets in Table 5–1, and cash and short-term government securities as a percent of working capital in Table 5–2 we can easily compute cash and short-term government securities as a percent of total assets. Just multiply the corresponding industry figures in each of the tables. For example, to find cash and short-term government securities as a percent of total assets for manufacturing multiply 0.47 times 0.12 to obtain 6 percent.

wholesale and retail trade have reduced their liquidity sharply in recent years.[3]

TABLE 5–1. Working Capital as a Percent of Total Assets for Major Industrial Groups (Ranked from Highest to Lowest)

| Industry group | Percent | Industry group | Percent |
|---|---|---|---|
| Total wholesale trade | 70% | Services | 31% |
| Total retail trade | 65 | Total mining | 28 |
| Construction | 57 | Agriculture, forestry, and fisheries | 27 |
| Total manufacturing | 47 | Total utilities | 8 |

SOURCE: U. S. Treasury Department, Internal Revenue Service, *Statistics of Income, 1969 Corporation Income Tax Returns* (Washington, D. C.: Government Printing Office, 1973, pp. 14ff). Working capital equals cash and short-term government securities plus receivables plus inventory.

TABLE 5–2. Cash and Short-Term Government Securities as a Percent of Working Capital for Major Industrial Groups in 1969 (Ranked from Highest to Lowest)

| Industry group | Percent | Industry group | Percent |
|---|---|---|---|
| Services | 30% | Construction | 18% |
| Total mining | 22 | Total manufacturing | 12 |
| Total utilities | 20 | Total retail trade | 11 |
| Agriculture, forestry, and fisheries | 20 | Total wholesale trade | 11 |

SOURCE: U. S. Treasury Department, Internal Revenue Service, *Statistics of Income, 1969, Corporation Income Tax Returns* (Washington, D. C.: Government Printing Office, 1973, pp. 14ff).

In the past firms have held excessive amounts of cash.[4] The excess cash permitted firms to grant liberal credit and receivables rose rapidly. In essence firms were granting interest-free loans. Cash accumulated during the 13-year period 1952–1964 because inventory increased little with rising sales. Also, profits rose, but the investment in fixed assets rose less rapidly than sales.

The overall liquidity position of U. S. corporations dropped sharply during the 1960s.[5] Between 1960 and 1965, for manufacturing the ratio of liquid assets to current liabilities shrank from 63 to 51.6 percent. By

---

[3] See A. E. Grunewald and Erwin Esser Nemmers, *Basic Managerial Finance*, 1st ed. (New York: Holt, Rinehart and Winston, Inc., 1970), p. 89 for the 1963 figures comparable to those appearing in Table 5–2.

[4] See J. A. Griswold, "How to Lose Money with Cash," *Financial Executive*, 34 (August 1966), pp. 28–34.

[5] "Bottom of the Till," *Barron's*, May 23, 1967, p. 5.

the end of 1966 it had dropped to 43 percent. The process speeded up as firms increasingly came to view liquidity as a constraining influence. The factors responsible for the drop in liquidity were rising capital outlays, rising receivables, inventory accumulation, and accelerated tax payments accompanied by a leveling off of profits and cash flow. Apparently firms had sufficient liquidity to absorb this drain. By the beginning of 1967, however, a flood of new corporate bond issues was hitting the market to replenish the "till." [6] High interest rates in the credit crunch of 1969–1970 again found firms short of cash but now reluctant to borrow long-term. As interest rates eased in 1971 and 1972 firms rushed to bring new issues to market to convert their short-term debt to long-term obligations but long-term rates decline slowly. Then there was a new cash squeeze with the sharp rise of interest rates in 1973, and steeper still in 1974.

### Balancing the Need for Cash and Its Cost

Cash is a strange asset. A firm seeks to receive it in the shortest possible time but hold as little of it as possible. The more cash a firm has available, the less need there is for recourse to the banks in the event of unexpected expenditures or a slowdown in collections. But then the firm will experience a lower rate of return on investment since a portion of these funds could be invested in plant and equipment that would yield expected profits. This is the opportunity cost of holding idle cash balances—balances loved by the banker. We speak in terms of expected profit since no guarantee exists that the funds if invested will return a profit.[7] On the other hand, if the firm commits the maximum amount of funds to fixed assets, its debt-paying ability is low and dependence on banks high. Then, when the firm is under financial strain and the economic outlook cloudy, banks may refuse to lend.[8] At a minimum, the inability to borrow will cause financial embarrassment to the firm and perhaps losses since then it must liquidate assets in an effort to raise the funds.

It is more profitable to maintain good credit sources than to hold extra cash or short-term securities against unexpected use. But the maintenance of rapidly available credit sources is not without cost. The size of the firm's bank balance determines the warmth of the banker's smile—and, hopefully, the strength of the banking relationship. Deposits are crucial to a bank, and the larger and less active the account, the greater the value

---

[6] Financial managers were being caught in a liquidity squeeze. Receivables and inventories kept rising while cash items showed little change. Current and quick ratios continued to decline. Contributing to the squeeze was the Treasury's tax plan to put firms on a pay-as-you-go basis. See "Corporations Scramble for Cash," *Business Week*, March 25, 1967, p. 151.

[7] For example, Penn Central and Yale Express went into receivership, Douglas Aircraft was "saved" through merging, and Lockheed through a $250 million government backed loan.

[8] It has been said that banks will lend you an umbrella on a sunny day and take it back when it begins to rain.

to the bank. But demand deposits do not earn a return for the firm.[9] As compensation for deposits, the banker can offer an active interest in the credit needs of the firm. During periods when banks have more funds than loan opportunities, the banker's interest will be of modest value to the firm. The banker can offer other services—tangible (credit information) and intangible (financial advice and business contacts). When banks have more loan opportunities than funds, they favor the applications of firms that maintain satisfactory balances. The customer's deposit balance is a major credit-rationing standard of banks. Since firms value their banking relationship and desire access to credit on short notice, profitable and well-established firms maintain substantial balances. The cost in lost income is felt to be worth the accommodation provided by the banker.

A minimum level of cash is necessary to carry on business activities. Operating expenses normally must be paid before the product is sold and the proceeds collected. Cash should be available to take trade discounts. Missing discounts is expensive short-term financing. A good credit rating and the availability and cost of credit are dependent upon an adequate cash position. Lending institutions and suppliers set financial standards they expect firms to meet. Ratios are the measuring technique and cash is the object measured. Finally, cash is a completely liquid asset, which can be given in exchange immediately. No uncertainty exists regarding acceptability. Cash also offers the ability to take advantage of special purchases of raw materials, to finance expansion, or even to acquire a subsidiary.

### Cash as a Working Asset

To this point we have described cash as contributing to the liquidity position of the firm and other assets as being the real producers of earnings. But in planning for the long-run survival of the firm we must seek to maintain adequate funds for each asset group to carry on efficient production and meet future requirements. All assets must be working assets and contribute to the maximization of the value of the firm. Hence, excess cash should be employed elsewhere.

## FACTORS INFLUENCING WORKING CAPITAL

"Working capital" is a widely used phrase. "Circulating capital" is more descriptive. It creates the image of funds flowing from cash to inventory, to receivables, and back to cash. The firm's fixed assets physically produce the items for sale, but working capital also is needed to market the production of the goods.

---

[9] Sentiment in favor of permitting banks to pay interest on demand deposits is increasing. There is currently tremendous movement of funds from demand deposits to savings vehicles and back. This activity would be reduced if banks were permitted to pay interest on demand deposits. However, it was exactly the phenomenon of paying interest on demand deposits that was held largely responsible for bank failures in the depression of the 1930s. This led to the rule of no interest on demand deposits. In finance as elsewhere, the lessons of history are soon forgotten.

### Seasonal Elements

The amount of working capital the firm holds as a portion of total assets depends on the nature of the industry, the firm's production policies, its rate of growth, the state of the economy, and seasonal fluctuations. A public utility requires a large amount of fixed assets and receives an almost continuous stream of cash from its bill-paying customers. Only a small working capital position is required. A wholesaler occupying a warehouse, carrying a large inventory, and selling on credit requires a large working capital position. A firm in a seasonal business finds that not only does the amount of working capital fluctuate from one season to the next, but also the composition of the working capital changes over the year. For example, a toy manufacturer during the spring and summer months[10] is engaged in large production. Cash, the firm's as well as the bank's, is converted to inventory. Working capital expands, and cash is reduced. In the fall, inventories are converted to receivables as shipments are made to merchants in anticipation of the Christmas shopping season. After Christmas the receivables are converted to cash as the merchants pay their bills. Total working capital is reduced as bank loans are paid off. The following spring the cycle begins anew.

### Production Policy

A toy manufacturer, for example, has the choice of maintaining fairly steady production throughout the year or concentrating production during a few months just before delivery time. With the more steady production plan a higher average amount of working capital is required to finance the longer holdings of inventory. In compensation, production costs are lower, and overtime in the last months is avoided. But concentrating production in the months just before delivery reduces the risk of missing the market. The firm can wait to the last minute to determine the toy trend for the year before entering production.

### Growth

Unless a rapidly growing firm is very profitable, permitting retained earnings to cover the increased financing, the firm will need to arrange larger bank loans to finance its always inadequate working capital position. When the bank refuses to increase loans further, the firm must turn to the leasing of assets or to the sale of securities to finance additions to plant and equipment and increased working capital requirements.

### Cyclical Swings

As the business cycle swings up, cash flows into inventory and receivables, short-term borrowing is arranged, and plant and equipment expand. Current assets increase and liquidity declines. On the down swing, inventory and receivables fall, and the funds invested in these assets are converted to cash. Capital replacements are deferred and funds generated

---

[10] Interesting developments are changing the traditionally seasonal nature of the toy industry. See "Christmas in July," *Barron's*, July 10, 1967, pp. 11ff.

from depreciation flow into cash. If the firm is operating profitably but at a reduced level of activity, short-term creditors are paid off, working capital is reduced, and liquidity of the firm improves.

## MOTIVES FOR HOLDING CASH

A firm has the same motives as an individual for holding cash—transactions, precautionary, and speculative motives.

### Transactions Motive

The transactions motive describes cash held to carry on its routine activities. Were inflows and outflows perfectly synchronized, the firm would need only a small cash balance; but this does not occur in the real world.

By analyzing its activities the firm can isolate the causes for normal discrepancies between the outflow and inflow of cash. One cause may be that the firm requires customers to pay by the 10th of the month following purchase but pays its own suppliers at the end of the month of purchase. Another may be extraordinary outflows, such as real estate, income taxes, and machinery purchases, and extraordinary inflows, such as the sale of securities, of unneeded machinery and equipment, and of surplus inventory.

### Precautionary Motive

Unpredictable discrepancies are met (in part) with precautionary cash reserves. Floods, strikes, and the failure of important customers are events that can interrupt the best-laid financial plans. Providing for the unpredictable is difficult. The amount provided is a function of the firm's willingness to assume this risk and of its reserve borrowing power. A firm wishing to avoid this risk holds large cash balances and maintains good banking relationships as a second line of defense. A somewhat less cautious or less affluent firm may activate most of its cash resources and depend on its line of credit for any unusual demands.[11] The firm willing to assume high risk or one in tight straits has most of its resources committed to productive activities, including a good portion of its borrowing power. Such a management's forecast and hope are that no sudden demand for funds will arise during a period of tight financial conditions. Once these conditions have passed and larger earnings have been generated, the firm will have taken the risk and won. It is now affluent and can maintain a solid working capital position. Most financial managers seek a middle course, maintaining some cash to meet the precautionary motive and keeping the firm's credit lines open to meet any large, unexpected demands for cash.[12]

---

[11] A revolving credit with a line of credit involves a commitment by the bank to lend to the firm funds as needed up to a predetermined limit; a credit line involves no commitment by the bank. To obtain a revolving credit with a line of credit the firm must usually pay a commitment fee.

[12] Financial managers usually have much to lose if the firm encounters severe financial difficulties and little to gain if the firm earns a few extra cents per share because of a policy of keeping cash balances at a minimum.

### Speculative Motive

The speculative motive for holding cash is a result of seeking opportunities, such as buying inventory at favorable prices either at depressed prices or at normal prices just before an anticipated rise. Generally, it is assumed that firms do not speculate on inventory purchases. It is not easy, however, to draw the line between shrewd buying of large quantities of inventory at what in retrospect are favorable prices and speculating on future inventory prices. It sounds good to say the financial manager should be primarily concerned with the profitable operations of the firm and not seek speculative opportunities. Yet the cost of raw materials inventory is such an important item in the cost structure of most firms that the acquisition of large inventory lots at favorable prices may mean the difference between profit and loss.

## CASH PLANNING THROUGH THE CASH BUDGET

Every firm must plan and control its use of cash. Failure to do so will at a minimum result in a reduced return on investment; at the extreme lies bankruptcy. The firm's cash balance at the end of any given period is the result of numerous interrelated activities. Planning is required, and the cash budget is the planning instrument. For efficient operation, management must know in advance when and how much cash will be needed to carry on the firm's activities. If more cash is needed than will be generated from operations, plans must be made to obtain the needed funds, from either short-term creditors or long-term investors. If a surplus of cash is expected, decisions must be made concerning the period for which the funds are to be invested and the kinds of securities to be purchased—Treasury bills, certificates of deposit, commercial paper, and so on. As the firm becomes more sophisticated in planning and controlling cash, the amount necessary to support any given level of operations is reduced.

The cash budget may be used either as a simple forecasting device or as a means of aggressive planning. When used as a forecasting device, operating projections are made, cash inflows and outflows matched, deficiencies provided for, and surplus funds invested. Aggressive planning involves estimating different levels of operations and juggling the inflows and outflows to obtain the mix that makes the greatest contribution to the profitability of the firm without involving too much risk.

The cash budget need not be a complex document. It is a formal statement showing estimated cash income and cash expenditures over the firm's planning horizon. The net cash position (excess or deficiency) of the firm as it moves from one budgeting subperiod to another is highlighted. The period of time covered by the cash budget may be 1 year, 6 months, 3 months, or some other period. The subperiods may be a day, a week, a month, or a quarter, depending upon the needs of the firm. If the firm's flow of funds is dependable, a cash budget covering a period of a year divided into quarterly intervals may be appropriate. Where substantial uncertainty is associated with the flow of funds, a quarterly cash budget broken into monthly or weekly intervals may be necessary.

The cash budget is the key to arranging needed funds on the most favorable terms available or to investing excess funds. With adequate time to study his firm's needs, the financial manager can afford to be selective.[13] Contrast this situation with that of a firm that has not forecast its cash requirements. Suddenly it finds itself short of funds. With the need pressing and little time to explore alternative avenues of financing, the financial manager must accept the best terms offered in a crisis situation. These terms will not be as favorable, since the lack of planning indicates to the lender that there is an organizational deficiency. The firm, therefore, represents a higher risk.

### Cash Budget Items

The cash budget includes only cash flows—in and out. Noncash items, such as depreciation, are excluded. But the effect of depreciation in reducing income taxes will be there. A classification of cash flows is given in Table 5–3.[14] The direction of the flow is the basis of the classification.[15]

## THE CASH BUDGET AS PART OF A FORECASTING SYSTEM

The sales forecast is the starting point of cash budgeting. In Chapter 8 we will discuss various methods of obtaining a reliable forecast, including environmental and break-even analysis.

TABLE 5–3. Typical Cash Flows

| *Cash outflows* | *Cash inflows* |
|---|---|
| Direct labor | Cash sales |
| Material and supplies | Collection of receivables |
| Administrative expenses | Interest income |
| Accounts payable | Dividend income |
| Repayment of bank loans | Tax refund |
| Retirement of loans outstanding | Bank loan |
| Repurchase of common and preferred stock | Sales of bonds and preferred or common stock |
| Interest payments | Sale of plant and equipment |
| Dividend payments | |
| Purchase of plant and equipment | |
| Tax payments | |

---

13 Bankers do not encourage shopping around. However, an informed financial manager is not likely to be paying more than the going rate.

14 We have included the opening cash balance and the disposition of excess or deficit cash in our cash budget. When a firm is larger, the cash budget stops with the determination of the excess or deficiency of cash, and a financial budget separately starts with the opening cash balance and reconciles the excess or deficiency with borrowings or repayments and security purchases or sales. In the case in which there also is a financial budget all interest and dividends paid or received are included in the financial budget rather than in the cash budget.

15 The source and application of funds statement is useful for studying the historical flow of funds and for tracing the firm's changing financial condition. The income and expenditure flows are important in examining the profitability of the firm and are best studied through analysis of the income statement. At this point, our main concern is with cash flows and the cash budget.

We now illustrate the use of the cash budget and *pro forma* financial statements as a forecasting instrument. The latter are derived from the cash budget data and provide an estimate of the firm's profitability over the period and its financial condition at the end of the period.

### An Example

Assume Hardy Tourist and Gift Shoppe is planning for the coming tourist season, which begins April 1 and closes September 30. The financial manager must estimate the monthly cash flows and arrange for any necessary borrowing. Management wishes to arrange for an adequate loan but does not wish to borrow excessively, knowing that the banker will be impressed with an orderly loan request supported by concrete estimates that will make the terms of the loan more favorable. Accordingly, the financial manager, beginning with the balance sheet of March 31 shown in Table 5–4, prepares a cash budget.

TABLE 5–4. Hardy Tourist and Gift Shoppe
Balance Sheet, March 31

| *Assets* | | | *Liabilities and Net Worth* | | |
|---|---|---|---|---|---|
| Cash | | $ 3,000 | Accrued salaries | $ 500 | |
| Inventory * | | 8,000 | Other liabilities | 2,500 | $ 3,000 |
| Equipment | $70,000 | | | | |
| Depreciation | 13,000 | 57,000 | Capital | | 65,000 |
| Total assets | | $68,000 | Total liabilities and net worth | | $68,000 |

* Composed of $2000 minimum inventory plus $6000 of inventory scheduled to be sold next month.

TABLE 5–5. Sales Forecast

| | | | |
|---|---|---|---|
| April | $10,000 | July | $50,000 |
| May | 20,000 | August | 40,000 |
| June | 30,000 | September | 20,000 |

TABLE 5–6. Salary Expense Budget

| | | | |
|---|---|---|---|
| April | $1,500 | July | $4,000 |
| May | 2,000 | August | 3,000 |
| June | 2,500 | September | 2,000 |

After consulting with the marketing manager, the financial manager estimates sales, as given in Table 5–5. After reviewing salaries and other major operating expenses in previous years and relating these to sales volume, he estimates salary costs, as given in Table 5–6. He estimates the other expenses will approximate 12 percent of sales. Depreciation is calculated at the rate of 1 percent per month on original cost. The Shop is expected to operate along the following lines:

1. Sales (scheduled in Table 5–7) will be 80 percent cash and 20 percent credit. The credit sales will all be collected in the following month, and no bad debts are expected.

2. The gross profit margin on sales will average 40 percent.

3. All inventory purchases will be paid for during the month in which they are made.

4. A basic inventory of $2000 (at cost) will be maintained. The Shop will follow a policy of purchasing enough additional inventory each month to cover the following month's sales.

5. A minimum cash balance of $3000 will be maintained.

6. New equipment orders of $20,000, scheduled for May 1 delivery, and $10,000, for June 1 delivery, have been made. Payment will be made at the time of delivery.

7. Accrued salaries and other liabilities will remain unchanged.

TABLE 5-7. Hardy Tourist and Gift Shoppe
Cash Budget

| | *Apr.* | *May* | *June* | *July* | *Aug.* | *Sept.* |
|---|---|---|---|---|---|---|
| Sales | $10,000 | $20,000 | $30,000 | $50,000 | $40,000 | $20,000 |
| *Inflows* | | | | | | |
| Cash sales | 8,000 | 16,000 | 24,000 | 40,000 | 32,000 | 16,000 |
| Collection of accounts receivable | | 2,000 | 4,000 | 6,000 | 10,000 | 8,000 |
| Total | $ 8,000 | $18,000 | $28,000 | $46,000 | $42,000 | $24,000 |
| *Outflows* | | | | | | |
| Inventory | $12,000 | $18,000 | $30,000 | $24,000 | $12,000 | |
| Salary | 1,500 | 2,000 | 2,500 | 4,000 | 3,000 | $ 2,000 |
| Expense | 1,200 | 2,400 | 3,600 | 6,000 | 4,800 | 2,400 |
| Equipment | | 20,000 | 10,000 | | | |
| Total | $14,700 | $42,400 | $46,100 | $34,000 | $19,800 | $ 4,400 |
| Net monthly cash gain or loss by end of month | ($6,700) | ($24,400) | ($18,100) | $12,000 | $22,200 | $19,600 |
| Cumulative cash gain or loss by end of month | ($6,700) | ($31,100) | ($49,200) | ($37,200) | ($15,000) | $ 4,600 |
| Cumulative borrowing necessary during the month | $ 7,000 | $32,000 | $50,000 | $38,000 | $15,000 | — |

8. Additional financing when necessary will be in multiples of $1000.
9. No taxes are due till after the close of the tourist season.

After gathering these figures together, the financial manager organizes them according to the direction of cash flow, as shown in Table 5–7. The difference between the cash inflow and outflow is the net cash inflow or outflow for the month. Cumulating these figures for each period after adding in the opening cash balance, he has the estimated cash on hand at the end of the period. In our example, the opening cash balance is exactly the planned minimum cash balance to be maintained during the tourist season. If the beginning level were below the minimum, the deficit would be supplied from an excess cash inflow or from additional borrowing. But if the beginning level were above the required minimum, the excess could be used to support an outflow of funds. Borrowing would not be necessary until this source was exhausted.

From the initial data and the cash budget figures we can now estimate the profitability of the coming tourist season by drawing up the *pro forma* income statement shown in Table 5–8 using the data above. The balancing figure is net profit.

TABLE 5–8. Hardy Tourist and Gift Shoppe
*Pro Forma* Income Statement
April 1–September 30

| Costs | | Sales | $170,000 |
|---|---|---|---|
| Cost of goods sold | $102,000 | | |
| Salary | 15,000 | | |
| Expenses | 20,400 | | |
| Depreciation * | 5,600 | | |
| Profit (pre tax) | 27,000 | | |
| | $170,000 | | $170,000 |

* Composed of depreciation charged at the rate of 1 percent per month on $70,000 for 6 months, 1 percent per month on $20,000 for 5 months, and 1 percent per month on $10,000 for 4 months.

TABLE 5–9. Hardy Tourist and Gift Shoppe
*Pro Forma* Balance Sheet
September 30

| *Assets* | | | *Liabilities and Net Worth* | | |
|---|---|---|---|---|---|
| Cash | | $ 7,600 | Accrued expenses | $ 500 | |
| Accounts receivable | | 4,000 | Other liabilities | 2,500 | $ 3,000 |
| Inventory | | 2,000 | Capital | $65,000 | |
| Equipment | $100,000 | | Retained earnings | 27,000 | $92,000 |
| Depreciation | 18,600 | 81,400 | Total Liabilities and Net Worth | | |
| Total Assets | | $95,000 | | | $95,000 |

Next we draw up the *pro forma* balance sheet as of the close of the tourist season, shown in Table 5–9. The cash on hand on September 30 is the sum of the beginning cash balance, $3000, and the cumulative cash gain, $4600—or $7600. Receivables will be 20 percent of September sales of $20,000; inventory will be the amount purchased during September plus the opening inventory of $2000; equipment will be the $70,000 plus the $30,000 purchased, minus the beginning depreciation of $13,000 and the accumulated depreciation of $5600. Accrued expenses, other liabilities and capital are assumed to remain constant. A pretax profit of $27,000 is anticipated.

### An Implicit Cash Budget Assumption: Even Cash Flows

Although the cash budget is a useful tool, the assumption of even cash flows within a period can lead to embarrassing miscalculations. This assumption and its implication are graphed in Figure 5–1. But cash flows usually are irregular because the firm buys from suppliers that demand payment on the same day, say the 10th of the month; or the firm itself extends credit that brings a concentration of payments at, say, the end of the month. To avoid such concentrations, some firms, notably department stores, have set up a cyclical billing system whereby a portion of the customers are billed on a certain day of each month. Banks also distribute the mailing of statements in this manner. To avoid miscalculation the financial manager must examine the individual cash flow characteristics of his organization, in order to determine whether the unevenness of the flows within a budget period is large enough to cause serious errors in decision making. The cash budgeting period or the minimum cash balance may be adjusted to reduce the impact of the uneven cash flows.

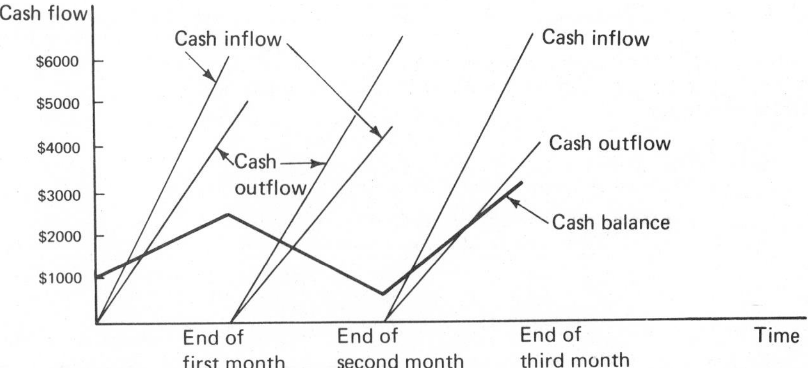


Figure 5–1 Even cash flows and resulting cash balance. The cash balance is cumulative. During the first month $5700 flows in and $4100 flows out. The cash balance is raised $1600, from $1000 to $2600. During the second month $4000 flows in and $6000 flows out; the net change amounts to $2000 and the cash balance is $600. During the third month $6000 flows in and $3600 flows out; the net change amounts to $2400 and the cash balance is $3000. The cash flows are not cumulative.

### The Cash Budget as a Planning System—an Example

The cash budget may also be employed in planning operations by altering what would otherwise happen. In the next example of cash budgeting we use a toy manufacturer and follow its operation over a one-year cycle. The details may vary from one firm to another but the principles are generally applicable.

*Setting* Rex Toy Company is a firm of limited resources operating in a high-risk industry subject to sweeping changes in the popularity of items. In the past, production has been scheduled directly in response to sales. In accordance with this policy, Rex minimizes its reliance on outside credit, keeps inventory down, and reduces its exposure to shifts in demand, but production fluctuates widely. During the first few months of the year the production level is low; before the year's end production runs for several months at capacity. As a result, the company experiences employee dissatisfaction, high labor turnover, substantial overtime payments, and loss of efficiency.

*Current Operating Characteristics* Sales are concentrated at the beginning of the month. Credit terms on sales require full payment by each month's end. No discounts for early payment are granted. Production anticipates sales by 30 days. The purchase of materials for cash precedes production by 30 days. The financial manager, wishing to estimate the coming year's borrowing requirements, draws up the cash budget shown in Table 5–10 and finds the need for cash fluctuates widely. In several months there is a large need for funds followed by a net inflow. Then comes another month of large outflow followed by a net inflow, which is again followed by an outflow; then comes a major inflow followed by 2 months of outflow. The last 3 months of the year show a net inflow. These wide fluctuations make cash management difficult, requiring the constant shifting of funds. Recalling the personnel and cost problems created by the "production in response to sale" policy, the financial man-

TABLE 5–10. Rex Toy Company
Cash Budget Forecast—Historical Production Pattern
(000)

| | Jan. | Feb. | Mar. | Apr. | May | June | July | Aug. | Sept. | Oct. | Nov. | Dec. |
|---|---|---|---|---|---|---|---|---|---|---|---|---|
| Production Schedule * | $300 | $400 | $400 | $600 | $600 | $800 | $800 | $900 | $1,000 | $1,000 | $1,000 | $200 |
| Cash Inflow | | | | | | | | | | | | |
| Cash from sales | $200† | $300 | $400 | $400 | $600 | $600 | $800 | $800 | $900 | $1,000 | $1,000 | $1,000 |
| Cash Outflows | | | | | | | | | | | | |
| Labor | $150 | $200 | $200 | $300 | $300 | $425** | $425 | $500 | $600 | $ 600 | $ 600 | $ 100 |
| Materials payments | 80 | 80 | 120 | 120 | 160 | 160 | 180 | 200 | 200 | 200 | 40 | 60‡ |
| Variable costs | 30 | 40 | 40 | 60 | 60 | 80 | 80 | 90 | 100 | 100 | 100 | 20 |
| Fixed costs | 10 | 10 | 10 | 10 | 10 | 10 | 10 | 10 | 10 | 10 | 10 | 10 |
| Selling and administrative expenses | 4 | 4 | 4 | 4 | 5 | 5 | 5 | 6 | 6 | 6 | 6 | 5 |
| Total outflow | $274 | $334 | $374 | $494 | $535 | $680 | $700 | $806 | $916 | $ 916 | $ 756 | $ 195 |
| Net cash change | —$74 | —$34 | +$26 | —$94 | +$65 | —$80 | +$100 | —$6 | —$16 | +$84 | +$244 | +$805 |

* Production figures are at selling price. Cost information: labor, 50 percent of current month's production; materials payments, 20 percent of next month's production; variable costs, 10 percent of current month's production; selling and administrative expenses, arbitrarily determined. These are all cash costs; no noncash charges such as deprceiation are involved.

† Production was $200,000 in December of the previous year.

‡ Production is assumed to be $300,000 in January of the next year.

** Overtime payments are made in June through November.

[A9838]

ager decides to determine the effects of a more level production program on both the firm's need for funds and on other costs, so he draws up the cash budget shown in Table 5–11.

TABLE 5–11. Rex Toy Company
Cash Budget Plan—A More Level Production Pattern
(000)

| | Jan. | Feb. | Mar. | Apr. | May | June | July | Aug. | Sept. | Oct. | Nov. | Dec. |
|---|---|---|---|---|---|---|---|---|---|---|---|---|
| Production Schedule * | $350† | $450 | $550 | $550 | $700 | $750 | $850 | $850 | $850 | $900 | $900 | $ 300 |
| Cash Inflow | | | | | | | | | | | | |
| Cash from sales (same as Table 5–10) | $200 | $300 | $400 | $400 | $600 | $600 | $800 | $800 | $900 | $1,000 | $1,000 | $1,000 |
| Cash Outflows | | | | | | | | | | | | |
| Labor | $175 | $225 | $275 | $275 | $350 | $375 | $425 | $425 | $425 | $ 450 | $ 450 | $ 150 |
| Materials payments | 90 | 110 | 110 | 140 | 150 | 170 | 170 | 170 | 180 | 180 | 60 | 70‡ |
| Variable costs | 35 | 45 | 55 | 55 | 70 | 75 | 85 | 85 | 85 | 90 | 90 | 30 |
| Fixed costs | 10 | 10 | 10 | 10 | 10 | 10 | 10 | 10 | 10 | 10 | 10 | 10 |
| Selling and administrative expenses | 4 | 4 | 4 | 4 | 5 | 5 | 5 | 6 | 6 | 6 | 6 | 5 |
| Total outflow | $314 | $394 | $454 | $484 | $585 | $635 | $695 | $696 | $706 | $ 736 | $ 616 | $ 265 |
| Net cash change | —$114 | —$94 | —$54 | —$84 | +$15 | —$35 | +$105 | +$104 | +$194 | +$264 | +$384 | +$735 |

* Production figures are at selling price. For cost information and method of computing costs, see note at bottom of Table 5–10. Under the more level production pattern, no overtime need be paid in in the later months of the year.

† Production in preceding December was $300,000.

‡ Materials payments for December are based on production at selling price of $350,000 in January of the next year.

[A9837]

*Planned Operations* This cash budget, based on a more level rate of production, shows a higher peak need for cash of $366,000 through June; under the "production in anticipation of sales" policy the peak need reaches only $191,000 in June. Further, by spreading production more evenly through the year, Rex would accumulate inventory in anticipation of the holiday season. If we consider sales and monthly inventory, we can calculate the additional inventory risk the firm assumes through adoption of the more level production pattern. Table 5–12 shows that Rex will accumulate approximately $400,000 additional inventory (at selling price). The financial manager can now weigh the increased borrowing cost and the inventory risk against reduced production costs and improved efficiency and employee morale.

TABLE 5–12. Rex Toy Company
Inventory Position * under the More Level Production Schedule of Table 5–11
(000)

| | Jan. | Feb. | Mar. | Apr. | May | June | July | Aug. | Sept. | Oct. | Nov. | Dec. |
|---|---|---|---|---|---|---|---|---|---|---|---|---|
| Month's opening inventory | $300† | $450 | $ 600 | $ 750 | $ 900 | $1,000 | $1,150 | $1,200 | $1,250 | $1,200 | $1,100 | $1,000 |
| Month's production | 350 | 450 | 550 | 550 | 700 | 750 | 850 | 850 | 850 | 900 | 900 | 300 |
| Total | $650 | $900 | $1,150 | $1,300 | $1,600 | $1,750 | $2,000 | $2,050 | $2,100 | $2,100 | $2,000 | $1,300 |
| Deduct month's sales | 200 | 300 | 400 | 400 | 600 | 600 | 800 | 800 | 900 | 1,000 | 1,000 | 1,000 |
| Month's ending inventory | $450 | $600 | $750 | $900 | $1,000 | $1,150 | $1,200 | $1,250 | $1,200 | $1,100 | $1,000 | $ 300 |
| Change from prior month's ending inventory | +$150 | +$150 | +$150 | +$150 | +$100 | +$150 | +$ 50 | +$ 50 | —$ 50 | —$100 | —$100 | —$700 |
| Cumulative change in inventory | 150 | 300 | 450 | 600 | 700 | 850 | 900 | 950 | 900 | 800 | 700 | 0 |

* All figures at selling price.

† Equal to production of prior December.

[A9835]

The production manager concerned with operating efficiency prefers long production runs and reduced set-up costs. He also likes the diminished scheduling problems of a more level rate of operations. The personnel manager approves the more stable labor force and better morale from production stability and points to reduced labor costs. The sales manager feels more comfortable having a large stock of inventory to meet customer demand promptly but he also feels uncomfortable about the risk of obsolescence in a large inventory. The higher risk and inventory-carrying costs are not welcome. To the financial manager, the reduced short-term borrowing charges and lower inventory-carrying costs of the *old* plan are real advantages. Through use of the cash budget, the financial manager has developed the issues whose resolution will lead to a plan for future operations.

The contribution of the financial manager need not end here. If the more level production plan is acceptable, he can return to the cash budget to determine ways of shifting the inflow and outflow of cash to reduce the firm's borrowing requirements. One way is to speed collections. Currently the toys are produced in one month, shipped at the beginning of the next month, and paid for by the end of that month. If the toys could be shipped at the end of the month in which they are produced and payment received shortly thereafter, the amount of short-term borrowing could be reduced. This acceleration of delivery and collection of receivables by about 30 days might be achieved through the granting of more generous trade discounts by the firm to its customers.

Alternatively, the financial manager might seek more rapid delivery of raw materials through a more rapid delivery system. Truck or partial shipment by air are possibilities. The objective would be to shift forward by 30 days (closer to time needed in production) the ordering, delivery, and payment dates for raw materials. With these policies (of accelerated collection and delayed ordering and payment) the cash budget and the cumulative cash flows would appear as in Table 5–13. This plan shows a steady net inflow of funds for all months except March and December, when there is a net outflow of $4000 and $55,000, respectively. If the financial manager were able to put this cash budget into effect, the firm

TABLE 5–13. Rex Toy Company
Cash Budget—Cash Flow Adjustments under the More Level Production Pattern
(000)

| | Jan. | Feb. | Mar. | Apr. | May | June | July | Aug. | Sept. | Oct. | Nov. | Dec. |
|---|---|---|---|---|---|---|---|---|---|---|---|---|
| Production schedule (same as in Table 5–11) * | $350 | $450 | $550 | $550 | $700 | $750 | $850 | $850 | $ 850 | $ 900 | $ 900 | $300 ‖ |
| Cash Inflow | | | | | | | | | | | | |
| Cash from sales † | $300** | $400 | $400 | $600 | $600 | $800 | $800 | $900 | $1,000 | $1,000 | $1,000 | $200 |
| Cash Outflow | | | | | | | | | | | | |
| Labor | $175 | $225 | $225 | $275 | $350 | $375 | $425 | $425 | $ 425 | $ 450 | $ 450 | $150 |
| Materials payments ‡ | 70 | 90 | 110 | 110 | 140 | 150 | 170 | 170 | 170 | 180 | 180 | 60 |
| Variable costs | 35 | 45 | 55 | 55 | 70 | 75 | 85 | 85 | 85 | 90 | 90 | 30 |
| Fixed costs | 10 | 10 | 10 | 10 | 10 | 10 | 10 | 10 | 10 | 10 | 10 | 10 |
| Selling and administrative expenses | 4 | 4 | 4 | 4 | 5 | 5 | 5 | 6 | 6 | 6 | 6 | 5 |
| Total outflow | $294 | $374 | $404 | $454 | $575 | $615 | $695 | $696 | $ 696 | $ 736 | $ 736 | $255 |
| Net cash change | +$6 | +$26 | −$4 | +$146 | +$25 | +$185 | +$105 | +$204 | +$304 | +$264 | +$264 | −$55 |

* Production figures are at selling price.

† Cash from sales figures are the same as those in Table 5–10 except they are assumed to flow in one month earlier.

‡ Materials payments figures are the same as those in Table 5–11 except they are assumed to flow-out one month later. Faster delivery means the raw materials arrive and are paid for in the month of production.

** Equal to production of prior December.

‖ The $300,000 produced in December is sold in January of the next year, so no net change in inventory occurs.

would have the best of both worlds—a more level production rate and no need to engage in extensive short-term borrowing. But these changes are achieved by a reduction in profit. In the first case, trade discounts granted might exceed the interest savings. In the second case, accelerated delivery costs might exceed the interest savings.

## THE MEANS OF MANAGING THE CASH FLOWS

We now consider methods for accelerating cash inflow and delaying outflow: the selection of individual banks, methods of communication, minimum balance requirements, means for transmitting funds, the investment of temporarily excess funds, and a method for coordinating the system activities. In monitoring the system the financial manager must be alert to discover ways of accelerating inflows and delaying outflows. More avenues are open in the former area.

Our firm may find its available funds shrinking since other firms sensitive to ways in which the collection of checks can be delayed will adopt methods to increase the "nonavailable" funds or "dead" float as it is called, consequently reducing the funds available to our firm. Not too long ago 10 days might elapse between the time a check sent to a distant supplier cleared the local bank upon which it was drawn. During this time the funds remain on deposit in the local bank thus contributing to the remitting firm's compensating balance [16] and in effect doing double duty—liquidating the payable obligation and at the same time maintaining the required bank balance. Today checks clear in a few days. Let us see why.

### Speeding the Inflow: A Network of Banking Connections and a Concentration Bank

Firms seek ways to speed up the collection of checks to make funds available sooner. Higher profitability per investment dollar results from reduced interest payments because of less borrowing, diminished reliance on bank lending, and perhaps even lower interest rates.

Commercial banks are interconnected through a series of correspondent banking relationships. Funds are transferred by wire among major banks. Federal Reserve banks, through which most commercial banks clear their checks, are also linked by a wire transfer system. A small firm may deal with only one bank located in its home community, where it deposits checks for collection. A national firm may have several hundred accounts in as many banks throughout the country to expedite check collection.[17] One bank in each area is selected to service the needs of one or several of the firm's branches. Funds are maintained there up to a certain point, and when the balance rises above this limit—generally through collection of receivables—the excess is transferred to a concentration bank located in a large city. The concentration banks are in turn linked to a control bank in the city of the home office. The control bank

---

[16] Bankers customarily require borrowers to keep on deposit from 15 to 20 percent of the amount borrowed. This deposit is called a compensating balance.

[17] See F. N. Anderton, "Centralized Cash Management for a Decentralized Company," *N. A. A. Management Accounting*, 47 (September 1965–August 1966), pp. 51–59, for a case illustration of a receipts-collection network.

works closely with the firm in meeting its liquidity requirements, in investing its temporarily idle balances, and in maintaining control of the firm's entire banking network.

The more banking relationships a firm establishes, the shorter the time span from mailing of the checks by the customer to deposit in a company account. However, since minimum balances must be maintained in each bank, the more bank accounts, the larger the total minimum balance maintained. The objective of control is to maintain balances at each bank sufficient to cover bank service charges and meet the operating needs of the division in that area. With daily information on current balances the financial manager shifts funds quickly by wire to any section of the country or the world or invests the balances not immediately needed. The overall time required to convert customers' checks to spendable cash depends on the extensiveness of the banking network, the methods by which funds are shifted, and the frequency with which they are shifted. The financial manager must judge the point at which the availability of the funds outweighs the cost of transferring them from one bank to another.[18]

### Lock-Box Banking

Firms wishing to speed the cash inflow and relieve themselves of clerical tasks have adopted the simple system of lock-box banking. The firm rents a post office lock box in every city where it has a servicing bank [19] designates the bank as its collection agent for that region, and notifies customers to mail payment to the lock box. The bank picks up the mail each day, deposits the checks, and sends the firm the deposit slip listing the checks deposited. Prearranged procedures are followed for nonconforming items, such as checks for incorrect amounts. Lock-box banking is recommended in an area where the firm has no regional office but desires a check collection point.

Customers who have built float time into their cash system will be unhappy with the introduction of a lock-box system. The collecting firm may encounter some difficulties where lock-box checks are deposited a day or so before the home office receives notification of payment. Credit cut-off of weak customers may occur due to delayed reporting.[20]

### Regulating the Outflow

The lock-box system that speeds the inflow of funds can also speed the outflow. But far fewer firms use multiple disbursing points. With

---

[18] The optimum use of cash, coordination of the divisions' cash requirements that fit in with the firm's financial planning, anticipation of cash deficiencies and surplus, minimization of interest and other charges, and more equitable banking relationships are the advantages claimed for centralized cash management. See Anderton, pp. 58–59.

[19] Banks actively solicit this business. The National Bank of Detroit carried an ad in the *Wall Street Journal* headed, "Patterns for Fast Cash", which described a kit permitting a firm to identify its most productive lock-box cities in order to speed the process of converting collections to spendable cash. *Wall Street Journal*, March 22, 1968, p. 32.

[20] F. E. Horn, "Managing Cash," *Journal of Accountancy*, 117 (April 1964), pp. 56–62. This article also discusses other procedures to speed up funds inflow.

a network of banks, the disbursing officer can transfer funds from one region to another as needed to cover checks presented for payment, thus reducing the total idle cash balances. Speeding the outflow reduces the firm's own funds by making them available more quickly to suppliers, but this can produce valuable goodwill.

A firm short of funds and wishing to maintain its float will not seek to speed payment. There are cases in which firms have maintained balances in distant banks in order to slow the payment process.

## MANAGING CASH IN EXCESS OF REQUIREMENTS

The firm may have excess cash balances—either temporarily idle funds accumulating or a permanent excess balance.

Long-term excess funds may accumulate because of factors such as a miserly dividend policy or an accounting policy reporting profits (and income taxes) down. These permanently excess funds can be employed in internal investment projects if the outlook is promising. If the firm is in a declining industry with limited investment outlets, serious consideration might be given to returning the excess funds to the shareholders as a return of capital. If the near-term outlook for the firm is not bright and the stock is depressed but better prospects lie ahead, the firm might repurchase its own stock.[21] If the stock is selling on a low price-earnings ratio and a high dividend-yield basis and internal investment opportunities are limited, stock repurchase is a sound alternate use of excess working capital. Later, when profitable investment opportunities appear, the shares can be reissued and the funds used to finance projects.

### Guides to Investing Temporarily Idle Working Capital

Temporarily excess cash may arise from many factors, such as a seasonal downswing, a spurt in the collection of receivables, or an improvement in inventory management. Or the firm may be accumulating funds in anticipation of some major outlay such as the initial payment on a new project, dividend payments, or partial debt retirement. Holding these funds as demand deposits would guarantee[22] their availability when needed. However, the funds can earn income in short-term obligations that offer safety of principal. Although firms may invest idle funds for only short periods of time, the amounts available for investment can be large enough to warrant investing them. Thus $10 million invested at 9 percent for 4 days, say over a long weekend, will earn over $9000. This income is generated with a small amount of additional administrative cost. The guides should be marketability *and* safety of principal, for exposure to risk for the sake of a slightly higher yield is a poor trade-off.

The safety policy eliminates from consideration the purchase of common and preferred stock and long-term bonds. The value of long-term

---

[21] See C. D. Ellis, "Repurchase Stock to Revitalize Equity," *Harvard Business Review*, 43 (July–August 1965), pp. 119–128; and L. A. Guthart, "More Companies Are Buying Back Their Stock," *Harvard Business Review*, 43 (March–April 1965), pp. 40–53 ff.

[22] This is normally so—but recall the San Francisco National Bank failure of 1965, which resulted in large losses to depositors.

government securities presents little risk if held to maturity, but even a small increase in the current interest rate will cause a significant drop in the market prices of the issue.[23] A trend has been developing since the early 1960s toward putting increasing amounts of idle funds into higher-yielding issues where there may be little risk. These issues include commercial paper, Japanese bankers' acceptances, and Euro dollars.[24]

### Treasury Securities—Outlet for Temporarily Excess Cash

Treasury securities are popular instruments for the investment of temporarily idle corporate funds. Their appeal derives from safety, liquidity,[25] and wide range of maturities. The principal types of Treasury securities are bills, tax anticipation bills, certificates of indebtedness, notes, and bonds.[26]

### Commercial Paper

For the firm desiring a yield above Treasury bills of the same maturity an alternative is high-grade commercial paper.[27] In recent years, commercial paper has carried yields equal to the prime rate on commercial bank loans.

---

23 The quotation on Treasury bonds, 4s, due August 1973 was 98.22 bid, 98.30 asked; for the 4s, February 1988–1993, the quote was 78.20 bid, 79.20 asked. *Wall Street Journal*, June 27, 1972, p. 28.

24 Jean Ross-Skinner, "The Profitable Art of Handling Corporate Cash," *Dun's Review and Modern Industry*, 79 (May 1962), p. 40.

25 Large blocks can be sold without influencing the market price.

26 Treasury bills are customarily issued each week and fall due in 91 days, but they are also offered as due in 182 days, and occasionally 1-year bills are issued. Tax anticipation bills mature approximately 1 week after the April, June, September, and December quarterly income tax due dates. Since they may be used to pay taxes on these dates at face value, the holder gains about 1 week's extra interest. All bills are sold at a discount and mature at face value, the yield being determined by the spread between the purchase price and the maturity value. Normally there are large amounts of bills outstanding and regular offerings. The bill market is active, resulting in a narrow spread between bid and offer.

Longer-term investments offering a higher yield are certificates of indebtedness, which mature in 1 year or less; notes, with an original maturity of 7 years; and bonds, which have a maturity of over 7 years. Certificates of indebtedness may be issued on a discount basis or carry a coupon. Both bills and certificates have been employed by the Treasury to raise funds in anticipation of tax receipts and may be used in the payment of federal income taxes. Because these obligations generally mature a few days after the income tax payment date, they afford the owner a few days' extra interest, since they may be tendered in payment of taxes on the due date. Though government notes and bonds are not ordinarily of interest to the financial manager, with the passage of time they enter the short-term class (maturity of 1 year or less) and sell on a yield basis approximately comparable to other short-term Treasury securities. Attractive purchase opportunities may present themselves to the alert financial manager who recognizes when an issue is selling outside of its regular yield curve pattern primarily because of market factors. Term to maturity and likelihood of an impending change in interest rates are the major factors in determining yield. This situation gives the financial manager the opportunity to ride the yield curve—ride the price up, sell off, and buy a slightly longer-term issue. This technique can bring big profits, perhaps to an annual return of 9 percent, but if the market interest rate changes upward in the middle of the procedure, the financial manager may be forced to hold to maturity to avoid a capital loss.

27 See Chapter 11 for a discussion of the characteristics and market for commercial paper.

### Repurchase Agreements

Under a repurchase agreement the firm arranges to purchase a substantial amount of Treasury obligations from a dealer who agrees to repurchase them at an agreed-upon price at a later date. Through this arrangement the firm earns a relatively good return on its funds,[28] though ordinarily not as high as on commercial paper, has collateral for its "loan" to the dealer, and helps the dealer carry his government security inventory. These repurchase agreements are tailored to the specific needs of the firm. Agreements may cover a period as short as overnight or some longer time span. Corporations have found repurchase agreements a desirable outlet for temporarily idle funds, and a large portion of the inventory of government securities dealers is financed through these money market instruments.[29]

### Certificates of Deposit (CDs)

Certificates of deposit represent time deposits in commercial banks for periods from 30 to 360 days that are interest-bearing, negotiable, and marketable. The yield varies according to maturity and the general level of interest rates as prices fluctuate in the secondary (resale) market. But, at original issue there is a maximum rate that banks can pay, regulated by the Federal Reserve System. Though they are of recent origin, CDs are now issued by banks across the nation. They are popular with financial managers because they offer a higher yield than do government securities, commercial paper, or repurchase agreements. The certificates compete directly with commercial paper and the rates are approximately equal. When a disparity arises due to market factors, funds flow from the lower-yielding to the higher-yielding instruments. But, when interest rates rise and the Federal Reserve does not raise the maximum allowable rate on CDs, the primary offerings are not competitive.

Many financial managers prefer the certificates of the larger banks because of their presumed greater safety and better marketability. As a result, the rates obtainable on the certificates of the smaller banks run to about one-fourth of 1 percent higher than those paid by the major banks in the financial centers. The rates are publicized by the banks and changed only infrequently to keep in step with money market conditions. Certificates are offered by some banks only in denominations of $1 million, but others offer them in denominations of as low as $1000.

## SUMMARY

Cash is the focal point of working capital flows. It is a perfectly liquid asset. Cash is held for transaction, precautionary, and speculative

---

[28] That is between ⅛ and ¼ percent above similar maturity Treasury obligations. See Donald P. Jacobs, "The Marketable Security Portfolios of Non-Financial Corporations, Investment Practices and Trends," *Journal of Finance*, 15 (September 1960), pp. 341–352.

[29] Government securities dealers in 1963 financed 41 percent of their requirements through repurchase agreements with nonfinancial corporations. See Louis Freeman, "The Financing of Government Securities Dealers," *Federal Reserve Bank of New York, Monthly Bulletin*, 46 (June 1964), pp. 107–116.

motives. The carrying of excess cash balances is costly since earnings on them are lost. Crisis borrowing is also costly; favorable terms can seldom be arranged under pressure. The cash budget provides a procedure for estimating cash flows and determining in advance the cash needs or surplus funds available. The cash budget may be used in aggressively planning the future operations of the firm.

Excess cash balances should be invested. Permanently excess funds might be invested in plant and equipment, the company's own stock, or a liquidating dividend payment. Temporarily idle funds should be invested in short-term, high-grade securities. Safety of principal and liquidity are the leading guidelines. Appropriate issues are Treasury bills and notes, certificates of deposit, and commercial paper.

## Study Questions

1. Review Tables 5–1 and 5–2. Explain why the various industries differ so widely with respect to working capital as a percent of total assets; and cash and short-term government securities as a percent of working capital. How do you explain the ranking of public utilities—last when taking working capital as a percent of total assets and third when taking cash and governments as a percent of working capital?
2. How do you explain the decline in liquidity suffered by corporations during the early 1960s? Why did the liquidity squeeze in 1969 and 1974 focus on cash? How could the federal government ease or intensify the situation?
3. Why do we say that cash is a strange asset? How does improvement in the speed of communications influence our thinking regarding cash?
4. Why is borrowing to meet short-term financial needs an economic use of resources? How is this activity assisted by a well-developed financial system?
5. Why is it desirable for a firm to invest its temporarily idle short-term funds? Would this be possible without a well-developed financial system? What forms of investment might a firm select? Is it in the national interest for firms to invest their temporarily idle funds? Should the government encourage it by legislation or otherwise?
6. Since cash does not "earn," can we still call it a working asset? Why? What are the motives for holding cash? How do they relate to cash as a working asset?
7. How can the cash budget be used as an aggressive planning system? What are the major uncertainties when drawing up a cash budget? How can the financial manager "allow" for these uncertainties?
8. How does the cash budget assist the financial manager in employing the resources of the firm in an optimum manner? How does this relate to arranging for timely borrowing or investing temporarily idle balances?
9. Under what conditions would a firm accumulate permanent excess working capital? Give examples of firms and industries in which excess working capital has been accumulated. Are these balances usually disposed of? Why or why not? How?

## Problems

1. As financial manager of Sky Rocket, Inc., a part of your responsibility is planning for the financial requirements during the peak season of January 1 to

June 30. A cash budget and *pro forma* income statement and balance sheet (Table 5–14) are normally prepared.

TABLE 5–14. Sky Rocket, Inc.
Balance Sheet
December 31

| | | | | |
|---|---|---|---|---|
| Cash | | $ 160,000 | | |
| Accounts receivable | | 100,000 | | |
| Inventory | | 490,000 | | |
| Fixed assets | $300,000 | | Common stock | $ 100,000 |
| Depreciation | 50,000 | 250,000 | Retained earnings | 900,000 |
| Total assets | | $1,000,000 | Total liabilities and net worth | $1,000,000 |

The sales forecast prepared by the marketing vice-president appears in Table 5–15.

TABLE 5–15. Sales Forecast

| | | | |
|---|---|---|---|
| January | $200,000 | April | $600,000 |
| February | 400,000 | May | 900,000 |
| March | 500,000 | June | 500,000 |
| | | July | 100,000 |

The operating department provided the estimates given in Table 5–16.

TABLE 5–16. Monthly Salary Expenses

| | | | |
|---|---|---|---|
| January | $30,000 | April | $ 90,000 |
| February | 50,000 | May | 110,000 |
| March | 70,000 | June | 60,000 |

Monthly selling and administrative expenses are expected to be 10 percent of sales. Depreciation charges are 1 percent per month.

Sky Rocket operates on the following terms:

1. Sales are on a net 30-day basis. The firm's customers seek to economize the use of cash, so sales made in one month are never collected until the next month.
2. Sky Rocket's suppliers demand cash for purchases.
3. The firm purchases enough inventory each month to cover the following month's sales.
4. The cost of goods sold is 60 percent of sales.
5. A basic inventory of $370,000 is maintained at all times to give customers prompt service.
6. A minimum cash balance of $100,000 is maintained.

*Additional Information*:

1. New equipment purchases of $50,000 are scheduled for March 1 delivery. Payment is made at the time of delivery.

2. Interest charged by the bank is at the rate of 1 percent per month. The amount needed as indicated by the cash budget is borrowed at the beginning of that month. Repayment is made at the end of the month. The interest is payable at the end of June when it is anticipated that the firm will have a net cash inflow. Borrowing is in $1000 units.

3. The income tax rate is at 50 percent and payable in July on the profit earned during the period January 1 to June 30. Recognize accrued income tax in the financial statements.

a. Prepare a cash budget for the period January 1 to June 30.

b. Prepare a *pro forma* income statement for the same period.

c. Prepare a *pro forma* balance sheet as of June 30.

d. Financial analysis:

(i) What is the month of peak borrowing needs?

(ii) Why do the borrowing requirements mount so rapidly?

(iii) If Sky Rocket's level of operation next year is approximately the same as this year's, what do you estimate its borrowing requirements to be?

(iv) Would you recommend that Sky Rocket sell stock to eliminate the seasonal borrowing at the high interest cost?

2. The Coordinate Instrument Company is studying the desirability of establishing a lock-box system in Texas to speed the inflow of spendable cash. Annual credit sales in that area currently total $18 million. Use of a lock-box system would reduce the dead float from 10 to 3 days. The bank in Houston would require a $60,000 minimum balance to service the account. Ignore administrative costs.

a. Assuming a 360-day year, calculate the net amount of funds freed through the establishment of the lock-box system.

b. If these freed funds would now be permanent excess working capital, would it "pay" the firm to install the system? On what factors would it depend?

c. If these funds would be only temporarily idle funds, would it be desirable to install the system now or wait until the funds are needed for the capital expansion program? Study a current issue of the *Wall Street Journal* and the *Federal Reserve Bulletin* and determine how much you could earn on these funds in a short period of time, say 90 days, 180 days, 6 months, 1 year.

3. Classify each of the following as a balance sheet item (B), a profit and loss statement item (P), a source and application of funds statement item (F), or a cash budget item (C). Some items may appear on more than one financial statement. Read each item carefully.

a. Collection of receivables.

b. Inventory.

c. Federal income taxes paid.

d. Equipment purchases.

e. Net profit (for the year).

f. Additions to plant.

g. Increase in receivables.

h. Proceeds from sale of common stock (for cash).

i. Reserve for depreciation.

j. Salary and wages paid in year.
k. Charge for depreciation.
l. Accrued dividends.
m. Decrease in cash.
n. Cumulative borrowing needs.
o. Cash dividends to stockholders.
p. Total current assets.
q. Decrease in inventory.
r. Cost of goods sold.
s. Selling and administrative expense accrued in year.
t. Sales.
u. Payment on notes payable.
v. Retained earnings.
w. Bank loan received.
x. Gross profit.
y. Interest paid.
z. Cash balance.

### Selected References


Anderson, P. F., and R. D. B. Harman, "The Management of Excess Corporate Cash," Financial Executive, 32 (October 1964), pp. 26–30 ff.

Baxter, N. D., "Marketability, Default Risk, and Yields on Money Market Instruments," *Journal of Financial and Quantitative Analysis,* 3 (March 1968) pp. 75–85.

Bloch, E., "Short Cycles in Corporate Demand for Government Securities and Cash," *American Economic Review,* 53 (December 1963), pp. 1058–1077.

Griswold, J. A. "How To Lose Money with Cash," *Financial Executive,* 34 (August 1966), pp. 28–34.

Horn, F. E., "Managing Cash," *Journal of Accountancy,* 117 (April 1964), pp. 56–62.

Jeffers, J. R., and J. Kwon, "A Portfolio Approach to Corporate Demands for Government Securities," *Journal of Finance,* 24 (December 1969), pp. 905–919.

Kraus, A., C. Janssen, and A. McAdams, "The Lock Box Location Problem," *Journal of Bank Research,* 1 (Autumn 1970), pp. 50–58.

Law, W. A., and M. C. Crum, "New Trend in Finance: The Negotiable C. D.," *Harvard Business Review,* 41 (January-February 1963), pp. 115–126.

Reed, W. L., Jr., "Profits from Better Cash Management," *Financial Executive,* 40 (May 1972), pp. 40–42 ff.

Ross-Skinner, J., "The Profitable Art of Handling Corporate Cash," *Dun's Review and Modern Industry,* 79 (May 1962), pp. 38–41 ff.

Sprenkle, C. M., "Is the Precautionary Demand for Money Negative?" *Journal of Finance,* 22 (March 1967), pp. 77–82.

Stancill, J. M., *The Management of Working Capital,* Scranton, Pa.: Intext Educational Publishers, 1971.

***Appendix E***

## PLANNING FOR UNEVEN CASH FLOWS

To explore the situation of uneven cash flows within the budget subperiods large enough to cause concern to the financial manager, we continue the example of the Hardy Tourist and Gift Shoppe.

Assume that the shop, in addition to selling to tourists, also serves as a wholesaler to three other gift shops. Two of these, L and M, always purchase a predetermined amount. Sometimes they take advantage of the slight discount and pay by the 10th of the month; at other times they pay by the end of the month. The third shop, Q, buys a variable amount each month but always takes advantage of the discount.

Assume that cash sales for April of $8000 include purchases by these three gift shops; that the amount not purchased by them is sold evenly throughout the month; that payments for inventory are due one-third on each the 10th, 20th, and 30th; and that salaries and other expenses are paid at the end of the month. The large orders placed by the L, M, and Q gift shops cause unevenness in the smooth flow of funds, and management is interested in estimating its borrowing requirements as of the 10th of the month. Beginning on April 1, with $3000 on hand, if cash sales had flowed smoothly, the firm would have taken in approximately $2700, ($8000/3 $\cong$ $2700) and would have had to pay out $4000, (Table 5–7) for inventory on the 10th, leaving it with a cash balance of $1700. Whether this balance should be reinforced by some borrowing depends on the probability that cash on hand will actually sink to this level and the extent to which the firm is willing to assume risk.

From previous experience the financial manager knows that sales to customer L will be $300 and to customer M $400 at the beginning of April. He also estimates that there is a 75 percent probability that L will pay by the 10th and a 50 percent probability that M will pay by the 10th. Thus there is a 25 percent probability that L will pay on the 30th and a 50 percent probability that M will pay on the 30th. The financial manager estimates customer Q will order by the 10th and pay for either $500 or $1000 worth of merchandise. Each size order is equally likely—a probability of 50 percent. The financial manager wants to know the probability that he will have sufficient cash on hand on the 10th of April to render borrowing at this time unnecessary. If the probable need for funds at this date is high, he will arrange for a loan beginning on that date, but if the probability is low, he might merely arrange a line of credit whose cost is substantially less than the actual loan would be. The commitment may cost as little as one-half of 1 percent of the line of credit.

Customer L buys and pays by the 10th of the month with a probability of $P_a^L$ and pays by the 30th with probability $P_z^L$. Then $P_a^L + P_z^L = 1.0$. Similarly for M, $P_a^M + P_z^M = 1.0$. At the 10th of the month there are four payment possibilities: both L and M pay, L does but M does not, M does but L does not, or neither L nor M pays. It is assumed that L and M pay their bills independently of each other. The probability that L and M pay by the 10th of the month can be defined as the joint probability $P_a^L \cdot P_a^M$. It follows that the probability that L will pay and M will not is $P_a^L(1-P_a^M)$, that M will pay and L will not, $P_a^M(1-P_a^L)$, and that neither will pay, $(1-P_a^L)(1-P_a^M)$. Table 5–17 shows these computations.

The table indicates that there is a 37.5 percent probability that both L and M will pay by the 10th, a 37.5 percent probability that L will pay and M will not, a 12.5 percent probability that L will not pay and M will, and a 12.5 percent probability that neither L nor M will pay by the 10th. This information, along with the amounts to be collected, is summarized in Table 5–18.

TABLE 5–17. Hardy Tourist and Gift Shoppe
Joint Probability Payment Distributions of Customers L and M

| Customer L \ Customer M | Probability of payment by the 10th $P_a^M = 1/2$ | Probability of nonpayment by the 10th $(1 - P_a^M) = 1/2$ |
|---|---|---|
| | Joint Probability | |
| Probability of payment by the 10th $P_a^L = 3/4$ | $P_a^L P_a^M = 3/8$ | $P_a^L(1 - P_a^M) = 3/8$ |
| Probability of nonpayment by the 10th $(1 - P_a^L) = 1/4$ | $P_a^M(1 - P_a^L) = 1/8$ | $(1 - P_a^L)(1 - P_a^M) = 1/8$ |

TABLE 5–18. Hardy Tourist and Gift Shoppe
Probability Distribution of Collections from Customers
L and M * on the 10th

| | L and M both pay | Only M pays | Only L pays | Neither pays |
|---|---|---|---|---|
| Probability | 3/8 | 1/8 | 3/8 | 1/8 |
| Collections | \$700 | \$400 | \$300 | \$0.0 |

* The joint probabilities are obtained from Table 5–17.

[A9816]

Customer Q is expected to purchase with equal likelihood either \$500 or \$1000 worth of merchandise and pay by the 10th. Table 5–19 shows the probabilities of the various lump-sum cash inflows by the 10th. This information is summarized in Table 5–20.

TABLE 5–19. Hardy Tourist and Gift Shoppe Joint Probability
Distribution of Customers L, M, and Q Receipts by the 10th

| Payment by Customers L, M, and Q | | | | | | |
|---|---|---|---|---|---|---|
| Customer Q purchase distribution | | Customers L and M payment distributions * | | | | |
| Probability | Payment | Probability<br>Payment | 3/8<br>\$ 700 | 1/8<br>\$ 400 | 3/8<br>\$ 300 | 1/8<br>\$ 0.0 |
| | | | Combinations of L and M with Q | | | |
| 1/2 | \$ 500 | | 3/16<br>\$1200 | 1/16<br>\$ 900 | 3/16<br>\$ 800 | 1/16<br>\$ 500 |
| 1/2 | \$1000 | | 3/16<br>\$1700 | 1/16<br>\$1400 | 3/16<br>\$1300 | 1/16<br>\$1000 |

* Figures obtained from Table 5–18.

[A9817]

There is a 75 percent probability that *at least* \$900 will flow from purchases by the three gift shops. If we assume that the remaining approximately \$6800 worth of gifts sold for cash is sold evenly throughout the month, we can estimate the firm will have a cash balance of about $2200 on hand on the 10th after collections and after paying one-third of the month's inventory purchases. Assuming that the minimum of $900, as stated above, is the amount purchased by the gift-shop customers, we see that Q has purchased $500 and L $400 and paid by the 10th. Customer M has purchased $300 of gifts but he will pay on the 30th. Subtracting this amount from our expected total April sales of $8000, we have $6800 to be sold to the regular tourists, or about $2300 the first 10 days. Adding this amount and the $900 purchased by Q and L to the beginning cash balance of $3000 and subtracting our first inventory payment of $4000, we arrive at a net cash balance of $2200 on the 10th. Since there exists a 75 percent probability that this amount will be available, the financial manager might well merely arrange for a line of credit to meet the borrowing need and plan to engage in borrowing by the 15th. Where discounts are substantial, the calculations would have to be refined to account for the reduced amount received from the customers who pay cash.

In our example we used three customers for illustrative purposes. This same procedure can be applied to a large enterprise having many customers by establishing classes of customers and treating the classes as we have the individual customers L, M, and Q.

TABLE 5–20. Hardy Tourist and Gift Shoppe
Probability Distribution of Receipts from Customers L, M, and Q by the 10th *

| | L and M both pay, Q buys $1,000 | Only M pays, Q buys $1,000 | Only L pays, Q buys $1,000 | L and M both pay, Q buys $500 | Neither pays, Q buys $1,000 | Only M pays, Q buys $500 | Only L pays, Q buys $500 | Neither pays, Q buys $500 |
|---|---|---|---|---|---|---|---|---|
| Probability | 3/16 | 1/16 | 3/16 | 3/16 | 1/16 | 1/16 | 3/16 | 1/16 |
| Receipts | $1,700 | $1,400 | $1,300 | $1,200 | $1,000 | $900 | $800 | $500 |

* Figures obtained from Table 5–19.

[A9818]

# 6

# The Inventory Management System

In the flow of funds from cash back to cash, inventories (and receivables) represent an intermediate stage in the cycle. Every manufacturer must acquire input material to make its products; every wholesaler and retailer must purchase finished goods to sell. And since purchases, production, and sale are seldom completely in step, firms generally are required to maintain stocks of inventory.

Inventory management is important both for short-run liquidity and long-term profitability. The overstocking of some items will result in excessive investment and costs. The understocking of other items will mean lost sales or production time. Either imbalance will adversely affect profits. Overstocking will, in addition, decrease liquidity. Investors will place a lower value on the firm than if its inventory is well managed.

Even when well managed, the investment by firms in inventory is substantial. Inventory constitutes a major percent of the working capital of many firms and often a significant portion of total assets. In retail and wholesale trade, inventory comprises about 32 percent of the total assets of the firm; in manufacturing about 19 percent.[1]

---

[1] U. S. Treasury Department, Internal Revenue Service, *Statistics of Income 1969*, Corporation Income Tax Returns, (Washington, D. C.: Government Printing Office, 1973), pp. 14 ff.

Some costs are incurred by a firm in maintaining its inventory while other costs that would be incurred if no inventory were carried can be avoided by carrying inventory. *Optimal inventory policy* maximizes the value of the firm, that is, it balances these costs to produce the lowest total cost of inventory.

## THE FIRM'S INVESTMENT IN INVENTORY

It is not unusual for a firm to carry thousands of different types of items in inventory ranging from those widely used to those that turn over slowly. We will examine those inventory items of sufficient volume to warrant the application of sophisticated inventory control methods aimed at providing the best customer service at the least cost.

### The Uncertain Value of Inventory

Unlike receivables and cash, inventory may have no easily determinable value. A dollar in cash can command a dollar's worth of goods and services. With receivables, the firm has a legal right to collect cash. Inventory, however, has value only to the extent it can be sold, and the amount for which the goods can be sold varies from day to day. Consider a department store stocking its toy inventory. Some days before Christmas the toys have considerable value; the day after Christmas, half their value has disappeared.[2] They are the same toys, but with the season over they can only be sold at reduced prices.

### Maintaining the Right Amount of Inventory

A firm must have the right inventory at the right time to meet demand so it can earn a profit. The flow of funds aspect is also important. The faster the inventory flows through sales into receivables, the less the dollar investment of inventory relative to sales. With the same dollar profit being earned on a reduced inventory, the rate of return on investment is increased. Further, inventory carrying costs (storage, handling, obsolescence and spoilage) are reduced with a high turnover. Driving inventory too low has undesirable results such as additional set-up costs for more frequent production runs, an increased number of raw material orders, underutilization of capital and labor when a shortage of a particular raw material halts production, and the loss of sales as a result of not being able to meet delivery schedules. Except during periods of intense economic activity, management typically must counteract prevailing pressures to prevent high inventories.[3]

---

[2] Some standard raw material and all fashion items are vulnerable to sharp price drops. For example, the price of copper scrap dropped from 59½ cents to 34½ cents a pound in about nine months. *The Wall Street Journal*, May 1, 1970, p. 20 and January 20, 1971, p. 20. Many high fashion shops suffered large inventory losses in 1970 when they tried to force calf-length dresses into style.

[3] See James I. Morgan, "Questions for Solving the Inventory Problem," *Harvard Business Review*, 41 (July–August 1963), pp. 95–110, for an exhibit showing the conflicting pressures on inventory levels.

The sales manager is oriented toward sales volume and customer satisfaction, and these are promoted by prompt delivery. Insufficient inventory is felt directly while a reduced return on investment due to carrying too much inventory is felt indirectly. The production manager wants long production runs to reduce the number of times fixed set-up costs are incurred thereby reducing per unit costs, but this raises the average level of inventory. The financial manager must establish policies leading to an optimum inventory; that is, he strives to balance low unit production and ordering costs through long production runs on one side against increased carrying costs for larger inventory on the other. Similarly, the stock of finished goods carried should be high enough to meet the demands of most customers but not the demand of all customers for all items at all times. A point is reached where the added profit to be generated from the added sales is more than offset by the marginal cost of carrying additional inventory.

### Industry Overview

Table 6–1 shows inventory as a percent of working capital for industry groups ranked from highest to lowest. A wide spread exists, with retail and wholesale trade and manufacturing at the top and construction, mining, and services at the bottom. Inventory as a percent of working capital is influenced by the type of industry, season of the year, stage of the business cycle, and growth trend and rate.

TABLE 6–1. Inventory as a Percent of Working Capital

| | | | |
|---|---|---|---|
| Total retail trade | 51% | Total utilities | 29% |
| Total manufacturing | 41 | Services | 25 |
| Total wholesale trade | 42 | Construction | 22 |
| Agriculture, forestry and fisheries | 44 | Total mining | 20 |

SOURCE: U. S. Treasury Department, Internal Revenue Service, *Statistics of Income, 1969, Corporation Income Tax Returns* (Washington, D.C.: Government Printing Office, 1973), pp. 14ff.

## FUNCTION AND COST OF CARRYING INVENTORY

The holding of inventory is costly.[4] What function does it serve? Unavoidably, while production continues some "goods in process" inventory exists. Inventory will be in transit, moving from one machine to another. For example, automobiles moving down the line are goods in process from the moment the chassis is hooked to the assembling line to the time the finished unit is driven off. But what of the raw material and finished goods inventory?

[4] Annual inventory carrying costs, according to a survey by the Research Institute of America, range from a low of 8.6 percent of the value of the inventory to a high of 40.5 percent. See Robert W. Arnold, "Inventory Management," *The Woman C.P.A.*, 22 (February 1960), pp. 3–5 ff. Reprinted in Edward J. Mock, *Readings in Financial Management* (Scranton, Pa.: International Text Book Company, 1967) pp. 353–358.

Raw materials inventory is maintained to assure the flow of production. A guaranteed flow of raw materials from our supplier at the rate being used in production would greatly reduce the need for a raw materials inventory. Similarly, if we could sell our finished products at the rate they are being produced, there would be a need to carry only a small finished-goods inventory. But the firm usually has little control over the rate at which its products are sold. A firm usually finds it more economical to order at one rate, produce at another, and sell at a third. The carrying of inventories at each of these three stages enables us to uncouple [5] the buying, producing, and selling functions to engage in each activity at its economic rate.

Fixed and variable costs influence the economic inventory level. Costs such as handling, taxes, insurance, record keeping, obsolescence, and spoilage are variable as is the cost of capital of the funds invested in the inventory. Depreciation, most of the cost of storing the inventory, and the cost of the capital invested in the inventory-handling equipment are fixed. These fixed and variable costs can be measured. But the different risks specifically associated with different kinds of inventory are difficult to measure.

## DETERMINING THE OPTIMUM INVENTORY LEVEL

A firm operating under certainty would experience little difficulty in determining the proper inventory level. Demand would be known in advance and likewise the profit: sales price per unit minus cost per unit times the number of items sold. Although occasionally demand is known with certainty—the number of diplomas at graduation—usually it is not and sales must be estimated. In the following discussion we assume sales are not influenced by any systematic causes but can be described by a random variable function.

### Estimating Demand and the Concept of Probability

If sales demand is a random variable, how do we estimate the inventory to be carried? To help solve the problem, we associate some probability of occurrence with each sales estimate. The individual probability assigned to each estimate must be equal to or greater than zero and equal to or less than 1.0. The sum of the probabilities assigned must equal 1.0.

The wheel of fortune shown in Figure 6–1 illustrates the basic probability concepts employed in solving this problem. The numbers at the edge of the wheel are the possible outcomes and correspond to the amounts won or lost on a one dollar bet. If at this point we were dealing with a business problem, the outcomes might correspond to the margin of profit per dollar of sales revenue.

---

[5] Elwood S. Buffa, *Modern Production Management*, 3d ed. (New York: John Wiley and Sons, Inc., 1969), p. 504.

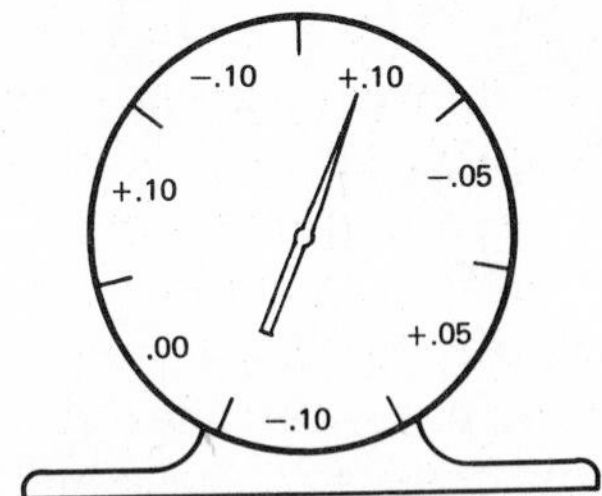


Figure 6–1 Wheel of fortune.

The numbers in each space indicate the amount won or lost for each dollar bet on the spin of the wheel.

If in Figure 6–1 the pointer stops at +0.10, the player wins 10 cents per dollar bet. He has realized a 10 percent return. If the wheel stops with the indicator on −0.05, he loses 5 cents per dollar bet; incurs a 5 percent loss.

Table 6–2 summarizes the characteristics of this wheel of fortune, the possible outcomes that can result from any spin of the wheel of fortune, the frequency with which each outcome appears, and the corresponding probability of a given outcome occurring.[6] A different wheel of fortune would involve a different probability distribution. The probabilities of immediate concern, however, are not those generated by a wheel of fortune but by some activity in the real world—the forces that generate the demand for the firm's product.

TABLE 6–2. Probability Distribution Represented by Wheel of Fortune

| *Possible outcomes* | *Frequency* | *Probability* |
|---|---|---|
| −0.10 | 2 | 2/7 |
| −0.05 | 1 | 1/7 |
| 0.00 | 1 | 1/7 |
| 0.05 | 1 | 1/7 |
| 0.10 | 2 | 2/7 |
| Total | 7 | 1.0 |

If we call each estimate of the daily demand for an item an *event*, we may assign probabilities to these events on the basis of experience, reasonable assumptions, or judgments. The various possible daily demand occurrences for an item can be transformed into a wheel of fortune, such as in Figure 6–1.

---

[6] The wheel of fortune may be thought of as a random variable function associating particular outcomes with the amounts won or lost on each spin of the wheel. The divisions of the wheel are all equal. The probability of each outcome is the same. And the algebraic sum of the possible outcomes is zero; this in an honest wheel.

### An Example

To illustrate, the demand for red roses sold by the Campus Florist may fluctuate within the limits of 7 to 10 dozen. The probability $p_i$ of selling $x_i$ dozen roses on any particular day is given in Table 6–3.

TABLE 6–3. Campus Florist
Probability Distribution of Demand for $x_i$ Dozen Red Roses

| | | | | |
|---|---|---|---|---|
| Probability ($p_i$) | 0.1 | 0.2 | 0.4 | 0.3 |
| Daily demand ($x_i$) | 7 | 8 | 9 | 10 |

The roses are long-stemmed, cost $5, and sell for $10 per dozen. They must be sold in one day or they become worthless. The florist can carry an inventory of 7, 8, 9, or 10 dozen roses. If an inventory of 7 dozen roses is carried, the sale of more than 7 dozen is impossible. It is quite probable however that calls for more than 7 dozen will occur; in fact there is a 0.9 probability.

Stocking 7 dozen roses costs $35, yields revenue of $70 when all are sold and a gross profit of $35. This profit will be earned with a probability of 1.0 or certainty. The results of the other inventory strategies are given in Table 6–4.

TABLE 6–4. Expected Profit Calculations of the Campus Florist
Using Probabilities and Demand, Shown in Table 6–3

| *Inventory strategy* $s_i$ | *Stock* $x_i$ *Dozen* | *Calculations* * | *Expected profit* |
|---|---|---|---|
| $s_1$ | 7 | 1.0($35) | = $35 |
| $s_2$ | 8 | 0.1($30) + 0.9($40) | = 39 |
| $s_3$ | 9 | 0.1($25) + 0.2($35) + 0.7($45) | = 41 |
| $s_4$ | 10 | 0.1($20) + 0.2($30) + 0.4($40) + 0.3($50) | = 39 |

* The expected profit for each inventory strategy is determined by the profit to be earned at each sales level multiplied by the probability of that level of sales occurring, and summing. For example, if we stock 8 dozen roses, there is a 0.1 probability that sales will reach 7 dozen and a 0.9 probability that sales will reach 8 dozen (or higher if we have the inventory). The profit on 7 dozen roses when 8 dozen are stocked is (7 × $10) − (8 × $5) = $30. The profit on 8 dozen roses when 8 dozen are stocked is (8 × $10) − (8 × $5) = $40. Multiplying by the respective probabilities, we have 0.1 ($30) + 0.9 ($40) = $39 expected profit from stocking 8 dozen roses.

Following our analysis, we would stock 9 dozen roses daily. Strategy $s_3$ will lead to the best average daily profit: $41.

The expected value of a probability distribution need not, as in this case, correspond to an actual outcome, nor does it necessarily represent the most likely event. It is simply a weighted average of the outcomes.

Note that we are assuming a 1-day lead time in order to get roses for our inventory. The problem would become more complicated if we were able to procure roses on a half-day's notice at a premium, say $6 a dozen.

## DETERMINING THE ECONOMIC ORDER QUANTITY (EOQ)

Determining the right inventory level necessitates the resolution of conflicting goals. A large inventory will assure continuous production and guard against stock-outs. But, associated with it are high carrying costs. A low inventory minimizes carrying cost but increases stock-out costs whether due to lost sales or to lost production. Buying or producing in large quantities reduces the order costs and set-up costs per period but raises the average inventory level and carrying costs. Smaller orders or shorter production runs reduce the carrying costs through reducing the average inventory level but raise the per-period reordering costs or set-up costs and increase the peril of stock-outs through bringing the inventory level more frequently to the action point. The benefits derived from inventory availability must be balanced against the costs of carrying that amount of inventory. This requires an analysis of the economic order quantity (EOQ) in the case of a merchandiser or the economic production run in the case of a manufacturer.

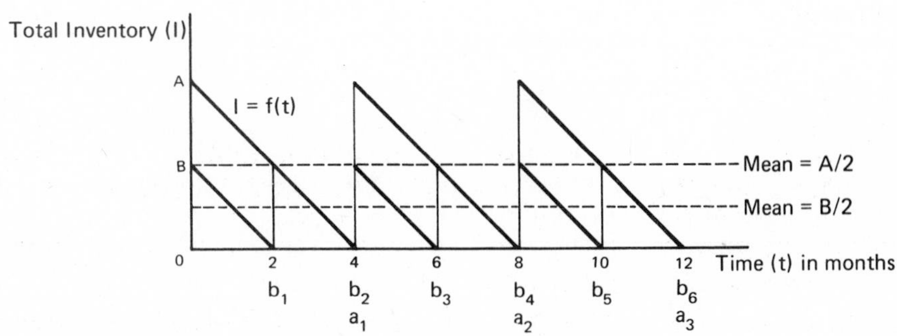


Figure 6–2 Inventory levels over time assuming two different order quantities *A* and *B*.

### The Inventory Cycle

The situation facing a merchandiser is graphed in Figure 6–2. Plotting inventory on the ordinate and time in months on the abscissa, we have inventory, $I$, as a function of time. Starting at time zero we assume a new order is placed and delivery immediately received. We are also assuming usage of the inventory is at a constant rate and continuous. If we order amount $A$ each time, twice $B$, we must place an order every 4 months, three orders per year. If we order amount $B$ each time, we order every 2 months, or six times a year and we incur twice the ordering costs that we would by ordering amount $A$ three times a year. If we order amount $A$ we will on the average carry twice as high an inventory as if we ordered amount $B$ each time. The average inventory for the order quantity $A$ is $(A/2)$; for the order quantity $B$ it is $(B/2)$. There is an optimum point between frequency of ordering and the carrying of inventory where the marginal cost of ordering just equals the marginal carrying cost.

### Economic Order Quantity—Graphic Solution

Assume Red Stick Paint introduces a new product called Kwik Kote. The demand and cost factors are summarized in Table 6–5. Using these data, the financial manager can compute the EOQ as shown in Table 6–6.

TABLE 6–5. Red Stick Paint Company—Kwik Kote Product. Symbols for annual demand, item cost, ordering cost, carrying cost, order size, and economic order quantity.

| | | Formula symbols |
|---|---|---|
| Demand per year | 3000 items | $D$ |
| Cost per unit other than carrying and order cost | \$1.00 | $b$ |
| Carrying costs per item for one year | \$0.20 | $k$ |
| Cost of placing each order | \$12.00 | $s$ |
| Number of items ordered each time | | $x$ |
| Economic order quantity | | $x_q$ |

TABLE 6–6. Red Stick Paint Company
Economic Order Quantity Determination
Annual Demand at 3000 Items

| | | | | | | | | |
|---|---|---|---|---|---|---|---|---|
| $bD$ | Cost of items purchased per year | $3000 | $3000 | $3000 | $3000 | $3000 | $3000 | $3000 |
| $x$ | Order size | 3000 | 1500 | 1000 | 600 | 500 | 300 | 100 |
| $D/x$ | Number of orders per year = demand per year/order size | 1 | 2 | 3 | 5 | 6 | 10 | 30 |
| $x/2$ | Average inventory = order size/2 | 1500 | 750 | 500 | 300 | 250 | 150 | 50 |
| $\frac{kx}{2}$ | Carrying costs = cost of carrying each unit for one year × average inventory | $ 300 | $ 150 | $ 100 | $ 60 | $ 50 | $ 30 | $ 10 |
| $s\left(\frac{D}{x}\right)$ | Ordering costs = cost per order × number of orders | $ 12 | $ 24 | $ 36 | $ 60 | $ 72 | $ 120 | $ 360 |
| $\frac{kx}{2} + s\left(\frac{D}{x}\right)$ | Total carrying and ordering costs | $ 312 | $ 174 | $ 136 | $ 120 | $ 122 | $ 150 | $ 370 |
| $Db + kx/2 + s\,(D/x)$ | Total cost | $3312 | $3174 | $3136 | $3120 | $3122 | $3150 | $3370 |

The graphic solution in Figure 6–3 shows the EOQ to be 600 items.[7] Red Stick should place five orders per year (3,000/600), incurring an annual combined inventory-ordering and carrying cost of $120. This cost would be less than any other ordering strategy. The EOQ occurs at the

[7] Note that the total cost curve is somewhat flat in the neighborhood of the EOQ. We could view the EOQ as a range rather than a point and order or produce at the most convenient level within this range with very little extra cost. See Arthur Snyder, "Principles of Inventory Management," *Financial Executive*, 32 (April 1964), pp. 15–16.

point where the carrying and ordering costs curves have equal slope but with opposite sign.

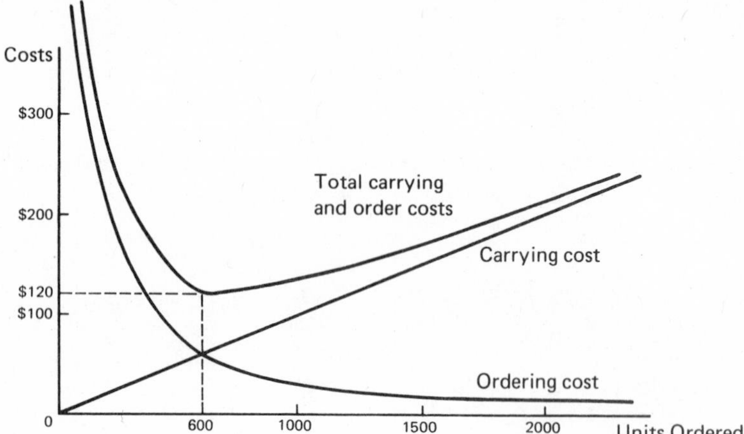


Figure 6–3 Red Stick Paint Company. Graphic determination of economic order quantity based on Table 6–6.

### Economic Order Quantity—Mathematical Solution

Total ordering and carrying costs of a given amount of annual demand are a function of two variables—the size of the orders and the frequency of the orders—all the other matters are constants. If we take the order quantity ($x$) as the independent variable and the costs incurred from ordering and carrying inventory as the dependent variables, the solution requires knowing the separate relationships between the two dependent variables and the independent so that we can combine the relationships of ordering and carrying.

At the quantity point where a small change in the independent variable results in an equal but opposite sign change in the dependent variables, the total of the ordering and carrying costs curve has zero slope. A line drawn tangent to this point on the total curve is horizontal. If that curve is convex to the origin the zero slope point is a minimum; if it is concave, it is a maximum. In our case the total cost curve is convex and hence the zero slope point is a minimum.

We now give the detail of the mathematical determination of the EOQ using the notation of Table 6–5. The total dollar cost per order (other than carrying and ordering) is $bx$ where $x$ is the number of items ordered at one time and $b$ the unit purchase price. Since $s$ is the cost per order, the total purchasing and ordering costs for a year are $s + bx$ times the number of orders placed per year ($D/x$)—the annual demand ($D$) divided by $x$, the number of items in an order. Thus, total inventory purchasing (but excluding carrying) and ordering costs per year is

$$(s + bx)\,\frac{D}{x}.$$

Next we determine the carrying costs. If $k$ equals the carrying cost per item and $x$ the number of units per order, the average inventory carried during the year is $x/2$ (assuming constant usage) and the inventory carrying costs are

$$\frac{kx}{2}$$

The total costs are then the cost of the items, the ordering costs, and the carrying costs. These costs are summarized as follows:

$$\underline{\text{Total costs}} = \underline{\text{Carrying costs}} + \underline{\left(\text{Order costs} + \text{Cost of inventory item} \times \text{items ordered each time}\right)} \times \underline{\text{Number of orders placed annually}}$$

$$TC = \frac{kx}{2} + \left( s + bx \right) \times \frac{D}{x}$$

$$= \text{Carrying costs} + \text{Total Order costs} + \text{Cost of items purchased}$$

$$= \frac{kx}{2} + \frac{sD}{x} + bD \qquad \text{[B2]}$$

We assume the annual quantity $D$ to be known and the cost figures $s$, $b$, and $k$ ascertainable from the records. We seek the economic order quantity $x_q$, which is the least total cost—the point of zero slope on the total cost curve. To determine this point we differentiate $TC$ with respect to $x$ and set the first derivative equal to zero.

$$\frac{d(TC)}{dx} = \frac{d}{dx}\left(\frac{kx}{2} + \frac{sD}{x} + bD\right)$$

Then

$$= \frac{k}{2} - \frac{sD}{x^2} = 0$$

$$\frac{k}{2} = \frac{sD}{x^2}$$

$$x^2 = \frac{2sD}{k}$$

and

$$x_q = \sqrt{\frac{2sD}{k}}$$

This is the economic order quantity formula [8] for the particular assump-

[8] Sometimes $k$, the cost per item for carrying for the period, is cast in the form $P \times I$, where $P$ equals the price of the inventory item and $I$ the percentage cost of carrying each dollar of inventory for the period. In this example $P = \$1$ and $I = 20$ percent.

tions we made about rate of inventory usage and other factors. Substituting in the formula we arrive at the same answer as in Table 6–6.

$$x_q = \sqrt{\frac{2 \cdot \$12 \cdot 3{,}000\text{-unit annual demand}}{\$0.20 \text{ per unit carrying costs}}}$$

$$x_q = \sqrt{\frac{\$72{,}000}{\$0.20}}$$

$$x_q = 600 \text{ units}$$

thus 600 units is the value of $x$ at which the total cost curve has zero slope.[9]

### Sensitivity Analysis

We are interested in knowing how changes in annual demand, order costs, and inventory-carrying costs affect the economic order quantity. As we have seen, the *price* of the item ($b$) does not affect the result since that price is a constant. The effect of each of the other changes we call sensitivity. What change in what variable produces what change in the result is the problem.

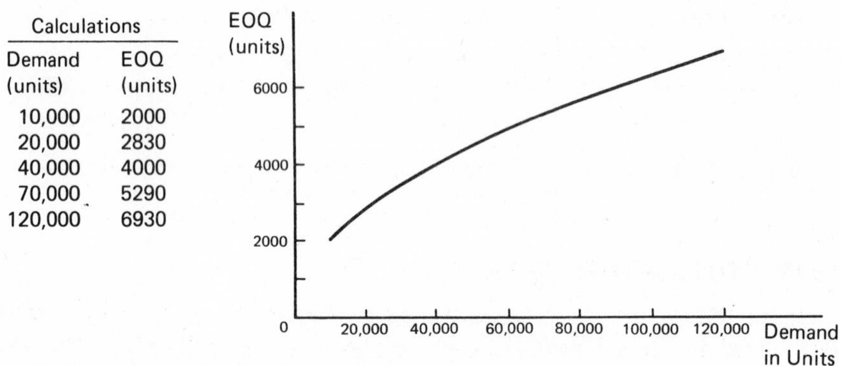


Figure 6–4 Situation 1: demand, $D$; independent variable, $S = \$20$; $K = 10$ cents.

We calculate the economic order quantity as a dependent variable for three separate situations: demand going from 10,000 to 120,000 units for the period, order costs from \$5 to \$80 per order, and inventory-

---

[9] Now we must take the second derivative with respect to x to know whether we have a maximum or a minimum at 600 units

$$\frac{d^2(TC)}{dx^2} = \frac{2sD}{x^3}$$

Since $s$, $D$, and $x$ are all necessarily positive,

$$sD/x^3$$

must be positive. Since the second derivative is positive 600 units is a minimum.

carrying costs from 5 cents to 50 cents per unit. In each situation the other variables are held constant. The calculations and the accompanying graphs are presented in Figures 6–4 through 6–6.

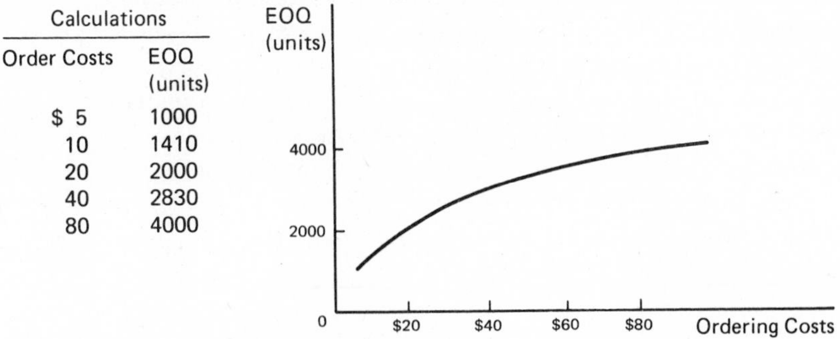

Calculations

| Order Costs | EOQ (units) |
|---|---|
| $ 5 | 1000 |
| 10 | 1410 |
| 20 | 2000 |
| 40 | 2830 |
| 80 | 4000 |



Figure 6–5 Situation 2: order costs, $S$; independent variable, $D = 10{,}000$ units; $k = 10$ cents.

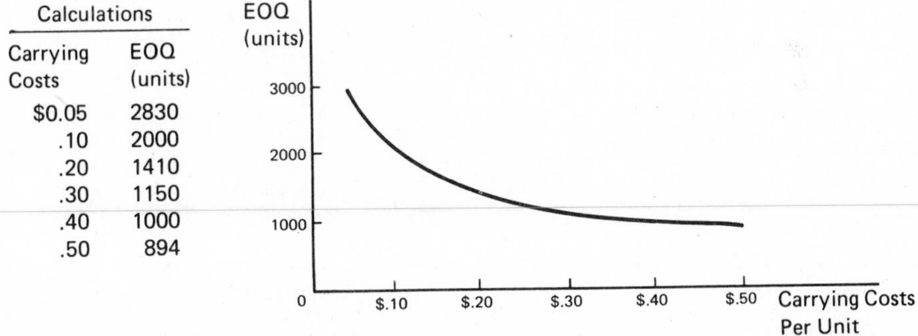

Calculations

| Carrying Costs | EOQ (units) |
|---|---|
| $0.05 | 2830 |
| .10 | 2000 |
| .20 | 1410 |
| .30 | 1150 |
| .40 | 1000 |
| .50 | 894 |



Figure 6–6 Situation 3: carrying costs, $k$; independent variable, $D = 10{,}000$ units; $S = \$20$.

## SAFETY STOCK:—WHY CARRY?

Up to this point we have assumed that when inventory is exhausted, a new order is placed and delivery is received immediately. In practice a lead time must be established to cover the span between the time an order is placed or production initiated and the time of scheduled arrival of the inventory. Hence, a safety cushion of inventory, or *safety stock*, is needed to absorb the demand between the time the old inventory actually runs out and the new inventory is available. Further delay in the actual receipt of the inventory may result because of strikes, floods, transportation delays, and so on. Or we may have unusually high demand between the action point and the actual delivery of the new inventory. Figure 6–7 depicts an inventory cycle illustrating unusual demand and delayed delivery for a merchandiser and a manufacturer. If all went smoothly during the interval following the action point indicated on the dashed line in Figure 6–7, there would be no need for safety stocks. Just as the last items from the previous shipment are being shipped out the front door the new shipment would arrive at the back door. However, in practice after the action point is reached either heavy demand builds up or delivery of incoming inventory is delayed. Either event may cause the firm to run out of inventory before the new shipment arrives unless a safety stock is present. The challenge is to estimate the *optimum safety stock level*—the point where the advantages obtained from carrying additional safety stocks just balances the cost of carrying this stock. Figure 6–7 shows that the range of choice falls between carrying no safety stock at level *a*, trusting all will run smoothly, and carrying level *ab* safety stock to be able to meet a customer's demand or have sufficient parts to continue production. Somewhere within this range lies the most economic level of safety stock. To determine this level requires that we balance the stock-out costs and their probability of occurring against the costs of carrying the *additional* inventory. The cross-hatched areas represent the invasion of safety stock and indicate sales lost were there no safety stock.

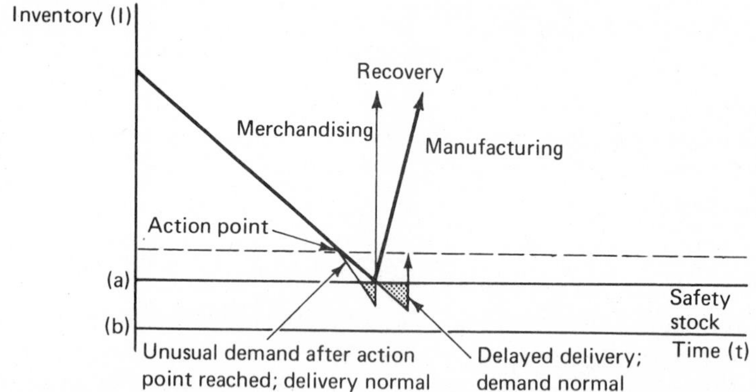


Figure 6–7 Safety stock cushioning, unusual demand, and delayed situations for a single cycle. Recovery refers to the buildup of inventory. For a merchandising firm, whether a wholesaler or retailer, the buildup to the predetermined level is immediate and is equivalent to the size of the order. For a manufacturer the inventory level buildup is slowed by the making of sales during the production run.

### Determining the Appropriate Safety-Stock Level—An Example

Assume that Strato-dyne manufactures electronic scanners. The firm requires 24,000 relay units per year, an average of 100 units per day. Assume the EOQ is 4000 units, thus requiring the placing of 6 orders per year. The normal lead time from the time the order is placed to delivery is 5 days. Remember the EOQ is dependent upon 3 variables, namely, the cost of placing each order, demand per year, and carrying cost per item per year.

In the past the firm carried a sufficiently large safety stock to prevent any stock-outs. Now the firm wishes to establish an optimum balance between the costs of carrying a safety stock and the cost of stock-outs. This problem is analogous to the EOQ problem.

Table 6–7 presents the results of studying the inventory record. We assume that the past use distribution will continue in the future. The table indicates, for example, that if the company places an order when the inventory level reaches 500 units and no safety stock is carried, the firm will be out of stock 26 percent of the time. These shortages could be reduced by carrying some safety stock.

TABLE 6–7. Strato-dyne Company
Probability of Stock-Outs when an Order is Placed at the Point That the Inventory Level Drops to 500 Units

| *Subsequent demand level* | *Probability of occurring* | *Carrying safety stocks* | *Percentage of the time having stock outs* |
|---|---|---|---|
| 500 units | 0.74 | 0 | 26 |
| 600 | 0.15 | 100 | 11 * |
| 700 | 0.07 | 200 | 4 |
| 800 | 0.03 | 300 | 1 |
| 900 | 0.01 | 400 | 0 |
| | 1.00 | | |

* For example, if there is a 0.89, (0.74 + 0.15), probability of demand reaching 600 units and we carry safety stocks of 100, we will be out of stock 11 percent (100% − 89%) of the time.

Stock-outs could be avoided entirely by carrying a safety stock of 400 units.

Assume out-of-stock costs are $4 per unit because we can obtain rapid partial delivery at $4 per unit. The cost of carrying one unit in inventory for the year is $2 whether or not it is sold during the year. This is a simplifying assumption. Table 6–8 develops the costs of being out of stock for the five safety stock courses of action, carrying 0, 100, 200, 300, or 400 units.

The stock-out costs in Table 6–8 are calculated as follows, using the 100-unit safety-stock level to illustrate. Carrying 100 units in safety stock, if demand reaches 600 items or less after the action point is touched, we have sufficient inventory to continue production. If the requirement reaches 700 units, we will be 100 units short, which must be procured at a premium cost of $4 per unit, or $400. This event occurs with a probability of 0.07. Since this outage could occur six times per year, we have a probable annual cost of $168, that is, ($400 × 0.07 × 6). The pattern for possible production requirements of 800 and 900 units is shortages of 200 and 300 units, respectively, which must be obtained at a premium of $4 per unit. Since these events can occur with a probability of 0.03 and 0.01, respectively, six times a year, we have probable costs of $144 and $72. Adding the total probable costs that can be incurred for a year if a safety stock of 100 units were carried, we get a total expected outlay of $384.

TABLE 6–8. Strato-dyne Company
Stock Cost Calculations (assuming regular [not safety-stock] inventory of 500 units)

| *Safety stock* | *Possible demand* | *Number of items short* | *Cost per unit of being out of stock* | *Probability of occurring* | *Number of times this can occur during the year* * | *Total annual stock-out costs* | |
|---|---|---|---|---|---|---|---|
| 0 | 500 units | 0 units | | 0.74 | | $ 0 | |
| | 600 | 100 | | 0.15 | | 360 | |
| | 700 | 200 | $4 | 0.07 | 6 | 336 | |
| | 800 | 300 | | 0.03 | | 216 | |
| | 900 | 400 | | 0.01 | | 96 | $1008 |
| 100 | 500 | 0 | | 0.74 | | $ 0 | |
| | 600 | 0 | | 0.15 | | 0 | |
| | 700 | 100 | $4 | 0.07 | 6 | 168 | |
| | 800 | 200 | | 0.03 | | 144 | |
| | 900 | 300 | | 0.01 | | 72 | $ 384 |
| 200 | 500 | 0 | | 0.74 | | $ 0 | |
| | 600 | 0 | | 0.15 | | 0 | |
| | 700 | 0 | $4 | 0.07 | 6 | 0 | |
| | 800 | 100 | | 0.03 | | 72 | |
| | 900 | 200 | | 0.01 | | 48 | $ 120 |
| 300 | 500 | 0 | | 0.74 | | $ 0 | |
| | 600 | 0 | | 0.15 | | 0 | |
| | 700 | 0 | $4 | 0.07 | 6 | 0 | |
| | 800 | 0 | | 0.03 | | 0 | |
| | 900 | 100 | | 0.01 | | 24 | $ 24 |
| 400 | 500 | 0 | | 0.74 | | $ 0 | |
| | 600 | 0 | | 0.15 | | 0 | |
| | 700 | 0 | $4 | 0.07 | 6 | 0 | |
| | 800 | 0 | | 0.03 | | 0 | |
| | 900 | 0 | | 0.01 | | 0 | 0 |

* Since 24,000 units are required in production annually and the economic order quantity is 4000 units, 6 orders annually must be placed.

### Total Safety-Stock Costs

Given the costs of being out of inventory (Table 6–8) and the annual cost of $2 per unit for carrying excess inventory, the total costs of various safety-stock policies are calculated in Table 6–9.

TABLE 6–9. Strato-dyne Company
Calculations of Cost of Alternative Safety Stock Levels

| *Strategies* | *Safety stocks* | *Cost of carrying safety stocks* | *Total probable stock-out costs* * | *Total costs per year of alternative inventory safety stock policies* |
|---|---|---|---|---|
| $s_0$ | 0 | $ 0 | $1,008 | $1,008 |
| $s_1$ | 100 | 200 | 384 | 584 |
| $s_2$ | 200 | 400 | 120 | 520 |
| $s_3$ | 300 | 600 | 24 | 624 |
| $s_4$ | 400 | 800 | 0 | 800 |

* Based on Table 6–8.

Strato-dyne should carry 200 units as safety stock,[11] resulting in additional carrying costs of $400 and total probable stock-out costs of $120 for a total cost of $520. Carrying a safety stock of 100 units would involve carrying costs of only $200, but the probable stock-out costs are $384 for a total cost of $584. Carrying a safety stock of 300 units would involve probable stock-out costs of only $24. But the carrying costs would rise to $600, resulting in total costs of $624. From the probabilities indicated in Table 6–7, one might intuitively arrive at the conclusion to carry about 200 units as safety stock by the following reasoning. Carrying no safety stock would result in stock-outs 26 percent of the time. By carrying an initial 100 units, stock-outs would be reduced 15 percent. However, another 100 units would reduce stock-outs by only 7 percent. We are approaching the margin. Deciding intuitively, the financial manager would probably recommend carrying 200 or 300 units of safety stock.

## SUMMARY

Holding inventory is necessary to uncouple purchasing, production, and selling, but it is also costly. The pressures to increase inventories are substantial and efforts must be made to keep inventories low. The EOQ occurs at the point where the slopes of the carrying and ordering cost curves are equal but of opposite sign. The total cost curve will have zero slope at this point. Under conditions of uncertainty we can make use of probabilities to establish the level of inventory that will yield the maximum profit.

[11] The answer may be obtained mathematically. See Erwin E. Nemmers *Managerial Economics*, rev. ed. (New York: John Wiley and Sons, 1964), problem 30 at the end of the book. (The pages at the end of the book are not numbered.)

Some inventory must be carried to cushion irregularities in shipments or absorb increased demand between the time the inventory is scheduled to run out and the time the goods are actually received. This is known as safety stock. The economic safety-stock level is found by determining the cost of carrying various safety-stock levels and comparing them with the costs resulting from being out of stock, taking into account probabilities of demand reaching various levels. The economic safety stock level is the level at which the expected cost is the lowest.

### Study Questions

1. Firms in the postwar period, preferring to hold receivables rather than inventory, have extended increasingly liberal trade terms. Explain the rationale for such action. What are the limits to such a policy?
2. Why does inventory represent such a high percentage of working capital for retailers and such a low percentage for service firms?
3. How do speed of communications and transportation affect the inventory level a firm must carry? Is this in the national interest? In what way?
4. How is proper inventory management linked (a) to the short-run liquidity of the firm? (b) to the long-run profitability of the firm?
5. How might a firm requiring scrap copper differ in its policy concerning its raw materials inventory from a firm requiring bicycle tires? Which firm might be tempted to speculate on its inventory? Why? Would you agree that the wider the fluctuation in the price of the inventory, the smaller the stock of inventory that should be maintained and the smaller each purchase order? Explain.
6. How can a knowledge of probability theory assist us in formulating proper inventory policies? Can we through the use of probability concepts eliminate the element of uncertainty from our inventory policy? Explain.
7. With demand constant, why is the average inventory carried always one half that ordered for the period? Would this also be true if the firm faced a seasonal demand?
8. What data are necessary for determining the EOQ? Why is the EOQ always at the point where the slopes of carrying costs and order costs are equal but of opposite sign? Is the same true for the carrying costs and set-up costs for a manufacturer seeking to determine the economic production run? Why?
9. What is the purpose of safety stock? Will the size of the safety stock be influenced by the firm's attitude toward risk? Why should this be so?
10. What tests can a firm apply to determine if its inventory position is in line with that of its competitors? What is to be gained and what are the dangers of applying such tests? Would they on balance be worthwhile?
11. How can probability theory help us to determine the proper level of safety stock? What advantages and dangers do you see in this approach? In what industries might it be particularly applicable?
12. The federal government since World War II has sought to even out the business cycle. As these efforts bear fruit, what will be the effect on the level of inventories carried by firms? When one firm slows its inventory buying, the production of suppliers may halt, causing wide business fluctuations. Will a policy among business firms of carrying smaller inventories assist in

evening out the business cycle? Is it possible that the actions of the federal government and the firms will reinforce each other?

13. As a firm grows in size will it tend to carry a larger or a smaller proportionate amount of inventory? Why? Would the variety of inventory items increase or decrease? Does the number of different inventory items a firm must carry affect the total size of the inventory? How?

## *Problems*

1. The Rinki-Dink Novelty Company carries a wide assortment of items for its swinging customers. One item, the matchless match, is particularly popular. Wishing to keep its inventory under control, management selects this item to initiate its new program of ordering only the economic quantity each time. You are given the following information. Help them solve their problem.

| | |
|---|---|
| Annual demand | 160,000 units |
| Price per unit | $4 |
| Carrying cost | 40 cents per unit, or 10 percent per dollar of inventory value |
| Cost per order | $5 per order |

a. Fill in the blanks. Identify the economic order quantity.

| | | | | | | |
|---|---|---|---|---|---|---|
| Size of order | | | | | | |
| Number of orders | 1 | 10 | 20 | 40 | 80 | 100 |
| Average inventory | | | | | | |
| Carrying cost | | | | | | |
| Order cost | | | | | | |
| Total cost | | | | | | |

b. Determine the economic order quantity by the use of the formula on page 139.

2. Rinki-Dink, looking to the future when the demand for matchless matches will mushroom, decides to establish its own production facilities and produce at the economic production run. The following information is given. You are asked to establish the economic production quantity for the next year. Use the formula on page 151.,

| | |
|---|---|
| Annual demand | 160,000 units |
| Production cost per unit | $1 |
| Factory set-up cost per time | $10 |
| Production rate per day | 1,000 |
| Sales per day | 500 |
| Carrying cost per dollar of inventory per year | 40 cents |

a. Determine the economic production run.

b. Why are the economic order quantity and the economic production run for Rinki-Dink different? Which is higher and why?

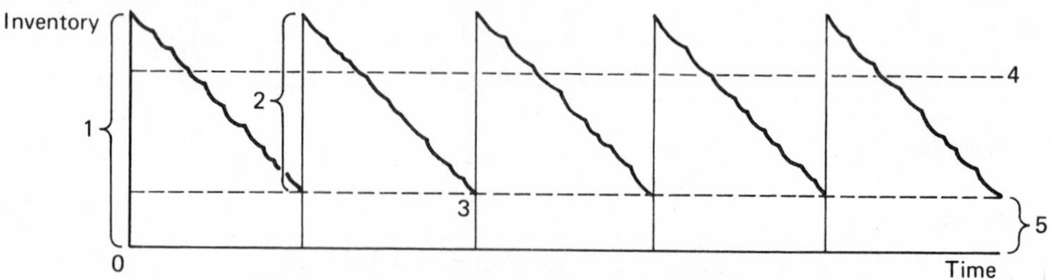


Figure 6–8 Successive inventory cycles.

**3.** Using Figure 6–8, match the numbered points with the following items: safety stocks carried; reorder point; quantity ordered; maximum inventory carried; quantity produced; ignoring safety stock: approximate average inventory carried; delivery time.

**4.** The Orange Blossom Bridal Shop stocks rolls of flowered ribbon. The annual demand reaches 8000 for these rolls. Each roll costs $10 and the order cost is $40 per order. Carrying costs are 10 percent, or $1 per roll. The Bridal Shop is currently ordering on an optimum basis.

Wholesalers, Slick & Company, in a sly effort to shift some of its inventory to the Bridal Shop, points to the high ordering cost of $40 and suggests that orders be placed only once a year. As an inducement Slick offers the management a 4 percent discount if the annual ordering policy is adopted.

a. Evaluate this offer and make a recommendation to accept or reject it. Show the calculations upon which you base your recommendation. Ignore interest on any borrowing that may be necessary to accept the offer.

b. If you reject the offer, what reasonable counteroffer might you make?

**5.** During the football season the Campus Florist stocks special victory mums. These are extra large mums dyed the school colors with a small "V" in the center. The flowers sell for $1 each and cost 40 cents. They are sold on the Saturday of the game, and on Sunday, win or lose, become worthless. The profitability from the sale has been erratic and you are called in for advice. Records of the Saturday sales over the past years reveal the following picture:

| Demand (units) | 200 | 300 | 400 | 500 | 600 |
|---|---|---|---|---|---|
| Probability | 0.20 | 0.20 | 0.30 | 0.20 | 0.10 |

a. You are asked to recommend the number of mums to stock to maximize the expected profit. Loss of good will is not a factor, since the enthusiastic fan's memory is always clouded by the results of the game. As a first step complete the following pay off matrix:

| Strategy \ Possible demand | 200 | 300 | 400 | 500 | 600 |
|---|---|---|---|---|---|
| $s_2$–200 | | | | | |
| $s_3$–300 | | | | | |
| $s_4$–400 | | | | | |
| $s_5$–500 | | | | | |
| $s_6$–600 | | | | | |

The second step is to apply the probabilities to the expected payoffs. Identify the economic order quantity.

| | *Possible demand Probabilities* | *200 (0.20)* | *300 (0.20)* | *400 (0.30)* | *500 (0.20)* | *600 (0.10)* | *Expected profit* |
|---|---|---|---|---|---|---|---|
| *Strategy* | | | | | | | |
| $s_2$—200 | | | | | | | |
| $s_3$—300 | | | | | | | |
| $s_4$—400 | | | | | | | |
| $s_5$—500 | | | | | | | |
| $s_6$—600 | | | | | | | |

[A9901]

b. The Campus Florist, always alert to ways of improving profits, offers a fellow-florist 50 cents a flower, 10 cents above wholesale cost, if he will provide delivery on demand. Again calculate the optimum inventory level to carry. Complete a new pay-off matrix and apply the probabilities to the expected pay offs. Identify the economic order quantity.

**6.** The economic order quantity formula, a method for controlling investment in inventory, is sometimes referred to as an inventory model. In order to build such a model we must first specify all inventory-associated costs that rise and that decline with higher levels of inventory. All such costs can be classified into three categories:

a. Costs associated with carrying inventory.

b. Costs associated with ordering and receiving inventory.

c. Costs associated with running short of inventory.

Give as many inventory-associated costs that fall into each of the above three categories as you can.

**7.** The management of cash can be viewed as an inventory problem involving the determination of the optimum cash balance. Note in our cash budgeting discussion we did not consider how to find an optimum cash balance. The similarity between the cash management problem and the inventory problem can be seen by correctly matching the statement in columns I and II.

| I. Inventory problem | II. Cash management problem |
|---|---|
| a. Carrying cost. | i. Brokerage costs of buying and selling securities. |
| b. Order cost. | ii. Cash revenue, borrowing, sale of securities. |
| c. Inflows of inventory (the orders). | iii. Cash purchases and expenses. |
| d. Outflows of inventory. | iv. Opportunity cost of having funds tied up in low or non-earning assets. |
| e. Safety stocks. | v. Minimum cash balance. |

### Selected References

Crankshaw, C. D., and R. J. Corlett, "Stock Inventory Control with Data Bases and Analysis," *Management Accounting,* (May 1970) pp. 26–28.

Eilon, S., and J. Elmaleh, "Adaptive Limits in Inventory Control," *Management Science,* 16 (April 1970), pp. B533–B548.

Gross, D., and A. Soriano, "The Effect of Reducing Leadtime on Inventory Levels —Simulation Analysis," *Management Science,* 16 (October 1969), pp. B61–B76.

Hofer, C. F., "Analysis of Fixed Costs in Inventory," *Management Accounting,* (September 1970), pp. 15–17.

Magee, J. F., "Guides to Inventory Policy: Functions and Lot Size," *Harvard Business Review,* 34 (January-February 1956), pp. 49–60.

———, "Guides to Inventory Policy: Problems of Uncertainty," *Harvard Business Review,* 34 (March-April 1956), pp. 103–116.

———, "Guides to Inventory Policy: Anticipating Future Needs," *Harvard Business Review,* 34 (May-June 1956), pp. 57–70.

Mao, J. C. T., *Quantitative Analysis of Financial Decisions.* New York: Macmillan Co., 1969, pp. 121–127.

Schussel, G., and S. Price, "A Case History in Optimum Inventory Scheduling," *Operations Research,* 18 (January-February 1970), pp. 1–23.

Shapiro, A., "Optimal Inventory and Credit-Granting Strategies under Inflation and Devaluation," *Journal of Financial and Quantitative Analysis,* 7 (January 1973), pp. 37–46.

Thurston, P. H., "Requirements Planning for Inventory Control," *Harvard Business Review,* 50 (March-April 1972), pp. 67–71.

### Appendix F

ECONOMIC PRODUCTION RUN WHERE REPLENISHMENT OCCURS OVER TIME

A manufacturer seeks to determine the economic production run: the point at which the increased savings to be obtained from a longer production run just balance the additional inventory carrying costs. Although inventory replenishment is a time-consuming process for a manufacturer, inventory is replaced instantly for a merchandiser upon arrival of the new shipment. The manufacturer's production-inventory level cycle traces the pattern shown in Figure 6–9.

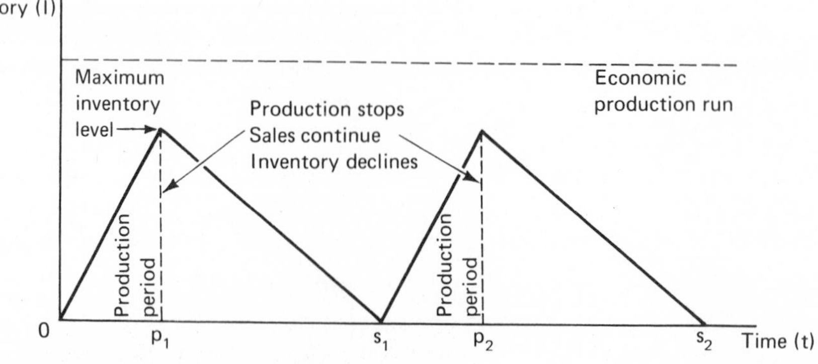


Figure 6–9 Inventory level: continuous sales and periodic production runs.

The EOQ model developed earlier can be adapted to solve the economic production run problem. The modification required is to take into account the sales being made while the inventory stock is being replenished through the time-consuming production process. We shall first illustrate the application of the model and then we shall derive it.

Sweet Green Grass Company produces a clamp costing \$5. The other figures necessary to determine the economic production run are given in Table 6–10.

TABLE 6–10. Sweet Green Grass Company
Vise-Grip Clamp Data

| *Item* | *Symbol* | *Amount* |
|---|---|---|
| Annual demand | $D$ | 5000 units |
| Production cost per unit | $c$ | \$5 |
| Factory set-up cost per set up | $s$ | \$80 |
| Production rate per day | $r$ | 100 units |
| Sales per day | $d$ | 20 units |
| Carrying costs per dollar of inventory per year | $k$ | \$0.20 |

Letting $x$ denote the economic size of the production run, we then have

$$x = \sqrt{\frac{2sD}{ck[1 - (d/r)]}}$$

$$= \sqrt{\frac{2 \times 5{,}000 \text{ units} \times \$80}{\$5 \times \$0.20 \times [1 - (20/100)]}}$$

$$= 1{,}000 \text{ units}$$

To derive this model note that at the EOQ point (Table 6–6 and Figure 6–3) the marginal reorder costs equal the marginal inventory carrying costs. Similarly, total production set-up and storage costs, are least when *marginal* set-up costs equal *marginal* carrying costs. Now, since $x$ equals the number of units in the economic production run and $r$ is the production rate per day in units, then $x/r$ equals the required number of days to produce the optimum number of units in one production run. With $d$ equaling the number of units sold per day, $xd/r$ equals the number of units sold during the production period. Then if from $x$ the optimum number of units produced in a production run we subtract the number of units sold during the production run, we have the maximum inventory level:

$$x - \frac{xd}{r}$$

If we divide by 2 (because we assume a uniform rate of sales) and factor, we will have the simplified expression for the average inventory level:

$$\frac{x}{2}\left(1 - \frac{d}{r}\right)$$

To find the total annual carrying cost in dollars for average inventory carried we multiply the average number of units of inventory by $k$, the carrying cost per dollar of inventory per year and then by the dollar cost of producing each unit of inventory, $c$:

$$ck\left(\frac{x}{2}\right)\left(1 - \frac{d}{r}\right)$$

As $D$ equals the total annual demand and $x$ the number of units in the optimum run, $D/x$ equals the number of times the production run must be set up. If $s$ equals the cost of each set-up, then $(D/x)s$ equals the total set-up costs for the year. Then, since at the optimum point the carrying costs equal the set-up costs, we have

$$\frac{Ds}{x} = ck\left(\frac{x}{2}\right)\left(1 - \frac{d}{r}\right)$$

$$x^2ck\left(1 - \frac{d}{r}\right) = 2sD$$

$$x^2 = \frac{2sD}{ck[1 - (d/r)]}$$

$$x = \sqrt{\frac{2sD}{ck[1 - (d/r)]}}$$

# 7
# The Receivables Management System

In selling goods and services the firm frequently extends *trade credit* to its customers because it is profitable to do so. Few buyers are willing to do business for cash on delivery (COD). Because a vendor is usually well acquainted with the business of his customers, he extends generous credit as compared to suppliers of other types of funds.

The level of receivables at any moment in time is determined by the volume of credit sales, terms of credit sales, standards for extension of credit, and collection pressure exerted. In managing the flow of receivables we seek to optimize the firm's investment in receivables. This requires effective trade credit management. The principle of trade credit is to stimulate sales and contribute to the overall profitability of the firm, not to eliminate all credit losses. If the latter were the best policy then the firm would extend no credit. Rather, the objective is to balance the cost of extending credit and bad-debt losses against the additional profit generated from extending credit to obtain the highest overall profit. Such a credit policy will contribute most to maximizing the value of the firm.

## A FIRM'S INVESTMENT IN RECEIVABLES

### Selling on Account

The composition of the receivables at a given time can be likened to a standing wave in a brook. A standing wave may be caused by water rushing past a partially submerged rock. The wave itself remains immobile but the water underneath changes. Similarly, the level of receivables may remain unchanged but individual accounts may change. With the passage of time and the changing of the underlying composition of the receivables, their overall quality and, hence, their collectibility changes. Just as the size of the wave changes with variations in the inflow of water into the brook, the level of receivables changes with sales.

Receivables arise when merchandise is sold and payment deferred. The seller, in effect, offers the purchaser a loan for a limited time such as 30 days. The seller may offer to discount the price 1 percent or more if payment is made within a shorter period.

The majority of credit sales are on open-book account, that is, the customer orders and the seller ships and invoices the buyer for the amount due but does not require a signed statement from the customer acknowledging his debt other than the buyer's original purchase order.

A signed note from the customer (the amount goes into notes receivables, not accounts receivable) gives rise to few rights additional to the seller's rights on an open-book account. If the bill is not paid, the note may constitute persuasive legal evidence if there is a dispute. However, in the absence of a note, the seller has the customer's purchase order, his own sales invoice, and in some cases shipping documents to support his claim.

Our remarks regarding the management of receivables are primarily directed toward the firm extending credit to other firms. However, many retail sales are made on credit, as evidenced by the familiar revolving 30-day charge and the installment account. Smaller retail items are generally sold on open-book account, but major durable goods such as automobiles are generally sold on the basis of an installment sales contract.

The extension of trade credit by a supplier to a purchaser is a well-established business practice. In the United States $580 billion of notes and accounts receivable were outstanding in 1969 for all corporate industrial groups.[1] These receivables represent about 37 percent of sales for the year.

For the selling firm, trade credit means that the flow of funds from cash back to cash does not cycle as rapidly as if credit were not offered. Inventory is converted into receivables instead of cash when a credit sale takes place. Clearly the total assets of the firm are larger by the amount of the receivables carried than if the firm sold on cash terms and the receivables did not have to be financed.

---

[1] U. S. Treasury Department, Internal Revenue Service, *Statistics of Income, 1969 Corporation Income Tax Returns* (Washington, D. C.: Government Printing Office, 1973), p. 17.

As a first approximation, the cost of these funds might be viewed as the cost of borrowing from a bank at a rate such as 6 percent. However, financing is a continuous process, and it is not possible to say which source of funds has financed which group of assets. The firm has some of its wealth tied up in receivables, and the cost of holding those receivables is the opportunity cost of earnings that might be generated if those funds were invested in other assets such as plant and equipment.

Four other costs are incurred when extending trade credit: the expense of investigating credit worthiness of the customer, the expenses of collecting the funds owed, losses incurred when some customers fail to pay, and any cash discount offered. Though particular nonpaying customers cannot be identified with certainty before credit is extended—if they could be the firm would require them to pay cash on delivery—the percentage that the aggregate of bad debts bears to aggregate credit sales can be predicted with fair accuracy.

### Benefits of Extending Trade Credit

Considering these costs you may wonder why firms extend credit so liberally. The reason is that credit extension boosts sales volume that is expected to add to total earnings. Though the return per unit of sales may decline due to the added costs of credit extension, total earnings may rise.[2] The shift from a cash on delivery (COD) basis to the extension of 30-day terms will result in increased sales, but will the increased sales volume be sufficient to offset the reduced profit per unit? Yes, if credit is carefully managed and the firm is not yet at economic capacity. But the extension of a further 30-day credit period might not produce a significant increase in sales and the added cost of the added credit might actually cause total earnings to decline.

### Trade Credit as a Positive Policy—An Example

Micro-Omega can sell for cash or extend credit for 30 or 60 days. Goods are currently being sold COD with Micro-Omega selling 100 electronic components a month at $10 each. The present cost is $8 per unit and profit per month is $200. The manager seeks to stimulate sales by trade terms of 30 days. Sales jump to 160 units generating revenue of $1600.

Production costs remain at $8 per unit (assuming the spreading of fixed costs is offset by other costs), and gross profit climbs to $320. However, this figure is not clear profit. The adoption of credit terms requires the firm to establish a new procedure to screen the credit worthiness of applicants and a collection procedure to watch the accounts and stimulate laggards into paying. In carrying out these activities, Micro-Omega incurs an additional cost of 50 cents per unit. Further, some of

---

[2] Many financial executives report that liberalizing credit terms boosts profits. See M. T. Welshans, "Using Credit for Profit Making," *Harvard Business Review*, 45 (January-February 1967), pp. 141–156. Unless the firm is operating at capacity, profits will not be maximized through a stringent credit policy. See R. M. Kaplan, "Credit Risks and Opportunities," *Harvard Business Review*, 45 (March-April 1967), pp. 83–88.

the accounts, despite the best efforts at collection, remain uncollectible. These amount to ¼ of 1 percent of sales. Despite the added costs, net earnings rise from $200 to $236, as shown in Table 7–1.

The manager, flushed with success at what 30 days of credit does, decides to go all the way and adopts credit terms of 60 days. If a little credit is a good thing, a lot of credit is better. True to expectations, sales again jump sharply. This time, however, the percentage increase in sales is not as great, and costs rise more than proportionately. Net earnings decline. The manager has overshot the mark. The tasks of investigating credit applicants and collecting become substantially more costly, since many marginal firms can now meet the more liberal trade terms and become heavily indebted before the collection process swings into action. Because of the higher proportion of marginal firms, the uncollectible receivables rise. Sales climb to 200 units, yielding a gross revenue of $2000, as appears in Table 7–1. Let us assume production costs remain at $8 per unit. But the collection expense rises from 50 cents to 80 cents per unit, whereas the bad-debt expense jumps from ¼ of 1 percent of sales to 1 percent. The resulting profit falls to $220, as shown in Table 7–1.

TABLE 7–1. Micro-Omega Company
Influence of Trade Terms on Sales and Profits

| | *Trade term options* | | |
|---|---|---|---|
| | *C.O.D.* | *30 days* | *60 days* |
| Sales (units) | 100 | 160 | 200 |
| Sales (dollars) | $1,000 | $1,600 | $2,000 |
| Cost of sales | $ 800 | $1,280 | $1,600 |
| Collection expense | — | 80 | 160 |
| Bad-debt expense | — | 4 | 20 |
| Profit | $ 200 | $ 236 | $ 220 |

## TRADE CREDIT TRENDS AND PRACTICES

Trade credit can be used in various situations to stimulate sales and expand profits. Some firms when introducing a new product grant especially liberal terms. The availability of excess capacity influences the extension of trade credit by some firms to high-risk customers. For other firms it is a high profit margin on the item sold that affects the credit extended to these customers. But the greatest pressure to liberalize credit comes from trade terms offered by competitors. As a result, receivables as a percent of sales and assets have grown significantly.[3] For 640 manufacturing companies representing 70 industries, receivables rose by 160 percent over the 13-year period 1952–1964, while over the same period inventory rose by only 80 percent.[4]

[3] The interest in inventory control has also pushed receivables up as firms strive to keep inventories down. Companies sell on especially attractive terms. The customer then holds the inventory and the firm the receivables.

[4] See J. A. Griswold, "How to Lose Money with Cash," *Financial Executive*, 34 (August 1966), pp. 28–30 ff.

#### Industry Overview

Receivables as a percent of total assets vary widely among industry groups. Wholesale trade has about 33 percent of its *assets* committed to receivables; utilities about 5 percent. Taking receivables as a percent of *working capital* (Table 7–2) we find greater uniformity. Construction has the largest percent with 60 percent, manufacturing, retail trade and agriculture, the least, with 47, 37, and 36 percent, respectively.

TABLE 7–2. Receivables as a Percent of Working Capital (Ranked by Major Industry Groups)

| | | | |
|---|---|---|---|
| Construction | 60% | Total utilities | 51% |
| Services | 56 | Total manufacturing | 47 |
| Total mining | 56 | Total retail trade | 37 |
| Total wholesale trade | 48 | Agriculture, forestry, and fisheries | 36 |

SOURCE: U. S. Treasury Department, Internal Revenue Service, *Statistics of Income, 1969, Corporation Income Tax Returns* (Washington, D.C.: Government Printing Office, 1973, pp. 14ff.

The relation between receivables and sales is determined to a large extent by the size of the selling firm and the resale value of its product. Large firms, with easy access to the capital markets and the ability to command favorable financing terms, grant liberal credit to smaller firms. Similarly, machinery and equipment firms extend liberal credit terms because equipment can be repossessed. Firms in the dairy and meat-packing industries carry a relatively low level of receivables to sales.

Some difference of opinion exists regarding who should set credit terms and police credit-granting and collection procedures.[5] The credit-granting and collection activities are sometimes the responsibility of the marketing department, but more often of the financial manager.[6] The argument for placing receivables management with marketing is that this department is close to the customer and can do a better job of extending credit and collecting after the goods have been shipped. The counter-argument is that the salesman does not want the customer's mind clouded by fear that he has come to dun for collection at the time when he has come to sell.

#### Trade Terms

When a firm sells merchandise on credit it is offering the purchaser a package consisting of two parts—the goods plus limited financing. The seller can also offer a discount for early payment. The purchaser then has

[5] Credit managers frequently complain that they are not consulted when credit terms are being set. To boost their corporate prestige they are increasingly talking in terms of the credit department as a profit center rather than of credit terms as a stimulant to sales. According to one survey, 41 percent of the respondents seldom had the opportunity to participate in planning sessions. See Welshans, pp. 152–153 and 155.

[6] G. G. Marrah, "Managing Receivables," *Financial Executive*, 38 (July 1970), pp. 41–44.

the option of obtaining his own financing in order to receive the discount or to let the seller carry the credit.

Trade terms commonly found in industry are 2/10/net 30; that is, a 2 percent discount is permitted on the price if payment is made within 10 days, with the full amount due at the end of 30 days.[7] The discount period may start with the date of shipping, the date of the invoice or the date of receipt of goods (ROG).

It is cheaper for the purchaser to take the 2 percent discount and borrow at say 6 percent to effect payment by the 10th. The 2 percent discount annualized is equivalent to 36.7 percent. The reasoning is as follows. The 2 percent discount is lost if the bill is not paid by the 10th, but in any event it should be paid by the 30th. The buyer exchanges the 2 percent discount for the use of the money for an additional 20 days. Since there are eighteen 20-day periods in a year, the effective annual rate is approximately 36 percent. Under 2/10/net 30 terms if the customer does not pay a $100 purchase by the 10th, he has the use of $98 for 20 days at a cost of $2. The annual effective interest cost is thus $(2/98) \times 18 = 36.7$ percent.

Extending cash discounts for early payment tends to increase sales, since the firm is, in fact, offering the goods at a reduced price. Under 2/10/net 30 terms the seller would carry the receivable for 10 days instead of 30 days. If the amount of the cash discount just offsets the savings from not having to carry the receivables the extra 20 days, the seller earns the normal margin between sales price and cost. If the discount exceeds the savings, the seller's margin of profit is reduced. In setting the trade terms we must be careful not to grant excessive discounts for early payment in order to capture a larger sales volume. The net result may be a reduction in total profit. Terms of 1/10/net 30 are equivalent to 18 percent per year and 2/10/net 30 to 36 percent per year. Some firms may earn 18 percent on their total assets, but few are able to earn 36 percent.

## HANDLING RISK IN THE RECEIVABLES SYSTEM

So far we have considered receivables management in a deterministic way assuming certainty. In the real world we can never be this sure. The anticipated results are estimates that involve probabilities. In discussing inventory management we faced the same kind of problem and treated demand as a random variable. Since a probability distribution for quantity demanded reflects the conditions in the real world, we therefore stocked the amount that maximized expected values. We can deal similarly with risk in managing receivables.

### Setting Optimum Credit Terms under Risk Conditions

Assume Micro-Omega operates in an industry that normally grants net 30-day credit terms but whose discounts for early payment vary. Man-

[7] Firms sometimes take the discount even when they mail the check several days after the discount date has passed; others skip the discount but wait until the 45th or 60th day to pay, depending upon the tolerance of the supplier's credit department.

agement, in seeking terms that optimize profits, directs the financial manager to study whether 1/10/net 30 should be extended or the no-discount policy continued. After examining the sales potential of electronic components, he concludes the demand levels and probabilities of reaching these levels under the 0 and 1 percent cash discount policies are those given in Table 7–3.[8]

TABLE 7–3. Micro-Omega Company
Sales Volume Potential with Various Trade Terms

| *Rate of discount if payment within 10 days* | *Potential demand in units* | | | | | | |
|---|---|---|---|---|---|---|---|
| | *100* | *110* | *120* | *130* | *140* | *150* | *160* |
| | | | | *Probability* | | | |
| 0.00 | 0.90 | 0.10 | | | | | |
| 0.01 | 0.10 | 0.20 | 0.40 | 0.30 | | | |
| 0.02 | | | 0.30 | 0.30 | 0.40 | | |
| 0.03 | | | | 0.30 | 0.40 | 0.20 | 0.10 |

Having established demand levels and probabilities, the financial manager can now recommend the credit terms to be extended and can link his credit recommendations to inventory policy in order to maximize profits.

Suppose the electronic units of Micro-Omega sell for $10 and cost $8, leaving a margin of $2 on each cash sale. Assume further that it costs 20 cents to carry either $8 of inventory or $10 of receivables for 30 days. If the component is not sold at the end of 30 days, additional carrying costs and other losses will total $1 per unit. The penalty cost for stock-out, including allowance for loss of customer goodwill, is $3 per unit. Table 7–4 shows the several inventory-level strategies along the left side, potential demand levels along the top, and profit to be earned at each sales level, given the inventory level.

TABLE 7–4. Micro-Omego Company
Sales Demand, Inventory Level, and Profit Matrix
Terms: Net 30 days

| *Inventory-level strategy (units)* | *Potential demand (units)* | | | |
|---|---|---|---|---|
| | *100* | *110* | *120* | *130* |
| | | *Potential profit* | | |
| *100* | $180 | $150 | $120 | $ 90 |
| *110* | 170 | 198 | 168 | 138 |
| *120* | 160 | 188 | 216 | 186 |
| *130* | 150 | 178 | 206 | 234 |

[A9814]

[8] You are invited to perform the corresponding computations for the 2 and 3 percent discount policy. You can check your computations against pages 151–153 of the first edition of this book.

Along the diagonal (upper left to lower right) is the maximum profit for each demand level if just the right amount of inventory is carried. No inventory losses, stock-outs, or excessive inventory carrying costs are incurred. The profit consists of the number of units sold times the selling price less the cost of production and the costs of carrying the receivables for the full 30 days. For example, if demand reaches 110 units and 110 units are stocked, a total revenue of $1100 would be generated, minus $880 for cost of goods sold, minus the receivables-carrying cost of $22—leaving a profit of $198. If 120 units were stocked, the same revenue and gross profit would be generated but the additional inventory-carrying costs of $1 per unit for the 10 extra units would pull earnings down to $188. If only 100 units were stocked with a demand level of 110 units, a gross profit of $200 would be earned, less a receivables-carrying cost of $20 and a penalty cost for understocking of $30, leaving a profit of $150.

### Applying Probability Estimates

Since the probability for each sales level under the differing credit terms is not the same, we need to determine the combination of credit and inventory policy that will maximize expected earnings. The bare minimum is an extension of net 30-day credit terms. If this policy is adopted we assume all customers will pay at the end of the 30-day period. Looking at our sales potential under these terms, we see there is a 0.90 probability that, on the average, demand will reach 100 units and a 0.10 probability that it will reach 110 units. If this trade policy is adopted the financial manager wants to know what level of inventory to carry to maximize expected profit.

TABLE 7–5. Micro-Omega Company
Expected Profit Determination
Terms: Net 30 days

| *Stock* | *Potential demand* (*a*) | *Probability* * (*b*) | *Profitability* † (*c*) | ($b \cdot c$) | *Expected profit* $\Sigma\ (b \cdot c)$ |
|---|---|---|---|---|---|
| 100 units | 100 | 0.90 | $180 | $162.00 | |
| | 110 | 0.10 | 150 | 15.00 | |
| | | | | | $177.00 |
| 110 units | 100 | 0.90 | $170 | $153.00 | |
| | 110 | 0.10 | 198 | 19.80 | |
| | | | | | $172.80 |

* From Table 7–3.
† From Table 7–4.

We assume no reaction by competitors to any shift by Micro-Omega away from its current no-discount policy. Such reaction might neutralize the benefits expected from a more liberal discount policy. Micro-Omega might counter with such nonprice competition tactics as improved quality control, faster delivery time, and increased advertising. But these involve added costs. Thus our analysis assumes no competitive reaction.

Table 7–5 shows that under net 30-day credit terms the most profitable strategy would be to stock 100 units. However, this is not the only trade credit option available. For example, there is 1/10/net 30.

### Extending a 1 Percent Discount

Because most of the firm's customers are in sound working capital position, the financial manager estimates that 90 percent will take advantage of a 1 percent cash discount if offered. Thus, the cost of carrying $10 of receivables will drop from 20 cents for the full 30 days to 7 cents (20¢/3 ≅ 7¢) for 10 days (for 90 percent of the receivables). But we must add back the discount of 1 percent or 10 cents per $10 of receivables to get a total cost for the cash discount alternative of 17 cents (10¢ + 7¢) per $10 of receivables, or an increase in profit of 3 cents per $10 of receivables (20¢ − 17¢). Under 1/10/net 30 terms the sales level would range from 100 to 130 units. The profit matrix for the various inventory-strategy levels, given the various sales levels, is presented in Table 7–6.

TABLE 7–6. Micro-Omega Company
Sales Demand, Inventory Level, and Profit Matrix
Terms: 1/10/Net 30; 90 Percent Will Discount *

| *Inventory-level strategy (units)* | *Potential demand (units)* 100 | 110 | 120 | 130 |
|---|---|---|---|---|
| | *Potential profit* | | | |
| *100* | $182.70 | $152.70 | $122.70 | $ 92.70 |
| *110* | 172.70 | 200.97 | 170.97 | 140.97 |
| *120* | 162.70 | 190.97 | 219.24 | 189.24 |
| *130* | 152.70 | 180.97 | 209.24 | 237.51 |

* Table 7–4 adjusted for 1 percent 10-day discount.

[A9831]

The profit when offering a 1 percent discount is calculated as follows: If we stock 100 units with a demand for 100 units, revenue is $1000 and production costs $800, leaving earnings before receivables cost of $200. Of the amount sold, 10 percent, corresponding to 10 units sold, will be carried as receivables to the end of the month at a cost of 20 cents per unit sold for a total of $2, and 90 percent, corresponding to 900 units sold, will be carried only to the 10th of the month at a cost of 7 cents per unit sold for a total cost of $6.30 (900 × 7¢). In addition, those paying cash receive a 1 percent discount, reducing earnings $9 ($900 × 1%). Subtracting these costs, we arrive at a profit figure of $182.70. If we understock by 10 units when potential demand is 110 units, the $3 per unit penalty will reduce earnings from $182.70 to $152.70. Overstocking by 10 units when potential demand is 100 units will reduce earnings from $182.70 to $172.20, as a result of the $1 per unit cost of storage charges.

The immediate problem is to determine the inventory-level strategy to adopt given this credit policy. The ultimate goal is to determine simultaneously the combined optimum credit policy and inventory strategy.

### Optimizing Credit Policy and Inventory Policy

It is apparent from Table 7–7 that the optimum inventory level under trade terms of 1/10/net 30 is 130 units. Furthermore the expected profit of $206 is higher than under the net 30-day terms (Table 7–5). Since we assumed no other alternative is available, we adopt the 1/10/net 30 terms and stock 130 units.[9] The credit policy optimum may conflict with the inventory policy optimum. Simulation is a technique that can be used to deal simultaneously with credit and inventory policy. This technique is discussed in the Appendix F at the end of this chapter. If we did not proceed simultaneously we would have to choose between optimizing receivables or optimizing inventory on the basis of the marginal profit at the receivables optimum versus the marginal profit at the inventory optimum.

TABLE 7–7. Micro-Omega Company
Expected Profit Determination

Terms: 1/10/Net 30; 90 Percent Will Discount
(to the nearest dollar)

| *Stock* | *Potential demand* (*a*) | *Probability* * (*b*) | *Profitability* † (*c*) | ($b \cdot c$) | *Expected profit* $\Sigma(b \cdot c)$ |
|---|---|---|---|---|---|
| 100 | 100 | 0.10 | $183 | $18 | |
| | 110 | 0.20 | 153 | 31 | |
| | 120 | 0.40 | 123 | 49 | |
| | 130 | 0.30 | 93 | 28 | $126 |
| 110 | 100 | 0.10 | $173 | $17 | |
| | 110 | 0.20 | 201 | 40 | |
| | 120 | 0.40 | 171 | 68 | |
| | 130 | 0.30 | 141 | 42 | $167 |
| 120 | 100 | 0.10 | $163 | $16 | |
| | 110 | 0.20 | 191 | 38 | |
| | 120 | 0.40 | 219 | 88 | |
| | 130 | 0.30 | 189 | 57 | $199 |
| 130 | 100 | 0.10 | $153 | $15 | |
| | 110 | 0.20 | 181 | 36 | |
| | 120 | 0.40 | 210 | 84 | |
| | 130 | 0.30 | 238 | 71 | $206 |

* From Table 7–3.
† From Table 7–6.

---

[9] We *assume* the profit on the additional sales above the marginal costs of producing and carrying the extra units in inventory and the additional receivables (when going from credit terms net 30 to 1/10/net 30) yields an adequate return on investment (ROI)—the trade-off between risk and return is favorable. We also *assume* the necessary funds for investment in the additional inventory and receivables are readily available and that management is willing to secure these funds.

## MANAGING THE FLOW OF RECEIVABLES

The three control points regulating the flow and level of receivables through the system after credit terms have been set are analysis of the customer's credit worthiness, matching his credit worthiness against the firm's standard, and collection procedure. The determinants of a firm's credit standard are trade practices in the industry, the firm's attitude toward credit risks, and the financial status of most of the firm's customers.

### Analyzing the Customer's Credit Worthiness

To evaluate the credit worthiness of a potential customer we consider character (the willingness of the customer to do his best to pay), capacity (the financial ability of the buyer, particularly liquidity), and current economic conditions. There are many sources of credit information. Perhaps the best known is Dun & Bradstreet, Inc., which makes available to its subscribers a reference book and written credit reports. The reference book rates about three million businesses of all types based on Dun & Bradstreet's credit appraisal of the firms and their estimated financial strength. The rating system is composed of a combination of letters and numbers. The estimated financial strength (net worth) of the firm is rated by letter. A number indicates Dun & Bradstreet's composite credit analysis of the firm. For example, a BA 2 rating indicates a firm with an estimated net worth of between $300,000 and $500,000 and a credit standing estimated as good. A rating of FF 4 indicates a firm with an estimated net worth of between $10,000 and $20,000 and a limited credit standing, as shown in Figure 7–1.

If additional information is desired, Dun & Bradstreet will supply a credit report that provides background on the history of the firm, its location, the nature of the business, and financial information, as shown in Figure 7–2. The report also shows the amount of credit some suppliers have extended, the amount currently owed these suppliers, whether discounts are taken, and whether payment is prompt or slow.

The weakness of the Dun & Bradstreet service is that, except for payment information furnished by suppliers of the firm and a few matters such as public records of judgments against the firm, Dun & Bradstreet passes on information furnished by the firm itself. The firm is hardly an unbiased source of information. In fact, matters frequently get down to whether the firm can "pull the wool over the eyes" of the Dun & Bradstreet interviewer. And when the firm is in difficulty, the incentive to do so is overwhelming.

In addition to Dun & Bradstreet, information may be obtained from commercial banks, particularly the customer's bank, local credit associations, the National Association of Credit Management, financial statements, releases by the customer, the firm's own salesmen, and personal interviews. The opinion of the salesmen, though frequently helpful, may reflect a desire to make a sale rather than concern for the collectibility of the account.

# Key to Ratings

| ESTIMATED FINANCIAL STRENGTH | | | COMPOSITE CREDIT APPRAISAL | | | |
|---|---|---|---|---|---|---|
| | | | HIGH | GOOD | FAIR | LIMITED |
| 5A | Over | $50,000,000 | 1 | 2 | 3 | 4 |
| 4A | $10,000,000 to | 50,000,000 | 1 | 2 | 3 | 4 |
| 3A | 1,000,000 to | 10,000,000 | 1 | 2 | 3 | 4 |
| 2A | 750,000 to | 1,000,000 | 1 | 2 | 3 | 4 |
| 1A | 500,000 to | 750,000 | 1 | 2 | 3 | 4 |
| BA | 300,000 to | 500,000 | 1 | 2 | 3 | 4 |
| BB | 200,000 to | 300,000 | 1 | 2 | 3 | 4 |
| CB | 125,000 to | 200,000 | 1 | 2 | 3 | 4 |
| CC | 75,000 to | 125,000 | 1 | 2 | 3 | 4 |
| DC | 50,000 to | 75,000 | 1 | 2 | 3 | 4 |
| DD | 35,000 to | 50,000 | 1 | 2 | 3 | 4 |
| EE | 20,000 to | 35,000 | 1 | 2 | 3 | 4 |
| FF | 10,000 to | 20,000 | 1 | 2 | 3 | 4 |
| GG | 5,000 to | 10,000 | 1 | 2 | 3 | 4 |
| HH | Up to | 5,000 | 1 | 2 | 3 | 4 |

CLASSIFICATION FOR BOTH
ESTIMATED FINANCIAL STRENGTH AND CREDIT APPRAISAL

| FINANCIAL STRENGTH BRACKET | EXPLANATION |
|---|---|
| 1 $125,000 and Over<br>2 20,000 to 125,000 | When only the numeral (1 or 2) appears, it is an indication that the estimated financial strength, while not definitely classified, is presumed to be within the range of the ($) figures in the corresponding bracket and that a condition is believed to exist which warrants credit in keeping with that assumption. |

**ABSENCE OF RATING DESIGNATION FOLLOWING NAMES LISTED IN THE REFERENCE BOOK**

The absence of a rating, expressed by two hyphens (--), is not to be construed as unfavorable but signifies circumstances difficult to classify within condensed rating symbols. It suggests the advisability of obtaining a report for additional information.

**EMPLOYEE RANGE DESIGNATIONS IN REPORTS OR NAMES NOT LISTED IN THE REFERENCE BOOK**

Certain businesses do not lend themselves to a Dun & Bradstreet rating and are not listed in the Reference Book. Information on these names, however, continues to be stored and updated in the D&B Business Data Bank. Reports are available on such businesses and instead of a rating they carry an Employee Range Designation (ER) which is indicative of size in terms of number of employees. No other significance should be attached.

KEY TO EMPLOYEE RANGE DESIGNATIONS

| | |
|---|---|
| **ER 1** | Over 1000 Employees |
| **ER 2** | 500 - 999 Employees |
| **ER 3** | 100 - 499 Employees |
| **ER 4** | 50 - 99 Employees |
| **ER 5** | 20 - 49 Employees |
| **ER 6** | 10 - 19 Employees |
| **ER 7** | 5 - 9 Employees |
| **ER 8** | 1 - 4 Employees |
| **ER N** | Not Available |



* Source: Courtesy of Dun & Bradstreet, Inc. [A9782]

Figure 7–1 Key to Dun & Bradstreet Ratings

**Dun & Bradstreet, Inc.** — BUSINESS INFORMATION REPORT

Please note whether name, business and street address correspond with your inquiry.

BASE REPORT

| SIC | D-U-N-S | © DUN & BRADSTREET, INC. | STARTED | RATING |
|---|---|---|---|---|
| 34 69 | 04-426-3226 | CD 13 APR 21 19-- | 1957 | DD1 |
| | ARNOLD METAL PRODUCTS CO | METAL STAMPINGS | | |

53 S MAIN ST
DAWSON MICH 49666
TEL 215 999-0000

SAMUEL B. ARNOLD )
GEORGE T. ARNOLD ) PARTNERS

SUMMARY

| | |
|---|---|
| PAYMENTS | DISC |
| SALES | $177,250 |
| WORTH | $42,961 |
| EMPLOYS | 10 |
| RECORD | CLEAR |
| CONDITION | STRONG |
| TREND | UP |

PAYMENTS

| HC | OWE | P DUE | TERMS | APR 19-- | SOLD |
|---|---|---|---|---|---|
| 3000 | 1500 | | 1 10 30 | Disc | Over 3 yrs |
| 2500 | 1000 | | 1 10 30 | Disc | Over 3 yrs |
| 2000 | 500 | | 2 20 30 | Disc | Old Account |

FINANCE

On Apr 21 19-- S. B. Arnold, Partner, submitted the following statement dated Dec 31 19--

| | | | |
|---|---|---|---|
| Cash | $ 4,870 | Accts Pay | $ 6,121 |
| Accts Rec | 15,472 | Notes Pay (Curr) | 2,400 |
| Mdse | 14,619 | Accruals | 3,583 |
| Current | 34,961 | Current | 12,104 |
| Fixt & Equip ($4,183) | 22,840 | Notes Pay (Def) | 5,000 |
| CSV of Life Ins | 2,264 | NET WORTH | 42,961 |
| Total Assets | 60,065 | Total | 60,065 |

Annual sales $177,250; gross profit $47,821; net income $8,204. Fire insurance mdse $15,000; fixt $20,000. Annual rent $3,000.
Signed Apr 21 19-- ARNOLD METAL PRODUCTS CO by Samuel B. Arnold, Partner.

-----0-----

New equipment purchased last Sep was financed by bank loan. Monthly payments on loan are $200.

Arnold reported sales for the three months ended Mar 31 were up 10% compared to the same period last year. Increase was attributed by management to additional capacity provided by new equipment.

Profit is being made and retained resulting in an increase in net worth. Current debt is light in relation to worth. Inventory turnover is rapid.

BANKING

Balances average high four figures. Loans granted to low five figures, secured by equipment, now owing high four figures. Relations satisfactory.

HISTORY

Style registered Feb 1 1965 by partners. S. ARNOLD, born 1918, married. 1939 graduate of Lehigh University. 1939-50 employed by Industrial Machine Corporation, Detroit, and 1950-56 production manager with Aerial Motors Inc., Detroit. Started this business in 1957. G. ARNOLD, born 1940, single, son of Samuel. Graduated in 1963, Dawson Institute of Technology. Served U.S. Air Force 1963-1964. Admitted to partnership Feb 1965.

OPERATION

Manufactures perforated metal stampings for industrial concerns. Sells on Net 30 day terms. Has twelve accounts. Territory greater Detroit area. Employs ten including partners. LOCATION: Rents 5,000 square feet in one story cinder block building in normal condition. Located in central business section of main street. Premises neat.
4-21 (803 77) PRA



* Source: Courtesy Dun & Bradstreet. This is a fictitious example.

Figure 7–2 Example of business information report.

Many firms when placing their first order with a new supplier volunteer as references a list of other suppliers who have extended credit.

Information-gathering activities are necessarily limited by time and cost.[10] If in a particular industry customers demand prompt delivery, a

---

[10] Inadequate information is a major problem facing financial managers at the time a credit decision must be made. A time sharing terminal hooked to a computer can be used to obtain analytical information quickly. D. W. Smith, "Efficient Credit Management with Time Sharing," *Financial Executive*, 39 (March 1971), pp. 26–30.

month is not available to make a credit investigation. The customer would become impatient and place his order elsewhere, perhaps never to return. If the order is small, it would hardly pay to spend a month gathering and analyzing credit information. Therefore, small orders are decided on the basis of a brief check.

### Matching a Customer's Credit Worthiness against the Firm's Standard

In judging the applicant's credit worthiness against the firm's standard we use ratio analysis and apply subjective "feel." Where the customer's credit standing is far above or below our standard the accept or reject decision is easy; where it is marginal, judgment is required. At this point the credit manager's years of experience are invaluable.

### Collection Procedure

For customers who pay promptly, no collection effort is required. But a certain percentage will be slow in paying and a smaller percentage of accounts will be noncollectible. The objective of the collection department is to speed up the slow payers and reduce the percentage of bad debts.

Extracting payment from slow-paying customers is a difficult art. The objective is to get payment without offending the customer and endangering future orders, particularly if slow payment is attributable to factors other than serious difficulty. For example, a firm may be seeking to stretch its current credit financing to the limit and thereby postpone raising new long-term capital, or a very profitable firm may be suffering from a lack of liquidity, a not uncommon phenomenon. If the collection department is too aggressive in pressing for payment, the customer may turn to other suppliers who are willing to carry this slow-paying account that promises to become a big customer in the future. Thousands of dollars of sales effort may later be required to win back an account rejected by a clerk. If the collection policy is too lenient, marginal customers will take advantage of the situation creating a substantial increase in the costs of credit extension and collection.

Customers are motivated to pay promptly, since they realize their habits will quickly become known in the industry and affect their credit standing. Furthermore, the fact that the seller can refuse to make new shipments until overdue accounts are paid exerts pressure on customers to pay promptly. Finally, if a customer refuses to pay, aggressive collection procedures, such as legal action, are in order.

If it is widely known that the customer is in serious financial difficulty, the threat of unfavorable publicity will have little effect. The creditor firm must then shift tactics. To force payment by legal action may accelerate failure of the customer, and little may be left after legal expenses to satisfy the claims of the creditors. Frequently, the best course of action is a compromise settlement of debts.[11]

---

[11] Chapter 26 on bankruptcy, reorganization, and dissolution and liquidation amply illustrates the wisdom of reaching a compromise settlement.

### The Flow of Receivables and External Factors

Decisions on credit extension to specific customers have little influence on the flow of funds into and out of receivables. This flow is determined by the credit policies of the firm. Likewise, factors external to the firm have a greater effect on the level of receivables than do the particular credits to specific customers. General economic conditions and the intensity of competition in the industry are the controlling elements. With a prosperous economy and reduced competition, a firm may adopt a higher standard of credit acceptability. But rosy conditions cause many customers' affairs to look better than they really are. As a result receivables turnover may tend to decline.

With a decline in the economy the level of receivables will fall with the decline in sales, but not as rapidly because some buyers increase their delay in payment. The problem with receivables is the same as with inventory. Excessive receivables and inventory are easier to correct in a high volume period than in a lower volume one when a longer time is needed to work off the excess.

### Evaluating the Flow of Receivables

The ratio of credit sales to receivables is one measure of the effectiveness of credit policy and of the credit department. A corresponding measure is days' credit sales outstanding as receivables. For example, if annual credit sales totaled $360,000 and today's receivables are $30,000, daily credit sales equal $1000: ($360,000/360) and receivables represent 30 days' credit sales ($30,000/$1000). Receivables turnover is 12 times, ($360,000/$30,000). These rough measures can be supplemented by an aging schedule such as Table 7–8 which summarizes receivables according to length of time outstanding.

TABLE 7–8. Aging Schedule of Receivables

| *Receivables outstanding* | *Amount outstanding* | *Percent* |
|---|---|---|
| Less than 30 days | $2,800,000 | 70.0 |
| 30–59 days | 700,000 | 17.5 |
| 60–89 days | 400,000 | 10.0 |
| Over 90 days * | 100,000 | 2.5 |
| | $4,000,000 | 100.0 |

* After 8 months receivables are written off as bad debts.

By computing the aging schedule of receivables at regular intervals, we detect trends toward a slowing or improvement in collection. The aging schedule is an early warning device regarding a deterioration in receivables and the increasing probability of large and unusual bad-debt losses. A significant rise in the percent of old receivables may be due to laxity in granting credit, to relaxation of past-due collections, or to external economic conditions.

An average-age-of-accounts-receivable figure may be obtained by taking the mid-age point of each age category (a simplifying assumption), multiplying by the percent that that age category bears to the total, and summing, as is done in Table 7–9.

TABLE 7–9. Determination of Average Age of Receivables in Table 7–8

| *Average age in category* | *Average age times percent in that category* |
|---|---|
| 15 days | 10.5 days |
| 45 days | 7.9 |
| 75 days | 7.5 |
| 165 days * | 4.1 |
| | 30.0 days. Average age |

* After 8 months the receivable is either collected or written off as a bad debt.

The credit terms of a firm heavily influence the average age figure. If in Table 7–9, for example, the firm sells net 30, the 30 days average age of receivables is a number biased by the firm's credit terms.

### Credit Insurance

A vendor extending trade credit may maintain an efficient credit and collection department and still get hit with unusual bad-debt losses. The profits of some of the vendor's customers may fall short, their overhead may get out of hand, or they may be unable to collect from their own customers. To guard against unusual bad-debt losses the vendor may take out credit insurance.

Under credit insurance a firm can only insure against abnormal credit losses. The firm cannot insure against normal or *primary* losses. If experience shows that credit losses normally reach one-half of 1 percent of sales, this is the primary loss and not insurable. To illustrate, if in a particular year we have sales of $10 million, we would then have to bear the first $50,000 of credit losses.

To contain enthusiasm for granting credit once a firm is insured, the insurance company imposes two constraints. First, the insurer restricts its coverage on individual accounts receivable. The restriction may be set in terms of a dollar limit for each account with a particular Dun & Bradstreet rating: $5000 for any account with a GG 3 rating. Second, the insurance company will require that the insured agree to coinsurance—participation in the insured credit losses. Depending on the credit risks, participation is usually from 10 to 20 percent.

The desirability of credit insurance depends on: (1) the trade-off between the insurance premium and the probability of unusual bad-debt losses, (2) the willingness of management to assume the risk of the unusual bad-debt losses. Most firms are willing to assume the risk, since the annual purchase of credit insurance is modest. In 1971 credit insurance premiums for the United States totaled $13.5 million and for Michigan, a "big" state, only $390,000.

Firms of all sizes carry credit insurance but most frequently the insured firms have annual sales of $1 to $50 million. The cost of insurance runs from 1/10 to 1/4 of 1 percent of sales. Large firms with diversified credit risks do not carry credit insurance. They self-insure, even though the cost of insurance is low, due to the small risk.

On the other hand, credit insurance protects financially weak firms or those with nondiversified credit risks. In both of these cases unusual bad-debt losses will really hurt. The likelihood is high that such losses may push the firm into bankruptcy.

### Captive Finance Companies

A captive finance company is a subsidiary that serves as the finance arm of the parent firm. This subsidiary buys the accounts receivable generated by the parent's sales. Frequently these sales involve machinery and heavy equipment, such as industrial lift trucks, tractors, and highway trailers, sold on time to dealers or at retail.

Many nonfinancial firms, such as Caterpillar Tractor, Clark Equipment, General Electric, ITT, Westinghouse, and White Motor, have formed captive finance companies. Many of these subsidiaries were formed in the 1950s and 1960s when sales were expanding and credit terms lengthening, thus increasing receivables beyond the abilities of firms to finance them internally. Rather than finance these burgeoning receivables through a stock issue, management decided to establish wholly owned subsidiaries to carry the receivables. The attraction of the captives is their ability to carry large debt to equity ratios and attract specialized lenders because of the limited risks, thereby lowering the cost of capital.

For captives, a relationship of $4 of debt to $1 of equity is not unusual. Such high debt to equity ratios are attainable because of the excellent collateral value of the captives' receivables. And since debt is generally cheaper than equity, the captives have a low cost of capital that translates into a low cost of carrying the receivables.

But note, by shifting the receivables from the parent to the captive the parent loses a portion of its liquidity and thereby a portion of its own debt-bearing capacity. In part the high debt to equity ratio of the subsidiary is made possible at the expense of the reduced debt-carrying capacity of the parent.

## SUMMARY

The strategic matters in the receivables system are: (1) credit period, (2) cash discount, (3) quality of account accepted, (4) collection efforts, (5) the seller's attitude toward this risk, and (6) the seller's cost of capital. Trade credit terms are an effective competitive instrument and rank as price concessions. Through liberalized credit terms sales can be stimulated, but added collection costs and bad-debt expense reduce profit.

The in-and-out flow of funds from the receivables account is controlled by investigation of the credit worthiness of the customer, matching the customer's financial standing with the standards of the firm and collection procedure. During prosperity these controls may fail because customers' affairs look better than they are and receivables rise faster than sales. In a declining economy, sales fall faster than receivables.

A vendor may use credit insurance to guard against unusual bad-debt losses. Coverage is restricted to rated receivables and the vendor must agree to share in the losses.

A captive finance company buys the receivables generated by the parent's sales. Captives carry a high debt to equity ratio and have a low cost of capital.

### *Study Questions*

1. Why does the extension of credit slow the flow of funds from cash back to cash? How can changing the credit terms affect the speed of the cycle?
2. Explain the complaint by a credit manager that when credit is being extended too cautiously the marketing department calls, when it is granted too liberally the treasurer calls, and when it is just right no one calls.
3. Why is it easier to pursue a credit policy that seeks to minimize bad-debt losses than one that seeks to make the greatest contribution to profits? Why are these goals incompatible?
4. What are the costs of extending trade credit?
5. How do you account for the rapid increase in receivables as a percent of sales in the postwar period? Why has so little attention been focused on receivables control relative to the heavy emphasis on inventory control? What would you expect the actions of the financial manager to be relative to receivables if credit should become tight and loan funds expensive?
6. Under what conditions might a firm make a rather intensive credit analysis? a token credit analysis? Is there a difference between the credit analysis undertaken by an industrial firm and that conducted by a bank? Explain.
7. Would a firm in the following circumstances tend to have generous or restrictive credit terms, and why: (a) has a high margin of profit; (b) is introducing a new product; (c) is short of working capital; (d) has a monopoly position in the market; (e) is in a period of declining economic activity?
8. How do the analysis of the customer's credit worthiness, the matching of the analysis against the financial standard required by the firm, and the collection procedure influence the inflow and outflow of receivables? How can these controls be adjusted to correspond with the level of economic activity? Is this a good idea?
9. Determine whether the cash discount a company offers its customers is likely to be increased, decreased, remain unchanged, or be indeterminate as a result of the following situations; explain your answer in each case: (a) new competition enters the field; (b) economic activity reaches capacity levels; (c) the price of raw materials increases; (d) the firm achieves a monopoly position; (e) a new credit manager is hired.

**Problems**

1. The Pine Knot Lumber Company has annual credit sales of $720,000. At year-end accounts receivable outstanding were $180,000. Pine Knot sells on net 30-day terms. Using the following formulas,

$$\text{Average credit sales per day} = \frac{\text{Annual credit sales}}{360}$$

$$\text{Days' credit sales outstanding as accounts receivable} = \frac{\text{Accounts receivable outstanding}}{\text{Average credit sales per day}}$$

a. Determine the number of days' credit sales outstanding as accounts receivable. Use a 360-day year.

b. Compare this with the credit terms of Pine Knot. What can you say about the firm's collection policy?

c. If the firm were to sell on net 45-day terms and hold to them, what would be the level of receivables? How much working capital would be freed for other uses?

2. Credit managers often claim the bad-debt losses come straight out of profit. The marginal cost of credit losses is considered to be the amount of the written-off bad debt. The credit manager of the Firefly Candle Company thinks this way. Last year the firm had $1 million in sales, $700,000 in cost of goods sold, $200,000 in selling and administrative expenses, sales included a sale with a potential bad-debt loss of $2000.

a. Following the credit manager's line of reasoning, calculate earnings before income taxes on a before and after bad-debt loss basis. What is the apparent marginal cost of the sale? Does this appear to be a fair way of presenting the cost of the bad-debt loss?

b. Suppose that analysis revealed the following about the $2000 bad-debt sale: variable costs on the shipment totaled $1400; the manufacturing cost of goods sold was $1200; and selling and administrative expenses were $200. The sale contributed $600 to profit.

Draw up the corrected comparative income statements showing the earnings before taxes on the basis of the sale not being made and on the basis of the sale being made but with the account uncollectible. What is the apparent marginal cost of the sale? Does this appear to be a reasonable way of presenting the bad-debt loss? Why?

c. Suppose that when the sale is made there exists a 50 percent chance that the customer will pay. What would be the expected value of the bad-debt expense? Calculate the income before taxes on the basis of the sale being made and the expected value of the bad-debt loss. What is the apparent marginal cost of the sale? Does this appear to be a more reasonable way of representing the bad-debt loss? Why? What would have to be the expected value of the bad-debt loss before it would pay Firefly to ship the $2000 worth of candles to the customer?

3. The Y. Askum Co. has annual credit sales of $144,000. Terms are net 30 days. Because of the firm's lax collection policy accounts are paid in 70 days on the average.

a. How much does the firm have tied up in receivables? Use a 360-day year.

b. What should the firm's investment in receivables be?

c. If the firm has an opportunity cost of investment in receivables of 10 percent, what would be the effect on profits of reducing receivables to a level corresponding to the firm's trade terms of net 30 days (other things equal)?

4. Shakey, Inc. sells to a limited number of customers. To protect itself against financial ruin the firm carries credit insurance. The cost of the insurance is ¼ of 1 percent of the firm's annual sales of $1 million. The insurance policy excludes the first $30,000 of loss per year and carries a 20 percent coinsurance clause on Dun & Bradstreet rated accounts. Coverage on each account, based on the customer's rating, is limited as follows:

| | |
|---|---|
| BB | $50,000 |
| CB | 45,000 |
| CC | 30,000 |
| DC | 20,000 |
| DD | 15,000 |

a. What is the dollar cost of the credit insurance?

b. How large a credit loss in a single year must the firm incur before the insurance policy begins to pay off?

c. During the year, four of Shakey's customers stumble into bankruptcy. Credit losses on these four accounts and the Dun & Bradstreet rating on each at the time the goods were shipped are as follows:

| | |
|---|---|
| CB | $25,000 |
| CC | 5,000 |
| DC | 15,000 |
| DD | 20,000 |

How much will Shakey collect on its credit insurance policy?

### Selected References

Bursk, E. C., "View Your Customers as Investment," *Harvard Business Review,* 44 (May–June 1966), pp. 91–94.

Davis, P. M., "Marginal Analysis of Credit Sales," *Accounting Review,* 41 (January 1966), pp. 121–166.

Kaplan, R. M., "Credit Risks and Opportunities," *Harvard Business Review,* 45 (March–April 1967), pp. 83–88.

Lane, S., "Submarginal Credit Risk Classification," *Journal of Financial and Quantitative Analysis,* 7 (January 1972), pp. 379–85.

Lewellen, W. G., "Finance Subsidiaries and Corporate Borrowing Capacity," *Financial Management,* 1 (Spring 1972), pp. 21–31.

———, and R. W. Johnson, "Better Way to Monitor Accounts Receivable," *Harvard Business Review* 50 (May–June 1972), pp. 101–109.

Marrah, G. L., "Managing Receivables," *Financial Executive,* 38 (July 1970), pp. 40–44.

Schiff, M. and Lieber, Z., "A Model for the Integration of Credit and Inventory Management," *Journal of Finance,* 29 (March 1974), pp. 133–140.

Smith, D. W., "Efficient Credit Management with Time Sharing," *Financial Executive,* 39 (March 1971), pp. 26–30.

Welshans, M. T., "Using Credit for Profit Making," *Harvard Business Review,* 45 (January–February 1967), pp. 141–156.

Wrightsman, D., "Optimal Credit Terms for Accounts Receivable," *Quarterly Review of Economics and Business,* 9 (Summer 1969), pp. 59–66.

Zelnick, J., "Credit Analysis by Computer," *Financial Executive,* 34 (June 1966), pp. 26ff.

## Appendix G

### JOINT INVENTORY AND CREDIT POLICY SIMULATION

The carrying of inventory and receivables requires funds. But available funds must be allocated among inventory, receivables, and other assets to optimize profit at a given level of risk. Thus, considering the firm as an entity, we seek a combined inventory—credit policy that will optimize profit rather than simply an optimum inventory where only inventory variables are considered or an optimum credit policy where only receivables are considered.

The Monte Carlo technique uses random numbers to simulate sales for various combinations of inventory—credit policy in order to observe the impact of a selected inventory—credit policy combination on sales and thus on profit. Using simulation we can predict the probabilities of various levels of sales given different combinations of inventory—credit policy, provided we know the separate probabilities of sales reaching various levels for different *independent* inventory and credit policies and that we introduce no new elements when combining the two policies. Then, knowing the probabilities of the various levels of sales we can by means of arithmetic convert these sales data to profit data.

The steps are as follows:

*Step 1.* Determine the probability distribution of sales for a selected inventory policy and the probability distribution of sales for a selected credit policy (as shown in Table 7–10).

*Step 2.* For each selected inventory policy and each selected credit policy, assign random numbers 00 to 99 (from Table 7–14) to each possible outcome in proportion to the probability of that outcome as indicated by the probabilty mass functions determined in Step 1 as shown in Table 7–10.

*Step 3.* Determine the size of the random number sample for each policy (in Table 7–11 we use a sample size of 20) and the number of samples to be drawn. This step requires intimate knowledge of the problem being analyzed.

*Step 4.* Proceed in some systematic manner through the random number table (Table 7–14) noting random numbers. Thus, in Table 7–11, the first random number for inventory policy is 62. Consulting Table 7–10, we find random number 62 is associated with sales of $200,000. The second random number is 14, which is associated with $100,000. We proceed similarly for all the random numbers in Table 7–11.

*Step 5.* Record in column 5 of Table 7–11 the lower sales figure for each simulated pair of sales levels, since for a given combination inventory-credit policy, the more restrictive of the separate inventory and credit policies is controlling. From column 5 of Table 7–11 compile the frequency distribution and the corresponding probability distribution of sales for the combined inventory-credit policy, as shown in Table 7–12.

Table 7–12 shows the resulting sales distribution likely to develop from the combined inventory and credit policies being simulated. We are interested, however, in the *profit* results. If we know the profit for each sales level, we can convert Table 7–12 into expected profitability, but in doing so the expected profit value must consider *separately* the profitability of each sales level, as is done in Table 7–13. For each level of sales in column 1 of Table 7–13 we assume the corresponding profit figure shown in column 2.

We should point out that this is a highly simplified model. One assumption is that a dollar's worth of sales added by credit policy is worth the same amount as a dollar's worth of sales added by inventory policy. When this assumption is relaxed, the computation becomes more complicated, specifically in Table 7–11 in columns 2 and 4. The profitability of each sales volume for inventory policy and credit policy would be shown rather than the sales volume, and column 5 would record the lower of these profitabilities.

We would next proceed to analyze another pair of inventory-credit policies. The pair with the highest expected profitability would be chosen if we assume risk constant.

**TABLE 7–10. Probability Distributions for a Selected Inventory and a Selected Credit Policy**

| Inventory policy $I_1$ | | |
|---|---|---|
| Sales | Probability | Random number assigned |
| $100,000 | 0.20 | 00–19 |
| 150,000 | 0.40 | 20–59 |
| 200,000 | 0.30 | 60–84 |
| 250,000 | 0.15 | 85–99 |
| **Credit policy $C_1$** | | |
| Sales | Probability | Random number assigned |
| $100,000 | 0.05 | 00–04 |
| 150,000 | 0.10 | 05–14 |
| 200,000 | 0.20 | 15–34 |
| 250,000 | 0.25 | 35–59 |
| 300,000 | 0.35 | 60–94 |
| 350,000 | 0.05 | 95–99 |

TABLE 7–11. Simulation—Sample 1

| Inventory policy $I_1$ | | Credit policy $C_1$ | | Combined policies |
|---|---|---|---|---|
| (1) Random number from Table 7–14, column 1 | (2) Corresponding demand from Table 7–10 | (3) Random number from Table 7–14, column 2 | (4) Corresponding demand from Table 7–10 | (5) Demand—lower of column (2) or (4) |
| 62 | $200,000 | 01 | $100,000 | $100,000 |
| 14 | 100,000 | 47 | 250,000 | 100,000 |
| 34 | 150,000 | 55 | 250,000 | 150,000 |
| 50 | 150,000 | 62 | 300,000 | 150,000 |
| 73 | 200,000 | 34 | 200,000 | 200,000 |
| 82 | 200,000 | 83 | 300,000 | 200,000 |
| 32 | 150,000 | 36 | 250,000 | 150,000 |
| 46 | 150,000 | 10 | 150,000 | 150,000 |
| 29 | 150,000 | 29 | 200,000 | 150,000 |
| 88 | 250,000 | 83 | 300,000 | 250,000 |
| 52 | 150,000 | 63 | 300,000 | 150,000 |
| 82 | 200,000 | 52 | 250,000 | 200,000 |
| 31 | 150,000 | 57 | 250,000 | 150,000 |
| 61 | 200,000 | 13 | 150,000 | 150,000 |
| 70 | 200,000 | 42 | 250,000 | 200,000 |
| 18 | 100,000 | 52 | 250,000 | 100,000 |
| 63 | 200,000 | 79 | 300,000 | 200,000 |
| 62 | 200,000 | 30 | 200,000 | 200,000 |
| 22 | 150,000 | 28 | 200,000 | 150,000 |
| 19 | 100,000 | 89 | 300,000 | 100,000 |

TABLE 7–12. Sales Results of Simulation—Sample 1

| (1) Frequency distribution of combined $I_1$ and $C_2$ (from Table 7–11, column 5) | | (2) Probability of sales of combined policies | (3) Weighted sales value column 1 × column 2 |
|---|---|---|---|
| Sales | Frequency | | |
| $100,000 | 4 | 4/20 = 0.20 | $ 20,000 |
| 150,000 | 9 | 9/20 = 0.35 | 52,500 |
| 200,000 | 6 | 6/20 = 0.30 | 60,000 |
| 250,000 | 1 | 1/20 = 0.05 | 12,500 |
| 300,000 | 0 | 0 = 0.00 | 0 |
| 350,000 | 0 | 0 = 0.10 | 0 |
| | | Expected sales | $145,000 |

TABLE 7–13. Conversion of Sales Results of Table 7–12 into Profitability Results

| (1) Sales (column 1 of Table 7–12) | (2) Profitability | (3) Probability (column 2 of Table 7–12) | (4) Weighted profitability column 2 × column 3 |
|---|---|---|---|
| $100,000 | −$ 5,000 | 0.20 | −$1,000 |
| 150,000 | 7,500 | 0.35 | 2,625 |
| 200,000 | 12,000 | 0.30 | 3,600 |
| 250,000 | 15,000 | 0.05 | 750 |
| 300,000 | 17,000 | 0.00 | 0 |
| 350,000 | 18,000 | 0.00 | 0 |
| | | Expected profitability | $5,975 |

TABLE 7–14. Random Number Table

| | | | | |
|---|---|---|---|---|
| 62 | 01 | 96 | 40 | 34 |
| 14 | 47 | 45 | 29 | 93 |
| 34 | 55 | 59 | 59 | 90 |
| 50 | 62 | 54 | 38 | 95 |
| 73 | 34 | 40 | 69 | 57 |
| 82 | 83 | 84 | 42 | 18 |
| 32 | 36 | 48 | 38 | 84 |
| 46 | 10 | 69 | 89 | 03 |
| 29 | 29 | 01 | 79 | 44 |
| 88 | 93 | 49 | 34 | 16 |
| 52 | 63 | 92 | 12 | 60 |
| 82 | 57 | 01 | 68 | 22 |
| 31 | 13 | 31 | 70 | 45 |
| 61 | 66 | 54 | 91 | 54 |
| 70 | 42 | 94 | 37 | 10 |
| 18 | 52 | 49 | 89 | 09 |
| 63 | 79 | 83 | 93 | 95 |
| 62 | 30 | 69 | 79 | 44 |
| 22 | 28 | 59 | 54 | 72 |
| 19 | 89 | 38 | 88 | 07 |

# PART THREE

# Profitability, Risk, and the Financial Environment

*

# 8

# Profit Planning and Control

Unexpected events can be fatal. At a minimum they are disruptive and usually bring losses. When the unexpected event occurs, there is often no "right" decision. The question at that late date is, how do we minimize our losses? Profit planning and sales forecasting, the basis of projecting the firm's financial requirements, can help avoid this predicament.

A study of the firm's financial statements not only provides a picture of its current position but also a clue to its future condition. In addition to statements, our tools include economic environmental analysis, moving average and exponential smoothing, regression analysis, break-even analysis, *pro forma* financial statements, and flexible budgeting. Although the cash budget is designed to assist management in meeting its liquid asset requirements, sales forecasting and profit planning relate to the need to generate profit and to forecasting the firm's future financial requirements.

Planning for profit requires that we forecast sales. We must know the various possible levels of sales and the resultant profitability in order to determine the "right" level of plant operation—how many units of each product to produce over a given time horizon—to earn an optimal profit. A tool frequently applied in profit planning, given a sales forecast, is break-even analysis. In Chapter 4 we introduced break-even analysis to examine the concepts of operating and financial leverage. Here we use break-even analysis to decide on the products and the number of units of each product to offer for sale.

Once the plans have been set and production begins, management must know the progress of the firm. The system of control provides this information.

To produce the variety of products and the different quantities of each to satisfy the anticipated sales demand requires a particular level and mix of assets: cash, receivables, inventory, fixed assets. This asset need must be financed. If sales are not expected to expand in the next period, the firm's existing stock of assets is probably adequate to carry out its production plans. Any needed small additions to assets can be financed by earnings of the period not paid out in dividends, but, if sales are expected to increase substantially, the firm then faces substantial asset and financing needs.

Proceeding from the sales and profit forecasts, the level of the financing needs of the firm can be planned. With such a forecast the financial manager can arrange both the amounts and the sources to supply the needed funds. Forward planning of this type reduces the risk of the firm, raises investor confidence, and increases the market value of the firm.

### Sales Forecasting

By forecasting we mean determining the effect that external and internal factors will have on the firm's sales and, hence, on its asset requirements. One method of environmental analysis involves determining some outside economic indicator that bears a close relation to and anticipates our sales. Knowing the level and trend of the economic indicator, we can forecast the *industry's* sales volume and prices with some reliability. Examples of economic environmental analysis are a building products manufacturer studying the supply of housing funds and family formations and a meat packer studying corn acreage plantings. But the industry forecast then forms the input to a forecast of our *company's* market share (if we have the capacity), our costs, and ultimately our profit.

### Profit Planning and Control

Actively planning for profits means aggressively adjusting the activities of the firm, such as shifting the product mix to meet anticipated external factors. Establishment of sales targets and cost limits is essential. These provide the guidelines for action and a control of performance. If actual sales and costs vary widely from the target figures, management must inquire into the reasons. Significant variations do occur and may be justified. To provide control and permit the information feedback mechanism to operate, it is important to reconcile promptly the budgeted with the actual figures. A flow of reports must be fed back to the decision makers, who are then in a position to revise decisions.

## PROFIT PLANNING THROUGH BREAK-EVEN ANALYSIS

Break-even analysis rests on the fact that some costs vary with production, while others remain fixed. When fixed costs are present, a firm will incur losses up to that minimum unit volume of sales that covers fixed costs. We seek a plan for operation above the break-even point.

### Operating under Conditions of Capacity Sales

Determination of a production schedule for available equipment when demand is sufficient to keep the plant operating at capacity is a simple matter. For example, in a high-fashion fabric-weaving plant, the mix of types of cloth to produce depends on the profit margin over variable cost that will be earned per hour of plant operation. The fabrics that promise the highest profits will be selected. A decision to switch from one fabric to another must take into consideration, in addition to earnings, the need for special equipment, the probability of the continuation of the earnings differential among the various types of fabric, and the effect of production changes on the firm's relations with its customers and suppliers. The financial manager in these favorable circumstances focuses on maintaining sufficient liquidity and keeping lines of credit open to the firm's banks.

### Operating at Less Than Capacity

The nature of profit planning changes when the firm is operating at less than capacity. The management of a paper mill, for example, meeting substantial competition from similar products being sold at lower prices has a number of options. Management might seek to discover new uses for its paper products, develop ways of making the product cheaper, or improve the product so it commands the necessary premium over the competitive item. Should none of these alternatives appear promising, management will be confronted with a major policy decision that will influence significantly the level of plant operations. The courses of action open are to reduce the price of the product, increase promotion and selling pressures, or to withdraw from the more competitive parts of the market by raising prices. The financial manager will seek the most profitable balance between price of the product, sales volume, and cost of production. For assistance he may turn to a study of the firm's cost-volume-profit relationships.

### Profit Planning through Break-even Analysis: An Example

Blue Light, Inc., manufactures a special-effects bulb that sells for \$2. The firm normally sells 100,000 of these bulbs per year and earns a net operating income (NOI) of \$30,000. Net operating income is income after operating costs but before income taxes.

Evidence of price-cutting in Blue Light's industry abounds. We are asked to estimate the combinations of selling price and volume necessary to maintain the existing net operating income level.

Table 8–1 shows the sales necessary to earn the target NOI should increasing competition dictate price reductions of 10 or 20 percent. Table 8–1 also indicates how much less need be sold if prices could be raised and certain sections of the market abandoned. Starting with these data, recommendations can be made regarding production levels, financing requirements, sales campaigns, and advertising budgets. Figure 8–1 casts the data in graphic form.

TABLE 8–1. Blue Light, Inc.
Sales, Cost, and Profit Estimates

| *Basic data* | *Price decrease* 20% | *Price decrease* 10% | *Current price* | *Price increase* 10% | *Price increase* 20% |
|---|---|---|---|---|---|
| Sales, units | 166,667 | 125,000 | 100,000 | 83,333 | 71,429 |
| Unit price | $1.60 | $1.80 | $2.00 | $2.20 | $2.40 |
| Sales, dollars | $266,667 | $225,000 | $200,000 | $183,333 | $171,429 |
| Variable costs, $1 per unit | 166,667 | 125,000 | 100,000 | 83,333 | 71,429 |
| Fixed costs | 70,000 | 70,000 | 70,000 | 70,000 | 70,000 |
| Total costs | $236,667 | $195,000 | $170,000 | $153,000 | $141,429 |
| Target net operating income | $ 30,000 | $ 30,000 | $ 30,000 | $ 30,000 | $ 30,000 |

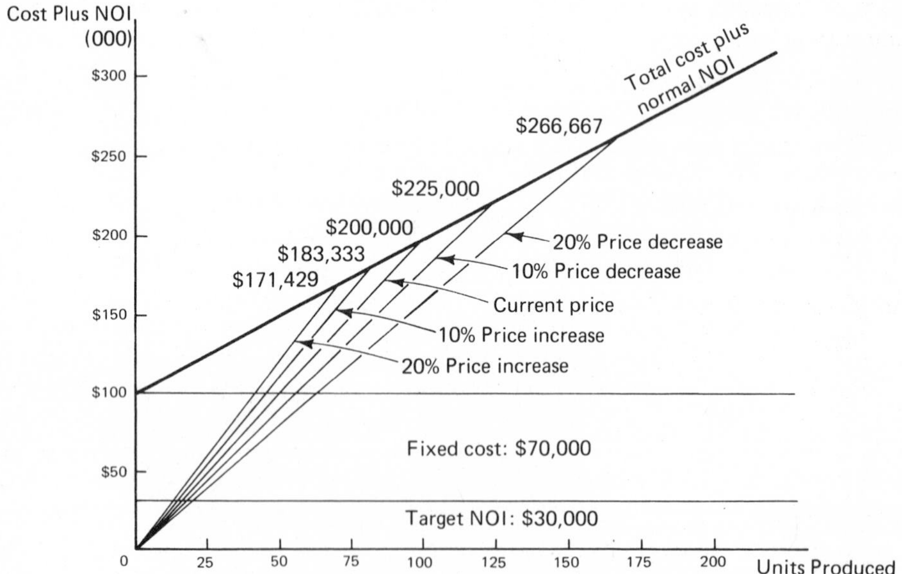


Figure 8–1 Blue Light, Inc. Volume required to yield target net operating income at various selling prices.

## Limitations of Break-even Analysis

Break-even analysis is easy to comprehend and useful in understanding the operating characteristics of a firm, but, its practical application in the real world as a method of predicting profit suffers from several limitations.

*First,* linear analysis assumes an unlimited demand for the firm's product at a fixed price and constant returns to scale. Actually, the number of units sold usually is a function of price. Furthermore, within a given range of output, the firm may experience economies of scale (declining variable cost per unit), and within another range, diseconomies of scale (rising variable cost per unit). This limitation and the demand assumption can both be overcome by using curvelinear relationships in break-even analysis.

*Second,* break-even analysis requires a strict classification of all costs into fixed and variable. But, in practice many costs are semivariable—that is, part fixed and part variable. A major judgmental element must then be applied to separate each of these costs into the fixed and variable portions. In addition, once all costs have been classified, it is assumed that the costs remain invariant over the relevant range. If the range is not wide, this may be true. But, if the firm, for example, is operating near capacity and considers bringing back into production a currently idle marginal plant, the assumption will not hold. This limitation can be met by establishing discontinuities in the relationship.

*Third,* the analysis assumes either a single product or an invariant product mix in the case of a multiple product firm. For the multiple product case the alternative of preparing a separate break-even analysis for each product or for various product mixes comes to mind. In practice the difficulty of allocating expenses common to several products may be insurmountable.

*Fourth,* obtaining the information inputs for the break-even analysis typically starts with an analysis of *historical* data. If the firm's operating configuration (decisions on prices, costs, products, volume) remains fairly stable from one planning horizon to the next, the information inputs may be based directly on the historical data. But, if the firm operates in a dynamic environment, the historical data may only roughly represent future conditions. Here major reliance on judgment is required to determine the necessary information inputs to the break-even analysis.

*Fifth,* the planning horizon for break-even analysis is short and reflects the status quo. Activities such as capital improvements and research and development that bring benefits over the longer term may not be reflected in a short-term horizon break-even analysis. And yet these long-term planning activities are the very activities vital to the long-run survival of the firm.

*Sixth,* the analysis assumes profits are a simple residual, but in the short-run profits are controllable to a considerable degree by management. There is wide latitude for manipulating the amount and timing of numerous operating costs related to past or future production and sale. Further, management pressure for efficient operation is not constant and profits will vary with the intensity of its drive to attain the least cost combination.

## FLEXIBLE (VARIABLE) BUDGETS

A budget is any formalized quantitative plan for allocating the firm's resources in a future period. A *fixed budget* is a plan containing revenue, production, and cost figures designed to meet a target level of output, say 100,000 units. A *flexible budget* is prepared for a range of activity and focuses on efficiency of operation. For a given level of operations, the flexible budget tells management what the costs will be. The actual performance of the firm will be influenced by external events over which management has little control and by the efficiency with which the firm operates in the budgeted range of activity.

Preparation of a flexible budget requires a sales forecast, a detailed classification of all costs, their separation into fixed and variable, and the establishment of responsibility (cost) centers. The centers permit grouping of costs and the assignment of each center to a manager for control. After assignment to a center, the controllable expenses are related to some measure of productive activity. Various yardsticks used include machine hours, direct labor hours, direct material costs, and units of output. With costs separated into fixed and variable, total costs for a given volume within the range budgeted by management may be computed.

Large firms have extended the idea of responsibility accounting by establishing investment centers that correspond to the divisions of the firm. For example, a large firm with a truck division, a farm equipment division, and a construction equipment division may designate each of these as an investment center. Each division has its own invested capital, is responsible for revenue and expenses, and its performance is measured by relating its net operating income to its invested capital. At the end of the period the budgeted amount is compared with the actual. If wide variations occur reasons are sought. The variation may have resulted because actual production differed widely from what had been budgeted.

Knowing why less was expended than budgeted is as important as knowing why more was spent. Perhaps savings are being accomplished at the expense of future operations through skimpy maintenance or inadequate staffing. The individual responsible for the center could be mistakenly rewarded if bonuses are based solely on currently measured efficiency for his department performance would be overstated.

Prompt feedback of information is necessary to make the flexible budgeting system work. The objective is to keep the actual in line with the budgeted. Once the actual is determined, the process of interpreting the variance from the actual should begin. When the cause of the variance is determined the information should flow back to those responsible for planning operations. The budget for the succeeding period may then incorporate the new information. The financial manager must take care not to overreact to every discrepancy between the actual and the budgeted. Only significant discrepancies should result in budget changes. Separation of significant from random discrepancies is an art and difficult at best.

## SALES FORECASTING SYSTEMS

The sales forecast is crucial to budgeting. From the sales forecast follows the estimate of cost of goods sold and decisions concerning inventory levels, purchases of raw materials, employment level, distribution and selling expenses, administrative and general expenses and financial requirements. These activities of purchasing, producing, selling, and administering are separate but must be planned as a system in relation to the sales forecast.

### Trend Extrapolation

To illustrate trend extrapolation—the use of a sales forecast to estimate future financial requirements, consider the data in Table 8–2 concerning actual sales, inventory, and inventory as a percent of sales figures for the period 1968–1972, and the target inventory requirement for 1977.

**TABLE 8–2. Relation between Inventory and Sales for a Firm in the Electrical Equipment Industry**

| Year | Sales | Inventory | Inventory as a percent of sales |
|---|---|---|---|
| 1968 | $100,000 | $35,000 | 35% |
| 1969 | 130,000 | 36,500 | 28 |
| 1970 | 160,000 | 38,400 | 24 |
| 1971 | 200,000 | 40,000 | 20 |
| 1972 | 250,000 | 42,500 | 17 |
| 1973 | — | — | — |
| 1974 | — | — | — |
| 1975 | — | — | — |
| 1976 | — | — | — |
| 1977 (estimated) | 600,000 | 60,000 | 10 |

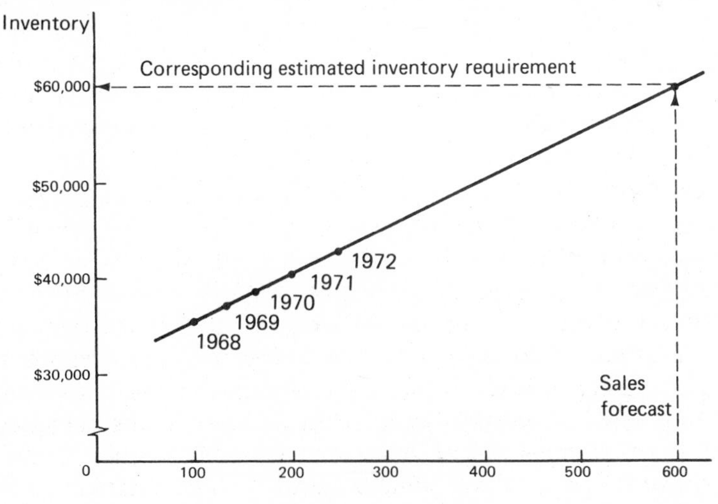


Figure 8–2 * Scatter diagram illustrating relation between sales and inventory.

* Based on table 8–2.

In Figure 8–2 the data of Table 8–2 are plotted on a scatter diagram and a freehand line fitted. Reading across the ordinate we obtain the estimated level of $60,000 inventory for 1977 estimated sales of $600,000. This is extrapolation of the historical pattern into the future. Trend extrapolation is the simplest forecasting practice. But extrapolation will never foretell the turn away from a trend.

### Moving Average

Another simple system used to make sales forecasts is the *moving average.* This system requires taking the most recent $n$ observations, where $n$ is a constant number, and calculating the average. The average is then taken as the forecast for the following period. For example, assume Delta Enterprises has experienced weekly unit demand $w_i$ for the previous five weeks, as given in Table 8–3. The average of the five observations and the forecast for the following week's demand, $F$, would be

TABLE 8–3. Delta Enterprises
Weekly Demand for Electronic Units

| *Week* $w_i$ | *Sales units* |
|---|---|
| $w_1$ | 1430 |
| $w_2$ | 1460 |
| $w_3$ | 1450 |
| $w_4$ | 1490 |
| $w_5$ | 1470 |

$$F = \frac{1}{n}\left(\sum_{i=1}^{n} w_i\right)$$

$$= \tfrac{1}{5}(7300) = 1460$$

Suppose that the actual demand for the sixth week, $w_6$, equals 1480 units. The demand was underestimated by 20 units $(1480 - 1460)$. This deviation may be meaningful or it may be random, that is, not produced by any systematic causes. Prompt feedback of the information permits early detection of any change in the factors generating the demand.

Examination of the data might reveal a new trend. To recognize this possibility, we can give greater weight to the more recent values. The moving average system, though adequate in a slowly changing situation, does not perform well under dynamic conditions. The impact of the more distant data could be eliminated by employing only the most recent observations, or we can weight recent values more heavily.

### Exponential Smoothing

In *exponential smoothing,* observations are weighted according to their age. Some weight is given even remote observations, but greater weight is given the more recent ones. The assumption is that more recent data have the greater relevance.

Exponential smoothing is initiated with a beginning forecast not prepared by exponential smoothing. The actual sales of this period are compared with the forecast and the difference weighted by a smoothing constant, designated by $\alpha$ (alpha), which is usually a value between 0 and 1. The weighting may be called *discounting* since only a fraction of the change from the prior period is recognized. The discounted difference is then added to the old forecast and the sum becomes the forecast for the next period.

If we let

$F_n$ = forecast made in the $n$th period for sales in the $n + 1$ period

$F_{n-1}$ = forecast made in the $n - 1$ period of sales in the $n$th period

$S_n$ = sales in the $n$th period

$\alpha$ = smoothing constant

we can write the new forecast as

$$F_n = F_{n-1} + \alpha(S_n - F_{n-1}) \quad (8\text{–}1)$$

Rearranging terms,

$$F_n = \alpha(S_n) + F_{n-1}(1 - \alpha) \quad (8\text{–}2)$$

The forecast $F_n$ for the next period is based on the forecast $F_{n-1}$ for the current period, the actual realized sales $S_n$, and the smoothing constant $\alpha$. The next period forecast could also be based on more than one previous forecast and on more than one prior period's actual sales. For example, initially we might let the forecast made in the third period, $F_3$, for sales demand in the next or fourth period be based on the actual sales realized in the third period, $S_3$, and on the forecast of sales for the third period, which was made in the previous period two, $F_2$. Then, employing a smoothing constant $\alpha$, we can write

$$F_3 = \alpha(S_3) + F_2(1 - \alpha) \quad (8\text{–}3)$$

But since

$$F_2 = \alpha(S_2) + F_1(1 - \alpha) \quad (8\text{–}4)$$

$F_3$ then becomes [by substituting Eq. (8–4) into Eq. (8–3)]

$$F_3 = \alpha(S_3) + (1 - \alpha)[\alpha(S_2) + F_1(1 - \alpha)] \quad (8\text{–}5)$$

$$= \alpha(S_3) + \alpha(S_2)(1 - \alpha) + F_1(1 - \alpha)^2 \quad (8\text{–}6)$$

Continuing, since

$$F_1 = \alpha(S_1) + F_0(1 - \alpha) \quad (8\text{–}7)$$

$F_3$ becomes [by substituting Eq. (8–7) into Eq. (8–6)]

$$F_3 = \alpha(S_3) + \alpha(S_2)(1 - \alpha) + \alpha(S_1)(1 - \alpha)^2 + F_0(1 - \alpha)^3 \quad (8\text{–}8)$$

Note $F_0$ is the initial forecast and not prepared by exponential smoothing but might be based on a previous moving average sequence, or might be the latest realized figure, or might be determined subjectively.

Generally, to determine the forecast in the $n$th period we can write

$$F_n = \alpha[(S_n) + S_{n-1}(1 - \alpha) + \cdots + (S_1)(1 - \alpha)^{n-1}] + F_0(1 - \alpha)^n. \quad (8\text{–}9)$$

The smoothing constant influences the weight accorded the older observation. The smaller the smoothing constant, the heavier the weight accorded the more distant data and the nearer the result will be to a simple moving average.

The smoothing constant may be selected by studying past sales data and determining the one that gives the best fit to the data. Normally, the smoothing constant selected will fall within the range $0.05 \leq \alpha \leq 0.30$. If the factors that generate sales demand are relatively stable, a small smoothing constant is appropriate. But whether the smoothing constant is large or small, the purpose of the system is to filter out random fluctuations. The assumption is that conditions generating sales demand are relatively stable and that any deviations from the moving average are random. If there appears a real shift developing in the process that generates sales demand, a switch to a large smoothing constant is desirable to obtain a faster response and to have the forecasts reflect more heavily the recent observations.

By observing the forecasting errors, changes in the process that generates sales demand can be detected. If no changes are taking place (the demand-generating factors are stable), the algebraic sum of the forecast errors should approach zero. Low forecast errors in some periods will be countered by high forecast errors in other periods. A growing sum of forecast errors indicates that conditions generating sales demand are undergoing a change. The smoothing constant being used should be examined and adjusted.

All three of the forecasting methods we have examined (trend extrapolation, moving average, and exponential smoothing) are classified as naive because they predict from the series itself.[1] More sophisticated methods such as regression analysis and simultaneous equation models involve identification of external variables determining the series being forecast.

#### Deviation Patterns

One of two patterns can occur throwing the exponential smoothing system off. A sudden spurt in demand that fades rapidly generates an

---

[1] R. K. Chisholm and G. R. Whitaker, Jr., *Forecasting Methods* (Homewood, Ill.: Richard D. Irwin, Inc., 1971), p. 8.

impulse pattern. A jump in sales demand to a new high level from which demand then continues to expand slowly generates a step pattern. When either of these patterns is detected adjustment of the α value is in order. Failure to recognize either the impulse or the step pattern will cause the forecasting system to yield the output shown in Figure 8–3.

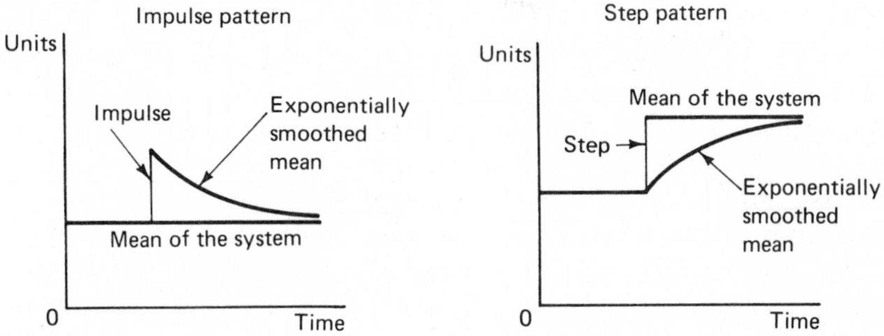


Figure 8–3 Delta Enterprise. Impact of a hypothetical impulse and step in weekly sales demand for electronic units on the output of the exponential smoothing forecasting system.

## CONTROL

One important part of financial management is review. In Chapters 3 and 4 we discussed financial ratios and showed how they could be used in combination to analyze the firm so no aspect of its operation gets out of balance. When using the flexible budget as an instrument of planning and control, other controls are available. One of these is the standard deviation.

After the budget is established, review and control are in order. Departure of actual costs from those budgeted will occur. Management requires some system for determining whether the departures warrant inquiry. The extremes are to investigate all departures or to investigate none. Some departures are too small; others are so large that they command inquiry. The limit may be either in terms of absolute size or in terms of relative magnitude. A probability test also has merit. We may be interested not only in the size of a given departure but also in the probability of its occurring.

Using a normal distribution, a simple system for signaling deviations that warrant inquiry can be developed.[2] To illustrate, assume Delta has budgeted $100,000 for the quarter for direct labor. This budgeted amount is a forecast. The actual amount spent will depart from this amount. The discrepancy may be caused by a shift in basic conditions (either internal to the firm or external) or by random events. To resolve this question we inquire into the probability of random departures of a given magnitude. Suppose we conclude there is a 50 percent chance that departures attributable to random events will approximate $10,000 or less. Now we

[2] If use of the normal curve is not justified, an alternative distribution can be adopted. The mechanics of the system are not altered by such substitution.

can evaluate the significance of any departure of the actual from the budgeted labor cost.

The estimate of a 50 percent chance that the actual will fall within $10,000 (either side) of the budgeted corresponds to a standard deviation of $15,000.[3] What is the probability that labor costs of, say $130,000 (a departure of $30,000 over budgeted) can occur randomly? Only 3 percent.[4] We would probably decide to inquire into the causes of the $30,000 deviation from the budget figure.

Since total variable cost changes with the level of production, the budgeted amount is not a fixed quantity in flexible budgeting but rather a variable amount. A fixed departure quantity then is not appropriate. A system of evaluating a departure must be used that ties the size of the departure to the level of production.

Assume in the case of Delta that the variability in production activity follows this relationship:

$$\sigma = \$15{,}000 + \$0.05x,$$

where $x$ is the difference between the actual unit volume of production and the expected level, and where $\sigma$ for the expected level is $15,000. If the actual and the budgeted coincide, $x = 0$; the problem remains as initially presented. As the actual increases over the budgeted, $\sigma$ will increase. For example:

| | Units |
|---|---|
| Actual production: | 120,000 |
| Normal production: | 100,000 |
| $x =$ | 20,000 |

$$\sigma = \$15{,}000 + \$0.05(20{,}000)$$

$$\sigma = \$16{,}000$$

Notice that we *independently* set $10,000 as the limit of random deviations that we would not investigate. There are two dangers in the control mechanism we just described. First, a deviation under $10,000 might be the sum of two significant deviations in opposite directions: a favorable deviation of $30,000 and an unfavorable deviation of $20,000, both of which would call for study. For example, the net deviation of $10,000 might have resulted from a 30 percent increase in output per manhour ($30,000/$100,000) and a 40 percent increase in overtime assuming overtime is paid a 50 percent premium. The production manager achieved

[3] A 50 percent chance that the actual amount will fall within $10,000 either side of the budgeted amount corresponds to $\pm\ \frac{2}{3}\sigma$ either side of the mean. If $\frac{2}{3}\sigma = \$10{,}000$, then $\sigma = \$15{,}000$.

[4] Using $z$ as the probability that costs will be between $130,000 and $100,000 we have $z = (\$130{,}000 - \$100{,}000)/\$15{,}000 = 2\sigma$. Since from a cumulative normal distribution table $2\sigma = 0.47$, then the probability that costs will randomly exceed $130,000 is $0.5 - 0.47 = 0.03$.

a $10,000 reduction in costs by firing a large part of the work force and going overtime with the balance of the force.

The second defect of this control mechanism is that it can stifle progress. We are implicitly judging our future performance by our past performance, but our past performance may have been very poor. With this control, as long as we do not get significantly poorer in performance, no investigation will result.

## *PRO FORMA* FINANCIAL STATEMENTS

*Pro forma* income statements and balance sheets provide management with a picture of the firm's profitability over the coming period and its financial condition at the end of the period, given certain assumptions. Management may also wish to plan operations over multiple periods of time, say five years. *Pro forma* statements involve estimating sales, expenses, profits, capital expenditures and other activities over each period and drawing up an income statement for the period and an ending balance sheet.

Two examples will illustrate planning for a single period and for multiple periods. The longer-range example highlights the need for maintaining control over the growth in cash, receivables, and inventory and fixed assets as sales rise. If the growth in these accounts is not controlled, an unnecessarily large amount of funds may be invested causing excessive financing and reducing the return on investment.

### Short-Term Planning

For the *pro forma* income statement we can obtain an estimate of sales from the moving average or exponential smoothing system. The direct raw materials and labor costs and the indirect manufacturing expense can be obtained from the flexible budget. Depreciation can be calculated from the plant and equipment figures and the applicable depreciation rates. The selling and administrative expense can be taken from the flexible budget.

The *pro forma* balance sheet figures that produce a forecast of financial requirements are estimated from the adjustments of the beginning balance sheet items using the *pro forma* income statement and cash budget. One simple way to obtain a forecast of new financial requirements is: (1) Identify the balance sheet items that will *vary with sales.* (2) Express each such item as a percent of sales. (3) Sum the percents on each side of the balance sheet and subtract the total credit (right-hand) percent from the total debit (left-hand) percent. The difference is the percent of each marginal dollar of sales that must be financed. (4) Then multiply the difference between the current sales level and the forecasted sales level by the percent found in (3). This is the amount of additional (or reduced) financing required.

To illustrate, assume the sales of Pastime Inc. are currently $2 million annually and are expected to go to $2.4 million next year. The firm is operating at economic capacity. How much additional financing is required to support the $400,000 higher sales level? Assume the relationship between the applicable balance sheet items and sales is directly proportional, and the firm earns 2 cents per dollar of sales and pays no dividend. Ignore income taxes.

Table 8–4 shows the applicable balance sheet items as a percent of current sales.

TABLE 8–4. Pastime Inc.
Balance Sheet Items as a Percent of $2 Million of Sales

| Assets | | Liabilities and Net Worth | |
|---|---|---|---|
| Cash | 3.0% | Accounts payable | 6.0% |
| Receivables | 7.0 | Accrued wages | 4.0 |
| Inventory | 10.0 | Common stock | na |
| Fixed assets (net of depreciation) | 15.0 | Retained earnings | na |
| | 35.0% | | 10.0% |

na = not applicable.

From Table 8–4 we see that for every marginal dollar increase in sales 35 cents of additional assets are required, of which 10 cents is financed by spontaneous sources of credit—thus 25 cents must be financed from external sources and profit from current operations. To support $400,000 of additional sales Pastime must obtain $100,000 ($400,000 × 25%) of "nonspontaneous" financing of which $48,000 is provided by current profit ($2.4 million × 2%).

To illustrate how this procedure can be used to indicate the possible internal financing, as well as total financing, requirement and the importance of maintaining control over working capital, consider a recently organized firm. The first cash that flows through the firm is supplied by owners. These funds, together with loans from the bank, finance most of the firm's initial fixed asset and working capital needs. The third source of funds is credit from suppliers for inventory purchases. The depreciation charge is in a limited sense a fourth source of funds. When the firm has been established, operating profits become an important source of capital to finance growth. Table 8–5 shows the opening balance sheet of Rainbow Tea Company.

TABLE 8–5. Rainbow Tea Company
Opening Balance Sheet
January 1, 1973

| Assets | | Liabilities and Net Worth | |
|---|---|---|---|
| Cash | $ 350 | Accounts payable | $ 150 |
| Inventory | 150 | Current liabilities | $ 150 |
| Total current assets | $ 500 | Common stock | $1350 |
| Plant and equipment | $1000 | | |
| Total assets | $1500 | Total liabilities and net worth | $1500 |

Assume the financial manager of the Rainbow Tea Company estimates sales, expenses, and profits for the first year, as shown in Table 8–6. Each item is expressed as a percent of sales. The net profit percent is used to estimate the firm's external financial requirements at the end of the period through indicating the amount of internal financing available. We assume the relationship between profit and sales is directly proportional.

The *pro forma* balance sheet for the end of the period (Table 8–7) shows the financial requirements: cash estimated at 3 percent of $5000 sales, receivables 30 days' sales (8 percent of sales), inventory 60 days (13 percent of sales), and accounts payable 36 days (8 percent of sales). Inventory and accounts payable are figured on the basis of cost of goods sold (COGS). Total plant and equipment is expected to remain at $1000, depreciation to rise by $50 and net worth to increase to $1500 from an opening figure of $1350. The difference or balancing item is a bank loan of $250. By showing estimated receivables, inventory, and payables in terms of turnover instead of just as percent of sales we can better evaluate the impact of changes in management efficiency on the financial requirements of the firm. We can conduct a sensitivity analysis showing the effect of changes in the turnover rates.

TABLE 8–6. Rainbow Tea Company
*Pro Forma* Profit and Loss Statement
January 1–December 31, 1973

| | | |
|---|---|---|
| Sales | $5000 | 100% |
| Cost of goods sold | 4000 | 80 |
| Gross profit | $1000 | 20 |
| Operating expenses | 700 | 14 |
| Profit before taxes | $ 300 | 6 |
| Taxes (50 percent rate) | 150 | 3 |
| Net profit | $ 150 | 3 |

TABLE 8–7. Rainbow Tea Company
*Pro Forma* Balance Sheet
December 31, 1973

| | | | | |
|---|---|---|---|---|
| Current assets | | | Current liabilities | |
| Cash (3 percent of sales) | | $ 150 | Accounts payable (10 ×, 36 days) | $ 400 |
| Accounts receivable (12 ×, 30 days)* | | 400 | Bank loan | 250 |
| Inventory (6 ×, 60 days)* | | 650 | | $ 650 |
| | | $1200 | | |
| Plant and equipment | $1000 | | Common stock | $1350 |
| Depreciation | 50 | $ 950 | Retained earnings | 150 |
| Total assets | | $2150 | Total liabilities and net worth | $2150 |

* Approximately.

The *pro forma* financial statements provide us with a picture of the impact of the expected production level during the coming period on the firm's financial requirements. As Table 8–5 shows, at the beginning of the period Rainbow Tea's assets totaled $1500, payables $150 and common stock $1350 with no bank loan. To support the $5000 sales results of Table 8–6, we would have total (asset) financial requirements of $2150. Since we have common stock of $1350 and payables of $150, we must raise $650. But $150 will be generated from retained earnings hence we must raise $500 externally either by an increase in the opening balance of $150 in payables or by a bank loan or both.

TABLE 8–8. Rainbow Tea Company
Five-Year Growth Pattern

| *Year* | *Sales* | *Net profit at 3 percent of sales* | *Plant and equipment at cost* | *Depreciation charged at 5 percent per annum* |
|---|---|---|---|---|
| 2 | $ 6,000 | $ 180 | $1,200 | $ 60 |
| 3 | 7,000 | 210 | 1,400 | 70 |
| 4 | 8,000 | 240 | 1,600 | 80 |
| 5 | 9,000 | 270 | 1,800 | 90 |
| 6 | 10,000 | 300 | 2,000 | 100 |
| Total | | $1,200 | | $400 |

## Long-Term Planning

Suppose after the first year's experience we are interested in looking five years ahead. The detailing of all expenditures to obtain a rough idea of the profitability and financial condition of the firm through estimating sales, profits, and plant and equipment requirements over the period is unnecessary. A simpler procedure is available.

Assume we expect sales to double during the next five years, plant and equipment purchases to keep pace with production output, net profits to continue at 3 percent of sales, and depreciation to be charged at 5 percent per annum. The five-year growth pattern of the firm appears in Table 8–8.

With a doubling of sales, receivables remaining at the 30-day level, inventory at the 60-day COGS level (COGS continuing at 80 percent of sales) and payables at the 36-day COGS level, the *pro forma* balance sheet of Rainbow Tea 5 years hence might appear as in Table 8–9. The expected retained earnings plus depreciation expense turn out to be almost enough to finance the expected growth. The bank loan need be increased only $200. The funds flow statement of Table 8–10 shows the detail.

TABLE 8–9. Rainbow Tea Company
*Pro Forma* Balance Sheet Five More Years Hence

| | | | | |
|---|---|---|---|---|
| Current assets | | | Current liabilities | |
| Cash (3 percent of sales) | | $ 300 | Accounts payable | |
| Accounts receivable | | | (10 ×, 36 days) | $ 800 |
| (12 ×, 30 days)* | | 800 | Bank loan | 450 |
| Inventory (6 ×, 60 days)* | | 1300 | | $1250 |
| | | $2400 | Common stock plus prior retained earnings | $1500 † |
| Plant and equipment | $2000 | | | |
| Depreciation | 450 | $1550 | New retained earnings | 1200 |
| Total assets | | $3950 | Total liabilities and net worth | $3950 |

* Approximately.
† From Table 8–7.

TABLE 8–10. Rainbow Tea Company
*Pro Forma* Funds Flow Statement for Five More Years

| *Additional funds required* | | *Additional funds provided* | |
|---|---|---|---|
| Cash | $ 150 | Accounts payable | $ 400 |
| Accounts receivable | 400 | Bank loan | 200 |
| Inventory | 650 | Retained earnings | 1200 |
| Plant and equipment | 1000 | Depreciation | 400 |
| Total funds required | $2200 | Total funds provided | $2200 |

Assume the management of Rainbow Tea wants to determine the effect on the financial requirements of the firm if a certain laxity in financial control were to creep in during the period. On a percentage basis assume receivables are allowed to rise and inventory to accumulate as sales increase. Table 8–11 indicates the effects of allowing receivables turnover to slow to 10 times or 36 days and inventory to 4 times or 90 days with COGS continuing at 80 percent of sales. To finance the expansion internally profits must reach $2100, or $900 above the planned $1200. If profits only reach the planned $1200 then the more than proportionate expansion of receivables and inventory will create a $900 deficit in funds. The funds flow statement of Table 8–12 points up the "deficit."

The situation would be further aggravated by any shrinkage in the profit margin. To the extent that retained earnings are reduced, the firm must resort to outside financing beyond that shown in Table 8–12.

TABLE 8–11. Rainbow Tea Company
*Pro Forma* Balance Sheet Five More Years Hence
(Lax Control)

| | | | | |
|---|---|---|---|---|
| Current assets | | | Current liabilities | |
| Cash (3 percent of sales) | | $ 300 | Accounts payable (10 ×, 36 days) | $ 800 |
| Accounts receivable (10 ×, 36 days) | | 1000 | Bank loan | 450 |
| Inventory (4 ×, 90 days) | | 2000 | | $1250 |
| | | $3300 | Common stock plus prior retained earnings | $1500 * |
| Plant and equipment | $2000 | | New retained earnings | 2100 |
| Depreciation | 450 | $1550 | | |
| Total assets | | $4850 | Total liabilities and net worth | $4850 |

* From Table 8–7.

TABLE 8–12. Rainbow Tea Company
Funds Flow Statement for Five More Years
(Lax Control)

| *Additional funds required* | | *Additional funds provided* | |
|---|---|---|---|
| Cash | $ 150 | Accounts payable | $ 400 |
| Accounts receivable | 600 | Bank loan | 200 |
| Inventory | 1350 | Profit | 1200 |
| Plant and equipment | 1000 | Depreciation | 400 |
| | | Additional funds necessary to finance the laxity | 900 * |
| Total funds required | $3100 | Total funds provided | $3100 |

* Either from external sources or retained earnings. See Table 8–11.

## SUMMARY

Planning and control are vital to a firm's long-run survival. Budgets provide management with a map of the road and serve as a standard of performance. Management can check the performance of the firm, evaluate the efficiency of operation, and modify its plans accordingly.

Break-even analysis is useful for profit planning. Postulating different selling prices, the financial manager can estimate the sales volume necessary to earn the planned net operating income. The element of risk can be accommodated by employing well-known statistical measures such as the standard deviation and the normal curve.

The crucial factor in budgeting is the sales forecast. Simple extrapolation, the moving average, and exponential smoothing are three naive methods of predicting sales. The moving average accords equal weight to each observation; exponential smoothing accords greater weight to the more recent events. The moving average performs well when the process that generates sales demand is changing slowly. Exponential smoothing is appropriate in a dynamic situation. But corrective action is required if an impulse or step is detected in the process that generates sales demand. All three of these methods are naive because each involves forecasting the series from itself.

Using *pro forma* financial statements management can estimate the profitability over the next period and the financial condition of the firm at the end of the period. If management is satisfied, the plans can be formalized and put into effect. Otherwise, new plans can be laid and the effect of the plans evaluated from a new set of *pro forma* statements.

### Study Questions

1. In the absence of adequate and reliable data, profit planning cannot be successful. Explain. In the absence of a mass of data in centuries past can we conclude that businessmen did not plan?
2. Why is it sometimes possible for a large firm to plan more successfully than a small firm? If a large firm were sufficiently influential to be able to modify its environment, how would its planning be improved?
3. The sales figure is the key figure in every forecast of operations level and profit. What guides would you use to estimate next year's sales for the following products: (a) baby carriages; (b) engagement rings; (c) automobiles; (d) mink coats; (e) earth-moving equipment?
4. How can break-even analysis assist in profit planning? Does the nature of the firm's operation influence its measure of profit planning success? How? Would lack of success invalidate the use of the break-even analysis in profit planning? Explain.
5. How does profit planning differ when a firm is operating at capacity and at less than capacity? Under which set of conditions is planning easier? Explain.
6. Uncertainty in a sales forecast can be recognized by thinking of the forecast for each product as a random variable. Explain. Why is this system superior to merely taking the best sales estimate?
7. Explain how the standard deviation can serve as a measure of the risk involved in marketing a particular product. How does a firm's attitude toward risk relate to the products it decides to promote?
8. A budget provides the firm not only with a glimpse of the future but also with a standard against which the firm's performance can be measured. Explain. Why is the prompt feedback of information regarding performance necessary for good control and improved decisions?
9. The moving average as a sales forecasting system is preferred in a slowly changing environment and exponential smoothing in a dynamic environment. Explain.
10. How can impulse and step patterns throw off a properly functioning exponential smoothing system?
11. How do projected income and balance sheet statements assist in financial planning? What do they provide that the budget does not? What are the dangers of relaxed control over accounts receivable and inventory?

### Problems

1. For the glamorous hostess the Fiesta Party Supply Company markets a disposable paper dress and napkins to match. The set is currently priced at $10

and Fiesta is selling 10,000 sets annually. Normal profit on the item before taxes is $10,000. Variable costs are $7 a set and fixed costs are $20,000. The possibility exists that competitive products may enter the market. The competition may fail, however.

a. Determine the sales volume required to maintain normal profit if the price were forced down to $7.50 a set; the sales volume required to maintain normal profit if prices could be raised to $13 a set. Supply the necessary figures in Table 8–13.

TABLE 8–13. Fiesta Party Supply Company
Sales, Cost, and Profit Estimates

| *Basic data* | *Price drop* | *Current price* | *Price increase* |
|---|---|---|---|
| Unit price | $ 7.50 | $ 10 | $ 13 |
| Required unit sales | — | 10,000 | — |
| Required dollar sales | — | $100,000 | — |
| Variable costs of $7 per unit | — | $ 70,000 | — |
| Fixed costs | $20,000 | $ 20,000 | $20,000 |
| Total costs | — | $ 90,000 | — |
| Normal profit | $10,000 | $ 10,000 | $10,000 |

b. After examining the data, how would you evaluate the significance of a forced price reduction to $7.50?

2. The Schnitzel Noodle Company had produced two brands of noodles, Super Fine and Common Ordinary, but because of limited production facilities only one brand can now be produced. The sales forecasts and their probability distribution are presented in Table 8–14. You are asked for recommendations.

a. The first step is to determine the expected sales level for each brand.

b. The next step is to determine the risk attached to marketing each product as measured by the standard deviation of the distribution, which you are asked to calculate.

c. Which brand has the highest sales potential? Which brand carries the greater risk? If Schnitzel Noodle were a risk-avoiding firm, which brand would it decide to produce?

d. Considering expected sales levels and risk and chance for high as well as as low sales, which brand would you recommend be produced?

TABLE 8–14. Schnitzel Noodle Company
Probability Distribution of Sales Estimates for Noodles

| *Possible sales level (pounds)* $x_i$ | *Super Fine* $p(x_i)$ | *Common Ordinary* $p(x_i)$ |
|---|---|---|
| 30,000 | 0.10 | 0.10 |
| 40,000 | 0.20 | 0.80 |
| 50,000 | 0.40 | 0.10 |
| 60,000 | 0.20 | |
| 70,000 | 0.10 | |

3. (Problem 1 continued.) Competition enters the party accessory field and Fiesta Party Supply is forced to reduce the price per paper dress and napkin set to $9. Variable costs remain at $7 and fixed costs at $26,000. The expected sales volume at the $9 price is 13,000 sets. The financial manager estimates that there is a 50 percent chance that sales will fall within 2000 units of present volume, which is equivalent to 0.68 standard deviations.

a. Determine the break-even point and the chance of Fiesta Party Supply at least breaking even.

b. What is the chance of Fiesta Party Supply selling 11,500 sets or more? What is the chance of the firm selling 8500 sets or less? What is the chance of the firm selling 15,000 sets or more?

4. Strohsack Baskets, Inc. wishes to install exponential smoothing into its sales forecasting system. The sales for the last 10 years have been selected for the purpose of determining a smoothing constant. The financial manager suggests a smoothing constant of 0.10, using the first period's sales and the initial forecast as a starting point. The opening forecast and the sales figures for the 10 years in units are given in Table 8–15.

TABLE 8–15. Strohsack Baskets, Inc.

Initial forecast: 10

| Year | Sales | Year | Sales |
|---|---|---|---|
| 1 | 11 | 6 | 11 |
| 2 | 10 | 7 | 12 |
| 3 | 11 | 8 | 14 |
| 4 | 13 | 9 | 12 |
| 5 | 12 | 10 | 13 |

a. Using the formula (with the terms defined as on p. 187)

$$F_n = \alpha(S_n) + F_{n-1}(1 - \alpha)$$

and a smoothing constant of 0.10, determine the forecasts for each of the years. Compare the forecasts with the actual sales figures and sum the deviations. Do the forecasts appear sensitive to the shift in sales?

b. Calculate the forecasts using a smoothing constant of 0.40. Compare the forecasts with the actual sales figures and sum the deviations. Do you find an improved fit?

5. The Ring-a-Ding Door Chime Company budgeted $40,000 per year for direct labor for the coming year. Sales are stable and the financial manager estimates that there exists a 50 percent chance that cost deviations attributable to random events will approximate $4000. At the end of the year actual labor cost figures total $58,000.

a. Would you recommend that the financial manager investigate the cause of the labor cost variation?

b. The next year sales are expected to climb sharply and, as a consequence, also labor costs. Instead of establishing a direct labor budget of $40,000 and a standard deviation of $6000, the following relationship is expected to hold, where $x$ is the difference between the actual unit volume of production and the expected normal production level:

$$\sigma = \$6{,}000 \pm \$0.20x$$

Normal production is 10,000 units. Production during the year rises to 15,000 units. With production up 50 percent, labor can also be expected to be up by 50 percent. Labor costs, however, rise to $63,500. What is the standard deviation at the higher level of production?

c. Does a labor figure of $63,500 warrant inquiry?

**6.** The sales of Molasses Inc. last year were $100,000. Sales for the current year are expected to rise 20 percent, to $120,000. The financial manager is asked to estimate the additional financing required to support the higher sales volume.

The recent balance sheet of the firm appears in Table 8–16.

TABLE 8–16. Molasses Inc.
Balance Sheet
December 31, 1972

| | | | |
|---|---|---|---|
| Cash | $ 5,000 | Accounts payable | $ 6,000 |
| Accounts receivable | 8,000 | Notes payable | 5,000 |
| Inventory | 15,000 | Bonds | 10,000 |
| | | Common stock | 15,000 |
| Fixed assets (net) | 32,000 | Retained earnings | 24,000 |
| Total assets | $60,000 | Total liabilities and net worth | $60,000 |

a. Observing that except for bonds, common stock, and retained earnings, the balance sheet items vary directly with sales, the financial manager asks that you express each such balance sheet item as a percent of last year's sales.

b. Estimate the total additional financing Molasses will require if sales go from $100,000 to $120,000.

c. Molasses earns a profit after income tax of 5 percent on sales and pays out 40 percent of its earnings in dividends. Income taxes are to be ignored. Determine the amount of additional external financing the firm will require to support sales of $120,000.

d. Construct a *pro forma* balance sheet as of December 31, 1973 based on sales of $120,000 for the year. As balancing items use "additional external financing needed," and "additional internal funds" under "retained earnings."

7. (Problem 6 continued.) Fiscal 1973 proves to be a good year. Sales of Molasses Inc. reach $125,000. The balance sheet of the firm at the close of the year appears in Table 8–17.

TABLE 8–17. Molasses Inc.
Balance Sheet
December 31, 1973

| | | | |
|---|---|---|---|
| Cash | $ 5,000 | Accounts payable | $10,000 |
| Accounts receivable | 12,500 | Notes payable | 15,500 |
| Inventory | 25,000 | Bonds | 10,000 |
| | | Common stock | 15,000 |
| Fixed assets (net) | 35,000 | Retained earnings | 27,000 |
| Total assets | $77,500 | Total liabilities and net worth | $77,500 |

a. Using the actual December 31, 1972 and December 31, 1973 balance sheets, compute each of the above balance sheet items as a percent of 1972 and 1973 sales, $100,000 and $125,000 respectively.

b. Given the estimated and actual 1973 sales figures, the *pro forma* and the actual December 31, 1973 balance sheets, and your answer to problem 7a, discuss the appropriateness of the percent-of-sales method of forecasting financial requirements.

### Selected References


Chambers, J. C., S. K. Mullick, and D. D. Smith, "How to Choose the Right Forecasting Technique," *Harvard Business Review,* 49 (July–August 1971), pp. 45–74.

Chisholm, R. K., and G. R. Whitaker, Jr., *Forecasting Methods.* Homewood, Ill.: Richard D. Irwin, Inc., 1971.

Dapuch, N., J. G. Birnberg, and J. Demski, "An Extension of Standard Cash Variance Analysis," *Accounting Review,* 42 (July 1967), pp. 526–536.

Jaedicke, R. K., and A. R. Robichek, "Cost-Volume-Profit Analysis under Conditions of Uncertainty," *Accounting Review,* 39 (October 1964), pp. 917–926.

Jensen, R. E., "A Multiple Regression Model for Cost Control—Assumptions and Limitations," *Accounting Review,* 42 (April 1967), pp. 265–273.

Morrison, T. A., and E. Kaczke, "A New Application of Calculus and Risk Analysis to Cost-Volume-Profit Changes," *Accounting Review,* 44 (April 1969), pp. 330–343.

Parker, G. C., and E. L. Segura, "How to Get a Better Forecast," *Harvard Business Review,* 49 (March–April 1971), pp. 99–109.


### Appendix H

## PROFIT PLANNING UNDER CONDITIONS OF RISK [5]

Our discussion of profit planning based on cost-volume-profit relationships has been in terms of certainty. We assumed the price, revenue, cost, and net operating income (NOI) figures would occur as predicted. In a dynamic business environment these figures are estimates. A firm may have little control over raw material prices and labor rates. It may have some control over product prices but frequently price is determined in the market place. The more standardized and competitive the product, the more nearly its price is determined in the market; the more unique the product, the closer the firm's pricing policy can approach cost plus profit. Cost and price forecasting can be undertaken with some confidence but estimates of dollar revenue (dependent on market share) are subject to larger errors. The following analysis focuses on the reliability of sales estimates. We abstract from reality by considering as certain: price, variable cost per unit, and fixed costs. Only revenue is treated as a risk-laden event.

### Quantifying Risk—The Certainty Equivalent Method

Though two products exhibit the same cost-volume-profit relationships, the financial manager can hardly be indifferent when the revenue estimate for one product is reliable and for the other the margin of error is large. Each product

[5] When conducting an analysis under conditions of risk it is assumed that the shape of the probability distribution is known. Under conditions of uncertainty little or nothing is known about the shape of the distribution.

has a different probability distribution attached to its sales forecast. One method of dealing with this problem is to develop certainty equivalents.

For example, assume Nifty Nities, Inc. produces two styles of sleep wear, "Daring" and "Reticent," having the same break-even point at 100,000 units and similar cost-volume relationships. Because of expanded demand and limited production facilities, a decision must be made to promote only one model. The financial manager develops the estimates of sales for each product and associated probabilities shown in Table 8–18. To determine the *expected* sales level of each product he multiplies each sales estimate by its probability. He seeks to maximize the expected value (or certainty equivalent) of the sales of his products, a goal consistent with the maximization of the market value of the firm. The higher expected sales level will produce the larger NOI, since both products have the same cost structure and break-even point, namely, 100,000 units. We assume the market will value the profits from both products on the same risk basis.

**TABLE 8–18. Nifty Nities, Inc.**

**Probability Distribution of Sales Estimates for Sleep Wear Models**

| *Possible sales levels (units)* | *Daring* | | *Reticent* | |
|---|---|---|---|---|
| $x_i$ | $p(x_i)$ | $x_ip(x_i)$ | $p(x_i)$ | $x_ip(x_i)$ |
| 90,000 | 0.15 | 13,500 | 0.05 | 4,500 |
| 110,000 | 0.20 | 22,000 | 0.90 | 99,000 |
| 130,000 | 0.30 | 39,000 | 0.05 | 6,500 |
| 150,000 | 0.20 | 30,000 | — | — |
| 170,000 | 0.15 | 25,500 | — | — |
| | 1.00 | | 1.00 | |
| Expected (or mean) sales level $\mu$ | | 130,000 | | 110,000 |

## Risk-Return Trade-off

Table 8–18 indicates that expected (mean) unit sales are higher for the Daring model, indicating that product is to be preferred. But an examination of the probability distribution of each model reveals more dispersion for the Daring model. There is a substantial chance that the firm may sustain a loss on Daring. The distribution shows a 0.15 probability that only 90,000 Darings will be sold, 10,000 below the break-even point. Hence the attitude of the firm toward risk becomes important.

If the firm is a risk-taker,[6] the Daring model will likely be preferred. The expected sales and NOI are higher and there is the possibility of a high NOI because of the 0.35 probability that sales will be 150,000 units or more. A risk-averting firm would select the Reticent model. The firm can be quite certain that operations will be profitable though not highly profitable. Maximization of the expected sales value would not be the criterion. The objective might still be the maximization of the market value of the firm. But, the risk in this case would be thought to outweigh the prospects for additional income; that is, that the stock market would not value income from the product associated with greater risk as highly as that from the safe product. The likelihood that the firm will

[6] A risk-taker is a firm that prefers an obligation promising a 10 percent return with a 0.5 probability and a 1 percent return with 0.5 probability to an obligation promising a 5 percent return with certainty.

operate at a loss if it promotes the Reticent model is small. This can be seen through calculating the standard deviation, $\sigma$, which measures the dispersion of each of the two probability distributions. Dispersion is one measure of risk, a subject more fully developed in Chapter 10.

Table 8–19 shows the standard deviation for the Daring model is 25,300 units and for the Reticent model 6300 units. Assuming a normal distribution, the probability that the firm will lose money in selecting Daring ($D$) can be calculated by determining the chance of sales falling below 100,000 units:

$$z = \frac{\text{Break-even point of } D - \text{Expected value of } D}{\sigma_D}$$

$$= \frac{100{,}000 - 130{,}000}{25{,}300} = -1.19.\sigma$$

With a difference of 1.19$\sigma$ from the mean, there is a probability of 0.119 that Nifty Nities, Inc., will operate at or below the break-even point. From the mean to $-1.19$ standard deviations includes 38.10 percent of the area under the lower one-half of the normal curve, hence 11.90 percent of the area is in the one tail below 100,000.

**TABLE 8–19. Nifty Nities, Inc.**

**Computations of Standard Deviation for Sales Estimates of Sleepwear Models**

| *Possible sales levels* | | *Daring* | | *Reticent* | |
|---|---|---|---|---|---|
| (000) $x_i$ | (000,000) $(x_i)^2$ | $p(x_i)$ | (000,000) $x_i^2p(x_i)$ | $p(x_i)$ | (000,000) $x_i^2p(x_i)$ |
| 90 | 8,100 | 0.15 | 1,215 | 0.05 | 405 |
| 110 | 12,100 | 0.20 | 2,420 | 0.90 | 10,890 |
| 130 | 16,900 | 0.30 | 5,070 | 0.05 | 845 |
| 150 | 22,500 | 0.20 | 4,500 | — | — |
| 170 | 28,900 | 0.15 | 4,335 | — | — |
| | | 1.00 | 17,540 | 1.00 | 12,140 |

$\sigma_D^2 = \Sigma x_i^2 p_D(x_i) - (\mu_D)^2$
$= 17{,}540{,}000{,}000 - 16{,}900{,}000{,}000$
$= 640{,}000{,}000$
$\sigma_D = 25{,}300$ units

$\sigma_R^2 = \Sigma x_i^2 p_R(x_i) - (\mu_R)^2$
$= 12{,}140{,}000{,}000 - 12{,}100{,}000{,}000$
$= 40{,}000{,}000$
$\sigma_R = 6{,}300$ units

Examining Reticent we find

$$z = \frac{\text{Break-even point of } R - \text{Expected value of } R}{\sigma_R}$$

$$= \frac{100{,}000 - 110{,}000}{6{,}300} = -1.59\sigma$$

and $-1.59$ standard deviations results in a probability of 0.0559 that the firm will incur a loss.

If we assume that both Daring and Reticent sell for \$10 each with fixed costs equal to \$200,000 and variable costs equal to 80 percent of selling price, we can develop the profit picture shown in Table 8–20. The decision whether to produce the Daring or the Reticent model would depend on the manager's evaluation of the trade-off between return and risk. Daring has the higher expected sales level, 130,000 units and profit of $60,000 but for Reticent, 110,000 units and a profit of $22,000. However, the risk of loss for Daring is also higher—one chance in eight as against one chance in eighteen. If the firm were a risk-taker, it would decide to produce the Daring model; if the firm were a risk-avoider, it would produce the Reticent model.

**TABLE 8–20. Nifty Nities, Inc.**
**Cost-Volume-Profit Computations**

| Sales volume in units | Profit $x_i$ | Daring | | Reticent | |
|---|---|---|---|---|---|
| | | $p(x_i)$ | $x_ip(x_i)$ | $p(x_i)$ | $x_ip(x_i)$ |
| 90,000 | ($ 20,000) | 0.15 | ($ 3,000) | 0.05 | ($ 1,000) |
| 110,000 | 20,000 | 0.20 | 4,000 | 0.90 | 18,000 |
| 130,000 | 60,000 | 0.30 | 18,000 | 0.05 | 3,000 |
| 150,000 | 100,000 | 0.20 | 20,000 | — | — |
| 170,000 | 140,000 | 0.15 | 21,000 | — | — |
| | | 1.00 | $60,000 | 1.00 | $22,000 |

## Alternate Method of Handling Risk

In planning future operations we might proceed in a more direct manner than was followed in the Nifty Nities illustration. Instead of calculating the mean expected sales volume and the standard deviation as a measure of the dispersion for the products, we might estimate the expected sales volume and the odds of attaining this level. Knowing the break-even point and given these figures we can determine the relative amount of risk associated with each product.

Assume that the financial manager of Blue Light, Inc. would like an estimate of the profit possibilities if the $2 price is continued. Variable costs are $1 per unit and fixed costs $70,000. The break-even point in units can be found by dividing fixed cost by the difference between the selling price and variable cost:

$$\frac{\$70{,}000}{(\$2 - \$1)} = 70{,}000 \text{ units: break-even point}$$

The expected unit sales volume at $2 per unit is 90,000 units. Suppose that after substantial analysis the financial manager feels there is a 50 percent chance that the actual unit sales will fall within 30,000 units of the expected sales: 60,000 to 120,000 units. Examining a normal probability distribution table, we see that a 50 percent chance is equivalent to $\pm\ 0.67\sigma$. Thus the financial manager is estimating that the standard deviation of the distribution is 45,000 units. The expected earnings can be derived as follows.

Let $E(E)$ = expected earnings

$E(U)$ = expected unit sales

$p$ = price

$v$ = variable cost

$F$ = fixed cost

$\sigma_u$ = standard deviation of expected unit sales = 45,000 units

$\sigma_e$ = standard deviation of expected earnings

We have

$$E(E) = E(U)(p - v) - F$$
$$= 90{,}000(\$2 - \$1) - \$70{,}000$$
$$= \$20{,}000$$

The standard deviation of the earnings distribution ($\sigma_e$) can now be derived[7] by multiplying the standard deviation for the unit sales distribution by the margin of price over variable costs.

$$\sigma_e = \sigma_u(p - v)$$
$$= 45{,}000(\$2 - \$1)$$
$$= \$45{,}000$$

By this process we convert the unit sales figure to a dollar profit figure. Since the break-even profit is zero earnings, knowing the standard deviation of the earnings distribution and the expected sales and earning level, we can compute directly the probability that Blue Light will at least break-even:

$$z = \frac{0 - E(E)}{\sigma_e} = \frac{-\$20{,}000}{\$45{,}000} = -0.444$$

The $-0.444$ standard deviations means that 15.5 percent of the area under the normal curve is included between the expected earnings of \$20,000 and zero earnings.

Continuing, the financial manager might be interested in evaluating the probability that the firm would incur a loss of \$25,000 or more or a profit of \$42,500 or more. Utilizing the formulations presented above and consulting a cumulative probability table, we find the probability of a loss of \$25,000 or more equals

$$P\left[E < \frac{(-\$25{,}000) - E(E)}{\$45{,}000}\,\sigma_e\right]$$
$$= P[E < -1\sigma_e \text{ from the } E(E)]$$
$$= 1 - P[E > -1\sigma_e \text{ from the } E(E)]$$
$$= 1 - 0.8413 = 0.1587.$$

Proceeding along the same lines we find that the probability of a \$42,500 or more profit equals

$$P\left[E > \frac{\$42{,}500 - E(E)}{\$45{,}000}\,\sigma_e\right]$$
$$= P[E > \tfrac{1}{2}\sigma_e \text{ from the } E(E)]$$
$$= 1 - P[E < \tfrac{1}{2}\sigma_e \text{ from the } E(E)]$$
$$= 1 - 0.6915 = 0.3085$$

---

[7] We rely on the relation $\sigma_{ax} + {}_b = a\sigma_x$ where $x$ is a random variable, $a$ is a coefficient, $b$ is a constant, and $a > 0$.

# 9

# The Capital Budgeting System

The future success of a firm depends on decisions made in the present. Among the most important are those dealing with capital outlays expected to generate returns extending beyond one year. Such an investment requires a current cash outlay but the benefits, if any, are received in the future. Examples include land, plant, equipment—fixed assets. Less obvious examples include increase in permanent working capital, expenditures on advertising, and research and development. We employ the system of capital budgeting to carry out the planning of these expenditures.

Capital budgeting focuses on two decisions regarding any investment: (1) the initial accept-reject decision and (2) the priority of those projects passing the accept-reject test. The first test identifies those projects that meet the firm's standard of acceptability, such as earning a specified return on investment. The second test narrows the group of acceptable projects to those the firm is willing and able to adopt. The limiting factor may be the amount of funds the firm has available for investment.

Examples of capital budgeting problems include: Is it profitable to expand capacity for an established market? Is it profitable to acquire different equipment to enter a new market? If the answer to these questions is "Yes," then should we do both? Similarly, is it attractive to intensify our investment in the domestic market and to diversify overseas, and, if so, can we do both? If we cannot do both, which project should be approved? A series of correct capital budgeting decisions will strengthen the competitive power and the profitability of the firm. A series of wrong decisions will put the firm on a downhill slide of loss of markets and profits.

The concept underlying several systems the financial manager might use to select the right projects is the *time value of money*—the widely accepted view tha ta dollar received today has greater value than a dollar received tomorrow. The "right" projects are those contributing most to maximizing the value of the firm. The formulas dealing with the time value of money can be grouped under the heading of the mathematics of finance and are discussed in Appendix I at the end of this chapter.

The dollar is the unit of measure of the time value of money. Hence, our first step in capital budgeting is to estimate the cash flows required by a project and the subsequent inflows it will generate. There is a second reason for focusing on cash flows. Investment for future profitability requires cash. Plant and equipment are paid for in dollars. And just because the accountant reports a profit from past operations is no assurance that needed cash will be available unless we plan for it. However, we do not disregard the accounting records. The way the accountant handles certain items for tax purposes is of interest to us because the treatment affects the cash flows.

## CAPITAL EXPENDITURE DECISIONS

Capital expenditures differ from operating expenditures (materials, labor, services) in the time period when benefits of the expenditures are to be received. The one year demarcation line is an arbitrary convenience, as it coincides with the most common accounting period.

Fixed assets represent a large percent of total assets of many firms, as may be seen from Table 9–1. Thus for many firms the management of fixed assets is a major problem. The importance of this problem is escalated by the fact that fixed assets contribute directly to profits.

TABLE 9–1. Depreciable and Depletable Assets Less Accumulated Amortization and Depreciation as a Percent of Total Assets

| Industry group | Percent | Industry group | Percent |
|---|---|---|---|
| Total utilities | 77% | Agriculture, forestry, and fisheries | 30% |
| Total mining | 46 | Total retail trade | 19 |
| Total services | 45 | Total wholesale trade | 13 |
| Total manufacturing | 31 | Construction | 11 |

SOURCE: U. S. Treasury Department, Internal Revenue Service, *Statistics of Income, 1969 Corporation Income Tax Returns* (Washington, D.C.: Government Printing Office, 1973), pp. 14ff.

### Capital Budgeting and Maximization of Firm Value

To remain efficient and meet competition a firm must: (1) replace worn and antiquated equipment, (2) modernize and expand capacity for current and new products, and (3) make strategic investments such as the acquisition of an important supplier to the firm. Both the appropriateness and the timing of the investment can be improved by capital budgeting.

Capital budgeting decisions depend on correct income and cost estimates of the project, the availability and cost of capital, and a yardstick for measuring the risk of the project. The theoretical standard is the minimum return required by those currently interested in trading the firm's securities (traders at the margin).

The firm makes capital investments, and investors evaluate the risks and returns associated with the projects and price the firm's shares at what they consider the appropriate price-earnings ratio. When risk enters, neither management nor investors can be certain of the expected future benefits from a project.

The capital budget in a given year is composed of a number of projects. Though all projects may promise a return above the required minimum, the risks associated with some projects may either reinforce each other or offset those of others. The optimal capital budget is of such size and comprises that group of projects offering a risk-return package that maximizes the market value of the firm.

In sophisticated capital budgeting systems the attractiveness of a project is measured in terms of the marginal cost of capital of the firm and the riskiness of the project. The element of risk is considered in Chapter 10 and the risk-adjusted cost of capital in Chapter 15.[1]

Our conclusions in a sense will be suboptimal—a best solution in one area may result in a lower degree of attainment in some other area. Similarly, when considering the management of working capital we sought optimal decisions in each area (cash, receivables, inventory) without directly considering the impact of the decisions on the firm's return on investment and market value of its stock.

If the objective in each area were independent of the objectives in other areas we would not have this problem. But we know earnings cannot be pursued without considering risk, maturing obligations, and a host of other variables. Thus, we should integrate the objectives in all the decision areas and relate them to maximization of the value of the firm. But the present development of financial management does not permit total optimization. The number of variables and their interrelationships are still too numerous and complex, though progress is being

---

[1] In this chapter we focus on identifying optimal capital budgeting decisions and assume as given the minimum required rate of return. The effect of financing "mix" decisions (debt and equity) and dividend (pay out ratio) decisions, as well as the portfolio effect (the mating of offsetting risks), are considered in Chapters 15 and 16.

made.[2] In the interim we seek to include as many variables as possible in each separate decision-making process.

### Risks of Capital Expenditure Decisions

*Risk of Bankruptcy.* Some investment decisions typically involve large expenditures that commit a major portion of the firm's assets at one time. A few wrong decisions and the firm may be forced into bankruptcy.

Many firms have established procedures for generating capital expenditure proposals and evaluating their attractiveness. The information feedback system that monitors the success of projects assists management in improving its investment decisions, but the risk of a wrong decision remains high because many major investment decisions are unique. No backlog of similar decisions exists, and the transferability of experience from one project to another is uncertain.

*Impact on the Character of the Firm.* Significantly, the riskiest projects and those in which prior experience is most lacking are those determining the nature of the firm and which change its character with the passage of time. Examples include products produced, scale of operations, the decision to "go international," to enter other industries, or finally, to become a conglomerate, that is, a widely diversified firm.

*Loss of Flexibility.* The long life of fixed assets means that once a decision is made, it is not easily reversed—management has lost its flexibility. Misinvestment results in lost opportunity earnings; underinvestment means inefficient equipment, under capacity, and lost customers.

*Need to Forecast.* Fixed asset acquisition is directly related to future sales, cash flow, and profit expectations. A decision to acquire an asset that is going to last 10 years requires a 10-year forecast; a failure to forecast correctly will result in overinvestment or underinvestment. Such errors can sometimes be corrected, but only at considerable expense.

*Need to Raise Funds.* The funds required for a major project are not available automatically. Plans must be made to raise the large sums required. These plans may be laid several years in advance and may include an adjustment in the dividend policy and arrangements for outside financing. This entails risk in that management cannot know with certainty the effect of a change in dividend policy or financing method on the market price of the firm's common stock.

### Hurdle Rate and Capital Rationing

The minimum acceptable capital budgeting hurdle rate (cutoff rate) is that rate which leaves the value of the firm unchanged.

In practice, however, some firms follow a policy of paying modest dividends and reinvesting the remainder. The amount of retained earn-

[2] Important progress is being made in the use of computerized corporate financial planning models. See J. B. Boulden and E. S. Buffa, "Corporate Models: On-Line, Real-Time Systems," *Harvard Business Review*, 48 (July–August 1970), pp. 65–83, and G. W. Gershefski, "Building a Corporate Financial Model," *Harvard Business Review*, 47 (July–August 1969), pp. 61–72.

ings sets a budget ceiling or constraint on the funds to be invested during the coming period. These firms measure the rate of return on proposed investments, rank them, and select the most attractive to the point permitted by the available funds.

These firms are reluctant to engage in external financing (debt or equity). The risk is felt to outweigh the restriction on the growth potential of the firm.

Other firms strive to maximize the value of the firm, pressing to the limit where marginal return from the least attractive project just equals the marginal cost of the funds. They seek external financing if internal funds are not sufficient to finance all attractive projects. To do this requires both a yardstick to measure the rate of return from the project and a hurdle rate. We propose as the hurdle rate the marginal weighted current cost of capital when adjusted for risk. The case for this standard is presented in Chapter 15.

## PRESSURES FOR CAPITAL EXPENDITURES

### Changes in Costs

Great pressures for capital expenditures stem from increases in variable costs. An upward shift in input costs, such as wages, narrows profit margins and reduces earnings. The availability of a machine that will do the work of high-priced workers at lower cost motivates the firm to undertake the capital expenditure. Resistance to such an expenditure is reduced if the present machinery is fully depreciated, for then no book losses are incurred. Though capital expenditures mean higher fixed costs, the objective is to reduce total cost so that the old margin is restored or increased.

### New Production Methods

Adoption of new production methods by competitors who cut prices puts pressure on a firm to undertake capital expenditures. Fearful of a smaller market share and lower profits, management seeks ways to trim costs.

Sometimes the availability of improved equipment coincides with rising costs on old equipment that is less efficient and requires increasing repairs that slow production and increase costs, thus squeezing profits.

### New Products

New and improved products of competitors exert pressure for capital expenditures. Maintenance of market share is a point of pride with some managements. A quick and sometimes cheap way to penetrate a new market is to acquire control of a firm already in the field. But whether funds are expended to acquire new equipment or to acquire another firm in the field, an analysis of return on investment is required.

New products flowing from a firm's research department also create pressures for capital expenditures. Management wants to take advantage of attractive opportunities.

### Growth

Finally, the demand for the firm's current products may be growing so rapidly as to force the firm to operate above *economic* capacity. Costs at this level are high, and the firm will be under pressure to expand to meet demand and reduce cost.

Figure 9–1 shows the effect of substituting capital equipment for labor, expanding capacity, rising maintenance costs, and the introduction of new production methods by competitors on a firm's break-even point and fixed cost-variable cost relationship. The substitution of equipment $c_1$ for labor will result in higher fixed costs but lower total costs, $c_{10}$ and will lower the break-even point from $e_1$ to $e_{10}$. New production methods of competitors will result in a drop in total revenue, $r_2$, if the firm is forced to reduce price, and raise the break-even point from $e_1$ to $e_2$. Increasing maintenance cost will result in an increase in total costs, $c_3$, and raise the break-even point to $e_3$. Modernization of plant and equipment that results in an improved product salable at a higher price will raise the total revenue curve, $r_4$, and lower the break-even point to $e_4$.

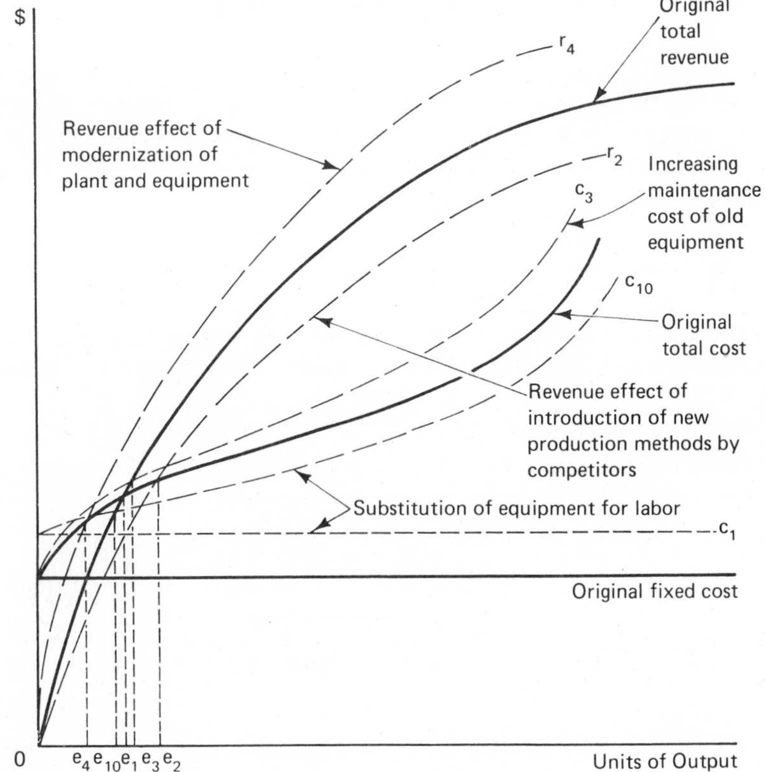


Figure 9–1 Effects of certain shifts on a firm's revenue and cost structure.

## EFFECT OF INCOME FLOW PATTERNS [3]

To illustrate the importance of the time pattern of cash flows, suppose we have two opportunities to invest $8300. One is the Bear Cat Oil Well; the other is the Desert Flat Gas Station. The first project is expected to realize a total of $10,000 over its 4-year life with no termination value; the second, $10,500. If both proposals promised a return of $2500 per year and we desired a 10 percent return, we would be indifferent between the investments and willing to buy both paying $7925 for each ($2,500 × 3.1699, the present value of $1 per year for 4 years discounted at 10 percent). But suppose the Bear Cat Oil Well is expected to produce annual cash returns of $4000, $3000, $2000, $1000 received at the end of each year and the Desert Flat Station, $1000, $2000, $3000, $4500 (Table 9–2).

TABLE 9–2. Bear Cat Oil Well versus Desert Flat Gas Station Value of Alternative Investments Based on the Discounting of the Income Streams at 10 Percent

| | Bear Cat Oil Well | | | Desert Flat Gas Station | | |
|---|---|---|---|---|---|---|
| Year | Cash inflow stream | Discount factor * | Discounted present value at 10% | Cash inflow stream | Discount factor * | Discounted present value at 10% |
| 1 | $ 4,000 | 0.9091 | $3,636.40 | $ 1,000 | 0.9091 | $ 909.10 |
| 2 | 3,000 | 0.8265 | 2,479.20 | 2,000 | 0.8265 | 1,652.80 |
| 3 | 2,000 | 0.7513 | 1,501.60 | 3,000 | 0.7513 | 2,253.90 |
| 4 | 1,000 | 0.6830 | 683.00 | 4,500 | 0.6830 | 3,073.50 |
| Total | $10,000 | | $8,300.20 | $10,500 | | $7,889.30 |

* Discount factors from Table A–1 at the back of the text.

What is the maximum price we should pay for each to earn a 10 percent return on our investment? That price is not more than $8300.20 for the oil well and not more than $7889.30 for the gas station. Paying $8300 for the oil well would yield 10 percent, but $8300 for the gas station would yield less than 10 percent, despite the added $500 received at the end of the fourth year.

[3] From this point on we assume the reader is familiar with the elementary mathematics of simple and compound interest and discounting as well as net present value. The appendix at the end of this chapter serves readers who seek review.

**PROBLEM OF THE HORIZON**

Much of the difficulty and dispute in capital budgeting centers in an area that can be called the "horizon problem". One view is that when an investment is made, the yield rate can only be determined by discounting the future income to eternity, including the income from the reinvestment of the funds as they are returned by the initial project. This is impractical. At any time the investor may decide to stop being an investor and consume the funds as they are returned by the initial project. If the investor does this, the only rate of return there can be is that determined by the discounted funds received from the project less the cost.

Another view is that when the future income of a project is discounted to establish the rate of return, we necessarily imply that the funds returned by the project are reinvested at the project rate. This also is an impractical approach. For example, suppose we invest in a real estate development project. Here the typical investing group is formed for this project only. As time goes by we receive income and principal repayments until all the lots are sold. The investing group then separates, each going his own way. Again, the only rate of return there can be is that determined by discounted future income from the project less the cost.

However, there are situations in which a firm undertakes expansion by more or less permanently committing an increase in funds that will first be invested in one project and later in other projects. Should the rate of return computed by discounting future income of the first project be considered as implying that the returned funds earn the same rate as the project rate? This raises several practical points.

If it is true that the increase of the firm's investment is permanent and if it is true that the first project is unusually good and that future projects using the returned funds cannot be expected to be that good, then the appropriate technique is to compound all funds as they return from the first project at the rate expected of future projects and to compound these returned funds to the expected termination date of the first project. The total *termination value* of all compounded returned funds is then discounted back to the inception date to get the rate of return of the first project. In this way we recognize that there is a "penalty" attached to the first project. Computed by the usual discounting method, the rate of return might be 15 percent, but future projects may be expected to earn only 10 percent and, hence, the earning on the returned funds will be 10 percent and the *average* earning of all funds (this project plus returned funds invested in future projects) will be more than 10 percent but less than 15 percent.

To illustrate, suppose that in the case of Bear Cat Oil Well and Desert Flat Gas Station (Table 9–2) the only alternative investment opportunity we have is 3 percent bonds. Then we could analyze the situation as in Table 9–3.

TABLE 9–3. Bear Cat Oil Well and Desert Flat Gas Station Where Future Opportunity Is Only 3 Percent Bonds

| | Bear Cat Oil Well | | | Desert Flat Gas Station | | |
|---|---|---|---|---|---|---|
| Year | Cash inflow stream * | Interest factor | Compounded at 3% to end of year 4 | Cash inflow stream * | Interest factor | Compounded at 3% to end of year 4 |
| 1 | $ 4,000 | 1.093 | $ 4,372 | $ 1,000 | 1.093 | $ 1,093 |
| 2 | 3,000 | 1.061 | 3,183 | 2,000 | 1.061 | 2,122 |
| 3 | 2,000 | 1.030 | 2,060 | 3,000 | 1.030 | 3,090 |
| 4 | 1,000 | 1.000 | 1,000 | 4,500 | 1.000 | 4,500 |
| Total | $10,000 | | $10,615 | $10,500 | | $10,805 |
| Discounted at 6% | | | 8,408† | | | 8,559† |
| Cost | $ 8,300 | | | $ 8,300 | | |

* Inflow assumed received at end of each year.
† Indicated rate of return obtained by discounting back is slightly over 6 percent in each case but greater for Desert Flat. Computed by taking 6 percent discount factor from Table A–1 at the back of the text at end of year 4, which is 0.79209 times $10,615 and $10,805 which produces $8408 and $8559.

[A9825]

In our earlier analysis (Table 9–2), Bear Cat Oil Well is preferred, because the cash inflow comes earlier, but this conclusion assumes we have another 10 percent investment available. However, in Table 9–3 Desert Flat Gas Station is preferable—exactly because the cash is returned later. It is preferable to have the apparently lower yield investment outstanding longer when the reinvestment alternative is 3 percent.

A word of caution is in order. If we apply the method just illustrated to a 2 percent project and the reinvested funds can earn 10 percent, the method will make the 2 percent investment show a higher figure than 2 percent. The average earning of the funds (over the original project plus reinvestment) will be higher than 2 percent because of the higher reinvestment rate.

These simple illustrations bring out clearly that the assumed conditions and alternatives are vital to capital budgeting analysis. What we seek is selection of the best alternative. What the rate of return of a project is depends on the assumptions.

Because of the necessity of assumed conditions and extending those conditions far into the future, most firms are not willing to make decisions based solely on an analysis of rate of return to the end of the "normal" life of the project, but make a series of analyses assuming the project is terminated at various points in time, such as at the end of 3 years, 5 years, and so on. This involves estimating the termination value (a better term is "resale value") of the project at each such termination date and including the termination value in the computation.

## WHEN SHOULD A PROJECT BE TERMINATED? [4]

Investment projects frequently have significant termination or *abandonment value.* The problem then is *when* to terminate or liquidate. It is wrong to assume that the optimal holding period is the "normal" life of a project.

Termination considerations suffer from the same lack of certainty as do all aspects of capital budgeting. Seldom is the termination value of a project known with certainty over its life.

Assume our firm has a 12 percent cost of capital and can regularly reinvest all available funds in projects yielding at least this minimum rate. Assume further that all projects, present and proposed, have the same risk. The adoption of any project does not change the business risk complexion of the firm. Also assume the project, whose data we will analyze in Table 9–4, entails an instant cash outlay, that the different cash recovery upon termination is instantaneous at the end of each year, and that the $1000 periodic cash inflows occur at year's end.

TABLE 9–4. Analysis of Termination Problem

| Project Data: | | | End at Years | | | | |
|---|---|---|---|---|---|---|---|
| Time | | 0 | 1 | 2 | 3 | 4 | 5 |
| Cash flows other than termination value | | − $3500 * | $1000 | $1000 | $1000 | $1000 | $1000 |
| Termination value | | — | 3100 | 2600 | 2000 | 1100 | 0 |

| Computations: Cash flows other than termination value | | Discount factor ‡ | Present value of project at 12% at time 0† if project terminated at end of year 1 | 2 | 3 | 4 | 5 |
|---|---|---|---|---|---|---|---|
| Year 1 | $1000 | 0.893 | $ 893 | $ 893 | $ 893 | $ 893 | $ 893 |
| Year 2 | 1000 | 0.797 | | 797 | 797 | 797 | 797 |
| Year 3 | 1000 | 0.712 | | | 712 | 712 | 712 |
| Year 4 | 1000 | 0.636 | | | | 636 | 636 |
| Year 5 | 1000 | 0.567 | | | | | 567 |
| Discounted termination value | | | 2768 | 2072 | 1424 | 700 | — |
| Total present value | | | 3661 | 3762 | 3826 | 3738 | 3605 |
| Cash outflow | | 1.000 | − $3500 | − $3500 | − $3500 | − $3500 | − $3500 |
| NPV of project at time 0 | | | $ 161 | $ 262 | $ 326 | $ 238 | $ 105 |

* Project cost.
† Considering separately the periodic cash inflows and the termination value of the project.
‡ Rounded. Applied to cost of project, periodic income, and termination value.

[A9902]

Holding the project for its full 5-year life, the net present value (NPV) of the project—that is, the present value of all cash inflows of the project minus the cost of the project—is $105 at a 12 percent discount rate. By terminating the project at an earlier date, the firm can realize in each year a higher NPV. The optimal holding period is 3 years where

[4] See A. A. Robichek and J. C. Van Horne, "Abandonment Value and Capital Budgeting," *Journal of Finance*, 22 (December 1967), pp. 577–89; E. A. Dyl and H. W. Long, "Abandonment Value and Capital Budgeting: Comment," *Journal of Finance*, 24 (March 1969), pp. 88–95; and A. A. Robichek and J. C. Van Horne, "Abandonment Value and Capital Budgeting: Reply," *Journal of Finance*, 24 (March 1969), pp. 96–97.

the NPV is the highest. By closing out the project at the end of the third year a NPV of $326 is realized.

## MUTUALLY EXCLUSIVE PROJECTS AND MULTIPLE SOLUTIONS

We have emphasized that assumptions and conditions are critical in capital budgeting analysis. We began with the Bear Cat Oil Well and Desert Flat Gas Station proposals (Table 9–2). Our first analysis showed that Bear Cat was a better investment because its cash receipts came in sooner. However, when we considered that our reinvestment opportunities were 3 percent bonds, we found Desert Flat better because we would not want the cash back sooner under that circumstance.

Now we will add additional facts and analyze the situation anew. Both Bear Cat and Desert Flat were available to us for $8300 each. In the first analysis we assumed we had at least $16,600 available to invest, so we could have bought both if we wanted to. The question was which investment was better if we were seeking a 10 percent return? Now let us assume we have nothing but borrowing power of $8300, so we can invest in only one of the two, but instead of shooting for a 10 percent yield we will seek to determine which of the two investments is more profitable *and at what rates of interest.* You will recognize this is very close to a sole proprietor who has all his equity committed and now can only borrow in order to invest.

Our new facts have created a mutually exclusive situation. We can take only one investment. This is a common situation in industry. Shall we build a 6-inch pipeline or a 12-inch one? Shall we buy a 2-ton truck or a 4-ton one? Shall we build a 16-story building or a 24-story one? The basic approach is marginal. Is the extra income worth the extra investment?

We need one additional fact to complete our problem. Let us suppose Bear Cat is available to us at $8300 but that Desert Flat is offered to us at $7500. Is Bear Cat worth the extra $800?

We begin our analysis by developing the increments of cash flows of Bear Cat over Desert Flat, as shown in Table 9–5.

TABLE 9–5. Incremental Cash (Outflows) and Inflows

| | Cost | 1st year | 2d year | 3d year | 4th year |
|---|---|---|---|---|---|
| Bear Cat | $(8300) | $4000 | $3000 | $2000 | $1000 |
| Desert Flat | (7500) | 1000 | 2000 | 3000 | 4500 |
| Increment | ( 800) | 3000 | 1000 | (1000) | (3500) |

Then we apply discounting (using various rates of interest) in Table 9–6. The net present values and discount rates of Table 9–6 are graphed in Figure 9–2.

TABLE 9–6. Discounting Incremental Investment and Incremental Cash Inflows at Various Rates

| Rate of discount | Cost | Cash inflows 1st year | 2d year | 3d year | 4th year | Total net present value † |
|---|---|---|---|---|---|---|
| 0% | ($800) | $3000 | $1000 | ($1000) | ($3500) | ($1300) |
| 5 | (800) | 2857 | 907 | (864) | (2879) | (779) |
| 10 | (800) | 2727 | 826 | (751) | (2391) | (389) |
| 15 | (800) | 2609 | 756 | (658) | (2001) | (94) |
| 18 | (800) | 2543 | 718 | (609) | (1805) | 47 |
| 20 | (800) | 2500 | 694 | (579) | (1688) | 127 |
| 40 | (800) | 2143 | 510 | (364) | (911) | 578 |
| 60 * | (800) | 1646 | 301 | (165) | (317) | 665 |
| 80 | (800) | 1348 | 202 | (91) | (143) | 516 |
| 100 | (800) | 1104 | 135 | (49) | (56) | 334 |

* For rates from 60 percent up, use continuous discounting from Erwin E. Nemmers, *Managerial Economics: Text and Cases* (New York: John Wiley and Sons, Inc., rev. ed., 1964), pp. 395ff.

† Negative net present values favor Desert Flat, positive ones favor Bear Cat.

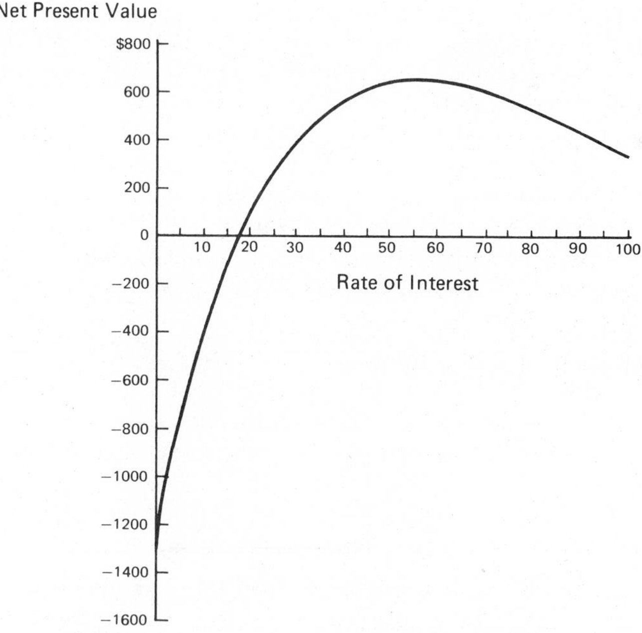


Figure 9–2 Net present values from discounting incremental cash outflows and incremental cash inflows at various rates of interest.

Examination of Table 9–6 and Figure 9–2 shows that Desert Flat is the preferred investment as long as we can borrow at rates of interest slightly under 18 percent. At such rates the incremental investment in Bear Cat yields a negative NPV. But at rates of interest above 18 percent, Bear Cat is the preferred investment, as shown by the positive NPV of the increment.

It is also apparent from Table 9–6 and Figure 9–2 that Desert Flat will again become the preferred investment at very high rates of interest above 100 percent. The reason is that the present value of the inflows goes to zero as the rate of interest becomes very high and the $800 added investment overrides the present value of the cash inflows.

The underlying reason for the results of Table 9–6 is that over time the undiscounted increments in Table 9–5 change from negative (the added cost) to positive (the first 2 years' cash inflow) to negative (the last 2 years' cash inflow). Whenever the incremental pattern over a time changes *sign* there will be a shift at an appropriate interest rate from preferring one investment to preferring the other.

Observe that in this example the net cash flows are regular—one or more periods of cash outflow followed by periods of cash inflow. Thus, if we are given the rate of discount, the more attractive project can be identified directly by computing for each project the ratio of the present value of the cash inflows to the cost of the project—the *profitability index.* We need not carry out the marginal analysis to identify the more attractive project.

In practice the value of the marginal analysis is two-fold. First, we may not be given the rate of discount. Thus, we will want to know at what rates of interest it will be attractive to adopt the project requiring the extra investment. Second, even if given the rate of discount, through this study of the marginal cash flows we obtain a sensitivity analysis of the two mutually exclusive projects analogous to that performed on the economic order quantity models discussed in Chapter 6. We can compare the relative attractiveness of the two projects and "see" the range of the rate of discount for which one project is more attractive than the other. From Figure 9–2 the height of the curve at any point as measured on the vertical axis indicates the relative attractiveness of the two projects, and the horizontal axis tells us the range of the rates of discount for which one project is more attractive than the other.

## SIZE AND COMPOSITION OF THE CAPITAL BUDGET

Most firms generate a multitude of investment proposals—many more than they are capable of financing. We need a method for ranking proposals and establishing a cut-off point. We will assume at this time that the projects have the same risk and that this risk is the same as the average of the firm. Later this constraint will be relaxed. The method will involve: (1) computing the dollar costs and benefits of the project, (2) evaluating the estimated net benefits by some measure of attractiveness, (3) ranking the projects according to this measure, and (4) establishing a cut-off point that tells how far down the list to proceed in approving projects.

A few proposals are automatically eliminated because they are *mutually exclusive,* as we just explained. Most proposals are *independent* of each other, representing projects capable of separate consideration. An automobile company may be considering a new computer, a new office building, a new body paint facility, and so forth. But even here the marginal analysis is useful: the *added* investment in the new computer compared to continuing with the old and the *added* benefits of the new computer compared to those of the old one.

Given a series of projects, one key element in the capital budgeting system is the cut-off rate. In Chapter 15 we will propose the marginal cost of capital adjusted for risk. Other cut-off rates found in industry include an arbitrarily determined rate, the marginal cost of capital with and without a risk premium, the weighted average cost of capital, the current rate of return earned by the firm on its investments, and the average earned by the industry. The standard we propose will enable the firm to maximize its value.

In Figure 9–3 we illustrate the ranking of projects as part of the capital budgeting problem. Seven projects are proposed. We assume all projects carry equal risk and that any combination of projects is as good as any other. Only Projects I, II, and III meet the minimum acceptable hurdle rate. If Amizade Inc. does not have sufficient funds to adopt all three projects, the funds should be raised externally. If excess funds are available, they may be used to retire debt, pay dividends, or repurchase the firm's own shares.

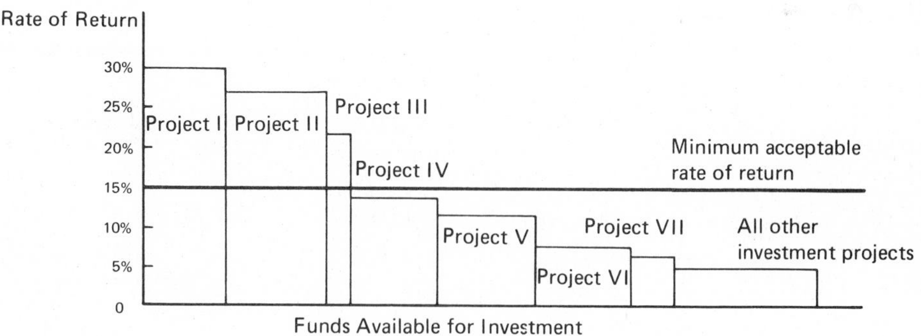


Figure 9–3 Amizade, Inc. Project proposals.

We deferred examining the various systems for ranking projects until we looked at several aspects of the Bear Cat and Desert Flat proposals so that we can give a more meaningful appraisal.

## SYSTEMS FOR RANKING INVESTMENT PROPOSALS [5]

Accurate inputs—sales, costs, and cash flows—are essential to the proper functioning of any capital budgeting system. The correctness of the project ranking can be no better than the input data.[6]

### Payback System of Ranking Projects

The *payback system* ranks projects according to the number of years required until after-tax income plus depreciation equals the original investment. There are two types of payback systems: one uses undiscounted flows and the other involves some form of time-adjustment (such as net present value or discounted cash flow). The first type is rejected as assuming a zero rate of interest and ignoring cash flows beyond the payback period.

Payback places great emphasis on the risk aspect. The further we look into the future, the greater the uncertainty of all our estimates. The payback system focuses on how quickly we recover our principal. The sooner that recovery, the less the risk of unforeseen changes. For example, Silver Tassle Uniforms, Inc. is considering a new piece of equipment costing $10,000. The machine has an estimated life of 5 years and discounted benefits, as shown in Table 9–7. The capital expenditure for the equipment is recaptured by the end of the third year—the payback plus the rate of return assumed in discounting.

TABLE 9–7. Silver Tassle Uniforms, Inc.
Project Data for Payback Illustration

| *Year* | 1 | 2 | 3 | 4 | 5 |
|---|---|---|---|---|---|
| Discounted cash inflow * | $3,000 | $3,000 | $4,000 | $3,000 | $2,000 |

* At a 0 rate of discount.

### Average Rate of Return System

The *average rate of return on investment,* also called the *accounting method,* is the average annual earnings *after* depreciation and taxes divided by maximum investment in the project. Another form uses average investment as the denominator. The latter form recognizes that the original outlay is recovered through depreciation charges over the project life and, hence, under straight-line depreciation, average investment is

[5] We implicitly assume that the probability for success for each project is the same. See A. E. Grunewald, "Capital Budgeting Strategy," *Management International Review,* Vol. 2–3, 1967, pp. 109–130, for a discussion of a unique capital budgeting system which takes into consideration the factor of a different probability of success being associated with each project.

[6] In an article based on research of small business investments, W. Warren Haynes and Martin B. Solomon, Jr. conclude that searching for investment opportunities, obtaining information about each, and carefully estimating the associated costs and income are preferable to stressing the refinements of computation, at least for small firms. See "A Misplaced Emphasis in Capital Budgeting," *Quarterly Review of Economics and Business,* 2 (February 1962), pp. 39–46.

equal to one-half the original capital commitment. Thus, if a \$10,000 project were to yield an average income net after taxes and depreciation of \$1000 per year for 5 years, the return on *maximum* investment would be

$$\frac{\$1000}{\$10{,}000} = 10\%$$

The return on *average* investment is

$$\frac{\$1{,}000}{\$10{,}000/2} = 20\%$$

Like payback, average return is easy to understand and calculate. It has the advantage of considering the income produced over the life of the project, but there is no recognition of the time value of money. There would be no difference in average return if the earnings of one project accrue in early years and those of the second in later years, where both have the same average income and same capital outlay.

### Internal Rate of Return System (IRR)

The *internal rate of return,* also called the *discounted cash flow system,* establishes that rate of discount, $r$, that equates the sum of the present value of future after-tax profits plus depreciation $A_t$ (where $t = 1, 2, \ldots$) and termination value to the capital outlay $C$:

$$C = \frac{A_1}{(1+r)^1} + \frac{A_2}{(1+r)^2} + \cdots + \frac{A_n}{(1+r)^n}$$

The IRR is calculated by trial-and-error discount rates applied to the cash inflow plus any termination value. These discounted quantities are summed and the sum compared with the capital outlay. If the sum is higher than the capital outlay, a higher discount rate is tried. If the sum is lower, a lower discount rate is tried. Interpolation is performed to get the true rate. After computing the rate of return on each project, the proposals are ranked in the order of rate of return. Provided the firm has sufficient funds to undertake the projects or is willing to raise additional funds, projects will be approved down to the cut-off rate of return.

To reduce the number of trial-and-error computations, the first trial rate may be selected by taking the reciprocal of the payback. For long-lived, level-earning projects in which the life of the project is somewhat greater than twice the payback period, this rate will give a rough approximation.

To illustrate the IRR system, suppose Silver Tassle Uniforms, Inc. decides to determine the IRR that new equipment promises. Table 9–8 shows trial rates of 12 percent, 16 percent, and 20 percent. The 12 percent discount rate produces a present value of \$10,960, which is too high;

20 percent, a present value of \$9147, which is too low; 16 percent is approximately the IRR.[7]

The internal rate of return system emphasizes the time-value of money and is capable of incorporating risk into the calculation, as we shall see in the next chapter. But the system is frequently abused by ignoring risk differences between projects.

TABLE 9–8. Silver Tassle Uniforms, Inc.
Project Data for Internal Rate of Return Illustration

| Year | Annual cash inflow | Discount factor (12%) | Present value | Discount factor (16%) | Present value | Discount factor (20%) | Present value |
|---|---|---|---|---|---|---|---|
| 1 | \$3,000 | 0.893 | \$ 2,679 | 0.862 | \$ 2,586 | 0.833 | \$ 2,499 |
| 2 | 3,000 | 0.797 | 2,391 | 0.743 | 2,229 | 0.694 | 2,082 |
| 3 | 4,000 | 0.712 | 2,848 | 0.641 | 2,564 | 0.579 | 2,316 |
| 4 | 3,000 | 0.636 | 1,908 | 0.552 | 1,656 | 0.482 | 1,446 |
| 5 | 2,000 | 0.567 | 1,134 | 0.476 | 952 | 0.402 | 804 |
| Present value | | | \$10,960 | | \$ 9,987 | | \$ 9,147 |
| Investment | | | − 10,000 | | − 10,000 | | − 10,000 |
| Net present value | | | \$ 960 | | \$−13≅0 | | \$ − 853 |

[A9840]

## Net Present Value System (NPV)

The net present value system (NPV) involves finding the total of the present value of future cash inflows discounted at an assumed rate of return $k$ and minus the cost of the project. If the remainder is positive, the project is adopted; otherwise it is rejected. Given two mutually exclusive projects both with a positive NPV, the project with the higher NPV is selected. The equation for the NPV system using the same symbols as the IRR system is:

$$\text{NPV} = \frac{A_1}{(1+k)^1} + \frac{A_2}{(1+k)^2} + \cdots + \frac{A_n}{(1+k)^n} - C$$

When NPV $= 0$, then $r = k$ and we have the internal rate of return. If we assume the hurdle rate in the Silver Tassle example is 10 percent, then Table 9–9 shows the NPV of the project is \$1500. The project promises a 10 percent return plus an additional return of \$1500 (\$11,500 − \$10,000). Projects are ranked by the size of the net present value.

---

[7] Given the present value for the project corresponding to the 12 and 20 percent discount rates, the approximate rate may be found by interpolation:
$12\% + \frac{10{,}960\,(20\% - 12\%)}{10{,}960 + 9{,}147} = 16.4\%$. The 16.4 percent is an approximate figure because interpolation assumes linear relationships but the relationship is really curvilinear.

TABLE 9–9. Silver Tassle Uniforms, Inc.
Project Data for Net Present Value Illustration

| *Year* | *Annual cash inflow* | *Discount factor (10%)* | *Present value* |
|---|---|---|---|
| 1 | $3,000 | 0.909 | $ 2,727 |
| 2 | 3,000 | 0.826 | 2,478 |
| 3 | 4,000 | 0.751 | 3,004 |
| 4 | 3,000 | 0.683 | 2,049 |
| 5 | 2,000 | 0.621 | 1,242 |
| Present value | | | $11,500 |
| Investment | | | − 10,000 |
| Net present value | | | $ 1,500 |

Like the IRR system, net present value emphasizes the time value of money and is exposed to the abuse of ignoring the differences in risk among the projects being ranked.

### Profitability Index System (PI)

If there are more projects with a positive net present value than funds available, ranking projects according to the size of the NPV of each project will not give the project ranking that maximizes the market value of the firm because not all projects can be implemented and normally the larger projects will show larger net present values even though they may be less attractive.[8] For example, Silver Tassle may have a second project, a modernization program, estimated to cost $100,000 that has a present value of $110,000 with a net present value of $10,000. Compare this with the net present value of $1500 for the smaller equipment project. The *profitability index* (PI), is a simple procedure for comparing the attractiveness of projects when computing the net present values of projects. The profitability index is calculated by dividing the present value of the project by the cost of the project. Comparing the modernization and the equipment projects, we have

$$\text{Modernization project: } \frac{\$110{,}000}{100{,}000} = 1.1$$

$$\text{Equipment project: } \frac{\$11{,}500}{10{,}000} = 1.15$$

The PI puts different-sized projects on a comparable basis. If the rate of return of the project is desired, we must compute the internal rate of return. Neither the net present value nor the profitability index provides that information.

[8] Some elementary texts consider it too complex to take the discussion beyond the net present value system. This shows the danger of being too elementary.

### Conflict of the IRR and NPV Systems

Independent investment proposals often require a simple accept or reject decision. The IRR or the NPV systems will yield the same ranking provided the cash flows are normal—one or more periods of cash outflow followed by periods of cash inflow.[9] But when two proposals promise substantially different cash flow patterns, the two systems may offer conflicting recommendations. For example, Crusty Baking Company is considering two new pie-filling machines carrying the trademarks CH (for "come hither") and HR for ("hit and run"). Each costs $10,000. The CH model produces a more costly but also fuller, tastier pie that is expected to win and hold customers over many years. The HR model produces a seemingly full but cheap pie that after 5 years will no longer be able to attract buyers. Table 9–10 shows the cash flow data and the conflict in ranking.

TABLE 9–10. Crusty Baking Company
Pie Machine Data for Mutually Exclusive Projects
Required Return on Investment, 10 Percent

| | | *Cash inflow per year for 19 years* | | | |
|---|---|---|---|---|---|
| *Model* | *Cost* | *1–5* | *6–19* | *Internal rate of return* | *Profitability index* |
| CH | $10,000 | $1,000 | $2,000 | 13% | 1.3 |
| HR | 10,000 | 3,000 | — | 15 | 1.1 |

Applying the IRR system, we find the HR model to be the clear choice. Applying the NPV system and calculating the PI we see that the CH model is preferable. Which project do we select? The decision should be governed by the estimate of the availability of attractive projects five years hence. If Crusty Baking is expected to have regularly available investment opportunities promising 15 percent, the HR model is the indicated choice. If projects that promise even a 10 percent return are becoming scarce, the CH model is the indicated choice. Depending on the pattern of the cash flows, the discount rate selected may also influence the results. With a low discount rate the timing of the cash flows is less important, and the higher nondiscounted cash flows assume greater importance.

## IMPACT OF DEPRECIATION POLICY ON PRESENT VALUE

A tax-free organization can evaluate the attractiveness of a project simply by comparing the present value of the cash inflows against the

---

[9] When the outlays are not conventional, that is, when there is an outflow in period 0 followed by an inflow in period 1 and a further outflow in period 2, it is possible for the internal rate of return system to yield two rates. See Harold Bierman, Jr., and Seymour Smidt *The Capital Budgeting Decision*, 3d ed. (New York: The Macmillan Company, 1971), pp. 43–46, for an example yielding internal rates of return of 10 and 25 percent and an explanation of the multiple yields.

necessary outflows, as we have been doing without considering depreciation. Depreciation is considered in the profit and loss statement but in evaluating benefits using a time-adjusting system, it is the cash flows that are significant. The discounting process allows for both the return of capital and the return on investment.

For example, a new investment for the tax-free Zippy Foundation is expected to cost $10,000 and generate a cash inflow of $5,000 a year for 3 years at year end and to have zero termination value. At a rate of discount of 5 percent, the present value of the stream of income is $13,-616. If, as appears in Table 9–11, undertaking the project requires a loan, it would be possible for Zippy to borrow the $13,616 from its bank, agree to pay the loan off in three annual installments of $5,000 plus 5 percent interest, invest $10,000 in the project, and make an immediate grant to a student of $3,616, as appears in Table 9–12.

**TABLE 9–11. Zippy Foundation**

Present Value of Income Stream of $5,000 Per Year at Year End for Three Years

| Year | Cash inflow | Discount Factor (5%) | Present value of cash flows |
|---|---|---|---|
| 1 | $ 5,000 | 0.9524 | $ 4,762 |
| 2 | 5,000 | 0.9070 | 4,535 |
| 3 | 5,000 | 0.8638 | 4,319 |
| Present value | | | $13,616 |
| Investment | | | − 10,000 |
| Net present value | | | $ 3,616 |

For a firm subject to income tax, the method of depreciation adopted —straight line, double declining balance, sum-of-the-years' digits—influences the attractiveness of a project because the timing of income tax due depends on the timing of depreciation charged, since the after-tax cash inflow figure is equal to gross receipts minus the cash costs of operation and income tax. Depreciation is excluded as a noncash cost. The income tax is equal to the tax rate times the difference between sales revenue and all costs of operation, including depreciation.

**TABLE 9–12. Zippy Foundation**

Loan Repayment, Principal and Interest

| *Year* | *Loan at beginning of period* | *Interest charge at 5%* | *Total due at end of period* | *Loan repayment* | *Amount of loan at end of period* |
|---|---|---|---|---|---|
| 1 | $13,616 | $681 | $14,297 | $5,000 | $9,297 |
| 2 | 9,297 | 465 | 9,762 | 5,000 | 4,762 |
| 3 | 4,762 | 238 | 5,000 | 5,000 | 0 |

To illustrate how depreciation policy influences cash flow and the attractiveness of an investment, consider the new equipment project of Rosy Optical. The equipment cost is $15,000, expected life 5 years, sales revenue minus cash expenses $7000 per year at year end, and there is no termination value. Rosy Optical's hurdle rate is 10 percent. Revenues, costs, and tax due under straight-line, double declining balance, and sum-of-the-years' digits methods of depreciation are summarized in Tables 9–13, 9–14, and 9–15. Income taxes are 50 percent. Though the totals of revenue, cash expenses, depreciation, and cash inflow are the same, the higher earlier depreciation charges reduce the tax liability in the early years, permitting the firm to retain a larger portion of the early-year cash inflows. In the later years under the accelerated methods of depreciation the income tax payments are higher as a result of the reduced depreciation charges. The result is reduced net cash inflow in later periods. But these later cash flows are not as valuable as the earlier cash flows. This explains the higher present value of the equipment under the accelerated methods of depreciation. The present value of the equipment using the double declining balance method is $19,337, using sum-of-the-years' digits $19,310, and under straight-line only $18,950.

TABLE 9–13. Rosy Optical Company
Income Tax Computation under Various Methods of Depreciation

| | | | *Tax payments due under different depreciation policies* | | | | | |
|---|---|---|---|---|---|---|---|---|
| | | | *Depreciation* | | *Depreciation* | | *Depreciation* | |
| *Period* | *Sales revenue* | *Cash expenses* | *Straight-line* | *Income tax* | *Double declining balance* | *Income tax* | *Sum-of-years' digits* | *Income tax* |
| 1 | $12,000 | $ 5,000 | $ 3,000 | $ 2,000 | $ 6,000 | $ 500 | $ 5,000 | $ 1,000 |
| 2 | 12,000 | 5,000 | 3,000 | 2,000 | 3,600 | 1,700 | 4,000 | 1,500 |
| 3 | 12,000 | 5,000 | 3,000 | 2,000 | 2,160 | 2,420 | 3,000 | 2,000 |
| 4 | 12,000 | 5,000 | 3,000 | 2,000 | 1,296 | 2,852 | 2,000 | 2,500 |
| 5 | 12,000 | 5,000 | 3,000 | 2,000 | 1,944 | 2,528 | 1,000 | 3,000 |
| Total | $60,000 | $25,000 | $15,000 | $10,000 | $15,000 | $10,000 | $15,000 | $10,000 |

[A9823]

TABLE 9–14. Rosy Optical Company
Cash Flow under Various Methods of Depreciation

| | | | *Taxes and cash inflow under various depreciation policies* | | | | | |
|---|---|---|---|---|---|---|---|---|
| | | | *Income tax* | | *Income tax* | | *Income tax* | |
| *Period* | *Sales revenue* | *Cash expenses* | *Straight-line* | *Net inflow* | *Double declining balance* | *Net inflow* | *Sum-of-years' digits* | *Net inflow* |
| 1 | $12,000 | $ 5,000 | $ 2,000 | $ 5,000 | $ 500 | $ 6,500 | $ 1,000 | $ 6,000 |
| 2 | 12,000 | 5,000 | 2,000 | 5,000 | 1,700 | 5,300 | 1,500 | 5,500 |
| 3 | 12,000 | 5,000 | 2,000 | 5,000 | 2,420 | 4,580 | 2,000 | 5,000 |
| 4 | 12,000 | 5,000 | 2,000 | 5,000 | 2,852 | 4,148 | 2,500 | 4,500 |
| 5 | 12,000 | 5,000 | 2,000 | 5,000 | 2,528 | 4,472 | 3,000 | 4,000 |
| Total | $60,000 | $25,000 | $10,000 | $25,000 | $10,000 | $25,000 | $10,000 | $25,000 |

[A9822]

TABLE 9–15. Rosy Optical Company
Determination of the Present Value of the Different Cash Flows Resulting from the Application of Various Methods of Depreciation
Rate of Discount, 10 percent

| | *Straight-line* | | *Double declining balance* | | *Sum-of-years' digits* | |
|---|---|---|---|---|---|---|
| *Period* | *Net cash inflow* | *Net present value* | *Net cash inflow* | *Net present value* | *Net cash inflow* | *Net present value* |
| 1 | $ 5,000 | $ 4,545 | $ 6,500 | $ 5,909 | $ 6,000 | $ 5,454 |
| 2 | 5,000 | 4,130 | 5,300 | 4,378 | 5,500 | 4,543 |
| 3 | 5,000 | 3,755 | 4,580 | 3,440 | 5,000 | 3,755 |
| 4 | 5,000 | 3,415 | 4,148 | 2,833 | 4,500 | 3,074 |
| 5 | 5,000 | 3,105 | 4,472 | 2,777 | 4,000 | 2,484 |
| Total | $25,000 | $18,950 | $25,000 | $19,337 | $25,000 | $19,310 |

[A9824]

Note in Table 9–13 the columns headed by the various methods of depreciation represent the amount of depreciation charged, whereas in Table 9–14 they show the amount of income tax liability that results when that particular method of depreciation is adopted.

## PROJECT CONTROL

The last steps in the capital budgeting information feedback system after a project has been approved are control of the expenditure of funds and audit of the performance of the project after completion.

Detailed cost records showing the data of the approved project, the authorized expenditures, the amount expended, the percentage of the project completed, and the estimated completion date are essential. If the project costs more than originally authorized, the additional expenditures must be included. These reports may be compiled monthly or quarterly, depending in part on the size of the project and the reliability of the original cost estimates. They aid us in cash planning, serving as an early warning system of possible difficulties and providing a guide to the accuracy of estimates of project costs. If the reports reveal that substantial overexpenditures may be anticipated, we will usually have the project reviewed. If warranted, additional funds can be requested or the project can be terminated.

Termination is probably adopted only infrequently—but sometimes quite spectacularly. The Ford Motor Company spent several hundred million dollars on the Edsel. After the production of a handful of cars the project was abandoned. Frequently a firm will establish a deviation standard such as 10 percent that requires the submission of a report to obtain additional funds when expenditures will exceed the originally budgeted funds. When the project is finished a completion report is drawn up. This report permits an evaluation of the cost-estimating accuracy of the capital budgeting system and will make suggestions for avoiding similar errors in the future. As a further check, some firms also require a report on the performance of a project after it has been in operation for several years.

Areas of interest in reviewing project audits are the generation of project proposals, development of cost and revenue estimates, evaluation of the attractiveness of the projects, and actual attractiveness of projects after completion and operation. Management might find, for example, that revenues are conservatively estimated—that is, projects are generating a higher yield than anticipated. Such information can be fed back to those responsible for developing the revenue estimates with a view to raising their level of optimism. Management itself might take a more liberal attitude in approving capital expenditure projects. Additional outside funds might even be raised to take advantage of the stream of projects that had previously been viewed too conservatively.

## SUMMARY

Correct capital budgeting decisions are essential to the success of every firm. The impact of these decisions extends far into the future, shaping the character of the firm. Capital budgeting decisions are not easily reversed. The acquisition of fixed assets entails a major outlay of funds and reduces management flexibility.

The acquisition of fixed assets involves exchanging a present estimated outlay for an estimated future stream of income. Fixed assets have value to the extent that they are capable of producing future income that is discounted back to the present.

The capital budgeting process requires determining the amount and timing of cash receipts. Mutually exclusive projects are evaluated on an incremental basis as to the amount of investment and the cash inflows. When using the average rate of return on investment for ranking proposals, receipts are earnings after depreciation and taxes—the conventional accounting concept of profit. Following payback, internal rate of return (IRR) or net present value (NPV) systems, receipts mean the difference in funds inflow between having the project and not having it—receipts after costs including taxes but before depreciation.

The method of depreciation is important in determining the fund flows and the profitability of a project that might be of marginal attractiveness under straight-line depreciation or attractive under accelerated methods of depreciation. The depreciation charge acts as a tax shield, increasing the early, more-valuable fund inflows and reducing the later, less-valuable inflows.

Of the various ranking systems, payback (number of years required to recapture the cost of the investment) is widely used. It is easy to calculate, can serve as a coarse screen for selecting attractive projects, tells a firm how long it will have its money tied up, and weeds out longer-term paybacks. A disadvantage is that it does not consider the flows of a project after the cost of the investment has been recovered. The average return on investment system relates the expected earnings (accounting definition) of the project to the required investment. This system considers the earnings over the life of the project but does not adjust for the time value of money nor, usually, for depreciation.

The IRR and the NPV systems consider depreciation and the time value of money. The IRR system requires the determination of the discount rate that causes the summed present values of the annual cash inflows to equal the cost of the project. The NPV system requires selecting a discount rate to use in evaluating projects, summing the present values of cash inflows at that rate, and subtracting the cost of the project. The profitability index (PI) is found by computing the ratio of the sum of the present values of the cash inflows (discounted at the required rate of return) to the cost of the project.

For a firm subject to income taxes, the method of depreciation affects the profitability of the project because the type of depreciation affects the timing of payment of income taxes. Heavy early depreciation gives a tax shield against early income tax payment thus deferring tax payments.

The capital budgeting system in practice represents a dynamic flow of decisions, actions, and events. Individuals formulating proposals and developing cost and income estimates are swept by moods of optimism and pessimism hurrying and slowing down project conception and approval. Economic events and political conditions can be assessed correctly or incorrectly. Thus, we find the flow of projects conceived, proposed, approved or rejected, audit reviews of project performance made, and recommendations advanced for adjustment and refinement surging and ebbing as the information feeds back to the individuals at the key decision points. The flow of information and decisions is not smooth and even but moves in waves, constantly raising and lowering the level of activity taking place in the capital budgeting system.

### *Study Questions*

1. Why is the future success of a firm heavily dependent upon correct capital expenditure decisions? What are the critical elements that lead to correct capital expenditure decisions? How can the quality of these decisions be improved?
2. Review Table 9–1. Explain the different proportions of fixed assets to total assets found in the various industries.
3. What pressures induce a firm to make capital expenditures? Are these capital expenditures in the national interest? Can or should the federal government encourage capital expenditures? If so what actions do you recommend?
4. Explain what is meant by the time value of money. Which capital budgeting systems take this concept into consideration? How is it possible for the capital budgeting systems that do not take it into consideration to lead to wrong decisions?
5. What are the advantages and disadvantages of the payback method? Why might a small firm find payback attractive?
6. Contrast the IRR and the NPV systems. Under what circumstances may they lead to comparable recommendations? To conflicting recommendations? Where these two systems lead to conflicting recommendations, what criteria should be used to select the project?

7. How can the time pattern of the income flows affect the relative ranking of a group of projects? Why under capital rationing is the NPV of a project not a reliable guide for ranking projects? What system may be used instead?

8. How can the method of depreciation affect the profitability of a project? What is the relation between the income tax bill, the desirability of an accelerated method of depreciation, and the attractiveness of a capital expenditure project?

9. Why is project control an important stage in any capital expenditure information feedback system? Of what significance is a cut-off point requiring the filing of detailed reports if expenditures will exceed the budgeted figure by this amount? How can detailed records lead to improved capital budgeting decisions?

### Problems

1. Compute the following:

a. The present value of $8000 to be received at the end of 15 years when discounted at 20 percent.

b. The present value of $8000 to be received at the end of 5 years when discounted at 20 percent.

c. The present value of $8000 to be received at the end of 15 years when discounted at 15 percent.

d. The present value of $8000 to be received at the end of 5 years when discounted at 5 percent.

e. The present value of $2000 per year for 5 years discounted at 10 percent.

f. The present value of $2000 per year for 15 years discounted at 10 percent.

g. The present value of $1000 per year for 9 years discounted at 10 percent plus the present value of $5000 to be received at the end of the tenth year discounted at 10 percent.

2. Unreal Casino in Las Vegas has just been put up for sale. The owner is asking $3,600,000 in cash or $6,000,000 with nothing down. The $6,000,000 is to be paid in five equal installments due at the end of each year.

a. What is your implicit rate of interest if you buy and do not pay cash?

b. Suppose you have the $3,600,000 in cash and also another investment opportunity that promises a 25 percent annual return over the next 5 years. Just on the basis of the data given, which is more attractive: pay cash for the casino or buy it "on the installment plan," and invest the $3,600,000 in the available opportunity? What other factor(s) might you consider in reaching a decision?

3. The Tart Foundation, a tax-exempt organization, owns various investment projects. One project is doing poorly and is being considered for replacement. Three mutually exclusive projects have been proposed. Funds are available for only one project. Management asks for your recommendation. The projects are coded Maple, Peach, and Rose. The projects are expected to each require a $40,000 outlay, have an estimated life of 5 years, 3 years, and 4 years, respectively, and have no termination value. The foundation's required rate of return is 12 percent. The anticipated cash inflows for the three projects are given in Table 9–16.

TABLE 9–16. Tart Foundation
Cash Inflows of Proposed Capital Expenditure Projects

| *Year* | *Project Maple* | *Project Peach* | *Project Rose* |
|---|---|---|---|
| 1 | $10,000 | $17,000 | $10,000 |
| 2 | 10,000 | 17,000 | 10,000 |
| 3 | 10,000 | 10,000 | 10,000 |
| 4 | 10,000 | — | 5,000 |
| 5 | 38,000 | — | — |

a. Determine the payback period for each project.

b. Determine the average return on total investment and on average investment for each project. Remember to deduct the required depreciation charge from each cash inflow figure to obtain the necessary net income figure. To simplify calculations use straight-line depreciation.

c. Determine the internal rate of return for each project.

d. Determine the present value of each project and its profitability index. Recall that the required rate of return is 12 percent.

e. Rank each project applying the methods of payback, average return on investment, internal rate of return, and profitability index.

f. Explain why the five capital budgeting systems yield conflicting answers.

g. What would be the profitability index if the internal rate of return equaled the required return on investment? What is the significance of a profitability index less than one?

h. Recommend the project to be adopted and give your reasons.

4. The Ham Bone Packing Company is planning a modernization of its production line, which is expected to result in savings before depreciation and taxes of $8000 per year. The cost of the equipment is $15,000. There is no termination value. Ham Bone requires a 15 percent return on investment. Income taxes are at a 50 percent rate. (See Table 9–17).

TABLE 9–17. Ham Bone Packing Company
Modernization Program Data

| Year | 1 | 2 | 3 | 4 | 5 |
|---|---|---|---|---|---|
| Savings before depreciation and taxes | $7000 | $7000 | $7000 | $7000 | $7000 |
| Depreciation, sum-of-years' digits method | 5000 | 4000 | 3000 | 2000 | 1000 |
| Taxable income | 2000 | 3000 | 4000 | 5000 | 6000 |
| Income tax (50%) | 1000 | 1500 | 2000 | 2500 | 3000 |
| Cash flow from operations | 6000 | 5500 | 5000 | 4500 | 4000 |
| Cost of equipment, $15,000 | | | | | |
| Required return on investment, 15 percent | | | | | |

a. Determine the profitability index.

b. Determine the internal rate of return.

c. Determine the profitability index and the internal rate of return if straight-line depreciation were required by tax law.

d. Compare your answers in parts (a), (b), and (c). How do you explain that the project appears less attractive when using straight-line depreciation than when the sum-of-the-years' digits method is employed? Why is the difference so small?

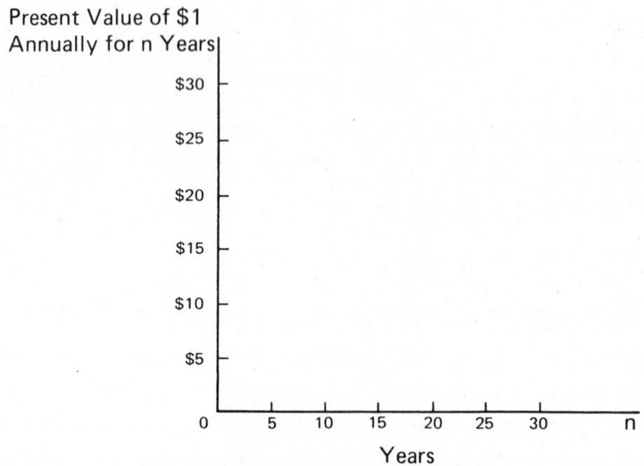


Figure 9–4 Present worth of a $1 per year annuity at various rates of discount.

5. Refer to Table A–2 at the end of the text and graph the present value of an annuity of $1 per year. Use discount rates of 1, 5, 10, and 20 percent.

a. Graph the points at 5-year intervals from 0 to 25 on Figure 9–4.

b. With reference to Figure 9–4 how do you explain the almost linear relationship between the number of years $1 is to be received per year and the value of that stream of income when discounted at 1 percent? How do you explain the very pronounced curvature of the 20 percent curve and the rapid approaching to a horizontal position?

6. Bongo-Bongo, Inc. is contemplating the introduction of a new instrument called the Rhythmette. The cost of the project, the required rate of return, and other pertinent data appear in Table 9–18.

TABLE 9–18. Bongo-Bongo, Inc.
Rhythmette Project

| *Year* | *0* | *1* | *2* | *3* | *4* | *5* |
|---|---|---|---|---|---|---|
| Outflow at year end | $10,000 | — | — | $10,000 | — | — |
| Cash inflow at year end | — | $5,000 | $5,000 | — | $10,000 | $20,000 |
| Termination value, $0 | | | | | | |
| Required rate of return on investment, 10 percent | | | | | | |

Management asks that you determine the profitability index.

7. The land of Vagalumee is planning to enter an exhibit in the coming world's fair. The initial cost of the exhibit is $8322. During the two years of

operation the exhibit is expected to generate a net cash inflow of $20,000 which may be considered centered at the end of the first year. The third year the exhibit will be dismantled and tour the country. The anticipated additional outlay is $12,000 at the end of the fair, see Table 9–19. Assume the benefit of the tour is valued at zero other than the cash inflow.

TABLE 9–19. Vagalumee World's Fair Exhibit Data

| *Year* | *0* | *1* | *2* |
|---|---|---|---|
| Outflow at year end | $8,322 | — | $12,000 |
| Cash inflow at year end | — | $20,000 | — |

a. Show that the internal rate of return is *both* 18 and 26 percent.

b. Determine the net present value of the exhibit at 0 and 50 percent discount rates. The present value of $1 to be received at the end of 1 and 2 years discounted at 50 percent is 0.667 and 0.444 respectively.

c. Determine the net present value of the exhibit at a 22 percent required rate of return. Is the net present value of the project positive or negative at this rate? Compare the sign of the net present value with that found in (b). What can you conclude about the attractiveness of the project when the required rate of return is less than 18 percent? between 18 and 26 percent? greater than 26 percent?

8. The Skinner National Bank, to meet increased competition, advertises that it will pay interest at 4 percent compounded continuously. The other banks in the area are currently also paying 4 percent interest, but compounding quarterly. The advertising campaign is structured to attract many small depositors.

a. Is the Skinner Bank really offering the small depositors a substantial incentive to open new savings accounts?

b. What do you think is the impression of the "average man on the street" regarding quarterly versus continuous compounding? Examine your own first reactions to continuous compounding. Do you think advertising "daily interest" is fair?

### Selected References

Bernhard, R. H., "Mathematical Programming Models for Capital Budgeting—A Survey, Generalization, and Critique," *Journal of Financial and Quantitative Analysis,* 4 (June 1969), pp. 111–158.

Bierman, H. Jr., and S. Smidt, *The Capital Budgeting Decision,* 3d ed., New York; The Macmillan Co., 1971.

Cheng, P. L., and J. P. Shelton, "A Contribution to the Theory of Capital Budgeting—The Multi-investment Case," *Journal of Finance,* 18 (December 1963), pp. 622–636.

Donaldson, G., "Strategic Hurdle Rates for Capital Investment," *Harvard Business Review,* 50 (March-April 1972), pp. 50–58.

Elton, E. J., "Capital Rationing and External Discount Rates," *Journal of Finance,* 25 (June 1970), pp. 573–584.

Klammer, Thomas, "Empirical Evidence of the Adoption of Sophisticated Capital Budgeting Techniques," *Journal of Business* 45 (July 1972), pp. 387–397.

Lewellen, W. G., H. P. Lanser and J. J. McConnell, "Payback Substitutes for Discounted Cash Flow," *Financial Management,* 2 (Summer 1973), pp. 17–25.

Mao, J. C. T., "Survey of Capital Budgeting: Theory and Practice," *Journal of Finance,* 25 (May 1970), pp. 349–360.

Myers, S. C., "Interactions of Corporate Financing and Investment Decisions," *Journal of Finance,* 29 (March 1974), pp. 1–25.

Sarnat, M., and H. Levy, "The Relationship of Rules of Thumb to the Internal Rate of Return: A Restatement and Generalization," *Journal of Finance,* 24 (June 1969) pp. 479–489.

Walter, James E., "Investment Planning Under Variable Price Change," *Financial Management,* 2 (Winter 1972), pp. 36–50.

## Appendix I

## MATHEMATICS OF FINANCE

Money has a time value. A dollar to be received one year hence is not worth as much as a dollar to be received immediately. If we hold a dollar we can put it in a savings account and earn, say, 4 percent in interest.

Thus a dollar to be received one year from now, assuming a 4 percent rate, must be worth today no more than the amount that, deposited in a bank at 4 percent, would bring our balance to \$1 one year from now. That figure is \$0.9615. How do we arrive at the figure \$0.9615?

*Simple Interest.* As on student loans, interest is earned (paid) only on the original amount deposited (borrowed). A person depositing amount $P$ and making no withdrawals for $n$ years, where $I$ equals the total dollar interest earned and $i$ the rate of interest, will have a future sum $S$ on account:

$$\begin{aligned} S &= \text{principal} + \text{total interest earned} \\ &= P + I \qquad (9\text{–}1) \end{aligned}$$

Since total interest earned is

$$\begin{aligned} I &= \text{principal} \times \text{years} \times \text{rate} \\ &= Pni \qquad (9\text{–}2) \end{aligned}$$

it then follows [substituting Eq. (9–2) in (9–1)] that

$$\begin{aligned} S &= P + Pni \\ &= P(1 + ni) \qquad (9\text{–}3) \end{aligned}$$

To illustrate, a \$1000 note due in 5 years with interest at 4 percent per year has a maturity value of

$$\$1000[1 + 5(0.04)] = \$1200$$

*Compound Interest.* Usually, when money is left on interest at a financial institution, interest accrued at the end of one period is added to the beginning balance of $P$ for the next period. In the succeeding period, interest is paid on the new balance, composed of the original deposit plus the interest earned. This form of interest is called *compound interest.*

An amount $P$ deposited with a bank paying interest compounded annually will grow to a future sum, $S$, according to the formula

$$\begin{aligned} S &= P + Pi \\ &= P(1 + i) \quad \text{for one year} \end{aligned} \tag{9–4}$$

For 2 years we have

$$\begin{aligned} S &= P(1 + i)(1 + i) \\ &= P(1 + i)^2 \end{aligned} \tag{9–5}$$

At the end of $n$ years the original sum deposited will grow to

$$S = P(1 + i)^n \tag{9–6}$$

Financial institutions usually compound interest more frequently than once a year; four times a year is standard practice. With interest compounded quarterly, the amount on deposit at the end of 3 months is

$$S = P\left(1 + \frac{i}{4}\right) \tag{9–7}$$

The balance at the end of 6 months is

$$\begin{aligned} S &= P\left(1 + \frac{i}{4}\right)\left(1 + \frac{i}{4}\right) \\ &= P\left(1 + \frac{i}{4}\right)^2 \end{aligned} \tag{9–8}$$

and at the end of 1 year,

$$S = P\left(1 + \frac{i}{4}\right)^4 \tag{9–9}$$

In general, if interest is compounded $m$ times per year, the amount on deposit at the end of $n$ years will be

$$S = P\left(1 + \frac{i}{m}\right)^{mn} \tag{9–10}$$

The number of times per year interest is compounded may range from once to continuously. The interest rate is usually stated on an annual basis and is known as the *nominal* rate. When the nominal rate is compounded more than once a year a higher rate of return results, known as the *effective* rate. The effective rate compounded once a year yields the same return as the nominal rate compounded $m$ times per year. If we let the effective rate be $j$ and the nominal rate be $i$, the relationship between $j$ and $i$ is given by

$$(1 + j) = \left(1 + \frac{i}{m}\right)^m, \quad \text{or} \quad j = \left(1 + \frac{i}{m}\right)^m - 1 \tag{9–11}$$

To illustrate, a nominal rate of 4 percent compounded four times a year yields an effective rate of 4.06 percent:[10]

$$(1 + 0.0406) = \left(1 + \frac{0.04}{4}\right)^4, \quad \text{or} \quad j = 1.0406 - 1 = 4.06\%$$

*Continuous Compounding.* Interest can also be compounded continuously. For a large $m$ in the term $(1 + \frac{i}{m})^m$ we have the relation[11]

$$(1 + j) = \lim_{m \to \infty} \left(1 + \frac{i}{m}\right)^m = e^i \cong (2.718)^i \tag{9–12}$$

and

$$j = e^i - 1 \tag{9–13}$$

For example, a nominal rate of interest $i = 4\%$ compounded continuously is equivalent to an effective rate of interest $j = 4.08\%$ compounded once per year or

$$j = (e^i - 1) = (2.718)^{0.04} - 1 = 0.0408 = 4.08\% \tag{9–14}$$

Using customary notation letting $g$ represent growth and $t$ (time) years, we can rewrite Eq. (9–10) (the general compound interest formula) in the following form. Our purpose is to develop the standard expression for continuous compounding, which is simply a special case of compounding.

$$S = P\left(1 + \frac{g}{m}\right)^{mt} \tag{9–15}$$

Then as $m$ runs to infinity we see from Eq. (9–12) that Eq. (9–15) reduces to

$$S = Pe^{gt} \tag{9–16}$$

In words, Eq. (9–16) says that an amount $P$ invested now will grow to the sum $Pe^{gt}$ at time $t$ when interest is compounded continuously at rate $g$.

---

[10] One dollar deposited at 4 percent compounded quarterly will accumulate over the four quarters as follows: \$1.01, \$1.0201, \$1.0303, \$1.0406.

[11] The irrational number 2.718 . . . is noted by the symbol $e$ and is the base of the system of natural logarithms. Therefore since $(1 + j) = e^i$ we can write $i = ln\,(1 + j)$. Or, under continuous compounding, \$1 deposited at 100 percent nominal interest will grow to \$2.72 at the end of the year having earned interest at the effective rate of 172 percent. When the nominal rate of interest is low, the gain from compounding declines sharply as $m$ becomes large. A \$1 deposited at 4 percent compounded quarterly grows to \$1.0406 at the end of a year. Compounding continuously adds only 0.02 of a cent or 0.0002 of \$1. See Eq. (9–14).

To further illustrate the relationship between nominal and effective interest rates under continuous compounding, in Eq. (9–16) let $P=1$ and $t=1$. Then from Eq. (9–12) we can write

$$(1+j) = e^{g} \tag{9–17}$$

where $j$ denotes the effective rate of interest and $g$ the specified rate of growth under continuous compounding. Then taking the natural logarithm ($ln$) of both sides of Eq. (9–17) we have (since $e$ is the base of the natural logarithms, $ln\ e=1$)

$$\ln(1+j) = g \tag{9–18}$$

If interest were compounded once per year at $j=0.25$ this is equivalent to continuous compounding at the rate

$$g = \ln(1+0.25) = 0.2231 \tag{9–19}$$

which may be found by consulting a table of natural logarithms. Or if under continuous compounding the rate were specified at 25 percent, the amount for any value of $t$ would be given by (see Eq. 9–17)

$$(1+j)^{t} \tag{9–20}$$

or by

$$e^{t\ln(1+j)} \tag{9–21}$$

Where $j=0.25$, these relationships are graphed in Figure 9–5.

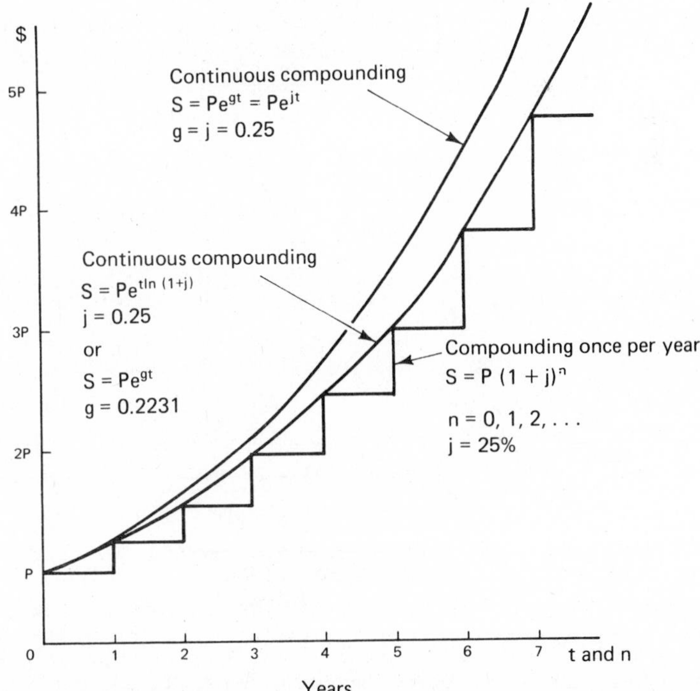


Figure 9–5 The value $S$ of an amount $P$, say, \$1000, compounded annually at rate of interest $j=0.25$, continuously at $ln(1=j)$ and continuously at $j$ per year.

Note from Figure 9–5 that Eqs. (9–20) and (9–21) give the same year-end values. Thus, if we are concerned only with year-end values, it makes no difference whether we compound once per year or continuously. Either method will yield the same result. But, starting with the rate of interest, the results are substantially different under annual and continuous compounding at high rates of interest—for example if $j = 0.25$ is used as a continuous compounding rate of $g = 0.25$. This is apparent from the widening spread between the two curves even after just a few years.

### Present Value Concept

When we buy a capital asset we exchange present dollars for expected future income from the asset. The value today of a capital asset is the sum of the future income the firm expects from the asset with each dollar of future income discounted at a given interest rate. This process of reducing future income payments to their present value is called *discounting.* The value today of the sum to be received in the future is called its *present value.*

### Discounting a Finite Income

*Single Payment.* Finding the present value (discounting) of a single payment is the reverse of compounding an initial sum over the same period of time. Dividing both sides of Eq. (9–6), $S = P(1 + i)^n$ by $(1 + i)^n$ where $S$ is the future sum, $P$ is the amount deposited, and $i$ and $n$ are defined as above, we have

$$P = \frac{S}{(1 + i)^n} \qquad \textbf{(9–22)}$$

Rearranging terms and substituting $PV$ for $P$ we have

$$\text{Present value} = PV = S\left[\frac{1}{(1 + i)^n}\right] \qquad (9–23)$$

The present value of \$10 to be received in 2 years discounted at 5 percent is

$$PV = \$10\left[\frac{1}{(1 + 0.05)^2}\right] = \frac{\$10}{1.1025} = \$9.07 \text{ (rounded)}$$

Computing the term in brackets is laborious and tables such as Table A–1 at the back of the book have been prepared for different values of $i$ and $n$. Using Table A–1 to find $PV$, go to the 5 percent column, move down to $n = 2$ and note the discount factor ($DF$): 0.90703. *Multiply* the $DF$ by the sum $S$ to be received at the future date.

Thus,

$$\begin{aligned} P &= S(DF) \\ &= \$10(0.90703) \\ &= \$9.0703 \end{aligned}$$

By using Table A–1 verify that the present value of \$10 to be received in 2 years discounted at *10* percent is

$$\begin{aligned} PV &= S(DF) \\ &= \$10(0.82645) \\ &= \$8.2645 \end{aligned}$$

Note that the higher rate of discount lowers the present value of the future sum.[12] The same holds as the year in which the sum is to be received is pushed farther into the future. The present value of $10 to be received in 20 years discounted at 10 percent is $1.49.

*Stream of Payments.* A typical investment yields a stream of periodic payments $A_1, A_2, \ldots, A_n$ to be received in the future. To find the present value of such a stream of payments we have the relation

$$PV = A_1\left(\frac{1}{(1+i)^1}\right) + A_2\left(\frac{1}{(1+i)^2}\right) + \cdots + A_n\left(\frac{1}{(1+i)^n}\right)$$

$$= \sum_{t=1}^{n} \frac{A_t}{(1+i)^t} \quad (t = 1, 2, \cdots, n \text{ years}) \qquad \text{(9–24)}$$

In Table A–2 at the end of the text you will find the *DF* needed to determine the present value of a stream of periodic payments. Provided the payments are uniform, the relation to use to find the present value is

$$PV = A(DF)$$

Suppose you are offered the opportunity to buy a note yielding $10 per year for 3 years. You demand a 5 percent return on your money. Go to Table A–2, the 5 percent column, move down to $n = 3$, and note the $DF = 2.7232$.

Thus

$$PV = \$10(2.7232) = \$27.23 \quad \text{(rounded)}$$

You will be willing to pay a maximum of $27.23 for the note.

The present value of $10 per year for 3 years discounted at 5 percent may also be found using Table A–1. Go to the 5 percent column and verify that the *DF* corresponding to the present value of $1 to be received after 1 year is 0.95238, after 2 years 0.90703, and after 3 years 0.86384.

Thus,

$$\begin{aligned} PV &= \$10(0.95238) + \$10(0.90703) + \$10(0.86384) \\ &= \$9.52 + \$9.07 + \$8.64 \\ &= \$27.23 \end{aligned}$$

Use Table A–1 when the payments are not uniform.

### Discounting an Infinite Stream of Income (Capitalization)

The simplest valuation case involves an asset such as noncallable preferred stock producing a steady income with no termination date—the limiting case of the discounting process where the periodic payments continue forever is known as *capitalization.*

Assume the $100 preferred stock of Zingo pays a $4 annual dividend and investors currently are demanding a 5 percent return on money invested in the type of risk represented by Zingo preferred. How much should they be willing to pay for the preferred? Letting $i$ equal the current rate of interest, $A$ the

---

[12] Conversely the lower the rate, the higher the present value. At a zero rate of discount the present value of a $1 to be received in $n$ years in the future is $1. And the present value of a stream of dollars to be received a $1 per year at the end of each year for $n$ years discounted at a zero rate of interest is $n$ dollars.

return to be received annually at the end of the year for an infinite number of years, and $PR$ price, we have

$$PR = \frac{A}{i} = \frac{\$4}{0.05} = \$80 \tag{9–25}$$

Investors should pay no more than $80 for the $4 preferred stock.

### Value of Distant Payments

We can now continue our discussion of discounting a finite stream of payments and show how we obtain the capitalization formula in Eq. (9–25).

The following example shows that sums to be received in the far distant future have relatively little value today—even when a modest rate of discount such as 5 percent is applied. Assume Zingo is considering the purchase of a machine expected to produce $4 per year for 10 years and then become worthless. The present value of this machine, or what is really being purchased—the present value of the stream of income of $4 per year for 10 years, is $30.88, as may be found using Table A–2 at the end of the text. Tables such as these are based on the formula

$$PV = A\left[\frac{1-(1+i)^{-n}}{i}\right] \tag{9–26}$$

To derive Eq. (9–26), recall from Eq. (9–24) that the present value $PV$ of a payment $A_t$ to be received at the end of each of $n$ periods discounted at rate of interest $i$ is given by the expression

$$PV = A_1\left[\frac{1}{(1+i)^1}\right] + A_2\left[\frac{1}{(1+i)^2}\right] + \cdots + A_n\left[\frac{1}{(1+i)^n}\right] \tag{9–27}$$

Now assume the stream of payments $A_t$ is uniform and agree to let

$$v = \frac{1}{(1+i)} \tag{9–28}$$

Then we can write the expression given in Eq. (9–20) as

$$PV = Av + Av^2 + Av^3 + \cdots + Av^n \tag{9–29}$$

Since the right-hand side of Eq. (9–29) is a geometric progression with a ratio of $v$ and with the first term equal to $Av$, we can write

$$PV = \frac{Av(1-v^n)}{1-v}$$

$$= \frac{A}{i}(1-v^n)$$

$$= A\,\frac{1-(1+i)^{-n}}{i}$$

To continue, if the machine were to last 30 years, the firm would be justified in paying $61.44; if it were to last 50 years, it would be justified in paying $73.02. As the life of the machine lengthens its value increases but does not grow infinitely large. As the life span extends to infinity, the value of the machine approaches a limit, the limit being the amount obtained by capitalizing at the appropriate rate of interest the annual income to be received. To show this, assume $A = \$1$ and put the formula in Eq. (9–26) in the following form:

$$PV = \frac{1}{i} - \frac{1}{i(1+i)^n} \tag{9–30}$$

As $n$ goes to infinity, the right-hand factor tends to zero and the factor $1/i$ is the capitalization formula Eq. (9–25). The first 30 years of income in our example account for more than 75 percent of the maximum possible value of the machine (\$61.44/\$80). Of the \$80 maximum value, the \$4 per year from the 51st year to infinity is presently worth only \$6.98 or (\$80 − \$73.02).

### Continuous Discounting

To determine the present value of a sum to be received in the future when applying continuous discounting, consider again Eq. (9–16), $S = Pe^{gt}$. Substituting $PV$ = present value for $P$, letting $k$ denote the discount rate under continuous discounting, and dividing both sides by $e^{kt}$ we obtain

$$PV = \frac{S}{e^{kt}} = Se^{-kt} \tag{9–31}$$

### Continuous Compounding and Discounting of a Stream of Payments

Recall, an amount placed on deposit $P$ with interest $i$ compounded annually will grow according to Eq. (9–6),

$$S = P(1+i)^n.$$

With continuous compounding at rate $g$, that amount $P$ will grow according to Eq. (9–16),

$$S = Pe^{gt}.$$

Instead of depositing a single amount, we have the possibility of depositing an amount $P$ at the end of each year and have the stream of payments grow with interest $i$ compounded annually. The accumulated sum at the end of the $n$th year is given by

$$S_n = P(1+i)^0 + P(1+i)^1 + \cdots + P(1+i)^{n-1} \tag{9–32}$$

$$= \sum_{t=1}^{n} P(1+i)^{t-1} \tag{9–32a}$$

Under continuous compounding at rate $g$ the stream of deposits will accumulate to a sum at the end of year $n$ that is given by

$$S_n = \int_0^N P_0 e^{gt}\,dt = P_0 \int_0^N e^{gt}\,dt \tag{9–33}$$

In words, to find $S_n$ we take the initial deposit $P_o$ and let it grow at the continuous rate $g$ for $t$ years.

$$P_t = P_0 e^{gt} \tag{9–34}$$

The expression in Eq. (9–34) traces a smooth curve. Then by means of integration we find the area under the curve between the limits of $t = 0$ to $t = N$. This area under the curve represents the value of $S_n$.

Recall further that the present value of a single payment $P$ (previously denoted by $S$) with annual discounting at rate of interest $i$ to be received $n$ years in the future is given by the expression

$$PV = P(1 + i)^{-t} \tag{9–35}$$

With continuous discounting at rate $k$ the present value of that single payment $P$ to be received $n$ years in the future is given by

$$PV = P_t e^{-kt} \tag{9–36}$$

The present value of a stream of periodic payments $P$ to be received for $n$ years with annual discounting at rate $i$ is given by

$$PV = P(1 + i)^{-1} + P(1 + i)^{-2} + \cdots + P(1 + i)^{-n} \tag{9–37}$$

$$= \sum_{t=1}^{N} P_n(1 + i)^{-t} \tag{9–37a}$$

Under continuous discounting at rate $k$ the present value of that stream of payments to be received for $n$ years is given by

$$PV = \int_0^N p_t e^{-kt}\, dt \tag{9–38}$$

Since from Eq. (9–34) we see that $P_t = P_o e^{gt}$ we can substitute in Eq. (9–38) and obtain

$$PV = \int_0^N P_0 e^{gt} e^{-kt}\, dt \tag{9–39}$$

$$= P_0 \int_0^N e^{-(k-g)t}\, dt \tag{9–39a}$$

Performing the integration yields the expression

$$PV = \left. \frac{-P_0 e^{-(k-g)t}}{k - g} \right|_0^N \tag{9–40}$$

Evaluating Eq. (9–40) for $t = \infty$ and $t = 0$ we have

$$PV = 0 - \left(-\frac{P_0}{k - g}\right) \tag{9–41}$$

$$= \frac{P_0}{k - g} \tag{9–41a}$$

In words, Eq. (9–41a) determines the present value of an infinite stream of periodic payments that begins with $P_o$, that will grow continuously at the rate $g$, and that will be discounted continuously at the rate $k$.

#### Termination Value

When the asset has a termination value, we must add to the present value of the future income stream the present value of the funds to be received at the distant date when the asset is sold. To illustrate, the present value of \$4 per year for 10 years discounted at 5 percent may be found using the expression

$$PV = \frac{\$4}{(1 + 0.05)^1} + \frac{\$4}{(1 + 0.05)^2} + \cdots + \frac{\$4}{(1 + 0.05)^{10}}$$

Or, more compactly:

$$PV = \sum_{t=1}^{10} \frac{\$4}{(1 + 0.05)^t}$$

Assume at the end of the tenth year that the machine generating that cash stream has a termination value of \$20. The present value of both cash flows may then be found using the expression

$$PV = \frac{\$4}{(1 + 0.05)^1} + \frac{\$4}{(1 + 0.05)^2} + \cdots + \frac{\$4}{(1 + 0.05)^{10}} + \frac{\$20}{(1 + 0.05)^{10}}$$

Or, combining terms:

$$PV = \sum_{t=1}^{10} \frac{\$4}{(1 + 0.05)^t} + \frac{\$20}{(1 + 0.05)^{10}}$$

To find the answer we use Tables A–1 and A–2 at the end of the text. Verify that

$$\begin{aligned} PV &= \$4(7.7217) + \$20(0.61391) \\ &= \$43.17 \text{ (rounded)} \end{aligned}$$

# 10
# Risk-Evaluation Systems

In the last chapter the return from each project was calculated and the projects ranked as though there were no doubt that the return would be realized. The analysis proceeded in the comfortable world of certainty. We assumed the acceptance of any project or group of projects did not change the total business risk character of the firm; but the riskiness of a project is important in capital budgeting. A project carrying high risk without a compensating high return will depress the price of the firm's shares.

A glaring characteristic of the area of capital budgeting is the wide difference between the actual return from a project and the forecasted return. Many projects, even after passing a rigorous screening procedure, simply fail to break even. In this chapter we will consider several concepts of risk and present methods of incorporating it into the capital budgeting system. The objective is to assist the financial manager in making better decisions in a very difficult area.

## CAPITAL BUDGETING AND RISK

### Risk of Ruin

Since future flows are only estimates, the return on a project is not a certainty. Some would have us think of risk as the mere variability of possible returns from the project. When the expected returns (means) from two projects are the same, then truly the project with the greater variability of possible returns *does* represent the higher risk. But when the expected returns from the two projects are not the same then we see that risk is more than mere variability of return. Concern about variability in itself *implies* that the return may be so low as to involve *default,* commonly called *the risk of ruin* or bankruptcy.

The concept of risk of ruin is not antagonistic to the popular concept of risk. To the man on the street risk means the chance of absolute loss or a return below some target rate of return. This view is both reasonable and reconcilable with the view of risk as variability of possible returns from a project.

To illustrate, suppose we are asked to evaluate the riskiness of several projects. Our firm has a cut-off rate of return, wishes to avoid an absolute loss on any project, and wishes to guard against ruin due to a series of unprofitable projects. Looking at one project we see that the expected rate of return (certainly equivalent) is very high, in fact, much higher than the cut-off rate of return. Examining the variability of the possible outcomes we see that it is also very high. But despite the large variability, the chance of the project yielding a rate of return less than the cut-off rate of return is slim. Thus, even the large variability of this project carries little risk for the firm.

Looking at a second project we find that the expected rate of return is only slightly above the cut-off rate of return. Examining the variability of the possible outcomes we see that it is quite narrow but that the chances of the project yielding a rate of return less than the cut-off rate of return are quite good. Thus, despite the modest variability of possible outcomes, the project carries substantial risk for the firm.

To generalize, where projects have different expected rates of return, the riskiness of a project must be evaluated in terms of both the expected rate of return from the project and the variability of possible outcomes relative to the cut-off rate of return and ruin. A project with high variability and a high expected rate of return may be less risky than another project with low variability and a lower expected rate of return. In these situations variability of possible outcomes alone is not a good measure of risk since what we seek is to avoid ruin.

If we analyze the risk of ruin, we find that it also depends on a third factor. The risk of ruin depends upon not only the chances for success of a particular project and the size of the gain to be achieved but also upon the size of the project in relation to the size of the firm. In a nutshell, the principle involved is the same as that involved at Monte Carlo. Assuming the gamble is not "rigged" and involves no skill, the man with the larger bankroll will "outlast" the man with the smaller bankroll. Thus, a man with 100 pennies is almost certain to outlast a man with 5 pennies in a game of "heads or tails" played until one or the other's fund is exhausted. In the early stages of the game a short run of unfavorable tosses will cause ruin for the man with 5 pennies. For the man with 100 pennies a long run of unfavorable tosses is necessary to cause ruin. The probability of a short run of unfavorable tosses occurring is substantially higher than the probability of a long run of unfavorable tosses. Correspondingly, the probability is small of a long run of favorable tosses permitting the man with the few pennies to obtain a large number of pennies thereby reducing his chances of ruin.

The interrelationship of three variables determines the risk of ruin; namely, the probability of success of the project, the size of the gain from the project, and the size of the commitment in the project in relation to the total funds.[1] In the example of matching pennies the probability of success is 50 percent on *each* toss and the size of the gain is *always* 100 percent. When all three variables are permitted to have different values for each project (or toss), the probability of ruin of the firm is shown in Figure 10–1, which is a nomograph. Here, by "success" we mean the project earns either the target rate or zero. With the probability of ruin set at 0.01, each line shows a given probability of success for a project that is associated with various capital ratios (the ratio of the total investment fund to the size of the proposed investment) on the $y$ axis and the different return ratios (the ratio of the net expected return to the proposed investment) on the $x$ axis.

For example, Figure 10–1 shows that a project with a 20 percent chance of success needs a capital ratio of 30 and a return ratio of 7 in order to keep the probability of ruin at 0.01. Further, a firm with a capital ratio of 2.5 needs a return ratio of 1 and a 90 percent chance of success in order to keep the probability of ruin at 0.01.

Despite the restrictive assumption (of target return or nothing), the principle illustrated is applicable in practice. The probability of ruin limits the size of projects that a smaller company can undertake as compared to a larger company. These companies must maintain protection against the possibility of a bad luck streak.

### Mere Variability a Plus, Not a Minus

Some projects involve no variability of return and no risk of default, such as the return from a 4 percent coupon short-term government bond. The only risks a government bond has are a change in the market interest rate or inflation, causing a change in the purchasing power of the dollar.

There is considerable confusion on the subject of risk. It is popular to assume the secret of success is risk aversion. It is assumed the government bond just described is to be preferred to another investment that has a mean return of 4 percent but where the return may vary from 3 percent to 5 percent at any one time. Exactly the opposite is true. The invest-

---

[1] For this purpose there are several possible measures of total funds of the firm: (1) current assets, (2) total assets, (3) capital structure (long-term debt plus equity) and (4) capital structure plus all potential additions thereto.

ment with greater variability but the same mean will sell for a higher price (price-earnings ratio) than the government bond,[2] provided the

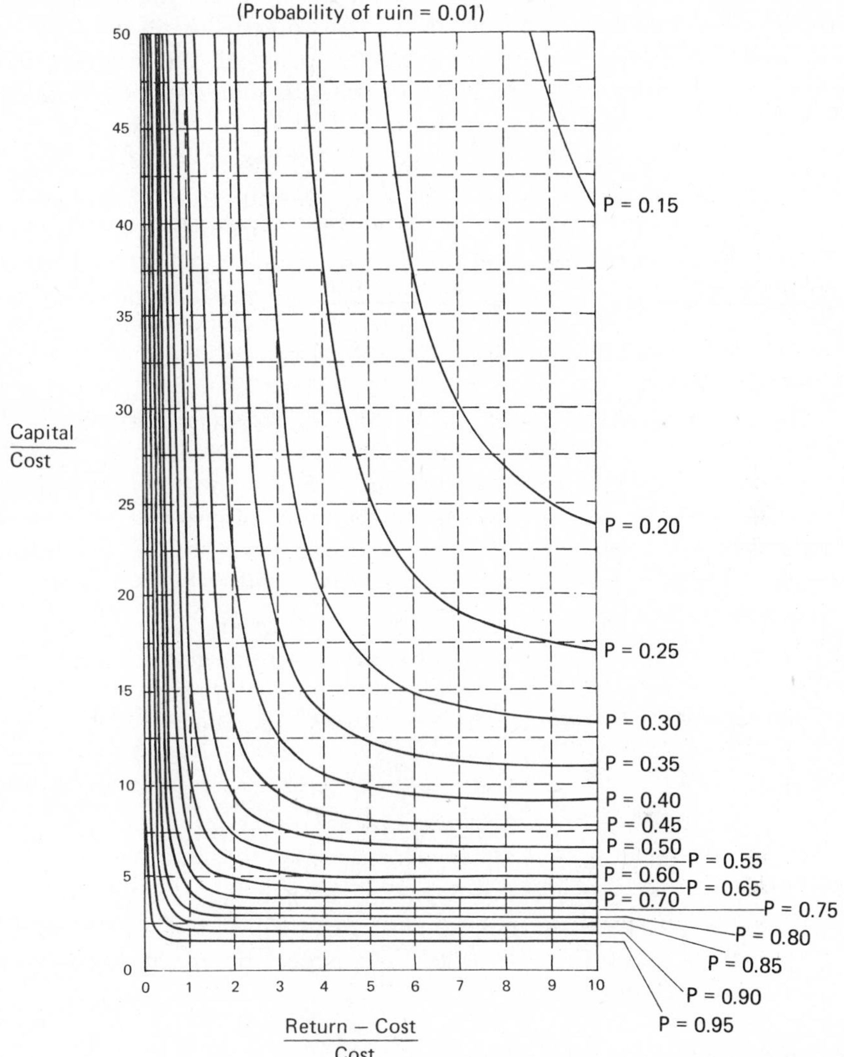


Figure 10–1 Lines of equal probability of success of a project when the probability of ruin is fixed at 0.01 for different capital and return ratios.

Reproduced from D. W. Miller and M. K. Starr, *Executive Decisions and Operations Research* (Englewood Cliffs, N.J.: Prentice Hall, 1960) with permission.

---

[2] Evidence to support this proposition appears in Haskel Benishay, "Attitudes Towards Characteristics of Common Stocks," 1968 Social Statistics Section, *Proceedings of the American Statistical Association*, pp. 318–337.

To quote E. M. Lerner and R. E. Machol, "Risk, Ruin, and Investment Analysis," *Journal of Financial and Quantitative Analysis*, 4 (December 1969), pp. 473–492, at p. 480: "It is clear that *other things being equal*, the probability of loss varies monotonically with variance. . . . However, that variance is monotonic with risk does *not* mean that variance is a measure of risk." For example, the wealth of the investor is relevant. Thus Lerner and Machol continue: "In fact, when the decision-making framework arising from this definition of risk (as measured by the variance) is applied to everyday problems, one can easily show that it leads to bizarre recommendations. For example, as between two investments, one of which returned 5 percent certain and the other 5 percent or 10 percent with probabilities ½, ½ a person with sufficiently high risk aversion risk of ruin has not been materially increased by the variability. The reason is that the investment with variability offers substantial opportunity for capital gains and investors are willing to pay a premium for this opportunity. We make only a routine profit where the return and price of the security are stable.[3] But when the price of the security moves (whether up or down does not matter) we can make extra capital gain if we can anticipate the price movement.

In any event, maximization of the value of the firm requires that we consider the riskiness of a project and evaluate the effect of the trade-off between risk and rate of return on the market price of the firm's shares. To apply this principle we need some system for explicitly recognizing the riskiness of a project, but first we will take up a terminological question.

#### Risk versus Uncertainty

Risk is associated with established probability distributions for such chancy events as the rolling of a pair of dice or spinning of a roulette wheel. When contemplating investment projects rather than games, we frequently are only able to estimate the probabilities for success of a particular project based on such historical data as exist. Some projects are so unique that there is little relevant historical data.[4]

The distinction we make is between certainty and lack of certainty; we allow the concepts of risk and uncertainty to merge,[5] whereas others distinguish between risk (which involves a known probability distribution)[6] and uncertainty (where the probability distribution is unknown).

#### Diversification

The phrases "spread the risk," and "don't put all your eggs in one basket," are commonplace. They suggest that investment risk is not associated with a single event but rather with a series of events; not with one stock purchase or adoption of one project but rather a portfolio of stocks or a group of projects. The expected benefit from diversification is reduction of risk.

---

would presumably prefer the former." Further, when the time dimension (more than one period) is added, studies show that *all* risky portfolios do better than the riskless investment available. But if a risky portfolio always returns more than a riskless rate, in what sense is the portfolio risky?

[3] It is true that given the same arithmetic average return the stable return compounds more rapidly over time than the variable return. Thus a return of 4 percent for certain, over multiple periods is superior to a 50 percent chance of 3 percent or 5 percent. Henry A. Latané and Donald L. Tuttle, *Security Analysis and Portfolio Management* (New York: Ronald Press Co., 1970), pp. 629–632.

[4] A bank setting up a network of branches would have information feedback regarding its estimates. A fairly reliable probability distribution of success can be developed in this and similar instances.

[5] J. Hirshleifer, "Inventory Decision under Uncertainty: Choice-Theoretic Approaches," *Quarterly Journal of Economics*, 79 (November 1965), pp. 509–536.

[6] We may also think of risk in terms of the chance of decline in the value of capital invested in a business due to its inability to earn a competitive rate of return. Many individual investors think this way. See W. A. Morton, "Risk and Return: Instability of Earnings as a Measure of Risk," *Land Economics*, 45 (May 1969), pp. 229–261.

Proper diversification, however, requires that we consider the relationship of the variability of returns of one investment with the variability of returns of each of the remaining investments. Adequacy of diversification does not depend simply on the number of stocks held or projects adopted. Owning 10 airline stocks may be little better than owning the shares of a single airline. What we need for proper diversification is some airline stocks that will rise when the economy is booming and some public utility stocks that will rise when the economy is slackening and airline stocks are falling. To reduce risk we must combine investments that are less than perfectly positively correlated. This is called *Markowitz efficient diversification.*[7] Appendix K, following this chapter, considers the implications of diversification for risk and return of a portfolio of projects.

The following analysis assumes projects are independent of each other. The adoption of a single project does not affect the risk complexion of the firm. In it the firm anticipates operating only one project over the next planning horizon.

### Measuring Risk

Given the same expected (mean) return, the tighter the distribution the less the risk of ruin, as in Figure 10–2 in which Project A involves less risk of ruin than Project B. Yet B will be preferred if its greater risk is more than offset by the premium the market pays for capital gains opportunities. The measure of risk usually adopted is the standard deviation denoted by $\sigma$ (sigma). But we should be clear that in using *the standard deviation we are assuming that $\sigma$ correlates perfectly with the risk of ruin.* Real life is not that simple, and the analysis becomes much more complicated.

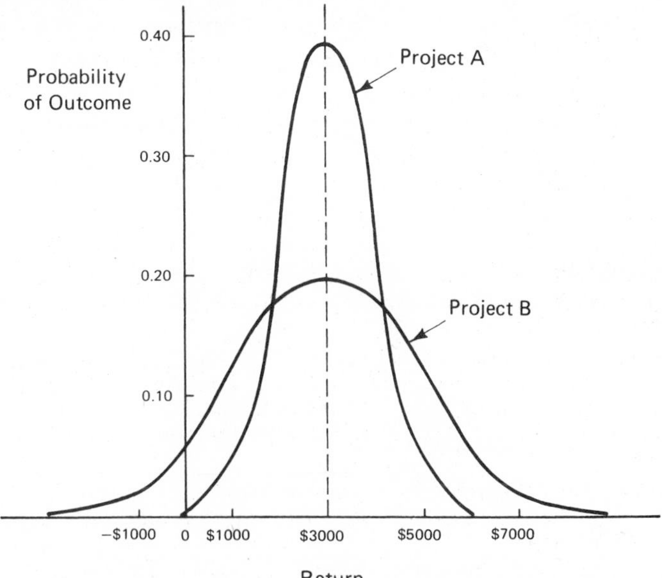


Figure 10–2 Risk of projects measured by probability distributions affecting the probability of ruin.

[7] Harry Markowitz, "Portfolio Selection," *Journal of Finance*, 7 (March 1952), pp. 77–91.

If two projects have the same cost and net present values, the riskiness of the projects can be judged by comparing their *standard deviations.* If the projects have the same cost but different NPVs, we compare the risk-return attractiveness of the projects by taking the ratio of the standard deviation for each project to its mean or expected NPV—computing the *coefficient of variation.* If the projects have different costs, we compare the attractiveness of the projects by taking the ratio of the standard deviation for each project to its profitability index—computing the *risk-return quotient.* Performing these latter two computations adjusts the projects for differences in NPV and cost respectively.

There are three reasons why these three measures—standard deviation, the coefficient of variation, and the risk-return quotient—as measures for comparison of *risk* are only crude approximations and can lead to bizarre results. First, such measures assume the investor has a constant utility of money [8] at various levels and, further, that the utility function of money for various investors is the same, even if not constant. Second, such measures assume normal distributions about an expected (mean) return. Finally, the implication that risk comparisons so made correlate with market values of the investments being compared is contrary to the evidence—which is that risky portfolios do better than "riskless" investments.

### Adjusting the Rate of Discount to Reflect Risk

If we define a riskless rate of return as the rate earned on an asset whose return may be determined with certainty then a risk premium commensurate with the risk of the project must be added to the risk-free rate when investing in a risky project. Following the IRR system the hurdle rate would be raised by this premium amount for projects carrying risk, and under the NPV system the cost of capital or return on assets rate of discount would be increased. For example, with the rate on short-term government bonds at 6 percent, a firm may require as adequate risk compensation a 15 percent return on additions to productive capacity, 25 percent on new products and 40 percent on Latin American investments.

Subjective adjustments have proved workable, and it is not possible to say that more sophisticated systems such as the standard deviation yield superior results.

## COMPUTING RISK AND RETURN

### Applying Variability of Returns as a Measure of Risk

If we decide to go the standard deviation route, we would develop a number of cash flow estimates. Each estimated cash flow stream is characterized by a net present value estimate and viewed as an element, $x_i$, of a normal probability distribution, with determinable mean and standard

[8] Utility of money at various income levels is examined later in this chapter.

deviation. This system keeps the information visible rather than suppressed.[9]

Assume the Sunrise Oil Exploration Company has limited funds to invest in one of several drilling sites. The cost of drilling the Sage River site is $150,000. The hurdle rate is 10 percent. Table 10–1 gives the net present value estimates for the project and their chances of occurring. A pessimistic financial manager might allow his drilling decision to be heavily influenced by the *lowest* possible return—$10,000. An optimistic type might be guided by the *highest* estimate—$50,000. A middle-of-the-roader might select the *median* value—$30,000, which in this case also happens to be the mean. An average person willing to be guided by the probabilities of the estimated net present value might be willing to accept the *expected return* (mean). In Table 10–2 we translate these estimates into a probability distribution and calculate the expected return.

TABLE 10–1. Sage River Site
Net Present Value Estimates

| $x_i$ | Estimate | Chance |
|---|---|---|
| $x_1$ | $10,000 | 1 chance in 10 |
| $x_2$ | $20,000 | 2 chances in 10 |
| $x_3$ | $30,000 | 4 chances in 10 |
| $x_4$ | $40,000 | 2 chances in 10 |
| $x_5$ | $50,000 | 1 chance in 10 |

TABLE 10–2. Expected Net Present Value Calculations
for Drilling on the Sage River Site

| Net present value estimate $x_i$ | Chance | Probability $p(x_i)$ | Weighted estimate $x_i\,p(x_i)$ |
|---|---|---|---|
| $10,000 | 1 in 10 | 0.1 | $ 1,000 |
| $20,000 | 2 in 10 | 0.2 | 4,000 |
| $30,000 | 4 in 10 | 0.4 | 12,000 |
| $40,000 | 2 in 10 | 0.2 | 8,000 |
| $50,000 | 1 in 10 | 0.1 | 5,000 |
| | | 1.0 | |

Expected (mean) net present value $= \mu =$ $30,000

[9] Objective forecasts may not be the rule in industry. Managers appear to gain most from entering conservative estimates. See Donald H. Woods, "Improving Estimates That Involve Uncertainty," *Harvard Business Review*, 44 (July–August 1966), pp. 93 ff.

TABLE 10–3. Cactus Gulch Site
Net Present Value Estimates

| $x_i$ | Estimate | Chance |
|---|---|---|
| $x_1$ | \$20,000 | 3 chances in 10 |
| $x_2$ | \$30,000 | 4 chances in 10 |
| $x_3$ | \$40,000 | 3 chances in 10 |

TABLE 10–4. Expected Net Present Value Calculations
for Drilling on the Cactus Gulch Site

| Net present value estimate $x_i$ | Chance | Probability $p(x_i)$ | Weighted estimate $x_i\, p(x_i)$ |
|---|---|---|---|
| \$20,000 | 3 in 10 | 0.3 | \$ 6,000 |
| \$30,000 | 4 in 10 | 0.4 | 12,000 |
| \$40,000 | 3 in 10 | 0.3 | 12,000 |
| | | 1.0 | |

Expected (mean) net present value $= \mu =$ \$30,000

To compare the prospects for drilling on the Sage River site with those for the Cactus Gulch site we have the data in Tables 10–3 and 10–4. The cost of drilling at Cactus Gulch is estimated at \$100,000. The Cactus Gulch site appears more attractive because the profitability index (PI) is 1.3, compared to 1.2 for the Sage River site [10] but we must consider risk as well as expected return. Having adopted the standard deviation as our measure of risk we perform the necessary calculations for both sites in Tables 10–5 and 10–6.

TABLE 10–5. Risk-Measure Calculations for Sage River Drilling Site

| Net present value estimate $x_i$ | Deviation from expected return $(x_i - \mu)$ | $p(x_i)$* | $(x_i - \mu)^2 p(x_i)$ | $\sigma = \sqrt{\Sigma (x_i - \mu)^2 p(x_i)}$ |
|---|---|---|---|---|
| \$10,000 | −\$20,000 | 0.1 | \$ 40,000,000 | |
| \$20,000 | −\$10,000 | 0.2 | 20,000,000 | |
| \$30,000 | 0 | 0.4 | 0 | $\sigma = \sqrt{120{,}000{,}000}$ |
| \$40,000 | \$10,000 | 0.2 | 20,000,000 | |
| \$50,000 | \$20,000 | 0.1 | 40,000,000 | |
| Variance ($\sigma^2$) of net present value | | | \$120,000,000 | $\sigma =$ \$10,950 |

* The probabilities are obtained from Table 10–2.

[10] Recall the PI is the ratio of the present value of a project to the cost of the project. The present value of total income from Sage and Cactus must be \$180,000 and \$130,000 respectively if the net present value of each is \$30,000.

TABLE 10–6. Risk-Measure Calculations for Cactus Gulch Drilling Site

| Net present value estimate $x_i$ | Deviation from expected return $(x_i - \mu)$ | $p(x_i)$* | $(x_i - \mu)^2 p(x_i)$ | $\sigma = \sqrt{\Sigma (x_i - \mu)^2 p}$ |
|---|---|---|---|---|
| \$20,000 | −\$10,000 | 0.3 | \$30,000,000 | |
| \$30,000 | 0 | 0.4 | 0 | $\sigma = \sqrt{\$60,000,000}$ |
| \$30,000 | −\$10,000 | 0.3 | \$30,000,000 | |
| Variance ($\sigma^2$) of net present value | | | \$60,000,000 | $\sigma = \$7,750$ |

* The probabilities are obtained from Table 10–4.

[A9907]

In this example the decision appears to be easy. At the same discount rate both projects promise to yield the same expected return, \$30,-000. But the drilling costs for the Cactus Gulch site are \$50,000 less (\$150,000 – \$100,000). Also, we might be tempted to say the risk of Cactus Gulch is less because its standard deviation of \$7,750 is less than Sage's \$10,950. However, the risk of ruin does not appear to be different for the two projects since there is no measured probability for loss in either case.

If Sunrise does not have enough funds to handle a large number of these projects, the possible low return of Sage may loom large in the decision made.

## Applying the Risk-Return Quotient (RRQ)

When a large number of projects must be evaluated, there will be variations in cost, expected NPV, and risk. Neither the absolute value of the standard deviation nor the coefficient of variation (standard deviation/mean) will be adequate guides to decision making. We need a better measure of relative attractiveness, one that considers these differences in the costs of projects, expected net present value, and risk. Such a measure is the *risk-return quotient.* It is superior to the net present value, internal rate of return, and profitability index measures. These do not consider risk. Even ignoring risk, the net present value method is dangerous as differences in the costs of projects are not considered. Similarly, use of the coefficient of variation is dangerous even considering risk, as differences in the costs of projects are again not considered.

Let us consider two projects, E–Z and Duro, costing \$100,000 and \$200,000, respectively. E–Z has a profitability index of 3 and Duro an index of 1, based on expected present values of \$300,000 and \$200,000, respectively. In both cases the standard deviation of net present values is \$10,000. If we consider only this standard deviation, the projects are equally acceptable. When looking at the PIs, E–Z is preferable. The two projects may be put on a comparable basis by computing the risk-return quotient (RRQ)—dividing the standard deviation of net present values by the profitability index.

The PI relates the present value to the cost of the project. Relating the standard deviation to the PI, we consider the amount of risk in relation to the expected return. The E–Z project has a RRQ of 3333.3, ($10,000/3), the Duro project 10,000, ($10,000/1). The project with the smaller RRQ is preferable.

### Converting to Percents

The risk-return attractiveness of projects may also be computed using estimates of *rates* of return on each project (Table 10–7) rather than using estimates of net present value for each project (Table 10–5). This makes project comparison more straightforward but requires calculating each rate of return that will equate the different estimated streams of income to the investment—the internal rate of return. Here the standard deviation of the rate of return distribution is divided by the expected (mean) rate of return to compute the risk-return quotient.

For the Sunrise Oil Exploration Company example, the expected rates of return of the two projects are given in Table 10–7 and the standard deviation for each distribution in Table 10–8. Using the data in Table 10–7 and Table 10–8, we compute the RRQ for the Sage River site as 0.37 (0.110/0.30) and for the Cactus Gulch site as 0.26 (0.077/0.30). The Cactus Gulch site again is more attractive.

Note that our RRQ has two meanings, namely

$$\frac{\sigma \text{ of expected net present value}}{\text{PI}}$$

and

$$\frac{\sigma \text{ of expected rate of return}}{\text{expected rate of return}}$$

The second meaning is the coefficient of variation computed for a distribution cast in terms of percents. It measures the risk-return attractiveness of a project without the necessity of computing the profitability index.

### Selecting the Risk-Return Combination

An examination of several projects will reveal that some have similar expected rates of return and others represent similar risks. Of the projects promising the same expected return we may prefer those carrying the lower risk;[11] of those representing the same risk we may prefer those promising the higher return. But, some projects may promise a higher expected return and represent more risk. Other projects may be less risky and

---

[11] Remember, as we pointed out earlier in this chapter, risky portfolios fare better than riskless portfolios when consideration is given to market values and performance.

TABLE 10–7. Expected Rates of Return for Drilling on Sage River and Cactus Gulch Sites

| Sage River | | | Cactus Gulch | | |
|---|---|---|---|---|---|
| Estimated rate of return † $x_i$ | Probability * $p(x_i)$ | Weighted rate $x_i\,p(x_i)$ | Estimated rate of return †† $x_i$ | Probability * $p(x_i)$ | Weighted rate $x_i\,p(x_i)$ |
| 10% | 0.1 | 0.01 | 20% | 0.3 | 0.06 |
| 20 | 0.2 | 0.04 | 30 | 0.4 | 0.12 |
| 30 | 0.4 | 0.12 | 40 | 0.3 | 0.12 |
| 40 | 0.2 | 0.08 | | | |
| 50 | 0.1 | 0.05 | | | |
| | | $\mu = 0.30$ | | | $\mu = 0.30$ |

* The same probabilities as those in Tables 10–2 and 10–4.

† Assume a timing of the inflows such that the NPV estimates given in Table 10–1 correspond to these estimated rates of return on the $150,000 investment.

†† Assume a timing of the inflows such that the NPV estimates given in Table 10–3 correspond to these estimated rates of return on the $100,000 investment.

Note: Tables 10–1 and 10–3 show NPV estimates not IRR. No time element is mentioned in Tables 10–1 and 10–3 or Table 10–7. The discount rate applied in the NPV example is 10 percent. There is no link between the estimated rates of return in Table 10–7 and the NPV estimates of Tables 10–1 and 10–3. The 10 percent rate applied in Tables 10–1 and 10–3 and the amounts of investment in the Sage River and Cactus Gulch sites are consistent with the estimated rates of return in Table 10–7.

TABLE 10–8. Risk Calculations for Sage River and Cactus Gulch Sites *

| | Sage River | | | Cactus Gulch | |
|---|---|---|---|---|---|
| Estimated rate of return $x_i$ | Deviation from expected rate $(x_i - \mu)$ | $(x_i - \mu)^2 p(x_i)$ | Estimated rate of return $(x_i)$ | Deviation from expected rate $(x_i - \mu)$ | $(x_i - \mu)^2 p(x_i)$ |
| 10% | −0.2 | 0.004 | 20% | −0.1 | 0.003 |
| 20 | −0.1 | 0.002 | 30 | 0 | 0 |
| 30 | 0 | 0 | 40 | 0.1 | 0.003 |
| 40 | 0.1 | 0.002 | | | |
| 50 | 0.2 | 0.004 | | | |
| | | $\sigma^2 = 0.012$ | | | $\sigma^2 = 0.006$ |
| | | $\sigma = 0.110$ | | | $\sigma = 0.077$ |

* The probabilities are obtained from Table 10–7.

[A9821]

promise a lower return. How do we choose? We are in deep and uncharted waters. The question is: How far out on the risk scale should we venture to reach for the higher expected return? The answer lies in judgment that is unfortunately frequently salted with emotion. If we are aggressive and confident of the future, we will reach for the higher expected return and slight the added risk. If we are cautious and pessimistic as to the future, risk will dominate judgment and high expected returns will hold little allure. These ideas may be formalized by a family of concentric circles on a coordinate chart with risk on the horizontal axis and return on the vertical axis, as shown in Figure 10–3. Each concentric circle represents some constant risk-return combination for various projects available during a capital budgeting period.[12] These concentric circles are mathematically described. Economically speaking, the portions of these concentric circles lie in the fourth quadrant, the arcs between $A$ and $B$. The arcs in quadrants 1 through 3 are usually neglected because they involve less return for more risk than combinations available in quadrant 4.[13]

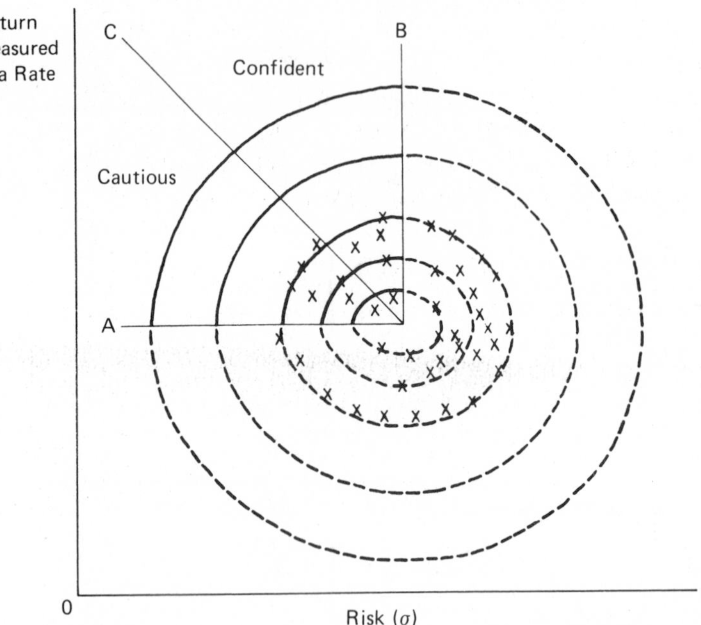


Figure 10–3 Equivalent risk-return combinations.

In selecting projects management would approve only projects lying within the $AB$ quadrant and on the outermost curve, encompassing a set of projects available that period. Within this $AB$ range projects carrying higher risk also promise a higher return. If management were cautious, the projects in the $AC$ range would be favored; if confident, those in the $BC$ range would be favored.[14]

---

[12] Mathematically, the concentric circles can be described by a quadratic function $f(R_1, R_2) = k$, where $R_1$ denotes the risk of a given project, $R_2$ the return from that project, and $k$ a constant value. For example, the concentric circles in Figure 10–3 might be described by the function $f(R_1, R_2) = 10R_1 + 10R_2 + 2R_1R_2 - 2R_1^2 - 2R_2^2$, and for appropriate pairs of values for $R_1$ and $R_2$ we might find that the outermost concentric circle is defined as $f(R_1, R_2) = 42$.

[13] Again, we must refer to our earlier discussion in which we showed that more risky (volatile) stocks command a disproportionately higher price because of the greater chance of capital gain, if we can anticipate price movements of the stock better than the market can. It is appropriate for management to consider this factor when the goal is to maximize the *market* value of the firm (not simply its return in dollars on its investment).

[14] This discussion assumes that the higher-risk projects yield the larger returns, an assumption not definitely established. A careful study of corporate *bond* performance for the period 1900 to 1943 found that *bond* investors who took the smaller risks realized the higher returns. H. G. Fraine, *Valuation of Securities Holdings of Life Insurance Companies* (Homewood, Ill.: Richard D. Irwin Inc., 1962), p. 46. But what is true of bond

## UTILITY OF MONEY AND RISK AVERSION

When discussing capital budgeting, we implicitly assumed a linear relationship between the return to be earned on a proposed investment and the utility to the firm of the additional dollars. However, upon examining the business scene we may find a prosperous and comfortably financed firm unwilling to assume a certain risk regardless of the expected returns and a firm on the verge of bankruptcy willing to assume any risk for another chance of continued survival. More formally, given a choice between two investments with identical expected returns, one firm may choose the safe investment and another may choose the risky investment.

The firm selecting the safe investment is a risk-averter; the firm selecting the risky investment a risk-taker. How do we explain these different preferences? The most widely offered explanation involves the theory of utility.[15]

### Unequal Utility of Successive Dollars

By observing the actions of individuals and firms we see that the utility of added dollars is not equal to prior dollars.[16]

Suppose we examine your own attitude toward risk *vis-à-vis* an investment. Suppose you had a total capital of $1000 and were offered the opportunity to invest $500 in a project that has a 0.60 chance of doubling your money in 30 days and a 0.40 chance that it will become worthless. The odds are distinctly in your favor, but probably you and most people with only $1000 would let the opportunity pass. However, if the opportunity were to invest $1 with the same odds and rate of return, probably you and most people would take it.[17]

Now consider two situations in which the odds are unfavorable. Most homeowners carry fire protection. The annual premiums are low compared to a loss, should it occur. The insurance company has substantial operating expenses. The premiums must be high enough to cover both the fire losses and expenses.

---

investors need not be true of stocks. Thus, under the illusion that any bond is more secure than any stock, the bond-seeker may reach for a higher yield—but he gets more risk than if he had taken a safe stock. Also see L. K. Richardson, "Do High Risks Lead to High Returns?" *Financial Analysts Journal*, 26 (March–April 1970), pp. 88–110. Even given that risk and return are related positively, the problem whether they are linearly related remains.

[15] Again we must look to an alternate explanation stating that more risky stocks command a disproportionately higher price if we feel we can outguess the market as to the future of a particular stock. In other words, the risk-taker firm is counting on the fact that most firms are risk-averters.

[16] The measurable preference among a variety of choices that an individual has in risk situations is called his *utility function*. See Ralph O. Swalm, "Utility Theory—Insights into Risk Taking," *Harvard Business Review*, 44 (November-December 1966), pp. 123–136, for the derivation of an individual's utility curve and samples of utility functions.

[17] If it were a monthly opportunity it would be unrefusable because on the average for every series of 100 one-dollar bets our winnings would be $20, ($120 – $100). We would win $2 for each $1 bet 60 percent of the time.

People are willing to exchange a small-known loss—the insurance premium—at unfavorable odds for the avoidance of a large but uncertain loss. In most lotteries only about one-half of the money from ticket sales is paid out in "winnings." Though the odds are clearly unfavorable, people will risk a small sum in exchange for the chance of winning a very large sum.

To generalize, depending in part on his wealth a sum of money has a different utility to an "investor." If the sum to be committed represents a large proportion of the individual's or the firm's total wealth, the opportunity is usually and rightly foregone even if the odds are favorable—perhaps even if they are very favorable. Conversely, a minor portion of one's wealth might readily be committed. Thus we see that the desire for additional money (utility) is not linearly related to the quantity of money one has.[18]

Most investors are risk-averters, an observation explained by the diminishing marginal utility of money. But others are risk-takers. Therefore, even if risk and return were linearly related, for most investors risk and the utility of additional dollars are not.

### Utility and Risk in Evaluating Capital Expenditure Projects

The utility of money to a firm must reflect the utility functions of its board of directors. When sitting as a director, an individual probably has a different utility function in mind than when acting for his personal account. The utility function probably tapers more slowly and might even rise. Since most of the money involved is other people's money, the temptation to gamble may be high.

To achieve a target level of earnings, the firm is willing to adopt projects representing a reasonable amount of risk, but excess earnings are of diminishing utility. Figure 10–4 presents a graph of the utility curve of Doggerel Publishing, Inc. The target earnings are $70,000 per

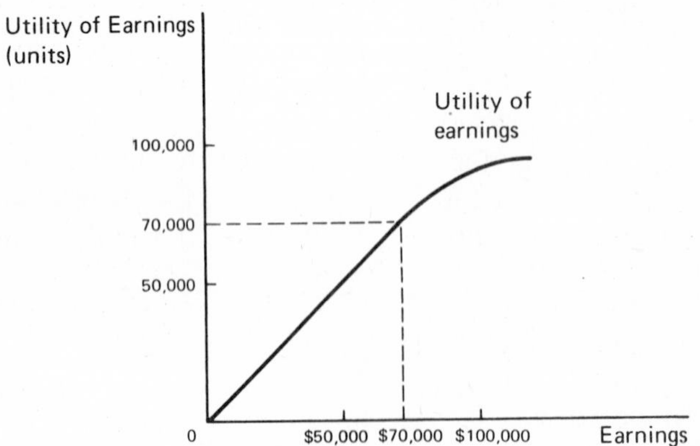


Figure 10–4 Doggerel Publishing, Inc. utility curve.

---

[18] The progressive income tax does not seem to reduce the incentive to earn. High-income individuals are as eager to earn as low-income persons—perhaps more so. But the income tax may reinforce the declining marginal utility of money in the case of risky investments.

year. In exceptional years $100,000 in earnings is possible. The utility of each additional dollar of earnings to the company is constant ($1 = 1 util) until the $70,000 mark is reached and then declines from $70,000 to $100,000.

The marginal and average utility for earnings above $70,000 are given in Table 10–9. For example, an additional $5000 of earnings above $70,000 has a utility of 96 cents per dollar of earning.

TABLE 10–9. Doggerel Publishing, Inc.*
Utility Schedule

| Marginal earnings | Marginal utility per dollar | Total earnings | Average utility of all dollars |
|---|---|---|---|
| First $70,000 | 1.0 | 70,000 | 1.0 |
| Additional $5,000 | 0.96 | 75,000 | 0.997 |
| Additional $10,000 | 0.90 | 85,000 | 0.986 |
| Additional $15,000 | 0.80 | 100,000 | 0.958 |

* Graphed in Figure 10–4.

Doggerel Publishing, Inc. uses a 24 percent cut-off rate. A manuscript entitled *Stirrings* is available and the firm is trying to decide whether to publish it. The earnings goal for the year seems assured. The expected cash inflow from *Stirrings* is $10,000 per year for 6 years, but an immediate cash outlay of $30,000 is required. The other manuscripts are expected to return profits substantially above the 24 percent mark. Applying a 24 percent discount rate to the cash flows from *Stirrings*, we have a present value of $32,205 ($10,000 × 3.2205) and a net present value of $2205 ($32,205 − $30,000). This means returns from the project are sufficiently high to permit recapture of our investment, earn a 24 percent return, and receive $2205 "to boot." But we are in the range at which an *additional* dollar of earnings above $70,000 no longer means an additional dollar of utility. Considering the reduced utility of earnings, that is, cash inflow beyond the cost of the project, is the project worth the risk? Applying the marginal utility figures for additional earnings in excess of $70,000 shown in Table 10–10, we find that *Stirrings* is not worth the publishing risk. The net present value is negative ($28,863 − $30,000 = $1137).

TABLE 10–10. Doggerel Publishing Inc.
Present Value Determination

| (1) Year | (2) Cash inflow | (3) Marginal utility per dollar * | (4) Discount factor (24%) | (5) Present value (2)×(3)×(4) |
|---|---|---|---|---|
| 1 | $10,000 | 1.0 | 0.806 | $ 8,060 |
| 2 | 10,000 | 1.0 | 0.650 | 6,530 |
| 3 | 10,000 | 1.0 | 0.524 | 5,240 |
| 4 | { 5,000 | 0.96 | 0.423 | 2,030 |
|  | 5,000 | 0.90 | 0.423 | 1,904 |
| 5 | { 5,000 | 0.90 | 0.341 | 1,535 |
|  | 5,000 | 0.80 | 0.341 | 1,364 |
| 6 | 10,000 | 0.80 | 0.275 | 2,200 |
|  |  |  |  | $28,863 |

* Based on Table 10–9.

## SUMMARY

The variability of possible returns from a project is termed *risk*. But true risk depends not on mere variability but on changes in the risk of ruin, which in turn depends on three variables: the probability of success of the project, the size of the possible gain from the project relative to the investment (the return ratio), and the size of the investment relative to the total fund for investment (the capital ratio).

Variability is described by a probability distribution and measured in terms of standard deviations. One way to accommodate the riskiness of an investment is to adjust the discount rate. Another is to assign probabilities to the cash flow estimates, to determine the expected (mean) return (certainty equivalent) and standard deviation of the distribution, and to take the standard deviation as the measure of the risk. This risk measure is not entirely satisfactory since it does not consider the magnitude of the expected net present value. Weighting the standard deviation by the size of the expected net present value gives the coefficient of variation that can be used if the projects have the same cost. If projects have different costs and different expected net present values, we can compare them by computing the risk-return quotient (RRQ), which is the ratio of the standard deviation of the distribution of net present values to the profitability index of the project, or, if using rates of return, the ratio of the standard deviation of the distribution of rates of return to the expected rate of return.

The utility of additional dollars is not the same for all firms or even for the same firm under different circumstances. A risk-taking firm may place more value on additional earnings than a risk-avoiding firm. A small firm with limited capital may decline to engage in a project that would absorb a large portion of its funds, even though the odds for success are very favorable, while a large firm for whom the same amount of funds represents only a small percentage of its assets might readily undertake a project, even though the odds are less favorable.

Most investors are risk-averters. This observation is explained by diminishing marginal utility. A firm can evaluate the risk-return trade-off of a project in terms of utility by attaching its subjective utility to the marginal income. The expected return on a project after discounting for the reduced utility of income at the margin can be compared with the cost of the project. If the net present value (NPV) still remains positive, the project should be accepted.

### *Study Questions*

1. What makes risk important in the selection of projects? Is a low-risk project expected to earn a 15 percent return more desirable than a high-risk project also expected to earn 15 percent?
2. What is the difference between risk and uncertainty? What difficulties stand in the way of developing methods for dealing with uncertainty?
3. Is it in the national interest for a firm to select high-yielding, low-risk projects? Can the federal government influence the degree of business risk? How?
4. Why may use of the standard deviation as a measure of risk lead to wrong decisions? What modification can be made to obtain an improved measure?
5. Why are income estimates for distant years usually less reliable than for more immediate years? How can this time factor be accommodated when evaluating the riskiness of a project?
6. When the NPV of a project is zero, what does this signify about the minimum anticipated rate of return and the IRR? When the IRR is less than the minimum anticipated rate of return, what does this signify about the NPV?
7. How is it possible for the risk attached to a combination of several projects to be less than that attached to any single project?
8. Why might the utility of an additional dollar of income not be as high to a prosperous firm as to a marginal firm?
9. How does willingness to risk a certain sum of money on a project relate to the size of the firm? Is this a rational attitude? Why?

### *Problems*

1. Waco, Inc is considering two mutually exclusive projects, A and B. Project A's investment is $10,000, Project G's is $12,000. Table 10–11 presents the net present value probability distribution for each project.

TABLE 10–11. NPV Probability Distribution of Projects A and B

| Project A | | Project B | |
|---|---|---|---|
| Probability | NPV Estimate | Probability | NPV Estimate |
| 0.1 | $1,000 | 0.2 | $1,000 |
| 0.4 | 2,000 | 0.3 | 2,000 |
| 0.4 | 4,000 | 0.3 | 4,000 |
| 0.1 | 5,000 | 0.2 | 5,000 |

a. Compute the expected net present value of projects A and B.

b. Compute the risk attached to each project, that is, the standard deviation of each probability distribution.

c. Compute the profitability index for each project.

d. Compute the coefficient of variation for each project.

e. Compute the risk-return quotient for each project.

f. Rank projects A and B according to expected net present value, risk, profitability index, coefficient of variation, and risk-return quotient.

2. The Peer Gynt Music Company is considering expanding its present downtown location. The project cost is $20,000. Table 10–12 gives appropriate net present value estimates and their probabilities.

TABLE 10–12. Peer Gynt Music Company
Net Present Value Estimates of Expansion Project

| *NPV Estimate* | *Probability* |
|---|---|
| $3000 | 0.2 |
| 4000 | 0.6 |
| 5000 | 0.2 |
| | 1.0 |

a. Determine the expected return of the project and the risk (standard deviation).

b. Determine the profitability index and the risk-return quotient.

Before any action can be taken the opportunity arises to establish a second store in the new Red Mill suburban shopping center. The project cost is $30,000. Table 10–13 presents the net present value estimates for the project and their probabilities.

TABLE 10–13. Peer Gynt Music Company
Net Present Value Estimates of Red Mill Shopping Center Project

| *NPV Estimate* | *Probability* |
|---|---|
| $11,000 | 0.3 |
| 12,000 | 0.4 |
| 13,000 | 0.3 |
| | 1.0 |

c. Determine the expected return of the shopping center project and the risk.

d. Determine the PI and the RRQ.

e. Comparing the expansion and Red Mill shopping center projects, which promises to be more profitable? Which carries the least risk? How would you decide which project to select?

3. (The material required to work this problem is found in Appendix J, which follows these problems.) The Relaxer Company has developed a new health

aid to improve muscular vitality. The project cost is \$2000 and is expected to yield \$1000 a year for 3 years. The discount rate is 20 percent. Relevant data are summarized in Table 10–14.

TABLE 10–14. Relaxer Company, Health Aid Project

| Project information | Year | Expected cash flow $\overline{A}_t$ | | Risk Measure $\sigma_t$ | Discount rate $i$ |
|---|---|---|---|---|---|
| Cost (cash outflow) | 0 | \$2,000 | | 0 | |
| Receipts (cash inflow) | 1 | | \$1,000 | 100 | |
| | 2 | | 1,000 | 100 | 20% |
| | 3 | | 1,000 | 200 | |
| Termination value, \$0 | | | | | |

a. Determine the net present value of the project.

b. Determine the project risk.

c. Determine the probability that the IRR will fall below the discount rate.

d. Express your opinion regarding the desirability of adopting the project.

4. (The material required to work this problem is found in Appendix K, following these problems.) The Flo Thro Corporation manufactures three perfume fragrances called Xmee, Yum-Yum, and Zingo, or $X$, $Y$, and $Z$, distilled from a single coal tar input. With Flo Thro's equipment any combination of the three fragrances can be produced. Recommend the proportions of the three fragrances to produce on the available equipment. The relevant data are summarized in Table 10–15.

TABLE 10–15. Flo Thro Corporation
Xmee, Yum-Yum, and Zingo Data

| *Fragrances* | | $X$ | $Y$ | $Z$ |
|---|---|---|---|---|
| Expected profit | | 3.0 | 3.30 | 4.00 |
| Variance | | 0.4 | 0.39 | 0.60 |
| Covariance ($XY$) | −0.4 | | | |
| Covariance ($XZ$) | +0.1 | | | |
| Covariance ($YZ$) | +0.3 | | | |

With the formulas

$$E(P) = aE(X) + bE(Y) + cE(Z)$$

where $a =$ proportion of fragrance $X$ produced
$b =$ proportion of fragrance $Y$ produced
$c =$ proportion of fragrance $Z$ produced
$E(P) =$ expected value of the perfume fragrance production

and $a + b + c = 1.00.$

$\mathrm{Var}(P) = a^2\mathrm{Var}(X) + b^2\mathrm{Var}(Y) + c^2\mathrm{Var}(Z) + 2ab\mathrm{Cov}(XY) + 2ac\mathrm{Cov}(XZ) + 2bc\mathrm{Cov}(YZ)$

determine the combination of fragrance production that will yield (a) the highest return on investment; (b) the lowest return on investment; (c) the variance and the associated expected return when equal portions of fragrances $X$, $Y$, and $Z$ are produced.

d. Scaling variance on the ordinate and expected return on the abscissa, calculate various combinations of the production of only fragrances $X$ and $Z$ and trace the outer boundary of combinations. Identify the unacceptable combinations—those combinations that promise a lower return and a higher variance. These are the combinations to the left of the minimum variance point. Suggestion: use intervals of tenths.

5. Joe Go-Go, an energetic young businessman, is interested in determining his utility function and turns to you for help. After some close questioning you determine the following facts.

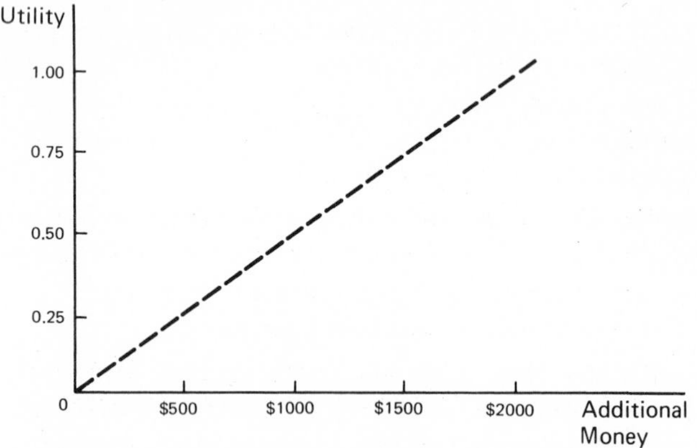


Figure 10–5 Joe Go-Go's utility curve for money.

Offered the opportunity to gamble $1000 with 50–50 odds of doubling his money or losing it, Go-Go would refuse to gamble. He would hold onto his $1000.

Offered the opportunity to gamble $500 with 50–50 odds of winning $1000 or losing the $500, he would gamble.

Offered the opportunity to gamble $700, with 50–50 odds of winning $1000 or losing the $700, he would be indifferent as to whether he gambled or not. The $700 certain would be equally attractive to him as the gamble with 50–50 odds.

You conclude that $2000 has a utility of 1.00 to Go-Go. No money, of course, has a zero utility. The $700 has a utility of 0.50, since Go-Go would be willing to accept 50–50 odds of doubling his $1000 fortune or losing $700 or not gambling at all and keeping the $700 safe. Given these three points, trace Go-Go's utility curve on the graph in Figure 10–5. If the relationship between utility and money were linear the curve would be a straight line, as indicated in the graph. Does the curve indicate that Go-Go is a risk-taker or a risk-avoider?

## *Selected References*

Arditti, F. D., "Risk and the Required Return on Equity," *Journal of Finance*, 22 (March 1967), pp. 14–36.

Benishay, Haskel, "Attitudes toward Characteristics of Common Stock," *Proceedings of the American Statistical Association* (1968 Social Statistics Section), pp. 318–337.

Blume, M. E., "On the Assessment of Risk," *Journal of Finance*, 26 (March 1971), pp. 95–117.

Breen, William J. and Eugene M. Lerner, "Corporate Financial Strategies and Market Measures of Risk and Return," *Journal of Finance* 28 (May 1973), pp. 339–351.

Brown, Rex, "Do Managers Find Decision Theory Useful?" *Harvard Business Review,* 48 (May-June 1970), pp. 78–89.

Fisher, I. M., and R. G. Hall, "Risk and Corporate Rates of Return," *Quarterly Journal of Economics,* 83 (February 1969) pp. 79–92.

Gentry, James and John Pike, "An Empirical Study of the Risk-Return Hypothesis Using Common Stock Portfolios of Life Insurance Companies," *Journal of Financial and Quantitative Analysis,* 5 (June 1970), pp. 179–186.

Hakansson, N. H., "Friedman—Savage Utility Functions Consistent with Risk Aversion," *Quarterly Journal of Economics,* 86 (August 1970), pp. 472–487.

Hertz, D. B., "Risk Analysis in Capital Investments," *Harvard Business Review,* 42 (January-February 1964), pp. 95–106.

Hirshleifer, J., "Investment Decision under Uncertainty: Applications of the State—Preference Approach," *Quarterly Journal of Economics,* 80 (May 1966), pp. 252–277.

Lerner, E. M., and R. E. Machol, "Risk, Ruin and Investment Analysis," *Journal of Financial and Quantitative Analysis,* 4 (December 1969), pp. 473–492.

Lintner, J., "Security Prices, Risk, and Maximal Gains from Diversification," *Journal of Finance,* 20 (December 1965), pp. 587–615.

Litzenberger, R. H., and Alan P. Budd, "Corporate Investment Criteria and the Valuation of Risk Assets," *Journal of Financial and Quantitative Analysis,* 5 (December 1970), pp. 395–419.

Magee, J. F., "How to Use Decision Trees in Capital Budgeting," *Harvard Business Review,* 42 (September-October 1964), pp. 79–95.

Markowitz, H., "Portfolio Selection," *Journal of Finance,* 7 (March 1952), pp. 77–91.

Morton, W. A., "Risk and Return: Instability of Earnings as a Measure of Risk," *Land Economics,* 45 (May 1969), pp. 229–261.

Näsland, B., "A Model of Capital Budgeting under Risk," *Journal of Business,* 39 (April 1966), pp. 257–271.

Richardson, L. K., "Do High Risks Lead to High Returns?" *Financial Analysts Journal,* 26 (March-April 1970), pp. 88–99.

Rubenstein, M. E., "A Mean-Variance Synthesis of Corporate Financial Theory," *Journal of Finance,* 28 (March 1973), pp. 167–181.

Stapleton, R. C., "Portfolio Analysis, Stock Valuation and Capital Budgeting Decision Rules for Risky Projects," *Journal of Finance,* 26 (March 1971), pp. 95–117.

Swalm, R. O., "Utility Theory—Insights into Risk Taking," *Harvard Business Review,* 44 (November-December 1966), pp. 123–136.

Virts, J. R., "Weighing Risk in Capacity Expansion," *Harvard Business Review,* 48 (May-June 1970), pp. 132–141.

Woods, D. H., "Improving Estimates That Involve Uncertainty," *Harvard Business Review,* 44 (July-August 1966), pp. 91–98.

### Appendix J

## EVALUATION OF RISK AND THE TIME DIMENSION

In Figure 10–2 we assumed risk constant over time; that the returns in a distant year could be estimated as precisely as for an immediate year. But the range of possible outcomes widens when we estimate returns further in the future. As Figure 10–6 shows, the probability distribution of returns over time broadens and flattens. The range of the standard deviation increases and the expected return (mean) for each year increases in variation. The last idea is only imperfectly shown in our two-dimensional graph.

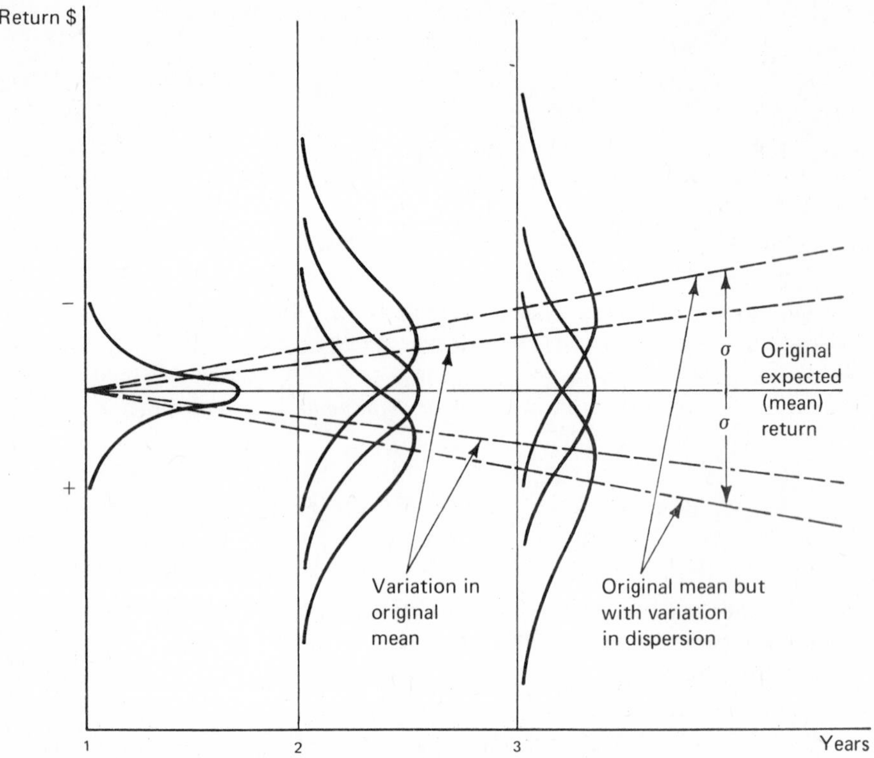


Figure 10–6 Increasing risk over time.

To develop the general formulation of this risk-evaluation system recall a few elementary propositions. The net present value (NPV) of an investment is defined as

$$\text{NPV} = \sum_{t=0}^{n} \left[ \frac{A_t}{(1+i)^t} \right]$$

where $i$ is the firm's desired return and $A_t$ the expected cash *outflow* or *inflow* during the $t$ th period.[19] The NPV instead of being considered a single-valued quantity, however, may be thought of as a random variable where each element

[19] The NPV of a project is equal to the discounted value of the estimated future cash receipts minus the cost of the project. Since in the formula the beginning of the series is at $t = 0$ and the cost of the project is negative, we obtain the NPV.

$A_t$ is actually the mean $\bar{A}_t$ of a cash flow estimate probability distribution for the $t$ th year. Thus we may think in terms of

$$\text{NPV} = \sum_{t=0}^{n} \left[ \frac{\bar{\mathbf{A}}_t}{(1+i)^t} \right]$$

The project will be undertaken if the NPV is greater than zero. Assume that the cash flows $A_0, A_1, \ldots, A_n$ for the years 0, 1, 2, . . ., $n$ are mutually independent.[20]

The variance of the NPV is given by

$$\sigma_{\text{NPV}}^2 = \sum_{t=0}^{n} \frac{\sigma_t^2}{(1+i)^{2t}}$$

A firm will avoid investment proposals that promise a rate of return less than $i$, the desired return on investment; that is, where the NPV is negative. A negative NPV will occur if the IRR is less than the desired rate of return $i$.[21] Thus the firm wishes to know the probability that IRR$<i$. This may be expressed as

$$\text{Prob}\{\text{IRR} < i\}.$$

For any given project and a fixed value $i$, the higher the estimated cash inflows, the higher the value of IRR. Knowing that the probability of the IRR is less than the desired return on investment $i$ gives the firm a measure of the project's risk. We may express these ideas in the form

$$\text{Prob}\{\text{NPV} < 0 \mid i\}$$

This says, "given a rate $i$, when applied to the cash flow stream, what is the probability that the NPV will be less than zero?"

Assume that Paul Revere Lantern, Inc. is considering a new project expected to cost $500. The expected cash inflows are $200 annually for 4 years. The firm's desired rate of return $i$ is 15 percent.

TABLE 10–16. Paul Revere, Inc.
Lantern Evaluation Project

| *Project information* | *Year$_t$* | $\bar{A}_t$ | | $\sigma_t$ | $i$ |
|---|---|---|---|---|---|
| Cost (cash outflow) | 0 | $500 | | 0 | |
| Receipts (cash inflow) | 1 | | $200 | 10 | |
| | 2 | | 200 | 20 | 15% |
| | 3 | | 200 | 30 | |
| | 4 | | 200 | $\sqrt{1000}$ | |
| Termination value | | | 0 | 0 | |

[A9843]

[20] See Frederick S. Hiller, "The Derivation of Probabilistic Information for the Evaluation of Risky Investments," *Management Science*, 9 (April 1963), pp. 443–457, for a discussion of the case where the cash flows may be independent in part and related in part.

[21] Recall, to raise the present value of a future stream of income we lower the discount rate.

Developing a new lantern is a risky affair. The cash flow estimates in the more distant years are less certain. Assume the expected cash inflow in each year is the same but that the dispersion increases as the years stretch from 1 to 4, as show in Table 10–16. Returning $200 per year for 4 years, discounted at $i = 15$ percent, the project has a NPV of $71. The IRR is 22 percent. Using a 22 percent discount rate the NPV is zero.

If the cash benefits stream fell such that IRR<$i$, the project would be returning less than the firm's desired rate of return. To determine the risk that this will happen we need the NPV of the project at $i$ equals 15 percent (which is $71), and the standard deviation of this distribution, which is

$$\sigma^2_{\text{NPV}} = \sum_{j=0}^{4} \frac{\sigma_t^2}{(1+i)^{2t}} = 0^2 + \frac{10^2}{(1.15)^2} + \cdots + \frac{(\sqrt{1{,}000})^2}{(1.15)^8}$$

$$= \$1{,}020.20$$

$$\sigma_{\text{NPV}} = \$32.00.$$

To find the probability of the cash benefits falling so low that the NPV is less than zero we compute

$$z = \frac{\text{NPV}}{\sigma_{\text{NPV}}} = \frac{\$71}{\$32} = 2.2\sigma$$

From a table of areas under the normal curve we find that only 2 percent of the area lies to the left of 2.2 standard deviations below the mean. Therefore,

$$\text{Prob}\{\text{NPV} < 0 \mid i = 15\%\} = 0.02$$

The odds are 49 to 1 the project will earn at least the desired return.

## Appendix K

### EVALUATING RETURN AND RISK OF AN ASSET PORTFOLIO

Up to now we have assumed that projects are independent of each other. Seldom can one project, however, be considered apart from the other projects a firm adopts. Adopting one group of projects will represent a different composite return and degree of risk than commitment of the same total capital to a different project mix.

*Return and Risk of a Group of Projects* The return from an asset portfolio may be considered the weighted average of the percentage of total funds invested in each project times the expected (mean) return from the project. But the risk of the portfolio is not simply a weighted average of the risk estimated to be associated with the individual projects. This is true only if the returns of the individual projects are perfectly positively correlated with each other. To the extent risks of individual projects offset each other, we can select an asset portfolio that yields the optimum risk-return combination.

If variation is our measure of risk, then the higher the variation the greater the risk of a portfolio. The variation of the portfolio is determined in part by the variability of the individual projects, in part by the extent to which the variability of individual projects tends to offset each other, and by the percent of total capital invested in each project (assume the projects are infinitely divisible). The variability of one project associated with the variability of another is called the *covariance*. For a project portfolio that may contain either one, the other, or both projects the net variation may range from zero, where equal amounts of funds are committed to two perfectly negatively correlated projects, to the variation of the highest-risk project if all the funds are invested in that one project.

*Perfectly Positively Correlated Projects* Assume the Pine Box Casket Company has a given sum to invest in either or both of two projects, new hand tools or additional advertising, in any amounts desired. If proportionately the returns on both projects rise and fall together, the projects are perfectly positively correlated. Then any combination of the two has the same expected return and carries the same risk. Suppose, for example, that each project has the cash flow estimates and corresponding probabilities shown in Table 10–17.

TABLE 10–17. Pine Box Casket Company

Expected Return, Hand Tools or Additional Advertising

| Probabilities $p_i$ | Cash flow estimates $x_i$ | |
|---|---|---|
| 0.2 | $2000 | $\mu =$ $3,000 |
| 0.6 | $3000 | $\sigma^2 =$ $400,000 |
| 0.2 | $4000 | $\sigma =$ $633 |

[A9842]

Since the returns of the two projects are perfectly positively correlated, their total may be treated as a single project. Regardless of the percentage of a fixed sum—say *M*—committed to the projects, the portfolio will yield the same expected rate of return and carry the same risk, provided the entire amount is invested. Should we have available 2*M* funds and decide to undertake fully both projects we will have the figures found in Table 10–18. Doubling the amount invested doubles the expected return and the standard deviation.

TABLE 10–18. Pine Box Casket Company

Expected Return, Hand Tools and Additional Advertising, Investment Doubled

| Probabilities $p_i$ | Cash flow estimates $x_i$ | |
|---|---|---|
| 0.2 | $4000 | $\mu =$ $6,000 |
| 0.6 | $6000 | $\sigma^2 =$ $1,600,000 |
| 0.2 | $8000 | $\sigma =$ $1,267 |

*Perfectly Negatively Correlated Projects* Suppose we have two perfectly negatively correlated projects. They are a new hearse and a new ambulance for the Friendly Funeral Home.[22] The cost of each vehicle is the same, namely $10,-800, and each vehicle is to be in service for 4 years and then junked at no salvage value. Three economic conditions may prevail, as shown in Table 10–19. If the first economic condition prevails (many deaths by suicide require a hearse but no ambulance) the hearse is expected to yield $6000 of revenue and the ambulance $2000; if the second condition prevails, the hearse and the ambulance can each be expected to earn $4000; and if the third condition prevails, the hearse can be expected to yield $2000 and the ambulance $6000. The expected return of this asset portfolio with an equal amount of funds invested in each project is $8000. The standard deviation of the portfolio is zero because the portfolio always returns $8000. Though each project individually involves some variation, the two risks perfectly offset each other.

---

22 In this community faster ambulance service means fewer hearse passengers.

TABLE 10–19. Friendly Funeral Home
Hearse and Ambulance Investment
Estimated Cash Flows and Probabilities under Three Possible Economic Conditions

| Possible economic condition $w_i$ | Estimated probability $p_i$ | Estimated return on individual projects: Ambulance | Hearse | Estimated return, combined projects |
|---|---|---|---|---|
| $w_1$ | 0.2 | \$2000 | \$6000 | \$8000 |
| $w_2$ | 0.6 | \$4000 | \$4000 | \$8000 |
| $w_3$ | 0.2 | \$6000 | \$2000 | \$8000 |

*Optimum Combination of Projects* Most asset portfolios consist of projects falling somewhere between being perfectly positively correlated and perfectly negatively correlated. Let us see how the percentage amounts invested in two projects affect the expected return and the risk from the portfolio.

Boothill Memorial Company has the opportunity to acquire additional quarrying rights. The historical record reveals a pattern of returns from granite and marble quarrying operations under a variety of economic conditions. With no startling technological developments on the horizon, we draw up the data in Table 10–20 for the two quarrying operations. We want to know the proportion of funds to invest in each project.

The expected return for the granite project is \$3000 and for the marble project \$3300. The expected return, $E(Q)$, of the total quarry operation is given by

$$E(Q) = aE(G) + (1 - a)E(M) \qquad (10\text{–}1)$$

$$= a(3{,}000) + (1 - a)(3{,}300).$$

where $a$ equals the percentage invested in the granite quarry and $(1 - a)$ the percentage invested in the marble quarry.

TABLE 10–20. Boothill Memorial Company
Estimated Cash Flows and Associated Probabilities for Granite and Marble Quarries

| Possible economic conditions $w_i$ | Probability $p_i$ | Estimated Cash Flows: Granite quarry $G_i$ | Marble quarry $M_i$ | $(G_i \times M_i)$* (000) | $p_i$ * |
|---|---|---|---|---|---|
| $w_1$ | 0.3 | \$4000 | \$2000 | \$ 8,000 | 0.3 |
| $w_2$ | 0.1 | 2000 | 3000 | 6,000 | 0.1 |
| $w_3$ | 0.1 | 2000 | 3000 | 6,000 | 0.1 |
| $w_4$ | 0.1 | 3000 | 3000 | 9,000 | 0.1 |
| $w_5$ | 0.2 | 2000 | 5000 | 10,000 | 0.2 |
| $w_6$ | 0.1 | 4000 | 3000 | 12,000 | 0.1 |
| $w_7$ | 0.1 | 3000 | 5000 | 15,000 | 0.1 |

* Used to facilitate identifying the joint probabilities in Table 10–23.

To determine the risk attached to any combination of the two-project portfolio we need the variance of each project and the covariance of the projects.

Table 10–21 shows the variance of the granite project and Table 10–22 the variance of the marble project. The covariance of projects $G$ and $M$ is given by

$$\text{Cov}(G, M) = E(GM) - E(G)E(M) \tag{10–2}$$

To find $E(GM)$ we draw up a joint probability table (Table 10–23) that is based on Table 10–20. Table 10–23 shows the probability of the granite project yielding \$4000 and the marble project yielding \$2000 at the same time, the probability of $G$ returning \$3000 and $M$, \$2000 at the same time, and so on.

TABLE 10–21. Boothill Memorial Company
Variance of the Granite Project

| $G_i$ * | $\Sigma p_i G_i$ † | $[G_i - \Sigma p_i G_i]^2$ (000) | $p_i$ * | $p_i[G_i - \Sigma p_i G_i]^2$ (000) |
|---|---|---|---|---|
| \$2000 | \$3000 | \$1000 | 0.4 | \$400 |
| 3000 | 3000 | 0 | 0.2 | 0 |
| 4000 | 3000 | 1000 | 0.4 | 400 |
| | | Variance of the granite project = | | \$800 |

* Computed from Table 10–20 as follows. There is a combined probability of 0.4 that \$2000 will occur, a 0.2 probability that \$3000 will occur, and a 0.4 probability that \$4000 will occur.
† Computed from Table 10–20.

TABLE 10–22. Boothill Memorial Company
Variance of the Marble Project

| $M_i$ * | $\Sigma p_i M_i$ † | $[M_i - \Sigma p_i M_i]^2$ (000) | $p_i$ * | $p_i[M_i - \Sigma p_i M_i]^2$ (000) |
|---|---|---|---|---|
| \$2000 | \$3300 | \$1690 | 0.3 | \$ 507 |
| 3000 | 3300 | 90 | 0.4 | 36 |
| 5000 | 3300 | 2890 | 0.3 | 867 |
| | | Variance of the marble project = | | \$1,410 |

* Computed from Table 10–20 as follows. There is a combined probability of 0.3 that \$2000 will occur, of 0.4 that \$3000 will occur, and of 0.3 that \$5000 will occur.
† Computed from Table 10–20.

In Table 10–23 the top row is the first column of Table 10–22 and the first column is the first column of Table 10–21. The number in the upper left-hand corner of each central box is the product of the numbers in the first column and the top row. Thus, in the upper left central box there is zero probability that \$4 million will result as the product of $G_i$ of \$2000 and $M_j$ of \$2000 (see Table 10–20). In the next box to the right there is 0.20 probability that a $G_i$ of \$2000 will occur with an $M_j$ of \$3000. And in the box under the first box discussed, there is zero probability that a $G_i$ of \$3000 will occur with an $M_j$ of \$2000. The bottom row sums the vertical probabilities and the last column sums the hori-

TABLE 10–23. Boothill Memorial Company Joint Probability Table

| $G_i$ (000) \ $M_j$ (000) | \$2 | \$3 | \$5 | $P_j$ |
|---|---|---|---|---|
| \$2 | 4 / 0 | 6 / 0.20 | 10 / 0.20 | 0.40 |
| \$3 | 6 / 0 | 9 / 0.10 | 15 / 0.10 | 0.20 |
| \$4 | 8 / 0.30 | 12 / 0.10 | 20 / 0 | 0.40 |
| $P_i$ | 0.30 | 0.40 | 0.30 | 1.00 |

zontal probabilities. The box in the lower right-hand corner sums the bottom row and the last column. The $M_j$ in this table corresponds to the $M_i$ in Tables 10–20, 10–21, and 10–22.

The expected value of $G$ times $M$ $[E(GM)]$ is obtained by multiplying the estimated cash flows from granite under different economic conditions (the $G_i$'s) by the estimated cash flows from marble under different economic conditions (the $M_j$'s) and multiplying the product by the corresponding probability (the $p_{ij}$'s). In other words, the $p_{11}, p_{12}, \ldots, p_{ij}, \ldots, p_{33}$ in the following equation represent the probability that the cash flows from $G_1$ and $M_1$ will occur simultaneously, the probability that $G_1$ and $M_2$ will occur simultaneously, and so forth.

$$E(GM) = p_{11}G_1M_1 + p_{12}G_1M_2 + \cdots + p_{ij}G_iM_j + \cdots + p_{33}G_3M_3 \qquad (10\text{–}3)$$

Plugging the data from Table 10–23 into the general expression given in Eq. (10–3) we obtain the expected return of the joint granite and marble quarrying projects:

$$\begin{aligned} E(GM) &= \$0.0 + \$0.0 + \$1{,}200{,}000 + \$2{,}000{,}000 + \$0.00 \\ &\quad + \$900{,}000 + \$1{,}500{,}000 + \$2{,}400{,}000 \\ &\quad + \$1{,}200{,}000 \\ &= \$9{,}200{,}000 \end{aligned}$$

and substituting in Eq. (10–2); $E(G) = \$3{,}000$, $E(M) = \$3{,}300$ and $E(GM) = \$9{,}200{,}000$

$$\begin{aligned} \text{Cov}(G, M) &= \$9{,}200{,}000 - (\$3{,}000)(\$3{,}300) \qquad (10\text{–}3a) \\ &= -\$700{,}000 \end{aligned}$$

The variance of the total quarry is determined by

$$\begin{aligned} V(Q) &= a^2\,\text{Var}(G) + (1 - a)^2\,\text{Var}(M) \qquad (10\text{–}4) \\ &\quad + 2a(1 - a)\,\text{Cov}(G, M) \\ &= a^2(\$800{,}000) + (1 - a)^2(\$1{,}410{,}000) \\ &\quad + 2a(1 - a)(-\$700{,}000) \\ &= \$800{,}000a^2 + \$1{,}410{,}000(1 - a)^2 \\ &\quad - \$1{,}400{,}000(a)(1 - a) \end{aligned}$$

Using Eq. (10–1) and Eq. (10–4) we can calculate the expected return and the risk for various combinations of the granite and marble quarry projects. We give the calculations for one combination:

$$G = a = 1.0$$

$$M = (1 - a) = 0.0$$

$$E(Q) = 1.0(\$3{,}000) + 0(\$3{,}300)$$

$$= \$3{,}000$$

$$V(Q) = \$800{,}000(1) + \$1{,}410{,}000(0) - \$1{,}400{,}000(1)(0)$$

$$= \$800{,}000$$

The remaining points are presented in Table 10–24. The expected return from quarrying varies from $3,000 to $3,300; the variance from $800,000 to $1,410,000. The least risk occurs when 60 percent of the available funds are invested in the granite project and 40 percent in the marble project. The data of Table 10–24 are graphed in Figure 10–7.

TABLE 10–24. Boothill Memorial Company Expected Returns and Variance for Different Mixes of Projects *G* and *M*

| *Proportions of* | | *Expected return from total quarry operations* * | *Variance* † (*Risk of quarrying*) (000) |
|---|---|---|---|
| *G* | *M* | | |
| 1.0 | 0.0 | $3000 | $ 800.0 |
| 0.9 | 0.1 | 3030 | 536.1 |
| 0.8 | 0.2 | 3060 | 334.4 |
| 0.7 | 0.3 | 3090 | 224.9 |
| 0.6 | 0.4 | 3120 | 177.6 |
| 0.5 | 0.5 | 3150 | 202.5 |
| 0.4 | 0.6 | 3180 | 299.6 |
| 0.3 | 0.7 | 3210 | 468.9 |
| 0.2 | 0.8 | 3240 | 710.4 |
| 0.1 | 0.9 | 3270 | 1,024.1 |
| 0.0 | 1.0 | 3300 | 1,410.0 |

* Computed by use of Eq. (10–1) where $E(G)$ is $3000 and $E(M)$ is $3300.
† Computed by use of Eq. (10–4).

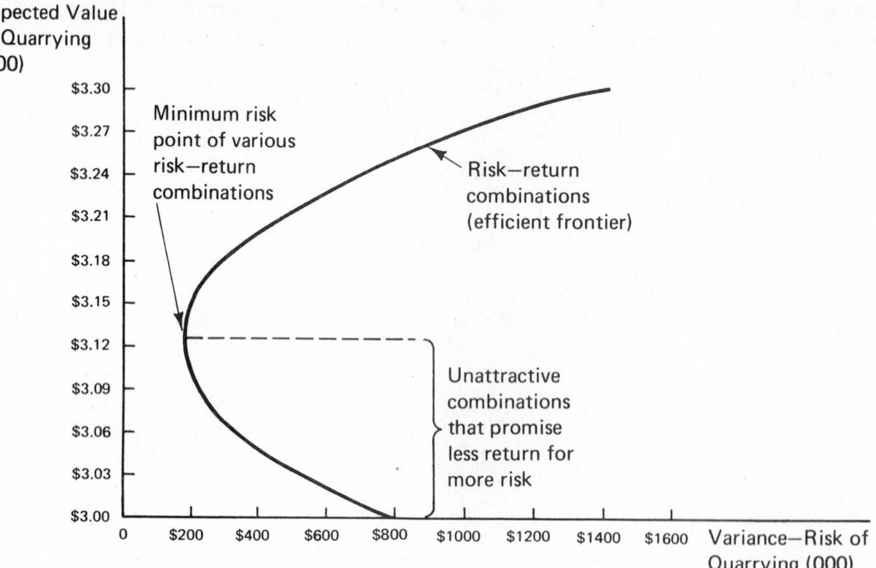


Figure 10–7 * Boothill Memorial Company. Risk and expected return associated with different mixes of the granite and marble projects.

* Based on table 10–24.

*Sensitivity Analysis—Varying the Correlation Coefficient* The risk of a portfolio of projects is determined by three factors: (1) the percentage amounts (weights) invested in each of the projects, (2) the variance (standard deviation) of each project, and (3) the covariance (correlation coefficient) between the projects. The variance of each project and the covariance between the projects remained fixed in the Boothill example as we showed how return and risk for the portfolio varied when varying the percent invested in each of the two available projects Granite and Marble. Now we will examine the effect on return and risk of a portfolio as we vary the correlation coefficient between two projects over the maximum possible range of +1 through 0 to −1.

Suppose we have two new projects $K$ and $S$ with expected returns of $E(K) = 0.20$ and $E(S) = 0.40$ and standard deviations of $\sigma_K = 0.10$ and $\sigma_S = 0.30$. The covariance between these two projects is given by

$$\text{Cov}(K, S) = \rho_{KS}\sigma_K\sigma_S \tag{10–5}$$

where Cov $(K, S)$ = the covariance between projects $K$ and $S$, $\rho_{KS}$ = the correlation coefficient between the returns of the two projects and $\sigma_K$ and $\sigma_S$ are the standard deviations of the returns from the two projects.

If the returns on projects $K$ and $S$ are perfectly correlated with each other we have a correlation coefficient of +1.0; conversely for −1.0, with zero indicating no correlation.

Combining projects $K$ and $S$ the expected return of the portfolio is given by

$$\begin{aligned} E(Q) &= aE(K) + (1 - a)E(S) \\ &= a(0.20) + (1 - a)(0.40) \end{aligned} \tag{10–6}$$

where $E(Q)$ denotes the expected return from the portfolio, $a$ equals the percentage invested in project $K$, and $(1–a)$ is the percentage invested in project $S$.

The risk of the portfolio is given by

$$\sigma_Q = \sqrt{a^2\sigma_K^2 + (1-a)^2\sigma_S^2 + 2a(1-a)\,\text{cov}(K, S)} \tag{10–7}$$

Substituting the expression for covariance given in Eq. (10–5) we have

$$\sigma_Q = \sqrt{a^2\sigma_K^2 + (1-a)^2\sigma_S^2 + 2a(1-a)\rho_{KS}\sigma_K\sigma_S} \tag{10–8}$$

To see how the return and risk combination of this portfolio changes with the correlation coefficient, assume 75 percent of our funds committed to project $K$ and 25 percent committed to project $S$. Then portfolio return $E(Q) = 25$ percent, as appears in Table 10–25. When $\rho_{KS} = +1$, the risk of the portfolio $\sigma_Q = 15$ percent, when $\rho_{KS} = –1$, the risk of the portfolio $\sigma_Q = 0$, and when $\rho_{KS} = 0$, the risk of the portfolio $\sigma_Q = 10.61$ percent.

Figure 10–8 following Table 10–25 presents graphically possible proportions invested in projects $K$ and $S$ for $\rho_{KS} = +1$, $\rho_{KS} = –1$, $\rho_{KS} = 0$.

TABLE 10–25. Portfolio Returns and Standard Deviations for Different Mixes of Projects $K$ and $S$ when $\rho_{KS} = +1$, $\rho_{KS} = –1$, $\rho_{KS} = 0$.*

| Proportions of | | Expected return | Standard deviation (risk) |
|---|---|---|---|
| $K$ | $S$ | $E(Q)$ | $\sigma_Q$ |
| | | $\rho_{KS} = +1$ | |
| 1.00 | 0.00 | 0.20 | 0.10 |
| 0.75 | 0.25 | 0.25 | 0.15 |
| 0.50 | 0.50 | 0.30 | 0.20 |
| 0.25 | 0.75 | 0.35 | 0.25 |
| 0.00 | 1.00 | 0.40 | 0.30 |
| | | $\rho_{KS} = -1$ | |
| 1.00 | 0.00 | 0.20 | 0.10 |
| 0.75 | 0.25 | 0.25 | 0 |
| 0.50 | 0.50 | 0.30 | 0.10 |
| 0.25 | 0.75 | 0.35 | 0.20 |
| 0.00 | 1.00 | 0.40 | 0.30 |
| | | $\rho_{KS} = 0$ | |
| 1.00 | 0.00 | 0.20 | 0.10 |
| 0.75 | 0.25 | 0.25 | 0.106 |
| 0.50 | 0.50 | 0.30 | 0.158 |
| 0.25 | 0.75 | 0.35 | 0.226 |
| 0.00 | 1.00 | 0.40 | 0.30 |

* Based on the expressions given in Eqs. (10–6) and (10–7).

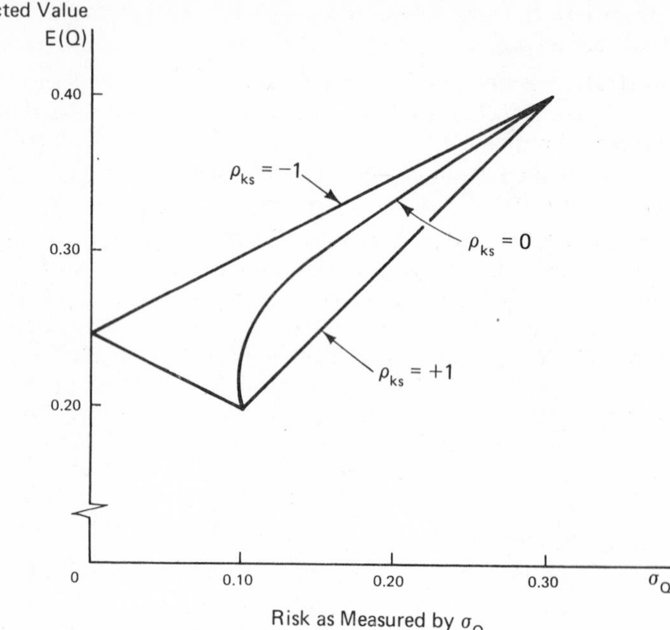


Figure 10–8 Risk and expected return for different mixes of projects $K$ and $S$, where $\rho_{KS} = 1$, $\rho_{KS} = -1$, and $\rho_{KS} = 0$.

***Appendix L***

## OTHER TECHNIQUES FOR HANDLING RISK

Many techniques attempt to deal with risk. All are based on the concept of probability. Two of these are decision trees and simulation.

### Decision Trees

Projects involve a sequence of decisions extending from the present into the future. For example, a foreign automobile manufacturer considers establishing a U.S. assembly plant. Before the project is completed or abandoned he might: (1) survey the U.S. supply-demand conditions; (2) if the survey is encouraging, he might build a modest-sized plant; (3) depending on continuing demand and profitability, he might expand the plant or build additional plants throughout the country.

Further, consider a firm planning to introduce a new product. Over time the following sequence of decisions might result: (1) After surveying the supply-demand conditions, the firm must decide whether (a) to introduce it regionally or (b) to introduce it nationally; (2) If (a) and a large regional demand develops, the firm must decide (c) to distribute regionally or (d) to distribute nationally.

A sequence of decisions and subsequent events can be diagrammed, giving the appearance of a tree with its base as the beginning decision point, which is represented by a "1" enclosed in a square shown in Figure 10–9. Branches (lines) extend from each decision point to risk events represented by A, B, C, and D enclosed in circles and called *nodes*. Each risk event produces two or more possible results that may or may not lead to subsequent decision points. Associated with each risk result represented by a branch departing from a risk node (as we move from left to right across the page) is a probability $p$ giving the chance of that result occurring.

To illustrate, assume our auto manufacturer has found the U.S. market favorable [1] and has the choice of expanding its U.S. plant Ⓐ or building an additional U.S. assembly plant Ⓑ. The optimal sequence is found by starting on the right-hand side of the page and working backward toward the beginning decision computing an expected NPV at each decision point and risk node.

The expected NPV at each risk event node is computed by taking the sum of the probability times the PV figure less the cost for all branches departing that node. The expected NPV at a decision node is computed for each branch departing that decision point to end. The highest NPV represents the best sequence of decisions and risk events from that decision point to end.

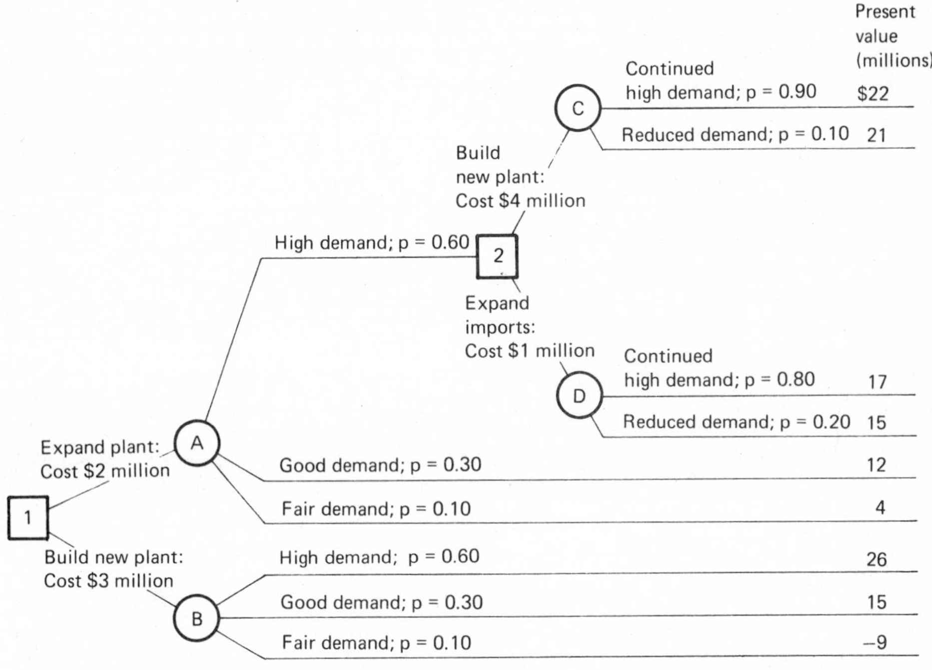


Figure 10–9 Decision tree use to analyze investment alternatives for auto assembly capability.

Thus, from Figure 10–9:

Expected NPV, risk event node Ⓒ $= 0.90(\$22) + 0.10(\$21) - \$4 = \$17.9$

Expected NPV, risk event node Ⓓ $= 0.80(\$17) + 0.20(\$15) - \$1 = \$15.6$

Expected NPV's at decision point [2] $= \$15.6$ and $\$17.9$

Arriving at point 2 the optimal decision is to build new plants since $\$17.9 > \$15.6$.

Expected NPV, risk event node Ⓐ $= 0.60(\$17.9) + 0.30(\$12) + 0.10(\$4) - \$2 = \$12.74$.

Expected NPV, risk event node Ⓑ $= 0.60(\$26) + 0.30(\$15) + 0.10(-\$9) - \$3 = \$16.2$.

Being at point 1, the optimal decision is to build new plants, since $\$16.2 > \$12.74$, but note from Figure 10–9 the wider range of outcomes if new plants are built than if initially the plant is expanded (a range of \$26 to − \$9 versus \$22 to \$4). Weighing the range of possible outcomes management might prefer the plant expansion route.

### Monte Carlo Simulation

Monte Carlo is only one form of simulation. It consists of random sampling from a probability distribution and is described in Appendix F at the end of Chapter 7. Most practical simulations are carried out by computer, but manual simulation, if size permits, is possible.

A simulation of a problem is conducted when (1) a mathematical model useful in analysis is impossible to build, (2) though a model can be built, it is so complex that mathematical solution is not possible, or (3) where we are interested not only in the final outcome but in the path to that outcome.

*An Investment Model* When computing the internal rate of return (IRR) of a project we obtain a single figure—a point estimate. We have no information on the riskiness of the project as represented by the probability distribution of the possible outcomes around the expected IRR. This would be useful information to have.

To obtain the probability distribution of the IRR for a project we proceed as follows:

*Step 1.* Select the variables important to the IRR computation. For simplicity suppose they are (1) market size *MS*, (2) share of the market *SM*, (3) operating cost *OC*, and (4) life of plant *LP*.

*Step 2.* Estimate the parameters of these four variables (Table 10–26) and assign probability density functions (no restriction on shape).

TABLE 10–26. Estimates of Investment Model Variables

| | Expected value | Standard deviation |
|---|---|---|
| Market size *MS* | \$5,000,000 | \$400,000 |
| Share of market *SM* | 20% | 3% |
| Operating cost *OC* | \$150,000 | \$ 10,000 |
| Life of plant *LP* | 10 years | 1 year |

The IRR of the project can then be expressed in the following functional form.

$$IRR = R(MS, SM, OC, LP) \tag{10–8}$$

*Step 3.* Generate values for the four random variables, market size, share of market, operating cost, and life of plant on a computer and substitute these values into Eq. (10–8) to obtain a single value for IRR. Repeat 25 times to generate a probability distribution of IRR for the project.

Figure 10–10 illustrates the process described in Step 3. The derived IRR distribution located in the lower right-hand corner is determined by keeping count of the number of times the various rates of return are computed using Eq. (10–8).

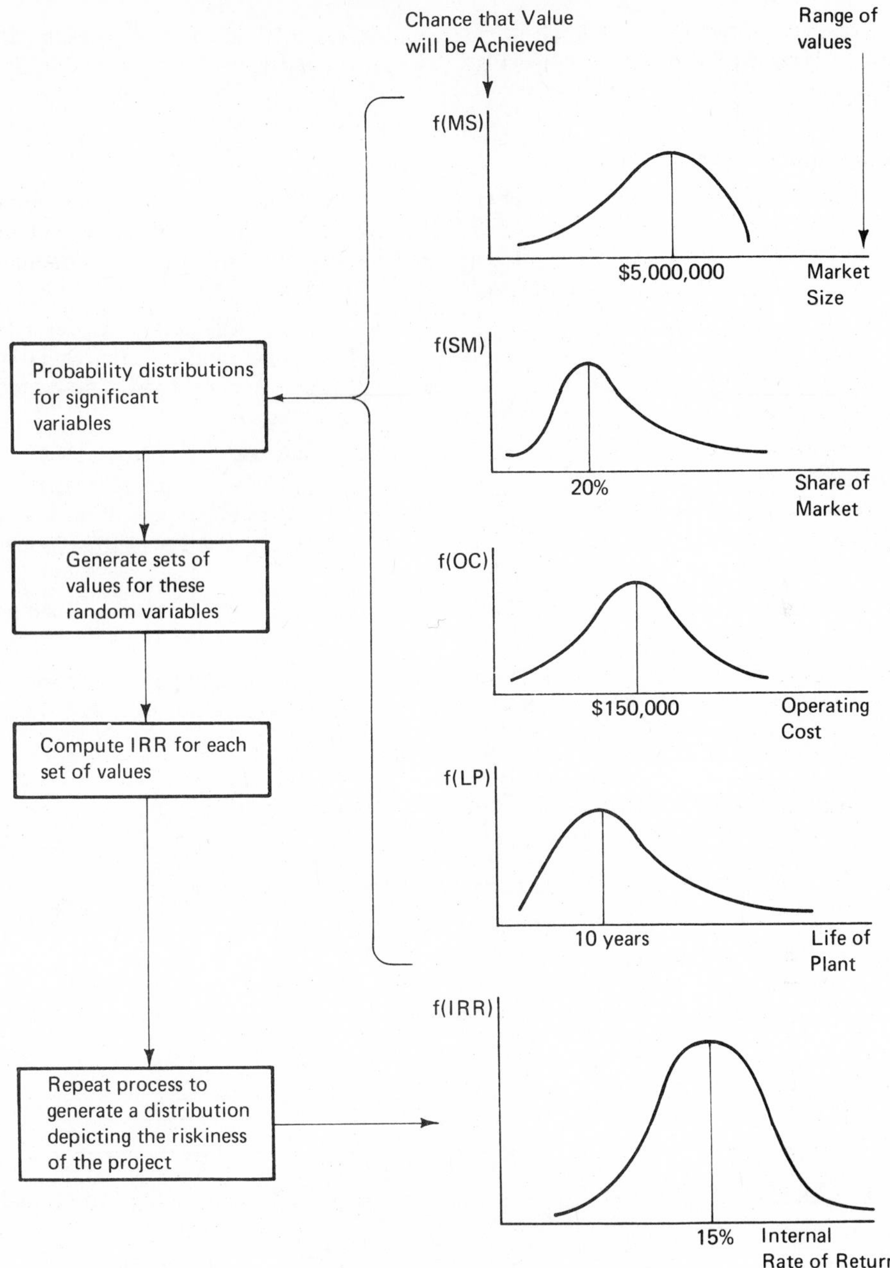


Figure 10–10 Simulated IRR for a project.

*Corporate Models* Investment models, while useful, treat only one decision area in the firm at a time. The same can be said for other financial, production, and marketing models. Recently, major firms have adopted the approach of building corporate simulation models that treat the firm as a total system. In these models the firm's production, marketing, finance and accounting, and control subsystems are considered as completely interdependent. Figure 10–11 depicts such a model.

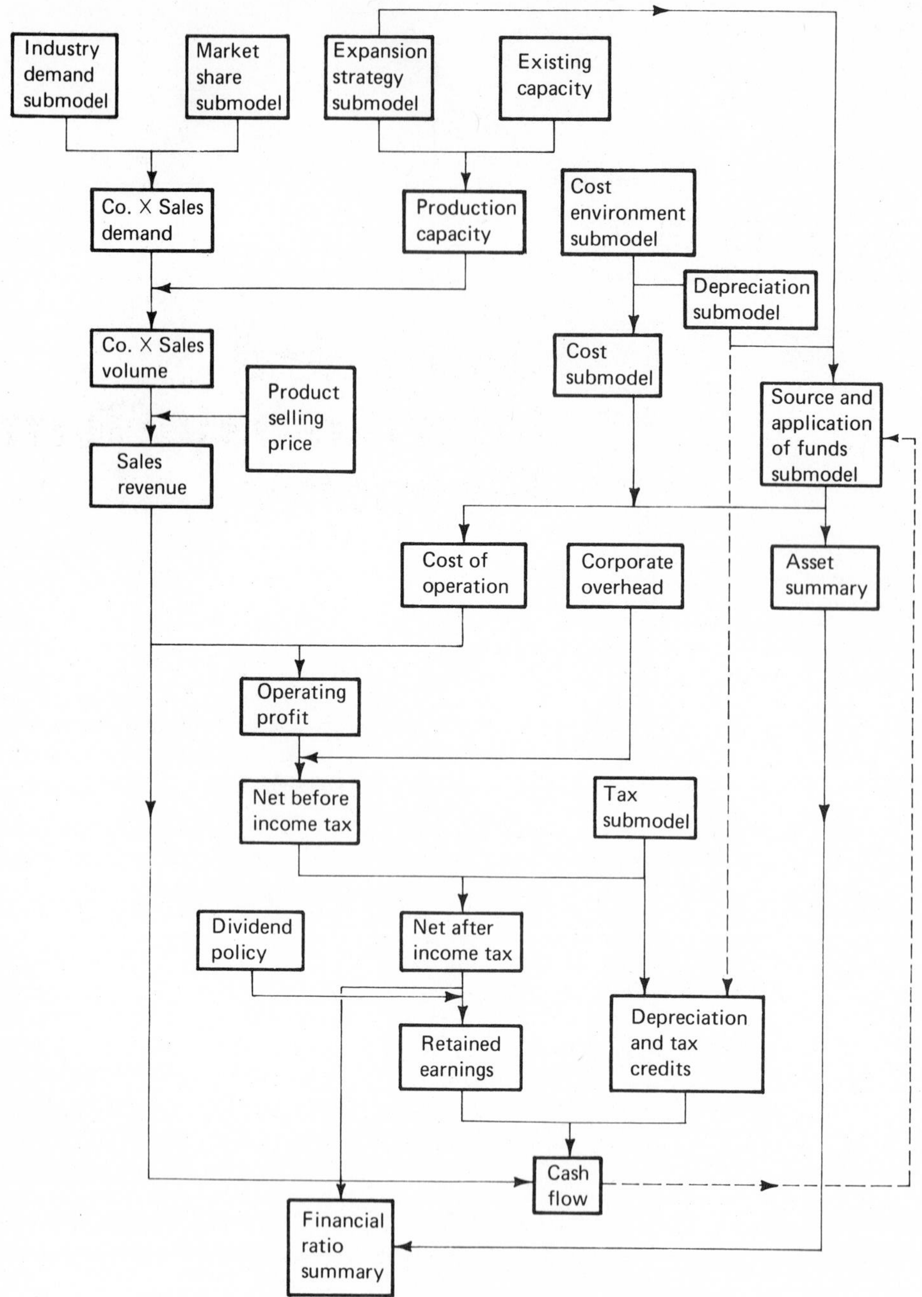


Figure 10–11 * Corporate simulation model.

* Based on David B. Hertz, "Risk Analysis in Capital Investment," *Harvard Business Review*, 42 (January-February 1964) pp. 95–106.

SOURCE: Adapted from T. H. Naylor, *Computer Simulation Experiments with Models of Economic Systems* (New York, John Wiley and Sons, Inc., 1971), p. 69.

# PART FOUR

# Short-and Intermediate-Term Financing

*

# 11

# Short-Term Financing Strategy and Unsecured Credit Sources

Financing alternatives may be classified according to debt or ownership sources. Debt may be short term (that is, up to 1 year),[1] term loan, or long-term. The distinction between term loan and long-term loan is not based solely on length of time, since both are for more than 1 year, but rather on the type of lender and repayment schedule. *Term loans* are privately placed with one or a few lenders and usually provide for periodic repayment. *Long-term loans* may be public or private but seldom provide for periodic repayment; rather, repayment is usually in a lump sum at maturity. There are no such time distinctions in ownership categories. In this chapter we consider those sources of short-term financing that do not require collateral. We will discuss the availability, cost, and risk of trade credit, commercial bank loans, and commercial paper. In the next chapter we will examine secured short-term and term loans.

---

[1] The 1-year number is not magic. Accounting theory recognizes that if the period of production is more than 1 year, then short-term or current assets and liabilities are to be classified on the basis of the period of production that may be 2 or 3 years. C. T. Horngren, *Accounting for Management Control,* 2d edition (Englewood Cliffs, N. J.: Prentice-Hall, Inc., 1970).

## MATCHING MATURITY TO THE TIME NEED FOR FUNDS

A firm seeks to obtain funds on favorable terms and for the time needed subject to prior prepayment with or without penalty. Whether prepayment provisions are included depends on alternative opportunities for the lender and the borrower. One principle of finance stipulates that short-term needs (for example, a seasonal increase in sales and, hence, inventories) should be financed by short-term borrowings and that longer-lived assets (for example, plant or a permanent increase in working capital) should be financed by longer-term borrowings or equity. Although loans can be classified by maturity, time will cause the term of a loan to shift from one maturity category to another. For example, a sudden upsurge in business may initially be thought to be temporary. Having obtained a short-term loan, the financial manager may find the upsurge permanent and press the banker to have the loan renewed for another 6 or 9 months, if it would be more favorable to engage in long-term financing at a later date. Or, an unexpected decline in sales may reduce receivables and inventory levels and cash requirements so a term loan can be repaid early.

Besides negotiated debt and equity sources, a firm obtains financing in the day-to-day course of its operations. These so-called *spontaneous sources of credit* include trade credit obtained from suppliers and accrued and deferred items. Modest trade credit from suppliers may be "cost-free" if the purchasing firm takes its discounts through timely payment. Sometimes vendors build a credit charge into the price and this charge is borne by those firms not taking their cash discounts. Trade credit and accrued and deferred items are called spontaneous sources of credit because they arise from and are directly geared to the buying and producing activities of the firm. Because trade credit is flexible, it is subject to a good deal of management—and mismanagement. Once the financial manager has decided the extent to which he is going to employ—or exploit—these cost-free sources of funds, the remaining asset requirements must be financed by other sources.

## TRADE CREDIT AS A SOURCE OF FUNDS

### How It Works

Recurring purchases of material by a firm are seldom paid by cash on delivery (COD). Trade credit is extended by the vendor to the purchasing firm.[2] The longer the credit period and the larger the volume of purchases, the larger the amount of credit received. Where our receivables can be collected about the time payment is due on payables, our supplier is financing both inventory and receivables. Then other financing need cover only fixed assets and cash balances. If a firm can sell its goods and

[2] Trade credit is the primary source of short-term funds for manufacturing firms. For the period 1950–1960 suppliers provided about 45 percent of the short-term capital of these firms. See "Financing Manufacturing Corporations, 1950–1960," *Monthly Business Review*, Federal Reserve Bank of Cleveland, February 1962, pp. 3–10. The figure was 40 percent in 1969. U. S. Treasury Department, Internal Revenue Service, *Statistics of Income, 1969, Corporation Income Tax Returns* (Washington, D. C.: Government Printing Office, 1973), p. 14.

collect substantially *before* payment to the vendor is due, the vendor is financing some of the *permanent* capital requirements of the purchaser.

For example, suppose our firm sells on the average $2000 of merchandise a day with an average collection period of 30 days. On any day the firm will have approximately $60,000 of receivables outstanding. If our firm buys $1000 of materials a day with an average payment period of 35 days, accounts payable will average $35,000. The difference between our receivables ($60,000) and payables ($35,000), or $25,000, is the amount of net credit our firm is extending that must be financed from other sources. If our average payment period to our supplier were 90 days the vendor would be financing $30,000, ($90,000 – $60,000) of our permanent capital requirements. Actually, the amount would be somewhat larger because we do not need to finance our profit (that part of receivables that is profit).

Trade credit arises in a simple manner. The purchasing firm sends a purchase order to the supplier for the goods desired. The supplier checks the firm's credit and if good, sends the merchandise, entering on his books the amount of the shipment and sending an invoice covering the items to be delivered, the cost, and terms of sale. This system is simple and flexible. The major portion of trade credit is extended on this "open-book" account basis.

#### The Cash Discount

Trade credit terms may extend a cash discount for payment within a specified period but full payment is due thereafter. Cash discounts should be distinguished from quantity discounts for the size of the order, and from trade discounts granted only to certain members of an industry group. Cash discount terms of 2/10, n/30 are usual. These terms mean the purchaser can deduct 2 percent if paid within 10 days. If payment is delayed beyond 10 days, the invoice amount is due within 30 days. The date triggering the discount period may be the invoice date, the shipment date, or the date of receipt of goods (ROG), as specified by the seller. The cost of not taking the 2 percent discount, or conversely, the cost of the extra 20 days' credit is substantial. Roughly, the purchaser is paying 2 percent for 20-days credit, and since there are eighteen 20-day periods in a year, the annual cost of using trade credit beyond the discount date but paying by the due date is roughly 36 percent (18 periods times 2 percent). The actual interest cost is slightly higher because it is only the face amount of the invoice less the discount that is being "borrowed" for the period between the discount day and the due date. The interest rates implicit in various credit terms are shown in Table 11–1.

Delaying payment beyond the 30th may not involve any immediate added cost to the purchaser but will result in a damaged credit reputation, reduced ability to obtain trade credit in the future, and worst of all, difficulty in obtaining inventory during periods of high demand. Suppliers will favor their better-paying customers. But delaying payment may not produce these consequences. It depends on the customs in the industry, the supplier, and the level of economic activity.

TABLE 11-1. Selected Trade Credit Terms and Their Respective Costs Computed Using the Formula. Annualized

$$\text{Interest Cost} = \frac{\text{Percent discount}}{1.00\text{—Percent discount}} \times \frac{360 \text{ days}}{\text{Credit period—Discount period}}$$

(payment is assumed made on the due date)

| Trade terms | Implicit annual interest cost |
|---|---|
| a. 1/10, n/30 | 18.18% |
| f. 1/10, n/60 | 7.27 |
| g. 2/10, n/30 | 36.72 |
| b. 2/10, n/40 | 24.48 |
| d. 2/10, n/60 | 14.69 |
| c. 3/15, n/60 | 24.72 |
| e. 6/10, n/90 | 28.71 |

### Stretching Payment beyond the Due Date

Though payment is due, in practice payment may be stretched beyond the due date. Some suppliers regard trade terms casually. When extending say 2/10, n/30 based on the invoice date they stiffly require payment by the 10th if the discount is to be taken, but do not enforce payment by the 30th. The supplier may permit accounts to become overdue without getting excited. When the account is 10 days overdue he may send a friendly notice requesting payment, and at the end of 20 days may send a stronger notice. Only after 30 days may the supplier press for payment. Knowing this policy, a buyer could plan his payments for the 50th day after purchase (20 days overdue). This would leave him with a little margin before the supplier hits the boiling point. Stretching payment in this manner will bring the cost of trade credit down substantially—in this case to approximately 18 percent. The principle is: If one cannot take the cash discount, the farther the payment can be pushed into the future, the lower the implicit cost of the trade credit.

The impact on the firm of stretching trade credit payments varies with the firm's general financial condition and the stage of the business cycle. A strong firm and good customer caught in a temporary cash squeeze may get away with postponing payment on accounts payable with relative impunity, whereas a small, weak firm and poor customer may have difficulty if payment is delayed a few days. During slow periods suppliers are anxious to keep their equipment operating and tend to be tolerant of customers' paying habits. Operating at reduced levels can leave a supplier—if not operating at a loss—in a liquid position.[3] This liquidity and reduced level of operations permits expansion of receivables and provides incentive to produce to cover variable cost and partially cover fixed cost. During a boom period things are different. Operating at capacity, the supplier is selling all he can produce; his working capital position is tight,

[3] This is so provided the firm had a good working capital position when previously operating at capacity levels.

and he is anxious to sell to customers who pay promptly. The supplier may even have trouble with his bank as he reaches his short-term borrowing power limit.

### Business Utilization of Trade Credit

Small manufacturing firms finance a greater percentage of their asset requirements through trade credit than do large firms. Examining the aggregate data in 1973, we find that for firms with assets of less than $1 million, trade credit equaled 17.5 percent of total assets. For firms of asset size $1 million to $5 million, trade credit dropped to 15.1 percent of total assets. For larger firms with assets of $250 to $1000 million, trade credit as a percentage of total assets was about 7.2 percent.[4]

Among manufacturing concerns in different industries, there is wide variation in the use of trade credit. Apparel firms and others that turn out consumer products tend to be heavy users of trade credit. Basic chemicals and allied products, and petroleum refining tend to be more moderate users.[5] The textile industry is characterized by many smaller firms that as buyers are heavy users of trade credit. The petroleum, auto, and chemical industries are characterized by large firms. The firms in these industries as buyers use proportionately less trade credit. Consequently, it is unclear whether the nature of the industry or the size of the firm most influences the heavy use of trade credit.

Trade credit can be an effective competitive inducement to buy. Hence, many large corporations that can borrow cheaply extend liberal trade credit to their customers.

Railroads and electric utilities are large enterprises but small users of trade credit. The services industries, such as laundries, credit cards, and motel chains, are small enterprises and are also small users of trade credit. The key factor here is not size but the extent to which inventory is needed. In both these situations the firms use little inventory, and hence need little trade credit.

### Management of Trade Credit

The primary cause of business failure is mismanagement. Frequently trade credit is mismanaged because it is easy to obtain, requires few formalities, and is flexible, expanding as inventory rises and contracting as purchases are reduced. Should the firm be a little late in paying a bill, no immediate harm may be apparent. If discounts are taken, the use of trade credit provides "cost-free" financing. Weighing the profit margin on the sale against the cost of reviewing the financial condition of each customer leads some manufacturers to be liberal in extending trade credit. After continued dealings with a customer the supplier develops experience regarding the firm's bill-paying habits. The customer in turn also acquires

---

[4] Federal Trade Commission, *Quarterly Financial Report, U. S. Manufacturing Corporations*, First Quarter, 1973, pp. 29, 30.

[5] Trade credit represented 17.8 percent of assets in the apparel industry and only 6.2 percent in basic chemicals. Federal Trade Commission, *Quarterly Financial Report, U. S. Manufacturing Corporations*, First Quarter, 1973, pp. 23, 25.

a feel for the collection policies of his suppliers. But the best strategy is to take discounts. The credit information exchange network operates efficiently and fast enough to make a firm's payment record widely known. A record of prompt payment lifts the firm's reputation and enhances its ability to obtain credit from banks and other lenders.

A firm relying heavily on trade credit because its financing ability is limited must engage in a difficult balancing act. Payment may be pushed as far into the future as suppliers will tolerate. Periodic clean-up on a rotating basis of all accounts due will tend to keep suppliers somewhat calm. The placement of orders with suppliers who are lax in collections will stretch the amount of trade credit obtainable. The other end of the balancing act is that suppliers may call a halt to further credit extension and force a long-term debt or equity issue at an inopportune time.

The manager of a shaky firm, therefore, must constantly guard against using too much trade credit. Regularly volunteering financial information to trade creditors boosts their confidence and willingness to extend credit. By watching the changing condition of his customer, a supplier may spot the deterioration in financial condition and stop further extension of credit before it is too late. This will force the customer to obtain additional equity financing. Actually, the supplier will have done his customer a favor, for once the firm is on the edge of bankruptcy such funds are obtainable, if at all, only by giving the firm away.

## ACCRUED AND DEFERRED ITEMS AS A SOURCE OF FUNDS

Accrued expenses such as wages, interest, and taxes, and deferred income such as advances by customers in part payment on special projects can be thought of as spontaneous sources of credit.

### Accrued Expenses

Employees provide their services and at the end of 1 week, 2 weeks, or 1 month receive their paycheck. During the interim the firm has both the services of the employee and the money due him. On pay day this source of credit falls to zero. The credit arising through accruals then builds up until the next pay day. Clearly the firm would require additional financing if it shifted from monthly to daily salary payment. The amount of this credit goes up and down with the volume of business.

### Accrued Taxes

Whenever a firm operates profitably it must share its profit with the government. All income taxes must be paid at the end of a prescribed period. In the period that taxes accrue, before the payment date, taxes are a source of funds. The maximum time lag between the earning of profit and the payment of income taxes is approximately three months but on the average is half that time. In the case of other taxes, such as property taxes, the maximum time lag may be more than a year.

### Deferred Income

Deferred income items consist of cash received before it is earned. The cash is added to the assets of the firm. The goods and services are deliverable at some future date. Customers who are required to make advance payments on orders are the primary suppliers of these funds.

## FINANCING BY COMMERCIAL BANK CREDIT

Commercial banks and finance companies are the principal sources of short-term negotiated credit. Since finance companies seldom make unsecured loans, discussion of them is deferred to the next chapter. Banks in the aggregate are a smaller source of short-term financing than is trade credit.[6] Notes payable to banks on the balance sheet of a firm usually indicate commercial bank borrowing.

### The Bank as a Lending Organization

The availability of bank credit is important to the success of a firm whether the firm is currently borrowing or not. A short-term loan can usually be arranged quickly with but a few more formalities than trade credit. Flexibility in the form of tailoring to the borrower's needs is an important advantage of bank borrowing. To the nonborrowing firm the bank can serve as a reserve source of funds.

A firm with a good credit reputation will be able to borrow from some bank when the need arises. The word "some" is emphasized because all banks do not have the same loan policies. Some are cautious and conservative, others aggressive and anxious to build new business; hence, the firm may be turned down by one bank but not by another. The financial manager should choose his banking connections so his firm's needs are met.

For a firm to hold idle reserve balances to meet every sudden unexpected cash drain is uneconomic. Both the firm's deposits and borrowing are valuable to the bank. The bank can use a portion of the deposit to loan to other firms or to purchase income-yielding securities. Borrowing by the firm generates income for the bank.

All financial managers are interested in obtaining bank credit to meet short-term needs. The more aggressive firms and many small firms are interested in obtaining as much bank credit as possible. Though the purpose of a bank is to make loans, it cannot assume much risk. While a bank is interested in earnings, its focus must be on safety of principal because the bank's assets must be sufficiently liquid to meet depositors' demands. In contrast, a firm is primarily concerned with profitability and is willing to take risks to achieve this goal. Thus, the borrowing firm and the lending banker do not see eye to eye—and the banker is in the stronger position because he has numerous alternatives for putting his money to work—

---

[6] Between 1950 and 1960 bank loans furnished 15 percent of the short-term capital needs of manufacturing firms. Roughly 14 percent of total capital additions and one-half of the external capital raised during this period was provided by short-term borrowing. See "Financing Manufacturing Corporations 1950–1960," *Monthly Business Review,* Federal Reserve Bank of Cleveland, February 1962, pp. 3–10.

for example municipal bonds that give a satisfactory tax-free return, or government bonds. Since municipal and government bonds involve little risk the banker must consider the trade-off between the risk-return of bonds against commercial loans.

The financial manager, in contrast, is often in urgent need of bank credit but with fewer alternative sources of cheap funds. Inventory purchasing may be necessary to meet a major selling season, receivables collection may be slowing, the purchase of new machinery or equipment may suddenly become desirable, or any one of a dozen needs for cash may arise. Accommodating these needs may mean profit while failure to accommodate them may result in losses. The banker does not find himself in this position.

### Industry Use of Bank Credit

Most small and many medium-sized firms rely heavily on short- and intermediate-term bank credit. Often this is a firm's only source of negotiated credit. Even for large firms bank credit is one of several alternative sources of credit to be tapped in time of need. In May, 1974 large commercial banks had commercial loans of $120 billion outstanding, of which maturities of 1 year or less accounted for about 60 percent.[7] In contrast several years earlier accounts payable for all active *corporations* were $99 billion.[8]

Small business accounts for a major portion of the *number* of bank business loans, but the average loan size is small—in the thousands of dollars. In contrast, large borrowers account for a small number of loans, but the average loan size is large—in the millions of dollars. Thus a firm, small or large, should first turn to its friendly banker for needed funds.

In 1973, manufacturing firms with assets of $250 million or less had short-term bank credit of about 6 percent of total assets. Firms in the $250 million to $1 billion range had 4.4 percent, and those in the class of above $1 billion had 2.6 percent.[9]

### Selection of the Bank and Banker

Banks vary widely in their view of risk and their role in the community.[10] Some follow a cautious lending policy, others are more liberal, and still others are quite aggressive. One bank may be stockholder oriented, seeking a good rate of earnings growth. Another may seek to establish

---

[7] *Federal Reserve Bulletin* (May, 1974), p. A25.

[8] U. S. Treasury Department, Internal Revenue Service, *Statistics of Income, 1966 Corporation Income Tax Returns* (Washington, D. C.: Government Printing Office, 1970), p. 14.

[9] Federal Trade Commission, *Quarterly Financial Report, U. S. Manufacturing Corporations*, First Quarter, 1973, pp. 31–33.

[10] See David C. Cates and Jay R. Olson, "Do Corporations Properly Analyze Banks?" *Financial Executive*, 34 (September, 1966), pp. 22–24 ff, for a low-budget procedure for measuring bank soundness. The authors suggest that the declining liquidity of banks makes analysis of a firm's banks more desirable. Though the chance of deposit loss is small, when it occurs it is highly embarrassing to the financial manager and to the firm.

itself as one of the "big" banks in the community, be willing to pay high rates on certificates of deposit to increase its pool of loanable funds and to make liberal loans at low rates to get customers and build volume to obtain larger profits later. Immediate profits may be secondary.

Several bankers within an institution may evaluate a loan application with reasonable care and yet not reach the same conclusion regarding the risk. Further, some bankers may emphasize service to the community and stimulation of its growth and prosperity.

*Size of the Bank.* For the firm, as both depositor and borrower, size of the bank is important. Among banks size and safety often go together, and the firm as depositor is interested in safety. Demand deposits are insured by the Federal Deposit Insurance Corporation (FDIC) to $20,000 but the bank balance of even a modest-sized firm would exceed this amount. Further, the size of a loan a bank may grant to a single borrower is limited by the bank's capital and surplus. National banks cannot make a loan to any one borrower in excess of 10 percent of capital stock and surplus. State banks have similar restrictions. This limit is 25 percent if the loan is secured by livestock, goods in storage, or government securities. Therefore, the firm as a borrower would also tend to favor a bank large enough to be able to accommodate its growing loan demands; yet in a smaller bank, the firm may get more personal attention. The loan may be arranged by the bank president himself. If the firm is satisfied with the safety of the bank, and the best loan accommodation can be obtained there, then that may be the bank to choose. Size alone is not a determining factor. The bank may have correspondents in other parts of the country who will take the amount by which the loan exceeds the legal limit of the bank's lending power.

A large bank may have a specialist in the firm's particular line of business. Being closer to the field the specialist may be more knowledgeable as to loan requests. Also, the specialist may be a source of information and extend expert advice on many aspects of the business.

*Bank Lending Policy.* Some insight into the lending policies of a bank and its ability to lend can be obtained by analyzing its financial position. A bank with a high deposit (that is, liability) to capital ratio has a thin equity position and must be cautious since it has little cushion to absorb losses and therefore should make only low-risk loans. Another measure of a bank's financial position is the loan to deposit ratio. Loans normally yield a higher return than securities but are less liquid. A high loan to deposit ratio may mean a bank is "loaned up"; a new loan would be hard to get. But it will also indicate the bank's policy of preferring loans. A low ratio may mean the bank could safely make additional loans or that the banker may be ultraconservative and interested only in prime risk-free loans; the slightest hint of risk may mean refusal. Finally, to meet sudden withdrawals of demand depositors, banks carry a substantial percentage of cash and government obligations, which are called reserves. An abnormally high ratio of reserves indicates the bank is preoccupied with safety rather than earnings, but a low ratio indicates earnings are important and the bank is aggressively making loans, particularly if the bank also has a high loan to deposit ratio.

The financial manager might favor the "middle of the road" bank. Obtaining even a low-risk loan from an illiquid bank is difficult. And the firm as a depositor avoids an illiquid bank because of concern with the safety of the firm's funds. But it may be equally difficult to obtain a loan that represents a fair amount of risk from a liquid bank unless the bank has a specialist in the firm's area of business or the financial manager makes contact with a skilled loan officer. A great deal may depend on the personalities involved. In any event, as depositor of a highly liquid bank, the financial manager would be able to sleep comfortably nights. Unless the firm is an old and valued customer (that is, carries large bank balances), illiquid, loaned-up banks should be avoided. The firm should prefer the bank that provides good protection for its depositors and follows a fairly aggressive loan policy.

*Other Factors to Be Considered in Selecting a Bank.* The interest rate on a prospective loan is one element to consider. Even though the anticipated profitability of the project is the major factor, the cost of a loan in these high interest times is important. Furthermore, all banks may not charge the same rate for a given loan for many reasons. One bank may feel that a certain firm is a better risk than other banks. Another bank may be loaned-up but willing to make room at a high price. Though it is usually not good practice to shop around for the lowest rate for a particular loan, it does make sense to do so before establishing banking connections. The firm that establishes a banking connection, but still keeps abreast of developments in the money and capital markets and makes broad contact with the banking community provides good insurance that poor loan service by the present bank will be detected, indicating that it is time for a change of banks.

Shopping for a rate on each loan, however, is usually poor practice for the same reasons that changing doctors for every illness would be: the benefits of prior analysis are lost, the possibility of misdiagnosis increases and so on.

The firm should also consider the charges levied for check handling, collection, and the availability and quality of services, such as the collection of notes and bills of exchange, the handling of foreign exchange, trust department services, and credit and business information services. All large banks are able to render good service at competitive rates in each of these areas. In the smaller banks not all these services are available directly but are obtainable indirectly through a correspondent bank. Where the services are provided directly, such as the management of securities under trust agreement, the quality of the service may depend largely on the skill of one or a few individuals rather than on the organization itself.

Finally, there is convenience of the bank's location. A firm in a small community will likely carry its account with the local bank. Even if the firm is large it will carry one account there. A firm located in a large metropolitan area containing many banks will select that institution with which it can work out a mutually satisfactory arrangement, and convenience of location may be one factor.

### Uses of Short-term Bank Credit

*Seasonal Financing.* Bank credit is excellent for financing seasonal bulges in inventory and receivables. These "self-liquidating" loans please the banker and most firms can expect to obtain bank credit for this purpose. The repayment proceeds are generated from the sale of the merchandise or the collection of the receivables and do not depend on the profitability of the firm.

For a stable firm any seasonal borrowing requirement can be readily established. But the expanding firm with a *growing* basic level of receivables and inventory will have more than a seasonal borrowing requirement. Here bank credit may be employed, either by design or inadvertently, to finance a part of the firm's permanent capital needs. This may go on until the bank realizes the situation and forces the firm to seek other financing. Besides its ready availability in the short run, bank credit is usually cheaper than long-term debt. But recently rising interest rates show it would have been cheaper to finance by long term at an earlier period rather than to finance continually by short term.

*Other Needs for Short-term Loans.* A weak firm or one employing its assets to the maximum may borrow monthly to take advantage of trade discounts—say, at the beginning of the month—and repay during the month as the receivables are collected. Though attractive to the firm, a loan arrangement of this kind might be difficult to obtain as the banker may feel that the firm is operating too close to the line. He may either refuse to lend or demand higher rates or even security. Since the passing of trade discounts puts additional pressure on the weak firm, such a bank loan, though costly, would still be desirable.

The financially strong and tightly run organization can weigh the cost of bank credit against long-term financing. Here bank credit may be strategically employed as interim financing while the firm is awaiting a more favorable period to undertake long-term financing. A typical example would be a firm that, for competitive reasons, must launch a major expansion project immediately but finds that rates for long-term financing are currently prohibitive.

### Borrowing Arrangements for Short-term Bank Credit

*Single Loan.* Occasional bank borrowing is done by signing a promissory note. Each borrowing requires a fresh analysis and a new negotiation. The note may be for 30 days to 1 year, but most notes are for 30 to 90 days although they may be renewed at maturity. Such a short maturity gives borrower and lender the opportunity to adjust the interest rate to new money market conditions. In today's world of "jumping" interest rates, many notes provide the rate will change automatically and on the same date as any change in the *prime rate*—which is the lowest rate a bank charges to its most credit-worthy customers. The loan may be repayable in a lump sum or in installments and may provide for payment before due date (prepayment) at no penalty or at a penalty.

*Line of Credit.* A firm with periodic borrowing requirements can eliminate negotiation each time a new loan becomes necessary by arranging for a *line of credit* with the bank, which is a formal (written)[11] or informal (oral) arrangement providing the bank will lend up to a predetermined limit as long as agreed conditions are maintained. The firm may "draw down" varying amounts as needed against the line up to the limit specified. A promissory note for the amount, showing interest and date of maturity, is drawn up each time a loan is made against the line of credit, which is usually renegotiated once a year.

A line of credit is not to be confused with a credit line, which is a simple statement by the banker that, in any event, he is not prepared to lend to the borrower in excess of a stated amount. A credit line involves no formal or informal commitment that any loan will be granted at any time. Two other important differences between a line of credit and a credit line are: (1) a line of credit may require the borrower to maintain a minimum deposit balance throughout the period of the line of credit, whether or not the loan is ever taken. The credit line exacts no such commitment by the borrower; and (2) the line of credit agreement frequently requires the borrower to pay a commitment fee at the rate of $\frac{1}{4}$ to $\frac{1}{2}$ percent per year; sometimes to the extent the maximum is not borrowed and other times on the amount of the line regardless of what is borrowed.

The line of credit is a sound financial planning arrangement. The firm can rely on it and can plan without having to know the exact amount of funds needed each month. The bank will provide the requested funds as long as the agreed conditions are maintained. These conditions usually include maintenance of a minimum working capital.

*Revolving Credit.* This is a formal line of credit secured by receivables or inventory. The term "revolving credit" implies that each new loan involves new receivables or inventory.

### Cost of Short-term Bank Credit

Interest rates vary by size of firm, industry, and section of the country. The bank's rate to the small firm is higher than to large firms,[12] although less than could be obtained elsewhere. The reason is that the costs of loaning to a small firm are larger *per loan dollar* because of the fixed costs of a loan. Furthermore, the risks are higher than for a larger firm. Public utilities, because of their stability, and large finance companies, because of their asset liquidity, receive favorable rates. Construction firms tend to pay the highest rates. The risk is high. Banks in the northern and eastern sections of the country charge lower rates than those in the South and West [13] because the supply of funds is greater and lending opportunities less in the northern and eastern sections.

---

[11] The provisions of an actual line of credit agreement appear in Erwin Esser Nemmers, *Cases in Finance* (Boston: Allyn and Bacon, Inc., 1964), pp. 82–86.

[12] Federal Reserve Board surveys consistently reveal that small bank loans carry higher rates than do large ones. Though size of loan and size of firm are correlated, this does not prove that banks discriminate against small businesses. The marginal cost of lending to small firms and risk are higher, justifying the higher rate. See George J. Benson, "Commercial Bank Price Discrimination against Small Loans: An Empirical Study," *Journal of Finance*, 19 (December 1964), pp. 631–643.

[13] See Theodore G. Flechsig, "The Effects of Concentration on Bank Loan Rates," *Journal of Finance*, 20 (May 1965), pp. 298–311. The differentials seem to have remained

Industry, size of firm, and location are factors management must recognize when seeking a loan. Timing often cannot be greatly altered. The funds must be obtained when needed, whether money is tight or loose. Consequently, to keep the interest cost down the borrower must maintain his firm healthy and keep the banker informed and friendly.

### Other Provisions Attached to Short-term Bank Credit

*Compensating Balance.* Banks usually require that to justify their business customers maintain a checking account balance or compensating balance of 15 to 20 percent of the loan.[14] The bank and the customer, when agreeing on the loan terms, settle on the compensating balance, which provides several advantages to the bank. First the compensating balance increases the effective interest rate. A 20 percent compensating balance raises the effective rate to 25 percent.[15] A customer requiring $10,000 must borrow $12,500. At simple interest, 5 percent on the $12,500 equals $625 interest, but since the firm can only use $10,000, the effective rate is 6¼ percent. However, the firm ordinarily has funds in its checking account and these funds count in the computation. Further, the computation is usually made in terms of the books of the bank. The borrower receives credit on "both ends" for the "float"—the period of time needed to collect checks deposited and checks drawn. Thus, the added amount of borrowing needed to maintain a compensating balance is reduced. If large balances are typically carried, that is, large enough to cover the bank's cost of clearing the borrower's checks and to meet the compensating balance requirement, the effect of the imposed requirement is nominal. Banks object to a firm's deposit balances doing double duty. "Trading on the float" can be done by a firm that writes checks against a deposit just made but not yet collected by the bank. If the checks just written come home to the bank before the bank has received the collection of the checks just deposited, the firm is using the bank's funds "for free."

Through the right of offset the bank reduces its risk by compensating balances if the firm should fail. The amount the firm has on deposit at the time of failure may be applied by the bank against the loan, thus reducing the amount of its unsecured claim against the firm. The bank's *reduced* claim will then rank as unsecured if the bank has no collateral and will participate proportionately with other unsecured creditors.

---

constant during the post-World War II period. See Richard G. Davis and Lois Banks, "Interregional Interest Rate Differentials," *Monthly Review*, Federal Reserve Bank of New York 47 (August 1965), pp. 165–174.

14 The required deposit level is normally defined in terms of average balances, thus permitting use of the required balance to meet working capital needs for some portion of the loan period. See Jack M. Guttentag and Richard G. Davis, "Compensating Balances," *Monthly Review*, Federal Reserve Bank of New York, 43 (December 1961), pp. 205–210.

15 Through link financing the added cost of compensating balances can be reduced. It works like this: A firm needs a full $100,000 loan and the bank requires a $20,000 compensating balance. The firm arranges for an insurance company to purchase a $20,000 certificate of deposit from the bank and pays the insurance company a supplemental amount. The firm has the full $100,000 loan, the bank has an additional $20,000 of funds, and the insurance company has a safe investment yielding a generous return.

Bankers argue that the maintenance of a compensating balance is in the firm's best interest as well as the bank's. A firm should follow conservative practices. For the bank this is so; for the risk-taking firm the matter is not so clear-cut. The bank is not interested in making risky loans but the firm may quite properly assume risk to attain profits and a more competitive level of operations.

*Annual Clean-up.* The requirement that the firm be "out of the bank" a minimum of 1 month each year at least superficially demonstrates that the firm is not using bank credit to finance long-term needs. Bank credit is extended to finance seasonal needs, and the annual clean-up provides some evidence that the loan is being used for its intended purpose.

Brief borrowing from another bank is one method of negating the annual clean-up provision but this is hard to do these days where the second bank is alert. Another dodge is to permit accounts payable to expand and after the clean-up to pay them quickly with newly borrowed funds. The problem here is that banks are afraid of being caught alone with a loan that goes sour. Consequently, if another bank has been willing to extend a firm credit, the second bank is reassured of the firm's credit worthiness and will be happy to lend even though the firm finances the annual clean-up through the second bank.

*Protective Provisions.* For smaller and weak firms a bank may set minimum working capital ratios, impose restrictions on dividends and salaries, and prohibit the repayment of insider shareholder loans. Though the risk associated with a short-term loan is substantially less than that attached to a long-term loan, the management of a sinking firm may try to salvage as much as possible before all is lost. Thus, the bank sets these restrictions to prevent the firm's assets from flowing out the back door.

## COMMERCIAL PAPER AS A SHORT-TERM SOURCE OF FUNDS

Short-term corporate unsecured promissory notes sold at a discount on the open market are known as *commercial paper.* These negotiable notes are in even amounts such as $10,000 (the minimum) and go to the millions. The total issue by one firm often runs into the millions of dollars and is seldom less than $100,000. Maturities are 20–270 days.[16] Commercial paper is an important source of credit to commercial, industrial, and sales finance firms although it totals only about one-fifth the amount of commercial loans by banks.[17]

### The Commercial Paper Market

The commercial paper market is well organized and restricted to firms with top-quality credit. Major sales finance companies such as Associates Investment Company and General Motors Acceptance Corporation sell their paper directly to investors. Other firms typically sell theirs through middlemen called *dealers.* Dealers are granted a marketing

[16] A longer maturity would require registration of the paper with the Securities and Exchange Commission. Securities Act of 1933, § 3a3.

[17] *Federal Reserve Bulletin,* (November, 1973) pp. A22 and A31.

spread of $\frac{1}{4}$ to $\frac{1}{2}$ or 1 percent. Purchasers of commercial paper include nonfinancial institutions, pension funds, and universities. Commercial paper provides these organizations with a low-risk, short-term, moderate return investment. The rate is higher than that on short-term Treasury securities but typically below the prime rate. The risk of loss is negligible.[18]

Firms issuing commercial paper are ordinarily willing to tailor maturity to the needs of the buyer who seeks to have the necessary funds available to meet dividend, tax, or other obligations falling due. Furthermore, finance companies usually issue commercial paper whenever there is a demand, thus permitting corporate investors to place their temporarily idle funds as they accumulate. The finance companies control the volume of paper issued by modifying the terms rather than by restricting the offerings. Generally, commercial paper is held to maturity by the purchaser. No secondary market for the paper exists. However, the major finance companies will usually repurchase the paper if requested, or, if the paper was originally purchased from a dealer, repurchase arrangements with that dealer can be negotiated.

Table 11–2 shows the volume of commercial paper outstanding in recent years. Note the steady rise in the first part of the period and the big jump in 1968 and 1969 as interest rates rose and top-quality borrowers scrambled for funds.

TABLE 11–2. Volume of Commercial and Finance Company Paper Outstanding, 1965–1973 (in billions of dollars)

| End of period | Placed through dealers | Placed directly | Total |
|---|---|---|---|
| 1965 | 1.9 | 7.4 | 9.3 |
| 1966 | 3.1 | 10.5 | 13.6 |
| 1967 | 4.9 | 12.2 | 17.1 |
| 1968 | 7.2 | 14.0 | 21.2 |
| 1969 | 11.8 | 20.8 | 32.6 |
| 1970 | 12.7 | 20.4 | 33.1 |
| 1971 | 11.4 | 20.7 | 32.1 |
| 1972 | 12.2 | 22.5 | 34.7 |
| 1973 | 13.0 | 28.0 | 41.0 |

SOURCE: *Federal Reserve Bulletin*, (May, 1974), p. A 27.

[18] The rapid expansion of the commercial paper market started in the latter part of the 1960s and was accompanied by a deterioration in the quality of the paper issued. This deterioration went unnoticed by some until mid-1970 when Penn Central Transportation Co. defaulted on its outstanding paper. The Penn-Central went into receivership with $87 million of commercial paper in trusting hands. Panic developed in the commercial paper market and Chrysler Financial Corp. was almost tipped over. *New York Times*, July 7, 1970, Section 3, pp. 1, 11. F. C. Schadrack and F. S. Breimyer, "Recent Developments in the Commercial Paper Market," *Federal Reserve Bank of New York—Monthly Review*, 52 (December 1970), pp. 280–291.

### Advantages and Disadvantages to the Borrower

Currently as a result of high interest rates, a large firm can obtain funds in the commercial paper market at a lower rate than the short-term prime bank rate and at less than its bonds would require.[19] And since compensating balances are not required the spread is even wider.[20] Another advantage is that large amounts of funds can be raised hourly without having to deal with a number of banks. The main disadvantage is that the commercial paper market is an impersonal market. Investors look solely for the best yield at the lowest risk. No extensions at maturity are possible; new paper must be sold.

## OTHER SOURCES OF UNSECURED SHORT-TERM FUNDS

A firm's officers, stockholders, friends, and suppliers may provide short-term loans. A supplier may make a loan to build customer goodwill and maintain an outlet for his product. Loans of this type are frequently used by small firms. The rates are lower than elsewhere and the funds are often unavailable from other sources.

Tax reasons exist for officers and shareholders extending loans to the firm instead of making their entire capital contribution in the form of equity. The interest paid on such a loan is a tax deductible expense for the firm, whereas dividends are not. The bank will not be concerned whether the capital contribution is in the form of debt or equity if the amount is subordinated to the bank loan. "Subordinated" means the lenders agree the bank must first be satisfied in full in the event of financial difficulty before these "insider" lenders receive any repayment on their loan. The Internal Revenue Service, however, frowns on deductibility for income tax purposes of interest on large insider loans. A discussion of the limits to which one may go in setting up and operating a "thin" or low-equity company in which lenders are really stockholders would lead us too far afield. What creates a thin company is the practice of shifting part of what is really equity to a subordinated debt position because the ownership of both is the same.

## SUMMARY

Trade credit is the most widely used form of short-term financing. It arises in the day to day operations of the firm as do other means of financing such as accrued interest, wages and taxes, and deferred income. Trade credit can be an expensive form of short-term financing if cash discounts are missed and full payment made a short time later.

Small firms typically employ relatively larger amounts of trade credit. The type of business activity also influences the firm's use of trade credit. The amount of inventory carried, its rate of turnover, and the competitive situation are other factors influencing a firm's use of trade credit. Trade

[19] Quote from the 1970 *Annual Report of Allied Chemical.*

[20] But the trade does require commercial paper issuers to maintain unused lines of credit equal to about 10 percent of their outstanding paper which to some extent offsets the benefit of no compensating balance.

terms may be used in the industry as an effective competitive weapon. During declining business activity buyers put pressures on sellers to relax trade terms. In a recovery sellers gradually tighten trade terms. Although prices remain the same, the real cost of doing business has increased.

Bank credit is a frequent source of short-term funds, but not as widely used as is trade credit. Self-liquidating loans, whether secured or not, are the specialty of the commercial banker.

The firm's banking connection should be chosen carefully. The bank's lending policies, services available, experience, size, and location should be compatible with the firm's deposit, borrowing, and collection requirements. Deposits are valuable to the banker. At the same time the attractive borrowing alternatives of a firm are limited. In contrast, a banker has numerous alternative investment opportunities. Large firms usually have easy access to bank credit. Small firms may have difficulty. A firm's best protection in the unequal contest with the banker is maintenance of an adequate deposit balance at a cooperative bank. When the bank ceases to be competitive, the firm should not hesitate to change banks.

Commercial paper is corporate unsecured short-term promissory notes sold in the open market. The selling firms are large with high credit ratings. The notes must be paid at maturity. The rate on commercial paper is currently below the prime rate making it cheaper than a bank loan. Financial institutions and firms with temporarily surplus funds purchase commercial paper. The rates are higher than those on short-term Treasury securities and the risk is small. As a result, they are attractive short-term investments.

### *Study Questions*

1. Trade credit is sometimes called a spontaneous source of short-term funds. Explain. What are some other spontaneous short-term sources of funds? Does bank credit belong to this group? Explain.
2. Give examples of trade credit terms. What is the amount of cash discount granted for early payment in each example?
3. Distinguish between cash discounts and trade and quantity discounts.
4. Passing cash discounts results in a high cost of short-term trade credit financing if payment is required shortly after the discount date. How may the implicit interest cost be reduced? How does this method operate?
5. What advantage does a firm have that sells on net 30-day terms and purchases on net 60-day terms? What problems would be created if the firm's suppliers tightened trade terms to net 30 days? to cash on delivery? How might the firm ease its tightened financial position?
6. What major factors influence a firm's use of trade credit? Is the state of the economy one of these? If so, how do economic conditions influence the use of trade credit? On balance do you think a firm would have a larger accounts payable balance during a period of economic boom or during one of recession? Explain.
7. The financial difficulties of many firms begin with the excessive use of trade credit. Explain. How can the firm extract itself from these difficulties?

Frequently the only remedy is bankruptcy. What conditions may exist that preclude rehabilitating the firm's financial condition?

8. Suppliers generally extend trade credit more quickly and more easily than bankers. Explain the reasons for the difference. How is it possible for a firm to obtain trade credit and be refused bank credit?
9. What are the rates charged on trade credit, bank credit, and commercial paper? How do you account for the differences? How do these rates relate to the bank prime rate? to the short-term Treasury bill rate?
10. Why is a firm's demand deposit account valuable to a banker? Why is it likely to be more valuable to one bank than to another?
11. What factors should be considered in selecting a bank? Why is shopping around for the best terms on a loan generally to be avoided by a firm? How can an alert financial manager sensitive to money market conditions save his firm the necessity of shopping around for the best terms?
12. Why do bankers enjoy making short-term self-liquidating loans? Why might a banker make a loan of this type even to a financially weak firm?
13. What is a bank line of credit? How does it differ from a straight bank loan? What are the advantages and disadvantages of a line of credit?
14. What do compensating balances offer the bank in the event the firm is forced into bankruptcy?
15. What is the annual clean-up and what purpose does it serve? How may this requirement be avoided? Why may a bank tolerate and even encourage this maneuver?

### Problems

1. The Razz-ma-Tazz Company purchases from numerous suppliers.

a. Calculate the implicit interest rate on an annual basis of failure by the company to take cash discounts when purchasing from its suppliers on the following terms (assuming payment must be made on the due date when the discount time passes). Use a 360-day year.

(i) 1/10, n/30
(ii) 2/10, n/40
(iii) 3/15, n/60
(iv) 2/10, n/60
(v) 6/10, n/90
(vi) 1/10, n/60
(vii) 2/10, n/30

b. Examine the implicit interest rates calculated above and compare the effect on the rate of doubling the discount offered with halving the time period within which payment must be made, given the same discount. Which is more powerful in raising the implicit annual interest cost of trade credit to the firm that cannot take trade discounts? Why does the result come out this way?

2. The Razz-ma-Tazz Company encounters financial difficulties and some discounts must be missed. You are called in to develop a strategy aimed at obtaining the maximum benefit from the discounts that can be taken, minimizing the financial effect from those that cannot be taken and keeping to a minimim the possibility of suppliers shutting off the flow of inventory. Of the seven suppliers in question 1a, which discounts would you recommend the firm take, which should be passed, and what tactics should the firm adopt to minimize the cost of trade credit and still keep the suppliers from closing in? Assume the firm can borrow at local financial institutions at rates ranging from 15 to 20 percent.

3. You have just been married and are purchasing your major appliances from Castle Stores. The terms are 3/10, n/90.

a. Should you not be able to pay by the 10th, what would be the rate you are paying for credit, on an annual basis, if you paid by:

(i) the 20th day after purchase

(ii) the 70th day after purchase

(iii) the 90th day after purchase

b. Examination of your financial condition reveals that you will not be able to pay for the appliances until one year from today. The friendly banker, eager to help, offers a loan of the necessary funds at 6 percent a year. You accept the offer, make the purchase, and resolve not to pay anyone more than 6 percent for the use of credit. From the date of purchase, for how many days must you delay payment to equal the bank loan rate? *Corollary:* The loan from the banker must be for how many days? At 6 percent, what would be the interest cost on a loan of $3,000 from the banker? Use a 360-day year.

4. Cold Start Cereals Company signs a one-year $20,000 note. Annual interest is 6 percent, discounted.

a. How much will the bank credit to the firm's account?

b. What is the effective rate of interest being paid on the loan?

5. The following year Cold Start decides to switch banks. The bank does not discount its loans but requires a 20 percent compensating balance. Interest is at 5 percent.

a. How much will the firm have to borrow to have available the required amount as calculated in question 4a?

b. Compute the annual dollar interest cost of borrowing this amount for one year at 5 percent. Remember that the loan is not discounted. Also compute the effective rate of interest.

c. Was it smart to switch banks? What savings, if any, were realized?

6. Cold Start fails and is forced to liquidate. The balance sheet upon liquidation is given in Table 11–3.

TABLE 11–3. Cold Start Cereals Company

Balance Sheet

| | | | |
|---|---|---|---|
| Cash on deposit | $ 20,000 | Accounts payable | $120,000 |
| Other assets | 90,000 | Bank loan | 50,000 |
| Deficit | 110,000 | Capital | 50,000 |
| Total assets | $220,000 | Total liabilities and net worth | $220,000 |

The assets in liquidation bring the stated balance sheet figures. One advantage to banks of compensating balances is the right of offset; should a firm fail, the amount it has on deposit with the bank can be used to offset the bank loan. It need not be thrown into the pot to help satisfy the claims of all the creditors.

a. How many cents on the dollar would the creditors receive if the bank did not have the right of offset?

b. How many cents on the dollar would the general accounts payable creditors receive if the bank has the right of offset?

c. With the right of offset, how much in absolute dollars will the bank receive?

d. With the right of offset, what is the percentage recovery that the bank makes? How does this compare with the other creditors?

7. You walk into a leading mail order store and purchase $100 worth of sporting equipment. The terms are cash in 30 days or after that, with 6 months to pay $110 in equal monthly installments. The carrying charge of $10 is added to the $100. Determine the approximate annual rate of interest you would be paying if a cash purchase were not possible. *Note:* Repayment in equal installments means that you have the use of only half of the funds for the period of time.

## Selected References


Agemian, C. A., "Maintaining an Effective Bank Relationship," *Financial Executive,* 32 (January 1964), pp. 24–28.

Brosky, J. J., *The Implicit Cost of Trade Credit and Theory of Optimal Terms of Sale.* New York: Credit Research Foundation, 1969.

Christe, R. A., "New Developments in the Commercial Paper Market," *Industrial Banker,* 35 (August 1969), pp. 10–13 ff.

Edwards, R. E., "Finance Companies and Their Creditors," *Journal of Commercial Bank Lending* 54 (October 1971), pp. 2–10.

Gibson, W. E., "Compensating Balance Requirements," *National Banking Review,* 2 (March 1965), pp. 298–311.

Gordon, R. L., "Talking Business with a Banker," *Financial Executive,* 35 (February 1967), pp. 10 ff.

Harris, D. G. "Rationing Credit to Business: More than Interest Rates," *Business Review—Federal Reserve Bank of Philadelphia* (August 1970), pp. 3–14.

———, "Some Evidence on Differential Lending Practices at Commercial Banks," 28 *Journal of Finance* (December 1973), pp. 1303–1311.

Hayes, D. A., *Bank Lending Policies: Issues and Practices.* Ann Arbor, Mich.: University of Michigan Press, 1964.

Levenson, A. M., "Interest Rate and Cost Differentials in Bank Lending to Small and Large Businesses," *Review of Economics and Statistics,* 44 (May 1962), pp. 190–197.

Nadler, P. S., "Compensating Balances and the Prime at Twilight," *Harvard Business Review,* 50 (January-February 1972), pp. 112–30.

Robinson, R. I., *The Management of Bank Funds.* 2d ed. New York: McGraw-Hill, Inc., 1962.

Schadrack, F. C., Jr., "Demand and Supply in the Commercial Paper Market," *Journal of Finance,* 25 (September 1970), pp. 837–852.

Stone, B. K., "The Cost of Bank Loans," *Journal of Financial and Quantitative Analysis,* 7 (December 1972), pp. 2077–86.

# 12

# Secured Short-Term Financing and Intermediate Financing

A lender normally does not extend credit if the risk of default by the borrower is high, nor does he demand security if the risk of default is low. The lender is concerned with safety of principal and a fair return. And the "cleaner" the deal, the lower the administrative costs of the loan. Rather than refuse a loan a lender may demand security to reduce the risk of loss.

With collateral the lender has both the cash-generating ability of the firm and the collateral of the pledged asset as sources of loan repayment. Should the borrower fail, the lender has a prior claim over other creditors to the collateral and the lender can force sale of the asset to repay the loan.

In this chapter we discuss short-term financing using receivables and inventory as security. But whether collateral is put up or not, the purpose of a short-term loan is to finance a seasonal need for funds with the loan being repaid from the proceeds of sale of merchandise and collection of receivables. With term loan financing (more than 1 year) the scene changes.

## COLLATERAL LOANS

### Secured versus Unsecured Borrowing

Businesses prefer to borrow on an unsecured basis. Pledging of security restricts further borrowing and is bothersome and costly. Firms are more anxious to pledge security if they receive a reduction in interest rate, but this seldom occurs. A weak borrower usually must either provide collateral or not receive the loan.

Many firms are not of sufficient financial stature to obtain unsecured credit from commercial banks. One study reported two-thirds of the outstanding business loans of national banks and one-half of the dollar volume represented were guaranteed by a third party or secured. Though commercial banks are the most important source of secured loans, the main function of organizations called *finance companies* is the granting of secured business loans.[1] Unlike banks, these institutions cannot accept deposits and do not serve as department stores of finance. They raise their funds in more specialized ways.

### Why Collateral May Be Necessary

A firm may be required to post collateral for several reasons. Usually the firm is too weak or too new to justify an unsecured loan, or the firm may be seeking more credit than the lender is willing to grant on an unsecured basis—for example, the firm may get $70,000 against a pledge of marketable common stocks but only $50,000 on an unsecured basis. Or the firm may want the funds for a longer time than the lender is willing to extend on an unsecured basis.

### Characteristics of Good Collateral

Legality of claim to the asset in the event the borrower defaults and the probable recovery value on the asset are the two most important characteristics of good collateral. Government securities left with the lender rank high on both counts. Should the borrower default, the lender simply sells the securities already in his possession. The recovery value is high because "governments" are stable in price, have a ready market, and a large block can be disposed of quickly without affecting price. The common stocks of listed corporations also make good collateral, but their wider price fluctuations result in lower loan value of these securities—typically 80 percent as against 90 percent on governments. At the other end of the spectrum are the shares of closely held companies. Such securities adequately fill the ownership protection requirement but not that of predictable recovery value. Lack of a market makes determination of their value difficult. The same is true for fixed assets such as machinery.

### Working Capital Assets as Collateral

Inventories of raw materials such as grain or steel are marketable collateral, have durability, and their value is quickly ascertainable. But

---

[1] Funds are available at some rate to most company borrowers because of the variety of financial institutions.

because they are portable and fungible (one specimen may be used in place of another in satisfaction of an obligation), they suffer from title or ownership protection weakness. Other inventory items, such as fresh fish or produce, while quite marketable, remain in that state for only a short time. Their lack of durability makes them poor collateral.

The title protection problem arises partly because the borrower may require the raw material in production, whereas the lender wants the inventory stored and controlled. Since the raw material cannot be in both places at once, a number of devices have been established to safeguard the title of the lender but permit release of the inventory when needed in production.

Work in process is infrequently pledged as loan collateral because it changes in form, lacks marketability, has uncertain recovery value, and has weak title protection. As the raw material is fed into the production stream, it is difficult to separate out the pledged parts from those claimed by the general creditors. When financial difficulty occurs, the general creditors want to find as many of a firm's assets unpledged as possible. The secured creditor, therefore, must make certain that no defect exists in his claim to a particular group of assets. The lender can avoid this difficulty by obtaining a security agreement that provides for a "floating" lien on the shifting stock—that is, one that shifts from one batch of raw material to the next. Even so, great reliance must be placed on the honesty of the borrower. The goods remain in his control and are not clearly identifiable. Commercial finance companies are the primary lenders in this area.

Finished goods such as appliances or automobiles serve as good collateral. Their durability, marketability, and predictable recovery value rank high, and they offer title protection. But the lender must be confident of the integrity of the borrower. The goods to be sold may be in the borrower's showroom. The borrower, has control over the merchandise, and when this is sold also has control over the proceeds of the sale. The lender, therefore, must spot check the dealer's showroom to determine whether the goods are still on the floor. If sold, the funds should be flowing to the lender to repay the loan made against that particular unit.

Receivables have good collateral qualities and are frequently pledged,[2] but there are difficulties. Keeping track of many receivables is costly. The borrower may pledge nonexistent accounts. Confusion may arise in identifying the pledged accounts in the event of the borrower's financial difficulty. Still worse, the customer owing the receivable may have counterclaims for defective merchandise or guaranteed life of equipment or may return the merchandise.

---

[2] Should the borrower default the lender may notify the customer whose account was pledged to send the checks to the lender. However, the customer would then be assuming the risk that the pledge was valid and therefore should not send the checks to the lender unless the borrower agrees.

## ACCOUNTS RECEIVABLE FINANCING

### Borrowing

Borrowing against receivables is based on an agreement, including a promissory note, setting forth the terms and procedures and sometimes providing for pledging of all or only specified receivables. A stack of invoices is placed with the lender for review and appraisal. Those that do not meet the lender's credit standards are rejected. Credit may be extended on the basis of an acceptable pool of receivables. Payment by customers of their accounts, returned merchandise and allowances for defects, and bad debts reduce the pool of credit available. The pool is expanded through replenishment with newly generated receivables. To protect against loss, the lender sets a prudent margin between the face value of the receivables and the amount of the loan, selects only sound receivables, and establishes a claim against the receivables pledged. To perfect his security interest the lender files a copy of the security agreement in one or more offices of the state, including the secretary of state of the state where the collateral is located.

The legal form used to borrow against receivables is standard. Thus, it pays for the borrower to shop for the most attractive package of percentage amount advanced and interest rate. Lenders extend from 50 to 90 percent of the value of the receivables pledged. The average is 75 to 80 percent.[3] Such characteristics as the financial position of the borrower, the credit standing of the customer, and the proportion of returns and allowances determine the actual proportion advanced. Commercial banks lend somewhat less on the average than finance companies such as Commercial Credit and CIT but charge lower rates. Commercial bank interest charges average 1 to 6 percent over the prime rate. Some banks levy an additional annual service charge of 1 percent on the balance outstanding. Finance company charges run from a daily rate of 1/40 of 1 percent or 9 percent annually for large accounts to 1/15 of 1 percent or 24 percent annually.

Most receivables financing is done on the *nonnotification plan*; the customer is not notified that the receivable has been pledged by the seller, but the receivables are pledged with recourse, that is, should the customer not pay, the lender can look to the borrowing firm for payment. Under the *notification plan,* the customer is informed by the seller that the account has been pledged and directed to make payment to the lender. Again, recourse is applicable. If the customer does not pay, the borrower must still pay the lender.

To prevent fraud and establish its claim to the collateral, the lender usually requests copies of the invoices, requires the borrowing firm to mark its receivables ledger to show the assigned accounts, and reserves the right to inspect the books. The borrower may also be required to deposit all customer payments in the form they are received thus enabling the lender to verify the receivables, note defective merchandise claims, and make certain the borrower is paying immediately.

---

[3] See "Accounts Receivable Lending—Credit at the Margin," *Business Conditions,* Federal Reserve Bank of Chicago (March 1958), pp. 5–12.

Many financially sound firms use receivables financing. We cannot state categorically that such financing is a sign of weakness. Its use is growing. Computer systems are reducing the administrative cost thus increasing its attractiveness. The method provides a flexible source of funds expanding and contracting with sales. Furthermore, though the cost is high, it may not be as high as it appears, since the interest cost is based on the daily outstanding balance and the finance company does not require a compensating balance, although a commercial bank may. The cost of receivables borrowing may be compared with the cost of the sale of additional common stock.[4] A small firm may find the sale of common stock possible only at a very high cost. Through borrowing against receivables the firm obtains capital and the advantages of leverage but with considerable risk. If the economy turns against the firm, little source of new funds is left. If the firm survives the risk—that is, makes profits aided by leverage sufficient to reduce indebtedness—the firm's value will increase substantially because profits will be improved and risk reduced.

### Factoring

Factoring involves the sale (not mere assignment) of receivables to a financial institution such as an *old line factor*—a commercial finance company or one of a few commercial banks who recently entered the field. The sale is usually without recourse; if the customer does not pay, the factor takes the loss. Consequently, the factor carefully selects the receivables purchased. Before shipping goods the firm can get the factor's approval of the credit of any customer whose receivable the firm expects to "factor." If the factor approves, the goods are shipped and the factor will buy the receivable. Should the factor not approve, the firm can still ship and assume the credit risk. When the receivables are sold the customer is notified and instructed to make payment directly to the factor. The receivables when sold no longer appear on the firm's balance sheet. A firm borrowing against receivables carries them on the balance sheet and footnotes their pledged status.

The factor performs a number of services for its client firm in addition to the lending service. This makes it difficult to compare the costs of factoring with borrowing against receivables. The factor serves as a credit department for the client firm, checking the financial condition of its customers. The factor also relieves the client of collection efforts. When the factor purchases the receivables he assumes the risk the customer will not pay. Only the last service is unique to the factor. The other services may or may not be furnished as part of ordinary accounts receivable financing.

Factors charge service fees (commission) of from 1 to 3 percent of the receivables purchased, the rate depending on the risk of the paper bought, the amount of business, the size and maturity of the receivables. These charges cover the cost of credit examination, collection expense, and bad-debt losses (risk-taking). A firm in the 1 percent category that turns its receivables 12 times a year is paying approximately 12 percent of the

---

[4] The cost of common stock will be developed in Chapter 15. For the present it will be sufficient to think in terms of what percentage of ownership must be given up for new money.

average dollar volume for having its receivables serviced. Interest at the rate of about 3 percent above prime is charged for funds withdrawn ahead of the normal collection or average due date, that is, from the date of the sale of the receivables to the average customer due date. Any funds not drawn by the firm before the customer's due date bear no interest charge and funds earn interest when collected by the factor but left with the factor after the customer due date.

The factoring agreement is renewable on an annual basis but may be canceled on short notice. When the process of factoring is continuous (as new receivables arise, they are regularly sold to the factor), then the factor provides not only credit for temporary or peak needs but is also financing a portion of the firm's permanent working capital. The factor is better able to handle the credit risk than the client firm because the factor diversifies and has wider knowledge of the industries served by the client firm.

### Finance Companies

Finance companies engage in many secured lending activities. Sales finance companies handle both wholesale and retail financing. They make loans to finance a dealer's inventory of automobiles or appliances and purchase the "paper" of the customers buying the merchandise on the installment plan. Commercial finance companies make loans to businesses that commercial banks cannot accept because of risk. These loans may be secured by any acceptable asset, receivables and inventory being most frequently pledged. Factors specialize in financing accounts receivables either by making secured loans or by purchasing the receivables. The assumption by commercial finance companies and factors of a degree of risk higher than that normally accepted by banks is the justification of their economic existence.

When making a loan, commercial finance companies and factors rely for safety primarily upon the collateral offered by the borrower and may lend many times his net worth or working capital. Often the firm is small or moderate-sized or was recently established and is growing rapidly and its management is relatively inexperienced. To keep losses tolerable, these financial institutions have developed complex procedures whose high cost is borne by the borrower in the form of interest and service charges.

## INVENTORY FINANCING

### Terms

Much business credit is secured by a pledge of inventory and commercial banks are the primary lenders. Approximately 10 percent of all secured loans by banks are backed by inventories. Large and medium-sized firms are the major clients. Small firms with less than $50,000 in assets obtain relatively little credit via this financing option.

A wide variety of products may be pledged as collateral for a loan. Raw materials and finished goods have the highest collateral value. Next come certain standard purchased parts that can be returned to the supplier at a discount. Finally, and almost without collateral value, is work in process. What little value this has concerns works that are almost finished.

The inventory may be on the borrower's site, in storage, or in transit. It may remain in the possession of the borrower or be stored with a third party. Title (ownership) of goods in transit is evidenced by a *bill of lading*; title to those stored in a warehouse is covered by a *warehouse receipt*. Grains and vegetable oils are examples of inventory secured by warehouse receipts. Title is the basis on which much inventory financing is done.

If inventory is the security, the lender considers the durability, the ability to identify, the salability, and the validity of his lien against the assets. When making the loan, the lender takes a margin of safety to protect against a decline in the value of the merchandise. Perishability, stability of market price, and cost of liquidation are the risks considered. The amount loaned ranges from 50 to 80 percent of the book value of the inventory. The exact percentage is a matter of judgment, bargaining, and trade-off against other terms of the loan, particularly the interest rate. One lender might be willing to grant a higher amount but also charge a higher rate; another a lower amount but a lower rate.

Although interest rates on inventory-backed loans made by commercial banks are lower than the rates charged by commercial finance companies, bank lenders may require a compensating balance of 15 to 20 percent. Other lenders may impose service charges to cover the cost of checking the inventory on the borrower's premises. If the inventory is placed in a public or terminal warehouse, that is, a warehouse that rents space to all comers, there will be charges to cover "in and out" handling costs. If a field warehouse is set up on the premises of the borrower, fixed or variable costs will be incurred. Generally the rates on the borrowed funds do not vary significantly, the major variation being the service charges that arise from the costs of checking and handling the merchandise and the length of time it is in storage.

### Who Holds the Collateralized Inventory?

Having reached an agreement with the lender on the terms of the loan to be secured by inventory, the firm is asked to sign a promissory note covering the loan of funds and a document evidencing title to the inventory serving as the collateral. These are the two basic pieces of paper underlying the deal. Because of the fixed costs of setting up such an arrangement, the loan is usually for a substantial sum and regularly renewed.

*Inventory in Borrower's Possession.* Appliances and automobiles are identifiable by serial number, and their presence on the showroom floor is necessary for their sale. Hence, they are usually left in the possession of the borrower. Protection of the lender is through a *security agreement* under which the borrower agrees to hold the units and the sale proceeds for the lender. The proceeds must be forwarded to the lender immediately upon sale of a unit. The lender protects himself against unsecured creditors by filing the security agreement in the county where the borrower's office is and in the state capitol and by requiring the borrower to keep the units properly insured. The lender makes periodic unannounced inspections to ascertain that the borrower still has the pledged units for which the lender has not yet received sale proceeds as repayment of the loan.

This *floor-plan arrangement* serves the firm by keeping paper work to a minimum and permitting display of the merchandise. The major disadvantage to the lender is dependence on the honesty of the dealer. If it is not imperative that the inventory remain in the borrower's possession, the lender can obtain greater safety by requiring the borrower to store the inventory in a warehouse.

*Inventory in Warehouseman's Possession.* Upon receipt of the goods the warehouseman issues a warehouse receipt[5] and releases the goods only upon presentation of this piece of paper. The lender is protected against the claims of unsecured creditors since the goods are segregated, and against the dishonesty of the borrower since the goods are no longer in his hands.

But loss may still be sustained. The warehouse receipt is subject to fraudulent use; an innocent holder of the receipt can claim the goods. The receipt does not warrant the quality or value of the goods nor provide for insurance. If the borrower does not have good title to the goods (as with stolen goods), the lender gets no title. Furthermore, the lender must satisfy himself that the goods are what they are purported to be—perhaps by opening the boxes to see that they actually contain cans of cherries and not of applesauce. Through the years some spectacular frauds running to millions of dollars have been based on fake warehouse receipts and nonexistent inventory.[6] Yet warehousing, and particularly field warehousing, remains a popular method for facilitating loans secured by inventory.

To carry out *field warehousing,* the premises of the borrower are used as a warehouse for the collateral pledged. The field warehouse may be a simple fenced-in area containing lumber, scrap iron, or coal awaiting use in the production process or sale. Or, it may be a building containing stored cotton, cases of canned goods, or tanks of salad oil. Signs are posted around the segregated area stating who has control. If the area is in control of a separate company which is bonded and has its own employees it is a true warehouse. However, "field warehousing" may not involve a separate warehouse company and may use employees of the borrower. Then there are risks.

Warehouse receipts may be negotiable or nonnegotiable.[7] Negotiable receipts are used primarily in connection with the storage of actively

---

[5] The warehouse receipt is not a guarantee of title. The lender must assure himself that the borrower had title before the goods were put in the warehouse. If a thief puts an article in a warehouse, the true owner can still get it.

[6] The Tino De Angelis, Billie Sol Estes, and McKesson Robbins cases are examples. See Thomas G. Greaves, Jr., " 'Salad Oil,' and Collateral Loans: Solutions to the Banker's Dilemma," *Robert Morris Associates Bulletin,* 47 (April 1965), pp. 370–378.

[7] Briefly, the distinction between "negotiable" and "nonnegotiable" is as follows. Transfer of a nonnegotiable paper means the new owner steps into the shoes of the prior owners and is exposed to all the claims made against them. However, if the paper is negotiable, then many claims are cut off, for example, a claim that one of the prior owners was not paid or that the goods were not as represented to him. There are two major exceptions; the claims of the immediate seller with whom the buyer (new owner) deals are not cut off, and the new owner is not free of a claim of forgery of the document or a claim that the goods were stolen at some point in the chain of changes in prior possession.

traded commodities such as wheat or corn. Title to the commodity is transferred simply by the receipt changing hands. Nonnegotiable receipts are usually employed for a loan financing raw materials required in production. Such receipts need not be so carefully guarded against loss and sometimes need not be presented to the warehouseman each time goods are to be withdrawn into the production process or for sale. A letter by the lender to the warehouseman authorizing withdrawal is sufficient. That letter is issued only after the borrower has made the appropriate payment on his loan.

*A Field Warehouse Financing Illustration.* A canner with sufficient capital to start the season may borrow from his bank later in the year, using the canned goods coming off the production line and flowing into the field warehouse on his property as collateral to keep the process going. His loan rises as the inventory increases. When the canner sells a carload of canned goods the bank releases the required amount of merchandise and the canner remits the proceeds of the sale.

A summary of types of secured short-term financing appears in Table 12–1.

## INTERMEDIATE FINANCING

All intermediate financing involves maturities beyond one year but the line on the other end is not drawn on a time basis but on the type of arrangements for the loan and its repayment.

Three major forms of intermediate financing exist: term loans, installment financing, and leasing. The first two we will consider presently. Leasing is sufficiently important to warrant separate treatment in the next chapter.

TABLE 12–1. Provisions of Secured Short-term Financing Arrangements

| Type of financing arrangement | Funds obtainable as a percent of value of asset | Interest rate | Other typical provisions |
|---|---|---|---|
| Receivables loan (bank) | 50–90% | 1 to 6 percent over prime rate | Service charge, compensating balance |
| Receivables loan (finance company) | 50–90% | 9–24% | Service charge |
| Factoring | 97–99% | 3% above prime | Interest earned on funds left with factor |
| Inventory loan | 50–80% | 1 to 6 percent over prime rate | Service charge, banks may require compensating balance |

### A Shift in Focus

Self-liquidating is the feature that characterizes most short-term loans. The proceeds for repayment come from the sale and collection of inventory and receivables. Profitability of the firm is not a major concern of the lender. Liquidity is the key to a short-term loan.

With intermediate financing the emphasis shifts to profitability. The longer loan span makes preoccupation with liquidity hazardous. Extended periods of unprofitable operation dissipate liquid assets, but if the firm is profitable, it generates values that repay the loan.

### Term Loans

Term loans are normally paid off in regular installments covering principal and interest and are privately placed with banks or insurance companies. This arrangement neatly fits the financing of a permanent increase in working capital or acquisition of a specific asset such as equipment. The increase in the firm's earning stream plus depreciation can be used for loan repayment. Maturity is tailored to the firm's expected earning power and cash-generating abilities. Funds are not raised for a longer period of time than needed, and idle funds need not be temporarily reinvested. Also, term funds may be obtainable at a lower rate than long-term debt funds, thus widening the leverage gain, and are usually cheaper and more quickly obtained than the selling of stock. Term financing is well suited to meeting the needs of smaller and growing firms.

There are also disadvantages. Financing a permanent need with term funds requires that the expected level of earnings be realized to amortize the loan as projected. The two time schedules (loan repayment and increased earnings) must mesh. Committing the firm to a sizable annual payment for a number of years is risky, but the risk is lessened if the firm has a good margin of safety between expected earnings and annual payments and if future earnings can be accurately predicted.

*Lenders.* Commercial banks and insurance companies are the leading sources of term loan funds. Bank term loans are generally 1 to 5 years and are given mostly to small firms that have $10 million or less in assets. Insurance company loans are frequently 5 to 15 years and are made to large firms. Many term loans involve the bank taking the short maturities of the loan and an insurance company the long maturities. Government agencies, such as the Small Business Administration (SBA), also lend to firms on a term loan basis where other financial institutions are unwilling to lend. Banks frequently participate in loans made by the SBA by making all or part of the loan subject to the guarantee of the SBA as to interest and principal repayment, with the borrower paying a fee to the SBA for this guarantee.

*Provisions.*[8] A note or a series of notes is executed by the borrower with staggered maturity dates for the several repayments. To reduce the risk arising from longer maturity and uncertainty of future earnings, the

[8] The provisions of an actual term loan agreement appear in Erwin Esser Nemmers, *Cases in Finance* (Boston: Allyn and Bacon, Inc., 1964), pp. 118–120.

lender makes a thorough financial analysis of the firm, requires the submission of future periodic financial statements, may or may not require collateral, but will impose protective covenants. The collateral taken is mainly stock, bonds, machinery and equipment, or other long-term assets. The protective covenants include provisions such as the maintenance of specified amounts of working capital and net worth; "key" man insurance on the lives of the top management; and prohibitions (unless the lender consents) against sale of assets, acquisition of further debt, repayment of existing debt (particularly loans by officers), the payment of dividends, increases in officers' salaries, or the reacquisition of the firm's stock. Most of these so-called negative limitations are designed to prevent taking assets "out the back door" and leaving the lender with a corporate shell.

Besides these protective provisions, the loan contract will contain the *acceleration clause,* which provides that in the event of any default (in payment or of any other provision of the loan) the entire note may be declared due and payable immediately. In the absence of this clause the firm is liable only for the installment currently due.

*Computing Payments.* Term loans are typically repayable in equal installments covering both interest and principal. Where these installments do not fully repay the loan at maturity, the last payment is larger and called a *"balloon" payment.* Balloons are not popular with lenders. Most term loans may be prepaid ahead of schedule but with a prepayment penalty (usually one year's interest on the prepayment).

To illustrate the determination of a term loan amortization schedule assume a firm borrows \$1000 for 5 years with interest at 8 percent. The \$1000 is really the present value of a stream of annual payments for 5 years discounted at 8 percent. We want to find the amount of each of these annual payments. From Chapter 9 we know that the present value $PV$ of a stream of uniform payments equals the annual payment $A$ times the discount factor $DF$ (Table A–2 at end of this book), or $PV = A(DF)$. Solving for $A$ we have $A = PV/DF$. Thus \$1000/3.993 ≅ \$250 where 3.993 is the $DF$ for 5 annual payments at 8 percent. The \$250 annual payment includes principal and interest. The first year's interest is \$80 (\$1000 × 8%) and principal repayment \$170 or (\$250 − \$80). The complete schedule for the five years is shown in Table 12–2.

TABLE 12–2. Computation of Term Loan Repayments per \$1,000 Over Five Equal Annual Installments at 8 Percent

| Year | (1) Annual payment ($A = PV/DF$) | (2) Interest | (3) Principal (1) − (2) | (4) Remaining balance at end of year \$1000 − (3) cumulated |
|---|---|---|---|---|
| 1 | \$ 250 or (\$1000/3.993) | \$80 or (\$1000 × 0.08) | \$170 or (\$250 − \$80) | \$830 |
| 2 | 250 | 66 or [(1000 − 170) × 0.08] | 184 or ( 250 − 66) | 646 |
| 3 | 250 | 52 or [(1000 − 354) × 0.08] | 198 or ( 250 − 52) | 448 |
| 4 | 250 | 36 or [(1000 − 552) × 0.08] | 214 or ( 250 − 36) | 234 |
| 5 | 250 | 19 or [(1000 − 766) × 0.08] | 231 or ( 250 − 19) | 0 * |
| Total | \$1250 | | | |

* Rounding error.

[B5]

*Cost.* The rate on term loan financing is on the average about 1 percent higher than for short-term credit lent the same borrower.[9] The financial standing of the borrower, the size of the loan, and the condition of the capital market determine the exact rate charged. A financially strong firm borrowing a large amount may pay only slightly more than the prime rate. A small firm might pay 4 or 5 percent over prime. On larger term loans the rate may change over the life of the loan with variations in the prime rate. This practice is growing. Likewise lenders are currently seeking part of their compensation in the form of options to buy common stock at a price fixed over some agreed-upon period. If the firm prospers and its stock rises above the option price, the lender can take capital gains.

### Installment Equipment Financing

The purchase of income-producing machinery or equipment on a plan providing for an initial down payment and installment payments amortizing the remaining balance is known as *installment equipment financing. Commercial finance companies* (sometimes the subsidiaries of the equipment manufacturer) are the primary source of this type of credit. Commercial banks are entering this area. The field has had rapid growth due to increasing mechanization of all phases of production, but is still small relative to other intermediate term financing.

The cost of this financing is normally high. Small firms or those with weak credit ratings are forced to follow a policy of pay-as-you-earn and, thus, use the collateral of the purchased equipment and the downpayment to induce the borrower to lend. The weaker the credit rating the larger is the downpayment required. Acquisition of equipment on the installment plan enables the firm to obtain a greater amount of credit than otherwise would be possible, and is attractive to the firm if future revenues can be expected to be substantially improved by the new asset.

The reasons for the high cost of installment equipment financing are the risk borne by the lender, the administrative cost of servicing the loan, and the poor bargaining power and limited alternatives of the purchaser-borrower. The downpayment on a piece of equipment—factory, farm, medical, bowling, hotel or restaurant, and so on—may range from 20 to 35 percent of the purchase price with the balance amortized over a 3- to 5-year period. The payments include principal and interest and are set to recover the amount of the loan substantially in advance of the estimated decline in the value of the equipment.

The lender looks to the recovery value of the equipment as protection for his loan but even more to the pressure on the borrower to meet the payment schedule in order to keep the equipment. The situation is analogous to the equipment trust certificate in railroading.[10] Without a

---

[9] The extra 1 per cent is principally protection for the lender against the risk of an increase in the market rate of interest during the loan period and also the longer period of exposure of the lender to the risk of default.

[10] The equipment trust certificate (to be discussed in Chapter 19) involves *ownership* of the equipment by the lender who leases it to the borrowing railroad with an agreement by the lender to deliver title when full payment has been made. The lender then sells shares of ownership participating in the deal: equipment trust certificates.

locomotive, the railroad stops. If the resale value of the pledged asset fails to cover the outstanding portion of the loan at any time the lender can seldom find other unmortgaged assets of the borrower to recover the difference. Hence, the repayment schedule may provide for uniform payments over the stipulated term or may follow the anticipated decline in market value of the asset.

The nominal interest rate charged is 7 to 9 percent per year but is based on the initial purchase price rather than the declining balance due. Since the firm makes a large downpayment and amortizes the remainder of the loan, the effective interest rate may range up to 24 percent.

Installment financing may be arranged either with the manufacturer or dealer selling the equipment or directly with a finance company. The basic document is a contract that retains title to the equipment in the lender until payment is completed. The manufacturer or the dealer arranging financing may either retain the paper himself or in turn may discount it with a finance company. Usually when the maufacturer or dealer sells the paper to a finance company it is stipulated that in the event of default the lender may repossess the equipment and return it to the manufacturer or dealer in order to recover full payment of the balance due. Then the manufacturer or dealer reconditions and sells the equipment, retaining any gain and absorbing any loss.

## SUMMARY

A pledge of assets may be required when there is substantial risk as to ability to repay. Both the borrower and the lender prefer an unsecured loan since the pledging of assets is costly and cumbersome. Receivables and inventory are the assets most frequently pledged by business firms for short-term loans.

The purpose of collateral is to minimize the lender's risk of loss. To achieve this the lender's claim to the pledged assets must be valid, the recovery value of the assets stable and ascertainable, and an adequate margin must exist between the sale value of the assets and the loan principal. Government securities make excellent collateral with loan value of 90 percent. Listed common stocks carry a loan value of 80 percent. Loans against receivables run from 50 to 90 percent and against raw material or finished goods from 50 to 80 percent. Work in process carries little loan value.

Receivables may be factored (sold) as well as pledged, usually with recourse. The factor examines the credit position of the firm's customers and decides which receivables to purchase. The firm selling the goods can withdraw the funds immediately or wait until the receivables' due date. When receivables are purchased the factor incurs less risk of title imperfection than when receivables are pledged. In the latter case, the lender must be sure the pledge of receivables is noted on the borrower's books and that all receivables are genuine.

Raw materials, such as grains or metals, serve as excellent loan collateral. Market prices can be checked daily against the loan amount.

Similarly, automobiles and appliances are readily acceptable. Some problems arise in assuring a valid claim by the lender to these assets. Raw material is frequently needed in production; the appliances and automobiles must be on the showroom floor. The lender retains title and control over the raw materials required in the borrower's production process by having them placed in a field warehouse. The loan is secured by the inventory in the field warehouse and the lender releases it to the firm as the firm makes payment on its loan. Automobiles and appliances are normally floor-planned. The dealer borrows against the units, holds them in trust for the lender, displays them for sale, and when sold remits the amount of the loan to the lender. The lender is trusting the borrower because at one moment in time the borrower has both the funds of the lender and of the customer who bought the goods. Lenders make frequent checks to be sure either the unit is on the floor or the funds are on the way to the bank.

Term loans and installment financing of equipment are forms of intermediate-term borrowing. This type of lending focuses on profitability. Term and installment loans are usually paid off in installments over the life of the loan. Term loans may be secured, and usually carry protective provisions designed to maintain the financial condition of the firm. Interest is charged on the unpaid balance. Small firms may find secured installment financing the only form of financing available. The cost is high. Interest charged is usually on the original balance and a large downpayment is required as well as installment payments, thus driving the effective rate of interest to as high as 24 percent.

### Study Questions

1. How does short-term credit differ from intermediate-term credit? Could an intermediate-term loan be self-liquidating? Why or why not? Cite examples on both sides of the argument.
2. What are the characteristics of good collateral? Give examples of good and "bad" collateral and show how each possesses or does not possess these characteristics.
3. Distinguish between borrowing against and factoring accounts receivable. Compare the effect each will have on the firm's balance sheet as measured by familiar ratios.
4. Should trade creditors be concerned if a firm pledges collateral for a loan? Why should pledging assets for a loan influence a firm's trade credit and unsecured borrowing limits?
5. What difficulties may arise in accepting raw material inventory as collateral for a loan? How may these difficulties be avoided?
6. What are warehouse receipts? How may they be used as collateral for a loan? What risks are present for a lender loaning against a pledge of warehouse receipts and how may the risk be minimized?
7. Distinguish between a public and a field warehouse. Which would be most convenient for a firm borrowing against needed raw materials?
8. What services does a factor perform? Why may some of these services be particularly advantageous to a small firm just getting started?
9. Distinguish between a term loan and an installment financing loan. Which is more likely to be unavailable to the smaller firm? Why?

10. Despite the fact that the cost of installment equipment financing is high, why may it still be advantageous for some firms to finance their equipment needs by this method?

11. What are some of the protective covenants in a term loan and what is their purpose? How does the acceleration clause protect the lender? Whom does the balloon payment provision benefit? How?

### Problems

1. The Deep Six Excavating Company purchases a new piece of equipment for $10,000 on the installment plan. Interest is charged at the rate of 6 percent on the purchase price and is added to the initial balance. A downpayment of $3,000 is required and the balance amortized at the rate of $650 per month over 1 year. What is the approximate effective rate of interest?

2. The working capital of the Deep Six Company has deteriorated in recent years and now stands as shown in Table 12–3.

TABLE 12–3. Deep Six Company
Working Capital Position

| Current Assets | | Current Liabilities | |
|---|---|---|---|
| Cash | $ 20,000 | Trade payables | $ 70,000 |
| Receivables | 50,000 | Notes payable | 30,000 |
| Inventory | 80,000 | | |
| Total current assets | $150,000 | Total current liabilities | $100,000 |

Note: since only the working capital portion of the balance sheet is presented, the statement need not "balance."

a. Compute the current and quick ratios.

b. A $30,000 short-term bank loan backed by a pledge of receivables is contemplated. Compute the liquidity ratios assuming the loan is made.

c. A sale of $30,000 of receivables to a factor is contemplated. Compute the liquidity ratios assuming the receivables are factored, the funds withdrawn immediately, and the notes paid off.

3. Nevada Snow Machine Company has experienced a rapid growth of sales in recent years. Control, however, has been lax and profits have not kept pace. The result has been a tightened financial condition. Further growth in sales is anticipated, and additional financing required. The financial condition of Nevada Snow Machine Company appears in Table 12–4.

TABLE 12–4. Nevada Snow Machine Company
Balance Sheet
December 31, 1973

| | | | | |
|---|---|---|---|---|
| Cash | | $ 60,000 | Accounts payable | $150,000 |
| Accounts receivable | | 200,000 | Bank notes | 350,000 |
| Inventory | | 240,000 | Common stock | 200,000 |
| Plant and equipment | $400,000 | | Retained earnings | 100,000 |
| Depreciation | 100,000 | 300,000 | | |
| Total assets | | $800,000 | Total liabilities and net worth | $800,000 |

Other pertinent data are:

Sales during the past year totaled $1,200,000. Sales are made evenly throughout the year.

Purchases are normally 50 percent of sales.

The inventory cost is 80 percent of sales.

The snow machines are sold on a net 30-day basis. All sales are on credit.

Inventory should equal a 45-day supply.

Purchases are also on a net 30-day basis.

a. Compute the liquidity ratios, the excess receivables and inventory being carried, and the extent to which Nevada is not paying its suppliers promptly.

b. Nevada Snow Machine plans to factor $150,000 of receivables, pay off its suppliers to the net 30-day level, and with the remaining portion pay off part of the unsecured notes payable. The banker has been exerting pressure for some payment. Compute the effect this plan will have on the liquidity ratios. How much of the bank loan can be repaid if the deal goes through? Do you see any difficulty in Nevada Snow Machine arranging this deal?

c. The factoring deal falls through. The bank reluctantly decides to go along for one more year provided management agrees to have the firm's working capital position at year's end in a satisfactory condition—receivables, inventory and payables at the above indicated normal levels. Sales are expected to be $1,-500,000, profit after income taxes 10 percent of sales, no dividends will be paid, replacements are to equal depreciation charges, and cash should be 5 percent of sales. Draw up the *pro forma* balance sheet and determine the extent of the bank's loan to Nevada Snow Machine. By what amount would the bank's loan be decreased or increased?

d. Draw up a source and application of funds statement to show the anticipated flow of funds.

e. Calculate the firm's liquidity ratios and comment on the anticipated working capital position.

f. Sales and earnings develop as anticipated, plant and equipment and depreciation remain the same, but cash drops to $50,000, receivables stand at 45 days, inventory at 90 days, and payables at 60 days. The bank has financed the expansion. Draw up the *pro forma* balance sheet showing the amount of bank loan now outstanding.

g. The bank now calls a halt and demands that by the end of the year its entire loan be paid off. In addition, $100,000 of new equipment must be purchased. Disregard depreciation. You are called in to recommend a plan of action to meet the bank's demand. Draw up a source and application of funds statement to highlight your recommendations.

## Selected References

Abraham, A. B., "Factoring—The New Frontier for Commercial Banks," *The Journal of Commercial Bank Lending,* 53 (April 1971), pp. 32–43.

Addison, E. T., "Factoring: A Case History," *Financial Executive,* 31 (November 1963), pp. 32–33.

Adler, M., "Administration of Inventory Loans under the Uniform Commercial Code," *The Journal of Commercial Bank Lending,* 52 (April 1970), pp. 55–60.

Alsobrook, G. H., "Small Business Term Loans by Banks," *Robert Morris Associates Bulletin,* 48 (October 1965), pp. 61–77.

Budzeika, G., "Term Lending by New York City Banks," *Monthly Review,* Federal Reserve Bank of New York, 43 (February 1961), pp. 27–31.

Daniels, F. L., S. C. Legg, and E. C. Yuille, "Accounts Receivable and Related Inventory Financing," *The Journal of Commercial Bank Lending,* 52 (July 1970), pp. 38–53.

Edwards, R. E., "Finance Companies and Their Creditors," *Journal of Commercial Bank Lending,* 54 (October 1971), pp. 2–10.

Fisher, D. J., "Factoring—An Industry on the Move," *The Conference Board Record,* 9 (April 1972), pp. 42–45.

Holmes W., "Market Values of Inventories—Perils and Pitfalls," *Journal of Commercial Bank Lending,* 55 (April 1973), pp. 30–36.

Nadler, P., "Compensating Balances and the Prime at Twilight," *Harvard Business Review,* 50 (January 1972), pp. 112–120.

Popma, J., "A Behind-the-Scenes Look at Factoring," *Credit and Financial Management,* 65 (May 1963), pp. 31–33.

Seiler, J., "Commercial Financing Risks Outlined for Bankers," *Burroughs Clearing House,* 56 (January 1972), pp. 22 ff.

Stone, B., "How Secure Is Secured Financing under the Code?" *Burroughs Clearing House,* 50 (April 1966), pp. 46 ff.

Wellman, M. T., "Field Warehousing—Protective Measures!" *Robert Morris Associates Bulletin,* 47 (March 1965), pp. 302–312.

# 13

# Lease Financing

The objective of control by the firm over an asset is to employ that asset most profitably. Although business assets are usually owned,[1] the firm has the alternative of leasing them. The alternative of owning or leasing fixed assets introduces another dimension into the already complex task of financial management. The choice requires comparing the aggregate costs of leasing against the costs of other financing to purchase the asset. For this we need an estimate of the rate of obsolescence or depreciation and the terminal value of the fixed assets in addition to the unusual financing costs.

A lease is a contractual arrangement whereby the lessor (property owner) grants the lessee (user) the right to the services of the property for a specified time period in return for periodic payments. The lessee

[1] The practice of leasing of equipment and real estate grew rapidly during the 1950s, but the rate of growth now seems to be slowing. See Richard S. Bower, Frank C. Herringer, and J. Peter Williamson, "Lease Evaluation," *Accounting Review*, 41 (April 1966), pp. 257–265.

may be given an option to renew the lease or an option to purchase, exercisable during the term of the lease or at its end.

The leasing of real property has long been a method of obtaining the use of this type of asset. During the past 20 years, the popularity of leasing has spread to other assets and grown rapidly, attracting many new firms as lessors offered a wide variety of deals—so diverse that the topic must be considered largely in general terms. The specific lease agreement is usually tailored to the requirements and bargaining position of the lessee *vis-à-vis* the lessor.

## LEASE ARRANGEMENTS

Leases may be classified as operating leases and financial leases. An *operating lease* involves some period less than the normal life of the asset and hence recovery from the first lessee of less than the asset's cost. A *financial lease* involves recovery of the full cost from the lessee. One variation of the financial lease is the *sale and lease-back arrangement* in which the present owner sells the asset to the leasing firm and immediately leases it back for some specified term.

Although our main concern is with financial leases, operating leases have become so important that they deserve comment.

### Operating Leases

An example of an operating lease is a contract for a jet plane to ferry the firm's executive team. The lease may give the firm the right to cancel before the lease expiration date. The lease will also provide for maintenance service by the lessor.

Computers, trucks, automobiles, and specialized equipment are typical assets involved in operating leases.

### Financial Leases

A financial lease is not cancelable and commits the lessee to make a series of payments whose sum is greater than the cost of the asset because included is a return on the investment. Maintenance is usually the obligation of the lessee.

Equipment and real estate are typical assets involved in financial leases. Specialized leasing companies are active in the equipment leasing field as are commercial banks since a 1963 Comptroller of the Currency ruling permitting national banks to acquire and lease assets to customers.

The customer selects the equipment, negotiates the terms with the manufacturer, arranges for the bank to purchase the equipment and immediately leases it from the bank. The same procedure is followed when dealing with a specialized leasing company. The many different kinds of assets and the competitiveness of leasing have led to considerable specialization. Some firms specialize in the leasing of vehicles, others in office equipment and computers, and still others in industrial equipment. Life insurance companies dominate the long-term real estate leasing market.

Leasing is not merely an alternative financing plan for the user but a sales tool for the manufacturer of the asset. Cash-short customers cause a manufacturer to form a leasing subsidiary which buys the equipment from the manufacturer for lease to customers thus promoting the sale of the manufacturer's equipment. The major profit is made on the sale of the equipment. The leasing operation is subservient to this objective.

The principal financial difference between an installment purchase and a financial lease lies in the length of time over which payments are made: the cost is paid in a much shorter period of time in installment purchasing. Other important differences are that the installment purchaser owns any residual value and likewise can resell while the lessee in a financial lease does not own the residual value at the end of the lease and cannot alter his situation as in a resale.

### The Financial Lease as a Form of Debt Financing

The financial lease creates long-term contractual obligations similar in some ways to debt financing. Length of time of the lease is not the determinative factor. By signing a lease, the lessee agrees to pay fixed rental fees, service the property, and maintain financial standards. A debtor-creditor relationship runs between lessee and lessor. It is sometimes argued that in a financial lease there are really two decisions that should be kept separate: the lessee's decision to invest in the asset or not and the lessee's decision how to finance: whether by debt or by lease. This is incorrect in that it is then proposed that the rate of interest on debt be used to discount the costs of the two financing methods with a view to preferring the method which shows the least cost *at this rate.* The *generally* correct rate to use is the marginal cost of capital which includes the cost of equity and is higher than the debt rate. As we saw in Chapter 9, different rates of discount may result in different choices depending on the pattern of cash flows.

The rental payments and protective provisions of a lease must be met as promptly and as fully as bond issue covenants but the consequences of defaulting on a realty lease differ from defaulting on straight debt. Under a lease the lessor may take possession of his property by a prompt court order in the event the lessee does not fulfill the terms of the agreement. The lessor's claim to damages is limited to 1 year's rent for realty in the event of bankruptcy and liquidation. If the firm is reorganized and the trustee in reorganization rejects the lease, the lessor is limited to a maximum of 3 years' rent for realty.[2] A bondholder, on the other hand, has a claim against the firm for the entire principal and unpaid interest. Even when his claim is secured by a mortgage, a creditor cannot upon default simply come in and take possession. A court order after a hearing is needed to foreclose a mortgage for the debt and the creditor collects only his debt; any surplus on a sale goes to the debtor or other cred-

---

[2] U.S.Code, Title 1, Chapter X, § 602 and Chapter XI, § 753. These statutory limitations of the Federal Bankruptcy Act apply only to leases for real property. Under an equipment lease the lessee is liable for all remaining lease payments.

itors. A court order after a hearing is also necessary for a lessor to take possession upon default by a lessee.

### Advantages of Leasing

Most firms have the alternative of leasing or buying assets through a wide variety of arrangements. Many advantages are given for leasing over the borrow-and-buy option. Leasing is sometimes said to be more expensive than borrowing because the implicit rate of interest in the lease is usually higher than the explicit rate of interest if the lessee were to borrow and buy. It is true that both leasing and borrowing chew up the debt-carrying ability of the firm—and both affect the firm's cost of capital. But we lack evidence whether leasing and borrowing have the same effect on the cost of capital. Yet even if both do have the same effect it is true as we have just said, different rates of discount may produce different decisions depending on the true pattern of the cash flows. A lower rate of discount favors the alternative where more cost is paid out sooner; a higher rate of discount favors the alternative where more cost is paid out later. This in itself may be an adequate explanation for the observable phenomenon that leasing is preferred when the cost of capital is higher.

### Avoidance of the Risks of Ownership through the Insurance Principle

Leasing avoids the risks of ownership and substitutes a fee for the risks of obsolescence and terminal value losses. Leasing real estate is desirable in an area likely to be subject to a rapid erosion of value due to such things as market, traffic, or population shifts. Similarly, leasing is desirable for the acquisition of high-technology equipment subject to rapid and sudden obsolescence. The lessor is usually more knowledgeable than the lessee regarding risk of obsolescence and includes in the rental payments a premium for this risk.[3]

The lessee gains from the insurance principle. Particularly as to specialized assets, the lessee might suffer a large loss due to technological change if he bought and owned. The lease enables him to shift this risk to the lessor. The lessor can spread the loss of a sudden technological change as to one piece of equipment over the many pieces that he has leased, provided these pieces are not all exposed to the same technological risk.

### Flexibility

If equipment becomes obsolete and is returned to the lessor before expiration of the lease, the lessee can substitute new equipment under a new lease for the obsolete equipment of the old lease.

The leasing of real estate for terms running from 20 to 100 years provides little if any flexibility over ownership. We have a heavy commitment in the property in either event. In fact, leasing may be less flexible

[3] One function performed by the lessor is to package all the costs connected with the leasing of a specific item of property and recover these costs through a stream of lease payments.

unless the lease is transferable. But if the lessee owned the property, he could terminate the situation by selling the asset. If the utility of leased property to the lessee declines, the firm must still make rental payments. Subleasing by the lessee is usually not prohibited as long as the original lessee remains secondarily liable—that is, the original lessee is liable to pay if the new lessee defaults.

Many business properties not earning a profit—a particular theater, for example—can seldom be made profitable simply by a change of ownership. Downward valuation of the property and wiping out some claims in bankruptcy usually is necessary before unprofitable property can again show a satisfactory return on investment.

Outright ownership of the property in a case such as the theater might provide more flexibility. Assuming we own a chain of theaters and one of these is no longer profitable, we can demolish it and construct a parking ramp. Leasing would tie us to the theater operation.

### Step-by-Step Financing

Some firms expand in stepwise fashion as in building a chain of supermarkets. Here lease financing can be utilized to advantage. As each new location is added, a lease can be arranged for constructing the building. Large sums obtained from earlier security issues are not left in low-yielding investments waiting for new locations to be identified. One alternative to leasing is short-term temporary financing or open-ended loans that permit additional borrowing as needed. Later the temporary loans can be refinanced. This "double" financing can be costly both in time and money and, ultimately, may be more expensive than lease financing.

### Raising a Larger Amount of Capital

Leasing may permit a firm to raise more "debt capital" than direct borrowing, given the firm's existing equity base. One reason is that title to the property remains with the lessor so that upon default the lessor simply reclaims his property. Court proceedings to replevy[4] the property are simpler than mortgage foreclosures, which may cost the lender one year's income due to the delay. More rapid write-off in equipment leasing is an advantage over debt expansion.

A second factor is that the debt burden created by a lease does not appear under existing accounting rules on the lessee's balance sheet. Consequently, less sophisticated lenders may extend more credit than they would if the obligation were evidenced by debt appearing on the financial statements. The Securities and Exchange Commission and many accountants, aware of this situation, have moved for full disclosure in financial statements of the lessee. Lenders are becoming increasingly aware of the implication of the lease form of financing and firms will find it more dif-

---

[4] The process of *replevin* applies only to personal property, which is all property except real estate. Replevin rests on the right to possession rather than on title or ownership. It is the matter of a claim to ownership involved in a mortgage foreclosure which takes more time in court than the right to possession.

ficult in the future to employ this device in an effort to overreach their normal borrowing power.

Leasing was one of the standard methods of avoiding the restriction in older bond agreements on the acquisition of additional debt. But this restriction has now been expanded in new bond issues to include the time-discounted value of leasing obligations as debt. Leasing is no longer available as a "back door" method for increasing the debt to equity relationship.

### Tax Advantage

A firm owning real estate can depreciate the building but not the land. But if the firm enters a sale and lease-back arrangement, it can deduct the entire rental payment for federal income tax purposes, thus including amortization of the cost of the land as well as buildings over the term of the lease. This maneuver is particularly attractive where the land component constitutes a high percentage of the total value of the real estate or where the building is already fully depreciated on the books of owner who sells and leases back. Any gain on the sale of real estate in the sale and lease-back is subject to capital gains tax. But this rate is 30 percent [5] while the rental payments are offset against income taxed at a rate of 48 percent.

Taxes are an important consideration in almost any decision and no action should be taken before checking the tax consequences. After all, unnecessary taxes resulting from poorly planned actions are little different from operating losses resulting from poor decisions. Both result in an unnecessary outflow of cash and a reduction of earnings.

Prior to the 1954 Revenue Act, leasing gave the taxpayer-lessee an attractive method for shifting the timing of tax deductions in his favor. Depreciation for tax purposes was chargeable only on a straight-line basis. Lease payments could be arranged so that the heavy payments occurred in the early years, shifting the tax liability to later years. This resulted in substantial savings of interest on the deferred tax liability. The 1954 Code permits accelerated depreciation and the Internal Revenue Service reduced the number of years over which equipment could be written off—although it lengthened the term on real estate, thus giving ownership, as well as the lease, about the same tax timing if accelerated depreciation is used. However, the investment tax credit [6] revived interest in leasing because the law permits the lessor and lessee to allocate the investment tax credit between themselves by agreement.

---

[5] *Internal Revenue Code*, §§ 56, 1201(a) for long-term capital gains up to $30,000 per year. (There are exemptions.) Capital gains over this amount are subject to a flat 10 percent preference tax.

[6] The investment tax credit is not merely a tax deduction but is applied as a dollar-for-dollar reduction of taxes due up to 7 percent of the investment expenditure. As a tax shelter, equipment leasing (typically aircraft, computers, rolling stock) by high-bracket individual taxpayers to corporations languished after the 1969 repeal of the 7 percent investment tax credit. Under the 1971 provisions reinstating the investment tax credit the noncorporate lessor is restricted in the extent to which he can claim the credit. *Internal Revenue Code*, § 46(d)(3).

### Leasing May Be the Only Alternative

We have assumed the firm has a choice. But a small or weak firm unable to secure the necessary funds for purchase may be forced to lease. Competitive pressures to expand may leave the firm little alternative when earnings are poor, credit sources dried up, and thus the debt market is closed to the firm.

One example is a railroad requiring rolling stock—cars and locomotives—and unable to get debt or stock financing. Leasing was the method originally employed by these weak railroads. Under the name "equipment trust certificates," the trustee or lessor-owner acquires rolling stock on its credit and then leases the equipment to the railroads. As the safety of these securities became apparent, the interest cost decreased and this method of financing spread even to stronger railroads.

Sometimes the owner of the asset refuses to sell. A computer manufacturer or shoe machinery producer wishing to retain ultimate control over the equipment may insist on lease terms. Or the owners of land may desire to hold the land for capital appreciation. But they may be willing to sell the timber or mineral rights, or permit the erection of a building. Furthermore, purchase of the asset may not be feasible considering the business of the firm. For an arts and crafts shop in midtown Manhattan, leasing space on the ground floor is the viable alternative to purchasing the skyscraper.

### What Rate of Discount Should Be Used in Analyzing Leasing?

In establishing the comparative costs of leasing against borrowing to buy [7] one approach suggests that the applicable rate of discount is the loan rate [8] rather than the higher weighted cost of capital [9] used in capital budgeting. Earlier in this chapter we endorsed the *general* use of the cost of capital.

The argument for using the loan rate is: Suppose in a tax-free world a company whose overall cost of capital is 10 percent sees a machine that will save $2400 per year in cash operating costs over its life of 4 years. There is no scrap value. The machine can be purchased for $6500 or leased at $2000 per year payable at the end of each year for 4 years. The following computation as to the benefits of leasing is then proposed:

| | |
|---|---|
| Annual cash operating savings | $2400 |
| Less lease payments | 2000 |
| Increase in cash flow per year | 400 |
| Outlay at time zero | 0 |
| Time adjusted rate of return | infinite |

[7] There is an additional option: purchase with equity funds, but then there is no income tax deduction for interest or rent.

[8] Harold Bierman, Jr., and Seymour Smidt, *The Capital Budgeting Decision*, 3d ed. (New York: The Macmillan Co., 1971), p. 216; and C. T. Horngren, *Cost Accounting, A Managerial Emphasis*, 3d ed. (Englewood Cliffs, N. J.: Prentice-Hall, Inc., 1972), pp. 522–524.

[9] Thus, if a firm's current cost of debt is 6 percent and of equity is 16 percent and we assume a capital structure of 50 percent debt, the weighted cost of capital is 11 percent.

To back things up, if we discount the lease payments at 10 percent (as a cost of capital) the present value of the payments is \$6340 (\$2000 × 3.170 from Table A–2 at the end of the text) compared to the \$6500 purchase price. The lease is favored.

Then, the general statement is made that "discounting of lease payments at the lessee's weighted-average cost of capital will lead to leasing rather than buying in *all* instances where the lessee's cost of capital exceeds the lessor's implicit contractual interest rate." [10] (Emphasis supplied.)

Finally, this analysis suggests that the first step in leasing analysis is to determine the lowest borrowing rate to purchase. Then, discount the rentals at this rate to determine an "equivalent purchase price." If the equivalent purchase price of leasing is less than the purchase price, we should lease. Thus assuming the loan rate is 6 percent in our example, the equivalent purchase price of the lease is \$6930 (\$2000 × 3.465). Purchasing is now favored. What the "equivalent purchase price of leasing" is depends heavily on the rate of discount. A higher rate of discount will favor leasing, a lower rate will favor purchasing.

It is proposed that we *then* take the cheaper form of financing in proceeding to determine the capital budgeting question of whether we will proceed with the project. That is, the cash outflows and inflows of the cheaper form of financing (determined in the way just discussed) will now be discounted at the firm's weighted cost of capital to determine whether we accept or reject the project.

The basic premise of this approach appears intriguingly sound. Both the loan and the lease are forms of debt and assuming the payment schedules in each case are reasonably close to each other, we choose the lower cost of debt.

But there are some problems with the approach. The first is that it is *assumed* that the annual payment patterns on lease or borrow-to-buy are approximately the same. If the annual payments differ substantially as would be true, for example, when the loan provides for a significant "balloon" payment at the end of the loan this approach will fail. In capital budgeting we rejected the idea that each project should use that rate of discount involved in the specific source of funds for that project (for example, 6 percent if debt funds, 8 percent if preferred stock funds). For the same reason, in the lease or purchase decision we use the weighted cost of capital of the firm. Each debt transaction (lease or purchase) uses up a piece of the debt carrying capacity of the firm.[11]

In the case of the "balloon" payment loan, the impact of the "balloon" arrangement on the weighted cost of capital must be considered. It is not just a matter of the rate of interest on *this* loan but what this loan does to the rate on *future* debt transactions we may enter. The "balloon" has the effect for example, of reducing the cash outflow in the immediate future years compared to leasing. This may be viewed by the firm's investors as reducing the risk of default particularly in a growth situation. Further-

---

[10] Horngren, p. 523.

[11] We are anticipating the discussion of the cost of capital that follows in Chapter 15.

more, the reduced immediate cash outflow of a loan-with-balloon may stave off new equity financing to a time when the growth firm enjoys a better price-earnings ratio for its common stock.

The lesson to be learned from this example of leasing analysis is that great care must be taken lest the *assumptions* of the analysis assume away the problem. The fact is there are different variables which dominate in different cases and hence no single format of analysis is possible.

## COST OF LEASING VERSUS OWNING

The final decision between leasing and owning rests on comparative costs. Interest cost and income tax deductions are only two factors in the comparison. The implicit interest cost of lease funds can run from ½ to 2 percent higher than on comparable term loans.[12] This differential can be partly attributed to an imperfect market situation and partly to the insurance principle where the lessor is expert at specific risks and seeks compensation for this service. Lessors may not adjust the implied interest rate on the lease for the residual value of the asset at the end of the lease, resulting in a higher lease cost. Under competitive pressures, the interest rate implied in a lease can approach that of comparable term loans. Much depends on the bargaining power of the respective parties.[13]

Our discussion of the rate of discount to use in leasing analysis indicates that the leasing-borrow comparison involves far too many variables to be reduced to a simple comparison of interest rates and tax benefits. For example,[14] suppose a substantial size company with $50 million in annual sales of heavy equipment needs major trucking services to deliver to customers throughout the country. The individual diesel tractor-trailer trucks put on 400,000 miles per year on an average. Six trucks are involved. Despite the best preventive maintenance, breakdowns occur and sometimes in remote parts of the country. If the firm owned the trucks the driver would have to hunt the repair garage to be called. If the firm leases, the driver calls the lessor's headquarters, which activates the appropriate garage. The difference between the repair costs of the two methods (which we might call the gouge) is so great that even if the interest rate implied in the lease were *double* that in borrowing-to-buy, the firm would make handsome savings by going the lease route. This example is typical. The *ceteris paribus* assumptions of most textbooks in which the only variables analyzed are the interest rate and the tax impact are atypical. Consequences of some variables are: (1) the use of accelerated depreciation favors owning; (2) the fact of rapid obsolescence favors leasing; (3) larger residual values favor owning; and (4) a higher implicit interest rate in the lease favors owning.

---

[12] But money costs are only one part of the cost of an operating lease and are difficult to separate from the service and maintenance benefits the lessor may supply. As a package the total lease cost may be lower than if the lessee purchased the benefits separately.

[13] Firms with a government (or other) cost plus contract may find leasing attractive if required equipment can be leased just for the term of the contract. Owning the equipment may require writing it off over a much longer term.

[14] This is an actual case, name withheld.

### Implied Interest Rate in Leasing

Under highly simplified assumptions, the interest rate implied in leasing can be calculated by equating the present value of the after-tax lease payments and the estimated after-tax terminal value of the equipment with its cost. The interest rate that does this is the internal rate of return. It is apparent that comparisons must be made over a specific time period because at different time cut-off points, the same terms will produce opposite decisions, as we saw in Chapter 9 when considering the abandonment problem in capital budgeting.

To illustrate, assume Gesundheit, Inc. requires a new pretzel-bending machine. The cost of the machine is $13,869. The firm can lease the machine at a rental of $3000 a year for 6 years. Consulting the present value tables at the end of the text we find that the cost of leasing is 8 percent assuming zero terminal value.[15] Should there be a terminal value of $3000 because of no major technological breakthroughs, the effective gross cost of the lease financing would jump to 12 percent. In this example we have not considered the role of income taxes.

### The Terminal Value Factor

Terminal value considerations are important in all cases. Suppose in the case of Gesundheit, the lessor estimates $2500 terminal value for the equipment and sets the rental payments at $2500 per year to earn a 6 percent return on his investment. If subsequently the actual terminal value of the equipment drops to $1000 the lessor earns a bare 4 percent.

Terminal values in real estate leasing are frequently in the distant future and, hence, their present value of less consequence. But major swings upward occur in real estate values and offset the futurity dimension. Equipment normally declines in value. The guessing concerns the rate of decline, the chances and timing of a technological breakthrough that will obsolete the equipment. But real estate values not only may decline substantially, but also appreciate tremendously. The range within which the terminal value of the real estate may fall is wider.

For example, a firm may find a lease or loan equally attractive to secure a shopping center location, given the estimated terminal value. The actual terminal value likely will *in retrospect* make either the lease or the loan the superior arrangement. A substantially high terminal value will favor ownership. If the property were leased, upon termination of the lease the firm must seek another location at high cost or remain at the same location at increased rental. On the other hand, a substantially lower terminal value would favor leasing. At termination the firm returns the property to the owner and seeks another, more desirable location or pays a lower rental.

Because of the wider range within which real estate terminal values may fall, the risk element is prominent in such lease or own decisions. One way to analyze the risk element is to cast the estimates of terminal value

---

[15] $13,896/$3,000 = 4.632. Table A–2 at the end of the text. Run your finger across the six-year row till you hit 4.6229 (4.632 ≅ 4.6229). Look to the top of the table and find 8 percent. This is the implicit interest cost.

as a probability distribution and to use the concept of expected value and its standard deviation to measure the confidence to place in the computations.

### Tax Aspects of Leasing or Owning

The most meaningful method of comparing leasing to borrowing is on an after-tax basis, but in practice comparisons are difficult because the required assumptions affect leasing and owning differently.

*An Example:* Assume Alpine Ski, Inc. wants to build new facilities. The financial position of the firm is good. Borrowing on a 6 percent term-loan basis is possible. The facilities cost $252,340;—$200,000 building and $52,340 land. The owner will sell the land for $52,340 and let the firm construct the building, or will construct the building and lease the entire facility to Alpine Ski at a rental of $22,000 a year for 20 years. Assuming zero terminal value of both land and building, the rental is sufficient to amortize the total cost of the property over the 20-year period and provide the lessor with a 6 percent return on his investment.[16] With income taxes at 50 percent, the net after-tax cash outflow of the firm will be $11,000. The $22,000 annual lease payment creates a tax shield of $11,000, since the entire rental is tax deductible.

Compiling a schedule of after-tax cash outflows under the borrowing alternative is more difficult. The entire annual payment cannot be tax deducted as an expense. Only the interest on the loan and the allowable depreciation on the building can be deducted for tax purposes.[17] The after-tax cash outflow under the borrowing alternative, to be compared with the after-tax lease payments, is calculated by deducting from the annual loan payments the tax shield created by the interest and allowable depreciation charge. The remainder is our net out of pocket cash costs. The calculations for the first few years are as follows.

*Calculating the Cost of Leasing versus Borrowing.* A loan of $252,340 is necessary to acquire the property. The first year's interest payment at 6 percent is $15,140. We know $22,000 per year for 20 years will amortize a loan of $252,340 and provide a yield of 6 percent. Thus, deducting from the $22,000 the $15,140 first year's interest payment, we find $6860 is return of principal. Only the $15,140 is tax deductible. To calculate the total tax shield we also need the depreciation charges. Alpine Ski charges depreciation on a straight-line basis. For simplicity, assume the life of the building is 20 years. New problems are raised when the term of the lease differs from the depreciable life under the loan.

Depreciation charges in the first and subsequent years are $10,000, ($200,000/20) per year. The total tax-deductible expense is $25,140 ($15,-140 + $10,000). The tax shield is $12,570 (income tax rate of 50 percent). The before-tax payment on the term loan is $22,000. Deducting the tax shield, the after-tax payment is $9430 ($22,000 − $12,570). This figure

---

[16] The reader should verify this by following the method shown in footnote 15.

[17] The annual cost of a maintenance contract could also be deducted if this were an equipment deal. Under leasing, the maintenance cost may be included in the lease payment.

compares with an after-tax payment of $11,000 under the lease arrangement, as shown in Table 13–1.

TABLE 13–1. Alpine Ski, Inc.
Net After-Tax Cash Outflow under the Term Loan Arrangement and Lease for the First Three Years

| | First year | Second year | Third year |
|---|---|---|---|
| *Term Loan* | | | |
| Loan amortization | | | |
| Principal | $ 6,860 | $ 7,271 | $ 7,707 |
| Interest | 15,140 | 14,729 | 14,293 |
| | $22,000 | $22,000 | $22,000 |
| Depreciation | $10,000 | $10,000 | $10,000 |
| Interest | 15,140 | 14,729 | 14,293 |
| Total expense | $25,140 | $24,729 | $24,293 |
| Tax shield (50 percent) | $12,570 | $12,365 | $12,147 |
| Before-tax loan payment | 22,000 | 22,000 | 22,000 |
| After-tax cash outflow | $ 9,430 | $ 9,635 | $ 9,853 |
| *Lease* | | | |
| After-tax cash outflow | $11,000 | $11,000 | $11,000 |

The rationale of the calculations is as follows. Under both the lease and the loan $22,000 a year must be paid. What we want to know is what part of the $22,000 is our cash outflow after taxes on the loan—that is, from our pocket as opposed to what the government is losing in tax revenue—as compared to the lease. In the first year the lease "costs" us $11,000, and the term loan $9,430. The remainder in both cases is the tax shield.[18]

From Figure 13–1 we see that, as the years progress, the interest portion of the annual $22,000 term loan payment becomes smaller and the principal repayment portion becomes larger. Thus, the total tax shield is higher in the early years under the term loan. Or, conversely, in the early years the after-tax cash outflow under the lease arrangement is larger than under the term loan. But at some point the after-tax cash outflow under the loan will be greater than under the lease. Since the "higher cost" term loan payments occur in later years, the present value of each dollar of differential is not as large as that of the higher lease payments that occur in the earlier years.

We want to know whether the lease or term loan involves the lower present value of after-tax cash outflows. *Under the simplifying assumptions we have made,* this will be the most attractive alternative. If there were a terminal value its discounted after-capital-gain tax would be included in the calculation.

[18] The tax shield is operative only if there is taxable income. Things take a different bent if the firm is running at a deficit before the depreciation charge. As further evidence of the tenuous character of lease analysis, income tax rates are assumed to remain constant throughout the period involved.

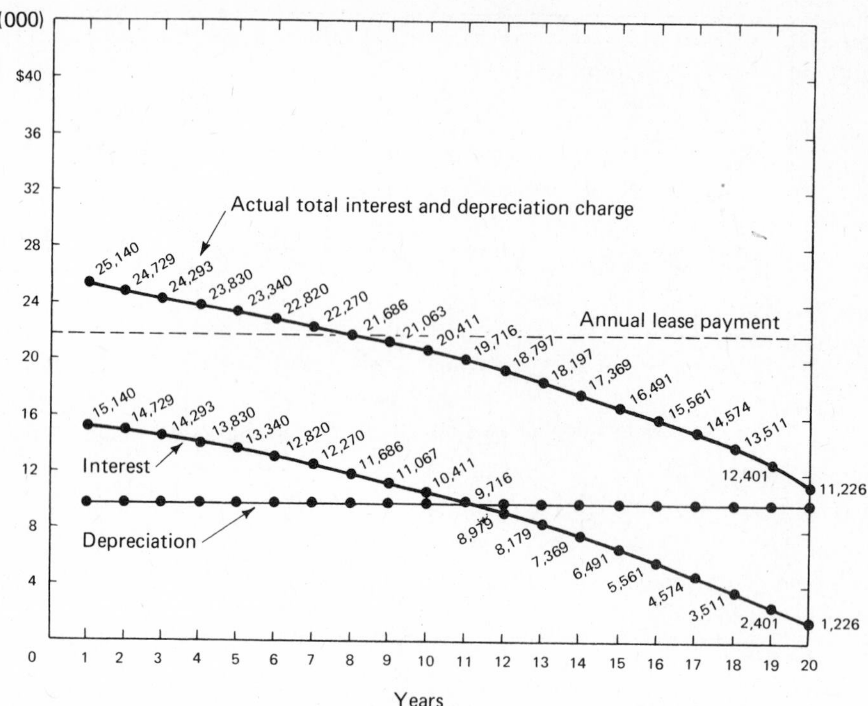


Figure 13–1 Alpine Ski, Inc. Undiscounted pretax annual interest and depreciation charges under the term-loan purchase (solid lines) and under leasing charge (dotted line).

Figure 13–2 shows the *time-unadjusted cumulative after-tax* cash outflows under the two financing proposals using a discount rate of 6 percent. Leasing requires an annual net after-tax cash payment of $11,000. Borrowing means a low net after-tax cash payment in the early years and high payments in the later years. The time-unadjusted totals are $220,000 for leasing and $246,190 for borrowing—a differential of $26,190 in favor of leasing—ignoring terminal value of the property.

Figure 13–3 presents the cumulative after-tax cash outflows of the two financing proposals on a *time-adjusted* basis using a discount rate of 11 percent—the weighted cost of capital (not the loan rate). Leasing is still favored although the difference is only $1428, ($89,021 – $87,593). Using the loan rate of 6 percent, the advantage of leasing is more than it is at the 11 percent rate.

*To Lease or to Borrow?* Is it more attractive to lease the property for 20 years, committing ourselves to pay $22,000 ($11,000 out of pocket) each year for a cumulative total on a time-adjusted basis of $87,593 and losing the property at the end of the period, or to take the term loan, also committing ourselves to paying $22,000 each year for a cumulative time-adjusted after-tax total of $89,021 and owning the property? [19]

[19] Under the property tax laws of all states, one can walk away from realty with no liability. The tax is levied against the realty, not the owner. Thus, owning the property at the end of 20 years is not a substantial hazard. If the property should turn out to be undesirable we simply walk away from it. The law is different for personal property. The owner is liable, even though the property cannot bring the amount of the tax on a sale.

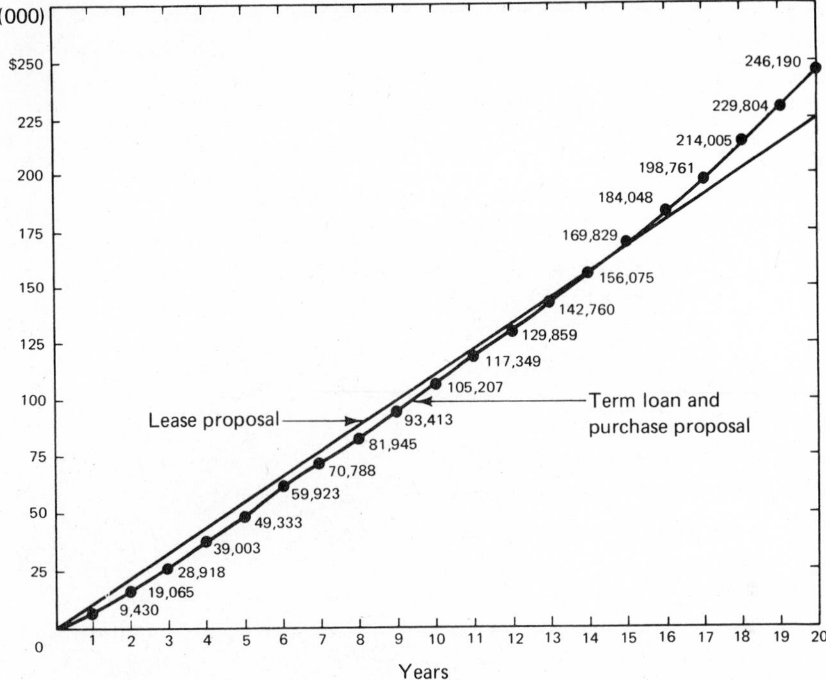


Figure 13–2 Alpine Ski, Inc. Undiscounted after-tax comparison of the cumulative after-tax cash outflow required under the term loan-leasing arrangement to finance $252,340 with loan interest at 6 percent. Based on Table 13–1 and data in Figure 13–1 and using the format in Table 13–1, the reader can determine the after-tax cash outflow required under the term loan for any single year.

The land is currently worth $52,340 and the building $200,000. Assume after 20 years that the building is worthless, the land worth $52,340, and that the firm requires at least an 11 percent return on its projects. Then looking back, borrowing to buy would have been more attractive than leasing since $52,340 discounted at 11 percent yields $6490, which is greater than the prior $1428 difference between leasing and borrowing. But the risk of the terminal value may be much greater than that of operation, warranting a higher rate of discount, say 20 percent. As shown in Table 13–2, taking $1428 and investing it at a 20 percent compounded rate for 20 years roughly equals the assumed terminal value of the land. In this case the choice is a toss up.[20]

The peculiar problem of Alpine is that site value is almost completely tied to ski use and skiing can dwindle fast in popularity—just as it rose fast.

*Sensitivity Analysis.* In the example we used straight-line depreciation and found the 11 percent time-adjusted net after-tax cash outflows were less for the lease than for owning when terminal value is zero. If we used accelerated depreciation, the taxes in the early years would be lower for a loan (higher tax shield), thus decreasing the net after-tax cash outflows in

[20] For simplicity, we have ignored any capital gains tax on terminal value. There would be none under our assumed conditions.

these years. Since the lease outflows are unaffected, the result would be to change the time adjusted net after-tax cash outflow differential between leasing and owning to favor owning. Considering only the net after-tax cash outflows, using a discount rate greater than 11 percent will tip the present value sums in favor of ownership. Compare Figures 13–2 and 13–3.

TABLE 13–2. Alpine Ski, Inc.
Comparative Cost Advantage of Owning versus Leasing

| (1) | (2) | (3) | (4) | (5) |
|---|---|---|---|---|
| Present value of net after tax cash outflow (total) | | Present value of leasing over owning at 11%, ignoring terminal value (1) − (2) | Assumed terminal value of property | Present value of owning, terminal value discounted at 20 percent |
| Lease | Term loan | | | |
| $87,593 | $89,021 | $1428 | $52,340 | $1360 |

Including some terminal value will favor ownership. The higher the terminal value *or* the lower the rate of discount applied to the terminal value, *or* the shorter the period, the greater the advantage to the ownership option in this example.

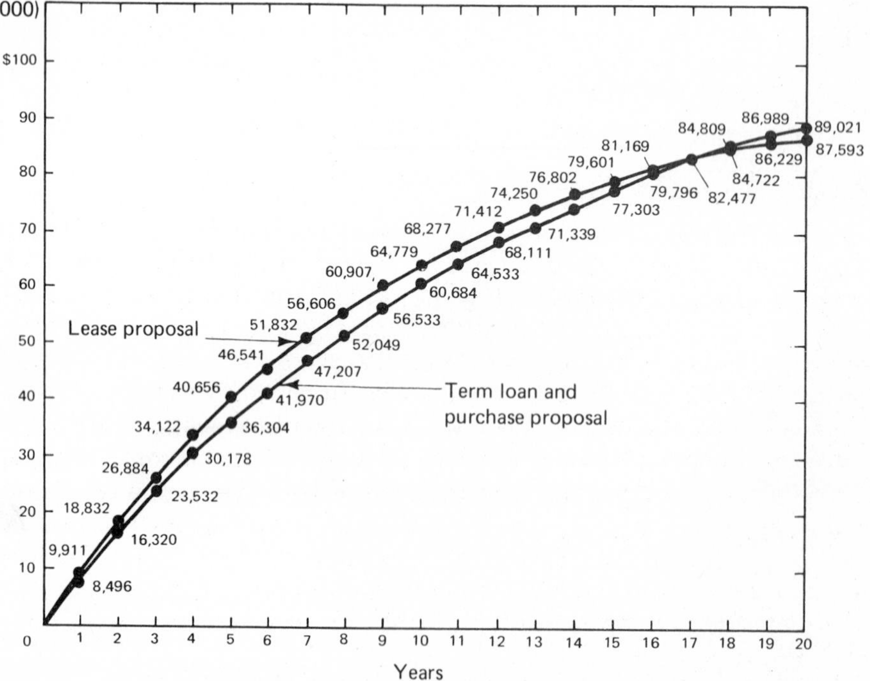


Figure 13–3 Alpine Ski, Inc. Time adjusted comparison of the cumulative after-tax cash outflow required under the term loan and lease arrangement to finance $252,340 with interest at 6 percent, considering only the financing options and ignoring terminal values. The net after-tax cash outflows are discounted at 11 percent.

## LEASE FINANCING AND FINANCIAL STATEMENTS

The financial burden created by lease financing normally does not appear on the balance sheet. The standard treatment is to footnote the lease payments. The analyst who reads footnotes may be unpleasantly surprised to find an apparently conservatively financed firm encountering serious financial difficulties because of high lease payments, which rank with interest payments in their claim on earnings.

The firm can add the lease payments to the interest charges to calculate the fixed charge coverage and can add the discounted total of the lease payments to debt to calculate the debt-to-equity relationship. An "outside" analyst may have available only the amount of the annual lease payments for the preceding year and the termination year of the longest-term lease currently on the books. To obtain a figure for the discounted total of the lease payments, he must estimate both the average annual lease payments and the average life of the leases.[21]

The mechanics of adjusting ratios for lease financing are shown in Table 13–3. The fact that leases can be avoided in bankruptcy but bonds cannot seriously weakens this method of adjusting for lease financing. The concern at this point is not so much what happens to the obligations of a firm that stumbles into bankruptcy but the likelihood of the firm going bankrupt. And a failure to meet lease payments operates just like a failure to meet interest payments in putting a firm into bankruptcy.

Adjusting for the lease financing reveals a less conservatively financed firm. The amount of the reduction in the apparent financial strength of the firm from the lease burden depends on the size of the lease relative to the long-term debt.

## LEASE FINANCING TRAPS

The drafting of lease agreements is no job for amateurs.[22] In a lease title to the property remains in the lessor and the entire amount of the lease payment may be deducted by the lessee for income tax purposes. Consequently, every lease agreement has two attackers—creditors and tax collectors. Creditors are only an intermittent threat; tax collectors are a constant threat. When a firm runs into financial difficulty, creditors of the lessee will take a hard look at the lease agreements, since the other assets are seldom sufficient to cover all the creditor claims. Consequently, to bolster their position creditors prefer to have the leased assets declared the property of the lessee rather than have the lessor simply repossess his property. Tax collectors, always on the lookout for the unwary and a chance to bring in some additional revenue, would like to see the lease payments as installment payments on an installment sales contract.

---

[21] The arguments against the accountant reflecting this information on the financial statements are given by Donald C. Cook, "The Case against Capitalizing Leases," *Harvard Business Review*, 41 (January-February 1963), pp. 145–150 ff.

[22] Courts have often held the lease to be the very form of transaction for which it was intended to substitute, namely an installment purchase. See Sidney J. Simon, "The Lease-Option Plan—Its Tax and Accounting Implications," *Journal of Accountancy*, 113 (April 1962), pp. 38–45.

This would permit the lessee firm to deduct only an imputed interest payment plus depreciation rather than all the rental payment. The remainder would be considered a payment of principal. The result would be higher annual income tax payments for the lessee firm and a larger tax "take" for the collector.

TABLE 13–3. Sarong, Inc.

Adjusting Debt-Equity Ratio and Times Charges Earned by Capitalizing Lease Financing with Annual Rental of $2500 per Year for 18 Years and Discounting Future Rentals of $2500 at 7 Percent for a Capitalized Value of $25,000

| | *Figures as per financial statements* | *Adjusted for lease financing* |
|---|---|---|
| *Balance sheet* | | |
| Long-term obligations | $25,000 | $50,000 |
| Common stock and surplus | 50,000 | 50,000 |
| Debt-to-equity ratio | 1 to 2 | 1 to 1 |
| *Income statement* | | |
| Earnings before interest and charges | $60,000 | $60,000 |
| Fixed charges | 12,500 | 15,000 |
| Times charges earned | 5 to 1 | 4 to 1 |

The single aspect of leasing most frequently seized upon by the tax collector to claim that the lease is a tax dodge to cover up a purchase is any option in the lease permitting the lessee to buy and have prior lease payments credited to the purchase price. If such an option exists, the lessee is in effect free to decide whether he has a lease or an installment sales contract. Such freedom, the tax collector argues, is intended only to bilk the taxing authority. If the option to buy exists, but without credit against the purchase price for prior lease payments, some of the tax collector's argument is negated. The way to reduce the risk that the transaction will be classified as an installment purchase is to have the option price implicitly allow for rental payments through a declining option price over time. However, the option price cannot be reset every year, or it will be easy for the tax collector to show what is really going on.

## SUMMARY

Leasing is an alternative to ownership for a firm to obtain the use of physical assets and has long been used in real estate. An early use in the equipment financing field is found in rolling stock leasing by railroads. Now leasing has spread to a wide variety of assets. Firms specialize in leasing certain types of equipment: computers, trucks, cars, and so on. The terms of the lease are tailored to the needs of the lessee.

The charges levied by the lessor are frequently higher than costs to borrow and buy, but leasing may provide other advantages. Restrictive bond covenants may be avoided; a higher percentage of the asset acquisition price may be financed; the borrowing power of the firm may be stretched; the risk of obsolescence is avoided and maintenance burdens may be shifted (both at a cost); and the problem of disposing of old equipment eliminated.

The effective cost of leasing can be substantially affected by the terminal value of the asset. Though not high when standardized equipment such as automobiles is involved, that risk rises rapidly for specialized equipment such as computers subject to rapid obsolescence or real estate where terminal values can rise significantly. Should a more rapid degree of obsolescence take place than contemplated in the lease payment schedule, the leasing option would be more attractive. When considering real estate, should a substantial and unforeseen appreciation in property value take place, ownership would be more attractive.

Lease rental payments are a fixed obligation. Failure to meet the lease provisions brings financial difficulties. The lessor has an advantage over the lessee's creditors, secured or unsecured. Upon default the lessor repossesses his property by a prompt court order. The secured creditor must wait longer for a court action before he can force the sale of the property in satisfaction of the debt, and then he gets none of the surplus if the property brings more than the debt. Thus, financial institutions are willing to lease equipment to small and weak firms but not to lend to these firms.

### *Study Questions*

1. Total lease payments normally exceed the lessor's cost of the property. What factors explain this differential? Since the lessor over the term of the lease is expected to recover at least his cost of the property, why should the credit worthiness of the lessee be of concern?
2. Why does the terminal value element impart a greater risk to the borrow-and-buy versus lease decision when real estate is involved rather than automobiles? Would the decision be tipped one way or the other if the financial manager anticipated a stepped-up rate of inflation if the firm were contemplating leasing real estate? automobiles?
3. Why may a firm find it possible to lease equipment and yet not be able to borrow at the bank? In what way can we say a lessor may be better protected than a secured creditor in the event of default? in what way less well protected?
4. Leasing lost part of its competitive advantage when accelerated depreciation was allowed for tax purposes. Explain.
5. What reasons exist for leasing?
6. The credit worthiness of the lessee is of greater importance to the lessor when specialized equipment such as a special-purpose machine is leased than when standardized equipment such as rolling stock is leased. Explain. Equipment trust certificates secured by rolling stock will be of the highest financial quality even if issued by a weak railroad. How does your answer to the first part of this question help explain this phenomenon?
7. The financial ratios will be different depending upon whether a firm leases or borrows and buys. Which ratios will be affected and how?
8. Borrowing agreements frequently carry provisions against the firm incurring additional indebtedness. What device comes to mind for avoiding such provisions? How can lenders protect themselves against such a maneuver?

9. The tax collector would always prefer to see lease payments as payments on an installment sales contract. Explain. Creditors, in the event of default, would prefer to see lease assets as ownership assets. Explain.

### Problems

1. Sarong Textiles, Inc. is planning to lease a piece of new equipment which sells in the market for $73,600. Lease payments are $10,000 per year, payable at the end of the year. The lease agreement runs for 10 years and is a net lease; that is, the lessee bears all maintenance, property taxes, and so forth.

a. If the equipment were worthless at the end of 10 years, what would be the effective rate of interest?

b. Sarong Textiles signs the lease and pays $10,000 per year rental for 10 years. The value of the equipment at the expiration of the lease is $53,100. What is the effective rate of interest that Leasing, Inc. earned on its investment?

2. Sarong Textiles, now convinced of the high cost of leasing, decides to borrow at 6 percent and purchase land and buildings costing $815,100. Leasing, Inc. offers to buy the real estate and lease it back to Sarong Textiles for 50 years at an annual rental of $50,000. Leasing, Inc. says it would be satisfied with a 6 percent return on its investment.

a. What is the terminal value of the property that Leasing, Inc. is anticipating? (The present value factors corresponding to 6 percent and 50 years are 0.054 and 15.762 in terms of Tables A–1 and A–2 at the end of the text).

b. Should the value of the property decline to zero at the end of 50 years, would the effective rate of return earned by Leasing, Inc. be materially affected? Give your reasons. (The present value of $1 to be received every year for 50 years discounted at 5 percent is 18.256.)

c. The terminal value of the property at the end of 50 years rises to approximately $10 million. What is the effective earning rate generated by the stream of payments of $50,000 per year for 50 years and a terminal value of $10 million in exchange for a present outlay of $815,100? Would borrowing at 6 percent have been a good use of leverage? Ignore capital gains tax adjustment. (The present value factors corresponding to 8 percent and 50 years are 0.021 and 12.233 in terms of Tables A–1 and A–2 at the end of the text.)

d. Sarong Textiles, Inc. can normally earn 10 percent on capital invested in its operating activities. Would purchase of the facilities with the 6 percent borrowed funds, in restrospect, have been a wise decision if the funds could have been invested in regular operations?

e. Would it have been attractive for Sarong Textiles to borrow at 6 percent and use the funds in operations and lease the real estate, even if the terminal value of the real estate were $10 million?

3. Pigskin Enterprises, Inc. requires a new piece of equipment in its production process to keep pace with the mounting demand for its products. The anticipated cost of the equipment is $100,000. Leasing, Inc., will lease the equipment to Pigskin for a rental of $25,000 per year for five years, at which time the equipment reverts to Leasing, Inc. The terminal value of the equipment is anticipated to be zero.

a. What is the effective interest cost of the lease arrangement to the nearest percent to Pigskin, Inc.?

b. Slippery Bank and Trust Company, hearing of Pigskin's financial requirements, offers to extend a five-year term loan repayable in equal installments with interest at 5 percent payable annually on the original balance. Compute the total annual payments and the effective rate of interest being charged by Slippery Bank and Trust Company.

**4.** Pigskin Enterprises, Inc. is uncertain which offer to accept—Leasing, Inc. or Slippery Bank and Trust Company—and you are called upon for a recommendation. Pigskin pays taxes at the rate of 50 percent and follows the double declining balance method of depreciation.

a. If Pigskin accepts the leasing arrangement, compute the net annual tax shield.

b. If Pigskin accepts the term loan arrangement, compute the net annual tax shield. On this piece of equipment Pigskin contemplates switching from the double declining balance method of depreciation to straight line in the fourth year.

**5.** To make a recommendation in the Pigskin case it is necessary to compute the present value of the tax shield created by the two financing arrangements.

a. Using an 8 percent rate of discount, compute the present value of the tax shield under the lease and term loan arrangements.

b. On the basis of these calculations, which financing arrangement would you recommend?

c. What one major factor accounts for this financing arrangement being the more favorable?

**6.** Green-Wood Timber, Inc. has been caught in a working capital squeeze at a time when its short term borrowing power is exhausted. Demand for its products is rising and additional working capital is needed. The latest financial statement of the firm appears in Table 13–4.

TABLE 13–4. Green-Wood Timber, Inc.
Balance Sheet

| | | | |
|---|---|---|---|
| Cash | $ 2,000,000 | Accounts payable | $ 4,000,000 |
| Accounts receivable | 3,000,000 | Notes payable | 6,000,000 |
| Inventory | 5,000,000 | | |
| Total current assets | 10,000,000 | Total current liabilities | 10,000,000 |
| Land, plant and equipment | | Long-term debt | 10,000,000 |
| (net) | 15,000,000 | Common stock and surplus | $ 5,000,000 |
| Total assets | $25,000,000 | Total liabilities and net worth | $25,000,000 |

a. Compute the current, quick, and long-term debt-to-equity ratios. How does the financial condition of the firm appear?

b. Green-Wood Timber plans to sell and lease back $10 million of its timber lands. The $10 million is to be used to pay off $2 million of accounts payable, $3 million of notes payable, and $5 million of long-term debt to ease the pressure being exerted by its creditors. Prepare a *pro forma* balance sheet giving effect to this transaction and calculate the current, quick, and debt-to-equity ratios. Does the financial position of the firm seem improved?

c. The timber lands, valued at $10 million are being leased at an annual rental of $1,100,000 for 25 years. The general opinion is that the terminal value of the land after the timber has been cleared is marginal. No reforestation is planned. What is the interest rate being charged on the lease assuming the terminal value is zero?

d. The leasing firm, however, anticipates a 15 percent return on its investment on this deal. What is the terminal value of the land being anticipated by the leasing firm?

### Selected References


Alexson, A. S., "Needed: A Generally Accepted Method for Measuring Lease Commitments," *Financial Executive,* 39 (July 1971), pp. 40 ff.

Bierman, Jr., H., "Accounting for Capitalized Leases: Tax Considerations," *Accounting Review,* 48 (April 1973), pp. 421–424.

Clark, D. C., "Leases as Loan Security," *Journal of Commercial Bank Lending,* 54 (April 1972), pp. 25–30.

Gordon, M. J., "A General Solution to the Buy or Lease Decision: A Pedagogical Note," *Journal of Finance,* 29 (March 1974), pp. 245–250.

Jenkins, D. O., "Purchase or Cancellable Lease: Which is Better?" *Financial Executive,* 38 (April 1970), pp. 26–31.

Johnson, R. W., and W. Lewellen, "Analysis of the Lease-or-Buy Decision," *Journal of Finance,* 27 (September 1972), pp. 815–823.

Roenfeldt, R. L. and J. S. Osteryoung, "Analysis of Financial Leases," *Financial Management,* 2 (Spring 1973), pp. 74–87.

Shapiro, H. D., "Just Because You Like Beer, Why Buy a Brewery?" *Corporate Financing,* 4 (March–April 1972), pp. 37–39 ff.

Vancil, R. F., "Lease or Borrow—New Method of Analysis," *Harvard Business Review,* 39 (September–October 1961), pp. 122–136.

———, "Lease or Borrow—Steps in Negotiation," *Harvard Business Review,* 39 (November–December 1961), pp. 138–159.

———, and R. N. Anthony, "The Financial Community Looks at Leasing," *Harvard Business Review,* 37 (November–December 1959), pp. 110–130.

Weeks, P. A., J. C. Chambers, and S. K. Mullick, "Lease—Buy Planning Decisions," *Management Science,* 15 (February 1969), pp. B295–B307.

Wilhelm, M. F., Jr., "Purchase or Lease: That Is the Question," *Management Accounting,* 51 (July 1969), pp. 43–46.

Zeher, L. A., Jr., "Investor Leasing Programs," *Financial Executive,* 38 (July 1970), pp. 62–64.

Zises, A., "Law and Order in Lease Accounting," *Financial Executive,* 38 (July 1970), pp. 46–54.

# PART FIVE

# Theory of Finance

*

# 14

# Enterprise Valuation

Valuation of a firm is a difficult matter for several reasons. First, valuation necessarily is concerned with estimating future earnings, and such an estimate has to do with uncertainty. This means that there is a probability distribution applicable to the earnings estimates. Second, valuation necessarily involves either directly estimating a capitalization rate for the estimated future earnings or indirectly doing so by making a comparison with the values of similar firms. Third, valuation is always undertaken for a specific purpose, for example, at the time of a merger, or to determine gift taxes; in each case there are specific restraints placed on the valuation process.[1] Thus, the law may govern the factors to be considered in arriving at a value.

---

[1] Even the very concept of the "value" sought—market value, fair market value, replacement value, value to the owner, and so on—is not uniformly the same in every valuation situation nor is there universal agreement regarding the proper concept of value to be sought in each group of valuation problems. See A. E. Grunewald, *Stock Valuation in Federal Taxation* (East Lansing, Mich.: Bureau of Business and Economic Research, Michigan State University, 1961), Chap. 2.

## SITUATION IN WHICH THE VALUATION PROBLEM APPEARS

Without attempting to make a complete list, we can point out a number of situations in which the valuation problem arises.

1. *Value of a new firm.* This problem is perhaps closest to determining the economic value of the firm; it presents an ideal framework for discussing the theory of valuation because this situation is not subject to the constraints placed upon the valuation problem in other contexts. It is the focus of the present chapter.

2. *Value in mergers.* Here primary concern is directed at the value of the fused enterprise (which may be greater than, equal to, or less than the sum of the separate values of the two firms) and at the division of that value between the owners of the two firms. This subject is taken up in Chapter 23.

3. *Value in recapitalization.* This problem concerns whether the value of the firm is affected by its capital structure and is closely related to the cost of capital and the theory of financial structure. The latter topics are discussed in Chapter 15.

4. *Value in reorganization.* This problem concerns whether a plan of reorganization is "fair and feasible." The starting point is the determination of a value for the firm. Chapter 26 considers the problems.

5. *Value in liquidation.* Here the problem is what can be realized in a relatively short period of time from the assets of a company being terminated either in bankruptcy or voluntarily. This problem is considered in Chapter 26.

6. *Value in rate regulation.* This problem involves a definition of "value" of public utilities under laws whose purpose is to assure that the profits resulting from rates charged are not excessive. A public utility is granted a monopoly in a specific area in return for its consent that profits may be controlled by the state.[2] Since the value of the firm depends on the profit (rates) allowed, there is an element of circular reasoning and there has been a marked tendency to abandon any effort to determine "value" and to substitute concepts such as cost or cost of reproduction.

7. *Value in taxation.* Many taxes, such as realty and personal property taxes, and gift, inheritance, and estate taxes, are based on value. The starting point for such taxation often is "market value." In most cases a market value does not exist; that is, no day-by-day transactions are available. But what may be considered in an effort to construct an estimate of market value is constrained by law.[3]

8. *Value of a majority or minority interest.* Another frequent problem is the valuation of less than the total firm. Although a minute share of the total firm may be valued as its proportion of the total firm, a sub-

[2] See Erwin E. Nemmers, "The Hope Case-Pandora's Box," *Illinois Law Review* (now called *Northwestern Law Quarterly*), 45 (September 1950), pp. 460–482.

[3] For an illustration of the problem of valuation for tax purposes see "The Sunburst Corporation—E Case," in Erwin E. Nemmers, *Cases in Finance* (Boston: Allyn & Bacon, Inc., 1964), pp. 353–373. Also see A. E. Grunewald, "Assets and Earnings as Bases of Taxable Value," *Tax Law Review*, 13 (November 1957), pp. 93–111.

stantial block of ownership may carry more or less than its proportionate part of the total firm. Thus, a majority interest or an interest representing effective control commands more than its proportionate share of the value of the total firm; conversely, for a minority interest.

Another aspect of the problem involves the dissenting stockholder in the case of many corporate decisions such as merger. Here the dissenter is entitled to be paid in cash his proportionate share of the value of the total firm before the merger.

### Usual Inadequacy of Book Value as a Measure of Value

We will consider value without the constraints that are associated with many of the specific situations in which valuation is considered.

Perhaps the most important point is that the value of a firm (or of an asset) can have little relation to its cost to the present owners, although value may clearly have a relation to the cost of replacing the asset. The replacement cost will place an upper limit on the value of an asset but will not guarantee the lower limit of value. The figure—book value per share—is not the answer to value in the case of most corporations since it is not consistently related to the market value of the assets after liabilities have been paid.

For a small group of companies, book value per share does have some meaning. These are largely financial institutions such as banks and insurance companies whose assets are largely limited to those involving money claims that carry a fixed income and are of low risk as to default. The major risk to the value of such assets is a sharp change in the interest rate. In the case of banks and insurance companies many specialized accounting rules are applicable, and hence, even here book value is usually quite different from market value.

Book value is relevant when the assets of a firm carry approximately their market value and the earnings of the firm are low. In this case the liquidating value of the firm may be above the value established by capitalizing its earnings.

### Volatility of Market Value

Market value is sometimes advanced as the true measure of value on the ground that it represents the current valuation (in the market place) to be placed on the future earnings of a firm at a capitalization rate that the market place finds satisfactory. But the market value of the securities of a corporation fluctuates even in a "normal" year. It is unlikely that the future earnings prospects of the company would have changed so much in so short a time. It is more likely that the capitalization rate changed during the year, and small absolute changes in the capitalization rate can produce large changes in the market value of a security.

What then accounts for the gyration in the market value of securities? In the case of speculative securities such as mining stocks, a single event, for example, an assayer's report, may produce radical changes in the expected income and hence in market value. Or, in the case of more seasoned stocks, an unusual event, such as credit control expected to exist for a considerable period of time or the announcement of a new product, may cause drastic changes. In this connection we should remember that if the capitalization rate is high (say, 20 to 40 percent), the value of the security is based largely on the expected earnings in the immediate few years, since the discounted value of more remote years is very little at high rates of discount.

Another reason for the volatility of the market value of a security is that a relatively small percentage of a given issue is traded in a period of time. In order for a mutual fund holding a large block of a given issue to sell its holdings, it is often necessary to begin selling well before the price of the security reaches its expected peak. Selling may proceed for many days while the price of the security moves up, reaches its peak, and moves down. The reason is clear. The seller desires to maximize the proceeds of selling, and this can be done by reducing the effect of the seller on the market. Sudden selling in enough quantity not only might cause the market to break sharply in price but also, once that has occurred, the market place can sense what has happened (if no other news has occurred to account for the break). Then the price is not likely to rise again to its old level because other buyers and sellers have been alerted.

## VALUE AS THE CAPITALIZATION OF EXPECTED EARNINGS

In Chapter 9 we discussed the use of discounted present value in evaluating investment opportunities. Essentially the same principle can be applied to establish the value of a firm. For the present we will assume the firm to be entirely equity financed.

Capitalization of earnings consists of dividing the expected annual earnings by an annual rate, called the *capitalization rate,* with the resulting quotient being the *capitalized value,* or what we consider the investment is worth. In other words, the capitalized value will then earn the annual expected earnings in perpetuity (no growth) at the rate we used; we selected that rate as satisfactory to us as a rate of return on the investment. This can be simply stated as

$$V = \frac{E}{k}$$

where $V$ = the value of the investment, $E$ the expected earnings, and $k$ the capitalization rate.

Expected earnings can be handled as a probability distribution with the degree of dispersion in this distribution reflecting risk to some degree. But dispersion does not adequately incorporate the risk of ruin: the chance that a major negative deviation in earnings may cause bankruptcy.

It is important that the expected future earnings take proper account of "regular" earnings and nonrecurring earnings. Often the estimate of future earnings is prepared by examining historical earnings. Care must be taken to separate out nonrecurring earnings.

It is apparent that the capitalization rate we use in our computation is critical, particularly because a small absolute difference in this rate appears to be magnified in its effect on the absolute difference in value.

Thus, if a firm is expected to realize $1000 in earnings and we capitalize at 5 percent, the firm has an investment value of $20,000 (or $1000/0.05), but if we capitalize at 6 percent, this value is only $16,667 (or $1000/0.06).[4]

Capitalization rates to be used for a proposed investment are frequently established by studying the earnings rates of other actual investments of the same type of risk measured against the market value of those investments. Thus, a 5 percent $1000 bond issued 10 years ago but with 20 years still to run will be valued well above par when 3 percent 20-year bonds of the same risk are being sold today at par. The exact value of the 5 percent bond will be the value of an extra $20 per year for 20 years discounted at 3 percent.[5] If the 5 percent bond had a longer maturity, its value would increase even more. Therefore, we can state that the longer the maturity of a bond (or lease), the greater the reaction to any given change in the capitalization rate (whether up or down).[6] We are assuming the loan is not callable before maturity. If the bond is callable, the computations will employ the call date if the current interest rate is above the coupon rate of the bond.

## THE THEORY OF THE TREND VALUE OF COMMON STOCKS

The capitalization process we have just examined is at work in the area of common stocks. It might appear, however, that when some stocks sell at a price-earnings ratio of 100 and others sell at a ratio of 5 there is something wrong in the theory. The stock selling at a price-earnings ratio of 100 is being capitalized at an apparent rate of 1 percent on an earnings basis; that selling at a price-earnings ratio of 5 is being capitalized at an apparent rate of 20 percent. Both may be well-established firms. Surely the risk differences are not that great.[7]

The explanation lies in an assumption we have been making. We have assumed that the expected earnings of the several firms would each continue to be the same indefinitely into the future. For many investments this is true, such as a long-term bond with fixed interest or a long-term lease with fixed rentals.

Many studies [8] have demonstrated that the values of common stocks have increased over long periods of time at an annual rate averaging ap-

---

[4] The change in rate from 6 to 5 percent is a 16.6 percent reduction; the decline from $20,000 to $16,667 is also a 16.6 percent reduction.

[5] In this case the extra value is $297.55:

$$V = \sum_{t=1}^{20} \frac{E}{(1+k)^t} = \sum_{t=1}^{20} \frac{20}{(1.03)^t} = \$297.55$$

[6] The reaction on a longer bond need not be exactly the same because the longer bond is exposed to the added risk of a change in the market interest rate during the extra time to maturity.

[7] This does not imply (as is often done) that the capitalization rate is the inverse of the current price-earnings ratio, as will be presently made clear. In addition to the capitalization rate, the price-earnings ratio incorporates the market's estimate of the growth potential of the stock.

[8] See, for example, John P. Herzog, "Investor Experience in Corporate Securities: A New Technique for Measurement," *Journal of Finance*, 19 (March 1964), pp. 46–62, which lists principal earlier studies. L. Fisher, "Some New Stock-Market Indexes," *Journal of Business*, 29 (January 1966), p. 191, concludes the annual rate of increase is 9 percent.

proximately 7 to 9 percent. Since common stocks are one way of protecting against the erosion of purchasing power due to inflation, their rate of growth in value must exceed the rate of inflation if they are to achieve this goal. But even the "real" value of common stocks has on the average increased. If the capitalization process is to be validly applied to common stocks, some adjustment is necessary to recognize the fact that earnings are not expected to remain the same in the future, as in the case of a bond or lease, but, rather, are expected to grow.

Before examining the adjustment for growth, common stocks present the question whether dividends or earnings should be used as the income to be capitalized. It is true that the emphasis placed on dividends or earnings in the market place appears to vary from time to time. Thus, in the period 1957 to 1968, more emphasis was placed on earnings than either before or since. There is one basis [9] for a possible distinction between the use of dividends and earnings in capitalization of income. This difference arises from the fact that dividends are taxable at ordinary income tax rates, but if the "would-be" dividends are not paid and are realized as a capital gain upon the sale of the stock they are taxable at the lower capital gains tax rates. Hence some investors in high income tax brackets may have a preference for common stocks currently paying no dividends. This is a minor point, and we will proceed in the analysis of common stock values with the use of dividends rather than earnings.[10] It is customary in finance to analyze earnings in terms of the *price-earnings ratio* but to consider dividends in terms of *yield*, which is dividend/price.

### Valuation of Common Stocks with Zero Rate of Growth

Common stocks with expected dividends that will not change present no difference from our previous case of valuation. Hence, value = dividend/rate of capitalization, or $V = D/k$.

---

[9] In addition to specific facts that controlling interest of a corporation may be valued higher than its proportionate share or that when a management is in control that intends to suppress dividends below customary levels, the market is unsure how long such management may be in control. The latter case is illustrated by Line Material, Inc. prior to its merger in the early 1950s into McGraw Edison Company.

[10] If further proof is demanded, the following is cited. Suppose you buy a common stock, intending to sell it one year later. The value as an investment today will be the discounted dividend you will receive plus the discounted price on sale. This can be expressed as

$$V_0 = \frac{D_1}{1+k} + \frac{P_1}{1+k}$$

where $V_0$ = today's value, $D_1$ the first year's dividend, $P_1$ the sale price one year from now, and $k$ the capitalization rate. Income taxes have not been considered, but it would be a simple matter to include them in the computation.

If we intend to hold for 2 years and the dividend remains constant, the value today would be

$$V_0 = \frac{D_1}{(1+k)^1} + \frac{D_2}{(1+k)^2} + \frac{P_2}{(1+k)^2}$$

Similarly, we can extend the period for any length of time. Thus, ultimately, investment value depends on dividends.

### Valuation of Common Stocks with Average Growth Rates

For convenience we have classified common stocks with expected growth into two classes: expected average growth and expected above-average rate of growth. The principle used is the same for both groups, but the classification will enable us to compare the values we generate with the real world.

The average growth rate of common stock value (measured in current rather than constant dollars) has been 7 percent a year. Thus, for a given company the dividend 1 year after today will be increased by the growth rate, or $D_1 = D_0\ (1 + g)$, where $D_0$ and $D_1$ are the dividends today and 1 year hence and $g$ is the annual growth rate of dividends. We assume dividends are paid once a year and payment is made at the end of the year.

Thus the total of all future dividends will be

$$V_0 = \frac{D_1}{(1+k)^1} + \frac{D_2}{(1+k)^2} + \frac{D_3}{(1+k)^3} + \cdots \qquad (14\text{–}1)$$

Then, since $D_1 = D_0\ (1 + g)$, we can substitute for $D_1, D_2, D_3, \ldots$ in Eq(14–1) and obtain

$$V_0 = \frac{D_0(1+g)}{(1+k)} + \frac{D_0(1+g)^2}{(1+k)^2} + \frac{D_0(1+g)^3}{(1+k)^3} + \cdots \qquad (14\text{–}2)$$

which results in

$$V_0 = \sum_{t=1}^{\infty} \frac{D_0(1+g)^t}{(1+k)^t} \qquad (14\text{–}3)$$

Using algebra,[11] this becomes

$$V_0 = \frac{D_0(1+g)}{k-g} \quad \text{or} \quad V_0 = \frac{D_1}{k-g} \qquad (14\text{–}4)$$

---

[11] The algebra is

$$V_0 = \frac{D_0(1+g)}{1+k} + \frac{D_0(1+g)^2}{(1+k)^2} + \frac{D_0\,(1+g)^3}{(1+k)^3} + \cdots \qquad \text{(i)}$$

We multiply by

$$(1+g)/(1+k):$$

$$V_0\frac{1+g}{1+k} = \frac{D_0(1+g)^2}{(1+k)^2} + \frac{D_0(1+g)^3}{(1+k)^3} + \cdots \qquad \text{(ii)}$$

we subtract (ii) from (i):

$$V_0 - V_0\frac{1+g}{1+k} = \frac{D_0(1+g)}{1+k} \qquad \text{(iii)}$$

$$V_0 = \frac{D_0(1+g)}{k-g} \quad \text{or} \quad V_0 = \frac{D_1}{k-g} \qquad \text{(iv)}$$

To express this verbally, the present value of a common stock is equal to the beginning dividend divided by the capitalization rate less the growth rate. We should point out that the no-growth case is simply a special case where the term for growth rate is zero.

### Valuation of Common Stocks with Above-Average Growth Rates

When we speak of a common stock with an above-average growth rate we are not speaking of a rate continuing indefinitely higher than the average of 7 percent. Rather, we are speaking of the common stock of a firm that will continue to enjoy an above-average growth rate for a period such as 10 years and then drop to an average growth rate. This has been the pattern of many new industries such as railroads, automobiles, television, and electronics. Sometimes the period has been somewhat longer than 10 years and sometimes it has been shorter.

As a first approximation, the valuation of the above-average common stock can be broken into two periods, the growth period and the mature period, represented respectively by the first and the second terms in the following:

$$V_0 = \sum_{t=1}^{t=N} \frac{D_0(1 + g_{aa})^{t-1}}{(1 + k)^t} + \sum_{t=N+1}^{\infty} \frac{D_N(1 + g_a)^N}{(1 + k)^t} \tag{14–5}$$

where $g_{aa}$ is the above-average growth rate and $g_a$ is the average rate.

Table 14–1 indicates what figures would be generated under this theory of the trend value of common stocks. Four different situations are analyzed:

1. The company that is slowly shrinking, as reflected in an annual decline of 2 percent in the dividend.

2. The company that shows no growth but is simply able to hold its dividend.

3. The company that grows at an "average" rate, which is taken to be an average annual increase in dividends of 7 percent. The average growth rate in the industrial production index appears to be about 6 percent.

4. The company that grows at an "above-average" rate, which is taken to be an average annual increase in dividends of 20 percent for 15 years, and thereafter at an average growth rate of 7 percent.

Given these situations, we need two further pieces of information to implement the analysis. The first is a capitalization rate, which we now understand is not just a rate of return but the rate required when the growth rate is zero. Since the rate on fixed-return bonds is currently near 6 percent, and since common stock involves a greater risk than bonds, we have used 9 percent. The other piece of information needed (to establish a price-earnings ratio) is a *payout percentage,* or the percentage of earnings that will be paid out in dividends. A very high percentage of payout ratios (defined as the percentage of earnings paid out as dividends) fall between 25 and 75 percent. We have used a payout ratio of 50 percent in the analysis summarized in Table 14–1.

TABLE 14–1. Values, Yields, and Price-Earnings Ratios

Assuming $1 Last Year's Dividend, 9 Percent Capitalization, and Various Growth Rates, and a 50 Percent Dividend Payout to Establish the Price-Earnings Ratio

| Type | $V_o = \frac{D_1}{k - g}$ | Value | Current dividend yield | P/E Ratio * |
|---|---|---|---|---|
| Negative growth: — 2 percent per year | $\frac{\$0.98}{0.09 - (-0.02)}$ | $ 8.91 | 11% | 4.46 |
| No growth | $\frac{\$1}{0.09}$ | $ 11.11 | 9% | 5.55 |
| Average growth: 7 percent per year | $\frac{\$1.07}{0.09 - 0.07}$ | $ 53.50 | 2% | 26.75 |
| Above-average growth for 15 years: 20 percent per year. Afterward, average: 7 percent per year | † (below) | $247.07 | 0.4% | 123.53 |

* The P/E ratio is the last year's earning per share divided into the current price. In the case of above-average growth the high P/E will drop to the average growth P/E as it becomes apparent the above-average growth will not continue.

† The value of the stock at end of year 15: [B6]

$$V_{15} = \frac{D_{16}}{k - g} = \frac{\$15.407}{0.09 - 0.07} = \$770.35 \quad \text{(i)}$$

Present value of the stock value at end of year 15:

$$V_{15}\left(\frac{1}{1 + 0.09}\right)^{15} = \$211.83 \quad \text{(ii)}$$

Present value of 15 years of dividends:

$$\sum_{t=1}^{15} \frac{1(1.20)^t}{(1.09)^t} = \$35.24 \quad \text{(iii)}$$

Present value of stock: $\text{(ii)} + \text{(iii)} = \$211.83 + 35.24 = \$247.07$ (iv)

**Detail of (iv):**

| Year | Dividend $1(1.20)^t$ | Discount factor $1/(1.09)^t$ | Dividend present value |
|---|---|---|---|
| 1 | $ 1.200 | 0.917 | $ 1.100 |
| 2 | 1.440 | 0.842 | 1.212 |
| 3 | 1.728 | 0.772 | 1.334 |
| 4 | 2.074 | 0.708 | 1.468 |
| 5 | 2.488 | 0.650 | 1.617 |
| 6 | 2.986 | 0.596 | 1.780 |
| 7 | 3.583 | 0.547 | 1.960 |
| 8 | 4.300 | 0.502 | 2.159 |
| 9 | 5.160 | 0.460 | 2.374 |
| 10 | 6.192 | 0.422 | 2.613 |
| 11 | 7.430 | 0.388 | 2.883 |
| 12 | 8.916 | 0.356 | 3.174 |
| 13 | 10.699 | 0.326 | 3.488 |
| 14 | 12.839 | 0.299 | 3.839 |
| 15 | 15.407 | 0.275 | 4.237 |
| | | | $35.238 |

The table suggests that the average capitalization rate may be somewhat lower than 9 percent for average companies included in the Dow Jones Industrial Average, and the average growth rate may be less than 7 percent, since the price-earnings ratios of the stocks included in the Dow Jones Industrial Average seldom go outside the range of 10 to 20, whereas the ratio for this category in Table 14–1 is 26.75. We should note that under the theory we have presented, the price-earnings ratio depends on the *difference* between the capitalization rate and the growth rate. Likewise, the assumption as to the payout ratio has a bearing. Thus, if the payout were cut from 50 to 25 percent for above-average growth companies, the price-earnings ratio would drop to 61.8. This suggests that a "growth company" might do well to increase its payout to drive up the price of its stock in order to procure funds for new projects by selling additional shares rather than by using retained earnings, *provided* that the company can continue thereby to maintain its earning and growth rates.

We must point out that it may appear necessary that $k > g$ or the stock would have an infinite price.[12] However, note that in the above-average growth case in Table 14–1, we have a $g$ of 20 percent and a $k$ of 9 percent. We avoided the mechanical problem of $g > k$ by our methods of computation. A *real* problem in this regard would arise only if we assumed $g > k$ for an infinite period. Such an assumption is clearly nonsense since it would require the investment to take over the whole world in a rather short period of time.

## SUMMARY

The determination of a proper concept of value and the selection of the method and relevant data for translating this concept into a dollar figure are the two fundamental problems that underlie the valuation of any

[12] David Durand, "The St. Petersburg Paradox and Growth Stock Valuation," *Journal of Finance*, 12 (September 1957), pp. 348–363.

property. We are primarily interested in determining the market value of a firm via the capitalization of earnings. Required, therefore, is a reasonably accurate estimate of the future earning power of the firm and an appropriate capitalization rate. The generation of a solid earnings estimate usually proceeds from a study of the past. The earnings record is examined and the relation of the firm's earnings to major economic movements is studied. The trends in the economy and the industry are then analyzed and the earnings projected based on the movements of these major factors in the economy and the industry. The determination of an appropriate capitalization rate is more difficult. A wide variety of opinion exists regarding the appropriate rate to apply in a particular situation. Such differences of opinion are what make horse races and markets of all kinds. The starting point is frequently the yield on riskless securities and the prices at which comparable companies are selling. The proper capitalization rate for a firm would be the riskless rate plus the premium for risk appropriate for that firm.

The valuation of a firm that is growing faster than the economy is significantly more difficult. The valuation formula is deceptively simple. Because a stock is worth what it will produce in income, an estimate must be made of the dividends the company will pay and the timing of those dividend payments. Starting with the dividend currently being paid, we must estimate the growth rate of those dividends and the length of time that the growth is expected to continue. When all the necessary factors have been determined one simply inserts them in the formula and then "turns the handle." A mathematically correct answer will come out. Whether or not it is correct financially will depend on the inputs. Time will provide the answer.

### *Study Questions*

1. What factors make valuation of a firm such a difficult task?
2. How are accurate valuation estimates linked to the proper allocation of resources in the economy? Why does it make a difference to the general welfare of a nation if valuation estimates are appropriate?
3. What are some of the areas in which the valuation problem appears? How does the valuation problem differ in each of these areas?
4. At one time an important measure, book value no longer is as significant as to the value of major industrial firms. What is the major determinant of the value of an industrial firm? Why is the book value figure not similarly disregarded in the valuation of financial institutions and small firms?
5. What would be the value of the Ritzee Hotel built in the middle of the Sahara desert in an inaccessible location at a cost of $10 million? How do you arrive at your estimate? What are your assumptions?
6. How will the rates on U.S. government securities affect the valuation figure placed on a firm?
7. Give several examples of stable stocks and growth stocks. Why are growth stocks more difficult to value than stable stocks? Are the wider market price fluctuations for growth stocks a reflection of this greater difficulty? Support your answer.
8. What is the payout ratio? Under what conditions might a firm increase its payout ratio and thereby increase the market price of its stock?

9. Of what importance is the "growth horizon" in valuing growth stocks? How does it affect the calculated value of the stocks?

***Problems***

1. Miss Muffit purchases an elegant pair of leather gloves for $15.00. Upon leaving the store she loses one of them. An unscrupulous person finds the glove. Since it is brand new, he believes the glove has considerable value and decides to try to sell it "in the market."

a. For what price do you think the glove can be sold in a normal market?

b. The finder discovers that Miss Muffit is the owner of the glove and decides to try to sell it back to her.

How much do you think Miss Muffit might be willing to pay for the glove?

c. Assuming Miss Muffit is willing to pay a good price for the glove, how do you reconcile her willingness to pay for the glove with what would normally be the market price for one glove?

2. The Mini-Machine Shop is expected to generate earnings of $1000 a year forever. Comparable firms are currently selling on a 10 percent capitalization rate basis.

a. How much can the owners of Mini-Machine expect to receive for their firm should they decide to sell?

b. The following year people's attitudes toward risk change. The market now is willing to buy such firms on a 5 percent capitalization rate basis.

How much can the owners of Mini-Machine now expect to receive for their firm?

c. A new product is introduced into the market and the sales of Mini-Machine plummet to zero. The equipment of Mini-Machine is still in perfect working condition, but being highly specialized, cannot be used for the manufacture of any other products.

What is the market value of Mini-Machine now?

3. What is the basis of the market value of an enterprise? Of the value of consumers' goods? How do your answers to these questions help to answer questions 1 and 2?

4. Mickey Mouse, Inc., an average light manufacturing firm is currently paying a dividend of $1 a share. Earnings and dividends are expected to grow at the rate of 5 percent per year. Comparable companies with no growth are selling on a 10 percent capitalization rate basis. Management is considering a stock issue.

a. Approximately what price per share can management expect to receive?

b. Management is reluctant to proceed because of new developments on the horizon. Several years later the firm introduces a new product which is expected to permit dividends to grow at the rate of 10 percent a year for 3 years. After this period the dividends will return to the normal growth rate of 5 percent. Over the past years dividends had remained at $1 per share. The firm required all its available funds to develop this new product. The market rate of capitalization had dropped to 9 percent.

Approximately what price per share can management now expect to receive should it decide to offer a new issue in the market?

c. Management decides to proceed and sells the new issue in the market for the price determined in (b). In fact, the issue is enthusiastically received. Shortly thereafter the threat of new competition appears. It is now expected that the $1 dividend will grow at the rate of 10 percent a year for only 2 years, and after that time growth will be at a rate of 4 percent per year. The market rate of capitalization is still 9 percent.

What is the new market price of the stock and how much did the investors lose that purchased the stock of Mickey Mouse, at the offering?

d. Compare the numbers derived from the calculations in parts (b) and (c). What was the relative influence of the shortened rapid growth horizon, from 3 to 2 years, and the reduced long-term growth rate, from 5 to 4 percent? Did these changes tend to offset or reinforce each other?

5. Ricochet, Inc., a small measuring instrument manufacturer, is currently earning $5 a share and paying a $1 dividend. The firm acquires through merger a medical electronics firm. With the combined capability the market expects the firm to grow at the rate of 20 percent a year for 10 years and then level off to 7 percent a year. The market rate of capitalization is 9 percent.

a. Based on these estimates, what is the current fair value of the stock?

b. If the stock actually sells at this price, what is the price-earnings ratio?

Ricochet has several projects that promise a return in excess of 20 percent. Internal funds are not available to undertake these projects. Accordingly, management plans to issue additional stock but feels the current price-earnings ratio is too low. Management feels a ratio of 30 to be appropriate.

c. What action would you recommend to management to raise the price-earnings ratio to this level?

d. What would be the indicated market price for the stock?

e. Is this a sustainable market price if the firm's earnings actually grow faster than 20 percent?

f. What will happen if the firm cannot maintain the anticipated 20 percent growth rate? Why?

### Selected References

Beranek, W., *Common Stock Financing, Book Values and Stock Dividends: The Theory and the Evidence,* Madison, Wisc.: University of Wisconsin, 1961.

Durand, D., "The St. Petersburg Paradox and Growth Stock Valuation," *Journal of Finance,* 12 (September 1957), pp. 348–363.

Fama, E. F. and M. H. Miller, *The Theory of Finance* (New York: Holt, Rinehart and Winston, 1972).

Gordon, M. J., *The Investment, Financing and Valuation of the Corporation.* Homewood, Ill.: Richard D. Irwin, Inc., 1962.

Heidrick, H. H., "Determining Utility Market Value," *The Appraisal Journal,* 38 (April 1970), pp. 253–272.

Herzog, J. P., "Investor Experience in Corporate Securities: A New Technique for Measurement," *Journal of Finance,* 19 (March 1964), pp. 46–62.

Kotler, P., "Elements in a Theory of Growth Stock Valuation," *Financial Analysts Journal,* 18 (March 1961), pp. 37–42.

Malkiel, B. G., "Equity Yields, Growth and the Structure of Share Prices," *American Economic Review,* 53 (December 1963), pp. 467–494.

Olson, I. J. "Valuation of a Closely Held Corporation," *Journal of Accountancy,* 128 (August 1969), pp. 35–47.

Walter, J. E., "Dividend Policies and Common Stock Prices," *Journal of Finance,* 11 (March 1956), pp. 19–47.

# 15

# The Cost of Capital and Capital Structure Management

The cost of capital[1] is an important element in determining which projects are to be undertaken and the composition of assets of the firm. At the moment of decision no capital expenditure proposal should be approved that does not promise an expected return at least greater than the cost of capital. Hence, it is important to minimize the cost of capital in order to maximize net return and growth. If the firm employs the net present value method, the cost of capital will be used as the discount rate to determine whether the project promises a positive net present value. If the internal rate of return method is employed, the internal rate will be compared with the cost of capital to determine if the internal rate of return is greater than the cost of capital. Other capital budgeting methods, such as the accounting method and the payout method, may also be used in con-

[1] A. A. Robichek and J. G. McDonald, "The Cost of Capital Concept: Potential Use and Misuse," *Financial Executive*, 33 (June 1965), p. 26.

junction with the cost of capital, but the results will not lead to the best decisions, since these methods do not take into consideration the time value of money.

## CAPITAL BUDGETING HURDLE RATE

The cost of capital when adjusted for risk is the earning rate needed to maintain the market value of the firm, if the firm is performing to the satisfaction of the owners. The "cost of capital" is commonly used to refer to the weighted marginal cost of debt and equity. Thus, if the debt-equity ratio is 1 and if *new* debt costs 6 percent and *new* equity 10 percent, the weighted marginal cost is 8 percent. The term "weighted average cost of capital" is used in this sense but is not to be confused with an average which includes, for example, existing debt at its rate. The cost of new equity is taken as $(D/V) + g$, as developed in Chapter 14.

Care must be taken or error can quickly creep into the analysis. As an example consider Swiftee, Inc., a firm of $100 capital, raised through selling 10 shares of stock at $10 each. The firm is in the 10 percent risk class, that is, the risks to which the firm is exposed are those facing other companies earning 10 percent return and with zero growth rate. All earnings are paid out in dividends and the firm earns $1.50 a share and sells at $15.00 a share. Swiftee plans to expand, selling 10 more shares at $15 each. If the firm invests the new funds, it would seem that it must earn a minimum of 10 percent on its investments—the cost of capital—if the market value of its stock and the firm as a whole is not to decline.[2] If the firm finances projects from depreciation charges on the original assets, the new projects must earn a minimum of 15 percent if the market value of the shares is not to decline. The reconciliation of this apparent conflict is as follows. The belief that the proceeds from the new shares must earn 10 percent ($1.50 per share on the price of $15 per share) in order for the per share value of the firm to be maintained is an illusion. The old shares (and new) are priced at $15 because the firm is able to earn $1.50 a share on assets of $10 a share. If the new assets earn only 10 percent, the price of the stock will fall. For the price of the stock to remain at $15 the new assets must earn 15 percent, which is the rate on the old assets (15 percent on $10 per share).

If a firm cannot generate a return on new assets equal to the cost of capital, the firm should not reinvest funds. Instead, the firm should either pay dividends or repurchase its own shares in the market, a practice that numerous firms have been following. For many well-established firms in mature industries with limited investment prospects the cost of capital may be higher than the present return on assets. In this case the cost of capital is the hurdle rate.

Firms frequently employ an arbitrarily determined rate, say, 15 or 20 percent, as their capital budgeting cut-off rate. Such a procedure abandons to luck the goal of maximizing the value of the firm.

In this chapter we will explore ways in which the cost of capital may be minimized through rearrangement of the capital structure to establish

---

[2] The adjustment for risk is reserved for Appendix N to this chapter.

the optimum mix of low-cost debt and high-cost equity. The financial manager seldom has an opportunity to build the capital structure of his firm from the beginning. He comes to a going concern that has a capital structure fashioned by those who went before. Within limits, he can slowly change the capital structure with the objective of minimizing the cost of capital to the firm.

### Definition of Key Concepts

At the outset, let us be clear about the definition of several key concepts. *Capital structure* refers to the long-term financing of the firm, namely, long-term debt and net worth. *Net worth* consists of preferred stock, common stock, capital surplus, retained earnings, and net worth reserves. *Financial structure* refers to all the financial resources marshaled by the firm, short as well as long term, and all forms of debt as well as equity.

The term "capital" has a number of meanings. We may speak of capital and labor as resources. Here the term refers to the physical means of production, but in finance, "capital" is most frequently used to refer to funds or liquid resources. It is true that we reserve the term "capital market" for long-term funds and use the term "money market" for short-term funds, but when we speak of the "cost of capital" we refer to either long or short-term funds.

## COST OF CAPITAL AND ALLOCATION OF RESOURCES

The funds for a particular capital expenditure may be obtained from a variety of sources. The firm may sell marketable securities it owns or other assets. The specific cost of these funds would be the foregone income earned had the assets been retained. The firm may also borrow from its bank, expand its current liabilities, sell bonds [3] or preferred or common stock, or retain a greater portion of its earnings. The cost of these funds to the firm may be determined with varying degrees of ease. The direct cost of a new bank loan or new bond issue is not difficult to calculate; the cost of foregone trade discounts due to allowing current liabilities to increase is only slightly more difficult to determine. On the other hand, the cost of new common stock and retained earnings is surrounded by uncertainty and controversy. But we are ultimately interested in the overall cost of capital. If we stop short of this and consider only the cost of funds from a specific source for a particular project, the cost of capital will fluctuate sharply as the firm finances one project with a bank loan, the next with an issue of common stock, and a third with a convertible debenture issue. Projects will be penalized or made to appear more favorable depending upon the source of funds tapped to finance that project at that particular time. Such a randomly fluctuating cost of capital will not lead

[3] Complete freedom, of course, does not exist for substituting bank loans for long-term capital in the financing of projects. Only with projects that have a relatively short life span, say, 5 years, is such substitution normally possible.

to as good decisions as will be possible when employing the overall cost of capital. But first we will consider why capital should have any cost at all.

## DEMAND FOR CAPITAL RESOURCES

Capital (that is, funds) is a scarce resource, and its allocation is achieved by the rationing process of the price system. If the market is not free and competitive, factors other than price may influence the rationing process. In the business sector, demand for funds stems from opportunities to invest. Such "investments" may be of two fundamentally different types: the purchase of physical resources, which is called "real" investment, and the purchase of the right of others to the earning of assets, such as purchase of shares of stock in a going business, which is called "financial" investment. The first has direct economic consequences in employment. The second has only indirect consequences. It is important to note that both types of investment create a demand for funds and compete in the same market for funds. Thus, the businessman seeking to build an addition to his plant finds he is competing for funds against his own bondholders who seek to acquire funds by selling those same bonds.

In addition to the demand for funds by the business sector, there are demands by the government sector and personal sector. The demand by the business sector is dominated by the marginal efficiency of capital, that is, the extent to which expectations of revenue inflows exceed the costs of the investment. Demand for funds by the government sector is heavily weighted with noneconomic considerations such as social objectives and national defense considerations. Demand for funds in the personal sector is dominated by a variety of factors such as the willingness of individuals to incur debt to satisfy current consumption, the expectations of these individuals as to future income to effect debt repayments, and the current debt levels and repayment schedules of such individuals.

## SUPPLY OF CAPITAL RESOURCES—THE ACTIVITIES OF THE FEDERAL RESERVE SYSTEM

Similarly, on the supply side of funds there is a diversity of factors affecting each individual or entity considering offering funds in the capital market. Thus, insurance companies as large suppliers of funds are influenced by the volume of incoming premiums and current repayment of loans as well as their expectations as to future interest rate patterns in deciding whether to offer such funds for longer-term investment or to sit on them in short-term paper, reinvesting the funds every 90 days until a decision is made to pursue long-term investment.

Besides the difference in motives among the three sectors, business, government and personal, there is one unique entity at work in the market for funds. In the United States this is the Federal Reserve System and in the case of other countries the central bank. The Federal Reserve System [4]

---

[4] For a brief explanation of the operations of the Federal Reserve System, see Board of Governors of the Federal Reserve System, *The Federal Reserve System, Purposes and Functions*, 5th ed. (Washington, D. C.: The Board, 1963).

is not operated for profit but, rather, seeks to influence the market for funds, including both the price of these funds and the quantity available. These efforts seek price stability, full employment, and economic growth as well as the solvency of the banking system.

The Federal Reserve System influences the price and quantity of funds through a number of tools such as (1) the rediscount rate, which is intended to affect the loan policies of banks; (2) the reserve requirements for demand and savings deposits, which are similarly directed; (3) open market operations (buying or selling federal obligations) to affect the price and quantity of funds in the market; and (4) specific regulations influencing the installment loan area (by downpayment and length of loan rules), the stock market (by margin requirements), and other areas. The Federal Reserve System affects the price and quantity of short-run funds directly and more importantly than long-term funds.

Thus, the factors that determine the cost of capital are numerous and their interaction complex, but from them the financial manager will gather much of the insight needed to interpret and forecast changes in the cost of capital to his firm.

In our mixed society a pure rate of interest is determined partly by supply and demand. The rate on U.S. government bonds might be considered as approximately the pure rate of interest.[5] In a sense the pure rate is a foundation for all the other charges for the use of capital. In fact, *availability* of funds rather than their price (the interest rate) is not unusually the controlling element in current transactions. When many desire funds, whether for consumption or production, the available *supply* of funds can reach the point where it is inelastic with reference to the interest rate. Further, labor, machines, and equipment may not be available except after long waiting periods. Here the *demand* for funds becomes interest inelastic. In deep depression, demand for funds may become interest inelastic or the demand curve for funds may shift drastically downward as profit opportunities shrink.

## QUALITY FACTORS INFLUENCING THE COST OF FUNDS

What factors cause the cost of funds from a particular source to be higher than the pure rate? The answer is risk differences. Risk implies the possibility of loss and the prospect of gain. Suppliers of capital, in addition to compensation for exchanging present funds for future funds, also require a chance for gain at least commensurate with the chance of loss. The risk element is composed of five aspects that are closely intertwined: business risk, financial risk (also called leverage), purchasing power risk, money rate risk (also called interest rate risk), and market (or liquidity) risk.

---

[5] Two classical references on the interest rate are Irving Fisher, *The Theory of Interest* (New York: The Macmillan Company, 1930), and Oskar Lange, "The Rate of Interest and the Optimum Propensity to Consume," *Economica* (New Series), 5 (February 1938), pp. 12–32.

### Business Risk

*Business risk* refers to the risk of default or variability in return of a particular venture. It concerns the changes in the income stream before capital claims. Lack of perfect foreknowledge raises doubts regarding future returns when liquid funds are used to buy brick and mortar. If the funds are invested in an electric utility through the purchase of its common stocks, the variability of return normally will not be great and the business risk premium then will not be large. On the other hand, if the firm is unable to keep its business risk down—if it is not in a stable industry and does not invest in uncorrelated projects—the business risk premium demanded by suppliers of funds will be high.

### Financial Risk

Financial or leverage risk refers to the proportion of debt and equity with which a firm is financed. When a firm is financed entirely by common stock, there are no fixed financial charges that must be met. The probability then is small that it may be forced into bankruptcy through inability to pay debts (there is no bond interest). Whenever prior claim securities, whether debt or preferred stock, are introduced into the capital structure, financial risk arises. All the suppliers of capital to the firm are then exposed to this risk in varying degrees. Bondholders are the least exposed since they have a senior claim. Common stockholders are the most exposed since they provide the cushion to absorb any shrinkage in earnings and would be the first to feel any adverse turn of the business. The phrase "trading on the equity" is commonly given to the use of prior claim securities. Suppliers of debt are willing to exchange their funds for the promise to pay interest because other investors provide an equity cushion to absorb normal losses; hence, the term "trading on equity." Prior claim securities give rise to a leverage effect: everything earned above that amount due prior claimants accrues to the benefit of the common stockholder. If the invested funds earn less than enough to pay all security holders, the amount promised prior claim securities is first paid in full, and thus the common stockholders' return is reduced. Leverage works both ways.

### Purchasing Power Risk

Purchasing power risk refers to changes in the purchasing power of money measured by price-level changes. Though all securities are affected by this risk, prior claim securities are especially affected. The premium to cover purchasing power risk is determined by investor expectations of future price level stability. For example, a prospective bondholder expecting prices to rise will demand a higher rate of return to cover the decline he expects in the purchasing power of money so that his *real* income is maintained. If the bond is already on the market, the money yield (a rate) must increase in order to maintain real income and hence the bond's price must fall. This is exactly what happens to the price of all prior claim securities when the price level rises. During a period of inflation, when all resources are fully employed and profits increase due to capacity operations, the common stock of a firm with a high percentage of debt may not decline in price because through trading on the equity earnings may actually rise faster than the premium for the decline in purchasing power is rising.

### Money Rate Risk

Money rate risk refers to the premium in yield demanded by suppliers of capital to cover the risk of an increase in future interest rates. As with purchasing power risk, prior claim security holders, particularly high-grade bondholders, are sensitive to this form of risk. As residual claimants to the income of the firm, common stockholders seek large returns but are also subject to the greatest risk since they are the buffer absorbing all fluctuations in income. The bondholder, on the other hand, since he has insulation against business and financial risk, is promised a lower return for the use of his capital, and even slight changes in expectations of future interest rates have an important effect on him.[6] Money market management may cause changes in the interest rate structure, or such changes may result from fundamental shifts in economic forces. Increases in wealth or postponement of current consumption make a larger supply of capital available for investment and move the entire structure of rates downward. On the other hand, marked increases in the productivity of capital increase the current demand for funds and shift the costs for funds upward.

### Market Risk

Market (or liquidity) risk refers to the ability of a supplier of funds to sell his holdings quickly. The owner of shares traded on an exchange is in a position to liquidate his holdings in minutes through a phone call to his broker. The holder of shares inactively traded on the over-the-counter market usually has greater difficulty disposing of his holdings at a price close to the last trade. In order to dispose of the shares quickly he may have to offer them at a bargain price. Although there is no study to establish the proposition, it is frequently stated that for comparable quality common stocks those traded in the over-the-counter market tend to sell at a little higher yield (dividend/market price) and lower price-earnings ratio than those traded on a stock exchange. Holders of assets such as real estate or machinery and equipment may require a longer period to realize a generally prevailing price for their assets. This risk of not being able to liquidate promptly except at a substantial discount from the prevailing market price is known as *market risk* and the supplier of funds expects a premium to compensate for this risk.

---

[6] In mid-1974 the market rate for high-grade municipal bonds (exempt from federal income tax) rose so high (index average nearly 7 percent) that earlier bonds of the same municipalities issued at par during the 1940s or earlier when the market rate was low (1.8 to 1.5 percent) fell in price to as low as $250 for a $1000 bond. How low the bond price fell depended in part on the length of time from 1974 to maturity of the bond.

## MEASURING THE COST OF DEBT, PREFERRED AND COMMON STOCK FUNDS

In investing funds management must ascertain their cost to decide whether the project should be undertaken. The principle we follow is that for any project to win support it must promise a return of at least the cost of capital.[7] This requirement applies whether the funds are obtained from external sources, such as the sale of new securities, or from internal sources, such as retained earnings and depreciation charges. The cost of capital from external sources includes the contractual payments on debt and preferred stock and dividends on the common stock. The cost of internally generated capital is the opportunity cost, or income the stockholder could earn on these funds if they were paid out in dividends rather than retained in the firm. Because of the personal income tax on dividends, the cost of retained earnings might be considered less than funds procured by a new common stock issue. The overall cost of financing depends in part on the proportion of debt and equity that a firm has in its capital structure. This ratio will influence the cost of new debt or equity issues and hence the overall cost of capital.

Before we proceed to measure the weighted marginal cost of capital, we must determine the costs of funds from the individual sources. What we seek to measure is the marginal cost by a *current* tapping of the several sources of funds. Costs of previously obtained capital are not relevant. The composition of the capital structure will be altered by the inflow of any new funds, since a firm will seldom find it economical or convenient to raise additional funds simultaneously from all sources. Because the capital structure mix will change with new financing, it can be expected that the weighted marginal cost of capital will also change.

### The Cost of Long-Term Debt

The cost of funds raised through direct placement of securities with pension funds, insurance companies, and other financial institutions is only slightly higher than the stated rate of interest, since these securities are usually placed at close to par value and expenses of private placement of a large issue are minimal. Since interest payments qualify as a tax deduction in determining net taxable income, all securities bearing interest have a tax advantage to the issuer over funds raised through equity securities. Debt securities sold to the public must be registered with the Securities and Exchange Commission. Registration and sale through an underwriter involve additional expenses thus raising the cost of capital obtained in this way. Furthermore, since the securities are traded in a market and both interest rates and the outlook for the firm may change, the price of the bond often soon departs from its issue price. In calculating the cost of the debt issue, we consider (1) the nominal rate of interest paid, (2) the flotation costs, and (3) the premium or discount at which the securities are currently selling.

A $1000 bond bearing a 4 percent interest rate sold to an investor for $1000 will result in a cost to the firm of 4 percent if there are no other

---

[7] In Appendix N to this chapter we develop a risk adjustment to the cost of capital.

costs. If the flotation costs are $10 per bond, the longer the term to maturity the closer to 4 percent will be the cost. If the bond runs for 1 year the cost of this debt will be 5 percent. If the bond runs infinitely long, the cost will be 4 percent. The same observations may be applied to any premium or discount.

Bond tables indicate the effective interest rate (the rate to maturity) a particular bond is yielding given the market price, the nominal interest rate, and the number of years to maturity. Lacking such a bond table, one can make a good approximation of the effective rate by adding to or subtracting from the stated interest amount the discount or premium reduced to an annual amortized basis and dividing by the average of the current market price for the bond and the face value. The rationale is that the annual amortized amount of the discount or premium accrues to the holder and that his investment is not the current market price but, rather, the average of the market price and the face value.

The formula[8] for approximating the effective interest rate for bonds selling at a premium or discount is

$$k_b = \frac{\text{Annual interest payment} \begin{pmatrix} + \text{ Discount/Years to maturity} \\ \text{or} \\ - \text{ Premium/Years to maturity} \end{pmatrix}}{(\text{Par of bond} + \text{Market price})\ /2}$$

The symbol $k_b$ refers to the cost ($k$) of bonds ($_b$)

[B7]

For example, assume the $1000, 4 percent bond we spoke of is a 25-year bond. Now 5 years after issue, due to a general shift upward in the structure of interest rates, the bond is selling at $900, so that if the firm issued a new 4 percent bond of the same maturity as the remaining life of the old bond, it could expect to get $900 per new bond before adjusting for the costs of financing. The effective rate of interest investors currently demand on their funds can be approximated by plugging the numbers into the formula and turning the handle:

$$k_b = \frac{\$40 + (\$100/20)}{(\$1{,}000 + 900)/2}$$

$$k_b = 4.73\%$$

To adjust for flotation costs, add to the numerator the flotation costs divided by the number of years to maturity. This gives the pretax cost of debt to the firm. The definiteness of the cost of funds raised through bonds disappears if they are callable, convertible into stock, or include warrants to buy stock. The problem relates to the fact that stock values look to the future and reflect investor estimates of earnings, dividends, and growth. We will consider these elements later when estimating the cost of common stock.

---

[8] Because at maturity there is a capital gains tax due on the discount and a capital loss for a premium, the discount or premium should be adjusted to an "after tax" basis.

### Cost of Short-Term Obligations

The cost of trade credit for the buyer is high if cash discounts are missed. If payment is made within the discount period, there is no explicit cost for the credit, though there may be more administrative costs to the firm in buying goods on credit rather than for cash. Also the seller may hide some of the credit costs in the price, but these can ordinarily not be ascertained or avoided.

Accrued liabilities carry no explicit cost to the firm and can be an important source of "free" capital. An example would be accrued taxes where a profitable firm may have outstanding average accrued taxes of $1 million as it moves from one quarterly tax payment to the next.

The nominal interest rate on a short-term loan appears as an annual rate in the loan agreement. The true interest rate, however, varies from the nominal rate, depending on whether the loan is discounted (that is, the interest is deducted in advance), whether the loan is repaid in equal installments, or whether there is a balloon payment at the end. Discounting a $1000 loan at 4 percent for one year makes available to the borrower only $960, and the effective interest rate is

$$\frac{\$40}{\$900} = 4.16\%$$

The $1.60 additional profit (4 percent on $40) to the banker appears to be negligible, but the $40 helps cover the reserve requirement of $160 which the banker must maintain for a $1000 loan when the reserve ratio is 16 percent.[9] If the loan were not discounted but the principal were repaid in 12 equal installments, the interest rate would be approximately double the 4 percent stated rate, or 8 percent. Formulas are available for calculating the rate exactly, but the thinking proceeds along the following lines. The $40 interest for the year is paid for the $1000 loan, but if the principal of the loan is repaid in equal installments, the borrower really has available for his use over the entire time only one-half of the funds.

In addition, there is the more significant compensating balance requirement by a bank. By *compensating balance,* we mean the amount of cash the banker requires the borrower to keep in his account at all times in connection with a loan. Thus, if the loan is $100,000 at 4 percent, but the banker requires the borrower to keep an average of $20,000 on deposit, the true interest rate is 5 percent (namely $4000/$80,000). In addition, the compensating balance reduces the bank's risk in the event of bankruptcy. The banker would then immediately seize the balance on hand (say $20,000) and still have a claim for $80,000. And, as was explained, the compensating balance also reduces the pressure on the banker for the reserve required for the loan.

---

[9] When a banker grants a loan, he does so by entering a credit in the borrower's account. At the same time, the loan is entered as an asset of the bank in the amount which the borrower promises to repay. The Federal Reserve System requires a member bank to maintain a reserve against deposits (including the credit granted on this loan). This reserve is typically 16 percent.

### Cost of Preferred Stock

The cost of noncallable preferred stock, since it carries no maturity date, is a function of the stated dividend, the current price, and flotation costs. A 5 percent preferred issued at par of $100 may at a later date sell in the market at $90. The new purchaser would receive a 5.55 percent return. The rise in this return may have resulted from a general rise in interest rates, a decline in the investment quality of the firm, or fear of inflation. The formula for determining the pretax cost of noncallable preferred stock capital is

$$k_p = \frac{\text{Dividend on the preferred}}{\text{Market price of the preferred} - \text{Flotation costs}}$$

If the firm has no preferred stock outstanding, it can search the market for a preferred stock of a reasonably similar company and by the formula calculate the cost of selling preferred. Adjustments would have to be made for any difference in risk between the two firms and for flotation costs. Also, an adjustment is in order for differences between the capital structures of the two firms. The firm would have to earn twice this dividend in order for the common stockholders not to be subjected to negative leverage, because the corporate tax rate is approximately 50 percent. A corporation must earn $2 for every $1 it pays to the preferred.

When we come to the cost of callable preferred, the stockholder receives a premium at the time the preferred is called. Preferred may be called when the interest rate falls sufficiently below the issue rate to enable the firm to absorb the premium. The risk of call for the preferred stockholder complicates the computation of the rate of return—and complicates the cost for the issuer. Almost all preferreds are callable. If the preferred is convertible into common stock or participates in additional dividends after receiving its stated dividend, the cost of preferred is further complicated.

### Cost of Common Stock

Debt and preferred stock involve contractual agreements between the firm and the investors providing for the payment of a fixed sum of interest or dividends. The cost of common stock capital is more indefinite, since the agreement provides only that the investor is to participate *pro rata* according to his holdings in the future fortunes of the company.

For example, a firm wishing to raise additional common stock capital will have to sell its shares at the going market price. But the reciprocal of the current price-earnings ratio at which the shares are sold is not the cost of common stock capital to the firm except in the case where the growth rate of the firm's earnings is zero.

The cost of common stock is determined by the pure rate of interest and the risk class to which the firm belongs. The anticipated growth rate of the firm is another important element affecting price. Risk affects both the cost of capital and the price-earnings ratio, but the rate of growth directly influences only the price-earnings ratio. The market price will reflect changes in growth and in risk, but the cost of capital will reflect only changes in risk, assuming no change in the pure rate of interest. We will have more to say about this shortly, but first let us consider the relationship between common stock earnings and prices.

## GROWTH AND THE MARKET PRICE OF COMMON STOCK

### Earnings and Price-Earnings Ratios

The offering price of a new issue of common stock reflects the estimated earning power per share and particularly the prospect for growth in such earnings. Past earnings performance, estimated future earnings, and the prices at which the shares of similar firms in the same industry are selling will all be considered. The major determinant will be anticipated earnings, which will provide the dividends and generate the capital gains the investor is seeking.

The prices of common stocks traded in the market reflect anticipated earnings and the price people are willing to pay for these earnings—the *confidence factor.* And since these earnings estimates and the level of confidence are subject to change with new information concerning the international and political situation, the domestic economy, the industry, or the company itself, the price of the common shares will also change to reflect this new information.

On the other hand, holders of existing bonds and preferred, being limited to a specified return, are more significantly affected by subsequent issues of debt or preferred paying a higher or lower rate, which produce an increase in financial or leverage risk when the firm assumes greater fixed charges.

### Dilution

The effect on the existing common is a major consideration when the firm is contemplating the sale of additional common stock. If future common stock earnings were always properly estimated, the prices of common stocks would not experience such wide swings of optimism and pessimism, but even the most casual observer can recognize that this is not the case. The economy proceeds through periods of high and low business activity. Common stock prices often reflect in an exaggerated manner nearer-term business conditions, pushing stock prices too high or too low. Thus, when a firm sells a new issue of common stock at a particular price, if the actual future earnings turn out to be much greater than anticipated, the price would, in retrospect, have been set too low and the old stockholders, those holding shares before the new issue, will suffer a loss in potential earnings since a higher price for the stock might have been realized. This process is called *dilution.* The earning power of the firm as distributed among shareholders existing at any time new shares are sold may be reduced when the new shareholders do not contribute sufficient capital to maintain the earning power of the firm at the old rate. Management attempts to avoid this dilution by not selling new common stock when market prices are unduly depressed. True, if the firm did not issue new shares these same investors could have purchased their shares in the open market. But the earning power of the firm is not affected by such purchases.

If the actual earnings after the sale of new common turn out to be substantially less than was anticipated, the price for the new common would, in retrospect, turn out to have been too high and the new shareholders will suffer a large loss. The old stockholders would benefit at the expense of the new shareholders.[10] To prevent such losses to disenchanted stockholders, some managements are reluctant to issue common stock at times when prices have been bid up by rosy optimism. Yet, it is just when the economy is operating at a high level that firms are most pressed for funds, and with stocks selling at high prices, what could be more natural than to issue common stock—especially since at this time the high demand for loans sends interest rates up. Thus, new issues of common stock are brought to market either by the firm or by insiders who wish to dispose of a portion of their holdings when business activity is high and earnings outlooks are good, and optimistic investors anxious and willing to pay high prices for stock. Even a superficial survey of the "new issues" calendar will reveal most selling occurs when the market is buoyant.

### Growth Rate and the Cost of Common Stock

Earnings generated by the firm accrue to the stockholders who can spend or reinvest that portion of the earnings paid out in dividends. Another way a shareholder may realize a return on his investment is to sell his shares at a higher price than that at which he purchased them, thus realizing a capital gain. Excluding consideration of capital gains for the moment, since common, like noncallable preferred, has no maturity date, we might calculate the cost of common in the same way as noncallable preferred. Thus,

$$k_c = \frac{\text{Dividend on the common}}{\text{Market price of the common} - \text{Flotation costs}}$$

If the current dividend on the common were not expected to change, this would be an adequate solution. Testing this formula in the market, we might expect to find common stocks selling on a dividend-yield basis of 8, 10, or 12 percent return depending upon the risk involved and upon the ratio of dividends paid out to earnings (the payout ratio).

This is not what we find. Instead, we find common stocks selling at modest yields of 5 percent, at very low yields of around 1 percent, or at zero yield where the stock has never paid a dividend. Do these low yields mean that common is less costly than preferred or even debt? Not in the least. Where common stocks are selling on such a low dividend-yield basis, investors are anticipating a growth in dividends such that the combined return of current dividend yield and the annual rate of growth will exceed the yield on prior claim securities. Investors anticipate high future dividends or capital gains from currently low or nondividend-paying shares.

In the short run, low or zero dividend-paying shares may be bid up to high prices on what might be called the "bigger fool theory." The theory runs something like this: "I will buy these shares at this inflated price because I am fairly certain a bigger fool will bid them away from me at

---

[10] But, as will be seen shortly in the discussion of Figure 15–1, even the old stockholders might suffer.

a higher price." When the earnings and dividends are not forthcoming, expectations evaporate and prices plummet. However, if the shares are to maintain the high prices to which they have been bid, earnings and dividends accompanied by a high growth rate must develop.

Since common stocks do not have a maturity date, we can either discount dividends into the far distant future, adding a growth factor, or discount those dividends for a shorter period, with a growth factor, and calculate the capital value of the shares at the end of the shorter period. The difference between the current market price and the later higher price would be the anticipated capital gain. Since that later price is itself a function of the discounted future dividends and growth, we will find it convenient to calculate common stock costs simply in terms of dividend yield and growth. Thus,

$$k_c = \frac{\text{Dividend on the common}}{\text{Market price of the common} - \text{Flotation cost}} + \text{Growth rate}$$

For example, suppose the Migrane Drug Company is paying a current annual dividend on common stock of 76 cents and is selling it at $38. Neglecting the growth factor, we see that the stock is selling on a current dividend-yield basis of 2 percent. If the firm were to accept 2 percent as its true cost of equity, sell large additional amounts of common stock at $38, and undertake projects with an expected return of around 2 percent (assume the firm has an all common stock capital structure), it would have many headaches. A major one would be to watch the price of its stock drop from $38 to around $8 (which would be a 10 percent yield) if no further growth in dividends were expected. A market price of $38 obviously reflects something more than the 2 percent current dividend yield, and that something is an anticipated annual growth rate of 8 percent or more.

But considerable risk surrounds future growth estimates. During a rising market period an anticipated growth factor of 12 to 15 percent would not be unreasonable for many common stocks, but on the average earning power grows at 5 percent per year.[11] Under these conditions, the firm should set at least 15 percent as a hurdle rate in its capital budgeting system. Any rate less than this would slow the earnings and dividend growth of the firm and result in a fall in the price-earnings ratio. Many examples can be found in the market to illustrate this fall in the price-earnings ratio when the growth rate has declined. Investors getting in at these high points would be distressed to see, after several years, that the earnings and dividends of their shares are higher than when they purchased them and yet the price per share is down sharply because the price-earnings ratio fell.

Note that Migrane cannot reduce its common stock cost of capital by increasing its growth rate.[12] An increased growth rate would be reflected

---

[11] Earning power is estimated to grow at the rate of about 5 percent per year because common stocks have typically earned an average *total* rate of return of 11 to 12 percent per year with a no-growth yield of 6 or 7 percent. See J. B. Cohen and E. D. Zinberg, *Investment Analysis and Portfolio Management* (Homewood, Ill.: Richard D. Irwin, Inc., 1967), pp. 231 ff.

[12] There is one qualification to this statement. If the growth rate is altered by a change in the payout ratio (dividend policy) then the firm may shift to a new risk class and *k* will be affected.

in a proportionately increased market price, which would reduce the dividend yield and leave the cost of equity unchanged. We compute the cost of common stock using dividend yield *and* growth, but Migrane cannot change its common stock cost of capital by changing its growth rate. To lower the cost of capital, Migrane must move to a lower-risk class, as we shall now illustrate.

A dollar of *return* from a growing company should be no more valuable to an investor than a dollar from a nongrowth firm. Consequently, in a perfect market, assuming constant growth, the increasing earnings from the growth firm should be appropriately discounted by the market, so the total returns from each firm—growth and nongrowth—in that risk class are the same. That is, the price and price-earnings ratio of the growth firm would be sufficiently higher—thus, the dividend yield would be lower—than that of the nongrowth firm, so investors in the stock of either firm will obtain the same overall return. Growth influences the price-earnings ratio, but in a perfect market growth will not influence the cost of capital.[13] This may be seen from a simple example. A growth firm $G$ and a nongrowth firm $N$, both in the same risk class, may have an equity cost of capital $k$ as follows:

$$k_G = \frac{D}{P} + g; \quad k_N = \frac{D}{P} + g$$

$$10\% = \frac{40¢}{\$10} + 6\%; \quad 10\% = \frac{\$1}{\$10} + 0$$

A drop in the growth rate of $G$ from 6 to 5 percent would not influence the cost of capital but would surely influence the market price, causing a drop from \$10 to \$8. Thus,

$$k_G = \frac{40¢}{\$8} + 5\% = 10\%$$

As a numerical illustration, Caprice, Inc. has three assets, A, B, and C, each represented by one share of stock and each generating \$1 of income annually. The stock normally sells at 10 times earnings. In the first period the A asset is replaced by one that will earn \$1.10 in the next period; in the second period the B asset is replaced by one that will earn \$1.10 in the next period; and in the third period the C asset is replaced by one that will earn \$1.10 in the next period. After this, earnings stabilize at \$3.30. The probable price-earnings ratio and price action of the stock are given in Table 15–1. As the market anticipates growth the price-earnings ratio moves up, and as growth disappears it falls again.

[13] We do not have perfect markets nor do we have constant growth rates. As a result, the market price of a firm is frequently bid up to spectacularly high levels not justified, in retrospect, by the firm's long-run earnings growth and the market prices of alternative investments at the time. The cost of equity capital of such a firm would then, in fact, be very low. In such a situation a rational firm will use its stock to raise funds to buy additional assets or use its stock to buy earnings via stock ownership in other companies. These earnings, when consolidated, will increase the market price of the stock, the amount of increase depending upon the relative price-earnings ratio of the two companies and the ratio of the additional earnings to the total earnings.

TABLE 15–1. Caprice, Inc.

The Rise and Fall of the Price-Earnings Ratio and of Market Price as Earnings Grow and Then Plateau

| Asset \ Period | Earnings 0 | I | II | III | IV | V |
|---|---|---|---|---|---|---|
| A | \$ 1.00 | \$ 1.00 | \$ 1.10 | \$ 1.10 | \$ 1.10 | \$ 1.10 |
| B | 1.00 | 1.00 | 1.00 | 1.10 | 1.10 | 1.10 |
| C | 1.00 | 1.00 | 1.00 | 1.00 | 1.10 | 1.10 |
| Total earnings | \$ 3.00 | \$ 3.00 | \$ 3.10 | \$ 3.20 | \$ 3.30 | \$ 3.30 |
| Price-earnings ratio | 10 × | 11 × | 12 × | 11 × | 10 × | 10 × |
| Price | \$30.00 | \$33.00 | \$37.60 | \$35.20 | \$33.00 | \$33.00 |

[B4]

Market imperfections exist. The stock of the growth firm may be overvalued or undervalued relative to its future growth. Investors are generally reluctant to buy stocks with very high price-earnings ratios. Hence, should such shares be undervalued, the firm should not raise any new capital via the common stock route. To do so would result in the dilution of the old shareholders' equity. Conversely, if the market is overdiscounting the future growth of the firm, that is, the price-earnings ratio of the stock is in the clouds, the sale of common stock to raise new funds might be seriously considered.

Let us analyze Caprice, Inc. in terms of our formula for determining the cost of equity:

$$P = \frac{D}{k - g}$$

where $P$ = market price
$k$ = cost of equity
$g$ = anticipated rate of growth, assumed to continue forever

Now, if we assume all the earnings are paid out in dividends in the following period, no growth is expected in period zero, and since Caprice belongs in the 10 percent risk class and pays a \$3 dividend, we have

$$P = \frac{\$3}{0.10 - 0.00} = \$30; \quad \text{P/E} = \frac{\$30}{\$3} = 10 \text{ times earnings.}$$

Then, starting in period 1 a growth rate of 0.9 percent forever is *anticipated* far into the future by investors (although there is a current actual growth rate of 3.3 percent, or 10¢ on \$3.00):

$$P = \frac{\$3}{0.10 - 0.0091} \cong \$33; \quad \text{P/E} = \frac{\$33}{\$3} = 11 \text{ times earnings.}$$

Starting in period 2 a growth rate of 1.7 percent forever is *anticipated* far into the future by investors (although there is a current growth rate of 3.3 percent again):

$$P = \frac{\$3.10}{0.10 - 0.017} \cong \$37.35;$$

$$\text{P/E} = \frac{\$37.35}{\$3.10} = 12 \text{ times earnings.}$$

The same format can be used to derive the given price-earnings ratios for periods 3 and 4.

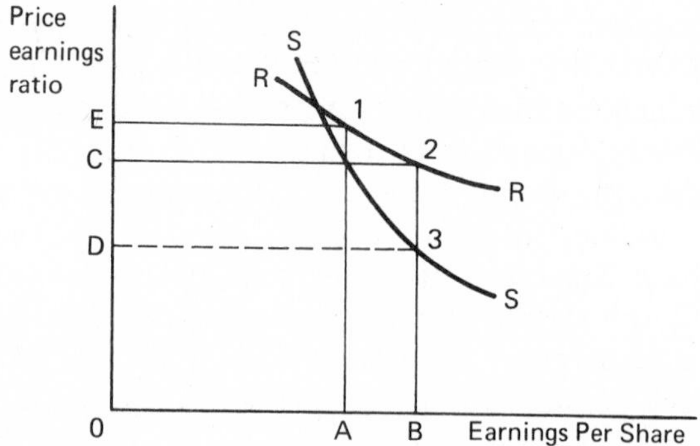


Figure 15–1 Elasticity of the price-earnings ratio with respect to earnings per share when a proposed project earns more that the cost of capital but less than the previous rate of return on assets of the enterprise.

## Elasticity of the Price-Earnings Ratio

It is possible for the market value of a firm to increase despite the fact that a proposed project will earn less than the 15 percent return we have just required. This is illustrated in Figure 15–1. Given a particular price-earnings ratio and earnings per share (such as point 1 in Figure 15–1), the price of a share can be viewed as the product of $(P/E) \times (E)$, or the area of the rectangle $OA1E$. It is clear that the proposed project (if its rate of return is above the cost of capital but below the present rate of return on assets) will add to the earnings per share, increasing that figure from $OA$ to $OB$. Associated with this increase in earnings per share will be a decrease in the price-earnings ratio, since the proposed project will earn a rate of return less than the present rate of return on assets of the firm. But the price-earnings ratio may fall to $C$ (point 2) or $D$ (point 3), depending on various factors such as the evaluation by the market of the profitability of the proposed project. If the price-earnings ratio drops only to point 2, price per share (the area of the rectangle $OB2C$) will rise, but if the price-earnings ratio drops to point 3, the price per share will fall. This phenomenon can be described as the elasticity of the price-earnings ratio in a manner parallel to the familiar concept of price elasticity of demand for a good. If the price-earnings ratio is relatively inelastic with respect to earnings (as indicated by the $RR$ curve), the addition of projects below average will not decrease the value of the firm immediately. If, on the other hand, the curve is relatively elastic (as with $SS$), the total value of the firm may fall. Note that the independent and dependent variables on the $x$ and $y$ axis are in accordance with normal research presentation (as opposed to the usual presentation in price theory) with the independent variable on the ordinate and dependent variable on the abscissa. As a result of the reversal of the coordinate axes, what appears to be an elastic curve, $RR$, is really inelastic, and conversely for the $SS$ curve.

Market prices reflect any expectation of growth, but this growth element is difficult to ascertain [14] except in approximate terms through the liberal application of judgment.

Let us emphasize again, we use dividend yield and the growth rate to *compute* the cost of common equity, but the pure rate of interest and the risk class *determine* the cost of capital. Dividend yield ($D/P$) is easily determined. The big question is, what rate of growth is the market discounting? A starting point might be the historical growth rate. If the firm has grown at the rate of 10 percent per year for the past five years and is selling on a 2 percent dividend yield basis, it might be reasonable to conclude that the firm's cost of common equity, as determined in the market place, is 12 percent. A comparison might also be made with firms —probably in the same industry—representing a similar degree of risk. By comparing growth rates and dividend yields an approximation may be reached regarding the firm's cost of equity. The difficulty with this approach is the absence of a definitive scale of risk classes; without such a scale it is not easy to identify the risk class to which the firm belongs. Whether easy or difficult, the financial manager must reach some conclusion regarding the cost of common equity to his firm.

## RETAINED EARNINGS AND COMMON EQUITY COST OF CAPITAL

### The Extent of Retained Earnings and Financing

Common stockholders universally anticipate—they would demand if they could—a large rate of return on the capital they have invested in a firm. When retained earnings are used to finance projects that yield an attractive rate of return, their reinvestment is generally favored over higher dividends. This action would then lead to higher future dividends and market price, both of which stockholders appreciate. Stockholders will object to retention of earnings where they feel they are not being wisely reinvested. The question that naturally follows is, how important are retained earnings as a source of funds to firms? Table 15–2 reveals that retained earnings provide a major share of new equity of many corporations. Further, these funds, unlike the sale of additional common stock, may be obtained without the requirement that management stand the test of the market place *before* making its decision. If the firm wishes to sell a new issue of stock, past management performance and future prospects will be reflected in the issue price, and the funds cannot be obtained except on that basis. Funds retained in the firm do not need to meet this test. Management has the option of retaining a part or all of the earnings without being required to meet any standard of performance, except that *after*

---

[14] Attempts have been made to measure growth rates. With a gross national product growth rate estimated at 3 to 4 percent, growth in earning power has been estimated at 4½ to 5½ percent. See Cohen and Zinberg, p. 229, and J. G. Cragg and Burton G. Malkiel, "The Consensus and Accuracy of Some Predictions of the Growth of Corporate Earnings," *Journal of Finance*, 23 (March 1968), pp. 67–84, for a study of predicting corporate earnings growth. Some available evidence suggests that earnings growth in the past period is not a very useful guide to predicting future earnings growth. Cragg and Malkiel, p. 83.

the decision is made the market place will pass judgment. The retention of some portion of earnings is normal, and the firm that pays dividends in excess of earnings for a considerable period would loudly call attention to itself.

TABLE 15–2. Nonfarm, Nonfinancial Corporate Business Sources of Funds 1959–1970 (in billions of dollars)

| | Internal Sources | | | | External Sources | | | | | | | | |
|---|---|---|---|---|---|---|---|---|---|---|---|---|---|
| | Total | Retained earnings | Inventory adjustment | Capital consumption allowance | Total | Stock | Bonds | Mortgages | Bank * loans * | Other loans | Trade debt | Tax liability | Other liability |
| 1959 | 35.0 | 12.6 | —0.5 | 22.9 | 22.9 | 2.2 | 3.0 | 3.0 | 3.5 | —0.3 | 5.5 | 2.4 | 3.6 |
| 1960 | 34.4 | 10.0 | 0.2 | 24.2 | 13.7 | 1.6 | 3.5 | 2.5 | 1.9 | 1.9 | 0.6 | —2.2 | 4.0 |
| 1961 | 35.6 | 10.2 | —0.1 | 25.4 | 21.0 | 2.5 | 4.6 | 3.9 | 0.7 | 0.6 | 5.4 | 1.4 | 1.7 |
| 1962 | 41.8 | 12.4 | 0.3 | 29.2 | 23.1 | 0.6 | 4.6 | 4.5 | 3.0 | 0.0 | 4.6 | 0.6 | 5.2 |
| 1963 | 43.9 | 13.6 | —0.5 | 30.8 | 23.2 | —0.3 | 3.9 | 4.9 | 3.7 | 0.2 | 5.3 | 1.9 | 3.7 |
| 1964 | 50.5 | 18.3 | —0.5 | 32.8 | 21.3 | 1.4 | 4.0 | 3.6 | 3.8 | 0.9 | 3.6 | 0.5 | 3.5 |
| 1965 | 56.6 | 23.1 | —1.7 | 35.2 | 36.5 | 0.0 | 5.4 | 3.9 | 10.6 | 0.6 | 9.1 | 2.2 | 4.6 |
| 1966 | 61.2 | 24.7 | —1.8 | 38.2 | 39.4 | 1.2 | 10.2 | 4.2 | 8.4 | 1.4 | 7.8 | 0.2 | 6.5 |
| 1967 | 61.5 | 21.1 | —1.1 | 41.5 | 35.2 | 2.3 | 4.5 | 4.5 | 6.4 | 1.4 | 4.9 | —4.7 | 5.6 |
| 1968 | 61.7 | 19.9 | —3.3 | 45.1 | 46.3 | —0.8 | 12.9 | 5.8 | 8.8 | 3.6 | 10.0 | 2.1 | 3.8 |
| 1969 | 59.5 | 15.8 | —5.5 | 49.2 | 58.6 | 4.3 | 12.1 | 4.8 | 11.0 | 7.0 | 19.7 | —1.9 | 1.7 |
| 1970 | 61.5 | 12.3 | —4.5 | 53.8 | 44.0 | 6.8 | 20.3 | 5.3 | 1.2 | 5.2 | 5.5 | —3.3 | 3.1 |

* Not elsewhere classified.

SOURCE: *Economic Report of President, 1972*, Table B–76, p. 284. Figures differ from national income and product accounts due to inclusion of net flow of funds to and from foreign countries and exclusion of farming corporations. Table not available on same basis in *Economic Report of President, 1973*.

Many well-recognized growth firms where earnings and dividends steadily march upward retain a large portion of their earnings. There are other firms with a good growth record whose management retains a more modest percentage of earnings. In contrast, there are firms that retain a large portion of their annual earnings—upward of 60 to 75 percent—and show little or only a very modest growth trend. These firms may be characterized as "fad" growth firms; they temporarily catch the attention of the investment community. In short, all growth firms reinvest a large portion of their earnings, but not all firms that retain a large portion of their earnings are growth companies. And though some managements look at retained earnings as cost free, these earnings do involve the problem of optimum allocation of resources and opportunity costs.

## Cost of Retained Earnings When Taxes Are Ignored

As we have said, if a firm were paying out all earnings and expected to neither grow nor decline, the cost of equity could be the earnings per share divided by the market price. Once we admit the possibility of retaining a portion of the earnings for reinvestment, we open the door to difficult problems. In capital budgeting a problem arises because of the need to put the retained earnings to work. An active but inconclusive controversy has for years turned on the question of the importance of retained earnings and whether investors look primarily to earnings or to dividends or to both in evaluating investments. If investors look to both, what respective importance do they attach to each? One answer reflects actual market conditions: "it all depends." When investors are evaluating growth stocks, earnings appear to be most important, but when considering mature firms, dividends seem to play the more important role. In the latter situation, a dollar of dividends seems to be valued more highly than a dollar of retained earnings.

We begin our analysis by assuming that (1) for a particular firm the current level of earnings will remain constant in the future; and (2) a decision has been reached to retain a percentage of these earnings, and we, as financial managers, are interested in determining the cost of this retained capital. If we ignore personal income and capital gains taxes and flotation costs, we can say that every dollar of dividends is worth a dollar to the investor, and it follows that every dollar retained by the firm should be so invested as to have a present value of at least a dollar. We assume that the quality of the new earnings in terms of risk is the same as the previous earnings, so the discount rate applied to the constant stream and the augmented stream is the same.

#### Cost of Retained Earnings When Taxes and Brokerage Fees Are Considered

The situation changes when we introduce the personal income tax factor. The part of the dividend that the stockholder is permitted to keep depends on his marginal tax bracket. If we assume a uniform marginal tax bracket for all stockholders of 40 percent, then if the firm normally earns 10 percent at a given level of risk and the shareholders could earn 10 percent after-tax dividends invested at the same risk, the firm could as a first approximation retain earnings and invest them at a minimum return of 6 percent. With this rate on retained earnings the shareholder is as well off as if the firm pays out the earnings in dividends and gives the stockholders the opportunity to pay 40 cents to the government in income taxes for every dollar of dividends received and then reinvest the remaining 60 cents at a 10 percent rate of return in either the shares of this firm or another firm.

A second element is present that reduces the cost of retained earnings, that is, brokerage fees. When the shareholder wishes to reinvest his dividends he normally purchases the additional shares through a broker and must pay commission charges in accordance with an established schedule. Assuming an average commission charge of 1 percent, the cost of retained earnings would be reduced to 5.94 percent. In symbols, if we let

$k$ = rate shareholders can earn on reinvested dividends

$k_r$ = cost of retained earnings

$t$ = taxpayer's marginal tax rate

$b$ = brokerage fees

we have

$$\begin{aligned} k_r &= k(1 - t)(1 - b) \\ &= 0.10(1 - 0.40)(1 - 0.01) \\ &= 5.94\%. \end{aligned}$$

As an illustration, consider Honeymoon, Inc., a firm with net after-tax earnings of $100,000. All of the firm's stockholders are in the 40 percent tax bracket, and upon reinvestment of their dividends the shareholders incur average brokerage costs of 1 percent. The directors are considering the proportion of earnings to pay out in dividends. To assist in the decision they determine that the rate the firm must earn on retained earnings should at least equal what the shareholders can earn on the reinvested dividends. The calculations are shown in Table 15–3. Assume that $100,000

TABLE 15–3. Honeymoon, Inc.
Retained Earnings Cost Calculation

| | | | |
|---|---|---|---|
| Dividends | $100,000 | Net amount available for investment | $59,400 |
| Taxes | 40,000 | | |
| After taxes | $ 60,000 | Stockholders' earnings rate | × 10% |
| Brokerage Fees | 600 | | |
| Net amount available for investment after taxes and brokerage fees | $ 59,400 | Additional stockholders' earnings on investment | $ 5,940 |

The minimum rate Honeymoon, Inc. must earn on retained earnings to generate $5,940 of incremental stockholder income:

$$\frac{\$\ 5{,}490}{\$100{,}000} = 5.94\%$$

of earnings is paid out in dividends and that shareholders can reinvest the after-tax dividends to yield a return of 10 percent for the same degree of risk as Honeymoon, Inc. The purchase of Honeymoon shares is included as a possible vehicle for the reinvestment of dividends.

The example assumes the stock is held forever—passed from heir to heir—and that no capital gains taxes are paid. If the stock were held a minimum of 6 months so as to qualify for capital gains treatment and then sold, the individual's tax rate would be 25 percent, or one-half the marginal tax rate, whichever is lower. In our example the capital gains rate would be 20 percent. On this basis the cost of retained earnings would be

$$\begin{aligned} k_r &= 0.10\ (1\text{–}0.20)\ (1\text{–}0.01) \\ &= 7.92\% \end{aligned}$$

But our analysis so far has been incomplete. We assumed the present stockholders are the only ones interested in the price of the common stock, and we viewed matters through their eyes. However, people who are *not* presently holders would cause the price of Honeymoon's stock to decline if we applied a cut-off rate of 5.94 or 7.92 percent. As they observe Honeymoon, what they see is a shrinking return on assets. The old 10 percent rate falls as we meld in more and more projects at 5.94 or 7.92 percent. For this reason it is customary to apply the common stock formula to all common equity: new issues and retained earnings.

### The Combined Cost of Common Stock and Retained Earnings

Hence, the cost of common equity, both new issues and retained earnings, can be stated as:[15]

$$k_e = \frac{D}{P} + g$$

## WEIGHTED MARGINAL COST OF CAPITAL

### Overall Cost of Capital Using Book Values as Weights

To this point we have developed measures for the cost of debt, $k_d$, preferred stock, $k_p$, and common equity, $k_e$.

TABLE 15–4. Zoozlee, Inc.
Cost of Capital Calculation Weighted by Book Values

| Capital structure | Book value | Percent of total | After-tax cost of capital | Weighted cost |
|---|---|---|---|---|
| Debt | $ 2,000,000 | 20% | 2% | 0.4% |
| Preferred stock | 1,000,000 | 10% | 4% | 0.4% |
| Common equity | 7,000,000 | 70% | 20% | 14.0% |
| | $10,000,000 | 100% | | 14.8% |

The determination of the weighted cost of capital is almost anti-climatic once the appropriate costs of debt, preferred, and common have been determined. We compute the percentage each source of capital bears to the total capital structure and multiply this percentage by the cost of that particular source of capital. The example in Table 15–4 illustrates this procedure.

The weighted marginal cost of capital for Zoozlee, Inc. is 14.8 percent. These calculations are based on book values of debt, preferred stock, and common stock. While these figures may be of historical interest, the firm's capital budgeting decisions are carried on in the present, and what we need is a current cost-of-capital figure. The use of market value weights rather than book value for the capital structure components achieves this objective.

### Overall Cost of Capital Using Market Values as Weights

Assuming Zoozlee, Inc. is a growth company, its stock sells substantially above book value. Using market value weights rather than book values in this situation increases the importance of the high-cost equity in the capital structure and thereby increases the overall weighted cost of capital structure as appears in Table 15–5.

---

[15] Note the switch in notation from $k_c$ to $k_e$. In the previous section we were concerned with $k_c$, the common stock cost of capital. We are now concerned with the cost of the entire common equity.

TABLE 15–5. Zoozlee, Inc.
Cost of Capital Calculation Weighted by Market Values

| Capital structure | Market value | Percent of total | After-tax cost of capital | Weighted cost |
|---|---|---|---|---|
| Debt | \$2,000,000 | 10% | 2% | 0.2% |
| Preferred stock | 1,000,000 | 5% | 4% | 0.2% |
| Common equity | 17,000,000 | 85% | 20% | 17.0% |
| | \$20,000,000 | 100% | | 17.4% |

The cost of capital using market values is 17.4 percent, substantially above the 14.8 percent if we used book value figures. In slowly growing firms, book and market values do not differ much. Here there is little danger that the financial manager will sharply underestimate the overall cost of capital. But where a company is growing rapidly and market values are far above book values, market values must be used to calculate the overall cost of capital in order to guard against underestimating the cost of capital. High price-earnings ratio stocks demand consistently high rates of growth in earnings.

## DIVIDEND POLICY AND THE COST OF COMMON EQUITY

One variable affecting the cost of common equity that will be considered in greater detail in Appendix O to Chapter 16, is dividend policy and specifically the payout ratio, that is, the percentage of earnings of a period paid out in dividends. If the payout ratio affects the cost of common equity, then there will be an optimum payout ratio.

It is important to note that in examining the payout ratio we will be considering the *same* earnings stream, and hence, when the payout ratio is increased, the added funds must come from other sources, such as the sale of new shares, and if the payout ratio is decreased, the extra funds may be otherwise expended as in repurchase of shares. Actually, the optimum combination of leverage, the growth rate, and dividend payout ratio requires a simultaneous solution.

Dividends, which we have denoted as $D$, can be expressed as $E$, (earnings) times the payout ratio. Thus, the cost-of-equity equation we have been using can be rewritten as

$$k_e = \frac{E \times \text{payout ratio}}{P} + g$$

Having translated the dividend form of the equation into the earnings form, we see that behind $D$ there are two variables at work: $E$ and the payout ratio, which is $D/E$. The complement of the payout ratio is the retention ratio, which is $(E - D)/E$. We can go one step further: $g$ (the growth rate) can be broken down into $b$ (retention ratio) times $r$ (expected rate of profitability) so that the equation reads

$$k_e = \frac{E \times \text{payout ratio}}{P} + (\text{retention ratio} \times \text{profitability rate})$$

## MANAGEMENT OF THE CAPITAL STRUCTURE

Firms generally can borrow funds up to a point, comparatively cheaply. Preferred, because of its junior position and the tax factor, usually costs more.[16] On the other hand, common equity seems an expensive source of funds. If nothing else entered the picture, the apparent conclusion would be the more prior claim securities in the capital structure and the less common equity the better. The best capital structure providing the lowest overall cost of capital would then be the one with the largest percentage of prior claim securities and the lowest percentage—just a few shares—of common stock. But the element of financial risk enters and with it the difficult question of determining the ideal capital structure.

Modigliani and Miller have seriously contended that in the absence of income taxes there is no ideal capital structure and that the overall cost of capital to a firm in a particular risk class will be the same regardless of the proportions of prior claim and equity capital.[17] In a perfectly competitive market where all risks and growth rates are properly evaluated and in the absence of taxes, it is reasonable to theorize that as a firm moves from an all-equity capital structure to one with a high percentage of prior-claim securities, the increases in earnings due to trading on the equity would be offset by higher interest rates demanded but lower price-earnings ratios required by suppliers of funds, so that the overall cost of capital would remain unchanged. But, we do have income taxes and we do not have perfect evaluation of the risk element or growth rates in the market. As a result, debt capital can be used but only up to a point to reduce the overall cost of capital.

### The Effect of Increasing Amounts of Debt

Many investors are willing to pay a premium to avoid risk, thus accepting the lower rate of return that goes with prior-claim securities. Starting from an all-equity capital structure, a firm can obtain some amount of debt at comparatively low rates. As the percentage of debt moves up sharply, the interest rate the firm must pay also rises. At first the rate rises slowly, but as the percentage of debt increases the rate rises faster until the point is reached where the firm for all practical purposes cannot obtain any additional debt. Lenders are simply not available at any price. Shareholders, after a point in the process of increasing debt, will also demand a higher return on their capital to compensate for the higher financial risk. If debt is available at relatively low rates, and if the firm is experiencing growth in earnings, the use of leverage will increase the growth rate and actually increase the price-earnings ratio of the stock. With a faster growth rate, investors are

---

[16] Because of the intercorporation dividend credit against income taxes the situation sometimes occurs that a corporate buyer of preferred stock will retain far more of preferred dividends than of interest. Such a corporate buyer then sometimes offers to buy an entire preferred issue with a lesser dividend rate than he would demand for debt securities of the same issuer.

[17] This matter is more fully examined in appendix M to this chapter.

willing to pay a higher price for the stock as long as the benefits of that growth rate exceed the increased financial risk of the increase in debt.

### Leverage and Its Effect on Earnings

The magic of leverage and how it works its wonders (and sometimes its catastrophes) on earnings per share and total market value can be illustrated by a numerical example. Let us consider the S–K Company model with four possible structures; Alpha, Beta, Gamma, and Delta. We will seek to develop a judgment as to the range where the optimum trading on equity might lie. This is the range where the overall cost of capital is at a minimum and the total market value of the firm is at a maximum. In Table 15–6, the total assets and the total book value of S–K in all four capital structure cases are the same. The capital structure in each case is assumed to be $200, split in different amounts between 5 percent interest-bearing bonds and $10 par common stock.

To avoid unnecessary complications, ignore the tax factor and the fact that the interest rate on the bonds would increase as the percentage of bonds increases. Assume the company is operating at the financial break-even point where it is earning 5 percent, or $10, on its total assets. Since the firm must pay a 5 percent return to its bondholders, the firm is neither gaining nor losing from trading on the equity. Earning 5 percent on its assets and paying 5 percent on its prior claim securities, the firm might carry a large or small percentage of debt capital and the common stockholders would neither benefit nor suffer, as Table 15–7 shows.

TABLE 15–6. The S–K Company
Four Possible Capital Structures

| Assets | Liabilities and Net Worth | | Assets | Liabilities and Net Worth | |
|---|---|---|---|---|---|
| | Alpha | | | Beta | |
| | | No bonds | | $ 50 | 5 percent bonds |
| | $200 | 20 shares $10 par common stock | | $150 | 15 shares $10 par common stock |
| $200 | $200 | | $200 | $200 | |
| | Gamma | | | Delta | |
| | $100 | 5 percent bonds | | $150 | 5 percent bonds |
| | $100 | 10 shares $10 par common stock | | $ 50 | 5 shares $10 par common stock |
| $200 | $200 | | $200 | $200 | |

TABLE 15–7. The S–K Company

Impact of Varying Degrees of Leverage at the Financial Break-even Point

| | Capital Structure | | | |
|---|---|---|---|---|
| | Alpha | Beta | Gamma | Delta |
| Operating income | $10.00 | $10.00 | $10.00 | $10.00 |
| Bond interest | 0.00 | 2.50 | 5.00 | 7.50 |
| Earnings available for the common stock | $10.00 | $ 7.50 | $ 5.00 | $ 2.50 |
| Earnings per share | .50 | .50 | .50 | .50 |
| Return on common stock | 5% | 5% | 5% | 5% |

In Table 15–8 we see that when a firm is operating above the financial break-even point, the greater the degree of leverage, other things being equal, the higher the earnings per share for a given level of operating income. This effect can be pushed to the point where earnings on the common stock can be made almost infinite if the amount of debt can be made large enough. However, other things do not remain equal. With the introduction of large amounts of debt the firm assumes a large amount of financial risk, and a small decline in operating income may be all that is necessary to shift the firm from a profit to a large loss position.

TABLE 15–8. The S–K Company

Impact of Varying Degrees of Leverage at an Operating Income Level of $20 Earnings

| | Capital structures | | | |
|---|---|---|---|---|
| | Alpha | Beta | Gamma | Delta |
| Operating income | $20.00 | $20.00 | $20.00 | $20.00 |
| Bond interest | 0.00 | 2.50 | 5.00 | 7.50 |
| Earnings available for the common stock | $20.00 | $17.50 | $15.00 | $12.50 |
| Earnings per share | $ 1.00 | $ 1.17 | $ 1.50 | $ 2.50 |
| Return on common stock | 10% | 11⅔% | 15% | 25% |
| Percent increase from financial break-even point | 100% | 133% | 200% | 400% |

By way of extreme illustration consider the example in Table 15–9 of Way-Out, Inc., financed 90 percent by 6 percent debt and 10 percent equity, or one $10 par share of common stock. Table 15–10 presents the effect during a year when Way-Out, Inc. earns $7, or 7 percent, on its assets and the following year when it earns only $5, or 5 percent on its assets, an earnings decline of about 28 percent but earnings *per share* falls 138 percent. The dramatic results of large amounts of leverage are evident. But when gains beckon so enticingly it is small wonder that firms often follow the siren call of large profits and turn a deaf ear to the possibilities of large losses.

TABLE 15–9. Way-Out, Inc.
Balance Sheet

| Assets | Liabilities and Net Worth | |
|---|---|---|
| | $ 90 | 6 percent bonds |
| | 10 | 1 share common stock |
| $100 | $100 | |

TABLE 15–10. Way-Out, Inc.
Income Statements

| | With 7% earnings on total assets | With 5% earnings on total assets |
|---|---|---|
| Operating income | $7.00 | $5.00 |
| Bond interest (6% on $90) | 5.40 | 5.40 |
| Earnings per share | $1.60 | $ .40 deficit |

In this example we use operating income, or income after fixed and variable costs (other than financial costs). If the firm had only variable costs, then it would require a 28 percent drop in sales to produce a 28 percent drop in operating income. But if the firm has a large amount of fixed costs, it would require a small drop in sales, say 10 percent, to cause a 28 percent drop in operating income.

### Minimization of the Weighted Marginal Cost of Capital and Maximization of the Value of the Firm

Let us now introduce some modified figures so our example may more closely approximate the actual situation. Assume that investors anticipate the operating income of the S–K Company will grow and are willing to pay 10 times earnings for the stock under the Alpha capital structure, 12 times earnings under the Beta capital structure because of the faster anticipated earnings per share growth, and 9 times and 7 times earnings per share under the Gamma and Delta capital structures, respectively, because of the large amounts of leverage. The interest costs for debt now are 5, 6, and 7 percent, respectively, for the Beta, Gamma, and Delta capital structures. At a level of operating income of $20 the market price of the stock and the total market value of the firm under the different capital structures are as appears in Table 15–11.

The table expresses in numerical form the earlier suggestion that the introduction of some amount of low-cost debt can increase the overall market value of the firm.

TABLE 15–11. The S–K Company
The Impact of Varying Degrees of Leverage on Market Values

| | Capital structures | | | |
|---|---|---|---|---|
| | Alpha | Beta | Gamma | Delta |
| Operating income | $ 20.00 | $ 20.00 | $ 20.00 | $ 20.00 |
| Bond interest | $ 0.00 | $ 2.50 | $ 6.00 | $ 10.50 |
| Common earnings | $ 20.00 | $ 17.50 | $ 14.00 | $ 9.50 |
| Number of shares | 20 | 15 | 10 | 5 |
| Earnings per share | $ 1.00 | $ 1.17 | $ 1.40 | $ 1.90 |
| Price-earnings ratio | 10 | 12 | 9 | 7 |
| Market price per share | $ 10.00 | $ 14.04 | $ 12.60 | $ 13.30 |
| Market value of total equity | $200.00 | $210.60 | $126.00 | $ 66.50 |
| Market value of bonds | $ 0.00 | $ 50.00 | $100.00 | $150.00 |
| Market value of total firm | $200.00 | $260.60 | $226.00 | $216.50 |

The introduction of debt causes the firm to move to a higher risk class. With the firm operating under conditions of favorable leverage, the earnings per share may rise more than the price-earnings ratio falls due to the increased risk, so that on balance the market price per share and the value of the firm go up. However this does not happen in going from Beta structure to Gamma in Table 15–11. Further, if the rate of growth is sufficiently enhanced, the price-earnings ratio may actually rise (despite the added debt) as appears in going from Alpha structure to Beta in Table 15–11.

Consider the following example. Turmaline, Inc., with no debt in its capital structure, is currently paying $1 per share dividend (with 100 percent payout), which is expected to grow at the rate of 5 percent per year; its stock is selling at $20 per share. Its cost of equity $k_e$ is

$$k_e = \frac{D}{P} + g$$

$$10\% = \frac{\$1}{\$20} + 5\%$$

Turmaline now introduces some debt into its capital structure. As a result of the added risk the cost of equity moves to 11 percent. But the increased earnings and dividends resulting from the favorable leverage and the stepped-up growth rate of 6 percent more than offset the added risk, so that the market price of the common actually rises.

$$k_e = \frac{D}{P} + g$$

$$11\% = \frac{\$1.10}{\$22} + 6\%$$

Again, higher growth will not reduce the cost of capital, but it will raise the price-earnings ratio, and if on balance the earnings rise faster than the cost of capital is increased by the added risk, the overall value of the firm will be increased. In this example, we assume the price-earnings ratio does not change.

In the S–K Company example the ultraconservative all-common stock capital structure yielded a market price per share of only $10 and a total market value for the firm of $200. With the introduction of low-cost debt to the extent of 25 percent of the capital structure, the market value per share rose to $14.04 and the total market value of the firm rose to $260.60. As increasing amounts of debt are added, both the market price per share and total market value of the firm decline. This is caused by the higher interest rates demanded by lenders and the lower price-earnings ratios investors are willing to pay for the shares. This illustration suggests that the total market value of the firm as a function of percent of debt in the capital structures is inverted saucer-shaped, with the total market value of the firm low at the extremes of all equity and heavy debt financing, and higher with moderate prior-claim financing, as appears in Figure 15–2.

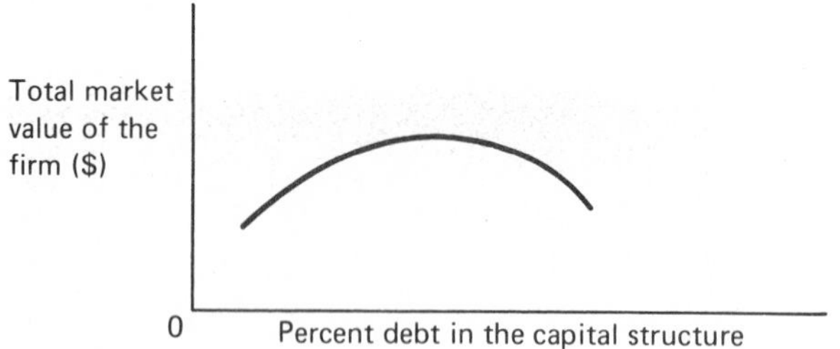


Figure 15–2 Total market value of the firm; possible curve.

The weighted marginal cost of capital, on the other hand, would be saucer-shaped, as in Figure 15–3. The highest cost of capital would be at the extreme of an all-common stock capital structure and heavy debt financing. Common stock normally carries the highest cost of capital. The initial introduction of much lower-cost debt will result in the cost of equity rising more slowly than the cheaper debt is pushing down the overall cost of capital. The net effect is to reduce the overall cost of capital. As we expand debt, however, the equity cost rises faster than more expensive debt can push down the overall cost of capital. At this point the subsequent introduction of additional debt will cause the overall cost of capital to rise. This pattern demonstrates that every time a company borrows it "uses up" a piece of its equity base. Thus the opportunity cost of debt is greater than appears in any computation of weighted marginal cost of capital.

We now push our analysis to the limit. The traditional view, reflected in Figure 15–3 holds that when debt is substituted for existing equity the marginal cost of capital first falls and then rises; the curve is U-shaped. But when the aggregate of debt *and* equity is changed it is more proper to speak of a new curve, as illustrated in Figure 15–3. For a particular weighted cost-of-capital curve such as (1) total capital remains constant. The marginal cost of capital will change along this particular curve as the percentage of debt in the capital structure is changed.

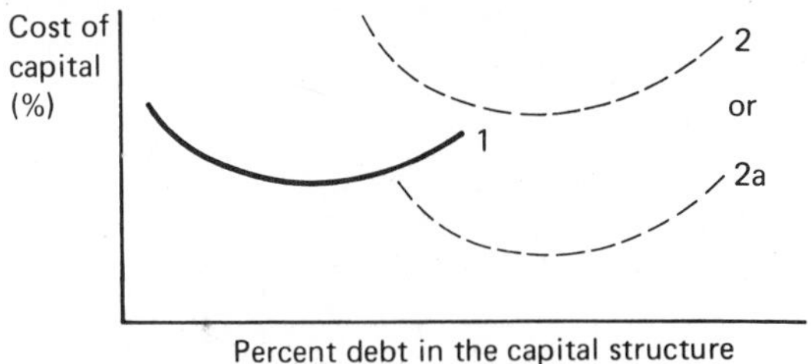


Figure 15–3 Marginal cost of capital curves.

When the size of the total capital structure, namely, debt plus equity, is changed, then the marginal cost-of-capital curve will most likely shift either up or down to positions (2) or (2a). When the size of the total capital structure is changed, the firm shifts to a new debt-acquiring position. The question at this point is, what will determine whether the new curve is higher or lower than the old curve? The answer depends on whether the firm's total capital structure is approaching or moving away from what the investment community considers the ideal level of *business risk* for a firm in that particular industry. If by changing the size of the capital structure the firm moves away from what the investment community considers the ideal business risk position for a firm in that particular industry, the marginal cost-of-capital curve will shift upward, and conversely if the change is favorable. Hence there is not only an optimal debt-equity ratio but also an optimal size of capital structure for a business operating in a particular industry.

### An Illustration of Optimal Debt-Equity Ratio

Continuing our S–K Company example of Table 15–11 when operating earnings remain at $20, of the four possible cases presented the Beta capital structure is the best. But what if earnings are to grow at 10 percent per year on the base of $20? We can see if we project into the future that leverage higher than Beta will pay off handsomely. If the firm bears the risk successfully, it will have earned large profits, can use the income to pay off some debt, and will have achieved the twin goals of high profitability and conservative financing. In other words, stepping into a high risk situation does not mean that the firm will forever after be locked into that position. From the initial point events can either take a bad turn, in which case the firm will find itself in serious difficulty, or things can turn out favorably, with the firm generating larger earnings that can be used to neutralize the risk. Taking a higher risk in the immediate future is warranted because the margin of error in forecasting the immediate future is less than that in forecasting more remote events.

From Table 15–12 we can see how under conditions of favorable income it would be possible over time to reduce a high-risk situation to one of moderate or even minor risk, having in the meantime generated exceptionally large profits. For the sake of brevity let us use EPS for earnings per share, MPPS for market price per share, MVE for market value of equity, and MVF for market value of the firm. In Table 15–12, the same assumptions are made as in Table 15–11 namely, price-earnings ratios of 10, 12, 9, and 7 for capital structures Alpha, Beta, Gamma, and Delta, number of shares outstanding as 20, 15, 10, and 5, respectively. Similarly the debt cost is 5, 6, and 7 percent for capital structures Beta, Gamma, and Delta with debt of 25 percent, 50 percent and 75 percent, respectively. Alpha has no debt.

TABLE 15–12. The S–K Company

Leverage and the Reduction of Risk under a Growing Stream of Operating Income

| | Operating Income | | | |
|---|---|---|---|---|
| | $20.00 | $22.00 | $26.00 | $30.00 |
| *Alpha* | | | | |
| EPS | $ 1.00 | $ 1.10 | $ 1.30 | $ 1.50 |
| MPPS | 10.00 | 11.00 | 13.00 | 15.00 |
| MVE | 200.00 | 220.00 | 260.00 | 300.00 |
| MVF | 200.00 | 220.00 | 260.00 | 300.00 |
| *Beta* | | | | |
| EPS | 1.17 | 1.30 | 1.57 | 1.83 |
| MPPS | 14.04 | 15.60 | 18.84 | 21.96 |
| MVE | 210.60 | 234.00 | 282.60 | 329.40 |
| MVF | 260.60 | 284.00 | 332.00 | 379.40 |
| *Gamma* | | | | |
| EPS | 1.40 | 1.60 | 2.00 | 2.40 |
| MPPS | 12.60 | 14.40 | 18.00 | 21.60 |
| MVE | 126.00 | 144.00 | 180.00 | 216.00 |
| MVF | 226.00 | 244.00 | 280.00 | 316.00 |
| *Delta* | | | | |
| EPS | 1.90 | 2.30 | 3.10 | 3.90 |
| MPPS | 13.30 | 16.10 | 21.70 | 27.30 |
| MVE | 66.50 | 80.50 | 108.50 | 136.50 |
| MVF | 216.50 | 230.50 | 258.50 | 286.50 |

A study of Table 15–12 indicates, as expected, that with operating income rising, *earnings per share* will rise for the higher leverage capital structure; the earnings will rise more than enough to offset the lower price-earnings ratio. If we compare the Beta and Delta capital structures we see that after the operating income hits $22, the market price per share ($16.10) under the Delta capital structure exceeds that under the Beta capital structure ($15.60). However, 75 percent debt, except for an electric utility, is excessive. Under the more reasonable capital structure Gamma, at the level of $30 operating income, the market price is less ($21.60) than under the Beta capital structure ($21.96). The point here is that the price-earnings ratio is an important and powerful aspect of the price of a stock, and in the case we have postulated a substantial rise in operating income is required to compensate for the fall in price-earnings ratio of 12 (Beta) to 9 (Gamma).

We should remember that while the price-earnings ratio is the result of dividing market price by earnings, investors in the market place handle the ratio as if it were an active force and not a resultant. Thus if investors consider the price-earnings ratio of a given stock too low, they will apply a higher ratio that they think appropriate and gradually bid the stock up to the price indicated by this higher ratio.

If the S–K Company elects, say, to assume a 50 percent debt structure (the Gamma case) and if through the skillful reinvestment of retained earnings pushes its earnings per share up to \$2.40 from \$1.40 and then employs perhaps \$1.40 per share, or \$14 total each year, to retire its debt, it would take but a few years to bring the debt ratio down to a conservative level.

In a static situation, the optimum debt position would be at the point where the price-earnings ratio begins to fall faster than the earnings per share are rising from the introduction of additional debt. This situation is illustrated in Figure 15–4. Given a certain level of operating income, the price-earnings ratio (PER) may rise or fall as the first debt is introduced, reflecting the desire of the investing community to see the management use some debt financing or none. When this is the case the ratio will trace a path somewhere in the shaded area *bcd* and market price per share (MPPS) would trace a path somewhere in the shaded area *fhg*. At *a* the price-earnings ratio would begin to turn down sharply, more than offsetting the rise in earnings per share, and market price would fall.[18] This would be the case for a static situation in which we postulate a fairly steady income level, and changes in the price-earnings ratio and in earnings per share are reflections of the proportion of debt in the capital structures.

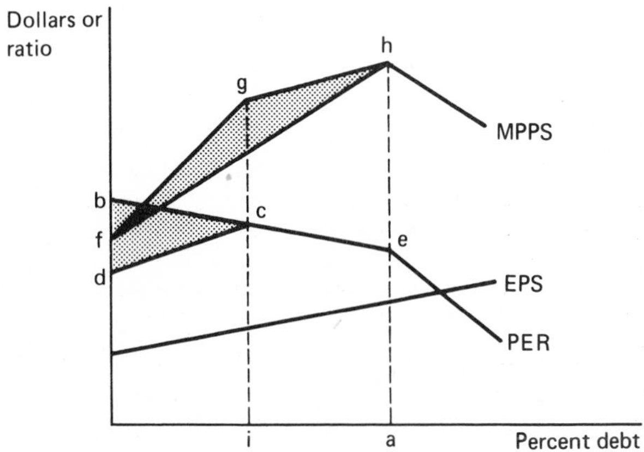


Figure 15–4 Leverage, earnings per share, and the price-earnings ratio in a stable situation.

[18] Because of the phenomenon examined in connection with Figure 15–1 earlier in this chapter, the "turning points" (*a*) and (*i*) of the MPPS curve need not be directly above those of the PER curve. The exact relationship of these two points depends on the slopes of the PER and EPS curves. This same comment is true for Figure 15–5.

The price-earnings ratio of a growth stock is normally at a high level because of the anticipated growth in earnings and dividends. The introduction of leverage increases the rate of growth in earnings per share and dividends, as appears in Figure 15–5. Hence, at least up to some point (*b* in Figure 15–5) every increase in debt causes an increase in earnings and dividends such that the price-earnings ratio rises. After this point is reached the ratio will begin to fall gently because the increased financial risk more than offsets the increased earnings per share. Then as added debt substantially increases the financial risk, the price-earnings ratio falls sharply.

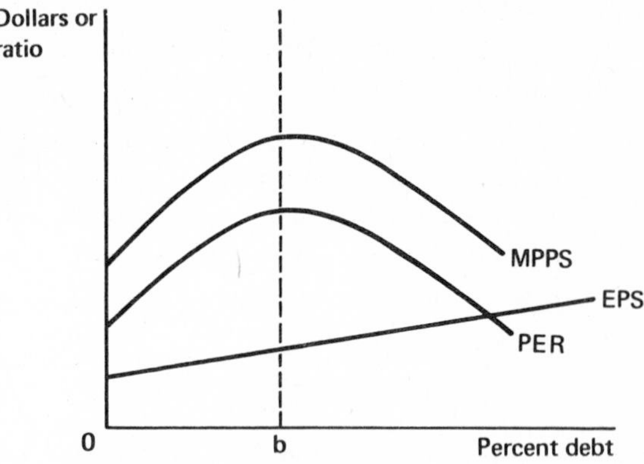


Figure 15–5 Leverage, earnings per share, and the price-earnings ratio in a growth situation.

The financial manager will have difficulty in setting the exact inflection points on the MPPS and PER curves, but insights may be obtained into the relationships we have here sketched by observing the practices of other companies and the market performance of their stock and studying the effects of the debt-financing.

### Measures of the Debt-to-Equity Relationship

Several ratios exist for measuring the proportion of debt in the capital structure. The one most frequently encountered expresses the ratio of long-term debt to total equity (preferred, common stock, and surplus). If the amount of debt exceeds the equity, the index will be greater than 1; if it does not, it will be less than 1. Another widely used ratio expresses long-term debt as a percentage of the total capital structure, that is, long-term debt plus equity. Short-term debt is frequently excluded from these calculations, though it also provides a leverage effect. Current liabilities in a large firm frequently represent only a small percentage of the total financing sources and to include them would not significantly affect the index. Firms in the wholesale and retail trade fields are an exception. A larger portion of their capital needs is financed with current debt because of seasonal sales fluctuations. For a medium or small firm, short-term debt often represents a major financing source and should be included in calculating the debt-to-equity relationship.

Inclusion of preferred stock with the common stock when measuring the safety cushion for outstanding debt is proper. All stock is junior to creditors in its claims to income and assets upon liquidation. The fixed dividend provision of preferred stock creates leverage, though usually not as much as debt, since the amount of leverage depends on the amount of prior claims and the spread between the rate being paid and the rate earned on the assets. The spread is narrower for preferred stock than it is for debt and preferred dividends are not tax deductible while interest is. Further, preferred stock carries a cumulative dividend provision. Failure to pay preferred dividends will result in arrearages, depressing the market price of all of the firm's oustanding securities. Thus the bondholders would be affected by preferred arrearage as would the common stock. If the firm needs additional equity when the market price of its common is unduly depressed, the raising of equity funds would be possible only on very unfavorable terms and all security holders would suffer.

Leasing also creates creditor obligations and introduces leverage into the capital structure. Consequently, leases must be considered even though not on the balance sheet. There is no principal value of a lease obligation. The lease provides merely for the regular payment of rentals and at the end of the term the premises may be purchased, a new lease drawn up, or the premises vacated. But a principal value for the lease may be imputed. This may be done by capitalizing the lease rental payments at an appropriate rate. For example, if a firm has $2 million of debt outstanding and $8 million of equity at book value, debt would constitute 20 percent of the capital structure. But the firm may lease part of its property on a *long-term basis* and make rental payments of $100,000 per year. Capitalizing these payments at 5 percent, we get an imputed principal value for the lease of $2 million.[19] Adding this imputed value to the outstanding debt, we get a somewhat different picture. Debt becomes 33 percent of the capital structure.[20] The failure of the lessee to meet one of the promises in the lease is an act of default and the lessor can force liquidation or reorganization.[21] But there is one great difference: debt has a principal amount due at maturity; a lease does not. Hence many analysts include the lease payment in tests of fixed charge coverage but do not include the imputed value of the lease for debt-equity computations.

The debt-to-equity relationship is most frequently calculated taking the common equity at book value rather than at market value. Creditors look to earnings for the payment of interest, but when earnings fail they look to assets to meet their claims on liquidation. When the price level has risen for a long time, historical cost figures for assets carry some protection because they represent the price paid years ago for the assets. For prosperous firms able to earn a generous return on their assets, us-

---

19 Note the lease is "on a long-term basis." Capitalizing the annual rental payments at some selected rate has the effect of discounting these rentals to infinity. If the lease is fairly short—as is the case in most industrial leases as compared to railroad leases—the equivalent debts created by the lease may be found by discounting the annual rental payments for the period of the lease to their present value.

20 Some lenders add the imputed lease value to both the firm's assets and liabilities in making their analyses.

21 The failure to meet lease payments involves somewhat different remedies for the lessor than an interest default as was explained in Chapter 13.

ing book values of equity may present too restricted a view of the debt-carrying capacity of the firm.

**Fixed Charge Coverage Test**

This test is sometimes called "times interest earned." It is more important than the debt-equity ratio because default usually occurs first in current payments due. Correctly computed, it is the ratio of earnings before fixed charges (primarily interest *and* lease payments) *and* income taxes to fixed charges.[22]

There also is the ratio times fixed charges and capital payments earned. Loan repayments are included in the denominator, particularly when scheduled on an annual basis. This ratio reflects the fact that a financial payment due is an obligation whether in the form of interest or principal and is more important when there are several lenders, since a default in principal repayment to one lender jeopardizes the other lenders the same as an interest default. Relating earnings available to service debt to the actual debt requirements over a period longer than a year generates information on the adequacy of earnings under various economic conditions. The more volatile the income fluctuations, the higher the coverage ratio must be. Interest charges must be covered at a minimum at least several times. Additional debt financing will prove difficult if after such financing the margin of safety fails to protect against such decline in earnings as can reasonably be anticipated. Debt financing, even if available, may prove risky for the firm. In the event of a sharp and prolonged decline in earnings, the common shareholders could lose their ownership position in reorganization or bankruptcy.

The larger the times fixed charges earned and the smaller the debt-to-equity ratio, the less financial risk embodied in the firm. An aggressive financial manager will not be content with safe ratios—the safest would be no fixed charge obligations—but will use debt intelligently to lift the per share earnings of the common stock without materially reducing the price-earnings ratio.

Appropriate debt limits vary among industries, over time, and from creditor to creditor. Stable and predictable industries such as electric utilities have a substantially greater debt-carrying capacity than firms, say, in the machine tool industry.

During periods of buoyant economic conditions creditors and owners alike are more optimistic and willing to go further down the debt path than during quieter periods. Further, financial institutions specializing in lending to particular industries may conclude that the debt limits of these firms can be pushed substantially further than other financial institutions lending to a wide variety of industries might feel possible.

Table 15–13 gives the 1969 debt-to-equity ratio and times interest charges earned for selected industries. Note the low total debt-to-equity ratios in mining (0.83) and manufacturing (0.91) and the high times

[22] Pretax computation has the merit of eliminating the effect of changes in income tax rates over time and the effect of acquiring another company with accrued losses that can be used to improve the future after-tax earnings of the acquiring company.

interest earned (6.95 and 5.38) ratios. These industries also exhibit a low long-term debt-to-equity ratio 0.44 and 0.42. Construction, generally regarded as a high-risk industry, shows a substantial long-term debt-to-equity ratio (0.93) but reveals a much higher total debt-to-equity relationship (2.63) because firms in this industry are typically highly leveraged with *current* debt. The times interest charges earned is low (4.28). Total utilities show a large amount of long-term debt-to-equity (1.00) and a relatively low times interest charges earned ratio (2.85). Utility companies, being typically stable in nature, are in a position to carry a large long-term debt burden, and the investment community does not require a large coverage.

These 1969 averages can be compared to recommended standards that industrials should earn their fixed charges before taxes on the average of 7 times, retail firms 5 times, and public utilities 4 times.[23] Bonds that meet high coverage standards relative to the industry group to which the firm belongs are judged to be of the best quality. Bonds that have a lower coverage ratio, a higher debt-to-equity ratio, and a weaker working capital position are judged of lesser quality and must offer higher yields.

TABLE 15–13. Relationship of Debt to Equity and Times Interest Charges Earned for Selected Industries in 1969

| | Agriculture, forestry, and fisheries | Total mining | Construction | Total manufacturing | Total utilities | Total wholesale trade | Total retail trade | Total services |
|---|---|---|---|---|---|---|---|---|
| Total debt to equity | 1.61 | 0.83 | 2.63 | 0.91 | 1.31 | 1.52 | 1.41 | 2.08 |
| Long-term debt * to equity | 0.70 | 0.44 | 0.93 | 0.42 | 1.00 | 0.38 | 0.48 | 1.17 |
| Times interest charges earned † | 2.24 X | 6.95 X | 4.28 X | 5.38 X | 2.85 X | 4.20 X | 3.82 X | 2.86 X |

* Bonds, notes, and mortgages maturing in one year or more and other liabilities and loans from shareholders.

† Earnings before interest and taxes to interest.

SOURCE: U.S. Treasury Department, Internal Revenue Service, Statistics of Income, 1969. Corporation Income Tax Returns (Washington, D.C.: Government Printing Office, 1973), Table 2, pp. 14 ff.

## Dividend Policy and the Cost of Equity Capital

The effect of dividend policy on the price of a firm's stock and thus on its cost of equity is of major importance to the financial manager. What we would like to know is whether by changing the dividend payout we can reduce the cost of capital—that is, change the value of shares with the same earnings stream by changing the mix between retention and payout.

Clearly, since we have set for ourselves the goal of maximizing shareholder wealth, we are interested in determining whether there exists an optimum payout ratio that maximizes the market price of a firm's shares, and if so, under what conditions such an optimum exists. These questions are not new, and much research has been devoted to finding definitive answers to them. Many views have been offered and the is-

[23] See Benjamin Graham, David L. Dodd, and Sidney Cottle, *Security Analysis*, 4th ed. (New York: McGraw-Hill Book Company, Inc., 1962), p. 373. Compare Cohen and Zinbarg, p. 373.

sues are still being debated. In Chapter 16 and Appendix O we will pursue these questions.

## SUMMARY

The appropriate capital budgeting hurdle rate is the weighted marginal cost of capital. In Chapter 4 we discussed return on investment; the present chapter is devoted to measuring the cost of capital—debt, preferred and common stock, depreciation, and retained earnings—and to determining the optimum capital structure so as to minimize the overall cost of capital. Consideration of the relation of the dividend payout ratio to the cost of capital is deferred to Chapter 16.

Risk is generally avoided by investors unless properly compensated. Bonds as a class carry less risk than preferred stock and the latter carry less risk than common stock. The qualitative factors influencing the cost of funds include business risk, financial risk, purchasing power risk, money rate risk, and market risk.

The cost of debt (before income tax) is the ratio of the interest cost, taking into consideration any premium or discount and flotation costs, to the debt funds currently obtainable. The cost of noncallable preferred stock is measured by the ratio of the preferred dividend to the market price of the preferred stock less flotation costs.

The measurement of the cost of common stock is more difficult and is determined by the pure rate of interest and the risk class to which the firm belongs. We measure cost of the common stock by dividing the current dividend by the market price, and adding the estimated dividend growth rate.

Growth is an important factor in determining the market price of a stock and, consequently, directly influences the price-earnings ratio. Risk affects both the cost of capital and the price-earnings ratio; growth directly influences only the price-earnings ratio.

Depending upon the elasticity of the price-earnings ratio, the market price of a stock may rise or fall if a firm adopts projects that promise a rate of return above the cost of capital but below the present return on assets.

The cost of retained earnings is measured by the rate of return investors can earn on the funds when invested in comparable risks if paid out in dividends, their marginal tax rate, and the brokerage fees. The difficult estimates needed to determine the cost of capital of retained earnings are avoided by substituting the cost of common equity.

The proper hurdle rate is the weighted marginal cost of capital. A slowly growing firm might use book value weights in determining its cost of capital because book value is close to market value. Rapidly growing firms with high price-earnings ratios must calculate the cost of capital based on market value weights to avoid underestimating the cost of capital.

Leverage is a key factor in determining the optimum debt-to-equity mix. The marginal cost of capital curve is saucer-shaped, first falling as debt is increased and then rising. The curve will shift upward or downward if the total of debt and equity is changed. When the firm undertakes such action it moves to a different borrowing plane. The cost of capital curve will shift upward or downward depending upon whether the firm is moving toward or away from the ideal business risk position in the industry.

The introduction of increasing amounts of debt will push earnings per share upward. With the introduction of increasing amounts of debt the price-earnings ratio may either start to fall immediately, reflecting the rising risk from the increasing amounts of debt, or may actually rise, reflecting the investment community's favorable reaction to seeing some debt in the capital structure. In either event, at first the market price per share will rise as earnings per share are rising and after some point will fall as the price-earnings ratio falls faster than the earnings per share are rising. The turning point of the market price per share curve represents the optimum percentage of debt in that capital structure.

### Study Questions

1. It is argued that prior claims are exposed only to the money rate and purchasing power risks and that common stock is exposed only to the business and financial risk? Do you agree? Explain.
2. Would you agree that the hurdle rate in capital budgeting should be the cost of capital? Why?
3. Can it be said that any part of the funds used by a firm is free? Explain.
4. Can the historical interest rate on outstanding bonds of the issuer be used to get the cost of debt capital for current capital budgeting decisions?
5. Would you agree that the cost of common equity is the reciprocal of the price-earnings ratio? What is the reasoning behind your answer?
6. Does dilution occur when more common shares are sold by a firm?
7. Do you agree that the price-earnings ratio will fall when an all-equity company accepts new projects with a rate of return on assets below that presently enjoyed by the company on its assets?
8. If a company knows that its future investment opportunities will be less rewarding than its recent record but the market place does not know this, would you advise the company to sell common stock at the present time?
9. How would you reconcile the statement that earnings determine the price of of a stock with the statement that dividends determine the price?
10. A company's growth rate will depend on the proportion of annual earnings together with depreciation that is reinvested and the earnings realized on these funds if no common stock is sold. Do you think this is a complete statement?
11. If financial risk did not exist, the optimal capital structure would include a minimum of common equity. Do you agree?
12. As a company increases its ratio of debt in the capital structure, it is argued that we can measure the cost of this debt by the change in the weighted marginal cost of capital. Do you agree?
13. Most discussions about an optimal debt-to-equity ratio assume that one (or some) variable(s) is fixed. What do you consider such variable(s) to be and what importance attaches to this?

14. In applying the times interest charges earned test would you use the most recent year's income data or would you use the lowest income year in the preceding 5 or 10 years?

15. The debt-to-equity ratio is not nearly as meaningful as the fixed charge coverage test because the ratio is computed on the basis of book value. Do you agree?

## Problems

1. No-no, Inc. sold $1000, 5 percent coupon bonds carrying no maturity date to the public several years ago at par. Interest rates have since risen, so that bonds of the quality represented by this firm are now selling on a 7 percent yield basis.

a. Compute the current indicated market price of the bonds (ignoring the capital gains tax).

b. Because of market imperfections the bonds of No-no are selling at $800. If the bonds have 10 years to run to maturity, compute the approximate effective yield an investor would earn on his investment (ignoring the capital gains tax).

c. The investment outlook for No-no, brightens so that the bonds are bid up to sell on a 5 percent yield basis. What is the current market price for the bonds?

2. The $7 noncallable preferred stock of F133, Inc. is selling to yield investors a 6 percent return on their money.

a. Compute the current indicated market price of the preferred stock.

b. Assume the $7 preferred stock of F133, which is of 6 percent yield quality, is callable at 110. Estimate the market price of the preferred and the indicated yield.

c. Why might F133 be reluctant to refinance its outstanding preferred if the situation were as in (a) above but anxious to refinance if the situation were as in (b) above?

3. The stock of Jumbo, Inc. is currently selling at $30 per share. The firm is paying $1 per share dividend annually and the investment community expects a growth rate of approximately 5 percent per year.

a. Compute the firm's indicated equity cost of capital.

b. Compute the indicated market price of the stock if the anticipated growth rate of the firm were to rise to 6 percent.

c. Compute the indicated market price of the stock if the firm's cost of capital were 9 percent, the anticipated growth rate 5 percent, and a $1 per share dividend were being paid annually.

4. a. It is dividend time. The management of Sweetie is considering a dividend distribution of $100,000. The stockholders are in the 60 percent marginal tax bracket and incur a brokerage fee of an average of 2 percent on the reinvestment of any dividends received. The stockholders are able to earn 10 percent on their investments, and the firm has one last capital budgeting project on which it can earn a 7 percent return. Management is uncertain whether to pay the dividend or approve the marginal capital budgeting project. Provide management with the answer and the necessary supporting information.

b. Assume that the stockholders are in the 40 percent tax bracket and are interested only in capital gains. As soon as six months have passed they sell their shares. Given this cause of investment behavior and that the dividend will not affect the stock price would it be advisable for Sweetie to declare the $100,000 extra dividend. The capital gains tax rate is half the regular rate.

5. Go-go, Inc., a recently organized drug company, has been launched with the capital structure shown in Table 15–14.

TABLE 15–14. Go-go, Inc.

| Assets | Liabilities and Net Worth | |
|---|---|---|
| | $ 200,000 | 6 percent, 20-year debentures |
| $1,000,000 | 300,000 | 7 percent preferred stock |
| | 500,000 | 50,000 shares of common stock |
| $1,000,000 | $1,000,000 | |

The investment community estimates that the firm will earn $50,000 annually after taxes but before preferred dividends and pay dividends of $25,000 on common. It is anticipated that dividends will grow at the rate of 5 percent per year. The stock was sold at $10 per share net to the company and is currently trading in the market at $10. The firm's marginal tax rate is 50 percent.

a. Compute the price-earnings ratio based on the anticipated earnings.

b. Compute the common dividend yield based on the $25,000 of dividends.

c. Compute the firm's weighted after-tax cost of capital using market-value weights if the bonds and preferred are selling at par.

6. Go-go is an instant success. Earnings and dividends grow rapidly. The market price rises. After several years of operation the firm is earning $100,000 annually after taxes but before preferred dividends, and paying out $50,000 in common dividends. The market price of the common stock is $100 per share and the book value is $20 per share. Stockholders' marginal tax rate is 40 percent and brokerage cost is 2 percent.

a. Compute the price-earnings ratio of the common stock based on current earnings.

b. Compute the dividend yield of the common based on the current dividend.

c. The firm's common stock cost of capital remains at 10 percent. Compute the anticipated growth rate.

d. Compute the firm's weighted after-tax cost of capital based on book value. Assume the bonds and preferred stock are selling at par.

e. Compute the firm's weighted after-tax cost of capital based on market value. Assume the bonds and preferred stock are selling at par.

f. How do you explain the higher weighted cost of capital when based on market value as compared to the calculation based on book value? What would you expect if the market price were below book value?

7. Go-go is planning to raise an additional $1 million of capital. Bonds to be sold on a 6 percent net yield basis to the company and common stock to be sold at $100 per share net to the company are the alternatives being considered. The firm is currently paying $1 per share dividend. The expansion is expected to carry the firm into a new, higher risk area. Both management and the investment community estimate the firm's cost of common stock will be 20 percent.

a. Compute the growth rate of the firm which the market is anticipating.

b. Management is anticipating a 19.2 percent growth rate. On this basis, at what price should the stock be selling?

c. Given the findings in (a) and (b) above, would you advise Go-go to sell bonds or common stock? Explain your answer.

d. Assume now that management is anticipating a growth rate of only 10 percent per year. What form of financing would you recommend?

8. The capital structure of Mr. Chips, Inc., on the eve of a major expansion program to be financed by the sale of new securities is as follows:

| | |
|---|---|
| First mortgage bonds, 5s of 79 | $1,000,000 |
| Debentures, 5½s of 88 | 2,000,000 |
| Preferred stock 6 percent | 3,000,000 |
| Common stock (100,000 shares) | 1,000,000 |
| Retained earnings | 3,000,000 |
| Total capital structure | $10,000,000 |

The first mortgage bonds were sold in 1955 at 101. The firm netted 100. The bonds are currently selling in the market below par. Investment bankers estimate that a comparable new issue could currently be brought out with a 5¾ percent coupon at a price of 100 net to the firm.

The debentures were sold in 1963 at 102 and the firm netted 100. The bonds are currently selling on the market substantially below par. The investment bankers estimate a comparable new issue could currently be brought out with a 6½ percent coupon at a price of 100 net to the firm.

The preferred stock was originally sold at $107 and the firm netted $100, the par value. Comparable issues are currently selling at $87. The costs incurred in bringing out a new issue would be the same as those incurred on the previous issue.

The common stock is earning $2.40 per share, paying a $1.20 dividend, and selling at 28 times earnings. The firm has historically paid out 50 percent of its earnings in dividends and plans to continue this policy. The market estimates that the earnings of the firm will grow at the rate of 10 percent per year. Underwriting and other costs associated with bringing out a new issue of common stock are expected to total $7.20 per share and are not tax deductible. The firm is in the 50 percent tax bracket. Compute the weighted after-tax cost of capital using market value weights.

### Selected References


Arditti, F. D., "The Weighted Average Cost of Capital: Some Questions on Its Definition, Interpretation and Use," *Journal of Finance*, 28 (September 1973), pp. 1001–08.

Barges, A., *The Effect of Capital Structure on the Cost of Capital.* Englewood Cliffs, N. J.: Prentice-Hall, Inc., 1963.

Baxter, N. D., "Leverage, Risk of Ruin and the Cost of Capital," *Journal of Finance* 22 (September 1967), pp. 395–404.

Beranek, W., *The Effects of Leverage on the Market Value of Common Stocks.* Madison, Wisc.: University of Wisconsin School of Commerce, 1964.

Breen, W. J. and E. M. Lerner, "Corporate Financial Strategies and Market Measures of Risk and Return," *Journal of Finance*, 28 (May 1973), pp. 339–352.

Brigham, Eugene F., and M. J. Gordon, "Leverage, Dividend Policy and the Cost of Capital," *Journal of Finance*, 23 (March 1968), pp. 85–103.

Cragg, J. G., and B. G. Malkiel, "The Consensus and Accuracy of Some Predictions of the Growth of Corporate Earnings," *Journal of Finance,* 23 (March 1968), pp. 67–84.

Durand, D., "Growth Stocks and the Petersburg Paradox," *Journal of Finance,* 12 (September 1957), pp. 348–363.

Elton, E. J., and M. J. Gruber, "The Effect of Share Repurchases on the Value of the Firm," *Journal of Finance* 23 (March 1968), pp. 135–149.

Fisher, I., *The Theory of Interest.* New York: The Macmillan Company, 1930.

Haley, C. W., "Taxes, the Cost of Capital, and the Firm's Investment Decisions," *Journal of Finance,* 20 (September 1971), pp. 901–917.

Kessel, R. A., "Inflation-Caused Wealth Redistribution: A Test of a Hypothesis," *American Economic Review,* 46 (March 1956), pp. 128–141.

Lange, O., "The Rate of Interest and the Optimum Propensity to Consume," *Economica* (New Series), 5 (February 1938), pp. 12–32. Reprinted in American Economic Association, *Readings in Business Cycle Theory.* Homewood, Ill.: Richard D. Irwin, Inc., 1951, pp. 169–192.

Lerner, E. M., and W. T. Carleton, *A Theory of Financial Analysis.* New York: Harcourt, Brace & Jovanovich, Inc., 1966.

Lewellen, W. G., *The Cost of Capital.* Belmont, Calif.: Wadsworth Publishing Co., Inc., 1969.

Lintner, John, "The Cost of Capital and Optimal Financing of Corporate Growth," *Journal of Finance,* 18 (May 1963), pp. 292–310.

Modigliani, F., and M. Miller, "The Cost of Capital, Corporation Finance, and the Theory of Investment," *American Economic Review,* 48 (June 1958), pp. 261–296.

———, "Dividend Policy, Growth and the Valuation of Shares," *Journal of Business,* 34 (October 1961), pp. 411–432.

———, "Taxes and the Cost of Capital: A Correction," *American Economic Review,* 53 (June 1963), pp. 433–444.

Porterfield, J. T. S., *Investment Decisions and Capital Costs.* Englewood Cliffs, N. J.: Prentice-Hall, Inc., 1963.

Robichek, A. A., and S. C. Myers, *Optimal Financial Decisions.* Englewood Cliffs, N. J.: Prentice-Hall, Inc., 1965.

Rubinstein, M. E., "A Mean-Variance Synthesis of Corporate Financial Theory," *Journal of Finance,* 28 (March 1973), pp. 167–181.

Schwartz, E., and J. R. Aronson, "Some Surrogate Evidence in Support of the Concept of Optimal Financial Structure," *Journal of Finance,* 22 (March 1967), pp. 10–18.

Sharpe, W. F., *Portfolio Analysis and Capital Markets.* New York: McCraw-Hill, Inc., 1970.

Solomon, E., *The Theory of Financial Management.* New York: Columbia University Press, 1963.

Stiglitz, J. E., "A Re-examination of the Modigliani-Miller Theorem," *American Economic Review* 59 (December 1969), pp. 784—793.

Vickers, D., "The Cost of Capital and the Structure of the Firm," *Journal of Finance,* 25 (March 1970), pp. 35–46.

## *Appendix M*

## THEORIES OF COST OF CAPITAL AND FINANCIAL STRUCTURE

In this chapter and preceding chapters we discussed the role of operating leverage and financial leverage and the theory of common stock valuation. These matters have relevance to the design of a financial structure for a corporation. But other factors must be considered before the final design of a financial structure can be set. Unfortunately, there is still dispute as to the role and significance of these other factors. Hence, we will consider the several proposed theories and the evidence cited by each.

The first theory we shall examine considers whether the real value and money value of assets [24] play a vital role in designing a capital structure.[25] The second theory we shall examine, which conflicts sharply with the first theory, argues that the relative use of debt and equity in the financial structure does not affect the total value of the firm except for the fact that our current environmental system favors the use of debt because of the deductibility of interest payments for income tax purposes and the nondeductibility of dividend payments. The third theory we shall examine concerns the role of the dividend payout ratio (dividends/earnings) in the value of a firm. This area is reserved for Appendix O, following Chapter 16.

*The Critical Phenomenon: The Price-Earnings Ratio.* The value of the firm depends heavily on the price-earnings ratio (or the earnings-price ratio, which can be called the earnings yield in analogy to the dividend yield). The earnings part of this ratio is determined by the ability of management to control sales and costs to produce earnings. We are concerned particularly with the price part of that ratio.

The argument centers on whether the ratio of real to money assets affects the price-earning ratio. R. A. Kessel argues that the ratio of real to money assets does affect the price-earnings ratio over time and specifically that lenders on the average underestimate future price-level changes.

In contrast to this theory Franco Modigliani and Merton Miller argue that as the percentage of debt in the financial structure changes, the prices of the debt and the equity change so as to maintain the total value of the firm at the same level (except for the effect of the tax deductibility of interest). Specifically, it is argued that the expectations concerning future price-level changes both by stock investors and lenders and by those who do the planning for firms correctly anticipate the future.

### Monetary Debtor-Creditor Theory

Briefly stated, the monetary debtor-creditor theory argues that each business firm is, on balance, a net monetary borrower or lender depending on its ratio

---

[24] The real value of an asset may be defined as the value of the asset in terms of constant dollars (where the variation in purchasing power due to changes in the general price level of the economy has been eliminated). Money value of an asset is the value in terms of current dollars. It is apparent that one asset, namely, cash, has a constant money value, but other assets such as plant have a value that is constantly shifting in money terms even though accounting rules take no recognition of this fact.

[25] The debt-equity composition of a capital structure is, as we have seen in this chapter, an important factor in determining the cost of capital of a firm. We do not mean to imply at this point that the real or money value of assets directly influences the cost of capital; rather, this influence occurs only indirectly through influencing the capital structure.

of real to money assets.[26] Those firms that are net monetary debtors can be expected to gain in an inflation by repaying their debts with cheaper dollars.[27]

To explore this hypothesis requires that all assets and liabilities be classified as monetary or real. The classification in Table 15–15 is proposed:

TABLE 15–15. Monetary Assets and Real Assets

| Monetary assets | Monetary liabilities and ownership | Real assets | Real ownership |
|---|---|---|---|
| Cash | Accounts payable | Inventory | Common stock |
| Marketable securities | Notes payable | Fixed assets | Surplus |
| Accounts receivable | Tax liability reserve | | |
| Tax refunds receivable | Bonds | | |
| Notes receivable | Preferred stock | | |
| Prepaid insurance | | | |

There are several troublesome balance sheet accounts. The first is preferred stock. While preferred stock is legally an ownership account, it carries a fixed monetary return (except in the unusual case of participating preferred stock, which might be classified as a real account). Other difficult items are convertible bonds and convertible preferred stock.

We can then examine the net position of each firm as a monetary debtor or creditor. If the firm is a net monetary debtor, we expect the price of the firm's stock to rise during a period of inflation relative to the price level and to fall during deflation.[28]

This can be illustrated by a firm that is half debt financed and half equity financed. Then if the volume of debt and the number of shares are not changed, a doubling of the price level implies that the equity value of the firm will triple.

Test samples of stocks listed on the New York Stock Exchange indicate that the samples perform as anticipated by theory using both the period of inflation 1942–1948 and the period of deflation 1929–1933. Further, the tests perform with considerable reliability in forecasting for the period 1940–1950.

No direct consideration was given to the role of financial leverage in this analysis by Professor Kessel. Not only can a firm be a net monetary debtor or creditor but at the same time it may have high or low financial leverage. Thus the balance sheets given in Tables 15–16 and 15–17 show monetary debtors and monetary creditors with high and low financial leverage.

---

26 The original testing of this hypothesis appears in R. A. Kessel, "Inflation-Caused Wealth Redistribution: A Test of a Hypothesis," *American Economic Review*, 46 (March 1956), pp. 128–141.

27 Originally economists argued that all business firms gain during inflation on the ground that business firms are debtors and debtors gain in inflation by repaying debts with cheaper dollars. See Irving Fisher, *The Purchasing Power of Money* (New York: The Macmillan Company, 1930), pp. 56–73 and 190–191, and J. M. Keynes, *Tract on Monetary Reform* (London: The Macmillan Company, 1923), p. 18.

28 This is the exact hypothesis tested by Professor Kessel, using several samples and applying the appropriate tests of statistical significance. The price level used was the wholesale price level.

TABLE 15–16. Firms That Are Monetary Debtors

| High leverage | | | | Low leverage | | | |
|---|---|---|---|---|---|---|---|
| Cash | 10 | Payables | 20 | Cash | 10 | Payables | 10 |
| Receivables | 30 | Notes | 20 | Receivables | 10 | Notes | 10 |
| Inventory | 30 | Bonds | 20 | Inventory | 40 | Bonds | 10 |
| Fixed assets | 30 | Equity | 40 | Fixed assets | 40 | Equity | 70 |
| Totals | 100 | | 100 | Totals | 100 | | 100 |
| Monetary debtor of 20 * (60 — 40). | | | | Monetary debtor of 10 * (30 — 20). | | | |

* Following the classification in table 15–15.

TABLE 15–17. Firms That Are Monetary Creditors

| High leverage | | | | Low leverage | | | |
|---|---|---|---|---|---|---|---|
| Cash | 20 | Payables | 20 | Cash | 20 | Payables | 10 |
| Receivables | 60 | Notes | 20 | Receivables | 60 | Notes | 10 |
| Inventory | 10 | Bonds | 20 | Inventory | 10 | Bonds | 10 |
| Fixed assets | 10 | Equity | 40 | Fixed assets | 10 | Equity | 70 |
| Totals | 100 | | 100 | Totals | 100 | | 100 |
| Monetary creditor of 20 * (80 — 60). | | | | Monetary creditor of 50 * (80 — 30). | | | |

* Following the classification in table 15–15.

Although Professor Kessel did not point out directly the combination of financial leverage with the net monetary position as we have just done, he did consider its effect when he performed tests in which he ranked the sample firms by the amount of their net monetary position and the change in stock price relative to the general price level; namely, the higher the monetary debtor position, the greater the rise in stock price relative to the price level in inflation and the greater the fall in deflation. For the monetary creditor position the converse is true.

Formally recognizing the role of financial leverage in this analysis enables us to add an additional insight that was not observed by Professor Kessel. Growth companies are typically high leverage, high monetary debtors. Mature companies are typically low leverage, high monetary creditors. This is a reinforcing reason for high price-earnings ratios for growth companies. Thus not only do earnings grow faster in growth companies but the debtor position helps them in inflation.

The analysis just presented is an adequate explanation of why on the *average* the increase in a stock price barely parallels the increase in the price level. First, there are about as many net monetary creditor firms as there are net monetary debtor firms.[29] Second, leverage is increased in periods of inflation by some net debtor firms but not by others.

[29] This explains why the original position of economists (referred to in footnote 27) that all business firms gain in an inflation is not true even though the basic insight of these economists as to the effect of debt was correct.

### Theory that the Cost of Capital Is Not Affected by the Debt-Equity Ratio in the Absence of Tax Advantage of Debt

In sharp contrast to the analysis of Professor Kessel, we have the position of Professors Modigliani and Miller[30] that followed shortly after Professor Kessel's analysis but oddly enough does not bother to consider the Kessel analysis. The Modigliani-Miller hypothesis is that, in the absence of the deductibility of interest for income taxes, the cost of capital to the firm will not vary with changes in the debt-to-equity ratio.

Orthodox theory argues that as financial leverage is used the cost of capital to the firm declines up to a point as leverage is increased, and that beyond that point increased leverage drives up the cost of capital. This point of the ideal debt-to-equity ratio and its minimization of the cost of capital to the firm will vary from industry to industry and from firm to firm within an industry primarily as the amount of business risk varies. Furthermore, it is at least implied in orthodox theory that the ideal debt-to-equity ratio for a firm will vary over time with the condition of the business cycle and particularly with such factors as the long-term interest rate and the average price-earnings ratio of the market for a constant package of stocks.

The basic position of Modigliani and Miller can be further stated as follows. While both the average and marginal cost of debt vary with the amount of leverage (increasing with the increase in leverage), the cost of equity moves in complementary fashion to exactly offset the cost of debt, so that the cost of capital to the firm stays fixed for its given risk. This position abstracts from the tax advantage of debt.

Modigliani and Miller might argue that their position can be reconciled with the analysis of Kessel by the matter of the assumptions made as to the expectations of investors and lendors. If investors and lenders correctly anticipate the effect of future price-level changes, as Modigliani and Miller assume, then this factor is of no concern in their analysis. Or to put it another way, for the analysis of Kessel to have significance, he must assume that lenders underestimate the degree of future price-level changes because if lenders correctly anticipate such changes they can adjust the return they demand to allow for the changes. Kessel found his hypothesis verified by the evidence.

In the following summary of the theory of Modigliani and Miller we adhere to the nomenclature they use so that the reader can pursue further study without the inconvenience of shifting symbols.

There are two main propositions in the theory of Modigliani and Miller. The first is concerned with net operating income[31] and establishes the value of a firm by capitalizing net operating income, which is taken to be the combined earnings of the debt and equity of the firm. This is simply stated as:

$$V_i = (S_i + D_i) = \bar{\mathbf{x}}_i \rho_k$$

where

$V_i$ = market value of all the firm's securities (debt and equity) or the market value of the firm

[30] Franco Modigliani and Merton Miller, "The Cost of Capital, Corporation Finance, and the Theory of Investment," *American Economic Review*, 48 (June 1958), pp. 261–296, and "Taxes and the Cost of Capital: A Correction," *American Economic Review*, 53 (June 1963), pp. 433–443.

[31] This proposition was previously established by David Durand, "Costs of Debt and Equity Funds for Business: Trends and Problems of Measurements," in National Bureau of Economic Research, *Conference on Research in Business Finance* (New York: National Bureau of Economic Research, 1952), pp. 215–247.

$S_i$ = market value of the common stock of the firm

$D_i$ = market value of the debt of the firm

$\bar{\mathbf{x}}_i$ = expected return on the firm's assets before income taxes: its net operating income

$\rho_k$ = capitalization rate appropriate to the risk of the firm

The argument is that as long as the relation of this equation does not hold for any pair of firms of the same risk, "arbitrage" will occur to restore the equality stated by the proposition. Thus a firm with higher leverage (but the same net operating income) would find its equity bid up in the market place, but its investors would sell those shares to gain shares of the unleveraged firm. And by borrowing for their personal account to do so they would gain the same leverage that they previously enjoyed when owning shares of the leveraged firm. Thus the market value of the shares of the leveraged firm would fall while the shares of the unleveraged firm would rise until equilibrium was restored.[32]

The second proposition of Modigliani and Miller is concerned with the net income of the equity and states that the expected yield of a share of stock is equal to the appropriate capitalization rate for a pure equity stream of the same risk plus a premium related to financial risk equal to the debt-to-equity ratio times the spread between the capitalization rate ($\rho_k$) and the interest rate ($r$). Or in equation form,

$$i = \rho_k + (\rho_k - r)\frac{D}{S_i}$$

where i = expected yield of common stock, namely, net income, $\pi$, divided by $S_i$
r = interest rate

and $\rho_k$, $D_i$ and $S_i$ are as previously defined.

Professors Lerner and Carleton have argued that the second proposition of Modigliani and Miller is nothing but a tautology and implies that the market value of the firm is equal to its book value.[33]

---

[32] The original study of Modigliani and Miller (see footnote 30) involved the erroneous statement that the market values of firms of the same risk class must be proportioned in equilibrium to their expected returns net of taxes. Actually the market values are a function not only of such expected after-tax returns but of the tax rate and the degree of leverage. In short, the tax effect of interest deductibility is not in proportion to the ratio of debt. This point is now generally recognized and need not detain us.

[33] Thus from the accounting identity that assets equal debt plus equity and the definition of profit available to common stock as net operating income less the amount paid on debt, we derive the second proposition of Modigliani and Miller by simple algebra:

$$\pi = \rho_k(D_i + S_i) - rD_i$$

First rearrange the terms:

$$\pi = \rho_k S_i + \rho_k D_i - rD_i$$

Then divide through by $S_i$:

$$\frac{\pi}{S_i} = \rho_k + (\rho_k - r)\frac{D_i}{S_i}$$

with $i$ defined as $\pi/S_i$. Eugene Lerner and Willard T. Carleton, *A Theory of Financial Analysis* (New York: Harcourt, Brace & Jovanovich, Inc., 1966), p. 93.

In support of their second proposition (earnings yield of common stock) Modigliani and Miller fitted a regression to the data of 43 electric utilities in 1947–1948 and found

$$z = 6.6 + 0.017b \quad r = 0.53$$
$$(\pm 0.004)$$

where $z =$ (earnings/price) $\times$ 100

$b =$ (market value of senior securities/market value of common stock) $\times$ 100

The sample included debt ratios ranging from less than 5 to over 40 percent.

In support of their first proposition (cost of capital), the regression equation for the same sample is:

$$x = 5.3 + 0.006d \quad r = 0.12$$
$$(\pm 0.008)$$

where $x =$ cost of capital, or (total earnings of debt and equity/market value of all securities) $\times$ 100

$d =$ (market value of senior securities/market value of all securities) $\times$ 100

In both cases the slope is slight, indicating little change in the earnings yield or in the cost of capital as the percentage of debt in the capital structure is varied.[34]

To examine further whether the cost of capital changes with the ratio of debt to equity, Modigliani and Miller tested the data by fitting a parabola [35] and found that the curvature of the parabola was not statistically significant. Orthodox theory would predict a parabola.

Following these tests, Professor Barges employed the data for railroads in 1956 and found that the average cost of capital and leverage are not independent [36] but that the U-shaped curve of traditional theory existed.[37]

Many criticisms of the Modigliani-Miller hypothesis have been made and a flood of literature has been generated by the controversy. The most basic attack is that the hypothesis and test ignore the fact that different companies of the same risk class have different growth rates [38] and different dividend payout policies. Another important problem, raised by Professor Solomon,[39] is that regardless of theory, the different industrial groups have developed optimal debt-to-equity ratios for each industrial group as if there were an optimal ratio for each group simply because the market believes in an optimal debt-equity ratio. If this is so, then empirical testing of the Modigliani-Miller hypothesis will be extremely difficult, since if people act on the basis of a "mistaken" proposition that they assume to be true, it is difficult to say what they would

---

[34] Modigliani and Miller also applied the same tests to the data of 42 oil companies in 1952–1953 and found the same general conclusions but with the oil companies earning a yield 2.5 to 3 percent higher, reflecting the higher risk class of an oil company compared to an electric utility.

[35] This simply involves adding a squared term to make the fitted equation read $y = a + bx + cx^2$, the general form of equation of a parabola.

[36] Alexander Barges, *The Effect of Capital Structure on the Cost of Capital* (Englewood Cliffs, N. J.: Prentice-Hall, Inc., 1963).

[37] Namely, with the debt-to-equity ratio on the horizontal axis and with cost of capital (total earnings after taxes plus interest/market value of all securities) on the vertical axis, a U-shaped curve fits with statistical significance.

[38] We considered the bearing of the growth rate on the value of common stock in Chapter 14 and found the growth rate to be vital to valuation.

[39] Ezra Solomon, *The Theory of Financial Management* (New York: Columbia University Press, 1963), p. 98.

do if they knew the "truth." The first empirical work in this area [40] indicates Professor Solomon's surmise to be correct, namely, that different industrial groups have developed typical financial structures that are (considered) optimal for their operational risks and asset structures and that they are significantly different from each other. This work proceeded with analysis of only four rather crude classes: railroads, gas and electric utilities, mining, and industrials.

*Response to Criticism.* Modigliani and Miller responded to the criticisms, in part, by opening up the role of payout ratio and growth.[41] Failure to consider the relevance of growth in their original tests means, as we have already indicated,[42] that the use of the current price-earnings ratio understates the cost of capital to a company with growth. What appears to be the cost of equity if we use the current price-earnings ratio (as Modigliani and Miller did) actually includes an offsetting factor based on the market's estimate of the likelihood of growth.

As a refuge from the criticism for failure to take account of growth and dividend policy, Modigliani and Miller fall back on the proposition that their hypothesis may not be observable in the real world because "other" forms of financing, notably retained earnings, may in some circumstances be cheaper still when the tax status of investors under the personal income tax is taken into account.[43]

This admission ties together the two broad categories of criticism of the Modigliani-Miller hypothesis that we have already noted, namely, a failure to recognize the role of growth (and dividend policy) and the fact that different parts of the investing public pursue different areas of interest to them (railroads, gas and electric utilities, mining, or industrials). These interests are not arbitrarily or even psychologically determined (by their attitudes toward risk) but are determined more importantly by the personal income tax situation of each investor. Collectively, these individual investors affect the supply of funds offered for investment purposes.

This leaves the area of dividend policy for theoretical consideration. We will examine this subject at the end of Chapter 16.

## *Appendix N*

## THE PORTFOLIO CONCEPT, THE CAPITAL ASSET PRICING MODEL AND THE COST OF CAPITAL

The mean level of risk (expected value) of a firm is not the sole determinant of the risk premium that is included in its cost of capital. Because there is uncertainty, risk is a distribution of possible outcomes and is not a single value. Thus the standard deviation about the mean level of risk will also affect the risk premium. Given two projects using the same amount of funds with the same mean risk (mean of expected value), the project with the larger standard deviation involves a greater probability of ruin on the "downside" of the probability distribution and the diminishing marginal utility of money on the "upside" of the probability distribution renders the return worth less than that of the project with the smaller standard deviation. The cost of capital for that project will be higher than for the project with the smaller standard deviation.

---

[40] E. Schwartz and J. R. Aronson, "Some Surrogate Evidence in Support of the Concept of Optimal Financial Structure," *Journal of Finance*, 22 (March 1967), pp. 10–18.

[41] Franco Modigliani and Merton Miller, "Dividend Policy, Growth and the Valuation of Shares," *Journal of Business*, 34 (October 1961), pp. 411–432.

[42] See Chapter 14.

[43] Modigliani and Miller, "*Taxes and the Cost of Capital*," p. 442.

There is, however, an offsetting factor which may reduce the cost of capital for the project with the larger standard deviation. Such a project if it is a common stock is likely to be more volatile in market price over time. Given a greater variation in market price, this common stock offers greater opportunity for capital gains if one can correctly anticipate its price changes. There is evidence [44] that the market pays some premium for this greater risk and greater opportunity for capital gain. Hence this is an offset to the higher cost of capital to be expected for a project with more variation in expected returns.

Further, given two projects with the same mean risk but one using more funds and yielding a higher return, the one with more funds can tolerate a somewhat larger standard deviation without having a higher cost of capital than the other. Thus the correct comparison of the risk of these two projects is to use the coefficient of variation, namely $\sigma/\bar{R}$, that is, the standard deviation of the project returns over the mean return of the project. Thus if $\sigma$ increases in proportion to $\bar{R}$, the cost of capital will not be affected. Or if $\sigma$ is the same for two projects but $\bar{R}$ is greater for one, that one will have a lower cost of capital. Or if $\bar{R}$ is the same for two projects, the one with the lower $\sigma$ will have a lower cost of capital.

### The Portfolio Effect

But this is not the end of the road. We may be able to offset the risks of one project by the risks of another—as when the two risks are *negatively* correlated. Then when the risk of one project is high, the risk of the other project is low and vice versa. We are in a position to *reduce* the overall cost of capital to the firm by a proper "mating" of projects. This is the whole point of diversification of investments. Successful diversification involves a mating of projects whose risks are negatively correlated. Mere diversification on a random basis will achieve only random results.

Professor Sharpe [45] has refined these ideas by separating the risk of an investment into two parts: the unsystematic risk (which can be eliminated by diversification involving negative correlation of projects) and the systematic risk (which cannot be so removed). If we use a common stock as the proposed investment, Sharpe measures the systematic risk of a firm by its correlation with an index of the *general* market.[46]

Thus we can correlate the possible returns from an investment $j$ with the possible returns of a general market index $m$ to get the coefficient of correlation ($r_{jm}$).

The covariance is $r_{jm}\sigma_j\sigma_m$, where $\sigma_j$ is the standard deviation of the returns of the proposed investment; and $\sigma_m$ is the standard deviation of the returns of the market index $m$. The ratio of the covariance to the variance of the market

---

[44] Haskel Benishay, "Attitudes Towards Characteristics of Common Stocks," 1968 Social Statistics Section, *Proceedings of the American Statistical Association*, pp. 318–337.

[45] W. F. Sharpe, *Portfolio Analysis and Capital Markets* (New York: McGraw-Hill Book Co., 1970) and his earlier articles such as "Capital Asset Prices: A Theory of Market Equilibrium Under Conditions of Risk," *Journal of Finance* 19 (September, 1964), pp. 425–27. In turn, work in this area stems from Harry Markowitz, *Portfolio Selection: Efficient Diversification of Investments* (New York: Wiley, 1959).

[46] Strictly speaking, the systematic risk involves a correlation of each proposed investment with every other in the group or portfolio. As soon as the number of projects becomes large, the number of correlations becomes astronomical. To simplify this, a general market index such as the Standard & Poor Index of 500 Common Stocks is used in a single correlation with the proposed project.

rate has been identified as Beta ($\beta_{jm}$) and represents the risk which cannot be diversified away. The higher the $\beta_{jm}$ of a project, the greater its risk and therefore the higher the expected return, $\bar{R}_j$, we demand.

It follows that the expected return of a project, $\bar{R}_j$, is equal to the risk-free rate ($R_f$) plus the excess of the expected return of the market index ($\bar{R}_m$) above the risk-free rate times the ratio of the covariance of the project's return to the variance of the market index return, or

$$\bar{R}_j = R_f + (\bar{R}_m - R_f)[(r_{jm}\sigma_j\sigma_m)/\sigma_m^2]$$

where the symbols are as defined above.

Using Beta ($\beta_{jm}$) for the ratio of the covariance to the variance of the market rate, this equation becomes:

$$\bar{R}_j = R_f + (\bar{R}_m - R_f)\beta_{jm}.$$

## The Capital Asset Pricing Model

A recent modification[47] of the use of the weighted marginal cost of capital in capital budgeting has begun the integration of the subject of risk into the decision process. This modification is called the capital asset pricing model.

Starting with the statement of the expected return of a project which we just developed,

$$\bar{R}_j = R_f + (\bar{R}_m - R_f)\beta_{jm},$$

if the risk-free rate is 4 percent and the average market return over a long period of time is accepted as an estimate of the expected future market return and this is 9 percent, and if $\beta_{jm}$ is 2, then the expected return of project $j$ after diversifying away nonsystematic risks is

$$\bar{R}_j = 0.04 + (0.09 - 0.04)2$$

$$= 14 \text{ percent.}$$

Referring now to Figure 15–6 if the weighted marginal cost of capital is 14 percent, this is represented by the horizontal dotted line. The market line begins at 4 percent, the risk-free rate, and increases with the risk. Suppose that the market line is such that for a $\beta$ of 2, the market requires an expected return of 14 percent. Then our project is just at the cut-off rate which is where the market line intersects the weighted marginal cost of capital.

Now if we examine project A in Figure 15–6 we find it satisfies both the market line test and the weighted marginal cost of capital test. Project C satisfies the weighted marginal cost of capital test but fails the market line test, the rate of return is not adequate for the risk. Accepting this project would raise the cost of capital. Project B would be accepted even though it fails the weighted marginal cost of capital test because its low risk will bring the cost of capital down since its return is above what the market requires for such a risk. Project D fails both tests.

---

[47] M. E. Rubinstein, "A Mean-variance Synthesis of Corporate Financial Theory." *Journal of Finance*, 28 (March 1973) pp. 167–181.

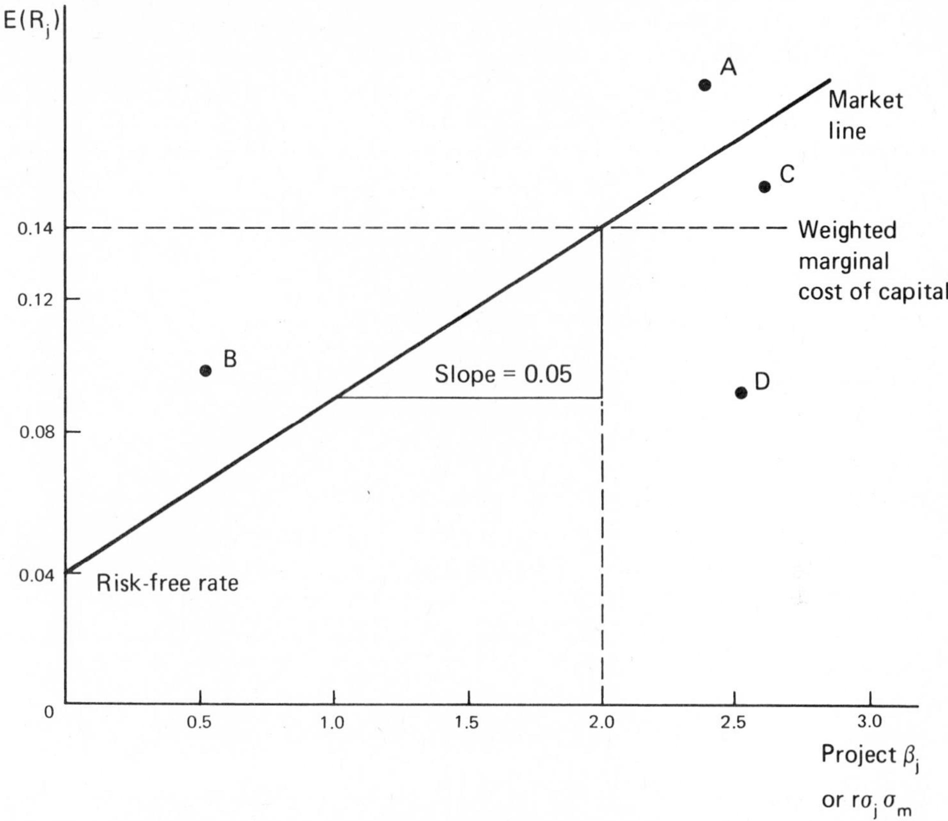


Figure 15–6 Market line for risk compared to weighted marginal cost of capital.

In Figure 15–6 notice that the slope of the market line is 0.05. For an increase in $\beta_j$ from 0 to 2, there is an increase in expected return from 4 percent to 14 percent. This slope is, of course, the risk premium of 5 percent appearing in the expected return equation as the excess return of the expected market rate ($\bar{R}_m$) over the risk-free rate ($\bar{R}_f$) or 9 percent less 4 percent.

The capital asset pricing model examines not only whether the project's return meets the weighted marginal cost of capital but also examines the effect of the risk of the project on the weighted marginal cost of capital.

## An Example Applying the Capital Asset Pricing Model

The following example illustrates the computations involved in the capital asset pricing model. In Table 15–18 we show the computation of the market variance, assuming probabilities for four possible outcomes of the market, which might range from depression to prosperity.

Using the expected market return of 5 percent with a standard deviation of 29 percent, we compute the expected return and covariance for a proposed project in Table 15–19 [48] faced with the same probabilities as to outcomes of the market.

---

[48] This computation of covariance assumes random variates and is not normalized, hence the coefficient of correlation (r) is not used.

TABLE 15–18

Computation of Expected Market Return and Market Variance

| Situation | (1) $p$ | (2) $R_m$ | (3) $pR_m$ | (4) $R_m - E(R_m)$ | (5) $[R_m - E(R_m)]^2$ | (6) $p[R_m - E(R_m)]^2$ |
|---|---|---|---|---|---|---|
| 1 | 0.2 | −0.4 | −0.08 | −0.45 | 0.2025 | 0.04045 |
| 2 | 0.2 | −0.1 | −0.02 | −0.15 | 0.0225 | 0.00450 |
| 3 | 0.3 | 0.1 | 0.03 | 0.05 | 0.0025 | 0.00075 |
| 4 | 0.3 | 0.4 | 0.12 | 0.35 | 0.1225 | 0.03675 |
| | | | $E(R_m) = 0.05$ | | | Var $R_m = 0.08245$ |
| | | | | | | $\sigma_{R_m} \cong 0.29$ |

TABLE 15–19

Computation of Expected Return and Covariance of a Proposed Project

| Situation | (1) $p$ | (2) $R_j$ | (3) $pR_j$ | (4) $R_j - E(R_j)$ | (5) $R_m - E(R_m)$ | (6) $[R_j - E(R_j)] \times [R_m - E(R_m)]$ | (7) $p(6)$ |
|---|---|---|---|---|---|---|---|
| 1 | 0.2 | −0.5 | −0.10 | −0.57 | −0.45 | 0.2565 | 0.0513 |
| 2 | 0.2 | −0.2 | −0.04 | −0.27 | −0.15 | 0.0405 | 0.0081 |
| 3 | 0.3 | 0.1 | 0.03 | 0.03 | 0.05 | 0.0015 | 0.0045 |
| 4 | 0.3 | 0.6 | 0.18 | 0.53 | 0.35 | 0.1855 | 0.05565 |
| | | | $E(R_j) = 0.07$ | | | Cov $(R_j, R_m) =$ | 0.11955 |

[B9]

The risk-free rate of return is assumed to be 4 percent and the market risk premium 5 percent.

The Beta of this project then is covariance jm/variance m or 0.11955/0.08245 = 1.45 and the measurement of the return required by the market line is $R_f + R_m B_{jm}$ or $0.04 + 0.05(1.45) = 11.25$ percent. Since the expected return of the project is 0.07, the excess return of the project is $(0.07 - 0.1125) = -.0425$.

The margin of the project's return over the risk-free rate, 7 percent − 4 percent, is not sufficient to meet the relatively high Beta of 1.45. The market demands an extra 7.25 percent for this risk (5 percent × 1.45) but the project achieves only 3 percent towards this risk.

# 16

# Internal Financing and Dividend Policy

Retained earnings are an important source of financing the investment requirements of firms. In the aggregate, a large percentage of each year's earnings is normally retained. And, little wonder. As we will show, retained earnings are a relatively cheap source of funds and create no obligation on the part of the corporation to pay interest or dividends, and involve no transaction or flotation costs.

## PAYOUT VERSUS RETENTION: A MAJOR PROBLEM AREA

We have set the goal of management as maximizing the market value of the firm. Since the market price of the common stock can be influenced by the division of earnings between "plow back" and payout,[1] divi-

[1] Under conditions of perfect capital markets, rational investors, and absence of tax discrimination between dividend income and capital appreciation, given the firm's investment policy, its dividend policy may have no influence on the market price of the company's shares. See Merton H. Miller and Franco Modigliani, "Some Estimates of

dend policy should not satisfy merely the existing group of shareholders. The split between retention and dividends should be such that potentially interested investors are attracted and, through purchasing the stock, bid up the market price to the highest attainable level.

The conflicts of interest between corporate management and stockholders and among different stockholders regarding the appropriate portion of earnings to be paid out highlight better than any other aspect of corporate activity the complications that arise when management is separated from ownership.

### The Sole Proprietorship and the Utilization of Earnings

In the sole proprietorship ownership and management are united. The owner directly manages the affairs of the business, receiving all the income and absorbing all the losses. The sole proprietor, however, is not freed from the conflict regarding the utilization of earnings to expand the business or increase his standard of living. As a businessman, expansion of the firm and pride in business success are important. On the other hand, the proprietor as an individual may be concerned with his present standard of living and may seek to increase his current level of personal expenditures. A conflict may rage within the individual regarding the appropriate division of earnings, and he may not be completely satisfied with the results after the decision has been made. But the important fact remains that he is the man that makes the decision; there is no conflict of owners versus management.

### The Partnership and the Utilization of Earnings

The partnership resembles the proprietorshp in that the owners decide directly the disposition of the earnings. No separation of management and ownership exists though there may be conflict among several of the partners. Some partners may favor more rapid expansion of the firm while others desire more current consumption. Tax considerations do not enter the picture. Partnership income is taxed as ordinary earned income whether it is retained or paid out. Partners must settle among themselves the same conflicts that beset the sole proprietor. Whatever the decision, in both the sole proprietorship and the partnership the benefits of expanding the firm and withdrawing profits flow directly to the owners.

### The Corporation and the Utilization of Earnings

In a corporation, separation of ownership and management creates a different situation. The owners (stockholders) control management through the election of a board of directors who immediately control management. The board of directors makes the decisions regarding the

---

the Cost of Capital to the Electric Utility Industry, 1954–57," *American Economic Review*, 56 (June 1966), p. 345. However, in the real world, the choice of dividend policy will, in fact, almost always influence the value of the company. See James E. Walter, "Dividend Policy: Its Influence on the Value of the Enterprise," *Journal of Finance*, 18 (May 1963), pp. 280–291.

disposition of earnings, namely, what part shall be paid in dividends and what part retained.

The corporation exists as a separate economic entity apart from both the managers and the owners. Furthermore, the actions of a corporation affect the public at large as well as labor, suppliers, and the consumer. Stockholders have conflicts both with management and among themselves. Management desires high salaries and even stock options while stockholders desire high dividends. One group of stockholders may desire rapid growth generated by heavy retention of earnings, and another group may favor slower growth and more liberal dividends. The same stockholder may even shift his position, favoring large retention and more rapid growth when he is younger or has a high salary and is in a stiffer tax bracket, and favoring slower growth and more liberal dividends during retirement. The demands on corporate income are heavy and the vested interests conflicting. In practice dividend policy often constitutes a compromise among these divergent interests. The board of directors in seeking to balance these interests may be chasing the proverbial will-o-the-wisp; the interests and attitudes of stockholders are not a static quantity but subject to frequent change. An application of the theoretical marginal principle to be discussed in the following section yields better results than if management merely negotiates a compromise.

## INTERNAL FINANCING DEMANDS

### The Marginal Principle of Earnings Retention

The marginal principle of earnings retention states that such earnings should be retained as can be invested at a higher rate of return, considering the risks, than that which the stockholders could obtain if the funds were paid out.[2] Ideally, in following this principle, the capital budget should mesh with the decision as to earnings retained. Dividends may mean the sale of stock or borrowing at a later date to cover what previously was paid out in dividends. Viewed in this light, is it proper that any dividends at all be paid by a firm that requires external financing? The answer to this question may be found in the marginal principle illustrated by the following example. The situation is presented first in static terms and then its application is traced over a period of years.

During the current year the Swing Company has earnings of $2,-500,000, which represent a 10 percent earning on assets, and has three projects promising a 20, 15, and 8 percent rate of return, respectively. Stockholders can invest their funds in other firms at the same degree of risk and earn a 10 percent return. The figures appear in Table 16–1. The marginal guide to dividend policy tells us that if we retain $1 million and invest in project A, our earnings will be lifted by $200,000 an-

[2] The objective is to maximize the return on the shareholders' investment. See James T. S. Porterfield, "Dividends, Dilution and Delusion," *Harvard Business Review*, 37 (November-December 1959), p. 57. Maximizing the profit of the firm is only one element. The other is the amount the stockholder can earn through reinvesting the dividends received.

nually; a marginal rate of 20 percent will be earned. Considering the risk of the project, the stockholders, if given the funds, could not do as well investing outside the firm. With project B, retaining $500,000 more, the firm will improve its earnings by $75,000 annually, earning a marginal rate of 15 percent on the retained earnings. Again the shareholders could not do as well outside the firm. Retention of the last $1 million to finance project C produces a different picture. Project C promises only an 8 percent return, lifting earnings by $80,000 annually. Since stockholders have open to them alternative investment opportunities of equal risk promising 10 percent, management should not retain the last

**TABLE 16–1.** Swing Company
Use of Earnings of $2,500,000 for
Capital Budgeting Projects, Dividend Payment, and Stockholder Returns

| Project | Cost of project | Marginal earnings increase from projects | Rate of return on project | Dividends paid | Cumulative retained earnings for projects |
|---|---|---|---|---|---|
| A | $1,000,000 | $200,000 | 20% | $1,500,000 | $1,000,000 |
| B | 500,000 | 75,000 | 15 | 1,000,000 | 1,500,000 |
| C | 1,000,000 | 80,000 | 8 | 0 | 2,500,000 |

$1 million to undertake project C. In the interests of shareholder wealth, maximization of the value of the firm, and optimum allocation of economic resources, management should retain $1,500,000 of the earnings of $2,-500,000 (a payout ratio of 40 percent). Retention of the last $1 million would cause a drop in the market price of the firm's stock, since the firm is currently earning 10 percent on assets. Thus total stockholder earnings would be reduced—compared to paying out $1 million on which stockholders could earn 10 percent directly. Through application of the marginal principle the firm will optimize the utilization of earnings, retaining that portion it can reinvest more profitably than the shareholders and paying out the remainder.

The marginal principle is simply illustrated; its application is difficult. The rate of return to be expected from the various capital budgeting projects must be calculated and estimates made of the rate of return on similar risks open to shareholders generally. These alternative projects open to shareholders are the *opportunity cost* of retained earnings.

### The Marginal Principle, Stockholders' Income Taxes and Future Financing Requirements

Dividend policy is clearly linked to capital budgeting policy.[3] It is also related to the debt-equity ratio and growth pattern of the firm.

[3] Eugene M. Lerner and Willard T. Carleton, "The Integration of Capital Budgeting and Stock Valuation," *American Economic Review*, 54 (September 1964), pp. 683–702.

Strict adherence to the marginal principle makes retained earnings the active variable and dividend payout the residual. This fact can be illustrated by a continuation of our example. Assume that next year the Swing Company has earnings of $3 million and two capital budgeting projects, one costing $2 million and the other $1 million. The anticipated returns are 25 and 20 percent, respectively. Alternative stockholder investment opportunities promise only 10 percent. Following the marginal principle, no dividends would be paid this year. The third year the firm earns $3,500,000 and the capital budgeting team comes up with only one attractive project, costing $1,500,000 and promising a rate of return of 20 percent. The firm this year retains only $1,500,000 and pays out $2 million.

With retention as the active variable the result is a very uneven dividend payout. But stability of dividends has a certain value in the market place. Also, when considering the maximization of the market price of the stock, the trade-off between a dollar of retained earnings and a dollar of dividends may not be equal. A dollar of dividends may be valued more highly by the investor than a dollar of retained earnings.

On the other hand, we have the matter of the income tax. The investor receiving a dollar of dividends does not get to keep the entire amount. If he is, for example, in the 40 percent marginal tax bracket, he is allowed to keep only 60 cents of each dollar. At the margin and *for him* a 6 percent return on an equivalent investment by the corporation matches a 10 percent return earned outside the corporation. But as we explained in Chapter 15, this income tax aspect cannot be permitted to influence the payout decision. To view the situation only through the eyes of *existing* shareholders is self-defeating. While the present stockholder in our case might prefer that the firm accept a 7 percent return project rather than pay him a dividend of which he can keep only 60 percent, it is clear that by admitting 7 percent projects, the firm will no longer appear in the market place as a 10 percent firm to *prospective* stockholders and the price of the firm's stock will fall.

Even with retained earnings as the active variable, retention should not be related solely to current capital budgeting requirements but also to those of the future. The firm might not have immediate need for some of the funds retained but may see a major project on the horizon that cannot be financed from the earnings retained for a single year. The firm could accumulate the required funds over a period of years, investing them in the interval in short-term securities of risk equal to that of the forthcoming investment. The alternative would be to pay out the funds not currently needed and go to the market to raise the funds when the time comes. If the funds were to be raised through the sale of bonds, the prior dividend policy would probably have little effect on the cost of debt capital, so long as some dividends were paid, because the rule of some states requires that dividends be paid annually on the common stock if the bonds are to qualify for a legal list. Certain financial institutions in these states must select their bond investments from the legal list. Thus a bond that can qualify for the list sells at a lower yield than one that does not. But if the funds for expansion are to be raised through a stock issue, a more generous dividend policy may raise the market price of the stock, thus requiring that fewer shares of stock be sold to obtain a given amount of money.

### Earnings Retention and Growth Pattern

We consider now the role of retained earnings in combination with these other sources of funds to finance firms caught up in different growth patterns.

A slowly growing firm will find that all the needed funds for expansion and renewal can be obtained from retained earnings. During periods when capital budgeting needs are low, funds can be accumulated and then applied when the need for funds jumps. A balance must be struck between the amount of funds currently needed, the amount to be accumulated against future needs, and the amount to be paid out to shareholders.

The declining firm will have no need for retained funds. But the replacement of assets at prices higher than original cost due to inflation may cause some difficulty. The declining firm can pay out a large percentage or all of its earnings in dividends. No corporate management, however, willingly lets a firm—and its job—pass out of existence. Earnings are retained and new opportunities sought that management hopes will return the firm to the growth group.

### Informational Value of Dividends

The growth firm will be faced with many high-return projects, usually more than can be financed from retained earnings. Such a firm will be under pressure to raise funds outside to finance its needs. Is it logical, then, to pay any dividends at all? Growth firms in practice pay a small but rising dividend, though a good case can be made for not paying any dividends, since the firm usually can reinvest earnings at a higher rate than can stockholders. Dividends have informational value. This is expensive information, however, since the government skims off a substantial percentage—depending on the taxpayer's marginal tax bracket—of what is paid out. But shareholders seemingly require the assurance given by some dividends that the retained earnings have been invested wisely. Confidence that retained earnings will produce a satisfactory rate in the long-run appears to be instilled through slowly but regularly raising the dividend.

### Retained Earnings Not Subject to Market Test

Table 15–2 at page 374 shows that internal sources in the 1960s were substantially larger than the amount of funds procured externally by corporations.

The large amount of funds retained by corporations causes concern about the efficient allocation of economic resources. The market is a fairly efficient allocator of economic resources, but earnings retained in the corporation are not subject to this market test.

The sole proprietor or the partners can directly compare the returns to be achieved from reinvestment of funds with other external investment opportunities and the added comforts of raising their standard of living. Separation of ownership and management in the corporation deprives stockholders of the opportunity of making this choice, and consequently the door is open to a misallocation of resources.

### Possible Inefficient Utilization of Resources

The officers and directors of a firm may or may not be substantial shareholders, but their position in the firm and their status in the industry as professional managers are always strong motivating factors. It is not easy for management to recognize, let alone accept, the fact that the company is going downhill and should be liquidated. Even if management consists of the controlling shareholders of a previously profitable firm now faced with significant financial difficulties, management is reluctant to sell out and sometimes waits until the last minute to sell, so strong is the desire to remain in command.

We live in a dynamic economy. This means that some companies producing for expanding markets will grow and others producing for declining markets will contract and eventually disappear. Funds should flow to the expanding firm and be withheld from the declining firm. But directors have full control over dividend policy and generally will bend all efforts to prevent a declining firm from dying through retaining a higher percentage of earnings than is justified by the firm's profit prospects.

## DIVIDEND STABILITY AND PAYOUT POLICY

Total corporate dividends exhibit greater stability than earnings. Figure 16–1 and Table 16–2 show fluctuations in earnings, dividends, and retained earnings since 1929. Earnings were substantially less than dividends during the Great Depression. During this period dividends were paid out of past accumulated earnings (surplus). Then earnings slowly began to rise and by the latter half of the 1930s more nearly approximated dividends. With the advent of World War II earnings rose sharply and dividends continued their slow but steady rise.

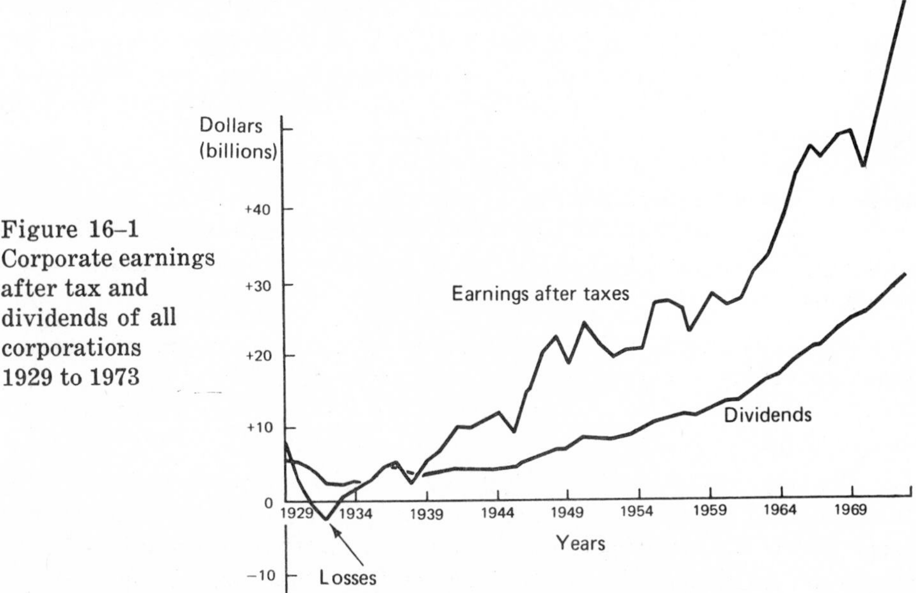


Figure 16–1
Corporate earnings after tax and dividends of all corporations 1929 to 1973

TABLE 16–2. Schedule of Earnings, Dividends and Payout Ratio for Corporations, 1930–1973
(in billions of dollars)

| Period | Earnings | Dividends | Payout Ratio |
|---|---|---|---|
| 1930–34 | ($1.3) | $21.3 | — |
| 1935–39 | 21.3 | 19.0 | 89.2% |
| 1940–44 | 50.7 | 21.7 | 42.8 |
| 1945–49 | 85.9 | 30.7 | 35.7 |
| 1950–54 | 107.1 | 44.2 | 41.3 |
| 1955–59 | 131.0 | 57.7 | 44.0 |
| 1960–64 | 156.9 | 76.2 | 48.0 |
| 1965–69 | 239.7 | 110.0 | 45.9 |
| 1970–73 | 212.5 | 103.6 | 48.8 |

SOURCE: *Economic Report of the President, 1974* (Washington, D.C.: Government Printing Office), Table C–74, p. 335.

These statistics, which are for all private corporations, cover a wide range; some firms pay no dividends at all, and never have. Others pay out a high percentage of earnings in dividends each year. Some firms continue to pay dividends in the face of declining earnings while others cut or suspend dividends immediately when earnings dip. Generally the electric utilities and telephone companies because of their steady and slowly rising earnings and ready access to external sources of funds pay a high and steadily increasing dividend. But rapid-growth utilities do not pay out a large percentage of earnings. The cyclical industries such as machine tools tend to pay out a high percentage of current earnings, but when earnings dip, dividends are quickly reduced. Often firms in the same industry will have widely different dividend policies, thus making it difficult to generalize about most industries.

## THE LEGAL BASIS OF DIVIDENDS

When a corporation makes a dividend payment it is distributing something it owns to its stockholders. All stockholders of a particular class must be treated equally. Cash is most frequently distributed as a dividend. Sometimes stock in another company is distributed. On occasion inventory of the firm may be distributed.[4] Cash, stock of another company, and inventory are known as *asset dividends*. The payment of these dividends has the effect of reducing the book value of the firm. Net worth, or more specifically, surplus, is reduced. It is popular to talk of a dividend being paid out of surplus, but in fact the debit is to surplus to record the portion of the stockholder's equity that has been withdrawn by the payment of the dividend. The credit is to cash, inventory, or the share of another company being held as an asset.

[4] A tobacco company may distribute packages of cigarettes or a cosmetic company bottles of its newly developed after-shave lotion.

### Directors Declare Dividends

The directors of a corporation have the discretionary power to declare dividends. The preferred or common stock contract cannot carry a provision obligating the firm to a fixed payment or face bankruptcy in the event of default. Owners assume fixed obligations to pay principal and interest on bonds or debt; they cannot meaningfully grant such obligations to themselves. Directors must vote to declare preferred and common stock dividends. But once declared, the dividend becomes a liability. Without action by the directors no dividend can be paid. And as long as they act in good faith, no legal means exist to force a dividend where none has been declared or to increase a dividend that the shareholders consider too small.

The nonpayment of dividends, or a decision to keep dividends low when the firm has fair but not rapidly rising earnings, may have unpleasant consequences for management. Stockholders dissatisfied with the entire corporate policy will have a strong talking point and increased chances for winning a proxy fight. Directors have been known to reinstitute dividends or to increase dividends and declare stock dividends or stock splits when threatened with a takeover.[5]

No legal rules require dividend declaration but legal rules do exist specifying the conditions under which dividends must *not* be paid. The corporate laws of the various states differ in detail, but the general rule is clear. Dividends may be paid only from retained earnings and unimpaired capital surplus. The rationale of this rule lies in protecting creditors and encouraging people with funds to extend credit. The rule protects creditors against withdrawal from the firm of the equity cushion they had originally relied upon when extending credit.

### There Must Be a Surplus

Dividends can legally be declared as long as a surplus exists. This means that dividends can be paid out of past as well as current earnings. During the early 1930s dividend payments exceeded current earnings by a wide margin. The dividends were paid against prior accumulated surplus.

Dividends once declared become a liability of the corporation and are owed to the stockholders. The stockholders have a creditor claim to the declared, but as yet undistributed, asset dividends. The same rule does not apply to stock dividends, which involve merely a change in the number of pieces of paper representing ownership.

Asset dividend distributions that impair capital are illegal and most state statutes provide that the approving directors be personally liable to the corporation for the amount of the illegal dividend, and in some states the firm can recover the amount from the shareholders. If the

---

[5] The attempted takeover of an electric utility by a utility holding company was thwarted in this way. The electric utility also hit upon the idea of requiring the shareholders to turn in their old shares in order to receive the new *split* stock. With the stock in the hands of the company, the stockholders who mailed in their shares could not deliver on the tender offer. In the case of a *stock dividend,* the additional shares are simply mailed to the stockholders.

directors acted in good faith and relied on the books of the firm, they may be absolved from liability.

### Contractually Assumed Dividend Restrictions

Important restrictions on the payment of dividends may be accepted by a firm when obtaining external capital either by loan agreements or by preferred stock contracts. Such restrictions may require the firm to maintain a certain current asset position or restrict surplus available for dividends to the amount existing at the time the agreement is made. The payment of a cash dividend in violation of a restriction would be an act of default in the case of a loan and the entire principal would become due and payable immediately through the inclusion of the acceleration clause in the contract.

## DIVIDEND POLICY IN PRACTICE

### Dividend Disbursement Procedure

Dividends are customarily paid quarterly by U.S. firms. The dividend item will appear at specific intervals on the agenda of the directors' meetings, and the directors decide both the form—cash or stock—and the amount of the dividend as well as the record date and the date of payment. Those whose names appear on the stockholder list on the record date will receive the dividend. The checks may be mailed on the date the dividend is payable or several days earlier so as to arrive on the payment date.

Stock is traded *ex-dividend* starting with the fifth business day before the record date. The purchase of the stock on or after the ex-dividend date will not carry with it the right to the dividend declared at the last directors' meeting; hence the name ex-dividend. Buying high-yielding stocks just before and selling just after the ex-dividend date is not a surefire way to make money. Other things being equal, the stock should drop in price on the ex-dividend date by the amount of the dividend. But other things do not always remain the same. The stock may fall more or less than the amount of the dividend or even rise in price. Everything depends on the supply and demand for the stock on the ex-dividend day, as it does on any trading day.

### Dividend Policy of Business Firms

The marginal principle that designates retained earnings as the active variable and dividends as the residual does not conflict with the legal rules regarding the payment of dividends. The legal rules merely require that there exist retained earnings—accumulated or current—out of which dividends can be declared. The *marginal principle* specifies that all earnings that cannot be reinvested at as attractive risk adjusted rates of return as exist outside the firm be paid out. In actual practice, corporate managers impart the impression that the marginal principle is not followed. The very concept of a dividend policy suggests a certain stability of cash dividend payments and implies that dividends are the active variable, not retained earnings. But firms following the marginal principle would act as though each dividend decision were quite independent of prior dividend decisions. The major consideration would be the availability of attractive investment projects.

One study of dividend policy found that in the majority of firms the current dividend decision is closely related to past dividend decisions.[6] The existing payments tend to be continued until the reasons for change are strong. Management is reluctant to give the impression that it acts hastily, an impression that might arise if dividends were adjusted frequently, particularly in our economy where stability and gradual increases are *the* goal.

Common stock carries no specified dividend rate but the strong predilection of corporate managers to favor the payment of a regular dividend generates an expectation among stockholders that the next dividend will closely approximate the last one. Since in practice directors start with the past dividend and continue it unless there are compelling reasons for change, this expectation among stockholders is justified. The major reason for dividend change is a shift in earnings, actual or anticipated. A drop in earnings will cause directors reluctantly to lower the dividend—usually only after the evidence of reduced earning power is overwhelming. The dividend is reduced to the level the directors believe can be maintained for a reasonable period of time.

A rise in earnings will cause directors to examine its strength and origin, and when convinced the increased earning power will be maintained for a reasonable period directors will raise the dividend. This is particularly true of growth companies that raise their dividend slowly in response to rising earnings. A slowing down in the rate of earnings growth of these firms is usually detectable only over a longer period of time and then only with much uncertainty. The price-earnings ratio then would decline only slowly. A cut in a dividend previously raised to an unmaintainable level by a growth firm would be a clear signal for all to see. The price-earnings ratio and the market price of the stock would plummet. Understandably, directors cautiously adjust dividends upward.

Examination of Figure 16–1, showing corporate earnings after taxes and dividends from 1929 to the present, clearly confirms the general policy of dividend stability and gradual adjustment to changes in earnings. Also noticeable is a fairly steady relation between earnings and dividends. It is apparent that directors believe there is an appropriate payout ratio to be maintained over time. The most popular payout ratio runs from 40 to 60 percent.

The actual payout ratio varies from year to year depending mainly on the current level of earnings. With a steady rise in earnings and maintenance of the same dividend the payout ratio falls. For example, a firm is earning $1.20 per share and paying dividends of 60 cents. If earnings slowly rise in the following years to $1.80 per share, and dividends remain at 60 cents, the payout ratio falls from 50 percent to 33⅓ percent. Directors, now convinced of the increased earning power of the firm, may

---

[6] John Lintner, "Distribution of Incomes of Corporations among Dividends, Retained Earnings, and Taxes," *American Economic Review*, 46 (May 1956), pp. 97–113.

belatedly increase the dividend to 90 cents. This cautious attitude results in the observable pattern of step-by-step dividend increases.

### Extra Dividends

Directors, not fully convinced of the increased earning power of the firm, but feeling a responsibility to pay out some of the increased earnings, may proceed to an intermediate stage. They may declare the regular dividend of 15 cents per quarter and in the last quarter of the year declare an extra dividend of 20 cents. The implication is that the extra dividend is added to the regular dividend in response to the increase in earnings for the current year, strictly a one-shot deal, with no suggestion that the extra will be paid again next year. Hence the extra dividend is seldom used. Because of the implication, the market price of the stock will not increase, which in turn leads to the feeling that the money paid out has been "wasted."

### Dividend Policy and the Marginal Principle

Initially the corporate practice of paying regular dividends does not appear to be consistent with the marginal principle. A policy of dividend stability implies that the directors determine an appropriate level of dividends, pay out that amount each year, and retain the remainder. But the marginal principle specifies that retained earnings be the active variable and dividends the residual. The reconciling fact is that a stable dividend policy enhances the price of the stock and reduces the cost of capital. Thus both the dividend policy and the marginal principle of earnings retention are active variables.

## ECONOMIC DETERMINANTS OF DIVIDEND POLICY

### Earnings Availability

The level of economic activity fluctuates from year to year and causes a certain instability in the earnings stream of every firm. This instability leads directors to establish a modest dividend policy that can be maintained over a reasonable period of time considering both the earning power of the firm and the availability of cash resources.

Retained earnings are usually invested in fixed assets and required working capital. Having become an integral part of the income-producing capital of the firm, these accumulated earnings are responsible for providing a portion of the current earnings. Directors would hesitate to reduce the firm's future earnings through liquidating a portion of its "earning" assets to pay dividends. Consequently, dividends normally represent some portion of the current level of earnings of the firm.

Dividends in any one year may exceed current earnings. This practice could not be continued very long without diminishing the firm's earning power and its capacity to pay dividends. Therefore, directors look ahead, anticipating future earnings, the need for capital, and the availability of funds for distribution of dividends.

### Cash Availability

Dividends are normally paid with cash. A firm may be legally entitled to pay a dividend and yet be unable to do so because of a deficient cash position. It is the current and future earnings that generate the cash enabling the firm to continue the payment of dividends, not past earnings that have been invested in brick and mortar.

We have seen that it is desirable to link dividend policy to the capital budget in order to promote the long-run profitability of the firm and to contribute to the optimum allocation of economic resources in the nation. Dividend policy must also be tied to the cash budget to provide for that dividend cash outflow. A given dollar amount of earnings generated in a period does not necessarily result in an equivalent sum of cash added to the bank balance. The dynamic firm experiencing a tight liquidity position will tend automatically to reinvest each dollar of revenue—the profit as well as the cost portion—in the working capital stream. Without fitting the dividend payments into the cash budget the firm will continually be strained to meet this outflow, and because of their noncontractual nature, common stock dividends will tend to be meager. Corporate management will see dividends as a diversion of funds from more productive uses and will explain the low dividend on the basis of the great need of the firm for funds. Better planning of all cash flows, including dividends, and the provision for a margin of liquidity would enable the firm to maintain an adequate dividend policy over time.

### Debt Management and Capital Market Accessibility

The repayment of outstanding debt obligations, if they are not to be refunded, also requires cash. Repayment may take the form of a regular sinking fund or periodic payments. Retained earnings provide protection for creditors in the event of default, but an adequate liquidity position is necessary to meet annual interest and principal payments that have a high priority claim against the available cash. Thus in setting dividend policy directors must look to current and future earnings not only as a source of new funds for reinvestment and dividends but also as the means for debt retirement. The target payout ratio should be set so that these demands on cash can be met from the future earnings flow.

A rapidly growing firm with a high rate of return will reinvest a large portion of its current earnings. If the firm has debt outstanding, it is likely that the debt will be refunded (renewed) or if stock market conditions are favorable will be replaced with a common stock issue.

A less rapidly growing firm may accumulate the funds needed for repayment out of earnings by keeping the target payout ratio down, particularly if the firm is small or speculative and does not have easy access to the capital markets. On the other hand, a large and well-established firm of modest growth rate is likely to pay out a higher portion of earnings in dividends. The easier access of the large firm to the capital markets may encourage directors to maintain a liberal dividend policy. Directors may feel that stockholders merit a greater share in the current earnings and that any existing debt should be refunded. If debt were to be retired through earnings, then the payout ratio would tend to be low even for a well-established firm of modest growth potential. But if debt is to be exchanged for a new common stock issue some time in the future, the directors may set a more liberal dividend for the purpose of pushing up the market price, since the higher the price the fewer the number of shares that have to be issued to raise the same amount of money provided the increase in the value of shares *to be sold* exceeds the added cash outlay for increase in dividends on all *outstanding* shares.

### Reinvestment Opportunities in a Fluctuating Economy

A growing firm has many alternative uses for funds. Its major problem is to uncover sources of funds at a reasonable cost, not how to put them to work. Dividends in such firms compete with the other uses of funds, and the directors must decide between making cash payments to the shareholders and employing the funds to increase the earning power of the firm.

Firms not in a long-term expansion phase will tend to find that their investment opportunities fluctuate with the level of economic activity. During a recession fewer profitable opportunities for investment exist. Corporate managers applying the marginal principle to the projects generated by the capital budgeting system will find that for all projects the scale of rates of return has moved downward. But during periods of reduced economic activity not only are the firm's investment opportunities reduced but the stockholders' alternative investment opportunities are also reduced. The reason for the higher dividend payout ratios during these periods is the better liquidity position of the firms. Reduced economic activity lowers working capital needs—cash, receivables, and inventory—and fixed assets are not replaced as rapidly as depreciation is charged. Therefore the "free" cash balance rises and dividends can remain at a high level while earnings fall. A fall in earnings to the dividend level, however, will force directors to consider a cut in the dividend.

A period of prosperity brings with it an increase in investment opportunities. Directors, anticipating the improved profitability of capital investments will hold dividends down, reinvesting all available working capital and current earnings as they are generated. Increase in dividends will lag behind the rising earnings. The dividend is not reduced; it is just not increased as fast as earnings are rising. What is often forgotten in the rush to reinvest is that shareholders' alternative investment opportunities have also improved.

### Inflation and Replacement of Fixed Assets

A period of inflation is characterized by rising prices of goods. The firm seeking to replace machinery will be forced to pay higher prices. Depreciation charged on the basis of the old, lower historical cost of the fixed assets is not adequate to provide for replacement unless improved efficiency offsets the higher price of the new asset. Consequently, net profit for the period, calculated on the basis of the inadequate depreciation figure, will result in an overstatement of profit. A portion of this accounting profit will have to be retained to maintain the real income-earning power of the firm. The payment of dividends in accordance with the accounting income, without considering the rising costs of replacing plant and equipment, would reduce the firm's command over goods and services.

For example, assume that we have a plant that produces 1000 popcorn machines a year and at the end of the year all equipment must be replaced. Assume, in addition, that we earn a net profit of $100 on each machine for a total annual income of $100,000. If all costs doubled and it were necessary to replace our equipment at the end of the year, charging depreciation at historical cost, we would be able to acquire a new popcorn machine plant with a capacity of only 50 machines per year. With all prices and costs doubled we would now be making a profit of $200 per machine, or still $100,000 per year profit. But the $100,000 now would buy the equivalent of only $50,000 worth of goods and services. If the firm were previously paying out all earnings in dividends, it would have to suspend all payments if it wished to maintain its former capacity of 100 machines. Only to the extent that the price of popcorn machines rose faster than the economic costs of producing them—that is, the margin of profit on each machine widened—should any dividends at all be paid. During a period of rising prices corporations are generally cautious in the payment of dividends on their accounting-determined profits. To the extent that a firm's depreciation charges are understated, net profit as well as federal income taxes are overstated. If prices of capital equipment doubled, a corporation paying a tax rate of 50 percent would have to carry down to net before taxes $2 for every $1 it needed to retain to make up the deficient depreciation charges.

Fortunately, matters are often not so bad as just described. Technological advances cut costs, and while replacing the old machine might cost much more, when the time for replacement comes the increase in efficiency of the new machine over that of the old machine often offsets the rise in the price level.

Inflation has a magnifying effect on the earnings of firms with high fixed costs and heavy investment in long-lived plant and equipment and/or with a large proportion of long-term debt in their capital structure. Rising prices and the larger proportion of fixed costs may result in a widened profit margin as an increased number of dollars of revenue produces a more than proportionate jump in earnings. These firms could quite properly raise their dividend payments during a period of inflation since, although the accounting income would be up sharply, the economic income of the firm would be up even more.

### Inflation and Operating and Financial Leverage

During inflation, if profit margins remain stable, firms with a large proportion of variable costs and/or with no leverage in their capital structure may find it necessary to reduce their dividend in order to maintain their economic position. Worse still, these firms may find themselves in a profit margin squeeze, with operating costs rising faster than prices, so that not only is their economic income way down but their accounting profit is also reduced. The historical record does not confirm the frequently held view that inflation is beneficial to *all* business and that *all* common stocks are a good hedge against inflation. Firms with a net debtor position benefit from inflation. But this situation is not true of all firms. Furthermore, inflation causes uncertainties among stockholders, inclining them to reduce the price-earnings ratios on the stocks they buy.

### Inflation and Working Capital

Common stock prices have performed well during periods of relative peace with a high level of economic activity and perhaps slightly rising prices to give the economy a certain stimulus. During these periods corporate earnings are high and rising, and the same can be said for price-earnings ratios. The double impact pushes stock market prices way up.

Working capital needs are also affected during inflationary periods. More dollars of cash and accounts receivable are needed to handle the higher dollar volume of business, though the physical quantity of goods may be the same. Inventory also presents a problem. On the one hand the same inventory item may cost more to replace, absorbing a larger portion of funds, and on the other hand the sale of the old inventory items carried on the books at a lower cost will result in an overstated accounting-income figure unless the last in, first out inventory method is used.

Assume, for example, that we are a wholesale distributor of popcorn machines. We buy the machines at $500 each and make a gross profit of $50 on each machine. We sell one machine a month and begin each month with two in inventory—we do not know on which day of the month we will sell the machine and we wish always to have one on hand to display. When the price of a machine rises to $600, we will either have to borrow or draw down our cash position by $100 to put the new machine in inventory. We now have $1100 tied up in inventory, whereas before this amount was only $1000. Then during the next month we sell one machine at a price reflecting the $100 increase in cost and take our normal mark-up of $30 per machine. If we keep our transactions on a last-in, first-out basis, we would record the normal $30 profit, but if we follow the first-in, first-out basis we would show a gross profit of $130 in the first month after the increase of price to $600, but a profit of only $30 thereafter.

Assuming prices stabilized at the $600 level for a number of months and the firm continued to earn its usual $30 per popcorn machine mark-up, we would then be showing a return on investment of only 2.7 percent per month—$30 of gross profit on $1100 of inventory instead of the gross profit of 3 percent on $1000 of inventory.

During periods of rising prices, dividends tend to lag behind rising reported earnings, and management quite properly permits the payout ratio to fall. The increased working capital required to do the same physical volume of business forces a greater retention rate. True, the accounting income may be rising, but the real or economic income may be stationary or actually falling. Since the federal government takes about 50 percent of all profits, real or imaginary, a firm will find it quite difficult to recoup understated depreciation charges out of retained earnings.

## DIVIDEND PAYOUT AND MARKET PRICE

The proper objective of corporate management is the maximization of the value of the firm. A question of crucial importance is whether the percentage division between payout and retention of each dollar of earnings can influence the market price of the company's stock.[7]

The marginal principle specifies that the *optimum dividend payout* is the point where the stockholders can earn as much on the funds as the firm can. If the firm retained less than this amount, the price of the stock might fall as the firm by-passed high income-producing projects, reducing earnings below buyers' expectations; if it retained more, the reduced earnings on the less profitable projects would cause buyers to pay less for the stock. According to the marginal principle, the market price might be at a maximum at this point of optimum payout.

A number of difficulties face management in attempting to apply the marginal principle. Not all stockholders have open to them the same alternative investment opportunities. Thus the question of what the shareholder's alternative investment opportunity rate is may be practically impossible to answer. Furthermore, there are two arguments, one favoring at least some, preferably stable, dividends and the other favoring a percentage payout lower than that suggested by the marginal principle. We will take up these arguments in order.

The firm may be able to retain a larger portion of its earnings than specified by the marginal principle and yet increase the market price of its stock as was explained in Chapter 15 in connection with Figure 15–1.

Assume that a company is earning $1 per share, is paying 60 cents in dividends, and its stock is selling at $20 with the dividend representing the optimum retention according to the marginal principle. Lowering the payout to 50 cents because management is not capable of reinvesting the additional 10 cents per share at a higher rate than the stockholder might be expected to lower the stock to, say, $19 per share; the price, instead of falling, may actually rise to $20.50 as the amount of earnings rises more than enough to offset the slight fall in the price-earnings ratio.

Nevertheless, an optimum dividend policy does exist, namely that which maximizes the value of the firm, but the optimum point is not likely to be the one specified by the marginal principle.[8]

---

[7] Since an asset dividend reduces the earning resources of the firm, it initially would seem that such a dividend would reduce the value of the common stock by the amount of the dividend. But increasing the dividend may actually increase the market price of the stock. No simple relation exists between the amount paid out in dividends and the market price of the stock.

[8] The goal of maximization of the stockholders' equity does not imply maximization of the firm's growth rate. Furthermore, the dividend yield plus the growth rate may overstate or understate the required profit rates on the incremental investments. See John Lintner, "Optimal Dividends and Corporate Growth under Uncertainty," *Quarterly Journal of Economics*, 78 (February 1964), pp. 89–94. Empirical studies relating stock prices to current dividends and retained earnings indicate that for nongrowth firms the higher dividend payout is usually associated with the higher price-earnings ratios. But in growth industries the opposite appears to be true. Irwin Friend and Marshall Puckett, "Dividends and Stock Prices," *American Economic Review*, 54 (September 1964), pp. 657–680.

## DIVIDEND POLICY AND MANAGEMENT CONSIDERATIONS

Focusing on a dividend policy rather than on a single dividend payment, we have seen that the market prefers a stable to a fluctuating dividend, that some firms can be expected to pay out a high percentage of earnings in dividends and others a low percentage, and finally, that changes in the payment influence the market price of the stock. Shareholders attach informational value to dividends, and when dividends are raised this is taken as evidence of the increased earning power of the firm. Accordingly, up to some point each dollar of dividends may be valued more highly than each dollar of retained earnings.

### New Stock Issue

Management, knowing that the market will respond to changes in dividend policy, is in a position to influence the market price of the firm's stock. If the stock is selling too low and management is contemplating a stock issue in the near future, raising the dividend will call favorable attention to the stock and most likely will result in an increase in the market price—particularly if the dividend increase is unexpected. If the new dividend rate is not maintainable, the action takes on the appearance of manipulation.

### Maintaining Control

In pursuing the goal of maximizing the market price of the firm's stock, dividend policy is a key variable, but sometimes management employs dividend policy as an effective instrument to maintain its position of command and control. Where an outside group is seeking to gain control of the firm, management has been known to declare stock splits and stock dividends or to increase or reinstate dividends in an effort to strengthen stockholder loyalty and raise the market price, making it more expensive for outsiders to acquire control. On the other hand, if management is securely in control, either through large holdings or through wide stock distribution and a favorable corporate image, it may seek to avoid all risk to its tenancy in office and shun debt financing, preferring retained earnings even though the firm might advantageously substitute debt financing for retained earnings and raise the market price of its stock.[9]

### Stock Options

Sometimes the factor guiding management is gaining large stock options and protecting large stock holdings. Management would then be particularly unhappy to see the market price fall and would be inclined to maintain dividends at the same level long after it has become evident that the earning power of the firm has declined. In the short run higher

---

[9] Management often prefers common stock and retained earnings to debt and preferred capital. See Charles D. Ellis, "Repurchase Stock to Revitalize Equity," *Harvard Business Review*, 43 (July-August 1965), pp. 119–128. On the trade-off between risk and return, management frequently avoids risk.

prices may be maintained in this way but where the dividend outflow significantly reduces the future expected rate of earnings, this will at some point be recognized in the market, and the price-earnings ratio will decline, reflecting the slower projected growth rate.

### To Whom Is Dividend Policy Geared?

The difficulty of ascertaining the optimum split between retention and dividends is the result of diverse investment goals and alternative investment opportunities of the current and potential shareholders. Since various groups of stockholders have different objectives and desires, we might let investors gravitate to that firm that combines the mix of growth and dividends they desire.[10]

Whether maximization of market value of the firm will result from a dividend policy designed to appeal to a segment of investors or from one geared to investors in general will depend upon dividend policies of other firms. Thus if at a given time there is a shortage of firms following a policy currently preferred by a substantial segment of investors (say, a particular mix of growth and cash dividends), the market will bid up the price of such stocks. This might, for example, happen as the result of personal income tax rate changes. A sharp increase in such rates increases the demand for high growth, no dividend stocks.

This is similar to the question of whether a firm should specialize or diversify. No simple conclusion is possible. If many firms are specializing, it may pay to diversify. On the other hand, as the recent history of the market shows, the first firms to become conglomerates skimmed the cream while latecomers in the movement gained nothing and, indeed, lost.

Optimum economic development of society will be served by diverse dividend policies as long as investors are permitted to have differences in objectives.

## SUMMARY

Retained earnings are an important source of financing. This source is relatively cheap—compared to issuing common stock—and does not increase exposure of the firm to financial embarrassment or of management to loss of control. Consequently, management usually looks upon retained earnings as an ideal source of funds. But the goal of management should be the maximization of the value of the firm's stock. The basic determinant of the market price of a company's stock, given the capital structure and degree of risk, is earning power, but the price of stock can be influenced by the division of the earnings between retention and payout.

The marginal principle holds that a firm retain all the earnings that it can reinvest at a rate in excess of the investment opportunities avail-

---

[10] It is a good practice for a firm to explain its policy on dividends and earnings retention, since different groups of investors have different objectives and such explanation will assist investors in their decision. Mere information cannot assure maximization of value but maximization cannot be achieved without releasing information.

able to its stockholders, current and prospective. The dividend policies of many firms over time can be at least roughly reconciled with this principle. During periods of economic expansion when attractive investment opportunities abound, earnings usually climb rapidly, but dividend increases are allowed to lag. The result is a declining payout ratio. When the economy levels off or begins to dip, earnings may decrease, but the dividend tends to be maintained and as a result the payout ratio rises. Firms in a growing industry have a higher retention rate than those in a mature industry. The investment opportunities are more numerous and attractive in a rapidly growing industry. Stockholders of firms in these industries prefer the accelerated growth rate and ordinary income is exchanged for capital gains.

Optimal dividend policy will maximize the market value of the firm's shares but this is likely to conflict with the marginal principle because of practical aspects. Thus dividends have informational value and a stable dividend policy has value. Firms in a declining industry represent the greatest departure from the marginal principle of retention and payout. Many factors motivate management: industry position, prestige, and continuation in a top management position. Consequently, management of such firms is tempted to reinvest as much as possible in an effort to turn the company around. Through branching out in new fields a company can be rejuvenated. The risk is great, however, and losses by firms venturing into new areas are frequent and large. The better course of action often would be paying out a substantial portion of earnings in dividends, repurchasing shares, or gradually liquidating the firm, depending upon the circumstances. Such a course of action would be beneficial to both the stockholders and the economy.

### *Study Questions*

1. How does the dividend policy of a firm influence the allocation of resources within the nation? What arguments can you cite to support or reject a proposal that firms be compelled to pay out all of their earnings in dividends?
2. Since the main determinant of the market price of a firm's stock is earning power, given the degree of risk, how is it possible for dividend policy to influence market price? Is setting the dividend policy to influence the market price of the stock really manipulation? How would you distinguish between constructive influence and manipulation?
3. Why do dividends exhibit a more stable pattern than earnings? What arguments can you give to support management's practice of maintaining the same dividend in the face of fluctuating earnings? Is it logical for stockholders to prefer stable to fluctuating dividends? Why or why not?
4. "A firm that pays dividends and subsequently raises equity capital through a "rights offering" is taking back with one hand what it distributed with the other. In view of the tax bite and brokerage commissions, a firm requiring common stock financing should never pay a dividend." Discuss.
5. The management of a particular firm may not wish to set the dividend policy in such a manner as to maximize the market value of the company's shares. How can such action be explained? What other factors may be motivating management?

6. One approach to dividend policy suggests that management set the percentage distribution at its discretion and investors will gravitate to those firms that offer the desired combination of current dividends and growth. Discuss the advantages and disadvantages of this approach.

7. Growth companies generally are justified in retaining a larger proportion of earnings in dividends than are mature companies. Why? Though supporting arguments can be marshaled, the management of a declining company is reluctant to pay out all earnings in dividends. Why?

8. Dividend declarations are usually made shortly before the date the dividend is to be paid. Since firms sometimes make earnings projections, would anything be wrong with declaring a dividend one year in advance?

9. Firms in some countries pay only one dividend annually. The practice in the United States is to pay dividends quarterly. Discuss the advantages and disadvantages of each procedure.

10. What legal restrictions exist regarding the payment of asset dividends? What contractual restrictions may a firm assume on the payment of dividends? What purpose do these restrictions serve? Are they not an infringement on management freedom? If so, how are they justified?

11. Why is it not possible for common stock to carry a meaningful fixed dividend clause? If the stock contract carried such a clause, would it still be a common stock even if the certificate stated common stock? Why or why not?

12. Why does management raise the dividend only slowly in response to rising earnings? Why is management usually even more reluctant to cut dividends than to increase them? Is this a rational attitude? Why or why not?

### Problems

1. The Hey Boy Company, a closely held firm has long geared its dividend policy to maximizing the market value of the firm. Accordingly, each year at dividend time the capital budget is reviewed in conjunction with the earnings for the period and the alternative investment opportunities of the shareholders. In the current year the firm reports earnings of $1 million. It is estimated that the firm can earn the indicated amounts on the retained earnings shown in Table 16–3 before taxes of 50 percent.

TABLE 16–3. The Hey Boy Company

| Dividends | Retain | Earnings on retention before taxes |
|---|---|---|
| — | $1,000,000 | $250,000 |
| $ 100,000 | 900,000 | 240,000 |
| 300,000 | 700,000 | 208,000 |
| 600,000 | 400,000 | 130,000 |
| 900,000 | 100,000 | 40,000 |
| 1,000,000 | — | — |

The stockholders have alternative investment opportunities that will yield them 10 percent.

a. Calculate the amount that Hey Boy should retain this year if it wishes to maximize the total earnings of the stockholders.

b. How much should Hey Boy pay out in dividends?

c. What would be the payout ratio?

2. The following year Hey Boy, which is in the glamorous medical electronics field, decides "to go public." Management holds all the present 400,000 shares and the firm sells 600,000 new shares of stock to the public at $60 per share. The estimated earnings for the year are $2 million.

a. What is the price-earnings ratio on the estimated earnings basis at which the stock was sold?

b. Hey Boy announces its intention at the time of the stock issue of paying a dividend of 60 cents a share. The market rate of capitalization for this firm is 11 percent. Given the market price of $60 per share and the 60-cent dividend, what is the growth rate anticipated for this firm by the market?

c. The capital budget is prepared for the coming period on the basis that the $2 million in earnings will actually be realized. It is estimated that thereafter the firm can earn the amounts on the retained earnings indicated in Table 16–4. The income tax rate is 50 percent.

TABLE 16–4. Hey Boy Company
Projection of Earnings on Retained Earnings

| Dividends | Retain | Earnings on Retention Before Taxes |
|---|---|---|
| — | $2,000,000 | $560,000 |
| $ 600,000 | 1,400,000 | 500,000 |
| 1,000,000 | 1,000,000 | 420,000 |
| 1,800,000 | 200,000 | 100,000 |
| 2,000,000 | — | — |

Hey Boy decides to reinvest all funds that will produce an earnings rate at least equal to the rate of capitalization. How much would the firm retain?

d. What is the payout ratio?

e. What is the rate earned by Hey Boy on its retained earnings?

3. In a few years Hey Boy is earning $4 million, or $4 a share, and paying a dividend of $1. During these intervening years the market rate of capitalization for this firm has risen to 21 percent and the anticipated growth rate is 20 percent.

a. What is the market price? The price-earnings ratio?

b. Management is distressed with the low price-earnings ratio at which the stock is selling and is of the opinion it should sell at about 40 times earnings. To what amount would the dividend have to be increased to achieve a PER of 40? Does this make sense? What else must occur if this is to be feasible?

### Selected References

Brennan, Michael, "A Note on Dividend Irrelevance and the Gordon Valuation Model," *Journal of Finance*, 26 (December 1971), pp. 1115–1121.

Brittain, J. A., *Corporate Dividend Policy*, Washington, D. C.: The Brookings Institution, 1966.

Ellis, C. D., "Repurchase Stock to Revitalize Equity," *Harvard Business Review*, 43 (July-August 1965) pp. 119–128.

Elton, E. J., and M. J. Gruber, "Marginal Stockholder Tax Rates and the Clientele Effect," *Review of Economics and Statistics*, 52 (February 1970), pp. 68–74.

Friend, I., and M. Puckett, "Dividends and Stock Prices," *American Economic Review*, 54 (September 1964), pp. 656–682.

Gordon, M. J., "Dividends, Earnings and Stock Prices," *Review of Economics and Statistics*, 41 (May 1959), pp. 99–105.

Harkavy, O., "The Relation between Retained Earnings and Common Stock Prices for Large Listed Corporations," *Journal of Finance*, 8 (September 1953), pp. 283–297.

Higgins, R. C., "The Corporate Dividend—Saving Decision," *Journal of Financial and Quantitative Analysis*, 7 (March 1972), pp. 1527–41.

Lintner, J., "Distribution of Incomes of Corporations among Dividends, Retained Earnings, and Taxes," *American Economic Review, Proceedings*, 46 (May 1956), pp. 97–113.

———, "Dividends, Earnings, Leverage, Stock Prices and the Supply of Capital to Corporations," *Review of Economics and Statistics*, 44 (August 1962), pp. 243–269.

———, "Optimal Dividends and Corporate Growth under Uncertainty," *Quarterly Journal of Economics*, 78 (February 1964), pp. 49–95.

Miller, M. H., and F. Modigliani, "Dividend Policy, Growth and the Valuation of Shares," *Journal of Business*, 34 (October 1961), pp. 411–433.

Pettit, R. R., "Dividend Announcements, Security Performance, and Capital Market Efficiency," *Journal of Finance*, 27 (December 1972), pp. 993–1007.

Porterfield, J. T. S., "Dividends, Dilution and Delusion," *Harvard Business Review*, 37 (November-December 1959), pp. 56–61.

Pye, Gordon, "Preferential Tax Treatment of Capital Gains, Optimal Dividend Policy, and Capital Budgeting," *Quarterly Journal of Economics*, 86 (May 1972), pp. 226–242.

Van Horne, J. C., and J. G. McDonald, "Dividend Policy and New Equity Financing," *Journal of Finance*, 26 (May 1971), pp. 507–519.

Walter, J. E., "Dividend Policies and Common Stock Prices," *Journal of Finance*, 11 (March 1956), pp. 19–41.

———, *Dividend Policy and Enterprise Valuation.* Belmont, Calif.: Wadsworth Publishing Company, 1967.

———, "Dividend Policy: Its Influence on the Value of the Enterprise," *Journal of Finance*, 18 (May 1963), pp. 280–291.

Whittingdon, G., "The Profitability of Retained Earnings," *Review of Economics and Statistics*, 54 (May 1972), pp. 152–160.

## Appendix O

### THEORY OF DIVIDEND POLICY

Dividend policy represents the link between the theory of capital budgeting and the theory of cost of capital.

There is little question but that the stockholder should prefer to have the firm reinvest the earnings if the rate of return upon reinvestment exceeds the rate of return he could obtain elsewhere. But there are stockholders who want some of the benefits of investment in common stocks (such as a hedge against inflation) and at the same time seek some immediate cash return.[11] But, each stockholder is subject to different personal income tax rates. Thus there are some rich stockholders who prefer a minimum dividend and who must seek to obtain the bulk of their share of earnings by selling their stock and realizing a capital gain.

Furthermore, we must clearly keep in mind the assumption under which the discussion proceeds. A model may be constructed to analyze the situation in a world of no corporate taxes and no personal income taxes. Or a model may be constructed to recognize no outside equity financing.

As the subject of dividend policy has developed in the academic journals of the past decade, it is fair to state that the cost of capital question has been thrust onto new and higher ground, or "escalated," to use the current phrase. Once dividends are introduced into the problem of maximizing value, we become concerned with dividing the stream of cash flows among debt repayment, dividends, and reinvestment in order to maximize the value of the business firm. The size of the stream itself is not to be taken as if given. We can add to the stream by issuing new debt or new equity. And additions to the stream are not simply the amount of water added, since new money can induce growth. It is as if new water were to cause new springs to come into action.

In this complex situation it is not surprising that diametrically opposed positions are taken. Thus Modigliani and Miller wash their hands of the dividend problem:

> Like many other propositions in economics, the irrelevance of dividend policy, given investment policy, is "obvious", once you think of it. It is, after all, merely one more instance of the general principle that there are no "financial illusions" in a rational and perfect economic environment. Values there are determined solely by "real" considerations—in this case the earning power of the firm's assets and its investment policy—and not by how the fruits of the earning power are "packaged" for distribution.[12]

Thus their position on valuation of the firm on a dividend basis is parallel to that on an earnings basis. As was noted in Appendix M to Chapter 15, the testing of the theories of Modigliani and Miller is difficult if the market place believes in a contrary theory.

On the other hand, Professor Walter's conclusion is that "the choice of dividend policies almost always affects the value of the firm." [13]

These conflicting conclusions cannot be tested by resort to experience because the theories assume perfect capital markets in which, for example, transaction costs, the informational value of dividends, and differential taxes on income from dividends and capital gains do not exist. The conflicting conclusions result from different assumptions. Specifically, the Walter formula recognizes that dividend policy cannot be separated from the investment policy of the firm while Modigliani and Miller assume the contrary.[14]

---

[11] A participating preferred stock offers some of the common stock benefits but does not give the basic inflation protection of common stock. In practice, the participating preferred stock seldom "participates."

[12] M. H. Miller and F. Modigliani, "Dividend Policy, Growth and The Valuation of Shares," *Journal of Business*, 34 (October 1961), p. 411 at 414.

[13] J. E. Walter, "Dividend Policy: Its Influence on the Value of the Enterprise," *Journal of Finance* 18 (May 1963), pp. 280–291.

[14] Michael Brennan, "A Note on Dividend Irrelevance and the Gordon Valuation Model," *Journal of Finance*, 26 (December 1971), pp. 1115–1121.

*Adjustment of Formula for Common Stock Value to Include Dividend Policy.* To adjust the formula for valuation of common stock that we gave in Chapter 15 as

$$V = \frac{D}{k - g} \tag{16–1}$$

where $V$ = value of a common stock

$D$ = initial dividend

$k$ = capitalization rate appropriate to the risk

$g$ = expected growth rate of earnings

to reflect earnings retention, we have

$$V = \frac{D}{k - rb} \tag{16–2}$$

where $b$ = percentage of earnings retained, $(E - D)/E$
$r$ = expected rate of profitability
$V$, $D$ and $k$ are as defined above

In other words, the rate of growth of dividends ($g$) is the product of the rate of profitability of retained earnings ($r$) muliplied by the earnings retention percentage ($b$).

*Translating Formula for Common Stock Value to Operational Form.* Equation (16–2) is basically accepted by almost all who have engaged in discussion of the theory of dividend policy, but it falls far short of being a complete treatment of all the variables affecting dividend policy, and it is not operational as it stands.

In an effort to put Eq. (16–2) into operational form, Walter [15] has developed the formula

$$V_c = \frac{D + (R_a/R_c)(E - D)}{R_c} \tag{16–3}$$

---

[15] J. E. Walter, "Dividend Policies and Common Stock Prices," *Journal of Finance* 11 (March 1956), pp. 29–41. The transition from Eq. (16–1) to Eq. (16–3) is as follows:

Restating Eq. (16–1) we have $k = \dfrac{D}{V} + g$

since $g = \dfrac{\Delta V}{V}$, $k = \dfrac{D}{V} + \dfrac{\Delta V}{V}$,

and since $\Delta V = \dfrac{R_a}{R_c}(E - D)$ and $k = R_c$

hence, $V = \dfrac{D + (R_a/R_c)(E - D)}{R_c}$

where

$V_c$ = market value of a share of common stock

$R_c$ = market capitalization rate

$R_a$ = rate of profit of retained earnings

$E$ = earnings per share

$D$ = dividends per share

In this formula the rate of capitalization ($R_c$) is taken as the rate of capitalization of a broad group of common stocks such as Standard & Poor's Index of 500 Common Stocks (see Table 16–5). The rate of profit on retained earnings can be measured as the increase in earnings per share of the firm over a recent period, such as three years, divided by the change in book value per share over that period. The other terms of the formula are readily available for any particular firm.

TABLE 16–5. Price-Earnings Ratio and Earnings-Price Percentage (Rate of Capitalization) of Standard & Poor's Index of 500 Common Stocks, 1957–1973

| | P/E | E/P |
|---|---|---|
| 1957 | 12.50 | 8.0% |
| 1958 | 17.04 | 5.9 |
| 1959 | 18.95 | 5.3 |
| 1960 | 18.75 | 5.3 |
| 1961 | 20.68 | 4.8 |
| 1962 | 15.93 | 6.3 |
| 1963 | 17.78 | 5.6 |
| 1964 | 18.67 | 5.4 |
| 1965 | 17.61 | 5.7 |
| 1966 | 14.74 | 6.8 |
| 1967 | 17.41 | 5.8 |
| 1968 | 17.54 | 5.7 |
| 1969 | 16.58 | 6.0 |
| 1970 | 17.22 | 5.8 |
| 1971 | 17.91 | 5.6 |
| 1972 | 18.39 | 5.4 |
| 1973 | 11.95 | 8.4 |

SOURCE: Standard & Poor's Index of 500 Common Stocks, 4th quarter.

The Walter formula (16–3) can be recast into the form

$$V_c = \frac{E}{R_c} + \frac{R_a - R_c}{R_c^2}(E - D) \tag{16–4}$$

for the purpose of bringing out the fact that the price or value of a share of a particular firm will deviate from what would be indicated by the price-earnings ratio of the average common stock according to the role played by the second term of Eq. (16–4). The second term of the right-hand side brings out the role of dividend policy and the earning rate on new investment.

It should be emphasized that both forms of the Walter formula given in Eqs. (16–3) and (16–4) assume that the rate of profitability of new investment ($R_a$) will continue indefinitely into the future. As a practical matter, this rate is likely to drop as the firm grows and diminishing returns set in. But if the drop in $R_a$ occurs far in the future, the effect is less because the drop will be time-discounted. Hence what is desired for use in the formula is a time-weighted average of $R_a$ far into the future. Furthermore, it is apparent that a change in dividend policy in the future will have a similar effect and hence what is desired is the average future dividend payout.[16]

Many companies have successfully pursued a policy to maintain $R_a$ at a constant figure, as Table 16–6 indicates.

TABLE 16–6. Target Rate of Return on Investment

| Company | Target rate |
|---|---|
| U. S. Steel | 8% |
| General Electric | 20% |
| Alcoa | 20%—higher on new products |
| General Motors | 20% |
| International Harvester | 10% |
| Sears Roebuck | 10–15% |
| Kroger | 20% before taxes |
| Johns-Manville | 15%—higher on new products |

SOURCE: Robert F. Lanzillotti, "Pricing Objectives in Large Companies," *American Economic Review*, 48 (December 1958), pp. 921–940.

Finally, the Walter formula permits the ready incorporation of two practical aspects. The first is the desire of stockholders for diversification. As an investment develops favorably, particularly if the stock is a large segment of an investor's portfolio, the investor will seek some diversification with the profits of the investment. This practice entails costs of diversification, which include commission and a capital gains tax. These costs, defined as $p$ and measured as a rate, can be readily incorporated into the basic formula to compute the value of the stock to the particular investor:

$$V_c = \frac{D + [R_a/(R_c + p)](E - D)}{R_c} \tag{16–5}$$

As this value falls below the market price, the investor will sell.

The second practical aspect involves the tax differential between the capital gains rate and the marginal rate of personal income tax on the ordinary income of the investor. To reflect this aspect, the formula becomes

$$V_c = \frac{D + [(t/s)R_c](E - D)}{R_c} \tag{16–6}$$

[16] These same observations are applicable to the determination of g in Eq. (16–2) and also to the basic equation for common stock value.

where $s = 1$ minus the special tax rate of capital gains
$t = 1$ minus the marginal rate on ordinary income[17]

*Illustration of the Interplay of Dividend Policy and Key Variables.* Case 1—Illustrations of Professor Walter's formula bring out the interplay of dividend policy and the key variables. Thus if a company's earning rate on recent investment ($R_a$) is 10 percent and the average market rate of common stock ($R_c$) is 10 percent and the company is earning \$4 per share with a 75 percent payout of \$3 per share, the indicated market value of a share using Eq. (16–3) is:

$$V_c = \frac{3 + (0.1/0.1)(1)}{0.1} = \$40$$

Then, if we shift the dividend payout to 50 percent or \$2 per share, the market value remains

$$V_c = \frac{2 + (0.1/0.1)(2)}{0.1} = \$40$$

Here we have an average company (its $R_a = R_c$), and shifting the dividend payout ratio will not affect the market value of a share of its stock. The stockholder would gain nothing by leaving retained earnings with the company, since such money earns only the average rate available elsewhere.

Hence it follows that in the case where retained earnings yield no more than the average of common stocks, the dividend payout policy will have no effect on the price or value of the particular stock.

Case 2—If we examine a growth company in which we leave all the values as they stood in our first case with $R_a$ now taken to be 20 percent (and we pay out 75 percent of earnings), we have

$$V_c = \frac{3 + (0.2/0.1)(1)}{0.1} = \$50$$

And if we cut the dividend payout to 50 percent, the market price becomes

$$V_c = \frac{2 + (0.2/0.1)(2)}{0.1} = \$60$$

This follows because earnings kept in the firm will earn double what they would if the stockholder received them in dividends and invested them at the market rate.

---

[17] Clearly this involves the statement that

$$R_a = \frac{t}{s} R_c$$

which simply means that to the particular investor the rate of profitability of reinvested funds is to be adjusted for the fact that a lower dividend payout ratio improves the tax position of the investor relative to his position under a higher payout ratio. Thus the individual investor seeks equivalence of the retention situation to his personal tax rate on ordinary income. This requires that

$$s\left(\frac{R_a}{R_c}\right) = t$$

This is the same as stating

$$R_a = \frac{t}{s}(R_c)$$

Then if we cut the dividend payout to 25 percent, the market price becomes

$$V_c = \frac{1 + (0.2/0.1)(3)}{0.1} = \$70$$

Hence it follows that if $R_a > R_c$, the value of the stock will vary inversely with the dividend payout percentage.

Case 3—If we examine a declining company in which earnings on new investment opportunities fail to meet the average rate of capitalization of common stocks and leave all the values as they stood in our first example but with $R_a$ now taken to be 5 percent (and we pay out 75 percent of earnings), we have

$$V_c = \frac{3 + (0.05/0.1)(1)}{0.1} = \$35$$

But if we shift the dividend payment to 50 percent of \$2 per share, the market value becomes

$$V_c = \frac{2 + (0.05/0.1)(2)}{0.1} = \$30$$

Hence it is apparent that if $R_a < R_c$, the value of the stock will vary directly with the dividend payout percentage.[18]

There has been little empirical work in the area of the dividend payout ratio and the value of stock [19] other than to examine large groups of stocks without distinguishing within each group those with an $R_a$ above average or below average.

---

[18] This clearly exposes the erroneous position taken by tax authorities when they argue that "the 'plowing back' of corporate profits gives rise not only to growth in the value of the corporation capital accounts but also to appreciation in the value of corporate securities." See U. S. Treasury Department, Tax Advisory Staff of the Secretary, *Federal Income Tax Treatment of Capital Gains and Losses* (Washington, D. C.: Government Printing Office, 1951), p. 15.

[19] One of the few studies is Oscar Harkavy, "The Relation between Retained Earnings and Common Stock Prices for Large, Listed Corporations," *Journal of Finance*, 8 (September 1953), pp. 283–297. Harkavy considers four "matched pairs" over the 20 years 1931–1950, namely, General Baking and Purity Baking, American Chicle and William Wrigley, Schenley and National Distillers, and Freeport Sulphur and Texas Gulf Sulphur. In three of these four pairs (except General Baking and Purity Baking) he observes that the higher percentage of retained earnings resulted in a greater return to the stockholder in the form of dividends plus capital gains.

*

# PART SIX

# Long-Term Financing

*

# 17

# The Capital Markets: Investment Banking and Private Placement

## TRADITIONAL INVESTMENT BANKING

Investment banking[1] is concerned with the merchandising of securities. Sometimes a distinction is drawn between investment banking and brokerage. The term "investment banking" is then restricted to the primary market—the underwriting of new security issues; that is, the investment banker buys a new issue of securities for his own account with the expectation of reselling quickly. The term "brokerage" covers the secondary market, serving as an agent on a commission basis in buying or selling securities for the account of another.

A third category falls between underwriting and brokerage, namely, acting as a dealer who functions in the secondary market. In this case the investment banker or broker buys shares of an existing issue of securities in the open market for his own account for later resale. A deal-

[1] The term "investment banker" can be misleading, first, because an investment banker does not "invest" but acts as a middleman between a buyer and a seller of securities; second, he is not a banker in that he receives no deposits. There is no such place as an "investment bank." While the term "investment banker" is used, the business is seldom carried on as a sole proprietorship but most often as a partnership or corporation.

er is seeking a greater profit than just a commission because he expects to sell at a higher price than he paid. The expected profit rewards him for the risk he takes that the price may fall rather than rise.

One particular aspect of the role of the underwriter that is too frequently ignored in textbooks is the maintenance of an "after-market" by the investment banker after the initial public offering in the case of a corporation whose securities are traded over the counter. If the investment banker merely completes the initial offering of the securities and then loses interest, an incomplete service has been furnished to both the corporation whose securities were marketed and to the buyers of those securities, since the latter will sooner or later want to sell them. Failure of the investment banker to maintain an adequate after-market may easily sour the issue.

Thus far we have viewed the investment banker as one who deals with the general public as buyer or seller of securities. In addition to serving this area, the investment banker also fills other roles. One is directly or privately placing securities with one or a few (as many as 30) large buyers, often insurance companies or pension funds. The investment banker serves in this area by bringing the selling corporation and the buyer(s) together without acting as agent for either. The rise and decline of direct or private placement are illustrated in Table 17–1. The table indicates that the use of this method grew from 20 percent of all new bonds issued in 1937 to more than 60 percent in 1964, declined to 16 percent in 1970 but rebounded to 60 percent in 1973.

TABLE 17–1. Estimated Gross Proceeds of Corporate Bonds Publicly and Privately Offered, 1937–1973 (in billions of dollars)

| | Total bonds | Amount privately offered | Percentage privately offered |
|---|---|---|---|
| 1937 | $ 1.6 | $0.3 | 20% |
| 1947 | 4.9 | 1.9 | 38 |
| 1957 | 10.0 | 3.8 | 39 |
| 1960 | 8.1 | 3.3 | 41 |
| 1961 | 9.4 | 4.7 | 50 |
| 1962 | 9.0 | 4.5 | 50 |
| 1963 | 10.9 | 6.2 | 57 |
| 1964 | 10.9 | 7.2 | 66 |
| 1965 | 13.7 | 8.2 | 60 |
| 1966 | 15.6 | 7.5 | 48 |
| 1967 | 15.0 | 7.0 | 47 |
| 1968 | 17.4 | 6.7 | 38 |
| 1969 | 18.3 | 5.6 | 31 |
| 1970 | 30.3 | 4.9 | 16 |
| 1971 | 31.9 | 7.1 | 22 |
| 1972 | 27.7 | 9.4 | 34 |
| 1973 | 22.5 | 13.6 | 60 |

SOURCE: Securities and Exchange Commission, *Statistical Bulletin*, monthly. Beginning with 1973, weekly.

One factor that had lent impetus to this movement is that direct placement avoids federal and state regulation, particularly by the Securities and Exchange Commission, which began federal regulation in 1933. Another reason for the growth in direct or private placement had been the accumulation of an increasing percentage of the total savings of individuals in financial intermediaries such as insurance companies and pension funds that can deal privately with the issuer. A third, and probably the most important, reason is the flexibility afforded in a direct placement that is not available in a public issue. In direct placement borrower and lender can modify the loan terms easily, while it is impractical to do this when there are thousands of bondholders. In addition, it is difficult to anticipate and provide for all possibilities over a 20-year period at the time of a bond offering.

One reason for the drastic decline of the percentage privately placed in 1970 is that while life insurance companies are normally the major buyers of private placements, with a rather stable amount of money to invest each year, these companies found their policyholders borrowing large amounts at the relatively low loan rates set in their policies when the market rates of interest were high in 1970. Then in 1973, the poor prices in the public market forced borrowers into private placements.

### Investment Counseling

Another important role of the investment banker is investment counseling. This service has many forms.

First, the investment banker may act as a financial adviser to corporations whose securities he has underwritten. Sometimes the investment banker carries out this role by being on the board of directors of the client corporation. Holding such a directorship may be questionable because it may give rise to a suspicion that dealings between the corporation and the investment banker are not at arm's length. Furthermore, the presence of the investment banker on the board makes him an "insider" with special access to information about the corporation while at the same time he may be dealing for his own account in the securities of that corporation. Thus the question of a conflict of interests arises, particularly in the case of a corporation whose securities are traded over the counter, between the role of the investment banker in maintaining the after market and his interest in turning a profit based on his evaluation of the future of the corporation, which depends in part on his information. It is true that whether the directorship is held or not, this potential conflict still exists.

Second, the investment banker offers his counseling services to individual and institutional investors. In this role he may furnish a wide spectrum of services, ranging from merely offering special reports and analyses of industries or of specific companies to agreeing to assume complete management of the investment account of the client once the client's investment objectives have been established. These objectives can be generally classified as safety, income maximization, and growth or capital gains maximization.

Third, the investment banker may enter a long-term agreement with a mutual fund to act as manager of the fund's assets. With the great growth of mutual funds after World War II some investment bankers have been attracted to this field and have "sponsored" funds, benefiting not only from the management fee but also from the commissions generated by the funds' transactions.

The investment banker offers a wide range of services, including management of an investment fund, record-keeping for tax and other purposes, custodial care of the securities, income collection, and disposition of rights or warrants. At the one extreme is the management contract with a mutual fund and at the other are limited services for accounts as small as $100,000 to $200,000.

In general, fees for such service start at one-half of 1 percent per year and ultimately slide down to one-quarter of 1 percent as the size of the fund increases. Fees vary not only with the size of the fund and with the type of service but also with the type of client, such as whether the account is individual or corporate, whether it is a pension or profit-sharing fund, and whether it is a charitable or educational institution.

## THE UNDERWRITING OPERATION

The heart of investment banking is the underwriting operation involving an original issue of securities by a corporation or an offering of a block of stock by large stockholders in a transaction called a secondary or "sell down." Table 17–2 presents the record of recent years as to new corporate registered public issues of bonds and preferred and common stocks. Basically the issue may be offered by a corporation that already has a publicly held issue or by one that is going public for the first time. This distinction is perhaps even more important than that of whether the corporation's securities are listed on an exchange or not.

**TABLE 17–2. Volume of New Registered Primary Corporate Issues by Security Type, and Flotation Costs, 1960–1973 (in millions of dollars)**

| | | | | | Underwriting commission | | Other expenses | |
|---|---|---|---|---|---|---|---|---|
| | Bonds | Preferred stocks | Common stocks | Total securities* | amount | percent | amount | percent |
| 1960 | $4,552 | $219 | $1,719 | $ 6,491 | $140 | 2.2% | $46 | 0.7% |
| 1961 | 4,715 | 212 | 3,055 | 7,983 | 161 | 2.0 | 60 | 0.8 |
| 1962 | 4,172 | 315 | 1,333 | 5,821 | 114 | 2.0 | 52 | 0.9 |
| 1963 | 4,118 | 150 | 1,007 | 5,275 | 77 | 1.5 | 31 | 0.6 |
| 1964 | 3,134 | 177 | 2,558 | 5,871 | 86 | 1.5 | 37 | 0.6 |
| 1965 | 4,762 | 377 | 1,811 | 6,951 | 104 | 1.5 | 38 | 0.5 |
| 1966 | 7,803 | 458 | 2,265 | 10,526 | 158 | 1.5 | 43 | 0.4 |
| 1967 | 11,462 | 494 | 1,484 | 13,441 | 276 | 2.5 | 70 | 0.5 |
| 1968 | 12,603 | 906 | 2,854 | 16,363 | | | | |
| 1969 | 10,818 | 515 | 5,949 | 17,282 | | (No longer | published) | |
| 1970 | 17,825 | 768 | 7,382 | 25,975 | | | | |
| 1971 | 23,329 | 3,564 | 7,091 | 36,282 | | | | |
| 1972 | 16,959 | 2,416 | 6,795 | 28,555 | | | | |
| 1973 | 13,039 | 2,343 | 4,487 | 23,603 | | | | |

* Includes equity securities other than common and preferred stock.

SOURCE: Securities and Exchange Commission, *Statistical Bulletin*, monthly; since 1973 weekly.

[B11]

Many observers have claimed that there is a "life cycle" of a firm. Actually, what they are referring to is the life cycle of the key managers of a firm. But in any event, many firms ultimately arrive at the point where they merge with other corporations. This is true whether they are listed on a national exchange or not. It is clear, then, that it is vital to the structure of the capitalistic system and to the national exchanges that new corporations mature, make public offerings, and seek listing as older ones merge or die.

Whether the new issue is by a corporation already publicly owned or by one that is going public for the first time, the process and documents used are the same, although the type of investment banker involved is often different. Few corporations go public for the first time through the services of a "national" house; most go public through a regional investment banker. Then as the corporation grows, additional issues usually are managed by a national house. Figure 17–1 shows the pattern of the second public offering of a corporation's stock and the proceeds to the corporation. The first public issue had been a secondary offered eight years previously by the regional underwriter who continued as a comanager on the second offering when a national house joined as comanager.

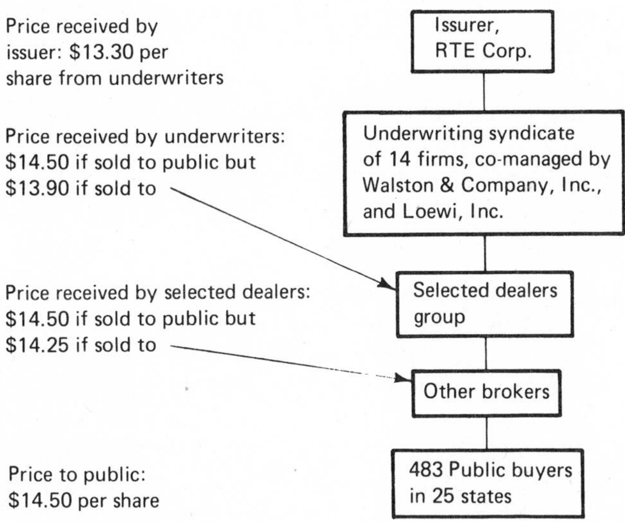


Figure 17–1 Second public offering of the RTE Corporation, November 21, 1966; 70,000 shares of no par stock at $14.50 per share.

### Planning for Underwriting and Timing the Offering

Before an underwriting occurs there is considerable planning and a series of conferences between the seller and investment banker. One of the most important matters to be settled is the timing of the offering. In order to achieve an optimum price for the issue, both the corporation and conditions in the capital market must be healthy. Sometimes the needs of the corporation require a sale of securities when either of these conditions is less than ideal. The result is a lower price. Often such temporary situations can be bridged with bank loans.

The underwriting may involve objectives beyond the raising of funds for the corporation, the most frequent being the establishment (and later the broadening) of a market for the corporation's securities. In the absence of a market value for the corporation's securities, all of the owners of the firm's securities are exposed to serious risks as to the sale value or as to the value that will be set by tax authorities in cases of gift, inheritance, and estate taxes.[2] In addition, establishing a market for the corporation's securities under favorable circumstances will bring benefits at a later date for other offerings. The market value of a security depends in part on the amount of seasoning that the corporation's securities have had.

During this preunderwriting period extensive investigations are carried on by accounting, legal, financial, and engineering experts to satisfy the investment banker as to the quality of the securities to be offered. In the case of a company going public for the first time, the underwriter may offer a set price before the registration process begins. That commitment would be subject only to major and unforeseen changes in either the capital market or the condition of the corporation. In the case of securities of a company that is already publicly held, the price will not be set until very shortly before the offering. Often this time will be the close of business the day before the offering. What the price will be involves a phenomenon called *underpricing*. For the issue to be successful the investment banker feels there must be an inducement to the public to buy the securities to be offered rather than the same securities in the open market. There is considerable variation in the amount of underpricing. In the case of stocks traded over the counter, the underpricing may be no more than to offer the stock at the bid price rather than at the average of the bid and ask prices. In the case of stocks listed on an exchange, a set differential from the closing price on the day preceding the offering may be used.

During the preliminary negotiations between the investment banker and the issuer an *upset price* may be agreed upon. An upset price is that price below which the issuer has the option not to proceed with the offering should the market price drop during the registration process.

Another phenomenon involved when a corporation is offering additional shares is *dilution*. If the new issue is to be equal to 10 percent of the total shares presently outstanding, some people believe that the price

---

[2] For an example of the viciousness of this risk, see Erwin E. Nemmers, *Cases in Finance* (Boston: Allyn & Bacon Inc., 1964), Sunburst Corporation, Case C, pp. 166–184.

of outstanding shares should fall by about 10 percent[3] *because the same earnings will now be spread over 10 percent more shares.* But the reason given reveals the fallacy. The new money received as a result of the offering may result in increased earnings. If this is the case, then dilution will be less than such a computation shows. Indeed, there may be no dilution. The question of whether there will be any dilution cannot be answered by examining the prospectus to see whether the company states that the proceeds of the stock issue will be applied to debt retirement or used for plant expansion or working capital. Even if the proceeds are to be applied to debt retirement, this is merely an accounting phenomenon. In anticipation of the issue management may already have entered a program of expansion and there may be very little lag in realizing the increased earnings necessary to prevent dilution. Such matters may be as subtle as adding new types of customers.

One benefit of delaying the pricing of an issue to the last minute (after the market place knows the size of the issue and other facts from the preliminary prospectus) is that the market will have assessed the problem of dilution and the answer of the market place will become available to the investment banker during the registration process.

### The Registration Process

The preliminary activities of underwriting, which may have extended over a period as long as several years (but seldom as short as several months), culminate in the registration process.

Since 1933 the *Securities Act* has required the registration with the Securities and Exchange Commission (SEC) of all publicly offered securities in amounts over $300,000 ($500,000 since January 1971), either offered interstate or through the U.S. mails.[4] Table 17–3 shows total registered issues and differs from Table 17–2 by including the registration of investment company offerings. Table 17–2 is on a calendar-year basis while Table 17–3 is based on a fiscal year ending June 30.

It is important to note that the federal act does not involve any qualitative judgment by the SEC. Rather, the federal act is directed solely at truthful and adequate disclosure of facts relevant to the proposed issue. This is in sharp contrast to the so-called *blue sky* legislation of some states, which purports to examine the quality of the issue and the fairness of the offering price.[5] In recent years many states have simplified the matter of compliance with state laws by permitting the filing of duplicate federal registration papers.

---

[3] Actually, the fall would be a little more than 9 percent. Thus if $100,000 in earnings is spread over 110,000 shares instead of 100,000, the amount earned per share drops from $1 to $.909.

[4] Even amounts under $500,000 are subject to the requirement of a prospectus (called an "offering circular") conforming to Regulation A if the U. S. mails are used or if the offering crosses state lines.

[5] Thus the states of Michigan and Missouri limit the price at which a common stock is offered to a maximum of 15 times the prior year's earnings.

TABLE 17–3. Issues Registered for Cash Sale, Total and by Type of Security, 1950–1973 (in millions of dollars)

| Year ended June 30 | Total | Debt | Preferred stock | Common stock |
|---|---|---|---|---|
| 1950 | $ 4,381 | $ 2,127 | $468 | $ 1,786 |
| 1951 | 5,169 | 2,838 | 427 | 1,904 |
| 1952 | 7,529 | 3,346 | 851 | 3,332 |
| 1953 | 6,326 | 3,093 | 424 | 2,808 |
| 1954 | 7,381 | 4,240 | 531 | 2,610 |
| 1955 | 8,277 | 3,951 | 462 | 3,864 |
| 1956 | 9,206 | 4,123 | 539 | 4,544 |
| 1957 | 12,019 | 5,689 | 472 | 5,858 |
| 1958 | 13,281 | 6,857 | 427 | 5,998 |
| 1959 | 12,095 | 5,265 | 443 | 6,387 |
| 1960 | 11,738 | 4,224 | 253 | 7,260 |
| 1961 | 12,260 | 6,162 | 248 | 9,850 |
| 1962 | 16,286 | 4,512 | 253 | 11,521 |
| 1963 | 11,869 | 4,372 | 270 | 7,227 |
| 1964 | 14,784 | 4,554 | 224 | 10,006 |
| 1965 | 14,656 | 3,710 | 307 | 10,638 |
| 1966 | 25,723 | 7,061 | 444 | 18,218 |
| 1967 | 27,950 | 12,309 | 558 | 15,083 |
| 1968 | 37,269 | 14,036 | 1,140 | 22,092 |
| 1969 | 52,039 | 11,674 | 751 | 39,614 |
| 1970 | 48,198 | 18,436 | 823 | 28,939 |
| 1971 | 58,452 | 27,637 | 3,360 | 27,455 |
| 1972 | 49,882 | 20,127 | 3,237 | 26,518 |
| 1973 | 44,034 | 24,841 | 2,578 | 26,615 |

SOURCE: Securities and Exchange Commission, *39th Annual Report* (June 30, 1973) p. 163. Includes investment company offerings.

In the registration process a prospectus [6] is prepared for distribution to prospective brokers and buyers. The prospectus covers such matters as:

1. The history of the company
2. The use of the proceeds of the proposed offering
3. The recent price range of the security (if previously traded)
4. The capitalization of the company before and after the proposed issue
5. The dividend history of the company
6. The profit and loss statement for at least the most recent five years and quarters of a year
7. The business activities of the company
8. The properties owned by the company

[6] A sample prospectus together with an agreement among underwriters and a purchase or underwriting agreement appear in Erwin Esser Nemmers, *Cases in Finance* (Boston: Allyn and Bacon, Inc., 1964), pp. 191–236.

9. Management personnel of the company and their compensation
10. Any stock option plans, employee stock purchase, deferred compensation, profit sharing, and similar plans
11. The principal holders of securities
12. The security proposed
13. The underwriting agreement proposed
14. Identification of those passing on legal and accounting questions
15. Financial statements, including a recent balance sheet, the profit and loss statements for the last five years, statement of retained earnings for the last three years, and supporting schedules covering depreciation, taxes, rents and royalties, and special items
16. The participating underwriters and the share of each

The preliminary prospectus is called a "*red herring*" because on it is printed vertically in red ink a statement indicating that while the prospectus has been filed with the SEC, it has not yet become effective. This serves to warn anyone receiving it that there may be changes in it or additions to it before it becomes effective.[7]

In addition to the prospectus, the issuer files a registration statement,[8] which contains among other items:

1. The proposed agreement among underwriters, the underwriting (or purchase) agreement, and any dealer agreements
2. The articles of incorporation and by-laws of the issuer
3. Any loan agreements of the issuer
4. Any stock option, profit-sharing, retirement, or other plans of the issuer
5. Any contracts with related persons

This registration statement (in most cases Form S–1) becomes effective 20 days after it is filed unless the SEC acts during this time. Invariably the SEC notes some items requiring clarification or amplification. In this case an amended registration statement is prepared and another 20-day waiting period is begun. The second waiting period can be accelerated.

While the SEC registration is in progress the issuer proceeds with the process of filing under the laws of each state in which the issue will be offered for sale so that both federal and state clearances will arrive at the same time.

---

[7] Where there are serious changes between the "red herring" and the final prospectus, the SEC may require that a second "red herring" be circulated. In any event, every ultimate purchaser of the security must receive a copy of the final prospectus.

[8] Copies of this statement may be obtained from the SEC by paying the cost of reproducing it.

### Formation of the Underwriting Syndicate

As soon as the registration statement is filed with the SEC, the managing underwriter sets about organizing the underwriting syndicate. The latter may have previously engaged in informal discussions concerning the proposed issue with other prospective underwriters, but the filing of the registration statement (which is reported in newspapers) sets the wheels in motion.

The *underwriting syndicate* consists of the managing underwriter and as many other underwriters as are needed to account for the entire offering. The agreement among underwriters may provide for a divided or an undivided syndicate. The *divided syndicate* is the most common and specifies the maximum number of shares for which each underwriter is liable. Most commonly there is a provision that, in addition to the participation of each underwriter as stated in the prospectus, each will be liable for an additional amount, often 10 percent, of his participation if fellow underwriters are unable to sell their agreed-upon share. In the *undivided syndicate* each underwriter is liable for any unsold securities in proportion to his participation regardless of how many he may have sold.

The underwriting syndicate is concerned with three basic documents:

1. The *agreement among underwriters,* which sets out the rights and liabilities of the underwriters among themselves.

2. The *purchase or underwriting agreement,* which sets out the terms of sale by the issuer to the underwriting syndicate. This includes the price to be paid to the issuer and the price at which the securities will be sold to the public. This price difference is called "the *spread.*"

3. The *selling group agreement,* which covers the purchase of securities by brokers in smaller quantities from the underwriting syndicate.

### Function of the Selling Group and Stabilization

The underwriters are, in effect, wholesalers who may retail part of their participation directly to the public and wholesale another part to brokers in smaller quantities. These brokers, called the *selling group,* then retail to the public. The subscription of each broker is made in a document that commits him not to sell to the public below the stated price; if securities sold by the broker are repurchased by the underwriters in the market in order to achieve stabilization prior to the termination of the syndicate, the broker is bound again to sell the securities or be liable for the costs of the underwriters in repurchasing and reselling.

*Stabilization* involves the maintenance by the managing underwriter during the period of the syndicate of such a bid price for the securities as will stabilize the market price no lower than the offering price for the issue. This prevents any cumulative downward movement of the price of the security during the selling or syndicate period.

Typically there is a distinction between brokers who enter the selling group and sign the document just described, called the *selected dealers agreement,* and other brokers who simply buy shares as agents of the public. The selected dealers receive a larger commission or concession from the underwriters. In the underwriting operation outlined in Figure 17–1, that commission was 60 cents per share, whereas the nonsigning broker received a concession of only 25 cents per share.

### Setting the Price, the Sale and Stabilization

The price of the stock to be offered is usually set by the managing underwriter after the close of business the day before the proposed offering. The price is usually set at or slightly under the "bid side of the market" at the close. That day is established against the expected letter from the SEC granting acceleration of the current 20-day waiting period after the most recent amendment of the registration statement has proven acceptable to the SEC.

The night before many things happen. The attorneys complete a price amendment to be filed with the SEC the next morning and a courier leaves by night plane to Washington, D. C. for the filing. High-speed presses grind out thousands of copies of the final prospectus, which move out by special delivery air mail or courier to be on hand the following morning around the country. Then as dawn is breaking in California, with Hawaii and Alaska still asleep, a telegram leaves the SEC declaring that registration has become effective. Similar telegrams are awaited from all the states where the offering is to be made. With the receipt of these telegrams, telephones start to jingle and selling of the securities commences all over the country.

Most offerings are subject to stabilization. This is usually carried out by *overselling* the issue. That is, if 100,000 shares are being offered, the managing underwriter authorizes the sale of say 105,000 shares or even more depending on market conditions and the strength of the offering. Then, in order to deliver the extra 5000 shares, the managing underwriter enters the market as a buyer and in so doing he supports the price. If the manager misjudged, he may have to pay more than the issue price to "cover" the short sales. Profits or losses from stabilization are shared *pro rata* by the underwriting syndicate. Once the manager judges the market for the issue stabilized, he declares the syndicate ended. For a successful issue this is usually the second or third day after the offering; for a "sticky" issue the time may be a week or ten days. Even if all the issue is not sold, the syndicate would then be declared terminated and each underwriter would be "stuck" with his *pro rata* share of unsold inventory.

### Is Stabilization Socially Desirable?

The argument is frequently advanced that stabilization, or "pegging the price" during the period of the syndicate, is bold price-fixing, which is forbidden elsewhere in the economy as a violation of the antitrust laws. The counterargument is that stabilization is more analogous to resale price maintenance agreements, which are an exception to the antitrust laws.

What is frequently overlooked in this debate is that the SEC rules forbid any promotional efforts on behalf of the securities for a period of 40 days after the public offering. Similarly, such activities are forbidden for an indeterminate period prior to the public offering. This period is usually considered to be from three to six months prior to the offering. These rules are designed to assure a free market price.

The question concerning stabilization can best be answered by pointing out that if price-pegging were forbidden, the risk to the underwriters would be increased. As a result, the underwriters would demand a larger spread. The question then would be whether the increase in the spread would come more from the hide of the issuer or the hide of the buying public. Because the price of the new issue must be competitive with the prices of other similar outstanding securities that are not now burdened with the spread problem, it is likely that the increase in the spread would come out of the hide of the issuer. This in turn means that the increase in the spread would be borne by all the stockholders of the issuer, including the purchasers of the new issue, on a *pro rata* basis.

## ALTERNATIVES TO UNDERWRITING

Instead of the underwriting procedure just discussed three alternatives are available to an issuer of securities:

1. A best-efforts or agency sale
2. Direct sale to the public by the issuer
3. Private placement

### Best-Efforts Sales, or Agency Sales, and Direct Sales to the Public

The *best-efforts sale* employs the services of the investment banker as a selling agent. Thus the full risk is on the issuer, and the unsold securities may be turned back to the issuer by the investment banker. Table 17–4 gives some idea of the relative importance of this channel.

TABLE 17–4. Volume of New Registered Corporate Issues, Total, Underwritten, and Agency Basis (by Types), 1960–1967 *
(in millions of dollars)

| | | Underwritten | | Agency basis | | | | |
|---|---|---|---|---|---|---|---|---|
| | Total registered corporate issues | Amount | Percent | Total amount | Percent | Bonds | Preferred stock | Common stock |
| 1960 | $ 6,491 | $ 5,610 | 86% | $136 | 2% | $ 9 | $13 | $114 |
| 1961 | 7,983 | 5,955 | 75 | 224 | 3 | 16 | 26 | 202 |
| 1962 | 5,821 | 5,065 | 87 | 417 | 7 | 56 | 4 | 357 |
| 1963 | 5,275 | 4,762 | 90 | 83 | 2 | 6 | 4 | 73 |
| 1964 | 5,871 | 4,093 | 70 | 127 | 2 | 13 | 6 | 108 |
| 1965 | 6,951 | 5,944 | 86 | 150 | 2 | 18 | 0 | 132 |
| 1966 | 10,526 | 9,585 | 91 | 112 | 1 | 23 | 0 | 89 |
| 1967 | 17,154 | 16,583 | 97 | 103 | 1 | 11 | 0 | 92 |

* Securities not underwritten or sold on agency basis were issued directly to existing security holders.

SOURCE: Securities and Exchange Commission, *Statistical Bulletin*, monthly. Publication of data for this table terminated with the year 1967.

[B8]

We might expect the commission for best efforts selling to be less than for underwriting because the risk of underwriting is absent. Table 17–5 shows that, interestingly, the commission for best-efforts selling is higher. No doubt this is because the effort in selling is greater.

Oddly enough, issuers at both ends of the quality spectrum tend to use the best-efforts procedure. Issuers of high quality appear prepared to take the negligible risk of some unsold securities. Such a case was the landmark offering in March 1935 by Swift and Company of $43 million of 3.75 percent bonds due in 1950. The commission was only four-tenths of 1 percent. On the other hand, very speculative small concerns, particularly in mining, cannot get an underwriter even for a spread of 20 to 30 percent and are forced to use the best-efforts or agency basis.

**TABLE 17–5. Underwritten Cost versus Best-Efforts Distribution Cost by Size of Issue, 1963–1965, for Primary Common Stock Offerings (expressed as percentage of gross proceeds)**

| Size of issue (in millions of dollars) | Number of issues | | Total cost | | Commission | | Other expenses | |
|---|---|---|---|---|---|---|---|---|
| | BE * | U * | BE | U | BE | U | BE | U |
| Under 0.5 | 26 | 24 | 19.3% | 17.3% | 12.2% | 10.0% | 7.0% | 7.4% |
| 0.5– 1.0 | 15 | 45 | 14.7 | 14.6 | 10.4 | 9.4 | 4.3 | 5.2 |
| 1.0– 2.0 | 24 | 93 | 10.7 | 11.8 | 8.3 | 8.7 | 2.4 | 3.1 |
| 2.0– 5.0 | 23 | 119 | 9.7 | 9.0 | 8.0 | 7.3 | 1.7 | 1.7 |
| 5.0– 10.0 | 12 | 57 | 10.0 | 7.0 | 9.3 | 6.0 | 0.7 | 1.0 |
| 10.0– 20.0 | 5 | 19 | 10.8 | 5.7 | 10.3 | 5.0 | 0.5 | 0.7 |
| 20.0– 50.0 | 0 | 11 | — | 5.6 | — | 4.9 | — | 0.8 |
| 50.0–100.0 | 0 | 2 | — | 3.2 | — | 2.9 | — | 0.3 |
| 100.0–500.0 | 0 | 1 | — | 2.3 | — | 2.0 | — | 0.3 |
| Over 500.0 | 0 | 0 | — | — | — | — | — | — |
| Total Issues | 105 | 371 | | | | | | |

* BE = best-efforts or agency selling; U = firm underwriting.

SOURCE: Securities and Exchange Commission, *Cost of Flotation of Registered Equity Issues, 1963–1965* (Washington, D. C.: Government Printing Office, 1970), p. 13.

[A9916]

The same situation exists for the alternative of direct selling by the issuer to the public without the use of any investment banker. Here high-quality issuers may proceed by a rights or warrant offering,[9] giving each stockholder the right to subscribe to the new issue at a price significantly below the current market price. This has been done by American Telephone and Telegraph Company. Such rights can be sold by the stockholders to others who wish to exercise them. At the other extreme a small concern occasionally will attempt to sell some of its securities by advertising in local newspapers. To avoid SEC registration such offers are limited to residents of one state and require the buyer to sign a statement that he is purchasing for investment and not for resale.

In connection with the rights offering just described, a "stand-by" underwriting agreement may be entered into by the issuer. Such an agreement provides that the underwriter will pick up all or some agreed maximum of the issue not sold by the exercise of rights.

## The After-Market

One matter of prime interest to the issuer if the securities are not listed on an exchange but are traded over-the-counter is what happens to the price of the securities after they have been issued. This will vitally affect the next issue of the corporation.

---

[9] Rights are discussed more fully in Chapter 21.

The managing underwriter should "make the after-market" in the security. Other investment bankers and brokers will turn to him for information about the affairs of the issuer and for a bid and ask quotation. In making the after-market an investment banker forms an estimate of what the security is worth in the current market and goes long or short in an effort to approximate that price. If he does not do this but merely acts as an agent, the price of the security will fluctuate more widely. Weakness on the part of the investment banker making the after-market will soon be detected by others and the security will be shunned.

The incentive to the investment banker to make the after-market lies in the opportunity to make a profit larger than the usual commission by adding a differential. To prevent abuses, the National Association of Security Dealers [10] limits this differential to 5 percent of the price of the last previous transaction.

### The Risks of a Public Offering

It is frequently stated that the public offering of securities is a risky business. On the other hand, attacks are frequently made on the size of the "spread" or underwriting commission received by investment bankers. Table 17–6 shows that the spread can average as much as 12 percent for small issues of common stock. There is some little-known evidence that helps place this conflict in perspective.

**TABLE 17–6. Comparison of Underwriting and Other Costs of Various Equity Types of Security, 1963–1965 Classified by Size of Issue (cost as a percentage of proceeds)**

| Size of issue (millions of dollars) | Convertible bonds | | | Preferred stock | | | Certificates of participation † | | | Common stock primary offering | | |
|---|---|---|---|---|---|---|---|---|---|---|---|---|
| | No. of issues | Cost | | No. of issues | Cost | | No. of issues | Cost | | No. of issues | Cost | |
| | | U * | E * | | U * | E * | | U * | E * | | U | E |
| Under– 0.3 | 2 | 10.2% | 6.7% | 5 | 6.7% | 9.8% | 0 | — | — | 21 | 8.7% | 8.0% |
| 0.3– 0.5 | 2 | 6.2 | 8 0 | 1 | 10.0 | 5.0 | 3 | 9.6% | 1.5% | 29 | 12.0 | 6.8 |
| 0.5– 1.0 | 4 | 6.3 | 3.6 | 1 | 8.0 | 3.1 | 9 | 6.7 | 2.0 | 60 | 9.7 | 4.9 |
| 1.0– 2.0 | 24 | 7.6 | 3.8 | 4 | 8.0 | 3.4 | 10 | 5.0 | 1.6 | 117 | 8.6 | 3.0 |
| 2.0– 5.0 | 33 | 4.3 | 1.9 | 6 | 4.8 | 1.2 | 6 | 7.6 | 0.5 | 142 | 7.4 | 1.7 |
| 5.0– 10.0 | 15 | 3.4 | 1.2 | 17 | 1.0 | 0.6 | 5 | 6.0 | 0.4 | 69 | 6.7 | 1.0 |
| 10.0– 20.0 | 5 | 2.3 | 1.2 | 11 | 1.4 | 0.4 | 1 | 7.7 | 0.6 | 24 | 6.2 | 0.6 |
| 20.0– 50.0 | 7 | 1.3 | 0.4 | 5 | 2.7 | 0.4 | 0 | — | — | 11 | 4.9 | 0.8 |
| 50.0–100.0 | 4 | 1.5 | 0.3 | 3 | 1.4 | 0.3 | 0 | — | — | 2 | 2.9 | 0.3 |
| 100.0–500.0 | 1 | 1.1 | 0.3 | 0 | — | — | 0 | — | — | 1 | 2.0 | 0.3 |
| Over 500.0 | 0 | 0 | 0 | 0 | — | — | 0 | — | — | 0 | — | — |
| Total | 97 | | | 53 | | | 34 | | | 476 | | |

* U = underwriting compensation, E = other expenses.

† Certificates of participation are discussed in chapter 21.

SOURCE: Securities and Exchange Commission, *Cost of Flotation of Registered Equity Issues, 1963–1965* (Washington, D. C. Government Printing Office, 1970), various tables.

[A9914]

---

[10] While each exchange regulates activity in trading securities it lists, trading in unlisted securities is policed by the National Association of Security Dealers (NASD), a voluntary association recognized by the SEC.

In the case of an issue of convertible debentures,[11] where the common stock (into which the bond is convertible) is selling at a price well above the conversion price, many corporations have felt compelled to enter into underwriting agreements with investment bankers before calling the bonds in an effort to force conversion. These agreements provide that the underwriters will take an amount of common stock equal to that represented by bonds turned in for payment because some bondholders decline to convert.

There are at least two risks to which the corporation issuing the convertible bonds is exposed when it makes a call. First, the call of the convertibles may result in so much selling of the common stock by "converters" as to disorganize the market in the stock. Second, the period (30–60 days) between the day of notice to bondholders of the call and the day when conversion rights cease is long enough that sizable changes may occur in the general securities market, with the possible result that the market price of the issuer's common stock may fall below the conversion price. Then all bonds would be surrendered to the issuer for cash.

The underwriting of calls of convertible debentures[12] illustrates a situation in which the risks to the issuer are typically far smaller than in the usual public offering, particularly the first public offering by a corporation. Yet underwriting is frequently sought by the issuer in the case of a call of convertibles with the size of the spread in proportion to the risk.

### Private Placement

The most important alternative to standard underwriting is private placement. Table 17–1 shows the great growth in the use of this channel in recent decades in the case of bonds. The same movement also exists in the case of preferred stock, where there is an added stimulus. If the private purchaser is a fully taxable corporation, 85 percent of the preferred dividends received are free of income tax under a section of the Internal Revenue Code, which softens multiple taxation of dividend income flowing between taxable corporations.

Corporate officers give four principal reasons for this shift from underwritten public offerings to private placement. First, they cite that the long waiting periods for registration with the SEC create a hazard that the market may shift in this period. As already pointed out, the underwriting agreement is not usually signed until the day before the public offering, and this risk of change in the market falls on the issuer.

---

[11] Convertible debentures are discussed in detail in Chapter 19. A *convertible debenture* is a bond that gives the holder the right to convert the bond into common stock at a price stated in the bond. The conversion right may run for the life of the bond or for a limited period. Conversion will tend to occur when the market price of the common stock rises above the conversion price, since the bondholder can make a profit by converting the bond and then selling the stock.

[12] Bismarck Williams and Marvin Letwat, "Underwritten Call of Industrial Convertible Securities, 1950–61," *Quarterly Review of Economics and Business*, 3 (Winter 1963), pp. 71–77.

Second, private placement avoids the costs of registration and the underwriting spread, as well as potential criminal and civil liabilities for the officers and directors for statements in the prospectus that may later be held to be false or misleading. With respect to such liability, it is important to remember that there is liability not only for statements made but for failure to make statements about matters that later appear to have been significant. Not all of the costs of underwriting are truly saved because, first, there are also costs in a private placement and, second, the buyer of the private placement may succeed in capturing a part of the cost saving by slightly adjusting the yield or price he offers.

The third reason advanced by the issuer in favor of private placement is the great increase in funds available in the hands of institutional investors. This situation not only creates pressure but also enables such institutions to buy larger parts of issues without violating the rule of investment diversification.

The fourth reason is that private placement permits modification of the terms of the loan during the period of the loan because of the small number of security holders whose consent is required. This cannot be done when there are thousands of bondholders except through the expensive process of calling the issue. The need for modification during the long period of a loan is greater for industrial borrowers than for utilities, whose patterns are more stable. Many industrial companies are currently reworking the terms of their long-term loans every two years.

There is one sticky point in private placement: When does a private placement cease to be private and become public (and hence subject to registration) because of the number of buyers of the security? Most state "blue sky laws" answer this problem by setting the maximum number of buyers for a situation entitled to exemption. Federal legislation and administrative practice have not done this but have permitted the question to be resolved on the basis of the number of buyers involved, the financial knowledge of the buyers, and other factors. The counsel's office of the SEC examines each case submitted and gives the issuer a statement that, if the question is raised, it will render an opinion to the SEC recommending that the transaction be or not be recognized as private or public depending on the facts of each case.

The vast growth in private placements has presented a challenge as well as an opportunity to investment bankers. Many investment bankers have turned to serving the new development as agents, brokers, or "finders," collecting a fee for bringing buyer and seller together.

## COST OF UNDERWRITING

Our discussion has indicated that considerable attention is focused on the costs of floating an issue of corporate securities. These costs to the issuer are easily classified into the underwriter's spread and the expenses of flotation.

Three generalizations are immediately apparent, as Table 17–6 indicates:

1. The costs of issuing common stock are substantially higher than those for issuing preferred stock, and the latter in turn is more expensive to issue than bonds. This reflects the difference in underwriting risk associated with the types of securities.
2. The costs of issuing are in inverse proportion to the size of the issue.
3. The expenses of an issue (other than the underwriting fee) fall more in proportion to the size of the issue than underwriting commissions fall.

The expenses (other than the underwriting spread) are primarily printing costs, legal fees, and accounting costs. These expenses are more fixed than variable with the size of the issue. Hence they decline as a percentage of proceeds. The other expenses are engineering investigation costs in the case of some issues, the filing fee of the SEC, the transfer agent's fees, the costs of qualifying under state blue sky laws, and miscellaneous expenses such as telephone and telegraph.

The reasons for the variation in costs with the size and type of issue are readily apparent. The smaller-sized issues, particularly those under $5 million, involve greater underwriting risk and less well-known companies. Common stocks as opposed to bonds and preferred stock represent smaller unit sales and hence greater selling efforts.

The expenses (other than the underwriting commission) of the offering of RTE Corporation in 1966, shown in Figure 17–1, are given in Table 17–7.

TABLE 17–7. RTE Corporation Cost of a Stock Offering of $1,015,000

| | |
|---|---|
| SEC filing fee | $ 224 |
| Legal fees | 6,500 |
| Auditor's fees | 3,750 |
| Transfer agent fees | 400 |
| Printing expense | 4,000 |
| State blue sky fees | 1,600 |
| Miscellaneous | 526 |
| Total | $17,000 |

These expenses were 1.7 percent of the gross proceeds ($1,015,000) compared to the average of 3.0 percent for this size offering for 1963–1965 (see Table 17–6). The underwriting commission, or spread, in this offering was 8.3 percent compared to the average of 8.6 percent for this size offering (see Table 17–6).

### The Dying Issue of Competitive Bidding

In 1941 the SEC adopted Rule U–50, requiring competitive bidding on all new issues of bonds of utilities subject to the Public Utility Holding

Company Act of 1935. Then in 1944 a similar rule was adopted by the Interstate Commerce Commission for railroad bonds. The Federal Power Commission and some state public service commissions also followed this rule. The practice of competitive bidding was taken from the area of state and municipal securities and U.S. Treasury bills where it has long been the rule.

In the period 1934–1939 some 57 percent of registered bond issues were floated by six investment banking firms.[13] This situation fostered the argument that there was unequal bargaining power when there were several hundred corporations issuing securities but only a handful of investment banking firms on the other side, with each one tending to its own clients. The percentage of registered bond issues handled by these six firms dropped to 40 percent during 1948–1951. The question is whether this drop was due to the competitive bidding requirement or to the growth of private placements and the disbanding of the utility holding company empires, thus reducing the relative size of issues offered. The holding company empires were gradually dismantled after the Public Utility Holding Company Act of 1935, and the smaller units that resulted enabled smaller investment bankers to seek out the financing deals.

In any event, the effort of the SEC to follow the mandate of its rule requiring competitive bidding on utility issues had led to rather useless rituals. Some utilities under the pressure of the rule sought, but were unable to get, more than a single investment banker willing to handle their public offerings.[14] In this situation the SEC backed down and authorized exceptions to the rule. Few investment banking firms can risk the costs of investigating a proposed utility issue of smaller size in competition with the investment banker who has maintained close contact with the utility. Thus the investment banker who handled the last offering of a utility already has an extensive file on the client that he has kept current in the ordinary course of business. For a new investment banker to spend the time and money to develop the information necessary to place an intelligent bid in competition with the investment banker who now serves the client is just one more risk he must add to those he must carry.

## SUMMARY

Investment banking is the merchandising of securities. It includes both underwriting new issues and trading in previously issued securities. The investment banker deals for his own account and also acts as agent in buying and selling securities for his customers. The issuance of new securities is subject to SEC regulation under the Securities Act of 1933, and trading on the stock exchanges is subject to the Securities Exchange Act of 1934.

---

[13] The data are taken from P. L. Howell, "Competition in the Capital Markets," *Harvard Business Review*, 31 (May–June 1953), pp. 88–93.

[14] See the case of Public Service Company of New Hampshire in Erwin Esser Nemmers, *Cases in Finance* (Boston: Allyn and Bacon, Inc., 1964), pp. 318–321.

Private placement is direct dealing between the issuer of the securities and the buyer and is not subject to regulation. Investment bankers assist in private placements and also furnish investment counseling service. The percentage of all bonds privately placed grew from 20 percent in 1937 to a peak of 66 percent in 1964 and in 1973 stood at 60 percent.

In the underwriting process the investment banker uses a prospectus of the issue, which must make full disclosure of all relevant facts concerning the issuer and the issue. The issuing company is required to file a registration statement with the SEC which includes much more detail than the prospectus. Underwriting is carried out by a syndicate of underwriters brought together to handle the particular issue. The underwriters organize a selling group to assist in the sale. Underwriting may involve (1) a firm commitment by the underwriters to buy the issue or (2) merely their "best efforts" to sell the issue. Ninety percent of the dollar volume of registered securities is sold through firm underwriting.

In the underwriting process the managers of the underwriting syndicate may stabilize the price of the securities by their own rebuying and reselling.

The costs of underwriting are classified into two categories: (1) the underwriting commission and (2) other costs, such as printing, legal, and accounting expenses. Both kinds of costs decline as a percentage of proceeds as the size of the issue increases. The costs of handling common stock are higher than those for handling preferred stock, and the costs for the latter, in turn, are higher than for bonds.

Competitive bidding is required only in the issuance of securities by public utilities and railroads. The terms of other issues are negotiated by the investment banker and the issuing company.

### Study Questions

1. As the financial officer of a company going public, would you recommend that the company invite a number of investment bankers to make bids and proposals or would you advise the company to concentrate on a single investment banker?
2. Would you recommend that a company pursue a policy of obtaining its debt financing through private placement but its equity financing through public offerings?
3. Would you accept the argument that competitive bidding is possible for government securities and public utility offerings because the risks of such securities are small and extensive information about them is publicly available but that such bidding is not feasible for industrials because the risks are higher and because such firms are not willing to broadcast information about their operations?
4. It is sometimes argued that investment banking is bound to traditional ways that have little rational basis currently, although there may be historical reasons for such ways. One example cited is the matter of the dominance of underwriting compared to the agency basis of marketing securities (see Table 17–4). Is it the issuer or the underwriter that is bound to tradition?
5. Why is there objection to the practice of stabilizing the price of securities when the seller of canned goods offers his merchandise at a constant price?

6. Is it naive and unrealistic for the SEC to permit brokers to deliver the final prospectus to the buyer of a security at the same time the buyer receives his bill for the purchase of the security? What difficulties would stand in the way of a requirement that no sale can be made until five days after the final prospectus is first made available? If the "red herring" is all that the buyer can see at the time he makes his decision whether to buy, what is the point in requiring a final prospectus?
7. Frequent reference is made in finance to the term "dilution." Define "dilution" so that the term is not misleading but actually reflects the situation in which the earning power of a share of common stock has been weakened by an increase in the number of shares of the issuer.
8. Prior to 1933 the functions of investment banking were frequently combined with commercial banking. Do you think the separation has been sound or that the divorce was dictated by weaknesses (both in investment banking and in commercial banking) that were corrected by legislation—for example, the Federal Deposit Insurance Corporation for bank deposits and the Securities Act for investment banking?
9. The costs of a full registration of an issue of securities with the SEC are substantial (see Table 17–6), but the costs of filing under Regulation A are much less. Might you still favor a full registration in a situation in which you have the option to file under Regulation A?
10. Some states under blue sky laws limit the maximum price-earnings ratio at which common stock may be offered. Do you think this is a sound proposition or would you favor limiting the underwriter's commission to a maximum percentage of the offering price as a more effective means of achieving the same objective?
11. A leading finance text expresses concern over the growth of private placement because: (a) "small life insurance companies are unable to participate in private placements"; and (b) "small corporations must sell their securities through investment bankers." What is your evaluation of this concern over the growth of private placements?
12. In some public offerings of securities the prospectus reveals that the underwriters as part of their compensation will receive options to purchase a stated number of additional shares for a stated period (often one year) at the net price to be received by the issuer for the shares presently offered for sale. Would you favor such a provision if you were the officer of the issuer? If you were considering purchasing the shares? If such a provision were not granted the underwriters, what might the alternatives be?
13. SEC rules require that a proxy statement show the number of shares held by each nominee for director, but they do not require such a showing for directors in the case of a prospectus covering public offering of securities. Is this an inconsistency? (A proxy statement is a summary of the affairs of the corporation that the SEC requires anyone soliciting a proxy to furnish to each shareholder whose proxy is solicited.) (See Chapter 21.)
14. Will the underwriting commission be larger for the first offering of the common stock of a closely held corporation than for the same size offering of a publicly owned corporation, assuming that the two companies are identical in all respects, that is, are in the same industry, have the same product lines and records and the same debt leverage, and so on? Would there be any difference if the offering were for bonds rather than for common stock?

***Problems***

1. Secure a recent prospectus from a broker or directly from an underwriter (whose name can be obtained from advertisements in the *Wall Street Journal* or on the financial pages of a metropolitan newspaper). From the prospectus and the use of investment manuals such as Moody's or Standard & Poor's determine the following:

   a. Is this an initial public offering or have the company's securities been publicly traded previously?
   b. Is the offering by the company only, by selling stockholders only, or jointly by the company and selling stockholders?
   c. What is the relationship of the offering price to prior prices for the security (if this is not a first issue) or to prices of securities of comparable and competing companies (if it is a first issue)?
   d. What is the pattern of the price of the security after the public offering (paying attention to the movement of the general securities market as measured by the Dow-Jones Industrial Average or some similar index)?
   e. What is the underwriting commission as a percentage of gross proceeds? Compare this commission with (1) those of similar-sized issues brought to market at the same time and (2) the average commission for the class size of the issue during 1963–1965 (see Table 17–6).
   f. What is the number of underwriters and the dollar amount and percentage of the issue that each underwriter assumed as well as the provision (if stated in the prospectus) covering the situation in which one of the underwriters may be unable to sell his amount and seeks to turn it back to the other underwriters?

2. On November 21, 1966, RTE Corporation of Waukesha, Wisconsin, sold an offering of 70,000 shares of common stock at $14.50 per share at a commission of $1.20 per share through a firm (not agency) underwriting syndicate of 14 firms whose home offices are in New York, Chicago, Milwaukee, Denver, Cleveland, Los Angeles, Kansas City, Des Moines, Philadelphia, New Orleans, and Fayetteville, N. C. (several firms had home offices in New York and Chicago). Two of the firms (Walston & Company, Inc., and Dempsey, Tegeler & Company, Inc.) were "national wire houses" with offices in cities throughout the country. The proceeds of the offering were applied to working capital.

In 1966 RTE was the fifth largest manufacturer of distribution transformers (after General Electric, Westinghouse, McGraw-Edison, and Allis-Chalmers). The firm produces only that product. A distribution transformer is the familiar small tank on the electric pole near residences and serves to step down electric power from thousands of volts to the 110 and 220 volts used by customers.

RTE went public in October 1958 by the offering of approximately 100,000 shares (adjusted for stock dividends) by selling stockholders through a single underwriter, Loewi & Company, Inc., of Milwaukee, at $6 per share. This was a firm underwriting with a commission of $57,000. Before this offering RTE had 60 stockholders and after it 400 stockholders. Between 1958 and 1966 the list of stockholders grew to 1200 (of whom more than 900 were located in Wisconsin) by sales of the original 60 stockholders. The 1966 offering increased the number of stockholders to 1700. The stock was traded over the counter, and after the 1966 offering there were 831,467 shares outstanding. The 10-year record of RTE appears in Table 17–8.

TABLE 17–8. RTE Corporation Stock Record, 1958–1967

| Year * | Sales (millions) | Earnings (thousands) | Earnings per share | Dividends per share | Bid ‡ per share High | Bid ‡ per share Low |
|---|---|---|---|---|---|---|
| 1958 | $ 4.3 | $ 311 | $0.41 | $0.08 | $ 8 | $ 6 |
| 1959 | 5.1 | 305 | 0.40 | 0.17 | 9½ | 6 |
| 1960 | 5.7 | 233 | 0.31 | 0.17 | 6 | 5 |
| 1961 | 6.6 | 309 | 0.41 | 0.17 | 5½ | 4½ |
| 1962 | 7.8 | 337 | 0.44 | 0.19 | 9½ | 4 |
| 1963 † | 7.3 | 195 | 0.26 | 0.15 | 6¾ | 3½ |
| 1964 | 9.4 | 603 | 0.79 | 0.23 | 11½ | 6½ |
| 1965 | 12.7 | 952 | 1.25 | 0.31 | 17¾ | 10 |
| 1966 | 15.0 | 970 | 1.27 | 0.50 | 16⅜ | 12 |
| 1967 | 21.4 | 1,590 | 2.03 | 0.60 | 55 | 13 |

* Fiscal year ended March 31.

† In this year industry prices collapsed as a result of the antitrust proceedings begun in 1960 involving most manufacturers in the electric power industry but not RTE.

‡ This information is on a calendar year basis.

Additional information is available in Moody's *Industrials* or Standard & Poor's *Manuals*. The only comparable companies (manufacturing electric power-type transformers only) were Central Transformer Company and Moloney Electric Company, both publicly owned during this period. These companies merged in October 1965. RTE stock was split 3 for 1 in August 1968.

The industry record of sales of the product manufactured by RTE and of the pricing of this product appears in Table 17–9.

TABLE 17–9. Industry Record of Sales

| | Sales (millions) | Transformer Price index (1949 = 100) | | Sales (millions) | Transformer Price index (1949 = 100) |
|---|---|---|---|---|---|
| 1950 | $138 | 102 | 1959 | $234 | 132 |
| 1951 | 230 | 115 | 1960 | 211 | 129 |
| 1952 | 167 | 111 | 1961 | 210 | 126 |
| 1953 | 183 | 116 | 1962 | 213 | 118 |
| 1954 | 178 | 128 | 1963 | 186 | 96 |
| 1955 | 222 | 128 | 1964 | 222 | 96 |
| 1956 | 250 | 132 | 1965 | 257 | 96 |
| 1957 | 230 | 141 | 1966 | 312 | 99 |
| 1958 | 205 | 138 | | | |

SOURCE: National Electric Manufacturers Association.

a. Why was a single underwriter used for the initial offering in October 1958?

b. How was the initial offering price probably determined?

c. Why was a syndicate of 14 underwriters used in November 1966?

d. How was the price determined in the second offering?

e. Why do you think the 1966 underwriting commission (as a percentage of gross proceeds) did not differ much from that in 1958?

f. Is the stock qualified for listing on the New York Stock Exchange (see listing requirements, p. 472)? on the American Stock Exchange (see listing requirements, p. 472)? on the Midwest Exchange?

g. Why do you think the stock is not listed?

h. Why did the price of the stock advance so sharply after the November 1966 offering?

3. On July 28, 1961, in the midst of the "hot issue" market that came to an end in the major stock market collapse of May 1962, 170,680 shares of common stock of W. A. Brown Manufacturing Company of Chicago were offered by two selling stockholders at a price of $7 per share to the public.[15] This was about 35 percent of the total of 490,680 shares outstanding. The company is the country's largest manufacturer of large-scale, precision cameras and other photo-mechanical equipment. Its products are sold by 300 dealers in the United States and Canada, including Eastman Kodak, American Type Founders, Harold W. Pitman, and Roberts & Porter. Previously all of the stock had been closely held. Of the 170,680 shares offered, 14,000 were reserved for purchase by officers, directors, and others interested in the company.

The underwriting commission was 70 cents per share, or 10 percent of the selling price. Other expenses totaled $35,400, or 3 percent of the gross proceeds of $1,194,760. Of these expenses, $30,500 was borne by W. A. Brown Manufacturing Company and $5000 by the selling stockholders. The members of the underwriting syndicate, under comanagers Loewi & Company, Inc., of Milwaukee, and Blunt Ellis & Simmons, of Chicago, are listed in Table 17–10.

TABLE 17–10. W. A. Brown Manufacturing Company
Underwriting Syndicate of Common Stock Issue, 1961

| *Underwriter* | *Shares purchased* |
|---|---|
| Loewi & Company, Inc., Milwaukee | 40,090 |
| Blunt Ellis & Simmons, Chicago | 40,090 |
| Paine, Webber, Jackson & Curtis, New York | 19,000 |
| Bache & Company, Chicago | 11,000 |
| G. H. Walker & Company, New York | 11,000 |
| Cruttenden, Podesta & Company, Chicago | 7,500 |
| Dempsey-Tegeler & Company, Inc., St. Louis | 7,500 |
| Straus, Blosser & McDowell, Chicago | 7,500 |
| Baker, Simonds & Company, Inc., Detroit | 4,500 |
| The Illinois Company, Inc., Chicago | 4,500 |
| Mullaney, Wells & Company, Chicago | 4,500 |
| Raffensperger, Hughes & Company, Inc., Indianapolis | 4,500 |
| Rodman & Renshaw, Chicago | 4,500 |
| Saunders, Stiver & Company, Cleveland | 4,500 |
| Total shares underwritten | 170,680 |

The agreement among underwriters provided for a concession of 35 cents per share to selected dealers signing the selling agreement and of 12½ cents per share to other dealers who were members of the National Association of Securi-

[15] The complete prospectus, agreement among underwriters, purchase agreement, and selling agreement (selected dealers agreement) appear in Erwin E. Nemmers, *Cases in Finance* (Boston: Allyn & Bacon, Inc., 1964), pp. 191–236. These documents are as filed with the SEC and the prospectus is photographically reproduced.

ties Dealers. The agreement also provided that the comanagers were to receive 10 cents per share for their management services. The agreement authorized the comanagers, according to their discretion, to change the public offering price and the concessions to dealers after the release of the stock for sale to the public. The agreement also authorized the comanagers to borrow for the account of each underwriter to cover his commitment for shares if payment was not on hand at the time of the purchase transaction. In the stabilization section of the agreement the underwriters agreed that the comanagers could sell short or buy long (overallot and cover such overallotments) provided the net commitment did not deviate by more than 10 percent from the amount of shares each underwriter had agreed to purchase. But the comanagers were not committed to stabilize the price, nor if they began stabilization, were they committed to continue it. The agreement was to terminate 30 days after the initial day of offering unless the comanagers terminated the syndicate sooner. Prior to termination of the syndicate any shares reacquired by the comanagers of the underwriting group resulted in the disallowance of the commission of the original selling member of the syndicate for those shares and his agreement to pay any costs incurred by the comanagers in such reacquisition.[16] Upon default by any of the underwriters each underwriter agreed to increase his allotment by not more than 10 percent and authorized the comanagers to bring in any new purchaser.

The purchase agreement (by the comanagers with the selling stockholders) provided that if on the contemplated date of sale underwriters for less than 10 percent of the shares to be purchased were in default, there could be a four-day delay. If underwriters of more than 10 percent of the shares to be purchased were in default, the other underwriters could proceed with the total purchase (but were not obligated to do so) and could within 24 hours substitute other underwriters, and within another 24 hours the selling stockholders could substitute other underwriters. Thereafter either side could withdraw. The selling stockholders also agreed not to dispose of any further shares within six months of this sale, unless the comanagers consented. The selling stockholders and the company agreed to indemnify the underwriters for any liability the underwriters suffered under the Securities Act of 1933 as a result of any untrue statement of a material fact (or omission of any material fact) in any documents filed with the SEC. After the execution of the purchase agreement (signed July 25, 1961, with the actual offering July 28, 1961), the underwriters could withdraw *only* in the event of (1) a major physical calamity to the company's facilities, (2) material litigation, (3) the cessation of trading on the New York Stock Exchange or the Midwest Stock Exchange, or (4) a banking moratorium.[17]

The selling agreement (selected dealers' agreement of the comanagers of the underwriters with various dealers) provided that the stock would be offered only at $7 per share until the agreement was terminated and that the selected dealer would receive 35 cents per share and could reallow 12½ cents per share to members of the National Association of Securities Dealers. Subscriptions by any dealers under this agreement were subject to acceptance by the comanagers of the underwriters and allocation or refusal in the event of oversubscription. In the event that the underwriters reacquired during the agreement any stock sold

[16] It is this provision that is designed to discourage any buyer in the general public (a "fast buck artist") who hopes to buy the security at the offering price and resell it to another member of the syndicate at a higher price. Such a buyer will cause a loss to the underwriter who sold shares to him and will be cut off by that underwriter as to future transactions.

[17] The purchase agreement did not contain the usual provision that withdrawal by the underwriters could occur if there was material, adverse development of prices on the New York Stock Exchange.

by the signing dealer, the dealer would forfeit his commission. This agreement was to terminate 30 days after the date it was signed unless it terminated sooner or was extended for another 30 days.

The earnings record of W. A. Brown Manufacturing Company prior to this issue appears in Table 17–11, and the balance sheet in Table 17–12.

TABLE 17–11. W. A. Brown Manufacturing Company
Earnings Record, 1956–1961

| *Year* * | *Sales (thousands)* | *Earnings (thousands)* | *Earnings per share* † |
|---|---|---|---|
| 1956 | $ 662 | $ 20 | $0.03 |
| 1957 | 863 | 39 | 0.05 |
| 1958 | 1,164 | 74 | 0.08 |
| 1959 | 1,608 | 115 | 0.12 |
| 1960 | 2,034 | 186 | 0.19 |
| First 6 months of 1960 | 980 | 85 | 0.09 |
| First 6 months of 1961 | 1,140 | 200 | 0.20 |

* Fiscal year ended October 30.
† No dividend has been paid on the shares.

Additional information is available in Moody's *Industrials* or Standard & Poor's *Manuals* prior to the merger of W. A. Brown Manufacturing Company into American Photocopy Equipment Company in 1964. There was no other comparable company whose securities were publicly traded. The principal competitors of W. A. Brown were Robertson Photo Mechanix, Inc., Lanston Unitronics, Inc., and the Nu Arc Company.

This stock offering was sold to about 700 stockholders in nine states.

a. Why were the underwriting commission and other expenses of this issue less than appear for the average of issues of this size in Table 17–6?

b. Why were the other expenses allocated between the company and the selling stockholders when only the stockholders were selling?

c. This is one of the smallest corporations (in either sales or assets) whose stock has ever been fully registered with the SEC. With a net worth of $415,000, the market value of the firm's shares at $7 per share was $3,434,760. Why would front-rank names of investment banking handle this issue?

d. Might this offering have been made at a higher price through less prominent investment bankers?

e. Why was such an offering not made?

f. Is the company qualified for listing on the New York Stock Exchange (see p. 472)? on the American Stock Exchange (see p. 472)?

g. It is customary in offerings of this kind for the underwriters to oversell the issue by 7 to 10 percent and to terminate the syndicate within a week after the offering. What determines the amount of oversale and the length of time the syndicate exists? Is there danger in overalloting?

h. What was the reason for omission of the usual provision in the purchase agreement permitting the underwriters to withdraw in the event of an adverse development of prices on the New York Stock Exchange?

i. What is the purpose of the clause restricting any further sales of stock by the selling stockholders for six months after this offering?

TABLE 17-12. W. A. Brown Manufacturing Company
Balance Sheet, April 30, 1961
(in thousands of dollars)

| *Assets* | | | *Liabilities* | | |
|---|---|---|---|---|---|
| Cash | | $146 | Trade accounts | | $ 80 |
| Accounts receivable | $217 | | Accrued expenses | | 39 |
| Less reserve | 10 | 207 | Federal income taxes | | 104 |
| Due from officer | | 8 | Other taxes | | 6 |
| Inventories | | | *Total current liabilities* | | $229 |
| Raw material | $ 96 | | | | |
| Work in process | 26 | | Stockholder investment | | |
| Finished goods | 28 | 150 | Common stock, $100 par, | | |
| Prepaid expenses | | 8 | 522 shares * | $ 52 | |
| *Total current assets* | | $519 | Additional paid-in capital | 6 | |
| | | | Retained earnings | 357 | |
| Deposits | | 16 | Total net worth | | $415 |
| Equipment | | | | | |
| Plant equipment | $144 | | | | |
| Office equipment | 19 | | | | |
| Automobiles | 12 | | | | |
| Leaseholds | 34 | | | | |
| | $209 | | | | |
| Depreciation and amortization | 100 | 109 | | | |
| Total assets | | $644 | Total liabilities and net worth | | $644 |
| | | | Long-term lease † | | |

* On June 5, 1961, the common stock was split 940 shares of no par, stated value 50 cents per share for each share of $100 par, resulting in a restatement of net worth as:

| | |
|---|---|
| Common stock, no par, 50 cents stated value, 490,680 shares | $245,000 |
| Retained earnings | 170,000 |

† The company leases its factory building from W. A. Brown and a personal holding company for an annual rental of $40,320 through April 30, 1971 and an adjoining parking lot for $3300 annually through September 30, 1969. The company also leases office space in Prudential Plaza, Chicago, for $10,525 annually.

j. What determined the price of the offering as $7 per share? What is the last year's price-earnings ratio on this basis? the current year's (annualized)?

k. What happened to the price of this security after offering?

### Selected References


Cohan, A. B., *Private Placements and Public Offerings: Market Shares Since 1945*. Chapel Hill, N. C.: University of North Carolina Press, 1961.

Commission on Money and Credit, *Private Financial Institutions*. Englewood Cliffs, N. J.: Prentice-Hall, Inc., 1963.

Corey, E. R., *Direct Placement of Corporate Securities*. Cambridge, Mass.: Harvard University Press, 1961.

Eiteman, D. K., "The S.E.C. Special Study and the Exchange Markets," *Journal of Finance*, 21 (May 1966), pp. 311–323.

Friend, Irwin, G. W. Hoffman, W. J. Winn, M. Hamburg and S. Schorr. *The Over-the-Counter Securities Markets* (New York: McGraw-Hill Book Co., 1958).

Friend, L., H. P. Minsky, and V. L. Andrews, *Private Capital Markets.* Englewood Cliffs, N. J.: Prentice-Hall, Inc., 1964.

Hayes III, S. L., "Investment Banking: Power Structure in Flux," *Harvard Business Review,* 49 (March-April 1971), pp. 136–152.

Howell, P. C., "Competition in the Capital Markets," *Harvard Business Review,* 31 (May-June 1963), pp. 88–93.

Investment Bankers Association of America, *Investment Banking.* Englewood Cliffs, N. J.: Prentice-Hall, Inc., 1949.

Life Insurance Companies of America, *Life Insurance Companies as Financial Institutions.* Englewood Cliffs, N. J.: Prentice-Hall, Inc., 1962.

Logue, D. E., "On the Pricing of Unseasoned Equity Issues: 1965–1969," *Journal of Financial and Quantitative Analysis,* 8 (January 1973), pp. 91–104.

Robinson, R. I., *Money and Capital Markets.* New York: McGraw-Hill Book Company, Inc., 1964.

Sears, G. A. "Public Offerings for Smaller Companies," *Harvard Business Review,* 46 (September-October 1968), pp. 112–120.

Securities and Exchange Commission, *Cost of Flotation of Corporate Securities, 1951–1955.* Washington, D. C.: Government Printing Office, 1957.

———, *Cost of Flotation of Registered Equity Issues, 1963–1965.* Washington, D. C.: Government Printing Office, 1970.

———, *Privately Placed Securities: Cost of Flotation.* Washington, D. C.: Government Printing Office, 1952.

———, *Special Study of Securities Markets.* Washington, D. C.: Government Printing Office, 1963.

Soldofsky, R. M., "The Size and Maturity of Direct Placement Loans," *Journal of Finance,* 15 (March 1960), pp. 32–44.

Stoll, H. R. and A. J. Curley, "Small Business and the New Issues Market for Equities," *Journal of Financial and Quantitative Analysis* 5 (September 1970), pp. 309–322.

Taft, R. W. "The Greening of the Red Herring Prospectus," *Financial Executive,* 39 (November 1971), pp. 73–76.

Waterman, M. H., *Investment Banking Functions,* Ann Arbor, Mich.: University of Michigan Press, 1958.

Williams, B. S., and M. Letwat, "Underwritten Calls of Industrial Convertible Securities, 1950–61," *Quarterly Review of Economics and Business,* 3 (Winter 1963), pp. 71–77.

# 18

# The Capital Markets: Security Exchanges and Markets

Organized security exchanges play a vital role in the functioning of the capital market. The New York Stock Exchange (called the Big Board) overshadows all other exchanges, as Table 18–1 indicates, with the American Stock Exchange, also located in New York City, outstripping the remainder. Only members can trade on the New York Stock Exchange. New firms become members by buying seats from old members. The transactions of the general public are executed through a member. A broker who is not a member arranges with a member to execute the order of that broker's customers.

There were 3377 corporations with 3923 stock issues and 2165 bond issues listed on these exchanges on June 30, 1973.[1] The majority of companies with issues listed on any exchange (52 percent of issuers and 90 percent of listed bond issues) were listed on the New York Stock Exchange. In market value of listed shares traded, the New York Stock Exchange led in 1972 with 78 percent of the total volume of $204 billion, followed by

[1] Securities and Exchange Commission, *39th Annual Report*, year ended June 30, 1973, p. 154f.

the American Stock Exchange with 10 percent. The other 12 exchanges had a total of only 12 percent in volume of shares traded. These 12 exchanges serve companies with regional interest and also duplicate some listings on the two New York exchanges.

In the 20 years from 1950 to 1970, for the New York Stock Exchange the percentage *value* of all listed stocks rose from 84.5 to 92 percent.

Stock exchanges are important to the corporate financial manager for a variety of reasons:

1. An exchange is an efficient and relatively inexpensive way of carrying on transactions in securities. Self-regulation as well as government regulation of the exchange guard against fraud and a host of other practices that would shake confidence. The practice of the members of the exchange in making good on any defalcation of a member adds significantly to the functioning of the exchange.[2]

2. Information on prices and trading volume is quickly and accurately transmitted, and the fact that such information is available is a stabilizing force. Price changes are smaller and more frequent on a continuously functioning exchange than would be true otherwise.

3. The improved marketability offered by an exchange creates higher collateral values for securities.

## SHORT SELLING AND MARGIN TRADING

Two specific practices of an organized exchange aid the effective functioning of the market. The first is *short selling*, or selling a security that is not owned by the seller at the time of the sale. In this case the seller expects to buy the security later at a lower price to "cover" the commitment. The seller in a short sale borrows the stock from the broker (who borrows it from another customer) in order to make delivery to the buyer, who actually receives the stock in the same way as if there had been an ordinary sale. When the one who sold short finally buys the stock, the shares are delivered to the broker from whom he borrowed the stock at the time of the short sale.

Much of the stock that is available to a broker to use in short sales arises from *margin trading*, which involves the use of credit to buy securities. In margin trading the broker holds the stock as collateral for the loan of part of the stock's unpaid purchase price. This stock is then available for lending to carry out short sales. When margin requirements are 50 percent the buyer can acquire stock by paying half of the price and borrowing the other half from his broker and paying interest on the loan.

Certain rules on short selling exist that limit the speculative dangers inherent in a downward spiraling of stock prices. One rule prevents short sales at a price lower than the last sale. A short sale is permitted only at a price higher than the last sale, or "on the up tick," as it is called. Another rule forbids short selling by officers or directors of a corporation.

---

[2] Mention should be made of the 1970 insolvency guarantee fund set up by the New York Stock Exchange after the Haupt failure following the salad oil swindle. Under federal legislation passed in 1970, individual accounts are insured up to $60,000 against defalcation by brokers.

Similarly, changing the margin requirements is a tool available to limit speculative excesses on the up side and to encourage investment on the down side.

TABLE 18–1. Number of Issues, Volume of Trading, and Value of Securities Traded on Registered Securities Exchanges, 1972

| | Stocks | | | Bonds | | |
|---|---|---|---|---|---|---|
| | No. of issues | Shares traded † | Dollar volume | No. of issues | Face value | Dollar volume |
| Exchange | | (millions) | | | (millions) | |
| New York | 2037 | 4496 | $159,700 | 1946 | $ 9168 | $8717 |
| American | 1404 | 1103 | 20,452 | 191 | 840 | 753 |
| All other * | 482 | 700 | 23,873 | 28 | 109 | 46 |
| Total | 3923 | 6299 | $204,025 | 2165 | $10,117 | $9516 |

* "All other exchanges" does not include duplicating of issues on the New York Stock Exchange and American Stock Exchange as to number of issues, but as to shares and dollar volume does include such duplicating issues. No issues are traded on both the New York Stock Exchange and American Stock Exchange.

† Does not include right and warrants of 144,723,000 units with dollar volume of $1.5 billion.

SOURCE: Securities and Exchange Commission, *39th Annual Report*, year ended June 30, 1973, pp. 154 and 159 (Washington, D.C.: Government Printing Office, 1973).

[A9917]

After the 1929 stock market crash it was argued that the speculative excesses that preceded the crash might have been reduced by controls over margin buying. As a result, the Board of Governors of the Federal Reserve System sets the current margin (downpayment) requirements for loans by both banks and brokers against the purchase of securities, and the SEC has the responsibility of enforcing these requirements.

The purchaser of securities on margin must not only meet the margin requirement at the time of purchase; if the price of the security falls drastically, he may have to post additional cash. How much *remargining*, as it is called, may be required is a matter of judgment by the broker or bank. If the purchaser is unable to post the additional funds, the broker will sell the securities to repay the loan.

One argument advanced for margin control is that speculators might easily overreach themselves, with the result that a relatively small change in the price might push them into a forced sale, thus precipitating sharp market movements. This possibility is supported by the computations in Table 18–2. Thus, the higher the margin requirement, the lower the incentive to speculate.

TABLE 18–2. Effect of Sample Margin Requirements

| | Margin requirement | | | |
|---|---|---|---|---|
| | 10% | 25% | 50% | 80% |
| Speculator's funds, or margin | $ 10,000 | $ 10,000 | $ 10,000 | $ 10,000 |
| Margin buyer can purchase | 100,000 | 40,000 | 20,000 | 12,500 |
| Profit (or loss) before interest on the loan if the price moves 5 percent | 50% | 20% | 10% | 6.25% |

The other argument is that there is a macroeconomic aspect to margin controls. Because of the matter of forced sales to meet margin requirements, the buying or selling of a given security may bear no relation to the long-run merits of the particular company and its securities. Hence, it is argued that applying higher margin requirements in a boom market will reduce the boom somewhat, and vice versa, in a slump. There is no evidence yet to support this argument.

It is true that some issues are less stable than others and that a selective margin requirement (different margins for different issues) might produce a greater equilibrium in the market. The New York Stock Exchange has applied such selective margin requirements by temporarily going to 100 percent margins for issues of great speculative interest. This means cash must be paid in full; no margin trading.[3] When the speculative interest wanes, the selective margin requirement is eliminated.

Brokers will not enter margin agreements for securities traded over-the-counter[4] but only for listed securities. However, commercial banks will loan against the collateral of over-the-counter securities.

## LISTING

The advantage of marketability gained by listing on an exchange can be overstated. Ultimately, marketability of a security depends more on the size of the issue, its distribution, and the character of its holders than on the mere fact of listing on an exchange. Many over-the-counter issues have a larger volume of trading than many listed issues. All exchanges maintain minimum listing requirements, which vary from time to time. These requirements are designed to insure that the security will have a sufficient volume of trading. Listing also involves a commitment by the corporation to release information regularly and to respond promptly to special inquiries by the exchange.

Premature listing by a corporation can be a disadvantage. In the over-the-counter market the commissions and therefore the likelihood of profit to the broker by dealing in the stock are larger than on the exchange, thus giving the incentive to the broker to bear the costs of promoting the security. When the stock is listed this incentive is removed.

There are potential dangers in listing. Wide distribution of a security may increase the possibility of loss of control of a corporation. It is possible for speculators to acquire control through corraling the smaller number of shares needed for control than would be necessary if ownership were more concentrated. Listing may also increase management's concern with security prices and thereby divert energies from regular business activities. Or management may become unduly concerned with the short-term effect of a decision on the price of its securities rather than with the long-run consequences of the decision.

---

[3] James A. Largay III, "100% Margins: Combating Speculation in Individual Security Prices," *Journal of Finance*, 28 (September 1973), pp. 973–986.

[4] Securities not traded on an exchange are referred to as traded over-the-counter. This market is considered later in this chapter and in Chapter 21.

## LISTING REQUIREMENTS

To be eligible for listing on the New York Stock Exchange, a company must currently (1974) have:

1. At least 2000 stockholders with 100 shares or more
2. At least 1 million shares publicly held
3. A minimum market value of $16 million for publicly held shares
4. Net tangible assets of $16 million
5. Pretax annual earnings of $2.5 million in most recent year and $2 million in the two preceding years

Bond and preferred stock issues do not have to show as wide a distribution, and the American and regional exchanges set less stringent standards for all types of securities. The requirements (1974) for listing in the American Stock Exchange are:

1. Net worth of $3 million
2. Net earnings in the last year of at least $300,000 and pretax earnings of $500,000
3. A minimum of 300,000 publicly owned shares (excluding shares owned by officers and directors and family-held shares)
4. A minimum of 900 public stockholders, including 600 with lots of 100 shares or more
5. A minimum aggregate market value of $2 million for publicly held shares
6. Shares selling at a minimum of $5 a share for a reasonable period of time prior to filing the listing application

The listing committee will not approve nonvoting common or preferred stock that does not provide for voting rights after more than 2 years of default in dividend payment. The listing committee will also examine conflicts of interests in an applying company.

In addition to meeting the eligibility requirements, the company must furnish the exchange with much of the same material as would appear in an SEC registration statement, for example, the charter and bylaws, so that information concerning the number of shares and classes of stock issued, the rights of classes of stockholders, and voting and annual meeting requirements is readily available. The company's financial history must be set out and information must be given concerning the firm's growth record, properties held, product lines, personnel, and like matters. Subsidiary and affiliated companies must be identified. Independently certified balance sheets and income statements must be furnished, and the company must agree to furnish financial statements to stockholders. The distribution among holders of the issue must be set out in detail so the exchange can satisfy itself that a substantial part of the issue is widely held and a free market will exist in the issue. If too large a part of the issue is closely held, it would be possible for manipulation to occur. Also, the company must maintain independent stock transfer facilities in the city of the exchange to facilitate transfers and to reduce the chances of fraudulent certificates. Engraving of certificates is required in order to reduce the possibilities of forgeries.

The SEC receives a duplicate of the listing application and must consent to the listing. Once the listing is effective, the process of removing the issue from listing may be difficult. Delisting requires SEC approval and is allowed only if the company has declined to the point where there is little trading interest.

Some issues are traded on exchanges although they are not formally listed. This *unlisted trading privilege*, as it is called, arises without any action by the issuing corporation. These issues are mainly of two types: those that carried the privilege at the time of the passage of the Securities Exchange Act of 1934 and those listed on an organized exchange but which received the unlisted privilege on regional exchanges because of local interest in the issue. The number of issues with unlisted trading privileges (not registered on another exchange) is continually declining [5]

### Secondary Distributions and Exchange Distributions

An important function of the organized exchanges is to handle the sale of large blocks of stock that otherwise might upset the price performance of an issue and trigger violent, although temporary, price action. A *secondary* is the sale of a large block of stock that originates with a security holder and not with the issuing corporation. The use of the secondary is an alternative to disposing of a large block of stock in small lots over a long period of time. In the case of a secondary, buying orders are solicited after the close of the market on one day in an effort to dispose of the entire lot before the opening the next morning. The consent of the exchange is necessary for such activity. The offering is usually at the closing price or slightly below. The buyer pays no commission, which is a bit of an incentive to purchase, but the seller pays a commission, ordinarily larger than the regular exchange commission, to compensate for the special effort. A group of buyers may purchase all or part of the block for redistribution at their risk, and securities dealers who are not members of the exchange may participate.

The secondary may require SEC or state blue sky registration. Thus, if the block is being sold by one in control of the issue (any holder of more than 10 percent of the issue), the seller is limited in a 6-month period to the sale of no more than 1 percent of the total issue or the average daily trading volume in the most recent 3-week period, whichever is less. If the seller wants to sell a block larger than this, the issue must be registered with the SEC.

---

[5] In the 7 fiscal years ended June 30, 1972, the list of issues with unlisted trading privileges (not registered on another exchange) declined from 132 to 57 and constituted less than 1 percent of all shares traded. Securities and Exchange Commission, *38th Annual Report*, year ended June 30, 1972, p. 162.

Unlisted trading in issues listed on other exchanges constituted a large part of all trading on regional exchanges, in year ended June 30, 1970—57 percent of shares on the Cincinnati Exchange, 78 percent on the Boston Exchange, 60 percent on the Pittsburgh Exchange, 35 percent on the Midwest Exchange, and 30 percent on the Pacific Coast Exchange. Securities and Exchange Commission, *36th Annual Report*, year ended June 30, 1970, p. 78.

A *special offering* is a technique that has been available since SEC approval in 1942. This is the offering of a block of stock smaller than a secondary and made during regular trading hours. It requires the consent of the exchange and is offered at a fixed price, with only the seller paying a special commission. The minimum size of a special offering is 1000 shares and $25,000 in market value. Since 1953 the special offering has been known as an *exchange distribution.*

Price stabilization is permitted in both the secondary and the special offering or exchange distribution.

### The Specialist

One important part of an organized exchange is the role of the specialist. Each listed security is assigned to at least one specialist and more active issues may have more than one specialist. Members of the exchange with buy or sell orders in a security go to the post of a specialist in that security who then executes or matches buy and sell orders. The specialist is responsible for maintaining an orderly market in that security.[6] In doing so he frequently trades for his own account, making profits or losses, but he must execute customers' orders before his own. He maintains files of all open orders (orders away from the market price) arranged in the sequence in which he received them. It is apparent that there must be an objective set of rules governing the sequence in which orders are filled, since the price of the security may move before all who want to do business at a stated price are taken care of. The simplest rule would be to handle all orders at a given price in the order in which they are received, regardless of the type of order. This is the rule but only within categories of types of orders. Without listing the complete rules governing priority of orders, we can cite some examples. A regular-way order (in which payment and delivery of the stock are due on the fifth business day following the transaction) takes precedence over a next-day order (in which payment and delivery are due on the next business day) at the same price. Or the larger of two orders received at the same time will be filled first. Or, in the case of identically sized orders received simultaneously, the flip of a coin will determine which is to be executed when both cannot be executed.

### The Odd Lot Dealer

In addition to a specialist, there is the *odd lot dealer.* With some exceptions for high-priced stocks, an *odd lot* is an order for less than 100 shares of a stock. To illustrate the handling of an odd lot, assume an odd lot sale order. When the price of a stock moves up, all of the odd lot orders at the *old* price will be filled. This is so because, in order to receive a given price for the sale of an odd lot, the market price must reach *more* than the desired price. The price is ⅛ of a point *more* for stocks selling under $55 and ¼ *more* for those selling at $55 and more. Then,

[6] Failure to do so may result in disciplinary action by the Exchange. The specialist in GM stock was censured for permitting the price to fluctuate widely on October 14, 1971—traded as high as $83¾ and closed at $81⅛.

even though the odd lot dealer has no matching buy order, he must execute the sell order by buying for his own account. The extra 1/8 or 1/4 compensates him for the risk he takes as well as the higher unit cost of executing the order compared to the round 100 shares.

## THE OVER-THE-COUNTER MARKETS

The over-the-counter markets are best described as all activities of trading securities through brokers that do not occur on the organized exchanges. The over-the-counter markets handle the great bulk of security issues. Although federal government bonds are listed, most of the trading in them is over-the-counter. Only a few state and municipal issues are listed, and the great bulk of them are traded over-the-counter. Almost all bank and insurance shares are traded over-the-counter, as well as about half of the corporate bond and preferred stock sales. Thus, listed securities predominate only in railroads, utilities, and industrial common stocks. Most new issues by corporations are by those whose securities are traded over-the-counter.

Quotations of the over-the-counter markets are published as representative bid and ask figures rather than as the price of actual transactions. These figures along with volume of trading of some issues, appear daily in metropolitan newspapers for securities of local interest. *The Wall Street Journal* publishes daily bid and ask figures for a large list of over-the-counter stocks. Currently the requirement for appearing in this list is 1500 or more stockholders. On Mondays this newspaper also publishes bid and ask figures regionally in several editions for securities that have a more limited distribution. All of these quotations originate with members of the National Association of Security Dealers and, specifically, with an investment banker making a market in the security. Ordinarily, this is the investment banker who was the manager of the last public offering of that security.

In addition, the National Quotation Bureau publishes the *National Daily Quotation Service* in regional editions containing security quotations together with the names of brokers who are interested in each issue. These editions are referred to by their colors:

| | |
|---|---|
| Eastern bonds | Yellow |
| Eastern stocks | Pink |
| Western bonds | White |
| Western stocks | Green or white |
| Pacific bonds | White |
| Pacific stocks | Blue or white |

State and municipal bonds offered for sale appear daily in *The Blue List.*

In the over-the-counter markets, brokers act not only as agents but also as principals, buying and selling for their own account. Thus their profit may include not only the commission, which follows the rates of the Big Board, but also some spread where they have bought the security at a somewhat lower price. To guard against dealer abuses of acting as principal, the National Association of Security Dealers has adopted a rule that a spread of more than 5 percent in an over-the-counter transaction in which a dealer buys at one price and sells at another "raises the question as to whether there is a violation of the rule" which binds them to trade at prices "reasonably related to the current price." [7]

While the SEC has jurisdiction over the over-the-counter markets, the actual policing is done by the National Association of Security Dealers with more than 3000 member firms under a system of self-regulation made possible by the Maloney Act of 1938. The most effective tool in this policing is the practice of limiting to members the price concessions from wholesalers to retailers at the time of a public offering. These concessions are vital to the profits of a broker.

In 1965 the SEC extended its jurisdiction over securities traded over-the-counter. Previously only public offerings of over-the-counter securities came under the SEC. Now the requirements of a proxy statement and the limitations on insiders, which had previously applied only to listed securities, are extended to all issues with 500 stockholders traded over-the-counter. An *insider* is defined as an officer, director, or one holding 10 percent of the security.[8] Insiders are prohibited from profiting by selling and buying within 6 months thereafter, or vice versa. Any profit from such an insider transaction is payable to the company. All transactions by insiders must be reported monthly to the SEC and are published monthly by the SEC in the *Official Summary of Security Transaction and Holdings* and appear in *The Wall Street Journal.* In the case of a listed security, insiders are also barred from selling short.

### The Third and Fourth Markets

The term *third market* has been applied to "off-board" trading through brokers of securities listed on the New York and/or American stock exchanges. Recently the term *fourth market* has been applied to direct trading between buyer and seller without the use of a broker.[9] There is no law requiring that transactions in listed securities go through an exchange although Exchange rules require members to do so. Table 18–3 shows the relative size of the third market. This activity is not solely directed at eliminating or reducing commissions but also at securing better prices for larger blocks of stocks. In essence the third market seeks to locate "potential" buyers and sellers, namely, those who might be willing to buy or sell but who do not presently have open orders on the exchange at prices for which they would be willing to do business. More than three-quarters of the third market sales are of securities that are principally traded on the New York Stock Exchange. In particular is-

---

[7] Securities and Exchange Commission, *10th Annual Report* (1944), p. 80.

[8] This is defined under the SEC rule 16b. By court decisions, the term "insider" also includes anyone with information not publicly known about the company.

[9] The "first market" is trading of listed securities on the stock exchanges. The "second market" is the trading of unlisted securities through brokers on the over-the-counter market.

sues at particular times the trading in the third market exceeds that on the exchanges.

TABLE 18–3. Third Market Sales of Common Stocks Listed on New York Stock Exchange Compared with Exchange Sales of Common Stocks, 1965–1972 (in millions)

| | Sales on exchange | | Third market sales | | | |
|---|---|---|---|---|---|---|
| Year | No. of shares | Value | No. of shares | Percent of total | Value | Percent of total |
| 1965 | 1809 | $ 73,200 | 48 | 2.7% | $ 2,500 | 3.4% |
| 1966 | 2204 | 98,555 | 58 | 2.4 | 2,873 | 2.9 |
| 1967 | 2886 | 125,329 | 85 | 2.9 | 4,151 | 3.3 |
| 1968 | 3299 | 144,978 | 120 | 3.6 | 5,983 | 4.2 |
| 1969 | 3174 | 128,663 | 155 | 4.9 | 7,228 | 5.5 |
| 1970 | 3213 | 103,063 | 210 | 6.5 | 8,021 | 7.8 |
| 1971 | 4265 | 147,098 | 298 | 7.0 | 12,383 | 8.4 |
| 1972 | 4496 | 159,700 | 327 | 7.3 | 13,581 | 8.5 |

SOURCE: Securities and Exchange Commission, *39th Annual Report* (June 30, 1973), p. 157, and *Statistical Bulletin*, monthly, beginning with 1973, weekly.

[B20]

## SUMMARY

Securities are traded either on the stock exchanges or on the over-the-counter market. By far the largest of the 14 organized securities exchanges is the New York Stock Exchange, which handles 92 percent of the dollar value of listed stocks, with the American Stock Exchange handling 7 percent. The other 12 exchanges handle only 1 percent of the total value of listed shares for companies listed with them exclusively. Each exchange is made up of member firms who act for themselves and for customers.

Short selling is the borrowing of stock from a broker in order to carry out a sale by one who expects to buy the stock later at a *lower* price in order to return the shares to the one from whom he borrowed them. Margin trading is the purchase or sale of stock but making only part payment while the broker makes a loan to the customer for the balance. Thus margin trading involves leverage.

Listing on an exchange requires the application of the issuer. The various exchanges have minimum standards for listing in order to reduce fraud and to assure the listing of only such securities as have a sufficiently broad interest among investors. The unlisted trading privilege applies to companies whose securities were traded on the exchanges before the Securities Exchange Act of 1934 and to trading on other exchanges of securities listed on one exchange.

Secondary distributions and exchange distributions involve the sale on an exchange of large blocks of stock in such a way as to preserve an orderly market. Many buyers are gathered to handle the purchase.

Much of the work of the exchange is carried on by the specialist who handles the transactions in a particular security and is responsible for maintaining an orderly market in that security. To do this the specialist will trade for his own account. Another important function is performed by the odd lot dealer, who handles less than round lots. In most cases a round lot is 100 shares.

The over-the-counter market handles the great bulk of security issues, including most of the volume in federal and municipal bonds, almost all the bank and insurance shares, and half of the corporate bond and preferred stock sales, as well as smaller common stock issues. This market is policed by the National Association of Security Dealers, whose membership includes more than 3000 investment bankers.

The third market involves "off-board" trading in listed issues and involves searching out buyers or sellers of large blocks of stock to be handled in a single transaction.

### *Study Questions*

1. The statement is sometimes made that short selling is a form of gambling and should be prohibited on all organized exchanges. Do you agree?
2. In some parts of the country the practice of delayed delivery has developed for stocks traded over-the-counter as an effort to approximate short selling on organized exchanges. Under this practice the buyer (usually a broker) agrees that the seller has a stated period of time (usually 90 days) in which to make delivery of the stock certificate. The seller usually makes a small concession in price (such as 2 percent) to effect the transaction and does not receive payment until he delivers the certificate. Would you favor permitting such a practice?
3. Why should margin trading be restricted to securities listed on an exchange? Why not permit margin trading of securities not listed but traded over-the-counter?
4. What problems might be encountered if selective margin requirements were made effective with varying margins required for different securities?
5. The role of the specialist in a listed security has been frequently criticized. Do you think specialists should be eliminated as part of the exchange picture? If so, what device would you recommend to perform the matching of buy and sell orders?
6. Would you favor a rule requiring that the practice of quoting bid and ask prices for securities traded over-the-counter should be replaced by a rule requiring the reporting of the high and low price for the day? If so, who should be designated to report such prices, since many brokers may trade the stock and prices are not collected in one place such as is true of the exchange? What rule would you apply if there were no trades on any given day?
7. Should the third market be subject to regulation such as applies to the organized exchange?
8. Does regulation of the securities markets increase or decrease the volatility of the price of securities? Before you leap to an answer, consider the argument that increased certainty about the absence of fraud, manipulation, and so on encourages people to take risks they otherwise might not take.

9. In the income tax laws of England and Canada, capital gains are not taxed on the grounds that they are not income but rather, are changes in one's capital account. On the other hand, some states (such as Wisconsin) tax capital gains at the same rate as ordinary income. Would a change in the federal income tax law (which taxes capital gains) to either the English-Canadian position of no tax on capital gains or to the full tax position of some states have a substantial effect on the prices of securities? In this connection, remember that a large part of the volume of present security transactions is accounted for by pension funds and other institutions that are not subject to income tax.
10. If a company is unwilling to make the commitments required by an organized exchange for listing, should the unlisted trading privilege be extended to owners of its securities or should the policy of the Securities Exchange Act of 1934 continue so that no new unlisted trading privileges are permitted?

### Problems

1. If you have $5000 with which to "play the market," what market value of listed securities can you buy if the margin requirement is 60 percent? What will your profit or loss be if you go the limit of your margin in purchasing securities and the price of the security moves 10 percent either way? What percentage will this be of your capital? How much additional money must you furnish if the price of the security falls 10 percent?

2. If you use your funds to acquire unlisted securities and borrow the necessary additional funds at a bank instead of from the broker, and the bank loans 80 percent of *current* market value, what will your profit or loss be if the security moves 10 percent either way? What additional money must you furnish if the price of the security falls 10 percent?

3. Take any issue of *The Wall Street Journal*, locate the page giving quotations for stocks traded over-the-counter, and select 20 stocks at random. How many of these would qualify for listing on the New York Stock Exchange (applying the standards appearing in the text at p. 472)? The necessary information for this purpose will be found in Moody's or Standard & Poor's manuals, except some information on the number of stockholders will not be shown, although information as to the number of shares publicly offered in issues registered with the Securities and Exchange Commission will appear. Using a rule of thumb that such offerings average 100 to 200 shares per purchaser, is it possible to estimate the number of shareholders added by the company in the process of such an offering? Be alert to stock splits and stock dividends.

4. Select one of the 12 regional exchanges and examine the stocks that are listed only on that exchange (exclude unlisted trading in securities listed on the New York and the American stock exchanges) to determine how many could qualify for listing on the New York exchanges.

The 12 exchanges are Midwest (Chicago), Pacific Coast (San Francisco), Boston, Philadelphia-Baltimore-Washington, Cincinnati, Detroit, Pittsburgh, Colorado Springs, Honolulu, Richmond, Salt Lake City, and Spokane.

You will find quotations of these exchanges in the appropriate metropolitan newspaper and can consult Moody's or Standard & Poor's manuals for data on individual companies.

Can you determine in the individual cases a likely reason why companies listed on one of the 12 exchanges have not sought listing on the New York or American exchanges?

### Selected References

Blume, M. E. and Frank Husic, "Price, Beta, and Exchange Listing," *Journal of Finance,* 28 (May 1973), pp. 283–299.

Cooke, G. W., *The Stock Markets.* New York: Simmons-Boardman Publishing Company, 1964.

Eiteman, W. J., C. A. Dice, and D. K. Eiteman, *The Stock Market,* 4th ed. New York: McGraw-Hill Book Company, Inc., 1966.

Fredman, A. J., and C. C. Johnson, "Effect of New NYSE Fee Structure on the Third Market," *Financial Executive,* 38 (October 1970), pp. 18–23.

Friend, Irwin and M. E. Blume, "Competitive Commissions on the New York Stock Exchange," *Journal of Finance,* 28 (September 1973), pp. 795–819.

Leffler, G. L., and L. G. Farwell, *The Stock Market,* 3d ed. New York: The Ronald Press Company, 1963.

Loll, L. M., Jr., and J. G. Buckley, *The Over-the-Counter Securities Markets: A Review Guide,* 2d ed. Englewood Cliffs, N. J.: Prentice-Hall, Inc., 1967.

McKinley, G. W., "Life Insurance Company Lending to Small Business," *Journal of Finance,* 16 (May 1961), pp. 280–290.

Schultz, B. E., *The Securities Market,* rev. ed. New York: Harper and Row, Publishers, Inc., 1963.

Securities and Exchange Commission, *Special Study of Securities Markets.* Washington, D. C.: The Commission, 1963.

Van Horne, J. C., "New Listings and Their Price Behavior," *Journal of Finance,* 25 (September 1970), pp. 783–794.

Walter, J. E., *The Role of Regional Security Exchanges.* Berkeley, Calif.: University of California Press, 1957.

# 19

# Long-Term Debt Financing

In this chapter we will examine corporate long-term financing. Strictly speaking, all debt maturing in more than 1 year is long term. In recent decades the category of intermediate-term debt has been recognized,[1] and generally the label "term loan" has been applied to it. Term loans are for more than 1 year but are characterized by the fact that they are made by private placement and usually involve periodic repayment of principal, whereas long-term debt financing does not involve such periodic repayment and may be a public offering or a private placement.

After examining the terminology of long-term debt we will proceed to the basic device of the indenture and the trustee, the key questions of priority, security, additional borrowing, and other rights, and the arguments for and against long-term debt. We will then focus on specialized areas such as convertible debt, warrants, and income bonds. Finally,

[1] The reader will recollect that intermediate-term debt financing was discussed in Chapter 12.

we will consider planning for maturity with the alternatives of retirement or refunding of the debt.

## TERMINOLOGY

If a debt issue over $1 million is offered publicly, there must be a trust agreement, called an *indenture*, between the borrowing corporation and a trustee who serves as a representative of all the buyers of the debt securities. The key points of the trust agreement are usually summarized in the debt security itself. The debt security issued under the indenture may be called a *bond* or a *debenture*. Financial usage does not draw a clear line between what is a bond and what is a debenture. The word "debenture," however, is usually used to identify a general obligation of the borrower that is not secured by a mortgage. If there is a mortgage as security, the document is called a bond. But unsecured debt securities are also called bonds. We can summarize this by stating that a debenture is a bond, but not all bonds are debentures.[2] If the debt instrument matures in less than 1 year from the time of issue, the security is called a *note*. All debt maturing in more than 1 year is called *funded debt*. This does not mean that there is a cash fund linked with the debt; rather "funded" is a financial term to describe debt with a maturity over 1 year.

A *mortgage* is a grant by the borrower to one class of creditors of preference or priority in a specific asset. In the event of any default by the borrower in paying the one holding a mortgage, or any other condition, the creditor holding the mortgage is entitled to force the sale of the specific asset and to receive full payment of his claim from the proceeds of the sale of the specific asset before any other creditors receive anything from such proceeds. At one time a borrower issuing a mortgage was required to transfer title to the mortgaged property to the lender. The borrower then had only the right to redeem or get the property back if he paid the debt. Today title is not transferred by the borrower to the lender, but the borrower simply puts the asset up as collateral to be seized if he defaults. The legal procedure by which the creditor forces the sale of the asset when the debtor defaults is called *foreclosure*. This is a proceeding for the protection of the debtor in which the creditor must prove in court that there is a debt, that there has been default in its terms, and that the debt is secured by a mortgage. Finally, the creditor asks the court to order the sale of the mortgaged asset, with the proceeds to be used to pay the lender's claim.[3]

---

[2] The securities issued in a term loan are also called bonds or debentures.

[3] When the asset put up as security for the debt is personal property, as distinguished from real estate, the relationship may be called a *pledge* rather than a mortgage. In general, a mortgage of personal property (called a *chattel mortgage*) involves the retention or possession of that property by the debtor, but a pledge requires the debtor to deliver possession of the property to the creditor. Even though the debt is unpaid, the creditor loses the pledge if he ever redelivers possession of the property to the debtor. These historical distinctions have been greatly reduced by the Uniform Commercial Code, which is now the law in many states.

### The Indenture and the Trustee

In the case of a short-term loan the main risks are known to the lender and are not likely to change significantly during the period of the loan. Furthermore, the few things that the lender considers important (such as maintenance of a given current ratio) can usually be set down in less than a dozen pages for all manner of possible developments. Borrower and lender remain in close contact. Unusual developments can be met by rewriting loan provisions. In contrast once bonds are issued (and many issues are in bearer form [4]), it will be impossible to assemble the bondholders to rewrite the agreement. Thus to meet every possible point, the indenture will usually run to hundreds of pages and will specify the duties and compensation of the trustee, the form of bonds to be issued, their number, amount, interest rate, maturity, a description of the property mortgaged as security if any, any call or redemption provisions, the terms upon which additional bonds may be issued, the percentage of bondholders needed to cause amendments of the agreements, conversion rights if any, sinking fund provisions if any, remedies of bondholders in the event of default, and protective provisions covering items such as paying taxes, maintaining insurance, limitation on other mortgaging, and condition under which the borrower may pay dividends.

The standard unit for a bond is $1,000 or multiples thereof and price is quoted as a percentage of par (but without a percentage sign). Thus if the bond quotation is 120, it means $1,200 for a bond of $1,000 par value. The bond is negotiable [5] and may be in: (1) full bearer form, that is, the bond and its attached interest coupons can be sold by whomever has possession of it; (2) registered form as to principal and bearer form as to interest coupons, or (3) fully registered form as to principal and interest. By registered we mean that the owner's name appears on the bond and that a register of owners is maintained by the trustee (or a separate institution acting as a registrar). Registered as to interest means there are no coupons attached but the owner receives the interest by check.

The trustee's main duties are: (1) to certify, that is, vouch for the authenticity of the bonds at the time they are issued; (2) to verify that all of the commitments of the borrower are carried out; and (3) to assert the rights of the bondholders in the event of default, such as to bring foreclosure. As a result of the laxness of trustees of bond issues in the Great Depression, bondholders frequently did not receive the benefits specified in the indenture. As a result, the Trust Indenture Act of 1939 gave the SEC jurisdiction over indentures so that the trustee must be independent of the borrower, have sufficient power to act for the bondholders, and can be held liable for his actions. Prior to the act it was common to include an "*exculpatory clause,*" which released the

---

[4] An instrument is in bearer form when it reads "payable to bearer," or if payable to a stated person, has been endorsed in blank by that person, that is the person to whom payable has simply signed his name with nothing more.

[5] This means that in law the buyer of the bond who receives it in good faith, having paid value for it before maturity and with no notice of any defect, will prevail over others who claim rights to it. A negotiable instrument can be recovered from a thief but not from one who bought it for fair value from a thief with no knowledge of the theft and prior to any default of the bond.

trustee from liability for his misactions, including negligence. Such a clause is now forbidden by the act, which applies to all issues over $1 million.

### Classification of Bonds

Bonds can be classified in many ways. A far from complete list of bonds shows 42 distinct types.[6] For our purposes we can identify the key bases of classification as: (1) what the priority position of the bond is; (2) what the security for the bond is; (3) what the rights of the borrower regarding the issuance of more debt are; and (4) what unusual rights the bondholder has.[7] Many categories of bonds involve merely an identification of the situation leading to the issuance of the bond rather than the substantive rights of the bondholder. Thus, a refunding bond may simply indicate it replaces a previously issued but now expired bond, or it may replace a bond that has been called in for payment before maturity.

Bond priority and security provisions affect the interest rate of the bond both directly as to what the underwriter of the bonds will seek and indirectly because of their effect on the bond rating (AAA, AA, A, and so on) which the issue will receive from Moody's or Standard & Poor's.

1. *Priority.* As to priority, the question always is, prior to what? Even unsecured bonds may have priority over some other debt, such as a subordinated debenture that has been subordinated to the bond and hence will be paid only after the bond is paid. If no contrary provision exists, all debt has equal priority, particularly over all ownership or equity interests. Most priority is concerned with specific property mortgaged as security for the particular bond issue. Such property may be real estate, leases, other securities, or any property. To the extent that the specific property is inadequate to pay off the bonds in full, the unpaid balance of the bonds qualifies as a general or unsecured debt.

It is sometimes difficult to determine the security behind a bond. This is true in the case of a railroad system that was put together by combining previously separate railroads. The system was put together with all old bond issues continuing to exist, each with its prior claim on some specific stretch of track. Thus, a first mortgage bond of the system may actually be a second mortgage bond on such separate pieces of track as were previously mortgaged. It often requires considerable study to identify accurately the true extent of priority that such bond issues have.

2. *Security.* It is apparent that the security for the bond issue may be linked to the priority of the issue. The security may be identified as certain parcels of real estate or it may include all real estate owned by the corporation. The bond may include a so-called *after-acquired property clause.* Under this provision all future property that the cor-

---

[6] See Erwin E. Nemmers, *Dictionary of Economics and Business,* 3d ed. (Totowa, N. J.: Littlefield, Adams & Company, 1973). Reproduced below at p. 697.

[7] Sinking fund and call provisions are discussed later in this chapter.

poration may acquire automatically becomes subject to the mortgage. The benefit of such a clause to the bondholder is dubious. The clause tends to be used to bolster what otherwise would be a weak issue, but as soon as the issue containing the clause has been sold, the first order of business for the borrower is to develop means to avoid the effect of the clause in hampering further financing.

There are many ways to defeat the after-acquired property clause. The most obvious way is not to buy more property but instead to lease it. The rights of the corporation (which issued the after-acquired property bonds) on this lease may become subject to the after-acquired property clause if the clause was worded broadly enough. But the lessor continues to own the leased property and has the first claim on it if the rent is not paid. The equipment trust certificate covering the rolling stock of a railroad is a classic example of this. The "lease" may be arranged in different forms, such as a conditional sale of the property to the corporation, or a trust may be used. All of the forms are directed at preserving the priority of the one financing the specific equipment.

Another method to avoid the after-acquired property clause is to create a subsidiary corporation to buy the property and give a mortgage on it. Thus, the parent corporation that issued the bonds with an after-acquired property clause becomes the owner of only the stock of the subsidiary.

Another way to avoid the after-acquired property clause is a *purchase-money mortgage.* Here the seller of the new property has a mortgage placed on it to secure the purchase price, and the buyer (the corporation that issued bonds with an after-acquired clause) gets only the equity in the new property. Thus, the bonds with the after-acquired clause get only a second mortgage.

Still another way to avoid the after-acquired property clause may be through a merger. Here the after-acquired clause may specifically state that it does not apply in mergers, or the merger statute of the state of incorporation may permit the alteration of the terms of bonds.

Last, the corporation may have included call provisions in the bond issue and, thus, will be able to refund the issue with a new issue that omits the after-acquired clause.

3. *Right of Borrower to Issue More Debt.* The bond indenture may contain various provisions covering the right of the borrower to issue more debt. The first question is whether more bonds may be issued against the same security and with equal rank. If this is true, the issue is called an *open-end mortgage bond.* Even in this case there will be a limit provided as to the total additional bonds that may be so issued. If at the time of first issue no more bonds may be issued against the security, the bonds are *closed-end mortgage bonds.* The right of the borrower to issue more bonds, whether or not against the particular security, may also be limited. There are many ways of achieving this objective. The obvious method, placing a specific dollar limit, is seldom used in public offerings because the bond issuer will object to the inflexibility.

In direct placements, however, the provision is common that no other bonds may be issued. This provision is paired with another stating that when additional bond money is sought by the borrowing corporation the lender will be given the first opportunity to purchase any new proposed bonds. Then if the lender is not interested, the borrower may solicit the additional money elsewhere on the same terms as were offered the lender. If the borrower can find a second lender on this basis, the first bond indenture contains specific provisions providing, for example, that the new bond issue will pay off the first bond issue (usually at some premium).

In addition to the control over the right of the borrower to issue additional bonds, the bond indenture can, at least indirectly, control the amount of short-term borrowing or trade credit that the bond issuer can obtain. This is done by provisions covering the maintenance of a minimum current ratio, minimum working capital, dividend conditions, and so on. These provisions will not only affect the right of the borrower to additional long- or short-term funds but also will specify the balance the borrower must maintain between current assets and fixed assets and the ratio of current assets to current liabilities.

4. *Additional Rights of the Bondholder.* Here we are concerned with the rights the bondholder may receive over and above the myriad provisions seeking to protect him against default.[8] The earliest of these rights to develop was the provision for voting in the event of default either in payment due or in any covenant of the agreement. There are many provisions possible, ranging from a provision for complete control of voting by the bondholders to some type of *pro rata* participation in voting with stockholders. However, a group of thousands of bondholders scattered across the country is hardly able to take effective action to improve matters over what stockholders (who are also quite interested) would decide.

Particularly since the end of World War II, a movement has developed to offer bondholders additional rights under the assumption that the borrower will prosper. These rights focus on conversion privileges and warrants to buy common stock and have become so prominent as to justify separate consideration later in this chapter.

## ARGUMENTS FOR AND AGAINST LONG–TERM DEBT

Having examined the institutional framework of long-term debt commitments, we are in a position to evaluate the arguments for and against long-term debt.[9]

From the viewpoint of the lender (the bondholder), it has been customary to speak of risk, income, and control as dominant factors, but

---

[8] One technical provision that should be mentioned is the *acceleration clause*, which provides that as soon as any default occurs all the obligations under the particular issue of the borrower become due immediately, particularly the payment of the principal.

[9] At this point we do not reconsider the theoretical aspects of debt financing, which were examined in the Appendix M to Chapter 15 in a consideration of the theory of capital structure.

this classification omits some matters of grave concern to the bondholder. Risk is often thought to include only two items, the risk of loss of principal or interest and the risk of call. Default has been discussed and the bondholder is more secure than other security holders, both as to earnings and in the event of liquidation. There is also the risk that he may lose a favorable investment by call before maturity, thus presenting him with the problem of reinvesting his money. But these are only two of the classical risks of investment. The others are: (1) the liquidity risk; (2) the risk of the change in the interest rate (or the capitalization rate in the case of equity); and (3) the risk of change in the purchasing power of money. It is the last that has dominated the scene (particularly for bondholders) since the end of World War II. Bondholders' concern with this risk has led to the increasing use of convertibles[10] and warrants. As to income, the bondholder is willing to forego participation in higher earnings in return for a steady flow of income and protection against dips in earnings. The matter of control over the investment by voting rights is surrendered by the bondholder for the covenants the borrower makes. From the viewpoint of the bondholder, there is little tax difference between bonds and stock: both involve ordinary income taxation of earnings and both present some capital gain or loss possibilities.

From the viewpoint of the borrower (the issuer of the bonds), the cost of debt funds is lower than that of equity funds[11] if for no other reason than because the interest is tax deductible. In addition, the borrower does not part with any control, and he gains financial leverage; the swing in earnings per share with a change in income of the corporation is heightened in both directions. Leverage is not only useful in heightening earnings at some increase in risk but it is also the basis for an issuer to diversify his risk. By passing some of the risk of the firm to creditors the issuer reduces his own funds committed to this venture and frees money for use in another firm in another venture. The use of debt with a call provision makes the borrower better able to expand or contract, although repurchase of shares can also achieve contraction for equity.

However, debt has a maturity date that the issuer must provide for. Long-term debt, in particular, involves covenants that are much more extensive than those required for short-term debt. Despite the best effort to anticipate and provide for all contingencies in the indenture, events may develop that would require a change in the covenants before maturity. It is difficult to devise methods for altering covenants. The most feasible solution is to call the issue and refund.

## CONVERTIBLE DEBENTURES AND CONVERTIBLE SUBORDINATED DEBENTURES

A *convertible debenture* is an unsecured obligation of a borrower carrying a rate of interest and providing the holder with the right to con-

---

[10] See Table 19–1 p. 490.

[11] The reader is reminded of the theoretical dispute (see Appendix M to Chapter 15) concerning whether the use of debt lowers the overall cost of capital to the company in the absence of the deductibility of interest for income tax purposes.

vert the debt into common stock of the issuer at a set price. The interest rate is lower than the rate for the same debenture without the conversion privilege because of the potential value of the privilege. The price of the common stock into which the debenture may be converted is set above the market price of the common stock at the time the debenture is issued, usually by 10 to 15 percent. A debenture usually has a call price, enabling the issuer to force conversion if the market price of the stock rises sufficiently. A *subordinated convertible debenture* usually provides that the debt will be subordinate to any other funded debt and to bank loans. Both types of convertibles may carry any of the other provisions commonly found in bonds and debentures. Convertibles have a maturity of from 10 to 30 years, with 20-year to 25-year maturities being the most common. A significant number of convertibles carry a *conversion price* step-up provision providing for periodic increases in the conversion price.

We noted earlier that a change in the purchasing power of the dollar is a major risk against which the bondholder has no protection except a conversion right or warrants.[12] A *bond warrant* is a right to buy common stock at a stated price. There are two types: one involves turning in the bond as payment for the stock, the other does not require the surrender of the bond but permits cash to be used as payment for the stock. The first type is equivalent to a convertible bond. The bondholder is also exposed to the risk of a change in the market rate of interest, but this risk is more limited. Convertible debentures are not a creation of the post-World War II period but were widely used in the 1920s, another period of a rising price level.

Several environmental factors also encourage the increasing use of convertible debentures. First is the legal restriction on insurance companies, banks, personal trusts, and some pension funds as to investment in common stocks. Also, there are large amounts of money under self-imposed restrictions of risk; for example, the restrictions imposed by the "balanced" objectives of some mutual funds. Convertible debentures offer such institutions an opportunity to participate in the capital gains afforded by common stock but with less risk than is associated with common stock. In the case of a trust or fund limited to bonds by law or contract, sacrificing some income by investing in a convertible debenture in the hope of a capital gain upon conversion is an example of a phenomenon more common in taxation: avoiding the letter of the law without being guilty of evading the law.

Another environmental factor that has encouraged the use of convertibles has to do with margin requirements. Until 1968 credit up to 90 percent could be obtained from banks for the purchase of debentures, while margin requirements on stock fluctuate and may permit as little as 30

---

[12] It may be argued that the bondholder accepts the risk that the purchasing power of the dollar will fall (or the price level will rise) as balanced by the likelihood that the purchasing power will rise (or the price level will fall). This argument must be rejected, because the long-run trend of the price level over several hundred years has been up and the periods of rise have been of much greater time duration than those of fall. Hence the risk of a price-level rise is only in small part offset by the likelihood of a price-level fall.

percent credit on stock purchases. In 1968 the Federal Reserve subjected banks to the same margain rules as brokers in the case of convertibles. But convertibles have a more secure price floor than stock, thus reducing the risk of a call for additional margin.

Finally, there has been a cyclical factor at work in the case of convertibles. This was apparent in the market of 1965–1969. After the severe collapse of the speculative stock market in May 1962, many investors became wary of stocks as an investment. Convertibles attracted large sums during the period 1965–1969 as investors saw them as a chance to have their cake and eat it too.[13]

What happened between 1962 and 1965–1969 appears to have been a change in the risk-aversion attitude of a significant number of investors. Underwriters sensed this shift and capitalized on it by offering subordinated convertibles.[14] Even prime credit firms were attracted to the supply of funds available in this market at this time. Table 19–1 shows the growth in the absolute and relative use of convertible debentures from 1963 through the first half of 1969.

A detailed consideration of convertibles is warranted, since as much as 60 percent of all publicly offered debt issues in any 1 year may be convertible.[15]

### Antidilution Provisions in Convertibles

Before examining the theory of convertibles, we should note the antidilution provisions commonly found in both convertible bonds and convertible preferred stock. Because the conversion price of the common stock is fixed at the time the convertible is issued, it is necessary to provide for the adjustment of this conversion price if the issuer later (1) declares stock dividends or splits, (2) makes capital distributions to the holders of common stock, (3) grants options at less than the conversion price of the common stock stated in the convertible, or (4) sells common stock at less than the market price at the time the convertible was issued,

---

13 This view has considerable validity up to the time the corporation calls the convertible and the investor must decide whether to "cash out" by selling the stock after conversion or hold the stock.

14 Of a small sample of 43 convertibles offered in 1961–1963, all but 2 were subordinated. See E. F. Brigham, "An Analysis of Convertible Debentures," *Journal of Finance*, 21 (March 1966), pp. 35–54. Whereas this sample showed only issues of $2.5 to $60 million, with the majority in the $5 to $20 million class, the issues of 1967 show many in the hundred million dollar and up class.

15 This was true in 1951. See C. J. Pilcher, *Raising Capital with Convertible Securities* (Ann Arbor, Mich.: University of Michigan Bureau of Business Research, 1955). This study covers convertibles from 1933 to 1952. In 1967, $4.1 billion was raised by 226 public issues of convertible bonds, as Table 19–1 shows. This was 40 percent of all publicly offered debt in that year and 20 percent of all underwritten public financing for the year. In contrast, in the entire 20-year period 1933–1952 there were only 182 issues of convertible bonds. Pilcher, p. 6. In view of the fact that convertibles have been used far less frequently by public utilities (except for telephone companies such as American Telephone & Telegraph and General Telephone), the use of convertibles is greater than overall figures suggest. The reason for the nonuse of convertibles by many utilities is probably tied to state rate regulation. The attitude of federal regulatory jurisdiction over the parent appears to be the reason why telephone companies have used convertibles.

either directly or through the use of rights. If there are no antidilution provisions, the holder of the convertible will find he has lost some of his bargain, since the capital gain on conversion will be less than it would be were there antidilution provisions.

### Dual Statement of Earnings

As soon as convertible debentures are employed, the problem of the correct statement of earnings per common share arises. The Securities and Exchange Commission requires that earnings per common share be shown on both an "as is" basis, that is, with the outstanding convertible debentures figured as debt, and then on a "fully diluted basis," assuming all the convertible debentures have been converted into common stock. In the process of computing the "fully diluted basis," the interest savings, due to the fact that the outstanding convertibles are assumed converted, are added back to pre-income tax profits in order to arrive at fully diluted earnings.

This dual statement must also include not only the effects of conversion of convertible debentures but also the effects of conversion of convertible preferred stock, the exercise of warrants (to be discussed shortly), and the exercise of options.

### Theory of Convertibles

An interesting study [16] of convertibles offers a convenient device for examining the theory of convertibles. A graphic presentation of what the history of a convertible issue might look like if the issue performs successfully is given in Figure 19–1.

TABLE 19–1. Growth in Relative Use of Convertible Debentures as a Security Type, 1963–1969 (amounts in millions of dollars)

| | Total securities | | Common stock | | Preferred stock | | Convertible bonds | | Other debt | |
|---|---|---|---|---|---|---|---|---|---|---|
| | Number of issues | Amount | Number of issues | Amount | Number of issues | Amount | Number of issues | Amount | Number of issues | Amount |
| 1963 | 475 | $ 5,275 | 280 | $1,007 | 27 | $150 | 46 | $ 226 | 122 | $3,892 |
| 1964 | 522 | 5,871 | 324 | 2,559 | 26 | 177 | 48 | 305 | 124 | 2,892 |
| 1965 | 598 | 6,951 | 376 | 1,811 | 26 | 377 | 60 | 900 | 136 | 3,863 |
| 1966 | 625 | 10,526 | 324 | 2,265 | 35 | 458 | 104 | 1,749 | 162 | 6,054 |
| 1967 | 1,006 | 17,154 | 466 | 1,935 | 50 | 794 | 226 | 4,075 | 264 | 10,350 |
| 1968 | 1,464 | 14,722 | 1009 | 3,890 | 41 | 586 | 208 | 2,371 | 206 | 7,875 |
| 1969 (1st half) | 1,137 | 10,075 | 883 | 3,840 | 21 | 310 | 119 | 1,899 | 114 | 4,026 |

Note: Common stock includes certificates of participation. This table includes only registered offerings for the account of the issuer and excludes foreign government issues, investment company issues, employees plans, warrants, and other miscellaneous issues.

SOURCE: Securities and Exchange Commission, *Cost of Flotation of Registered Equity issues, 1963–1965* (Washington, D. C.: Government Printing Office, 1970) p. 2.

[B19]

It is important to note that many important variables in the situation have been held constant for convenience, so that we can examine what would be expected to happen if these variables remained constant. In Figure 19–1, important variables held constant are the market attitude toward risk and the market rate of interest. Furthermore, it is assumed there is some earnings growth by the issuer; otherwise the price of the

[16] Brigham, pp. 35–54.

common stock would not rise and the conversion privilege would have no value.

Several of the curves present no problem. The issue price and maturity price of the convertible are the same, namely, par.[17] The call value curve starts above par (usually by the amount of 1 year's interest) and steps down to par at maturity. The debt-only curve starts below par because the convertible carries a lesser interest rate than a debenture with no conversion rights. As this curve approaches maturity it rises to par because the total remaining interest disadvantage keeps shrinking over time.

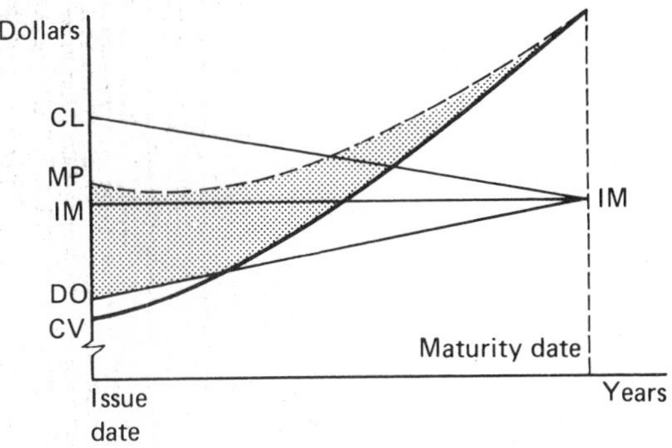


Figure 19–1 The history of a successful convertible debenture issue. $IM$ = issue-maturity price; $DO$ = debt-only price if there were no conversion privilege; $CL$ = call price; $CV$ = conversion value; $MP$ = market price of security.

Reproduced from E. F. Brigham, "An Analysis of Convertible Debentures," *Journal of Finance*, 21 (March 1966), p. 37, with permission.

Two curves remain to be explained: the conversion price of the common stock is normally set at 10 to 15 percent above the market price of the common stock at the date of issue of the convertible debenture. Thus, the conversion value of the debenture will start 10 to 15 percent below par (the issue price), since it is determined by multiplying the market price of the common stock at the time of issue of the convertible by the number of shares for which the convertible can be exchanged. The starting conversion value is usually below the starting debt-only value, but the situation might be reversed, as we shall see, depending on the trade-off of interest rate against conversion rate.

Following the theory of common stock value discussed in Chapter 14, the common stock value is expected to grow, as indicated by the equation

$$V_t = \frac{D_{t+1}}{k - g}$$

where $V_t$ is the value of the common stock at any date, $D_t$ is the dividend at that date, $k$ is the capitalization rate, and $g$ is the expected growth rate.

---

[17] The issue price deviates from par occasionally because of inability of the underwriter to work out the precise arithmetic. Most interest rates are quoted in eighths of a percent. The only other variable available to adjust to market conditions is the date of the issue, since the bonds will be offered by the underwriters at par plus accrued interest from a given date.

It follows, then, that the conversion value of the convertible will reflect the growth rate of the common stock value. Thus, where $CV_t$ is the

$$CV_t = V_0(1 + g)^t CR$$

conversion value of the convertible at any date, $V_o$ is the value of the common stock at the time of issues of the convertible, $g$ is the growth rate of the common stock value, the exponent $t$ is the number of years after issues, and $CR$ is the conversion ratio (that is, the number of shares of common stock available per debenture.)

The heavy line in Figure 19–1 indicates that in the early years the debt-only value may be above the conversion value. The higher of the two values is the value that will influence the market price of the convertible. The heavy line sets the floor for market price. There are three reasons why the *MP* curve (market price of the convertible) will be above the floor set by the heavy line (the higher of the *DO* and *CV* curves). First, the conversion right has a positive value, assuming that the issuer did not estimate a growth rate higher than the market place is willing to apply to the common stock. The right gives the debenture owner a chance at a capital gain. Second, the convertible enables the holder to reduce risk. Owning the common stock would also give him the chance at a capital gain, but it would expose him to the risk that the common stock might fall drastically in value. The convertible reduces this risk by setting a floor (the value of the convertible as a debt security) against the impact of a drop in market value of the common stock. The floor will not hold against a rise in the market rate of interest.

The last reason for a market value higher than the debt-only or conversion values is the institutional environment. We have previously noted that legal restrictions on some investors cause them to bid up the market for convertibles.

This leaves us with exploring why the *MP* and *CV* curves will converge as time passes. The most important reason is the existence of a call price on the convertible. If the issuer calls the convertible, the holder of the debenture must decide whether to "cash out" or to become the holder of common stock. A call will terminate the down-side risk protection that the owner of the convertible found attractive. The likelihood of call increases as the years go by (for reasons we will shortly examine) and as the common stock value rises. Second, if as the years go by the market price of the convertible were too much above the higher of the call price or the conversion value at the time one purchased the convertible, the risk of loss upon an immediate call would not be worth the chance for future profit if the call were delayed. The last reason for the closing of the gap is that the dividend rate of the common stock is growing but the interest on the convertible is fixed. The value of the common stock as well as the convertible is based on dividend or interest plus a capital gain, and the capital gain component will be the same for both the common stock and the convertible once the conversion price is reached. The effect of the upward movement of the dividend on the common stock while the interest on the convertible is fixed will cause the gap between the market price of the convertible and the conversion value to close.

### When Will a Convertible Be Called? Why Was It Issued?

Little evidence is available concerning the policy of corporations with respect to calling convertibles.[18] Many policies might be adopted: call as soon as you are sure of conversion (which would be when the market price is far enough above the call price); or let the holder of the convertible decide in view of dividend increases on the common stock; or call only if necessary to present a favorable capital structure at the time when additional new debt is needed.

The policy on calling will most likely be related to the reason for issuing the convertible. If the issuing company needs funds but considers its stock currently undervalued by the market place, either because the entire equity market is depressed or because the market is pessimistic about this particular company, the company should resort to debt. But the company may already have exhausted its possibilities for straight debt, or the cost of debt may also be high at this time. The convertible offers a lower interest cost than straight debt (because of the trade-off against the value of the conversion right) and presents the likelihood of the shift from debt to equity, with the corporation realizing a better price for the equity to the extent that the conversion ratio is above the market price of the common stock at the time the convertible is issued.

If the company's stock is currently overvalued in the market, the company should proceed to issue common stock for new money, but the use of a convertible would be preferable to straight debt.

These are reasons for convertibles from the company's point of view. But the relative preferences of the market place must be considered. As noted earlier, the extent of risk aversion in the market varies from time to time, as do margin requirements and the interest of restricted institutions in capital gains. As a result, the market may offer much more attractive terms for convertibles than for straight debt or equity.

The fact that the common stock of a company is selling at a certain price in the market place does not mean that underwriters would be willing to handle an offering at anywhere near that price. At the same time that the market could not stand the issue of common stock, it is quite possible for the market to have a substantial interest in convertibles. Conversely, at a time when the company wants to issue debt, the market may reject straight debt except at higher interest rates and insist on conversion rights as a sweetener.[19] This leads to an examination of the trade-off between the reduced interest rate of the convertible and the conversion ratio.

### The Trade-Off between Reduced Interest Rate and Reduced Conversion Price

One convenient way for analyzing the trade-off between the interest rate and the conversion ratio is presented in Figure 19–2. In negotiating

[18] Brigham notes (footnote 14) that in a sample of 42 companies which had issued convertibles he got 22 answers to the question of what the call policy was. Only 5 companies indicated that they intended to call as soon as they felt sure that conversion would occur.

[19] This was true for 5 of the 22 replies received for the period 1961–1963 by Brigham. See Brigham, p. 51, Table 2.

a convertible debenture issue the company may try to drive the interest rate down compared to a straight-debt offering. This can be done by reducing the conversion price to make it closer to the market price. Little empirical work has been done in this area.[20] It is apparent, however, that any analysis must proceed with recognition of the fact that the expected growth rate of the common stock (as well as the appropriate capitalization rate) are factors that must be held constant. A mere plot of $I_{DO}/I_C$ against $V_C/V_M$ for many different companies would ignore the effect of the different expected growth rates for the different common stocks.

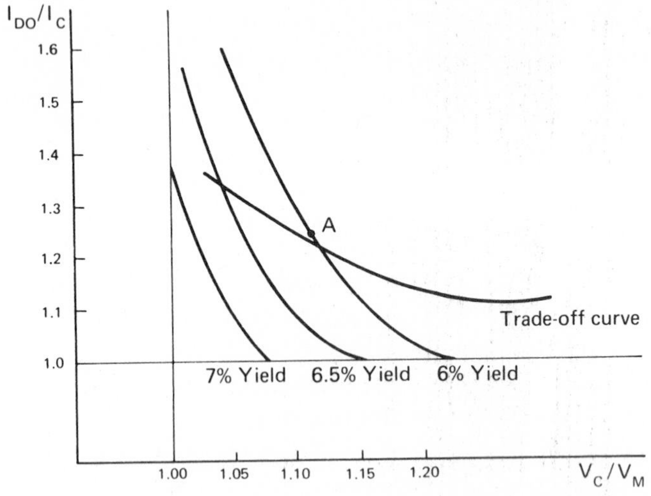


Figure 19–2 The trade-off between the interest rate at issue and the conversion ratio in convertibles, assuming a 4 percent growth rate of common stock for all yield curves and a call when the bond reaches a conversion value of \$1200 (on a par of \$1000). $I_{DO}$ = interest rate for debt-only issue; $I_C$ = interest rate for convertible debenture issue; $V_C$ = conversion price of common stock specified in convertible debenture; $V_M$ = market value of common stock at time of issue of convertible debenture.

Reproduced from E. F. Brigham, "An Analysis of Convertible Debentures," *Journal of Finance*, 21 (March 1966), p. 37, with permission.

The iso-yield curves of Figure 19–2 are constructed by assuming a market rate of interest for straight debt, say 4.5 percent. Then, if we have an interest rate of 3.6 percent on the convertible, $I_{DO}/I_C$ will equal 1.25, as appears at point $A$ on the 6 percent yield curve in Figure 19–2. If the market price of the stock is \$45, then with a conversion price of \$50, $V_C/V_M$ will equal 1.1. Assuming a 4 percent growth rate for the stock and a call when the conversion value (not the market price) of the deben-

[20] Brigham's study reports the combinations of $I_{DO}/I_C$ and $V_C/V_M$ for only five companies. The difficulty is the $I_{DO}$ is not available unless the negotiators of the convertible issue actually considered this alternative and the parties are willing to reveal what is was. As a poor substitute, the debt-only interest rate of contemporaneous issues of straight debt, thought to be of about the same risk, is used. Such information about the straight-debt rate of individual issues of convertibles is published in Moody's *Bond Survey*.

ture reaches $1200 on a $1000 bond, there will be a yield of about 6 percent (assuming no income taxes). The computation involves determining the number of years necessary to compound the market price of the common stock at the time of issue of the convertible to a conversion value of $1200 assuming 4 percent growth [21] and then substituting the number of years into a rate of return equation to find the yield.[22] In this manner we can generate the iso-yield curves appearing in Figure 19–2.

If we examine these iso-yield curves, we can see that the trade-off curve between interest rate differences and conversion ratio differences would not be expected to follow the yield curve, because the higher up on the vertical axis we go (reducing the convertible interest rate more and more), the greater the capital gain necessary to maintain the given yield. But this increase in capital gain can be achieved only by greatly increasing risk. Hence, the trade-off curve must have a "flatter" shape, such as is drawn in Figure 19–2. Such trade-off curves must be developed empirically.

## SUBORDINATED DEBENTURES

Many convertible debentures are subordinated. In fact, any debt can be subordinated. When debt is subordinated, that debt ranks *after* the specific debt to which it is subordinated in priority on liquidation. Usually debt is subordinated only to bondholders, bank loans, and other debt to financial institutions, but not to general creditors.

Suppose that we have the situation on liquidation given in Table 19–2, where the subordination agreement provides only for subordination to bank debt and where the mortgage is not held by the bank.

TABLE 19–2. Sample Subordination Situation

| Proceeds | | Amount Owed | |
|---|---|---|---|
| All assets except building | $12,500 | Accounts payable | $ 15,000 |
| Building (mortgaged) | 75,000 | Bank debt (unsecured) | 25,000 |
| Total | $87,500 | Mortgage loan | 150,000 |
| | | Subordinated debt | 10,000 |

The proceeds in Table 19–2 are applied on liquidation of the debt in Table 19–2 as shown in Table 19–3.

[21] Using the symbols of this chapter, we have (where $N$ is the number of years and $I_M$ is the interest rate to maturity, or yield):

$$N = \frac{(\log V_C - \log V_M) + (\log 1200 - \log I_M)}{\log(1 + g)}$$

[22]

$$I_M = \sum_{t=1}^{N} \frac{I_C}{(1 + y)^t} + \frac{1200}{(1 + y)^t}$$

where $y$ is a particular rate, such as 6 percent.

TABLE 19–3. Application of Proceeds upon Liquidation

| (1) Class of debt | (2) Amount of claim | (3) First allocation | (4) Second allocation | (5) Third allocation | (6) Percent of claim paid (5)/(2) |
|---|---|---|---|---|---|
| Bank debt | $ 25,000 | | $ 2,500 | $ 3,500 | 14% |
| Mortgage debt | 150,000 | $75,000 | 82,500 | 82,500 | 55 |
| Accounts payable | 15,000 | | 1,500 | 1,500 | 10 |
| Subordinated debt | 10,000 | | 1,000 | 0 | 0 |
| Total debt | $200,000 | | $87,500 | $87,500 | 43.75% |

The first allocation is to pay the mortgage debt to the extent the proceeds of the mortgaged property are adequate. If the mortgage proceeds are inadequate the unpaid mortgage debt becomes a general claim. If the mortgaged proceeds exceed the mortgage debt, the excess becomes general assets.

The second allocation takes the general assets and distributes them *pro rata* over all now unsatisfied debt. In Table 19–3 that debt is $75,000 of mortgage and $50,000 of other debt. With $12,500 of general assets now available, the distribution is 10 percent on each dollar. The mortgage receives an extra $7500 on its still unsatisfied $75,000.

The third allocation takes whatever the subordinated debt received in the second allocation and transfers as much of that as necessary to make whole the debt to which it is subordinated.

## BONDS WITH WARRANTS, NONDEBT SECURITIES WITH WARRANTS, AND WARRANTS INITIALLY SOLD SEPARATELY

A *warrant* is a long-term option (usually for several years) to purchase a stated number of shares of a particular security (usually common stock) at a stated price (in some cases the price steps up as time goes on) for a stated period of time (some are perpetual). A warrant is not to be confused with a *stock right*,[23] which is a short-term option, usually for 10 to 20 days, to buy stock at less than market price and distributed to present stockholders. Warrants are used as a sweetener for long-term debt and recently even as a sweetener in deals that do not involve debt. As an option, a warrant carries no voting right, interest, or dividends.

Warrants may be detachable or nondetachable. A *detachable warrant* may be separated from the bond and sold. A *nondetachable warrant* must be passed along to the buyer when the bond is resold and can be detached only when the holder exercises the warrant to buy stock. Recently warrants have also been used with nondebt securities and even sold separately.

[23] Although stock rights are sometimes created by documents called warrants. This illustrates the lack of uniformity in financial terminology. Stock rights are discussed in Chapter 21.

Warrants are an alternative to the convertible debenture as a sweetener for an issue of debt. Although detachable warrants are used on publicly offered issued and some are traded on the New York and American stock exchanges, the device is largely used in private placements. The reason is that the insurance company or other institutional long-term lender wants to continue with the debt issue. In the case of a convertible the debt issue is terminated by the act of conversion.

As a sweetener, the warrant enables a company to sell its debt at lower rates of interest than straight debt, and in some cases a company can place debt with warrants where it otherwise could not find a lender. It is apparent that there will be a trade-off between reduced interest rates and the option price in the warrant similar to that of the convertible trade-off just discussed.

The warrant differs from the convertible in this respect: cash (the option price) is paid to the corporation at the time the warrant is exercised. In the case of a convertible this is not usually the case, although a convertible can provide for the payment of additional cash as part of the conversion.

Warrants have grown in popularity in recent years. The 18 listed in 1967 on the American Stock Exchange grew to 60 listed on the New York and American Stock Exchanges in 1971. The New York Stock Exchange did not list warrants until the American Telephone and Telegraph Company warrants were listed in 1970.

#### Determination of the Arbitrage Value of Warrant

The arbitrage value [24] of a warrant at any time depends directly on (1) the difference between the market price of the common stock less the cash required by the option price of one share, times (2) the number of shares each warrant can purchase. In equation form

$$AV_W = (MV_S - OP)S_W$$

where $AV_W$ is the arbitrage value of the warrant, $MV_S$ is the market value of the common stock, $OP$ is the option price of one share of common stock, and $S_W$ is the number of shares that can be bought with one warrant.

The market value of a detachable warrant will not drop below the arbitrage value because one could buy the warrant, exercise it, and sell the stock into which it is convertible for an immediate profit. But the market value of a detachable warrant often rides above the arbitrage value. The reason is that a warrant has great leverage: the chance for a large capital gain can be had for relatively little investment.

#### Leverage in Warrants

Leverage in the case of warrants can be explained by an example. Using a warrant with the right to one share of common, assume the common stock is at \$20, the option price is \$10, and the market price of the warrant is \$10. If the common price rises to \$40, the stockholder has a 100 percent gain, but if the common price rises to \$40, the warrants must rise to at least

[24] The latest terminology continues to use "theoretical value" rather than "arbitrage value". However, "theoretical value" is a misnomer. Theory does not say the arbitrage value is anything but a floor to market price.

$30, since the option price plus the warrant price must at least equal the common price. The gain on the warrant is 200 percent (from $10 to $30). The leverage of a warrant is greatest when the common is near the option price, which is also called the *striking price.*

If the common were to rise an additional $20 to $60, the stockholder would realize a 50 percent gain. The warrants would rise at least $20 to at least $50, but now the gain is only 66 percent. At this point the warrant holder has a greater risk on the downside (reverse leverage) plus, by the time the stock has tripled in value, the common is likely carrying a substantial dividend that the warrant holder will not receive while in turn the warrant holder must consider the financing cost of holding the warrant.

Because a detachable warrant does not require the purchase of its associated bond once it is detached, nor the purchase of the bond as in a convertible, the detached warrant by rule of thumb is valued at 1.5 times the same privilege in a nondetachable or convertible case.

### Other Factors Affecting Value of Warrants

A number of factors in addition to leverage and dividends on the common into which the warrant is convertible will affect the market value of the warrant. One of these is the margin requirement. Warrants can be bought on margin just like other listed securities, but in the case of warrants there is leverage upon leverage. First there is the leverage of the warrant itself, which we have just explained. Then there is the leverage of buying on margin which we explained in Chapter 18. Finally, because the warrant sells for only a fraction of the price of the common, the possible loss to a warrant holder (say, in the event of bankruptcy) is far less than for the common until the common reaches a price well above the option price. Thus, every time margin requirements increase (or decrease) the market interest in warrants increases (or decreases).

Warrants also offer a tax advantage over convertibles. When the warrant has a market value at the time of issuance of the debt to which it is attached, the value of the warrants can be treated as a cost of the debt, thereby reducing the principal of the debt for the issuer and creating a discount that can be amortized as a deduction for tax purposes. In turn, the gain on the sale of the warrant is a capital gain for the holder.

Three other factors affect the value of the warrant. The first is the length of time to the warrant's expiration, particularly when less than 2 years. The longer the period of the warrant, the greater the probability, *ceteris paribus,* that the common will at some time in the period hit a high price and give arbitrage value to the warrant. Second, if the warrant is listed on the American Exchange or the New York Stock Exchange, it has more value than if traded over-the-counter. This is due in part to the availability of margin financing and the ability to sell short offered only by listed securities. Third, the higher the dividend yield of the common stock, the lower the warrant value. This dividend effect is small but consistent; the logic is that a higher dividend causes the common price to be higher, which in turn increases the financing cost of carrying the warrant for the warrant holder, compared to a no-dividend common.

Another factor affecting the value of the warrant is the outlook for its associated common stock, particularly the volatility of the common price.

An argument is made that warrants constitute a "dilution" of ownership. Whether there is "dilution" depends on what the earnings will be on the new money paid in upon exercise of the warrants compared to the earnings on the old money. To consider that there is "dilution" just because there are more shares, without realizing that there could not be more earnings without the increase in shares, is fantasy. Yet this use of the term "dilution" frequently occurs. On the opposite side we should note that both warrants (with bonds) and convertibles are attractive compared to straight common stock financing, since the debt will enable the company to build up the new earnings so that when the exercise of the warrants or conversion takes place there will be a minimal temporary impact on earnings per share and, hence, on the price of the common stock.

#### Example of the Market Value of a Warrant in Relation to Its Common Stock

To illustrate our statements about market value of a warrant we have selected the TWA warrant for two important reasons: (1) TWA common has recently swung over a wide price range from well above the option price to well below it and back again; and (2) This swing has occurred in the relatively short time of 6 years. The shorter the time period studied, the more likely homogeneity exists.

Warrants are sophisticated securities. The TWA warrant was issued June 8, 1961, 27 detached warrants for each $1000 of 6.5 percent subordinated debenture due June 1, 1978 with the option price at $20 to June 1, 1965 and at $22 to December 1, 1973—the expiration date. The warrant is of the CD type, that is, either cash or the debentures themselves can be used as payment upon exercise of the option. In the high market interest rate period of 1969 to 1971, the debenture was selling at a discount as high as 56 percent from par and when bought to pay for stock purchased by the warrant had the effect of *reducing* the option price of $22 by 56 percent compared to cash. Other warrants have other "gimmicks" such as being callable or the *issuer* having the right to reduce the option price. These "gimmicks" may affect the premium the buyer will pay.

Table 19–4 shows the market prices of TWA common and TWA 6.5 percent debenture (both listed on the New York Stock Exchange) and the TWA warrant (listed on the American Stock Exchange), for the period April 1966 to April 1972. Thus we can study the relation of the arbitrage value of the warrant (gross, using cash, and net, using bonds) and the market price of the warrants and arrive at the premium paid by the market for the warrants (gross, using cash, and net, using bonds). The dates were selected to reflect changes of price of $5 to $10 of the common stock except that more readings were taken when the stock was near the option price.

TABLE 19–4. TWA Common Stock, Warrant and Bond (When at a Discount) Prices from April 1966 to April 1972, together with Gross and Net Arbitrage Values and Gross and Net Premiums

| Date | (1) Market price of common | (2) Option price | (3) Gross arbitrage value of warrant (1) — (2) | (4) Warrant price | (5) Gross premium for warrant (4) — (3) | (6) Bond price if at discount | (7) Adjusted option price of common (2) × (6) | (8) Net arbitrage value of warrant (1) — (7) | (9) Net premium for warrant (4) — (8) |
|---|---|---|---|---|---|---|---|---|---|
| 4/29/66 | $ 85⅞ | $22 | $63⅞ | $66¼ | $ 2⅜ | AP | $22 | $63.87 | $2.37 |
| 6/22/66 | 100⅝ | 22 | 78⅝ | 81 | 2⅜ | AP | 22 | 78.62 | 2.37 |
| 3/2/67 | 79½ | 22 | 57½ | 59 | 1½ | AP | 22 | 57.50 | 1.50 |
| 5/24/67 | 71⅝ | 22 | 49⅝ | 51½ | 1⅞ | AP | 22 | 49.62 | 1.87 |
| 8/31/67 | 60⅞ | 22 | 38⅞ | 44⅛ | 5¼ | $96 | 21.12 | 39.75 | 4.37 |
| 12/26/66 | 50¾ | 22 | 28¾ | 35⅛ | 6⅜ | 87½ | 19.25 | 31.50 | 3.62 |
| 12/30/68 | 42¾ | 22 | 20¾ | 30⅝ | 9⅞ | 83 | 18.26 | 24.49 | 6.12 |
| 5/1/69 | 34½ | 22 | 12½ | 24⅞ | 12⅜ | 85½ | 18.81 | 15.69 | 9.18 |
| 9/3/69 | 28 | 22 | 6 | 15¼ | 9¼ | 71 | 15.62 | 12.38 | 2.87 |
| 1/2/70 | 23⅞ | 22 | 1⅞ | 13⅞ | 12 | 68½ | 15.07 | 8.80 | 5.07 |
| 2/26/70 | 19½ | 22 | 0 | 11⅜ | 11⅜ | 67½ | 14.85 | 4.65 | 6.72 |
| 5/1/70 | 14¾ | 22 | 0 | 7⅝ | 7⅜ | 65½ | 14.41 | 0.34 | 7.28 |
| 7/9/70 | 10 | 22 | 0 | 5⅛ | 5⅛ | 50 | 11.00 | 0 | 5.12 |
| 9/1/70 | 14¼ | 22 | 0 | 7¼ | 7¼ | 56⅛ | 12.35 | 1.90 | 5.35 |
| 10/30/70 | 11¾ | 22 | 0 | 6 | 6 | 51½ | 11.33 | 0.42 | 5.58 |
| 12/30/70 | 14¼ | 22 | 0 | 6⅜ | 6⅜ | 44⅛ | 9.71 | 4.54 | 1.83 |
| 2/26/71 | 18⅞ | 22 | 0 | 10⅞ | 10⅞ | 53⅞ | 11.85 | 7.02 | 3.85 |
| 3/31/71 | 19¼ | 22 | 0 | 10⅝ | 10⅝ | 57 | 12.54 | 6.71 | 3.91 |
| 4/8/71 | 22⅜ | 22 | ⅜ | 13½ | 13⅛ | 65 | 14.30 | 8.08 | 5.42 |
| 4/15/71 | 26 | 22 | 4 | 16 | 12 | 68¾ | 15.13 | 10.87 | 5.13 |
| 4/21/71 | 24⅝ | 22 | 2⅝ | 15½ | 12⅞ | 66¼ | 14.58 | 10.04 | 5.46 |
| 5/3/71 | 30⅞ | 22 | 8⅞ | 19⅝ | 10¾ | 65⅞ | 14.49 | 16.38 | 3.24 |
| 6/29/71 | 27½ | 22 | 5½ | 17 | 11½ | 62⅝ | 13.78 | 13.72 | 3.28 |
| 9/1/71 | 32⅛ | 22 | 10⅛ | 21 | 10⅞ | 70½ | 15.51 | 11.99 | 4.01 |
| 10/29/71 | 36½ | 22 | 14½ | 22⅜ | 7⅞ | 76¼ | 16.78 | 15.35 | 7.02 |
| 12/30/71 | 42½ | 22 | 20½ | 25¾ | 5¼ | 84⅛ | 18.51 | 23.99 | 2.76 |
| 4/3/72 | 52¼ | 22 | 30¼ | 35⅛ | 4⅛ | 91½ | 20.13 | 32.12 | 3.00 |

Note: All prices are closing prices. AP = above par.
SOURCE: *Wall Street Journal.*

The TWA warrant during 1966 to 1972 furnishes an ideal situation to examine the impact of the probability of ruin on the price of the warrant. The probability of ruin has not been considered in the extensive literature on warrants with the result that the warrant price curve in Figure 19–3 is represented as having a substantial intercept. In the year 1970, there was fear that TWA might be forced into receivership and the price of the common stock fell sharply and likewise this price of the convertible debenture. The debt-only value of the debenture had also fallen because of high interest rates and the tight-money market.

In this situation, the warrant is less secure than the common stock. The likelihood that a warrant will survive reorganization is less than the chance of survival of the common stock. Accordingly, the probability of ruin rises faster for the warrant. In addition, the leverage advantage of the warrant is shrinking as the common stock goes further down from the option price.

Figure 19–3 shows that the correct curve to fit to the warrant price is a quadratic (with two flex points) rather than a cubic with only a single flex point. In nonmathematical terms, there is a "hump" in the warrant price curve at the option price. This point is brought about more clearly if we rearrange the data of Table 19–4 from its chronological order to an order of magnitude. We must be assured that this rearrangement does not introduce a new element in the analysis.

In support of the validity of this rearrangement, the warrant prices on Figure 19–3 are identified as to whether they occur when the common stock price is rising (hollow dot) or falling (solid dot). Figure 19–3 indicates that this factor does not appear material.

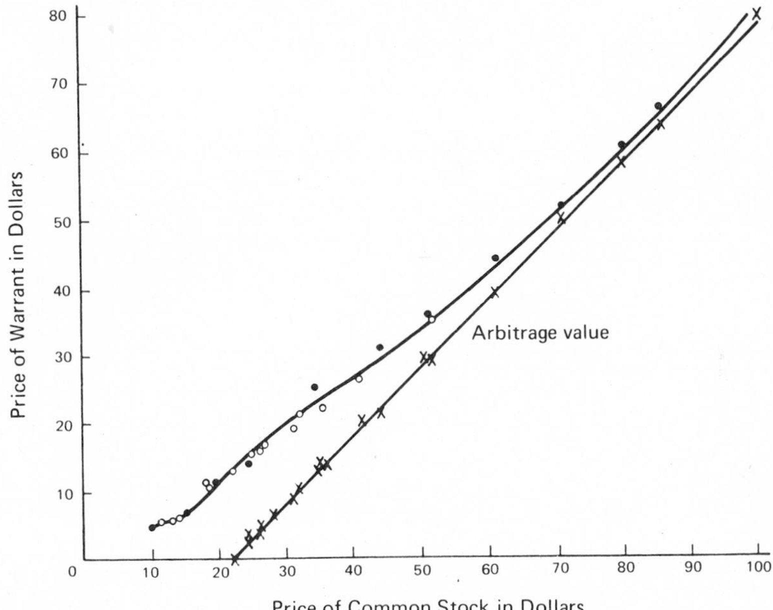


Figure 19–3 Sample of TWA common stock and warrant prices (on way down, solid dot; on way up, hollow dot) and gross arbitrage values (x), April 1966 to April 1972.

SOURCE: Table 19–4.

TABLE 19–5. TWA Common Stock and Warrant Prices with Gross and Net Arbitrage Values and Gross and Net Premiums Arranged by Stock Prices Rather Than Chronology

| | Value of warrant | | | Premium of warrant | |
|---|---|---|---|---|---|
| Price of stock | (1) Gross arbitrage | (2) Net arbitrage | (3) Market price | (4) Gross (3)–(1) | (5) Net (3)–(2) |
| $ 10.00 | $ 0 | $ 0 | $ 5.12 | $ 5.12 | $ 5.12 |
| 11.75 | 0 | 0.42 | 6.00 | 6.00 | 5.58 |
| 14.25 | 0 | 4.54 | 6.37 | 6.37 | 1.83 |
| 14.25 | 0 | 1.90 | 7.25 | 7.25 | 5.35 |
| 14.75 | 0 | 4.54 | 7.62 | 7.62 | 1.83 |
| 18.87 | 0 | 7.02 | 10.87 | 10.87 | 3.85 |
| 19.25 | 0 | 6.71 | 10.62 | 10.62 | 6.72 |
| 19.50 | 0 | 4.65 | 11.37 | 11.37 | 3.92 |
| 22.37 | 0.37 | 8.08 | 13.50 | 13.12 | 5.42 |
| 23.87 | 1.87 | 8.80 | 13.87 | 12.00 | 5.07 |
| 24.62 | 2.62 | 10.04 | 15.50 | 12.87 | 5.46 |
| 26.00 | 4.00 | 10.87 | 16.00 | 12.00 | 5.13 |
| 27.50 | 5.50 | 13.72 | 17.00 | 11.50 | 3.28 |
| 28.00 | 6.00 | 12.38 | 15.25 | 9.25 | 2.87 |
| 30.87 | 8.87 | 16.38 | 19.62 | 10.75 | 3.24 |
| 32.12 | 10.12 | 11.99 | 21.00 | 10.87 | 4.01 |
| 34.50 | 12.50 | 15.69 | 24.87 | 12.37 | 9.18 |
| 36.50 | 14.50 | 15.35 | 22.37 | 7.87 | 7.02 |
| 42.50 | 20.50 | 23.99 | 25.75 | 5.25 | 2.76 |
| 42.75 | 20.75 | 24.49 | 30.62 | 9.87 | 6.42 |
| 50.75 | 28.75 | 31.50 | 35.12 | 6.37 | 3.62 |
| 52.25 | 30.25 | 32.12 | 35.12 | 4.87 | 3.00 |
| 60.87 | 38.87 | 39.75 | 44.12 | 5.25 | 4.37 |
| 71.62 | 49.62 | 49.62 | 51.50 | 1.87 | 1.87 |
| 79.50 | 57.50 | 57.50 | 59.00 | 1.50 | 1.50 |
| 85.87 | 63.87 | 63.87 | 66.25 | 2.37 | 2.37 |
| 100.62 | 78.62 | 78.12 | 81.00 | 2.37 | 2.37 |

SOURCE: Table 19–4.

Table 19–5 and Figure 19–4 (rearrangement of Table 19–4 and Figure 19–3) are consistent with a number of conclusions:

1. The premium is not affected substantially by whether the stock is going up or down.
2. The premium is erratically affected by the CD privilege [25] because, until shortly before the expiration of the option period, warrants are bought to be traded and not for conversion by the current buyer. The more erratic behavior of the net premium compared to the gross premium supports this conclusion. Furthermore there is a tax dis-

[25] This conclusion coincides with the results of a study by D. F. Rush and R. W. Melicher, "An Empirical Examination of Factors Which Influence Warrant Prices," presented at the Midwest Finance Association Meeting, April 22, 1972, at St. Louis, Mo.

advantage in the use of the bond as payment. If the warrant is held for 6 months and sold, there is a long-term capital gain. If the warrant is exercised, the common must be held for a new 6 month period or there will be a short-term capital gain upon its sale. Using the bond as payment excludes the possibility of only one six month period to realize a capital gain.

3. The variation in premium is overwhelmingly determined by the variation in leverage over the range from the option price to $60 per share, or from the option price to about triple the option price. In the range under the option price, leverage is substantial. It is off-set, however, by increased risk of ruin, and the warrant premium shrinks sharply.

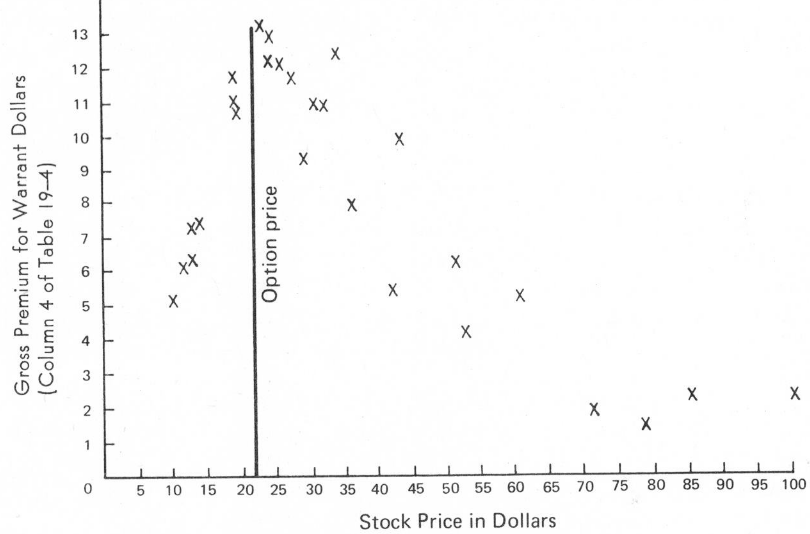


Figure 19–4 The effect of leverage and risk of ruin on gross premium of a warrant.

SOURCE: Table 19–5.

In April of 1972 there were still more than 1 million warrants unexercised despite the rapidly approaching expiration date of December 1, 1973. The impact of volatility of the common price on the value of the warrant can only be determined from a comparison of a number of different warrants rather than the study of one warrant over time.

Figure 19–4 shows the gross premium variation as the common stock price varies. The largest warrant premium occurs when the common is at the option price, reflecting the optimization of the combination of leverage and risk of ruin at this point.[26]

[26] Since these are propositions new in the literature, we should state that the patterns of TWA common and its warrants are confirmed by a study of a number of other warrants such as Pacific Southwest Airlines and Loew's as well as Leasco, which has two warrants, one with an option price of $16.50 and the other $34.80.

It is true leverage has been recognized in various studies but only in a limited form, such as the ratio of the option price to market price of the common as an independent variable in regression, with the ratio of warrant price to option price as the dependent variable, in a cross-sectional study of many warrants at one point in time. In this effort to adjust or normalize differences between companies in common stock prices and dif-

### Use of Leverage in Practice

There is one aspect of warrants that has been largely omitted in all published work except that of Thorp and Kassouf,[27] namely, the use of a warrant as a hedge against its common stock by making use of the differences in leverage between the warrant and the common (just discussed), particularly in the range where the common is priced ± 75 percent of the option price. Thus, if we buy the warrant when the common is near the option price and short sell the common, we can buy at almost any time to cover the common and sell the warrant at a net profit if the common rises and if we sell the same *dollars worth* of common as we bought *dollars worth* of warrants. Conversely, if the common falls, we can buy warrants and convert to cover at a profit the common sold short, since the warrants have fallen more percentage-wise than the common has (see Figure 19–4), thus offsetting our loss on the warrants we still hold. If there is a 50–50 chance that the common will go up or down from the option price where we take the initial steps, we are almost sure to profit no matter which way the common goes.

There is no surefire way to get rich—unless you are the *first* to discover it. Since the warrant has been analyzed by practitioners, the leverage aspect we have just discussed has been *partly* built into the market price of warrants (inflating their price). This makes it harder to detect by routine cross-sectional methods of scientific analysis that academicians employ, but enough of leverage still survives so that its effects can be observed in Figures 19–3 and 19–4.

## CHICAGO BOARD OPTIONS EXCHANGE

Until recently, warrants and convertibles have been the only listed options available to investors. In 1972, the new Chicago Board Options Exchange established the first organized market for puts, calls, straddles, spreads, strips, straps, and other options. Until this market was established, these functions were carried out for many years by individual securities dealers offering these agreements on an individual basis.

To define these transactions briefly: a *put* is a contract under which the holder can, for a fee, sell a given security at a fixed price in stated quantity within a stated period and the buyer will accept. A *call* is a contract under which a nonowner of a security can, for a fee, demand a security at a fixed price for a stated quantity within a stated period. A *spread* is a combination of a put and call with the owner of the spread either able to buy or sell a stated quantity of a given security for a given period at a fixed price. A *straddle* is a combination of a put in one security with a call in another security.

Since Chicago is the principal center in the United States in which "futures," of *commodities* are traded (corn, wheat, cotton, and so on, sold

ferences between companies in option prices, researchers have ignored the great differences in risk-profit combinations between companies in the effort to hold the state of the stock market as a whole constant.

[27] E. O. Thorp and S. T. Kassouf, *Beat the Market* (New York: Random House, 1967).

today at an agreed price for future delivery), it is logical that Chicago should tackle the matter of options in securities.

## INCOME BONDS AND ADJUSTMENT BONDS

An *income bond* is a bond providing for the payment of interest only when it is earned. The term *adjustment bond* is a descriptive term identifying the bond as arising out of a reorganization. Income bonds may arise out of reorganization but are used by healthy corporations as well.

One main attraction for issuing income bonds is the deductibility of the interest for income tax purposes. An income bond is similar to preferred stock, and if it is made too similar, the Internal Revenue Service will deny the tax deductibility of the "interest" payments. However, the use of provisions peculiar to bonds as opposed to preferred stock will usually satisfy tax authorities. These provisions include the use of a sinking fund, the denial of voting rights except in limited situations such as a period of nonpayment, and some type of security (mortgaged property). In addition, a bond has a maturity date, whereas a preferred stock does not. Even these provisions can be challenged. A sinking fund is similar in effect to a redemption schedule for preferred stock. Voting rights are frequently denied to preferred stock except in limited cases such as the existence of arrearage. Preferred stock can contain a commitment that there be no mortgaging by the corporation. And, finally, the maturity date of the income bonds can be thrown so far into the future as to be of little concern. This leaves one vital difference: the dividend on preferred stock need not be paid even if it is earned. Every dividend requires a decision by the board of directors, and no amount of dividend arrearage can form the basis for bankruptcy proceedings. However, under a properly drawn income bond indenture the interest if earned becomes payable and is a liability which, in turn, can be used to initiate bankruptcy proceedings if the interest is not paid.

Income bonds can provide for cumulation of an arrearage when the interest is not earned, so that whenever earnings occur the interest will be payable; or the income bond may be noncumulative in this respect.

## PLANNING FOR THE MATURITY OF LONG-TERM DEBT

Any discussion of long-term debt that does not consider plans for the maturity of the debt is like a discussion of laws defining crimes that does not consider the penalties for law violation.

Planning for the future of long-term debt involves a number of alternatives:

1. Provision for a sinking fund
2. Use of serial bonds
3. Use of series bonds
4. Use of call provisions and premature retirement or refunding
5. Refunding at maturity

6. Indirect control of the situation by a specific covenant in the bonds, such as depreciation requirements, *negative pledge* clause, and dividend restriction.

1. *Sinking Fund.* A sinking fund may be defined as a segregation of funds to be applied to debt reduction, usually by the trustee under the indenture but sometimes directly by the corporation.

The sinking fund offers a wide variety of provisions designed to carry out this purpose. While a provision for periodic loan repayments may not be considered a sinking fund provision, the effect is much the same. In the case of direct private placements this is the form the sinking fund will take. As to publicly held bonds, we can classify sinking funds into two broad classes. First, there is the type of provision requiring the company to repay some bonds pursuant to a schedule set in the indenture agreement. Thus, the provision may be that annually a stated amount or percentage will be chosen by lot for repayment (with or without a premium for the bonds so chosen). Or there may be the infrequent provision that annually the corporation will set aside a stated amount of funds which will be invested in stated types of securities by a trustee for ultimate use in bond repayment.

The existence of sinking fund requirements helps maintain a market for the bonds, since the company must reacquire the necessary bonds. The use of a call provision prevents exorbitant prices in connection with the sinking fund requirements. Some indentures specify two call prices, one for general use and a lower one (by lot) to meet sinking fund requirements. Care must be taken that the sinking fund requirement, designed to protect bondholders, is not the very event that causes insolvency. Hence, some provision for flexibility may exist and this is usually tied to earnings. Termination of dividends when earnings shrink may afford as much protection to bondholders as is wise. The sinking fund is not designed to extinguish all bonds but will leave a final amount due at the maturity date. This amount is known as the *balloon.*

2. *Serial Bonds.* Instead of a sinking fund provision the entire issue may be arranged as serial bonds with varying amounts maturing each year. Such an arrangement presupposes either considerable stability of future income of the company or a readily predictable depreciation of the fixed assets to which the proceeds of the bond issue are to be applied. The principal advantage of the serial bond is interest saving, since the shorter-term bonds will normally carry a lower interest rate than longer-term bonds. Theoretically, a parallel sinking fund provision should lower the average interest rate just as a serial bond, but the serial bond increases the size of the market by adding banks as buyers of the short-term part of the bonds. On the other hand, serial bonds do not create a market for the bonds such as results from purchases by the company to meet sinking fund requirements. And if the market rate of interest should rise compared to the rate on the bond issue, the sinking fund method would result in gains to the company through purchase of bonds at prices lower than par without invoking the call provision. Conversely, the selling bondholder suffers.

3. *Series Bonds.* Series bonds are separate issues of bonds made at different points in time and with different maturities, often under a "master" indenture. In the case of larger companies, the maturity problem can be dealt with by a series of issues so planned that there are frequent maturities but each for only a small part of the total long-term debt. In this way unfavorable market conditions at the time of individual maturities can be met with short-term funds. Such issues may be formally identified as series bonds or may simply appear under an open-end agreement as having different issue dates and different maturities.

4. *Call Provisions and Premature Retirement or Refunding.* We have already indicated that the call provision is useful in forcing conversion of convertible bonds and in protecting the company in meeting its commitments for sinking fund purposes. The call provision is also useful in accomplishing premature retirement where the company generates excess funds due to contraction in the volume of business, such as occurred after World War II when many producers of war goods reverted to their usual peacetime production. Or the excess funds may develop as a result of good earnings and a conservative dividend policy adopted in an effort to accelerate debt retirement.

Premature refunding might occur for several reasons. A substantial drop in the market rate of interest affords a company the opportunity to refund and reduce interest costs after paying the costs of refunding.[28] Let us suppose a 40-year bond issue is entering its last 10 years. Rather than wait until the maturity date and assume the risk as to what the interest rate will then be, the company may seize the opportunity offered by low interest rates at this time and carry out the refunding prematurely. Or premature refunding may occur because the corporation is expanding and requires increased debt funds. In this situation, rather than "patching on" another issue, any outstanding issue would be called and the total debt requirement met by a single new issue.

5. *Refunding at Maturity.* As maturity approaches the balloon that will become due after the reduction of the issue by sinking fund payments may be handled in several ways. If during the period of the issue the corporation has prospered and the ratio of long-term debt to total capital structure has declined, the corporation may be willing to take the risk of an unfavorable long-term market for refunding at the time of the due date and will seek to cover this possibility with short-term money from banks or with a privately placed term loan. The risk in this case is really one of a sharply unfavorable interest rate rather than of default. If the company has not seen much growth in profitability during the first part of the life of the bond issue, it should move earlier on the matter of premature refunding in order to avoid the problem of an unfavorable market coinciding with the due date of the balloon.

6. *Indirect Control by Specific Covenants.* Up to this point we have been examining the problem of planning for the maturity of the debt from the point of view of the borrower. However, the lender is

---

[28] An illustration of the computation of the gains of refunding is presented in Chapter 22.

well advised to consider the problem. We have examined the covenants in the indenture as protection to assure timely interest payments and to control risks such as the depreciation of the mortgaged asset at a rate faster than the reduction of the debt.

Covenants can also be used to control the risk of the situation of the borrower at maturity. Indeed, covenants can be used to induce premature refunding. Instead of the greater risk to the borrower of an unfavorable market at a single future point in time (the maturity date), we can substitute the lesser risk of an unfavorable market over a longer period by stepping up the protective requirements during the last five years of the issue. Thus the covenants can increase the liquidity requirements during this period or can raise the required ratio of net fixed assets to long-term debt. Such a situation would put pressure on the borrower to seek premature funding.

### Restriction on Prepayment of Debt Issued under Tight Money Conditions

When tight money conditions develop, as they did in 1966 to 1974, lenders often seek restrictions on prepayment rather than still higher interest rates. The reason is simply that the lender may otherwise earn the extra 1 or 2 percent in interest for only a year or two. As money eases the borrower will refund. Accordingly, lenders may obtain provisions that the debt cannot be refunded for a minimum period of 5 years and thereafter only at the cost of a prepayment penalty, which might start at 1 year's interest and decline one-half of 1 percent per year. To sweeten this clause, the lender may agree that if the borrower seeks additional funds on any set of terms and first offers the new loan to the lender and it is rejected, the borrower may then procure the funds elsewhere on such terms and may prepay the existing loan on a much reduced penalty basis. Here we have an illustration of the greater flexibility available in private placement. It would be nearly impossible to administer such provisions in the case of a publicly offered issue.

## SUMMARY

Long-term debt financing involves bond issues with a maturity of more than 15 years. Such financing may be by a public offering of bonds or by direct placement. In either case the basic agreement is called an indenture. In the case of a public bond issue the indenture provides for a third party, designated as a trustee, to act on behalf of the bondholders to assure that the company issuing the bonds conforms to the terms of the agreement. In the event of default the trustee acts for the bondholders.

There are more than 75 different types of bonds, which vary according to the provisions of the bonds and the circumstances giving rise to their issue. Bonds are rated largely on the basis of their amount relative to equity, their priority, security, the borrower's right to issue more debt, the times interest earned, and the stability of the issuer's earnings.

Long-term debt from the point of view of the bondholder involves several risks: default, call, liquidity, change in the market rate of interest, and change in the purchasing power of money. The bondholder accepts a lower anticipated rate of earning than equity in return for improved certainty of the reduced earning and greater safety of his principal. The borrower gains financial leverage and does not part with any control.

A substantial part of the dollar volume of all bonds is in the form of convertible debentures, which give the bondholder the right to convert into common stock at a set price. If the price of the stock moves above this price the bondholder can take a profit. In return for this option the bondholder receives a lower interest rate than would apply to straight debt of the same borrower. From the viewpoint of borrower or lender there is a trade-off between a reduced interest rate and the conversion price. Convertibles appeal to a substantial part of the investing market that is legally required to invest almost entirely in bonds. Because of their attractiveness to investors, convertibles are usually subordinated to other funded debt of the borrower. Some control over the situation is maintained by the borrower's right to call the issue. If the stock is selling at or above the conversion price, the borrower can force conversion by calling a bond. A floor to the market value of the convertible is set by the bond's value as straight debt. The market price of the convertible will tend to rise above this floor as the price of the stock rises above what it was at the time the convertible was issued. The conversion value of the convertible depends on the current and expected price of the stock into which the bond is convertible.

Instead of a convertible bond the borrower may issue bonds with detachable warrants (rights to purchase stock at a fixed price). In this case the bond is not terminated when the warrants are exercised, whereas in the case of a convertible the bond is terminated upon conversion. Detachable warrants also bring cash to the issuer when the warrant is exercised. These warrants offer great leverage and their value depends on many variables, but most important is the price of the associated common stock.

Income bonds provide for the payment of interest only during years in which the debtor earns that amount. Income bonds are similar to preferred stock but carry no voting rights and are not cumulative, although interest paid on them is tax deductible.

Planning for the future of long-term debt involves a choice of: (1) sinking fund, (2) serial bonds, (3) series bonds, (4) call provisions, (5) refunding, and (6) indirect control by specific covenants.

### Study Questions

1. Do you think that the premium (defined as the difference between market price and arbitrage value) of a warrant would, stated as a percentage of market value, be greater than the premium of a convertible debenture?
2. Rank the following "protective" provisions of bonds in their order of importance to you as an investor. Then rank them from the point of view of the issuer: (a) sinking fund provision; (b) mortgage; (c) dividend limitation; (d) minimum net working capital provision; (e) after-acquired property clause; (f) call provision; (g) limit of ratio of funded debt to total assets; (h) pledge to insure, repair, and pay taxes. Would you expect the order of your two rankings to be the same?

3. Do you think that the real reason for a mortgage is not to give priority as to the specific asset covered by the mortgage but to prevent the debtor from incurring additional indebtedness?
4. Thirty years ago and earlier industrial companies seldom had long-term debt in excess of 5 percent of their capital structure. Why is it that many industrials today have much more substantial ratios of long-term debt?
5. The use of a convertible bond results in the buyer paying more for the bond than it is worth as a straight bond and also paying more for the common stock than he would pay for it as common stock. Why then would a buyer be willing to buy a convertible?
6. The issuer of a convertible bond gets money at a lower rate than for straight debt and gets more for the common stock than an offering of common stock would realize. Why would a company issue straight debt rather than convertible bonds?
7. Do you think that the call price of a bond should be lower when the bond is called for sinking fund purposes than when it is not called for that purpose? Why?
8. Do you think that bonds should contain a provision restricting the call provision so that the bonds are not callable during an initial period (such as 5 or 10 years)? Why?
9. It is sometimes said that conversion of a convertible bond can be stimulated by (a) calling the bond at the call price, (b) providing in the bond that the conversion price will increase with time, or (c) increasing the dividend of the common stock into which the bond is convertible. If you were the financial manager of the issuer of the convertible, which of these stimulants would you favor? Would your choice depend on the type of business in which you were engaged? What type of business would favor which type of conversion stimulant?
10. One finance test states: "There appears to be no case on record in which a firm, having failed to meet sinking-fund requirements but having paid the interest on the debt, has been forced into bankruptcy." Assuming that this statement is true, do you agree with this text, which then states: "The trustee, acting under the so-called *prudent-man rule*, would do more harm to the bondholders by forcing the company into bankruptcy if the firm did not meet the sinking fund payments on its debt while still being able to meet its interest"? You may assume in your answer that the text is in error in stating that the prudent-man rule is related to the problem confronting the trustee. The prudent-man rule is related only to the investment policy of a trustee of funds for investment and is not concerned with what action a trustee of a bond issue will take upon default of an investment unless the indenture specifies that standard.

### Problems

**1.** It has been suggested that a company should use the economic order size formula to establish the ideal balance between the costs of a major financing and the cost of carrying excess cash (inventory). Thus, the economic order size (of a financing) would be

$$Q = \sqrt{\frac{2CU}{K}}$$

where $Q$ is the size of financing, $C$ is the cost of financing (a trip to the well), $U$ is the annual usage or demand for cash, and $K$ is the cost of carrying the inventory of cash.

In finance the cost of carrying the inventory is the interest the company pays to the lender (say, 6 percent) less the earning the company gets by investing the excess cash in short-term notes (say, 2 percent).

Suppose that the costs of a financing are $20,000, that the company will need an annual increment of $1 million for several years, and that it can borrow at 6 percent but that the earning of short-term money is 2 percent. What is the ideal size of the loan? [See William Beranek, *Analysis for Financial Decisions* (Homewood, Ill.: Richard D. Irwin, Inc., 1963), pp. 345–396.]

2. In problem 1, once the company has borrowed the ideal amount, the next question is how frequently to make withdrawals from short-term funds if the act of withdrawal has a fixed cost (as would be true if the short-term notes must be sold before maturity in order to get cash). In this case we can use the short-term earning rate (2 percent) as the cost of carrying cash and again employ the economic order size formula to determine how large the withdrawals should be. What will the optimum size withdrawal be if there is a brokerage charge of $150 on each sale of short-term notes?

3. Suppose a company has a mortgage debt of $4 million, general creditors of $1 million, bank loans of $3 million, subordinated debentures of $1 million (which are subordinated to any bank debt), and common stock with par value of $5 million. Unmortgaged assets are $3 million and mortgaged assets $3 million. How will distribution be made in bankruptcy?

4. Suppose the bond indenture of a company specifies that the company must maintain a ratio of bond debt to the sum of subordinated debt plus net worth of 0.75:1, that subordinated debt provides its ratio cannot exceed net worth in the ratio 0.8:1 and that the preferred stock provides the maximum ratio to common stock be 0.5:1.

What total amount of money can the company raise if $1.25 million of new common stock is sold?

5. Torgerson Company has an open-end bond issue that permits more bonds to be issued as long as total interest due after the increase in bonds is covered at least three times by the sum of earnings before income taxes plus depreciation in the year preceding the increase in bonds. Furthermore, the total bonds after the increase cannot exceed 60 percent of the preceding year's net worth and the original cost of the security of the total bonds must equal 150 percent of the bonds to be outstanding.

Presently the company's records show:

| | |
|---|---|
| Last year's depreciation plus earnings before income tax | $ 300,000 |
| Previously outstanding 6 percent bonds | 1,500,000 |
| Last year's net worth | 2,700,000 |
| Cost of presently mortgaged land and buildings | 3,000,000 |
| Cost of proposed building addition | 400,000 |

How much in additional 6 percent bonds might be issued?

6. Oscar Goodman, Inc., has an outstanding issue of 4 percent, 25-year bonds sold at par and convertible into common stock at $50 a share. The bonds are callable at $108. The bonds as straight debt would have carried 5 percent at the time of issue. At the time of issue the common stock was selling at $42 and paying $1.50 dividend per year. The bonds still have 20 years to run and carry no provision for increase in conversion price, although there are the customary provisions for adjustment of conversion price in the event of stock dividends,

splits, and so on. New bonds of similar quality but without conversion rights currently bear 6 percent. The stock is currently selling at $40 a share and is still paying $1.50 dividend. There is no reason to expect that the price of the stock will advance in the near future. Give your best estimate of what the market value of the bond might be.

7. Guthmann Corporation has 6 percent convertible bonds due in 10 years. The present conversion price is $40 per share of common stock. In several weeks the conversion price will change to $50. The call price is $108. Nonconvertible bonds of the same type are presently yielding 6 percent. The current market price of the common stock is $50, and the shares pay an annual dividend of $2.40 per share. Will the bondholders likely convert?

8. Howard Industries has outstanding a 5 percent convertible bond issue, which carries the privilege of conversion into common stock at $25 per share. The bond is callable at $105. Bonds of similar quality but without the conversion privilege are being issued on a 5 percent basis. The common stock is presently selling at $30 and the dividend rate has just been increased from $1.25 to $1.50 a share. Will the bondholders likely convert?

9. Examine the following summaries of offerings of convertible subordinated debentures:

a. One of the offerings is on rights and one is on nonrights. Do you consider the rights offering less costly to the issuer? Do you think that the evidence on the matter of the costs of rights versus nonrights in a convertible subordinated debenture issue is applicable to the same question in common stock offerings?

b. How do you account for the differences in the underwriting agreements between the two offerings?

c. Moody's *Bond Survey* shows the straight-debt cost of these two bonds at the time of issue to have been:

| | | |
|---|---|---|
| National Cash Register | 4¼s | 5.65% |
| Lockheed Aircraft | 4¼s | 5.95% |

How do you account for the apparent inconsistencies if we measure an "inconsistency" by the *difference* between the coupon rate and the straight-debt yield? All the bonds were issued at par.

*Sale of Convertible Subordinated Debentures by Rights, National Cash Register Company* [29]

*Offering.* The offering was $88,696,700—4.25 percent convertible subordinated debentures due April 15, 1992, at $100 plus accrued interest from April 26, 1967; convertible into common stock at a price of $100 per share on or before April 15, 1982. The capitalization of NCR is in Table 19–7 and the earnings summary in Table 19–6. The common stock price range appears in Table 19–8.

*Rights.* On April 12, 1967, NCR issued to common stockholders of record a transferable warrant granting 1 right for each share of stock, with 10 rights re-

[29] This material is taken from the prospectus, dated April 12, 1967.

quired to purchase each $100 debentures and with subscription possible only in round multiples of $100. The rights expired April 26, 1967.

TABLE 19–6. NCR Earnings Summary (millions)

| | *1962* | *1963* | *1964* | *1965* | *1966* |
|---|---|---|---|---|---|
| Income | | | | | |
| Sales | $463 | $474 | $519 | $560 | $654 |
| Service and rental | 101 | 118 | 147 | 177 | 218 |
| Miscellaneous | 12 | 13 | 13 | 15 | 14 |
| Total | $576 | $605 | $679 | $752 | $886 |
| Costs and expenses | | | | | |
| Costs of goods and service | 261 | 275 | 307 | 334 | 395 |
| Selling and general | 202 | 212 | 239 | 273 | 319 |
| Research | 19 | 20 | 22 | 25 | 30 |
| Depreciation | 31 | 38 | 45 | 50 | 62 |
| Interest | 7 | 9 | 9 | 10 | 13 |
| Total | $520 | $554 | $622 | $692 | $819 |
| Profit before taxes | $ 56 | $ 52 | $ 57 | $ 60 | $ 67 |
| U.S. income taxes | 13 | 11 | 12 | 11 | 11 |
| Foreign income taxes | 15 | 15 | 17 | 18 | 22 |
| Total | $ 28 | $ 26 | $ 29 | $ 29 | $ 33 |
| After-tax profit | $ 29 | $ 25 | $ 28 | $ 31 | $ 34 |
| Less minority interest | 2 | 2 | 2 | 2 | 2 |
| Less foreign nonremittals * | 3 | 2 | 4 | 4 | 5 |
| Less foreign write downs | 3 | 1 | — | — | — |
| | $ 8 | $ 5 | $ 6 | $ 6 | $ 7 |
| Net income | $ 21 | $ 20 | $ 22 | $ 25 | $ 27 |
| Earned per share | $2.37 | $2.30 | $2.56 | $2.81 | $3.10 |
| Dividends per share | 1.14 | 1.14 | 1.14 | 1.16 | 1.20 |
| Net sales, service income and rentals outside the U.S. included above | $244 | $262 | $297 | $331 | $390 |

* NCR policy is to report only overseas income remitted to the United States.

The subscription agent, if requested, sold any rights (not more than 100) and bought up to nine rights for any stockholder, with NCR absorbing all brokerage fees, taxes, and expenses, provided the subscription agent could find buyers or sellers. All rights sold or bought on any day would be at the average price for all rights handled by the agent on that day.

No warrants were mailed to stockholders with record addresses outside the United States and Canada or to those whose addresses indicated military or other government service in such areas but were held by the First National City Bank until noon of the day of expiration for the stockholder's instruction. If no instructions were received, the rights would be sold if feasible and the proceeds remitted to the stockholders.

*NCR Business.* The firm began business in 1884. The company has become the largest manufacturer of cash registers in the world and one of the leading manufacturers of electromechanical and electronic accounting machines as well as electronic data processing equipment. The company also markets a line of pressure-sensitive coated papers which make duplicate copies without the use of carbon, and in 1966 entered the microfilm field for business records.

The prospectus does not detail the product mix of the company as is usually done in a prospectus but lists plant facilities in seven foreign countries.

TABLE 19–7. Capitalization of NCR after This Issue

| | |
|---|---|
| Long-term debt | |
| 3.25 percent sinking fund notes due 3/1/77 | $ 8,570,000 |
| 3.75 percent sinking fund notes due 3/1/80 | 8,125,000 |
| 4.75 percent sinking fund debentures due 6/1/85 | 37,600,000 |
| 4.375 percent sinking fund debentures due 4/1/87 | 47,000,000 |
| 5.6 percent sinking fund debentures due 6/15/91 | 60,000,000 |
| 4.25 percent convertible subordinated debentures | 88,696,700 |
| Common stock | 8,869,663 shares |

*Price of Rights.* The rights fluctuated in value from a high of 1½₁₆ and a low of 13⁄16 on April 12, 1967, to a high of 1 9⁄16 and a low of 1½ on April 26, 1967, the expiration date. The high on the last day was the highest price at any time during the period. The low on the first day was the lowest price at any time during the period. The stock moved from a low of 85¼ on the third day of the period to a high of 97 on the fourth, last day of the period and closed the period at 94⅝.

TABLE 19–8. NCR Common Stock Price Range

| | *High* | *Low* |
|---|---|---|
| 1962 | $132¾ | $66¾ |
| 1963 | 85⅜ | 65 |
| 1964 | 84⅜ | 63 |
| 1965 | 91¾ | 69 |
| 1966 | 91½ | 59 |
| 1967 | 96 | 67⅛ |
| Last sale on April 11, 1967, $89 | | |

*Underwriting Terms.* The underwriters received a minimum of $1.125 per $100 principal of bonds (an aggregate of $997,837 on the total issue) if required to take no bonds, and $1.875 per $100 principal of bonds (an aggregate of $1,663,063 on the total issue) if required to take all the bonds, with a sliding scale for quantities in between. The purchase or underwriting agreement provided that in the case of default of one or more underwriters involving 9 percent or more of the unsubscribed debentures, then less than all unsubscribed debentures could be sold. But if 9 percent or less of the debentures were not taken by defaulting underwriters, the other underwriters had their allotments increased *pro rata.* In the event the unsubscribed debentures were less than $8,869,700, Dillon, Read & Company would use its best efforts to sell such at prices above subscription price and to pay NCR any excess if the unsubscribed debentures were not more than $2,660,900 or 50 percent of the excess if the unsubscribed amount were between $2,660,900 and $8,869,700 but not less than 26,609 times the average excess over $100 principal of the bonds.

The underwriters may allow up to 1 percent to selected dealers and such dealers could reallow up to ¼ percent to other dealers.

There were 95 underwriters, with the manager (Dillon, Read & Company) taking 10 percent of the issue, 3 underwriters taking 2.7 percent each, 17 taking 2 percent each, 4 taking 1.25 percent each, and 23 taking 1 percent each.

Prior to and after expiration of the warrants the underwriters were authorized to offer debentures on a "when issued" basis or otherwise subject to the restriction that the price on any day could not be increased more than once and could be no higher than the highest price at which nonparticipating dealers were quoting over the counter, or after the debentures were admitted to trading on the New York Stock Exchange, not more than the greater of the last sale price or current offering on the exchange.

*Results of NCR Offering.* Of the total of $88,696,000 in convertibles, $86,857,000 was purchased by the exercise of rights and $1,839,000 was purchased by the underwriters.

*Sale of Convertible Subordinated Debentures without Rights, Lockheed Aircraft Corporation* [30]

*Offering.* The offering was $125,000,000—4.25 convertible subordinated debentures due 1992 at 100 percent plus accrued interest from March 1, 1967; convertible into common stock at a price of $72.50 per share.

*Lockheed Business.* Lockheed began business in 1932. The company makes aircraft of all types, military and commercial, is a manufacturer of missiles for the space program, is engaged in shipbuilding, construction, electronics, and propulsion, and other activities. The sales, capitalization, earnings and common stock prices of the business are given in Tables 19–9 through 19–12.

TABLE 19–9. Sales and Revenues of Lockheed
(millions)

| | *1962* | *1963* | *1964* | *1965* | *1966* |
|---|---|---|---|---|---|
| U.S. Government | | | | | |
| Aircraft | $ 584 | $ 930 | $ 780 | $ 978 | $1,187 |
| Missiles | 454 | 478 | 365 | 331 | 371 |
| Space | 370 | 324 | 272 | 269 | 278 |
| Shipbuilding and construction | 35 | 39 | 58 | 67 | 24 |
| Electronics, propulsion | 19 | 21 | 38 | 41 | 50 |
| Total | $1,462 | $1,792 | $1,513 | $1,686 | $1,910 |
| Foreign governments | $ 237 | $ 109 | $ 51 | $ 63 | $ 65 |
| Commercial | 54 | 29 | 39 | 69 | 110 |
| Total | $1,753 | $1,930 | $1,603 | $1,818 | $2,085 |

[30] This material is taken from the prospectus, dated March 21, 1967.

TABLE 19–10. Capitalization of Lockheed after This Issue

| | |
|---|---|
| Long-term debt | |
| 4.5 percent debentures due May 1, 1975 | $ 16,865,000 |
| 4.25 percent, convertible subordinated debentures | 125,000,000 |
| | $141,865,000 |
| Capital stock, $1 par value | 11,153,078 shares |

TABLE 19–11. Lockheed Earnings Summary (millions)

| | *1962* | *1963* | *1964* | *1965* | *1966* |
|---|---|---|---|---|---|
| Sales | $1,753 | $1,930 | $1,603 | $1,818 | $2,085 |
| Other income | 2 | 3 | 2 | 2 | 2 |
| | $1,755 | $1,933 | $1,605 | $1,820 | $2,087 |
| Costs and expenses | | | | | |
| Cost of sales | $1,553 | $1,713 | $1,386 | $1,557 | $1,810 |
| General expenses | 100 | 109 | 106 | 115 | 132 |
| Research and development | 18 | 23 | 26 | 43 | 36 |
| Interest | 5 | 3 | 1 | 2 | 2 |
| | $1,676 | $1,848 | $1,519 | $1,717 | $1,980 |
| Earnings before tax | 79 | 85 | 86 | 103 | 107 |
| Income taxes | 42 | 42 | 40 | 49 | 48 |
| Earnings | $ 37 | $ 43 | $ 46 | $ 54 | $ 59 |
| Capital gain net of tax | 13 | | | | |
| Earnings | $ 50 | $ 43 | $ 46 | $ 54 | $ 59 |
| Earned per share | $4.83 | $4.06 | $4.26 | $4.89 | $5.29 |
| Dividends per share | 0.90 | 1.30 | 1.60 | 2.00 | 2.20 |

TABLE 19–12. Lockheed Common Stock Price Range

| | *High* | *Low* |
|---|---|---|
| 1962 | 42 | 25⅞ |
| 1963 | 44 | 33⅜ |
| 1964 | 40⅞ | 31¾ |
| 1965 | 69⅝ | 36⅝ |
| 1966 | 73 | 49 |
| 1967 to March 20 | 65¼ | 57½ |
| Last sale March 20, 1967, $61.125 | | |

*Underwriting Terms.* The underwriters received 1⅛ percent, or an aggregate of $1,406,250. The purchase or underwriting agreement provided that if any debentures were purchased all would be purchased. The underwriters offered selected dealers a concession up to 0.5 percent, and other dealers 0.25 percent. There were 189 underwriters, with the managing underwriter (Blyth & Company, Inc.) taking 19 percent and the next 18 largest taking 1.6 percent each.

### Selected References

Bacon, P. W., and E. L. Winn, Jr., "The Impact of Forced Conversion on Stock Prices," *Journal of Finance,* 24 (December, 1969), pp. 871–874.

Baumol, W. J., B. G. Malkiel, and R. E. Quandt, "The Valuation of Convertible Securities," *Quarterly Journal of Economics,* 80 (February 1966), pp. 48–59.

Bladen, A., *Techniques for Investing in Convertible Bonds.* New York: Salomon Bros. & Hutzler, 1966.

Brigham, E. F., "An Analysis of Convertible Debentures," *Journal of Finance,* 21 (March 1966), pp. 35–54.

Broman, K. L., "The Use of Convertible Subordinated Debentures by Industrial Firms, 1949–59," *Quarterly Review of Economics and Business,* 3 (Spring 1963), pp. 65–75.

Chen, A. H. Y., "A Model of Warrant Pricing in a Dynamic Market," *Journal of Finance* (December 1970) pp. 1041–1059.

Cohan, A. B., "Yields on New Underwritten Corporate Bonds, 1935–58," *Journal of Finance,* 27 (December 1962), pp. 595–605.

Halford, F. A., "Income Bonds," *Financial Analysis Journal,* 20 (January 1964), pp. 73–79.

Hayes, S. L., "New Interest in Incentive Financing," *Harvard Business Review,* 44 (July–August 1966), pp. 99–112.

———, and H. B. Reiling, "Sophisticated Financing Tool: the Warrant," *Harvard Business Review* 47 (January–February 1969), pp. 137–150.

Jen, F. C., and J. E. Wert, "The Value of the Deferred Call Privilege," *National Banking Review,* 3 (March 1966), pp. 369–378.

———, and ———, "The Effect of Call Risk on Corporate Bond Yields," *Journal of Finance,* 22 (December 1967), pp. 637–651.

Johnson, R. W., "Subordinated Debentures: Debt That Serves as Equity," *Journal of Finance,* 10 (March 1955), pp. 1–16.

Kassouf, S. T., "Warrant Price Behavior," *Financial Analysis Journal,* 24 (January-February 1968), pp. 123–126.

McKenzie, R. R., "Convertible Debentures, 1956–65," *Quarterly Review,* 6 (Winter 1966), pp. 41–51.

Poensgen, O. H., "The Valuation of Convertible Bonds: Part I: The Model," *Industrial Management Review,* 6 (Fall 1965), pp. 77–92, and "Part II: Empirical Results and Conclusions," 7 (Spring 1966), pp. 83–89.

Pye, G., "The Value of the Call Option on a Bond," *Journal of Political Economy,* 74 (April 1966), pp. 200–205.

———, "The Value of Call Deferment on a Bond: Some Empirical Results," *Journal of Finance,* 22 (December 1967), pp. 637–651.

Robbins, S. M., "A Bigger Role for Income Bonds," *Harvard Business Review,* 33 (November-December 1955), pp. 100–114.

Samuelson, P. A., and R. C. Merton, "A Complete Model of Warrant Pricing that Maximizes Utility," *The Industrial Management Review,* 10 (Winter, 1969), pp. 17–46.

Shelton, J. P., "The Relations of the Price of a Warrant to the Price of Its Associated Stock," *Financial Analysts Journal,* 23 (May-June and July-August 1967), pp. 88–89 and 143–151.

Walter, J. E. and A. V. Que, "The Valuation of Convertible Bonds," *Journal of Finance*, 28 (June 1973), pp. 713–732.

Weil, R. L, Jr., J. E. Segall, and D. Green, Jr., "Premiums on Convertible Bonds," *Journal of Finance*, 23 (June 1968), pp. 445–463.

Weingartner, H. M., "Optimal Timing of Bond Refunding," *Management Science*, (March 1967), pp. 511–524.

Winn, W. J., and A. Hess, Jr., "The Value of the Call Privilege," *Journal of Finance*, 14 (May 1959), pp. 182–195.

# 20 Preferred Stock Financing

As is true throughout the field of finance, the classical distinctions of years ago have been blurred by modern refinements. Thus, what once was the rather sharply defined area of preferred stock is today a rainbow of provisions producing a security that goes from the income bond at one end of the spectrum to a security at the other end whose preference is so denuded as to be little more than a class of common stock.

To be considered a preferred stock the security must represent ownership, that is, it must have no due date and must be entitled to dividends only as they are declared by the board of directors rather than as an interest payment legally enforcible on a set date. In addition, the stock must have at least some preference over common stock in the payment of dividends and may or may not have preference to assets in the event of liquidation or reorganization. Under present federal income tax law, the dividend paid on preferred stock is not deductible by the issuer, but, as we shall see later in this chapter, a fully taxable corporation owning the preferred stock can claim tax deduction at 85 percent of the preferred dividend that it receives.

In the case of bonds, we found it necessary in considering priority to ask the question, prior to what? In the case of preferred stock we must ask, preferred to what? Only an examination of the specific situation can answer that question.

The provisions governing preferred stock are normally found in the corporate charter and in the resolution of the board of directors authorizing the issue. These provisions may be summarized on the stock certificate. There is no indenture or trustee such as is customary for a bond issue.

## PRINCIPAL PROVISIONS ON PREFERRED STOCK

Before we consider the role of preferred stock in finance, we must examine the principal provisions associated with preferred stock.

### Priority as to Some Earnings Over Common Stock

Preferred stock enjoys some priority as to earnings over common stock. This priority is limited to a stated percentage or amount per share on an annual basis. If the preferred stock has par value,[1] this priority as to earnings over common stock may be a figure such as $6, or 6 percent annually in the case of a par value of $100. However, the fact that the company "earned" the amount of this priority does not assure that it will be paid. The order for payment must issue from the board of directors, and their decision must rest on a number of factors, one of which is the liquidity position of the company. The board is also entitled to consider

---

[1] Par value means little more than the value printed on the stock certificate and the value for the stock shown in the capital account on the balance sheet of the issuer. In the case of a bond, par can be defined as the dollar amount the corporation is obligated to repay, but in the case of a stock, the meaning of par value is less certain, particularly because of the alternative of no par stock. A "share" of stock means that the owner shares *pro rata* (share for share) with other owners of the same class of stock. Because of the problem of what par value means, some states forbid the issuance of no par preferred stock. In the case of no par stock, most states of incorporation require the corporation to set a "stated value" for the no par stock.

What "par" means as applied to stock ultimately depends on the law of the state of incorporation. How the state law defines the term has to do with the legal requirements of the state concerning what a share of stock can be sold for in terms of price and whether cash, goods, or services are permitted as payment. The early legal rule that stock could be sold only at or above par gave way to the realities of the situation. Originally the rule was intended to prevent dilution of the principal amount paid to the company by previous purchasers. But sale by the company to subsequent purchasers at less than par had to be realistically permitted when the stock was no longer worth par.

The origin of the difficulty is that the law was ignorant of the fact that the "principal" of an equity is nothing but the capitalized future earnings of that equity.

Thus, in the final analysis par (and stated value in the case of no par) is a figure the corporation is required by law to set so that the rules of law applicable to a host of problems can use this figure as a starting point. These rules are concerned with what prices are permissible for stock sales at the time of issue, under what conditions par or stated value can be increased or decreased, and when dividends can be paid or shares repurchased.

In states where the legal rule that stock cannot be sold by the company below par still has teeth, the rule is avoided by lowering the par value by appropriate stockholder action.

that even if cash is available payment would work to the disadvantage of the corporation as a whole, as might be true if there were an immediate investment opportunity requiring cash.[2]

As protection against this discretion of the board of directors, preferred stock typically carries a *cumulative* clause providing that, if the dividend is not paid, it accumulates and must be paid before any distribution to the common stockholders. Where the company experiences prolonged difficulty, these arrearages may pile up to such an extent that the firm may seek to make a compromise that would give consenting[3] preferred stockholders a package in lieu of the arrearage. The package might include some cash, some notes, and some stock.

### Participation by Preferred Stock

Most preferred stock is limited to the dividend for which it has priority over the common stock. A number of issues of preferred stock carry the right to participate in any additional dividends that may be paid by the company. The most common provision of such *participating preferred* is the right to receive an additional dividend on the same basis, share for share, as is received by the common stock after the common has received the same dividends as the initial preferred dividend.

### Call, Protection, and Redemption Provisions

Most preferred stock contains a provision entitling the company to call in the preferred stock for payment. The call premium may be a set amount or may be scaled against time. Without a call provision the company may be caught when the market rate on preferred drops sharply below the rate that prevailed at the time the preferred was issued. Without a call provision the company has the problem of retrieving the preferred in this situation in order to "refund" at a lower rate. The only way for the company to do this is to repurchase the stock on the open market. However, the market will have capitalized the difference between the higher rate on the preferred and the current market rate,

---

[2] This appears to be exactly what happened in the case of Virginia-Carolina Chemical Corporation. As of 1946 the firm's $100 par 6 percent cumulative participating preferred stock had an arrearage of $92.50 accumulated from depression years. This arrearage was cut by dividends to $73.50 in 1949. From 1950 through 1958 the company paid $6 per year on the stock but then stopped the preferred dividend even though in the years ending June 30, 1960, 1961, and 1962 the company earned $15.48, $10.80, and $20.83, respectively, per share of preferred stock. On June 30, 1962 the arrearage stood at $96 per share. In August 1962 the company offered each preferred share a package of 1 share of $100 par common stock (which had never paid a dividend), 1.3 shares of a new 5 percent preferred at $50 par, and 1 share of new 5 percent preferred $50 par convertible into 1.1 shares of common. This package had an estimated market value of $153 and was offered for each preferred share whose preference then stood at $196. Just prior to the vote on the package, the company paid $6 per share of preferred. Some 72 percent of the voting preferred stockholders voted to accept the package, and 1 year later the 5 percent prior preferred was called. In 1963 Virginia-Carolina was acquired by Socony Mobile Oil Company. A complete recital of the facts appears in J. B. Cohen and S. M. Robbins, *The Financial Manager* (New York: Harper & Row, Publishers, Inc., 1966), pp. 844–848.

[3] The problem of the rights of preferred stockholders who do not accept the package offer is considered in Chapter 23.

and the price the company would have to pay to repurchase would eliminate any gain in refunding at the then-current market rates.

Preferred stock resembles debt in that earnings are limited, except in the case of participating preferred. Likewise, preferred has a priority as to earnings and sometimes as to assets on liquidation. Hence, protective provisions of various kinds can be expected. In addition to the cumulative dividend provision, there often is a provision that no stock of equal or prior standing may be issued without the consent of the preferred stockholders. Otherwise the company may issue *prior preferred* carrying priority over the preferred already issued. To attempt to assure liquidity for dividends a current ratio provision may exist. And to attempt to assure availability of earnings for dividends, a provision may be included requiring the maintenance of a minimum earned surplus before dividends may be paid on the common stock.

To assure preferred priority in earnings it will be necessary to insert a provision classifying the repurchase of common stock as the same as a dividend on the common. Many states now have statutes limiting the repurchase of common shares to the amount of surplus that is available for dividends.[4]

Redemption provisions, parallel to a sinking fund for debt, are frequently found in connection with preferred stock. These provisions may specify either the call by lot or the repurchase in the open market of a stated amount of preferred stock per year. The company may be bound to use the cheaper of the two methods. Then if the market price of the preferred stock falls below par (as would occur when the market rate of dividend on preferred stock increases), redemption will furnish a market for the stock. If the market rate decreases, the company would call shares by lot because the market price would be above call. There is a trade-off between increased redemption provisions and a reduced dividend rate for the preferred stock.

Another method of protection conserves the company's cash by not requiring redemption but simply "freezing" an amount of surplus each year, thus rendering that part of surplus unavailable for common stock dividends.

### Voting Rights and Priority as to Assets

Preferred stock may have full voting rights (on an equal basis, share for share with the common stock), no voting rights, or limited voting rights. *Limited voting rights* typically grant all (or share for share with the common) voting rights to the preferred stock in the event of a default or arrearage for several years. Such voting rights terminate as soon as the default is cured. More often, upon default the preferred stockholders are given the right to elect some of the directors.

In recent years many state statutes have been amended to require a separate vote by *classes* of stock in order to authorize amendments of the corporate charter affecting classes differently. In such cases the

---

[4] This topic is developed more fully in Chapter 22.

law of the state of incorporation takes precedence over any contrary provisions in the stock.

Most preferred stock issues provide for priority of the par value plus unpaid arrearages over the common stock in the event of liquidation or reorganization. Sometimes liquidation preference is given to one class of common stock even though the class is not designed preferred.

### Convertibility

Preferred stock may be made convertible into common stock in a manner analogous to the convertibility of bonds.[5] Although several decades ago preferred stock carried convertibility rights in only 25 percent of the listed issues outstanding, that percentage has been increasing.

### Income Tax Deductibility of Intercompany Preferred Stock Dividends

One important income tax provision supports a large part of the market for preferred stock. A fully taxable corporation owning preferred stock of another (unrelated) corporation is entitled to deduct 85 percent of the preferred dividends it receives in determining its income subject to income tax.[6] Thus, the owning corporation receiving 7 percent on bonds of another company will net 3.64 percent (after taxes of 48 percent), but on 7 percent preferred dividends will net 6.496 percent (after a 48 percent tax on 15 percent of the dividend). In order to be entitled to the deduction of 85 percent of the preferred dividends received, the corporation receiving the dividend must be a fully taxable corporation.

The enormous impact of the intercompany exemption of 85 percent of stock dividends is shown in Table 20–1, which reports the *average* yield (return on current market price, not the coupon or dividend on par) of AAA rated industrial bonds compared to the yield of high grade industrial preferred stocks from 1960 through 1972. It is clear that the corporate investor fears the income tax more than a junior position as to assets and income, but for *individual* investors, there is no income tax advantage of preferred stock over bonds. The corporate exemption is allowed to prevent multiple taxation at the *corporate* level.

This tax exemption produces a double effect: the higher the bond yield relative to the preferred yield, the more *individual* investors desert preferred for bonds while fully taxable corporations will pursue their preference for preferred stock. Except for one factor, this movement might continue until bond yields would be almost double preferred yields (as long as corporate income taxes remain at 50 percent and this intercompany exemption of 85 percent of dividends continues) *provided* fully taxable corporate investors continue to be a large enough segment of all investors.

---

[5] See the discussion of convertibility of bonds in Chapter 19.

[6] This provision is examined in Chapter 24. In the case of affiliated companies intercompany dividends are not taxed when a consolidated return is filed.

The one additional factor is corporate *issuers* will prevent the bond yield from reaching double the preferred yield because the issuer is willing to pay some price (increased after-tax cost) for preferred rather than debt, since a defaulted preferred dividend can never place the issuer in bankruptcy, but defaulted interest can.

Table 20–1 shows a reversal in 1971 and 1972 of the phenomenon just discussed. This change reflects the increase in the supply of new preferreds in 1971 and 1972 shown in Table 17–3 (p. 448) without proportionate increase in demand.

TABLE 20–1. Impact of Intercompany Dividend Exemption on Yields of Bonds and Preferred Stock, 1960–1972

| Year | AAA Industrial bond yields | High-grade industrial preferred stock yields | Excess of preferred yields over bond |
|---|---|---|---|
| 1960 | 4.28% | 4.71% | 0.43% |
| 1961 | 4.21 | 4.60 | 0.39 |
| 1962 | 4.18 | 4.47 | 0.29 |
| 1963 | 4.14 | 4.29 | 0.15 |
| 1964 | 4.32 | 4.28 | −0.04 |
| 1965 | 4.45 | 4.30 | −0.15 |
| 1966 | 5.12 | 4.85 | −0.27 |
| 1967 | 5.49 | 5.18 | −0.31 |
| 1968 | 6.12 | 5.65 | −0.47 |
| 1969 | 6.93 | 6.31 | −0.62 |
| 1970 | 7.77 | 7.48 | −0.29 |
| 1971 | 7.05 | 7.05 | 0.00 |
| 1972 | 6.97 | 7.01 | 0.04 |

SOURCE: *Moody's Industrial Manual*, 1973.

## ADVANTAGES AND DISADVANTAGES OF PREFERRED STOCK FOR FINANCIAL MANAGEMENT

The advantages of preferred stock are parallel to those of debt. Leverage is achieved where the earning of the preferred is less than the earning of the common stock. The risks of achieving this leverage by debt include the maturity date and the fixed interest payments. Default in either respect would lead to insolvency in the case of debt. Avoiding this risk by the use of preferred stock involves the financial manager in the payment of a higher rate on preferred stock than on bonds and the tax disadvantage of the nondeductibility of preferred dividends compared to the deductibility of interest on bonds.

Lesser advantages are that preferred stock offers the opportunity of preserving assets free from mortgage and available for future financing and may avoid parting with voting rights if the preferred is nonvoting as long as there is no arrearage. Furthermore, the use of the call provision offers the same flexibility that exists in the case of bonds. This flexibility is not available for the issuance of common stock except to a limited extent through the repurchase of common stock.

The tax disadvantage of preferred stock compared to debt severely limits the use of preferred, because the after-tax cost of preferred is almost twice that of debt.[7]

TABLE 20–2. New Corporate Security Issues by Types, 1931–1951, 1960–1966, and 1968–1972 *
(billions)

| | 1931–1951 | | 1960–1966 | | 1968–1972 | |
|---|---|---|---|---|---|---|
| | Amount | Percent | Amount | Percent | Amount | Percent |
| Bonds | $26.6 | 75% | $33.3 | 68% | $125.8 | 72% |
| Preferred Stock | 4.1 | 12 | 1.9 | 4 | 9.7 | 5 |
| Common Stock | 4.5 | 13 | 13.8 | 28 | 39.2 | 23 |

* These figures exclude investment company offerings.
SOURCES: 1931–1951, H. C. Guthmann and H. F. Dougall, *Corporate Financial Policy*, 3d ed. (Englewood Cliffs, N. J.: Prentice-Hall, Inc., 1955), p. 169; 1960–1966 and 1968–1972, Securities and Exchange Commission, *Statistical Bulletin*, monthly.
[B10]

Table 20–2 illustrates the dramatic shift away from preferred stock as corporate income tax rates continued high after World War II. In the early years of the period 1931–1966, income taxes were lower than they are today, and although they were high during World War II, there was an expectation that they would ultimately revert to prewar levels. In the latter part of the period it became apparent that corporate income taxes would not fall to prewar levels. By way of explanation, bond figures point to considerable refunding during the 1930s and to a lesser extent so do the preferred stock figures. It must be remembered, too, that a high percentage of new funds for companies is retained earnings.[8]

No research is available on the extent to which even the current showing of preferred stock financing rests on the 85 percent intercompany tax deduction for preferred dividends, but there are cases where "lending" corporations have been willing to buy preferred issues of companies whose bonds would not be of interest to the lender. Such purchases have been motivated by the tax deductibility of the intercompany preferred dividend to the "lender."

One factor favoring the use of preferred stock in public utility financing is that the tax disadvantage is largely removed by the legal rule that the allowable return for a public utility is determined *after* income taxes.[9] Thus, regulating commissions must increase rates charged to utility customers sufficiently so that the after-tax earning is the same whether preferred stock or debt is used even though the use of debt would result in lower rates to customers than the use of preferred stock.

---

[7] Assuming an income tax rate of approximately 50 percent and a preferred dividend rate slightly above the bond rate.

[8] For the 5 years 1946–1951, retained earnings were $56 billion, and in the period 1968–1972 they were $107 billion. *Economic Report of the President 1973* Table C–73, p. 278.

[9] Under the rule of *Galveston Electric Co. vs. Galveston*, 258 U.S. 388 (1922).

The financial manager must always consider not only the effect of the proposed financing on his company but how investors will react. Investors are attracted by the higher earnings offered by preferred stock in comparison to bonds. The fact that the market price of preferred stock fluctuates more than that of bonds and the fact that sometimes dividend arrearages are not paid out in cash have not been important deterrents to investors.

## MANAGEMENT OF PREFERRED STOCK AFTER ISSUANCE

After the preferred stock has been issued problems of management arise that are similar to those associated with bond issues except that the financial manager does not face the maturity problem in the case of preferred stock.

As market rates on preferred stock move in a downward direction, opportunities arise for replacing the preferred stock with another issue at lower rates, or for replacing the issue with more favorable covenants. The changing affairs of a business and of the market place may produce situations in which protective provisions of the original issue become onerous and place constraints on the firm.

For example, market conditions at the time of issuance may have forced the inclusion of a clause severely limiting the amount of debt. The company may now wish to take advantage of subordinated convertible debentures to increase the amount of common stock through conversion at prices much more favorable than a direct issue of common stock. But a covenant in the preferred stock setting debt limits may stand in the way.

In computing the saving of a replacement issue it is important to compare the results after taxes. The fact that preferred stock has no maturity date simplifies the rate of return computation to a comparison of the first year after-tax saving against the after-tax investment (some costs of replacement are tax deductible and some are not). If, however, the preferred issue has a redemption schedule, the rate of return computation for the proposed new preferred issue will involve using present value tables.

One special problem is the replacement of noncallable preferred or of an issue with a very high call premium.[10] While noncallable preferred is not issued today, there are still some noncallable preferred issues outstanding that were issued in the 1920s. At the time of issuance, few people anticipated the severe drop in the long-term interest rate that developed in the 1930s, and fewer still anticipated the high corporate tax rates that began in the 1940s.

Except for the possibility of eliminating preferred stock afforded by a merger [11] and the obvious case of elimination in bankruptcy reorganization, the only way to terminate a noncallable preferred stock issue is

[10] Bucyrus Erie in 1952 replaced a 7 percent $100 par preferred issue callable at $120.

[11] This device is explained in Chapter 22.

through tenders by the issuer or repurchase in the open market. Noncallable 6 and 7 percent preferred issues stood around $150 in the market place from the 1930s to the 1960s. The most important single factor that deterred repurchase by issuers was not the high premium in itself but the prospect that the long-term interest rate might rise shortly after the issuer replaced the preferred. This would enable much less expensive replacement. Ultimately this did happen when in late 1966 and early 1967 many of these noncallable issues fell in the market place to the range of 100–110. In 1974 these issues fell to the range of 60–70.

One illustration of this feeling of frustration is the replacement of the noncallable $100 par 7 percent preferred by U.S. Steel in 1965. When the plan was announced in August 1965 the preferred stock stood at $152. U.S. Steel offered $175 in principal of 4⅝ percent 30-year debentures for each share of preferred stock. To be effective a tender must be somewhat above the market. The replacement, effected in December 1965, netted U.S. Steel an annual increase of $10 million in earnings available to common stockholders. This increase in earnings was predicated on 1965 federal income tax rates. Barely 1 year later this replacement could have been carried out on much better terms in the tight money world of 1966. The principal of bonds offered would have been nearer $100 rather than $175. The extra $75 principal is not tax deductible by U.S. Steel. The interest rate would have been higher, but it is tax deductible and the period of the higher interest rate even if no call were inserted would be limited to 30 years. Having waited so long, U.S. Steel would have benefited greatly by waiting one more year.

## RECENT USE OF CONVERTIBLE PREFERRED STOCK IN MERGERS

In recent years until an accounting change in 1970, a new phenomenon was taking place which promised to revitalize the slipping popularity of preferred stock. This was the frequent use of convertible preferred stock in mergers, particularly the conglomerate merger.

Of a total of 335 issues of preferred between 1960 and 1967 by firms that had securities listed on the New York Stock Exchange during that period, some 292 issues arose in mergers, and all of those issues were convertible.[12]

There are a number of reasons for this development. First, there was the desire of the acquiring company to use the "pooling of interests" method of accounting[13] for mergers. To qualify for this accounting treatment, the preferred had to be convertible, voting, carry no significant sinking fund provisions, and not be redeemable until after the initial

---

[12] G. E. Pinches, "Financing with Convertible Preferred Stock, 1960–1967," *Journal of Finance*, 25 (March 1970); pp. 53–63.

[13] The pooling of interests method of accounting is explained in the discussion on mergers in Chapter 23. Briefly, pooling permits the acquiring company to add the earned surplus of the acquired company to its own earned surplus and to account for any excess of the purchase price over the book value of the acquired company by a charge to capital surplus. Neither of these benefits is available under the alternative "purchase" method of accounting.

conversion date.[14] Pooling of interests could be used when the acquiring company issues common rather than convertible preferred. What was the motivation for using the convertible preferred? One important reason is to equalize the difference in dividends between the two companies. Many stockholders would oppose a merger if their dividends were altered. The easiest way to meet this problem is to create a new class of stock preserving the higher dividend for the acquired company. Furthermore, the acquired company might think itself of superior quality and thus seek the priority of a preferred both as to assets and dividends. Both of these purposes are legitimate. A third and not so legitimate a purpose may be to hide the "dilution" of earnings that may ultimately result when the preferred is converted into common stock. To deal with this abuse, the accounting profession[15] now requires that earnings per share of common stock be stated both on the basis of actually outstanding common stock and on the basis of "full dilution," assuming the conversion of all securities convertible into common stock and the exercise of all outstanding options for common stock.

The future use of convertible preferred in mergers has been hampered by the recent accounting ruling that when convertible preferred is used in a merger, the purchase method of accounting must be used.[16]

In some cases the real basis for the merger is the fact that the management of the acquired company has grown old and stagnated or the controlling owners are torn in irreconcilable conflict.[17] The acquired company may have a modest percentage of its shares publicly owned but may be unable to market additional shares at a price comparable to that available in merger. In some cases the owners of the acquired company may feel that their business involves less risk than that of the acquiring company; or the selling owners may be more interested in current income than prospective capital gains while the acquiring company sees growth potential in the acquired business if new and aggressive management is installed. Preferred stock can serve as a convenient vehicle to reconcile all of these objectives on both sides. The tax disadvantage of preferred stock pales in the plans of the acquiring company, which frequently does not have available cash and may have used (or seeks to preserve) its borrowing capacity to the limit. As a clincher, the acquiring company makes the preferred stock convertible into common stock.

---

[14] J. H. Fisch and Martin Mellman, "Pooling of Interests: The Status of the Criteria," *The Journal of Accountancy*, 126 (August 1968), p. 43.

[15] Accounting Principles Board Opinion No. 15, *Earnings per Share* (New York: American Institute of Certified Public Accountants, 1969); R. W. Melicher, "Financing with Convertible Preferred Stock: Comment," *Journal of Finance*, 26 (March 1971), pp. 144–147; and C. R. Sprecher, "A Note on Financing Mergers with Convertible Preferred Stock," *Journal of Finance*, 26 (June 1971), pp. 683–685.

[16] Accounting Principles Board Opinions No. 16 and No. 17, *Business Combinations,* (New York: American Institute of Certified Public Accountants, 1970). The purchase method of accounting is described in Chapter 23.

[17] This appears to have been the reason Automatic Sprinkler was able to acquire George J. Meyer Manufacturing Company, the country's largest producer of bottling machinery. *The Milwaukee Journal*, March 31, 1968.

## SUMMARY

Preferred stock is ownership with no maturity but a priority as to earnings and/or liquidation rights over common stock. It carries no due date for dividends, which are payable only when the board of directors so determines, although most preferred issues provide for accrual of unpaid dividends.

Some preferred issues are participating, that is, after the stated amount per share has been paid the preferred and an equal amount per share is paid the common, then both classes participate equally in further dividends during that year. Other forms of participation may be specified.

Almost all preferred stock carries call and redemption provisions as well as various protective covenants. Some preferred stock has regular voting rights while other issues have no voting rights until dividends are in arrears. Some preferred issues are convertible into common stock at a stated price per share.

While dividends on preferred stock are not tax deductible to the issuing corporation, such dividends are 85 percent exempt from taxation when received by another taxable corporation.

The advantages of preferred stock parallel those of debt with respect to leverage but without the disadvantages of a maturity date and fixed interest payments. On the other hand, preferred stock carries a higher rate and lacks tax deductibility to the issuer for dividends paid. The tax disadvantage reduces the use of preferred stock in high tax periods compared to low tax periods.

After issuance of the preferred stock the financial manager is faced with the question of refunding if the market rate on preferred stock falls. Because preferred has no maturity date, the computation of the profitability of refunding is simplified to a comparison of the results in the first year of refunding unless the preferred issue has a redemption schedule. If the preferred is noncallable, the refunding is carried out by repurchases in the open market or tenders to stockholders. One problem of refunding is timing. If refunding occurs too soon, the costs of a second refunding will bar taking advantage of further declines in the preferred rate.

In recent years convertible preferred stock has frequently been issued in mergers for a wide variety of reasons. The tax disadvantage of preferred stock is outweighed in the eyes of the acquiring company by the potential it sees in the acquisition. Furthermore, the acquiring company seeks to avoid using its debt capacity (or may have already exhausted it). A recent accounting rule specifying the purchase method of accounting for a merger where convertible preferred is used now limits the popularity of convertible preferred in mergers.

### *Study Questions*

1. What factors should determine the amount of preferred stock that a company will issue?

2. Do you think that voting rights are important to preferred stockholders? Would size of the company have a bearing on the importance you attribute to the voting rights?
3. Rank the following types of "protective" provisions found in preferred stock in the order of their importance to you as an investor. Then rank them in the reverse order of desirability to the company (that is, least desirable first, and so on). Is the order of the two rankings the same? How do you account for this?
   a. Cumulation.
   b. Limiting the ratio of debt to net worth.
   c. Limiting the earnings that can be paid to common stock as dividends and the amount of common stock that can be repurchased by the company.
   d. Sinking fund provisions for the preferred.
   e. Putting a lower limit on the current ratio.
   f. Granting voting rights that expand upon arrearage.
   g. Priority in liquidation.
4. Would your order of ranking be affected by: (a) the type of industry in which the company is (for example, a public utility versus a machine tool manufacturer), (b) the amount of the preferred dividend, or (c) whether the preferred was convertible or participating? Remember there are two orders of ranking involved, yours as an investor and the issuing company's.
5. Do you think that preferred stock arrearages should appear on the company's balance sheet? in the liabilities section? in the net worth section? If you would put arrearages on the balance sheet, what account would you debit?
6. As an investor do you favor a high or a low call price on preferred stock? Why? As an issuing corporation would you favor a high or a low call price? Why?
7. What type of situations, if any, would cause a company to favor shifting from debt to preferred stock? Would the reverse of these same elements cause a company to shift from preferred stock to debt?
8. The Supreme Court has ruled that whether a security is an income bond or a preferred stock will not be decided for income tax purposes by the "label" that appears on the security. Would you apply the same principle for questions other than income taxes?

### *Problems*

1. From Moody's or Standard & Poor's investment manuals or from the offering prospectus determine the following points with respect to the offering on May 18, 1965, by Control Data Corporation of 489,448 shares of 4 percent cumulative convertible preferred stock, par value $50 per share.

   a. What is the conversion price and what is its relation to prior prices of the common stock?
   b. What other financing was the company doing at the same time?
   c. What use was made of the funds secured at this time?
   d. What was the debt-to-equity ratio after these offerings?
   e. Why did the company use expensive preferred stock (the dividends are not tax deductible) rather than secure all the funds at this time by debentures? Why did it not omit the preferred offering?

f. Why did the company sell a convertible preferred stock rather than common stock?

g. What protective provisions were offered to the preferred?

h. What is the call provision in the preferred?

i. The offer was on rights on the basis of 1 share of preferred for each 15 shares of common. The underwriters received 65 cents a share for all shares offered and an additional 55 cents for each share they acquired as a result of failure of rights to be exercised. Do you consider the underwriting commission out of line? See Tables 21–1 and 21–2, pp. 555 and 556.

j. What antidilution provisions were included?

2. In 1973 Sno-Go Products had before its board of directors the matter of a possible conversion of its preferred stock into common stock. The company began in 1965 with the production of small snow blowers.

In 1965 Sno-Go had issued 1825 shares of $100 par preferred stock with $5 per year cumulative dividend, callable at $105. At the same time Sno-Go sold 1125 shares of common stock with $100 par value. The first 2 years of operation showed a loss of $82,500. Although losses during the starting period were anticipated, the loss exceeded expectations.

The intention had been to pay preferred dividends during the starting period despite losses. As the situation developed Sno-Go suspended preferred dividends after the payment of $3.33 per share in 1965. In the succeeding years Sno-Go prospered; the record appears in Table 20–3.

TABLE 20–3. Sno-Go Products
Dividends and Earnings

| | Preferred Stock | | Common Stock | | |
|---|---|---|---|---|---|
| Year | Paid per share | Arrearage at year end | Earned per share after preferred dividend | Paid per share | Book value after preferred arrearage |
| **1969** | $ 0 | $11.67 | $57.55 | 0 | $ 74.93 |
| 1970 | 5.00 | 11.67 | 73.94 | 0 | 157.00 * |
| 1971 | 5.00 | 11.67 | 42.96 | 0 | 201.85 |
| 1972 | 2.50 | 14.17 | 24.94 | 0 | 226.22 |
| 1973 | 19.17 | 0 | 87.54 | 0 | 314.33 |

* In 1969 Sno-Go bought back $40,500 in preferred stock at par, the sellers waiving the arrearage.

A temporary setback in 1972 caused the board to interrupt preferred dividends, but the resounding success in 1973 eliminated the arrearage completely. During the 5 year period 1969–1973 the shortage of cash prevented Sno-Go from paying more on the arrearage. In addition, Sno-Go had moved from leased quarters to its own plant.

The balance sheet at year-end 1972 and 1973 is given in Table 20–4.

TABLE 20–4. Sno-Go Products
Comparative Balance Sheet
December 31

| | *1972* | *1973* |
|---|---|---|
| *Assets* | | |
| Cash | $ 19,247 | $ 81,026 |
| Receivables | 201,878 | 289,085 |
| (Receivables reserve) | (15,000) | (15,000) |
| Inventory | 287,866 | 378,891 |
| Prepaid expenses | 10,500 | 12,068 |
| Total current assets | $504,491 | $746,070 |
| Other assets | 14,351 | 4,752 |
| Land and buildings | 37,203 | 117,429 |
| Equipment | 79,636 | 105,734 |
| Leasehold improvements | 29,076 | — |
| Depreciation and amortization | (31,842) | (36,593) |
| Net fixed and other assets | $128,424 | $191,322 |
| Total Assets | $632,915 | $937,392 |
| *Liabilities and Net worth* | | |
| Notes payable | $100,640 | $104,099 |
| Accounts payable | 79,398 | 221,396 |
| Income taxes | 23,157 | 71,421 |
| Total current liabilities | $203,195 | $396,916 |
| Mortgage loan | 13,107 | 44,850 |
| Preferred stock, 1,420 shares, $100 par | 142,000 | 142,000 |
| Common stock, 1,125 shares, $100 par | 112,500 | 112,500 |
| Retained earnings | 162,113 | 241,126 |
| Net worth | $416,613 | $495,626 |
| Total liabilities and net worth | $632,915 | $937,392 |

What do you think would be an appropriate exchange ratio of preferred for common? Who decides what the ratio will be? What factors determine the ratio?

3. In the Great Depression of the 1930s many preferred stocks developed large arrearages in cumulated dividends. To a lesser extent this situation develops today when an individual company experiences a prolonged depression in earnings while the rest of the economy enjoys relatively good earnings.

The Bradley Knitting Company had a history of good growth from its beginning in 1903, benefiting particularly from a good volume of activity in World War I. After a sharp inventory loss in the depression of 1920 the company forged ahead in the prosperous 1920s, acquiring another knitting company as it grew. During the 1920s the company avoided the use of debt but did employ two issues of preferred stock. At the end of 1933 (the depth of the depression) the company's capital structure was as follows:

| | |
|---|---|
| 7 percent preferred, 15,000 shares, $100 par, authorized, callable at $110, annual sinking fund of 3 percent, issued and outstanding 10,795 shares | $1,079,500 |

| | |
|---|---|
| 7 percent participating second preferred, cumulative after retirement of first preferred, $100 par, authorized 5000 shares, issued and outstanding 4824 shares | $ 482,400 |
| Common stock, no par, authorized 20,000 shares, 15,501 shares issued and outstanding | $ 367,000 |

At this time the law did not require that no par stock be shown at a stated value. Hence, surplus is combined with capital in the statement of common stock. The preferred stock had received no dividends after December 1, 1931. The record of earnings and dividends appears in Table 20–5.

The preferred stock was originally issued in the full amount of 20,000 shares in 1922, and in the 1920s the company had carried out a program of retiring the preferred. The participating preferred had also been reduced by retirement of 176 shares in the 1920s. The common stock had also been reduced by the repurchase of 4449 shares for $243,537 in 1926.

The preferred stock was nonvoting except in the event of arrearage and provided that current assets be maintained equal to 120 percent of outstanding preferred and that no mortgages (other than purchase money mortgages) could be entered into unless three-quarters of the preferred consented.

The participating noncumulative (nonvoting except after one year of no dividends) second preferred provided that it would succeed to the provisions of the preferred as soon as the preferred was retired.

TABLE 20–5. Earnings and Dividend Record of Bradley Knitting Company

| | *Earnings* | *Total Dividends Paid* | | *Earnings* | *Total Dividends Paid* |
|---|---|---|---|---|---|
| 1926 | $107,000 | $160,000 | 1931 | ($168,000) | $77,000 |
| 1927 | 178,000 | 154,000 | 1932 | ( 441,000) | 0 |
| 1928 | 174,000 | 150,000 | 1933 | ( 306,000) | 0 |
| 1929 | 222,000 | 149,000 | 1934 | 64,000 | 0 |
| 1930 | (112,000) | 154,000 | 1935 | 195,000 | 0 |

The company used unsecured bank debt from 1929 to 1933, peaking at $490,000 in 1931. By 1934 the company was "out of the bank" but was factoring accounts receivable. The company in 1934 proposed a mortgage loan with the Reconstruction Finance Corporation, a federal agency created in the 1930s to grant loans to firms trapped in financial difficulty during the Great Depression. The required three-quarters consent of preferred failed by 1 percent. The minority demanded payment of their arrearage.

In early 1936 the company repurchased 809 shares of first preferred at an average price of $6.17 per share. The balance sheet at the end of 1935 is given in Table 20–6.

TABLE 20–6. Bradley Knitting Company, Balance Sheet
December 31, 1935
(thousands)

| Assets | | Liabilities and Net Worth | |
|---|---|---|---|
| Cash | $ 247 | Accounts payable | $ 34 |
| Receivables | 25 | Accrued expenses | 83 |
| Inventories | 565 | Liability reserves | 49 |
| Total current assets | $ 837 | Total current liabilities | $ 166 |
| Investment in subsidiary | 332 | Net worth | |
| Land | 81 | 1st preferred, 10,795 shares, | |
| Buildings | 786 | $100 par | 1,080 |
| Machinery | 1,351 | 2d preferred, 4,824 shares, | |
| Fixed assets (cost) | $2,218 | $100 par | 482 |
| Depreciation | (1,342) | Common stock, 15,501 shares, | |
| Net fixed assets | $ 876 | no par and surplus | 367 |
| Deferred charges | 50 | Net worth | $1,929 |
| Total assets | $2,095 | Total liabilities and net worth | $2,095 |

In late 1936 matters came to a head and the management proposed a plan for eliminating the arrearages, which then totaled $35 per share for the first preferred, or an aggregate of $377,825. Operations for 1936 were profitable but were expected to produce only about 60 percent of the 1935 profit.

The plan called for the payment of 10-year noninterest-bearing subordinated notes of $20 for each $35 of arrearage. Each note was convertible into 1.25 shares of common stock. The company offered to buy such notes immediately at 50 cents on the dollar. The dividend rate of the preferred would be reduced from 7 to 5 percent, current asset coverage reduced from 120 to 65 percent, and the sinking fund requirement reduced from 3 to 2 percent per year. The second preferred would receive four shares of common for each share of second preferred.

Common stock would not be altered, but the authorized number of shares would be increased to 50,000.

a. Do you approve of the high dividend payment ratio in the late 1920s?

b. Was an excessive amount of preferred stock issued?

c. What defect (if any) do you see in the protective provisions of the preferred?

d. Why did the company repurchase preferred stock in early 1936 rather than start paying the arrearage?

e. Would you as a (first) preferred stockholder accept the offer made? Would you cash in the notes? If not, what is your recourse?

f. What division of voting would you expect on this proposal?

g. Is the second preferred the "forgotten man" in this situation?

### Selected References


Bildersee, J. S., "Some Aspects of the Performance of Non-Convertible Preferred Stocks," *Journal of Finance*, 28 (December 1973), pp. 1187–1201.

Buxbaum, R. M., "Preferred Stock—Law and Draftsmanship," *California Law Review*, 42 (May 1954), pp. 243–309.

Donaldson, G., "In Defense of Preferred Stock," *Harvard Business Review*, 40 (July-August 1962), pp. 123–136.

Elsaid, H. H., "Non-convertible Preferred Stock as a Financing Instrument 1950–1965: Comment," *Journal of Finance*, 24 (December 1969), pp. 939–941.

Fergusson, D. A., "Preferred Stock Valuation in Reorganizations," *Journal of Finance*, 13 (March 1958), pp. 48–69.

Fisher, D. E., and G. A. Wilt, Jr., "Nonconvertible Preferred Stock as a Financing Instrument 1950–1965," *Journal of Finance*, 23 (September 1968), pp. 611–624.

———, "Recent Trends in Electric Preferred Stock Financing," *Public Utilities Fortnightly*, 78 (September 15, 1966), pp. 19–31.

Melicher, R. W., "Financing with Convertible Preferred Stock: Comment," *Journal of Finance*, 26 (March 1971), pp. 144–147.

Pinches, G. E., "Financing with Convertible Preferred Stock, 1960–1967," *Journal of Finance*, 25 (March 1970), pp. 53–64.

———, "Financing with Convertible Preferred Stock, 1960–67: Reply," *Journal of Finance*, 26 (March 1971), pp. 150–151.

Santow, L. J., "Ultimate Demise of Preferred Stock as a Source of Corporate Capital," *Financial Analysts Journal*, 18 (May-June 1962), pp. 47–50.

Sprecher, C. R., "A Note on Financing Mergers with Convertible Preferred Stock," *Journal of Finance*, 26 (June 1971), pp. 683–685.

Stevenson, R. A., "Retirement of Non-callable Preferred Stock," *Journal of Finance*, 25 (December 1970), pp. 1143–1152.

Weygandt, J. J., "A Comment on Financing with Convertible Preferred Stock, 1960–67," *Journal of Finance* 26 (March 1971), pp. 148–149.

Williams, C. M., "Senior Securities—Boon for Banks?" *Harvard Business Review*, 41 (July-August 1963), pp. 95–110.

# 21
# Common Stock Financing

## THE STRUCTURE OF A CORPORATION

The ownership of a corporation is called the *equity*.[1] Stockholders, each of whom owns one or more "shares" of the corporation, own the equity. Shares are evidenced by stock certificates stating the number and type of shares and the owner's name as it appears on the books of the corporation or its transfer agent. Partly for convenience and sometimes to shield the identity of the real owner, stock may be carried in "*street name*," that is, in the name of an investment banking firm. The firm holds the stock for the benefit of the true owner. A certificate in street name makes transfer of ownership easier. If the certificate is in the name of the individual owner, transfer must be accompanied by the guarantee of a bank or broker of

[1] The term "equity" originates from the fact that the internal affairs of a corporation were originally administered in a court of equity as opposed to a court of law. This is also the origin of the term "equity" when speaking of the ownership of property that has been mortgaged for a debt, whether by a corporation or an individual. Here the ownership is the "equity of redemption," which can be cut off only by foreclosure in a court of equity.

the owner's signature endorsing the certificate for transfer, whereas the endorsement of the investment banking firm is well known. There is some danger in the event of insolvency of the investment banking firm. Although street certificates are not the property of that firm and cannot be reached by that firm's creditors, the certificates may no longer be on hand at the time of insolvency.[2]

Stock certificates are transferable but not negotiable.[3] Negotiability cuts off many of the claims of prior owners of a security.

A brief statement of the legal status of a corporation aids understanding many of the niceties of finance. A corporation is a creature of the state of incorporation [4] and subject to its laws. Ever since the Dartmouth College case in the early nineteenth century, corporation charters under general corporation statutes have been granted subject to the right of the state to change the applicable laws.

### Corporate Charter

The *corporate charter,* also called the *articles of incorporation,* is usually kept as simple as possible because of the difficulty of procuring the required two-thirds consent of shares to amend the charter when ownership is widespread. The charter usually gives the name of the corporation; the location of its principal office (where legal papers may be served); a statement of its purposes (usually very broad) and duration (usually perpetual); a statement of the classes of stock and numbers of shares of each class that are authorized and a statement of the "preferences" of any class; and a statement of the initial number of directors and who the incorporator(s) is. In some states the charter must also deny certain rights or they are presumed to exist. Chief among these are the *preemptive right* [5] and voting rights for all classes. The charter may also include any other provisions not in conflict with the law of the state. One provision frequently inserted in the case of small corporations is that before the stock can be sold it must first be offered to the corporation on the terms of sale that will be proposed to others.

### Bylaws

After the state corporation law and the corporate charter, the basic document is the bylaws of the corporation. The *bylaws* are the rules of operation given in sufficient detail to permit the corporation to operate effectively. Thus the bylaws specify the current number of directors; information concerning both stockholders' and directors' meetings, for example, time, place, quorum, notification procedure; the officers (to be

---

[2] The newly established federal insurance protects individual accounts to the extent of $60,000.

[3] The requirements for negotiability are explained on p. 483, n. 5.

[4] Only a few corporations are federally chartered. These include national banks and federal savings and loan associations. There is no federal general corporation act such as each state has.

[5] The preemptive right is the right of a stockholder to maintain his proportion of ownership in the corporation by buying his proportion of any new stock issued by the corporation.

elected by the directors) of the corporation and their duties; provisions governing the handling of cash and other assets; and many specific provisions, for example, who can authorize the purchase of fixed assets.

It is basic to corporation law that the power to manage and control rests with the *board of directors* (more strictly, with what the *majority* of the board decides). For this reason a resolution of the board of directors is necessary for many actions. Thus, the issuance of stock and debt must be authorized by resolution of the board of directors. Dividend payments can be authorized only by the board of directors.

All of this discussion identifies the scope of the stockholder whose action is limited to electing the directors and voting on those matters reserved by the state statutes to stockholders. These matters are amendment of the corporation charter, merger, consolidation, dissolution, sale of substantially all assets, reduction of the par or stated value of stock, and a few other matters that vary from state to state. The most important variation is whether stockholder consent is need for long-term debt and mortgaging of assets.

### Policy as to Choice of Directors

The entire management of a corporation is the responsibility of the directors. Officers administer the day-to-day affairs of a company but they are legally subject to the control of directors. In many corporations, the role of the board of directors is perfunctory and officers assume the role of the directors. No man can serve on many boards and do justice to his responsibility unless he is a "professional" director—one whose entire business efforts are expended in the capacity of being a director for many companies. Such a man is called a "working director," and he is paid accordingly.

These problems raise the fascinating question of what constitutes an "ideal" board of directors. Experience has led to the formula that one-third of the board should be active managers of the company and two-thirds of the board should not be active in the day-to-day affairs of the company. This has led to the expression: one-third "inside" directors and two-thirds "outside" directors.

The merits of this rule are apparent. The decision of the board of directors is determined by majority vote. But the "inside" directors have a biased position—their jobs are involved. Hence, discretion dictates that potential control be not placed in their hands but in the hands of the outside directors.

Thus, in examining a corporation, the focus is placed on the qualifications and performance of the "outside" directors. A corporation without an active board of directors is little more than a legalized sole proprietorship or partnership—and there are many corporations of this type both large and small. Such corporations are limited and stunted in their potential. The strength of a corporation lies in its harnessing of the *abilities* of many individuals and in the *resource* of many individuals. Controlling the reins of this harness is the board of directors.

### Voting

There are three methods of voting—regular, common law, and cumulative. *Regular voting* accords one vote to each share of a voting class. *Common law voting* (usually limited to cooperatives and special types of corporations) accords one vote to each owner regardless of the number of shares owned. *Cumulative voting* is applicable only to the election of directors and is designed to assure minority representation on the board of directors if the minority votes its shares effectively.[6] Each share owned receives as many votes as there are directors to be elected and each shareholder can distribute those votes for such director or directors as he wishes. All directors are voted on at once, with those receiving the greatest number of votes elected.[7] Under regular voting each director is elected separately and the majority elects all directors.

### Eligibility to Vote, Voting Trusts, Classified Stock

For convenience and orderly procedure the bylaws of the corporation usually provide for the establishment by the board of directors of a "record date" for determining eligibility to vote and again to determine stockholders who will receive a dividend. The record date is usually 10 to 20 days before the meeting date (or date the dividend is payable). If stock is sold after the record date but before the meeting date, the seller of the stock delivers a proxy to the buyer. This proxy is irrevocable [8] and gives the buyer the right to vote.

In many cases corporations have experienced periods when the stockholders have been divided on basic questions of policy. Sometimes the

---

[6] Cumulative voting is highly controversial. The Illinois constitution requires it (21 other states also require it); the Wisconsin statutes (by indirection) forbid it.

[7] The formula to determine the minimum number of shares needed to elect a certain number of directors (*if* all the minority shares are cast *evenly* for *only* these directors *and if* the majority casts its votes *evenly* for its maximum) is:

$$\frac{(\text{Total } \textit{shares voting}) \times (\text{Number of directors desired})}{\text{Total number of directors to be elected} + 1} + 1$$

Any fractional share in the answer is dropped. This formula is frequently misstated. For example, some texts state total number of shares *outstanding* in the numerator. Other texts misstate the numerator in the same way but compound the error by requiring an *agreement* by factions that the formula includes only shares voted. No such agreement is needed.

It is quite possible (and it has occurred) that a minority can seize control by organizing its votes rigidly while the majority *attempts* to elect *more* directors than its votes can assure. This happens not only because the majority's votes are disorganized but because the majority may not know how many votes the minority has. A further complication is that some votes may be cast by stockholders acting independently of the majority or the minority groups.

One method for the majority to use to avoid the result of cumulative voting is to amend the bylaws to reduce the number of directors. On this vote the majority must prevail. By reducing the board to three (the legal minimum) the majority will make minority representation impossible unless the minority controls at least 25 percent of the votes cast. It is clear that cumulative voting properly belongs in the area of game theory.

[8] Ordinary proxies are revocable despite the fact that they may contain a statement that they are irrevocable. The proxy given to the buyer of stock by one selling after the record date is an exception to this rule of law.

conflict has involved efforts to "raid" the corporation in which "outsiders" seek control. Because stockholders are free to change their position from one meeting to the next,[9] a basic instability may develop. This instability can threaten the entire future of the corporation, mainly by creating a reluctance of many groups to share the uncertainty. These groups would include the firm's executives, principal customers, suppliers, and the commercial banks and financial institutions interested in the corporation. One means of dealing with this uncertainty is the voting trust.

The *voting trust* is a device by which stockholders may surrender their right to vote by transferring their stock to the voting trustees named in the trust document.[10] In return the stockholders receive certificates of beneficial interest in the voting trust. Only the right to vote is transferred in this process. Following a period during which the courts were somewhat hostile toward the device, most state statutes now authorize the voting trust and surround it with limitations designed to prevent abuse.

The voting trust is adaptable to resolving uncertainty and is, in addition, one basis for creating a "leverage of control" by which the majority *within* the voting trust can now control.[11]

The voting trust is not the only device available for continuity of control. Many corporation laws authorize classified directors. Under this provision only some of the directors (usually one-third) are elected each year. Thus each director holds office for 3 years. Since only one-third is elected each year, another type of leverage of control results. Another possible provision in the corporate charter under the laws of some states is that election of a director may require more than a majority vote.

In considering the voting procedure, we must bear in mind the basic legal rule that until new directors are elected, the current directors continue to hold office. It is obvious, then, that any effort which prevents the establishment of a quorum for a meeting will continue the current control.

Another device related to voting control is the use of classified common stock. One class is created without voting rights, with this class being sold to investors. The other class with voting rights is retained by the controlling stockholders.

### Proxy Fights

Despite efforts to centralize voting control and sometimes because no steps have been taken in this direction, a proxy fight may develop. A proxy is simply a written authorization to another to exercise the right to vote.

---

[9] In addition, in some states, such as Wisconsin, stockholders have the right at any time to convene a meeting and recall any or all directors, replacing them with new directors.

[10] An actual voting trust agreement can be found in Erwin E. Nemmers, *Cases in Finance* (Boston: Allyn & Bacon, Inc., 1964), pp. 137–140.

[11] This is true except in the rare case of a single voting trustee. Most voting trusts provide for democratic voting within the membership. Hence control rests in half of the voting trust, which may in turn have half of the total votes of the corporation. In short, there is a "holding company" of voting. Some state corporation laws require that the voting trust be revealed on the stock records of the company. This simple requirement is a powerful limitation on the possibility of abuse.

Although generally one can orally appoint another to act for him, there are several areas of law where the authorization must be in writing.[12]

The power to appoint another as agent includes the right to revoke that power before the agent has acted. Thus, except in the case of stock that has been sold after the record date, the proxy is revocable. Hence the proxy signed at the later date governs in cases where more than one proxy has been signed.[13] Likewise, the stockholder who appears personally at the meeting can revoke a proxy.

As a practical matter, in preparing for a meeting of stockholders, the disputing groups will begin by gathering proxies. The solicitation of proxies by the management of a company and by others is subject to SEC control.[14] If persons other than management seek to solicit proxies, they may rely on the required information previously furnished to stockholders. In the event no solicitation of proxies by management or any one else is undertaken, the company is still required to furnish stockholders prior to the annual meeting with the same information as would be required in a proxy statement. In addition to this information, each stockholder must receive an annual report and adequate means to register his instructions as to how his proxy should be voted on issues known in advance. If the stockholder signs but does not indicate his vote, he must be advised how the proxy will be voted. The proxy statement must include the following:

1. A statement as to revocability of the proxy.
2. Any dissenter's rights as to any matter to come before the meeting.
3. A statement as to who solicits the proxy and who is paying the costs of solicitation and the name of any director who dissents if the proxy is solicited by management.
4. A statement concerning the interests of any officer or director in any matters to be acted on.
5. A statement as to the number of voting securities by class, the record date for voting, and the holders of 10 percent or more of voting securities.
6. The names of all nominees for director and their other positions with the company or principal employment for the prior five years, together with the number and class of equity securities owned by each.
7. The names of each director receiving compensation over $40,000, and the total compensation of all officers and directors as a group. The same applies for options over $10,000 to any officer or director or over $40,000 for the group.

---

[12] And even witnessed and acknowledged before a notary public, as is true of real estate transactions.

[13] In the case of co-owners of stock, the signature of either for the other is presumed to be authorized until the contrary is proved.

[14] Under Regulation 14A all securities listed on organized exchanges and all over-the-counter securities which are held by more than 500 stockholders are subject to the proxy statement requirement.

8. A statement concerning any indebtedness over $10,000 by an officer, director, or nominee or any associate of such to the company or any material interest (over $40,000) in any transaction with the company.
9. The name and interest of any auditor to be selected at the meeting.
10. Information concerning any bonus, profit sharing, pension, retirement, options, or other remuneration plans to be acted on.
11. A statement concerning any securities to be authorized or issued at the meeting and the terms of any proposed transaction involving the securities.
12. Information relating to any modification or exchange of securities to be acted on, any merger, consolidation, acquisition, or similar matters to be acted on, or any property acquisition or disposition or restatement of accounts to be acted on.
13. Any proposed amendments to charter, bylaws, or other documents.

In the event of a proxy fight over the election or removal of directors, special rules apply.[15] Those who seek to challenge the management for proxies are required to furnish each security holder and to file with the SEC a statement listing the following:

1. The name and address of the solicitor of the proxy together with his background of residence and all occupations in the prior 10 years.
2. Any other proxy contests in which the solicitor has been involved in the prior 10 years and the outcome of such contests.
3. Any convictions or criminal proceedings in the prior 10 years.
4. The amount of securities of the company owned by the solicitor and the amounts and dates of any acquisitions during the prior 2 years (including whether such acquisitions were financed by borrowing and how much is still owed).
5. The name, address, and holdings of anyone associated with the solicitor of the proxy.
6. The terms of any arrangements concerned with the securities of the company in which the solicitor is or was involved in the prior year.
7. Any material dealing with the company in the past year and any understandings about employment transactions with the company.
8. The amount to be contributed by the solicitor to further the solicitation of the proxy.

[15] Rule 14a–11 of the Securities and Exchange Commission Regulation 14A.

## ADVANTAGES AND DISADVANTAGES OF COMMON STOCK FOR FINANCIAL MANAGEMENT

The prime advantage of common stock is that it involves no fixed charges or commitments. It carries no maturity date and no obligation to pay dividends.[16]

The increase in value of the common stock increases the credit of the business in all respects: trade credit, bank credit, and long-term credit.

The sale of common stock makes available to the company the funds of that part of the money of investors which is seeking higher returns and protection against the erosion of inflation. Protection against inflation arises from the increase in the value of the real assets of the company and the increasing returns in dividends, providing profit margins are not squeezed by rising costs. Inflation protection for the common stock of a company with little debt may do little more than keep pace with the inflation. But to the extent that the company uses debt, there may be a *real* gain for the common stock. The holders of debt funds that are invested in real assets by the company will not share in the increase in money value of the assets. All of this increase in value will accrue to the common stockholders. Conversely, in times of deflation the brunt will fall on the common stock and not on the debt.

The disadvantages of the use of common stock center on the "dilution" of voting rights and the sharing of earnings with the new owners. We have already indicated that classified common stock is a device for retaining voting rights. The new common stock to be sold may be classified as nonvoting. The sharing of profits with new owners has to be weighed against the lower cost and leverage of debt as well as the risk created by debt.

Lesser disadvantages of common stock include the fact that underwriting costs are higher than for debt or preferred stock. This higher cost follows in part from the smaller unit sales of common stock than in the case of debt or preferred stock where institutional buyers take large

---

[16] In very rare cases a court may intervene where the controlling group of a corporation is not paying dividends. Perhaps the strongest statement about intervention was given in a New Jersey court case in which the directors and officers of a *closely held* paper company were pursuing a policy for years of using profits to expand the business. Upon suit by a stockholder to force dividends, the directors defended themselves on the ground that in their discretion they were pursuing profitable expansion.

But the court admonished the directors: "They should bear in mind that the only sure benefit to the stockholders to be derived from the successful prosecution of the corporate business must come from the distribution of dividends in cash, and that the piling up of a surplus, which remains undistributed, may in the end go wholly to future creditors of the corporation!" *Reynolds vs. Diamond Mills Paper Co.*, 69 New Jersey Equity Reports 299, 60 Atlantic Reports 941.

It is easier to force dividends when a company is closely held and a stockholder has no alternative. When the company is publicly owned there is at least the opportunity of selling the stock and realizing some of the accrued surplus in a capital gain. In such a case the proof to support forcing of dividends has shown that distribution was withheld because of an adverse interest or wrongful purpose or bad faith or willful abuse of discretion. See Henry W. Ballantine, *Ballantine on Corporations*, rev. ed. (Chicago: Callaghan and Company, 1946), p. 554.

units. Furthermore, the risks for the underwriter both at the time of issue and in the "after-market" [17] are greater because of the greater volatility of common stock prices.

Common stock usually yields the buyer a higher return than debt and thus "costs" the company more. But with the emphasis on growth and the inflation of recent years, common stocks have been bid up to high prices, so that bond yields have actually been higher than common stock yields. Thus, this disadvantage of common stock relative to debt has varied considerably as far as the company seeking funds is concerned.

## MANAGEMENT OF COMMON STOCK

Taking a company from the point of its inception, we shall examine various problems of managing its common stock position and the institutions that the market has developed for dealing with these problems. Since these problems do not necessarily follow a logical (or even a chronological) order, it should not be presumed that they will arise in the order in which they are presented here. The order of discussion of these problems will be (1) par, no par, and "optional" stock, (2) going public, and (3) listing on an exchange.[18]

### Par, No Par, and "Optional" or Blank Stock

The use of, or switching between, par or no par stock is largely a matter of the "cultural lag" of the laws of some states. The starting point of earlier laws was the idea that the purchase price paid by the initial stockholders was, in some sense, principal or value. Since value is simply the capitalized future earnings of a firm, there is an important distinction between the concept of principal as applied to debt and that of principal as applied to equity or ownership. In the case of debt, principal means the amount of money the borrower is obligated to repay at a specific point in time, namely, the maturity date. In the case of equity or ownership, principal at best can mean the amount of money that was paid to the corporation by the purchaser of common stock. There is no maturity date.

Because the law was proceeding on the premise that the amount of money paid by the initial stockholders was principal in the same sense as

---

[17] The "after-market" is a term used by investment bankers to describe their activities and risks in "making a market" for unlisted securities after the issuance. Since only 3500 corporations have securities listed on one or more of all the exchanges, the great bulk of issues involve an investment banker who "takes a position" (buys long for inventory or sells short) in order to provide the owner with a ready market for his security. If the security owner allows the broker some time to find a buyer, the price is likely to be higher than if he demands an immediate transaction. The reputation of an investment banker depends in part upon his astuteness in conducting the after-market for a security. This factor particularly influences companies as to repeat business. When a company is considering a second issue it is likely to scrutinize the performance to date of the investment banker who handled the first issue.

The investment banker cannot be expected to control or support the price of a security he underwrote, but he can be expected to maintain an orderly and realistic market for the security.

[18] One problem that might also be considered at this point is the repurchase of the company's own stock. However, we have elected to defer the consideration of this problem to Chapter 22.

principal in the case of debt, the law followed the rule that additional shares could not be sold for less than par value. Otherwise the new purchasers would be taking advantage of the existing owners. The law made an initial purchaser of par stock who bought for less than par liable for the deficiency.

The law overcame its cultural lag with the first use of no par stock in New York State in 1912. The lag was closed by the legislature and not by the courts. No par stock permitted the company to sell stock at different times at different prices. As long as the price of any sale was close to the then market value and there was no bad faith or self-dealing by the directors, no liability would arise.

But the answer to this problem created new problems. No par stock created the problem of what should be shown on the balance sheet as capital stock in contrast to surplus. For a long period there was uncertainty in the law until the statutes came to incorporate definite accounting concepts. Stated value designates the amount of no par stock to be shown as capital stock on the balance sheet. Any amount received by the company in excess of stated value is reported in paid-in surplus. Stated value cannot be reduced in most states except by stockholder action but can be increased by action of the board of directors. In the case of the sale of no par stock at a price below stated value, the deficiency would be made up by a reduction in paid-in surplus and to the extent paid-in surplus is not available by a charge against earned surplus.

At the practical level, the initial decision as to par or no par common stock or the shifting of the common stock of a corporation from par to no par status or vice versa is often motivated by quirks in the franchise tax statute of the state of incorporation that discriminate in favor of either par or no par status.

Recently, many states have authorized what we can call optional or blank stock. We use the term "optional" because the statute authorizes the *board of directors* to vary some provisions of the stock, such as dividend rate, par or no par status, priority or conversion privileges, from one issue to the next. Until this recent development, the articles of incorporation set out the rights of each class of stock and left no room for decision by the board of directors except as to price of the issue. The appearance of optional stock was forced by the growth of mergers and the need to tailor each stock issue to each merger.

### Going Public

Chapter 17 considered the role of the underwriter but in terms more applicable to issues by companies already publicly owned. The first public offering of a company presents a different emphasis.

If sufficient time is allowed, it is possible for a company to become publicly owned without going through the process of a public offering. The term "publicly owned" does not have an exact definition. We might define public ownership as the status of being listed in the daily over-the-counter quotations in *The Wall Street Journal.*[19] This would be too high a standard, since there are many issues sponsored by an investment banker appearing in the list quoted once weekly in the regional issue of *The Wall Street Journal.*[20] Further, we might define public ownership as the status of appearing in the quotations published in any metropolitan newspaper, or as the status of any stock handled by any investment banker.

It is possible for the ownership of a firm's stock to spread by the natural process of large holders now and then selling off some shares. This process involves risk, since the selling stockholder might be found by regulatory bodies to be conducting a marketing or offering and therefore subject to filing requirements.

### Federal Filing

We will outline the various possibilities for a smaller company to market its stock without violating state or federal laws governing the sale of securities. The federal legislation applicable to stock and administered by the SEC is found in the Securities Act of 1933. The law is based on the philosophy of full and truthful disclosure rather than any evaluation of the soundness of the stock,[21] or of its pricing. It is not enough that what is said must be truthful; the issuer must also disclose all that is relevant. The SEC has evolved rules concerning what it considers the minimum relevant data, and it is authorized to issue a "stop order" if it finds that the information submitted is inadequate.

There are several exemptions from the federal act available to the small company. The first is the so-called private sale as opposed to the public offering. The matter of what is private and what is public is not decided on the basis of the number of buyers; rather, the SEC places heavy emphasis on whether the buyers are knowledgeable in financial matters generally and on the reputation of the company whose stock is involved.[22] Thus, 30 insurance companies buying an entire issue could easily be found to be a private placement, but a newspaper advertisement that produced only a handful of ordinary citizens as buyers would be a public offering.

The second exemption covers an offering that is intrastate only. Here the issuer avoids the use of the U.S. mails and requires each buyer to sign a statement that he is a resident of the same state as that in which the is-

---

[19] Currently admission to this status requires the recommendation of a committee of the National Association of Security Dealers, who in turn recommend a stock held by at least 1500 stockholders and having the interest of several investment bankers.

[20] All companies who have had an issue fully registered (Form S-1) with the SEC would appear in this list as a minimum. The number of stockholders might be as few as 400.

[21] As is sometimes said, any garbage can be legally sold as long as it is plainly marked for what it is.

[22] This matter is normally handled by submitting a full statement of facts to the general counsel for the SEC, who then states the recommendation he would make to the commission if these facts were submitted to him. If his decision is that he would advise the commission that no illegality is involved, the letter he writes back to the company is called a "no action" letter.

suer is incorporated and otherwise goes to considerable lengths to make certain that no state lines are crossed.

Finally, the SEC provides for a minimum amount of filing where the offering is of an amount totaling less than $500,000 in any one year.[23] In this connection it is important that the SEC requires as part of the filing the advance submission of copies of all material to be used in solicitation and requires the issuer to furnish an offering circular to all buyers.

### State Filing

In addition to federal regulation, the smaller company faces state regulatory bodies. The philosophy of most state regulation is quite different from that of the federal act. These state statutes, popularly called blue sky laws,[24] authorize the state agency to pass on the merits of the proposed transactions, namely, whether the stock represents something feasible and whether the proposed price is fair. While this might seem to be an extremely difficult assignment for the state agency, many practical working rules have been developed which aid in culling out a high percentage of proposals that have little, if any, merit. Some of these rules have been enacted by the legislature, thus leaving the agency with no discretion.

To cite a few of these rules, the lowest permissible quality of securities may be required to have clearly printed on the stock certificate and on all material of solicitation the legend, "These are speculative securities." Or limits are set concerning the maximum commission or expense that will be allowed in connection with the sale of any security. To deal with the matter of fair pricing, some states set a maximum price-earnings ratio that will be allowed even for the offering of securities of the most highly regarded corporations.[25]

It is clear that the task of the financial manager of a small but growing business in navigating his way through regulatory problems is not easy, particularly when we consider the vulnerability of the earnings of the small company to the vicissitudes of the business cycle, the competition of established businesses in the same field, and the risks inherent in a "thin" management.

---

[23] Such offerings are governed by Regulation A, which is discussed in detail in Ezra Weiss, "Regulation A under the Securities Act of 1933—Highways and Byways," *New York Law Forum* 8 (March 1962), pp. 3–131. Regulation A (Rule 257) provides for a further reduction in filing requirements if the offering is less than $50,000 in 1 year.

In the year ended June 30, 1972, there were 1087 offerings, for a total of less than $400 million under Regulation A, of which 497 did not use an underwriter. This figure compares with the 3712 offerings (including investment companies) totaling $62.5 billion that were fully registered. The fully registered figures include offerings of about $14 billion by investment companies. See *Securities and Exchange Commission*, 38th Annual Report, June 30, 1972, pp. 163 and 166.

[24] The term is usually taken to have come from the claim that the legislation is intended to prevent naive people from buying a piece of the blue sky.

[25] This limit in some states is a price-earnings ratio of 15. We should note that in the last decade the average price-earnings ratio of the 30 industrial stocks in the Dow Jones average has frequently been above 15. As a result, in some of these states—for example, Missouri and Michigan—the issue may be barred, but buyers in these states use various devices to get the stock if they want it.

Advantages of going public accrue to both the corporation and its stockholders. For the corporation, going public means a reduction of uncertainty in future equity financing. The market place will assess the strengths and weaknesses of the company and evolve a price for the company's stock. Thus the foundation is laid for future equity financing. In the absence of the guideline furnished by even a thin market for a stock, the investment banker considering an initial issue must increase the protective margin that he seeks.[26]

For the stockholder, going public means that his investment has marketability. In turn this has many benefits, ranging from value as collateral for loans to some certainty of valuation for gift and inheritance tax purposes.[27]

There are disadvantages to going public. Labor unions and competitors gain access to information they would otherwise not have, and the company comes under the jurisdiction of new regulatory agencies.

### Letter Stock

In recent years, banks, trust companies, insurance companies, and other institutions have felt pressure from their accounts for the higher earnings and inflation protection offered by common stocks. Because these institutions deal in blocks of shares, a new market has opened up for unregistered securities. If the buyer of shares is a sophisticated investor and if that buyer gives the seller (either the primary issuer or a selling stockholder) an "investment letter" stating that the purchase is for purposes of investment and not for distribution, then the sale is not subject to the requirement of registration. Such stock is called "letter stock." The buyer can resell to another who furnishes a similar letter. Under existing practice, if the buyer holds for 2 years he can resell without getting a new letter.

In "letter" deals, the buyer frequently protects himself by requiring the seller to agree to pay registration costs if the buyer wants to sell within the 2-year period. In turn the seller may satisfy the buyer by offering a "piggy-back" registration, that is, combining the registration of the letter stock with another registered offering made by the original seller.

### Listing—Advantages

Having achieved the status of a publicly held company and having grown, particularly in number of stockholders, to the point where its stock is quoted daily in the *Wall Street Journal,* the company is now ready to consider listing on one of the 14 organized exchanges.[28]

---

[26] To the extent that a company has become larger and well known as a closed corporation, this risk may be reduced to the point that the investment banker feels secure in pricing the offering against the prices prevailing for the stock of any competitive company that is publicly owned.

[27] For an example of the vicious tax-valuation problem for the taxpayer in the case of a closely held corporation, see the case of Sunburst Corporation in Erwin E. Nemmers, *Cases in Finance* (Boston: Allyn and Bacon, Inc., 1964), pp. 353–373.

[28] Number of issues listed, trading volume, and similar data of the national exchanges appear in Table 18–1. The 1974 requirements for listing on the New York Stock Exchange appear on p. 472 and those for the American Stock Exchange on p. 472.

Listing in itself will not assure active trading of a security. Ultimately trading will depend on the size of the security issue, how widely it is distributed, and the type of holder who is attracted to the issue. It is the last attribute that has given rise to the phrases "glamour stock," "high flyer," and "speculative stock."

Listing offers the financial manager greater marketability for the company's securities, even though the corporation cannot market its new issues on the exchange.

One specific gain of listing is the ability to engage in equity financing through the use of rights. The over-the-counter market offers no way for an underwriter to dispose of an unsold balance of rights. In this market, rights are usually limited to an amount equal to 1 or 2 years' dividends.

Listing also furnishes an attraction in merger. The listed company offers the unlisted one a better price than it could get elsewhere, because the listed company tends to have a higher market value.

To the investor, listing means that he can meet emergencies more easily by selling because of the greater liquidity of the stock. Likewise, his ability to use stock as collateral for borrowing is greatly improved if the stock is listed. The lender feels he can allow a higher percentage against the stock because of the speed with which it can be sold if that becomes necessary. Brokers will loan the investor funds on collateral of listed securities but not on unlisted ones.[29] Collateral value can be additionally important to the investor in enabling him to avoid the immediate payment of the capital gains tax that would follow his selling the security and later rebuying it. Furthermore, the investor avoids the risk that the market will move up during the interim.

#### Listing—Disadvantages

Listing also entails disadvantages. Just as listing advertises the security and its issuer more than if the company were not listed, so during adverse conditions the same spotlight focuses on the company. A collapse in the price of a security may cause a reaction on the customers of the issuer and even on its short-term credit. This reason is often given by banks (with the exception of Chase Manhattan) for their unwillingness to list. If public confidence were shaken, despositors would be likely to react.

Listing also presents a problem of control. The cost to outsiders of gaining control will depend on the publicly owned proportion of shares of the stock outstanding and the price per share. Speculators are attracted, particularly as the price falls. Merger tends to become an increasing possibility as the firm's business slumps. There is a point before the firm reaches the reorganization or bankruptcy stage at which another, stronger company may be able to turn the situation around.

To avoid the control problem in listing, many companies shift to two classes of common stock, one voting and the other nonvoting, with only

[29] Both brokers and banks are subject to the margin (downpayment) requirements of the Board of Directors of the Federal Reserve System.

the nonvoting shares offered to the public. However, the New York Stock Exchange will not list nonvoting common stock.

Listing is also thought to increase the hazard of speculative manipulation of the stock. Many factors favor speculation on the exchange. The availability of margin transactions and improved collateral value give the speculator great leverage. Only listed securities can be sold short. This raises the question of whether speculation serves an economically useful purpose. Informed speculators are attracted by deviations from "sound" values. If a security is overpriced or underpriced, the speculator becomes interested because he expects the price to move toward the "sound" value. Uninformed speculators can accentuate the overpricing or underpricing and may exceed the actions of the informed speculators, thus causing the pricing extremes to continue and grow.

Another disadvantage of listing is that the stock may lose some of the promotional efforts of the investment bankers who were making a larger profit on each transaction when the security was traded over the counter because of their ability to command a price differential up to 5 percent away from the last transaction (in addition to the usual commission). This additional source of profit is removed when the stock is listed and with it the funds to pay for producing and circulating reports which the investment bankers had been sending out for the over-the-counter security.

Finally, listing may bring with it an unhealthy interest in the current price of the security. Management may become overconcerned with the immediate effect of its business decisions on the price of the security, and its judgment may be impaired. Thus, major changes that are sound from a long-range point of view may be deferred for fear the current price of the security will be affected. The delay may mean that the projected change will become more costly later on or may even mean disaster for the firm.

## FINANCING THROUGH RIGHTS

While bonds are underwritten and sold, common stock is frequently sold through the device of rights. A financing through rights is not done on the exchange, but the fact that a stock is listed makes it feasible to use financing with rights. The use of rights for financing in the case of over-the-counter stocks is limited to small amounts, such as 1 or 2 years' dividends because of the difficulty of handling unused rights.

A *right* is an option to buy a given security from the issuing corporation during a stated period at a stated price. The use of the rights procedure may be required because of the existence of a preemptive right,[30] or the right may be granted even though preemptive rights do

---

[30] A *preemptive right* is the right of a stockholder to maintain his proportion of ownership by participating in any new issue of stock. Preferred stock does not normally carry the preemptive right even when the common stock does. Preemptive rights are a creature of the common law, but today all but two state statutes permit a corporation to deny the existence of preemptive rights by an appropriate statement in the corporate charter. More than half of all corporations have acted to cut off preemptive rights.

not exist. A right[31] is evidenced by a stock warrant or certificate issued to the stockholder and stating the number of such rights that his present ownership can claim. The warrant is distributed by the company to its stockholders and is transferable. Almost half of the number of new registered issues result from rights offerings.

An issue of rights must be registered with the SEC just as any other offering. The filing of the registration establishes the first relevant date. As already indicated, registration takes a minimum of 20 days. Hence, the price of the new shares offered will be set at the effective date of the registration statement. This date is followed by the record date, used to determine what stockholders will receive the rights, which begins the trading period for rights, usually from 10 to 20 days. The trading period ends with the expiration date of the rights.

### Formulas for Determining the Value of Rights

The valuation of rights has given rise to considerable theoretical speculation. The earliest approach was the development of formulas for determining the value of a right both before and after the record date. The most convenient way to develop the present discussion is by an example.

Let us assume that a company seeks to increase its equity funds by $2 million. The firm has 500,000 shares outstanding, and the current market price is $20 per share. One might conclude that the sale of 100,000 shares at $20 per share will yield $2 million. Since there are 500,000 shares outstanding and we seek to sell 100,000 shares, it would appear that it will take five rights to buy one share. However, it is necessary to give value to the rights or there will simply be an offering of 100,000 shares at the market price, which would depress the price. In addition, we would be using a cumbersome device to try to carry out the offering. Thus, in order to give them value, rights carry a subscription price for new stock that is lower than the current market price. One target may be a subscription price 20 percent under the market price, say $16 per share. Then to get $2 million we need to sell 125,000 shares ($2 million/$16), and it will take four rights to buy one share. What will one right be worth?

Once the rights are being traded (that is, the stock is now *ex* rights) the value of one right depends on three factors: (1) the market price of a share of stock, (2) the subscription price, and (3) the number of rights needed to buy one new share:

$$R = \frac{M_e - S}{N} \qquad \textbf{(21–1)}$$

where $R$ is the value of one right, $M_e$ is the market price of the stock *ex*

---

[31] We will be using the term "right" in the sense of a "New York" right, namely, the right that goes with one share of existing stock. There is another nomenclature, a Philadelphia right, which is the right to buy one new share. Thus, a Philadelphia right is worth the value of the New York right times the number of such rights needed to buy one new share.

rights, $S$ is the subscription price, and $N$ is the number of rights needed to buy one new share.

It is clear that if the right has value, then the market price of the stock must drop by the amount of the value of one right on the day the stock goes *ex* rights,[32] or where $M_c$ is the market price of the stock *cum* rights (or "rights on"):

$$M_e = M_c - R \tag{21–2}$$

Hence, we can arrive at the value of one right in terms of the market price of the stock *cum* rights by substituting Eq. (21–2) into Eq. (21–1) to get

$$R = \frac{M_c - R - S}{N} \tag{21–3}$$

which simplifies to

$$R = \frac{M_c - S}{N + 1} \tag{21–4}$$

Using our illustrative numbers, we get the value of one right when the stock is *cum* rights by substituting in Eq. (21–4)

$$R = \frac{\$20 - \$16}{4 + 1} = \$0.8$$

The market price of a share of stock will change over the record date [by substituting in Eq. (21–2)]:

$$M_e = \$20 - \$0.8 = \$19.2$$

Finally, the value of the right after the record date by substituting in Eq. (21–1) is

$$R = \frac{\$19.2 - 16}{4} = \$0.8$$

While we have pursued the determination of the value of a right, it is clear that the same formulas may be used to compute the fall that can be expected in the market price of the stock after the record date.

### Why the Values Given by the Formulas Seldom Occur

One reason the values given by the formulas seldom actually occur is that the formulas are derived on assumptions that are not true. In developing the formulas we assumed that the new money to be raised would be invested by the company and would behave in *exactly* the same manner as the total company was performing before the new money was added. Thus, we assumed that the marginal earning of the new money and the marginal risk of the new money would be the same as the previous average earning and average risk. Actually, the new money is likely to carry a higher earning (as in a growth company) or a lower earning (as in a mature company). To the extent that the market place expects

[32] This will be the fifth business day before the record day, since regular delivery of stock is due on the fifth day after the sale of the stock.

above- or below-average performance by the new money, the market price of the stock *cum* rights will be disturbed immediately.[33]

The other reasons the formula values seldom occur involve environmental factors. First, many stockholders are uncertain what the evaluation of the market will be for the new phenomenon of additional funds and investment by the company. Hence, a sizeable number of stockholders simply wait during the early part of the trading period to see what the initial reaction of the market will be. This will tend to create a shortage of rights offered for sale and to drive the price up during the early days of trading; hence, the well-known maxim of the market place—sell rights early in the trading period and buy them late.

A second environmental factor is the preferential treatment accorded rights financing under the margin requirements set by the Federal Reserve System. Customarily margin requirements provide a substantially smaller margin (downpayment) for rights offerings than for regular offerings. Thus, the current (1973) margin is 65 percent for stock but only 25 percent for rights offerings. Prospective buyers therefore find it much easier to finance new rights offerings.

A third environmental factor is the alternative method available for handling rights for income tax purposes. First, the income tax law permits the taxpayer to elect that rights be treated as having zero cost basis. The profit on the sale of the rights would be a capital gain. The investor can thus use the short-term capital gain[34] to offset short-term capital losses or can report the gain as ordinary income. As an alternative the investor can allocate the cost basis of his original shares over the original shares plus the rights. This is done by dividing the market price of the right by the market price of the common stock to establish what percentage of the market price of a share of common stock is attributable to the value of a right. This percentage is then applied to the cost basis of the common stock in order to determine the cost basis of the right. The cost basis of the original shares is then adjusted by deducting the cost basis of the rights. Hence, when either the original stock or the rights are sold, the capital gain of each is separately determined. This flexibility in income tax treatment is a tax advantage to the investor and accordingly an attraction for the rights method of financing.

A fourth environmental factor is the conduct of investment bankers. Under the old pattern underwriters of a rights offering merely stabilized the price of the stock or of the rights or of both.[35] Any stock they acquired

[33] An outstanding example of this occurred with the rights offering in 1957 by International Business Machines. When the market price of the common stood at $228 per share, IBM announced a rights offering of 1,050,000 shares at $220 per share. During the rights trading period the market price went to $337 per share. The reason was simply that the market knew that computer sales were then growing at 50 percent per year and the new money was expected to enable the company to pursue this growth. The value of the rights shot up accordingly.

[34] This is because all trading periods in rights are far short of the 6 months required to establish a long-term capital gain for income tax purposes.

[35] We have not yet mentioned (but will immediately consider) the fact that rights offerings may be underwritten; that is, the underwriter may agree (for a fee) to exercise all rights not otherwise exercised, thus assuring the company of the funds it set out to get.

by virtue of their underwriting commitment would then be offered later—too late to deal with any problems of an unsuccessful offering. More modern practice involves the underwriter in taking action immediately during the trading period of the rights in order not to stabilize the price of the stock or of the rights but to assure the success of the offering and, thus, to minimize the risk that after the trading period has elapsed he will have unsold stock to market.

The fifth environmental factor affecting rights offerings is that from 1 to 3 percent of the outstanding shares [36] on a rights offering will never act despite the fact that there would be a profit in selling the rights at any time during the offering period. This fact arises from the absence of the stockholder from home during a relatively short period of time, ignorance, or other reasons.

### Flexibility of Rights Offering

A rights offering presents great flexibility for the financial manager. He may schedule the offering with or without underwriting. In the event of no underwriting he may estimate the amount of rights that will not be exercised and increase the amount of the actual offering accordingly. Or he may seek a "standby" underwriting agreement under which the underwriter (for a fee) [37] will agree to pick up any stock not purchased upon the rights offering. Standby underwriting fees will be smaller than the underwriting fee that would be charged for the entire offering. *Oversubscription* rights may be used; that is, those receiving the rights may be allowed to subscribe for additional shares beyond those covered by the right. In this case, all right holders who oversubscribe will participate *pro rata* in any shares not taken up by the exercise of rights in the event that the oversubscription exceeds the shares unsubscribed. Or the financial manager can avoid an underwriting fee by arranging for the purchase of unsubscribed shares by employees of the offering company [38] or some other interested group. In this case the proposed purchasing group is functioning as an underwriter.

In addition to the flexibility offered by a standby underwriting, a rights offering may be combined with a stock split. Thus, by offering a subscription price far below that required for a successful rights offering, the financial manager may achieve both a stock split and a rights offering at some saving in underwriting and clerical costs. The unsophisticated investor may believe that he is receiving a bonanza when the company offers the low subscription price as part of the rights offering. He may receive a substantial amount of cash by the sale of his rights, but the fact remains that the price of the original stock will be reduced from what it would otherwise have been if the subscription price had not been so low.

---

[36] E. A. Grimm, "The Money You Save May Be Your Own," *Exchange*, 16 (December 1955), pp. 17–20.

[37] A standby agreement usually provides for a flat fee for the underwriter and an additional fee based on the number of shares he is required to purchase. See the NCR case at the end of Chapter 19 where a convertible debenture offering was made by rights with a standby underwriting fee.

[38] This technique has been used in recent years by companies such as Wisconsin Electric Power Company.

A rights offering also gives the financial manager protection against his wrong estimates of what the market reaction will be to the proposed expansion. By setting the subscription price low enough, the financial manager with no thought of a stock split achieves protection against the possibility that the market may place a lower evaluation on the expansion than he has. If the market does not agree with his estimate, the value of the right will be positive, although not as large as he expected. As long as the value of the right remains positive, the offering will be successful. Thus, the financial manager has been his own underwriter. Instead of doing business for an underwriting fee, which is determined in advance by the underwriter's *estimate* of the market reaction, the financial manager is settling for what the market's actual reaction will be. That reaction may be better than the manager (or underwriter) expects or worse. In a sense, then, the use of a rights offering means that the financial manager is substituting the actual market reaction for the underwriter's estimate of the market reaction, and the financial manager can blend these two positions by using standby underwriting.

### Costs of Rights Offering and Regular Underwriting; Costs of Primary and Secondary Offerings

Another factor considered by the financial manager when comparing a rights offering with a regular underwriting is cost.

TABLE 21–1. Comparison of Registered Common Stock Flotation Costs in 1963–1965, Rights and Nonrights Offerings, Classified by Size of Issue (Cost as a Percentage of Proceeds but Underpricing Not Reckoned as a Cost)

| Size of issue (millions of dollars) | Number of issues | | Underwriting cost | |
|---|---|---|---|---|
| | Nonrights | Rights | Nonrights | Rights |
| Under 0.3 | 10 | 1 | 9.4% | 1.7% |
| 0.3– 0.5 | 14 | 6 | 9.9 | 8.3 |
| 0.5– 1.0 | 45 | 11 | 9.4 | 3.6 |
| 1.0– 2.0 | 93 | 24 | 8.7 | 5.4 |
| 2.0– 5.0 | 119 | 22 | 7.3 | 2.9 |
| 5.0– 10.0 | 57 | 9 | 6.0 | 3.6 |
| 10.0– 20.0 | 19 | 8 | 5.0 | 1.2 |
| 20.0– 50.0 | 11 | 7 | 4.9 | 2.0 |
| 50.0–100.0 | 2 | 1 | 2.9 | 1.4 |
| 100.0–500.0 | 1 | 2 | 2.0 | 1.9 |
| Total: | 371 | 91 | | |

SOURCE: Securities and Exchange Commission, *Cost of Flotation of Registered Equity Issues, 1963–1965* (Washington, D. C.: Government Printing Office, 1970), p. 26.

Some rights offerings are undertaken at a larger discount with no underwriting. Others are undertaken at a small discount in the subscription price with underwriters acting in a standby arrangement. Here the typical underwriting commission is ⅛ percent on the whole issue plus 0.75 percent on the unsubscribed shares the underwriters pick up. The underwriting commission in regular underwriting varies considerably. The average for all registered securities (including bonds) offered by corporations in 1967 was 2.5 percent.[39] Table 21–1 shows that underwriting costs of common stock offered through the use of rights are consistently less for all sizes of issue than are the underwriting costs of nonrights offerings. However, these figures cannot be directly compared. Most utility financing is carried out by rights offerings with a small price discount from current market price. Risk in this industry is low; earnings and security prices are stable. The opposite is true of most industrials. We must compare the costs of the two methods in the same risk situation.

Unfortunately, the most recent (1970) study by the SEC does not focus on underwriting costs of rights and nonrights offerings but rather, on whether the costs of nonrights offerings are greater when offered by the issuer contrasted with secondary offerings by stockholders.

TABLE 21–2. Comparison of Common Stock Flotation Costs in 1963–1965, Underwritten Primary and Secondary Offerings, Classified by Industry and Size of Offering (Cost as a Percentage of Proceeds)

| Size of Issue (millions of dollars) | Industry | Primary Offerings | | | Secondary Offerings | | |
|---|---|---|---|---|---|---|---|
| | | No. of issues | Under-writing | Other expenses | No. of issues | Under-writing | Other expenses |
| Under 0.3 | Manufacturing | 5 | 9.7% | 10.9% | 3 | 11.4% | 2.3% |
| 0.3– 0.5 | | 13 | 12.1 | 6.9 | 5 | 10.7 | 2.2 |
| 0.5– 1.0 | | 12 | 10.2 | 6.8 | 14 | 7.7 | 3.0 |
| 1.0– 2.0 | | 52 | 8.7 | 3.1 | 62 | 8.1 | 2.5 |
| 2.0– 5.0 | | 56 | 7.1 | 1.7 | 85 | 6.7 | 1.4 |
| 5.0– 10.0 | | 25 | 6.5 | 1.2 | 41 | 5.6 | 0.9 |
| 10.0– 20.0 | | 11 | 5.0 | 0.7 | 29 | 4.5 | 0.7 |
| 20.0– 50.0 | | 4 | 5.0 | 1.3 | 12 | 3.9 | 0.4 |
| 50.0–100.0 | | 0 | — | — | 1 | 0.3 | 0.3 |
| 100.0–500.0 | | 0 | — | — | 6 | 3.2 | 0.2 |
| Over 500.0 | | 0 | — | — | 0 | — | — |
| All | | 178 | | | 258 | | |
| Under 0.3 | Utilities | 0 | — | — | 1 | 3.0 | 6.7 |
| 0.3– 0.5 | | 0 | — | — | 0 | — | — |
| 0.5– 1.0 | | 3 | 8.0 | 3.5 | 1 | 7.0 | 5.3 |
| 1.0– 2.0 | | 4 | 4.8 | 1.8 | 5 | 6.5 | 1.8 |
| 2.0– 5.0 | | 11 | 5.6 | 1.4 | 2 | 1.3 | 1.4 |
| 5.0– 10.0 | | 8 | 3.3 | 0.6 | 6 | 5.4 | 1.3 |
| 10.0– 20.0 | | 4 | 4.3 | 0.7 | 2 | 3.4 | 0.4 |
| 20.0– 50.0 | | 4 | 4.0 | 0.7 | 0 | — | — |
| 50.0–100.0 | | 1 | 2.6 | 0.3 | 0 | — | — |
| 100.0–500.0 | | 1 | 2.0 | 0.3 | 0 | — | — |
| Over 500.0 | | 0 | — | — | 0 | — | — |
| All | | 36 | | | 17 | | |
| Under 0.3 | Extractive | 0 | — | — | 0 | — | — |
| 0.3– 0.5 | | 1 | 15.0 | 5.7 | 0 | — | — |
| 0.5– 1.0 | | 2 | 9.7 | 4.6 | 0 | — | — |
| 1.0– 2.0 | | 0 | — | — | 1 | 6.3 | 1.9 |
| 2.0– 5.0 | | 1 | 8.0 | 1.9 | 2 | 7.3 | 0.7 |
| 5.0– 10.0 | | 1 | 2.6 | 1.1 | 0 | — | — |
| 10.0– 20.0 | | 1 | 7.5 | 0.7 | 2 | 3.3 | 0.5 |

[39] See Table 17–2, p. 444. This is the latest year available.

TABLE 21–2 (continued)

| Size of Issue (millions of dollars) | Industry | Primary Offerings | | | Secondary Offerings | | |
|---|---|---|---|---|---|---|---|
| | | No. of issues | Under-writing | Other expenses | No. of issues | Under-writing | Other expenses |
| 20.0– 50.0 | | 0 | — | — | 0 | — | — |
| 50.0–100.0 | | 0 | — | — | 0 | — | — |
| 100.0–500.0 | | 0 | — | — | 0 | — | — |
| Over 500.0 | | 0 | — | — | 0 | — | — |
| All | | 6 | | | 5 | | |
| Under 0.3 | Financial | 3 | 7.9 | 8.3 | 0 | — | — |
| 0.3– 0.5 | | 3 | 13.9 | 11.3 | 1 | 15.0 | 3.8 |
| 0.5– 1.0 | | 18 | 9.1 | 10.0 | 4 | 6.9 | 4.1 |
| 1.0– 2.0 | | 29 | 7.7 | 9.9 | 4 | 7.6 | 2.1 |
| 2.0– 5.0 | | 40 | 8.0 | 7.7 | 14 | 6.7 | 2.1 |
| 5.0– 10.0 | | 22 | 8.1 | 7.2 | 11 | 5.8 | 1.1 |
| 10.0– 20.0 | | 6 | 9.6 | 7.3 | 11 | 5.5 | 0.6 |
| 20.0– 50.0 | | 2 | 7.0 | 3.5 | 2 | 7.1 | 1.1 |
| 50.0–100.0 | | 1 | 3.2 | — | 0 | — | — |
| 100.0–500.0 | | 0 | — | — | 0 | — | — |
| Over 500.0 | | 0 | — | — | 0 | — | — |
| All | | 124 | | | 47 | | |
| Under 0.3 | Other | 13 | 3.4 | 7.3 | 3 | — | 6.0 |
| 0.3– 0.5 | | 12 | 2.8 | 7.7 | 3 | 3.8 | 4.9 |
| 0.5– 1.0 | | 25 | 4.3 | 4.8 | 12 | 4.1 | 3.4 |
| 1.0– 2.0 | | 32 | 2.7 | 3.2 | 32 | 2.1 | 2.9 |
| 2.0– 5.0 | | 34 | 1.6 | 1.8 | 47 | 2.1 | 1.8 |
| 5.0– 10.0 | | 13 | 1.0 | 0.8 | 24 | 1.1 | 1.0 |
| 10.0– 20.0 | | 2 | 9.5 | 0.7 | 6 | 0.6 | 1.7 |
| 20.0– 50.0 | | 1 | 0.8 | 0.2 | 3 | 1.1 | 0.4 |
| 50.0–100.0 | | 0 | 0.3 | — | 0 | — | — |
| 100.0–500.0 | | 0 | — | — | 0 | — | — |
| Over 500.0 | | 0 | — | — | 0 | — | — |
| All | | 132 | | | 150 | | |
| Under 0.3 | All Industries | 21 | 8.7 | 8.0 | 7 | 8.3 | 4.5 |
| 0.3– 0.5 | | 29 | 12.0 | 6.8 | 9 | 10.5 | 3.1 |
| 0.5– 1.0 | | 60 | 9.7 | 4.9 | 31 | 8.2 | 3.4 |
| 1.0– 2.0 | | 117 | 8.6 | 3.0 | 104 | 7.8 | 2.6 |
| 2.0– 5.0 | | 142 | 7.4 | 1.7 | 150 | 6.7 | 1.6 |
| 5.0– 10.0 | | 69 | 6.7 | 1.0 | 82 | 5.8 | 1.0 |
| 10.0– 20.0 | | 24 | 6.2 | 0.6 | 50 | 4.7 | 0.7 |
| 20.0– 50.0 | | 11 | 4.9 | 0.8 | 17 | 4.2 | 0.6 |
| 50.0–100.0 | | 2 | 2.9 | 0.3 | 1 | 0.3 | 0.3 |
| 100.0–500.0 | | 1 | 2.0 | 0.3 | 6 | 3.2 | 0.2 |
| Over 500 | | 0 | — | — | 0 | — | — |
| All | | 476 | | | 457 | | |

SOURCE: Securities and Exchange Commission, *Cost of Flotation of Registered Equity Issues 1963–65* (Washington, D. C.: Government Printing Office, 1970), pp. 49–53.

Table 21–2 shows the costs of primary (issue) offering compared to secondary (stockholder) offering, holding size of issue, industry type, and the fact of underwriting constant. From Table 21–2, it appears that secondary offerings typically "cost" less in underwriting commissions than primary offerings. This is as expected because a primary offering involves the risk associated with the results to be expected from the investment of "new money." This risk (called dilution) is not present in a secondary offering. Furthermore, Table 21–2 indicates that the underwriting commission and other expenses are lower for the larger-sized issues. The underwriting commission is lower for larger issues because more underwriters share the risk and because the larger issue originates with a larger company, which usually carries less risk. The other expenses are lower for the larger offering because these expenses are largely fixed. Finally, as shown in a companion table in a prior edition of this book,[40] in 1955 the percentage of underwriting commission and other expenses was less for larger companies (regardless of the size of the offering) than for smaller companies and less for public utilities than for manufacturing companies.

Table 21–2 further shows that the flotation costs of common stock are typically higher for manufacturing companies than for financial companies, which in turn have higher flotation costs than utilities when size of the issue is held constant. This reflects the hierarchy of risk.

## CERTIFICATES OF PARTICIPATION

*Certificates of participation* are expanding in usage and serve the same function as common stock but typically involve a limited partnership rather than a corporation. The certificate of participation goes under several names: a limited partnership interest, a unit of participation, or an investment contract. The certificate of participation is like common stock in that it represents ownership in the business and is a residual claimant to earnings but unlike common stock carries no voting right, it being agreed that *all* management rights reside in the general partners. Another important difference from common stock is that each holder of a certificate reports his *pro rata* share of profits or losses—whether distributed or not—on his personal income tax return, thus picking up depreciation and depletion allowances immediately. The tax avoidance motive is powerful.

The certificate of participation is ordinarily issued in minimum units of $5000 and, typically, the venture involves high risks such as oil and other "wildcatting," theatrical productions, real estate ventures, and breeding operations. More than 90 percent of these certificates are offered directly by firms whose assets are less than $1 million. The costs of issuance are less than for common stock (as appears in Table 17–6), because the ventures are new and have no prior accounting records to be certified, need no expensive engineering reports on reserves (if in "wildcatting"), involve reduced printing and engraving costs, and are typically not underwritten. But the issue must be registered under the Securities Act of 1933 if it exceeds $500,000 and crosses state lines. In 1963–1965, there were 146 such issues, involving $376 million, with more than 60 percent of the issues in the extractive industries. In contrast, underwritten preferred stock offerings of all industries were $598 million in this period.

## SMALL BUSINESS INVESTMENT COMPANIES AND SMALL BUSINESS ADMINISTRATION

In contrast to certificates of participation, which appeal to individuals prepared to take high risks in larger amounts, Small Business Investment

---

[40] Table 22–2 in the first edition of this book based on the older study, Securities and Exchange Commission, *Cost of Flotation of Corporation Securities*, 1951–1955 (Washington, D. C.: Government Printing Office, 1957), p. 60, Table 18.

Companies (SBICs) draw in part upon federal government financial help to provide debt and other financing to small businesses which are otherwise unable to borrow or obtain financing. The incentive to the SBIC is to lend via a convertible debenture or to secure warrants as part of a loan transaction in order to get equity participation where the venture succeeds. The SBICs have had a checkered history despite many tax advantages granted them. For example, losses on SBIC stock are not capital losses but fully deductible against ordinary income.

The Small Business Administration (SBA) supervises SBICs as well as itself engaging in direct assistance to small business. The principal financial activity of the SBA is to guarantee loans made by regular financial institutions to small businesses or to directly make such loans. Since the SBA does not compete with private financial institutions, it will enter the picture only after proof that private lending is not available unless SBA will guarantee the loan.

## SUMMARY

Corporations exist under charters, or articles of incorporation, granted by a state and subject to the laws of the state, including future changes in the laws. The articles are usually kept brief to reduce the need for amendment by stockholder vote. More detailed rules applicable to the corporation are found in the bylaws. While stockholders vote on directors, amendment of articles, merger, dissolution, and a few other matters, the board of directors has the power of managing the affairs of the corporation.

Majority vote controls both stockholders' and directors' meetings. A minority may secure representation on the board in states that permit cumulative voting. Control of a corporation may be achieved by a voting trust, which is a type of "holding company" of votes. Classified common stock is also used to narrow voting control by providing that only one class has voting rights.

All voting stock entitles the holder to designate an agent or proxy to cast his votes. A proxy fight is a battle to gain sufficient votes to achieve control of the corporation. The solicitation of proxies in the case of all corporations (except those with less than 500 stockholders) is governed by SEC rules.

Common stock involves no fixed charge and no maturity date. Financing the needs for increased funds with common stock may involve dilution of voting rights or dilution of earnings. Dilution of voting rights can be limited by the preemptive right, which gives each common stockholder the right to his *pro rata* share of new stock. But the preemptive right may be denied in the corporate charter. Dilution of earnings can be variously defined, but the most meaningful definition applies to the investment of funds from new common stock in projects that will earn less than the present earning rate of the corporation on its assets.

The management of common stock involves such questions as the use of par or no par stock and decisions concerning when to have public offerings and whether to seek listing on an exchange. No par common stock was first used in New York State in 1912 to avoid many legal rules as to what price must be obtained by a corporation for its stock. Recent state statutes permit the board of directors to specify some of the rights of each new issue of stock instead of the older law that the corporate charter fixes the rights for all issues of each class of stock.

A major decision for the financial manager is when to go public. Ideally, this occurs when the company is in optimum operating condition and the stock market is in optimum condition as to common stock prices. Going public may involve sale of stock by the company or by selling stockholders or a combination of both. Usually the offering of company securities is subject to full registration with the SEC. Exceptions exist if the offering is (1) private, (2) intrastate only, or (3) of a smaller amount (such as under $500,000). In addition to federal requirements, which pursue "full disclosure," there are the requirements of each state in which the securities are offered for sale. State blue sky laws set some minimum standards as to the "quality" of the proposed offering in addition to full disclosure.

The new phenomenon of "letter stock" particularly involves institutions that buy unregistered stock and give a letter stating they have no intention of making a distribution of the stock.

Whether to list on an organized exchange becomes a problem for relatively few financial managers. Listing aids the marketability of a security but does not create a market. The amount of trading in a security depends on how widely the issue is distributed and the type of holder attracted by it. Listing offers the company the opportunity to use rights for financing. For the stockholder, listing means improved collateral values for borrowing to meet emergencies rather than selling and later repurchasing the security. Listing also offers the investor improved conditions for installment (margin) purchase of securities. On the other hand, listing focuses attention on adverse developments in the company, may intensify problems of maintaining control of the company, and may expose the company to "raiding parties." In addition, the firm that is listed loses its attractiveness to sponsoring investment bankers who may earn a greater profit by dealing in unlisted securities.

Financing through rights involves issuance to stockholders of rights to purchase new shares at a price below the current market price of the stock. This option given to existing stockholders has value and can be sold. Almost half of new issues of common stock of listed companies are sold in this way. The value of such a right can be determined by theoretical formula, but the market price of such a right is usually different because of the following factors not considered in the formula: (1) many stockholders wait to see the value put on rights in the market, creating a short supply during the early part of the rights period, (2) rights are given preferential margin treatement, (3) rights are flexible in income tax determination, (4) investment bankers stabilize prices, and (5) some stockholders ignore rights.

Although the average of rights offerings costs less than underwritten issues, this may merely mean that better quality issues use rights as a method rather than that rights as a method are cheaper for an issue of a given quality.

Common stock offerings by the company typically have higher flotation costs than secondary offerings by stockholders because the dilution risk is present in the former and not in the latter.

Certificates of participation are proportionate interests in unincorporated ventures and are similar to common stock.

Small Business Investment Companies (SBICs) get government funds in addition to their own equity which they in turn invest in small businesses not able to get funds from other private financial sources. The Small Business Administration (SBA) regulates SBICs and itself guarantees loans of private institutions to businesses that could not otherwise get loans, or the SBA may itself make a loan to such businesses.

### *Study Questions*

1. If the modern tendency is to reject the preemptive right for stockholders, why are there so many rights offerings of corporate securities by companies that have denied the preemptive right to stockholders?
2. If a corporation does not provide for effective control by a stable group, it is exposed to raiding parties by those who are tempted by the prospect of acquiring control easily and then milking the assets. What devices are available to deal with this problem and under what circumstances is each device appropriate?
3. Will the ownership of common stock protect the investor against the erosion of inflation if the company makes no use of debt in its financing?
4. Is the truth and full disclosure theory of federal security legislation a better policy than the qualitative standard specified by state blue sky legislation? Are the quality and effectiveness of the agency administering the legislation more important than what the legislation is?
5. If you were employed by an investment banker to price the stock of a company going public for the first time, list in the order of importance the factors you would consider.
6. It is a fact that the offering of common stock through rights is limited to stocks listed on an exchange except that small rights offerings (limited to the amount of one or two years' dividends of that stock) occasionally are made by companies whose securities are traded over the counter. Is there a sound reason for the practice of investment bankers in setting such a limit to rights offerings of over-the-counter stocks?
7. It is a fact (see Table 21–1) that *on the average* rights offerings involve substantially lower underwriting commissions than nonrights offerings. It is also a fact that the costs other than the underwriting commissions are most frequently larger for rights offerings than for nonrights offerings. Can you reconcile this situation? (*Hint*: Examine the rights offering and the nonrights offering presented in the problems on pp. 512–517.)
8. Do you think that the formulas for the theoretical value of a right have any usefulness in predicting what the market value of a right will be, given the market price of the stock and the number of rights needed to acquire one unit of the new issue of a security? Would the formula for the theoretical value of a right have to be different in a situation in which the rights cover a convertible debenture offering rather than an offering of common stock? In this connection, examine the data as to the rights offering of convertibles by the National Cash Register Company (pp. 512–517).

9. Should a company seek to list its securities as soon as it can meet the minimum listing requirements of an exchange? If you think the company should wait beyond that time, what criteria should determine the ideal time for listing?

### *Problems*

1. The term "dilution of equity" has many different meanings, but all of them refer to an effect on common stock:

a. Dilution of equity is sometimes said to occur when the issue of additional shares results in a lower book value per share.

b. Dilution is sometimes said to occur when the effect of an issue of additional shares reduces the market price of the shares.

c. Dilution is sometimes said to occur when conversion (of a preferred stock or of a debenture) occurs at less than the market price of a share.

What is the dilution (in the first sense above) when the company's balance sheet before an issue is as follows and the company sells 1000 shares at $60? at $100? at $500?

| | | | |
|---|---|---|---|
| Current assets | $100,000 | Current liabilities | $ 50,000 |
| Fixed assets | 600,000 | Debt | 150,000 |
| | | Capital stock, stated value $100, 2,500 shares | 250,000 |
| | | Surplus | 250,000 |
| Total assets | $700,000 | Total liabilities and net worth | $700,000 |

2. What is the dilution (in the second sense given in problem 1) when the company offers rights to stockholders to buy one added share for each ten now held at a price of $60 per new share when a share was selling at $100 before the announcement?

3. What is the dilution (in the third sense given in problem 1) when the company sells $100,000 in convertible debentures for $98,000, convertible into common at $10 per share, the predebenture market price was $12, and the company's balance sheet has been as follows:

| | | | |
|---|---|---|---|
| Current assets | $100,000 | Current liabilities | $ 50,000 |
| Fixed assets | 70,000 | Capital stock, $10 par, 10,000 shares | 100,000 |
| | | Surplus | 20,000 |
| Total assets | $170,000 | Total liabilities and net worth | $170,000 |

4. It is argued in the text that the only meaningful use of the term "dilution" is to measure whether the additional (marginal) money will earn the average of the invested money of the company. Reverting to problem 1 and its facts, indicate whether the sale of 1000 additional shares at $60 results in dilution if the company applies the proceeds to a project that will annually earn $16,000 after taxes when the present (preissue) company is annually earning $70,000 after taxes?

Would you expect the price of the stock to rise if the project carries the same risk as the rest of the company's operations?

**5.** It is argued in the text that the traditional method of determining how many shares are needed to control a corporation under cumulative voting (assuming majority control of the board of directors is control of the corporation) is sharply in error because computations are based on the number of voting shares *issued.* Test the argument by considering the following facts:

The corporation has 1 million voting shares outstanding, with each share entitled to one vote times the number of directors to be elected. By studying the record of the corporation's meetings you determine it is highly probable that 15 percent of the shares will not be present in person or by proxy. This has been the case in the past when no pressing contest was apparent. You are counseling dissident stockholders and advise them not to push matters to the point where the majority believes there will be a showdown in votes. In this manner you believe you can rely on a total vote of only 85 percent of the shares entitled to vote.

Furthermore, the present nine-man board is supported by the majority stockholder group which no doubt expects to reelect the board. The dissident stockholders tell you that two members of the board would be responsive to the thinking of the dissident group if the latter were in control.

You propose to the dissident group that they nominate a full slate of nine directors against the majority's slate but that they vote evenly only for the number of directors they feel their shares can elect with certainty if the majority votes evenly for its full slate.

To execute the strategy you propose that some of the minority submit their (revocable) proxies in due course but revoke them at the meeting. The balance of the minority will submit no proxies but will appear in person at the meeting. The purpose of this strategy is to conceal the true size of the minority from the majority and thus to induce them to vote evenly for their nine-man board.

How many shares would the minority need (a) to elect five of their own directors if the minority counts on 15 percent not voting and; (b) to elect three who could be combined with the two present directors sympathetic to the minority's position if there is 100 percent voting?

**6.** The text indicates that a voting trust is a type of holding company of voting power, creating leverage in voting. In a situation such as that in problem 5 where there are nine directors and the applicable law (or articles of the corporation) provides for cumulative voting, how many shares of the voting trust would you have to control in order to be reasonably sure of controlling the board of directors if there is one voting trustee? if you assume there are five voting trustees and the trust document provides for cumulative voting in the election of voting trustees?

**7.** The proxy rules of the SEC require that anyone soliciting a proxy of a stockholder in a corporation subject to regulation must reveal considerable information in a statement he is required to furnish to anyone whose proxy he solicits.

You have been retained to advise the company with regard to its financial operations. There has been a dispute among the directors as a result of the current year's operations, which have been less profitable than those of previous years. In prior years the company has dutifully complied with SEC regulations in the solicitation of proxies. Under SEC rules the company would be required to reveal any dissenting director, and several directors have indicated that they wish to be noted as dissenting in the solicitation of any proxy on behalf of management.

The management group is not certain that it can command a majority of the votes of stockholders and consults you as to what to do. This group believes the company's setbacks are temporary and will be corrected in the normal course of business in the next year.

What would you advise?

8. a. What is the theoretical value of a right if the stock is trading *ex* rights and selling for $100 when the subscription price is $80 and the number of rights needed to buy one share is 10?

b. If you should find that the price of a right is selling for $3, how do you explain the deviation from your answer to (a)?

c. If investment bankers are willing to enter a rights financing with a company, do you think that the commission they will seek will be greater if this company prefers a direct (nonrights) underwriting agreement? Before you answer, study the two cases of subordinated convertible debentures given on pages 512–517.

### Selected References

Bacon, P. W., "The Subscription Price in Rights Offerings," *Financial Management*, 1 (Summer 1972), pp. 59–64.

Beranek, W., *Common Stock Financing, Bank Values and State Dividends:* The *Theory and the Evidence.* Madison, Wis.: University of Wisconsin School of Commerce, 1961.

Blume, M. E. and Frank Husic, "Price, Beta and Exchange Listing," *Journal of Finance*, 28 (May, 1973) pp. 273–282.

Evans, G. H., Jr., "The Theoretical Value of a Stock Right," *Journal of Finance* 10 (March 1955), pp. 55–61; and "Comment," by S. H. Archer and W. Beranek, *Journal of Finance*, 11 (September 1956), pp. 363–370.

Flink, S. J., *Equity Financing for Small Business.* New York: Simmons-Boardman Books, 1962.

Furst, R. W., "Does Listing Increase the Market Price of Common Stocks?" *Journal of Business*, 43 (April 1970), pp. 174–180.

Keane, S. M., "The Significance of the Issue Price in Rights Issues," *Journal of Business Finance*, 4 (September 1972), pp. 40–45.

Logue, D. E., "On the Pricing of Unseasoned Equity Issues: 1965–1969," *Journal of Financial and Quantititative Analysis*, 8 (January 1973), pp. 91–104.

Lynch, T. E., "Accounting for Equity Securities," *Financial Management*, 2 (Spring 1973), pp. 41–47.

McDonald, J. G. and A. K. Fisher, "New Issue Stock Price Behavior," *Journal of Finance*, 27 (March 1972), pp. 97–102.

Nelson, J. R. "Price Effects in Rights Offerings," *Journal of Finance*, 20 (December 1965), pp. 647–660.

Stevenson, H. W., *Common Stock Financing.* Ann Arbor, Mich.: University of Michigan Press, 1957.

Weiss, E., "Regulation A under the Securities Act of 1933—Highways and Byways," *New York Law Forum*, 8 (March 1962), pp. 3–131.

# 22

# Timing: Refinancing, Recapitalization, and Share Repurchase

*Refinancing* involves the sale of securities of the issuer to replace existing securities. *Recapitalization* involves changing the form or the amount of outstanding securities in a voluntary exchange, or with stockholders' consent, or unilaterally by action of the board of directors. *Reorganization,* on the other hand, involves changes in the capital structure that occur because of insolvency either in the equity sense (inability to meet debts as they mature) or in the bankruptcy sense (excess of liabilities, excluding capital account, over assets).

There are three types of refinancing: (1) funding, that is, the conversion of short-term debt into long-term debt; (2) refunding, that is, the replacement of maturing long-term debt or the calling of long-term debt for the purpose of replacement; and (3) the calling of preferred stock for replacement with new preferred bearing a lower rate or with other features different from the outstanding preferred. There is also the possibility of replacing the debt or preferred stock with common stock.

## THE IMPORTANCE OF TIMING

Although timing is always important in finance, it is particularly so in refinancing and recapitalization. Timing is important, as we have already seen, in the public offering of securities. In that case we indicated that the important matter is to make the public offering at a time when the state of both the company and the capital market is optimum.

One factor that affects timing is whether the industry in which the company is classified leads, coincides, or lags behind the general business cycle. Another factor is that, in general, the stock market leads the business cycle of the economy. Many analysts believe this lead is about 6 months, although there are exceptions. (The stock market drop in 1962 anticipated nothing—or what it anticipated was headed off.) A third factor involved in timing is that investors or speculators shift funds from the bond market to the stock market, and vice versa, making bond or stock financing easier at different times.

Also important are the monetary and fiscal policies that are pursued by government in order to head off extreme economic conditions—namely, lower rates and easier money in recessions and higher rates and tighter money during inflationary periods. The latter was illustrated in 1969–1970 when money rates of all types reached the highest points since 1929. At the same time the stock market had steadily declined so that in May of 1970 both the bond market and the stock market were in poor condition for any new issue, with respect to both costs and the availability of funds. Despite a temporary let-up in 1971, the capital markets continue in poor condition into 1974.

Both stock and bond yields are indicators of the availability of funds. High bond yields are associated with a relative scarcity of debt money. With stock the same situation is likely to exist, namely, low price-earnings ratios on stocks are an indication of a relative scarcity of equity funds.

There is still another aspect of timing that we dealt with in discussing capital budgeting; that is, the internal rate of return. What the internal rate of return from a project will be depends in part on *when* the project is undertaken. If the project materializes just as demand for the product involved is strong, the early return flow of funds is higher; the rate of return is higher; and perhaps a somewhat higher cost of capital can be profitably tolerated, the differential increase in the rate of return being more than the differential in the cost of money. It is foolhardy for a financial manager to chase the lowest cost of money only to find that he has procured the funds at bargain rates when the time for their usefulness has passed.

One aspect of timing that has drawn considerable attention in recent years is the *term structure of interest rates.* By term structure is meant the increase or decrease in the interest rate for a given debtor at any point in time as the maturity of the debt is extended.

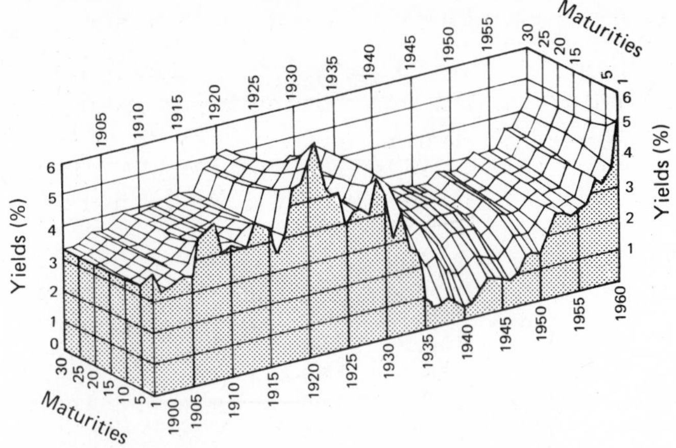


Figure 22–1 Basic yields of corporate bonds by maturity, 1900–1960. Perspective 1. (Yields are derived from Table 22–1.)

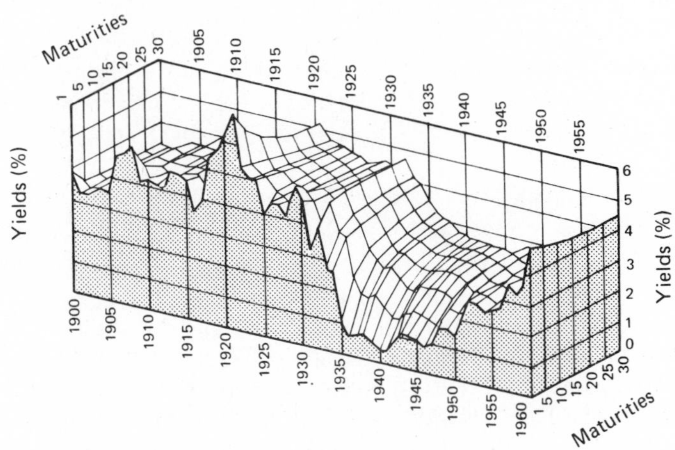


Figure 22–2 Basic yields of corporate bonds by maturity, 1900–1960. Perspective 2. (Yields are derived from Table 22–1.)

Figures 22–1 and 22–2 show two views of the same three-dimensional construction that relates three variables: the interest rate (yield), the maturity of the loan, and the time period from 1900 to 1960. The shortest maturity yields are nearest the viewer and the longest maturity yields are at the back of each figure. Figure 22–1 moves from left to right from 1900 to 1960, and in it the great decline in yields from 1930 to 1940 is hidden from the eye. Figure 22–2 shows the same construction from a different angle and emphasizes the parts hidden in Figure 22–1. Both figures are based on Table 22–1. As Sidney Homer has described the construction: "These charts suggest a rip tide as the powerful currents

TABLE 22–1. Basic Yields by Maturity—Prime Corporate Bonds

| | Years to maturity | | | | | | |
|---|---|---|---|---|---|---|---|
| *Feb.* | *1* | *5* | *10* | *15* | *20* | *25* | *30* |
| **1900** | 3.97% * | 3.36% * | 3.30% | 3.30% | 3.30% | 3.30% | 3.30% |
| 1901 | 3.25 | 3.25 | 3.25 | 3.25 | 3.25 | 3.25 | 3.25 |
| 1902 | 3.30 † | 3.30 † | 3.30 † | 3.30 † | 3.30 † | 3.30 † | 3.30 † |
| 1903 | 3.45 | 3.45 | 3.45 | 3.45 | 3.45 | 3.45 | 3.45 |
| 1904 | 3.60 | 3.60 | 3.60 | 3.60 | 3.60 | 3.60 | 3.60 |
| 1905 | 3.50 | 3.50 | 3.50 | 3.50 | 3.50 | 3.50 | 3.50 |
| 1906 | 4.75 * | 3.67 * | 3.55 | 3.55 | 3.55 | 3.55 | 3.55 |
| 1907 | 4.87 * | 3.87 * | 3.80 | 3.80 | 3.80 | 3.80 | 3.80 |
| 1908 | 5.10 * | 4.30 * | 4.02 * | 3.95 | 3.95 | 3.95 | 3.95 |
| 1909 | 4.03 | 3.97 | 3.91 | 3.86 | 3.82 | 3.79 | 3.77 |
| 1910 | 4.25 | 4.10 | 3.99 | 3.92 | 3.87 | 3.83 | 3.80 |
| 1911 | 4.09 | 4.05 | 4.01 | 3.97 | 3.94 | 3.92 | 3.90 |
| 1912 | 4.04 | 4.00 | 3.96 | 3.93 | 3.91 | 3.90 | 3.90 |
| 1913 | 4.74 | 4.31 | 4.12 | 4.06 | 4.02 | 4.00 | 4.00 |
| 1914 | 4.64 | 4.45 | 4.32 | 4.22 | 4.16 | 4.12 | 4.10 |
| 1915 | 4.47 | 4.39 | 4.31 | 4.25 | 4.20 | 4.17 | 4.15 |
| 1916 | 3.48 | 4.03 | 4.05 | 4.05 | 4.05 | 4.05 | 4.05 |
| 1917 | 4.05 | 4.05 | 4.05 | 4.05 | 4.05 | 4.05 | 4.05 |
| 1918 | 5.48 | 5.25 | 5.05 | 4.91 | 4.82 | 4.77 | 4.75 |
| 1919 | 5.58 | 5.16 | 4.97 | 4.87 | 4.81 | 4.77 | 4.75 |
| 1920 | 6.11 | 5.72 | 5.43 | 5.26 | 5.17 | 5.12 | 5.10 |
| 1921 | 6.94 † | 6.21 | 5.73 | 5.46 | 5.31 | 5.22 | 5.17 |
| 1922 | 5.31 | 5.19 | 5.06 | 4.95 | 4.85 | 4.77 | 4.71 |
| 1923 | 5.01 | 4.90 | 4.80 | 4.73 | 4.68 | 4.64 | 4.61 |
| 1924 | 5.02 | 4.90 | 4.80 | 4.73 | 4.69 | 4.67 | 4.66 |
| 1925 | 3.85 | 4.46 | 4.50 | 4.50 | 4.50 | 4.50 | 4.50 |
| 1926 | 4.40 | 4.40 | 4.40 | 4.40 | 4.40 | 4.40 | 4.40 |
| 1927 | 4.30 | 4.30 | 4.30 | 4.30 | 4.30 | 4.30 | 4.30 |
| 1928 | 4.05 | 4.05 | 4.05 | 4.05 | 4.05 | 4.05 | 4.05 |
| 1929 | 5.27 | 4.72 | 4.57 | 4.49 | 4.45 | 4.43 | 4.42 |
| 1930 | 4.40 | 4.40 | 4.40 | 4.40 | 4.40 | 4.40 | 4.40 |
| 1931 | 3.05 | 3.90 | 4.03 | 4.08 | 4.10 | 4.10 | 4.10 |
| 1932 | 3.99 * | 4.58 * | 4.70 | 4.70 | 4.70 | 4.70 | 4.70 |
| 1933 | 2.60 † | 3.68 | 4.00 | 4.07 | 4.11 | 4.14 | 4.15 |
| 1934 | 2.62 † | 3.48 | 3.70 | 3.83 | 3.91 | 3.96 | 3.99 |
| 1935 | 1.05 | 2.37 | 3.00 | 3.23 | 3.37 | 3.46 | 3.50 |
| 1936 | 0.61 | 1.86 | 2.64 | 2.88 | 3.04 | 3.14 | 3.20 |
| 1937 | 0.69 | 1.68 | 2.38 | 2.72 | 2.90 | 3.01 | 3.08 |
| 1938 | 0.85 | 1.97 | 2.60 | 2.81 | 2.91 | 2.97 | 3.00 |
| 1939 | 0.57 | 1.55 | 2.18 | 2.50 | 2.65 | 2.72 | 2.75 |
| 1940 | 0.41 | 1.28 | 1.95 | 2.34 | 2.55 | 2.65 | 2.70 |
| 1941 | 0.41 | 1.21 | 1.88 | 2.28 | 2.50 | 2.61 | 2.65 |
| 1942 | 0.81 | 1.50 | 2.16 | 2.47 | 2.61 | 2.64 | 2.65 |
| 1943 | 1.17 | 1.71 | 2.16 | 2.45 | 2.61 | 2.65 | 2.65 |
| 1944 | 1.08 † | 1.58 | 2.20 | 2.54 | 2.60 | 2.60 | 2.60 |

TABLE 22–1 (continued)

| | Years to maturity | | | | | | |
|---|---|---|---|---|---|---|---|
| *Feb.* | *1* | *5* | *10* | *15* | *20* | *25* | *30* |
| 1945 | 1.02 | 1.53 | 2.14 | 2.45 | 2.55 | 2.55 | 2.55 |
| 1946 | 0.86 † | 1.32 | 1.88 † | 2.26 | 2.35 | 2.40 | 2.43 |
| 1947 | 1.05 † | 1.65 | 2.08 † | 2.30 | 2.40 | 2.46 | 2.50 |
| 1948 | 1.60 | 2.03 | 2.53 | 2.66 | 2.73 | 2.77 | 2.80 |
| 1949 | 1.60 | 1.92 | 2.32 | 2.54 | 2.62 | 2.68 | 2.74 |
| 1950 | 1.42 † | 1.90 † | 2.30 | 2.40 | 2.48 | 2.54 | 2.58 |
| 1951 | 2.05 † | 2.22 † | 2.39 | 2.51 | 2.59 | 2.63 | 2.67 |
| 1952 | 2.73 † | 2.73 † | 2.73 | 2.81 | 2.88 | 2.94 | 3.00 |
| 1953 | 2.62 † | 2.75 † | 2.88 | 2.97 | 3.05 | 3.11 | 3.15 |
| 1954 | 2.40 | 2.52 | 2.66 | 2.78 | 2.88 | 2.95 | 3.00 |
| 1955 | 2.60 | 2.70 | 2.80 | 2.88 | 2.95 | 3.00 | 3.04 |
| 1956 | 2.70 | 2.78 | 2.86 | 2.93 | 2.99 | 3.04 | 3.09 |
| 1957 | 3.50 † | 3.50 † | 3.50 | 3.50 | 3.50 † | 3.60 | 3.68 |
| 1958 | 3.21 † | 3.25 † | 3.33 | 3.40 | 3.47 | 3.54 | 3.61 |
| 1959 | 3.67 | 3.80 | 4.03 | 4.10 | 4.10 | 4.10 | 4.10 |
| 1960 | 4.95 | 4.73 | 4.60 | 4.55 | 4.55 | 4.55 | 4.55 |
| 1961 | 3.10 | 3.75 | 4.00 | 4.06 | 4.12 | 4.16 | 4.22 |
| 1962 | 3.50 | 3.97 | 4.28 | 4.37 | 4.40 | 4.41 | 4.42 |

* Estimated by interpolation and therefore subject to error.
† More than usually subject to error.
SOURCES:
1900–1942: David Durand, *Basic Yields of Corporate Bonds, 1900–1942* (New York: National Bureau of Economic Research, Technical Paper 3, 1942).
1943–1947: David Durand and Willis J. Winn, *Basic Yields of Bonds, 1926–1947: Their Measurement and Pattern* (New York: National Bureau of Economic Research, Technical Paper 6, 1947).
1948–1952: *The Economic Almanac, 1953–1954* (New York: Thomas Y. Crowell Company, 1953).
1953–1958: David Durand, "A Quarterly Series of Corporate Basic Yields, 1952–57, and Some Attendant Reservations," *Journal of Finance,* XIII, 3, September 1958.
1959–1962: Estimates prepared by the use of methods similar to those employed by Durand.
Table reproduced from Sidney Homer, *A History of Interest Rates,* pp. 374 f with permission.

TABLE 22–2. Prime Bank Loan Rate and Rediscount Rate, New York Federal Reserve Bank, 1937–1974

| *Prime bank loan rate (%)** | *Date of rate change* | *Rediscount rate, N.Y. Fed. Res. Bank (%)†* |
|---|---|---|
| 1.5 | Aug. 27, 1937 | 1.0 |
| | Oct. 30, 1937 | 0.5 |
| | Apr. 25, 1946 | 1.0 |

* *Wall Street Journal.*
† *Federal Reserve Bulletin.*

TABLE 22–2 (continued)

| Prime bank loan rate (%)* | Date of rate change | Rediscount rate, N.Y. Fed. Res. Bank (%)† |
|---|---|---|
| 1.75 | Dec. 15, 1947 | |
| | Jan. 12, 1948 | 1.25 |
| 2.0 | Aug. 10, 1948 | |
| | Aug. 13, 1948 | 1.5 |
| | Aug. 21, 1950 | 1.75 |
| 2.25 | Sept. 22, 1950 | |
| 2.5 | Jan. 5, 1951 | |
| 2.75 | Oct. 17, 1951 | |
| 3.0 | Dec. 18, 1951 | |
| | Jan. 16, 1953 | 2.0 |
| 3.25 | Apr. 27, 1953 | |
| | Feb. 5, 1954 | 1.75 |
| 3.0 | Mar. 17, 1954 | |
| | Apr. 16, 1954 | 1.5 |
| | Apr. 15, 1955 | 1.75 |
| 3.25 | Aug. 4, 1955 | |
| | Aug. 5, 1955 | 2.0 |
| | Sept. 9, 1955 | 2.25 |
| 3.5 | Oct. 14, 1955 | |
| | Nov. 18, 1955 | 2.5 |
| 3.75 | Apr. 13, 1956 | 2.75 |
| 4.0 | Aug. 21, 1956 | |
| | Aug. 24, 1956 | 3.0 |
| 4.5 | Aug. 6, 1957 | |
| | Aug. 23, 1957 | 3.5 |
| | Nov. 15, 1957 | 3.0 |
| 4.0 | Jan. 22, 1958 | |
| | Jan. 24, 1958 | 2.75 |
| | Mar. 7, 1958 | 2.25 |
| | Apr. 18, 1958 | 1.75 |
| 3.5 | Apr. 22, 1958 | |
| | Sept. 12, 1958 | 2.0 |
| 4.0 | Sept. 15, 1958 | |
| | Nov. 7, 1958 | 2.5 |
| | Mar. 6, 1959 | 3.0 |
| 4.5 | May 18, 1959 | |
| | May 29, 1959 | 3.5 |
| 5.0 | Sept. 2, 1959 | |
| | Sept. 11, 1959 | 4.0 |
| | June 10, 1960 | 3.5 |
| | Aug. 12, 1960 | 3.0 |
| 4.5 | Aug. 24, 1960 | |
| | July 17, 1963 | 3.5 |
| | Nov. 24, 1964 | 4.0 |
| 4.75 | Apr. 20, 1965 | |
| | Dec. 6, 1965 | 4.5 |

* *Wall Street Journal.*
† *Federal Reserve Bulletin.*

TABLE 22-2 (continued)

| *Prime bank loan rate (%)** | *Date of rate change* | *Rediscount rate, N.Y. Fed. Res. Bank (%)†* |
|---|---|---|
| 5.0 | Dec. 7, 1965 | |
| 5.5 | Mar. 11, 1966 | |
| 5.75 | June 30, 1966 | |
| 6.0 | Aug. 17, 1966 | |
| 5.75 | Jan. 26, 1967 | |
| 5.5 | Mar. 23, 1967 | |
| | Apr. 16, 1967 | 4.0 |
| | Mar. 19, 1967 | 4.5 |
| 6.0 | Nov. 21, 1967 | |
| | Mar. 21, 1968 | 5.0 |
| | Apr. 18, 1968 | 5.5 |
| 6.5 | Apr. 21, 1968 | |
| | Aug. 30, 1968 | 5.25 |
| 6.25 | Sept. 25, 1968 | |
| 6.5 | Dec. 2, 1968 | |
| | Dec. 18, 1968 | 5.5 |
| 6.75 | Dec. 19, 1968 | |
| 7.0 | Jan. 7, 1969 | |
| 7.5 | Mar. 17, 1969 | |
| | Apr. 4, 1969 | 6.0 |
| 8.5 | June 9, 1969 | |
| 8.0 | Mar. 25, 1970 | |
| 7.5 | Sept. 21, 1970 | |
| 7.25 | Nov. 12, 1970 | |
| | Nov. 13, 1970 | 5.75 |
| 7.0 | Nov. 20, 1970 | |
| | Dec. 4, 1970 | 5.5 |
| 6.75 | Dec. 22, 1970 | |
| 6.5 | Jan. 6, 1971 | |
| | Jan. 8, 1971 | 5.25 |
| 6.25 | Jan. 15, 1971 | |
| 6.0 | Jan. 18, 1971 | |
| | Jan. 22, 1971 | 5.0 |
| | Feb. 13, 1971 | 4.75 |
| 5.75 | Feb. 16, 1971 | |
| 5.5‡ | Mar. 11, 1971 | |
| 5.25 | Mar. 19, 1971 | |
| 5.5 | Apr. 23, 1971 | |
| 6.0 | July 7, 1971 | |
| | July 16, 1971 | 5.0 |
| 5.75 | Oct. 20, 1971 | |
| 5.5 | Nov. 4, 1971 | |
| | Nov. 19, 1971 | 4.75 |
| | Dec. 17, 1971 | 4.5 |
| 5.25 | Dec. 31, 1971 | |

* *Wall Street Journal.*
† *Federal Reserve Bulletin.*
‡ Selective change began March 11, 1971. In many cases from this point on in time, more than one rate was in effect. The predominant rate and its date are then shown.

TABLE 22–2 (continued)

| *Prime bank loan rate (%)** | *Date of rate change* | *Rediscount rate, N.Y. Fed. Res. Bank (%)†* |
|---|---|---|
| 5.0 | Jan. 24, 1972 | |
| 4.75 | Jan. 31, 1972 | |
| 5.0 | Apr. 5, 1972 | |
| 5.25 | June 26, 1972 | |
| 5.5 | Aug. 29, 1972 | |
| 5.75 | Oct. 4, 1972 | |
| 6.0 | Jan. 4, 1973 | |
| | Jan. 15, 1973 | 5.0 |
| | Feb. 26, 1973 | 5.5 |
| 6.25 | Feb. 27, 1973 | |
| 6.5 | Mar. 26, 1973 | |
| 6.75 | Apr. 18, 1973 | |
| | May 4, 1973 | 5.75 |
| 7.0 | May 7, 1973 | |
| | May 11, 1973 | 6.0 |
| 7.25 | May 25, 1973 | |
| 7.5 | June 8, 1973 | |
| | June 11, 1973 | 6.5 |
| 7.75 | June 25, 1973 | |
| | July 2, 1973 | 7.0 |
| 8.0 | July 3, 1973 | |
| 8.25 | July 9, 1973 | |
| 8.5 | July 18, 1973 | |
| 8.75 | July 30, 1973 | |
| 9.0 | Aug. 6, 1973 | |
| 9.25 | Aug. 13, 1973 | |
| | Aug. 14, 1973 | 7.5 |
| 9.5 | Aug. 22, 1973 | |
| 9.75 | Sept. 2, 1973 | |
| 10.0 | Sept. 18, 1973 | |
| 9.75 | Oct. 24, 1973 | |
| 9.5 | Jan. 29, 1974 | |
| 9.25 | Feb. 11, 1974 | |
| 9.0 | Feb. 18, 1974 | |
| 8.75 | Feb. 25, 1974 | |
| 9.0 | Mar. 22, 1974 | |
| 9.25 | Mar. 29, 1974 | |
| 9.5 | Apr. 3, 1974 | |
| 9.75 | Apr. 5, 1974 | |
| 10.0 | Apr. 15, 1974 | |
| 10.25 | Apr. 19, 1974 | |
| 10.5 | Apr. 25, 1974 | 8.0 |
| 10.75 | Apr. 27, 1974 | |
| 11.0 | Apr. 29, 1974 | |
| 11.25 | May 14, 1974 | |
| 11.5 | May 17, 1974 | |
| 11.75 | June 20, 1974 | |
| 12.0 | July 3, 1974 | |

* *Wall Street Journal.*
† *Federal Reserve Bulletin.*

of rising and falling interest rates cut across equally powerful currents of change in the relationship of long-term to short-term interest rates."[1]

The figures indicate that in periods of depression low short-term rates rise sharply with increased maturity. On the other hand, in boom periods high short-term rates taper to lower rates as maturity is increased. This leads to what has been called the *positively sloped term yield curve* (with yield on the vertical axis and maturity on the horizonal axis) and the *negatively sloped term yield curve.*

The figures suggest the use of short-term money in a period of depression and of long-term money in a period of boom. However, before we accept that conclusion let us examine another dimension not revealed in these figures.

As Tables 22–2 and 22–3 and Figure 22–3 indicate,[2] the evidence seems to be that the long- and short-term rates move together. Remember that if we had plotted *average* quarterly (or annual) data in Figure 22–3

TABLE 22–3. Moody's AAA New Corporate Bond Yields, Monthly, 1952–1973 (in percents)

| | 1952 | 1953 | 1954 | 1955 | 1956 | 1957 | 1958 | 1959 | 1960 | 1961 | 1962 | 1963 | 1964 | 1965 | 1966 | 1967 | 1968 | 1969 | 1970 | 1971 | 1972 | 1973 |
|---|---|---|---|---|---|---|---|---|---|---|---|---|---|---|---|---|---|---|---|---|---|---|
| Jan. | 3.20 | 3.18 | 3.19 | 2.95 | 3.15 | 4.30 | 3.24 | | 5.03 | | 4.50 | 4.21 | 4.53 | 4.37 | 4.83 | 5.35 | 6.18 | 6.97 | 8.44 | 7.29 | 7.09 | 7.36 |
| Feb. | | | | 3.12 | 3.09 | 4.17 | 3.77 | 4.31 | 5.01 | 4.32 | 4.52 | 4.28 | | | | 5.31 | 6.32 | 7.02 | 8.59 | 7.07 | 7.26 | 7.30 |
| Mar. | | | | | 3.35 | 4.25 | 3.94 | 4.29 | 4.88 | 4.32 | | 4.23 | | | | 5.37 | 6.59 | 7.38 | 8.59 | 7.34 | | 7.625 |
| Apr. | 3.05 | | 2.98 | 3.12 | 3.40 | 4.31 | 3.68 | 4.60 | 4.80 | | 4.23 | | 4.48 | | | 5.35 | 6.70 | 7.30 | 7.77 | 7.50 | 7.39 | 7.43 |
| May | 3.11 | 3.74 | 2.98 | | 4.57 | 4.34 | 3.82 | | 4.80 | 4.64 | 4.27 | 4.33 | 4.45 | 4.50 | | 5.77 | 6.72 | 7.25 | 8.91 | 7.98 | 7.29 | 7.625 |
| June | 3.10 | 3.74 | 3.00 | | 3.50 | 4.77 | | | 4.78 | 4.68 | 4.30 | 4.27 | | 4.55 | 5.49 | 5.91 | 6.68 | 7.71 | 8.96 | 7.78 | 7.45 | 7.71 |
| July | 3.15 | 3.92 | 2.96 | 3.17 | | 4.43 | 4.00 | | 4.75 | 4.64 | 4.39 | 4.36 | 4.39 | 4.58 | 5.69 | 5.79 | 6.50 | 7.79 | 8.53 | 7.94 | 7.40 | 8.06 |
| Aug. | | 3.42 | 2.95 | | 3.94 | | 4.30 | 4.67 | 4.54 | 4.60 | 4.39 | 4.31 | | | 5.75 | 5.92 | 6.25 | 7.83 | 8.61 | 7.82 | 7.39 | 8.20 |
| Sep. | 3.12 | 3.60 | 3.01 | | | 4.73 | 4.41 | 5.17 | 4.54 | | | | | 4.68 | 5.98 | 6.01 | 6.34 | 8.15 | 8.56 | 7.52 | 7.47 | 7.91 |
| Oct. | | | 2.95 | 3.20 | 3.90 | 4.70 | 4.40 | 5.13 | 4.66 | | 4.30 | | | 4.64 | | 6.02 | 6.59 | 8.00 | 8.86 | 7.38 | 7.39 | 7.79 |
| Nov. | | | | 3.21 | | 4.65 | | | 4.72 | | | | | 4.67 | 5.96 | 6.47 | 6.83 | 8.38 | 8.55 | 7.36 | | |
| Dec. | | 3.22 | | 3.30 | 4.24 | 3.98 | 4.48 | 5.17 | 4.78 | | | 4.43 | | | 5.79 | 6.65 | 6.92 | 9.10 | 7.60 | 7.38 | | |

Note: Blanks indicate no new issues
SOURCE: Moody's *Bond Survey*.

[A9940]

[1] *A History of Interest Rates* (New Brunswick, N. J.: Rutgers University Press, 1963), p. 380.

[2] We would like to point out why we used the prime bank rate and Moody's yield on new corporate AAA bond issues. It is basic to scientific work (in business as well as in the natural sciences) that the data be (1) homogeneous and (2) the best measure of what we seek to measure. There are many series of average interest rates; these are averages of loans of widely varying risks, and the "mix" of the risks over time is not constant. The prime rate is more homogeneous than such averages. But there are some other series that are equally homogeneous. Second, the prime rate measures the greatest single segment of what we want to look at: the money available to, and used by, business. Thus, the high-grade municipal rate, while equally homogeneous, reflects not the demand for money by business but a complicated array of factors determining municipal investment activities.

There is a lack of homogeneity in the series of Moody's yield on new corporate AAA bond issues. Thus, no attempt is made to hold maturity, among other things, constant even though average maturity has fluctuated sharply from year to year and maturity is an important factor affecting the rate of interest. See A. B. Cohan, "Yields on New Underwritten Corporate Bonds, 1935–1958," *Journal of Finance*, 17 (December 1962), pp. 585–605.

the dispersion of the long-term rate about the prime rate would be reduced.

Thus, the financial manager can move into and out of short-term debt at appropriate times in order to optimize his situation with respect to long-term debt and equity. In fact, there is much to recommend a policy of using short-term debt this way even though short-term rates might fluctuate widely. We must remember that the high rate of interest on a short-term loan will be paid for a much shorter period of time than the saving would be on a properly timed long-term debt issue.

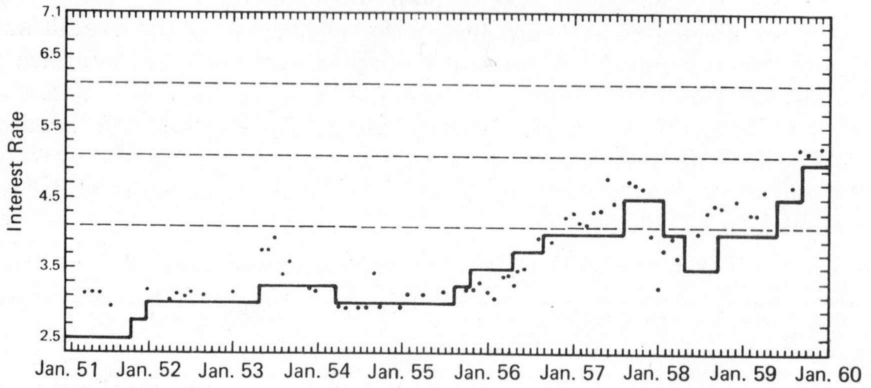


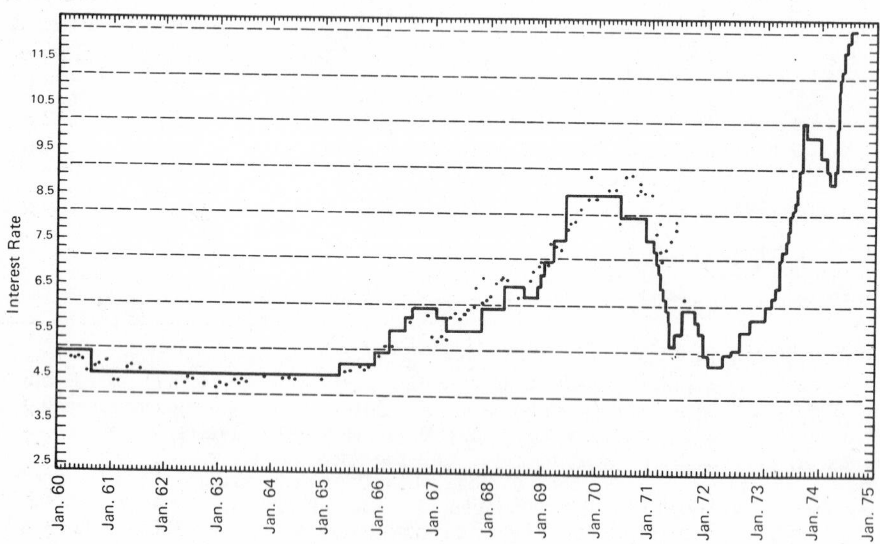


**Legend: Figure 22–3.** Yield on Moody's new AAA corporate bonds monthly; and the prime rate, 1951–1974. Key: Prime rate = ——; Moody's AAA new bonds = . . Data from Tables 22–2 and 22–3.

Finally, the financial manager is concerned with the cost of money to a particular company in a particular industry. But this cost will, in part, be determined by the overall situation with respect to capital. Despite the fact that the use of funds in housing was very low in 1969, as indicated by a rate of new housing starts less than half that of the previous 15 years, the general tight money condition assured high interest rates for those funds. In the case of housing the situation is complicated by the practice of the federal government in making money specially available to, or withholding it from, the housing area without the usual relation to whether the interest rate is high or not.

The financial manager can keep himself abreast of the overall situation in the capital and money markets through various publications. Table 22–4 gives a summary which appeared in *Business Week* that reflects the estimates of Bankers Trust Company and Salomon Brothers & Hutzler. Note that the requirements of the U.S. Treasury were not estimated, since fiscal policy would determine those amounts and fiscal

TABLE 22–4. How Bad Will the Capital Shortage Be?

| *Money needed (billions of dollars)* | | | |
|---|---|---|---|
| *1958* | | *1959* | |
| *Borrowers raised these amounts* | *for these purposes* | *The forecasts are* | |
| | | Bankers Trust Co. | Salomon Bros. & Hutzler |
| $ 9.0 | Domestic corporate, foreign financing | $ 8.0 | $ 7.9 |
| 14.8 | Real estate mortgages | 15.7 | 13.3 |
| 5.9 | State and local government finance | 5.9 | 4.6 |
| 2.9 | U.S. Treasury bond issues | ? | ? |
| $32.6 | Total | $29.6 | $25.8 |
| *What regular lenders supply* | | | |
| *1958* | | *1959* | |
| *These amounts* | *were supplied by these lenders* | | |
| $ 6.5 | Savings and loan associations | $ 6.7 | $ 5.5 |
| 2.5 | Mutual savings banks | 2.3 | 2.2 |
| 5.6 | Life insurance companies | 5.6 | 4.7 |
| 1.2 | Fire, casualty insurance companies | 1.7 | 1.3 |
| 2.9 | Corporate pension funds | 3.2 | 3.3 |
| 1.6 | State and local gov't retirement funds | 1.7 | 1.6 |
| 8.4 | Other | 4.2 | 1.0 |
| $28.7 | Total | $25.4 | $19.6 |
| *Additional amounts needed* | | | |
| $ 3.9 | | $4.2? | $6.2? |
| | | (plus Treasury's needs) | |

SOURCE: "How Bad Will the Capital Shortage Be?" *Business Week*, March 14, 1959, p. 50.

policy is heavily determined by expectations concerning the condition of the private sector of the economy. It is important that this forecast in *Business Week* of March 14, 1959, correctly called the upturn of the short-term interest rate in 1959. The issue of May 14, 1960 then correctly forecast the decline in this rate in 1960, and the issue of December 24, 1960 correctly predicted the upturn in 1961.

In this overall picture of the capital and money markets, consideration must be given not only to fiscal policy (taxes, budget surplus or deficit, and so on) but also to Federal Reserve bank policy as expressed in the rediscount rate, reserve requirements, open-market operations, and selective credits controls (such as margin requirements and real estate and consumer credit).

## STRATEGY RULES FOR THE FINANCIAL MANAGER

### Flexibility

To develop rules of strategy for the financial manager is not an easy assignment. First we must realize that every rule has its exception. This reminds us of the success stories of men who have made millions although without particular formal education. Such men, among other things, have been careful observers. For example, in a long period of rising prices they may have learned the profitability of buying, holding, and then selling at a profit. Without a rational approach as to when the price level will change direction (or even that it will change), they are caught by the change, and not understanding its significance, they lose all and start again with the next period of rising prices. During a lifetime they may go through several such cycles, and whether death finds them rich or poor is a matter of chance. On the other hand, the man with formal education may fail too, but the amplitudes of his cycles will probably be less and the likelihood that he will die poor will be less. How successful he will be will depend on how well he understands generalizations and how well he recognizes the exceptions.

It is with this philosophy that we approach these rules of strategy. The first rule and the one with the fewest, if any, exceptions is flexibility.

The financial manager must keep himself in a situation where he can change position. Flexibility, however, can be achieved only at a cost. When a financial manager achieves flexibility it means that the party on the other end of the transaction is foregoing something, and for doing this he wants a price.

To use a simple example, a noncallable preferred stock can be sold at a lower actual rate than a callable preferred stock. The nominal rates on the two issues might be the same, but then we must consider the call premium. On the other hand, a noncallable preferred stock issued near all time lows may make the matter of a call premium an academic point. Thus Wisconsin Electric Power Company issued in the 1930s $26 million of a still-outstanding 3.6 percent preferred stock at close to par and callable at $101.[3] On the other hand, this same utility had issued

[3] This issue fell as low as 36 in the tight money market of 1974.

a noncallable 6 percent preferred in 1899 which reached an all time high of $160 and an all time low of $65, with some $4.45 million of an original $4.5 million then outstanding.

In 1969 and again in 1974 the opportunity presented itself to repurchase the 6 percent preferred in the open market and either replace it temporarily with short-term funds or include this need for coverage in the proceeds of a common stock sale. This plan could easily be carried out, since there have been several recent common stock sales and another will occur shortly. The $10 par common in 1969 was priced at $20 to $26 per share in the market, earning $1.88 per share, and paying $1.38. To be sure, the company could also attempt to repurchase the 3.6 percent issue on about the same yield basis. In both cases some period of time would be needed to carry out the transaction without disturbing the market, and the consent of the public service commission would be needed. However, the penalty for failure to have included a call option in the 6 percent issue is clear. In the 1930s the issue might have been replaced by low-cost debt or even by another preferred issue if there had been a call provision.

Situations such as this raise the vital point that financial questions are not the only, nor even the dominant, concerns of a business. Whether calling the 6 percent issue in the 1930s (if that had been possible) might have triggered a rate-reduction case [4] is one question. We must remember that in the 1930s the total capital structure was much smaller. These were difficult times for utility management, particularly with the "tough" public service commission that Wisconsin had at that time. The costs of rate litigation in resisting a cut in rates plus the costs of getting the rates up later could easily exceed the "savings" we are considering. One such rate-reduction case in Wisconsin at this time cost the company $2 million and eight years to win before it was finally adjudicated.[5]

Whether rebuying this 6 percent preferred issue in the 1930s would have given rise to "savings," which labor leaders would immediately have sought to claim for wage increases, is hard to answer. It is a fact that at this time Wisconsin Electric Power Company had serious labor problems involving strikes with considerable violence.

### The Effective Use of Short-Term Funds

We have hinted that the use of short-term funds is a focal point of financial strategy. Call provisions in preferred stocks, options for prepayment of long-term debt, and the purchase of firm lines of credit for short-term commitments at the cost of a standby fee are all devices for maintaining flexibility. But one can buy more flexibility than is justified by the price, since each of these devices costs something in the interest rate.

The dramatic growth of term loans is one evidence of the philosophy of using short-term funds. When a company appears to have maximized its use of short-term funds, there is an exposure to the risk that there is

---

[4] That is, the rates charged consumers of electric power.

[5] *Wisconsin Telephone Co. vs. Public Service Commission,* 232 Wis. 274 (1939).

no margin of safety for more short-term funds. Term loans exist to meet this possibility by enabling the borrower to keep some unused short-term capacity without using long-term funds to do so.

### Staggered Maturities

We have reasoned that staggered maturities reaching into the future can present the ideal of flexibility. If it then becomes necessary to bridge temporary conditions prevailing in the longer-term markets, short-term funds can be used even at high cost. But this relatively high cost will be more than compensated for by the ability of the firm to choose the advantageous point for long-term commitments.

### Today's Gap between Form and Fact

It is a fact that currently many privately placed intermediate and long-term debt commitments are being "reset" every two years. In this resetting process the amount of the loan is frequently increased, repayment schedules are altered, interest rates revised, and protective provisions modified to reassure the lender but to avoid strangling the borrower. This pattern suggests a failure to anticipate the growth rate of the economy or the company or both. Such resetting also indicates the greater bargaining strength of lenders. Borrowers probably anticipate the growth that actually develops but reluctantly sign commitments that represent serious underestimates of their requirements because of their confidence that lenders will renegotiate the commitments. Lenders in this way feel they hold a veto power that can be more effective than efforts to control the borrower's conduct by mere protective provisions such as maintenance of required ratios, minimum working capital requirements, dividend limitations, and similar covenants.

## REFINANCING: REFUNDING

Having considered the various aspects of timing, we can focus on the problem of refunding a bond issue. As one basis for the decision whether to call a bond issue, we will want to know the "profitability" of doing so. We do not say that the decision to refund will rest solely on a simple computation of annual cash savings. This is so since if we refund now rather than later we may prevent ourselves from realizing a more profitable refunding later because there are considerable costs in each refunding that must be absorbed before we can speak of a gain from refunding. Thus refunding is essentially an investment decision and subject to analysis by capital budgeting techniques.[6]

Let us suppose that we have an issue of $1 million 6 percent 30-year bonds callable at 105 which have just ended their tenth year. There remain unamortized issuance expenses of $30,000 and an unamortized bond discount of $40,000 (the issue having been sold originally below par). The market interest rate may have fallen since the issue date or our credit may have improved so as to warrant a lower interest rate or both events

[6] E. A. Spiller, Jr., "Time-Adjusted Break-Even Rate for Refunding," *The Financial Executive*, 31 (July 1963), pp. 32–35.

may have occurred. We now can call[7] and refund this issue with 4 percent bonds which are salable at a discount of 2 percent and with issue costs of $40,000. For simplicity we may assume the new bonds would run for the unexpired life of the old issue: namely, 20 years.[8]

In a refunding operation both issues are usually outstanding for 30 to 60 days in order to facilitate the transaction. There may be a delay in registration of the new issue. This duplicate interest can be reduced by investing the proceeds of the new issue in Treasury bills or other short-term securities until the funds are needed to pay off the bonds of the old issue.

Both cash and noncash aspects are involved in the proposal, as the analysis in Table 22–5 indicates.

TABLE 22–5. Expenses for Tax Purposes and Cash Flow of Proposed Refunding

| | Expenses for tax purposes | Cash flow |
|---|---|---|
| Retirement of old bond principal | | ($1,000,000) |
| Call premium | $ 50,000 | ( 50,000) |
| Issue cost of new bonds | | ( 40,000) |
| Net overlapping interest (pre-tax)* | 2,500 | ( 2,500) |
| Unamortized bond discount, old bonds † | 40,000 | |
| Unamortized issue costs, old bonds † | 30,000 | |
| Totals | $122,500 | ($1,092,500) |
| Tax savings | 61,250 | 61,250 |
| After-tax expense | $ 61,250 | |
| After-tax cash outlay | | ($1,031,250) |
| Receipts of new issue | | 980,000 |
| Cash outlay to refund | | ($ 51,250) |

* Overlapping interest is computed as follows, assuming a 30-day overlap:

| | |
|---|---|
| Extra 30 days interest of old issue | $5000 |
| Offsetting 30-day Treasury bill income of 3 percent | 2500 |
| Pre-tax cost of extra 30 days' interest | 2500 |

† These items can be handled in any of three ways acceptable to accountants: (1) expensed during the year of refunding; (2) amortized over the life of the new bonds; (3) amortized over what would have been the remaining life of the old bonds. We have used the first method.

[7] Because of this disadvantage to the bondholder, callable bonds sell at a lower price (higher yield) than if the same bond were not callable. F. C. Jen and J. E. Wert, "The Effects of Call Risk on Corporate Bond Yields," *Journal of Finance*, 22 (December 1967), pp. 637–652, and G. Pye, "The Value of Call Deferment on a Bond: Some Empirical Results," *Journal of Finance*, 22 (December, 1967), pp. 623–636.

[8] If the maturity date of the new issue extends beyond the maturity of the old issue, we have the case of a strict refunding combined with additional financing for the period beyond the original maturity date. This might be handled by determining the rate for a refunding due at the original maturity date and attributing the difference between that rate and the rate for the extended maturity as the cost of the additional financing.

We can summarize this analysis by stating that for an investment of $51,250 (computed in Table 22–5) we can secure an annual cash gain of $10,750 (computed in Table 22–6) or a return of roughly 20 percent annually for 20 years. Put in this way we see that the problem is one in capital budgeting. If our weighted marginal cost of capital is below 20 percent, the refunding decision would be viewed favorably. If our weighted marginal cost of capital is above 20 percent, we may still accept the project because of its low risk.[9]

TABLE 22–6. Annual Cash Gains Resulting from Refunding

| | *Expenses for tax purposes* | *Cash flow* |
|---|---|---|
| *Old bonds* | | |
| Interest on retired bonds | $60,000 | $60,000 |
| Amortization of bond discount | 2,000 | |
| Amortization of issue cost | 1,500 | |
| Total expense | $63,500 | |
| Less income taxes | 31,750 | 31,750 |
| After-tax expense | $31,750 | |
| Annual cash outlay | | $29,250 |
| *New bonds* | | |
| Interest on new bonds | $40,000 | $40,000 |
| Amortization of bond discount | 1,000 | |
| Amortization of issue cost | 2,000 | |
| Total expenses | $43,000 | |
| Less income taxes | 21,500 | 21,500 |
| After-tax expense | $21,500 | |
| Annual cash outlay | | $18,500 |
| Annual gain in cash outlay $29,250 − $18,500 = $10,750 | | |

Essentially the same approach is applicable to calling preferred stock for replacement by a new issue of preferred except that preferred has no maturity such as a bond has.

[9] This matter was examined in Appendix N to Chapter 15.

Some analysts state that the refunding decision involves no risk because the annual gain of refunding is certain. Some even go so far as to argue that the savings of refunding should be discounted not at the weighted marginal cost of capital but at the *after-tax* rate of the new debt. This is wrong for several reasons: (1) the interest must be paid even if it is not earned and in that case there is no income tax advantage to having debt, but rather, there would be "reverse" leverage; (2) investment in refunding takes funds away from alternative investment opportunities which, after risk adjustments, may well earn more than the after-tax cost of new debt; and (3) future credit rating improvements of the firm or declines in the interest rate would offer new refunding chances, and many of the current costs of refunding would be duplicated with a resulting loss. Witness the mistiming by U.S. Steel in the refunding described in Chapter 20 at p. 527. Cf. J. F. Weston and E. F. Brigham, *Managerial Finance*, 4th ed. (New York: Holt, Rinehart and Winston, Inc., 1972) pp. 442 ff. and E. J. Elton and M. J. Gruber, "Dynamic Programming Applications in Finance," *Journal of Finance*, 26 (May 1971), pp. 473–506 at p. 483.

## RECAPITALIZATION

### Changes in the Capital Stock Account to Reflect the New Status of the Business

Over a period of time the affairs of a firm may prosper or decline to the point where the old capitalization is no longer appropriate even though no new securities have entered the capital structure.

In the case of declines, many companies in the Great Depression piled up sizable deficits over a number of years. The accrued deficits wiped out what earned surplus had existed. Dividends had ceased. The volume of business had been greatly reduced. To recognize the fact that the capital stock account no longer represented an existing investment value, the par value (or stated value in the case of no par shares) in many cases was reduced in an amount sufficient to eliminate the accrued deficit and perhaps by an additional amount to create a modest capital surplus.

In most states such a change requires the approval of two-thirds of the stockholders in the case of par or no par stock and an amendment of the corporate charter in the case of par stock. But two additional questions are involved. There may be loans or bond indentures outstanding which forbid the reduction of capital stock. Consent of the lender or bondholders is then required. The more important point concerns the resumption of dividend payments. Some reductions in capital stock are motivated by the desire to wipe out deficits in earned surplus and thus to accelerate the day when dividend payments can be resumed. The law protects creditors in existence at the time of the reduction if resumption of dividend payments impairs the payment of their claims.

### Stock Dividends and Stock Splits

The reverse situation exists when the business has grown and reached new plateaus, meanwhile developing a very large earned surplus through a policy of low dividend payout. To indicate that part of this swollen earned surplus is not a true surplus but is permanently committed to the business and to give creditors the assurance that this part will not be available for dividends, a large stock dividend may be declared by the board of directors.[10] This would increase the number of shares without changing the par or stated value of a share and effect the transfer of surplus to the capital account. If the stock dividend is less than 25 percent, New York Stock Exchange rules require that an additional amount of earned surplus equal to the difference between the market value of the dividend shares and the par or stated value of those shares be transferred to paid-in or capital surplus. A stock dividend over 25 percent is treated as a stock split[11] and only the amount of par or stated value is transferred to capital.

---

[10] Unlike the reduction in capital stock, which requires the consent of two-thirds of the stockholders, the increase in capital stock can be effected by sole action of the board of directors if there are sufficient authorized but unissued shares.

[11] The line of demarcation is drawn at 20 percent by the American Institute of Certified Public Accountants in *Restatement and Revision of Accounting Research Bulletins* (New York: American Institute of Certified Public Accountants, 1953) Chap. 7, Sec. B. There is further the practical matter that despite threats and cajoling, some stockholders never will turn in their shares in the case of a stock split and the transfer agent will sit holding the new shares for exchange.

In a true stock split the par or stated value of existing shares is reduced in the amount necessary to cover the new shares issued in the split, so that the dollar amount of the new total of shares is the same as before but the unit amount of par or stated value per share is reduced.[12] Because of the reduction in par or stated value per unit, a two-thirds stockholder consent is required.

In both the stock dividend and the stock split, the issuance of the new shares is not a taxable event as far as the stockholder is concerned on the theory that the ownership position of the stockholder is not changed. But a dividend in other than common stock on common stock is likely to be taxable as income to the stockholder because the ownership position of the stockholder has changed. Although a dividend of common stock on common stock is not a taxable event, the basis of the old share for income tax purposes is reduced by the percentage of the stock dividend with that percentage of the old basis assigned to the new shares.

There is a rare phenomenon called a reverse split or split-down in which the par of stated value of each share is increased and the number of shares is reduced to keep the total capital stock account the same.

In addition to the recognition of the larger commitment to capital stock that occurs in a stock dividend but not in a stock split, there is a second result in both cases—namely, the market price per share will be reduced in proportion to the increase in the number of shares. This is true if nothing else occurs at the same time such as a dividend increase.

The reduction in market value of a share pursuant to a stock dividend or stock split appears to have an additional purpose. Studies of the New York Stock Exchange have indicated that there is a tendency for the number of stockholders to increase after such a reduction in share

---

[12] The accounting entries are different for a stock split than for a stock dividend. If there is a split in which two shares of $50 par common stock are substituted for one share of $100 par common stock, neither the dollar amount of the capital stock account nor the dollar amount of the surplus account is changed. But in the case of a stock dividend of 10 percent, there will be a transfer from earned surplus of the "fair value" (market value if there is a market) of the number of shares of the dividend to the capital account. Thus the aggregate amount of par value or stated value (in the case of no par stock) of the shares will be transferred to the capital stock account, and the difference between fair value and par (or stated value) will be transferred to capital or paid-in surplus. The New York Stock Exchange has the additional requirement that the earnings of the period of the dividend must at least equal the fair value of the dividend.

Thus if a company has 10,000 shares of $1 par stock, earned surplus of $200,000, and declares a stock dividend of 10 percent and the market value of the stock is $10 per share at the time, ownership will appear as follows:

| Before stock dividend | | After stock dividend of 10 percent | |
|---|---|---|---|
| Common stock, 10,000 shares, $1 par | $ 10,000 | Common stock, 11,000 shares, $1 par | $ 11,000 |
| Earned surplus | 200,000 | Paid-in surplus | 9,000 |
| | | Earned surplus | 190,000 |

[A9903]

Under the laws of some states the board of directors may direct what the accounting entries shall be.

price. This may be because more people can deal in round lots of 100 shares as a result of the lower price per share. The adjustment of the shares may also have advertising value. Attempts to measure whether there has been a permanent value to stock dividends have been fraught with difficulty and are inconclusive.[13] The arguments advanced for the stock dividend have been that (1) cash is conserved, (2) stock ownership is broadened, (3) underwriting fees are avoided, and (4) the total market value of all shares is increased. However, the costs of administering a stock dividend are ten times as large as for a cash dividend.

### Recapitalization to Conserve Cash

One of the chief reasons advanced for stock dividends is the conservation of cash, yet there exists a more clear-cut way to achieve this objective. This can be done by creating two classes of common stock, one paying cash dividends and the other paying stock dividends. It may happen that this policy also serves the personal interests of stockholders. Thus the stockholders in high tax brackets seeking capital gains could buy the class that pays stock dividends. Those in lower brackets or seeking income could buy the class that pays cash dividends. Equity between the classes would be easily maintained by declaring the stock dividend that is indicated by dividing the cash dividend by the market price of the stock at the dividend declaration date. The market price of the two classes can be kept parallel by permitting the stockholders of the class that pays stock dividends to convert to the class that pays cash dividends. Citizens Utilities Company did what has just been described in 1955,[14] and the objectives sought by the program have been achieved.

---

[13] See, for example, J. C. Bothwell, Jr., "Periodic Stock Dividends," *Harvard Business Review*, 28 (January 1950), pp. 89–100; C. A. Barker, "Effective Stock Splits," *Harvard Business Review*, 34 (Jan.-Feb. 1956), pp. 101–106, and "Stock Splits in a Bull Market," *Harvard Business Review*, 35 (May-June 1957), pp. 72–79; and K. B. Johnson, "Stock Splits and Price Change," *Journal of Finance*, 21 (December 1966), pp. 675–686.

This book proceeds on the assumption of "rational" conduct by investors—that they are motivated by profits, analyze risks, and so on. However, it is unrealistic to ignore what many brokers report—namely, that many people dealing in securities in more modest amounts consider their activity as one way of spending money. Thus they enjoy appearing at a cocktail party and stating that they bought this or that security and otherwise conveying the impression of status. Such people have little interest in whether they make any profit. The funds they allot to this activity are considered spent in the same sense that they spend money for the pleasure of being seen at an expensive ball although they do not enjoy dancing. If this type of reaction accompanies a stock dividend, there may well be an increase in total market value of the corporation associated with stock dividends.

[14] Charles S. Lourimore, Jr., "Two Classes of Common Stock: One Gets Cash, One Stock Dividends; a Useful Tax Planning Tool," *Journal of Taxation*, 4 (May 1956), pp. 312–313.

This action was taken under a ruling by the Internal Revenue Service that the exchange of a share of one class of common stock for a share of either of the two new classes is a tax-free exchange and that the stock dividend on the class of stock paying only stock dividends is a tax-free stock dividend under the rule of *Eisner vs. Macomber*, 252 U.S. 189 (1920). In that case the Supreme Court stated, a stock dividend shows that the company's accumulated profits have been capitalized instead of being distributed to the stockholders, or retained as surplus available for distribution in money or in kind should opportunity offer. Far from being a realization of profits by the stockholder, it tends rather to postpone such realization, in that the fund represented by the new stock has been transferred from surplus to capital, and is no longer available for actual distribution. (footnote continued on next page)

### Recapitalization Incident to a Sale of Securities

Often the first public offering of a corporation involves a "sell down" by selling stockholders. Sometimes this is combined in the same offering with the procurement of additional funds for the corporation. Until the public offering such a corporation has been closely held and the matter of the value of a single share has not in itself been of concern. From the beginning days of the corporation when only a few thousand shares were outstanding, there has been no need for adjustment, particularly where growth has been achieved through the use of debt and retained earnings. Each share may now be worth thousands of dollars while it may have sold for only $100 at the time of incorporation.

At the time of going public the expected market value of the total equity of the corporation is determined by appropriate capitalization of the earnings at a rate developed by comparison with similar companies. The desired price range of a single share of the offering is then determined. This price of a single share is then divided into the total value of the equity to determine the number of new shares, and the ratio of the total number of new shares to the total number of old shares determines the size of the split, which often is 400 for 1 or even more.

At the same time the selling stockholders may decide not to sell straight equity and particularly not to part with the proportionate voting rights. In this event the recapitalization might involve two classes of common stock, one with voting rights and the other without voting rights. The selling stockholders then exchange their stock for the two new classes of common, and the shares of the nonvoting class are offered to the public while the selling stockholders retain the shares of the voting class.

The technique of issuing two classes of common stock for a young company at the time of going public is frequently used to reduce cash drains. In this case the class of stock publicly offered carries cash dividends while that retained by the principal owners carries no dividends but is convertible into the class that pays cash dividends according to a timetable. Thus in the public offering of AMT Corporation in 1961 conversion of the no-dividend stock followed this schedule: 1962, none; 1963, 20 percent; 1964, 25 percent; 1965, 33⅓ percent; 1966, 50 percent; 1967, all. These percentages apply to the percentage owned each year, and this amount is a

---

Not all stock dividends are tax free. Under the older rule the test of taxability was whether the stockholder's proportionate interest was changed by the stock dividend. If it was not, there was no taxable event. *Koshland vs. Helvering*, 298 U.S. 441 (1936). However, the amendments of the Internal Revenue Code have changed this rule, particularly to eliminate the "preferred stock bail out" (see p. 638). But the basic rule still survives that a common stock dividend payable in common stock is tax free. Likewise, Section 1036a of the Internal Revenue Code (1954) specifically provides that an exchange of one common stock for another common stock in the same corporation is tax free.

Despite the clarity of the law, no other corporation has been willing to follow the path of Citizens Utilities Company because the U. S. Treasury Department announced in 1956 that it was considering proposing a regulation that would make stock dividends issued under such a two-stock plan taxable. *Journal of Taxation*, 5 (September 1956), p. 178. The Treasury Department, however, has never issued such a regulation.

The evidence we have presented raises interesting questions concerning the timidity of financial managers.

constant 20 percent per year of a stockholder's original shares if conversion is maximized each year.

The large number of possible combinations of securities that can be created prior to the sell down is limited only by the variety of objectives the selling stockholders may seek to achieve and the creativity and competence of the corporate counsel they retain to carry out their objectives.

### Changes in the Capital Stock Account to Reflect New Status—Mergers

Another major category of recapitalization changes concerns companies involved in a merger or consolidation. The purposes to be achieved may vary considerably. In a very simple case the exchange might involve adjustments of the capitalization of either or both companies so that a simple one-for-one exchange of shares is the ultimate proposal submitted. A more complicated case might involve the acquisition of a small but publicly owned company with a record of rapid growth and high profitability by a larger concern with prospects of earnings drifting downward.[15] The larger company might offer attractive terms well above the market price, but the stockholders of the smaller company might want a priority position in the larger company's capital structure. Still greater complications such as avoiding (not evading) income taxes or security registration may dictate much more elaborate recapitalization changes such as the creation of holding companies and intermediate transactions.

### Recapitalization to Eliminate Accrued Preferred Dividends or to Change the Position of Preferred Stock

One interesting problem that occurred frequently as an aftermath of the Great Depression involved accrued preferred dividends. After a period of seriously reduced earnings or in a situation in which an undue amount of senior securities has been created in the capital structure or heavy sinking fund commitments have been made, a cumulative preferred stock on which dividends have not been paid for some time may have an arrearage of as much as $75 to $100 and more per $100 share. If there is an improvement in earnings, the corporation may be under pressure for dividends by common stockholders. But such dividends may well be many years away if the arrearage must first be discharged in cash.[16]

This problem raises fundamental questions concerning the nature of the rights of preferred stock. There is no question but that a bankruptcy court can make alterations in the rights of bondholders and stockholders, but in the case of arrearages on preferred stock there is no basis for a bankruptcy court to intervene. Short of bankruptcy, the contract specifying the rights of stockholders cannot be constitutionally altered without the consent of each stockholder.[17] This rule of law [18] threatened to stymie cor-

---

[15] For example, the offer by Bucyrus-Erie Company for all the convertible debentures and a large block of common stock of Racine Hydraulics & Machinery, Inc. was $1310 for each $1000 bond and $26 for each share, which had a market price then of $20. *Wall Street Journal*, March 8, 1967, p. 25.

[16] For full presentation of such facts see the case of Bradley Knitting Company in Erwin E. Nemmers, *Cases in Finance* (Boston: Allyn & Bacon, Inc., 1964), pp. 374–386.

[17] Only one state (Wisconsin) holds to the contrary. See Erwin E. Nemmers, "Accrued Preferred Dividends," *Wisconsin Law Review*, May 1943, pp. 417–424, for the

porate finance until the loophole was found. Accrued preferred dividends can be altered as part of the merger process. The stockholder must have always been aware of the possibility of merger, which requires only two-thirds vote of each class of stock. Thus many mergers have been brought about to lift the burden of the preferred arrearages. However, most states grant dissenters' rights in mergers. This is the right of each dissenter to a merger to be paid in cash for the appraised value of the security. Many mergers have been aborted because of the inability of companies—even large and well-known ones—to come up with the cash to meet this requirement.

Since the merger route requires cash, the corporation with accrued preferred arrearages is well advised to attempt a straightforward but tempting proposal to induce the consent and surrender of the preferred stockholders. There are myriad possibilities.

While we have presented the discussion in terms of preferred dividend arrearages, all of the principles apply to efforts to change the position of the preferred stock itself whether there are arrearages or not.

## REPURCHASE BY A CORPORATION OF ITS OWN SHARES

The difficult but widespread problem of the repurchase by a corporation of its own shares is classified under recapitalization because this activity has many of the same consequences.[19] For example, the cushion of the creditors is seriously reduced.

One reason the problem of repurchase is difficult is that the law on the subject is complicated [20] and has led to many recent state statutes attempting to unravel the difficulties.[21] In a general way the law of most states in this area can be summarized as follows:

1. In no case may repurchase jeopardize the corporation's ability to pay debts as they mature.
2. There are many repurchases that are exempt from additional restrictions: repurchase of shares sold to employees under a repurchase plan, preferred stock redemption programs, repurchase to fulfill the rights of dissenting stockholders in mergers or other activities requiring stockholder approval.

---

curious history of how Wisconsin arrived at this unique conclusion by a 4 to 3 vote of its supreme court.

[18] The rule has a sound basis. How would a court decide whether the arrearage had been created in bad faith if there were a rule permitting adjustment of arrearages?

[19] C. D. Ellis, "Repurchase Stock to Revitalize Equity," *Harvard Business Review*, 43 (July 1965), pp. 119–128; and L. A. Guthart, "More Companies Are Buying Back Their Stock," *Harvard Business Review*, 43 (March 1965), pp. 40–53.

[20] For a full discussion of the difficulties, see Erwin E. Nemmers, "The Power of a Corporation to Purchase Its Own Stock," *Wisconsin Law Review*, March 1942, pp. 161–197.

[21] See Erwin E. Nemmers, "The Treasury Stock Sections of the [new] Wisconsin Business Corporation Law," *Wisconsin Law Review*, May 1953, pp. 480–490. Repurchased shares are called treasury shares because they may be reissued. The term "treasury shares" is sometimes misused to describe authorized but unissued shares.

3. Also exempt from additional restriction is repurchase if the corporate charter contains specific authority on the matter or if two-thirds of the stockholders, each class considered separately, consent to the repurchase.
4. In all other cases repurchase is limited to the amount of earned surplus that the company has, and each repurchase freezes earned surplus, dollar for dollar, until the shares are resold.

The reasons for the legal restrictions on repurchase are several: (1) repurchase represents a reduction in capital stock and of the protective cushion, thus posing a threat to creditors (and to preferred stock if the repurchase is of common), (2) repurchase can be used as a preferential liquidation system through paying the withdrawing shareholder more than is due him (the question is, what repurchase price is permissible?), and (3) repurchase in the case of a closely held company with no market price to serve as a guide raises the opposite question—whether the withdrawing stockholder has been defrauded.

The subtlety of this subject is recognized by the Internal Revenue Service, which originally took the position that no gain or loss would be recognized for the corporation in any repurchase transactions whether or not any resale of these shares by the corporation occurred.[22] This has been changed to a rule that whether gain or loss to the corporation will be recognized is dependent on an individual analysis of the "real nature of each transaction."[23] No guidelines for such analysis are stated.

In the case of the stockholder who sells his shares back to the corporation, there is a capital gain (at lower tax rates than ordinary income). Such a selling stockholder takes out his share of surplus at advantageous rates compared to the receipt of dividends.[24] But, proportionate repurchase of shares from all stockholders would clearly be recognized as, in effect, a dividend, and would be taxable as ordinary income.

If a corporation develops excess cash and has no senior securities and lacks normal earnings opportunities, it is a prime candidate to repurchase its shares. To continue the payment of dividends will merely increase income taxes for its stockholders. The corporation cannot develop the liquidating dividend exemption from income taxes for its stockholders as long as earned surplus is available. Hence repurchase is indicated. Some corporations feel that a formal call for tenders by stockholders is in order, or at least notice to all stockholders that the corporation is a buyer.

The question of repurchase also arises for the corporation with only normal earnings opportunities. In this case the corporation may find the price of its own stock such that it is a better "investment" than any other

---

[22] Income Tax Regulations 74 (1928), article 66.

[23] Income Tax Regulations 111 (1943), sec. 29.22(a), 15.

[24] Harold Bierman and Richard West have argued that the only rational basis for repurchase of shares is the tax advantage for the stockholders that the distribution of surplus via repurchase has over distribution via dividends. Assuming a tax rate of 70 percent on ordinary income and a capital gains tax rate of 25 percent, they demonstrate that with the interest rate at 4 percent an infinite flow of repurchases rather than dividends would triple the value of a firm. "The Acquisition of Common Stock by the Corporate Issuer," *Journal of Finance*, 21 (December 1966), pp. 687–696.

proposal available. Again repurchase is indicated. One method of testing a proposed repurchase is to develop a *pro forma* earnings per share after repurchase for comparison with current earnings per share.

Another reason for share repurchase is a form of leverage. When shares are repurchased the number of outstanding shares is reduced and the market value of each share may well increase. This situation is in contrast to the use of the same amount of funds by the corporation to pay a dividend. After any dividend is paid the number of shares has not been reduced. Thus the "leverage" we are describing is in terms of the position of the stockholder who does not sell.

Other companies have used repurchase to reduce stockholder expenses in the case of small holdings which cost more to service than the dividends they receive.[25]

Unless the company cancels the repurchased stock, its problems have only begun.[26] Upon resale the SEC claims the same jurisdiction as over any issue. The law is in conflict as to whether preemptive rights are applicable to the resale of repurchased shares. There is no clear legal or accounting authority as to whether any gain or loss on the resale of the shares is to appear in earned or capital surplus,[27] and the Internal Revenue Service will examine taxability in the light of "the real nature" of the transaction.

### Disclosure of Repurchase by Corporation When Control Is at Issue

The Williams Act of 1968 authorized the SEC to make rules requiring the disclosure of pertinent information in connection with the repurchase by a corporation of its outstanding equity securities when it is involved in a battle for control of the corporation.

## SUMMARY

Timing in finance involves having the company's affairs in optimum condition when the market is in optimum condition for procurement of funds. Timing is affected by the industry in which the company functions and whether it leads, coincides with, or lags the general business cycle. Timing further involves the type of security (debt or equity, for example) being offered. Optimum conditions for debt financing seldom coincide with optimum conditions for equity financing and either or both seldom coincide with optimum conditions in the economy as a whole.

---

[25] The classic case is United Cigar-Whelan Stores Corporation, which in 1954 offered to buy all holdings of ten shares or less at $4 per share. The corporation had 9000 stockholders but 2500 had ten shares or less for an aggregate of 9600 shares of a total of more than 2 million shares outstanding.

[26] The repurchased shares are authorized and issued but not outstanding. They may become "not issued" if the board of directors cancels them.

[27] Conservative practice might be to report gains in capital surplus but charge losses to earned surplus.

The term structure of interest rates refers to the increase or decrease in the interest rate for a given debtor at any point in time as the maturity of the debt is extended. In depression low short-term rates taper to higher rates as maturity is increased.

The financial manager's rules must include (1) maintenance of flexibility, (2) effective use of short-term funds to achieve long-term financing goals and timing, and (3) maintenance of staggered maturities.

Refinancing involves the sale of new securities to replace existing securities. One form of refinancing is refunding a bond issue either at maturity or prematurely. In determining whether to refund prematurely the after-tax earning on the cash outlay for (or investment in) refunding costs is compared with discounted future savings due to the lower interest rate of the new issue in order to establish a rate of return on the cash outlay.

Recapitalization involves changing the form and/or the amount of outstanding securities in a voluntary exchange or with stockholder consent or unilaterally by action of the board of directors. Recapitalization may take many forms: (1) reduction of the capital stock account by a reduction of par or stated value, (2) increase in the capital stock account through a stock dividend, (3) change in the number of shares without a change in the amount of capital by a stock split, (4) reclassification of stock accounts for merger or other purposes, and (5) elimination of accrued preferred stock dividends.

Repurchase of its own shares by a corporation is frequent practice today. The reasons usually advanced for repurchase are: (1) repurchase offers the best investment opportunity available to corporations with limited investment opportunities; (2) it makes possible the achievement of a leverage effect for remaining stockholders that cannot be otherwise achieved; (3) there are significant tax advantages to stockholders by distributing corporate assets in this way rather than as dividends.

Share repurchase is hedged about by legal rules designed to avoid corporate illiquidity after the purchase and to prevent reduction of the equity cushion of creditors (through limiting repurchase to the amount of earned surplus). There are some exceptions to the latter of these two rules in the case of employee stock repurchase agreements, preferred stock redemption provisions, elimination of fractional shares, compromise of corporate debts, and the statutory rights of dissenters from some corporate actions such as merger.

The Williams Act of 1968 requires disclosure of repurchases when there is a battle for control of a corporation.

**Study Questions**

1. With respect to timing in the field of finance, do you think it is more important that the firm be in optimum condition or that the market be in optimum condition when the time comes for new financing for the firm?

2. If a smaller company has never resorted to long-term borrowing, should it make the effort to fund as soon as possible at current market rates, wait for what is thought to be a low point in interest rates in the current short-run business cycle, or depend on what terms it can get for funding at the time it needs funds?

3. The local broker says that he likes to see stocks priced in the range of $10 to $20 a share because then the average man can buy 100 shares without as much strain on the family budget as would be required if the price per share were higher. Likewise, the commission rate is less for a round lot than for an odd lot. The broker thinks that companies should split their stock to keep the price in this range and take advantage of the strong preference by the average man for 100 shares. Do you agree?

4. A well-known text states, "It should be noted that if our objective is to lower the market price of the stock, we could probably achieve the same result at a lower cost through a stock split [rather than through a stock dividend]." Do you agree?

5. The argument is advanced that as long as a company has cash it should repurchase its common stock whenever the market price falls below book value. Do you agree?

6. A stockholder proposes that the company reduce its cash dividends and use that amount to repurchase its own stock, thus cutting the tax bill for each stockholder. Do you agree?

7. If you were framing the provisions of a preferred stock issue would you specify that sinking fund purchases of the stock should take precedence over preferred dividends or vice versa? Would the company's position on this matter be different from that of the investor?

8. The argument is advanced that any company will do better in the market for funds by focusing its efforts on one segment of the capital market rather than by compromising in an attempt to appeal to everyone. Thus the company might pursue a policy of no cash dividends, as has Litton Industries, and appeal to those who seek capital gains. Is this a sound policy?

9. Would you recommend that a company try to tailor the type of security it offers in order to capitalize on the type that currently has the strongest market appeal? To be specific, in 1967 convertible subordinated debentures enjoyed great favor in the market. Would you favor refunding your company's capital requirements accordingly if the refunding were profitable by the usual computations?

### Problems

**1.** The Westfall Manufacturing Company has just completed its fourth year of producing electronic gear. The company rents its plant and office space and uses many standard parts with considerable subcontracting of other components. The essence of the business is design engineering and the assembling and testing of the final products, which are sold to a diversified group of larger companies for use in machinery of many types. Tables 22–7 and 22–8 present the firm's comparative balance sheets for 1972 and 1973 and its income statement for 1973.

TABLE 22–7. Westfall Manufacturing Company
Comparative Balance Sheets

| | *Dec. 31, 1972* | *Dec. 31, 1973* | | *Dec. 31, 1972* | *Dec. 31, 1973* |
|---|---|---|---|---|---|
| Assets | | | Liabilities and Net Worth | | |
| Cash | $ 75,273 | $ 20,852 | Notes payable | $131,095 | $209,447 |
| Receivables | 339,807* | 435,246† | Accounts payable | 65,681 | 99,152 |
| Inventories | 189,404 | 358,690 | Accruals | 75,438 | 84,330 |
| Prepaid | 2,176 | 4,013 | Income taxes | 96,000 | 52,876 |
| Total current assets | $606,660 | $818,801 | Total current liabilities | $368,214 | $445,805 |
| | | | Capital stock, 1,000 shares, $100 par | 100,000 | 100,000 |
| Other assets | 14,213 | 31,234 | | | |
| Net fixed assets | 34,871 | 55,786 | Retained earnings | 187,530 | 360,016 |
| | | | Net worth | $287,530 | $460,016 |
| Total assets | $655,744 | $905,821 | Total liabilities and net worth | $655,744 | $905,821 |

* $260,500 pledged to secure loan.
† $255,821 pledged to secure loan.

[A9966]

TABLE 22–8. Westfall Manufacturing Company
Income Statement
Year Ended December 31, 1973

| | |
|---|---|
| Sales | $2,304,957 |
| Cost of goods | 1,564,846 |
| Gross profit | $ 740,111 |
| Expenses | 424,290 |
| Operating profit | $ 315,821 |
| Other income | 13,852 |
| Net profit before taxes | $ 329,673 |
| Income taxes | 167,187 |
| Net profit | $ 162,486 |

[A9967]

The company is about to apply to insurance companies and banks for a 10-year loan.[28]

a. As the financial manager of Westfall what provisions do you expect will be required in the loan agreement?

b. Will the loan be secured by a mortgage?

c. What size loan do you believe you can obtain?

d. What is the weakest aspect of this company?

e. The company states that up to now its philosophy has been to "keep its money in a satchel." Do you agree with this policy?

2. What will be the cash outlay to refund an issue of $3 million 5 percent 30-year bonds callable at $105 that have an unamortized bond discount of $60,000 and unamortized expenses of $90,000 after five years of the life of the bonds if we can replace the $3 million issue with 4 percent 25-year bonds sold at par with issue costs of $50,000, callable at $104? You may further assume an overlapping net interest cost of $5000 for 30 days. Assuming the tax rate is 50 percent, what will be the annual cash saving?

3. Compute the rate of return and the profitability index (the ratio of the present value of the annual cash gain to the present value of the cash outlay) for the refunding proposal in problem 2. Assume the company's cost of capital is 10 percent.

4. What would be the break-even interest rate on the new issue in the case presented in problems 2 and 3? *Hint:* If $x$ is the break-even *amount* of interest, then the annual cash outlay on the new bonds is that amount of interest less the tax on that interest plus the amortization of issue cost:

$$x - 0.5(x + 2{,}000), \quad \text{or} \quad 0.5x - 1{,}000$$

and the annual cash gain of the new issue is equal to the annual cash outlay of the old bonds less the annual cash outlay on the new issue (defined above):

$$72{,}000 - (0.5x - 1{,}000), \quad \text{or} \quad 73{,}000 - 0.5x$$

Furthermore, the break-even point is where the profitability index equals 1.0.

5. A closely held company is preparing to go public and will recapitalize in an effort to offer shares in the $20 to $30 price range. The firm's earnings in the most recent three years have been $400,000, $450,000, and $500,000. The underwriters believe the stock can be sold at a price-earnings ratio of 20 times the average of the most recent three-years' earnings. There are now 1000 shares outstanding. What stock split is indicated?

---

[28] Representative term loan provisions can be studied in Erwin E. Nemmers, *Cases in Finance* (Boston: Allyn & Bacon, Inc., 1964), pp. 118–120, where a typical loan agreement is set out.

6. The Astro Company is engaged in manufacturing. Its balance sheet at the end of its third year appears in Table 22–9.

TABLE 22–9. Astro Company
Balance Sheet, December 31, 1973

| Assets | | Liabilities | |
|---|---|---|---|
| Cash | $ 62,453 | Notes to bank | $ 36,227 |
| Receivables | 400,458 | Short-term part of SBA loan | 60,000 |
| Bad-debt reserve | (14,230) | Payables | 141,440 |
| Inventory | 167,553 | Accruals | 68,751 |
| Prepaid | 3,712 | Income taxes | 9,444 |
| Total current assets | $619,946 | Total current liabilities | $315,862 |
| Deposits | 23,295 | SBA loan less current | 145,000 |
| Machinery | 36,769 | Preferred stock, 1390 shares, | |
| Leaseholds | 7,652 | $100 par, $5 dividend | 139,000 |
| Depreciation and | | Common stock, 11,560 shares, | |
| amortization | (14,001) | no par, $1 stated value | 11,560 |
| Net fixed assets | $ 30,420 | Earned surplus | 62,239 |
| | | Net worth | $212,799 |
| Total assets | $673,661 | Total liabilities and net worth | $673,661 |

The company makes electric controls, uses leased space to reduce financial requirements, and subcontracts considerable work in order to conserve cash.

In the early months of 1974 the four top managers, who each own 1500 shares of the common stock, fall into sharp and irreconcilable dispute on policy questions. The four split into two camps of two each. A proxy war ensues. The two winning managers remove the other two and an audit is performed as of the day of the changeover. During the period of the dispute the affairs of Astro disintegrated badly, as is indicated in the comparative income statements given in Table 22–10. There is no appreciable seasonal element in the business.

TABLE 22–10. Astro Company
Comparative Profit and Loss Statements

| | *Year ended Dec. 31, 1973* | *Percent* | *Jan. 1 to May 12, 1974* | *Percent* |
|---|---|---|---|---|
| Gross sales | $2,089,414 | 100 | $693,898 | 100 |
| Freight and commissions | 214,937 | 10 | 81,206 | 12 |
| Net sales | $1,874,477 | 90 | $612,692 | 88 |
| Cost of sales | 1,504,859 | 72 | 517,368 | 74 |
| Gross profit | $ 369,618 | 18 | $ 95,324 | 14 |
| Operating expenses | 295,705 | 14 | 88,794 | 13 |
| Operating profits | $ 73,913 | 4 | $ 6,530 | 1 |
| Other income | 1,018 | 0 | 22 | 0 |
| Profit before tax | $ 74,931 | 4 | $ 6,552 | 1 |
| Income taxes | 37,714 | 1.8 | 4,300 | 0.7 |
| Net profit | $ 37,217 | 1.8 | $ 2,252 | 0.3 |

At the same time that profitability slipped during the dispute, and the condition of the balance sheet deteriorated, as Table 22–11 indicates.

TABLE 22–11. Astro Company
Balance Sheet, May 12, 1974

| Assets | | Liabilities | |
|---|---|---|---|
| Cash | $ 50,127 | Notes to bank | $ 32,868 |
| Receivables | 455,604 | Short-term part of SBA loan | 185,000 |
| Bad-debt reserve | (16,648) | Payables | 213,464 |
| Inventory | 171,425 | Accruals | 66,467 |
| Prepaid expenses | 2,518 | Income taxes | 1,031 |
| Total current assets | $663,026 | Total current liabilities | $498,830 |
| Deposits | 21,071 | Preferred stock, 1,390 shares, $100 par, $5 dividend | 139,000 |
| Machinery | 35,961 | | |
| Leaseholds | 8,158 | Common stock, 11,560 shares, no par, $1 stated value | 11,560 |
| Depreciation and amortization | (14,335) | Earned surplus | 64,491 |
| Net fixed assets | $ 29,784 | Net worth | $215,051 |
| Total assets | $713,881 | Total liabilities and net worth | $713,881 |

The two remaining managers decide the company should buy out the stock of the two who were removed. They believe it best that the corporation repurchase these shares in order that none of the other stockholders become disturbed. Repurchase will have the effect of increasing each stockholder's share of the business, since except for the four managers who owned 6000 shares, the stock of the corporation had originally been sold as a package of one share of preferred with four shares of common. If any one stockholder or group of stockholders acquired the shares, the other stockholders would be unhappy with the shift in position of the buying stockholders.

Preferred stock dividends are in arrears $3.75 per share.

a. Do you believe it is legally possible for Astro to repurchase these shares?

b. Is it true that upon repurchase each stockholder's share of the business will be increased in proportion to his holdings before the repurchase?

c. What would be a fair price (or price range) for the repurchase of these shares?

7. The Hartzfeld Corporation is considering the use of a stock split or a stock dividend to reduce the price of its stock, which is currently trading at $400 per share. The company's balance sheet appears in Table 22–12.

TABLE 22–12. Hartzfeld Corporation
Balance Sheet, December 31, 1973

| | | | |
|---|---|---|---|
| Cash | $110,000 | Current liabilities | $100,000 |
| Receivables | 140,000 | Long-term debt | 500,000 |
| Inventory | 400,000 | Preferred stock, $100 par, 1000 shares issued | 100,000 |
| Fixed assets, net | 300,000 | Common stock, $100 par, 1000 shares issued | 100,000 |
| | | Paid-in surplus | 50,000 |
| | | Retained earnings | 100,000 |
| Total assets | $950,000 | Total liabilities and net worth | $950,000 |

What is involved if the company wants to bring the market price of the shares down to $25 by either a stock dividend or a stock split?

### Selected References

Barker, C. A., "Effective Stock Splits," *Harvard Business Review,* 32 (January–February 1956), pp. 101–106.

———, "Stock Splits in a Bull Market," *Harvard Business Review,* 35 (May–June 1957), pp. 72–79.

Beranek, W., *Common Stock Financing, Book Values and Stock Dividends: The Theory and the Evidence.* Madison, Wisc.: University of Wisconsin School of Commerce, 1961.

Bierman, H., and R. West, "The Acquisition of Common Stock by the Corporate Issuer," *Journal of Finance,* 21 (December 1966), pp. 687–696.

Bothwell, J. C., Jr., "Period Stock Dividends," *Harvard Business Review,* 28 (January 1950), pp. 89–100.

Bowlin, O. D., "The Refunding Decision: Another Special Case of Capital Budgeting," *Journal of Finance,* 21 (March 1966), pp. 55–68.

Brigham, E. F., "The Profitability of a Firm's Purchase of Its Own Common Stock," *California Management Review,* 7 (Winter 1964), pp. 69–76.

Ellis, C. D., "Repurchase Stock to Revitalize Equity," *Harvard Business Review,* 43 (July–August 1965), pp. 119–128.

Elton, E. J., and M. J. Gruber, "The Effect of Share Repurchases on the Value of the Firm," *Journal of Finance,* 23 (March 1968), pp. 135–150.

Fergusson, D. A., "Preferred Stock Valuation in Recapitalizations," *Journal of Finance,* 13 (March 1958), pp. 48–69.

Guthart, L. A., "More Companies Are Buying Back Their Stock," *Harvard Business Review,* 43 (March–April 1965), pp. 40–53.

Hausman, W. H., R. R. West, and J. A. Largay, "Stock Splits, Price Changes and Trading Profits, A Synthesis," *The Journal of Business,* 44 (January 1971), pp. 69–77.

Homer, S., *A History of Interest Rates.* New Brunswick, N. J.: Rutgers University Press, 1963.

Irving Trust Company, *The Calculation of Savings in Bond Refunding.* New York: Irving Trust Company, 1962.

Johnson, K. B., "Stock Splits and Price Change," *Journal of Finance,* 21 (December 1966), pp. 675–686.

Merrill, E. S., "A Guide to Bond Refunding, "*Public Utilities Fortnightly,* 70 (September 27, 1962), pp. 385–394.

Nemmers, E. E., "Accrued Preferred Dividends," *1943 Wisconsin Law Review* (May 1943), pp. 417–424.

———, "The Power of a Corporation to Purchase Its Own Stock," *1942 Wisconsin Law Review* (March 1942), pp. 161–197.

Spiller, E. A., Jr., "Time-Adjusted Break-even Rate for Refunding," *Financial Executive,* 31 (July 1963), pp. 32–35.

Sussman, M. R., *The Stock Dividend.* Ann Arbor, Mich.: University of Michigan Press, 1962.

Young, A., and W. Marshall, "Controlling Shareholder Servicing Costs," *Harvard Business Review,* 49 (January–February 1971), pp. 71–78.

# PART SEVEN

# Management Problems in Long-Term Financing

*

# 23

# External Growth Through Acquisitions: The Merger and the Holding Company

No subject in American finance is more controversial than that of mergers. Even textbooks make many assertions concerning mergers that cannot be documented, and in the world of finance discussions of the subject often proceed as if the antitrust laws did not exist or were innocuous.

Growth is essential to the health of a firm because it creates the opportunities that draw and challenge superior management, and makes possible the opportunities for promotion that are necessary to retain that management.

A firm can grow horizontally by enlarging its market share in the industry and by moving into related product lines and industries. A firm can also grow vertically by invading the industries that supply it and by invading the industries that supply the ultimate consumer if the firm does not presently serve them. It is also possible for a firm to grow by moving into products or processes that are unrelated to its industry or even to its industry classification, for example, a consumer goods company merging with a capital goods firm. Such mergers are called *conglomerate mergers.*

There are three formal devices for carrying out acquisitions: (1) *merger,* which involves the combining of two or more companies so that only one of the original companies survives, with the other being dissolved, (2) *consolidation,* in which a newly formed company takes over two or more companies which are then dissolved, and (3) the *holding company,* which acquires the stock of the companies being united, so that all the corporate entities continue to survive. There is a fourth category which might be recognized, namely, *affiliation,* in which firms join together to an extent by contractural arrangements, by stockholders common to the firms, by interlocking directorates, or by other ways.

## ACCOUNTING RULES

Two different accounting methods are practiced in such combinations. The first is the *purchase* or "scientific" method, which reflects the actual terms of the acquisition. Thus if the surviving company pays more than book value for the acquired company, this increment is recognized as goodwill on the asset side of the balance sheet and as acquisition surplus on the liability-ownership side by the acquiring company. This goodwill [1] must be written off over a period of not more than 40 years and not directly against the surplus account but through the income statement.

Another alternative is that the acquired assets be appraised at more than their book value in the hands of the acquired company. Then the increase in value of these assets replaces what would have been goodwill on the books of the acquiring company. If this increase in asset values is real, the Internal Revenue Service will allow the acquiring company to use these values for depreciation.

The other method, the so-called *pooling of interests,* combines the assets and liabilities of the separate balance sheets, and any differences between the terms of the merger and book values of net worth are directly accounted for in the capital surplus of the combined companies.[2]

---

[1] The handling of goodwill arising from mergers is covered by Accounting Principles Board, Opinion 17 (1970).

[2] Under the purchase method of accounting the earned surplus of the acquired company is transferred to capital surplus, but under the pooling of interests method the earned surplus of the acquired company is added to the earned surplus of the acquiring company.

Accounting Principles Board, Opinion 16 (1970) states the guidelines for corporate merger accounting. Pooling of interest is permitted only when:

1. The acquired firm's stockholders continue as owners in the acquiring firm.
2. Each firm was autonomous for two years prior to the plan to combine. Ownership of more than 10 percent of either firm's stock by the other shows lack of independence.
3. The accounting basis for assets of the acquired company is continued.
4. A single transaction is involved (no contingent payouts).
5. No significant part of the two companies' assets is disposed of within two years after merger.
6. The acquiring firm issues only common stock of its voting class of common for substantially all (at least 90 percent) of the voting common of the acquired company.

Thus the use of preferred stock requires the purchase method of accounting.

## INTERNAL GROWTH VERSUS EXTERNAL GROWTH

As Table 15–2 indicates, the expansion of American firms has been largely carried out by funds internally procured (depreciation and retained earnings). Guthmann and Dougall argue as follows:

> These general financial principles [to be recited in next sentence] are best observed where the business is able to grow from earnings, which explains why managements of American business corporations have depended so heavily upon earnings as a source of funds. The corporation expanding with such funds enjoys the simplest of capital structures, avoids both interest and preferred dividends as financial charges, reduces to a minimum claims that might weaken working capital position, has no problem of sharing voting control with outsiders, and enjoys a maximum of financial strength to meet the vicissitudes of the business cycle.[3]

If these financial principles are sound, then it follows that most growth will be internal. Mergers would be limited to cases where they can be carried out with no complication of capital structure, no increase in fixed charges, no weakening of working capital position, and no parting with voting control. There would still be room for some mergers, for example, by purchase for cash.

External growth is not a phenomenon of the post-World War II era. Periods of prosperity in the past have been times of much external growth. Thus in the 1920s the notorious amalgamation of electric and gas companies into public utility holding company empires reflected the external growth concept. There is no question but that the failure rate of companies involved in extensive external growth efforts greatly exceeds that of companies emphasizing internal growth. It must be conceded, further, that it is difficult to carry on any significant external growth without violating the financial principles succinctly summarized by Guthmann and Dougall.

In the conflict between internal and external growth, the advocates of external growth have crystallized the following arguments for merger:

1. *Speed.* The merger device increases the speed of growth. By a merger a company can acquire a going concern more quickly than it can put one together internally. It takes time to organize a production process. But two points must be remembered: the seller who put the operation together knows its value and by increasing his selling price will deprive the buyer of a good part of the advantage of entering the field by purchase as against putting together his own operation. Second, if the buyer is purchasing a "mature" operation, he has simply acquired a new problem of how to make it grow, and if he is acquiring a smaller, more rapidly growing operation that is still in its development stage, he assumes higher risks and still has the problem of continuing the development. In this case, price is the issue, not speed.

---

[3] H. G. Guthmann and H. E. Dougall, *Corporate Financial Policy*, 4th ed. (Englewood Cilffs, N. J.: Prentice-Hall, Inc., 1962), p. 516.

2. *Cost or price.* Is it cheaper to acquire than to grow internally? That is *the* question and it is a matter of what price the seller seeks. In particular cases a low-priced seller can be found. However, one factor must be remembered. The time to buy a business is early in the upswing of the business cycle. No doubt many acquisitions in the period immediately following World War II have worked out advantageously to the buyer. But what of acquisitions made late in the upswing and at the peak or plateau of the cycle? Can we postulate that there will be no major downturn in the next decade?

3. *Offsetting cyclical or seasonal instability.* Many companies are acutely aware of the cyclical or seasonal weaknesses of their own operations. This leads them to seek "mates" with compensating instability: match your peak with the valley of the new business, and vice versa. Offsetting seasonals is the easier objective to achieve. It is more difficult to offset cyclicals because the cycle of each business and particularly the relation of the cycles to each other are much less regular than are seasonal patterns. And in a major downturn, *all* the cycles of various businesses drop, though in differing degrees.

4. *Economies of diversification and large-scale operation.* When this argument is advanced we are no longer pursuing the question of internal versus external growth but are examining the merits of diversification and large-scale operations, both of which can be achieved by internal or external growth.

5. *Tax advantages.* A 1951 study by Butters, Lintner, and Cary found that tax considerations of sellers were a major factor favoring the sale of one-fourth of the companies and one-fourth of the assets of all selling companies with assets over $1 million.[4] The main tax interest of stockholders of the selling corporation is to liquidate the accrued earnings of the selling corporation at capital gains tax rates rather than as ordinary income. Taxes are less frequently a motive for the buyer, although we are all aware of the notorious cases in which a company with large and recently accrued losses is picked up in order to take advantage of the loss carry-forward provisions of the income tax law. Recently the tax laws on the use of this device have been tightened considerably. Even in this case the seller knows what he has and bargains a piece of it away from the buyer.

Thus it appears that arguments for external growth rather than internal growth are reduced to the single matter of price—as is usually the case in economic questions. We submit that the *true* price is not the *nominal* price of the transaction but rather that price *plus* the cost to the acquiring company of deviating from the "general financial principles" summarized by Guthmann and Dougall. Many of today's mergers involve such deviations, and the cost of these deviations is difficult to estimate.

---

[4] J. K. Butters, J. Lintner, and W. L. Cary, *Effects of Taxation: Corporate Mergers* (Boston: Harvard Graduate School of Business Administration, 1951). This study is based on 1990 mergers and consolidations between 1940 and 1947. More recently, in a study of 72 mergers using convertible preferred stock from 1962 through 1967, tax advantages were a consideration in 71 percent of the mergers. C. R. Sprecher, "A Note in Financing Mergers with Convertible Preferred Stock," *Journal of Finance*, 26 (June 1971), pp. 683–685.

### Example of Anti-trust Aspects

At the beginning of this chapter we pointed out that assertions are made concerning mergers that cannot be documented and that discussions of the subject sometimes proceed with no mention of the antitrust laws. We cite one such instance in order to serve as a springboard for a brief consideration of antitrust aspects of merger. Professors Weston and Brigham have stated:

> Market control may be obtained more rapidly and with less risk through mergers than by internal expansion. The merger of two large firms may result in market dominance by the combined firms. Coordinated price and output policies that might be illegal in separate firms may be achieved legally by a single, consolidated enterprise.[5]

Much evidence can be adduced that this statement is quite misleading. On March 16, 1967, the Federal Trade Commission in a consent order announced that W. R. Grace & Company was barred from acquiring any more chocolate and cocoa products firms for ten years without prior Commission approval. On October 20, 1964, Grace, with sales in excess of $1 billion, had acquired virtually all of the assets of the relatively small Ambrosia Chocolate Company for 116,000 shares of Grace common stock with a market value of $6.7 million. Grace is widely diversified in transportation, manufacturing, agriculture, banking, food products, brewing, and other areas. The firm is sixth in world chocolate companies but had no production facilities in the United States until buying Ambrosia. In 1965 there were 11 *independent* chocolate manufacturers in the United States plus even more "captive" operations. Grace had sought to acquire Fanny Farmer Candy, Inc., another relatively small company, as a market outlet for the output of Ambrosia. The Federal Trade Commission order barred this effort.

The acquisition of Fanny Farmer in addition to Ambrosia would hardly have given the "market control" that Weston and Brigham believe mergers can achieve while internal growth cannot legally do so. On the other hand, there is little doubt but that Grace will now legally enter the marketing of Ambrosia chocolate through internal expansion.

In sharp contrast, Aluminum Company of America quite legally, as the courts held, achieved by internal growth a 95 percent monopoly of basic aluminum production and fabrication in pre-World War II days. This monopoly was sharply cut down after World War II by the sale of government-owned aluminum facilities built during the war. Such sales by the government were made to companies such as Kaiser and Reynolds and at such low prices as to make certain that these firms could effectively compete against Alcoa.

---

[5] J. F. Weston and E. F. Brigham, *Managerial Finance*, 2d ed. (New York: Holt, Rinehart and Winston, Inc., 1966), p. 638. The same idea is restated at page 642: "The Sherman Act of 1890, which prohibits combinations or collusion in restraint of trade, gave impetus to holding company operations as well as to outright mergers and complete amalgamations, because companies could do as one company what they were forbidden to do, by the terms of the act, as separate companies.

These are just two instances of many that could be cited to support the proposition that under the antitrust laws market dominance is much more easily achieved by internal growth than by external growth. The reason lies in the very nature of the events. The antitrust laws are directed against two areas: (1) activity in restraint of trade and (2) activity tending to monopolize. The claim that internal growth is so directed must be proved by a *pattern* of conduct, or a series of events. The claim that external growth is so directed can be focused on a *single* event, namely, the acquisition, known to all the world. To ferret out proof of a pattern of conduct is much more of a problem, since it is difficult even to know where to look.

Many surviving companies in mergers have been forced to unscramble the legal aspects of the merger years after it has taken place. The acquiring company is often placed under legal mandate to conduct a forced sale, to say nothing of triple-damage claims it may face.

The mechanics of merger are the province of the legal expert, and many finance texts contain garbled versions of hearsay, outmoded law, and plain inaccuracy. Thus until 1950 the Clayton Act limited the jurisdiction of the Federal Trade Commission in antitrust matters to stock-for-stock acquisitions, and we find the statement in some textbooks that the antitrust laws could be avoided until 1950 by an acquisition for cash. But enforcement of the antitrust laws is not limited to the Federal Trade Commission, since the Justice Department and private persons (including corporations) may proceed under it, as is demonstrated by the hundreds of private cases that have arisen following the Philadelphia decision procured by the Justice Department in the electric utility equipment industry in the early 1960s.

## THE MECHANICS OF EXTERNAL GROWTH: MERGERS AND CONSOLIDATIONS

A merger can be effected by the acquiring company paying cash, stock, or a combination of the two for the stock or assets of the acquired company. In some cases the merger may involve acquisition of only part of the selling company.

The statutes of many states contain a separate provision covering the sale of all assets and a separate provision covering a merger involving the trade of stock for stock. The main purpose of the state statutes is not to distinguish a merger carried out by stock for stock from one using stock for assets. Rather, the purpose of the separate statute on the sale of assets is to make it applicable not only where mergers occur but to "any sales, lease, mortgage or pledge" of all "or substantially all" of the assets "when, not made in the usual and regular course of business." In brief, the sale of assets section applies to many types of transactions other than mergers.

Similarly, there is no significance as far as state statutes are concerned between merger and consolidation. The requirement is simply that the plan specify which company will survive and whether that one is to be a new one created for the purpose.

Likewise, there is little significant difference between the three methods (stock for assets, stock for stock, or consolidation) with respect to either the rights of creditors or the rights of dissenting stockholders to be paid in cash at the appraised value of their shares. One difference sometimes mentioned is that in the stock-for-assets purchase the buying corporation may avoid assuming the liabilities of the selling corporation, but in the stock-for-stock merger such assumption is automatic by statute.[6] Without going into legal analysis, we can say that the avoidance of the seller's liabilities is a very dubious proposition. The law is far from settled on what rights each group of creditors has in the situation. By "each group of creditors" is meant not only the creditors of the surviving corporation in contrast to those of the corporation to be dissolved but also other groupings such as secured and unsecured creditors of each firm. This says nothing about the conflict of state laws when one corporation is incorporated in one state and the other in another state.[7]

#### The Securities and Exchange Commission and the Internal Revenue Service

There are two agencies that draw distinctions between the various mechanics of mergers—the SEC and the IRS.

*Sale of Assets for Stock.* Under the method of sale of assets by the selling corporation for stock of the surviving corporation, the selling corporation agrees not to compete and in the case of the sale of all its assets to dissolve after distributing the survivor's stock to the stockholders of the selling corporation. If properly carried out,[8] this is a tax-free distribution for stockholders of the selling corporation until they sell the new stock.[9] The SEC has no registration jurisdiction, since there is no public offering of stock by the selling corporation, but it has jurisdiction to the extent of any proxy statement issued by the selling corporation in the case of reporting companies (those with 500 stockholders, assets over $1 million, and engaged in interstate commerce).

On the other hand, if the surviving corporation offers cash in whole or part for all stock of the selling corporation, there is an immediately

---

[6] J. K. Butters and W. L. Cary, "Motives Affecting Form of Sales and Purchases of Businesses," *Harvard Law Review*, 64 (March 1951), pp. 697–726.

[7] It is amazing that nonliability for the seller's obligations was found to be the most important nontax reason for use of the stock-for-assets merger in acquiring small concerns. Butters, Lintner, and Cary, pp. 335–336.

The way in which the buyer for cash attempts to protect himself against the liabilities of the selling corporation is to secure the seller's affidavit as to a complete list of the seller's creditors and then to verify the payment of these creditors. However, the real risk lies in unrecorded liabilities of the seller.

[8] Unless Section 337 of the Internal Revenue Code is satisfied, the sale results in taxation of the profit to the selling corporation. Dissolution and liquidation of the selling corporation within one year is required to satisfy Section 337.

[9] Butters, Lintner, and Cary, at page 315, quite properly observe: There are, in fact, few areas in which tax considerations more completely dominate business actions and in which the tax penalties for ill-advised decisions are more pronounced. Potential sellers of a successful enterprise, in particular, would be foolhardy to commence negotiations for the sale of their business without first ascertaining the tax consequences of each move and then scrupulously observing the ceremonials prescribed by counsel in carrying out the sale.

taxable event for the selling stockholders but no SEC jurisdiction. If the surviving corporation offers cash for only some of the stock of the selling corporation but stock of the surviving corporation for the balance of the stock of the selling corporation, only the stockholders receiving cash have incurred a taxable event.

*Stock for Stock.* If there is a stock-for-stock transaction other than under the merger statute of the state of incorporation, then the SEC has full registration as well as proxy statement jurisdiction because a public offering is being made to the selling stockholders. But if the stock-for-stock merger is undertaken pursuant to merger statutes, Rule 133 of the SEC recognizes that no registration is required on the questionable theory that the transaction is not completely "voluntary," since any minority is not free to do otherwise. If a single individual or small group is in control of either corporation in a statutory merger, the SEC may require registration. In both cases there is a tax-free exchange if the transaction is properly executed.

There can also be different tax consequences between these methods of acquisition for the surviving corporation depending on whether the acquisition is a purchase or a pooling of interests for accounting purposes. The determining factor is the values at which assets go onto the books of the buying corporation, which, in turn, determine allowable depreciation and losses on inventory.

## THE MECHANICS OF EXTERNAL GROWTH: THE HOLDING COMPANY

The term "holding company" can be used to describe a corporation that owns (1) any significant amount of stock of another company, (2) an amount of stock sufficient to constitute effective control of another corporation, or (3) nothing but stock of another corporation or corporations. It is apparent that the term presents difficulties,[10] but we will use it generally to describe a company at least one of whose activities is holding effective *control* of at least one other company. The emphasis is on control.

The differences between the holding company technique for combination and merger and consolidation can be summarized as follows. There are no dissenter rights for minority holders when a holding company gains control. At the same time, there is a relatively easy means for the holding company to dispose of the stock when there is a desire to switch investments. Thus an operating company in a declining industry such as an independent malting company (since breweries are more and more integrating malting into their brewing operation) may first turn itself into an investment company and then become an operating company in another industry over several decades as it recovers depreciation on its plant and phases out the malting operation.[11]

---

[10] For example, an investment company may be technically classified as a holding company under many definitions even though its interest is strictly that of investment and no purposes of control are involved.

[11] This is being done by Froedtert Malting Company through creation of a parent holding company, Basic Products. The parent has now been renamed Sola Basic and has become an electrical equipment manufacturer.

Perhaps the most widely recognized advantages of the holding company are (1) minimization of the amount of money needed to get control and (2) the leverage achieved by pyramiding. Suppose, for simplicity, that there are five operating companies each with the balance sheet given in Table 23–1.

Assume that the after-tax income of each operating company is $212,000, of which $12,000 is due the preferred stock. Assume that the common stock can be bought at book value.[12] Control may require buying at most 51 percent of the common. If we create a new company whose assets are the controlling stocks of the five operating companies and finance the acquisition with bonds and preferred as well as common stock, the balance sheet might be as given in Table 23–2, assuming we acquire 50 percent of the common stock of each operating company at book value. Now with $150,000 of the holding company's common stock we control $5 million in assets of the operating companies and claim $500,000 of earnings of the operating companies (assuming they pay out 100 percent of earnings). Of the $500,000 we apply $24,500 to holding company bonds and $8000 to the preferred stock (both of which carry higher rates than these securities of the operating companies because their income depends on the common stock earnings of the operating companies). If the holding company owns 80 percent or more of the operating company's voting

TABLE 23–1. Balance Sheet of Each Operating Company

| Assets | | Liabilities | |
|---|---|---|---|
| Operating assets | $1,000,000 | Current liabilities | $ 200,000 |
| | | 5 percent bonds | 300,000 |
| | | 6 percent nonvoting preferred stock | 200,000 |
| | | Common stock | 100,000 |
| | | Surplus | 200,000 |
| Total assets | $1,000,000 | Total liabilities and net worth | $1,000,000 |

TABLE 23–2. Balance Sheet of Holding Company

| Assets | | Liabilities | |
|---|---|---|---|
| Investment in operating companies ($150,000 of common equity in each of 5 operating companies) | $750,000 | 7 percent bonds | $350,000 |
| | | 8 percent nonvoting preferred stock | 100,000 |
| | | Common stock | 300,000 |
| Total assets | $750,000 | Total liabilities and net worth | $750,000 |

[12] If this assumption is unpalatable, reduce the earnings or increase the price of the stock and pursue the following transactions with other figures. The principle illustrated will be the same.

stock, no income tax is due because the intercompany dividends are exempt. But here we own only 50 percent, and hence only 85 percent of the intercompany dividends are exempt. At a tax rate of 48 percent the effective tax rate on the holding company receipts is $0.48 \times 0.15$, or 7.2 percent. Here 15 percent of the $500,000 is taxable, or $75,000. But since the bond interest of $24,500 of the holding company is deductible, $50,500 is taxable. This drives the effective tax rate below 7.2 percent in this case. Where the common stock of the operating companies earns 66 percent ($200,000 on $300,000), the common of the holding company earns 150 percent ($449,760 [13] on $300,000).

We have considered the use of only one level of holding company. Above this level the leverage increases.

Besides the advantages of avoiding dissenters' rights, minimizing the investment needed for control, and achieving leverage, the holding company presents two other advantages: (1) selective insulation of risks and (2) facility in financing. Both of these advantages are not clearcut. If there are intercompany transactions in the system, the courts may easily refuse to recognize the distinction of the corporations. But if the distinction between the holding company and the operating companies is maintained, the decline of one operating company may not affect the holding company as seriously as it affects the operating company. Facility in financing may follow from the superior standing of the system compared to the lesser status the individual operating companies would have.

The operating economies that might come from a system would also be available to other forms of combination.

### Abuses of the Holding Company Technique

A number of abuses have come to be identified with the holding company technique, particularly because of their frequent occurrence during the 1920s and early 1930s in the public utility area.

*Excessive Use of Leverage.* In the eight-layered Insull empire the leverage was so great that the Federal Trade Commission found that the West Florida Power Company was controlled by one-tenth of 1 percent of its securities [14] measured at book value. In view of the leverage effect already discussed, it is easy to see how defaults in holding company bonds quickly occurred, with the serious drops in operating income of the 1930s. Not only were excessive layers used but excessive debt was used in each layer.

---

[13] Computed as $500,000 less $24,500 bond interest, $8000 preferred stock dividends, and $17,740 income taxes (22 percent on first $25,000 and 48 percent on $25,500). We invite the reader to determine how low operating income can fall before the holding company common drops to the 66 percent income at which operating income started its fall. Note that at the operating company level assets of $5 million earn $1,135,000 (adding back the interest), or 22.7 percent, while at the holding company level $750,000 of assets earns $449,760 or 60 percent.

[14] Federal Trade Commission, *Utility Corporations* (1934), report under Senate Resolution 83, 70th Cong., 1st Sess., p. 160.

*Excessive Property Valuation.* Because operating companies were the basis for building the electric company empires, competitive bidding for their common stock led to such stocks being greatly overvalued as assets in the hands of the holding company. This practice is commonly called "watering" the securities.

*Excessive Charges for Expert Services and Profit on Construction Activities.* The holding company system in theory made possible economies in the use of specialized services spread over a number of operating companies, but in practice this area was abused and the cost of services increased. Similarly, in the area of construction, in theory economies flow from scheduling many projects of operating companies to keep construction activity constant and to establish facilities that can be jointly used to effect savings. But in practice there is evidence that in this area, too, excessive profits were taken.

*Upstream Loans.* An *upstream loan* is a loan by an operating company to the parent holding company. The theory of the holding company device is that the larger and better-known parent can get funds more cheaply than smaller operating companies, and the parent can in turn pass these savings on to the operating companies by lending them funds. But because of excessive leverage, as already explained, a decline in operating company income means a magnified decline in the earnings of the common stock of the holding company. In order for the holding company to maintain its financial standing by continuing to pay dividends, the holding company caused the operating company to lend funds to the holding company to be used for such dividends. This steady drain of funds led to the situation in which the holding company was paying dividends on its common stock when the operating company had already ceased paying dividends on its stock—both that part held by the public and that part held by the holding company. Further, such intrasystem loans would not appear on the consolidated statement of the system under the accounting rule that intercompany transactions are eliminated in preparing a consolidated statement.

#### Remedial Legislation

The abuses just described led to the Public Utility Holding Company Act of 1935. The effect of this act may be summarized as follows:

1. The SEC was granted jurisdiction over all gas and electric holding company systems with properties in more than one state. This jurisdiction extended regulatory powers to all aspects of the business, including all financial transactions. A holding company was defined as any corporation owning 10 percent or more of the voting stock of an operating electric or gas utility.

2. Two specific provisions struck hard at key abuses. Utility systems had to be directed to a unified geographic area rather than be scattered over large regions and had to be limited in size so as not to "impair the advantages of localized management." In addition, gas and electric utility had to be divorced so that their operations could be analyzed separately. All of these provisions were summed up in the expression, "the

*death sentence*." The other provision required that the levels of corporations in a holding company structure be no more than three. This provision was termed the "*grandfather*" clause, since an operating utility could have no more than a parent holding company and a grandfather holding company.

Competent administration by the SEC over a long enough period of time has resulted in an orderly dismantling of the complicated holding company structures that had been created in the 1920s.

Somewhat parallel problems in the bank holding company area led to the Bank Holding Company Act of 1956. The provisions of this act may be summarized as follows:

1. Existing bank holding companies may continue but may not own nonbanking assets. New bank holding companies owning 25 percent or more of two banks need a permit from the Board of Governors of the Federal Reserve System. Such a permit is also required for the merger of two bank holding companies.

2. Bank holding companies cannot cross state lines unless the state into which the system seeks to extend affirmatively authorizes such a move (and no state has).

3. Bank holding companies cannot borrow under "upstream loans" from subsidiaries, and "horizontal lending" by one subsidiary of the system to another is forbidden, although "downstream loans" by a parent to a subsidiary are permitted.

Abuses other than the tendency to monopoly were not widespread in the bank holding company development. The recent rapid growth in bank holding companies and in bank mergers led to the Bank Merger Act of 1960, which applies the limitations of the Bank Holding Company Act to the bank merger situation. The merger act requires consent for bank mergers from each of the Board of Governors of the Federal Reserve System, the Federal Deposit Insurance Corporation, and the Comptroller of the Currency. Both the Bank Holding Company Act and the Bank Merger Act were amended in 1966.

The existence of these two acts does not imply that banks are free of the antitrust provisions of the Sherman Act and the Clayton Act,[15] and the Department of Justice has attacked a number of bank mergers in recent years despite the blessing conferred on them by the various federal agencies under the Bank Holding Company Act and the Bank Merger Act.

Legislation in the public utility and bank area is of general interest, because such legislation may be extended to apply to all mergers.

---

[15] This point was settled in *U. S. vs. Philadelphia National Bank*, 374 U.S. 321 (1963), which held Section 7 (including stock acquisition as well as asset acquisition) of the Clayton Act applicable to bank mergers, and *U. S. vs. First National Bank*, 376 U.S. 665 (1964), which held Section 1 (restraint of trade) of the amended Sherman Act applicable to bank mergers.

## THE TERMS OF MERGERS

Having considered merger from various aspects and having come to the conclusion that price is critical, we now consider the terms of a merger. In the case of a combination of two companies, price is expressed as the number of shares the acquiring company gives up for the shares of the acquired company. There is no reasonably comprehensive information available on the percentage of merger proposals that fail to be finalized or of the reasons for the failure, but disagreement on price is certainly a major factor.

It is sometimes said that the principal determinants of the terms of a merger are (1) earnings, (2) market value of the firms, (3) dividends, (4) book value, and (5) net current assets.

It is clear that if we distribute securities in the new firm in proportion to any one of these bases, there will be a conflict with a distribution that uses any other of the bases except in an extremely fortuitous case.[16] Such a conflict suggests the question of what weight is to be attributed to each of these bases of comparison.

Before we examine the interplay of the different bases of valuation of a firm at the practical level, we must emphasize that the pie to be divided is not the total of the two separate pies as they have existed. What is being divided is the pie that is *expected* from the fusion of the two separate pies, and the new pie is expected to be greater than the sum of the two old pies. This is called the *synergistic effect*. Thus in merger negotiations there is always discussion of (1) the improvement of total receipts that can be anticipated beyond the sum of the separate earnings, (2) the savings or cost reductions expected from the fusion, and (3) the impact of both of these factors on the market value of the securities that would result from the merger. To illustrate the complexity of the problem, even if there were no increase in earnings by fusion and no cost savings, it is quite possible that the merger would result in a price-earnings ratio higher than the separate price-earnings ratios of the two companies, for example, due to offsetting risks. Hence we see that *historical* earnings or price-earnings ratios are usually inadequate as the principle of merger.

It follows, then, that much of the popular analysis of mergers is based on faulty assumptions, namely, that (1) the past record and valuation of each separate entity is indicative of its separate future records and (2) the future record and valuation of the fusion is the sum of the separate (even future) records and valuation of the separate firms.

Let us assume that it is agreed that the future valuation of the fused firms is what is to be divided. We might propose that this value should be divided between the two firms in proportion to the present value of each firm (or the market value ratio). But such a proposal assumes that each firm contributes to an improvement in the total value of the new firm in proportion to its separate market value.

---

[16] For a case in which the several bases lead to a close (but not exact) agreement, see the merger of two investment companies, Capital Administration Company and Tri-Continental Corporation, described in Erwin E. Nemmers, *Cases in Finance* (Boston: Allyn & Bacon, Inc., 1964), pp. 342–352.

Actually one or the other of the merging companies may have more opportunities to merge at high values with other companies. This is sometimes described as bargaining power and it affects not only the division of the increment of the fused value over the sum of the values of the two separate firms but can extend so far as to shift part of the original value of one of the firms to the other as a result of the ratio of shares in the fused firms.

### Illustration of the Problem of Merger Terms

The quantitative data most readily available and most frequently used to evaluate merger terms in the practical world are, as already indicated, earnings, dividends, market value, book value, and net current assets.

Assume the data given in Table 23–3. It is apparent that computations on a per share basis are convenient and this is the customary procedure. A look at the data suggests that Company X is a so-called growth company and Company Y is mature. If an exchange of one for one were to occur and if the market were to place no higher value on the fused operation than on its two separate parts and Company Y were the surviving company, the results might be those given in Table 23–4.

TABLE 23–3. Proposal to Merge Company X into Company Y

| | Company X | Company Y | Exchange rate (Y for X) indicated if only 1 factor were considered and no increase in earnings or P/E for fused firm |
|---|---|---|---|
| Total earnings | $20,000 | $50,000 | |
| Shares of common stock outstanding | 10,000 | 10,000 | |
| Earnings per share | $ 2.00 | $ 5.00 | 0.4 |
| Price-earnings ratio | 20 | 10 | |
| Market value per share | $40.00 | $50.00 | 0.8 |
| Dividends per share | $ 0.20 | $ 4.00 | 0.05 |
| Book value per share | $ 8.00 | $20.00 | 0.4 |
| Net current assets per share * | $ 0.50 | $ 3.00 | 0.17 |
| Expected annual growth rate of earnings | 10% | 5% | |

* Net current assets is the term used in Moody's *Manuals* and is the same as net working capital, which is the Standard & Poor's term. Both terms describe current assets less current liabilities.

TABLE 23–4. Possible Results of One for One Merger of Company X into Company Y

| | |
|---|---|
| Total earnings | $70,000 |
| Shares of common stock outstanding | 20,000 |
| Earnings per share | $ 3.50 |
| Price-earnings ratio | 12.8 |
| Market value per share | $45.00 |
| Dividends per share | $ 2.10 |
| Book value per share | $14.00 |
| Net current assets per share | $ 1.75 |

One thing immediately apparent is that all of the per share figures are the arithmetic means of the separate company figures but that the new price-earnings ratio is not an average of the old price-earnings ratios. A price-earnings ratio is determined by the price and the earnings; price is not determined by the price-earnings ratio and earnings.

Notice also that *none* of the single-factor exchange rates is one or greater. The exchange rate of one for one cannot be arrived at by some weighting of the several factors set out. However, in many cases after the exchange rate is established the result can be arithmetically equated to a number of different weighting systems applied to the several factors.

By now the reader is doubtful that the proposed one for one exchange is realistic, or he infers that some factor or factors are missing from our list, although this list includes the five factors that have received the greatest emphasis in arriving at merger terms.

Before going further, notice that a one for one exchange ratio offers the acquired company more than its present market value, but the reverse is true for the acquired company, which may lead to the problem of paying off dissenters in cash. This is basic. Unless the acquiring company is in a position to come up with the necessary cash, merger may not result.

In addition to the dissenter problem, what might account for the apparently high exchange ratio? There are a host of qualitative factors and we will mention just a few.

1. Company Y may be listed on the New York Stock Exchange [17] and Company X traded over the counter, with little prospect of qualifying for the Big Board and with major holders seeking the better marketability for large blocks that the exchange offers.

2. Top management of Company X may be a dynamic young team. Executive "head hunting" has been done through mergers. The procurement of individual executives does not guarantee that a team will result.

---

[17] A corporation with the small number of shares we assumed could not be listed, but if we add two zeros to the earnings and number of shares figures in our example the matter is taken care of.

3. We made one weak assumption in our case, although it is one commonly made in analysis by those who do not have access to the information that is exchanged behind closed doors, namely, that the earnings of the fused operation will not exceed the sum of the separate earnings. Here is one problem posed by the SEC regulatory process. If we are involved with a corporation that is procuring new money, the SEC requires the prospectus to state how the new money will be used and to show the *pro forma* capital structure after the issuance of the securities. But in a merger speculative projections of the effect of the merger are barred from use in solicitation, yet how else can the investor evaluate the effect of the merger? A few definite items can be stated and indeed must be, such as a plan to close a plant as a result of the merger. But what is definite is seldom sufficient to form a reasonable judgment.

Thus far we have not considered the impact of the different growth rates shown in Table 23–3 for the two companies in relation to the merger terms. Figure 23–1 shows that Company Y's earnings per share will be initially reduced by the terms of the merger but that after a period of 26.4 years, Company Y's earnings will be higher than they would have been without the merger. The converse is true for Company X but the number of years until this happens will not, except by coincidence, be the same.

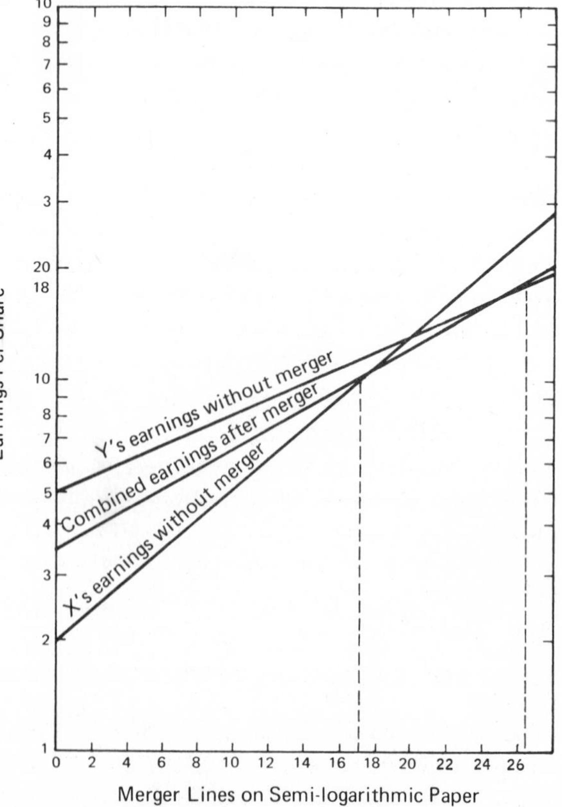


Figure 23–1
Showing growth in earnings per share of X and Y Companies separately and after merger.

We can determine how long this time period will be by solving the following equation for $N$:

$$E_1(1 + g_1)^N = E_2(1 + g_2)^N$$

where $E_1$ and $g_1$ are the earnings and growth rate before merger and $E_2$ and $g_2$ are the earnings and growth rate after merger and $N$ is the break-even number of years. The growth rate after merger is the average of the separate growth rates, weighted by the *total* earnings of each company. In our case $g_2$ is $[0.10(20{,}000) + 0.05(50{,}000)]/70{,}000$, or 6.43 percent. Thus Company Y is trading a current earning of $5 per share with a growth rate of 5 percent for a current earning of $3.50 per share and a growth rate of 6.43 percent. Conversely, Company X is trading a current earning of $2 per share with a growth rate of 10 percent for a current earning of $3.50 per share and a growth rate of 6.43 percent.

Substituting in this equation, $N$ turns out to be 26.4 years for Company Y and 17 years for Company X.[18] Thus as to Company Y, the decline in earnings in the merger from $5 per share to $3.50 per share will be equalized after 26.4 years where the earnings have risen to $18.13 per share [computed as log 5 + 26.4 (log 1.05) or log 3.5 + 26.4 (log 1.0643)]. Similarly the increase from $2 per share to $3.5 per share for Company X in the merger will be equalized after 17 years when earnings will be at $10.10 per share [computed as log 2 + 17 (log 1.1) or log 3.5 + 17 (log 1.0643)].

Figure 23–1 illustrates what the analysis of Table 23–3 made clear: that the exchange ratio of one for one appears to favor Company X—if we can extrapolate the growth rates of Companies X and Y as we have done. However if the mature Company Y cannot maintain its growth rate for long, then Company Y will recover its earnings position much sooner than 26.4 years.

### Situations in Which Each of the Five Factors Is Likely to Dominate

1. *Market Value.* Market value as we have suggested, will dominate when there are dissenter problems. Great deviation from market value threatens to result in litigation beyond the problem of raising the cash needed for dissenters. However, when "market" values represent a thin or even a supported market, only the naive company will be trapped into recognizing "market" value.

2. *Book Value.* Book value is likely to be dominant first in the case where liquidity carries a premium. This might occur, for example, at any time when the capital market and/or the economy as a whole have slowed down and new securities of any kind are difficult to market at anything approximating a reasonable price. A second situation where book value will be dominant is where the market value of the assets of one company is well above the market value of its stock.

3. *Dividends.* Dividend rates of the two companies are not likely to influence the terms of the merger but can be expected to affect the form of securities used. Dividends depend on earnings and policy as to payout. But in a merger every effort will be spent to use a type of security which

---

[18] In computing form: $\log E_1 + N \log (1 + g_1) = \log E_2 + N \log (1 + g_2)$.

will preserve existing cash dividends for stockholders of the acquired company. The payout policy of the fused operation cannot be readily determined in advance except where the policies of both companies have been nearly the same, thus creating an expectation that the same pattern will continue.

4. *Earnings.* Earnings are sometimes stated to be the dominant single factor, and "earnings" in such a statement means historical earnings. The relevant earnings, however, are expected future earnings, and these are reflected in market value. Variability of earnings is a factor to be considered, but this is reflected in the market value and appears in the price-earnings ratios, which reflect risk as well as growth prospects.

Earnings are inevitably a factor for discussion in a merger in connection with the use of market value in establishing the exchange ratios. When the price-earnings ratios of the two companies are different the result is the so-called earnings dilution for one company and an earnings accretion for the other company, which we have already described in connection with Figure 23–1.

### Capital Structure Adjustments: The "Scientific" Method of Reconciling Asset and Earnings Differences

A merger often brings with it problems of adjusting the capital structure of the fused firms to incorporate the outstanding senior securities (bonds and preferred stock) of each company before the merger. This need for realigning priority positions also furnishes an opportunity to reconcile the differences between the merger terms that would result from considering relative assets only and those that would emerge as a result of looking only at relative earnings.

Out of this situation has developed the "scientific" method [19] of merger, which gives senior securities for tangible assets and common stock for earning power. With this method there is typically an increase in the capital structure of the fused firms over the combined capital structures of each company. The method was further refined to apportion long-term debt of the fused firm in proportion to net current assets contributed by each company, preferred stock in proportion to fixed assets, and common stock in proportion to earnings.

While the "scientific" method was in vogue early in this century, modern practice has shifted to analysis of the factors we have already discussed. However, the older method focused attention on some important matters that modern merger analysis tends to overlook. These matters center on accounting practices. The fact that modern accounting statements have eliminated fraud and other gross practices does not mean that the earnings figures of the companies are immediately comparable. Thus the practice of showing assets at cost less accrued depreciation tells nothing about the time (and price level) at which fixed assets were purchased. While the SEC requires that accounting statements reveal the

---

[19] The method dates back to John Moody, "Preferred Stocks as Investments," *Annals of the American Academy of Political and Social Sciences*, Vol. 35 (May 1910), pp. 545–553, at p. 548. This is the same John Moody who founded Moody's *Manuals.*

lives used for asset categories and whether single or double rates are used, nothing of this sort appears in financial sources such as Moody's and Standard & Poor's. Thus the asset values of a company that uses faster depreciation can be seriously understated relative to those of another company. At the same time the earnings are also seriously understated in the comparison because of heavier depreciation expenses. Other areas of accounting that can give rise to such discrepancies are bad debts, repairs, and research and development expenditures (whether capitalized or expensed).

### Management: The Vital Factor Difficult to Measure

Textbooks rarely consider the effect that the quality of management has on the terms of a merger. Management abilities of companies are difficult to measure. Often the difference between the actual terms and those that analysis of the five factors would suggest can be accounted for by the management factor. For example, one of the companies may have a new management whose efforts have not yet appeared in improved earnings, although there may be agreement that the new management has made many substantial changes whose effects on earnings can already be estimated. This situation merely emphasizes again that what is relevant in all valuation problems is the future or expected earnings stream and not the historical record.

### Risk Differences

Another important factor to be considered in determining merger terms is the difference in the risk associated with each firm. In our discussion of risk in Chapter 10 we indicated that the heart of the matter lies in risk of ruin and variability in performance associated with the firm.

Of the five factors that are actually weighted to set merger terms, only market value of the securities includes an estimate of risk. This, then, is one reason that market value dominates in mergers. It should also be noted that the older "scientific" method has a key weakness at this point. By directly comparing assets and earnings of the two enterprises with no attention given to market value of the securities, the method assumes that the risk element is the same for both companies.

### The Earn Out

As the merger phenomenon has grown more popular in recent years, specialized techniques have been developed. One of these is the *earn out* which is used to deal with high-risk acquisitions. For example, a small firm with attractive products under development may catch the eye of a mature firm. Both firms have considerable confidence in the new products. But the selling firm wants a price based on the potential value of the firm if the products succeed. The buying firm is willing enough to pay handsomely *if* the products succeed. This dilemma is quickly resolved by a downpayment and a later second payment based on the earnings (if any) actually achieved. The downpayment will be in the amount of the fair market value of the selling firm today.

Various formulas can be devised to determine the "earn out" or second payment. Most formulas involve two factors to determine the agreed-upon additional payment: the earnings *increase* in a specified period after the acquisition over the earnings at the acquisition date times a multiplier (price-earnings ratio). Then there is a fork in the road. This agreed-upon amount is to be paid either in shares of the buyer valued at the date of the acquisition or valued at the date of payment. The former denies the selling firm the "P/E play" that develops in the buyer's stock after the acquisition; the latter permits the selling firm to participate in the rise (or decline) of the buyer's price-earnings ratio after the date of the acquisition.

It is basic to an earn out that the selling firm must have autonomy during the earn out period. If the terms are set right, the selling firm has everything to gain by optimum performance. Interference by the buying firm during the earn out period can only lead to possible lawsuits. The terms of the deal must also spell out with great care the accounting practices to be followed, particularly as to expensing or capitalizing many costs such as research and development and depreciation rates.

### Dissenters' Rights: The Foe of All Mergers

For every merger proposal that becomes an actual fact there are many that never come to fruition. There are no statistics in this area, but one factor that torpedoes many merger proposals is the right of any dissenting stockholder to demand payment in cash of the fair value of his stock *prior* to the proposed merger.[20] The inability of the liquidity position of the two companies to handle this drain of cash can easily bring further maneuvers to a halt. Because it is difficult to determine the number of stockholders likely to claim dissenters' rights, the merger agreement provides that if more than a stated percentage (usually 5 percent) of the stock held by the stockholders of either corporation (with dissenters' rights) dissents, the agreement may be canceled.

---

[20] Not all state statutes provide for the right of the dissenting stockholder to be paid in cash, but the number that do has been increasing. The states that make provision for cash payment to dissenters in the case of mergers or consolidation usually provide the same right for stockholders that dissent on other basic changes in the life of the corporation, such as the sale, lease, or exchange of substantially all of the assets of the corporation.

Sometimes the historical accident that the laws of the state of one corporation provide for the rights of dissenters to be paid in cash while those of the state of the other corporation provide no such right determines whether the merger proposal becomes a fact.

It should be noted that dissenters' statutes provide for payment to the dissenter of the market value of his shares the day before the merger becomes effective, not the day before the merger is announced. Hence, strictly speaking, the dissenter is stuck with the *immediate effect* of the merger on market price, since the market price will start to move to the merger terms as soon as the merger proposal is announced. How much the market values of the two companies move toward the proposed exchange ratio depends on market estimates of the likelihood that the merger will occur.

Bondholders continuue to hold their rights after a merger. Here it becomes important whether the bonds are secured by a mortgage; if so, then their priority in the collateral continues.

### Tender Offers

In recent years, the *tender offer* has been increasingly used by one corporation to "take over" another. In earlier years the classical method to achieve a take-over was a proxy fight to gain control of the board of directors. As explained in Chapter 21, the SEC has tight rules as to disclosure when proxies are solicited and special rules for the proxy fight situation. To avoid these rules, the acquisitive (and smart) corporation resorts to the tender offer, which consists of a full-page ad in major newspapers stating the price and terms upon which that corporation will acquire shares of the "victim" corporation. Usually the tender offer is stated to be not effective unless a stated percentage of the shareholders accept the offer and deliver their shares to an agent named in the offer. The tendering corporation seeks out victims with current difficulties, which in turn have caused the price of the shares of the victim corporation to decline sharply. At the extreme, a tendering corporation may be a "raider" whose purpose is to liquidate the victim for a quick profit. Another abuse of the tender offer takes the form of "short tendering." Here the tendering corporation specifies that actual stock need not be tendered if a bank or broker guarantees delivery of the shares.

The Williams Act of 1968 authorizes the SEC to make rules covering tender offers, which had up to that time been a "loophole" in SEC jurisdiction. Under the Act as amended in 1970, the SEC requires a filing in all cases where a successful tender would result in the tendering corporation acquiring more than 5 percent of any class of equity securities.

## SUMMARY

Growth is essential to the health of a firm. It can be achieved (1) by expansion of the existing firm through increasing its market share or expanding forward or backward into new products and markets (internal growth), or (2) by acquisition of other businesses (external growth). Whether the better choice is the first, called internal expansion, or the second, called external expansion, depends on the price demanded by the selling firm and environmental factors such as the antitrust laws.

External growth is effected in any of three ways: (1) merger, in which one firm takes over another and dissolves the acquired firm, (2) consolidation, in which a new firm replaces both the acquiring and the acquired firm, and (3) the holding company, which acquires the stock of another firm but does not proceed to dissolve the acquired firm. Sometimes two or more firms "affiliate" by contract, interlocking directorates, or other methods that fall short of full control.

In the case of merger, the acquiring company may use the purchase method by buying the assets of the acquired company or may follow "statutory" merger, which involves the exchange of stock of the acquiring company for stock of the acquired company.

Accounting for a merger may follow either of two methods: purchase in which "goodwill" appears on the asset side of the acquiring company to represent the payment of more than book value for the acquired company, or pooling of interests, in which the assets and liabilities of the two firms are combined and any differences between the terms of the merger and the combined book net worth of the two firms is recognized directly in capital surplus of the combined companies. Use of the pooling method has recently been restricted.

Expansion by internal growth rather than external growth (mergers) offers advantages in keeping the capital structure simple, avoiding financial charges, maintaining a strong working capital position, avoiding dilution of voting control, retaining maximum financial strength to meet the business cycle, and minimizing the danger of antitrust charges.

Expansion by external growth (mergers) may offer the advantages of (1) speed in entering a given market, (2) a lower cost for entering the market area (depending on the price paid for the firm acquired), (3) economies of diversification or large-scale operation, or (4) tax advantages.

Merger raises potential antitrust problems either under the section relating to restraint of trade or under that relating to the tendency to monopoly. Merger tends to focus antitrust problems on a specific event, namely, the merger, whereas internal growth proceeds in an inch-by-inch manner and is hard to pin down.

Both the SEC and the IRS are involved in mergers. If the IRS does not declare the proposed transaction a tax-free reorganization, the merger will most likely not proceed. In the case of the sale of the assets of the selling corporation for stock of the buying corporation, the SEC has no jurisdiction over the sale because there is no public offering of securities, although it does have jurisdiction over any proxy statement used by the selling corporation.

In the case of a stock-for-stock merger under the statutes of the states of the two corporations, Rule 133 of the SEC recognizes that there is no federal jurisdiction because the transaction is not voluntary as to any minority. The rule is different if a single person or small group is in control of either corporation.

Instead of formal merger the proposed union may be carried out by the holding company technique. Then there are no dissenters' rights, the acquiring company can easily reverse the acquisition by selling the stock, the amount of money needed to acquire control is reduced, leverage is achieved, and there is selective insulation of risks and increased facility in financing. But the holding company technique is exposed to the claim that the two companies have not been kept separate.

The holding company technique lends itself to abuses, such as (1) excessive leverage, (2) excessive valuation of the properties of operating companies, (3) excessive profits on construction by operating companies and excessive charges for expert services to the holding company, and (4) "upstream loans" by the operating company to the holding company. These abuses, particularly in the case of public utility companies, led to the Public Utility Holding Company Act of 1935, giving the SEC the authority to require that holding companies be restricted to a unified geographical area and involve no more than three levels of corporations.

The use of the holding company technique has also resulted in special legislation in the area of banking.

Merger terms involve a consideration of the two companies as to (1) earnings, (2) market value of the stock, (3) dividends, (4) book value, and (5) net current assets. The earnings accretion to one company and the dilution to the other company will erode with time. The relevant question is not the values of the two companies separately considered but the division of the value of the combined firm that the union creates. Actual merger terms reflect the relative "bargaining power" of each company.

Regardless of manipulation of these quantitative measures, some qualitative factors have been omitted, such as listing of the securities of one company and the skill and age of the respective managements.

The "scientific" method of merger involves the use of senior securities to reflect the relative asset position of each company and of equity to reflect the differences in earning power.

Stockholders who do not want to go along with proposed mergers are entitled to be paid in cash for the market value of their holdings. These dissenters' rights create cash requirements that defeat many merger proposals.

The tender offer is a public offer to all stockholders of a "victim" company inviting those stockholders to tender their stock pursuant to the offer made. The SEC now has jurisdiction over tender offers under the Williams Act of 1968.

### *Study Questions*

1. It is sometimes said that a company cannot afford to merge if its price-earnings ratio is low. Do you agree?
2. A well-known text states, "A particularly difficult problem regarding business combinations has been whether to treat the new company as a purchase or as a pooling of interests." Do you think this is a problem, or do you believe accounting is a branch of history that records events but does not shape them?
3. What basis would you use to determine the terms of merger of a small, rapidly growing, high-profit company into a large company with good earnings but poor growth prospects if neither company's securities are publicly traded?
4. If you were the financial manager of a company that has determined to make some acquisitions because it has excess cash and lacks internal investment opportunities, rank the following aspects of companies to be acquired in the order you would favor:
   a. A company with sound management regardless of the industry in which the company operates.

b. A company with a record for rapid growth and good profits.

c. A company that operates in a field closely allied to your company's field.

d. A company whose seasonal swing offsets that of your company.

Would your ranking depend on the strengths and weaknesses of your company? If so, what strengths and what weaknesses? Would you consider merger an expensive way to correct the weaknesses in your company?

5. Would you prefer to acquire another company by the use of a holding company or by a statutory merger? What would be the advantages of using a holding company and later performing the actual merger?
6. The "scientific" method was the first approach to establishing merger terms but has fallen into disfavor. Why has this happened?
7. A well-known text states, "The existence of long-term debt in a company's financial structure affects its valuation for merger purposes." Do you agree?
8. It is commonly stated that a pure (nonoperating) holding company is exposed to the risk that its only asset is the stock of other companies. Is there any way of compensating for this risk? Is there any relevance in the common proverb: "bulls and bears make money but pigs don't"?

### Problems

1. Using the holding company system given in Table 23–5, develop the earnings applicable to the common stock of the several companies. You may assume an income tax rate of 50 percent, with bond interest deductible, and an 85 percent exemption of intercompany dividends. Likewise, assume all earnings available to common stock are paid in dividends and that holding company acquisitions were made at book value.

TABLE 23–5. Holding Company System
Operating Company A
Balance Sheet

| | | | |
|---|---|---|---|
| Assets | $3,000,000 | 6 per cent bonds | $1,000,000 |
| | | 5 percent nonvoting preferred stock | 500,000 |
| | | Nonvoting common stock | 1,000,000 |
| | | Voting common stock | 500,000 |
| Total assets | $3,000,000 | Total liabilities and net worth | $3,000,000 |

Operating Company B
Balance Sheet

| | | | |
|---|---|---|---|
| Assets | $5,000,000 | 5 percent bonds | $2,000,000 |
| | | 6 percent nonvoting preferred stock | 1,000,000 |
| | | Nonvoting common stock | 1,500,000 |
| | | Voting common stock | 500,000 |
| Total assets | $5,000,000 | Total liabilities and net worth | $5,000,000 |

Holding Company X
Balance Sheet

| | | | |
|---|---|---|---|
| Voting common stock of operating Company A | $250,000 | 6 percent bonds | $200,000 |
| Voting common stock of operating Company B | 250,000 | 7 percent nonvoting preferred stock | 100,000 |
| | | Nonvoting common stock | 150,000 |
| | | Voting common stock | 50,000 |
| Total assets | $500,000 | Total liabilities and net worth | $500,000 |

Holding Company Y
Balance Sheet

| | | | |
|---|---|---|---|
| Voting common stock of holding Company X | $25,000 | 7 percent bonds | $10,000 |
| | | 8 percent nonvoting preferred stock | 5,000 |
| | | Nonvoting common stock | 8,000 |
| | | Voting common stock | 2,000 |
| Total assets | $25,000 | Total liabilities and net worth | $25,000 |

| Operating Company A | Case 1 | Case 2 | Case 3 |
|---|---|---|---|
| Earnings on assets before bond interest and taxes | 20% | 15% | 10% |
| Earnings before taxes and interest | $600,000 | $450,000 | $300,000 |
| Deduct bond interest | ______ | ______ | ______ |
| Taxable income | ______ | ______ | ______ |
| Deduct tax | ______ | ______ | ______ |
| Net income | ______ | ______ | ______ |
| Paid to bonds | ______ | ______ | ______ |
| Paid to preferred | ______ | ______ | ______ |
| Paid to nonvoting common | ______ | ______ | ______ |

| Operating Company B | Case 1 | Case 2 | Case 3 |
|---|---|---|---|
| Earnings on assets before bond interest and taxes | 15% | 10% | 5% |
| Earnings before taxes and interest | $750,000 | $500,000 | $250,000 |
| Deduct bond interest | ______ | ______ | ______ |
| Taxable income | ______ | ______ | ______ |
| Deduct tax | ______ | ______ | ______ |
| Net income | ______ | ______ | ______ |
| Paid to bonds | ______ | ______ | ______ |
| Paid to preferred | ______ | ______ | ______ |
| Paid to nonvoting common | ______ | ______ | ______ |
| Paid to voting common | ______ | ______ | ______ |

| Holding Company X | Case 1 | Case 2 | Case 3 |
|---|---|---|---|
| Earnings before taxes and interest | ______ | ______ | ______ |
| Taxable dividends | ______ | ______ | ______ |
| Deduct bond interest | ______ | ______ | ______ |
| Taxable income | ______ | ______ | ______ |
| Taxes | ______ | ______ | ______ |
| Net income | ______ | ______ | ______ |
| Paid to bonds | ______ | ______ | ______ |
| Paid to preferred | ______ | ______ | ______ |
| Paid to nonvoting common | ______ | ______ | ______ |
| Paid to voting common | ______ | ______ | ______ |
| **Holding Company Y** | | | |
| Earnings before taxes and interest | ______ | ______ | ______ |
| Taxable dividends | ______ | ______ | ______ |
| Deduct bond interest | ______ | ______ | ______ |
| Taxable income | ______ | ______ | ______ |
| Taxes | ______ | ______ | ______ |
| Net income | ______ | ______ | ______ |
| Paid to bonds | ______ | ______ | ______ |
| Paid to preferred | ______ | ______ | ______ |
| Paid to nonvoting common | ______ | ______ | ______ |
| Paid to voting common | ______ | ______ | ______ |

2. The Active Corporation acquires the Passive Corporation and issues stock in the amount required by the comparative market values of the common stock of the firms before the merger. Active decides to handle the transaction by the purchase method of accounting rather than by a pooling of interests.

The balance sheets of the firms are given in Table 23–6.

Make the necessary adjusting entries and develop a *pro forma* balance sheet. To do this you will need to fill in the blanks in the balance sheets. What is the dilution or accretion to each company if the combined earnings continue unchanged? What is the dilution or accretion if earnings of the combined operation increase 30 percent?

TABLE 23–6. Balance Sheets of the Active and Passive Corporations

| | Active | Passive | Adjustments Debit | Adjustments Credit | *Pro forma* balance sheet |
|---|---|---|---|---|---|
| Current assets | $600,000 | $200,000 | ______ | ______ | ______ |
| Fixed assets | 300,000 | 500,000 | ______ | ______ | ______ |
| Goodwill | ______ | ______ | ______ | ______ | ______ |
| Total assets | $900,000 | $700,000 | ______ | ______ | ______ |
| Current liabilities | $200,000 | $100,000 | ______ | ______ | ______ |
| Long-term debt | 200,000 | 100,000 | ______ | ______ | ______ |
| Common stock | 100,000 | 300,000 | ______ | ______ | ______ |
| Capital surplus | 100,000 | 100,000 | ______ | ______ | ______ |
| Retained earnings | 300,000 | 100,000 | ______ | ______ | ______ |
| Total liabilities and net worth | $900,000 | $700,000 | | | ______ |
| Par value of share | $10 | $6 | | | ______ |
| Net income | 100,000 | 50,000 | | | ______ |
| Current price-earnings ratio | 15 | 12 | | | ______ |
| Number of shares | ______ | ______ | | | ______ |
| Book value per share | ______ | ______ | | | ______ |
| Earnings per share | ______ | ______ | | | ______ |
| Market value per share | ______ | ______ | | | ______ |

3. Assume the same facts as in problem 2 except that the Active Corporation will apply pooling of interests as the method of accounting.

4. You are confronted with the proposed merger of the Electric Company and the Static Company. You may assume that the combined operation is expected to continue to perform as the sum of the separate companies. The balance sheets and earnings of the two firms are given in Table 23–7.

What exchange ratio would you recommend? What would be the dilution or appreciation for the shares of each firm in the event of merger at your calculated exchange ratio?

TABLE 23–7. The Electric Company and the Static Company

| | Electric Company | Static Company | Adjustments Debit | Adjustments Credit | Pro forma balance sheet |
|---|---|---|---|---|---|
| Current assets | $2,000,000 | $1,000,000 | ____ | ____ | ____ |
| Fixed assets | 3,000,000 | 1,000,000 | ____ | ____ | ____ |
| Goodwill | ____ | ____ | ____ | ____ | ____ |
| Total assets | $5,000,000 | $2,000,000 | | | |
| Current liabilities | $1,000,000 | $500,000 | ____ | ____ | ____ |
| Long-term debt (5 percent) | 1,000,000 | 500,000 | ____ | ____ | ____ |
| Common stock, $5 par | 2,000,000 | 800,000 | ____ | ____ | ____ |
| Capital surplus | 500,000 | 0 | ____ | ____ | ____ |
| Earned surplus | 500,000 | 200,000 | ____ | ____ | ____ |
| Total liabilities and net worth | $5,000,000 | $2,000,000 | ____ | ____ | ____ |
| Earnings | 200,000 | 100,000 | ____ | ____ | ____ |
| Price-earnings ratio | 15 | 20 | | | |
| Book value per share | ____ | ____ | | | ____ |
| Earnings per share | ____ | ____ | | | ____ |
| Market value per share | ____ | ____ | | | ____ |
| Net current assets per share | ____ | ____ | | | ____ |
| Dividends per share if Electric payout is 40 percent and Static is 80 percent | ____ | ____ | | | ____ |
| Return on assets (including interest) | ____ | ____ | | | |

5. *Acquisition of Moloney Electric Company by Central Transformer Corporation as of September 30, 1965.*[21]

In this merger the smaller company (whether measured by sales or net worth) acquired the larger company in a statutory merger. Both companies are engaged in the manufacture of electric distribution and power transformers for sale to electric power companies. The merger terms provide that each Moloney share (whether class A or class B) would receive two shares of Central together with one share of 5 percent second preferred $55 par stock.

*Reasons Stated for Merger.* Central needs additional production space. Moloney has excess plant capacity, including the ability to make transformers of a larger size than Central's present equipment. Central makes two-thirds standard transformers and one-third special, while Moloney makes two-thirds special and one-third standard. Central has plants in Arkansas, Florida, and California. Moloney has only one plant in Missouri. Most firms in this industry are multiplant, and there are freight savings from multiplant operations as well as sales

[21] The following information is taken from the proxy statement, dated August 20, 1965.

TABLE 23–8. Capital Structures of Moloney Electric Company and Central Transformer Corporation, March 31, 1965

| Title of class | Central | Moloney | After merger *pro forma* |
|---|---|---|---|
| 5.5 per cent mortgage note | 450,000 | ——— | $ 450,000 |
| 5.25 percent mortgage note | 7,342 | ——— | 7,432 |
| 5.5 percent sinking fund note | ——— | ——— | 1,006,000 * |
| 4.5 percent sinking fund note | ——— | $1,172,000 * | ——— |
| 5 percent 1st preferred stock, $100 par | 2,094 shares | ——— | 2,094 shares |
| 5 percent 2d preferred stock, $55 par | ——— | ——— | 68,046 |
| Common stock, $1 par | 472,243 shares | | 608,335 shares |
| Class A, no par | ——— | 31,046 shares | ——— |
| Class B, no par | ——— | 37,000 shares | ——— |
| Paid-in surplus, 3/31/65 | $1,544,948 | $ 137,882 | ——— |
| Earned surplus, 3/31/65 | $1,999,163 | $5,072,858 | $6,118,750 |

Note: Moloney class A is entitled to noncumulative $5 per year priority over Moloney class B, but class A has no voting rights. After $4 is paid on class A and $4 on class B, both classes share equally. Class B is closely held.

* The 4.5 percent note will be refunded by this 5.5 percent note.

TABLE 23–9. Over the Counter Bid Prices of Central and Moloney Stock

| | Central common | | Moloney class A | |
|---|---|---|---|---|
| Quarter ended | High | Low | High | Low |
| Sept. 30, 1963 | $ 7⅞ | $ 7 | $24 | $23 |
| Dec. 31, 1963 | 8½ | 7 | 22 | 22 |
| Mar. 31, 1964 | 8½ | 8 | 32 | 28 |
| June 30, 1964 | 8 | 7½ | 30 | 26 |
| Sept. 30, 1964 | 8 | 7⅝ | 26⅛ | 26 |
| Dec. 31, 1964 | 8½ | 7⅝ | 27 | 27 |
| Mar. 31, 1965 | 8¾ | 7¾ | 31 | 30 |
| June 30, 1965 | 12½ | 7¾ | 58 | 30 |
| August 16, 1965 | 12⅞ asked | 12⅜ bid | 65 asked | 61 bid |

Note: Both stocks had traded at substantially higher prices before September 30, 1963. The record can be found in Moody's *Industrials.*

TABLE 23–10. Central and Moloney, Per Share Earnings and Dividend Records

| | Central common, year-end 9/30 | | Moloney Class A year-end 12/31 | |
|---|---|---|---|---|
| | Earned | Dividends | Earned | Dividends |
| 1960 | $0.55 | $0.39 | $( 4.68) | None |
| 1961 | 0.41 | 0.40 * | (17.22) | None |
| 1962 | 0.81 | 0.40 | (35.06) | None |
| 1963 | 1.01 | 0.40 | (57.00) | None |
| 1964 | 1.01 | 0.40 | (29.60) | None |
| Six months ending 3/31/64 | 0.44 | 0.20 | (10.88) † | None |
| Six months ending 3/1/65 | 0.48 | 0.20 | 1.00 | None |
| Three months ending 6/30/64 | 0.18 | 0.10 | ( 4.46) | None |
| Three months ending 6/30/65 | 0.22 | 0.10 | 3.22 | None |

* Plus 2 percent stock.
† Moloney had a production strike from August 19, 1963 to February 24, 1964.

advantages of reciprocity with customers. Moloney has some patents Central can use. Moloney needs working capital and credit, which Central believes it can supply. Central also offers Moloney more modern management and research facilities. Although not stated as a reason for the merger, Moloney has an accrued tax loss carry forward of $8,057,156 as of December 31, 1964, which will expire as follows if not utilized: 1966, $9,397; 1967, $2,358,691; 1968, $3,305,544; 1969, $2,383,524.

TABLE 23–11. Central and Moloney Sales Records (millions)

| | Central | Moloney |
|---|---|---|
| 1960 | $7.5 | $28.3 |
| 1961 | 6.9 | 21.5 |
| 1962 | 8.3 | 22.0 |
| 1963 | 9.3 | 13.4 * |
| 1964 | 9.8 | 14.2 * |
| Six months ending 3/31/64 | 4.2 | 1.0 * |
| Six months ending 3/31/65 | 4.9 | 5.8 |
| Three months ending 6/30/64 | 2.5 | 2.9 |
| Three months ending 6/30/64 | 3.0 | 6.5 |

* Moloney had a production strike from August 19, 1963 to February 24, 1964.

*Additional Facts.* Central was not involved in the Philadelphia price-fixing scandal of the electric industry in the early 1960s. Moloney was involved, and as of August 3, 1965 has paid $447,318 of a liability of $766,442, with the balance accrued. In addition, legal expenses in this connection were $258,571. There still remain unsettled liabilities and legal fees. Moloney is also a codefendant with five others in an unsatisfied judgment of $2 million. The other defendants, all financially able to do so, have agreed to indemnify Moloney on this judgment. Moloney and some of its directors are also codefendants in a minority stockholders' suit alleging mismanagement, and Central has agreed to indemnify Moloney directors up to $50,000 for their costs of defending the suit but not for any judgment.

The laws of Arkansas (applicable to Central) and of Delaware (applicable to Moloney) permit dissenters from the merger proposal to demand fair value of their shares in cash. The merger terms provide that if more than 5 percent of the stock of either company claims dissenters' rights, Central shall have the option not to proceed with the merger.

The first preferred stock (the old Central preferred) has the right to elect the majority of the board of directors of the merged corporations if there is any default in its dividend or if the aggregate of capital, capital surplus, and earned surplus is less than $400,000.

TABLE 23–12. Central and Moloney Balance Sheets, March 31, 1965 (thousands)

| | *Central* | *Moloney* | *Pro forma entries* | *Pro forma combined under merger terms* |
|---|---|---|---|---|
| ***Assets*** | | | | |
| Current | | | | |
| Cash and securities | $ 19 | $ 508 | | $ 527 |
| Receivables (net) | 1,128 | 3,368 | | 4,496 |
| Inventories | 4,333 | 7,818 | | 12,151 |
| Prepaid expenses | 35 | 43 | | 78 |
| Total current assets | $5,515 | $11,737 | | $17,252 |
| Investments | 46 | 31 | | 77 |
| Property, plant, and equipment | 2,917 | 10,787 | ($7,951) | 5,753 |
| Less depreciation | 1,242 | 7,951 | ( 7,951) | 1,242 |
| Net fixed assets | $1,675 | $ 2,836 | | $ 4,511 |
| Deferred charges | 88 | — | | 88 |
| Total assets | $7,324 | $14,604 | | $21,928 |
| ***Liabilities*** | | | | |
| Current | | | | |
| Bank overdraft | $ 176 | $ — | | $ 176 |
| Notes payable | 1,500 | 4,000 | | 5,500 |
| Current long-term | 60 | 166 | | 226 |
| Payables | 398 | 2,241 | | 2,639 |
| Accruals | 271 | 348 | | 619 |
| Income taxes | 228 | — | | 228 |
| Total current liabilities | $2,633 | $ 6,755 | | $ 9,388 |
| Long-term debt | 396 | 1,006 | | 1,402 |
| Deferred liabilities | — | 390 | | 390 |
| Deferred credit | 70 | — | | 70 |
| Excess fair value over cost of net assets purchased | — | — | ($1,078) | 1,078 |
| Capital stock, A and B | — | 1,299 | 1,299 | — |
| 1st preferred | 209 | — | | 209 |
| 2d preferred | | — | ( 3,742) | 3,742 |
| Common stock | 472 | — | ( 136) | 608 |
| Paid-in surplus | 1,545 | 138 | 138<br>( 1,497) | 3,042 |
| Retained earnings | 1,999 | 5,073 | 5,073 | 1,999 |
| | $4,225 | $ 6,510 | $1,135 | $ 9,600 |
| Less treasury stock at cost | — | 57 | ( 57) | — |
| Total net worth | $4,225 | $ 6,453 | $1,078 | $ 9,600 |
| Total liabilities and net worth | $7,324 | $14,604 | $ — | $21,928 |

| Comparative book values: | Central common | $ 8.50 per share |
|---|---|---|
| | Moloney A and B | 94.84 per share |
| | Combined *pro forma* | 9.29 per share |

TABLE 23–13. Income Statements of Central, Year Ending September 30, 1964 and of Moloney, Year Ending December 31, 1964, and Pro Forma Combination of Such Statements (thousands)

| | *Central* | *Moloney* | *Pro forma combined* |
|---|---|---|---|
| Net sales | $9,756 | $14,242 | $23,998 |
| Cost of sales | 7,506 | 14,088 | 21,594 |
| Gross profit | $2,250 | $ 154 | $ 2,404 |
| Selling and general expenses | 1,158 | 2,039 | 3,197 |
| Operating profit | $1,092 | ($ 1,885) | ($ 793) |
| Other deductions | | | |
| Interest on long-term | 29 | 53 | 82 |
| Other interest | 14 | 96 | 110 |
| Miscellaneous, net | 37 | (20) | 17 |
| | $ 80 | $ 129 | $ 209 |
| Earnings before taxes | $1,012 | ($ 2,014) | ($ 1,002) |
| Income taxes (historical) | 523 | — | 523 * |
| Historical earnings | $ 489 | ($ 2,014) | ($ 1,525) |
| Preferred dividend | 10 | — | 197 † |
| Applicable to common | $ 479 | ($ 2,104) | ($ 1,722) |
| Earnings per share | $1.01 | ($ 29.60) | ($ 2.83)‡ |
| Dividends | $0.40 | $ — | $ 0.31 |

* Actual historical taxes paid.
† Preferred dividend requirements of merger terms.
‡ Giving effect to merger terms, one Moloney share would report a loss of $2.91, namely, two shares of new common stock at a loss of $5.66 less the earnings of $2.75 on one share of preferred. During the first two months of 1964 Moloney was on strike.

Moloney has no stock options outstanding. Central has the following stock options outstanding which will survive the merger:

1. Warrants for 10,000 shares expiring in 1971 at $15.25 per share held by its 5.5 percent noteholders. These warrants are adjusted to 10,200 shares at $14.95 as part of the merger.

2. Warrants for 9000 shares expiring in 1967 at $15.25 per share, or 13 times the preceding year's earnings, whichever is greater, held by its financial adviser.

3. Warrants for 13,000 shares to officers and employees at $8 per share, with 9000 shares expiring in 1968 and 4000 expiring in 1969.

Moloney has pension plans with unfunded past service liability of $2,713,500, which will continue after the merger. Central has no pension plan but has a profit-sharing plan.

TABLE 23-14. Income Statements of Central and Moloney for Three Months Ended March 31, 1965, and Combined Statement for Same Period (thousands)

| | *Central* | *Moloney* | *Pro forma combined* |
|---|---|---|---|
| Net sales | $2,755 | $5,815 | $8,570 |
| Cost of sales | 2,074 | 5,125 | 7,199 |
| Gross profit | $ 681 | $ 690 | $1,371 |
| Selling and general expenses | 344 | 568 | 912 |
| Operating profit | $ 337 | $ 122 | $ 459 |
| Other deductions | | | |
| Interest on long-term | 7 | 12 | 19 |
| Other interest | 15 | 45 | 60 |
| Miscellaneous, net | 5 | (3) | 2 |
| | $ 27 | $ 54 | $ 81 |
| Earnings before taxes | $ 310 | $ 68 | $ 378 |
| Income taxes (historical) | 154 | — | 154 |
| Historical earnings | $ 156 | $ 68 | $ 224 |
| Preferred dividend | 3 | — | 49 * |
| Applicable to common | $ 153 | $ 68 | $ 175 |
| Earnings per share of common | $ 0.32 | $ 1.00 | $ 0.29 † |
| Dividends per share | $ 0.10 | — | $ 0.08 |

* Preferred dividend requirements of merger terms.

† Giving effect to merger terms, one Moloney share would earn for the quarter: $0.6875 on the new preferred stock plus $0.29 on each of two shares of common, or a total of $1.27.

It is agreed in the merger that the surviving corporation will have 13 directors, with 7 to be present Central directors, 4 to be present Moloney directors, and 1 each to be nominated by Central and by Moloney.

No income statements are available for the three months ended June 30, 1965, but the following summary is available:

| | *Central, 3 months ended* | | *Moloney, 3 months ended* | |
|---|---|---|---|---|
| | *June 30, 1965* | *June 30, 1964* | *June 30, 1965* | *June 30, 1964* |
| Sales | $2,957,794 | $2,546,012 | $6,459,853 | $2,870,561 |
| Earnings | 104,628 | 85,598 | 219,322 | (303,590) |
| Earnings per share | $0.22 | $0.18 | $3.22 | ($4.46) |

The merger plan was approved by the directors of both Central and Moloney on June 15, 1965, at which time the price of Central was $12 per share and the price of Moloney $58.

Compute the terms of the merger that would prevail if the preceding merger were effected on: (1) an earnings basis, (2) a market price basis, (3) a dividend basis, (4) a book value basis, (5) a net current assets basis.

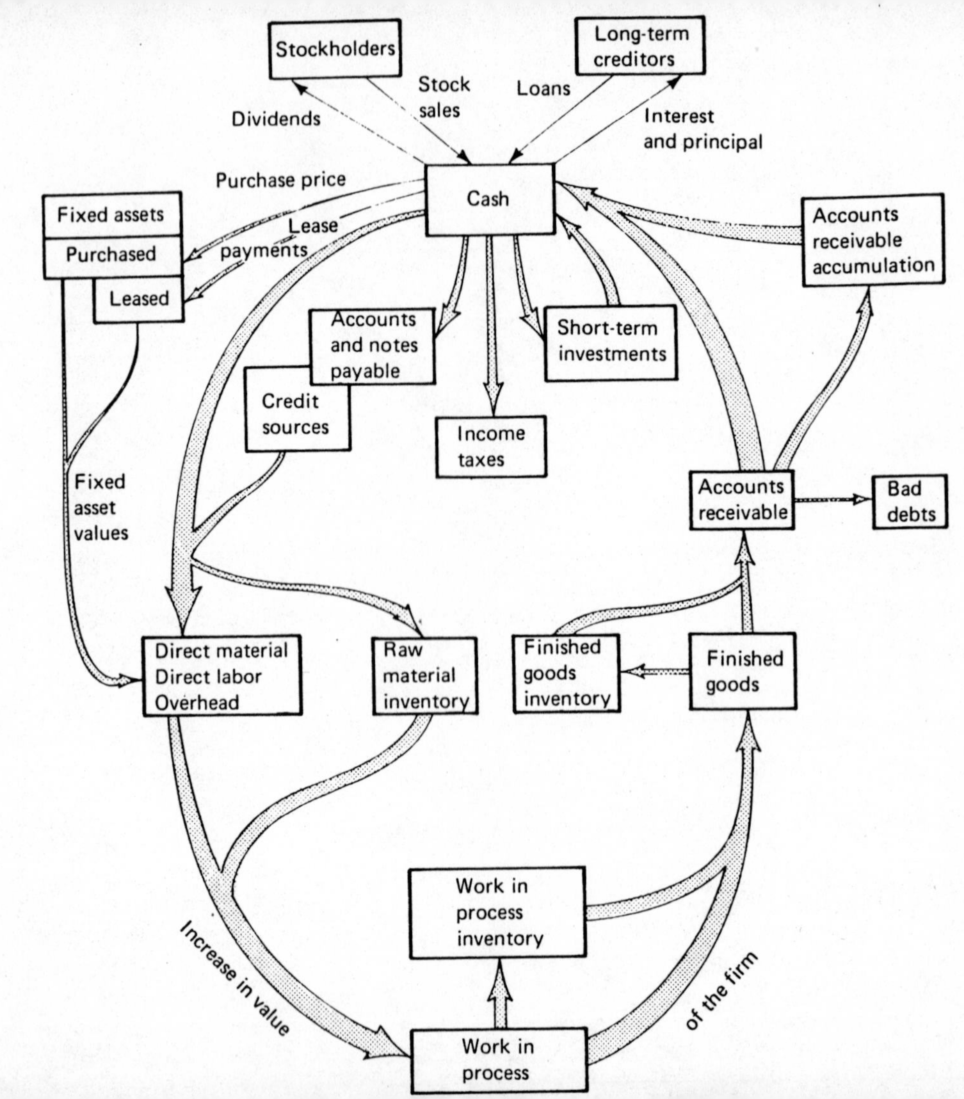

Stockholders
Long-term creditors
Stock sales
Loans
Dividends
Interest and principal
Purchase price
Cash
Fixed assets
Purchased
Leased
Lease payments
Accounts receivable accumulation
Accounts and notes payable
Short-term investments
Credit sources
Income taxes
Fixed asset values
Accounts receivable
Bad debts
Direct material
Direct labor
Overhead
Raw material inventory
Finished goods inventory
Finished goods
Work in process inventory
Increase in value
of the firm
Work in process

a. How do you arrive at the actual merger terms? That is, what specific factors do you think determined these terms? Furthermore, what is the origin of the proposal of $55 in preferred for each Moloney share?

b. Do you think the merger terms were affected by any information not set out? If so, what specifically might this information be?

c. Why did the smaller company swallow the bigger one?

d. Which company got the better of the terms?

e. What role do you think was played by nonquantifiable factors in this merger? What are such factors? Does the use of two classes of stock (in the case of Moloney), one voting and the other nonvoting, suggest any problem?

### Selected References


Alberts, W. W., and J. E. Segall, eds., *The Corporate Merger.* Chicago: University of Chicago Press, 1966.

Butters, J. K., and W. L. Cary, "Motives Affecting Form of Sales and Purchases of Businesses," *Harvard Law Review,* 64 (March 1951), pp. 697–726.

Butters, J. R., J. Lintner, and W. L. Cary, *Effects of Taxation: Corporate Mergers.* Cambridge, Mass.: Harvard Graduate School of Business Administration, 1951.

Cheney, R. E., "What's New on the Corporate Takeover Scene," *Financial Executive,* 40 (April 1972), pp. 18–21

Cohen, M. F., "Takeover Bids," *Financial Analysts Journal,* 26 (January–February 1970), pp. 26–31.

Crowther, J. F., "Peril Point Acquisition Prices", *Harvard Business Review,* 47 (September–October 1969), pp. 58–62.

Gort, M., *Diversification and Integration in American Industry.* Princeton, N. J.: Princeton University Press, 1962.

Gort, M. and T. E. Hogarty, "New Evidence on Mergers," *Journal of Law and Economics,* 13 (April 1970), pp. 167–184.

Hogarty, T. F., "The Profitability of Corporate Mergers," *Journal of Business,* 44 (July 1970), pp. 317–327.

Jaenicke, H. R., "Management's Choice to Purchase or Pool," *Accounting Review,* 37 (October 1962), pp. 758–765.

McCarthy, G. D., *Acquisitions and Mergers.* New York: The Ronald Press Company, 1963.

MacDougal, G. E., and F. V. Malek, "Master Plan for Merger Negotiations," *Harvard Business Review,* 48 (January–February 1970), pp. 71–82.

Mace, M. L., and G. G. Montgomery, Jr., *Management Problems of Corporate Acquisitions.* Cambridge, Mass.: Harvard University Press, 1962.

Melicher, R. W. and D. F. Rush, "The Performance of Conglomerate Firms: Recent Risk and Return Experience," *Journal of Finance,* 29 (May 1973), pp. 381–388.

Patton, E. J., "Tax Implications of Mergers and Acquisitions," *The Financial Executive,* 31 (January 1963), pp. 33–34.

Reinhardt, V. E., *Mergers and Consolidations: A Corporate-Finance Approach,* Morristown, General Learning Press, 1972.

Reum, W. R. and T. A. Steele, III, "Contingent Payouts Cut Acquisition Risks," *Harvard Business Review,* 48 (March-April 1970), pp. 83–91.

Rockwell, W. F., Jr., "How to Acquire a Company," *Harvard Business Review,* 46 (May–June 1968), pp. 121–132.

Scharf, C. A., *Techniques for Buying, Selling and Merging Businesses.* Englewood Cliffs, N. J.: Prentice-Hall, Inc., 1964.

Shick, R. A., "The Analysis of Mergers and Acquisitions", *Journal of Finance,* 27 (May 1972), pp. 495–504.

Sprecher, C. R., "A Note on Financing Mergers with Convertible Preferred Stock," *Journal of Finance,* 26 (June 1971), pp. 683–685.

Weston, J. F., *Planning for Corporate Mergers.* Los Angeles, Calif.: University of California at Los Angeles, 1963.

Wyatt, A. R., "Inequities in Accounting for Business Combinations," *Financial Executive,* 40 (December 1972), pp. 28–35.

# 24

# Tax Management of Enterprise Financial Affairs

Taxes are important considerations in almost all business decisions and particularly those in the area of financing. Inventories, fixed assets, selling and credit policies, and wages are also influenced by taxes.

Today federal, state, and local taxes take an amount equal to slightly more than 25 percent of gross national product, with 58 percent of total taxes going to the federal government. These figures do not include the current federal deficit nor the federal funds transferred to state and local government, which equal 12 percent of state and local taxes.

Taxation is a vast subject. The concerns of the financial manager in this area may be outlined as follows:

1. Activities directed to avoiding multiple taxation and to shifting ordinary income into capital gains to take advantage of the tax rate differential.[1]

[1] Throughout this chapter the term "capital gains" refers to long-term capital gains, that is, when the asset has been held more than six months and is not of the type that is held by the business for generating ordinary income. Under the Tax Reform Act of 1969 as amended in 1970, long-term capital gains carry the advantage of being subject

2. Activities directed to delaying tax payment, thus creating interest-free loans by the government to the taxpayer (accelerated depreciation and sale and leaseback are examples).

3. Activities directed to averaging income over the years to offset income in one year against losses in another.

4. Inventory problems.

5. Merger and reorganization problems.

6. Foreign activities.

7. State and local taxation.

8. Tax minimization as a possible overriding consideration.

Federal corporate income tax rates on ordinary income are 22 percent on the first $25,000 of annual income and 48 percent on income above $25,000. Individual income taxes are as shown in Table 24–1 except that "earned" income carries a maximum rate of 50 percent.

TABLE 24–1. Federal Personal Income Tax Rates, 1973

| Single taxpayers | | | | Joint returns | | | |
|---|---|---|---|---|---|---|---|
| Taxable Income | Tax | Plus percent | Of amount over | Taxable Income | Tax | Plus percent | Of amount over |
| — $ 1,000 | — | 14% | — | — $ 500 | — | 14% | — |
| $ 1,000– 2,000 | $ 140 | 15% | $ 1,000 | $ 500– 1,000 | $ 70 | 15% | $ 500 |
| 2,000– 3,000 | 290 | 16% | 2,000 | 1,000– 1,500 | 145 | 16% | 1,000 |
| 3,000– 4,000 | 450 | 17% | 3,000 | 1,500– 2,000 | 225 | 17% | 1,500 |
| 4,000– 8,000 | 620 | 19% | 4,000 | 2,000– 4,000 | 310 | 19% | 2,000 |
| 8,000– 12,000 | 1,380 | 22% | 8,000 | 4,000– 6,000 | 690 | 21% | 4,000 |
| 12,000– 16,000 | 2,260 | 25% | 12,000 | 6,000– 8,000 | 1,110 | 24% | 6,000 |
| 16,000– 20,000 | 3,260 | 28% | 16,000 | 8,000– 10,000 | 1,590 | 25% | 8,000 |
| 20,000– 24,000 | 4,380 | 32% | 20,000 | 10,000– 12,000 | 2,090 | 27% | 10,000 |
| 24,000– 28,000 | 5,660 | 36% | 24,000 | 12,000– 14,000 | 2,630 | 29% | 12,000 |
| 28,000– 32,000 | 7,100 | 39% | 28,000 | 14,000– 16,000 | 3,210 | 31% | 14,000 |
| 32,000– 36,000 | 8,660 | 42% | 32,000 | 16,000– 18,000 | 3,830 | 34% | 16,000 |
| 36,000– 40,000 | 10,340 | 45% | 36,000 | 18,000– 20,000 | 4,510 | 36% | 18,000 |
| 40,000– 44,000 | 12,140 | 48% | 40,000 | 20,000– 22,000 | 5,230 | 38% | 20,000 |
| 44,000– 52,000 | 14,060 | 50% | 44,000 | 22,000– 26,000 | 5,990 | 40% | 22,000 |
| 52,000– 64,000 | 18,060 | 53% | 52,000 | 26,000– 32,000 | 7,590 | 45% | 26,000 |
| 64,000– 76,000 | 24,420 | 55% | 64,000 | 32,000– 38,000 | 10,290 | 50% | 32,000 |
| 76,000– 88,000 | 31,020 | 58% | 76,000 | 38,000– 44,000 | 13,290 | 55% | 38,000 |
| 88,000– 100,000 | 37,980 | 60% | 88,000 | 44,000– 50,000 | 16,590 | 60% | 44,000 |
| | | | | 50,000– 60,000 | 20,190 | 62% | 50,000 |
| 100,000– 120,000 | 45,180 | 62% | 100,000 | | | | |
| 120,000– 140,000 | 57,580 | 64% | 120,000 | 60,000– 70,000 | 26,390 | 64% | 60,000 |
| 140,000– 160,000 | 70,380 | 66% | 140,000 | 70,000– 80,000 | 32,790 | 66% | 70,000 |
| 160,000– 180,000 | 83,580 | 68% | 160,000 | 80,000– 90,000 | 39,390 | 68% | 80,000 |
| | | | | 90,000– 100,000 | 46,190 | 69% | 90,000 |
| 180,000– 200,000 | 97,180 | 69% | 180,000 | 100,000– — | 53,090 | 70% | 100,000 |
| 200,000– — | 110,980 | 70% | 200,000 | — — | — | — | — |

to a maximum tax rate of 25 percent (30 percent in the case of corporations) on up to $50,000 per year with the excess taxable at 35 percent. In addition, a special additional "preference" tax of 10 percent applies to the difference between the half of the long-term capital gain not taxed and the capital gains tax. There is an annual specific exemption of $30,000 plus income tax paid from this last 10 percent tax. Gains on assets held for six months or less constitute short-term capital gains and are taxed at regular income tax rates.

The purpose of the new capital gains provisions is to close almost completely the gap between the tax rate on ordinary income and that on *large* capital gains.

In the use of cash or accrual basis the rules are the same for a corporation and a sole proprietorship. But in a partnership a partner's share of accrued income must be included on his personal return even though not paid to him. Although in general all "ordinary and necessary expenses" are allowable as deductions from revenues in order to determine taxable income, Congress can constitutionally eliminate any and even all classes of deductions and can, in addition, change the tax rate for the year that has passed.[2]

## MULTIPLE TAXATION

Interest on debt has always been allowed as a deduction to the corporation and the individual while dividends on stock have always been denied as a deduction to the corporation. Thus corporate dividends are subject to double taxation—once as equity income of the corporation and again as personal income to the stockholder.

### Intercompany Dividends: Preferred Stock

The Internal Revenue Code prevents double taxation in one case: where one taxable corporation pays dividends to another taxable corporation. Here the second corporation pays a tax on only 15 percent of the dividends so received, with 85 percent of the dividends free of tax.[3] Another provision permits consolidated tax returns by several corporations where one corporation owns 80 percent or more of the others. In this case all intercompany dividends are tax free.

The 85 percent exemption of intercompany dividends has important consequences in the capital market. Dividends received by a corporation on the preferred stock of another corporation enjoy a tax advantage over interest similarly received on bonds. The interest is fully taxable while only 15 percent of the preferred dividends is subject to tax. Thus to an investing corporation a preferred stock with adequate provisions limiting the prior debt may be more attractive than a bond. The same exemption is applicable to common stock dividends received by a second corporation. In addition, if almost all income is paid over to the shareholders, then investment companies, savings and loan associations, and cooperatives are virtually exempt from corporate taxes. Mutual insurance companies were once in this category but now are partially taxable.

## DEVICES TO AVOID MULTIPLE TAXATION OR TO RECLASSIFY INCOME TO CAPITAL GAINS

A number of other devices may be employed to avoid multiple taxation or to change the classification of income from ordinary income to capital gains income. Some of these have been classified as loopholes and have been rendered ineffective by amendments of the law. Others still survive and some are newly created.

---

[2] This occurred in February 1919 for application to the year 1918.

[3] Refer back to the discussion at p. 523.

### Collapsible Corporations

One of the earliest devices was to create a corporation to develop a specific opportunity. This corporation would then withhold all its earnings from the stockholders. After successfully completing its mission the corporation would be dissolved and its assets distributed to the stockholders, who would then sell the assets and claim a capital gain. The shareholder's tax liability would thus be less than the amount that would have been due if the profits of the corporation had been distributed as dividends. This device has been rendered ineffective by amendments to the income tax law.

### Preferred Stock Bail Outs

In the early case of *Eisner vs. Macomber* the Supreme Court held stock dividends not taxable in cases where the proportions of ownership were maintained and no rights were altered. This decision afforded an opportunity to arrange a nontaxable preferred stock as a dividend on common stock. The stockholders would then sell the preferred to outsiders and thus get the profits out as a capital gain. The outsiders in turn could get their money back by having the preferred stock called and redeemed. This device has also been rendered ineffective by amendments to the law.

### Election of Corporation to Be Taxed as Partnership

While many loopholes have been plugged, a new method has been created for a corporation to elect treatment as a partnership, with each stockholder reporting his share of the corporation's earnings without any income tax payable by the corporation. This device is limited to a corporation with not more than ten shareholders, all of whom must be individuals or estates. Such exemption is not applicable if the corporation is foreign or if it received more than 80 percent of its receipts from foreign sources or more than 20 percent from security income or from profit on transactions in securities, rents, royalties, or annuities. This section was enacted in response to pressure to give "small businesses" the benefit of the limited liability of a corporation and all the benefits available to shareholder-employees such as pension plans and stock options. However, the device has no limit as to size of net worth or volume of sales.

### Personal Holding Companies

The income tax law defines a personal holding company as one that derives at least 60 percent of its gross income from security income, profits on transactions in securities, rents, royalties, or annuities and in which over 50 percent of the stock is owned by not more than five persons. In addition to the regular (current) corporation income tax of 48 percent, a personal holding company pays a penalty tax of 70 percent on its *undistributed* income. The personal holding company was used as a device for individuals in high income tax brackets to transfer property to a corporation where the income would be taxed at only 48 percent.

### Unreasonable Accumulation of Earnings

Instead of trying to get income out of a corporation without paying a corporate tax or attempting to take income out of the corporation by a sale of stock now and taxed at capital gain rates, one might resign himself to leaving the income in the corporation indefinitely, paying the corporate tax and *delaying* the personal capital gains tax that would ultimately be due upon the sale of the stock. To block this loophole section 531 of the Internal Revenue Code (still commonly referred to by its earlier number, section 102) taxes *unreasonably* accumulated income. The first $100,000 of such accumulated surplus is exempted but the tax is 27.5 percent on the next $100,000 and 38.5 percent on any further amounts. However, this section of the law is difficult to administer, since any active corporation always has plans for retained earnings and, in view of the tax, may well entertain areas of investment that its management might otherwise reject.

### Taking Dividends Out in Disguises

One basic method of removing income from a corporation to avoid the corporate income tax is to find a disguise for what is really a dividend. The word "disguise" is well chosen because the possibilities in this area are numerous. An obvious one is for members of management to take money out as excessive salaries, which are deductible by the corporation, instead of as dividends, which are not. In this case there is not only the likelihood that the Internal Revenue Service will unmask the disguise but there also exists the problem of suits by stockholders who are not participating in these "dividends." Other disguises are low-interest loans to stockholders, excessive fees for professional-type services where the value of the services performed is difficult to establish, excessive rentals or other payments for fixed property or inventory (and, conversely, selling out fixed property or inventory at excessively low prices), personal expenses run through the corporation's books as business expenses, and repurchase of shares by the corporation at excessively high prices.

### Income Bonds

While preferred stock offers no tax advantage to the issuing corporation (although as we pointed out, there is a benefit to the taxable corporation that buys preferred stock), income bonds present possible tax savings to the issuing corporation. The terms of an income bond can be drawn so as to be different from preferred stock in name only. Owners of an income bond can have voting rights upon stated conditions without the Internal Revenue Service being able to pin down the issue as preferred stock. Income bonds can provide for cumulation or noncumulation of "arrearages."

## DELAYING BOTH THE TAXABLE EVENT AND THE PAYMENT OF THE TAX

Another category of devices is aimed primarily at delaying the payment of the income tax. Any legal delay in payment of a tax is an interest-free loan by the government to the taxpayer. If the delay extends for 20 or 30 years, the interest saving is substantial. There is also another aspect to this subject: income tax rates change from time to time and delaying the tax may enable the taxpayer to set the "taxable event" [4] into a low-rate year. The variation in federal income tax rates has been great. From a starting corporate rate of 1 percent in 1909 the rate increased to 12 percent in World War I, dropped back to 10 percent in the 1920s, increased to 17 percent in the 1930s, peaked at 80 percent in World War II (including the excess profits tax in this rate), varied in the 1950s between 30 and 52 percent, and stood from 1954 to 1963 at 52 percent on amounts over $25,000. The rate dropped to 50 percent in 1964 and to 48 percent for 1965 through 1967 but increased to 52 percent in 1968 and 1969, dropped to 49 percent in 1970 and to 48 percent for 1971, 1972 and 1973.

### Locked-in Stockholders and Estate Planning

There are many taxpayers who are "locked in," that is, unwilling to sell or realize a capital gain until favorable tax circumstances develop. This situation has probably contributed to bolstering security prices since the 1930s because large blocks of securities are locked in. There is an inducement for individual taxpayers to remain locked in until they die. In this way the capital gains tax can be completely avoided on the gain up to the time of death, since those who inherit the assets will take as their basis, or cost, the value on death of the one from whom they receive the property. On the other hand, if the taxpayer transfers the asset by gift during his lifetime, the donee receiving the property takes the basis of the donor but if gift taxes were paid these are added to the basis. Gift tax rates are only about three-quarters of estates or inheritance tax rates and offer additional exemptions. Federal estate and gift taxes are set out in Tables 24–2 and 24–3. There are also state gift and succession (estate or inheritance) taxes. There is a trade-off point at which the gift tax plus an eventual capital gains tax is matched against an estate and inheritance tax.

---

[4] Income tax laws must have a specific point in the income-generating process at which the income or gain becomes taxable. In general, the income must be "realized" to become taxable.

TABLE 24–2. Federal Estate Tax Rates, 1973

| *Net taxable estate* | *Tax* | *Plus percent* | *Of amount over* |
|---|---|---|---|
| $ 0–$ 5,000 | $ 0 | 3% | $ 0 |
| 5,000– 10,000 | 150 | 7 | 5,000 |
| 10,000– 20,000 | 500 | 11 | 10,000 |
| 20,000– 30,000 | 1,600 | 14 | 20,000 |
| 30,000– 40,000 | 3,000 | 18 | 30,000 |
| 40,000– 50,000 | 4,800 | 22 | 40,000 |
| 50,000– 60,000 | 7,000 | 25 | 50,000 |
| 60,000– 100,000 | 9,500 | 28 | 60,000 |
| 100,000– 250,000 | 20,700 | 30 | 100,000 |
| 250,000– 500,000 | 65,700 | 32 | 250,000 |
| 500,000– 750,000 | 145,700 | 35 | 500,000 |
| 750,000– 1,000,000 | 233,200 | 37 | 750,000 |
| 1,000,000– 1,250,000 | 325,700 | 39 | 1,000,000 |
| 1,250,000– 1,500,000 | 423,200 | 42 | 1,250,000 |
| 1,500,000– 2,000,000 | 528,000 | 45 | 1,500,000 |
| 2,000,000– 2,500,000 | 753,200 | 49 | 2,000,000 |
| 2,500,000– 3,000,000 | 998,200 | 53 | 2,500,000 |
| 3,000,000– 3,500,000 | 1,263,200 | 56 | 3,000,000 |
| 3,500,000– 4,000,000 | 1,543,200 | 59 | 3,500,000 |
| 4,000,000– 5,000,000 | 1,838,200 | 63 | 4,000,000 |
| 5,000,000– 6,000,000 | 2,468,200 | 67 | 5,000,000 |
| 6,000,000– 7,000,000 | 3,138,200 | 70 | 6,000,000 |
| 7,000,000– 8,000,000 | 3,838,200 | 73 | 7,000,000 |
| 8,000,000– 10,000,000 | 4,568,200 | 76 | 8,000,000 |
| 10,000,000 and up | 6,088,200 | 77 | 10,000,000 |

Exemptions and deductions of estate tax:
Expenses of administering estate deducted.
Charitable gifts deducted.
Marital deduction of up to one-half if that is left to spouse.
Specific exemption of first $60,000.
Limited credit for state inheritance taxes.

An individual taxpayer can minimize estate taxes over several generations (and, as already indicated, avoid capital gains taxes) by the use of a trust, or of what attorneys call a *legal future interest.* The latter is accomplished by providing that each succeeding generation shall receive only the income during its lifetime. Upon the death of each generation the next generation takes up its right to the income without the payment of any estate or inheritance tax. In addition, each generation is barred from disposing of the principal of the estate. In some states a limit is set on this process by the rule against perpetuities,[5] but in other states, for example, Wisconsin, there is no limit as long as no specific

[5] Under the rule against perpetuities future estates are limited to those vested, that is, determined and made unconditional, during lives in being at the time of death of the one initiating the estate plus 21 years (the period of minority). Thus in states having this rule estates can validly be created only for such children, grandchildren, and great grandchildren as are alive or will be born within the lifetime of lives in being at the time of the death of the one initiating the tax umbrella plus 21 years.

asset is prevented from being sold, with the proceeds of the sale to be re-invested.

TABLE 24-3. Federal Gift Tax Rates, 1973

| *Gift* | *Tax* | *Plus percent* | *Of amount over* |
|---|---|---|---|
| $ 0–$ 5,000 | $ 0 | 2.25% | $ 0 |
| 5,000– 10,000 | 112.5 | 5.25 | 5,000 |
| 10,000– 20,000 | 375 | 8.25 | 10,000 |
| 20,000– 30,000 | 1,200 | 10.5 | 20,000 |
| 30,000– 40,000 | 2,250 | 13.5 | 30,000 |
| 40,000– 50,000 | 3,600 | 16.5 | 40,000 |
| 50,000– 60,000 | 5,250 | 18.75 | 50,000 |
| 60,000– 100,000 | 7,125 | 21.0 | 60,000 |
| 100,000– 250,000 | 15,525 | 22.5 | 100,000 |
| 250,000– 500,000 | 49,275 | 24.0 | 250,000 |
| 500,000– 750,000 | 109,275 | 26.25 | 500,000 |
| 750,000– 1,000,000 | 174,900 | 27.75 | 750,000 |
| 1,000,000– 1,250,000 | 244,275 | 29.25 | 1,000,000 |
| 1,250,000– 1,500,000 | 317,400 | 31.5 | 1,250,000 |
| 1,500,000– 2,000,000 | 396,150 | 33.75 | 1,500,000 |
| 2,000,000– 2,500,000 | 564,900 | 36.75 | 2,000,000 |
| 2,500,000– 3,000,000 | 748,650 | 39.75 | 2,500,000 |
| 3,000,000– 3,500,000 | 947,400 | 42.0 | 3,000,000 |
| 3,500,000– 4,000,000 | 1,157,400 | 44.25 | 3,500,000 |
| 4,000,000– 5,000,000 | 1,378,650 | 47.25 | 4,000,000 |
| 5,000,000– 6,000,000 | 1,851,150 | 50.25 | 5,000,000 |
| 6,000,000– 7,000,000 | 2,353,650 | 52.5 | 6,000,000 |
| 7,000,000– 8,000,000 | 2,878,650 | 54.75 | 7,000,000 |
| 8,000,000– 10,000,000 | 3,426,150 | 57.0 | 8,000,000 |
| 10,000,000 and up | 4,566,150 | 57.75 | 10,000,000 |

Exemptions of gift tax:

Annual exclusion of $3,000 for each donee, or $6,000 if donor is married and other spouse makes no gift to that donee.

Marital deduction of one-half of gift to the other spouse.

Specific exemption thereafter of first $30,000 by each donor.

Charitable gifts excluded.

The gift tax is accumulative through the lifetime of the donor to determine the bracket for any one gift in any one year.

## Accelerated Depreciation

Another device for delaying the tax is the use of accelerated depreciation methods, which have been available since 1954 for assets with a minimum life of four years. The two principal methods are the double rate declining balance method and the sum-of-the-years' digits method. The former is the only method of depreciation that uses cost and does not require determination of a salvage value. Under all other methods expected salvage is deducted from cost to establish the depreciable amount. The double rate declining balance method is as follows. If an asset has an expected life of ten years, *straight-line depreciation* would deduct annually 10 percent of cost less salvage. Under the *double rate declining balance method,* 20 percent is deducted annually of the undepreciated balance at the start of each year. Therefore in the first year 20 percent of cost is deducted, in the second year 16 percent of cost (20 percent of the balance of 80 percent), in the third year 12.8 percent (20 percent of the balance of 64 percent), and so on. Thus in the first three years 48.8 percent of full cost would be recovered rather than the 30 percent of cost less salvage by straight line. The *sum-of-the-years' digits method* in this case would establish the sum of the numbers one through ten, since the life is ten years (this is 55) and deduct 10/55 of cost less salvage in the first year, 9/55 in the second, 8/55 in the third, and so on. Here 27/55, or 49.1 percent, of cost less salvage would be recovered in the first three years. At any time the taxpayer can shift to a slower depreciation method. But once having done so, he cannot revert to the accelerated basis unless the government consents.

The stated purpose of the government in 1954 in recognizing accelerated depreciation was that these methods reflect more accurately the pattern of the declining economic value of fixed assets. At the same time, the government shortened the allowable life periods for various assets.[6] There was a deeper reason, however, for the change. A niggardly depreciation allowance for tax purposes encourages business to continue to hold antiquated assets, since their early retirement involves a capital loss rather than recovery as a deduction against ordinary income. Some European countries, notably England, found their industrial plants antiquated in World War II. One of the reasons for this was a low depreciation allowance, since in England capital losses (and gains) are not recognized for income tax purposes.

In addition to these methods of accelerated depreciation, there is a category of special certificates issued by the government establishing even shorter life periods (usually five years). These apply if the proposed assets have defense significance.

It should be noted that even though the benefits of accelerated depreciation are claimed for tax purposes, the company is free to elect regular depreciation for financial reporting, and some companies are following this practice. When this is done an appropriate reserve for tax reconciliation on the right-hand side of the balance sheet offsets the higher values at which the assets appear on the left-hand side of the balance sheet. As time passes this reserve is periodically reduced, since the ordinary depreciation method arrives at the same net figure that the accelerated depreciation method had earlier established.

### Sale and Leaseback: Lease Rather Than Purchase

Another method of delaying tax payment is the sale and leaseback, or the leasing of property rather than purchasing. The most important reason supporting the use of the lease technique is the tax-saving possible to the lessee, or the company using the asset, since lease payments are tax deductible. One potential disadvantage to the lessee is that the effec-

[6] The taxpayer can use a shorter life than the allowable life if he can demonstrate that his assets deteriorate at a faster rate.

tive rate of interest implied in the lease agreement may be higher than the lessee could get on a loan to finance the purchase.

One tax advantage of the lease is that the life of the lease can be shortened compared to the depreciable life otherwise allowable if the company purchased the asset. Thus there is a delay in paying taxes and, in effect, an interest-free loan by the government to the extent of the delay in taxes. This advantage was, of course, reduced by the 1954 amendments to the Internal Revenue Code, which recognized accelerated depreciation methods. However, there is still the aspect that any loss on premature obsolescence of the asset is fully allowable against ordinary income through the continued rental payments due, whereas disposing of the asset at a loss while owned results in only a capital loss (with its lower effect because of the 25 to 35 percent tax limit on capital gains).

Another tax advantage of the lease is the opportunity to, in effect, depreciate otherwise nondepreciable assets. The principal asset of this type is land. The lease rental covers the cost of the land, which thus becomes deductible.

One possible disadvantage of the lease is that the lessee loses his right to continue to have the asset when the lease expires. However, this is easily handled by giving the lessee the option or a series of successive options to renew the lease for a much reduced rental payment. There is one caution. An option in the lessee to purchase the asset at the expiration of the lease for a small sum can be fraught with danger. The Internal Revenue Service is then in a position to argue that the lease was really an installment purchase contract, resulting in the disallowal of all prior rental payments.

There is also a unique possibility in leasing. If the lessor is an organization exempt from income taxes such as a college or university it can exploit its tax position. Such a lessor is otherwise limited to equity opportunities where an income tax has been paid before the investment income can be obtained by the university. But in a lease such a lessor is able to share some of its tax advantage with the leasing company by paying the company a higher purchase price for the asset. The company further benefits by paying at capital gain rates on this profit rather than at ordinary income tax rates.[7]

A note of caution is in order concerning one advantage claimed for leasing, namely, that leasing improves the working capital and current ratio of the lessee company by comparison to its owning the asset.[8] The accounting profession is currently concerned with how to get the liability involved in leasing onto the balance sheet. In earlier days when leasing was less common the use of a footnote to the balance sheet was considered adequate. Today all financial agreements carry provisions classifying major lease commitments as corporate debt and provide some basis for

---

[7] For an illustration see the Arrester case in Erwin E. Nemmers, *Cases in Finance* (Boston: Allyn & Bacon, Inc., 1964), pp. 310–317.

[8] See J. B. Cohen and S. M. Robbins, *The Financial Manager* (New York: Harper & Row, Publishers, Inc., 1966), p. 783.

discounting the total future rental payments in order to establish a present value of the liability.

## OPERATING LOSS CARRY BACK AND CARRY FORWARD

The matter of averaging income over a number of years has had a checkered history with respect to taxation laws, and provisions covering this area have varied greatly over the last 50 years. Essentially the problem arises from the fact that income taxes are assessed on an annual basis yet the ordinary income of some taxpayers fluctuates from year to year more than that of others, resulting in an inequity. Fluctuations in capital gains and losses create much less sympathy in Congress.

The most readily available device for meeting this problem is the operating loss carry back and carry forward. Since 1959 the federal tax law permits operating losses to be carried back three years and carried forward five years to be used to offset operating profits in such years and thus in effect to produce a tax on an average of the income. This type of provision, when considered in conjunction with the techniques for fusing two companies, creates substantial possibilities for avoiding taxes. Corporations that have accrued sizable losses and have no prospects for improvement have a ready value in reducing the taxes of the successful corporation. The case for denying tax benefits is easy for the tax authorities where such a "loss corporation" is acquired and dissolved promptly after the ritual has been completed. The 1954 amendments to the Internal Revenue Code also reached out to bar cases in which more than 50 percent of the stock changes hands within two years after purchase. The use of the device of a loss corporation is usually carried out by the successful corporation purchasing the stock of the loss corporation and then filing consolidated returns. The purpose is clearly to avoid contaminating the successful corporation with hidden liabilities of the loss corporations which would occur in the case of a statutory merger.

The other method of averaging income involves the manipulation of a delayed taxable event so that taxes are due on the event in a year in which the corporation would otherwise have a loss. During the period when the tax laws severely limited loss carryovers this was the more sophisticated device used.

## INVENTORY PROBLEMS

The Internal Revenue Code does not require any specific form of accounting for inventory but insists that whatever method is used must clearly reflect income and must be used consistently. No change in method (except a shift to last in, first out) can be made without the commissioner's consent; and before that consent is given the commissioner must be satisfied that as a result of the change no income will escape taxation and no delay in taxation will occur. If either will occur, a tax must be paid currently to adjust for the changeover.

Differences in inventory methods can have an important effect on the profit and loss statement and on the balance sheet but do not affect cash flows before income tax payments, although the source and application of funds statement will be affected.

The principal methods of inventory accounting are (1) average cost, (2) average cost or market, whichever is lower, (3) first in, first out (FIFO), and (4) last in, first out (LIFO). The best way to observe the effects of the different methods is to follow a simple illustration. We will dispense with the second method where market is taken as the bid price on the inventory date because its effects are readily understood once we know the other three methods.

Suppose we commence a simple trading operation with the following balance sheet.

Northwestern Trading Company
Balance Sheet, January 1, 1974

| | | | |
|---|---|---|---|
| Cash | $1,000 | Common Stock | $1,000 |

During the year we made purchases of goods to be resold:

| | | |
|---|---|---|
| January | 100 units | $1.00 each |
| March | 100 units | 2.00 each |
| May | 100 units | 2.40 each |

and we sold 210 units in June at $3 each.

What is our profit and what will our balance sheet look like? Under average cost we paid $540 for 300 units, or $1.80 per unit. Units sold cost $378, our profit is $252 (or $630 minus $378), and ending inventory is $162 (or $540 minus $378).

Under FIFO, the units sold cost $324 (100 at $1, 100 at $2, and 10 at $2.40), our profit is $306 (or $630 minus $324), and ending inventory is $216 (or $540 minus $324).

Under LIFO, the units sold cost $450 (100 at $2.40, 100 at $2, and 10 at $1), our profit is $180 (or $630 minus $450), and our ending inventory is $90 (or $540 minus $450).

Neither sales nor purchases were affected by the difference in accounting method but cost of sales, profit, and ending inventory all were affected. In all cases the cost of goods sold plus the value of ending inventory must equal purchases. This can be used as a check on the computation.

One proposition is clear. In a rising price level FIFO gives the higher profit and inventory values and LIFO gives the lower profit and inventory figures with average cost in between. The converse is also true: in a falling price level FIFO gives the lower profit and inventory figures and LIFO gives the higher profit and inventory figures with average cost again falling in between.

Our example was simple and reflected only changes in unit costs of "raw materials." If this had been a manufacturing operation, we would also be involved with different unit costs of labor and manufacturing overhead for each month's operations. These differences in unit costs would be handled in the same way and might have moved in the same direction or in the opposite direction from raw materials cost changes.

There are two points in our illustration to note carefully. The amount by which the earnings of FIFO are larger than LIFO exactly matches the amount by which the FIFO inventory exceeds the LIFO. The "larger" earnings finance the "larger" inventory—but this will not be true when we have to pay an income tax on the "larger" profit. Thus not only do we have an "inventory profit" as part of our total profit under FIFO but we also have to come up with financing in the amount of the increase in our tax bill. We may be forced to cut dividends in order to pay the increase in taxes. This is probably why the historical dividend payout percentages for the total economy dropped from 65 percent in the period before World War II to about 50 percent in recent years. Two pressures were at work: inventory profits, which cannot be used to pay dividends, and the cash drain from higher taxes brought about by the inventory profits.

## MERGER AND REORGANIZATION PROBLEMS

It is difficult to consider the tax implications of recapitalization, mergers, consolidations, and reorganization without a full discussion of the other problems involved in these activities. Hence tax implications are considered in Chapters 22, 23, and 26 where these areas are developed.

## FOREIGN ACTIVITIES

An increasing number of American businesses are becoming involved in various foreign enterprises. In general, the income of a U.S. corporation is subject to the U.S. corporate income tax regardless of where that income is earned.[9] At the same time, individuals who are out of the country for a minimum of 18 continuous months are not taxed on income earned abroad up to $20,000 and after 3 years up to $25,000.

Until 1962, however, foreign corporations, although controlled by U.S. individuals or corporations, were not subjected to the U.S. corporate income tax until the income was paid over to the U.S. stockholder. Such "tax haven" corporations might escape U.S. taxation, furnish funds for foreign living, or result in the earnings being brought to the United States and taxed at capital gain rates. Or the income earned by a tax haven corporation in one foreign country might be channeled to another foreign country to furnish the capital to start a new business.

Thus until 1962 three situations existed: (1) foreign branches of U.S. companies fully and currently taxed by the United States, (2) foreign subsidiaries of U.S. companies with U.S. taxes deferred until repatriation of the income, and (3) *tax haven corporations* where income might completely escape U.S. taxation.

[9] See W. F. O'Connor, "United States Taxation of Earnings of American-Controlled Foreign Corporation," *Taxes*, 42 (September 1964), pp. 588–637.

The device for reaching foreign income has been to *attribute* undistributed income and tax it to U.S. owners of controlled corporations. A foreign corporation is considered controlled if more than 50 percent of its voting stock is U.S. owned, provided at least one U.S. owner holds 10 percent of the voting stock. In an effort to get at the shuffling of funds from one foreign corporation to another, the new legislation taxes "foreign-based company income," which is defined as security income, rents, royalties, and income from sales and services acquired from other persons or corporations in another foreign country.

In an effort to deal with the multiple taxation question, all the income of the controlled foreign corporation is considered distributed if a minimum percentage of net profits, varying with the foreign tax rate, is distributed. If the foreign tax rate is less than 10 percent, 90 percent of the foreign income is considered distributed, and scaling down to no income is considered distributed if the foreign tax rate is 43 percent or more. Thus no income is to be attributed when the sum of the U.S. tax on distributed earnings and the foreign tax on total earnings is 90 percent of the tax that a domestic U.S. corporation would have paid.

In addition, the 1962 act classified any gains realized by a U.S. shareholder owning 10 percent or more of any foreign corporation as ordinary dividend income regardless of the form of the transaction. Likewise, the sale of a patent, copyright, or similar asset by a U.S. parent corporation to a subsidiary controlled by more than 50 percent U.S. ownership is ordinary income.

Finally, U.S. corporations either can deduct from their income the foreign taxes paid or can credit against U.S. taxes due on the foreign income the income tax paid to a foreign country (up to the U.S. tax due on the foreign income). For this purpose all foreign income and foreign taxes paid are lumped together. Prior to 1961 each foreign country was separately considered, thus working to the U.S. taxpayer's disadvantage in that the income of a high-tax foreign country could not be set off against the income of a low-tax foreign country.

In an effort to equate foreign subsidiaries with foreign branches of U.S. corporations, the U.S. corporation must "*gross up*" its foreign subsidiary income by using the preforeign tax income in order to claim the credit for foreign taxes paid.

Preferential treatment is accorded foreign corporations in two areas: less-developed countries (except those of Western Europe and Canada, Australia, Japan, and South Africa) and Western Hemisphere Trade Corporations. U.S. corporations are not required to "gross up" income from less-developed countries. In the case of Western Hemisphere Trade Corporations, which now number about 700, the U.S. corporate tax rate is limited to 15.6 percent of the first $25,000 (instead of 22 percent) and 34 percent of the excess (instead of 48 percent). Credit for foreign income taxes paid is applicable to reduce these amounts. To qualify as a Western Hemisphere Trade Corporation, the company must be chartered in the United States, 95 percent of its gross income must originate outside the United States, and 90 percent of its gross income must come from a trade or business.

## STATE AND LOCAL TAXATION

While state and local taxation adds up to 42 percent of the total of federal, state, and local taxes, state corporate income taxes are only about 2 percent of total state and local taxes. Property taxes, sales taxes, license fees, and similar monies constitute the bulk of state and local taxes. Personal state income taxes are only about 4 percent of total state and local taxes.

State corporate income taxes average 6 percent of income, but the state income tax is deductible on the federal tax, reducing the effective rate to 3 percent. Individual states, such as Wisconsin, have rates as high as 14 percent.

The main concern of the state corporate income tax for the financial manager lies in the matter of plant location. Prior to 1959 corporate income was generally taxed only by the state of incorporation. A few states such as Massachusetts, Wisconsin, and Minnesota had anticipated the rule that has ultimately developed and were taxing the income of out-of-state corporations under a formula allocating to the taxing state that proportion of the out-of-state corporation's income determined by the average of:

1. The ratio of the sales of the company in the state to the company's total payroll
2. The ratio of the payroll of the company in the state to the company's total payroll
3. The ratio of the property of the company in the state to the company's total property.

In 1959 the Supreme Court ruled that states might tax the income from state sales of out-of-state corporations even though the out-of-state corporation did nothing more than send salesmen into the state. Congress promptly canceled this decision by enacting the Interstate Income Tax Law returning the situation to that prior to the court decision and requiring a warehouse, plant, or other basis more substantial than merely sending in salesmen.

The formula just given for determining the proportion of the income of an out-of-state corporation taxable by each state is not exactly the same in each state having a corporate income tax law. Hence to a limited extent there may be overlapping of income and multiple taxation or, conversely, a gap of untaxed income.

## TAX MINIMIZATION AS A POSSIBLE OVERRIDING CONSIDERATION

Where tax structures reach excessively high rates, tax minimization can become *the* overriding consideration. Thus in Sweden personal income taxes are so high that individuals cannot be significant suppliers of equity to business firms. On the other hand Swedish tax policy permits businesses to write off buildings over 23 years (compared to 40 in the United States) and *all* other fixed assets over no more than 5 years. The result is that Swedish corporations are encouraged to adopt improvements quickly and to be risk-takers—becoming tough and effective competitors in the world market. The result also is that when ecological expenditures and benefits are considered, the Swedish standard of living may be the world's highest.

The consequence for Swedish business finance has been a heavier reliance on retained cash as the source of financing. Hence Swedish firms carefully select investments with those growth rates, rates of return, investment mixes that offset risks and heavy capital requirements so that taxes are minimized. Volvo, for example, is estimated to pay no more than 20 percent in taxes on pre-depreciation income by minimizing taxable income while maximizing cash flow and turnover.

Even in the United States, firms can minimize somewhat external equity requirements by accelerated depreciation and a *sustained* growth rate. If the growth rate can be maintained indefinitely, the day of tax reckoning can be postponed indefinitely because of the heavy deductions for tax purposes in the early years of a capital-intensive investment. Dividends can be kept to a minimum and the great bulk of the profit taken out via the tax-free merger route while the securities received in the merger are liquidated gradually over time at capital gains rates, thus avoiding the new preference tax on large capital gains. Information about such planning is kept ultra secret in the United States because of the ardor of the Internal Revenue Service. There is a lack of a national policy encouraging risk-taking and new investment except in the so-called tax shelter areas of oil and real estate. The investment tax credit is a feeble step and used only cyclically.

## SUMMARY

Taxes are a vital factor in financing decisions. The main areas of taxation of interest to a financial manager are (1) avoiding multiple taxation and shifting ordinary income to capital gains, (2) delaying tax payments to secure interest-free use of funds (accelerated depreciation and sale and leaseback), (3) averaging income and losses over a period of years, (4) inventory problems, (5) merger and reorganization problems, (6) foreign activities, and (7) state and local taxation.

The exemption of 85 percent of intercompany dividends from income taxation gives particular attractiveness to preferred stock for taxable corporate investors. But two devices are no longer effective: collapsible corporations and preferred stock bail outs. Corporations with no more than ten shareholders can elect to be taxed as partnerships. The use of personal holding companies and unreasonable accumulation of earnings as devices to avoid taxation are subjected to punitive taxes. The withdrawal of dividends under other disguises is difficult for tax authorities to detect.

Stockholders who own shares that were bought at low prices but that are now greatly increased in value are said to be locked in because of their unwillingness to pay the capital gains tax that would be due upon sale of the stock. Upon death of the stockholder this increase in value is free of capital gains tax. On the other hand, making gifts will reduce the estate tax due, but in this case the donee accepts the cost or other basis of the donor and the capital gains tax on the increase in value is not avoided.

Accelerated depreciation is one of the principal ways of delaying the date of tax payment. Another is the sale and leaseback.

Averaging income and losses over a period of years is done through the operating loss carry back (three years) and carry forward (five years).

Inventory methods affect the amount and due date of taxes by determining what income is received in what period. In a period of rising prices FIFO results in the higher profits and taxability but in a period of falling prices LIFO gives the higher profits and taxability.

Before 1962 foreign corporations controlled by U.S. individuals or corporations were taxed only when the income was repatriated, but branches of U.S. firms were fully taxed. Since 1962 legislation has attempted to equalize the tax situation for the various forms in which U.S. corporations do business abroad.

State and local taxes are particularly important in determining plant location.

Taxes can reach such proportions that tax minimization reaches overriding importance.

### Study Questions

1. Do you think taxation should be a factor for the financial manager to consider in making his decisions or should he permit taxation to enter his thinking only after he has made his decision and then only for the purpose of deciding how and when to execute what he has decided to do?
2. Can a financial manager assume that tax rates or tax rules will remain constant? For example, should he assume that the income tax laws will always distinguish between ordinary income and capital gains? If not, how should he proceed to deal with tax questions in planning?
3. Do you consider the limited liability aspect of a corporation more important than the avoidance of double taxation by using a noncorporate form of business? Would your attitude be influenced by whether you were a rich man or a poor man?
4. Do you think it is wise to place in the minutes of a corporation's board meetings elaborate detail of proposed activities in order to avoid any claim by the Internal Revenue Service of unreasonable accumulation of earnings?
5. Would you as a financial manager favor the use of double-rate depreciation (in any of its several forms)? Do you think the stock market recognizes the consequences of differences in depreciation policies? What evidence is there to support your answer to the preceding question?
6. As a financial manager would you be impressed with the accrued losses of any proposed acquisition because of the tax carry back and carry forward provision of the income tax law? What is the other side of the coin?
7. Examine the summary of the public offering of National Cash Register subordinated convertible debentures issued in 1967 (p. 512) and comment on the foreign income tax situation of the firm, particularly the effect of the radical 1962 changes in U.S. tax law.

8. In view of the fact that over the long run periods of rising price levels have been of much greater duration than periods of falling price levels, what inventory-valuation principle would you recommend to a corporation? Why?

### Problems

1. Arro, a fully taxable financial corporation, is examining proposed investments. The current market rate of interest for the type of bond issue that the borrower, Ruff Company, seeks is 7 percent for a 20-year issue. From the point of view of Arro, what is the break-even rate of preferred stock of Ruff to which Arro could dip if Arro ignores the priority of bonds over preferred stock? Assume a tax rate of 50 percent.

2. In problem 1 what is the break-even rate on a bond issue that Ruff Company can accept if Arro quotes its break-even point on the preferred stock of Ruff?

3. An individual stockholder holds $1 million of current market value of stock of a corporation (such as IBM) which he bought for $10,000 many years ago. The current dividend on this stock is $10,000, and the taxpayer is in the 50 percent income tax bracket. The stockholder has confidence in the future of the corporation. He understands that if he sells at present he is liable for $197,925 in taxes at capital gains rates (25 percent on first $50,000, 35 percent on excess plus a preference tax of 10 percent on the excess of $495,000 over the sum of $30,000 plus capital gains tax paid of $168,250.) Further, he will be presented with the problem of how to invest the remaining $802,075 which might be placed in tax-exempt municipal bonds at a yield of 5 percent in 1972 (if he accepts a lower rating such as Moody's BAA for New York City bonds).

What is your advice to the stockholder?

4. The Catalpa Corporation has a pre-tax earnings record as follows:

| | |
|---|---|
| 1964 | $100,000 |
| 1965 | 100,000 |
| 1966 | (400,000) |
| 1967 | — |
| 1968 | 50,000 |
| 1969 | 50,000 |
| 1970 | 100,000 |
| 1971 | 75,000 |
| 1972 | (75,000) |

What is the total federal income tax of Catalpa for these years? Assume a tax rate of 50 percent.

5. The Western Corporation deals in wheat. The purchase and sale record during the year is set out below. What is the income tax and value of ending

| | |
|---|---|
| Jan. 10, bought | 100,000 bushels at $1.25 a bushel |
| Jan. 26, bought | 5,000 bushels at $1.00 a bushel |
| Jan. 31, sold | 10,000 bushels at $1.15 a bushel |
| Feb. 6, bought | 30,000 bushels at $0.90 a bushel |
| Feb. 20, bought | 5,000 bushels at $1.10 a bushel |
| Mar. 10, sold | 20,000 bushels at $1.20 a bushel |
| Mar. 16, sold | 10,000 bushels at $1.00 a bushel |
| Mar. 20, sold | 50,000 bushels at $1.10 a bushel |

inventory if Western uses the FIFO inventory method? What is the tax if LIFO is used? Assume the tax rate is 22 percent on the first $25,000 and 48 percent on the excess over $25,000.

6. The Oliver Company acquired effective control of Eskimo, Inc., but less than 80 percent of the stock, for a price of $200,000 in 1970. Eskimo developed favorable earnings of $50,000 and Oliver sold the stock in 1972 for $250,000 after receiving $25,000 in dividends.

a. What is Oliver's income tax liability for these events (assuming it is already in the 50 percent tax bracket)?

b. Would it have been beneficial if Oliver had received an added dividend of $25,000 and accepted a reduction of its sale price from $250,000 to $225,000?

7. Gusto Enterprises has experienced unprofitable operations for several years as follows:

| | | | |
|---|---|---|---|
| 1970 | loss of | $100,000 | |
| 1971 | loss of | 50,000 | |
| 1972 | loss of | 10,000 | (estimated) |

Bright Company has earned $500,000 per year in each of these years. The market value of the assets of Gusto is estimated at $125,000 against a depreciated cost on Gusto's books of $250,000. The total liabilities of Gusto are estimated at $60,000. Bright Company believes it can manage Gusto so as to achieve at least cash break-even operation for several years (excluding depreciation charges). Income taxes are 50 percent on corporate incomes over $25,000 and 22 percent on the first $25,000.

a. What is the maximum price that Bright Company could pay for Gusto and still break even if it buys Gusto in late 1972?

b. What is the maximum price that Small Company, with earnings of $25,000 per year (which it expects will continue), can pay for Gusto and break even, assuming all other facts are the same?

8. In 1974 John Tebbutt is thinking about his current status. As president and principal stockholder of Electro, Inc. he receives salary and bonus of $60,000 a year. His current dividend income on his holdings in Electro is $40,000 per year. His holdings of Electro stock have a current market value in the over-the-counter market of $2,500,000. He has a wife and four sons, a $75,000 home in Evanston, Illinois, and $100,000 in life insurance. His other assets are of small amount. His wife has no separate assets but is joint owner of the Electro stock and the home. His sons are in their twenties, married, and starting their own families, with two children in each family.

a. Approximate Tebbutt's income tax computation, assuming his deductions for tax purposes are $10,000.

b. Approximate Tebbutt's federal estate tax liability if he were to die in 1974 and his will leaves one-half of his estate to his wife with the balance to be divided equally among his four sons. Assume administrative costs for the estate are 10 percent. Tebbutt's wife contributed nothing to the purchase of her interest in the stock or home, and under tax law Tebbutt's estate is taxable on the full value of each asset, although if Mrs. Tebbutt dies first her half of the stock and home is taxable in her estate.

c. Under federal tax law if Tebbutt terminates the joint ownership with his wife by giving her one-half, there is a taxable gift of the half ownership so transferred, but the half is no longer within Tebbutt's estate when he dies. If

Tebbutt makes this transfer but changes his will to leave all of his half to his four sons, what will be the effect on taxes? (Tebbutt might have elected to pay a gift tax on the value of one-half when he created the joint ownership, but he did not do so).

d. Being dissatisfied with the results of the course of action proposed in (c), Tebbutt decides to explore the possibility of annual gifts of $6000 in stock to his wife, each of his four sons, each of their wives, and each of his grandchildren. In addition, he proposes to give his wife their home in the present year. If Tebbutt follows this practice for ten years and the value of the stock and home do not change, what would the tax situation be if Tebbutt in his will continues to give one-half to his wife and the other half to his children and grandchildren? List all the other tax benefits or handicaps you can see in the proposed action. A gift of $6000 is tax-free under the marital deduction provision if the wife makes no gift to the same donee as her husband does.

### Selected References

Barboli, F. P., "United States Taxation of International Business," *Business Topics*, 12 (Summer 1964), pp. 55–62.

Brittain, J. A., "The Tax Structure and Corporate Dividend Policy," *American Economic Review*, 54 (May 1964), pp. 272–287.

Butters, J. K., J. Lintner, and W. L. Cary, *Effects of Taxation: Corporate Mergers.* Cambridge, Mass.: Harvard University Graduate School of Business Administration, 1951.

Davidson, S., and D. F. Drake, "Capital Budgeting and the 'Best' Tax Depreciation Method," *Journal of Business*, 34 (October 1961), pp. 442–452; and "The 'Best' Tax Depreciation Method—1964," *Journal of Business*, 37 (July 1964), pp. 258–260.

Harley, C. E., "Dealings between Closely Held Corporations and Their Stockholders," *Tax Law Review*, 25 (January 1970), pp. 211–341.

Holzman, R. S., *Tax Basis for Managerial Decisions.* New York: Holt, Rinehart and Winston, Inc., 1965.

Miller, M. H., "The Corporation Income Tax and Corporate Financial Policies," in Commission on Money and Credit, *Stabilization Policies.* Englewood Cliffs, N. J.: Prentice-Hall, Inc., 1968.

O'Connor, W. F., "United States Taxation of Earnings of American-Controlled Foreign Corporation," *Taxes*, 42 (September 1964), pp. 588–637.

Shelton, J. P., and C. C. Holt, "The Implications of the Capital Gains Tax for Investment Decisions," *Journal of Finance*, 16 (December 1961), pp. 559–580.

Smith, D. T., *Effects of Taxation on Corporation Financial Policy.* Cambridge, Mass.: Harvard Graduate School of Business Administration, 1952.

Weinrobe, M. D., "Corporate Taxes and the U. S. Balance of Trade," *National Tax Journal*, 24 (March 1971), pp. 79–86.

# 25

# Employee Stock Purchase Plans, Stock Options, Profit-Sharing, and Deferred Compensation

The corporation can be viewed as a stool supported by three legs: the customers, the employees, and the stockholders. One might add a fourth leg: the suppliers. A consideration of executive stock options and employee stock purchase plans might seem to be out of the field of finance, since these devices are primarily forms of compensation. However, they are closely tied to the values of stock. A poor plan can injure stockholders while a good plan can increase profits for all stockholders.

## EMPLOYEE STOCK PURCHASE PLANS

Employee stock purchase plans have a long history.[1] At first such agreements involved isolated individual employees. The motivation of the corporation in encouraging employee purchases varies considerably. Stimulating thrift, protecting retirement income against inflation, pro-

[1] As early as 1911 an employee of the Parish-Stafford Company sued to enforce the agreement of the company to repurchase his shares when he left the company. *Strodl vs. The Parish-Stafford Company*, 145 Appellate Division 406, 130 N.Y. Supplement 359 (1911).

moting the free enterprise system, reducing labor turnover, increasing labor productivity, broadening stock ownership, and raising funds without underwriting costs are among the reasons advanced.

There was a rapid growth of employee stock plans in the 1920s. At the same time, a number of customer ownership plans were introduced in the public utility field. It was difficult at that time to anticipate some of the dire problems that arose with such plans in the 1930s. Typically, such stock purchase plans involved an installment purchase, sometimes over many years. As the economy slumped in the Great Depression, the employee-purchaser frequently found that he still owed more for the unpaid balance than the stock was worth in the current market. Some employees had relied on dividends to help pay for the purchase, but dividends ceased. Many of the stock plans contained various types of agreements that the company would repurchase the stock either when the employment terminated or at any time. Some repurchases were in the form of options (of either the company or the employee) and some were in the form of commitments. Such proposed repurchases by the corporation of its own stock ran afoul of the legal restrictions on share repurchase [2] which we discussed in Chapter 22. Some sympathetic courts were able to find that the employee "purchases" were options or even agreements for "sale or return" so as to relieve the employee of the remaining indebtedness. For the employee to lose both his job and his stock was a double blow.

Today many state statutes provide special rules for employee repurchases, but no law can grant an employee-purchaser equality with creditors—much less priority—in cases of insolvency.

An employee stock plan can be implemented either by the issuance of shares by the corporation [3] or by the purchase of shares by the corporation in the open market as agent for employees. Many plans provide for a discount to employees in the price of the stock from the going market price.[4] Tax law permits a maximum discount of 15 percent on employee shares without depriving the employee of the later tax advantage of a capital gain rather than ordinary income. The discount furnishes a cushion against employee dissatisfaction if the market price of the stock dips.

Employee stock purchase plans expanded rapidly in the 1950s and 1960s and have achieved greatest popularity among financial institutions.[5]

---

[2] Erwin E. Nemmers, "Employee Stock Repurchase Agreements," *Marquette Law Review*, 26 (June 1942), pp. 187–196, reprinted in *Current Legal Thought*, 9 (October 1942), pp. 3–6.

[3] In this event some states provide for the suspension of the preemptive right if one exists in the particular company. Or stockholder action may remove the preemptive right.

[4] If the corporation purchases the shares in the open market, there are few legal restrictions on the resale price. Some state statutes provide an exemption for employee shares from the rule requiring the new shares be sold no lower than fair market price.

[5] There is no agreement as to what constitutes an employee stock purchase plan. The data of Tables 25–1 and 25–2 exclude plans that (1) do not cover rank and file employees, (2) result in delivery of stock after retirement, or (3) are awarded by the company without purchase by the employee.

TABLE 25–1. Percentage of Companies Listed on New York Stock Exchange Having Employee Stock Purchase Plans in 1960 and 1966

| Industry | Percent of companies with employee stock purchase plans | |
|---|---|---|
| | 1960 | 1966 |
| Manufacturing | 12% | 22% |
| Utilities | 26 | 41 |
| Retail Trade | 9 | 23 |

SOURCE: Mitchell Meyer and Harland Fox, *Employee Stock Purchase Plans*, Studies in Personnel Policy No. 206 (New York: National Industrial Conference Board, 1967), p. 5.

Thus, in 1966, 36 percent of a sample of 141 stock insurance companies with 200 or more employees had plans and 25 percent of a sample of 171 commercial banks with deposits over $100 million had plans. These two samples included slightly more than half of the insurance companies and banks of such size. In the case of companies whose securities were listed on the New York Stock Exchange, in the spring of 1966 some 251, or 21 percent, had employee stock purchase plans, representing an increase in all types of industry, as indicated in Table 25–1.

Employee stock purchase plans are more numerous among larger companies, as Table 25–2 indicates.

Another study by the exchange indicated that 21 percent of the 30.9 million shareholders in 1970 bought their first shares under an employees stock purchase plan, and that the number of shareholders making their

TABLE 25–2. Percentage of Companies Listed on New York Stock Exchange Having Employee Stock Purchase Plans in 1966, Classified by Industry and Size of Company

| *Industry* | *1965 sales volume of company* | *Percentage of companies with plan* |
|---|---|---|
| Manufacturing | $1 billion and over | 46% |
| | $400–$999 million | 29 |
| | $100–$399 million | 22 |
| | Under $100 million | 12 |
| | All manufacturing | 22 |
| Utilities | $200 million and over | 53% |
| | Under $200 million | 32 |
| | All utilities | 41 |
| Retail trade | $300 million and over | 33% |
| | Under $300 million | 21 |
| | All retail trade | 23 |

SOURCE: Mitchell Meyer and Harland Fox, *Employee Stock Purchase Plans*, Studies in Personnel Policy No. 206 (New York: National Industrial Conference Board, 1967), p. 5.

first purchase through their employer increased 77 percent between 1965 and 1970.[6]

Employee stock purchases have also been melded into employee savings programs.[7] Under such plans the employer contributes to the savings fund, usually in an amount equal to the employee's contribution. The fund is invested partly in the company's stock and partly in fixed-income investments, usually government bonds. One purpose of such plans is to modify the effect of any fall in the market price of the stock; another achieves a reduction in labor turnover, since if the employee leaves he takes only his own contributions, which were invested in fixed-income investments.

To illustrate the importance of employee stock purchase plans to the financial manager, we can cite the stock-savings plan of Sears, Roebuck and Company which began in 1916 and today owns about 25 percent of the company's outstanding stock. The market value of the company's stock is approximately $3 billion. The Sears plan is limited to a maximum of 5 percent of the employee's salary, up to $500 when he joins. On the other hand, American Telephone & Telegraph Company in recent years has permitted employees to subscribe for amounts in excess of 30 percent of their annual salary.

## STOCK OPTIONS

A stock option is a right granted most often to management-level employees to buy the stock of the employing company at a set price close to the market price at the time the option is granted. The employee pays nothing for the right, which continues for a number of years and then expires. If the market value of the stock advances during the option period, the employee can exercise his right to purchase at the set price and either retain the stock or dispose of it at a profit. The motivation to the employee is that he will participate in the fruits of his work. This can also be achieved by any profit-sharing arrangement. The particular attraction of the stock option is that the gain may be taxable at the lower capital gains rate rather than the higher rates applicable to ordinary income.

The stock option is a relatively recent phenomenon compared to the stock purchase plan. The reason for the tardy development of the stock option device lies in income tax rules. Until 1939 the Internal Revenue Service regarded all employee stock options as a form of compensation subject to taxation as ordinary income. Then until 1945 the difference between the option price and the market value at the time the option was exercised was taxed as ordinary income only to the extent that this amount could be considered compensation for services. In 1945 the United States Supreme Court ruled that the recipient of an option was tax-

---

[6] New York Stock Exchange, *Shareownership—1970* (New York: The Exchange, 1970), p. 3.

[7] One study of this aspect is Harland Fox and Mitchell Meyer, *Employee Savings Plans in the United States*, Studies in Personnel Policy No. 184 (New York: National Industrial Conference Board, 1962).

able on the "paper profits" he realized on the differences between the market price of the stock at the time the option was granted and the option price.[8] This effectively terminated the stock option as an attraction.

In 1950 Congress created the concept of a *restricted stock option.* If the option met the requirements set by Congress, no tax was due when it was created and none was due when it was exercised, and only a capital gain would result when the option stock was sold.[9]

Without disturbing the restricted stock options already granted, Congress in 1964 tightened the rules for *qualified stock options* to allow for tax-free status when granted and to qualify for only a capital gains tax when the stock is sold. Rules now require that the option price be equal to market value at the time of the grant. The one receiving the option must exercise it within five years and must be an employee (or within three months of terminating employment), and the stock must be held until three years after the date of the grant for the ultimate gain to qualify as a capital gain. In addition, the one receiving the option must own less than 5 percent of the stock except for companies with less than $2 million in equity. Furthermore, options must be exercised (or expire) in the order in which they were granted.[10]

The 1964 Act also requires stockholder approval of the stock option plan. This is the first time the tax law attempted to provide some protection for stockholders.

The 1969 Tax Reform Act represents the latest and most serious tightening of the tax benefits of stock options for executives. A special tax of 10 percent is imposed at the time the option is *exercised* to the extent the then-unrealized gain exceeds an annual exemption of $30,000.[11] Finally, there will be a regular capital gains tax due at the time the stock is sold. Because the capital gains rate increases to 35 percent over $50,000 in any one year plus the 10 percent preference tax and another special tax of 1.5 percent may then be due, the total tax on an option gain can reach 46.5 percent. On the other hand, if the executives receive a cash bonus

---

[8] *Commissioner vs. Smith,* 324 U.S. 177 (1945).

[9] The most important requirements were that the option price could not be less than 85 percent of market price at the time the option was granted. If the option was at least 95 percent of market price, the ultimate gain would be a capital gain. If the option price was between 85 and 95 percent, the difference between the option price and the market price when the option is granted (or the market price at exercise if that is less) would be ordinary income and any gain thereafter would be a capital gain. Furthermore, the option must expire in ten years and be exercised while still an employee, or within three months after leaving employment. Stock acquired under the option must be held until two years after the option was granted to qualify for capital gains treatment. No recipient of such an option could own 10 percent of the stock except under further restrictions.

[10] If the stock option qualifies for preferential treatment in the hands of the one receiving the option, there is no deduction for the corporation. If the stock option does not qualify for preferential treatment, the company is allowed a deduction as compensation paid.

[11] To the exemption of $30,000 is added an additional exemption in the amount of the regular income tax paid that year. On the other hand, the untaxed half of any long-term capital gains in that year also is chargeable against this exemption.

instead of the option gain, in years after 1971, this maximum tax on such earned income (regardless of amount) is 50 percent. Furthermore, the corporation receives a deduction for the cash bonus but no deduction for the option gain.[12]

Hence, except for smaller options where the unrealized gain at time of *exercise* is under $30,000 in that year and the employee has no long-term capital gains in that year, the 1969 Tax Reform Act has effectively terminated the tax benefits of stock options.

Many companies have moved to "phantom" stock options, which give the employee as a cash bonus the amount of gain which the employee would have had if he had a stock option. In short, this is a bonus based not on profits but on "market action" of the stock.

### Performance Stock

The stock options just described depend for their value not only on the efforts of the individual receiving the option but also on (1) the efforts of other employees and (2) many events over which the holder of the option has no control. Performance stock is a device to establish a more direct relation between the effort of the employee and his reward. Thus a stated number of shares may be issued at no cost to the employee upon achievement of a specific goal such as attainment of a given level of profit over a number of years in his division. Such stock is treated as ordinary income at its market value when received and is deductible by the corporation as compensation.

This detailed treatment of stock options is warranted by their importance (until recently) in the area of executive compensation.[13] However it appears that the performance of the stock of companies with stock options does not differ from that of companies without stock options.[14]

Some companies, for example, Allied Chemical, have shifted away from the stock option to granting employees "dividend units," which are simply varying bonuses measured by the amount of dividends the employee would receive if he owned a given number of shares. This substitutes the lesser risk (for the employee) of a change in the dividend rate for the greater risk of a change in the market value of a share. Such bonus amounts are taxable as ordinary income to the employee but are tax deductible by the corporation, whereas ordinary dividends are not.

## PROFIT-SHARING AND DEFERRED COMPENSATION

Having examined employee stock purchases and stock options, we can briefly view the principal alternative devices: profit-sharing and de-

[12] This is so except in the unusual case where the executive sells his shares in the same year as he exercises the option, thereby incurring a short-term capital gain.

[13] G. E. Lent and J. A. Menge, "The Importance of Restricted Stock Options in Executive Compensation," *Management Record*, 4 (June 1962), pp. 6–13, present evidence that exercised and exercisable options as a percentage of after-tax salary stood at 91 percent in 1956 but dropped to 64 percent in 1960.

[14] Emmet Wallace, *Appraisal of Stock Options as an Incentive Device*, unpublished Ph.D. dissertation, Columbia University, 1961.

ferred compensation. Profit-sharing can be of two types, providing for either immediate cash payment to the employees or for a deferred payment. The immediate cash payment type is simply a bonus. We will consider the deferred payment type, which has financial implications to the corporation.

Guthmann and Dougall have described the usual profit-sharing plan as "profit-sharing without investment" [15] to point out that employee stock purchase plans involve an investment by the employee. In the typical profit-sharing plan the company's contribution is stated as a percentage of profits before income taxes, since the company's contribution is itself tax deductible if the plan qualifies under the Internal Revenue Act.[16]

Profit-sharing has had a rapid growth, from only 37 such plans in existence in 1940 to 3565 plans in 1950 and 33,222 plans in 1963.[17]

Since profit-sharing contributions are tax deductible, the cash drain of the corporation is only half what it would be if employees received an equal amount in dividends.

Deferred profit-sharing requires the annual payment of the shared profit to an independent trustee who administers the fund under the provisions of the plan. The trustee may invest by buying shares of the company's stock. In this case we have the same result as an employee stock purchase plan but with several added and important advantages. The corporation gets tax deductibility for the purchase price of the shares and the employee's tax payment is deferred until he receives a distribution, which may be at retirement. In addition, the earnings of the trust fund are tax free, resulting, in effect, in another deferment of tax. In fact, if the employee dies before retirement or if he terminates employment and the entire amount due him is paid within one year, the entire amount is recognized as a capital gain rather than as ordinary income.

In lieu of investment in the shares of the company the trustee may purchase property which is then leased to the corporation.[18] Here we have the company maintaining the *availability* of cash with which it parted at the time of the profit-sharing payment. The availability is not cost free, since the company will be paying for the use of these funds, but it will have had the advantage of deducting the profit-sharing payment for tax purposes, thus making the amount of available cash twice what would exist in the form of retained earnings.

---

[15] H. G. Guthmann and H. E. Dougall, *Corporate Financial Policy*, 4th ed. (Englewood Cliffs, N. J.: Prentice-Hall, Inc. 1962), p. 433.

[16] The main requirements under the Internal Revenue Act are that the plan not favor officers and highly paid employees and that there be no possibility of return of the fund to the company when the profits are not to be immediately distributed but are to accumulate in a program that provides for payment to the employee after retirement. The Internal Revenue Service limits tax deductibility by the corporation to 15 percent of the annual compensation of covered employees in the case of deferred plans. Employees have no taxable income until they receive actual distribution.

[17] B. L. Metzger, *Profit-sharing in Perspective in American Medium-sized and Small Business* (Evanston, Ill.: Profit Sharing Research Foundation, 1964), p. 6.

[18] The lease must be an "arm's length transaction" or the transaction will run afoul of the Internal Revenue Service, which could result in denial of the tax deductibility of the profit-sharing payments.

*Deferred compensation* is the term used to describe the postponement of the payment of salary that would otherwise be currently payable. Deferred profit-sharing is a form of deferred compensation but is not considered within the meaning of the term "deferred compensation." Deferred compensation is used to offer a tax advantage to one in a high tax bracket. When the deferred part of the salary is paid at a later date (often after retirement) the taxpayer expects to be in a lower bracket. However, the corporation is not allowed a current tax reduction[19] for the amount of deferred compensation but must wait until actual payment is paid before gaining the deduction. Another reason sometimes advanced for deferred compensation is that the corporation may not be in a position currently to pay the salary requirements of a sorely needed executive.

Deferred compensation presents a number of problems to the executive-recipient. First, tax rates may advance between the current year and the year in which payment is scheduled, thus wiping out part of the original tax motives. Second, the executive is deprived of the investment opportunities to which he might currently apply the after-tax salary. This can be partially remedied by adjusting the deferred compensation upward by a compound rate to the date of payment. Third, the executive is exposed to the risks of inflation as to the unpaid balance of his salary. This can be dealt with by agreement to adjust this balance by the use of a price index. Finally, the executive becomes a creditor-investor of the business and assumes the risk of bankruptcy.[20]

From the corporation's point of view these difficulties with deferred compensation may damage the incentive of the executive and defeat its purpose.[21] Despite these problems, 28 percent of the companies in a sample survey in 1963 reported the use of deferred compensation.[22]

## SUMMARY

Special compensation methods create varying financial consequences for financial managers, since there is an effect on the value of the shares of stock.

Employee stock purchase plans have a long history. In the 1930s repurchase agreements by the corporation and unpaid installment purchases caused serious problems. Currently such plans are increasing, and in 1966 21 percent of all companies listed on the New York Stock Exchange had such plans, with larger companies showing an even higher percentage.

---

[19] This is because deferred compensation does not meet the nondiscriminatory test (referred to in footnote 16) to qualify as a deferred profit-sharing, in addition ot the fact that the agreement is not contingent on the existence of profits.

[20] While unpaid wages are entitled to priority in bankruptcy, the amount entitled to priority is limited to a maximum of $600 earned in the three months preceding bankruptcy. Any amount in excess of this priority is treated as an unsecured creditor.

[21] G. H. Foote, "When Deferred Compensation Doesn't Pay," *Harvard Business Review* 42 (May-June 1964), pp. 99–106.

[22] Harland Fox, "Deferred Compensation for the Executive," *Business Management Record* (July 1963), pp. 10–21. This periodical changed its name to *Conference Board Record*, a monthly, and began with Volume 1 in 1964.

Stock options are used to increase the incentive to management. The particular attraction of options is that they result in capital gains for the holder rather than in ordinary income. A 1945 Supreme Court decision hindered the use of options by holding that any difference in price of the option from the market value of the shares at the date of grant was ordinary income. In 1950 Congress created the concept of a restricted stock option which negated this decision. The rules were tightened in 1964 to provide for qualified stock option plans. Then the 1969 Tax Reform Act limited the tax advantage to small amounts.

Profit-sharing involves no investment on the part of the employee, in contrast with employee stock purchase plans. The company's contribution is tax deductible if the plan meets tax standards and does not exceed 15 percent of eligible employee compensation. The number of profit-sharing plans has grown from 37 in 1940 to 33,222 in 1963.

Deferred compensation involves no current tax deduction to the employing corporation but a deferment of tax to the employee until he actually receives the compensation, which is usually after retirement, thus leveling the income of the employee over the years.

Both profit-sharing funds and deferred compensation funds may be invested in the shares of the employing corporation or may be used to purchase assets for lease to that corporation.

### *Study Questions*

1. As an employee, would you favor a profit-sharing plan or a pension plan if the company is willing to contribute in the current year the same amount toward either plan? You may assume that in the past your company has grown in both profits and sales at a better than average rate.
2. As a company, would you favor the adoption of an employee stock purchase plan or a profit-sharing plan, assuming that the company is willing to contribute the same amount to either plan?
3. As an executive, would you favor a company's program for deferred compensation for yourself if you are 55 years old, earning a large salary, and have accumulated a substantial estate? The deferred compensation is proposed as an alternative to increasing your salary, with a provision that the deferred salary will be increased by an appropriate interest rate to the date of payment.
4. What do you think are appropriate provisions of a profit-sharing plan on the following points:
   a. Who should decide what the investments of the fund will be?
   b. When should the share of each member of the fund be subject to withdrawal?
   c. Should the provision for withdrawal of a member's share provide for a penalty, such as a provision that after one year the forfeiture should be 50 percent, after two years, 40 percent, and so on, until final "vesting" of all of the amount in the employee?
   d. What factors (salary, seniority, and so on) should determine the share of each employee in the profit-sharing total?
5. As a stockholder, do you favor the use of stock options as an incentive to key employees? Would your thinking be influenced by the degree to which the

employee can affect the profitability of the enterprise by his performance? Or do you think his value is already reflected in his salary?

6. It is sometimes argued that deferred compensation is to be preferred by an employee because he assumes no risk as to the amount of his deferred compensation while under profit-sharing he is exposed to the vicissitudes of the business. Would you therefore prefer deferred compensation?

7. From the point of view of the company, which type of program would you prefer: the employee stock purchase plan, the stock option, the profit-sharing plan, or the deferred compensation plan?

## Problems

1. Prepare the terms that you would include in an employee stock purchase plan, covering provisions (if any) that you would include on the following subjects. Give reasons for each position you take.

a. Whether the company or an independent party such as a bank should handle the administration of the plan.

b. Whether shares to be purchased under the plan should be issued by the company or bought in the open market.

c. Whether the plan should be limited to purchase of the company's shares or combined with a savings aspect involving some investment in government bonds or similar assets.

d. Whether the company should contribute to the plan, and if so, how much and on what basis.

e. Whether employee funds should be collected by payroll deductions or volunteered from time to time by employees.

f. Whether there should be any provision for repurchase of the shares by the company, and if so, at what price and at what times.

g. Whether the plan should permit purchase of shares on credit with installment payment later or should provide for accumulation of money until sufficient funds are on hand for the proposed purchase.

h. Whether the plan should have a maximum limit per employee.

i. Whether the plan should require that the employee continue in employment in order to obtain full right to any company contribution.

j. Any additional provisions.

2. Prepare the terms that you would include in a qualified stock option plan, covering provisions (if any) that you would include. What provisions must be included in order to meet Internal Revenue Service requirements to qualify for delayed capital gain treatment?

3. Prepare the terms of a profit-sharing agreement, including any provisions that would be necessary for the plan to meet the requirements of the Internal Revenue Service.

## Selected References

Baker, J. C., "Stock Options at the Crossroads," *Harvard Business Review,* 41 (January–February 1963) pp. 22–31.

Foote, G. H., "When Deferred Compensation Doesn't Pay," *Harvard Business Review,* 42 (May–June 1964), pp. 99–106.

Fox, H., "Deferred Compensation for the Executive," *Business Management Record* 9 (July 1963), pp. 10–21. (Name of journal changed in 1964 to *Conference Board Record,* monthly, beginning with Volume 1.)

———, and M. Meyer, *Employee Savings Plans in the United States, Studies in Personnel Policy, No. 184,* New York: National Industrial Conference Board, 1962.

Goldman, D., "Stock Options—Where to Now?" *Financial Executive,* 39 (March 1971), pp. 51–57.

Holland, D. M., and W. G. Lewellen, "Probing the Record of Stock Options," *Harvard Business Review,* 40 (March–April 1962) pp. 132–150.

Lewellen, W. G., *The Ownership Income of Management.* National Bureau of Economic Research, Fiscal Studies 14. New York and London: Columbia University Press, 1971.

Meyer, M., and H. Fox, *Employee Stock Purchase Plans,* Studies in Personnel Policy No. 206. New York: National Industrial Conference Board, 1967.

Monahan, J. P. and K. B. Monahan, "Company Contributions to Discretionary Profit-Sharing Plans: A Quantitative Approach," *Journal of Finance,* 29 (June 1974), pp. 981-994.

Nemmers, E. E., "Employee Stock Repurchase Agreements," *Marquette Law Review,* 26 (June 1942), pp. 187–196; reprinted in *Current Legal Thought,* 9 (October 1942), pp. 3–7.

# 26
# Bankruptcy, Liquidation and Dissolution

There are varying degrees of financial failure. But the most useful distinction, and one recognized by the law, is that between insolvency in the *equity* sense and insolvency in the *bankruptcy* sense. Insolvency in the equity sense means inability to pay debts as they become due, and in the history of the law this might place one under the supervision of a court of equity. Insolvency in the bankruptcy sense means either the performance of stated acts while insolvent in the equity sense or the performance of stated acts while liabilities (excluding any ownership interest) exceed assets. The detail of these stated acts will be discussed later in the chapter.

The financial manager even of a successful company must understand the area of failure if for no other reason than because his company lives in a world where failure is a fact. Failure may involve customers of his firm and thus affect, for example, the accounts receivable. Failure may involve competing firms in his industry and thus unstabilize pricing and other aspects of business vital to his company. Failure may involve a supplier of his firm and jeopardize the flow of incoming materials. There are many points at which failure of another firm may impinge on the financial manager.

It is unfortunately true that as soon as failure is suspected, the typical reaction of the financial manager and of the other executives of outside firms is to seek to withdraw and write off the situation. This in turn leads a firm confronted with financial problems to "cover up" as long as possible, since it is aware of the dire consequences of full disclosure.

A firm's financial problems can almost always be traced to inadequate management. To proceed as if recessions do not occur, to assume that markets do not shift, to ignore the fact that there is a probability distribution associated with every decision—these are the hallmarks of inadequate management.

It has been suggested that accounting entries are the first type of remedy available to deal with financial failure in its mildest form. This may involve such entries as reducing capital stock to create capital surplus and then charging accrued losses appearing as a deficit in retained earnings against the capital surplus. These accounting entries may be associated with a writing down of asset values. The obvious purpose of this manipulation is to accelerate the date when dividends can legally be paid.

## EXTENSION AND COMPOSITION

Both extension and composition involve *voluntary* actions on the part of the firm's creditors. The essential difference between an *extension* and a *composition* is that the former involves the agreement by one or more of the creditors to delay the date of payment of their claims while the latter involves the agreement of *all* the creditors to accept partial payment in full satisfaction of their debts. If only one creditor agrees to partial payment, the arrangement is called an *accord.*

In the case of a small business where the creditors are few and they have confidence in the management and the difficulties appear to be temporary, it is possible that an extension and/or composition may be worked out. The incentive to the creditors, obviously, must be that the successful liquidation of their claims plus the potential future profits of the business they expect to do with the debtor warrant the extension. This can be quickly tested. If the principal creditors feel justified in advancing sufficient funds to pay off lesser creditors in full, then the operation of revitalizing the company may be successful. If the principal creditors feel they cannot go this far, then their future activities in participating in the reorganization are self-deluding.

The analysis so far focuses on several items. First there is the need for the consolidation of smaller claims in order to avoid the threat of litigation (any three or more unpaid creditors with provable claims totaling $500 can force a company into bankruptcy by proving an act of bankruptcy). The channel often used to consolidate debts in this manner is a loan by a financial institution, and the creditors are paid with the proceeds of this loan. Presumably the debtor has exhausted his possibilities with banks and even with commercial credit companies, who accept risks beyond the limits of banks. Presumably also the debtor has exhausted the loan possibilities of assets that can be mortgaged or pledged, such as real estate and accounts receivable. In addition, the cash account has been run down.

It is clear that even if an extension can be established or a composition agreed upon, the business will be without current funds to purchase inventory, meet its payroll, finance receivables, and so on. Unless some assets can be promptly liquidated and new credit or new funds procured on some basis, the prospects will not be encouraging.

The successful use of the *creditors' committee*, especially during the recession of 1920–1922, is sometimes cited. The key fact in the case of the creditors' committee is not the committee but the replacement of the debtor as manager of the business with a temporary professional manager who may succeed in a relatively short time in revitalizing the business. New credit may be immediately available to the temporary manager, whose competence is established. The creditors' committee relates to an environment of American business that no longer exists: the corner grocery store, the neighborhood jeweler, and so on. The manufacturer of that era had relations with a thousand or more small establishments who were outlets of his goods, and he could be relied upon to come forward with the needed temporary manager.

## RECEIVERSHIP IN EQUITY AND BANKRUPTCY (PRIOR TO 1933)

The legal system at one time had developed a device to deal with the problems of incipient failure. This device was the *receivership* under the control of a court of equity. When the business was too large to be the subject of friendly adjustment either directly with creditors or through the use of a creditors' committee, one of the creditors (often with the consent of management) applied to a court of equity to appoint a receiver to administer the affairs of the debtor. One immediate result of the appointment was that due dates on unsecured debt were, in effect, suspended.

The equity receivership worked out the device critical to a successful recovery: the ability of the receiver to get the needed new funds by issuing a certificate with court-granted priority over all unsecured claims.[1] The success of the receivership would also depend upon the management ability of the receiver and the ability to procure the necessary correction in management talent to enable the business to continue. In addition to the need for new funds and management ability, there is the need to scale down the fixed charges and rearrange the capital structure.

The equity receivership was essentially a temporary device to permit time to decide whether the business could be revitalized or should be liquidated. During the receivership, operations continued under the control of the receiver and subject to the direction of the court. The immediate problem was to formulate and evaluate plans for the reorganiza-

[1] In effect, the certificate had priority to all *income* even as against secured claims, which had priority only over the proceeds from the sale of the specific asset that was mortgaged or pledged.

tion. The several classes of creditors formed protective committees to represent them. The receiver conducted an audit and determined the status of all claimants in order to arrive at a realistic balance sheet as a basis for developing a plan.

### Absolute and Relative Priority Rules

If no plan of reorganization could be developed in the old equity receivership, the matter would be thrown into bankruptcy. Until the Supreme Court decision in 1939 [2] there were two priority rules that were variously applied by the courts—absolute priority and relative priority. Absolute priority requires that each level of claims be paid in full before anything is paid to the next level. Relative priority merely requires that each level of claims be paid relatively more than the next lower level. A simple illustration will make the point. Assume that a business has assets worth $300,000. Assume, further, that there are bonds of $200,000, preferred stock of $100,000, and common stock of $300,000, with no debts other than bonds. Absolute priority requires that the bonds and preferred stock be paid in full. Relative priority would permit paying 90 cents on the dollar to bonds, 80 cents on the dollar to preferred stock, and applying the balance to common stock, which in this case would give the common stock 13 cents on the dollar. Instead of cash payment the distribution would be made in new securities, reflecting these values. To soften the blow the plan might then give the bonds and the preferred stock a bit of common stock. Under absolute priority the common stock would receive nothing, since the position of the bonds and preferred stock would exhaust the assets.

In the *Los Angeles* case the court made clear that the absolute priority rule must be observed.[3] In further application this means that the security behind each type of secured obligation must be separately valued, and to the extent the security is inadequate, the balance of the secured claim becomes an unsecured claim.

One way of attempting to kill two birds with one stone was for the court to order a sale of the business. At this sale one of the bidders (usually the only one) would be the reorganization committee of the old business with its plan. In this way creditors were assured the benefits of a sale and a plan and could not argue on appeal that if the court had not approved the plan they might have gotten more out of a sale.

### The "Upset Price"

To assure a modicum of protection to all interests the court would normally set an "upset price," or the value below which bids for the business would be rejected. It is important to note that at such a sale each claimant could bid and offer payment to the extent of his claim instead of cash. This follows the theory that the more of his claim he extinguishes in this way, the less the deficiency of assets to cover the remaining claims.

---

[2] *Case vs. Los Angeles Lumber Products Company*, 308 U.S. 106 (1939).

[3] See H. G. Guthmann, "Absolute Priority in Reorganizations," *Columbia Law Review*, 45 (September 1945), pp. 739–754.

One glaring defect of the equity receivership—and that led to legislation—was that many plans were not feasible and the new company was back in receivership shortly. In addition, dissenters could not be cut off by the proceeding and hence had to be paid off in cash.

## SALE AND MERGER AS AN ALTERNATIVE

With the exception of public utilities, one answer to the problem of financial difficulty is to sell or merge the business. In the case of public utilities this answer is not feasible. First, the sale or merger would require the consent of a regulatory agency such as the Interstate Commerce Commission or state public service commissions. Second, the purchaser or surviving company in the merger usually contemplates radical surgery upon the old company such as terminating product lines or selling off facilities. Such surgery on a public utility is not possible without extensive and time-consuming proceedings before abandonment of lines or types of service is permitted.

It is not surprising, then, that most of the cases involving receivership are public utilities and particularly railroads and transit companies. Almost all industrial companies took the sale and merger route rather than receivership.[4]

## MODERN REORGANIZATION AND BANKRUPTCY

The Great Depression brought to a head the festering inadequacies of the law governing reorganization and bankruptcy, particularly in the case of railroads. Bankruptcy is made a matter for federal courts by the U. S. Constitution. It is true that there can be matters such as an assignment for the benefit of creditors which may be settled in state courts, but any unhappy group of three creditors with claims totaling $500 can march the proceedings over to the federal court. After four months in the state court without such a move, however, the federal law concedes jurisdiction to the state court. One important thing that no court but a federal court can grant is a discharge in bankruptcy which terminates all claims. Whatever a state court may do, the debtor's liability cannot be terminated. In the case of a corporation, this is not important, since the corporation can be abandoned.

The Bankruptcy Act of 1898 stood unamended until a hasty amendment for railroads in 1933 and the final amendment in 1938 known as the Chandler Act. In essence, there are now two channels, known as Chapter X and Chapter XI. Section 77, which applies only to railroads, largely follows the pattern of Chapter X and need not be separately discussed. Section 77 was amended in 1948 by the Mahaffie Act.

---

[4] One classic case of the law of receivership is the Keeshin Companies case, summarized in Erwin E. Nemmers, *Cases in Finance* (Boston: Allyn & Bacon, Inc., 1964), pp. 400–411. In this case the record suggests that Keeshin had a disagreement with a major creditor and decided to have his claim "adjusted" in receivership. But once the court gets jurisdiction, the court and not the debtor decides what will be done and whether the debtor can have his company back. The long and strange history of what followed was surely not contemplated by Keeshin.

### Chapter XI Proceedings

Chapter XI purports to deal with milder situations and euphemistically identifies the process as an "arrangement." The proceeding is begun only by voluntary petition of the debtor and involves only the unsecured creditors. The court may or may not appoint a trustee or receiver. The proceeding is applicable to corporate or noncorporate debtors. Hearings are held and a plan is developed which may or may not scale down claims and may or may not authorize the issuance of bonds or stock to the creditors for their claims. Any plan requires the majority approval by number and amount of each class of creditors and binds even dissenting creditors. One principal purpose of Chapter XI is to bring to a halt all actions by creditors who are individually tearing the business apart. Hopeless cases under Chapter XI may be ordered to proceed under Chapter X.

### Chapter X Proceedings

Chapter X is the traditional bankruptcy section. Proceedings may be begun voluntarily by the debtor or forced (involuntary) by petition of three or more creditors with provable claims totaling at least $500 who can prove that one of the six acts of bankruptcy occurred in the preceding four months. These acts of bankruptcy are:

1. Transferring or concealing assets with intent to defraud creditors.

2. Transferring property to a creditor with intent to prefer him while insolvent (excess of liabilities over assets).

3. Permitting a creditor to obtain preference in legal proceedings, such as obtaining a lien or judgment while insolvent (excess of liabilities over assets).

4. Making a general assignment for benefit of creditors.

5. Permitting a receiver to take charge while insolvent in either sense.

6. Admitting in writing inability to pay debtors and willingness to be adjudged bankrupt on that ground.

Pending the hearing on the bankruptcy petition, the court may appoint a receiver. Once court jurisdiction is established, the court appoints a disinterested party as trustee, although a person from the old business may be appointed a co-trustee. A meeting of creditors is held and all claimants are required to file and prove their claims. The trustee and any other interested party may propose reorganization plans and hearings are held on all plans. The SEC renders an advisory report to the court on the plans.

### Fair and Feasible Plan of Reorganization

The critical words are that any reorganization plan that is to be approved must be "fair and feasible." Fairness presents no problem. A plan is fair only if it meets the rule of absolute priority that we have already discussed. But what meets the standard of feasibility is a difficult question indeed.[5] The plan, if approved by the court, requires a two-thirds vote of each class of creditors by value. Only a majority of the stockholders is required if assets exceed liabilities. If no fair and feasible plan is found, then the matter proceeds to liquidation and dissolution.

Feasibility of a reorganization plan is best handled by examining a number of cases, and this chapter ends with a series of thumbnail sketches of actual situations. However, we can indicate generally some of the issues involved. A business under the control of a bankruptcy court clearly involves greater uncertainty as far as forecasting its future is concerned[6] than would be true if the heavy hand of the law were not upon it. The statute specifying that the plan of reorganization must be "feasible" does not offer one word of explanation. By the time proceedings in the case have reached the point of considering feasibility, heavy expenses of administration have been incurred and the willingness to prolong litigation has weakened. Many plans have gone into operation despite serious doubts as to their feasibility because the exhausted parties have been unable to see much marginal value in trying to improve the feasibility of the plan.

Feasibility of a plan no doubt involves a probability distribution. The statute specifies no standard of probability, but the law falls back on the vague standard of a "reasonable" probability when the statute says nothing.

In all considerations of feasibility it is clear that forecasting the future revenues and expenses of conducting the business under the plan is a basic problem. Even if such forecasts can be made, problems remain about what type of capital structure is feasible given the assumed future revenue and expense forecast.

The feasibility of a proposed capital structure is examined first in terms of the appropriate capitalization rate to apply to estimated income in order to establish the total of the capital structure. Then the division of the capital structure among debt, preferred stock, and common stock is considered together with some examination of the problem of annual variability in the forecasted income stream.

Because of the high level of uncertainty involved in this whole process, an attempt may be made to mollify the parties and grease the plan through by using warrants to purchase future common stock. Such warrants appear attractive to the various parties because if the estimates on which the plan is based later turn out to have been pessimistic, then some kind of equity will prevail for those who were (mistakenly?) frozen out in the reorganization plan. They will have a chance to recoup their losses.

---

[5] An earlier consideration of the question of feasibility appears in F. J. Calkins, "Feasibility in Plans of Corporate Reorganizations under Chapter X," *Harvard Law Review*, 61 (May 1948), pp. 763–781.

[6] See F. J. Calkins, "Corporate Reorganization under Chapter X—A Post Mortem," *Journal of Finance*, 3 (June 1948), pp. 19–28. Calkins follows up on the estimates of future earnings by the SEC and finds that the SEC's estimates in a period of four to six years after reorganization varied between one-seventh and one-third of the actual earnings that developed.

But this method of proceeding has been challenged by the SEC in its advisory reports.[7] First the SEC argues that the rule of absolute priority is being violated because things of value (warrants) are being given to those who have no value or position in the reorganization. A watered-down version of the relative priority rule is being permitted to come in the back door. Second, the SEC objects that future financing is being hampered—at least future common stock cannot be sold on as favorable terms as it could if no warrants were outstanding. To this extent the (future?) feasibility of the reorganization plan is being jeopardized.

The infinite variety of the question of feasibility is demonstrated in the Northeastern Steel Corporation case.[8] Here the proposed plan involved the taking over of the defunct Northeastern Steel by Carpenter Steel, and the discussion shifted to how feasible Carpenter's capital structure might be after acquisition on the terms proposed by Carpenter.

### Theory of Receivership, Reorganization and Bankruptcy

Until recent years, little work has been done in the theory of corporate failure. Initial effort [9] has been directed at determining the variables that indicate impending corporate failure. It is important that modern theoretical work in this area begins with ratio analysis so widely used by practitioners in finance but downgraded as arbitrary rules of thumb by many theorists.

Tests of various ratios suggest [10] the most reliable ratios indicating impending failure are, in order of reliability: (1) retained earnings/total assets, (2) earnings before interest and taxes/total assets, and (3) working capital/total assets.

These results are not surprising. As a firm begins to slip, its retained earnings feel the first impact as the directors are reluctant to cut dividends. As earnings decline further, liquidity problems increase even though dividends have been terminated.

The debt/equity ratio (as a measure of financial leverage) and the sales/total assets ratio (as a measure of capital-turnover) are valuable *when used in conjunction* with the first three ratios. The higher the debt/equity ratio and the lower the capital turnover, the greater the risk of bankruptcy.

---

[7] The SEC renders advisory reports to federal courts on proposed reorganization plans under section 1738, Chapter X, of the Bankruptcy Act.

[8] Securities and Exchange Commission, "In the Matter of Northeastern Steel Corp., August 25, 1957." 38 SEC Decisions and Reports, 41–62. See also Corporate Reorganization Release 107.

[9] K. Cohen, T. Gilmore and F. Singer, "Bank Procedures for Analyzing Business Loan Applications", in *Analytical Methods in Banking*, K. Cohen and F. Hammer (eds.) (Homewood, Ill.: R. D. Irwin, Inc., 1966), pp. 218–251; W. H. Beaver, "Financial Ratios as Predictors of Failure," Empirical Research in Accounting: Selected Studies, supplement to *Journal of Accounting Research* (1966), pp. 71–111; and E. I. Altman, "Financial Ratios, Discriminant Analysis and the Prediction of Corporate Bankruptcy," *Journal of Finance*, 23 (September 1968), pp. 589–609.

[10] E. I. Altman, pp. 594–597.

Further study [11] has sought to include the risk of bankruptcy in the valuation formulas discussed in Chapters 14 and 15. Specifically, the variable measuring the stockholder's investment might be the amount he *could* have received had he sold prior to bankruptcy (or *would* have invested had he bought prior to bankruptcy). Alternatively, an investor holding for a long time prior to bankruptcy might compute his return as including pre- and post-bankruptcy dividends.

## VOLUNTARY LIQUIDATION AND DISSOLUTION UNDER CORPORATION STATUTES

The theoretical basis for liquidating a company is that the assets of the business, when sold for cash, will yield more than the same assets employed in the business. But the legal rules of reorganization and bankruptcy protect creditors when their position is threatened. In the case of stockholders the courts have repeatedly held that a corporation that is steadily losing money cannot be forced to liquidate unless the stockholders by the required statutory vote of two-thirds decide to dissolve. There is only one qualification to the rule, namely, that those in control must be proceeding in good faith, free of fraud and self-dealing. Ignorance is not evidence of bad faith. It is not enough to offer clear proof that the buildings and other assets of the firm can be sold for two and three times the amount at which they are carried on the books of the losing company. The reasoning of the law is quite simple: corporate stock is a train ticket to wherever the majority wants to go, provided the statute permits the trip and subject only to specific rules of the statute.

However, once the corporation has become entangled with Chapter X of the Bankruptcy Act, the court, under existing legislation, must proceed to liquidation and dissolution if no fair and feasible plan can be proposed.

Voluntary dissolution would be followed in the belief that more can be realized by a piecemeal sale of the assets by the existing management than by a sale of the entire business as a unit. The corporation laws of the various states specify how dissolution is to be carried out.[12] A resolution of dissolution is adopted first by the board of directors and then by a two-thirds vote of the stockholders present at the meeting. A plan of dissolution is then adopted, again by a two-thirds vote of the stockholders present after written notice setting forth the plan has been distributed to all stockholders. Under the statutes the plan of dissolution may provide (after payment of all liabilities or adequate provision therefor) either for the distribution of the excess to the stockholders *or* for any other distribution if the articles and bylaws do not specify return to the members.

---

[11] E. I. Altman, "Corporate Bankruptcy Potential, Stockholder Returns and Share Valuation," *Journal of Finance*, 24 (December 1969), pp. 887–900. An earlier study is Lawrence Fisher, "Determinants of Risk Premiums on Corporate Bonds," *Journal of Political Economy*, 67 (June 1959), pp. 217–237.

[12] The following outline of dissolution statutes is based on the laws of Wisconsin (*Wis.Stats.*1973, Chaps. 181.50–181.55) but is representative of modern state corporate statutes.

The reason for setting out what appears to be detail is to emphasize that a corporation is a creature of the state and that its conduct must conform to statutes. Thus if two-thirds of the stockholders desire to forgo the return of their money and desire to dispose of it otherwise, the remaining third has no choice in the matter. Indeed, failure to follow the statute creates liabilities. Likewise, such failure results in the forfeiture of benefits granted by the statute, such as the shortening of the period of the statute of limitations on claims.[13]

Thus finance textbooks are misleading when they recommend that voluntary dissolution be carried out by a common law assignment or a statutory assignment or an assignment with settlement, stating that such procedures are superior to bankruptcy. An assignment can never result in a discharge of the debtor's liability. The debtor can be haunted by creditors as long as the statute of limitations permits. Furthermore, it is clear that an assignment for the benefit of creditors is itself an act of bankruptcy. In an effort to avoid the expense and delay of bankruptcy, such a maneuver plays into the hand of bankruptcy. The only reason that the practice of assignment continues in the case of corporations is that no one seems to care what the liabilities of a corporation are once its assets are gone. But even here there is danger, since those who receive the assets in the case of an assignment can be forced to give them up so that a bankruptcy proceeding can examine who is entitled to them.

The state has specified a simple, direct way for a corporation to liquidate. In the case of a sole proprietorship or partnership, the use of an assignment is also to be avoided. Even when the debtor obtains a release from every creditor in such a program, claims can continue to be made until the final toll of the statute of limitations. Since the statute does not run during infancy, incapacity, or absence of the defendant from the state, that toll may be a lifetime away. In addition, in the case of a sole proprietorship or partnership, all of the assets of the owners are subject to claims of the business and not just business assets. The only exceptions are the small exemptions allowed by statute in each state. Thus an assignment for the benefit of creditors which does not include every asset of the debtor is a fraudulent act and all the releases obtained are subject to being set aside.

## LIQUIDATION IN BANKRUPTCY

As indicated in the preceding chapter, when a Chapter X proceeding has reached the point where the court has determined that no plan of reorganization is fair and feasible, the case proceeds to liquidation. At this point all claims will have been determined and appraisals completed, both being prerequisites to the decision concerning whether a fair and feasible plan of reorganization is possible.

All that remains are the sale of assets and the distribution of proceeds. Despite the best efforts of competent appraisers, the sale of assets

---

[13] A statute of limitations defines the period within which a claimant must act in court or lose his claim. Dissolution statutes provide for a shortening of this period (in many cases from six to two years) if the statute is followed.

usually produces surprises.[14] The assets are offered for bid individually, in various combinations, and finally as an entire unit. That set of bids will prevail which yields the greatest cash total. There may be problems when mortgaged property is involved and the proceeds of the sale of the mortgaged property are insufficient for the secured debt. If offered as part of the total business, the mortgaged property may increase the total proceeds compared to a separate offer. How should this increase be allocated between secured and unsecured creditors?

The sale must be confirmed by the court and may be set aside if the court for any reason is dissatisfied.

The order of priority of distribution of the proceeds of the sale to satisfy claims is as follows:

1. The costs of administering the proceedings and of operating the property during proceedings, including any trustee's certificates for new money granted priority by the court.

2. Unpaid wages up to $600 per person if earned within three months before the date of filing of the petition.

3. Unpaid taxes due the United States or any state or subdivision thereof.

4. Secured creditors to the extent of the proceeds of the specific property mortgaged, and as to any balance due, the secured creditors qualify as general creditors.

5. General or unsecured creditors.

6. Stockholders, with any stock having preference coming first.[15]

The sale having been confirmed and the proceeds distributed, the case is now ready for the issuance of a discharge in bankruptcy. Only one such discharge can be granted to the same person in any six-year period.

## SUMMARY

Failure in finance is a matter of degree. Insolvency in the equity sense means inability to meet debts as they mature. Insolvency in the bankruptcy sense means excess of liabilities over assets.

Insolvency in the equity sense subjects the company to supervision by a court of equity. Before this occurs creditors may extend their due dates. If all creditors agree to an extension of their maturities and to acceptance of partial payment, the transaction is called a composition. In view of the great changes in American business in recent years, the prospects for a composition are slim.

In the old equity receivership the hopes of creditors rested on new funds entitled to priority and correction of management deficiencies

---

[14] For one of the few cases in print giving the detailed results of such a sale, see the case of Saukville Canning Company in Erwin E. Nemmers, *Cases in Finance* (Boston: Allyn & Bacon, Inc., 1964), pp. 422–435.

[15] In state proceedings the order of priority is generally the same except that (2) and (3) are reversed, namely, taxes come before wages and (4) comes even before (1).

while the court-appointed receiver managed the business. Unless a plan of reorganization could be worked out, the company was thrown into bankruptcy for liquidation.

There are two rules of priority: absolute and relative. Under absolute priority (enforced as the law since a Supreme Court decision in the 1930s) bonds must be paid in full in the order of their priority before anything is paid to stock. In short, the priorities agreed to in securities are enforced. Under relative priority each prior class must merely receive relatively more than each succeeding class even though it is not paid in full (as provided in its security) before anything passes to the next lower level of priority.

As an alternative to reorganization, a company may consider merging before the more drastic losses of bankruptcy set in.

Milder problems are dealt with currently under Chapter XI of the Bankruptcy Act in a process called an "arrangement." This process can be begun only by voluntary petition of the debtor and involves only the unsecured creditors. A plan is developed after majority approval by creditors and it binds even dissenting creditors.

Liquidation is in order when the assets of a business are worth more when sold than when used in the business.

Legal rules govern liquidation to make certain that creditors received their priority. But a corporation that is meeting its obligations cannot be forced to liquidate no matter what its losses unless two-thirds of the stockholders at the meeting vote to liquidate. This is on the assumption the corporation commits none of the acts of bankruptcy.

Liquidation may be ordered once the company is in bankruptcy if no fair and feasible plan of reorganization can be developed. But liquidation may be voluntarily undertaken by a two-thirds vote of the stockholders even if no losses have been suffered.

If liquidation will not yield sufficient funds to pay all debts, an individual should proceed through bankruptcy in order to obtain a discharge, which can only be granted by a *federal* court. Otherwise the individual continues to be liable for unpaid debts. In the case of a corporation there is less concern, since only the corporation (not the stockholders) continues to be liable if there is no discharge by a federal court.

The order of priority in liquidation is:

1. Expenses of administration
2. Wages up to $600 per employee for the prior three months
3. Taxes
4. Secured creditors
5. Unsecured creditors

If no such plan can be developed under Chapter XI, the matter proceeds to bankruptcy under Chapter X. Or proceedings may be initially started voluntarily or involuntarily (by three or more creditors) under Chapter X upon proof of any of six acts of bankruptcy.

Under Chapter X any proposed reorganization plan must be "fair and feasible." If no plan can be had, liquidation is in order. To be "fair" a plan must follow the absolute priority principle. To be "feasible" it must offer a reasonable probability that the firm will not return to the bankruptcy court. The heart of any plan involves forecasting the future income of the reorganized company and the use of a realistic rate of capitalizing such income. Given these conditions, a financial structure can often be designed that provides reasonable coverage for any senior securities involved in the plan.

### Study Questions

1. The argument supporting the prevailing practice of firms in shunning any firm involved in financial difficulty is that their time and energy are more profitably employed in pursuing their normal activities rather than in trying to improve the amount that can be salvaged from a firm in financial difficulty. Is there social waste in permitting business firms to follow this policy?
2. Would you favor a law prohibiting accounting entries that reduce the capital stock account to wipe out accrued losses so that dividend payments can be resumed as soon as earnings improve? Is there any disadvantage to the investor in permitting this practice?
3. Should a company in financial difficulty concentrate its management talent on developing favorable merger opportunities or should management focus on rehabilitating the company?
4. In the old (pre-1933) equity receivership the emphasis was on the temporary character of the financial difficulty, and there was no way of dealing with a dissident minority objecting to a proposed plan other than to pay this group off in full. Has remedial legislation succeeded in improving the situation? If not, what do you think is the key problem in attempting to deal with financial failure or incipient failure, and is it susceptible to legislative remedy?
5. Considering the "efficient" view as to where to apply management's efforts when another firm is in financial difficulty, do you think that present-day management is being inefficient in pursuing the area of mergers rather than that of internal expansion, particularly when the typical merger involves one partner of the merger who is in a weak position financially?
6. Would it be possible to list criteria by which to judge the feasibility of a plan of reorganization? What do you think such criteria might be?
7. In view of the record of the SEC in seriously underestimating future earnings of reorganized corporations (see footnote 6 in this chapter), do you think there is merit in preparing a second reorganization plan based on more optimistic assumptions and then attempting to provide common stock warrants for those security holders excluded in the original plan but having values under the more optimistic plan?
8. Do you believe that merging two unsuccessful companies can produce a profitable company or would it merely compound the failure? Explain your position.
9. Should the court give weight to the current market value of the several types of securities of a debtor corporation when considering proposed reorganization plans?
10. It has been said that attempting to effect a composition is like poking your finger into a balloon—it merely gives somewhere else. The metaphor refers to the fact that the last few persons to sign an agreement of composition

realize that nothing will happen if they fail to sign. Realizing this, they are aware that they might demand payment in full. Does this mean that all efforts at composition are wasteful?

11. If a corporation faces a serious threat of bankruptcy, what alternatives does it have?
12. Why would any corporation be dissolved when its accrued losses are a valuable asset for tax purposes to any successful corporation?
13. Can you advance any reason why a corporation would realize more out of a liquidation sale than it could out of its earlier efforts to merge?
14. As the financial manager of a creditor, what are your reactions when you are called by other creditors who seem interested in pushing the debtor into a liquidation?
15. If you are the financial manager of a company and someone in the company proposes buying assets from a company that is liquidating, what are the considerations that enter your mind for evaluation?
16. Why do some firms not liquidate when their present assets are worth more in the market place than the values at which they are carried on the books of the firm, especially if their earnings are subnormal?
17. A prominent financial text asks: "Why do liquidations of all types usually result in losses for the creditors or the owners, or both?" Do you agree that "liquidations of all types usually result in losses for the creditors or the owners, or both"? If you do agree, then why do firms voluntarily liquidate?

### Problems

1. Swinger Enterprises landed in reorganization. Fundamentally, growth had not been controlled. In an effort to move too quickly the company acquired assets for expansion too far ahead of its ability to finance the increase. By the time the officers understood what they had done the possibility of procuring additional equity was reduced to very unfavorable terms. The owners preferred to go through the wringer rather than dilute ownership on such unfavorable terms.

The current balance sheet is given in Table 26–1.

TABLE 26–1. Swinger Enterprises
Balance Sheet

| *Assets* | | *Liabilities* | |
|---|---|---|---|
| Cash | $ 1,000 | Bank loan | $300,000 |
| Receivables | 99,000 | Accounts payable | 120,000 |
| Inventory | 400,000 | Accrued expenses | 100,000 |
| Total current assets | $500,000 | Accrued taxes | 60,000 |
| Prepaid expenses | $ 10,000 | Total current liabilities | $580,000 |
| Land | 40,000 | | |
| Buildings, net | 300,000 | Net worth, 1000 shares, $100 par | $100,000 |
| Machinery, net | 130,000 | | |
| | | Retained earnings | 300,000 |
| | | Total net worth | $400,000 |
| Total assets | $980,000 | Total liabilities and net worth | $980,000 |

The building account represents a $300,000 expansion of the old building but only $200,000 of the expansion has been finished. The contractor ceased work when progress payments were not maintained and threw Swinger into reorganization for the unpaid balance of $60,000 currently due him. Accrued taxes of $60,000 include $30,000 in taxes past due. The bank holds a pledge of the accounts receivable and a mortgage on the land and buildings. The mortgage is of doubtful validity, since it was taken in recent months as added security. The confused state of Swinger's finances has caused a drop in Swinger's current sales as doubt has spread regarding the firm's ability to meet delivery schedules.

The receiver has developed several proposals.

First, half of the land is held for future expansion. The receiver has procured a buyer willing to pay $20,000 for this half of the land and willing to grant an option to repurchase it at $30,000 at any time in the next two years.

Second, the receiver has procured a tenant willing to occupy the unused space in the new building for warehouse purposes at an annual rental of $7500 for the next two years payable monthly at the end of each month.

Third, the receiver has obtained an offer to buy the finished-goods inventory of $100,000 at $110,000.

Fourth, the bank has agreed that if these steps are taken it will advance $60,000 for working capital on the security of the receiver's certificates (granted priority by the court) provided all other cash realized is applied to payments, first to past due taxes and then to other accounts payable and accrued expenses.

Fifth, the contractor has agreed to accept notes due in 18 months secured by a mortgage having priority over the bank's claim. The owners have agreed that no dividends will be paid and no shares repurchased without the bank's consent. The officers have agreed to a 25 percent salary cut for the next two years, totaling $12,000, and will receive favorable options on stock in lieu thereof.

a. Evaluate the situation in view of the proposals. Assume a 50 percent income tax rate applicable to all profits.

b. What is the most important missing piece of information?

c. What motivated the bank in its agreement?

d. Which asset valuation do you consider most critical in the proposed situation?

2. Achiever Corporation, a manufacturer of toys, is in financial difficulty but it will be some time before the company will be faced with a formal reorganization. At present bankruptcy is still a shadow on the horizon. Robert Achiever is board chairman and the major stockholder. He is nearing retirement. His financial officer is an aggressive young man who has proposed that the company resort to the use of commercial finance companies to obtain financing at premium rates.

In the midst of this situation you are examining the firm with a view to reaching a decision whether you should recommend to your employer, Ajax, the purchase of Achiever and if so at what price.

Achiever furnishes you with the income statement of his company, given in Table 26-2 and prior earnings shown in Table 26-3. The comparative balance sheet is shown in Table 26-4.

TABLE 26–2. Achiever Corporation
Comparative Income Statement
(thousands)

| | *1973* | *1972* |
|---|---|---|
| Sales | $11,472 | $15,753 |
| Cost of sales | 9,596 | 12,040 |
| Gross profit | $ 1,876 | $ 3,712 |
| Selling and general expenses | 2,792 | 2,994 |
| Operating income | $ (916) | $ 718 |
| Interest expense | 192 | 123 |
| Other income | (11) | (14) |
| | $ 181 | $ 109 |
| Net income (loss) | $(1,097) | $ 609 |
| Provision (credit) for income taxes | (482) | 274 |
| | $ (615) | $ 335 |
| Extraordinary write off, less applicable income tax | (240) | — |
| Net income (loss) | (885) | 335 |
| Per share | ($1.34) | $0.52 |

During the last year the long-term lender called its loan for default in the covenants. This was replaced with short-term notes to commercial finance companies.

In the last half of 1973 operations were on a break-even basis after a heavy loss in the first half of 1973.

The company ceased paying dividends in 1972.

TABLE 26–3. Achiever Corporation
Prior Earnings Records

| | *Earned per share (average number of shares in year)* | *Sales* | *Profit on sales* |
|---|---|---|---|
| 1973 | $(1.34) | $11,472,000 | (7.71)% |
| 1972 | 0.52 | 15,753,000 | 2.13 |
| 1971 | 0.62 | 14,143,000 | 2.75 |
| 1970 | 0.03 | 12,732,000 | 0.16 |
| 1969 | 0.66 | 13,586,000 | 3.00 |
| 1968 | 1.08 | 10,873,000 | 6.15 |
| 1967 | 1.25 | 9,685,000 | 6.28 |
| 1966 | 0.49 | 5,810,000 | 3.80 |
| 1965 | 0.20 | 2,962,000 | 3.11 |
| 1964 | 0.32 | 2,571,000 | 5.57 |
| 1963 | (0.28) | 1,392,000 | (8.89) |

TABLE 26–4. Achiever Corporation Balance Sheet
Year Ending December 31

| | *1973* | *1972* |
|---|---|---|
| Assets | | |
| Cash | $ 238 | $ 107 |
| Federal tax refund * | 512 | — |
| Receivables—trade, after reserves of $107,000 in 1973 and $150,000 in 1972 | 3,425 | 4,328 |
| Other receivables | 11 | 46 |
| Inventories—finished and in process | 1,109 | 1,404 |
| raw materials | 678 | 1,267 |
| Prepaid tool and die costs | 405 | 683 |
| Prepaid expense | 31 | 35 |
| Total current assets | $6,409 | $ 7,870 |
| Plant and equipment, cost | | |
| Land | $ 139 | $ 139 |
| Building | 1,289 | 1,265 |
| Machinery | 2,138 | 1,959 |
| Leased equipment | 135 | 284 |
| Leaseholds | 43 | 24 |
| | $3,744 | $ 3,671 |
| Depreciation | 1,800 | 1,503 |
| Net fixed assets | $1,944 | $ 2,168 |
| Other assets | | |
| Investment in subsidiary † | — | $ 200 |
| Intangibles, net of amortization | $ 60 | 66 |
| CSV ‡ life insurance, less loans of $16,000 | 51 | 50 |
| Property not used in operations | — | 18 |
| | $ 111 | $ 334 |
| Total assets | $8,464 | $10,372 |

* Exhausts the use of all federal income tax carry back or carry forward.

† Investment in subsidiary written off during the year. Some recovery on this investment is likely to occur.

‡ Cash-surrender value.

TABLE 26–4. Achiever Corporation Balance Sheet Year Ending December 31—Continued

| | *1973* | *1972* |
|---|---|---|
| Liabilities | | |
| Notes payable § | $2,494 | $ 1,323 |
| Current part of long-term debt | 96 | 220 |
| Accounts payable | 1,826 | 2,577 |
| Accrued liabilities | 434 | 498 |
| Accrued income tax | — | 175 |
| Total current liabilities | $4,850 | $ 4,793 |
| Long-term debt | | |
| Leases, less current part ** | $ 139 | $ 214 |
| Equipment note | 16 | — |
| 5.25 and 5.5 percent notes payable, less current part | — | 1,050 |
| Total long-term debt | $ 155 | $ 1,264 |
| Stockholder investment | | |
| Common stock | $ 638 | $ 638 |
| Paid-in surplus | 2,051 | 2,051 |
| Earned surplus | 770 | 1,626 |
| Total stockholder investment | $3,459 | $ 4,315 |
| Total liabilities and net worth | $8,464 | $10,372 |

Throughout this period the company had Robert Achiever as chief executive officer but he stepped aside in mid-1973 and relinquished active management to a new man.

The difficulties in early 1973 involved many areas. The company had in the preceding 24 months diversified into product areas that were new to it. It has since decided to withdraw from these areas and concentrate entirely in the area in which the company grew to its present size. Lateness in delivery of dies meant that the company missed part of the market. A dearth of product innovation was also a factor. Corrective measures have been taken in all of these areas.

Capitalization rates for the toy business showed a wide dispersion among companies at any one time and in the record of any one company over time.

There are 637,863 shares of $1 par stock outstanding. In late 1967, 230,000 shares were publicly offered and the price of the stock has been as follows:

| | *Low* | *High* |
|---|---|---|
| 1968 | $14 | $24 |
| 1969 | 10¼ | 30 |
| 1970 | 7 | 13 |
| 1971 | 6¾ | 10 |
| 1972 | 6 | 8⅞ |
| 1973 | 2¾ | 7¼ |

Do you recommend purchase and at what price?

§ Bearing interest rates from 7.5 to 13 percent, secured by mortgage of receivables and inventory.

** Does not include building leases with total annual rentals of $50,000.

3. *Windermere Hotel Company.*[16] The SEC on January 31, 1962, rendered an advisory opinion to the federal court for the northern district of Illinois on two reorganization plans proposed in the involuntary reorganization of Windermere Hotel Company.

In September 1960 a group of holders of $2,371,800 of a total of $3,196,000 first mortgage bonds of Windermere filed under Chapter X of the Bankruptcy Act. Windermere had owned two neighboring hotels in the Hyde Park area of Chicago near Lake Michigan and the University of Chicago. The once fashionable area had deteriorated badly, but Windermere continued to be a prestige residential hotel. Windermere West was built in 1888 and demolished in 1959. Windermere East was built in 1923 as a 12-story building with 590 rooms, of which 120 were for transients and the rest for permanent residents.

There was a reorganization in 1932 when the present 5 percent first mortgage income bonds were issued, due June 1, 1961. The balance sheet on October 31, 1961, is given in Table 26–5.

TABLE 26–5. Windermere Hotel Company Balance Sheet
October 31, 1961
(thousands)

| | | |
|---|---|---|
| *Assets* | | |
| Cash | | $ 138 |
| Other current assets | | 60 |
| Total current assets | | $ 198 |
| Land | | 376 |
| Buildings | $2,947 | |
| Less depreciation | 2,541 | |
| Net | | 406 |
| Furniture and equipment | $1,728 | |
| Less depreciation | 1,390 | |
| Net | | 338 |
| Other realty | | 8 |
| Total fixed assets | | $1,128 |
| Other assets | | 44 |
| Total assets | | $1,372 |
| *Liabilities and Net Worth* | | |
| Current liabilities | | $1,118 |
| 1st mortgage 5 percent income bonds due 6/1/61 | | 3,196 |
| Accrued interest to 10/31/61 | | 1,960 |
| Federal taxes on unpaid interest | | 34 |
| Total liabilities | | $6,308 |
| Excess of liabilities over assets | | 4,936 |
| Common stock | | 3,263 shares |

[16] Based on 40 SEC Decisions and Reports, 970–985 (1962) and 1115–1118 (1962), and the file in the U.S. District Court, Northern District of Illinois.

The income statement for the last five fiscal years, ending October 31, is given in Table 26–6.

TABLE 26–6. Windermere Hotel Company Income Statement (thousands)

| | *1957* | *1958* | *1959* | *1960* | *1961* |
|---|---|---|---|---|---|
| Room revenue | $895 | $931 | $915 | $924 | $895 |
| Direct room expense | 304 | 321 | 329 | 336 | 339 |
| Gross profit on rooms | $591 | $610 | $586 | $588 | $556 |
| Gross profit of other operations | 37 | (10) | 10 | (1) | (23) |
| Store rentals | 7 | 6 | 5 | 5 | 5 |
| Total gross profit | $635 | $606 | $601 | $592 | $538 |
| Indirect expense | 447 | 480 | 505 | 532 | 494 |
| Income before depreciation and interest | $188 | $126 | $ 96 | $ 60 | $ 44 |

Until 1944 interest was not paid or payments were 3.5 percent or less per year. Full interest was paid in 1944, 1945, and 1946. Beginning with 1947, annual interest of 4 percent was paid, except for 4.5 percent in 1956 and 1.5 percent in 1960. Annual depreciation has averaged $144,000. About $800,000 of accrued loss is available for carry over for income tax purposes during the next five years.

*Proposed Reorganization Plans—The Goodman Plan.* Two competing reorganization plans were presented to the court. The first was proposed by the Goodmans, owning $2,371,800, the other by Schlensky, owning $30,000 in bonds.

The Goodman plan called for a new corporation to take over the assets and all liabilities except the old bonds. The new company would issue $1 million in 6 percent 20-year first mortgage bonds, of which $900,000 would be spent on capital improvements and the balance would be held as working capital. The bonds would be repayable on a level-payment basis over the 20 years, combining principal and interest in a constant annual amount. Subordinated debentures of $1,598,000 and 31,960 shares of $1 par value common stock were to be issued to the old bonds of $3,196,000 principal on the basis of $50 in debentures and one share of common stock for each $100 principal of old bonds. The old common stock would receive nothing.

Goodman proposed to offer all other holders ($3,196,000 minus $2,371,800 equals $824,200) $70 cash for each package of $50 in debentures with one share of common stock. Those who failed to elect otherwise would receive the $70 in cash.

The new debentures would carry 5 percent interest, mature in 20 years, be callable at any time at par plus accrued interest, and would provide an annual sinking fund of 5 percent to the extent of available net earnings. Such available net earnings were defined as annual net income before depreciation but after payments due the first mortgage bonds and after a cumulative $20,000 a year for capital improvements. Sinking fund payments would be first applied to repurchase of bonds held by persons other than the Goodmans except that such bonds as Goodman acquired for cash would be entitled to sinking fund benefits. The new common stock would have preemptive rights and would provide for cumulative voting, as required by the Illinois constitution. The common stock would be attached to each debenture and could not be separately transferred until the debenture was retired.

The plan also required that at least 10 percent of the "public" old bonds (or 38.77 percent of holders other than Goodman) must elect to take securities, otherwise all public holders would be paid in cash at $70 per $100 of old bonds.

*The Schlensky Plan.* Under the Schlensky plan the new company would issue 31,960 shares of $1 par common stock for the outstanding old bonds at the rate of one share for each $100 of bond principal. For each such share the present bondholders, other than Schlensky, would receive either $70 cash or $20 cash plus $50 principal of new first mortgage bonds bearing 5 percent interest and due in 15 years. Bondholders not electing otherwise would receive the second option. Schlensky would furnish all the money and receive all the new common stock. The old common stock would receive nothing. Schlensky made no specific proposals for future capital improvements.

If a public auction was proposed, Schlensky guaranteed a bid of not less than $70 per $100 principal of old bonds provided he obtain the first $25,000 (or any part) that the bidding produced over the figure of $70 per $100.

*Appraisal of Properties.* A court-appointed appraiser valued the hotel on three different bases and then averaged these values.

The first value was obtained by capitalizing earnings. The appraiser estimated annual earnings of $221,523 before interest and depreciation under efficient management and without capital improvements. This estimate was made by comparison with operating statistics of some 100 hotel properties. He estimated a capitalization rate of 10.86 percent, which yielded a value of $2,093,000 when applied to his estimated earnings.

The second method of valuation was reproduction new less depreciation for the building (that is what it would cost if built today and depreciation applied to this figure) together with estimated land value and furniture and equipment. This value was $2,098,000.

The third method was a computation of market value based on an actual sale in 1960 of another hotel property and its earnings. This value was $1,975,000 but was changed under cross-examination to $2,732,000.

The appraiser averaged these three values at $2,050,000, to which was added a value of $130,200 for the other real estate owned by the hotel.

In contrast, the $70 offer of Goodman and that of Schlensky applied to the old bonds of $3,196,000 represent a value of $2,237,200.

*The SEC's Analysis of the Feasibility of the Plans.* Goodman had estimated future annual earnings before interest and depreciation at $260,395 *after* capital improvements of $1 million (of which $900,000 would be proceeds of the new first mortgage bonds). Annual interest for all indebtedness would be $139,900 in the first year and then decline.

The SEC found the interest margin of 1.9 times to be "fair" but the combined interest and principal payment of $245,800 in the first year to be "onerous" in view of the estimate by Goodman that annual cash expenditures for improvements would be $35,000. The SEC objected that Goodman would subsequently be able to dispose of his debentures to the public. The SEC considered that Goodman might have been seeking the income tax benefits of interest deductibility but that he was jeopardizing financial stability to do so. The SEC considered that only $600,000 of the proposed $1,598,000 in debentures was warranted. This would allow 1.8 times coverage for interest and debt amortization.

The SEC also objected to the feasibility of the Schlensky plan. If all the old bondholders accepted the Schlensky option for securities, there would be $1,583,-000 of new mortgage bonds. Schlensky offered no estimate of future earnings and declined to give details of the capital improvements he believed were needed or the financing except to state that the funds would be procured "without putting the bondholders in a subordinate position." The SEC found the plan to lack feasibility until this information was furnished and proposed to limit the total debt to $1.6 million, consisting of $1 million of new money plus the maximum of $600,000 in debentures to the old bondholders, as it indicated in its comment on the Goodman plan.

The SEC also found that both plans lacked feasibility in that they failed to provide for payment of reorganization expenses. It further advised that the court require a bond of either Goodman or Schlensky to assure the performance of their commitments. The SEC also pointed out that although the court has authority to put the Schlensky plan into effect despite a negative vote by Goodman with 74 percent of the old bonds, this might be unwise where Goodman's cash offer was equal to Schlensky's and provided for participation in the common stock by public owners while Schlensky's plan did not.

*The SEC's Analysis of the Fairness of the Plans.* Both plans were considered fair in making no provisions for the old common stock, since the total claim of the old bondholders (both principal and interest) was $5,156,316.

The SEC found the total cash offer of $2,237,200 by each plan to be fair but advised that the Schlensky plan be amended to provide for cash payment in the event an old bondholder fails to elect for the securities option.

The SEC found that in order to be fair the Goodman plan should provide for priority in sinking fund retirement of publicly owned bonds over all bonds held by Goodman, whether his initial share or acquired for cash by him. Because the new debenture holders were also stockholders, the failure to provide a call premium on retirement was fair.

The SEC also called for an indenture provision limiting the amount of debt senior to the new debentures and limiting dividends on the common stock to net income after the date of the debentures.

The SEC found that the Goodman plan should be amended to provide that two thirds (not just 61.23 percent) of the public holders must vote for cash in order to bind a minority seeking securities.

The SEC also found that the Goodman plan for a five-man board of directors, with three to be named by Goodman and two to be named from a list submitted to and approved by the court, should be amended to state that two directors would be selected by the court from a list submitted exclusively by the minority security holders.

*Amendment of Plans.* After the SEC report amendments were made to the proposed plans and these were again submitted to the SEC for a supplementary report.

Both amended plans recognized that the court might direct a public auction of the property as part of the plan. Accordingly, the Goodman plan proposed a minimum cash upset price of $2,285,000 for the assets, excluding cash, receivables, prepaid expenses, and proceeds from a condemnation of some of the realty owned by the hotel. These items were estimated at $241,000 and were to be retained by the new company. Goodman tendered 10 percent of the $2,285,000 as earnest money, and his plan would require any other bidder to tender 10 percent of his bid in cash. Any bidder might tender not more than 60 percent of the principal of any bonds against the purchase price. The final payment would have to be made within 60 days of the sale. Initial distribution to the bondholders would be 60 percent of their principal. After payment of the operating liabilities of the trustee (estimated at $156,000) and the expenses of administration, the remaining cash would be distributed *pro rata* among bondholders.

The Schlensky plan was amended to accept the SEC limit of total debt to $1.6 million and the recommendation that bondholders receive the cash option unless they signified otherwise. Schlensky also agreed to supply the cash for administration expenses and initial capital improvements of $100,000.

The SEC's *Analysis of the Amended Plans.* On April 25, 1962, the SEC reported to the court on the amended plans. The SEC noted that the upset price of $2,285,000 of the Goodman plan plus the net assets not sold of $85,000 ($241,000 less $156,000) totaled $2,370,000, and if bondholders were to receive $70 per $100 of principal, this would leave only $133,000 for the expenses of administration.

The SEC found the amended Goodman plan fair and feasible.*

The SEC also found the amended Schlensky plan fair and feasible except to note that the attempt to capture the first $25,000 of any bid higher than the Schlensky minimum offer was inappropriate and could not be used in an attempt to foreclose better bids.

a. If you were the judge in the Windermere Hotel case, would you be guided by the advisory opinion of the SEC? Remember that the court is not bound to accept such advice.

b. If you were the judge, would you order a sale pursuant to the proposals of the plans or would you accept the minimum offer of either plan?

c. If you accepted one plan, which would it be? Note that in essence the Goodman plan provides for the sale of the assets while under the Schlensky plan the bidder in effect buys the stock of the old company.

4. Canned Foods, Inc., decided to liquidate voluntarily and consented to a receiver taking over its assets on June 21, 1972. At that time the company owed the Citizens Bank a first mortgage loan of $25,000 secured by its real estate and dated April 1, 1969, carrying 5 percent interest. Accrued interest is $3,342 to date. The company also owed the bank on a loan of $44,939 dated March 15, 1969, carrying 5 percent interest on which interest of $4,841 is accrued to date. This loan was secured by a second mortgage on the real estate and warehouse receipts covering the company's inventory of 7507 cases of canned corn. The total indebtedness of the first mortgage loan to its date of payment from sale proceeds was $28,342. The total indebtedness on the other loan to its date of payment was $49,780.

The company owed wages and taxes of $3127 and general claims of $26,931 on June 21, 1972. Wages totaled $540, due one man for the last two months of work.

The receiver had expenses as follows during his operation:

| | |
|---|---|
| Receiver's fee | $ 1,600 |
| Attorney's fee | 1,500 |
| Advertising expense | 807 |
| Auction expense | 313 |
| Real estate taxes | 4,655 |
| Personal property taxes | 596 |
| Miscellaneous | 2,479 |
| Storage charges | 3,013 |
| Cost of corn sales | 3,656 |
| Total | $18,619 |

* Although the SEC made no note of its prior objection to the lack of margin on the interest and principal payments, it must be assumed that Goodman reduced the rate of principal repayment on the new money in his revised plan.

The sales conducted by the receiver produced the following results:

| | |
|---|---|
| Real estate | $ 45,000 |
| Machinery sale | 19,000 |
| Corn sales | 39,000 |
| Warehouse rent | 600 |
| Sale of supplies | 4,285 |
| Insurance proceeds | 1,835 |
| Total | $109,720 |

What distribution should the receiver make?

5. Gungho Manufacturing Company was placed in bankruptcy by some of its employees who had unpaid wages due them. At that point in time the company's balance sheet was as given in Table 26–7.

TABLE 26–7. Gungho Manufacturing Company
Balance Sheet

| *Assets* | | | *Liabilities* | |
|---|---|---|---|---|
| Cash | | $ (670) | Accounts payable | $41,282 |
| Accounts receivable | | 3,450 | Accrued expenses | 27,620 |
| Inventory | | 27,413 | Accrued taxes | 7,380 |
| Total current assets | | $30,193 | Total current liabilities | $76,282 |
| Prepaid insurance | | 602 | | |
| Fixed assets | | | Realty mortgage loan | 27,132 |
| Building | $31,117 | | Net worth | |
| Equipment | 6,830 | | 200 shares $100 per common stock | 20,000 |
| | $37,947 | | | |
| Depreciation | 5,320 | 32,627 | Deficit | (59,992) |
| Total assets | | $63,422 | Total liabilities and net worth | $63,422 |

The accounts payable include one item of $4662 due a supplier who also owes Gungho $2815. The accrued expenses include the following:

| | | |
|---|---|---|
| John Starr | $ 753 | Wages for last two months |
| Bill Oar | 840 | Wages, of which $520 is for last three months and $320 previously |
| Oscar Goodman | 300 | For booking service ("Mail me Monday") |
| Marion Crost | 458 | Wages for last three months |
| Priscilla More | 210 | Wages disputed for six months ago |
| | $2,561 | |

Bankruptcy expenses to date have been $4315.

Upon sale of the assets, the proceeds given in Table 26–8 are realized (two sets of assumed figures).

TABLE 26–8. Gungho Manufacturing Company
Proceeds upon Sale of Assets

| | Assumption one | Assumption two |
|---|---|---|
| Receivables, other than the one supplier who owes Gungho $2,815 | $ 320 | $ 0 |
| Inventory | 15,000 | 680 |
| Prepaid insurance | 380 | 380 |
| Building | 27,222 | 23,146 |
| Equipment | 4,500 | 6,000 |
| | $47,422 | $30,206 |

Prepare the distribution of proceeds under each assumed set of facts.

**6.** Orange, Inc. has gone into bankruptcy. The court has found that no fair and feasible plan is possible because of the deteriorated condition of the business and the inability of a majority of the creditors to agree that the business should continue. At the time of bankruptcy the balance sheet was as given in Table 26–9.

TABLE 26–9. Orange, Inc.
Balance Sheet

| *Assets* | | | *Liabilities* | |
|---|---|---|---|---|
| Cash | | $ 1,000 | Secured bank loan | $ 78,000 |
| Accounts receivable, | | | Priority claims | 60,000 |
| $100,000 pledged | | 150,000 | General | 454,000 |
| Inventory | | 819,000 | Total current liabilities | $ 592,000 |
| Total current assets | | $ 970,000 | Long-term debt | |
| Land and building | $800,000 | | First mortgage bonds * | 200,000 |
| Less depreciation | 300,000 | 500,000 | Accrued interest | 10,000 |
| Machinery | $600,000 | | Second mortgage bonds † | 100,000 |
| Less depreciation | 470,000 | 130,000 | Accrued interest | 8,000 |
| | | | Debentures | 100,000 |
| | | | Accrued interest | 15,000 |
| | | | Net worth | |
| | | | Preferred stock | 160,000 |
| | | | Common stock | 400,000 |
| | | | Retained earnings | 15,000 |
| | | | Total net worth | $ 575,000 |
| Total assets | | $1,600,000 | Total liabilities and net worth | $1,600,000 |

* Secured by land and building.
† Secured by second mortgage on land and building and first mortgage on machinery.

[A9973]

Upon sale the assets bring the following proceeds (in addition to cash on hand):

| | *Assumption one* | *Assumption two* |
|---|---|---|
| Pledged accounts receivable | $ 50,000 | $ 90,000 |
| Unpledged accounts receivable | 40,000 | 40,000 |
| Inventory | 400,000 | 200,000 |
| Land and building | 240,000 | 140,000 |
| Machinery | 65,000 | 100,000 |
| Totals | $795,000 | $570,000 |

Administration expenses are $25,000.

Prepare the distribution of proceeds under each assumed set of facts.

### Selected References

Altman, E. I., "Financial Ratios, Discriminant Analysis and the Prediction of Corporate Bankruptcy," *Journal of Finance*, 23 (September 1968), pp. 589–609.

———, "Corporate Bankruptcy Potential, Stockholder Returns and Share Valuation," *Journal of Finance*, 24 (December 1969), pp. 887–900.

———, *Corporate Bankruptcy in America.* Lexington, Mass.: Heath Lexington Books, 1971.

Ballantine, H. W., *Ballantine on Corporations*, rev. ed. Chicago: Callaghan & Company, 1946.

Beaver, W. H., "Financial Ratios as Predictors of Failure," Empirical Research in Accounting: Selected Studies, Supplement to *Journal of Accounting Research* (1966), pp. 71–111.

Calkins, F. J., "Corporate Reorganization under Chapter X—A Post Mortem," *Journal of Finance*, 3 (June 1948), pp. 19–28.

———, "Feasibility in Plans of Corporate Reorganizations under Chapter X," *Harvard Law Review*, 61 (May 1948), pp. 763–781.

Coben, K., J. Gilmore, and F. Singer, "Bank Procedures for Analyzing Business Loan Applications," in *Analytical Methods in Banking*, K. Cohen and F. Hammer (eds.). Homewood, Ill.: R. D. Irwin, Inc., 1966, pp. 218–251.

Edmister, R. O., "An Empirical Test of Financial Ratio Analysis for Small Business Failure Prediction," *Journal of Financial and Quantitative Analysis*, 7 (March 1972), pp. 1477–1493.

Gordon, M. J., "Towards a Theory of Financial Distress," *Journal of Finance*, 26 (May 1971), pp. 347–356.

Murray, R. F., "Lessons for Financial Analysis," *Journal of Finance*, 26 (May 1971), pp. 327–332.

Van Arsdell, P. M., *Corporation Finance.* New York: Ronald Press, 1968, chaps. 48–53.

Walter, J. E., "Determination of Technical Insolvency," *Journal of Business*, 30 (January 1957), pp. 30–45.

*

# APPENDIX

## Glossary of Financial Terms*

The following definitions are taken from Erwin E. Nemmers, *Dictionary of Economics and Business* 3d ed. (Totowa, N.J.: Littlefield, Adams & Company, 1974). Used by permission.

ABSOLUTE PRIORITY. The right of senior creditors and stockholders to be paid in full before any junior issues receive anything. For example, if there are $500,000 in assets, $100,000 in bonds, $500,000 in preferred stock, and $500,000 in common stock, the bondholders are paid in full, the preferred stockholders get 80 cents on the dollar, and the common stockholders nothing. See *relative priority*.

ABSTINENCE THEORY OF INTEREST. An explanation of interest as the price paid by the borrower to the lender for the latter's abstaining from consumption of part of current income. See *agio theory of interest, liquidity preference theory of interest, loanable funds theory of interest, marginal productivity theory of interest, time preference theory of interest*.

* Italicized words are defined elsewhere in the glossary. This glossary distinguishes between "see" and "same." "See" refers to related terms or to the place where explanation is set forth. Where an abbreviation of a term exists, the term appears under the abbreviation.

ACCELERATED DEPRECIATION. Depreciation at a faster rate than usual. In recent years the term has been used to refer to *tax amortization certificates,* which (upon government consent) allow writing off an asset in five years for income tax purposes regardless of its life. Also recently used to describe *sum-of-the-years' digits method of depreciation, constant percent of declining balance method of depreciation* and *double declining balance method of depreciation.*

ACCOUNTING METHOD OF RETURN (IN CAPITAL BUDGETING). The ratio of the increase in future average annual net income from an investment to the cost of that investment. Cf. *present value method, yield method.*

ACCOUNT PAYABLE. A debt, owed by an enterprise, that arises in the normal course of business dealings and has not been replaced by a note payable of a debtor. For example, bills for materials received but not yet paid. See *account receivable.*

ACCOUNT RECEIVABLE. A debt, owing to an enterprise, that arises in the normal course of business dealings and is not supported by negotiable paper. For example, the charge accounts of a department store. But income due from investments (unless investments are the business itself) is not usually shown in accounts receivable. See *account payable.*

ACCOUNTS RECEIVABLE FINANCING. The use of *accounts receivable* to obtain *working capital* either through a loan secured by such accounts or through *factoring* them.

ACCOUNTS RECEIVABLE TURNOVER. The ratio of credit sales of a period to the average (daily) amount of accounts receivable outstanding. See *collection period.*

ACCRUED INTEREST. Interest that has been earned but is not yet paid or payable.

ACCUMULATED DIVIDEND. A dividend on cumulative preferred stock that has not been paid on the date due.

ACID TEST RATIO. Same as *quick ratio.*

ACQUIRED SURPLUS. In general, surplus arising from changes of the capital structure of one or more businesses. More narrowly, surplus arising from the purchase of one business by another business. Recapitalization surplus arises from changing the par or stated values of various classes of stock. Reorganization surplus arises from bankruptcy proceedings and a changing of the par or stated values of stock.

ACQUISITION. A generic term covering all forms of acquiring another firm, such as *consolidation, holding company, merger,* purchase of assets by cash or stock.

ADJUSTMENT BONDS. Bonds arising out of the reorganization of a corporation. Also called reorganization bonds.

AFTER-ACQUIRED PROPERTY CLAUSE. A clause in a mortgage providing that any property acquired by the borrower after the date of the loan and mortgage will automatically become additional security for the loan.

AFTER-MARKET. The term describing the market for a security after it has been initially sold by the issuer through *underwriters.*

AGING OF ACCOUNTS. Arranging the accounts (such as receivables or payables) in chronological order and grouping the accounts by intervals, such as accounts less than 30 days old, 30 to 60 days old, and so on.

AGIO THEORY OF INTEREST. An explanation of interest as the result of postponement of present consumption to future consumption and the payment of an *agio* (premium) for the postponement. See *abstinence theory of interest, liquidity preference theory of interest, loanable funds theory of interest, marginal productivity theory of interest, time preference theory of interest.*

AMORTIZATION. A reduction in a debt or fund by periodic payments covering interest and part of principal, distinguished from (1) depreciation, which is an allocation of the original cost of an asset computed from physical wear and tear as well as the passage of time, and (2) depletion, which is a reduction in the book value of a resource (such as minerals) resulting from conversion into a salable product.

AMORTIZED VALUE. In finance, certain bonds bought at a premium may be carried on financial statements at their amortized value rather than current market value in the case of banks, insurance companies, and similar institutions. This amortized value is the cost amount of the bond less (or plus) that part of the premium (or discount) that may be allocated to the time expired from the date of acquisition to the present, using the total period from acquisition to maturity as the basis for allocation.

ANNUITY BOND. A bond without a maturity date, that is, perpetually paying interest.

ANTIDILUTION PROVISION. In finance, part of the terms of an *option, warrant, convertible debenture,* or other security with exercise rights at a stated price in the future. The provision is designed to provide adjustment of the stated price to preserve its relative position at the time of issuance in the event more shares or rights are issued in the future, particularly if such issuance is at a lower price than the stated price of the security being protected against *dilution.*

APPRAISAL SURPLUS. Same as *appreciation surplus.*

APPRECIATION SURPLUS. The addition to *net worth* appearing in *surplus* as the result of a revaluation upward of the value at which assets are shown on the books of an enterprise.

APPROPRIATED SURPLUS. That part of the surplus of a corporation that has been set aside by the board of directors for a specific purpose other than to recognize an existing liability. The appropriation can be reversed by the board.

ARRANGEMENT. In law, the term applied to the plan resulting from a *receivership* proceeding under Chapter XI of the Bankruptcy Act.

ASSENTED BONDS. Bonds deposited by the owner with a trustee or intermediary pursuant to the owner's agreement to accept voluntarily a change in securities of a corporation.

ASSESSABLE STOCK. Stock subject to assessment, that is, the stockholder may have to pay more than his original investment if the affairs of the corporation so require.

ASSET AND LIABILITY STATEMENT. Same as *balance sheet.*

ASSET DIVIDEND. In finance, a dividend paid to stockholders in the form of an asset, usually cash but sometimes a product of the company, such as bottles of whiskey.

ASSET TURNOVER RATIO. The ratio of sales to *net operating assets.*

ASSUMED BONDS. Bonds of the original debtor that have been made the liability of the second debtor who voluntarily assumed them.

AUTHORIZED ISSUE. The total number of shares of capital stock that a charter permits a corporation to sell. Also the total number of bonds that may be sold under a given mortgage. Additional shares after the original amount is exhausted are authorized by charter amendment.

AVERAGE AGE OF RECEIVABLES. The weighted average age of receivables computed by summing the products of the number of days from date of each unpaid invoice to date of computation times the dollar amount of each invoice. This sum divided by the dollar total of receivables gives the average age.

BANK LINE. A *line of credit* offered by a bank to a borrower.

BANK MERGER ACT. Legislation in 1960 applying the limitations of the *Bank Holding Company Act* of 1956 to bank mergers.

BANKRUPTCY. A legal method by which a debtor may be relieved of his financial obligations. A court, through a trustee, takes the debtor's property and distributes it among his creditors in proportion to their respective claims against him. Bankruptcy is subject to federal law and may be voluntary or involuntary. There are six acts, any one of which constitutes bankruptcy: (1) making a general assignment for creditors, (2) admitting in writing inability to pay debts, (3) concealing or conveying property with intent to defraud creditors; and the following three acts if done while insolvent: (4) preferring one creditor, (5) failing to discharge a lien within 30 days, or (6) permitting a receiver to take over while unable to meet debts as they mature.

BAROMETER STOCK. On the stock market a term applied to a widely held stock of a leading company whose price movement is taken to reflect general market conditions.

BASIS POINT. In government securities one one hundredth of 1 percent (or of one unit) change in the yield (or price) of the security. Because government securities move less in absolute dollar amounts than other securities, though relatively the movement in their price may be more significant, the term "basis point" has come into use as a shorthand method of referring to absolute changes that would be more cumbersome to express in customary terms.

BEARER BONDS. Bonds payable to the person having possession of them. Such bonds do not require indorsement to transfer ownership but only the transfer of possession.

BEAR MARKET. A market in which prices are falling or are expected to fall. See *bull market.*

BEAR RAIDING. Driving the price of a stock down by a series of *short sales* in order to buy in at the lower price to cover. Regulations now control this possibility by requiring that a short sale be at a price one eighth higher than the last sale and also that the prior sale shall not have been a short sale.

BEST EFFORTS. In securities *underwriting*, an agreement by an *investment banker* to apply his best efforts to selling an issue of securities but with the right to turn back unsold securities.

BIG BOARD. A popular term referring to the board showing the current prices of securities listed on the New York Stock Exchange.

BLANKET MORTGAGE. A mortgage covering all the fixed assets of a borrower rather than specifically named assets.

BLANK INDORSEMENT. The signature (without more) of the owner or one whose name appears on a financial document.

BLANK STOCK. Stock whose terms need not be set forth in the articles of incorporation but may be established by the board of directors at the time of issue.

BLUE SKY LAWS. State laws governing securities. So called because they are designed to protect investors from purchasing a piece of the blue sky (worthless securities). Different in principle from the current federal legislation directed only at disclosure. Blue sky laws may also extend to determination of the legitimacy of the proposed financing.

BOARD LOT. The trading unit on a stock exchange. The unit on the New York Stock Exchange is ordinarily 100 shares. Also called a *round lot*.

BOND. (1) A written promise to pay the holder a sum of money at a certain time (more than one year after issue) at a stated rate of interest. A debt due in less than one year from the date of issue is usually called a note. (2) In suretyship the obligation of a guarantor to pay a second party upon default by a third party in the performance the third party owes to the second party.

BONDS, TYPES OF. See the following specific terms as to bonds (promises to pay a debt):

*adjustment bond*
*annuity bond*
*assented bond*
*assumed bond*
*bearer bond*
*callable bond*
*chattel mortgage bond*
*collateral trust bond*
*consolidated bond*
*consolidated mortgage bond*
*continued bond*
*convertible bond*
*coupon bond*
*debenture bond*
*discount bond*
*equipment trust bond*
*extended bond*
*extension bond*
*general mortgage bond*
*guaranteed bond*
*income bond*
*indorsed bond*
*interest bond*
*leasehold mortgage*
*mortgage bond*
*open-end mortgage bond*
*optional bond*
*overlying bond*
*participating bond*
*perpetual bond*
*profit-sharing bond*
*redeemable bond*
*refunding mortgage bond*
*registered bond*
*reorganization bond*
*serial bond*
*series bond*
*sinking fund bond*
*term bond*
*terminal bond*
*treasury bond*
*underlying bond*

BONDHOLDERS. The holders or owners of the bonds of a corporation or government. They are lenders or creditors.

BOND RATIO. The total face value of the bonds of a corporation divided by the total face value of bonds, preferred stock, common stock, reserve, and surplus.

BONUS STOCK. Stock given as a premium in connection with the sale of other stock.

BOOK VALUE. (1) The value of an outstanding share of stock of a corporation at any one time, determined by adding the par (or stated) value of the stock outstanding to the surplus applicable to that class of stock and dividing by the number of shares of that class outstanding. (2) The valuation at which assets are carried on the books, that is, cost less reserve for depreciation.

BOOK VALUE METHOD (IN CAPITAL BUDGETING). Same as *accounting method of return.*

BORROWING RATE IN CAPITAL BUDGETING. The rate an investor must pay in the market for funds. This rate is usually (but not always) above the rate the investor can secure for lending funds to the market. See *lending rate in capital budgeting.*

BREAK–EVEN POINT. There are three break-even points: the *cash break-even point,* the *financial break-even point,* and the *profit break-even point.* When only the term "break-even point" is used, profit break-even point is the one intended. The formula is BE = FC/(1 − variable cost ratio), where FC is the fixed cost in dollars for any output and the variable cost ratio is the ratio of variable costs in dollars to sales in dollars for any output.

BROKER. An agent of a buyer or a seller who buys or sells stocks, bonds, commodities, or services, usually on a commission basis.

BULL MARKET. A market in which prices are rising or are expected to rise. See *bear market.*

BUSINESS RISK. In finance, the risk of default or variability of return arising from the type of business conducted.

CALL. (1) An option permitting its holder (who has paid a fee for the option) to call for a certain commodity or security at a fixed price in a stated quantity within a stated period. The broker is paid to bring the buyer and seller together. The buyer of this right to call expects the price of the commodity or security to rise so that he can call for it at a profit. If the price falls, the option will not be exercised. The reverse transaction is a *put.* (2) A demand by a corporation for payment against stock subscribed but not fully paid. (3) Notice by a corporation that it will redeem securities on a given date.

CALLABLE. The right of a corporation or government to call bonds or notes for payment before they are due. Preferred stock may also be callable.

CALL PREMIUM. The amount over *par* or *face value* payable by the issuer of the security upon calling a security in for payment or redemption.

CAPITAL. (1) In accounting the amount invested in a business. (2) In economic theory there are several meanings. "Capital" may be used to mean (a) capital goods, that is, the tools of production, (b) the money available for investment, or invested, (c) the discounted value of the future income to be received from an investment, (d) the real or money value of total assets. (3) In law "capital" means capital stock.

CAPITAL BUDGET (PRIVATE BUSINESS). A period-by-period statement of beginning capital assets, planned acquisitions and disposals, and the resultant ending capital assets together with the sources and disposition of funds so involved.

CAPITAL BUDGETING. The analysis of investment projects to determine the *rate of return* of the investment and the *cost of capital* required to undertake the investment so as to compare the proposed investment with other opportunities and to decide under all the circumstances whether to make the investment commitment. Differences in risks are important in the computation.

CAPITAL GAINS TAX. A provision in the income tax that profits from the sale of capital assets are taxed at separate (lower) rates than the rate applicable to ordinary income.

CAPITALIZATION. In finance the total of bonds and the par value of stock outstanding. In the case of *no par stock* the number of shares is used because the dollar amount of *stated value* has little significance. Sometimes the term excludes bonds and is then used to refer to net worth. See *capital structure.*

CAPITALIZATION OF INCOME. The process of taking the net income of a business and dividing this figure by the appropriate *capitalization rate* to establish the value of the business.

CAPITALIZATION RATE. The rate of earning appropriate to apply to the net income of a business to establish its value.

CAPITALIZED VALUE. The money valuation set upon the assets of a business by dividing the annual profits by an assumed rate of earning, which is usually the current rate for similar risks.

CAPITAL MARKET. The market for long-term investment funds. Thus primarily investment bankers, savings banks, insurance companies, pension funds, and trust companies are involved. See *money market.*

CAPITAL RATIO. In *capital budgeting* the ratio of the total investment fund (in dollars) to the particular investment (in dollars) being analyzed.

CAPITAL STOCK. The shares of ownership of a corporation. Such shares may have a *par value* or *no par value.*

CAPITAL STRUCTURE. In finance the total of bonds (or long-term money) and ownership interests in a corporation, that is, the stock accounts and surplus. See *capitalization* and *financial structure.*

CAPITAL SURPLUS. Surplus that arises from "capital" transactions and not from usual business profits, for example, surplus from writing down the *par value* of capital stock.

CAPITAL TURNOVER. See *investment turnover.*

CASH BREAK–EVEN POINT. Assuming a plant organized for a given ideal volume of output, if units of output are put on the $x$ axis and total dollars on the $y$ axis, the cash break-even point is the intersection of the total cash revenue curve with the cash outlay curve.

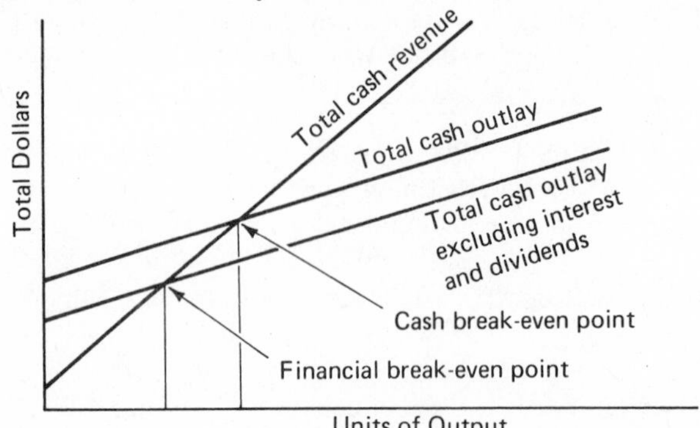


Figure A—Cash and financial break-even points

CASH BUDGET. A period-by-period statement of opening cash on hand, expected cash receipts, expected cash disbursements, and resulting expected cash balance at the end of each period.

CASH CYCLE. The time lapse between purchase of materials and collection of *accounts receivable* for finished product sold.

CASH DISCOUNT. A discount allowed for payment of a debt in advance of a due date. For example, 2/10, net 30 means a 2 percent discount if paid within 10 days, the net price if paid after 10 but before 30 days.

CASH FLOW. The *net profits* of a business plus the charges of the accounting period for *depreciation, depletion, amortization,* and extraordinary charges to reserves not paid in cash. This is the cash generated in a period if all other accounts do not change. In addition, decreases in assets, increases in liabilities, and new capital added are sources of cash, while increases in assets and decreases in liabilities and net worth are applications of cash.

CASH POSITION. The ratio of cash on hand and in banks to bank loans. Other ratios carry this name, for example, the ratio of cash to total assets.

CASH POSITION RATIO. The ratio of cash and marketable securities to current liabilities.

CASH TO DAILY PURCHASES RATIO. The ratio of cash to average daily purchases. Used as a test of the liquidity position of a firm.

CERTIFICATE OF PARTICIPATION. A certificate issued instead of shares of stock to show a proportionate interest in an unincorporated business or in the ownership of debt of a corporation.

CHATTEL MORTGAGE. A conveyance of personal property as security for the payment of a debt.

CHATTEL MORTGAGE BONDS. The bonds of a business which are secured by a mortgage on its movable property. See *equipment trust certificates.*

CLASS A AND B STOCK. During recent years it has been the practice of some corporations to issue common stock in two general classes, A and B, with the holders of only one class having voting power or with one class having preference. Also called classified common stock.

CLASSIFIED COMMON STOCK. See *Class A and B stock.*

CLASSIFIED DIRECTORS. A system of electing a percentage of the board of directors (usually one-third) each year for a period more than one year (usually three years) so that any attempted take-over of a corporation will be slowed.

CLEAN-UP PROVISION. In bank loans, an agreement by the borrower that at lease once a year he will have repaid all bank loans and be "out of the bank" for a stated period, usually 30 days.

CLOSE CORPORATION. A corporation whose stock is owned by a few people.

CLOSED-END MORTGAGE. A *mortgage* that does not permit additional borrowing.

COLLATERAL TRUST BONDS. Bonds of one corporation secured by its holdings of stocks, bonds, and/or notes of another corporation.

COLLATERAL TRUST CERTIFICATE. A security issued by a trustee pursuant to an agreement under which the trustee holds stocks and bonds of a number of companies for the benefit of the holders of the collateral trust certificate.

COLLECTION PERIOD. The average number of days needed to collect an *account receivable.* To compute, divide average daily credit sales into accounts receivable outstanding.

COMMERCIAL BANK. A bank, one of whose main functions is acceptance of deposits and creation of credit through short-term loans mainly for business purposes. See *investment banking.*

COMMERCIAL FINANCE COMPANY. Same as *sales finance company* or *commercial credit company.*

COMMERCIAL PAPER. (1) Promissory notes, commercial drafts, trade acceptances, and similar documents issued by business firms. (2) In banking, loans arising from transactions covering purchases of goods. See *financial paper.*

COMMITMENT FEE. The amount (such as ½ or ¼ percent) paid by a borrower to a lender for a loan in addition to interest on the loan. The fee may be against the total amount of the loan or against the unborrowed balance of a loan commitment or *line of credit* and may be paid once or annually.

COMMON STOCK. Shares in a corporation that have no fixed rate of dividends. They are the last to secure a share in the property when the corporation is dissolved.

COMMON STOCK RATIO. Par or stated value of common stock plus surplus reserves and surplus divided by the total value of bonds, preferred stock, common stock, surplus reserves, and surplus.

COMPENSATING BALANCE. In banking the balance a borrower from a bank is required by the bank to keep in his account. Typically, 15 percent of the borrowed amount.

COMPETITIVE BIDDING. The process of preparation of a security issue through the solicitation by the issuing company of the highest bids from competitive groups of investment banking firms and awarding the issue to the highest bidder. Since 1941 the required method for public utility holding companies and their subsidiaries unless exempted by the *SEC*. See *negotiated purchase.*

COMPOUND INTEREST METHOD OF DEPRECIATION. Taking the initial cost of a capital asset, deducting the expected salvage value at the time it is expected to be discarded, and spreading the difference in equal installments per unit of time over the estimated life of the asset but then reducing the depreciation charge for each period by the amount of interest that such a charge would earn from the period of the charge to the time of discard.

CONDITIONAL SALE. A security transaction in which the seller retains title to the property until the buyer has made full payment.

CONGLOMERATE. A company with widely diversified *product lines* which comes about through *merger* of many companies.

CONSOLIDATED BONDS. Bonds issued to replace two or more outstanding issues and thus to bring such indebtedness together into one issue. Also called unified bonds.

CONSOLIDATED MORTGAGE. A mortgage created to replace or unify several mortgages already existing. It may be the unification of several mortgages of one creditor or the unification of the mortgages of several creditors.

CONSOLIDATED STATEMENTS. The financial reports for a group of affiliated corporations or enterprises, eliminating intercorporation debts and profits and showing minority stockholders' interests.

CONSOLIDATION OR FUSION. A union of several corporations into a new one, the old ones ceasing to exist. See *merger.*

CONSTANT PERCENTAGE OF DECLINING BALANCE METHOD OF DEPRECIATION. Taking the initial cost of a capital asset, deducting the expected salvage value, and spreading the difference by a constant percentage of the undepreciated balance, so that at the end of the expected life the undepreciated balance equals the salvage value. The percentage is determined as $1 - \sqrt[n]{s/c}$ where $n$ = the number of periods, $s$ = the salvage value, and $c$ = the cost.

CONTINUED BOND. A bond that may be presented for payment at maturity or held by the bondholder at his option for a further definite or indefinite period as the bond provides.

CONVERSION POINT. The price (adjusted for accrued dividends) at which stock into which a bond is convertible will just equal the current market price of the bond plus accrued interest on the bond.

CONVERSION PRICE. The price stated in a bond or stock at which it can be exchanged at the option of the bondholder or stockholder for another security.

CONVERTIBLE BONDS. Bonds that may be converted into stock at the option of the owner.

CONVERTIBLE STOCK. Preferred stock that may be converted into common stock at the option of the owner.

CORPORATION. An association of stockholders created under law and regarded as an artificial person by the courts. The chief characteristics are (1) limited liability of stockholders, (2) continuity in existence, and (3) easy transferability of ownership interest.

CORPORATION CHARTER. A document issued by the state or federal government giving a group of persons the right to act as a legal person in the conduct of an enterprise and specifying at least some of the conditions of operation.

COST OF CAPITAL. In *capital budgeting* the cost to the investor of the funds to be committed to a proposed investment. This cost includes not only the "nominal" rate paid for the funds but the net effect (plus or minus) on the investor's cost of funds compared to not making the investment.

COST OF GOODS SOLD. Determined for any period by subtracting the value of the ending inventory from the sum of the value of the beginning inventory plus the cost of goods bought or manufactured during that period.

COST OR MARKET, WHICHEVER IS LOWER, METHOD OF INVENTORY VALUATION. Valuing inventory after physical count (or balance from a control account) on the basis of cost or market price per unit, whichever is lower. The cost price is commonly determined under the *cost method (average) of inventory* or under the *first in, first out method of inventory.* Market price is determined by current quotations or by averaging *bid* and *ask* quotations.

COUPON BONDS. Bonds provided with coupons, one for the amount of interest due on each interest date. Upon surrender of the coupon on the maturity date the bondholder receives the interest payment.

CREDIT INSTRUMENT. Any written or printed paper by means of which funds are transferred from one person to another. The most common are checks, drafts, money orders, promissory notes, and letters of credit.

CREDIT LINE. The maximum amount a lender agrees to lend a borrower. See *open credit.*

CREDITORS' COMMITTEE. In law, when a firm is in financial difficulty, the creditors may select a committee of representatives to work with the owner in attempting to solve his problems.

CUM RIGHTS. Latin for "with rights." Stock sold with rights of subscription to a current new issue of a corporation. See *ex rights.*

CUMULATIVE DIVIDEND. A dividend that if not paid annually (or periodically as provided in the stock certificate) will ultimately have to be paid before any common stock dividend can be paid. The arrearage is said to accumulate.

CUMULATIVE PREFERRED STOCK. Preferred stock whose dividends are to continue to accumulate even though they are not earned, or if earned are not declared; any arrears on this stock must be paid up before any dividend can be paid on noncumulative stock. In the event of liquidation the accumulated dividends may or may not take precedence over inferior stock, depending on the provisions of the stock.

CUMULATIVE VOTING. In a corporation a method of voting for directors involving the simultaneous election of all directors, with each stockholder receiving as many votes as he has voting shares multiplied by the number of directors to be elected. This assures some representation on the board for the minority if they cast all their votes for a limited number of directors. The number of shares needed to elect one director is determined by this formula (dropping fractional shares) *provided* all stockholders vote only for the number of directors who can be elected by their shares.

$$\frac{(\text{Total shares voting}) \times (\text{number of directors desired})}{\text{Number of directors to be elected} + 1} + 1$$

CURRENT ASSETS. Any property that will be converted into cash in the normal operation of business at an early date, usually within one year.

CURRENT DEBT. Debt due within one year.

CURRENT LIABILITY. A liability that will be paid in the normal operation of a business at an early date, usually within one year.

CURRENT RATIO. Current assets divided by current liabilities. The "normal" ratio for a business is 2 to 1. See *quick ratio, cash position ratio.*

CURRENT YIELD. The ratio of the current income from an investment to the purchase price or the current price of the investment.

DEAD FLOAT. Checks and items for collection in process of collection or not yet collected and hence the proceeds not yet available.

DEALER. (1) One who purchases goods for resale to final consumers. (2) In securities one who acts for his own account rather than as an agent for another.

DEBENTURE BONDS. Bonds not secured by any specific property but issued against the general credit of a corporation or government.

DEBT COVERAGE RATIO. The ratio of total assets to total debt of a firm. Sometimes stated inversely as ratio of total debt to total assets.

DEBT SERVICE. The interest and charges currently payable on a debt, including principal payments.

DEFERRED BONDS. Bonds on which interest payment has been postponed for a definite period by agreement of debtor and creditor.

DEPLETION RESERVE. An account recording periodic charges to income to reflect the decrease in value of an asset in the form of a natural resource that is exhausted in obtaining the income.

DEPRECIATION. (1) In accounting the allocation of the cost (purchase price minus salvage) of an asset that will be used up over a long period of time by charging a portion of the cost to each period of expected life. (2) More generally, any drop in value.

DEPRECIATION, METHODS OF. See the following specific terms.

*compound interest method of depreciation*
*constant percentage of decreasing balance method of depreciation*
*double declining balance method of depreciation*
*retirement method of depreciation*
*sinking fund method of depreciation*
*straight-line method of depreciation*
*sum-of-the-years' digits method of depreciation*
*unit cost method of depreciation*

DEPRECIATION RESERVE. An account recording periodic charges to income to reflect the portion of the cost of a long-lived asset recovered. If the amount is kept in cash or a specific asset, it is referred to as a fund. When an asset is disposed of, the account is credited with all the depreciation charges previously made for that asset.

DERIVATIVE SUIT. In corporation law a suit by a stockholder on behalf of the corporation. The stockholder alleges that the officers of the corporation have failed to act to protect the interest of the corporation, and therefore he is suing on behalf of the corporation.

DILUTION. In finance, crudely used to describe the reduction in the proportion of a corporation owned by old shareholders when new shares are sold. More accurately, dilution occurs only when the proceeds of the new shares earn at a lesser rate than the earning rate just before the new shares are issued.

DIRECT FINANCING. The securing of funds by direct negotiation by the borrower with the investor rather than through the use of an *underwriter.*

DIRECT PLACEMENT. The negotiation by a borrower, such as an industrial or utility company, directly with the lender, such as a life insurance company or group of companies, for an entire issue of securities. No *underwriter* is involved and the transaction is exempt from SEC filing.

DIRECT-REDUCTION MORTGAGE. A mortgage under which the borrower periodically pays interest and makes payments against the principal at the same time; the mortgage debt is thus reduced, with interest payable by the borrower only on the unpaid balance.

DISCHARGE IN BANKRUPTCY. At the termination of a *bankruptcy* case in federal court, the debtor receives a discharge, that is, he no longer is liable for debts listed in the proceeding.

DISCOUNT BOND. A bond sold for less than face or maturity value. No interest is paid annually, but all interest accrues to the maturity date when it is paid.

DISCOUNTED CASH FLOW. In capital budgeting a method of analysis emphasizing the time factor in considering receipts and outlays and further emphasizing that receipts are to be considered as after income tax but with depreciation charges "added back." The time factor is recognized in the form of a rate of interest (or discount) applicable to both outlays and receipts. Two methods are common: the *yield method* and the *present value method.*

DISSOLUTION. As applied to a partnership or corporation, the termination of the business with the assets distributed according to priorities to the creditors and owners.

DIVERSIFIABLE RISK. Investments whose returns are not systematically related to the market as a whole carry a diversifiable risk. Cf. *nondiversifiable risk.*

DIVIDED SYNDICATE. In finance, the *underwriting agreement* is divided when the maximum number of shares for which each underwriter is liable is specified. Cf. *undivided syndicate.*

DIVIDEND. (1) The earnings or profits that a corporation, upon the order of its board of directors, pays to its stockholders. The dividend may be in cash, property, securities, or any combination of these. Dividends can also, in some states, be declared out of nonearnings, for example, out of paid-in surplus. (2) Special types of businesses (for example, cooperatives and insurance companies) also declare dividends. In this case the "dividend" is a refund due to overpayment of the sales price or premium.

DIVIDENDS, TYPES OF. See the following specific terms:

*accumulated dividend*
*asset dividend*
*cumulative dividend*
*scrip dividend*
*stock dividend*

DIVIDEND–PRICE RATIO. The ratio of the current dividend to the market price of the stock.

DIVIDEND YIELD. The current annual dividend divided by the market price per share.

DONATED STOCK. Stock given to the corporation by stockholders, usually for resale. Originally used as an evasive device because different rules of law applied to price on the original sale and on resale.

DONATED SURPLUS. Surplus created by the gratuitious return by stockholders to the corporation of stock previously sold them or by the contribution of assets such as might be given by a municipality as an inducement to locate a plant.

DOUBLE DECLINING BALANCE METHOD OF DEPRECIATION. Spreading the initial cost of a capital asset over time by deducting in each period double the percentage recognized by the *straight-line method* and applying that double percentage to the undepreciated balance existing at the start of each period. No salvage value is used in the calculation.

DOUBLE LIABILITY. In the period before the 1930s, bank stock was subject to additional assessment of an amount equal to the original price.

EARNEST MONEY. A sum of money paid by a buyer at the time of entering a contract to indicate the intention and ability of the buyer to carry out the contract. Often the contract provides for forfeiture of this sum if the buyer defaults.

EARNINGS MULTIPLIER. Same as *price-earnings ratio.*

EARNINGS PER SHARE. One common measure of the value of common stock. The figure is computed by dividing the net earnings (after interest and prior dividends) by the number of shares of common stock. See (1) as to bonds, *times interest earned,* (2) as to preferred stock, *times preferred dividend earned.*

EARN OUT. A type of *merger* agreement in which all or a part of the price received by the acquired company is dependent upon the future earnings of that company.

EBIT. Abbreviation for "earnings before interest and taxes."

ECONOMIC LOT SIZE. Same as *optimum lot size.*

EFFICIENT FRONTIER. The set of securities that minimizes the *variance* of a *portfolio.*

EMPLOYEE STOCK REPURCHASE AGREEMENT. A plan under which stock in a corporation is sold to employees, with an agreement providing for repurchase by the corporation. Many variations are possible.

EPS. Abbreviation for "earnings per share."

EQUIPMENT TRUST CERTIFICATE. A device widely used in the railroad, airline, and trucking fields by which corporations can get new equipment.

The equipment is held by a trustee who leases the equipment to the corporation. Thus the equipment does not become subject to claims against the corporation. The equipment must be plainly marked as to true ownership, however, to make this device effective. The trustee issues certificates similar to shares of stock to those who put up the money to finance the trustee's purchase of the equipment. The rent from the lease becomes the income distributed to the certificate holders. When rental payments total purchase price plus interest, the equipment is turned over to the lessee. Three forms of contract may be used: the *chattel mortgage*, the *conditicnal sale*, or the *lease*.

EQUITY CAPITAL. The total fund invested in a business by the owners. See *net worth*.

EQUITY OF REDEMPTION. The interest of one who has mortgaged property for a loan. In so-called "title" states the lender owns the mortgaged property and the borrower has only the right (equity) to get it back (redeem it) upon payment of the debt. In *"lien"* states the mortgagor still retains title to the property and the mortgage is a lien.

EXCESS PRESENT VALUE. The difference between the purchase price of an asset and its *present value* at some assumed rate of discount of future income.

EXCHANGE DISTRIBUTION. In finance, the sale of a block of stock on a stock exchange by a holder (not the issuing corporation) during regular hours at a fixed price. Only the seller pays a commission. Cf. *secondary offering*.

EXCULPATORY CLAUSE. A provision in an agreement which excuses one of the parties from liability for any negligence he may commit. Made illegal as to trustees of a bond indenture by the *Trust Indenture Act of 1939*.

EXPECTED RETURN. The *mean* value of a probability distribution of possible returns each weighted by its probability.

EXPECTED VALUE. The *mean* value of a probability distribution, that is, the average of the respective values each weighted by its probability.

EX RIGHTS. Literally, without rights. Stock sold *ex* rights is sold without privileged subscription rights to a current new issue by a corporation. See *cum rights*.

EXTENDED BOND. A bond whose maturity date has been delayed with the consent of the bondholder.

EXTENSION BOND. A bond secured by a mortgage on an addition or extension of a railroad.

EXTERNAL FINANCING. Procurement of funds for a firm from sources outside the firm, for example, by the sale of new bonds or stock. Cf. *internal financing*.

FACE VALUE. The value stated on the face of a security or insurance policy. This is the value at maturity or death.

FACTORING. Sale of *accounts receivable* of a firm to a *factor* at a discounted price.

FEDERAL RESERVE SYSTEM. A system of 12 central banks created in 1913 and controlled by the Board of Governors of seven men in Washington, D. C. National banks must belong and state banks may. A member bank must invest 6 percent (of which only 3 percent or half has currently been called) of its own capital and surplus in the stock of its regional Federal Reserve bank and must also keep a minimum reserve of 12 percent if a country bank and 16.5 percent if a Reserve-city bank of its demand deposits in the Reserve bank or in vault cash and 4 percent of its time or savings deposits. The Board of Governors has the power to vary these percentages from a minimum of 7 for country banks and 10 for Reserve-city banks to a maximum of 14 and 22, respectively. The 12 cities in which the Federal Reserve banks are located are: (1) Boston, (2) New York, (3) Philadelphia, (4) Cleveland, (5) Richmond, (6) Atlanta, (7) Chicago, (8) St. Louis, (9) Minneapolis, (10) Kansas City, Mo., (11) Dallas, and (12) San Francisco. There are also 25 branch offices.

FINANCE COMPANY. Any company (other than a bank) engaged in lending money, usually against the security of goods.

FINANCIAL BREAK–EVEN POINT (See Fig. A, p. 700). Assuming a plant organized for a given output, if units of output are put on the $x$ axis and total dollars on the $y$ axis, the financial break-even point is the intersection of the total cash revenue curve and the total cash outlay curve, excluding interest and dividends.

FINANCIAL BUDGET. The plan for securing the deficit of cash from future operations or employing the excess of cash from future operations. Starting with the *cash budget,* the financial budget plans the borrowing or investing required by the cash budget balances, as well as interest or dividends.

FINANCIAL INDIFFERENCE POINT. With debt at a given rate of interest, and the income tax rate constant, there is a level of earnings before interest and taxes at which the resulting earnings per common share will be the same regardless of the percentage of debt and equity. There is one such point for each combination of interest rate and income tax rate. (See p. 96).

FINANCIAL INTERMEDIARIES. Financial institutions such as *commercial banks,* insurance companies, and *investment companies* that act as an intermediary between lenders (and savers) and borrowers. In national income accounting the fact that services and cost are offset (such as no interest on a checking account but "free service" allowed) requires inputing values to such situations.

FINANCIAL LEASE. Such a lease as provides for rental payments that cover the full repayment of original cost of the asset plus interest (with zero terminal value) and is noncancellable. Cf. *operating lease.*

FINANCIAL LEVERAGE. The use of the fact that the interest rate on debt is different from the earning rate of assets. If the rate on debt is lower than the earning rate, the leverage is favorable. Cf. *leverage factor, operating leverage.*

FINANCIAL PAPER. Accommodation paper, this is, a short-term loan not supported by a specific commercial transaction or transfer of goods. See *commercial paper.*

FINANCIAL PLAN. The financial plan of a corporation is the pattern of stocks and bonds issued at the time the corporation is organized, or after failure when it is reorganized.

FINANCIAL RISK. In investments used in contradistinction to *interest rate risk* and *purchasing power risk* to refer to the risk of default in performing the obligations of a security.

FINANCIAL STATEMENT. Any report summarizing the financial condition or financial results of an organization on any date or for any period. The two principal types of financial statements are the *balance sheet* and the *profit and loss statement.*

FINANCIAL STRUCTURE. All of the financial resources of a firm, short term and long term, debt and equity. Distinguished from *capital structure,* which includes only long-term resources.

FINISHED–GOODS TURNOVER. *Cost of goods sold* during a period divided by the average finished-goods inventory at cost of that period.

FIRST IN, FIRST OUT METHOD OF INVENTORY. Under the first in, first out rule (FIFO) items of inventory issued are priced out at the purchase price of the oldest batch in stock, then the purchase price of the next oldest batch, and so on. Inventory value is thus computed by assuming that goods on hand are those most recently purchased and are valued at the successively latest purchase prices. See *inventory valuation methods.*

FIRST, SECOND, OR THIRD MORTGAGE. The words "first," "second," or "third" applied to a *mortgage* indicate the priority of the interest of the *mortgagee* in the property given as security for a debt. Mortgages are ranked in the time order in which they are made unless earlier mortgagees consent otherwise.

FIXED ASSET. Any property used in carrying on the operation of a business, which will not be consumed through use or converted into cash during the current fiscal period, usually the year.

FIXED ASSET TURNOVER. See *plant turnover.*

FIXED BUDGET. A *budget* or estimate of receipts and expenditures that is not altered once it is established and does not recognize the effects of changes in the volume of sales or production or in product mix. See *variable budget.*

FIXED–CHARGE COVERAGE. The ratio of earnings before interest and taxes to fixed charges (total interest on all debt and any debt amortization commitments).

FIXED CHARGES. The expenses that have to be borne whether any business is done or not. The chief items are the company's interest on bonds, some taxes levied by the government, insurance payments, and depreciation due to obsolescence.

FIXED CREDIT LINE. Same as *irrevocable credit.*

FIXED DEBT. Same as *funded debt.*

FIXED OBLIGATION. An obligation that is fixed at the time the agreement is made and continues to run during the life of the agreement, for example, interest on bonds except *income* or *adjustment bonds.*

FLEXIBLE BUDGET. A *budget* that provides estimates for varying levels of sales and hence of cash requirements, profits, and financing needs for these several levels. Also called *variable budget.* See *fixed budget.*

FLOAT. (1) In banking practice checks and other items in the process of collection. (2) In manufacturing the amount of goods in the process of production, usually measured in terms of the number of units in process divided by the number of finished units produced per average day and expressed as, for example, "six days float." (3) In finance the unsold part of a security issue or (4) the number of shares actively traded.

FLOATING CAPITAL. That part of capital in *current assets* such as inventory and receivables.

FLOATING DEBT. Any debt not yet funded, that is, not formally evidenced by a bond issue. See *funding a debt.*

FLOOR PLANNING. Any method such as a *trust receipt* by which the borrower keeps possession of goods pledged as security for a loan and is able to sell such goods.

FLOTATION COST. The expenses of selling securities such as underwriting *spread*, legal and accounting fees, and printing and engraving charges.

FORECLOSURE. (1) The legal procedure that provides for the sale of mortgaged property when the mortgagor fails to pay the debt. The proceeds of the sale are then applied to the mortgage debt. Any excess of proceeds over the debt is refunded to the debtor; and deficiency is charged against the debtor in a *deficiency judgment* if that is asked for. (2) Strict foreclosure involves forfeiture of the mortgaged property upon default.

FOUNDERS' STOCK. Stock given promoters and management personnel at the time of incorporation for services rendered.

FULL–PAID STOCK. Same as *paid-up stock.*

FULLY DILUTED EARNINGS. In accounting, the adjustment of current earnings per share to show the result if all options and conversion privileges of bonds and preferred stock were exercised.

FUNDED DEBT. The indebtedness of a business or government that has been formally evidenced, as in a bond issue. Usually the line is drawn at debt due more than one year hence.

FUNDING. (1) The process of converting accounts payable or other short-term debt into fixed obligations with a maturity date and ordinarily represented by formal documents such as bonds. (2) The process of establishing an amount of securities as a reserve or for a specific purpose.

GENERAL MORTGAGE BOND. A bond secured by a general mortgage on the borrower's property, but it may be outranked as to individual assets by other bonds secured by prior mortgages on those assets.

GOING PUBLIC. A colloquial term describing the first offering of the stock of a company for purchase by the general public.

GRANDFATHER CLAUSE. (1) In general, a provision in new regulations exempting existing business from the new requirements. (2) In the Public Utility Holding Company Act, the prohibition of more than three tiers of utility corporations, that is, the limit is one *holding company* with stock of another holding company. Cf. *death sentence.*

GROSS PLANT TURNOVER. *Net sales* divided by gross plant, that is, undepreciated plant.

GROSS PROFIT. The difference between sales and the *cost of goods sold* before allowance for operating expenses and income taxes.

GROSS PROFIT MARGIN. Same as *gross profit ratio.*

GROSS PROFIT RATIO. The ratio of the difference between sales and the *cost of goods sold* to sales.

GROSS PROFITS TEST. In auditing a method of verifying the book valuation of a closing inventory. Having determined the *gross profit* (sales less *cost of goods sold*) of a previous period, the auditor takes the sales of the current period and applies the gross profit percentage of the previous period to obtain a theoretical cost of goods sold. Then taking the opening inventory, adding purchases during the current period, and deducting this theoretical cost of goods sold should yield a figure approximating the closing inventory shown on the books. This method is also used in settling fire losses where no inventory records exist or survive.

GROSS SPREAD. In finance the difference between the price paid by an investment banker for an issue and the price paid by the buying public.

GROSS UP. Colloquial term in taxation of U.S. international businesses under which U.S. corporations must "gross up" any income from foreign subsidiaries, that is, include pre-foreign tax income in U.S. income tax returns in order to claim credit against U.S. income taxes for foreign income taxes paid.

GUARANTEED BONDS. Usually arise when one corporation leases some property of another one and guarantees the principal or interest, or both, of the bonds of the corporation whose property is leased.

GUARANTEED MORTGAGE. A mortgage whose principal and/or interest payment is guaranteed by a guarantor. Today most guarantees are by the Federal Housing Administration or the Veterans Administration, but some are by a mortgage guarantee corporation.

GUARANTEED STOCK. Stock whose dividends are guaranteed by a corporation other than the corporation that issued the stock.

HIDDEN RESERVE. By undervaluing assets or overvaluing liabilities a hidden reserve is created, that is, the surplus amount thus created is not apparent from an examination of a financial statement.

HOLDING COMPANY. A corporation that controls the voting power of other individual corporations for the purpose of united action. A holding company may also be an operating company, as the American Telephone and Telegraph Company, which operates long distance lines and controls local telephone companies.

HURDLE RATE. In *capital budgeting,* the minimum *rate of return* acceptable to a firm on an investment. Also called *cutoff rate.*

HYPOTHECATE. To pledge something as security for a debt. Technically there is no pledging, since possession is not transferred but only the right to order sale upon default.

IMPAIRED CAPITAL. A negative surplus account. Hence the amount represented by the capital stock of the corporation has been reduced below what it was at the time the stock was issued.

INCOME BASIS. The ratio of the dollars of interest or dividend to the price paid for the security rather than to the face or par value. See *maturity basis* and *yield to maturity.*

INCOME BONDS. Bonds that receive interest only when it is earned during any one year. Ordinarily other fixed charges are paid first, then the income bonds, and then dividends on stocks.

INDENTURE. (1) Any written agreement. The term derives from the former practice of tearing the edges of two copies of a document so that later matching of the torn edges would establish the identity of the copies. (2) The contract between an apprentice and his master. (3) Historically the indentured servant contract of Colonial times, which provided for a term of personal service by a servant to his master.

INDEX OF PROFITABILITY. The ratio of the *present value* of an asset to its purchase price.

INDORSED BOND. Same as *assumed bond,* that is, bonds of an original debtor that have been assumed by a second debtor who indorses them.

INSIDER. In security regulation, anyone who has knowledge of facts not available to the general public. Specifically includes directors, officers, and holders of more than 10 percent of a corporation's stock who must report all transactions to the SEC if the stock is listed on an exchange or there are more than 500 stockholders.

INSOLVENCY GUARANTEE FUNDS. There are three major insolvency guarantee funds: (1) FDIC guaranteeing to $20,000 per account, deposits in insured banks; (2) FSLIC guaranteeing to $20,000 per account in insured savings and loan associates; and (3) federal insurance guaranteeing to $60,000 per account, individual accounts with brokers. In addition, as to brokerage accounts, the New York Stock Exchange has unlimited protection covering accounts with its member firms.

INSTALLMENT EQUIPMENT FINANCING. Buying equipment for a *downpayment* with an agreement to pay installments thereafter until the account is settled.

INTERCOMPANY DIVIDENDS. Dividends from one corporation fully taxable under the income tax law paid to another fully taxable corporation are excluded as to 85 percent of such dividends from taxable income of the receiving corporation.

INTEREST BOND. A bond issued in payment of interest on other bonds because of a shortage of cash to pay the interest.

INTEREST RATE RISK. In investments used in contradistinction to *financial risk* and *purchasing power risk* to refer to the risk that the interest rate may change, thus affecting the market value of a security even though its obligations continue to be met.

INTERMEDIATE FINANCING. Sometimes defined in terms of length of time to maturity, such as more than one year but less than five or ten years. However, intermediate financing is not merely a matter of time to maturity but rather of the type of arrangement, namely a *private placement,* which allows easy refinancing arrangements.

INTERNAL FINANCING. Securing the funds needed by a firm from retained earnings and depreciation rather than going outside the firm to borrow or sell stock. Cf. *external financing.*

INTERNAL GROWTH. The expansion of a firm from increased sales of its products rather than by acquiring new firms through *merger.*

INTERNAL RATE OF RETURN METHOD. Same as *yield method.*

INVENTORY TURNOVER. *Cost of goods sold* during a period divided by the average inventory at cost of that period.

INVENTORY VALUATION METHODS. See the following specific terms:

*cost or market, whichever is lower, method of inventory*
*first in, first out method of inventory*
*last in, first out method of inventory*
*retail method of inventory*
*standard cost method of inventory*

INVESTED CAPITAL. In finance the same as *capital structure,* namely, the total of long-term debt plus net worth.

INVESTED CAPITAL TURNOVER. *Net sales* divided by *invested capital.*

INVESTMENT. (1) The purchase of stocks, bonds, and property that, upon analysis, promise safety of principal and a satisfactory return. These factors distinguish investment from speculation. (2) In economic theory investment means the acquisition of means of production (including goods for selling) with money capital.

INVESTMENT BANKING. *Underwriting* and selling primarily new issues of stocks and bonds to investors.

INVESTMENT COMPANY. A corporation or trust organized for the purpose of dealing in securities. Shares in the company are sold to the public. The supporting argument is that this device "spreads the risk" and cost of handling by pooling the investments of many people.

INVESTMENT LETTER. A letter given by a buyer of stock to the seller stating that the purchase is for investment with no intent to reoffer the stock. Then registration of the stock with the SEC may not be required. Cf. *letter stock.*

INVESTMENT TAX CREDIT. Federal legislation designed to stimulate purchase of capital goods by allowing a percentage of the purchase price as a credit against taxes due and not merely as a deduction from taxable income. The percentage is in addition to *depreciation.*

INVESTMENT TURNOVER. The ratio of sales to the total of bonds and *net worth.* Also called *capital turnover.*

INVESTOR'S METHOD. Same as *yield method* (in capital budgeting).

IRR. Abbreviation for "*internal rate of return.*"

IRREVOCABLE CREDIT. A credit that cannot, before the date it expires, be cancelled, revoked, or withdrawn without the consent of the person in whose favor the credit is given.

ISSUE. (1) Used as a noun, all of the stocks or bonds sold by a corporation at a particular time. (2) In law either the children who are conceived by parents or ancestors or a material question raised by the pleadings.

JOINT STOCK COMPANY. An organization whose capital has been divided into shares transferable among its members, who, however, have the personal liability of partners for the debts of the concern. In use in England but not generally in the United States.

LAST IN, FIRST OUT METHOD OF INVENTORY. Under the last in, first out rule (LIFO) items of inventory used are priced out at the latest purchase prices of the goods. Inventory value is thus computed by assuming that goods on hand are those remotely purchased and are valued, at the successively most remote purchase prices.

LEASEHOLD MORTGAGE BOND. A bond secured by a building constructed on leased real estate. This bond is subject to the compliance by the lessee (who issues the bond) with the terms of the lease; upon default in the terms of the lease the lessor of the leased real estate has priority over the holders of the leasehold bonds.

LENDING RATE IN CAPITAL BUDGETING. The rate an investor can get in the market for his funds. This rate is usually (but not always) below the rate the investor pays for borrowing funds from the market. See *borrowing rate in capital budgeting.*

LETTER STOCK. Stock not registered under the Securities Act of 1933, where the buyer gives the seller a letter stating the buyer intends to hold for investment purposes and does not contemplate reoffering the stock to others. Cf. *investment letter.*

LEVERAGING EARNINGS. Changing the return on *equity* by issuing debt or preferred stock.

LEVERAGE FACTOR. (1) In finance the extent to which a corporation can effect, by the use of bonds and preferred stocks, proportionate changes in return to common stock greater than the changes in operating income. If the bulk of the corporation's capital is represented by bonds and preferred stock, the corporation has a high leverage factor. The process of using the leverage factor is called trading on the equity. (2) The increase in the rate of profit that follows an increase in the volume of sales or production when fixed costs are spread over more units. Called "operating leverage" to distinguish (1), which is financial leverage.

LIEN. A right by way of security against real estate or personal property for the satisfaction of a debt. May be created by specific act of the individual (for example, a *mortgage*) or by operation of law (for example, a mechanic's lien for work done or vendor's lien for the unpaid purchase price). A lien is lost when possession is surrendered, but a court of equity may impose an equitable lien where possession has been lost.

LIMITED LIABILITY. Restriction of the liability of an investor to the amount invested. In a *limited partnership* the limited partners, and in a business corporation all the stockholders, have such limited liability. Formerly, in the case of a bank, liability of stockholders extended to double the par value of stock owned. This was double liability.

LIMITED PARTNERSHIP. A partnership that has one or more partners whose loss is limited to the investment in the business. The name of a limited partner cannot be used in the firm name unless identified as limited. The limited partner cannot engage in business for the partnership. The limited partnership must also have one or more general partners who have unlimited personal liability for the debts of the partnership. Under the Uniform Limited Partnership Act the agreement of partnership must be publicly recorded.

LINK FINANCING. An arrangement by a bank borrower for an insurance company to purchase a *certificate of deposit* to be posted with the bank as the *compensatory balance* for the loan of the bank to the borrower.

LIQUIDATION. (1) The winding up of affairs, selling assets for cash. (2) More narrowly, the termination of liabilities or the selling of assets even though there is no winding up.

LIQUIDITY PREFERENCE. The schedule of the amount of resources valued in terms of money or of wage units that an individual wishes to retain in the form of money in different sets of circumstances.

LIQUIDITY PREFERENCE THEORY OF INTEREST. An explanation of the rate of interest as the price adjusting (a) the *liquidity preferences* of individuals, which determine demand for money, and (b) banking policy, which determines the supply of money. See *abstinence theory of interest, agio theory of interest, loanable funds theory of interest, marginal productivity theory of interest, time preference theory of interest.*

LIQUIDITY RATIOS. The principal liquidity ratios are: *acid test, cash-to-daily-purchases, current ratio* and *quick ratio.* These ratios measure the ability of a firm to meet its debts as they come due.

LIQUIDITY RISK. Same as *market risk.*

LIQUIDITY TRAP. The point at which the demand for money (liquidity) is infinitely elastic with respect to the interest rate and further increases in the supply of money yield no fall in the interest rate. Such a situation arises when the yield on earning assets is so low that the risk of holding such assets is (or is thought to be) so high that investors prefer to hold any increases in the money supply in liquid form.

LISTED SECURITY. A security that has met the requirements of a stock exchange for listing. Such requirements include submitting financial reports, consenting to certain supervision, and so on.

LISTING. (1) In real estate, the contract of an owner authorizing a broker to sell the owner's real estate. (2) In securities, the contract between a firm and a stock exchange covering the trading of that firm's securities on the stock exchange.

LOANABLE FUNDS THEORY OF INTEREST. An explanation of interest as the price adjusting the demand for and the supply of loanable funds available at any particular time, with demand determined mainly by investment opportunities and supply by savings and credit creation. See *abstinence theory of interest, agio theory of interest, liquidity preference theory of interest, marginal productivity theory of interest, time preference theory of interest.*

LOCK–BOX FINANCING. The operation of a system of lock boxes in post offices in many cities with instruction to customers of a firm to mail payments to the nearest city in order to speed the collection funds. A bank in each city collects the contents of each box at frequent intervals.

LOCKED IN. In the stock market a term describing an investor who owns securities on which he has a profit but which he is unwilling to sell because of the *capital gains tax.*

LOMBARD STREET. The street in London where most financial institutions are located. The British equivalent of *Wall Street.*

MALONY ACT. Passed by Congress in 1938 as an amendment to the *Securities Exchange Act* and providing for registration with the SEC of all brokers dealing in the over-the-counter market except those dealing exclusively intrastate or in exempt securities. Regulation occurs cooperatively with the *National Association of Securities Dealers.*

MARGIN. (1) In commercial transactions the difference between the purchase price paid by a middleman or retailer and his selling price. Also called *gross margin.* (2) In trading, the purchase of a stock or commodity with payment in part in cash (called the margin) and in part by a loan. Usually the loan is made by the broker effecting the purchase.

MARGINAL EFFICIENCY OF CAPITAL. The relation between the prospective yield of a capital asset and its supply price or replacement cost. Also the rate of discount that would make the present value of a series of annuities given by the returns expected from the capital asset during its life just equal to its supply price.

MARGINAL PRODUCTIVITY THEORY OF INTEREST. An interest theory explaining the interest rate as tending under competitive conditions to equal the marginal addition to output by the last unit of capital when the amount of available capital is assumed fixed. See *abstinence theory of interest, agio theory of interest, liquidity preference theory of interest, loanable funds theory of interest, time preference theory of interest.*

MARGINAL PROPENSITY TO INVEST. The ratio between (a) the increase in new capital formed which follows on a small increase in income and (b) that small increase in income.

MARGINAL PROPENSITY TO SAVE. The ratio between (a) the increase in income not spent on consumption which follows on a small increase in income and (b) that small increase in income.

MARGIN CALL. A demand by a broker to put up money or securities upon purchase of a stock, or if the stock is already owned on margin, to increase the money or securities where the price of the stock has fallen since purchase. The last process is remargining.

MARKET ORDER. An order to buy or sell on a stock or commodity exchange at the current price when the order reaches the floor of the exchange. See *open order.*

MARKET–OUT CLAUSE. A clause in some *underwriting* agreements permitting the underwriter to withdraw if the market becomes unfavorable.

MARKET RISK. In finance, the risk of being unable to sell securities or assets at a price near the last price.

MASSACHUSETTS TRUST. A form of business organization under which the control and management of a business as well as the legal title to the property of the business are in the hands of a trustee or group of trustees, while the ownership and equitable title to the property of the business are in beneficiaries whose ownership is evidenced by trust certificates. The device originated in Massachusetts because the laws of that state forbade ownership of real estate by a corporation. This trust has limited liability, like a corporation, for the beneficiaries (or the investors).

MATCHED AND LOST. On the stock market when the bids at a fixed price equal or exceed the stock offered, the flip of a coin decides which bid is successful; likewise for two asks.

MATCHED ORDER. An order to buy and sell the same stock, the purpose being artificially to raise or lower the price of the given security.

MATURITY BASIS. The ratio of the dollars of interest payable on a bond to the maturity value, thus ignoring any premium or discount at the time of acquisition. See *yield to maturity* and *income basis.*

MECHANIC'S LIEN. See *lien.*

MERGER. (1) In a broad sense, the combination of two or more corporations by any of several devices. (2) The acquisition by one corporation of the stock of another corporation. The acquiring corporation then retires the other corporation's stock and dissolves it. Cf. *consolidation, holding company.*

MINIMAX. The principle of selecting strategies under the regret criterion: that the decision-maker should select that alternative with the least of the maximum regrets possible.

MONEY DESK. The department at a bank buying and selling short-term funds.

MONEY MARKET. The institutions and practices through which short-term funds are channeled to borrowers and entrepreneurs. See *capital market.*

MONEY RATE OF INTEREST. Same as *nominal interest rate.*

MONEY RATE RISK. Same as *interest rate risk.*

MORTGAGE. A conveyance of property as security for the payment of a debt. The mortgage may specify that the property is now conveyed subject to redemption by payment of the debt or that upon nonpayment of the debt the property is to be conveyed automatically.

MORTGAGES, TYPES OF. See the following specific terms:

- *blanket mortgage*
- *chattel mortgage*
- *closed-end mortgage*
- *consolidated mortgage*
- *direct-reduction mortgage*
- *first, second, and so on, mortgage*
- *leasehold mortgage (bonds)*
- *open-end mortgage*
- *overlying mortgage*
- *purchase-money mortgage*
- *refunding mortgage (bonds)*
- *straight mortgage*
- *underlying mortgage*

MORTGAGE BONDS. Bonds for which real estate or personal property is pledged as security that the bond will be paid as stated in its terms. May be first, second, refunding, and so on.

MORTGAGEE. The one receiving the *mortgage,* that is, the one who is loaning money and receiving the mortgaged property as security. See *mortgagor.*

MORTGAGOR. The one issuing the *mortgage,* that is, the one who is putting up his property as security for a loan. See *mortgagee.*

NARROW MARKET. The market situation in which the volume of trading is small. Also called thin market.

NATIONAL ASSOCIATION OF SECURITIES DEALERS. An association of more than 3,000 American *investment bankers* who police the *over-the-counter market.*

NATURAL INTEREST RATE. The interest rate at which the demand for loanable funds just equals the supply of savings. The interest rate that keeps the flow of money incomes constant rather than the one that keeps the price level constant.

NEGATIVE PLEDGE CLAUSE. A clause in a mortgage providing that the borrower will not pledge any of his assets or will pledge his assets only if the notes or bonds outstanding have certain protection.

NEGOTIABLE. (1) In a popular sense the term means transferable by delivery. (2) In law, however, a document is negotiable when it meets certain legal formalities (for example, it must be in order or in bearer form). Then, as a consequence, one taking such a document is relieved of certain claims that could otherwise be made against him, provided the document has been received in good faith, for value, before maturity, and without knowledge of any defect in it. The other requirements of form to make a document negotiable are: (1) it must be in writing and signed by the maker or drawer, (2) it must be payable on demand or at a fixed or determinable time, (3) it must be an unconditional promise or order to pay a definite amount of money, and (4) if a bill of exchange, the drawer must be named or identified.

NEGOTIATED PURCHASE. The sale of a security issue of the issuing company by negotiation with the underwriting investment banking firms. See *competitive bidding.*

NET CURRENT ASSETS. Same as *net working capital.*

NET OPERATING ASSETS. The assets, net of depreciation and bad debts, employed in the ordinary course of business. Hence, excludes investments in stocks and bonds owned by a manufacturing company, for example.

NET OPERATING INCOME. Income before interest and income taxes but after depreciation produced by *operating assets.*

NET OPERATING MARGIN. *Net operating income* divided by sales for the period.

NET PRESENT VALUE. The difference between future cash inflows of an investment discounted to the present at an assumed rate and all cash outflows similarly discounted.

NET PROFIT. Deducting the *cost of goods sold* from sales gives the *gross profit.* Deducting the operating expenses (overhead) from gross profit gives the *operating profit.* Deducting income taxes from operating profit gives the net profit.

NET WORTH. The total assets of a person or business less the total liabilities (amounts due to creditors). In the case of a corporation net worth includes both capital stock and surplus; in the case of a partnership or single proprietorship it is the original investment plus accumulated and reinvested profits.

NET YIELD. The income of a bond less annual amortization if bought at a premium but plus annual accumulation if bought at a discount divided by purchase price.

NEW YORK STOCK EXCHANGE. An unincorporated association of 1,375 members founded in 1792 and handling the purchase and sale of corporate stocks for themselves and others. The largest security market in the United States.

NO–ACTION LETTER. An opinion issued by the attorney for a governmental agency that if facts stated in a request for a ruling are later presented, the attorney will advise the governmental agency not to act, that is, that the facts do not warrant a prosecution.

NOMINAL INTEREST RATE. The rate of interest stated in a security as opposed to the actual interest yield that is based upon the price at which the interest-bearing property is purchased and the length of time to maturity of the obligation.

NOMINAL YIELD. The rate of return specified in a security. This is calculated on the face or par value.

NONCUMULATIVE PREFERRED STOCK. A stock that has no right to unpaid and undeclared dividends of past years, but only a prior claim to any dividends declared during the current year.

NONDIVERSIFIABLE RISK. The systematic tendency of a stock (or investment) to move in price (or rate of return) with the market as a whole. Cf. *diversifiable risk.*

NONNEGOTIABLE. Frequently misunderstood to mean not transferable. Correctly, nonnegotiable means wanting in one of the requirements of a *negotiable* instrument, and as a consequence not entitled to the benefits of negotiability such as freedom from many defenses that could otherwise be raised by the maker, for example, fraudulent inducement. A nonnegotiable document is transferable by assignment. To prevent transfer the label nontransferable should be used.

NONNOTIFICATION LOAN. A loan made by a bank or *sales finance company* on the security of *accounts receivable.* The original debtor is not notified that the account has been pledged; the loan is made with recourse, that is, if an account receivable is not paid, the borrower still remains liable for the amount loaned against the receivable.

NONOPERATING INCOME. The income a business concern receives from investments it holds, either earnings on the investment or income derived from *capital gains.*

NONRECOURSE LOAN. A loan under the U.S. agricultural program to farmers on the security of surplus crops which are delivered to the government and held off the market. The loan must be liquidated as provided by the government's program, but the government has no recourse against the farmer for a deficiency if the security fails to bring the amount of the loan.

NO PAR STOCK. Stock without par value but which represents a proportionate share of the ownership of a corporation based on the number of shares. One issue of stock in a corporation may have par value and another issue may have no par value. New York was the first state to pass a no par value law in 1912.

NPV. Abbreviation for "net present value."

ODD LOT DEALERS. Members of a stock exchange who handle transactions in less than the usual trading unit. The ordinary unit on the stock exchange is 100 shares although a few inactive stocks have smaller units.

OFF-BOARD SECURITY. Same as *unlisted security.*

OFF-BOARD TRADING. Buying and selling a security listed on an exchange without routing the transaction over the exchange. Cf. *third market.*

OPEN CREDIT. A credit established by a bank (or a business house) permitting a borrower (or customer) to make withdrawals (or buy goods) up to a stated amount without depositing security (or making payment for the goods).

OPEN-END MORTGAGE. A *mortgage* that allows the borrowing of additional sums, usually providing that at least the stated ratio of assets to the debt must be maintained.

OPEN-END MORTGAGE BOND. A bond secured by a *mortgage* that authorizes the issuance of additional bonds against the same mortgage.

OPEN LINE. A *line of credit* which may be cancelled by the creditor as opposed to a *standby line,* which is noncancellable.

OPEN-MARKET OPERATIONS. The purchase or sale of government bonds and bills of exchange by the Federal Reserve System for several possible objectives: (1) to support the market price of government bonds, (2) to affect member-bank reserves and thus their lending policy. In the second case purchasing by the Federal Reserve makes possible the expansion of credit through the increase of reserves, and vice versa for selling.

OPEN-MARKET PAPER. Bills of exchange or notes drawn by one with high credit standing, made payable to himself and indorsed in blank. These are sold to financial institutions other than banks.

OPEN-MARKET RATE. The interest or discount rate for *commercial paper* in the open market.

OPEN MORTGAGE. (1) A mortgage of property against which the mortgagor can increase his indebtedness, thus reducing the percentage of security. See *closed-end mortgage.* (2) A mortgage whose note has passed maturity with an unpaid balance due.

OPEN ORDER. In finance an order to buy or sell on a stock exchange at (or above or below) a stated price whenever the order can be filled. Subject to cancellation if the order has not been fulfilled at the time it is cancelled. See *market order.*

OPEN TRADE. In securities and commodities the term to describe partially completed deals, for example, an uncovered *short* sale.

OPERATING ASSET TURNOVER. The ratio of sales to average tangible *operating assets.*

OPERATING ASSETS. The assets that contribute to the regular income from the operations of a business. Thus stocks and bonds owned, unused real estate, loans to officers, and so on, are excluded from operating assets.

OPERATING COSTS. *Cost of goods sold* plus operating expenses.

OPERATING EXPENSES. Commercial overhead; those expenses other than direct labor, materials, and manufacturing expense and other than financing expenses and income taxes.

OPERATING LEASE. Such a lease as provides for rental payments covering less than the full cost of an asset plus interest assuming zero value at the end of the lease. May or may not provide for the lessor to bear costs of maintenance. Cf. *financial lease.*

OPERATING LEVERAGE. The increase (or decrease) in rate of profit following any increase (or decrease) in volume of sales or production due to fixed costs. Cf. *financial leverage.*

OPERATING MARGIN. Net *operating income* divided by sales for the period.

OPERATING PROFIT. Deducting the *cost of goods sold* from sales gives *gross profit.* Deducting the *operating expense* (overhead) from the gross profit gives the operating profit.

OPERATING RATIO. The total of expenses of operation divided by the total of operating revenues. Usually this includes only the ratio of *cost of goods sold* plus selling, administrative, and general expenses to net sales.

OPERATING STATEMENT. Often used as the equivalent of the *profit and loss statement.* Technically, the operating statement reports only the results of the operations of a business and thus excludes income from other sources, such as investments held, or expenses, such as financing costs.

OPTIMUM SIZE LOT. That size of purchase that equalizes the cost of carrying inventory against the cost of processing additional orders so as to minimize the cost of feeding a production line. The equation is $x = \sqrt{2tu/c}$, where $x$ = minimum cost quantity size, $t$ = reorder cost, $u$ = annual usage in units, and $c$ = annual cost of inventorying one unit for one year.

OPTIONAL BOND. A bond that may be redeemed at the option of the issuer.

OVERCAPITALIZATION. In finance the term generally means the issuance of (1) securities with a stated value in excess of the market value of the net worth of an enterprise, or (2) securities bearing a rate of return above that which the income of the enterprise can maintain. See *watered stock.*

OVERISSUE. The issuance of more securities than are authorized by the articles of incorporation or by the action of the board of directors.

OVERLAPPING DEBT. In municipal finance that portion of the debt of governmental units for which the residents of a particular community are responsible. For example, the residents of a city that is part of a large sewer district (which itself is a municipal entity) and part of a county (an even larger unit) would be liable for the city's proportionate share of the debt of the sewer district and the county.

OVERLYING BONDS. Bonds subject to the prior claim of other bonds. See *underlying bonds.*

OVERLYING MORTGAGE. A *mortgage* subject to the claim of another mortgage, for example, when speaking of the first mortgage, the second mortgage is overlying.

OVERSOLD. (1) In securities or commodities the situation in which the amount of *selling short* is excessive in relation to the available items. (2)

More generally, any businessman who has committed himself for more than he can do.

OVER-THE-COUNTER MARKET. Generally applied to security transactions which take place outside of an organized stock exchange whether the securities are listed on an organized exchange or not.

OVER THE COUNTER SECURITIES. Those securities *not listed* on an organized exchange.

PAID-UP STOCK. Any share for which stockholders have made full payment due.

PAID-IN SURPLUS. Surplus that is contributed by the stockholders and does not arise from profits. Frequently in opening a bank, surplus is paid in at the time of organization. The sale of stock by a corporation at prices above the par value results in paid-in surplus equal to the excess of the sale price over par value.

PAPER PROFITS. Profits that would exist at a given moment if a person closed transactions of sale or purchase. For example, a house was purchased for $5,000. The present price if it were to be sold would be $8,000. There is a "paper profit" of $3,000.

PARTICIPATING BOND. A bond that shares in earnings but in any event receives a minimum stated amount as interest.

PARTICIPATING PREFERRED STOCK. *Preferred stock* that entitles the owner after receiving the regular preferred dividend to share the profits declared as dividends with the holders of common stock, either immediately or after a stipulated amount has been paid to the holders of common stock.

PARTNERSHIP. An association of two or more persons who own a business jointly for profit. The chief characteristics of a partnership are: (1) unlimited liability of all members (except for a limited partnership), (2) nontransferability of ownership unless the other partners consent, (3) instability of existence (death and other events can terminate the partnership). See *limited partnership.*

PAR VALUE. In the case of bonds and stock, the face value appearing on the certificate is the par value. Those stocks not containing such a statement have no par value. See *stated value.*

PAYBACK PERIOD. In *capital budgeting,* the cost of an investment divided by the annual cash inflow from the investment gives the number of years to recover the cost of the investment. An alternate form computes the payback period using profit earned rather than cash return.

PAYBACK RECIPROCAL. Approximation of the rate of return when the project life is at least twice the *payback period* and cash inflows are uniform.

PAY-OFF MATRIX. A matrix (table) with "states of nature" (situations that may develop) classified by rows (or columns) against available strategies (alternatives) classified by columns (or rows) for the purpose of analysis in view of the probabilities attaching to each of the states of nature.

PAYOUT PERIOD. In *capital budgeting* the ratio of the original investment to the average annual cash earnings (after income taxes) plus depreciation. The result is in units of years.

PAY-OUT RATIO. The ratio of dividends paid to earnings in a given period.

P/E. Abbreviation for *"price-earnings ratio."*

"PEGGING" PRICES. Prices are spoken of as pegged when they are artificially held at a given level usually through governmental action.

PERFORMANCE STOCK. Shares of stock in a corporation offered to a key employee at zero cost on the basis of achievement of specific objectives. Contrasted with *stock options,* which specify some payment for stock and are directed at general objectives such as increased earnings per share.

PERPETUAL BOND. Same as *annuity bond,* that is, without a maturity date.

PERSONAL HOLDING COMPANY. A holding company that under income tax law derives at least 80 percent of its gross income from royalties, dividends, interest, annuities, and sale of securities and in which over 50 percent of the outstanding stock is owned by not more than five persons.

PLANT TURNOVER. Net sales of a period divided by fixed assets before depreciation.

POINT. (1) A unit amount of money is referred to in different markets as a point. Thus in the stock market a point is one dollar, in foreign exchange a point is one-hundredth of a cent, and in commodity markets a point is one one-hundredth of a cent per pound. See *basis point.* (2) A change of one unit in an average such as the Dow-Jones industrial average.

POOLING OF INTERESTS. That method of accounting for a *merger* in which the asset and liability accounts of each company are combined with any difference between the merger terms and the book values of net worth accounted for in the *capital surplus* account of the combined companies. The *earned surplus* of the acquired company is added to the earned surplus of the acquiring company. Cf. *purchase method of accounting.*

PORTFOLIO. In investments the collective term for all the securities held by one person or institution.

PORTFOLIO EFFECT. The offsetting of the risk of one project with the risk of another whose returns fluctuate in the opposite direction from the first project. Thus the combined risk (variation in return) of the portfolio is smaller than of the individual items in the portfolio.

PREFERRED CREDITOR. A creditor whose claim by law enjoys a priority in bankruptcy, for example, a mortgage, a wage claim, or a tax claim.

PREFERRED STOCK. Stock with a claim to earnings and/or assets of a corporation prior to that of some other class of stock.

PREFERRED STOCK RATIO. The stated or par value of preferred stock divided by the total amount of bonds, preferred stock, common stock, reserves, and surplus.

PREFERRING CREDITORS. A solvent debtor may prefer his creditors, that is, pay them as he sees fit. An insolvent debtor who has within four months before bankruptcy paid creditors who did not *at the time of payment* give full consideration is presumed to have preferred them, and the payment may be recalled unless it can be shown that the payment did not defraud the other creditors. Even payments prior to four months may be proved to be fraudulent preferences, but the burden of proof is on the party claiming fraud.

PREPAYING. Paying before the date on which payment is due.

PRESENT VALUE. The sum of future payments due discounted back to the present date at an assumed rate of interest.

PRESENT VALUE METHOD (IN CAPITAL BUDGETING). The determination of the net excess (or deficiency) of cash inflows received from an investment over (or under) the cash flows laid out for an investment when applying a given rate to discounting (and accruing) both of these cash flows. See *yield method* (in capital budgeting).

PRICE–EARNINGS RATIO. The market price of a security divided by the earnings per share.

PRICING OUT OF THE MARKET. Colloquial term for a price set so high as to result in a very small number of sales.

PRIMARY EARNINGS. In accounting, the actual and unadjusted earnings per share. Cf. *fully diluted earnings.*

PRIMARY MARKET. In finance, the market where the initial sale by the issuer of securities occurs. Cf. *secondary market.*

PRIME RATE. In banking, the rate of interest charged the most credit-worthy customers for short term loans.

PRIOR PREFERRED STOCK. A preferred stock that has priority over other preferred stock.

PRIVATE DEBT. In national income accounting total corporate debt less duplicating corporate debt owed by one part of an economic system to another.

PROFIT. (1) In accounting *net profit* or *gross profit.* (2) In economics the remainder after all factors of production have been fully compensated. It is the compensation for uncertainty (pure or competitive profit) or for monopoly (monopoly profit or rent) or a windfall.

PROFITABILITY INDEX. In capital budgeting, the ratio of the *net present value* of a project to the cost of the project. Puts different-sized projects on a comparable basis.

PROFIT AND LOSS ACCOUNT. In this account are recorded transfer entries from all the income and expense accounts. The balance of the profit and loss account closes into the surplus account of a corporation or the capital account in a single proprietorship or partnership.

PROFIT AND LOSS STATEMENT. A statement summarizing the income and expense of any organization to show net profit or loss for the fiscal period involved.

PROFIT BREAK–EVEN POINT. Assuming a plant organized for a given ideal volume of output, units of output are put on the $x$ axis and total dollars on the $y$ axis. The profit break-even point is the intersection of the total income curve (including accruals) and the total cost curve (including accruals).

PRO FORMA. Latin for "for the sake of form." Used to describe accounting, financial, and other statements or conclusions based upon assumed or anticipated facts.

PROSPECTUS. A statement issued by a corporation at the time that securities are offered. The prospectus gives the details of the various issues of the corporation and other financial data such as comparative balance sheets and operating statements.

PROTECTIVE COVENANTS. In finance, provisions in a loan arrangement designed to reduce the risk of the lender such as restrictions against increase in officers' salaries and dividends.

PURCHASE AND LEASEBACK. Same as *sale and leaseback.*

PURCHASE GROUP. In security underwriting the group of investment banking firms that buys an entire issue of securities from the issuing company, each member of the group buying a stated amount. The part each member of the group cannot sell is then turned over to a syndicate manager who sells the remaining securities to the other members of the purchase group or to the members of the *selling group.* See *competitive bidding.*

PURCHASE METHOD OF ACCOUNTING. That method of accounting for a *merger* in which any difference between the merger terms and the book value of the acquired company is accounted for as goodwill on the asset side of the balance sheet and as *acquired surplus* on the liability side. The *earned surplus* of the acquired company is added to the *capital surplus* of the acquiring company. Cf. *pooling of interests.*

PURCHASE MONEY MORTGAGE. The reconveyance of property by the purchaser to a third party or to the seller at the time of purchase to secure the payment of the balance of the purchase price.

PURCHASING POWER RISK. In investments used in contradistinction to *financial risk* and *interest rate risk* to refer to the risk that the price level may move, thus affecting the market value of bonds, for example, relative to common stock.

PUT. An option permitting its holder to sell a certain commodity at a fixed price for a stated quantity and within a stated period. Such a right is purchased for a fee paid the one who agrees to accept the goods if they are offered. The buyer of this right to sell expects the price of the commodity to fall so that he can deliver the commodity (the put) at a profit. If the price rises, the option need not be exercised. The reverse transaction is a *call.*

PYRAMIDING. (1) In finance the narrowing of the amount of capital needed to control a business through the use of a number of *holding companies,* making use of the principle that ownership of 50 percent of the voting stock of a corporation gives control. (2) In the stock market an increase of holdings of a particular stock financed out of the margin created by a rise in the price of shares already owned.

QUALIFIED STOCK OPTION PLAN. A plan for the issuance of *stock options* to key employees of a corporation. The plan must qualify under section 422 of the Internal Revenue Code in order for employees to gain the benefit of *capital gains* tax rates when they exercise the option, that is, hold the shares for six months and sell. Prior to January 1, 1964, such a plan was called a restricted stock option plan under section 424 of the Internal Revenue Code.

QUANTITY THEORY OF MONEY. A theory that the price level is determined by the quantity of money in circulation and the velocity of circulation of that money. The leading statement is $PT = MV$, Fisher's equation, where $P$ is the general price level, $T$ is the volume of transactions, $M$ is the quantity of money, and $V$ is the velocity of money.

QUICK ASSET. Cash, marketable securities, accounts receivable, or other assets that can be immediately converted into cash with a minimum loss. Inventories are normally excluded.

QUICK RATIO. The ratio of cash, accounts receivable, and marketable securities to *current liabilities*. Also called the *acid test ratio*.

RATE OF RETURN (IN CAPITAL BUDGETING). That rate which makes the discounted cash receipts of an investment just equal to the discounted cash outlays.

RATIO ANALYSIS. In finance, the use of various ratios (such as *asset turnover*) for comparison with the ratios of the same firm earlier in time or with those ratios of other firms to establish the progress or deterioration of a firm as to liquidity, profitability and other aspects.

RATIOS, TYPES OF. See the following specific terms:

*acid test ratio*
*asset turnover ratio*
*benefit cost ratio*
*bond ratio*
*capital-deposit ratio*
*capital-output ratio*
*capital ratio*
*capital turnover ratio*
*cash position ratio*
*cash to daily purchases ratio*
*common stock ratio*
*concentration ratio*
*coverage ratio*
*current ratio*
*debt coverage ratio*
*deposit ratio*
*deposit-capital ratio*
*expense ratio*
*fixed charge coverage ratio*
*gross plant turnover*
*gross profit ratio*
*inventory turnover ratio*
*invested capital turnover*
*loss ratio*
*market ratio*
*merchandise turnover ratio*
*mint ratio*
*operating ratio*
*operating margin*
*plant (or fixed asset) turnover ratio*
*preferred stock ratio*
*price-earnings ratio*
*quick ratio*
*raw materials turnover ratio*
*receivables turnover ratio*
*return ratio*
*tangible asset turnover*
*total asset turnover*
*working capital turnover*
*work in process turnover ratio*
*yield ratio*

RAW MATERIALS TURNOVER. The amount of goods going into process during a period divided by the average raw materials inventory.

REAL INCOME. (1) Money income measured in terms of purchasing power. (2) Commodities and services that a person receives in kind plus what can be purchased with his monetary income.

REALIZATION. (1) The disposal of assets for cash. See *liquidation*. (2) In income taxation the tax is not levied until the income is "realized," that is, the income-yielding process has reached a point where the law considers the income definite enough to tax.

RECAPITALIZATION. A voluntary readjustment of the bonds and stocks of a corporation. For example, replacing debentures with mortgage bonds or replacing part of the common stock by an issue of second preferred stock. Does not imply financial embarrassment of the corporation. See *reorganization*.

RECAPITALIZATION SURPLUS. The surplus resulting upon a *recapitalization*, which usually arises from reduction in the par value of stocks and the exchange of bonds for securities of lesser value.

RECEIVABLES TURNOVER. See *accounts receivable turnover*, *collection period*.

RECEIVER'S CERTIFICATE. A short-term note issued by a receiver, after approval by the court that appointed the receiver, for the purpose of carrying out orderly liquidation or reorganization. This certificate has first priority on the assets not otherwise mortgaged.

RECEIVERSHIP. A legal proceeding involving the appointment by a court of a person (the receiver) to administer the affairs of a person or firm unable to meet its debts as they mature. The receiver administers matters until a decision is made to reorganize or to liquidate. If the decision, by court or by owners, is to liquidate, the receiver carries out the liquidation, although his title is changed to trustee in bankruptcy.

RECORD DATE. In corporation matters the date established by the board of directors as the closing time to establish the "record" of stockholders (those shown on the books as stock owners) to receive a dividend, having voting rights for a given meeting, or some other benefit.

REDEEMABLE BOND OR PREFERRED STOCK. A bond or preferred stock which can be called in by the issuer at a fixed price.

"RED HERRING." In finance an advance copy of the statement (prospectus) to be filed with the *SEC* preceding an issue of securities. The copy is marked in red ink, "not a solicitation, for information only."

REFINANCING. Replacing an existing financial structure of bonds or stocks with a new one, usually at a lower rate of interest or dividend.

REFUNDING. (1) In finance the replacement of an outstanding issue or issues of bonds by a new issue either at or before maturity. Usual purposes are the extension of the loan period or the reduction of the interest rate. (2) In general, the repayment of all or part of money paid previously.

REFUNDING MORTGAGE BONDS. Any mortgage bond issue that replaces an existing bond issue or issues. Sometimes the term is abused to describe the funding of short-term debt under a high-sounding title.

REGISTERED BONDS. A bond entered on the books of the issuing corporation or of its transfer agent in the name of the purchaser, whose name also appears on the face of the bonds. Either principal alone or both principal and interest may be registered.

REGISTRATION STATEMENT. The statement required by the Securities Act of 1933 to be filed with the *SEC* in the case of securities (some exceptions) sold in interstate commerce or through the mails. The registration statement must contain complete information about the issue and the issuer. A condensed form of this statement (called the *prospectus*) is made available to the investor. If the statement is not satisfactory, a *stop order* may be issued. Some state laws now require registration statements.

REGULAR–WAY DELIVERY. On the stock market delivery and payment are to be made on the fifth business day after a transaction except that for government bonds the following business day is used.

RELATIVE PRIORITY. A principle of reorganization under which each group of creditors and stockholders, based on seniority, survives the reorganization but the losses of each group are inversely proportional to its seniority. For example, if there are $500,000 in assets, $500,000 in bonds, $500,000 in common stock, and $500,000 in preferred stock, the reorganization might give the bondholders 75 cents on the dollar, the preferred stockholders 20 cents on the dollar, and the common stockholders 5 cents on the dollar. See *absolute priority.*

REMARGINING. Where securities have been purchased on *margin,* a subsequent change in the market prices of the securities will change the ratio of the margin to the new prices of the securities, and the process of restoring the original margin ratio is remargining. See *margin call.*

REORGANIZATION. The legal readjustment of bonds and stocks of a corporation, usually eliminating some of the securities which have become worthless because the value of the firm's assets has fallen. Cf. *recapitalization.*

REORGANIZATION BOND. Same as *adjustment bond.*

REORGANIZATION SURPLUS. See *acquired surplus.*

RESERVED SURPLUS. See *appropriated surplus.*

RESIDUAL VALUE. The market value of an asset after the lapse of a period of time.

RETAIL STOCK OPTION PLAN. The older (pre-1964) term for *qualified stock option plan.*

RETAIL METHOD OF INVENTORY. A method of approximating inventory by records kept at retail prices rather than at cost. The cost is estimated by applying to the inventory at retail value a percentage which is the complement of the average rate of gross profit (original mark up plus additional mark up minus mark downs).

RETENTION RATE. The ratio of *retained earnings* to total earnings of a given period.

RETIREMENT METHOD OF DEPRECIATION. An older system formerly used by railroads and public utilities under which many smaller unit assets were dealt with by charging the entire replacement amounts each year as depreciation on the ground that the rate of replacement was relatively stable from year to year.

RETURN ON INVESTMENT. (1) The annual income from an investment divided by the amount of the investment. (2) The average annual income from an investment over its life divided by the cost of the investment.

RETURN RATIO. In capital budgeting the ratio of (1) the difference between the expected return (in dollars) from a proposed investment and the proposed investment (in dollars) divided by (2) the proposed investment in dollars.

REVERSE SPLIT. The issuance of one share of stock in exchange for a number of shares of stock now outstanding. See *stock split.*

REVOLVING CREDIT. A credit established by a bank (or business house) permitting a borrower (or customer) to make new withdrawals (or purchase of goods) equal to payments made on prior accounts.

REVOLVING FUND. A fund from which withdrawals are made either as loans or as disbursements, with the obligation of repaying the fund (with or without interest) to keep the fund intact.

RIGHTS OFFERING. The issuance of new shares by distributing *stock rights* to existing stockholders.

RISK. The chance or possibility of gain or loss. (1) Risk may be economic, moral, physical, and so on. In finance, risk is classified as *business risk, financial risk, market risk, money rate (interest rate) risk,* and *purchasing power risk.* (2) See *probability of ruin* for the likelihood of surviving a consecutive series of adverse events. (3) Risk is frequently measured by the *standard deviation;* the greater the standard deviation (or variability) of a series, the greater the risk.

RISK INDEX. The ratio of the present value interest factor for a riskless cash flow to the present value interest factor for the risky flow.

RISK PREMIUM. The excess earnings of an investment with a variable return over an asset with a certain return.

ROI. Abbreviation for "return on investment."

ROUND LOT. The term applied to the unit of trading on the New York Stock Exchange, namely, 100 shares in the case of stock and $1,000 par value in the case of bonds except for some special instances.

SAFETY FACTOR. (1) In finance, the ratio of interest on funded debt to net income before taxes but after such interest has been deducted. (2) A numerical multiplier of the forecast error to determine the level of safety stock to reduce outages.

SALE AND LEASEBACK. A sale of an asset to a vendee who immediately leases back to the vendor. The usual objectives are (1) to free cash in the amount of the purchase price for other uses by the vendor, (2) for benefits not otherwise available such a deduction by the vendor of the full value of the property for income tax purposes as rental payments over a period of time shorter than would be in depreciation where the base period is the allowable depreciable life. The rental payments total the purchase price plus interest less an estimated salvage value.

SALES FINANCE COMPANY. A company whose principal business is purchasing the *accounts receivable* of other businesses at a discount. Usually there is recourse by the sales finance company against the seller of the goods if the buyer defaults on payments.

SCRIP OR SCRIPT DIVIDEND. A dividend paid by *scrip* and not by cash or stock. The scrip itself may or may not have a maturity date and may or may not bear interest.

SEC (SECURITIES AND EXCHANGE COMMISSION). A federal agency created in 1934 to administer the *Securities Act of 1933* and the *Securities Exchange Act of 1934.* The commission also administers the *Public Utility Holding Company Act of 1935,* the *Investment Company Act of 1940,* and the *Trust Indenture Act of 1939.*

SECONDARY DISTRIBUTION. In finance, the sale of a large block of stock on a stock exchange by a holder (not the corporation) after the close of business for the day. Only the seller pays a commission. Cf. *exchange distribution.*

SECONDARY MARKET. In finance, the market where resale occurs of securities already issued. Cf. *primary market.*

SECONDARY OFFERING. The sale of a block of securities by a large stockholder.

SECURED LOAN. A promise to pay by a person, corporation, or government. Against the promise are pledged specific assets, usually by means of a mortgage.

SECURITIES. A collective name for all kinds of written instruments in the form of mortgages, bonds, stocks, bills of exchange, bills of lading, stock warrants, warehouse receipts, certificates of ownership, acceptances, and so on.

SECURITIES ACT OF 1933. Federal legislation providing for registration of securities offered for sale to the public in interstate commerce or through the mails. The purpose of registration is to furnish complete and accurate information to investors. The commission has authority to stop issues until proper information is furnished.

SECURITIES EXCHANGE ACT OF 1934. This act provides for the regulation of securities exchanges and over the counter trading through the SEC. It also provides for publication of information regarding the condition of corporations whose securities are listed on an exchange.

SECURITY MARKET. The places for sale and purchase of stocks and bonds; on the organized exchange (see *stock exchange*) and in the unorganized market (see *over-the-counter market*).

SELL DOWN. The offering of a large block of securities by a large stockholder. Hence a *secondary offering.*

SELLING AGAINST THE BOX. The practice (typically by a large stockholder who desires to shield his selling of his shares) of *selling short* and delivering borrowed certificates rather than the shares the seller holds in his strong box.

SELLING GROUP. In finance the group working for underwriters of a stock or bond issue in selling to customers. The selling group ordinarily acts as agent and can turn back any stock remaining unsold. See *purchase group.*

SELLING SHORT. The agreement to deliver at a future date a security or commodity the seller does not own but which he hopes to buy later at a lower price. See *buying long.*

SERIAL BONDS. A serial bond issue consists of a number of bonds issued at the same time but with different maturity dates (serially due), usually with interest rates varying for the different maturity dates. To be distinguished from *series bonds.*

SERIES BONDS. Groups of bonds (for example, series A, series B) usually issued at different times and with different maturities but under the authority of the same indenture. To be distinguished from *serial bonds.*

SERVICE LEASE. Same as *operating lease.*

SHERMAN ANTITRUST ACT. Passed by Congress in 1890 with the purpose of barring acts or contracts "in restraint of trade" or "tending to monopoly." Provides for recovery of treble damages upon conviction. Amended by Clayton Act, Robinson-Patman Act, Miller-Tydings Act, Webb-Pomerene Act.

SHORT. See *selling short.*

SHORT COVERING. The purchase of a security or commodity by a trader who has earlier gone short, that is, sold at an agreed price for future delivery.

Short covering thus constitutes taking the profit or accepting a loss in an effort to avoid further loss.

SINKING FUND. (1) In general accounting segregated assets that are being accumulated for a specific purpose. (2) In governmental accounting, a fund established to accumulate resources for the retirement of bonds but not for the payment of interest, which is handled through the general fund or a special revenue fund.

SINKING FUND BOND. A bond to be paid from a sinking fund, that is, from segregated assets gradually accumulated for that purpose.

SINKING FUND METHOD OF DEPRECIATION. Taking the initial cost of a capital asset, deducting the expected salvage value at the time it is expected to be discarded, and spreading the difference in equal installments per unit of time over the estimated life of the asset, but with recognition of interest to be earned on the amount of depreciation from a fund actually established. Thus the net charge for each period is reduced by the interest to be earned with the interest deduction computed as either (a) the interest on the annual charge, which will bring the charge to full amount at maturity, or (b) the interest this year on all prior changes.

SLOW ASSET. An asset that will take a considerable period of time to convert into cash.

SOLVENCY. This term is used in two different primary meanings: (1) An enterprise is solvent when it is able to meet its obligations as they become due. This is the equity sense. (2) An enterprise is solvent when the total of its assets exceeds the total of its liabilities. This is the bankruptcy sense.

SOURCE AND APPLICATION OF FUNDS STATEMENT. A statement of the sources of funds of a business and the uses or applications of such funds during any given period. Sources of funds are (1) increases in liabilities, (2) increases in net worth, and (3) decreases in assets. Applications of funds are (1) decreases in liabilities, (2) decreases in net worth, and (3) increases in assets.

SPECIALIST. In finance a member of the stock exchange who handles for other brokers orders with limits above or below the current market price, and who may deal for his own account. The specialist usually confines himself to one or a few issues.

SPECIAL OFFERING. On the New York Stock Exchange, the offering of a block of securities during the regular trading session at a fixed price with no commission payable except by a seller. Cf. *secondary offering.*

SPECULATIVE MARKET. An organized exchange where speculative buying and selling regularly occur.

SPLIT. See *stock split.*

SPREAD. (1) In general, the difference between the total cost of production and the selling price to consumers. In this sense, the mark up. (2) In underwriting the difference between the buying price of the underwriter and the selling price to the public. (3) On exchanges the difference between present spot or cash prices and present prices for future delivery. (4) On exchanges a combination of a *call* and a *put,* so that the purchaser of the spread may at his option demand delivery from or make delivery to the seller of the spread. The *put* and the *call* are for different prices. If they are for the same price, it would be a *straddle.* (5) The difference between *ask* and *bid* prices.

STANDARD COST METHOD OF INVENTORY. Valuing manufactured goods on the basis of predetermined standards set for the materials, direct labor, and manufacturing overhead. These standards are separately determined for each product by analysis of prior records with adjustment for changed conditions. The differences between costs so determined (called standard costs) and the actual costs are collected in variance accounts.

STANDARD-GAMBLE METHOD. The central idea is that if a decision-maker faces a series of choices among which he must select, and if he indicates his preferences for the results of the choices by weighting, then by use of the probabilities that attach to each choice it is possible to select the choice that will maximize the value of the expected outcome for the particular decision-maker, since the value of each expected outcome is the product of its probability times its preference rating.

STANDBY LINE OF CREDIT. A *line of credit* which guarantees funds will be available when needed as opposed to an *open line* which can be canceled by the creditor.

STANDBY UNDERWRITING. The purchase pursuant to agreement by investment banking firms of the unsold portion of an issue offered by the issuing company directly to its own security holders or some other restricted group.

STATED VALUE. In the case of no par shares of stock the stated value of a share is the dollar amount per share set aside by resolution of the board of directors or by the charter as capital and therefore unavailable for dividends until the stated value is reduced. See *par value.*

STATUTORY MERGER. A merger or combination of two businesses pursuant to the statute of the state of incorporation under which one company survives and the other is absorbed. If a new company replaces the two merging companies, this is called a *consolidation.*

STEP-BY-STEP FINANCING. Any system, particularly leases, by which a firm enters a temporary commitment contemporaneously with acquiring an asset rather than making financial commitments in advance of acquiring the asset.

STOCK. (1) The certificates of ownership interests in a corporation. (2) The capital acquired through the sale of shares by a corporation. (3) An accumulation of raw materials, semifinished goods, or goods ready for sale.

STOCKS, TYPES OF. See the following specific terms:

*assessable stock*
*authorized stock*
*barometer stock*
*blank stock*
*bonus stock*
*callable preferred stock*
*capital stock*
*class A and B stock*
*classified common stock*
*common stock*
*convertible stock*
*cumulative preferred stock*
*donated stock*
*founder's stock*
*full-paid stock*
*guaranteed stock*
*half stock*
*inactive stock*
*interim stock*
*letter stock*
*listed security*
*noncumulative preferred stock*
*no par stock*
*paid-up stock*

*par value*
*participating preferred stock*
*performance stock*
*preferred stock*
*prior preferred stock*
*redeemable preferred stock*
*treasury stock*
*unissued stock*
*unlisted security*
*voting stock*
*watered stock*

STOCK CERTIFICATE. Written evidence of the ownership of one or more shares of the capital stock of a corporation.

STOCK DIVIDEND. Distributing stock as a dividend. If the dividend is common stock declared on common stock, the only result other than to reduce the value of each share of common and to maintain the proportionate interest of each stockholder is to transfer part of surplus to the stock account. To be distinguished from *stock split.*

STOCK EXCHANGE. (1) A place where stocks and bonds are bought and sold through brokers under definite rules and at regular hours. (2) The organization constituting the exchange.

STOCKHOLDERS. The holders of stock, the owners or proprietors of the corporate enterprise. Also called shareholders.

STOCK REPURCHASE AGREEMENT. An agreement by a corporation at the time the stock is issued to repurchase the stock on demand. Particularly used in the utility field for sales to employees or customers. Also used as an incentive that allows employees to own the stock during the period of employment but requires them to resell the stock to the employer upon termination of employment.

STOCK OPTION. The right to purchase shares of a corporation upon set conditions. The term "stock option" is used when the right is issued other than *pro rata* to all existing shareholders. When so issued to existing stockholders, the option is called a "stock right." See *qualified stock option plan.*

STOCK RIGHT. A right to purchase stock issued *pro rata* to existing shareholders. Sometimes issued on a "when, as, and if" basis; that is, the holder can buy the stock when it is issued, on such basis or of such kind as is issued, and if it is issued. The theoretical value of a New York right (the right that goes with one existing share) is determined by the following formula *before* the *ex* rights date:

$$\frac{\text{Market price} - \text{subscription price}}{\text{Number of rights needed to buy one share} + 1}$$

After the *ex* rights date the 1 is dropped from the formula. A Philadelphia right is the right to buy one share of the new issue and is worth the value of a New York right times the number of such rights needed to buy one new share.

STOCK SPLIT. The issuance of a number of shares for each share of stock now outstanding. The purpose of a stock split is to reduce the market price per share in order to make for wider trading and a larger price for the same ownership. See *reverse split.*

STOCK SPLIT-DOWN. Same as *reverse split.*

STOCK SUBSCRIPTION. An agreement to purchase the stock of a corporation *from* the corporation.

STOCK WARRANT. In finance, an option to purchase stock from the issuer at a fixed price for a stated period. When the period is less than 30 days, the option is called a *stock right.*

STRADDLE. A combination of a *call* and a *put* permitting the call and the put to be exercised at the same price (if both for the same goods), which is approximately the market price. Also used generally to refer to a call in one commodity and a put in another. See *spread.*

STRAIGHT-LINE METHOD OF DEPRECIATION. Taking the initial cost of a capital asset, deducting the expected salvage value at the time it is expected to be discarded, and spreading the difference in equal installments per unit of time over an estimated life of the asset.

STRAIGHT MORTGAGE. A mortgage under which the borrower is obligated to pay interest during the term of the mortgage, with the full amount of the principal to become due at the end of the mortgage term.

STREET CERTIFICATE. A stock certificate with a *blank indorsement* by an owner whose signature is guaranteed so that the stock can be transferred by delivery without the formality of transfer on the books of the corporation.

STREET NAME. The name of a broker or bank appearing on a corporate security with *blank indorsement* by the broker or bank. The security can then be transferred merely by delivery since the indorsement is well known. Street name is used for convenience or to shield identity of the true owner.

STREET PRICE. In securities trading the price for a stock delivered outside the stock exchange process.

STRIKING PRICE. With respect to a *stock warrant,* the exercise price at which the holder can call for stock.

SUBORDINATED BONDS OR DEBENTURES. *Bonds* or *debentures* which yield priority in liquidation to other (senior) debt of a corporation. Usually such bonds or debentures are not subordinate to general creditors but only to debt owed to a financial institution.

SUBSCRIBED CAPITAL. The total *capital stock* contracted for. When paid for, it becomes *paid-in capital.*

SUBSCRIPTION CONTRACT. (1) A contract for the purchase of stock from a corporation issuing its own stock. (2) Colloquially, any agreement to purchase by a buyer.

SUBSCRIPTION RIGHT. See *stock right.*

SUM-OF-THE-YEARS'-DIGITS METHOD OF DEPRECIATION. Taking the initial cost of a capital asset, deducting the expected salvage value at the time it is expected to be discarded, and spreading the difference over the life of the asset, deducting each year that fraction of this difference determined in the following way: Add the numbers of the number of years of life of the asset (thus for an asset of 4 years life, add 1, 2, 3, and 4 to get 10) and use each of these numbers as the numerator of fractions whose denominator is the sum of the digits (thus $1/10$, $2/10$, $3/10$, $4/10$). The fractions are then used in reverse order (the first year's depreciation would be $4/10$).

SURPLUS. (1) In a financial statement the excess of assets over creditor liabilities and capital stock. When accumulated from profits it is called earned surplus. If from other sources, it is called capital surplus. Sometimes the capital surplus account is broken down into categories, e. g., paid-in surplus, revaluation surplus, etc.

SURPLUS, TYPES OF. See the following specific terms:

*acquired surplus*
*appraisal surplus*
*appreciation surplus*
*appropriated surplus*
*capital surplus*
*donated surplus*
*earned surplus*
*paid-in surplus*
*recapitalization surplus*
*reorganization surplus*
*reserved surplus*

SURPLUS RESERVE. An amount of surplus or net worth set up as a reserve to indicate it is considered not available for withdrawal in dividends.

SWITCH TRADE. On a commodity exchange if a broker cannot execute an order for a particular month but executes it for another month and reports the trade executed as ordered, it is a switch trade and the broker is liable to his principal for any profit so made.

SYSTEMATIC RISK. The tendency of the return and price of an investment to move with the general market. Hence, *nondiversifiable risk.* Cf. *unsystematic risk.*

TANGIBLE ASSET. (1) In law and taxation an asset that has physical, material substance. (2) In accounting and finance the term is used in a broader sense to include securities, notes, and claims but not good will, patent, copyrights, trademarks, secret processes, and like items, which are considered intangibles.

TANGIBLE ASSETS TURNOVER. *Net sales* divided by *tangible assets.*

TANGIBLE NET WORTH. The *net worth* of a business excluding such assets as good will and patents in calculating.

TAX HAVEN CORPORATION. Any corporation used to avoid or reduce income taxes, particularly, a foreign corporation whose income may not be taxed to its U. S. stockholders until paid over to them as dividends. Legislation has largely closed this loophole.

TAX SELLING. In the stock market the phenomenon of deliberate selling of securities that presently have a lower market value than their cost (or other basis) to the taxpayer for the purpose of offsetting this capital loss against other capital gains and thus reducing income tax liability.

TAX SHIELD. In *capital budgeting* some expenditures that are deductible for income tax purposes (such as start-up costs for a new plant) are recognized as reducing (shielding against) income taxes that otherwise would be due. Depreciation acts similarly.

TENDER OFFER. In finance, an offer to purchase shares made by one company direct to the stockholders of another company, with a view to acquiring control of the second company. Used in an effort to go around the management of the second company, which is resisting acquisition.

TENOR. In finance the period of time between inception and maturity of an obligation.

TERM BOND. A bond of an issue in which all the bonds have a single maturity. See *serial bond.*

TERMINAL BOND. A bond issued to finance the construction of a rail, truck, or air terminal.

TERM LOAN. A loan to a business for a term, usually 1 to 10 years, and usually repayable in installments.

THIN CORPORATION. In income taxes, a thin corporation is one with little equity relative to debt in an effort to take out as deductible interest what is really a dividend where the debt and equity are held in the same proportion by each individual holder.

THIRD MARKET. In securities, the purchase and sale of securities listed on a stock exchange without routing the transaction through the exchange. Called *off-board trading.*

TIME-ADJUSTED RATE OF RETURN. That rate of discount which equates the *present value* of expected cash inflows from a project to the present value of expected cash outflows of that project.

TIME BARGAIN. In finance a firm contract to deliver securities at a set future date; not an option.

TIME LOAN. A loan for a stated period of time. To be distinguished from *call loan.*

TIME PREFERENCE THEORY OF INTEREST. An explanation of interest as the price people are willing to pay for immediate possession of goods as opposed to future possession. See *abstinence theory of interest, agio theory of interest, liquidity preference theory of interest, loanable funds theory of interest,* and *marginal productivity theory of interest.*

TIMES INTEREST AND PREFERRED DIVIDEND EARNED. A common measure of the earnings protection carried by preferred stock. The figure is computed by dividing the net earnings per year (after taxes) by the sum of the interest and preferred dividend requirements.

TIMES INTEREST EARNED. A common measure of the earnings protection carried by a bond. (1) The number of times the interest requirement of a business was earned in a period and hence a measure of the degree of safety enjoyed by the owner of the debt. Computed as the amount available to pay interest to all creditors divided by the interest requirements of all debts with equal or prior standing. (2) An alternate method (called the prior-deductions basis) is available where there are debts with priority. This is to take the total amount available for all interest charges, deduct the interest charges of debts having priority, and divide the remainder by the interest requirements of the junior debt to get the times interest earned for the junior debt. The first method is preferred.

In addition to these two methods, each method can use either (1) the amount available to pay interest before income taxes or (2) the amount available to pay interest after income taxes. As long as interest is deductible in determining income taxes, the former is the preferred method.

TOTAL ASSET TURNOVER. The ratio obtained by dividing total assets into sales, but more correctly, dividing total *operating assets* into sales, since funds devoted to outside investments do not affect sales but produce an independent income.

TRADER. One who buys or sells for his own account for a short-term profit.

TRADING DIFFERENCE. In finance the fraction of a point in price charged for shares bought or sold in *odd lots*.

TRADING ON MARGIN. See *margin*.

TRADING ON EQUITY. See *leverage factor*.

TRANSFER AGENT. The one designated to keep the record of stocks and bonds of a corporation. Often the original of this record is not kept by the corporation but by an independent specialist in these matters such as a bank, trust company, or other agent.

TREASURY BILL. An obligation of the U. S. Treasury with a maturity date less than one year from the date of issue and bearing no interest but sold at a discount. To be distinguished from a *certificate of indebtedness*, which likewise is of a maturity of one year or less but bears interest.

TREASURY BONDS. Used in three senses: (1) issued bonds that have been reacquired by the corporation from the bondholders, (2) bonds issued by the U. S. Treasury, (3) authorized but unsold bonds still in the "treasury" of the corporation.

TREASURY CERTIFICATE. An obligation of the U. S. Treasury, usually with one year maturity and paying interest on a coupon basis.

TREASURY NOTE. An obligation of the U. S. Treasury with maturity one to five years from the date of issue.

TREASURY STOCK. (1) Issued stock that has been reacquired by the corporation from stockholders. (2) Less commonly, authorized but unissued stock that is still in the "treasury" of the corporation.

TREASURY WARRANT. An order on the U. S. Treasury in ordinary bank check form. It is the instrument by which all treasury disbursements are made.

TRUST COMPANY. A corporation organized primarily to act as trustee for estates, as guardian of minors, and as custodian of property held in trust. Also to buy and sell securities for customers and to advise them in regard to investments and in creating estates.

TRUSTEE IN BANKRUPTCY. The person or persons appointed by the court to liquidate the assets of a bankrupt or to supervise reorganization, although the one performing the latter function is usually called a receiver.

TRUST INDENTURE. The written document containing the terms and conditions binding the trustee and his conduct. The document is signed by the person or persons establishing the trust (called the settlor) and by the trustee.

TRUST INDENTURE ACT. Passed by Congress in 1939, this law regulates some of the terms and conditions of trust arrangements in connection with corporate security issues.

TRUST RECEIPT. A document indicating that the entruster has advanced money to the trustee for the purchase of goods, with the trustee to hold the goods in trust until the debt is paid. The trustee is authorized to sell in regular course of trade.

TURNOVER. Generally, the number of times that a cycle takes place in a given unit of time. For example, an inventory turnover of 5/year means that, with inventory at a stable figure throughout the year, five times the inventory is sold in a year.

TURNOVER, TYPES OF. See the following specific terms:

*asset turnover*
*accounts receivable turnover*
*capital or investment turnover*
*finished-goods turnover*
*fixed asset turnover*
*gross plant turnover*
*inventory turnover*
*invested capital turnover*
*operating asset turnover*
*plant (or fixed asset) turnover*
*raw materials turnover*
*receivables turnover*
*tangible assets turnover*
*working capital turnover*
*work in process turnover*

TWISTING. (1) In insurance, persuading a policy holder to drop one policy and take another for the purpose of the additional commission received by the agent. (2) In finance, shifting from long-term debt to short-term or vice versa to take advantage of interest rate changes which affect either long term or short term more than proportionately.

UNADJUSTED RATE OF RETURN METHOD (IN CAPITAL BUDGETING). Same as *accounting method of return.*

UNDERCAPITALIZED. A business with insufficient ownership funds for the scale of operations it is carrying on.

UNDERLYING BONDS. That bond issue, in the use of a company with several bond issues, which stands prior as to income (or security).

UNDERLYING MORTGAGE. A mortgage prior in claim to another mortgage; for example, when speaking of a second mortgage, the first mortgage is the underlying mortgage.

UNDERPRICING. The policy common in the public offering of securities. As an incentive to the prospective buyer, the underwriter (or issuer) of new securities either as to (1) an issue already publicly held or (2) an issue of a company being offered to the public for the first time deliberately seeks to offer the issue at a discount of up to 10 percent below the underwriter's estimate of the probable price at the time of issuance.

UNDER THE RULE. In the stock market the purchase or sale of securities by an officer of the exchange to complete the transaction of a delinquent trader.

UNDERWRITER. (1) Any person, banker, or syndicate that guarantees to furnish a definite sum of money by a definite date to a business or government in return for an issue of bonds or stock. (2) In insurance the one assuming a risk in return for the payment of a premium.

UNDERWRITING SPREAD. See *spread.*

UNDERWRITING SYNDICATE. A combination of underwriters joined together to undertake the purchase of securities from the issuer for resale at the risk of the underwriters.

UNDIVIDED SYNDICATE. In finance, the absence of a limitation in an *underwriting* agreement upon the number of shares for which each underwriter is liable and hence each underwriter is liable for his proportion of any shares on which other underwriters default.

UNFUNDED DEBT. (1) The indebtedness of a business or government that lacks formal evidence such as a bond. (2) Usually the line is drawn that unfunded debt is all debt due within one year. See *floating debt.*

UNIT COST METHOD OF DEPRECIATION. To *sinking fund depreciation* is added interest on the asset and estimated cost of operation of the asset, including repairs and maintenance, and the combined charges are distributed on the basis of the number of units produced in a period as a percentage of total units expected to be produced over the expected life of the asset.

UNLISTED SECURITY. A security that is not traded on a recognized stock exchange.

UNLISTED TRADING. Trading in securities not fully listed on a stock exchange. Although they appear on the board, the stocks do not meet listing requirements. This unlisted privilege is limited to stock that had the right prior to 1934 (the date of the Securities Exchange Act). The term is also applied to trading on the regional exchanges in stocks listed on a national exchange.

UNSECURED CREDITOR. A lender whose loan or debt is not secured by any collateral or *mortgage*. See *secured loan.*

UNSYSTEMATIC RISK. The absence of correlation of the return and price of an investment with the general market. Hence *diversifiable risk.* Cf. *systematic risk.*

UPSET PRICE. A provision in most foreclosure laws providing that what is being sold must bring more than a minimum amount established by the court or it cannot be sold. A guard against collusion by the debtor with others to defeat his creditor. Also protects the debtor from a creditor who is interested in bidding in at a very low price.

UPSTREAM LOAN. A holding company with poor credit using its subsidiaries as a source of funds. Such lending by the subsidiary to a parent will not appear on a consolidated statement of the parent and the subsidiaries.

VALUATION RESERVE. An amount deducted from an asset to indicate by estimate that the market value of the asset is less than the full amount of the asset (for example, an account receivable), or in the case of a liability, to indicate the estimate that the liability may be greater (for example, income taxes) than stated on the books.

VARIABLE BUDGET. Same as *flexible budget.*

VENDOR'S LIEN. See *lien.*

VOTING. In corporations voting may be of three types (depending on the law and on the articles and by-laws): (1) common law voting—one vote to each person regardless of the number of shares held; (2) cumulative voting—applicable to the election of directors, permitting the individual to cumulate all his votes for one candidate or to spread them as he sees fit (for example, if nine directors are to be elected and one share of voting stock is held, the nine votes can all be cast for one candidate or divided); (3) ordinary voting—one vote for each share of voting stock, with all directors to be elected one at a time.

VOTING TRUST. A legal device by which the owners of voting stock (usually the common stock) assign the shares for a definite period of time to a group known as voting trustees and receive in return certificates of beneficial interest in the trust. Designed to concentrate control of a corporation and improve continuity of policy.

WALL STREET. A short narrow street in lower New York City. It is the chief financial center of the United States and has become synonymous with financial interests and money markets.

WATERED STOCK. The situation in which a corporation issues more stock than the true value of its assets. The purpose may be to hide heavy earnings or to give promoters a profit.

WHEN ISSUED. The practice of trading in securities on the new basis, as in the case of stock splits, as soon as the new basis is authorized but before the new shares are actually issued.

W. I. Abbreviation for "*when issued.*"

WORKING CAPITAL. Total *current assets.* See *working capital (net).*

WORKING CAPITAL (NET). (1) In accounting the difference between current assets and current liabilities. (2) In public utilities the amount of cash required by a business to carry on operations.

WORKING CAPITAL TURNOVER. The ratio of sales to current assets.

WORK IN PROCESS TURNOVER. The amount of work in process transferred to finished products during a period divided by the average work in process inventory of that period.

WORK-OUT LOAN. A loan granted to a borrower in a distressed financial condition pursuant to a plan to "work out" of the difficulty. Accordingly, many restrictions are imposed to assure the achievement of the purpose.

YIELD. In the case of stock the ratio of dividends per share in dollars to the purchase price per share in dollars.

YIELD (GROSS). In the case of bonds the ratio of interest in dollars to the purchase price. See *yield to maturity.*

YIELD CURVE. In finance, with time to maturity plotted on the $x$ axis and interest rate on the $y$ axis, the curve tracing the variation in interest rate for a given security (or given quality of security) for various maturities.

YIELD METHOD (IN CAPITAL BUDGETING). The determination of that rate which will equate the cash inflows received from an investment with the cash flows laid out for an investment. See *present value method (in capital budgeting).*

YIELD TO MATURITY. The calculated return of a bond, giving effect to (1) the dollars received in annual interest payments, (2) the amortization of the difference between the purchase price and the redemption value, and (3) the number of years to maturity.

A simple approximation formula is

$$Y = \frac{100 - P}{T} + \frac{I}{P}$$

where $P$ = price paid or current price
$T$ = years to maturity
$I$ = face rate of interest in dollars per year

See *current yield.*

# Tables

**TABLE A–1. Present Value of One Dollar Due at the End of *N* Years**

| N | 1% | 2% | 3% | 4% | 5% | 6% | 7% | 8% | 9% | 10% | N |
|---|---|---|---|---|---|---|---|---|---|---|---|
| 01 | .99010 | .98039 | .97087 | .96154 | .95238 | .94340 | .93458 | .92593 | .91743 | .90909 | 01 |
| 02 | .98030 | .96117 | .94260 | .92456 | .90703 | .89000 | .87344 | .85734 | .84168 | .82645 | 02 |
| 03 | .97059 | .94232 | .91514 | .88900 | .86384 | .83962 | .81630 | .79383 | .77218 | .75131 | 03 |
| 04 | .96098 | .92385 | .88849 | .85480 | .82270 | .79209 | .76290 | .73503 | .70843 | .68301 | 04 |
| 05 | .95147 | .90573 | .86261 | .82193 | .78353 | .74726 | .71299 | .68058 | .64993 | .62092 | 05 |
| 06 | .94204 | .88797 | .83748 | .79031 | .74622 | .70496 | .66634 | .63017 | .59627 | .56447 | 06 |
| 07 | .93272 | .87056 | .81309 | .75992 | .71068 | .66506 | .62275 | .58349 | .54703 | .51316 | 07 |
| 08 | .92348 | .85349 | .78941 | .73069 | .67684 | .62741 | .58201 | .54027 | .50187 | .46651 | 08 |
| 09 | .91434 | .83675 | .76642 | .70259 | .64461 | .59190 | .54393 | .50025 | .46043 | .42410 | 09 |
| 10 | .90529 | .82035 | .74409 | .67556 | .61391 | .55839 | .50835 | .46319 | .42241 | .38554 | 10 |
| 11 | .89632 | .80426 | .72242 | .64958 | .58468 | .52679 | .47509 | .42888 | .38753 | .35049 | 11 |
| 12 | .88745 | .78849 | .70138 | .62460 | .55684 | .49697 | .44401 | .39711 | .35553 | .31863 | 12 |
| 13 | .87866 | .77303 | .68095 | .60057 | .53032 | .46884 | .41496 | .36770 | .32618 | .28966 | 13 |
| 14 | .86996 | .75787 | .66112 | .57747 | .50507 | .44230 | .38782 | .34046 | .29925 | .26333 | 14 |
| 15 | .86135 | .74301 | .64186 | .55526 | .48102 | .41726 | .36245 | .31524 | .27454 | .23939 | 15 |
| 16 | .85282 | .72845 | .62317 | .53391 | .45811 | .39365 | .33873 | .29189 | .25187 | .21763 | 16 |
| 17 | .84438 | .71416 | .60502 | .51337 | .43630 | .37136 | .31657 | .27027 | .23107 | .19784 | 17 |
| 18 | .83602 | .70016 | .58739 | .49363 | .41552 | .35034 | .29586 | .25025 | .21199 | .17986 | 18 |
| 19 | .82774 | .68643 | .57029 | .47464 | .39573 | .33051 | .27651 | .23171 | .19449 | .16351 | 19 |
| 20 | .81954 | .67297 | .55368 | .45639 | .37689 | .31180 | .25842 | .21455 | .17843 | .14864 | 20 |
| 21 | .81143 | .65978 | .53755 | .43883 | .35894 | .29415 | .24151 | .19866 | .16370 | .13513 | 21 |
| 22 | .80340 | .64684 | .52189 | .42195 | .34185 | .27750 | .22571 | .18394 | .15018 | .12285 | 22 |
| 23 | .79544 | .63416 | .50669 | .40573 | .32557 | .26180 | .21095 | .17031 | .13778 | .11168 | 23 |
| 24 | .78757 | .62172 | .49193 | .39012 | .31007 | .24698 | .19715 | .15770 | .12640 | .10153 | 24 |
| 25 | .77977 | .60953 | .47761 | .37512 | .29530 | .23300 | .18425 | .14602 | .11597 | .09230 | 25 |

**TABLE A–1. Present Value of One Dollar Due at the End of *N* Years—Continued**

| N | 11% | 12% | 13% | 14% | 15% | 16% | 17% | 18% | 19% | 20% | N |
|---|---|---|---|---|---|---|---|---|---|---|---|
| 01 | .90090 | .89286 | .88496 | .87719 | .86957 | .86207 | .85470 | .84746 | .84034 | .83333 | 01 |
| 02 | .81162 | .79719 | .78315 | .76947 | .75614 | .74316 | .73051 | .71818 | .70616 | .69444 | 02 |
| 03 | .73119 | .71178 | .69305 | .67497 | .65752 | .64066 | .62437 | .60863 | .59342 | .57870 | 03 |
| 04 | .65873 | .63552 | .61332 | .59208 | .57175 | .55229 | .53365 | .51579 | .49867 | .48225 | 04 |
| 05 | .59345 | .56743 | .54276 | .51937 | .49718 | .47611 | .45611 | .43711 | .41905 | .40188 | 05 |
| 06 | .53464 | .50663 | .48032 | .45559 | .43233 | .41044 | .38984 | .37043 | .35214 | .33490 | 06 |
| 07 | .48166 | .45235 | .42506 | .39964 | .37594 | .35383 | .33320 | .31392 | .29592 | .27908 | 07 |
| 08 | .43393 | .40388 | .37616 | .35056 | .32690 | .30503 | .28478 | .26604 | .24867 | .23257 | 08 |
| 09 | .39092 | .36061 | .33288 | .30751 | .28426 | .26295 | .24340 | .22546 | .20897 | .19381 | 09 |
| 10 | .35218 | .32197 | .29459 | .26974 | .24718 | .22668 | .20804 | .19106 | .17560 | .16151 | 10 |
| 11 | .31728 | .28748 | .26070 | .23662 | .21494 | .19542 | .17781 | .16192 | .14756 | .13459 | 11 |
| 12 | .28584 | .25667 | .23071 | .20756 | .18691 | .16846 | .15197 | .13722 | .12400 | .11216 | 12 |
| 13 | .25751 | .22917 | .20416 | .18207 | .16253 | .14523 | .12989 | .11629 | .10420 | .09346 | 13 |
| 14 | .23199 | .20462 | .18068 | .15971 | .14133 | .12520 | .11102 | .09855 | .08757 | .07789 | 14 |
| 15 | .20900 | .18270 | .15989 | .14010 | .12289 | .10793 | .09489 | .08352 | .07359 | .06491 | 15 |
| 16 | .18829 | .16312 | .14150 | .12289 | .10686 | .09304 | .08110 | .07078 | .06184 | .05409 | 16 |
| 17 | .16963 | .14564 | .12522 | .10780 | .09293 | .08021 | .06932 | .05998 | .05196 | .04507 | 17 |
| 18 | .15282 | .13004 | .11081 | .09456 | .08080 | .06914 | .05925 | .05083 | .04367 | .03756 | 18 |
| 19 | .13768 | .11611 | .09806 | .08295 | .07026 | .05961 | .05064 | .04308 | .03669 | .03130 | 19 |
| 20 | .12403 | .10367 | .08678 | .07276 | .06110 | .05139 | .04328 | .03651 | .03084 | .02608 | 20 |
| 21 | .11174 | .09256 | .07680 | .06383 | .05313 | .04430 | .03699 | .03094 | .02591 | .02174 | 21 |
| 22 | .10067 | .08264 | .06796 | .05599 | .04620 | .03819 | .03162 | .02622 | .02178 | .01811 | 22 |
| 23 | .09069 | .07379 | .06014 | .04911 | .04017 | .03292 | .02702 | .02222 | .01830 | .01509 | 23 |
| 24 | .08170 | .06588 | .05322 | .04308 | .03493 | .02838 | .02310 | .01883 | .01538 | .01258 | 24 |
| 25 | .07361 | .05882 | .04710 | .03779 | .03038 | .02447 | .01974 | .01596 | .01292 | .01048 | 25 |

| N | 21% | 22% | 23% | 24% | 25% | 26% | 27% | 28% | 29% | 30% | N |
|---|---|---|---|---|---|---|---|---|---|---|---|
| 01 | .82645 | .81967 | .81301 | .80645 | .80000 | .79365 | .78740 | .78125 | .77519 | .76923 | 01 |
| 02 | .68301 | .67186 | .66098 | .65036 | .64000 | .62988 | .62000 | .61035 | .60093 | .59172 | 02 |
| 03 | .56447 | .55071 | .53738 | .52449 | .51200 | .49991 | .48819 | .47684 | .46583 | .45517 | 03 |
| 04 | .46651 | .45140 | .43690 | .42297 | .40960 | .39675 | .38440 | .37253 | .36111 | .35013 | 04 |
| 05 | .38554 | .37000 | .35520 | .34111 | .32768 | .31488 | .30268 | .29104 | .27993 | .26933 | 05 |
| 06 | .31863 | .30328 | .28878 | .27509 | .26214 | .24991 | .23833 | .22737 | .21700 | .20718 | 06 |
| 07 | .26333 | .24859 | .23478 | .22184 | .20972 | .19834 | .18766 | .17764 | .16822 | .15937 | 07 |
| 08 | .21763 | .20376 | .19088 | .17891 | .16777 | .15741 | .14776 | .13878 | .13040 | .12259 | 08 |
| 09 | .17986 | .16702 | .15519 | .14428 | .13422 | .12493 | .11635 | .10842 | .10109 | .09430 | 09 |
| 10 | .14864 | .13690 | .12617 | .11635 | .10737 | .09915 | .09161 | .08470 | .07836 | .07254 | 10 |
| 11 | .12285 | .11221 | .10258 | .09383 | .08590 | .07869 | .07214 | .06617 | .06075 | .05580 | 11 |
| 12 | .10153 | .09198 | .08339 | .07567 | .06872 | .06245 | .05680 | .05170 | .04709 | .04292 | 12 |
| 13 | .08391 | .07539 | .06780 | .06103 | .05498 | .04957 | .04472 | .04039 | .03650 | .03302 | 13 |
| 14 | .06934 | .06180 | .05512 | .04921 | .04398 | .03934 | .03522 | .03155 | .02830 | .02540 | 14 |
| 15 | .05731 | .05065 | .04481 | .03969 | .03518 | .03122 | .02773 | .02465 | .02194 | .01954 | 15 |
| 16 | .04736 | .04152 | .03643 | .03201 | .02815 | .02478 | .02183 | .01926 | .01700 | .01503 | 16 |
| 17 | .03914 | .03403 | .02962 | .02581 | .02252 | .01967 | .01719 | .01505 | .01318 | .01156 | 17 |
| 18 | .03235 | .02789 | .02408 | .02082 | .01801 | .01561 | .01354 | .01175 | .01022 | .00889 | 18 |
| 19 | .02673 | .02286 | .01958 | .01679 | .01441 | .01239 | .01066 | .00918 | .00792 | .00684 | 19 |
| 20 | .02209 | .01874 | .01592 | .01354 | .01153 | .00983 | .00839 | .00717 | .00614 | .00526 | 20 |
| 21 | .01826 | .01536 | .01294 | .01092 | .00922 | .00780 | .00661 | .00561 | .00476 | .00405 | 21 |
| 22 | .01509 | .01259 | .01052 | .00880 | .00738 | .00619 | .00520 | .00438 | .00369 | .00311 | 22 |
| 23 | .01247 | .01032 | .00855 | .00710 | .00590 | .00491 | .00410 | .00342 | .00286 | .00239 | 23 |
| 24 | .01031 | .00846 | .00695 | .00573 | .00472 | .00390 | .00323 | .00267 | .00222 | .00184 | 24 |
| 25 | .00852 | .00693 | .00565 | .00462 | .00378 | .00310 | .00254 | .00209 | .00172 | .00142 | 25 |

TABLE A–1. Present Value of One Dollar Due at the End of *N* Years—Continued

| N | 31% | 32% | 33% | 34% | 35% | 36% | 37% | 38% | 39% | 40% | N |
|---|---|---|---|---|---|---|---|---|---|---|---|
| 01 | .76336 | .75758 | .75188 | .74627 | .74074 | .73529 | .72993 | .72464 | .71942 | .71429 | 01 |
| 02 | .58272 | .57392 | .56532 | .55692 | .54870 | .54066 | .53279 | .52510 | .51757 | .51020 | 02 |
| 03 | .44482 | .43479 | .42505 | .41561 | .40644 | .39754 | .38890 | .38051 | .37235 | .36443 | 03 |
| 04 | .33956 | .32939 | .31959 | .31016 | .30107 | .29231 | .28387 | .27573 | .26788 | .26031 | 04 |
| 05 | .25920 | .24953 | .24029 | .23146 | .22301 | .21493 | .20720 | .19980 | .19272 | .18593 | 05 |
| 06 | .19787 | .18904 | .18067 | .17273 | .16520 | .15804 | .15124 | .14479 | .13865 | .13281 | 06 |
| 07 | .15104 | .14321 | .13584 | .12890 | .12237 | .11621 | .11040 | .10492 | .09975 | .09486 | 07 |
| 08 | .11530 | .10849 | .10214 | .09620 | .09064 | .08545 | .08058 | .07603 | .07176 | .06776 | 08 |
| 09 | .08802 | .08219 | .07680 | .07179 | .06714 | .06283 | .05882 | .05509 | .05163 | .04840 | 09 |
| 10 | .06719 | .06227 | .05774 | .05357 | .04973 | .04620 | .04293 | .03992 | .03714 | .03457 | 10 |
| 11 | .05129 | .04717 | .04341 | .03998 | .03684 | .03397 | .03134 | .02893 | .02672 | .02469 | 11 |
| 12 | .03915 | .03574 | .03264 | .02984 | .02729 | .02498 | .02287 | .02096 | .01922 | .01764 | 12 |
| 13 | .02989 | .02707 | .02454 | .02227 | .02021 | .01837 | .01670 | .01519 | .01383 | .01260 | 13 |
| 14 | .02281 | .02051 | .01845 | .01662 | .01497 | .01350 | .01219 | .01101 | .00995 | .00900 | 14 |
| 15 | .01742 | .01554 | .01387 | .01240 | .01109 | .00993 | .00890 | .00798 | .00716 | .00643 | 15 |
| 16 | .01329 | .01177 | .01043 | .00925 | .00822 | .00730 | .00649 | .00578 | .00515 | .00459 | 16 |
| 17 | .01015 | .00892 | .00784 | .00691 | .00609 | .00537 | .00474 | .00419 | .00370 | .00328 | 17 |
| 18 | .00775 | .00676 | .00590 | .00515 | .00451 | .00395 | .00346 | .00304 | .00267 | .00234 | 18 |
| 19 | .00591 | .00512 | .00443 | .00385 | .00334 | .00290 | .00253 | .00220 | .00192 | .00167 | 19 |
| 20 | .00451 | .00388 | .00333 | .00287 | .00247 | .00213 | .00184 | .00159 | .00138 | .00120 | 20 |
| 21 | .00345 | .00294 | .00251 | .00214 | .00183 | .00157 | .00135 | .00115 | .00099 | .00085 | 21 |
| 22 | .00263 | .00223 | .00188 | .00160 | .00136 | .00115 | .00098 | .00084 | .00071 | .00061 | 22 |
| 23 | .00201 | .00169 | .00142 | .00119 | .00101 | .00085 | .00072 | .00061 | .00051 | .00044 | 23 |
| 24 | .00153 | .00128 | .00107 | .00089 | .00074 | .00062 | .00052 | .00044 | .00037 | .00031 | 24 |
| 25 | .00117 | .00097 | .00080 | .00066 | .00055 | .00046 | .00038 | .00032 | .00027 | .00022 | 25 |

TABLE A–2. Present Value of One Dollar per Year; *N* Years at *R* Percent

| Year | 1% | 2% | 3% | 4% | 5% | 6% | 7% | 8% | 9% | 10% | Year |
|---|---|---|---|---|---|---|---|---|---|---|---|
| 1 | .9901 | .9804 | .9709 | .9615 | .9524 | .9434 | .9346 | .9259 | .9174 | .9091 | 1 |
| 2 | 1.9704 | 1.9416 | 1.9135 | 1.8861 | 1.8594 | 1.8334 | 1.8080 | 1.7833 | 1.7591 | 1.7355 | 2 |
| 3 | 2.9410 | 2.8839 | 2.8286 | 2.7751 | 2.7232 | 2.6730 | 2.6243 | 2.5771 | 2.5313 | 2.4868 | 3 |
| 4 | 3.9020 | 3.8077 | 3.7171 | 3.6299 | 3.5459 | 3.4651 | 3.3872 | 3.3121 | 3.2397 | 3.1699 | 4 |
| 5 | 4.8535 | 4.7134 | 4.5797 | 4.4518 | 4.3295 | 4.2123 | 4.1002 | 3.9927 | 3.8896 | 3.7908 | 5 |
| 6 | 5.7955 | 5.6014 | 5.4172 | 5.2421 | 5.0757 | 4.9173 | 4.7665 | 4.6229 | 4.4859 | 4.3553 | 6 |
| 7 | 6.7282 | 6.4720 | 6.2302 | 6.0020 | 5.7863 | 5.5824 | 5.3893 | 5.2064 | 5.0329 | 4.8684 | 7 |
| 8 | 7.6517 | 7.3254 | 7.0196 | 6.7327 | 6.4632 | 6.2098 | 5.9713 | 5.7466 | 5.5348 | 5.3349 | 8 |
| 9 | 8.5661 | 8.1622 | 7.7861 | 7.4353 | 7.1078 | 6.8017 | 6.5152 | 6.2469 | 5.9952 | 5.7590 | 9 |
| 10 | 9.4714 | 8.9825 | 8.5302 | 8.1109 | 7.7217 | 7.3601 | 7.0236 | 6.7101 | 6.4176 | 6.1446 | 10 |
| 11 | 10.3677 | 9.7868 | 9.2526 | 8.7604 | 8.3064 | 7.8868 | 7.4987 | 7.1389 | 6.8052 | 6.4951 | 11 |
| 12 | 11.2552 | 10.5753 | 9.9539 | 9.3850 | 8.8632 | 8.3838 | 7.9427 | 7.5361 | 7.1607 | 6.8137 | 12 |
| 13 | 12.1338 | 11.3483 | 10.6349 | 9.9856 | 9.3935 | 8.8527 | 8.3576 | 7.9038 | 7.4869 | 7.1034 | 13 |
| 14 | 13.0038 | 12.1062 | 11.2960 | 10.5631 | 9.8986 | 9.2950 | 8.7454 | 8.2442 | 7.7861 | 7.3667 | 14 |
| 15 | 13.8651 | 12.8492 | 11.9379 | 11.1183 | 10.3796 | 9.7122 | 9.1079 | 8.5595 | 8.0607 | 7.6061 | 15 |
| 16 | 14.7180 | 13.5777 | 12.5610 | 11.6522 | 10.8377 | 10.1059 | 9.4466 | 8.8514 | 8.3125 | 7.8237 | 16 |
| 17 | 15.5624 | 14.2918 | 13.1660 | 12.1656 | 11.2740 | 10.4772 | 9.7632 | 9.1216 | 8.5436 | 8.0215 | 17 |
| 18 | 16.3984 | 14.9920 | 13.7534 | 12.6592 | 11.6895 | 10.8276 | 10.0591 | 9.3719 | 8.7556 | 8.2014 | 18 |
| 19 | 17.2261 | 15.6784 | 14.3237 | 13.1339 | 12.0853 | 11.1581 | 10.3356 | 9.6036 | 8.9501 | 8.3649 | 19 |
| 20 | 18.0457 | 16.3514 | 14.8774 | 13.5903 | 12.4622 | 11.4699 | 10.5940 | 9.8181 | 9.1285 | 8.5136 | 20 |
| 21 | 18.8571 | 17.0111 | 15.4149 | 14.0291 | 12.8211 | 11.7640 | 10.8355 | 10.0168 | 9.2922 | 8.6487 | 21 |
| 22 | 19.6605 | 17.6580 | 15.9368 | 14.4511 | 13.1630 | 12.0416 | 11.0612 | 10.2007 | 9.4424 | 8.7715 | 22 |
| 23 | 20.4559 | 18.2921 | 16.4435 | 14.8568 | 13.4885 | 12.3033 | 11.2722 | 10.3710 | 9.5802 | 8.8832 | 23 |
| 24 | 21.2435 | 18.9139 | 16.9355 | 15.2469 | 13.7986 | 12.5503 | 11.4693 | 10.5287 | 9.7066 | 8.9847 | 24 |
| 25 | 22.0233 | 19.5234 | 17.4131 | 15.6220 | 14.0939 | 12.7833 | 11.6536 | 10.6748 | 9.8226 | 9.0770 | 25 |

TABLE A-2. Present Value of One Dollar per Year; *N* Years at *R* Percent—Continued

| Year | 11% | 12% | 13% | 14% | 15% | 16% | 17% | 18% | 19% | 20% | Year |
|---|---|---|---|---|---|---|---|---|---|---|---|
| 1 | .9009 | .8929 | .8850 | .3772 | .8696 | .8621 | .8547 | .8475 | .8403 | .8333 | 1 |
| 2 | 1.7125 | 1.6901 | 1.6681 | 1.6467 | 1.6257 | 1.6052 | 1.5852 | 1.5656 | 1.5465 | 1.5278 | 2 |
| 3 | 2.4437 | 2.4018 | 2.3612 | 2.3216 | 2.2832 | 2.2459 | 2.2096 | 2.1743 | 2.1399 | 2.1065 | 3 |
| 4 | 3.1024 | 3.0373 | 2.9745 | 2.9137 | 2.8550 | 2.7982 | 2.7432 | 2.6901 | 2.6386 | 2.5887 | 4 |
| 5 | 3.6959 | 3.6048 | 3.5172 | 3.4331 | 3.3522 | 3.2743 | 3.1993 | 3.1272 | 3.0576 | 2.9906 | 5 |
| 6 | 4.2305 | 4.1114 | 3.9976 | 3.8887 | 3.7845 | 3.6847 | 3.5892 | 3.4976 | 3.4098 | 3.3255 | 6 |
| 7 | 4.7122 | 4.5638 | 4.4226 | 4.2883 | 4.1604 | 4.0386 | 3.9224 | 3.8115 | 3.7057 | 3.6046 | 7 |
| 8 | 5.1461 | 4.9676 | 4.7988 | 4.6389 | 4.4873 | 4.3436 | 4.2072 | 4.0776 | 3.9544 | 3.8372 | 8 |
| 9 | 5.5370 | 5.3282 | 5.1317 | 4.9464 | 4.7716 | 4.6065 | 4.4506 | 4.3030 | 4.1633 | 4.0310 | 9 |
| 10 | 5.8892 | 5.6502 | 5.4262 | 5.2161 | 5.0188 | 4.8332 | 4.6586 | 4.4941 | 4.3389 | 4.1925 | 10 |
| 11 | 6.2065 | 5.9377 | 5.6869 | 5.4527 | 5.2337 | 5.0286 | 4.8364 | 4.6560 | 4.4865 | 4.3271 | 11 |
| 12 | 6.4924 | 6.1944 | 5.9176 | 5.6603 | 5.4206 | 5.1971 | 4.9884 | 4.7932 | 4.6105 | 4.4392 | 12 |
| 13 | 6.7499 | 6.4235 | 6.1218 | 5.8424 | 5.5831 | 5.3423 | 5.1183 | 4.9095 | 4.7147 | 4.5327 | 13 |
| 14 | 6.9819 | 6.6282 | 6.3025 | 6.0021 | 5.7245 | 5.4675 | 5.2293 | 5.0081 | 4.8023 | 4.6106 | 14 |
| 15 | 7.1909 | 6.8109 | 6.4624 | 6.1422 | 5.8474 | 5.5755 | 5.3242 | 5.0916 | 4.8759 | 4.6755 | 15 |
| 16 | 7.3792 | 6.9740 | 6.6039 | 6.2651 | 5.9542 | 5.6685 | 5.4053 | 5.1624 | 4.9377 | 4.7296 | 16 |
| 17 | 7.5488 | 7.1196 | 6.7291 | 6.3729 | 6.0472 | 5.7487 | 5.4746 | 5.2223 | 4.9897 | 4.7746 | 17 |
| 18 | 7.7016 | 7.2497 | 6.8399 | 6.4674 | 6.1280 | 5.8178 | 5.5339 | 5.2732 | 5.0333 | 4.8122 | 18 |
| 19 | 7.8393 | 7.3658 | 6.9380 | 6.5504 | 6.1982 | 5.8775 | 5.5845 | 5.3162 | 5.0700 | 4.8435 | 19 |
| 20 | 7.9633 | 7.4694 | 7.0248 | 6.6231 | 6.2593 | 5.9288 | 5.6278 | 5.3527 | 5.1009 | 4.8696 | 20 |
| 21 | 8.0751 | 7.5620 | 7.1016 | 6.6870 | 6.3125 | 5.9731 | 5.6648 | 5.3837 | 5.1268 | 4.8913 | 21 |
| 22 | 8.1757 | 7.6446 | 7.1695 | 6.7429 | 6.3587 | 6.0113 | 5.6964 | 5.4099 | 5.1486 | 4.9094 | 22 |
| 23 | 8.2664 | 7.7184 | 7.2297 | 6.7921 | 6.3988 | 6.0442 | 5.7234 | 5.4321 | 5.1668 | 4.9245 | 23 |
| 24 | 8.3481 | 7.7843 | 7.2829 | 6.8351 | 6.4338 | 6.0726 | 5.7465 | 5.4509 | 5.1822 | 4.9371 | 24 |
| 25 | 8.4217 | 7.8431 | 7.3300 | 6.8729 | 6.4641 | 6.0971 | 5.7662 | 5.4669 | 5.1951 | 4.9476 | 25 |

| Year | 21% | 22% | 23% | 24% | 25% | 26% | 27% | 28% | 29% | 30% | Year |
|---|---|---|---|---|---|---|---|---|---|---|---|
| 1 | .8264 | .8197 | .8130 | .8065 | .8000 | .7937 | .7874 | .7813 | .7752 | .7692 | 1 |
| 2 | 1.5095 | 1.4915 | 1.4740 | 1.4568 | 1.4400 | 1.4235 | 1.4074 | 1.3916 | 1.3761 | 1.3609 | 2 |
| 3 | 2.0739 | 2.0422 | 2.0114 | 1.9813 | 1.9520 | 1.9234 | 1.8956 | 1.8684 | 1.8420 | 1.8161 | 3 |
| 4 | 2.5404 | 2.4936 | 2.4483 | 2.4043 | 2.3616 | 2.3202 | 2.2800 | 2.2410 | 2.2031 | 2.1662 | 4 |
| 5 | 2.9260 | 2.8636 | 2.8035 | 2.7454 | 2.6893 | 2.6351 | 2.5827 | 2.5320 | 2.4830 | 2.4356 | 5 |
| 6 | 3.2446 | 3.1669 | 3.0923 | 3.0205 | 2.9514 | 2.8850 | 2.8210 | 2.7594 | 2.7000 | 2.6427 | 6 |
| 7 | 3.5079 | 3.4155 | 3.3270 | 3.2423 | 3.1611 | 3.0833 | 3.0087 | 2.9370 | 2.8682 | 2.8021 | 7 |
| 8 | 3.7256 | 3.6193 | 3.5179 | 3.4212 | 3.3289 | 3.2407 | 3.1564 | 3.0758 | 2.9986 | 2.9247 | 8 |
| 9 | 3.9054 | 3.7863 | 3.6731 | 3.5655 | 3.4631 | 3.3657 | 3.2728 | 3.1842 | 3.0997 | 3.0190 | 9 |
| 10 | 4.0541 | 3.9232 | 3.7993 | 3.6819 | 3.5705 | 3.4648 | 3.3644 | 3.2689 | 3.1781 | 3.0915 | 10 |
| 11 | 4.1769 | 4.0354 | 3.9018 | 3.7757 | 3.6564 | 3.5435 | 3.4365 | 3.3351 | 3.2388 | 3.1473 | 11 |
| 12 | 4.2785 | 4.1274 | 3.9852 | 3.8514 | 3.7251 | 3.6060 | 3.4933 | 3.3868 | 3.2859 | 3.1903 | 12 |
| 13 | 4.3624 | 4.2028 | 4.0530 | 3.9124 | 3.7801 | 3.6555 | 3.6381 | 3.4272 | 3.3224 | 3.2233 | 13 |
| 14 | 4.4317 | 4.2646 | 4.1082 | 3.9616 | 3.8241 | 3.6949 | 3.5733 | 3.4587 | 3.3507 | 3.2487 | 14 |
| 15 | 4.4890 | 4.3152 | 4.1530 | 4.0013 | 3.8593 | 3.7261 | 3.6010 | 3.4834 | 3.3726 | 3.2682 | 15 |
| 16 | 4.5364 | 4.3567 | 4.1894 | 4.0333 | 3.8874 | 3.7509 | 3.6228 | 3.5026 | 3.3896 | 3.2832 | 16 |
| 17 | 4.5755 | 4.3908 | 4.2190 | 4.0591 | 3.9099 | 3.7705 | 3.6400 | 3.5177 | 3.4028 | 3.2948 | 17 |
| 18 | 4.6079 | 4.4187 | 4.2431 | 4.0799 | 3.9279 | 3.7861 | 3.6536 | 3.5294 | 3.4130 | 3.3037 | 18 |
| 19 | 4.6346 | 4.4415 | 4.2627 | 4.0967 | 3.9424 | 3.7985 | 3.6642 | 3.5386 | 3.4210 | 3.3105 | 19 |
| 20 | 4.6567 | 4.4603 | 4.2786 | 4.1103 | 3.9539 | 3.8083 | 3.6726 | 3.5458 | 3.4271 | 3.3158 | 20 |
| 21 | 4.6750 | 4.4756 | 4.2916 | 4.1212 | 3.9631 | 3.8161 | 3.6792 | 3.5514 | 3.4319 | 3.3198 | 21 |
| 22 | 4.6900 | 4.4882 | 4.3021 | 4.1300 | 3.9705 | 3.8223 | 3.6844 | 3.5558 | 3.4356 | 3.3230 | 22 |
| 23 | 4.7025 | 4.4985 | 4.3106 | 4.1371 | 3.9764 | 3.8273 | 3.6885 | 3.5592 | 3.4384 | 3.3254 | 23 |
| 24 | 4.7128 | 4.5070 | 4.3176 | 4.1428 | 3.9811 | 3.8312 | 3.6918 | 3.5619 | 3.4406 | 3.3272 | 24 |
| 25 | 4.7213 | 4.5139 | 4.3232 | 4.1474 | 3.9849 | 3.8342 | 3.6943 | 3.5640 | 3.4423 | 3.3286 | 25 |

## TABLE A–2. Present Value of One Dollar per Year; *N* Years at *R* Percent—Continued

| Year | 31% | 32% | 33% | 34% | 35% | 36% | 37% | 38% | 39% | 40% | Year |
|---|---|---|---|---|---|---|---|---|---|---|---|
| 1 | .7634 | .7576 | .7519 | .7463 | .7407 | .7353 | .7299 | .7246 | .7194 | .7143 | 1 |
| 2 | 1.3461 | 1.3315 | 1.3172 | 1.3032 | 1.2894 | 1.2760 | 1.2627 | 1.2497 | 1.2370 | 1.2245 | 2 |
| 3 | 1.7909 | 1.7663 | 1.7423 | 1.7188 | 1.6959 | 1.6735 | 1.6516 | 1.6302 | 1.6093 | 1.5889 | 3 |
| 4 | 2.1305 | 2.0957 | 2.0618 | 2.0290 | 1.9969 | 1.9658 | 1.9355 | 1.9060 | 1.8772 | 1.8492 | 4 |
| 5 | 2.3897 | 2.3452 | 2.3021 | 2.2604 | 2.2200 | 2.1807 | 2.1427 | 2.1058 | 2.0699 | 2.9352 | 5 |
| 6 | 2.5875 | 2.5342 | 2.4828 | 2.4331 | 2.3852 | 2.3388 | 2.2939 | 2.2506 | 2.2086 | 2.1680 | 6 |
| 7 | 2.7386 | 2.6775 | 2.6187 | 2.5620 | 2.5075 | 2.4550 | 2.4043 | 2.3555 | 2.3083 | 2.2628 | 7 |
| 8 | 2.8539 | 2.7860 | 2.7208 | 2.6582 | 2.5982 | 2.5404 | 2.4849 | 2.4315 | 2.3801 | 2.3306 | 8 |
| 9 | 2.9419 | 2.8681 | 2.7976 | 2.7300 | 2.6653 | 2.6033 | 2.5437 | 2.4866 | 2.4317 | 2.3790 | 9 |
| 10 | 3.0091 | 2.9304 | 2.8553 | 2.7836 | 2.7150 | 2.6495 | 2.5867 | 2.5265 | 2.4689 | 2.4136 | 10 |
| 11 | 3.0604 | 2.9776 | 2.8987 | 2.8236 | 2.7519 | 2.6834 | 2.6180 | 2.5555 | 2.4956 | 2.4383 | 11 |
| 12 | 3.0995 | 3.0133 | 2.9314 | 2.8534 | 2.7792 | 2.7084 | 2.6409 | 2.5764 | 2.5148 | 2.4559 | 12 |
| 13 | 3.1294 | 3.0404 | 2.9559 | 2.8757 | 2.7994 | 2.7268 | 2.6576 | 2.5916 | 2.5286 | 2.4685 | 13 |
| 14 | 3.1522 | 3.0609 | 2.9744 | 2.8923 | 2.8144 | 2.7403 | 2.6698 | 2.6026 | 2.5386 | 2.4775 | 14 |
| 15 | 3.1696 | 3.0764 | 2.9883 | 2.9047 | 2.8255 | 2.7502 | 2.6787 | 2.6106 | 2.5457 | 2.4839 | 15 |
| 16 | 3.1829 | 3.0882 | 2.9987 | 2.9140 | 2.8337 | 2.7575 | 2.6852 | 2.6164 | 2.5509 | 2.4885 | 16 |
| 17 | 3.1931 | 3.0971 | 3.0065 | 2.9209 | 2.8398 | 2.7629 | 2.6899 | 2.6206 | 2.5546 | 2.4918 | 17 |
| 18 | 3.2008 | 3.1039 | 3.0124 | 2.9260 | 2.8443 | 2.7668 | 2.6934 | 2.6236 | 2.5573 | 2.4941 | 18 |
| 19 | 3.2067 | 3.1090 | 3.0169 | 2.9299 | 2.8476 | 2.7697 | 2.6959 | 2.6258 | 2.5592 | 2.4958 | 19 |
| 20 | 3.2112 | 3.1129 | 3.0202 | 2.9327 | 2.8501 | 2.7718 | 2.6977 | 2.6274 | 2.5606 | 2.4970 | 20 |
| 21 | 3.2147 | 3.1158 | 3.0227 | 2.9349 | 2.8519 | 2.7734 | 2.6991 | 2.6285 | 2.5616 | 2.4979 | 21 |
| 22 | 3.2173 | 3.1180 | 3.0246 | 2.9365 | 2.8533 | 2.7746 | 2.7000 | 2.6294 | 2.5623 | 2.4985 | 22 |
| 23 | 3.2193 | 3.1197 | 3.0260 | 2.9377 | 2.8543 | 2.7754 | 2.7008 | 2.6300 | 2.5628 | 2.4989 | 23 |
| 24 | 3.2209 | 3.1210 | 3.0271 | 2.9386 | 2.8550 | 2.7760 | 2.7013 | 2.6304 | 2.5632 | 2.4992 | 24 |
| 25 | 3.2220 | 3.1220 | 3.0279 | 2.9392 | 2.8556 | 2.7765 | 2.7017 | 2.6307 | 2.5634 | 2.4994 | 25 |

## TABLE A–3. Future Value of One Dollar N Years Hence

| N | 1% | 2% | 3% | 4% | 5% | 6% | 7% | 8% | 9% | 10% | 12% | 14% | N |
|---|---|---|---|---|---|---|---|---|---|---|---|---|---|
| 01 | 1.010 | 1.020 | 1.030 | 1.040 | 1.050 | 1.060 | 1.070 | 1.080 | 1.090 | 1.100 | 1.120 | 1.140 | 01 |
| 02 | 1.020 | 1.040 | 1.061 | 1.082 | 1.102 | 1.124 | 1.145 | 1.166 | 1.188 | 1.210 | 1.254 | 1.300 | 02 |
| 03 | 1.030 | 1.061 | 1.093 | 1.125 | 1.158 | 1.291 | 1.225 | 1.250 | 1.295 | 1.331 | 1.405 | 1.482 | 03 |
| 04 | 1.041 | 1.082 | 1.126 | 1.170 | 1.216 | 1.262 | 1.311 | 1.360 | 1.412 | 1.464 | 1.574 | 1.689 | 04 |
| 05 | 1.051 | 1.104 | 1.159 | 1.217 | 1.276 | 1.338 | 1.403 | 1.469 | 1.539 | 1.611 | 1.762 | 1.925 | 05 |
| 06 | 1.061 | 1.126 | 1.194 | 1.265 | 1.340 | 1.419 | 1.501 | 1.587 | 1.677 | 1.772 | 1.974 | 2.195 | 06 |
| 07 | 1.072 | 1.149 | 1.230 | 1.316 | 1.407 | 1.504 | 1.606 | 1.714 | 1.828 | 1.949 | 2.211 | 2.502 | 07 |
| 08 | 1.083 | 1.172 | 1.367 | 1.469 | 1.477 | 1.594 | 1.718 | 1.851 | 1.993 | 2.144 | 2.476 | 2.853 | 08 |
| 09 | 1.094 | 1.195 | 1.405 | 1.423 | 1.551 | 1.689 | 1.838 | 1.999 | 2.172 | 2.358 | 2.773 | 3.252 | 09 |
| 10 | 1.105 | 1.219 | 1.344 | 1.480 | 1.629 | 1.791 | 1.967 | 2.159 | 2.367 | 2.594 | 3.106 | 3.707 | 10 |
| 11 | 1.116 | 1.243 | 1.384 | 1.549 | 1.710 | 1.898 | 2.105 | 2.332 | 2.580 | 2.853 | 3.479 | 4.226 | 11 |
| 12 | 1.127 | 1.268 | 1.426 | 1.601 | 1.796 | 2.012 | 2.252 | 2.518 | 2.813 | 3.138 | 3.896 | 4.818 | 12 |
| 13 | 1.138 | 1.294 | 1.469 | 1.665 | 1.886 | 2.133 | 2.410 | 2.720 | 3.066 | 3.452 | 4.363 | 5.492 | 13 |
| 14 | 1.149 | 1.319 | 1.513 | 1.732 | 1.980 | 2.261 | 2.579 | 2.937 | 3.342 | 3.798 | 4.887 | 6.261 | 14 |
| 15 | 1.161 | 1.346 | 1.558 | 1.801 | 2.079 | 2.397 | 2.759 | 3.172 | 3.642 | 4.177 | 5.474 | 7.138 | 15 |
| 16 | 1.173 | 1.373 | 1.605 | 1.873 | 2.183 | 2.540 | 2.952 | 3.426 | 3.970 | 4.595 | 6.130 | 8.137 | 16 |
| 17 | 1.184 | 1.400 | 1.653 | 1.948 | 2.292 | 2.693 | 3.159 | 3.700 | 4.328 | 5.054 | 6.866 | 9.276 | 17 |
| 18 | 1.196 | 1.428 | 1.703 | 2.036 | 2.407 | 2.854 | 3.380 | 3.996 | 4.717 | 5.560 | 7.690 | 10.575 | 18 |
| 19 | 1.208 | 1.457 | 1.754 | 2.107 | 2.527 | 3.026 | 3.617 | 4.316 | 5.142 | 6.116 | 8.613 | 12.056 | 19 |
| 20 | 1.220 | 1.486 | 1.806 | 2.191 | 2.653 | 3.207 | 3.870 | 4.660 | 5.604 | 6.728 | 9.646 | 13.743 | 20 |
| 21 | 1.232 | 1.516 | 1.860 | 2.279 | 2.786 | 3.400 | 4.141 | 5.034 | 6.109 | 7.400 | 10.804 | 15.558 | 21 |
| 22 | 1.245 | 1.546 | 1.916 | 2.470 | 2.925 | 3.604 | 4.430 | 5.437 | 6.659 | 8.160 | 12.100 | 17.861 | 22 |
| 23 | 1.257 | 1.577 | 1.974 | 2.465 | 3.072 | 3.820 | 4.741 | 5.871 | 7.258 | 8.954 | 13.552 | 20.362 | 23 |
| 24 | 1.270 | 1.608 | 2.044 | 2.563 | 3.225 | 4.049 | 5.072 | 6.341 | 7.911 | 9.850 | 15.189 | 23.212 | 24 |
| 25 | 1.282 | 1.641 | 2.094 | 2.666 | 3.386 | 4.291 | 5.427 | 6.848 | 8.623 | 10.834 | 17.000 | 26.462 | 25 |

## TABLE A-3. Future Value of One Dollar N Years Hence—Continued

| N | 15% | 16% | 18% | 20% | 22% | 24% | 28% | 30% | 34% | 38% | 40% | N |
|---|---|---|---|---|---|---|---|---|---|---|---|---|
| 01 | 1.150 | 1.160 | 1.180 | 1.200 | 1.220 | 1.230 | 1.280 | 1.300 | 1.340 | 1.380 | 1.400 | 01 |
| 02 | 1.322 | 1.346 | 1.392 | 1.440 | 1.488 | 1.538 | 1.638 | 1.690 | 1.796 | 1.904 | 1.960 | 02 |
| 03 | 1.521 | 1.561 | 1.643 | 1.728 | 1.816 | 1.907 | 2.097 | 2.197 | 2.407 | 2.628 | 2.744 | 03 |
| 04 | 1.749 | 1.811 | 1.939 | 2.074 | 2.215 | 2.364 | 2.684 | 2.856 | 3.224 | 3.627 | 3.842 | 04 |
| 05 | 2.011 | 2.100 | 2.288 | 2.488 | 2.703 | 2.932 | 3.436 | 3.713 | 4.320 | 5.005 | 5.378 | 05 |
| 06 | 2.414 | 2.436 | 2.700 | 2.986 | 3.297 | 3.635 | 4.398 | 4.827 | 5.789 | 6.907 | 7.530 | 06 |
| 07 | 2.660 | 2.826 | 3.185 | 3.583 | 4.023 | 4.508 | 5.630 | 6.275 | 7.758 | 9.531 | 10.541 | 07 |
| 08 | 3.059 | 3.278 | 3.759 | 4.300 | 4.908 | 5.590 | 7.206 | 8.157 | 10.395 | 13.153 | 14.758 | 08 |
| 09 | 3.518 | 3.803 | 4.435 | 5.160 | 5.987 | 6.931 | 9.223 | 10.605 | 13.930 | 18.152 | 20.661 | 09 |
| 10 | 4.046 | 4.411 | 5.234 | 6.192 | 7.305 | 8.594 | 11.806 | 13.785 | 18.666 | 25.049 | 28.926 | 10 |
| 11 | 4.652 | 5.117 | 6.176 | 7.430 | 8.912 | 10.657 | 15.112 | 17.92 | 25.012 | 34.568 | 40.496 | 11 |
| 12 | 5.135 | 5.936 | 7.288 | 8.916 | 10.872 | 13.215 | 19.343 | 23.298 | 33.516 | 47.703 | 56.694 | 12 |
| 13 | 6.153 | 6.886 | 8.599 | 10.699 | 13.264 | 16.386 | 24.759 | 30.288 | 44.912 | 65.831 | 79.372 | 13 |
| 14 | 7.076 | 7.988 | 10.147 | 12.839 | 16.182 | 20.319 | 31.691 | 39.374 | 60.182 | 90.846 | 111.120 | 14 |
| 15 | 8.137 | 9.266 | 11.974 | 15.407 | 19.742 | 25.196 | 40.565 | 51.185 | 80.644 | 125.368 | 155.568 | 15 |
| 16 | 9.358 | 10.748 | 14.129 | 18.488 | 24.085 | 31.243 | 51.923 | 66.542 | 108.063 | 173.008 | 217.795 | 16 |
| 17 | 10.761 | 12.468 | 16.672 | 22.186 | 29.384 | 38.741 | 66.461 | 86.504 | 144.804 | 238.751 | 304.913 | 17 |
| 18 | 12.376 | 14.463 | 19.673 | 26.623 | 35.849 | 48.039 | 85.070 | 112.455 | 194.038 | 329.476 | 426.879 | 18 |
| 19 | 14.232 | 16.777 | 23.214 | 31.948 | 43.736 | 59.568 | 108.890 | 146.192 | 260.011 | 454.677 | 597.630 | 19 |
| 20 | 16.367 | 19.461 | 27.393 | 38.338 | 53.358 | 73.864 | 139.380 | 190.050 | 348.414 | 627.454 | 836.683 | 20 |
| 21 | 18.822 | 22.575 | 32.324 | 47.005 | 65.096 | 91.592 | 178.406 | 247.065 | 466.875 | 865.886 | 1171.36 | 21 |
| 22 | 21.645 | 26.186 | 38.142 | 55.206 | 79.418 | 113.574 | 228.360 | 321.184 | 625.613 | 1194.92 | 1639.90 | 22 |
| 23 | 24.892 | 30.376 | 45.008 | 66.247 | 96.889 | 140.831 | 292.300 | 417.539 | 838.321 | 1648.99 | 2295.86 | 23 |
| 24 | 28.625 | 35.236 | 53.109 | 79.497 | 118.205 | 174.631 | 374.144 | 542.801 | 1123.35 | 2275.61 | 3214.20 | 24 |
| 25 | 3.2919 | 40.874 | 62.669 | 95.396 | 144.210 | 216.542 | 478.905 | 705.641 | 1505.29 | 3140.34 | 4499.88 | 25 |

[A9972]

## TABLE A-4. Future Value of One Dollar per Year N Years Hence *

| N | 1% | 2% | 3% | 4% | 5% | 6% | 7% | 8% | 9% | 10% | 12% | 14% | N |
|---|---|---|---|---|---|---|---|---|---|---|---|---|---|
| 01 | 1.000 | 1.000 | 1.000 | 1.000 | 1.000 | 1.000 | 1.000 | 1.000 | 1.000 | 1.000 | 1.000 | 1.000 | 01 |
| 02 | 2.010 | 2.020 | 2.030 | 2.040 | 2.050 | 2.060 | 2.070 | 2.080 | 2.090 | 2.100 | 2.120 | 2.140 | 02 |
| 03 | 3.030 | 3.060 | 3.091 | 3.122 | 3.153 | 3.184 | 3.215 | 3.246 | 3.278 | 3.310 | 3.374 | 3.440 | 03 |
| 04 | 4.060 | 4.122 | 4.184 | 4.246 | 4.310 | 4.375 | 4.440 | 4.506 | 4.573 | 4.641 | 4.779 | 4.921 | 04 |
| 05 | 5.101 | 5.204 | 5.309 | 5.416 | 5.526 | 5.637 | 5.751 | 5.867 | 5.985 | 6.105 | 6.353 | 6.610 | 05 |
| 06 | 6.152 | 6.308 | 6.468 | 6.468 | 6.802 | 6.975 | 7.153 | 7.336 | 7.523 | 7.716 | 8.115 | 8.536 | 06 |
| 07 | 7.214 | 7.434 | 7.662 | 7.662 | 8.142 | 8.394 | 8.654 | 8.923 | 9.200 | 9.487 | 10.089 | 10.731 | 07 |
| 08 | 8.286 | 8.583 | 8.892 | 9.214 | 9.549 | 9.897 | 10.250 | 10.637 | 11.029 | 11.436 | 12.300 | 13.233 | 08 |
| 09 | 9.369 | 9.755 | 10.159 | 10.583 | 11.027 | 11.491 | 11.978 | 12.488 | 13.021 | 13.580 | 14.776 | 16.085 | 09 |
| 10 | 10.462 | 10.950 | 11.464 | 12.006 | 12.578 | 13.181 | 13.816 | 14.487 | 15.193 | 15.937 | 17.549 | 19.337 | 10 |
| 11 | 11.567 | 12.169 | 12.808 | 13.486 | 14.207 | 14.972 | 15.784 | 16.646 | 17.560 | 18.531 | 20.655 | 23.045 | 11 |
| 12 | 12.683 | 13.412 | 14.192 | 15.026 | 15.917 | 16.870 | 17.889 | 18.977 | 20.141 | 21.384 | 24.133 | 27.271 | 12 |
| 13 | 13.819 | 14.680 | 15.618 | 16.628 | 16.613 | 18.882 | 20.141 | 21.495 | 22.953 | 24.523 | 28.029 | 32.089 | 13 |
| 14 | 14.957 | 15.974 | 17.086 | 18.292 | 19.599 | 21.015 | 22.551 | 24.215 | 26.019 | 27.975 | 32.393 | 37.581 | 14 |
| 15 | 16.106 | 17.293 | 18.599 | 20.029 | 21.579 | 23.276 | 25.129 | 27.152 | 29.361 | 31.773 | 37.280 | 43.842 | 15 |
| 16 | 17.258 | 18.639 | 20.157 | 21.825 | 23.658 | 25.673 | 27.888 | 30.324 | 33.003 | 35.950 | 42.753 | 50.980 | 16 |
| 17 | 18.430 | 20.012 | 21.762 | 23.698 | 25.840 | 28.213 | 30.840 | 33.750 | 36.964 | 40.545 | 48.884 | 59.118 | 17 |
| 18 | 19.614 | 21.412 | 23.414 | 25.645 | 28.143 | 30.906 | 33.999 | 37.450 | 41.301 | 45.599 | 55.750 | 68.394 | 18 |
| 19 | 20.810 | 22.841 | 25.117 | 26.561 | 30.539 | 33.760 | 37.379 | 41.446 | 46.019 | 51.159 | 63.440 | 78.969 | 19 |
| 20 | 22.019 | 24.297 | 26.870 | 29.778 | 33.066 | 36.786 | 40.996 | 45.762 | 51.160 | 57.275 | 72.052 | 91.025 | 20 |
| 21 | 23.249 | 25.783 | 28.677 | 31.969 | 35.719 | 39.993 | 44.865 | 50.423 | 56.765 | 64.003 | 81.699 | 104.768 | 21 |
| 22 | 24.571 | 27.299 | 30.537 | 34.248 | 38.505 | 43.392 | 49.006 | 55.457 | 62.873 | 71.403 | 92.503 | 120.436 | 22 |
| 23 | 25.716 | 28.845 | 32.453 | 36.618 | 41.431 | 46.996 | 53.436 | 60.893 | 69.532 | 79.543 | 104.60 | 138.297 | 23 |
| 24 | 26.973 | 30.422 | 34.427 | 39.083 | 44.502 | 50.816 | 58.177 | 66.765 | 76.790 | 88.497 | 118.16 | 158.659 | 24 |
| 25 | 28.243 | 32.030 | 36.459 | 41.646 | 47.727 | 54.865 | 63.249 | 73.106 | 84.701 | 98.347 | 133.33 | 181.871 | 25 |

* Compounding deferred for one year. To obtain the value of one dollar per year N years hence with compounding from the beginning of year 1, multiply your figure in Table A-4 by $(1 + i)$ where i is the given rate of interest.

TABLE A–4. Future Value of One Dollar per Year N Years Hence—Continued

| N | 15% | 16% | 18% | 20% | 22% | 24% | 28% | 30% | 34% | 38% | 40% | N |
|---|---|---|---|---|---|---|---|---|---|---|---|---|
| 01 | 1.000 | 1.000 | 1.000 | 1.000 | 1.000 | 1.000 | 1.000 | 1.000 | 1.000 | 1.000 | 1.000 | 01 |
| 02 | 2.150 | 2.160 | 2.180 | 2.200 | 2.220 | 2.240 | 2.280 | 2.300 | 2.340 | 2.380 | 2.400 | 02 |
| 03 | 3.473 | 3.506 | 3.572 | 3.640 | 3.708 | 3.778 | 3.918 | 3.990 | 4.136 | 4.284 | 4.360 | 03 |
| 04 | 4.993 | 5.067 | 5.215 | 5.368 | 5.524 | 5.684 | 6.016 | 6.187 | 6.542 | 6.912 | 7.104 | 04 |
| 05 | 6.742 | 6.877 | 7.154 | 7.442 | 7.740 | 8.048 | 8.700 | 9.043 | 9.766 | 10.539 | 10.946 | 05 |
| 06 | 8.754 | 8.977 | 9.442 | 9.930 | 10.442 | 10.980 | 12.136 | 12.756 | 14.086 | 15.544 | 16.324 | 06 |
| 07 | 11.067 | 11.414 | 12.142 | 12.925 | 13.740 | 14.615 | 16.534 | 17.583 | 19.876 | 22.451 | 23.853 | 07 |
| 08 | 13.727 | 14.240 | 15.327 | 16.499 | 17.762 | 19.123 | 22.163 | 23.858 | 27.633 | 31.982 | 34.395 | 08 |
| 09 | 16.786 | 17.519 | 19.086 | 20.799 | 22.670 | 24.713 | 29.369 | 32.015 | 38.029 | 45.135 | 49.153 | 09 |
| 10 | 20.304 | 21.433 | 23.521 | 25.959 | 28.657 | 31.643 | 38.593 | 42.720 | 51.958 | 63.287 | 69.814 | 10 |
| 11 | 24.349 | 25.733 | 28.755 | 32.150 | 35.062 | 40.239 | 50.399 | 56.405 | 70.624 | 88.336 | 98.739 | 11 |
| 12 | 29.002 | 30.850 | 34.931 | 39.581 | 44.874 | 50.895 | 65.510 | 74.327 | 95.637 | 122.904 | 139.235 | 12 |
| 13 | 34.352 | 36.786 | 42.219 | 48.497 | 55.746 | 64.110 | 84.853 | 97.625 | 129.153 | 170.607 | 195.929 | 13 |
| 14 | 40.505 | 43.672 | 50.818 | 59.196 | 69.010 | 80.496 | 109.612 | 127.913 | 174.065 | 236.438 | 275.300 | 14 |
| 15 | 47.580 | 51.660 | 60.965 | 72.035 | 85.192 | 100.815 | 141.303 | 167.286 | 234.247 | 327.284 | 386.420 | 15 |
| 16 | 55.718 | 60.925 | 72.939 | 87.442 | 104.035 | 126.011 | 181.868 | 218.472 | 314.891 | 452.652 | 541.988 | 16 |
| 17 | 65.075 | 71.673 | 87.068 | 105.931 | 120.020 | 157.253 | 233.791 | 285.014 | 422.954 | 625.659 | 759.784 | 17 |
| 18 | 75.836 | 84.141 | 103.740 | 128.117 | 158.405 | 195.994 | 300.252 | 371.518 | 567.758 | 864.410 | 1064.70 | 18 |
| 19 | 88.212 | 98.603 | 123.414 | 154.740 | 194.254 | 244.033 | 385.323 | 483.973 | 761.796 | 1193.89 | 1491.58 | 19 |
| 20 | 102.444 | 115.380 | 146.628 | 186.688 | 237.989 | 303.601 | 494.213 | 630.165 | 1021.81 | 1648.56 | 2089.21 | 20 |
| 21 | 118.810 | 134.841 | 174.021 | 225.026 | 291.347 | 377.465 | 633.593 | 820.215 | 1370.22 | 2276.02 | 2925.89 | 21 |
| 22 | 137.632 | 157.415 | 206.345 | 271.031 | 356.443 | 469.056 | 811.999 | 1067.28 | 1837.10 | 3141.90 | 4097.24 | 22 |
| 23 | 159.276 | 183.601 | 244.487 | 326.337 | 435.861 | 582.630 | 1040.36 | 1388.46 | 2462.71 | 4336.83 | 5735.14 | 23 |
| 24 | 184.168 | 213.978 | 289.494 | 392.484 | 532.750 | 723.461 | 1332.66 | 1806.00 | 3301.03 | 5985.82 | 8033.00 | 24 |
| 25 | 212.793 | 249.214 | 342.603 | 471.981 | 650.955 | 868.092 | 1706.80 | 2348.80 | 4424.38 | 8261.43 | 11247.2 | 25 |

[A9971]

*

# NAME INDEX

Basic Man.Finance 2d Ed. CTB—48

*

# SUBJECT INDEX

END OF VOLUME